of

FOSSILS

&

FOXES

THE
OFFICIAL HISTORY OF
LEICESTER CITY FOOTBALL CLUB
By
Dave Smith and Paul Taylor

Published by
POLAR PUBLISHING (LEICESTER) LTD

DEDICATED
TO THE MEMORY OF

John Goodman of Littlethorpe, a Fosse supporter
and
Doug Simpson of Glenfield, a City fan.

DUST COVER PICTURE KEY:

Front (clockwise): Arthur Chandler; Jim Melrose and Gary Lineker celebrate a City goal; Frank Worthington; Fosse v Leeds City in February 1914 - Herbert Bown collects with Harold Burton and Jimmy Harrold looking on;

Back (clockwise): John Duncan; Ian King and Jimmy Walsh attack the Spurs goal during the 1961 FA Cup Final; Hughie Adcock; Arthur Rowley; Alan Smith in action against Arsenal.

First published in Great Britain by
Polar Publishing (Leicester) Limited
852, Melton Road, Thurmaston, Leicester LE4 8BT.
England.
© Polar Publishing 1989

ISBN 0 9514862 0 9

All rights reserved. No part of this publication may be reproduced, stored in a retrieval system, or transmitted, in any form or by any means, without permission of the publisher.

Dust Cover Design
Eamon C. Heighway

Edited by
Julian Baskcomb

Designed & Typeset by
Polar Publishing (Leicester) Limited

Printed by
Printstream Limited
33, Ashville Way, Whetstone, Leicester.

CONTENTS

ACKNOWLEDGEMENTS

This book has been a collaborative work in every sense,
and it is no longer possible to point to any section of the research or writing and ascribe it wholly to one or other of the authors. Both of us, however, are very much indebted to countless other individuals for assistance and enthusiastic support. Some have found us a single piece of information, others have pointed out unforeseen directions our sleuthing might take, a few have embraced the tasks of checking and challenging various preliminary drafts of our manuscript. In this latter respect we must offer sincere thanks to Mike Davage in particular, for work above and beyond the call of duty in providing assistance with the 'Who's Who' section of this work.

Fellow members of the Association of Football Statisticians have proved incredibly helpful, while relatives and friends of former players, or indeed, the players themselves, have been in many cases kind enough to provide memorabilia or cherished photographs for us to copy. In particular we should thank Charlie Adam, Jenny Blackhurst and Jack Curtis for their contributions in this area.

Also, to those pioneering football historians already in print, whose relevant works we have ransacked and rechecked, heartfelt thanks are offered for their unwitting contributions.

The man who instigated this collaboration was John Eastwood, who suggested we pool the resources we were separately expending on basically identical projects; his encouragement was crucial to us.

We both owe a considerable debt to the patience and ever helpful assistance of numerous librarians, as we have pored over virtually every daily Leicester newspaper from 1884 to date, and several other publications besides, in the Leicester Central Reference Library and in the British Library's Newspaper Library at Colindale.

We also must thank the Leicester Mercury who made available to us their collection of sports writers' notebooks dating back to the 1920s, and also were always willing to assist us in uncovering photographs from their excellent archives, many previously unpublished, and granting us permission to make use of them. For this assistance we especially thank John Aldridge, Bill Anderson, Steve England and Jenny Schofield.

Other photographic credits are due to three main sources: to Bill Barradell of Michael Stockton Photography, to Colorsport, and especially to Neville Chadwick Photography, who have an outstanding collection of club photographs available. Special thanks are due to Neville Chadwick for all his assistance in unearthing photographs to satisfy all kinds of unusual requests; without his help this volume would indeed have been the poorer.

For some of the photographs used, we have been unable to establish clear copyright. The publishers would be pleased to hear from anyone whose copyright has been unintentionally infringed.

Naturally, we must also thank the staff of Leicester City Football Club. Secretary Alan Bennett and the Board of Directors are due much gratitude for allowing us unique access to a number of old club minute books and to such material of historical interest as is still in their possession. Karen Levens and Joanna Pool are sincerely thanked for their readiness to assist in unearthing such material.

Polar Publishing have been superbly supportive since taking on this venture: we could not have hoped for a better relationship in terms of access to joint decisions over questions of editorial, illustration, presentation, production and promotion. Julian Baskcomb, Julia Byrne, Janice Greenop and Eamon Heighway have all proved genuine collaborators on this volume: their perspective, and their expenditure of time and enthusiasm has re-invigorated us over the past year as the project neared completion.

Our respective families will now doubtless sigh with relief at a return to domestic normality. We thank them sincerely for their forbearance and support over all the years we've been incommunicado over hot typewriters and dusty files.

Finally to a list of individuals not mentioned above who have all contributed crucially to the cause:
Liz Ashforth and colleagues at the Football League, John Belton, Graham Blackwood, John Borthwick, Steve Botting, Colin Boulter, John Byrne, Denis Clarebrough, Tom Coates, Alan Craft, Ian Crosland, Steven Day, Derek Deadman, David Dennison, Bill Donnachie, Michael Gardner, Ian Garland, John Garner, John Gaustad, Stan Goddard, Roger Harris, John Hayes, Charles Hine, Sam Holmes, Bill Hume, Gerald Hutchinson, Trefor Jones, Doug Kemp, Ray Kirby, David Kirkby, Douglas Lamming, Syd Lee, John Litster, Colin Martin, Wade Martin, Clive Major, Brian Mellowship, J. M. Melrose, Gerald Mortimer, Balbi Murrell, John Northcutt, G. H. Park, Geraint Parry, Jim Pennington, Steven Phillips, Paul Plowman, Ed Pointon, Rosemary Simpson, Ray Spiller, Barbara Taylor, Paul Taylor (no relation), Len Walker, Ian Weller, Richard Wells, Mike Wilbur, Ernest Wiles, Alex Wilson … and anyone else we have inadvertently overlooked.
Thank you one and all.

If anyone has any further information, memorabilia, etc., which may be of interest or use in subsequent works, they should contact the authors via Polar Publishing, as any contributions will always be gratefully received.

FOREWORD

LEN SHIPMAN CBE

Leicester City F.C.:
Director 1939-1979
Chairman 1948-1956 & 1970-1973
Life Member since 1979

Football League:
Committee 1955-1963
Vice-President 1963-1966
President 1966-1974
Committee 1974-1977
Life Member since 1978

Having followed the fortunes of Leicester City for more than 60 years, I am delighted to have been given the chance to write the foreword to this excellent book on the history of the Football Club. It is a most comprehensive and well illustrated publication which I am sure will be of enormous interest to all our supporters, both young and old.

No doubt memories will be stirred of a particular player or match, and I am often asked which period during my long association with the club has thrilled me most. Having watched from the terraces as a boy over half a century ago, I hope I can at least speak with some authority about the various up's and down's experienced by the team and its supporters over the years.

It was a particularly exciting era during the 1920's when Leicester City were a First Division force to be reckoned with, and the team contained such marvellous players as Arthur Chandler and Adam Black and, indeed, my most memorable match comes from those days when City met Tottenham Hotspur in an FA Cup fifth round tie at Filbert Street in 1928. We lost 0-3, but the game was watched by a record crowd of more than 47,000 and the whole day still stands out in my memory as a quite wonderful event.

I clearly remember my first Board meeting back in 1939, and it was also my honour to be Chairman of the club in 1949, the year we played Wolverhampton Wanderers in the FA Cup Final after a marvellous 3-1 semi-final win at Highbury over the hot favourites Portsmouth.

On reflection however, I would have to say that I have never seen such exciting and skilful football at Filbert Street as when the late Jimmy Bloomfield was manager. There were some outstanding individual players who were admired by clubs throughout the country, and even the great Bill Shankly of Liverpool made no secret of the fact he had studied and been most impressed by Leicester City's style and tactics.

Leicester City have produced some fine players over the years, but many of them have subsequently left the club. The answer why is simple, and in the end boils down to money. All too often we could not afford the wages other wealthier clubs were prepared of offer. In my early days on the Board a player's top wages were £20 per week, and although I am not advocating a return to that, it is my personal opinion that the players freedom of contract system has done the game in general a disservice, with the bigger clubs able to unsettle and tempt away the crowd-pulling stars from more modest clubs.

What of the future? Despite all the problems and difficulties, football remains a tremendously popular sport, and I am sure that Leicester City will continue to add to the pages of their history which has been so well chronicled here, and will strive for even greater heights and achievements. In David Pleat I am convinced we have a very astute manager, who, given the time, will get things right and take the club back into the First Division.

I wish both him and the club every success.

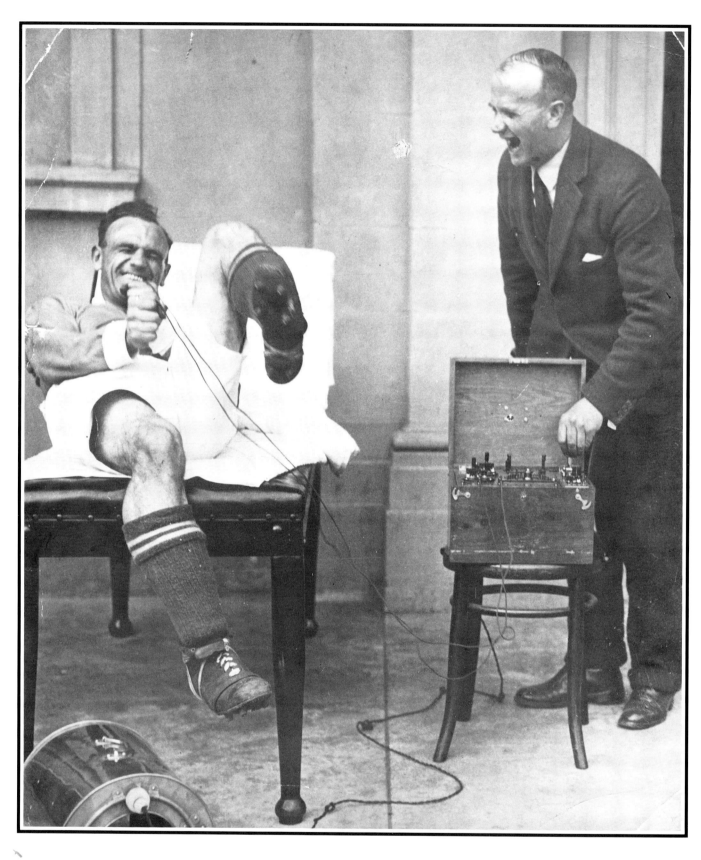

Leicester City clearly provided the very latest in physiotherapy technology to spark
Arthur Chandler's *electric goalscoring performances*
during the 1920's!!

NOTES
ON THE
TEXT AND TABLES

This book is essentially divided into three parts: a narrative history of the club; a statistical and records section; and a biographical index to players, managers, coaches and administrators. Hence, aspects of the same story are related from three different perspectives - making the authors acutely conscious of the necessity of avoiding undue repetition.

The bulk of the narrative is carried forward in season-by-season fashion. There is clearly no need for a match-by-match commentary, as the bare facts of every senior competitive game the club has ever played are tabulated in the statistical section. Likewise, there has been no temptation to mention every single player's arrival or departure in this part of the book, for fuller career details on each follow in the third section, as do retrospective summaries of each manager's period of control. Instead there is a concentration on context, development, salient incident and, hopefully, flavoursome anecdote.

It is beyond the remit and the competence of the authors to flesh out the purely sociological context of the story in any but the most sketchy of terms; and we acknowledge that as great a leap of imagination on the part of the reader will be required to picture, say, the everyday Victorian life of Leicester and its people (including those associated with the Fosse), as will be needed to envisage the game of football itself of that era: played to still-changing rules, and in differing tactical formations, on seemingly oddly-marked pitches, before spectators whose world-view and expectations we can barely guess at.

Accordingly, speculations about the vital varying relationships between The People and The People's Game have not really been attempted. We have had to limit ourselves to a book *for* Leicester's supporters, rather than *about* them; though the present authors would dearly love to see someone, someday, attempt that intriguing project.

The match-by-match statistical section - incorporating team line-ups and scorers for every first-class match played by Fosse and City - is substantially grounded in the painstaking research carried out by Dave Smith and presented in copy form to the club on the occasion of its Centenary in 1984. It has subsequently been minutely rechecked and marginally amended, and both authors are confident of its factual accuracy - as well as of its value for settling the sort of arguments that eternally arise whenever supporters or old players begin to match rather misted memories.

The attempt to construct a full career biography for every player to have represented Fosse and City in senior competition has thus far been an eleven-year task (principally on the part of Paul Taylor), doomed probably, never to be definitively completed; yet, for the authors, it represents perhaps the most exciting detective work involved in this book's genesis. Research difficulties have been legion; outside assistance immense. We sincerely hope this publication of what we accept is only a first - albeit substantial - draft of the project will prompt readers to supply any additional information they may have on any of the 700-plus individuals whose footballing lives we have here tried to encapsulate.

We hope similarly that no individual mentioned in this section feels remotely slighted by the brief informational assessments on their contribution to the Leicester cause. In the case of some 250-odd players, subjective criteria have intruded (i.e. the authors have assessed that contribution from the Filbert Street terraces and stands, in as opinionated a fashion as any other fan); while for the remainder we have distilled information and insight from as many sources and testimonies as possible.

All records and data are correct up to the end of the 1988/9 season.

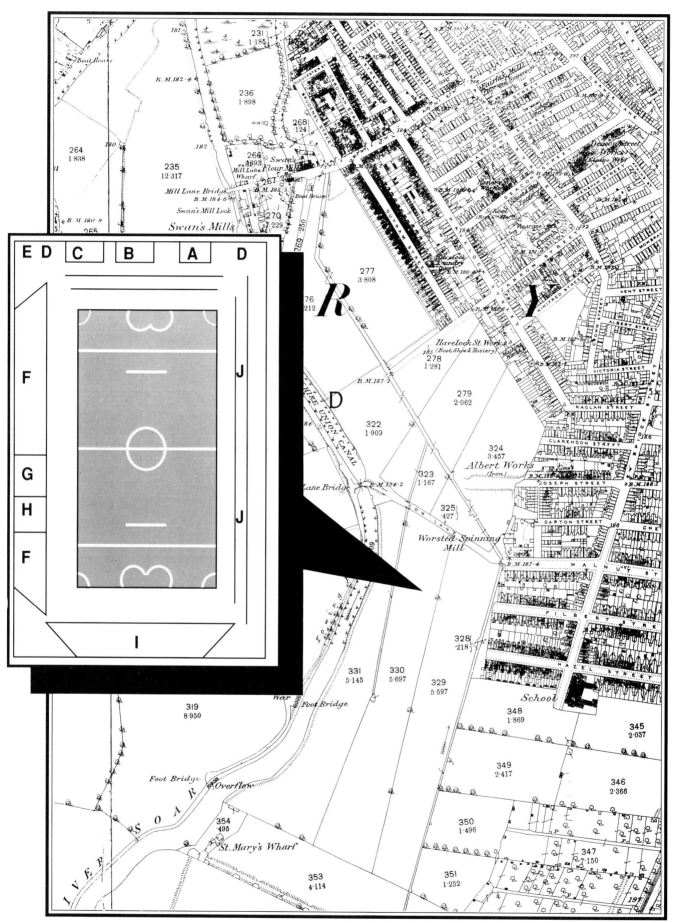

The **Filbert Street** and **Mill Lane** areas of Leicester in the mid-1880's. The playing areas were merely fields adjacent to the canal at that time. Inset is a plan of the ground in the mid 1890's.
KEY : A = Ground Entrance; B = Refreshment Room; C = Secretary's Office; D = Exits; E = Members Entrance; F = Members Stand; G = Subscribers Reserved Seats; H = Press & Committee; I = Open Stand; J = Unreserved.

FRIENDLY

FOSSILS

From a contemporary vantage of uncertainty over the future of Football As We Know It - especially regarding the sort of repressive governmental legislation that may soon make soccer synonymous with criminal activity in the public imagination - it is difficult to suppress an ironic smile in citing one of the earliest known records of The People's Game in Leicester and environs.

For almost 400 years ago, in April 1592, the game and the law were in similarly ludicrous, if more localised, conflict. The local magistrates were exercised by the case of one Matthewe Puchin, who, with eleven others, had been summoned for playing football on a Sunday at Oadby. Sensibly, they dismissed the charge.

The sport Puchin and his fellow pioneer miscreants were indulging in was doubtless barely recognisable as the game of today. Every locality at that time had its own variant on the basic notion of opposing teams (or mobs) projecting some vaguely spherical object towards some sort of 'goal': such rural folk-forms of football still exist today as quaint feast-day traditions in many parts of the country, and are still associated with notions of disorderly conduct.

The development of the 'modern' game - and its rise to a long-guarded respectability - really got underway in the second half of the nineteenth century. The impetus came from the universities and the public schools,where the knack of the youthful leisured classes lay in codifying rules for their competitive sport; and sanction came from the church, via then-popular notions of 'muscular Christianity' - a healthy mind in a healthy body, and all that. The social and moral benefits of well-ordered team sport were thus propounded with due missionary zeal by way of the grammar schools, the Sunday Schools, the temperance societies and similar avenues of influence, and quickly took root throughout the social fabric, especially - in the case of association football - among the men of the urban working class, many of whom were now being granted Saturday half-holidays for the first time.

The context for this development in Leicester was little different from that pertaining elsewhere in England. For years the term 'sport', especially as used in the press, referred exclusively to horse racing, although there was occasional acknowledgement of cricket as the pastime of the gentlemen of the county during the summer months. By the mid-nineteenth century, however, cricket matches had become frequent on parks and village greens, and the growing interest in competitive rivalry had led the local

press regularly to print scorecards of the more important games.

The Leicestershire County Cricket Club was organised into its present-day form in February 1879, and by 1884 had regular fixtures with the MCC as well as meetings with the touring Australians. Within a further year they would become officially part of the County Championship. They were also fortunate enough to have a private ground to play on at Grace Road, (where they would remain until 1900, and where they would return in 1946, having played in the interim at Aylestone Road).

When the cricket season ended each autumn, and only then, the parks were given over to winter games. Rugby was the premier pastime for the men of Leicester at this time. The first clubs appeared in the county in the 1860s, but the Leicester Football Club, the now famous Tigers, did not come into existence until 1880. In their initial season they played their home fixtures on the Belgrave Road Sports Ground, a venue long since demolished, but subsequently moved to Victoria Park. By 1884, they had established a sizeable following there, with fixtures against the likes of Moseley, Coventry, Northampton and Bedford - all leading Midland clubs who exploited the new ease of transport to broaden their sporting horizons.

In contrast, the round-ball game was struggling to gain a foothold within the town. The local press only gave room to match reports when the handling code did not fill all available space (and even then hardly in graphic detail), and it was clear that players, then drawn primarily from the well-educated middle classes, outnumbered spectators on most occasions. These diehards maintained a limited local fixture list - even the town's premier rugby club ran a subsidiary soccer team for three years - and took their cue from the national scene to await optimistically for reinforcements.

For the London-based Football Association had been formed in 1863; had instituted their English Cup in 1871/2; and had finally agreed a uniform set of Laws of the Game in 1877. Professionalism amongst some players was a covert fact from the mid 1870s, and would be legalised in 1885. And, by the 1880s, club rivalries were spilling across city, county, and even international boundaries as 'football fever' spread at a remarkable rate. Leicester, a thriving town at the heart of an expanding rail nexus, could not remain a soccer backwater for long...

The formation of the Leicester Fosse Football Club is believed to have taken place in the spring of 1884. The event was regarded as possessing little significance at the time, and was certainly not recorded in the local press. While it is certain that a number of Old Wyggestonians were amongst the founders, and that several of these were additionally members of the Bible class of the old Emanuel Church in New Parks Street (thus giving the club a wholly typical background for the period in emerging from the rugged philosophies of private education and 'muscular Christianity'), we have only folklore to trust for the enduring suggestion that the decision to form the club was reached at a meeting in a garden shed just off the old Roman Fosse Road.

Frank Gardner was elected as the first secretary and treasurer, and it is to him that the naming of the club is generally attributed. It is open to question whether he actually ever did utter the oft-quoted, prophetic statement -"As the Fosse is known throughout the land, so the new club shall be known to the future" - but, nevertheless, the football club was to be sustained through many a trial and tribulation by just such optimistic enthusiasm.

Messrs. Ashby, Bromwich and West additionally formed the first club committee - they were, of course, also players - and the captaincy was voted into the hands of W.Johnson. All members donated ninepence each towards a ball, and a further ninepence each as subscriptions. A local carpenter was engaged to make a set of goalposts, which he is reputed to have painted amber and black, and preparations were made for an inaugural fixture.

The first game to be played by Leicester Fosse actually took place on November 1st, 1884, the venue being a private field off the Fosse Road, and the opposition being Syston Fosse (the new club's name, as can be seen, was hardly unique). Leicester wore black jerseys with a diagonal blue sash and long white trousers, and goals from West (2), Dingley and H.Johnson (2) steered the club to an initial triumph by 5-0. The way in which the team lined up for that historic fixture, as detailed in the local press, shows the tenacious influence of rugby on tactical thinking at that time:

E.Smith *(goal)*;
F.Burdett *(three-quarter back)*;
E.Johnson,W.Johnson, F.Gardner *(half-backs)*;
(forwards) H.Johnson, B.Lewitt *(right-wing)*,
A.West, F.Bromwich *(centres)*,
A.Ashby, S.Dingley *(left-wing)*.

One of the earliest 'old chestnuts' associated with the club's history is the assertion that this initial game was a 12-a-side affair. This claim first appeared in a pamphlet about the club produced in 1893, and has been oft-repeated since. In fact, the fourth fixture that the club played was the 12-a-side game; the confusion arising from the fact that this time the opponents were Syston St.Peters.

For the rest of that initial 1884/5 season, Leicester

Fosse played their fixtures on either Victoria Park or the Racecourse - then the two principal venues for soccer in the town - but at no time did they record such a spectacular scoreline again as in that opening match. One incident, in March 1885, demonstrates the lack of organisation in the game in those days, for, when facing Wyggeston Boys School, Fosse were having particular problems coping with the opposition until a half-time tally-up established that the School team had actually fielded 13 men throughout the first period!

During that debut season, Fosse also played the odd game under the Union code. Local sources claim that two fixtures were probably played, but only one appears to have been reported - in February, when Holy Trinity Band of Hope provided the opposition, scoring one try to the four minor points achieved by the Fosse. All soccer opposition consisted of local clubs, with Mill Hill House, Melbourne Hall and St.Mary's swelling the remainder of the fixture list. By the end of that first campaign, the new club had actually made a profit of one shilling and tenpence.

For 1885/6, Victoria Park had become the club's established venue, although most spectators continued to turn their backs on the Fosse's efforts and watch Rugby Union on the adjoining pitches. The weekly tactical and selection meetings initially took place in the West Bridge coffee house, but later switched to the Eastgates coffee house, overlooking the Clock Tower in the centre of town. W.Johnson was again captain, but subscriptions had been raised to three shillings, together with a joining fee of a further shilling. Even these early examples of inflation couldn't balance the Fosse's books, though, and the season ended with the club two shillings and a ha'penny in the red.

The campaign itself was very poorly reported in the local press, as indeed, curiously, was that of the Rugby Union club. Sport was definitely not deemed fashionable reading during the winter of 1885/6. Of the games which did get noted, a record 6-0 victory was logged when Trinity Band of Hope were entertained at Victoria Park; revenge therefore being well and truly exacted for the previous season's defeat at the oval ball game. At the end of January, when playing Mill Hill House, the Fosse suffered their first recorded instance of completing a fixture with only ten men.

The fixture list was again predominantly local, but a game was secured with a team from Market Harborough. Another fixture, in March, was due to be played in Loughborough, with Old Loughburians scheduled to provide the opposition. However, Fosse could not find their hosts' ground, and are popularly believed to have spent the afternoon at the races instead.

By the start of the 1886/7 campaign, the club membership had increased to 40, and a reserve team, Leicester Fosse Rovers, was founded. The club colours had changed to chocolate and blue halved shirts, and the first 'outsider' joined the club. He was Sam Sudbury, from Lincoln, who had recently moved to the Leicester area when he was spotted by Frank Gardner kicking a ball about on Spinney

Hill Park. By the following weekend he was playing for the Fosse's first eleven!

The fixture list was gradually encompassing opposition from further afield. Barwell, Coalville, Loughborough and even Nottingham were all visited during the campaign, though not always with success. In November, the Coalville team walked off the pitch before the end of the game in disagreement with a decision made by the umpire. The same month, at Belgrave, Fosse turned up with only ten men, but persuaded a spectator to make up their numbers. Twice during the season Fosse met opposition made up of only ten men - first St.Marks and then Belgrave in the return fixture. Once again a record victory was established, Wyggeston School Past & Present being thrashed 9-0 at Victoria Park in March. Off the field, the AGM was presented with a balance sheet showing a credit of £1.12s.9 $^{1}/_{2}$d. Things were beginning to look up.

So much so that for the 1887/8 season membership had risen to 65 and the club was able to field three teams. Another pointer to the steady rise in the status of the club was the decision to move to a private ground. The Belgrave Road Sports Ground was hired, although it did not possess changing facilities. The teams got ready and later washed down, in fact, at the White Hart Hotel, almost a mile away from the enclosure. The arrangement of matches against the likes of Kettering, Burton Swifts and Notts County Reserves also indexed the club's growing esteem; and it was the November fixture with Burton Swifts that saw another landmark notched in the club's history, with gate money being taken from home spectators for the first time. Some things did not change, however, and on December 10th, when Castle Donington failed to put in a scheduled appearance, Fosse were reduced to playing a full-scale practice match against their own reserves, which ended in a 1-1 draw.

FRANK GARDNER

The other significant happening of this season was the formation of the Leicestershire Football Association, reported in the local press in September, and the institution of the Leicestershire Association Challenge Cup. Again, Frank Gardner had been a leading light in agitation to form the LFA, partly to regularise fixture organisation in the county, and he was soon to be honoured with the Association's Presidency.

Fosse of course entered the new cup competition, but soon hit trouble. Their first round tie with St.Saviours, at Belgrave Road, resulted in a 4-2 victory, but the result was declared void after a protest from the visitors over the poor light in which the game was completed. When the tie was replayed, Fosse were clearly in the mood to stifle further argument, and ran out winners by five clear goals. Rivalry between the Leicester town clubs and those based in the Loughborough area was particularly keen, and when Fosse were paired with Shepshed Albion in Round Two anticipation ran high. In the event, it took three attempts to settle the issue in favour of the North Leicestershire club, who subsequently went on to become the first holders of the trophy, defeating Mill Hill House 8-0 at Kegworth, after a 1-1 draw at Coalville.

By the end of the season Fosse's membership had crept up to 72, total gate receipts for the season amounted to £8.4s.0d., and the club was in credit with a balance of £2.13s.4 $^{1}/_{2}$d. showing on the books. Reporting of football in the local press had also improved considerably, and one regular correspondent was responsible for dubbing the club with their first pair of popular nicknames - 'The Fossils', of obvious derivation, or 'The Ancients', which contrived to imply a club of rather longer traditions than a mere three or four years. In fact, 'Old Fossil' was to become the pen-name of the reporter himself as he continued to log the club's deeds over many years in the old 'Daily Post'.

April 17th 1888 was a date of major significance in football history. On that day the second meeting called by Aston Villa committee man William McGregor ended in the formation of the Football League, initially to comprise twelve of the strongest clubs from the North and Midlands. In Leicestershire, however, there were other summer events to claim the sporting headlines. Firstly, the County Cricket Club became the toast of the land when their first ever victory over the touring Australians was hailed as the sensation of the season. Then, unfortunately for Fosse, they were outbid for the use of the Belgrave Road Grounds by the Rugby Union Club, who had become somewhat jealous of their upstart soccer rivals' rise in prestige. The Tigers were, in fact, to remain at this ground until September 1892, when they would move to the Welford Road site that they still occupy today, but the turn of events left a crestfallen Fosse with no alternative but to return to Victoria Park for the 1888/9 season.

To call this retrogressive move a body blow for the ambitious soccer club would be an understatement, and the first effect was the immediate defection to rivals Loughborough, who possessed a private ground, of skipper T.S.Ashmole and goalkeeper T.DeVille. In the reshuffle, G.A.Knight was made captain and W.Johnson assumed the role of assistant secretary. They did their best to ensure that performances on the field did not suffer and, to show that the club was still progressive in spite of setbacks, Fosse engaged the first professional to don their colours. His name was Harry Webb, and he was lured from Stafford Rangers with the promise of 2s.6d. per week plus travelling expenses.

Webb's debut came against Coalville Town on October 13th, but his biggest impact was made a month later in the first round of the Leicestershire Association Challenge Cup. Syston Wreake Valley provided the opposition and Webb scored six times as Fosse ran up a club record victory by 12-1. This was, however, to prove a false dawn in the Cup as, after receiving a bye in Round Two, Fosse were despatched 0-2 at Loughborough at the next hurdle. Despite the drawbacks of the parks pitch, the fixture list continued to expand and gain in quality, and games were played during the season against Long Eaton Midland, Bulwell United, Sawley Rangers and Nottingham Forest Reserves.

If the Fosse were to continue to pursue their intention of becoming the premier town club, it was imperative that a private ground be found for 1889/90. This was duly secured with the rental of a pitch on Mill Lane, owned by the Town Council. The season itself did not kick off in an auspicious fashion as, for the opening fixture at Bulwell, two Fosse players missed the train and the team had to complete the match with only nine men. This occurrence was actually repeated in December, when Grantham was the venue. Unsurprisingly, both games ended in 0-3 reverses. Still, nine men was better than none at all, which was what Long Eaton Midland contrived to deliver to Mill Lane just after Christmas. This resulted in the first occasion on which Fosse had to refund all gate money to the disgruntled spectators.

Not all though was doom and gloom, for meetings with the reserve teams of both Notts County and Nottingham Forest were retained on the fixture list, and the likes of Grantham Rovers, Stafford Rangers and Sheffield Montrose added. Jimmy Johnson had taken over as club captain, and it was to him that the honour would fall of lifting the club's first ever trophy.

The Leicestershire FA had decided to run two Cup competitions for their Senior and Junior members, reflecting the massive growth of the game throughout the county as it had taken hold of the working population's imagination, and Fosse were at last to make their mark in the Senior Cup. Rivalry with Loughborough was becoming more intense, and when the two clubs were paired in the semi-final, fireworks were expected. In the event, all the playing pyrotechnics came from Fosse, who won 4-0, though there was an acrimonious sequel when the Luffs put in a protest over the eligibility of J.Eggleton in Fosse's team. The accusation was that Fosse had illegally approached the amateur player after he'd appeared for Hinckley against Fosse Rovers, had paid him excessive travelling expenses, and had provided him with tea; but no substantive evidence was placed before the adjudicating Cup committee, and Eggleton himself had left the area to live in the south by the time of the hearing. Fosse were censured for obtaining no receipt for his expenses, but allowed to face Coalville Town in the final - ironically to be played at Loughborough. A 1-1 draw in the first clash was followed by a 4-0 replay victory for Fosse, and silverware was in the hands of the youthful Ancients at last.

Fosse's home pasture at Mill Lane was chosen as the venue for the first Junior Cup final, between Gresley Rovers and Loughborough Athletic, the Luffs' reserve team, as well as for an inter-Association match between Birmingham and Leicester. These extra fixtures did not though, swell the coffers appreciably, so despite their success the club still made a loss of £6.7s.10d. on the season. The AGM, undaunted, resolved that the club should consolidate its status by applying for membership of the Football Association. Fosse were duly accepted by the national body on July 21st 1890 and immediately lodged their initial entry for the English Cup.

The Mill Lane ground was retained for 1890/1, and Fosse started the season with their first-ever 'guarantee' game, away to Boston Town, who had offered a minimum of £5 plus refreshments to secure the fixture. The first English Cup tie came at Mill Lane on October 4th. Hopes were high and gate receipts totalled £15 as Fosse took the field against Burton Wanderers, but the visitors, steeled by regular competitive football in their second season in the new Midland League, ran out rather easy victors by 4-0.

Fosse's own friendly fare now encompassed meetings with the original Northampton Town club, the reserves of both Aston Villa and Derby County and, at Christmas, with London Casuals. Yet most interest was still aroused by the local derbies with Loughborough, for by now Fosse could rightly claim to be the premier club in the town, while the Luffs were top of the heap in the county surrounds. A crowd of 2,500 paid £23.3s.0d. at Mill Lane on December 13th to witness a 1-1 draw between the rivals. Not that they were able to witness very much - for the game was completed in a heavy fog. Local legend has it that Charlie Walker, the Fosse goalkeeper, was left on the pitch at the end of the game, and only discovered missing from the dressing room some 20 minutes later. When found still in his goalmouth he is reported to have been under the impression that the game was still in progress, and that Fosse were exerting heavy pressure at the other end!

Because this fixture was spoiled by the weather, the two clubs agreed to play a charity match over the Christmas period. This was staged at the Belgrave Road Grounds and £27.13s.3d. was raised as the teams again drew 1-1. For the third meeting of the local rivals on February 7th at Loughborough, some 1500 fans travelled to cheer on the Fosse on the first-ever 'football special' train to run from Leicester. It was all to no avail, though, as the Luffs recorded a comfortable 3-1 victory.

To round off the campaign, the Fosse committee invited the beaten English Cup finalists from Notts County to Mill Lane. A record crowd paid nearly £30 to watch Fosse's first opponents from the Football League being held to a 2-2 draw. Turnover for the season had risen to £334 and the club showed a profit of £15, while the Leicestershire Senior Cup had been retained with a 2-0 victory over Gresley Rovers at Loughborough.

Clearly, if the club was to continue to improve its standing, steps had to be taken towards an eventual application to join the Football League. With this ambitious goal in mind, Fosse took intelligent stock of the immediately achievable, applied to be granted a place in the Midland League and, on May 23rd 1891, were duly accepted (as, indeed, were Loughborough). In just seven short years of the club's existence so much progress had been achieved already, and future prospects looked nothing but golden.

THE MIDLAND LEAGUE

1891 - 1894

The Midland League was one of the most prestigious of several senior competitions established in the wake of the acknowledged success of the Football League, and had already completed two seasons (in which Lincoln City and Gainsborough Trinity had finished as champions) by the time it accepted Fosse into its ranks.

Twelve teams were to compete in season 1891/2, though Staveley would resign early in the campaign, so Fosse's first experience of 'a fixity of fixtures' eventually gave them a 20-game league programme, to be faced in their newly adopted colours of white shirts and navy blue shorts, and under the captaincy of 'Snooks' Nuttall. This initial adventure was not exactly to be a roaring success but, in mitigation, there were several severe handicaps to be overcome along the way.

The most serious cloud over the start of the campaign was the recurrent problem of a home ground. The Mill Lane enclosure was required by the Leicester Corporation for building purposes, and Fosse were stymied until graciously offered temporary use of the Aylestone Road cricket ground as an interim headquarters. It was here that Fosse started their still substantial supplementary programme of friendlies with a home defeat by Derby County; here that the first Midland League game against Derby Junction (with a 4.50pm kick-off) was won by a single goal from star winger Jimmy Atter; and here that Fosse received their first-hurdle FA Cup mauling at the hands of Small Heath, by 2-6. The eighth and final game at Aylestone Road was a 6-1 friendly win over Notts Olympic, as the hectic search for a permanent playing base had at last come to an end.

Open land nearby - between Aylestone Road and Walnut Street - had been earmarked (at the suggestion of, legend has it, a Miss Westland, niece of Fosse committee-man Joseph Johnson), and three and three-quarter acres secured on lease from the Corporation to serve as Fosse's new home. Mr.Johnson (who had seen four sons turn out for Fosse at various times) himself guaranteed the rent, and work proceeded apace to lay out a pitch and a rudi-mentary enclosure, bounded at one end by Filbert Street. It was initially deemed that few potential patrons would know the whereabouts of this relatively minor thorough-fare, so advertisements drew the crowds to what was called the Walnut Street Ground for the inaugural game, a friendly on November 7th against Nottingham Forest's reserve side. Jimmy Atter was again the scorer in a 1-1 draw.

Loughborough were the initial Midland League guests on the new ground, but it was not until January 9th that Fosse fans could cheer a League victory at Walnut Street, when champions-to-be Rotherham Town succumbed by 4-1. Indeed, it had long been apparent even by this juncture that Fosse were ill-equipped in playing terms for the regular competitive challenge. They had done little to strengthen their squad from the previous campaign and a succession of reverses and dents to morale was topped in the return game at Rotherham, when a ten-man Fosse shipped eleven goals without reply. Outside-left Atkins was the man who failed to turn up for this fixture, on only the second occasion he'd been selected.

The season ended with Fosse sharing the wooden spoon with Derby Junction. They had failed to win any of their final eight fixtures, and would have finished rock-bottom had goal-average or goal-difference then entered the calculations. Gate receipts had amounted to only £599, but both the financial and playing state of the club had come under intense discussion on March 18th, when a public meeting at the Co-operative Hall chaired by J.T.Hincks had been called "to consider the question of raising the standard of association football in Leicester, and the best means of helping the Fosse Football Club to attain this end". A fund-raising committee was elected, and an immediate infusion of £200 added to club coffers.

Public support for the novelty of regular competitive soccer was not yet massive, but at least it was whole-hearted. Competing demands for patronage included such events as a week of performances on the Belgrave Road Grounds by Buffalo Bill's Wild West Show,which coincided with the start of Fosse's season. There was to be no turning back to less rigorous local football for Fosse.

Neither was there the prospect of an under-strength team representing the club for 1892/3. Close-season dealings by newly-elected honorary secretary E.A.Marson had brought several new faces to Leicester, including former Notts County goalkeeper Jimmy Thraves and dashing winger Billy Dorrell, who helped demolish his former Singers' (Coventry) team-mates by 10-1 in Fosse's initial friendly. The club had now switched its official headquarters from the Victoria Hotel to the Freeman's Arms Hotel, and had also invested in considerable improvements to the Walnut Street ground, so that a record crowd of 13,000 (paying £254) could be accomodated when Fosse met Loughborough late in the Midland League campaign.

Two heavy defeats heralded the start of competitive fare, but Fosse soon perked up with a record 7-1 win over Newark and more than held their own, finishing the 24-game league season in a commendable fourth place. Rotherham Town were again champions and, as an encouraging sign to increasingly ambitious Fosse, were immediately elected to the Second Division of the Football League.

Fosse also registered their first FA Cup success this term. In the Qualifying competition, they removed both Rushden and Notts Olympic by 7-0 scorelines (the latter in a replay) before bowing out rather disappointingly to Buxton. Indeed, the growing respect for the club beyond the confines of town and county was indexed by the selection of Thraves, Dorrell and Nuttall to represent the Midland League in inter-league competition, and by the selection of Leicester to host the AGM of the Midland League executive.

Another pointer to the season's satisfactions was the increased turnover of £1,640. Admission charges had been amended in October: they were 4d for Midland League games, and 3d for friendlies. There was however, still some hedging over the relative 'pull' of Fosse in their home town, as the scheduled home and away fixtures with Gainsborough Trinity were switched to avoid the Walnut Street encounter clashing with the Tigers v.Guys Hospital rugby match in January.

Nineteen professionals were on Fosse's books for the start of season 1893/4, ready for a concerted attempt on

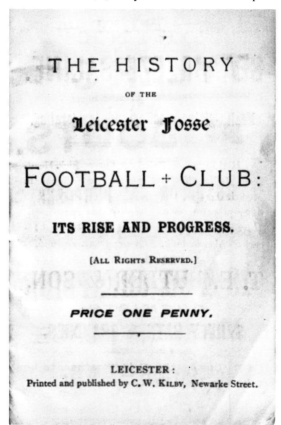

THE HISTORY

OF THE

Leicester Fosse

FOOTBALL + CLUB:

ITS RISE AND PROGRESS.

[ALL RIGHTS RESERVED.]

PRICE ONE PENNY.

LEICESTER:
Printed and published by C. W. KILBY, Newarke Street.

*The very first **Club History**, published for the tenth anniversary season of 1893/4.*

the Midland League championship. An opening-day defeat by Burton Wanderers was soon shrugged off but would, in the long run, prove crucial, For Fosse, Burton and Loughborough soon turned the title chase into a three-horse race. An attractive, free-scoring Fosse won 15 of their 20 fixtures, and lost only 3, but Burton remained unbeaten all term to take the title despite having two points docked for fielding an ineligible player in one game. Fosse did, however, pip their county rivals for runners-up spot.

Dorrell and Thraves were still starring weekly, and the gradual addition of ex-League expertise was helping consolidate Fosse's progressive reputation. Defender Arthur Henrys had arrived from Newton Heath before the end of the previous season, while influential Scotsman Jimmy Brown was recruited from Aston Villa in October to display his playmaking and goalscoring versatility, and centre-forward William McArthur signed on from Bolton Wanderers in April. Fosse had opened the campaign with a new Members' Stand, holding 1,400 patrons, adding a prestigious air to their home enclosure. Indeed, it was probably the seeking of prestige on all fronts which cost Fosse the coveted championship.

Their supplementary programme of friendlies now took in sapping encounters with League teams of the calibre of West Brom, Sheffield United, Newcastle and Wolves, and both the famous amateur Corinthians and mighty Glasgow Rangers were also added to the home fixture list for the first time. In addition, the FA Cup campaign this season also stretched resources, despite attracting wholly unaccustomed national acclaim to the club.

Three Qualifying rounds had to be surmounted, and Mansfield Town, Mansfield Greenhalgh's and local rivals Loughborough were each despatched without a goal conceded - though the latter tie was a fraught affair, which drew from the Leicester press accusations of 'downright ruffianism' against the Luffs, and involved a 34 minute delay while Luffs defender Kent - still lying on the pitch - had his broken leg set by a doctor. These successes saw Fosse in the First Round Proper for the first time, and a home tie with South Shore (later to amalgamate with their neighbours Blackpool) produced a 2-1 win.

In the Second Round, the might of Derby County (3rd in the First Division that season) had to be faced at Walnut Street, and 12,000 squashed in to witness Fosse come close to a shock result. They could not quite breach the Rams' rearguard, however, and the goalless draw was followed by an honourable exit by 0-3 in the replay. Later, a little consolation silverware was captured in the shape of the Kettering Charity Cup, after Wolverton L&NWR had been vanquished at Kettering.

By far the most exciting and rewarding of Fosse's three seasons at Midland League level, this term ended with two serious decisions made by the club committee. The first saw Fosse at last succumb to the lure of a hefty transfer offer of around £250 from Aston Villa for Billy Dorrell. This was sad, but comparatively minor as the second concerned Fosse's assessment of their own potential for continued progress. Would they continue to seek success in the Midland League or risk an application to play on the truly national stage represented by the Football League? The verdict was unanimous: Fosse would stand for election to the Second Division.

ELECTION TO RE-ELECTION

The Fosse committee, having definitively set their sights on Football League status for the club, spent a hectic couple of months in the 1894 close season lobbying their counterparts among existing League members, and their representatives travelled to the AGM on May 21st in confident mood. The fifteen-club Division Two, now two seasons old, was to be extended to a membership of sixteen regardless, and Northwich Victoria had resigned from the competition; while the fact that Ardwick (newly reconstructed as Manchester City) and Rotherham Town were seeking re-election meant that four places were being contested by eight applicants.

Joy among the Leicester contingent was unrestrained when the election figures were announced: both Fosse and Manchester City had garnered a maximum 20 votes, and were to be joined in Division Two by Bury and Burton Wanderers (17 votes each). Rotherham Town (15), Blackpool (8), Accrington (7) and Rossendale (nil) were the disappointed candidates, but in fact Rotherham regained their place only a week later when Middlesbrough Ironopolis folded.

Team-building for the new challenge (at a time when no player signed anything longer than a season's contract, and wholesale personnel changes in the close season were the norm) became a priority for secretary Mr.Lee and his committee-men, though a lot of faith was riding on the Midland League stalwarts. The fixture calendar was negotiated directly with the new opposition, and September 1st impatiently awaited by the likes of trainer Bob Roberts and skipper James Brown...

1894 - 95

In a season highlighted, naturally enough, by a series of 'firsts', Fosse kicked off their initial Football League encounter at Grimsby Town's Abbey Park ground. Newcomer David Skea claimed Fosse's opening goal, but a close tussle ended in a 3-4 defeat. A friendly victory over First Division Derby County on the following Monday boosted confidence, and the club's first points came from their first home game, with Skea claiming a hat-trick in a 4-2 result against Rotherham Town.

Alarm bells sounded when a subsequent run of four League defeats followed, but a remarkable 13-0 cakewalk against minnows Notts Olympic in the First Qualifying Round of the FA Cup (still the club's record score in the competition) heralded a turnaround in fortunes. A week later, Fosse were 0-4 down against Newcastle United but fought back to draw, and would have claimed both points had centre-forward Miller not missed the first penalty awarded the club at League level.

Fosse didn't lose again until Christmas Day, when they conceded their first hat-trick to Bury's Henderson, and in the interim both the first successful penalty (by Skea against Notts County) and the first own goal (by Burton Swifts' Hackett) had been recorded to Leicester's credit. A gate of around 10,000 had seen the first of three ties with Loughborough as Fosse continued their progress through the Cup's Qualifying rounds, but this run, too, came to an end at Bury in the First Round proper.

A League win by 9-1 over Walsall Town Swifts (who were only 0-2 down at the interval) established one seasonal record, while a 2-8 defeat at Darwen set its opposite, though this game was something of a farce. The original fixture on December 30th had been abandoned after only two minutes when the goalposts were blown down by a gale, and a 50-minute friendly substituted (which a bedraggled Fosse lost 0-6); while the rematch was deemed playable only by the referee, who allowed one set of posts to be moved back onto the adjacent cricket pitch, the playing field to be hastily re-marked, and the Darwen players to strap their boots in swathes of felt to help them traverse the mud, puddles and sand! The scoreline seems almost respectable considering a half-time deficit of seven goals.

Cricket pitches played quite a part in Fosse's season: they met Notts County at their then home, Trent Bridge; played Woolwich Arsenal on the Essex CCC ground at Leyton while their hosts' own Plumstead enclosure was under closure by FA order; and later faced Sheffield United at Bramall Lane in a United Counties League fixture. This latter competition was a supplementary first-XI league which had initially been set up for senior clubs who had made early FA Cup exits: Fosse's only season in contention was in fact the league's last.

The Football League, though, was soon appearing a less daunting arena for Fosse. Unbeaten in their final thirteen games, they came within a whisker of qualifying for the Test Matches which then decided promotion and relegation between the First and Second Divisions. Finishing fourth with 38 points, they were but a single point behind second-placed Notts County, and had only their appalling start to the season to blame. David Skea took top scorer's honours with 23 League strikes and eight in the Cup as an ever-present inside-left, while goalkeeper Jimmy Thraves was the other Fossil not to miss a game.

Perhaps ironically, Fosse hosted the crucial Test Match between Derby and Notts, in which a 2-1 win for the Rams kept them in Division One. Earlier, the Walnut Street ground had been the venue for the semi-final of the Birmingham Cup, when Loughborough crashed 2-6 to Aston Villa, who themselves had been one of Fosse's most notable scalps of the season when Leicester had triumphed 2-1 in the Bass Charity Vase semi-final. Fosse unfortunately fell in extra time of the final of this prestig-

ious competition to Burton Wanderers, who were also their conquerors in the final of the Kettering Charity Cup.

It was left to the reserve team to claim the season's silverware, adding the Wellingborough Cup to their championship trophy from the Leics. & Northants League.

Overall, though, Fosse's first season as a League club had been the cause of quiet satisfaction. On the field, they were clearly not out of their depth, though there was a worrying note intruding from the accounts book, which showed a £200 loss on a season which had seen gate receipts of £2,587.9s.11d., and an expenditure on wages of £1,434.9s.10d. There had been only one brush with authority, when the FA had censured the club in November over an illegal approach to Wrexham's Welsh international forward Trainer. 1894/5 was barely over, however, before Trainer was legitimately signed for the next assault on the promotion goal.

1895 - 96

The omens looked good for Fosse after their inaugural near-miss, but events were soon to sour. Near-neighbours and old rivals Loughborough had joined Fosse in Division Two, guaranteeing a couple of derby fixtures, and there were five new players in the opening line-up, prepared for the fray by a new trainer, Joe Newton. In fact, Fosse had celebrated a double over the Luffs by the middle of November (5-0 at home and 4-1 away), but there had been few other victories to cheer, and in that month secretary Lee resigned. He was presented with a gold medal by the players, with whom he had been extremely popular, and replaced by former West Bromwich Albion administrator Henry 'Swin' Jackson.

Quite what was going on in the background was unclear, as regular half-back Arthur Henrys was twice suspended by the committee for indiscipline, but it was evident that Fosse had lost their on-field consistency. A win over champions-to-be Liverpool and a draw at Woolwich Arsenal were followed seven days later by a humbling home FA Cup exit at the hands of Midland Leaguers Kettering.

Fosse were removed from three lesser cup competitions in January, and only climbed to mid-table League

respectability with a revival in March which coincided with the return of old hero Billy Dorrell. Dorrell in fact missed his train to the home fixture with Rotherham Town, in which a reshuffled Fosse scored eight without reply (Trainer belatedly coming good with a nap hand), but he was unfortunate enough to be present at Grimsby for the season's final game, when leading scorer William McArthur was experimented with at centre-half, and the Mariners' hot-shot Tommy McCairns helped himself to a six-goal haul from a 1-7 debacle.

The reserves again took the championship of the Leics. & Northants League, but their triumph was a little hollow, as only nine teams competed, and the league itself was disbanded in May. Fosse's home ground was chosen to host the FA Amateur Cup final on March 28th, when Bishop Auckland scraped a 1-0 win over Royal Artillery (Portsmouth). Finally, it was noted that the finances were getting little better: gate receipts had dropped by over £200, and the players' wage bill had risen by almost the same amount. May 25th saw Fosse promote a Sports Day, one of many such fund-raising events held during this period.

Fosse in 1890's action (opposite & below):
note the first Filbert Street members' stand.
*(Inset: An 1895 **Season Ticket**.)*

1896 - 97

New faces abounded as Fosse anticipated their third season of League combat. Club President Frank Ashwell stepped down from office (six months before his death in December 1896) and was replaced by J.F.L.Rolleston, while club trainer Joe Newton departed for Dundee. Six new players graced the Fosse line-up for the opening game against Darwen, and three of them got on the scoresheet in a 4-1 win, on the first occasion that neutral linesmen became mandatory.

Poor away form soon scuttled hopes of a promotion challenge, though, and a mid-table placing was on the cards from early in the season. All too typical inconsistency saw League victories over higher placed Newton Heath and Newcastle (5-0) bracketing a second successive Cup surrender to Kettering, for whom Fossil-to-be Alf Ball claimed a crucial goal.

Wages for the team who took Fosse to their lowest-yet placing of 9th were now up to £1,834, while gate receipts had fallen again to £2,344, with 10% of that total accounted for by the Christmas Day home derby with Loughborough (who were again dispatched home and away). A week-long Bazaar had been organised by the club at the Floral Hall in October to boost depleted funds, but the only substantial boosts to depleted spirits were the capture of both the Burford and Rushden Cups.

In the former, more highly regarded competition, Fosse humbled Nottingham Forest 3-0 in the semi-final and beat Second Division champions Notts County with two Billy Dorrell goals in the final, while the latter pot was secured with a 4-0 final win over Rushden themselves. Fosse's reserves, meanwhile, had claimed runners-up spot in the Leicestershire Senior League, won by Hinckley Town.

Back at League level, goalkeeper Jimmy Thraves bowed out in February after not having missed a senior game since 1892; and outside-right Willie Freebairn disgraced himself by becoming the first Fossil sent off in the League when he harangued a linesman at Lincoln.

Chatter of a more positive nature came in the early weeks of the close season. There had been several pre-meetings in smoke-filled rooms in the run-up to the club's AGM on May 26th, 1897, at the Temperance Hall, and a substantial motion was on the agenda as a result. Mr.Rolleston chaired the meeting, and from the floor a Mr.Boylan held forth on the failure of the current committee - 'hamstrung by cliques', as he put it - and proposed the setting up of a Limited Company. His motion was seconded by existing committee member S.Hudson, and eventually passed, amidst some acrimonious argument.

1897 - 98

The behind-the-scenes shuffles of the summer meant Fosse now had their first board of directors, with Mr.Hudson in the chair, and a new secretary in William D.Clark, formerly with Derby County. The latter's first innovation was to promote an exhibition game of baseball at Filbert Street - when Crystal Palace met Derby on August 21st - and a series of 100-yard handicap races for footballers, eventually won by Billy Dorrell. When he turned to soccer, it was to put out a reshaped Fosse side as Luton Town's first-ever opponents in the League, but the home draw achieved brought Fosse their sole point from

the first five matches.

Fosse's season thereafter was a matter of fits and starts, with a seven-game unbeaten run putting them back on course for another mid-table finale, though this time in the improved position of 7th. Clark's eye for a novelty led him to precede the Darwen home game with a 440-yard challenge race between Dorrell and visiting American half-miler C.H.Kilpatrick, which won the Fosse flyer £10, but which presumably tired him out for the game in hand, which was lost 0-1.

Only a week or so later, the board's response to

indiscipline and insubordination on the part of some players led to six of them being suspended indefinitely, and indeed several were never again heard of in a Football League context. (The fact that Fosse retained their registrations for that competition suitably indexed the then-pertaining state of 'soccer slavery' professionals found themselves in).

By this time Fosse were out of the FA Cup as well as the hunt for League honours. Though trainer Jackson's special regime for the Cup-tie at Southampton rather charmingly included 'paperchasing', the strong Southern League outfit proved too good on the day of Fosse's first automatic entry to the First Round proper. The Burford Cup was also surrendered during the season (to Nottingham Forest in the final), as was the Rushden trophy (again in the final, but this time to little Wellingborough).

The closing stages of the season were brightened in one regard for Fosse however, when left-half Dick Jones and reserve forward Alfred Watkins together won Welsh caps against Scotland, the first international honours to be won by players while on Fosse's books.

1898 - 99

Transfer activity around the Fosse was, if anything, noticeably less hectic than the close season norm during the summer months of 1898. The departure of trainer Jackson to Brighton United and his replacement by Bob Dunmore initially occasioned more comment than any movement of players. It was therefore quite a surprise just how much dust and dirt was kicked up in the early weeks of September as William Clark's dealings came under official scrutiny.

First, rivals Loughborough charged Fosse with poaching goalkeeper Godfrey Beardsley, but then withdrew the accusation, and accepted £25 and the promise of a friendly game. This climbdown pleased neither the FA, who instigated an enquiry, nor the outvoted chairman and secretary-manager of the Luffs, who both resigned. Fosse director E.A.Marson also resigned, and secretary Clark was suspended pending the FA's findings. But a second bombshell was to fall almost immediately, for Clark had signed former England 'keeper (and more recently Stoke secretary) William Rowley for the opening League game at Lincoln, and had paid him an illegal signing-on fee.

It was October before the FA delivered their judgement. For the Rowley affair, Fosse were fined £10, and both Rowley and Clark were suspended for 12 months from all involvement with football; for their part in the Beardsley matter, Fosse were fined £50, and Clark suspended *sine die*.

Fall-out from these upheavals was still felt some time later, as Fosse chairman S.Hudson resigned in January 1899, and director T.Staines was suspended for eight months from April, when Clark's first appeal against his sentence was unsuccessful. (It was eventually lifted in October, after which Clark took up a post with Burton United).

While all this was going on, replacement secretary George Johnson was marshalling his inherited forces into credible promotion challengers. A run of twelve wins in fifteen games ended in late January with Fosse atop the Second Division chart for the first time ever. A home win over Barnsley actually put them there, though a remarkable 6-1 win at Luton the week before had set them up. That was a game marred by crowd disturbances and attempts by the home fans to assault referee Kingswell; Luton's ground was closed for a fortnight as a result.

Another instance of disciplinary ground closure came to light a fortnight later, for as Fosse were being toppled from their lofty perch with a 0-4 defeat at Gainsborough, Filbert Street hosted another Division Two game, between Loughborough and Blackpool. The long-suffering Luffs' fans had apparently demonstrated their agitation rather too strongly for the FA, and not for the last time were forced to travel to Leicester to watch another 'home' defeat, by 1-3.

Fosse took their best receipts of the season (£344) from the February home game with Manchester City, but the result heralded a series of draws which cost Fosse dear, and it was another draw, at Newton Heath with two games to go, which finally stymied their promotion hopes.

The penultimate game brought an impressive win over New Brighton Tower which killed off that team's hopes, but Fosse finished a point adrift of second-placed Glossop in the first season that automatic promotion and relegation had taken the place of Test Matches. Few were more disappointed than Alfred Watkins, now a regular first-teamer, who turned down a further Welsh cap against Ireland to aid Fosse's cause.

Right-half Alf Ball (ever-present for the second season), Dick Jones and left-back and skipper George Swift were the defensive stalwarts of Fosse's vain struggle, while forwards Tommy Galbraith, Watkins and Rab King all reached double figures on the scoresheet as

Fosse negotiated their first 34-game season with an unbeaten home record. The FA Cup, in which Fosse were forced to plough through the Qualifying rounds once more, brought almost predictable disappointment in the shape of a replay defeat by bogey team Kettering.

A season which had seen Fosse shrug off its backstage embarrassments so well, and come so close to elevation, could surely have no other sequel but a successful promotion bid next time round? Fosse were poised to consult the timetables to First Division venues at the new Great Central Station (opened in March 1899), but, as someone surely must once have said, football's a funny game....

1899 - 1900

Fosse were certainly smiling during the opening weeks of the new season. With only centre-half Herbert Dainty and centre-forward Tommy Brown added to the previous term's squad, the team sailed through the first eleven games without defeat, at which point they were level at the top of the table with Sheffield Wednesday. In fact, the eleventh fixture saw Wednesday as the Filbert Street visitors in front of a record crowd of 12,000 paying customers and several thousand more who got in when the gates gave way.

A goalless draw meant Godfrey Beardsley had only conceded four in eleven games, but it was Wednesday who maintained their momentum throughout the campaign to finish as champions, while Fosse inexplicably fell away to fifth place. They would have finished higher, had it not been for two disastrous final games.

The penultimate match, at home to New Brighton Tower, ended in 1-2 defeat - Fosse's first home reverse in two full seasons - while the final game once more saw the team thrashed at Grimsby. McCairns may have gone, but both Hemingfield and Ratcliffe notched hat-tricks on behalf of the 6-1 victors.

Some Fosse supporters may have been tempted to blame the club's change of colours for the reverse in fortunes - this was the first season that the white shirts and black breeches had given way to an ensemble of Cambridge blue shirts and dark blue shorts - but a lack of punch up front was in the long run costly, and could not be compensated for by a defence which maintained admirable tightness until its familiar collapse at Grimsby.

Even when inside-forward Herbert Lyon was chosen to replace the injured Beardsley in goal for the crucial home fixture with Bolton Wanderers, he kept a clean sheet behind a consistent, experienced set of full and half-backs.

Back on the opening day of the season, Filbert Street had again hosted a Division Two game for the temporarily 'locked out' Loughborough, in which the Luffs had been beaten 2-3 by Bolton Wanderers, and this term unfortunately marked the last round of intra-county rivalry at League level. Fosse were far from the only team to claim a double off the Luffs this season, for their neighbours garnered only one win and eight points from the entire campaign. Finishing rock bottom for the second time in three seasons, Loughborough predictably failed to gain re-election in May, and in fact folded a month or so later, with massive debts. In five seasons of derby games, Fosse had taken 19 of the 20 available League points.

Another pair of notable fixtures at Filbert Street this season were provided first by the friendly encounter with a touring South African side, The Kaffirs (said to consist of "two Hottentots and nine Basutos"), which Fosse won 7-3; and secondly by the FA's choice once more of the Fosse ground for the Amateur Cup final in March, which Bishop Auckland again won, this time by a convincing 5-1 margin against Lowestoft Town.

Fosse's own Cup hopes had again been dashed at the First Round proper stage, when Sheffield United's Beer had claimed the lone goal of the tie, and the massive, 20-stone-plus goalkeeper Willie Foulke barred the way to an equaliser.

1900 - 01

Ground improvements were on the Filbert Street agenda during the summer of 1900, with the pitch being slightly enlarged and the wooden terracing replaced by earthwork banking at what would soon become known, in reference to the hill battle of the Boer War, as the Spion Kop end. But improvements to the playing blend were harder to achieve.

Four new Fosse forwards faced League newcomers Stockport County in the opening fixture of the term, yet the team's goalmouth failings were amplified and accentuated this year. Despite Johnny McMillan and Archie Brash each claiming four goals in a game at different stages, and Tommy Brown notching a hat-trick later, Fosse amassed their lowest goal-haul to date as they slipped to a moribund 11th place. In fact goals were at a premium all round for dedicated Fosse-watchers: the 34 League games produced 39 for and 37 against, and featured 12 matches in which Fosse failed to score at all (including six goalless draws).

Not only chances were getting away. Wragg, McMillan and Henderson were all transferred to Small Heath during the season, and helped the Brummies to promotion, while former Fosse favourite Rab King was quick to rub his ex-comrades' noses in the mud with a strike in Glossop's 3-1 win.

In a campaign that took an unexpected mid-season break in late January and early February - as the entire fixture list was cancelled for two weeks following the death of Queen Victoria - the only thing Fosse were first to do was complete their calendar.

George Swift marked yet another ever-present record by scoring from the half-way line in the season's-best 5-0 win over Walsall, and Brown completed his triple in this match by dribbling round an over-adventurous goalkeeper at the same spot and proceeding unmolested to the goal-line.

Only one goal came from close season signing Harry Hammond, but in fairness he was sidelined for nearly six months after his transfer with typhoid fever, and did not make his debut until the FA Cup tie at Nottingham Forest, which the Reds won easily by 5-1, with the help of a Calvey hat-trick.

One honour came the way of a Fossil this season, but right-back Mick Cochrane was perhaps not in any mood to celebrate it. The former Distillery player was chosen at left-half to win his eighth cap for Ireland, but Scotland rather spoilt his day by winning 11-0 in Glasgow!

1901 - 02

Change, perhaps inevitably, was in the air after Fosse's recent disappointments. Nationally, the maximum wage for professional footballers at League level had come into force, and allowed only a £10 signing-on fee, a wage of no more than £4 per week, and no match bonuses whatsoever. Against this background, Fosse's directorate, through secretary George Johnson, announced they would follow a policy of assembling a 'cheaper' team than had been the case with the previous term's collection of 'stars'. (Leicester businessmen knew all about relativity before Einstein theorised it!). Additionally, the Fosse team would appear in new strip; a rather attractive two-tone combination of dark blue shirts with light blue collars and sleeves, and white knickers.

The campaign began with a routine series of home wins and away defeats, but form in general was uninspired, home gates fell fairly alarmingly (a late December fixture with West Brom attracted an all-too-characteristic 2,034 patrons), and Fosse soon languished nearer the bottom of the table than the top. Indeed, they were to finish in fourteenth place, not far enough above the re-election places for total comfort.

*The **Fosse Sports** were a major local attraction by the turn of the century. This programme was for the 11th such event - held this time on the county cricket ground at Aylestone Road.*

December saw a first-hurdle FA Cup exit (in the Intermediate Round) at the hands of Glossop, for whom veteran player-manager John Goodall scored the only goal; and also the indefinite suspension of Tommy Brown, for a serious breach of Fosse's training rules.

Fosse's lack of firepower was illuminated in March in the home game with Blackpool: the visitors' goalkeeper missed his train, their secretary T.A.Barcroft stood in between the sticks, and only a long-range fluke by George Swift beat him all afternoon. The first-team forwards even failed when Fosse and Barnsley agreed to play the nominal Midland League reserve games between them at full strength; a goalless draw and a 0-6 defeat resulted, though the Tykes did provide Fosse with their only double at normal Second Division level.

Desperation was evident in several spheres. Not only were several local youngsters and amateurs inappropriately boosted into the League fray, but the club also felt the need for a little gimmickry in presentation. On April 26th an exhibition friendly with Kettering was played over 30 minutes each way, and followed by an archery tournament!

Forward Rab King, in his second spell with the club, and left-half Arthur Roulston were Fosse's ever-presents, but no-one overtook the meagre total of nine goals collected by Tommy Brown before his suspension.

1902 - 03

Under new trainer Alick Stewart, who had scored for Burnley against Fosse the previous season, a Leicester side which featured seven new faces, and included an entire forward line making its debut, fell to an inauspicious home defeat by Small Heath on the campaign's opening day. After five games had brought only one win - and that, against Burnley, aided by another flukey up-and-under from the half-way line by full-back Andrew Mills - it was clear that Fosse's decline had yet to bottom out.

There were spasmodic signs of recovery, especially when Tommy Brown returned to become top scorer, but consistency was always elusive, and Fosse ended the term grateful for a marginal improvement in their away form. Finishing in the dangerously low position of fifteenth, their record included five wins both at Filbert Street and on their travels.

One away win, by 3-1 at Burnley, would have been more comprehensive had not a shot by Tom Simpson hit a stray dog on the goal-line and rebounded clear; while another, 2-1 at Glossop, was prompted by an opening goal and inspirational performance from trainer Stewart, coaxed out of retirement for the occasion. This latter game, incidentally, was the only one of the final seven fixtures in which Fosse managed to score at all. Luckily, three goalless draws closed the campaign, and the point so gained in the penultimate match, at home to Lincoln, finally ensured Fosse's avoidance of a re-election slot.

The Cup brought no relief from Fosse's misery. It was back to the Qualifying rounds route this time out, and while Fosse squeezed through on a roped-off, standless field at Irthlingborough, they then departed the slightly less modest surroundings of Wellingborough with jeers ringing in their ears after a ludicrous 1-4 defeat, marked by Andrew Mills' second penalty miss in two weeks.

Injuries took their toll of Fosse's already fairly ragged forces: Mills was sidelined after being carried off during a Welsh international trial in February; while promising triallist Sandy Simpson broke his collarbone in a reserve game at Whitwick, and attendant Fosse director Tom Collins reacted with such 'improper conduct' that he was subsequently suspended for a month by the FA.

Fosse reserves in fact did nothing to alleviate the Filbert Street gloom: in their fourth season in the Midland League, they ended rock bottom for the second time, and subsequently withdrew to the less strenuous competition of the Leicestershire Senior League.

The standard contract for all footballers in pre-World War One days was a one-year affair, from 1st May to 30th April. This accounted for the frequent wholesale changes of playing staff from one season to another.
*This example was for **Tom Belton** in 1903.*

Fosse tried a new change of kit as 1903-04 got underway - turning out for the first time in the blue shirts/white shorts ensemble we now think of as traditional - but they met with little change in fortune. Despite the presence of a new on-field 'general' in veteran Scottish international Jimmy Blessington, League form dipped from bad to worse.

It was November, and the tenth fixture, before a win was recorded, and that, surprisingly, away from home at Blackpool. Already, a stinging 0-8 reverse had been experienced at Woolwich Arsenal, where future Fossil Tommy Shanks had helped himself to a hat-trick, and it was not long before a former Fossil, Johnny McMillan, repeated the feat for Bradford City.

Fosse's mixture of ageing veterans and callow youngsters could hardly be called a blend, and Second Division sides ruthlessly exploited the team's lack of defensive cohesion. Glossop's Goodall, Preston's P.J.Smith and Lincoln's O'Donnell were others to plunder hat-tricks as Fosse slumped to the bottom of the table and there took root until the season's end.

The board voted to extend its composition from seven to ten members in February as they desperately cast around for an infusion of ideas and capital; all they got however, was an early lesson of how a football team often gets kicked when it's down, as respected amateur full-back Ernest Vickerstaffe was drafted in for the away match at Burslem Port Vale, and promptly suffered a serious leg-break on his debut. In December, Fosse had fought for a 2-1 lead at Manchester United, only for the game to be abandoned 12 minutes from time because of fog. By the time the rematch was played in April, Fosse had already known for three weeks they would have to seek re-election.

They had no FA Cup run to point to in mitigation: while Market Harborough had been slammed to the tune of double figures, and revenge extracted from Wellingborough, a three-game marathon with Burton United, abandoned during extra-time in the Leicester replay, was finally settled in the Brewers' favour on Derby County's ground.

Yet Fosse clearly had the goodwill of most of the football community. Only a single vote went against them in the League's re-election poll, which they topped with 33 votes. Glossop were also re-elected with 27 votes, but Stockport County, who had finished two League places above Leicester, garnered only 11 responses to Doncaster Rovers' 21, and lost their status to the Yorkshiremen. Crewe Alexandra, with 10 votes, were the other unsuccessful candidates.

Fosse sighed with relief at their reprieve, and George Johnson set about the annual task of rebuilding the senior squad on an almost wholesale basis. Goalkeeper Walter Smith had been a promising discovery of the previous term, but in front of him on the opening day at Blackpool were no less than seven newcomers, including former England centre-half Billy Bannister. Two days later, a friendly at Northampton spelt the beginning and end of the Fosse career of young outside-left A.Sullivan, who broke his collarbone in this sole appearance.

Overall, though, there was a slight upswing in Fosse's fortunes. The fans were slow to rally round as Fosse battled to a mid-table slot, and there was a falling-away in results once survival appeared secure, but a final placing of fourteenth at least showed the corner had been turned. Fighting spirit manifested itself in several ways; though not all were positive, as Walter Robinson (at Barnsley) and both Bob Pollock and Ike Evenson (at Bolton) were sent off in the course of the campaign. The severely-depleted Fosse (Hubbard was stretchered off in the same game!) still though managed a valuable win at Burnden.

The defence was again too charitable on occasions: Liverpool's Robinson scored all four at Anfield, and Manchester United's Peddie and Preston's O'Donnell (for the second season running) helped themselves to hat-tricks, while Fosse had only Evenson as a three-goal man in the League this season.

ARTHUR COLLINS

Saw Fosse through their struggles after the turn of the century before moving to Fulham in July 1905. He later returned to play for the club during World War One.

There were, however, goals galore in the FA Cup, from which Fosse at last earned a bit of giant-killing glory. The Qualifying run started with another ten-goal hammering of minnows (Linby Church on this occasion), and eventually led Fosse into an Intermediate Round encounter at West Bromwich Albion. The form book suggested an easy passage for the Baggies, but Fosse overturned it with a superb 5-2 away victory. Three of their goals came in a whirlwind four minutes, and 'Pecker' Mounteney completed a hat-trick in 16 minutes. The subsequent draw for the First Round proper was hardly kind to Fosse, though, and they bowed out at that stage by 1-5 to a still-aristocratic Aston Villa in front of 26,091 at Villa Park.

Fosse's own gates were, however, still too low to make economic sense of League competition, and Director W.H.Squires wrote an open letter to the 'Leicester Mercury' in January inviting stay-away grumblers to put their money where their mouths were. This was somewhat ironically mocked only days later when the FA added to Fosse's financial woes by fining the club one guinea. This nominal penalty was also levied on Bolton Wanderers after some over-zealous official had noted that when the two teams met at Filbert Street in December, the players' knickers had been too short - an arcane rule of the time demanded they cover the knees!

As ever, a concerned group of fans were keen to assist the club through its monetary travails. In May 1905, George Johnson addressed the subscribers of the Fosse Supporters Fund, and explained the vicious circle in which the poverty-stricken club was apparently trapped. Basically, Fosse had to borrow to pay summer wages (when there was no gate income) and, therefore, always in debt at the start of the season, were unable to invest in players to fill any weak spots that might become noticeable. Yet only playing success could tip the balance sheet into the black. Maybe next year...?

1905 - 06

Division Two was extended to a twenty-club competition for the new season, and one of the newcomers, Clapton Orient, travelled to Leicester for their inaugural League game, only to be sent away on the wrong end of an inhospitable 2-1 scoreline. Fosse remarkably found the weather against them the next week, as they splashed through 75 minutes at Burnley before the referee called a halt. A few nervy performances followed - including the gifting of their first League win to newly-elected Leeds City - before Fosse got into an unaccustomed points-gathering stride.

In fact, a seven-match unbeaten run either side of Christmas raised hopes of a genuine promotion challenge, and a further eight-game spell without defeat from late January to mid-March kept Fosse on the fringes of the race. However, hopes were pitched too high, and a subsequent miserable haul of only two points from the final seven games saw the club finish in a creditable but disappointing seventh place.

The rot set in when Bradford City visited Leicester, brought 3,000 supporters with them on their 'annual club trip', and escaped with a 4-2 win, courtesy of a hat-trick from Wallace Smith, himself later to join Fosse. A further hat-trick the following week by Manchester United's Peddie (for the second successive season) merely emphasised Fosse's frailties at a time when they should have been gearing up for a final challenge.

By far their best performance of the season had come with a win at Ashton Gate in February. Bristol City were runaway divisional champions, and this defeat by a ten-man team (Oakes being badly injured) was the only one they suffered all term after the opening fixture.

Close-season signing Harry Ashby, at right-back, was a significant success in a consistent Fosse defence which featured centre-half Bannister and goalkeeper Smith as ever-presents, while up front it was left to local youngster 'Ranji' Hubbard to claim the lion's share of the goalscoring burden.

Fosse's Cup exploits of the previous season had won them immunity from the Qualifying competition this time round, but the draw was again unkind, pitting them against Liverpool at Anfield. A ding-dong battle ensued, which Fosse lost 1-2, but not before Walter Smith had distinguished himself by saving two penalties, and Bannister had blotted his copybook by missing one for Fosse.

WALTER SMITH

An early example of the club's great goalkeeping traditions, he excelled in the 1906 FA Cup tie at Anfield and was sold in the summer to Manchester City for a club record fee of £600.

1906 - 07

Before the new season got underway, Walter Smith had departed to Manchester City for a welcome incoming record fee of £600, and Tal Lewis, better known as a Somerset cricketer, took up his place between the Fosse sticks. Other new faces to bolster an optimistically resurgent Fosse included left-back Joe Blackett, wing-half Billy Leech, and forwards Harry Wilcox and Frank Middleton, with Irish schemer Tommy Shanks being added to the squad in October.

A nine-point haul from the opening five games registered notice of intent on Fosse's part and established them amongst the early divisional leaders. The crowds flocked back at this hint of success and, for once, Fosse maintained much of their momentum. They were beaten just once at home all season, and then only in their final Filbert Street fixture, when champions Nottingham Forest lowered their colours by the odd goal of three. But eventually Leicester had to be satisfied with third place, nine points behind runners-up Chelsea.

The lack of a consistent marksman was the main factor in keeping Fosse down. Wilcox was the only forward to reach a double-figure tally, with 14. The defence was generally sound, with 'keeper Lewis an ever-present in his only Fosse campaign. Harry Ashby was the unluckiest Fossil of the season; a broken leg sustained at Hull in March brought his career to a tragically premature conclusion.

Fosse had to travel again in the Cup - they had still yet to be drawn at home in the competition proper since becoming a League club, despite qualifying on seven occasions - and this time returned from Sunderland well beaten by 1-4.

The reserve side were once again the club's only trophy-winners. They had now spent four seasons in the Leicestershire Senior League, and this year completed a hat-trick of successive championship titles, after an initial term in the runners-up spot behind Loughborough Corinthians. Henceforth, they would compete again in the stronger Midland League.

The upsurge of interest in Fosse's League challenge was reflected in the accounts book at the end of the term, when a club record profit of £1,167 was announced. Leicester fans now looked forward to seeing it wisely invested in additional players who could take their club at least one placing higher in the League table next year, and on to the heights of the First Division.

1907 - 08

There was a staunch conviction in the air that this would be Leicester Fosse's year. Season-ticket sales had run at an all-time record, quality new players in the shape of left-back Harry Thorpe and forwards Jimmy Donnelly and Percy Humphreys had been signed up, and commerce climbed aboard the anticipated bandwagon. Clothiers W.H.Thompson of Granby Street offered a free mackintosh to the best Fosse player of each month - a change of tack, as their previous offer of a coat for each first-team hat-trick had remained unclaimed for two seasons!

The Great Central Railway now offered regular rail excursions to away matches (a day return fare of 2s.9d to Grimsby was typical), and local publishers, Messrs.Hill Brothers of Gallowtree Gate, even attempted to launch a weekly sports paper called 'Half Time' onto a market already saturated by three local dailies, the 'Post', the 'Mail' and the 'Mercury'. 'Half Time' itself only lasted until Christmas, but hardly endeared itself to Fosse fans in the interim with an editorial suggestion that the club follow a policy of signing only local players, and withdraw entirely from the transfer market!

Fosse certainly kicked off full of self-belief. They lost only one of their first eleven games, but then wavered a little. An exchange deal brought popular centre-forward Fred Shinton from West Brom to stiffen the challenge - after a bid for Middlesbrough's Steve Bloomer had failed - and even though the free-scoring Humphreys was allowed to move to Chelsea in February for £350 (the amount of a short-lived ceiling on fees imposed by the League), and illness removed Thorpe from the fray, Fosse were by then into unstoppable stride.

They only lost once in their final eighteen games as they pressed towards the promotion target, but nevertheless, a top-two placing was always tantalisingly out of their grasp, and Fosse were still in third position after the final scheduled Saturday of the season, behind Bradford City and Oldham Athletic, but with a game in hand.

Bradford, whom Fosse had already thrashed 5-1 away (a feat which earned them a brass band reception back in Leicester), were sure of the championship with 54 points. Oldham, whom Fosse had held to a crucial draw on the previous Tuesday at Boundary Park, were on 50 points with a goal average of 1.809. Fosse also had 50 points, but a lesser goal average of 1.511. They also had to face Stoke, away from home on Monday 27th April - needing at least a point to reach their cherished goal.

As it turned out, they claimed both points from the nail-biter at Stoke, thanks to a solitary goal from Tommy Shanks and a characteristically solid performance from newly capped England 'keeper Horace Bailey. By the time the Fosse party arrived back at the Midland Station in

LEICESTER FOSSE F.C. DIRECTORS 1908
Back : F.W.Wright, W.E.Stevens, W.Smith, O.J.Wright, J.S.Blackwell.
Front : S.W.Matthews, F.C.Norman, W.H.Squires (Chairman), G.Johnson (Secretary), E.J.Benn.

Leicester at 10.25 that evening, the surrounding streets overflowed with a delirious throng, and the players were cheered and sung to for hours as they negotiated London Road and celebrated at The Grand Hotel.

The promotion effort was a triumph for professionalism - the players had been taken away to sample the restful delights of such places as Matlock, Quorn, Skegness and Hornsea before important matches - yet the season had not been without its reminders that the pre-World War One game belonged to a different world. Fosse had started the match at Barnsley in December with only ten men - Fred Shinton arrived on a delayed train in time to play only the last 60 minutes! They had also played several matches without star goalkeeper Bailey - never thinking of denying him the chance of an amateur cap, and thereby innocently contributing to his rapid elevation to the full England team. Furthermore, amidst all the relatively high financial dealing of the season, the board saw fit to award the takings of the home League

game with Grimsby to stalwart defender Bob Pollock as his benefit payment.

The Cup might well have proved a costly diversion this season, so there were few tears shed when Fosse made a dignified exit in the Second Round, and were left to concentrate on their League challenge. They had proved a point to themselves by toppling First Division Blackburn Rovers, and took consolation that the Portsmouth goal which defeated them at Fratton Park was scored very much against the run of play.

Ultimately, there would seem to be no more appropriate way to close comment on this happy season than to quote the self-conscious hyperbole of 'Old Fossil' from the May 2nd edition of the 'Leicester Daily Post':

"In port! Tempest-tossed and weather-beaten, the stout old barque of the Fosse F.C. has at long last negotiated the shoals and rocks of the Second League, and reached a land of smiling promise - Division One."

1908 - 09

About 15,000 spectators gathered at Filbert Street on September 1st for their initial glimpse of Fosse in First Division action, and saw a goal from Jimmy Donnelly earn a point from a 1-1 draw with Sheffield Wednesday. Fosse's first win came almost three weeks later, at Preston, but already a cloud had shadowed the sunny prospect of the season. Full-back Harry Thorpe had failed to recover from the illness he contracted during the promotion push, and had died on September 15th at his Chesterfield home. He was buried by many of his former team-mates.

Lesser omens of gloom also accumulated. Former Liverpool half-back Jim Gorman was injured on his debut at Manchester City and sidelined for many months, while former England goalgetter Billy Garraty failed to settle at all with Fosse, and soon moved on. Amateur forward Sidney Owen was often kept out of the reckoning by business commitments, and it was soon clear that the oft-changed team would not set the Division alight.

On a brighter note, 'keeper Horace Bailey took time out in October to help the United Kingdom to gold-medal victory in the Olympic Games football tournament.

What really darkened the horizon, though, was the appalling run of results from late November, when Fosse picked up only three draws from a run of fourteen matches without a win. Not unnaturally, this sequence sent Fosse to the bottom of the table (prompting a programme request that spectators not barrack the players), and a brief revival in March was not sustained enough to lift them from the wooden spoon position. New centre-half and captain Andy Aitken inspired this flurry, and was rewarded at the end of the season with the post of player-manager, but he had arrived rather too late to substantially alter Fosse's fate.

Instant relegation was settled long before the fixtures were finished; but it would not have been characteristic of a Leicester team to merely accept their destiny quietly. On April 17th, they beat Cup finalists Manchester United 3-2, a week before United beat Bristol City to take the trophy. Then, only four days later, Fosse contested (if that's the right word) the game which put them into the record books for all the wrong reasons.

Nottingham Forest put twelve goals past a bewildered Bailey, and might have had more but for a spectacular display by the custodian; there was certainly little in the display of the ten men in front of him to pose a credible barrier to the Trentsiders' plundering, which featured hat-tricks from each of Spouncer, Hooper and West. Questions were bound to be asked after such a lacklustre display, meaningless though the result may have been in League placing terms, and it was the Football League that asked them, hastily convening a commission at Leicester's Grand Hotel, chaired by J.J.Bentley.

HORACE BAILEY
An Olympic gold medallist, he turned in a gallant goalkeeping display as Fosse suffered their record 12-0 defeat at Forest, and then represented the players at the subsequent enquiry.

The answers presented by Fosse's representatives (secretary George Johnson, director Orson Wright, and players Horace Bailey and George Hedley) centred on the fact that the Fosse team had rather overdone the celebrations on the day before the game, after former team-mate 'Leggy' Turner - recently transferred to Everton - had got married in Leicester. Accordingly, the League accepted that their dozy performance by the Trent could be put down to a collective hangover.

Other oddities peppered this season. Back in October, Fosse met Blackburn Rovers at Peel Croft, Burton in a floodlit game. This experimental friendly, which Rovers won 3-1, was Fosse's first experience of night-time football, played "by the light of electric arc lamps suspended around and *over* the ground". Then the Fosse reserves experienced a unique case of a referee's ignorance being officially acknowledged. Their away Midland League fixture with Sheffield Wednesday had to be replayed in its entirety after the official had awarded Fosse a last-minute penalty and then blown for time before it could be taken.

Fosse's pot-hunting aspirations drew mixed success this year. They got past Watford after a replay in the FA Cup, then drew 22,000 to Filbert Street for the Second Round tie with Derby County, who spoilt the party with a 2-0 win. A relaxed Fosse did, however, pick up the Bass Charity Vase in April, with a 2-0 final victory over Southern League Coventry City.

Little, though, could compensate for the loss of top-flight status for which the club had waited so long. 'Old Fossil', still waxing lyrical, but now in mournful vein, should once more have the last word on Fosse's predicament :*"Brief and transient has been their period of exaltation, and woeful their experience"* ....

ANDY AITKEN
This early cigarette card features Fosse's Scottish international , appointed player-manager in April 1909.

1909 - 10

The close season of 1909 was marked by a new spirit of activism amongst members of the Players' Union, and when negotiations over a limited form of freedom of contract met a stonewall from League representatives, a strike was threatened. As the due date for the campaign's opening drew near, each club's players were asked to declare their loyalty to their employers and the FA, and Fosse's less-than-radical professional muster duly complied - though the mooted strike itself never materialised.

Such matters hardly impinged, then, on Fosse's preparations for a renewed attempt to struggle out of the Second Division. Full-backs Billy Henry and Dick Pudan and forwards Fred Threlfall and John Lang joined the senior squad under the supervision of new player-manager Andy Aitken and trainer Harley Thompson, but there was never quite enough conviction to Fosse's challenge for the top spots.

They notched up some impressive results, and Fred Shinton alone claimed four hat-tricks during the season, but there was yet again a serious tailing-off in form over the latter stages, with not a single win coming from the last nine games, and Fosse eventually trailed in 5th, some nine points behind the three teams separated by goal average immediately above.

An early home victory over Clapton Orient was enlivened by the unedifying half-time spectacle of an Orient player fighting a spectator, while a Filbert Street goal-feast around Christmas time brought eighteen goals for Fosse in three games, half of them in a 9-1 mauling of Gainsborough Trinity, who lost their goalkeeper when the score was a mere 5-1. Dave Walker bagged four goals in this game, which also contributed one of top-scorer Shinton's trebles. Old Fosse goalkeeper Teddy Daw came out of retirement for the game at Stockport, but rustily conceded six.

The FA Cup provided the highlights of the season, though, with Fosse reaching the giddy heights of the quarter-finals (Round Four) after never previously having attained the Third Round. A fine 4-1 win at Birmingham started the run, then Fosse collected receipts of £565 and a 3-2 win from the home tie with First Division Bury. A trip to Southern League Leyton, for whom ex-Fossil Jamie Durrant was now starring, produced a 1-0 win, but Fosse finally exited at St. James' Park, where Newcastle gradually wore down a Leicester side reduced to ten men after Shirley Hubbard broke his collarbone, and added two late goals to their opener for a 3-0 victory. The Magpies went on to win the Cup.

Otherwise, interest briefly shifted to the international arena, where Sidney Owen claimed several amateur caps for England as a goalscorer, and where Andy Aitken revived his Scotland career at centre-half in their 2-0 beating of the Auld Enemy.

1910 - 11

Tragedy clouded Fosse's preparations for the new campaign. They were determined not to overreach themselves in the transfer market, but had pulled off a useful looking deal by persuading the 33-year-old former Wolves and West Brom centre-half Ted Pheasant to sign in July. However, within two weeks of his transfer, Pheasant died of peritonitis in Leicester Infirmary.

With the due period of mourning over, minds had to be concentrated once more on the game. At first, with Andy Aitken leaving himself out of the team to give Teddy King a run of games in the pivotal position, Fosse looked as if they might put together a renewed promotion challenge. They claimed six victories from the opening nine games, but soon slumped alarmingly. Neither of the new forwards, Jack Hall nor George Travers, showed much firepower, and Fosse were soon forced into blooding a set of local youngsters of decidedly variable quality.

Results accordingly see-sawed, even when crowd favourite Fred Shinton returned from a brief spell with Bolton Wanderers, until the by now traditional end of season slump saw only one win garnered from the final eight games. A placing of 15th left Fosse only five points above the re-election zone. With such a lack of charisma about the side, it was something of a surprise when Andy Aitken was awarded his final two Scottish caps during the campaign and, indeed, entrusted with his national side's captaincy against England, shortly before announcing his impending homeward return.

There was little cheer from the Cup this year, either. Southampton were despatched at Filbert Street in front of a 13,500 crowd, but First Division Middlesbrough disappointed 14,000 Leicester fans with a replay win in extra time after Fosse had returned from Ayresome with a goalless draw. Faithful goalkeeper Jonty Starbuck stood down after this game, to be replaced by well-travelled Fred Mearns, whom Fosse secured in an exchange deal with Barnsley which saw Travers depart.

Meanwhile Fosse reserves were seemingly intent on mirroring their seniors' in-and-out form: on the final day of October they walloped Worksop by 8-0, with Tommy Benfield netting six; while three days later they succumbed to Barnsley reserves by 2-9. They performed a home-and-away double over Chesterfield, then languishing in the Midland League after failing re-election in 1909, yet finished only two places off the bottom of the table.

Pretty much at a loss to explain Leicester failings this year was chairman W.H.Squires, though he had his own lengthy weekly column in the local 'Mail', headlined 'Doings of the Fosse', in which to try.

1911 - 12

Mr.Squires, with his column now redubbed 'Fosse Fancies', never quite resorted to the old football cliche on this being a season of two halves, but he would have been justified in doing so. None of the four experienced imports who saw Fosse to a deceptive opening burst of two wins were in the side by the end of the season, for a dangerous nosedive in results up to the turn of the year prompted the directors, now back in charge of team selection, to declare a policy of pinning their faith on youth, and it was a predominantly locally-recruited squad who saw Fosse to the safety of 10th place.

By early February, Fosse had just completed a run of eleven League games without a win, and were out of the Cup. As if this were not enough, the directors were prompted to their public policy statement by a couple of other events in January. On the 5th, long-serving secretary George Johnson announced his resignation to concentrate on his printing business, leaving director S.Scattergood to take up the reins on a *pro tem* basis, and only a day later Fosse were involved in a bizarre spectacle at Grimsby.

In appalling conditions of rain, sleet and gale-force wind, the referee refused to do the expected and abandon the game, which had turned into a farce with 15 minutes left and Grimsby holding a single-goal lead. At this point King and Thompson left the field exhausted, to be followed five minutes later by Harper, Clay and Rollinson, and in the final minute Allman joined them in the shelter of the dressing room, leaving only five Fossils on the pitch. Unsurprisingly, the game ended in a 4-0 win for Grimsby, and there was an equally inevitable sequel when the League ordered an enquiry. Each of the six players was fined £5, but more controversially, trainer Harley Thompson was suspended for two months for allegedly enticing them off. This apparent injustice followed hard on the FA suspension of Fosse's young Cockney forward Billy Mills for having dared to play football on a Sunday.

The Cup ties of January were also to have a longer-term effect on Fosse. They found themselves two down away to Southern League side Croydon Common before fighting back to draw, and though they took the replay honours by 6-1, they had been mightily impressed by the opposition. They soon signed centre-forward Harry Sparrow, arranged a further friendly meeting, and then on March 20th appointed 34-year-old Croydon boss John William Bartlett as their new secretary-manager - the youngest in the League. An advertisement for the post in the 'Athletic News' had brought 102 applications, but Mr.Laing of Darlington was the only other candidate interviewed at the Fosse offices; then still in Stanley Chambers, Gallowtree Gate, rather than at the ground.

Fosse had in the interim experienced their Cup exit at Barnsley, where full-back Sam Currie had a penalty saved, but revived admirably in the League thanks largely to the efforts of right-back Tommy Clay, inside-forward Fred Osborn, and wingers Tommy Benfield and George Harrison.

There were also a couple of minor talking points thrown up this season. Back in September, there had been much muttering over crowd behaviour: seven Chelsea supporters had been arrested on breach of the peace charges after the match at Filbert Street. Officials were also in the news; the Croydon Common Cup ties had been refereed by Mr.J.Talks, who at 4ft.9ins. was the smallest on the senior list, while the whistler for the home game with Hull failed to put in an appearance until half-time. His role was assumed by a linesman, and that gentleman's flag taken over by Wallace Smith, the former Fosse forward, then on Hull's injury list. Finally, the season was extended into May for the first time when a series of friendlies for the Titanic Disaster Fund were sanctioned by the FA. Fosse drew 3-3 with a Leicestershire XI in helping to boost the charitable coffers.

1912 - 13

New boss Bartlett had begun recruiting players to his squad before the 1911/12 season was over, and it was perhaps to be expected that a combination of Fosse's budgetary stringency and his own background should lead him to concentrate on men from both professional and amateur non-League circles in the South. However, his reshaping of the Second Division team paid few dividends, and this was very much a campaign of struggle for Fosse.

Right-half Douglas McWhirter (an Olympic gold-medallist from his summer jaunt in Stockholm) and, later, winger George Douglas and centre-half Jim Harrold (both also England amateur internationals) were among the few Bartlett signings who convincingly made the step up to the demands of League football. Once more it was predominantly a case of the locally-produced stars keeping Fosse's heads above the water-line of the re-election zone. Fred Osborn was top scorer with 14 goals, and George Harrison the only ever-present, but both were snapped up at season's end by First Division clubs, with the former going to Preston and the latter to Everton, on his way to England recognition.

Fosse had few alternatives but to sell their most valuable players. Attendances had fallen again, to the point

—AND "CROWDS" AT LEICESTER.

—for our "Dollar" or "Double Dollar" Prize.

The Victorious Preston Team.

Taylor, the Preston Goalie.

Sparrow, the Fosse Centre, gets in some clever head work.

Mearns, the 'home' goalie.

"more RINGS"

There was a record number of copies of "Lotinga's" in the crowd, and wherever our camera pointed they were held aloft for the "Double Dollar." Unfortunately, some of the enthusiasts, in the excitement of the moment, held the paper *in front* of their faces, making identification impossible.

—(with photo and autograph) in NEXT week's issue.

EXCLUSIVE PICTURES OF THE PLAY—

See if you and your friend are ringed—

The Fosse Team.

EXCLUSIVE PICTURES BY OUR OWN PHOTOGRAPHERS

A shot a track on the Fosse goal. Mearns (the goalie) clears with difficulty.

Dollar & Double Dollar Winners

Above is the result of our photographer's visit to Leicester on Saturday, on the occasion of the "Fosse's" match with Preston North End. The "home" supporters were provided with a capital game, the only drawback being the result—3-0 in favour of Preston North End.

—"Celebrities" in EVERY sport give their experiences—

where an appeal was made to season-ticket holders to voluntarily pay at the gate for the final two home games, to help alleviate the financial straits. The loss on the season was £634, contributing to an alarming accumulated deficit of around £7,700.

There had certainly been few Filbert Street highlights to attract the fans. Osborn shot four past Stockport, but the season was on its last legs by then. Cup hopes had been extinguished at the first glimmer. Southern League Norwich City had already given Fosse a scare when the first attempt to play the tie was aborted after 65 minutes in the midst of a snowstorm, with the game goalless. But Fosse failed to take the hint in the re-match, as they slid on a treacherous surface to a humiliating 1-4 defeat.

One rather cruel commentator claimed that the best football seen all season at Leicester had been that played in the benefit match held on behalf of former secretary George Johnson on March 6th, when First Division Bradford City had beaten Steve Bloomer's XI of all-stars by 2-0.

Fosse's fortunes, in both monetary and metaphorical terms, may have been at a low ebb in the summer of 1913, but spirits were briefly raised by an invitation for the club to undertake its first ever foreign tour. Whether because of their residual reputation, or simply because they had just given a season's worth of competitive

(reserve and friendly) football to international wing-half Karl Gustafssen, Fosse were offered an all-expenses-paid trip to Sweden by that country's FA, and set off on June 16th for a 46-hour sea-and-rail journey to Gothenburg and a whirlwind five-match tour.

What looked suspiciously like over-confidence at the outset actually paid off, for while Fosse took only eleven players (plus three directors) on the exhausting jaunt, and played their first game only two hours after arrival, they managed to avoid injuries and completed their schedule with five straight wins in ten days, culminating in a second 4-2 victory over the full Swedish international side at Rosunda, where Prince Eugene was amongst the crowd. New forward Mortimer scored in every game; all the matches were refereed by Danish international Nils Middleboe (just about to commence a nine-year playing career at Chelsea); and arrangements were made for another young Swedish international, H.Ekroth, to follow Gustafssen's path to Filbert Street during the following season.

Fosse clearly enjoyed their spell as ambassadors of English football, and the diversion was adjudged a diplomatic triumph, even if the FA at home - suspiciously aware of Fosse's otherwise impecunious circumstances - took some of the icing off the cake by demanding to see a full set of expense accounts when the party returned!

1913 - 14

Fosse at least made a bit of publicity capital out of their dire financial situation. As the season got underway, they were known nationally as 'The £105 Team', for only three members of their early selections had cost a fee: Sparrow £90, Mills £5, and newcomer Tom Waterall £10. Ironically, their initial away game was the first match to be played at Highbury, into which Arsenal's backers were sinking thousands of pounds in a gamble on North London support being more substantial than that found at their former Plumstead base.

Fine amateur 'keeper Ronald Brebner was now between the sticks, but sadly his career came to an abrupt end with a Boxing Day injury at Lincoln, and a few fellow recruits from the unpaid ranks found the Second Division going generally too tough. Indeed, Fosse as a whole were almost out of their depth this season. A few choice results in the early weeks provided much-needed insurance cover, for a sequence of only three wins from 21 mid-season games had disaster beckoning, and eventually Fosse escaped having to apply for re-election by the narrowest margin possible - goal average.

With three games to go, a 2-0 home win over Lincoln City proved crucial, though it was a point gained with a Whitfield goal at Bury on the following Saturday, while Lincoln were losing at home to promotion-chasing Bradford, that actually allowed Fosse to finish above the Sincil Bank club. Both sides had a meagre 26 points, Fosse finishing with a goal average of 0.737 to Lincoln's 0.545. It was little cause for complacency when both Lincoln and bottom club Nottingham Forest later duly

secured re-election.

Not unnaturally, Fosse's on-field problems were accompanied by much backstage activity. The board, under chairman W.Smith, had made itself unpopular with the Leicester public in January when prices for the Cup tie with Spurs were raised appreciably, and had also scored something of an own goal, as the smaller than expected crowd paid only £543, not much above the minimum guarantee Spurs were offering to host the tie at White Hart Lane.

Then the club fell foul of an FA commission, being fined £10 for making an illegal approach to an Ilford player, F.J.C.Blake, via an agent. Clubs at this time often used third parties to negotiate transfer deals, but the practice was frowned on by the authorities, and they were always on the lookout for breaches of rule. In this instance the agent, Bert Fish, was banned for life from entry to any FA-affiliated ground.

Only a week later, on March 1st, J.W.Bartlett resigned. Director J.M.Hawkes was temporarily installed in his place, but April saw the appointment to the secretary-manager's role of Louis Ford, a veteran administrator with both West Bromwich and Walsall.

Almost his first act was to sell Tommy Benfield to Derby to raise cash, for Fosse's finances were still in a critical state, with a further seasonal loss of £365 being reported despite the sale earlier in the campaign of the likes of Clay and Sparrow. Both these promising players went to Spurs immediately after the Cup ties, in which the Londoners gained a 2-0 replay triumph following a remarkable 5-5 draw at Filbert Street which Fosse had come very close to shading.

Though Fosse's seniors closed their campaign with a sigh of relief, it must have been one less exhausted than that uttered by their second string. The reserves had been switching Leagues quite regularly, most recently from the Midland League in 1911/12 to the Central Alliance the following term. For some reason, though, they had supplemented their 30 Central Alliance fixtures this term with an additional 40-game calendar in the South Eastern League. Remarkably, they finished 5th of 16 in the former competition, and 19th of 21 in the latter, with a composite goals record of 130 for, 129 against. They still found the energy to win the Leicestershire Senior Cup, beating Holwell Works 2-1 in the final at Coalville!

*Fosse prepare to meet Tottenham Hotspur in an FA Cup first round replay
in January 1914. They suffered a 2-0 defeat following a dramatic 5-5 draw at Filbert Street.
Left to right : **Stoodley, Douglas, McWhirter, Sparrow, Harrold, Currie, Burton, Bown, Clay, Mortimer, Waterall.***

1914 - 15

In Leicester as much as around the rest of the country, it was a matter of much heated debate whether or not this League season should take place. Britain was already embroiled in the Great War, and the first casualty lists were being published when the League and FA jointly decided on business as usual. Outraged commentators either saw the continuance of professional sport at home as an insult to those fighting abroad, or believed that men able-bodied enough to play football should automatically demonstrate their patriotism by enlisting for the front. Those in favour of the kick-off argued that the game would provide a sorely-needed diversion at a time of crisis. No-one, of course, knew at this time just how long the conflict would continue, or the likely dimensions of its carnage.

The War evidently put Fosse's problems into stark perspective, but it could not hide the club's own crisis entirely. Summer team-building had, as was now customary, been done on the cheap, but at least Louis Ford and his directors had spread their net a little more widely for professionals from Glasgow, the North-East and the South-West.

The new-look Fosse only briefly flattered to deceive. After gaining three points from the opening two games, they were beaten in six successive matches, and were soon shipping goals alarmingly. Wolves and Leeds City both claimed seven, Arsenal and Derby County six apiece. Fosse were removed from the Cup by lowly Southern League Swansea Town (in their last-ever appearance at the Qualifying stage), and spirits dropped terribly. In fact the Football League Management Committee were asked to advise on Fosse's internal problems when they met at Leicester on January 19th.

Their communique, published locally on February 2nd, contained the claim that they had been able to "adjust difficulties" in the relationship between the club and its players, but noted ominously that here was a "club shrouded in an atmosphere of pessimism, lacking vitality and confidence". The implied criticism was of the directors, but it was Louis Ford who resigned in the hiatus between the League meeting and the issuing of its statement. Director H.Linney took over the secretarial duties.

No change however in playing fortunes ensued. Fosse had only Glossop below them in the Second Division table, and were trailing the rest by some margin for the remainder of the campaign, which they finished five points behind 18th-placed Nottingham Forest.

What turned out to be Fosse's final League game under that title was a 0-2 defeat away to Clapton Orient, but at least they had said farewell to Filbert Street in this context with a 5-1 win over Leeds City a week earlier. Reconstruction, though an obvious remedy to Fosse's perpetual problems, would have to wait until the war was over. In the short term, thoughts strayed anxiously to the League AGM at which re-election had to be sought.

That AGM decided that League football would henceforth be suspended for the duration of the War, but not until after the voting had taken place to settle the membership. Fosse came top of the poll with 33 votes, Glossop bottom with only one. Stoke (21) were elected, and the other unsuccessful applicants were South Shields (11), Chesterfield (8) and Darlington (4). The immediate future for Fosse was one of uncertainty - but at least they had a future.

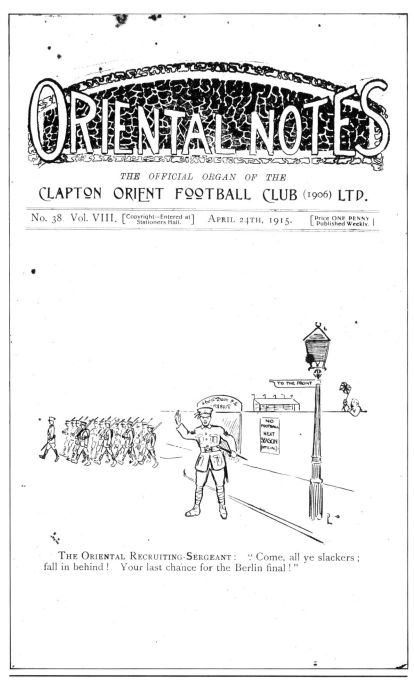

The programme for Fosse's final League game.
By the time the Football League had resumed, after World War One,
the club would be playing under the name of Leicester City.

FOSSE
AT WAR

1915 - 1919

The decision to suspend the Football League programme was in many ways overdue. The public could not really raise much enthusiasm for sporting events whilst so many of the country's young men were giving up their lives in the carnage just across the Channel.

Leicester Tigers had ceased their Rugby activities immediately upon the outbreak of hostilities in August 1914 and the Welford Road ground was actually acting as headquarters for two artillery units and a pioneer corps. Rugby was not resumed until Boxing Day 1918. The outbreak of war had also caused the cancellation of Leicestershire's final cricket fixture of the summer of 1914, and there would be no more first class cricket at Aylestone Road until 1919. This ground, too, was pressed into war-related service, being used as HQ for the 53rd A.S.C and for the Leicestershire Volunteer Regiment.

In contrast, Filbert Street was to remain open throughout the war years, as the Fosse continued to compete in the Regional League that had been created to replace national competition. However, in deference to the seriousness of the war effort, there were no cups to be played for, no medals to be awarded, and even league points were officially eliminated. This latter ruling was largely lost, however, on the popular press, who continued to publish league tables every weekend. No wages were paid to footballers during this period, though, and the only recompense to which they were entitled was for genuine out-of-pocket expenses.

The first obvious change for Fosse during 1915/16 was in their playing strip. Nominally because blue dye was hard to obtain, the now traditional blue shirts were abandoned in favour of blue and white stripes, an arrangement which continued until the end of the 1921/2 season. Fosse competed in the Midland Section of the League that first winter, achieving a moderate degree of success in eventually finishing fifth of the fourteen teams taking part - not that there were any official tables, of course. In a subsidiary tournament running through March and April, third place out of six was the end result.

As might be expected at such a time of disruption, the campaign did not pass without incident. Matches were compulsorily reduced to 80 minutes duration during December, but, due to inclement weather, the home clash with Bradford City on December 4th only lasted 73

minutes, and without any half-time break at that. Such matters were entirely at the discretion of the referee.

The introduction of compulsory military service in 1916 brought about the official introduction of the guest player system in football. However, guests were being used regularly some time before that as clubs struggled to field full-strength teams. Some players returned to the seat of their families during the hostilities, whilst those in the forces could be stationed anywhere in the country. Consequently, guests who appeared in wartime football constituted a wide mixture of ages and allegiances, as well as a range of abilities from that of local enthusiast to international star.

Two old Fossils who had last represented the club over a decade earlier, but who found themselves treading the Filbert Street turf again, were Sep Atterbury of Plymouth Argyle and Arthur Collins of Norwich City. Another to return in the early weeks of 1915/16 was George Harrison, who actually missed the train for what would have been his final appearance, at Bradford Park Avenue on October 16th. Accordingly, a friend of Gibson's, named Cope, who had gone along as a spectator, was press-ganged into donning a Fosse jersey for the afternoon. This sort of occurence was oft repeated throughout the wartime seasons.

The necessity to field an eleven-man team was no respecter of reputations or positions. So, when Fosse arrived two men short for the January 22nd fixture with Leeds City, the home club provided one guest, Fox, from their reserves, while Fosse had to persuade W.Green, the former Burnley goalkeeper, to step from the crowd and chase up and down their right wing. Among other notable guests who represented Fosse in that 1915/16 season were Alec Donaldson of Bolton Wanderers, Jimmy Leach of Aston Villa, Neddy Freeman of Northampton Town, and the Birmingham pair of Gibson and Walker.

Walker had the honour of recording Fosse's first wartime hat-tricks - at home to Leeds City on October 23rd and Hull City on January 29th - both 4-0 victories. He eventually finished the term as the club's leading marksman, finding the net on 13 occasions in 26 matches. There were no ever-presents for the 36 fixtures, but leading the appearance chart were Sep Atterbury and Teddy King on 32, with Arthur Collins just one behind.

As the 1916/17 season got underway, teams were beginning to come to terms with the specific demands of wartime football. As more and more of Britain's young men were called up for military service the guest player system flourished, and Fosse would eventually call upon 72 players to see them through their 36 fixtures. Even this figure looked frugal compared to Blackburn Rovers, who used no less than 95 different players throughout the campaign! The Football League altered regulations for the winter months, and the 80 minute match duration was now in force from mid-November to mid-January.

None of these circumstances seemed to help Fosse in any way as, after remaining unbeaten over their first six matches (five of which were drawn), their form fell away badly and they eventually finished in the penultimate position of the 16 teams in the Midland Section. Throughout November and December, the club actually recorded a sequence of ten successive defeats. Incredibly, the circumstances surrounding the trip to Grimsby on January 6th, the day on which the sequence was broken, were perhaps the most unfavourable of the season. The team were not only three players short on arrival at Blundell Park, but were also minus their kit, which had been lost somewhere on the journey. Eventually Fosse managed to secure the services of three guests - B.Pykett of Notts County, George Padley of Worksop Town and Colin Stainsby from a local Grimsby team - as well as to borrow a set of strip from a local club. The borrowed kit may well have dazzled the opposition, for it was described as 'all magenta', and certainly the guests played their part, as goals from Padley and Stainsby, together with an own goal, clinched an unlikely 3-1 win for Fosse.

In fact, the earlier home fixture with Grimsby Town that season provided another headache, with Fosse playing one man short for the opening quarter of an hour, until former Fossil 'Nigger' Trueman was spotted in the stand and persuaded to make up the full complement. One mystery remaining from 1916/17 is the true identity of 'A.Newman' who played at outside-right for Fosse in the home game with Lincoln City on October 28th. This time-honoured pseudonym was increasingly adopted by players attempting to keep their identities secret, especially from either the police or military authorities, who may have had other ideas as to how the individual should be spending his time. League records log an appearance for Tommy Benfield in this match.

The six fixtures played in the subsidiary tournament at the end of the season brought about an upturn in the team's fortunes. A finish with a flourish, resulting in four successive victories, enabled Fosse to finish in fourth place out of the sixteen entrants. Of those who represented Fosse throughout the campaign, goalkeeper Herbert Bown was not only the sole ever-present, but also managed to get himself onto the scoresheet. At Hull on March 3rd he scored from the penalty spot in a 1-2 defeat. Full-back Sam Currie only missed two games, whilst Teddy King and Jimmy Leach were the others who regularly supplied the backbone of the team. A Coalville youngster named Cliff Price was brought into the side in January and went on to become leading goalscorer with a mere 7 strikes.

By the time the 1917/18 season began, much of the original public hostility towards wartime football had disappeared. Travel arrangements, however, continued to

cause major headaches, and on December 22nd, when Fosse visited Bradford Park Avenue, the train carrying the team arrived so late that the match only lasted 52 minutes before darkness set in. The referee was so impatient to make a start that he ordered the kick-off to take place as soon as Fosse had their statutory first eight players changed and ready to begin.

Overall, the season's record showed an improvement on the previous winter. A final placing of seventh out of fifteen was achieved thanks mainly to a haul of eleven wins at Filbert Street. A slump followed in the end-of-season subsidiary tournament, though, and the club eventually ranked twelfth out of sixteen.

Guests were less numerous than in the previous season, but one who reappeared to figure in an unusual incident was Bolton's Alec Donaldson. When Sheffield United visited on February 9th, he netted direct from a corner kick. Unfortunately, the rules of the game as then applied did not allow this, so only a goal-kick resulted.

HERBERT BOWN

Once again, Herbert Bown was the only ever-present, and his season did not pass without incident either. Against Sheffield Wednesday at Filbert Street on October 6th he missed from the penalty spot, and such a panic ensued that he was not entrusted with the duty again. Two weeks later, when visiting Bradford City, he was involved in an even more bizarre event. A dog happened to run from the crowd behind Bown just as he prepared to take a goal-kick, and the 'keeper unwittingly landed his hefty punt on the canine intruder instead of the ball. Luckily, no permanent damage was done to either man or beast. A number of other players turned out in 30 or more games, with Currie, Donald, Draycott, Leach, Price and Storer contributing to the more settled aspect of the side. Cliff Price was again top scorer, this time notching 14 goals.

The season of 1918/19 was destined to be the last of regional fare, as hostilities drew to a close and the Armistice was signed in November. With so many players in transit around the end of the war, the guest system again flourished, and 57 players were used to see Fosse through their fixture list. Unsurprisingly, Fosse again failed to make any substantial impact in the Midland Section, finishing tenth out of sixteen. Results in the subsidiary tournament evened out rather more, and a ranking of second in a group of four was achieved with three wins and three defeats.

The season did prove to be just as haphazardly eventful as previous ones during wartime and, once again, the trip to Grimsby was to prove jinxed. This time no less than four players missed the train and local substitutes had to be drafted in. In fact, Fosse played for the first 40 minutes with only ten men, so the 1-4 defeat was no real shock. There was also another instance of the club literally losing their shirts, as the kit went astray en route to Hull, and a spare set had to be borrowed from the home side.

The popularity of the game, once peace was declared, was further increased, and this was particularly demonstrated at Filbert Street on Boxing Day when the gates were stormed and hundreds of fans managed to gain a free viewing of the game against Birmingham. Fosse gave them value for their non-contribution by losing 0-4.

SAM CURRIE

For the third consecutive season, Herbert Bown topped the appearance chart, taking part in 35 of the 36 fixtures. His remarkable wartime sequence of 94 consecutive appearances, stretching from the opening day of the 1916/17 season to February 8th, 1919, was finally interrupted when he had to withdraw from the trip to Sheffield United because he was needed to help out at home during his wife's illness. Sam Currie and Teddy King were, again, the most regular of the outfield players, whilst Cliff Price made it a hat-trick of seasons as leading marksman. The movement of Allied troops throughout the season brought about the appearance of one interesting guest. Henri Vlamynck of the Belgian Army played in four matches in November, and his three goals included a brace in the 7-3 victory over Sheffield Wednesday.

Throughout the four seasons of regional football, Fosse had played 142 matches in total, winning 55 but losing 64. Four individual players managed to reach three figures in terms of appearances: Sam Currie topped the chart with 123, followed by Teddy King 121, Herbert Bown 112 and Jimmy Leach (still officially a Villa player) with 102. Cliff Price was the club's top marksman during the period with 33 in 75 matches; though the striker of this era subsequently to build the biggest footballing reputation was Tom Roberts, who moved from Leicester via Southport Vulcan to Preston North End, and on to England international honours.

Leicester Fosse Football Club Co., Limited, 1918.

PRESIDENT—M. J. RICE, ESQ   VICE-PRESIDENT—A. RICE, ESQ.

DIRECTORS—

CHAIRMAN—MR W. H. SQUIRES   VICE-CHAIRMAN—MR. C. CROSSLAND.

MR. W. E. STEVENS.   MR. H. COLLINS.
„ L. H. BURRIDGE.   „ S. SCATTERGOOD.
„ W. SMITH.   „ H. LINNEY.
„ E. J. BENN.   „ J. M. HAWKES.

AUDITORS—MESSRS. ASPELL & BARNES, 3 Welford Place, Chartered Accountants.

REPORT OF THE DIRECTORS.

THE decision of your Directors to continue the playing of football under War time conditions cannot but be considered a wise one, as apart from the recreative standpoint our loss on the past season has been kept down to the moderate amount of £236 11s. 9d., including the depreciation allowance on Stands, &c. Our standing charges are approximately £500 per annum, not including any depreciation allowances, so it can therefore readily be seen, from a financial standpoint, that the discontinuing of football, even for a season, would be disastrous to the Club.

Considerable trouble was experienced from time to time in placing a regular eleven on the field of play, and it redounds highly to the credit of our players in having achieved and won the position they did, and our best thanks are extended to them for services so generously rendered.

The playing and working expenses are only £7 more than last season, a sure proof that every care has been exercised in meeting the general increase in the cost of almost every item under those headings.

Our President, M. J. Rice, Esq., has once again shown his sympathy and practical support in generously providing a number of footballs for Leicestershire men serving with various regiments at home and abroad.

The retiring Directors are Messrs. S. Scattergood and W. Smith, who are eligible and offer themselves for re-election.

Messrs. Aspell & Barnes, Auditors, and Mr. C. Davies, Shareholders' Auditor. retire and offer themselves for re-election.

On behalf of the Board,

W. H. SQUIRES, Chairman.
H. LINNEY, Hon. Secretary,

The Directors' report for 1918
alludes to the financial difficulties that the club was suffering during the period of hostilities.

More significant than these dry figures however were those of the balance sheet, which made no better reading than in the pre-war days of Fosse's pauperdom. Off-field events in the summer of 1919 would revolve around something more serious than a mere casual preparation for the return of peacetime Football League competition. Rather more substantial processes of transition were being negotiated.

RECONSTRUCTION - 1919

The front pages and editorial leaders of the local press were full of satisfied comment on the implications of the first change; the sports pages took longer (and much less column space) to interpret the upheaval which is more the concern of this narrative.

A concerted campaign to whip up parochial pride was mounted for the impending visit of King George V and Queen Mary on June 10th, as speculation was rife that this event would portend Leicester's restoration to the status of a City, after an interval of some 700 years. In fact it was four days after the flag-waving royal reception that the Home Secretary wrote to the Mayor confirming the restoration. There would soon be capitalisation on this event by the Football Club, but not until a more radical reconstruction had been carried out at Filbert Street.

By the end of the 1918/19 season, Fosse owed the United Counties Bank the sum of £3,150.3s.3d, and there seemed little chance of raising cash infusions for an essentially moribund business set-up. Accordingly, a winding-up and take-over by a new company was mooted at an extraordinary general meeting of the shareholders on May 16th, at the offices of Messrs Herbert, Simpson and Bennett, solicitors. The resolution (proposed by chairman W.H.Squires) was carried unanimously, and a liquidator appointed. A creditors' meeting at the end of May was told that, after realising the club's assets, there was still a deficiency to meet the claims of unsecured creditors of £940.18s.10d, and the resolution passed by the shareholders was confirmed. The take-over plans were set in motion.

The new company was ready for business by mid-July, by which time the change in status of Leicester itself had taken place. On July 5th, the new directors gained the assent of the Football League Management Committee for the club to change its name to Leicester City.

The following text, extracted from the share prospectus issued by the new concern, explains the terms of the take-over:

> "...The Fosse club enjoyed a considerable measure of popularity, and became well known in Football circles throughout England, but for some time past it has been suffering from financial difficulties by reason of the adverse conditions under which it has had to be carried on, and it is felt that the time has arrived when in the interest of true sport, and for the credit of the City of Leicester (with the name of which the Fosse has always been associated), some effort should be made to free the Club from its embarrassments and reorganise the same on a better basis. It was therefore decided to wind up the affairs of the old Company and to reorganise the Club under the auspices of a new Company which has been registered under the name of The Leicester City Football Club Company, Limited."

> "In order to accomplish this object and to make the Club worthy of the City of Leicester, it is considered that a sum of £10,000 will be required, and the Directors whose names appear at the head of this prospectus ask for sympathetic consideration and support, and trust that the people of Leicester will respond to the appeal to provide that sum."

> "...The Directors have arranged for the purchase of the old Company's assets (including the value of the players' transfers) from Mr John Fowler Beale ... the liquidator of the Leicester Fosse Football Club Company, Limited, at the price of £4,500, payable in cash out of this issue. Nothing is being paid for goodwill..."

The new board consisted of five former Fosse directors (W.H.Squires, L.H.Burridge, H.Collins, C.Crossland and H.Linney), plus four new men - W.A.Jennings, A.Needham, W.Tompkins and a former player, A.E.Pudan - though for some time the FA were to block the last-named from acting in his new capacity. The directors stated they would strengthen the team, embark on a series of ground improvements, and renegotiate the lease of Filbert Street with the City Corporation; while the new Articles of Association they signed seemed to cover almost any eventuality in terms of having amongst the club's 25 stated objects a paragraph enabling it to promote the practice and play of Football, Cricket, Lacrosse, Lawn Tennis, Hockey, Bowls, Bicycle and Tricycle riding, running, jumping, the physical training and development of the human frame, and other athletic sports, games and pastimes and exercises....

The new club offices were set up at 17, Market Place - where they remained until a move to the ground in June 1920 - and Harry Linney retained his role of honorary secretary until a professional appointment could be made. A sidelight on the times is provided by the fact that one of the numerous legal documents Leicester City had to file before they could commence business was a declaration under The Trading With The Enemy Amendment Act! Paperwork done, though, a return to sporting combat for the new-look club was less than a month away.

CITY'S HALCYON DAYS

The newly re-formed City's first ever Board of Directors.
Back : **P.Hodge** (Secretary), **W.Tompkins, A.Needham, A.Pudan, C.Crossland, L.Burridge, H.Collins.**
Front : **H.Linney, W.Squires, M.Rice** (President), **W.Jennings** (Chairman), **A.Rice.**

1919 - 20

August 1919 found a strange mixture of moods around Leicester. The euphoria that accompanied the restoration of peace was dying down, and intimations of social strife were growing (especially among returning servicemen and the unemployed, who were all too often one and the same). The elevation of the borough to City status satisfied the civic pride of the great and good, but offered no tangible benefit to anyone else. While the reconstruction of the Football Club - focus of interest for the bulk of Leicester's sporting public - encouraged a rather wary and quizzical response.

Would the new set-up be able to break the cycle of economic and playing poverty which had bedevilled the Fosse? Would the re-election trauma of the last pre-war League season be experienced again? Would the new board cleave like its predecessors to a style of amateurish administration of its professional playing staff?

It was a couple of weeks into the new season before the third question was answered first, with the appointment of Peter Hodge to the key post of secretary-manager. The former Raith Rovers and Stoke boss was to be given full responsibility for team matters, and was to prove an astutely inspired choice to lead the new club towards unparalleled success. His initial tasks, however, were more modest - to assess and alter the balance of playing strengths (between veterans of the Fosse's final struggles and a posse of largely untried youngsters), and aim at Second Division consolidation.

The squad he inherited was, characteristically for the time, an odd blend of experience and callowness. Remaining from pre-war campaigns were Herbert Bown, Sam Currie, George Douglas, Teddy King, Norman Whitfield and skipper Jim Harrold; while former Fossils Billy Thomson and Shirley Hubbard had also been persuaded to re-sign after spells away. More recent discoveries, untested beyond the bounds of wartime competition, included Sid Harrold, Ike Smith, Billy Barrett and Cliff Price; while 'name' players fixed up by the directorate before Hodge's arrival included Irish international James Macauley and former Newcastle and Arsenal stalwart George Jobey. It was around this nucleus that Hodge began his long-term team-building exercise, though neither he nor trainer Dave Gardner were tardy in recognising the need for short-term shoring-up.

City's first season opened with a home defeat by Wolves in front of an expectant crowd estimated at 10,000. George Douglas became the first scorer for the new club, but goals from Bate and Harrison negated his effort. The first victory did not arrive until the fifth fixture, when Fulham were beaten 3-2 at Filbert Street. Teddy King claimed the decisive goal, but was less happy in the return fixture a week later when sent off for fighting in a 0-5 defeat which featured a Donald Cock hat-trick. Goalscoring was an early problem for City, and the centre-forward position proved hard to fill effectively. Hodge made a double signing from Arsenal in October of forwards Harry King and Billy Spittle, but both suffered injuries, and it was December before a genuinely consistent striker was bought. Jock Paterson arrived from Dundee for a reportedly 'hefty' fee, and soon proceeded to justify it.

It was he who claimed City's first hat-trick (in a 4-0 home win over Lincoln City), just a couple of weeks before he became the new club's first full international, playing at inside-left for Scotland against England on the Wednesday's ground at Sheffield. Jock finished the season as the side's undisputed top marksman, with 11 League goals from his 20 appearances, and one more in the Cup. Only one signing this term was, eventually, to outshine that of Paterson, and that came in January, when Hodge secured a young full-back from Bathgate, named Adam Black.

Despite all Hodge's experimentation with personnel (no less than 30 players made senior appearances during the season) and the concomitant inconsistency of results,

City comfortably secured a mid-table position. Leicester crowds apparently appreciated the City's efforts, with around 17,000 turning up on Christmas Day to see the 1-0 win over Birmingham which produced the club's first ever match receipts total of over £1,000.

Crowd and receipts records were both to be quickly updated, though, in the course of a Cup run which took City into the last 16. The board made efforts to get Southern League strugglers Newport County to switch their first round tie with City to Filbert Street, but were rebuffed despite offering a £600 guarantee. The team, however, ensured the Leicester public would get to see them through by drawing 0-0 on Welsh soil. The replay drew 20,212 (£1,202) for a 2-0 win, and then 23,115 turned up to watch First Division Manchester City despatched 3-0, paying £1,945 for the privilege. What they did not see was the heroism of Jim Harrold. Concussed in the first half, he played on throughout, despite fainting at half time. City made their exit at Stamford Bridge, where no less an honoured spectator than King George V watched a bad-tempered game in which City tumbled to three second-half goals.

One trophy did though make its way to Filbert Street, with the Reserves taking the Leicestershire Senior Cup via a record 11-2 final win over Moira United in April. Earlier, they had remained unbeaten in the Central Alliance until November 22nd, but had then fallen away in a competition they were to dominate for the next three seasons.

However, the biggest smiles around Filbert Street in the close season of 1920 were those of the new board. The return on their investment and optimism had resulted in a profit of £463.18s.1d, and earned the club the rare accolade of an editorial comment of congratulation from the 'Daily Post'. A year of glancing back fearfully at the past struggles of the Fosse was over; the firm foundations of the City had been laid; Peter Hodge could start to dream of promotion and perhaps even more for his new club.

1920 - 21

The consolidation process continued this season; progress to a final position of 12th in the Second Division represented a leap of two places over the previous term, while Peter Hodge's influence - and especially its Scottish tinge - became ever more apparent.

Young Adam Black - in the early stages of creating the club record for League appearances - quickly established himself as a regular first-choice full-back, the amateur Roxburgh brothers were given sporadic chances in the forward line, and in mid-season a schemer from the classic Caledonian mould arrived in the shape of Harry Graham from Hearts. Jock Paterson was still the main scoring threat (claiming 16 League goals and one in the Cup); while the Reserves - who took the Central Alliance championship - instituted the distinctly Scottish practice of giving triallists the pseudonymn of 'Newman'. The Reserves, in fact, hogged many of the local headlines over the course of the season, due to the outstanding

scoring prowess of newcomer Albert Pynegar, an inside-forward who celebrated the season's opening day with a six-goal haul against Derby County, and finished with 49 goals from 25 second-team appearances. The Senior Cup was also retained by City's shadow-squad, with Loughborough Corinthians beaten 3-0 in the final at Filbert Street.

Back in Division Two, the first team's efforts were significantly held back by a poor away record, with only two victories registered on their travels, at West Ham and Nottingham Forest. At Filbert Street, the record League attendance was increased twice before Christmas, as 19,681 saw Fulham take a point and 21,228 cheered a win over Cardiff City. It was however, again left to the FA Cup to generate the major interest of the season. Only one tie was played, but what a game! The visitors to Filbert Street were League leaders Burnley, who were in the middle of their record-breaking run of 30 League games without defeat, and well on the way to the championship. They drew a record crowd of 29,149, who payed a record £2,323.10s.0d to witness a scintillating display in which Burnley triumphed by 7-3.

At the other end of the attendance scale came the final League game, away to Stockport County on May 7th. County's own Edgeley Park ground had been closed by order of the FA, so the fixture was arranged to be played at Old Trafford as part of a 'double-header', immediately following the First Division game between Manchester United and Derby County. The official attendance at the City match was a League record low of 13. However, this figure merely represented those who paid for entry between the two games, and masks an overall attendance estimated at around 2,000. Such is the stuff that some carelessly-quoted 'records' are made of!

Off the pitch, the most significant development at Filbert Street was the erection of the new main stand, built behind the existing structure at a cost of £24,000, to plans drawn up by Leicester architect W.E.Moore. The pitch itself would be moved ten yards towards the new edifice before the official opening ceremony in the following November.

Two effective changes to the City board occurred towards the end of the season. In March, the FA finally sanctioned the appointment of former player Dick Pudan as a director, while in April came news of the untimely death of chairman W.A.Jennings, at the age of 49. A self-made boot and shoe manufacturer and prominent Liberal, Jennings was borne to his grave by six City players.

JOCK PATERSON

Earlier, other harsh realities of the time had touched more briefly on the club. A friendly fixture at Merthyr in November had to be cancelled when the home club were almost crippled by the effects of a coal strike, while in the same month Filbert Street hosted a women's football match between the famous Dick Kerr's Ladies and St.Helens Ladies (won 4-0 by the former) which raised £700 for the Leicester Unemployment Fund.

1921 - 22

If Peter Hodge had been subject to a school report, his assessment by the end of this season might well have read 'steady progress maintained'. The club was now established in the top half of Division Two and remained on the fringe of the promotion battle throughout the season, but never really mounted a serious challenge, and finally finished the campaign in ninth place. The defence was much tighter than in previous seasons but the attack was still far from prolific. No-one reached a double-figure goal tally, with Jock Paterson and Alex Trotter claiming eight apiece, and deficiencies in marksmanship were primarily responsible for the high number of away draws which drained City's upward aspirations.

It is probable that Paterson would have led the charts on his own for a third year, but his City days were cut short in March, when Sunderland stepped in to effect his transfer. Indeed, he netted another five goals for the Rokerites in a dozen appearances this season.

Both the noteworthy scoring feats of City's campaign unfortunately occurred at the wrong end of the field. The New Year's Eve defeat at West Ham was sustained as a result of the first own goal registered by a City player since the war, with Ernest Walker bearing the red face; while the three-goal defeat at Leeds was the single-handed work of United centre-forward Bill Poyntz, who celebrated his marriage earlier that day!

A fortnight after Paterson's departure, City themselves parted with a substantial fee. The target was inveterate wanderer Mick O'Brien, latterly the QPR centre-half, but a fine player, who immediately added to his tally of Irish caps with appearances against Scotland and Wales.

City's Cup campaign consisted of a trio of meetings with clubs from the capital. Clapton Orient and Fulham were both despatched at Filbert Street, but Arsenal at Highbury were too sharp for Leicester.

On the international scene, Filbert Street was chosen as the venue for an amateur international between England and Ireland on November 12th. Disappointingly, the game had to be abandoned because of thick fog, but it was replayed two days later, England winning 4-1.

Two weeks later, on November 26th, the main stand was officially opened by John McKenna, the President of the Football League, before City's 1-1 draw with Coventry City. Season tickets for the new structure had been available from the start of the campaign at three guineas (ladies two guineas) for the reserved section, and two guineas (ladies one guinea) for the unreserved seats.

While the first team consolidated their position, the Reserves again dominated the Central Alliance, retaining their title with a haul of 58 points from their 34 fixtures.

The close season of 1922 saw the next and, so far, most significant piece added to Peter Hodge's jigsaw. In July, John Duncan was tempted to leave Hodge's old club, Raith Rovers, to try his luck south of the border. A goal-scoring inside-forward, he was to be the pivotal figure around whom City's first major promotion campaign revolved. He scored twice on his debut, a spectacular 5-4 win away to Stockport County and, at last, the goals which had dried up in previous seasons began to flow. Centre-forward George Waite (another former Raith player, as were Harry Graham and John Duncan's brother, Tom) also began to find the net regularly, and even Albert Pynegar enjoyed a brief resurgence, culminating in a four-goal haul in March as Wolves were humbled 7-0 at Filbert Street.

By the end of the season, City were the leading goalscorers in Division Two but, ironically, were to be denied promotion by virtue of an inferior goal average to that of West Ham United. City's record of 65 goals for and 44 against resulted in an average of 1.477 while the Hammers recorded 63-38 for an average of 1.657.

Indeed, the eventual position of third was a huge disappointment to Leicester supporters, for promotion had looked likely for much of the season. A 2-0 home win over Bradford City on October 14th had taken the club to the top of the table, and they rarely dropped out of the top three from then onwards. On April 28th, after 41 matches, City again stood in top spot, but a 0-2 reverse at Bury on the final day (with John Duncan out injured) denied them glory. Beaten Cup-finalists West Ham won a game in hand on Monday April 30th to lead the table on goal average from City and Notts County; then, on that final day, the Hammers lost at home to the Magpies, who themselves clinched the title, leaving City to ponder on might-have-beens. Head of the hindsight list of 'if only's' must have been the February home game against the Hammers, lost by a clear six goals.

However, Hodge's pattern was beginning to take shape. Reg Osborne and Norman Watson were introduced to the first team during the latter weeks of the season, whilst, during March, a youngster named Hugh Adcock joined the club from Loughborough Corinthians. He would not make his debut until the following season, but his role would be significant in City's future. By the end of the campaign Adam Black and goalkeeper George Hebden had become the club's first 'ever-presents' since the reconstruction.

Away from League business, the Filbert Street record attendance was again broken as 35,690 people paid £2,805 to witness the second round Cup exit at the hands of Cardiff City, and, for the third consecutive season, the Reserve team clinched the championship of the Central Alliance.

This set of caricatures depicted City's visit to Crystal Palace in September 1922. Note the mistaken spellings of Roxburgh and Hebden.

*A rare aerial view of the **Filbert Street** ground in the mid-20's. The new main stand has been constructed, but work has yet to begin on the Double Decker. This photograph was taken from a newspaper cutting found in an old scrapbook rescued from a rubbish tip in New Zealand!*

The disappointments of the near-miss campaign were, of course, tempered by optimistic expectations among City supporters that elevation to the top flight would almost certainly ensue this season, and such hopes were bolstered in the summer with news of Peter Hodge's acquisition of a new centre-forward. Arthur Chandler had not been a particularly prolific goalscorer with Queens Park Rangers, but Hodge had spotted clear potential in his robust style - though it is doubtful that even the manager could have imagined in June 1923 just what an impact on City's history his new signing eventually would have.

Chandler and Adcock both made their debuts in the opening game, a 1-1 draw at Hull, and both registered their first goals two days later, as Stoke were thrashed 5-0 at Filbert Street. Optimism seemed indeed well founded as the goals continued to flow from City over the early weeks of the season, and the club fringed the promotion race for a spell. But a bad crop of injuries, and a series of inconsistent performances away from home, saw the team's challenge fade badly. Eventually, a position of 12th had to be settled for, with Hodge utilising the second half of the season to further his team-strengthening exercise in earnest. Only 'Channy' finished the term as an ever-present, hitting the first two of his seventeen City hat-tricks on the way to a chart-topping goals total of 24. Introduced around him at various stages of the campaign were Pat Carrigan, John Bamber, George Carr, Billy

Newton and Albert Godderidge, as the formidable team of the mid-20s began to take discernible shape.

There would henceforth be no place for Mick O'Brien, who had succeeded Jim Harrold as club captain and who had been capped twice more this year for Ireland; or for Teddy King, who had been on the club's books since the summer of 1906, and was about to take up the new position of club coach after a couple of seasons lending his vast experience to the Reserves. That team had just completed its first season in the Southern League, Eastern Section, to which it had switched in search of sterner opposition, and where it had to settle for runners-up spot, behind Peterborough & Fletton United. The second team also regained the Leicestershire Senior Cup by defeating Barwell United 5-1 in a replayed Final, and ran up their all-time record score of 22-0 in an earlier round against the hapless Ibstock Colliery.

Strangely enough, in view of the generally deflating aspects of their campaign, the final day of the League season had, for the second season running, involved City's seniors in high drama. They were at the Baseball Ground, where Derby knew they required a 5-0 win to pip Bury for the second promotion place on goal average. City, in no mood for over-neighbourly gestures after their own high hopes had died, somehow contrived to keep the bitterly frustrated Rams down to four unanswered goals!

IMPRESSION OR RATHER EXPRESSION OF GEORGE CARR WHEN THINGS ARE RUNNING TO HIS LIKING.

The final game of this season would produce far from hollow glory, for at the end of it City were in possession of the Second Division championship shield, and contemplating life among the elite.

During the close season of 1924 the final pieces of Peter Hodge's jigsaw were nudged into place. Two key signings were made, full-back Harry Hooper from Southampton and outside-left Harold Wadsworth from Liverpool, while, in recognition of his motivational role, John Duncan was appointed club captain in succession to O'Brien.

The season did not get off to a particularly auspicious start, with only three points taken from the opening five fixtures, but once Black and Newton regained their places forfeited through pre-season injuries, events took a distinct upturn, and goals began to flow with consummate ease, particularly from the boots of Duncan and Chandler.

The former claimed 30 League and 4 Cup goals, while the latter notched 32 in the Second Division and a further 6 in the knockout competition. Duncan set a club record with six goals in the 7-0 Christmas Day thrashing of Port Vale, whilst Chandler failed by only one goal to equal the feat as Barnsley were crushed 6-0 on February 28th. Chandler's consistency as a marksman was most amply demonstrated in mid-season when he scored in eight successive games, and actually found the net in 14 out of 15 consecutive matches. The odd game out, a 0-2 League defeat by Blackpool, immediately preceded a record unbeaten run which proved the crux of the championship effort.

From December 6th to March 30th there stretched a magnificent run of 18 League games without defeat, 14

of which were won. After this, only an aberrant sequence of goalless draws postponed City's celebrations. A George Carr goal in the penultimate game, at home to Bradford City, finally sealed promotion, and a 4-0 cakewalk in the last home game against Stockport (marred only by an elbow injury to Duncan after he'd scored twice) guaranteed the top spot. Other club records amassed along the way included those for number of League wins, number of goals scored, and number of points attained.

Success, however, was not confined solely to League matters. In the FA Cup, the club equalled its best ever performance by reaching the quarter-finals, and dreams of a first Wembley trip were still very much alive when Cardiff City grabbed a last-minute winner at Ninian Park with a goal scored direct from a corner kick. As this was, in fact, the first time the feat had been achieved since a rule change had allowed for the possibility, much confusion followed. As no time had remained in which to restart the tie, several City players left the field in the genuine belief that they had earned a replay.

City ever-presents were Chandler and Wadsworth, and six other players missed three games or less, so the consistency was in marked contrast to the tribulations of the previous season. There was also a surprise at the lower end of the scorers' list as Adam Black had briefly assumed the mantle of penalty taker and successfully converted three spot-kicks. This apparently unremarkable feat is put into its proper perspective when it is considered that in a career spanning 557 games for Leicester, Adam only managed four goals in total!

With the club having now reached Division One for only the second time in its history, the question was whether this time the elevated status could be maintained for longer than a single season?

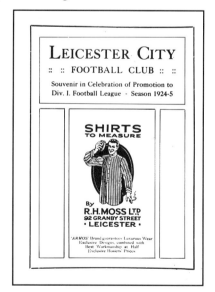

LEICESTER CITY
:: :: FOOTBALL CLUB :: ::
Souvenir in Celebration of Promotion to
Div. I. Football League - Season 1924-5

SHIRTS
TO MEASURE

By
R.H. MOSS LTD
92 GRANBY STREET
· LEICESTER ·

'ARMOS' Brand guarantees Luxurious Wear
Exclusive Designs, combined with
Best Workmanship at Half
Exclusive Hosiers' Prices

To celebrate promotion in 1925, a special
Handbook *was issued. This was the forerunner of*
regular issues during the 20's and 30's.

The efforts of the previous season had brought the players of Leicester City to public notice, and attracted the predatory attention of several bigger clubs. Everton had enquiries for Duncan, Chandler and Carr rejected, and Preston North End received short shrift when chasing Adam Black. If City were indeed to consolidate amongst the elite, they would require every bit of the class, character and consistency represented by this quartet, and would almost certainly need to augment it.

An opening-day home win over Liverpool sent hopes soaring, and City were denied two points from their first away game, at Highbury, only by a Norman Watson own goal. But a hat-trick for Burnley by ex-Fossil Tom Roberts initiated a sequence of five consecutive defeats, plunging City towards the depths. Their resources were then severely stretched when George Carr broke a leg in the home defeat by Leeds and ruled himself out for the rest of the season. Nevertheless, City crowds remained loyal, and a new record gate of 37,483 was registered at Filbert Street for the October game with Aston Villa.

*City skipper **John Duncan** with his Scottish International jersey and cap.*

*During the 20's, City were successful in several charity cup competitions. The players are seen here with one such trophy, believed to be the Hull Hospital Cup. Pictured left to right are **Duncan, Black, Chandler, Watson** and **Bamber**.*

October also saw Peter Hodge's first significant foray into the transfer market. A record outlay of £3,300 was required to entice Manchester United to part with inside-forward Arthur Lochhead. The intelligent Scot, who had already scored against City at Old Trafford this season, netted twice on his debut in compensation. However, despite Lochhead's impact, the introduction of Scottish international 'keeper Kenny Campbell and Chandler's continued goalscoring consistency, City remained locked in the relegation struggle throughout the first half of the season.

Again, Hodge was allowed to chase and secure a major signing; expending another £3,000 on Barnsley

marksman Ernie Hine. And, again, a two-goal debut was the immediate reward - though Hine blotted the margin of his copybook by missing a penalty late in the same game. With results picking up, a mid-table finish seemed likely, but a couple of late slips left the club in 17th place at the season's conclusion. Still, it was the highest League ranking ever achieved by a Leicester side, and the promise was of better to come.

Amidst all the activity of October 1925, John Duncan had won his sole Scottish cap, scoring once in a 3-0 demolition of Wales; and Arthur Chandler had become the first Leicester player to notch 100 consecutive appearances. Injury interrupted Chandler's run after 118 games, though he was again City's top scorer with 26 League goals. Mystery however, surrounds the failure of the Scottish selectors to further recognise Duncan's genius. The popular view of Leicester as 'unfashionable' is something the likes of Chandler, Sep Smith and later Arthur Rowley would also have to contend with as they endured the disparity between their evident weekly achievements and a dearth of international honours.

There were, however, matters of greater weight and immediacy on the minds of all concerned with Leicester at the close of this term. Peter Hodge had done perhaps more than anyone to strengthen both the club's self-esteem and their status, and had guided City from the embers of wartime to hitherto undreamed-of heights. Consequently, it came as a great shock to everyone concerned with the club when, in May 1926, he resigned to take over as manager of relegated Manchester City.

Shocked and distressed though the City board may have been, they wasted no time in finding a replacement for Hodge. Their choice in July was Willie Orr, a former Scottish international left-half who had become a successful manager with Airdrieonians; and by mid-September they must have been toasting themselves on their clear sightedness.

With the new, less restrictive offside rule in operation, the season opened with an avalanche of goals all round, and City were quick to claim their share. On the evening of September 18th, Orr and everyone at the City experienced a wholly new and heady sensation. City, three goals down at half-time at Goodison, had stormed back to win 4-3, and attain top place in Division One:

	P	W	D	L	F	A	Pts
Leicester City	**7**	**3**	**4**	**0**	**23**	**17**	**10**
Birmingham	6	4	1	1	11	7	9
Sheffield United	6	4	1	1	12	9	9
Arsenal	7	3	3	1	12	12	9
Burnley	6	3	2	1	18	13	8
Huddersfield Town	7	2	4	1	12	10	8

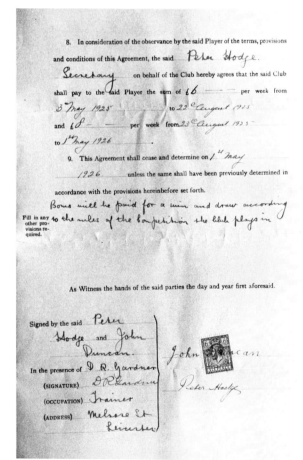

John Duncan's contract :
He was one of several City stars paid the maximum allowable wage at the time of £8 per week during the season and £6 per week during the summer.

*Caricatures of **Bell, Watson, Osborne** and **Black** as published in 'All Sports Weekly' in October 1926.*

On the following Monday, Birmingham beat Everton 1-0 to take over the top spot. Then, on the next Saturday, City crushed Blackburn Rovers 4-0 to regain the pinnacle, but one week later, a 3-5 reverse at Huddersfield dropped the team to third place. The goal rush at both ends of the park continued, but City could not quite maintain the impetus of their title bid, and eventually a disappointing final month to the season meant the club had to settle for 7th position, ten points behind champions Newcastle.

There could, though, be no complaints about entertainment value this season, and memorable individual performances dotted the campaign. Chandler notched a hat-trick on the opening day, and later twice achieved five-goal hauls; while the returning George Carr banished unhappy memories of the previous season's injury against Leeds by claiming a hat-trick off them this time. At the other end of the pitch, Kenny Campbell saved two penalties at St. James' Park as City drew 1-1, but conceded two strikes from George Camsell in the Cup as City bowed out 3-5 and the Middlesbrough forward barged on towards a seasonal record of 64 goals.

Billy Lane scored for Spurs against City at Filbert Street and then arrived as cover for Chandler, scoring on his debut against Derby. The latter match also marked the initial City appearance of Sid Bishop, the classy former West Ham skipper who was Willie Orr's first major purchase, and won England caps before the season's end.

Also gaining a representative honour at last was Arthur Chandler, who led the line for the Football League against the Scottish League in March in Filbert Street's second 'Auld Enemy' tussle of the season. The first-ever amateur international between England and Scotland had also been hosted by Leicester on December 18th.

In an attempt to further improve the quality of young players coming through the ranks, the Reserves - who the previous season had completed a hat-trick of Senior Cup wins - were entered into the London Combination as well as the Southern League. Undaunted by their strenuous programme, they eventually finished as runners-up in the former competition and, from then onwards, continued in that League only.

There was no doubt by this time that Leicester City had become a First Division force to be reckoned with. They were well respected throughout the land, and despite manager Willie Orr's failure to land an eve-of-season transfer coup when Motherwell rejected his enquiry for Bob Ferrier, another good start to the season was exactly what the supporters demanded. They were not disappointed, for, after four games, City once more sat atop the early League table, holding off Arsenal on goal average.

Their reign, however, was to be short lived (of two days duration, to be exact!), and a subsequent run of four successive defeats rather comprehensively took the gloss off the early success. To compound the problems skipper Duncan suffered a dislocated elbow and broken arm and was missing until the New Year.

Orr was quick to respond to the setbacks. The captaincy passed to Reg Osborne and a new-look half-back line was introduced. Billy Findlay, Norman Watson and George Carr took over from the injured Duncan and the out-of-form Carrigan and Bishop. The forward-line, too, was strengthened, with the acquisition of outside-left Len Barry from Notts County for a £3,450 fee. It all had the desired effect, as City showed new steel to climb back into the top half of the table and eventually to the fringe of the championship battle. Such was the extra competitive edge shown that Adam Black was severely censured by the FA for an 'improper expression' made to Arsenal's Charles Buchan during the October fixture!

By the end of the season City had to settle for third place, five points adrift of champions Everton. They had, however, established a new record goal tally of 96 - of which Chandler contributed 34, including two hat-tricks and one four-goal haul at Newcastle. (In the debit column, incidentally, was included a hat-trick from Dixie Dean, one-twentieth of his record seasonal goal-haul). International recognition was also forthcoming for City players, with Reg Osborne performing for England against Wales and Len Barry donning the white shirt in the games against France and Belgium. In fact, City's willingness to allow their stars to appear in representative games cost them dearly, for they lost a couple of important League matches while Bishop (Football League), Duncan and Lochhead (both in the Scottish trial) were absent.

Osborne was one of three players granted a benefit that season; Duncan and Watson being the others. By a strange quirk of fate, all three were injured and unable to play in their respective benefit matches.

Filbert Street by this time was beginning to take on the aspect of the ground we know today. Completing a major scheme of ground improvements, the Double Decker Stand was officially opened on November 26th, when Newcastle United were the visitors. Coincidentally, this was six years to the day since the official opening of the main stand, which might have disappeared in December had not a fire in the trainers' room been spotted early enough. Fortunately, the only damage was to kit, for which the insurance company paid up £130.

The addition of the Double Decker increased the official capacity of the ground to around 45,000, but even that was insufficient to accommodate all those who wanted to see the Fifth Round FA Cup tie with Tottenham Hotspur in February. By the time the gates were closed on the heaving throng, a ground record crowd of 47,298 had paid £4,702.10s.6d to witness City's exit by 0-3.

Such was the enhanced status of Filbert Street that it was chosen to stage the FA Cup Semi-Final between Arsenal and Blackburn Rovers on March 24th. A disappointing turn-out of 25,633 saw Rovers win 1-0, on their way to a surprise Final win over Huddersfield Town. Blackburn actually brought the Cup with them for the final League game of the season at Leicester, and went home with a 6-0 thrashing from an unimpressed City. Also unimpressed, or perhaps even slighted, were the City board, who summarily rejected an application for the summer use of Filbert Street for greyhound racing!

Other questions for the board to debate at the season's end were the more usual ones concerning prospective transfer moves. Hearts were given short shrift when cheekily chasing Arthur Chandler, but lengthy negotiations with Chelsea ended in the sale of Sid Bishop for £3,800, after the apparently homesick Londoner had attempted to get permission to live in the capital and commute to City's games.

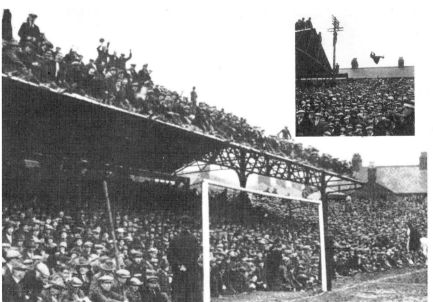

Fans in the record crowd for the FA Cup tie with Tottenham Hotspur even braved sitting on the roof of the stand at Filbert Street.
(Inset) : A daring spectator climbs in via a telegraph wire!

Both Willie Orr and his directors were now further determined to hold on to the spine of the City squad for a renewed title challenge. Enquiries from Manchester City for Watson and from Everton for Duncan were rebuffed, and while protracted negotiations continued with Falkirk to set up a deal which would see classy left-half George Ritchie replace Bishop, overtures from the Scottish club to take either Carrigan or Watson in part-exchange were also refused. Eventually, Ritchie arrived in late September, with City reserves Russell and Wyness going as makeweights in the complex transaction.

Oddly enough, in what was to turn out to be City's finest and most convincing challenge for the title, the club never actually reached the top of the table at any time during the season. After suffering mixed fortunes in the early weeks of the campaign and finding themselves down in 14th position after ten games, City effectively launched their championship bid on October 20th, when Portsmouth were the visitors to Filbert Street.

City ran in five goals in the first half, with Chandler collecting a hat-trick in the space of 14 minutes. After 70 minutes, as 'Channy' collected his fifth and City's seventh, five swans flew over the ground as if to mark the occasion. A few minutes later, after Hine added number eight, a sixth swan from the nearby canal straggled overhead. The crowd were quick to call for another Chandler special, and the popular centre-forward duly obliged to equal John Duncan's club record of six goals in a game. Eventually Ernie Hine completed a hat-trick of his own and City had registered their record League victory, by 10-0. They even burst the ball as well!

With this boost to their morale, and despite never winning more than four games in succession throughout the campaign, City rapidly climbed the table and continued to chase hard for the title. By the morning of April 27th, they stood in second place. Sheffield Wednesday had already completed their fixtures, compiling 52 points (goal average 1.39), whilst City, with two games left to play, had 48 points and a goal average of 1.37. Two victories would surely have brought the title to Filbert Street at last.

Alas, City's one-goal lead at Huddersfield that afternoon was cut back by an equaliser from George Brown, and the 1-1 draw meant the dream was shattered. Even a 6-1 spree in the final fixture against Bolton Wanderers (FA Cup winners after edging City out in the Fifth Round) proved little consolation as the club finished in the runners-up spot, just one point adrift of the Owls.

City could not even mark their achievement with any proper reward for the players. A request from the directors to the Football League in May that they be allowed to show their appreciation to the twelve regulars by way of a gift to the approximate value of £10 was refused out of hand! And even though the club were in demand abroad, the directors themselves felt unable to accept offers to tour either Denmark or Sweden on the grounds of finance.

At least Hughie Adcock *(caricature pictured right)*

*Arthur Chandler in action against Liverpool at Filbert Street with **Hugh Adcock** and **Ernie Hine** in support.*

and Len Barry managed to tour Europe with England at the end of a season in which Ernie Hine also won his first cap, but there was still no international call for Arthur Chandler, despite his impressive performance in the trial match. Chandler and Hine had both topped the 30-goal mark for City as the club equalled their 96 goals of the previous season, and Adcock completed a new record run of 119 consecutive appearances in February. In remaining unbeaten at home throughout the campaign, City had equalled the feat of the Fosse in the shorter 1898/9 season, and set a record the club has still to parallel to this day.

There was, of course, an optimistic train of thought that City would automatically continue their recent progression through the top three positions of the First Division, and at last capture the Championship trophy in 1930. Such hopes, though, were soon to be dashed. And hindsight would prove that City's heyday as a consistent contender for the highest football honour was unfortunately at an end.

City entertain Sunderland at Filbert Street on 17th November 1928.
Arthur Chandler, *who scored the winner in a 1-0 success, puts pressure on the visitors' goal with* **George Ritchie.**

1929 - 30

By most yardsticks, a season which resulted in a final position of eighth in Division One should be looked back on with some degree of satisfaction, but in view of what had happened in the previous two years, the campaign was largely one of disappointment for City's followers.

Defeat at Huddersfield in the opening fixture, where a Jack Brown own-goal proved the decisive one of five, and where the youthful Sep Smith made an unexpected debut, heralded a shaky start in which only one victory was gained from the first six outings. A commendable recovery ensued, to quickly banish any relegation fears, and the top half of the table was soon reached. But fifth place in March was the summit of City's achievement, and they never looked likely to effect a realistic challenge for honours.

Goals again flowed freely, with Chandler once more topping the 30 mark (and claiming four hat-tricks to set alongside the one scored by his deputy, Lovatt), but it was the goals conceded column which gave most cause for concern. The total of 90 goals against was the highest since the relegation season of 1908/9, and was a foretaste of things to come. In January, City visited Sheffield United and received a 1-7 hiding, with Irishman Jimmy Dunne notching four to set alongside his Filbert Street hat-trick. A week later they returned to Bramall Lane on FA Cup duty. The 1-2 defeat suffered that day (with Dunne restricted to a single goal) seemed almost a good result in the circumstances, but it also served notice that the club had to come to terms with an unfamiliar lack of

interest in the later stages of the season.

The highlights of the campaign unsurprisingly revolved around high-scoring games. A double was achieved over Everton with both games incredibly ending 5-4, whilst Cup-finalists Arsenal came to Filbert Street in April to share in a League record 6-6 draw. David Halliday, later destined to become a City manager, scored four goals for the Gunners that day, including a hat-trick in the space of five minutes, yet was left out of their Wembley side the following week.

Newcomers to the City scene included centre-half Albert Harrison, bought for a substantial fee from Nottingham Forest in December, and wing-half Roger Heywood, who was immediately ruled out by injury after signing from Chorley, while no less than four goalkeepers took turns between the City sticks. Forward stalwarts Adcock and Hine each added two more England caps to their tally, but, behind the scenes, rumblings of discontent were beginning to be heard.

In January, George Carr approached the board to ask for permission to open a greengrocer's shop and off-licence in the city. As any business interests concerning the sale of alcohol were specifically banned by the directors, permission was refused. Carr's immediate transfer request attracted only a derisory £1,000 bid from Grimsby, which was rejected, but it was April before Carr patched up his differences with the club. This case, however, proved to be the forerunner of a major dispute that would rock the club during the summer.

At a board meeting on August 12th, it was reported that club captain John Duncan had taken over the licence of a public house in Leicester. As this was against club policy, it was agreed the player was deemed to have automatically terminated his agreement with Leicester City, without prejudicing the club's rights to retain his registration or any transfer fee which might accrue. Northampton Town were the only club to show any interest in Duncan. In September their offer of £800 fell far short of City's valuation of £2,500, but, the following month, a bid of £1,000 was accepted. However, the player could not agree personal terms, and decided instead to retire to concentrate on his new business. City, of course, continued to maintain the name of one of their greatest-ever players on their official open-to-transfer list for another year.

George Ritchie took over as club captain for 1930/1, but Duncan's departure definitively signalled that City's brief golden era was over. There was never really a whiff of disaster about the term, as City bobbed around in mid-table before settling into 16th place, but vital sparks were clearly missing. Ernie Hine passed the 30-goal target and also took a well-earned benefit during the season, as did Findlay and Lochhead, but he generally lacked support. Chandler was not as prolific as in recent seasons, whilst the goals conceded total - 95 - continued to rise.

Both regular goalkeepers suffered their share of criticism - Jim McLaren conceded eight goals at Grimsby and John Beby was beaten seven times by Arsenal at Filbert Street. Grimsby's Coleman, with four goals, and Arsenal's Lambert, Villa's Beresford, Blackpool's Hampson, Manchester United's Bullock and Sheffield Wednesday's Ball, each with hat-tricks, were among First Division forwards who enjoyed field-days against City's oft-changed rearguard, in which only Adam Black was a fixture.

The most evident sign of slipping standards at Leicester, though, came with the embarrassment of a Third Round Cup exit at home to Brighton & Hove Albion, from the Third Division (South), in front of a 25,722 crowd.

At the end of the campaign, the board once more rejected on cash grounds the opportunity of a summer tour, this time to Holland, yet also rejected two requests to lease Filbert Street for boxing tournaments during the close season.

Arthur Chandler and Ernie Hine take a break during a training session at Filbert Street.

Len Barry and Arthur Chandler after a paddle in the sea on one of City's special training trips to Skegness.

1931 - 32

If the campaign of 1930/1 had seemed near-disastrous to some eyes, it was as nothing compared to what followed. The events of the opening day might well have been heeded as portents. The train which took the City team to their away fixture at Villa Park arrived late at Birmingham station, and then the charabanc driver who transported the party from the station to the ground took the wrong route. The game eventually kicked off eleven minutes late, an ill-prepared City lost 2-3, and a detailed explanation had to be supplied to the Football League to avert a hefty fine.

Early results were far from encouraging and team spirit inevitably suffered throughout the club. This was amply demonstrated before a reserve match at Brentford in

Arthur Chandler takes the field at Filbert Street.

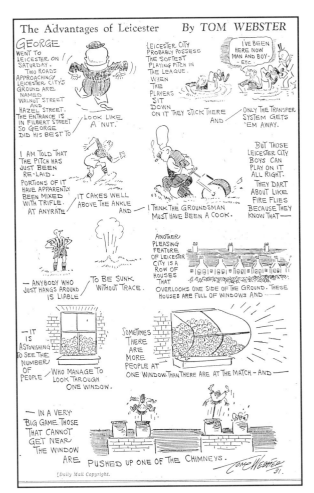

A visitor's view of Filbert Street - reproduced from the Daily Mail of 23rd November 1931.

November when two of the fringe members of the first-team squad, John Beby and Billy Jackson, were involved in a petty dispute over changing room pegs, which escalated to blows. Jackson was ruled the aggressor and fined £5 by the board, whilst Beby was severely censured. The fine was subsequently reduced to £2 when Jackson proffered a letter of apology, but the incident was symptomatic of the atmosphere within the club.

Matters really came to a head in January when Willie Orr resigned as secretary-manager. Dave Gardner, the club's long-serving trainer, had suffered a heart-attack playing golf at Longcliffe and died the previous November, so the team had, within a short space of time, lost both its main guiding influences. A string of atrocious results, including a 2-9 defeat at Goodison in which Dixie Dean claimed four goals and a 3-8 home defeat by Aston Villa in which George Brown went nap, bore eloquent testimony to the lack of leadership. (Incidentally, those present for the latter game unwittingly watched history made: never before or since has any other Football League game finished with a 3-8 scoreline in favour of the away team).

In their hour of need, the board turned to their former mentor, Peter Hodge. He agreed to take up his old managerial post in March, much to Manchester City's chagrin, and immediately set about the task of ensuring top flight survival. At the very end of the season a return of three wins and a draw enabled City to finish in 19th position, five points clear of relegation.

Hodge also embarked on a rebuilding programme and sizeable fees were paid for Ernest Keeley (£1,700), James Paterson (£1,025), Joe Calvert (£1,200), Danny Liddle and Edward Lowery (together £1,320). Considering the club's financial state, this money had to be recouped from somewhere, and the most marketable possession was new skipper Ernie Hine, who had again been capped by England during the season. The £6,000 price tag set by City attracted enquiries from both Bradford Park Avenue and Huddersfield Town, although when the latter duly signed Hine in May, the accepted fee was only £4,000. Hine had ended his final City season once more as the

A light-hearted moment during training at Filbert Street.

club's leading goalscorer and, in January, had joined Duncan and Chandler in a select band who had scored five goals in a game for City - a feat he achieved in the 7-0 thrashing of non-League Crook Town in the FA Cup Third Round.

Perhaps the saddest departure, though, was that of Teddy King, whose position as club coach was deemed redundant - an unfortunate end to a 26-year association with the club.

1932 - 33

Try as he might, Peter Hodge could not reverse the downward trajectory of City's fortunes this season. Osborne took over again as club captain, but was soon replaced by Black, now nearing the veteran stage himself. Adcock was still a regular but had lost some of the sparkle of his youth, and Chandler could no longer command a regular place. Lochhead, too, was coming towards the end of a distinguished playing career. So often, great teams that have grown up together also grow old together, and this was happening to Leicester. They did possess, however, one rising star in Sep Smith, whose cultured displays at half-back or inside-forward prompted a rapidly-rejected enquiry from Bradford City.

City were marked down early as relegation candidates, and had only gained one win by Christmas, yet managed thereafter to pick themselves up sufficiently to maintain slim hopes of avoiding the drop, before a remarkable run of three successive victories in the final three fixtures once again ensured safety, this time with just two points to spare.

Hodge had, in fact, made two further significant signings. Inside-forward Arthur 'Digger' Maw had arrived from Notts County back in July, while Scottish international 'keeper Sandy McLaren was bought for £2,500 from St.Johnstone in February. Both were introduced into the team in the later stages of the campaign, and both played their part in the final escape, as did full-back Sandy Wood, newly repatriated from the United States.

Maw collected seven goals in those final three fixtures as City uncharacteristically crushed Sunderland (4-2), Birmingham (4-0) and West Bromwich Albion (6-0), and actually ended the season as the club's leading marksman, albeit with a tally of just 14 goals. This was the first time since 1921/2 that no City player had reached the 20-goal mark for the season.

Despite their decline, City were still in demand abroad, and were offered the opportunity to tour South America during June. Once again, though, the financial position of the club led the board to pass up the invitation.

At least the Reserves began to enjoy some success again as they retained the Leicestershire Senior Cup, defeating Loughborough Corinthians 3-0 in the final at Filbert Street. The previous season they had brought the trophy back to the club by overcoming the challenge of Market Harborough in a replayed final at Springfield Road. The Thirties was to be a decade in which City Reserves would dominate this particular competition.

1933 - 34

In the wake of 1949 and 1969, City may have gained something of a reputation for overturning the form-book when it came to FA Cup exploits, but there was no precedent for their Jekyll and Hyde act this season. During the club's heyday in the Twenties they had never met with much success in the Cup, reaching the quarter-finals only once. Now the team was struggling each season against relegation, and going through a desperate transitional period, yet City found themselves only 90 minutes from Wembley in their first ever Semi-Final. More of that in a moment.

With Chandler no longer the force he was in the previous decade, Hodge's main priority was to find a replacement centre-forward. As City again battled to keep out of the drop zone throughout the season, much of the behind-the-scenes activity surrounded this subject, together with the eventual fate of 'Channy' himself.

As early as September, City made enquiries for Jack Bowers of Derby and Middlesbrough's George Camsell, but both were rejected. City then baulked at the £3,000 asking fee for Arsenal's Jack Lambert. The following month, Gurney of Sunderland was the target, but the price tag of £5,000 was also beyond City. By November, with pressure mounting in the local press, the board went back to Sunderland with an offer of £3,500, but this was rejected by the Rokerites.

By February, Hodge had turned his attention north of the border. George Mutch of Arbroath (and later Preston) was watched, but eventually Archie Gardiner of Hearts was signed for a £1,000 fee. He exploded onto the Football League scene with four goals on his debut, a 5-3 win at Portsmouth, and recorded another hat-trick two weeks later as Arsenal were toppled 4-1 at Filbert Street, and indeed his goals did help keep City up.

In the meantime, Chandler had often looked set to end his association with the club. Millwall made an enquiry for his services in September but were dissuaded by the £1,000 fee. The following month, Norwich City sniffed, City asked £750, and the Canaries promptly lost interest. The following week it was Bournemouth who were after 'Channy'. This time City asked £600, but the Dean Court club would not agree. By the end of November, City received a letter from Norwich City offering to take Chandler off their hands for free. The assistant secretary, George Smith, was asked to draft a reply acknowledging their impertinence! Eventually, in May 1934, Queens Park Rangers came up with an offer of £500 to buy back their former centre-forward. The two clubs agreed terms, but Chandler himself rejected the move, stating that he would prefer to end his career with Leicester, for whom he had

*City's first appearance in the FA Cup Semi-Finals ended in defeat at the hands of Portsmouth. Mackie, the Pompey full-back here clears from the incoming **Arthur Chandler**.*

developed so much affection over the years.

Before leaving the topic of transfers, there was one further incident, back in October, which was worthy of note. One of the directors had been sent to Stoke to watch a fledgling outside-right named Stanley Matthews. He reported back that the youngster seemed to be of above average ability, but no further action was recommended - the rest, as they say, is history!

Back on the field, City once more managed to cling on to their First Division status - by a safety margin of four places and five points - but it was definitely a case of the 'cup that cheered' in 1934.

The Third and Fourth Round ties saw City emerge victorious at home to Lincoln City and away to Millwall, the two clubs who would eventually be relegated from Division Two. Scorelines of 3-0 and 6-3 resulted, with the recalled Chandler netting a brace at The Den. Next up was a trip to Birmingham, one of the few First Division clubs to finish below City this season, and Chandler again scored twice to clinch a 2-1 victory. City's reward was another away tie. This time the opposition was high-flying Preston, later destined to fill one of the promotion places from Division Two. Once more it was 'Channy', with the only goal of the game, who saw City through.

Thus the big day came on March 17th. St.Andrews, Birmingham was the venue and Portsmouth the opposition. Three of the footballing Smith brothers were on the pitch (Sep for City; Jack and Willie for Pompey), but it was the Portsmouth centre-forward Weddle, one of the survivors of their 0-10 defeat in 1928, who emerged as the hero. He collected a hat-trick as City's Wembley dream was dashed 1-4. It would be another fifteen years before City extracted their sweet revenge.

As for the rest of the season's happenings, Roger Heywood had taken over from Black as captain and he

OPPORTUNISM PAYS PORTSMOUTH

LEICESTER CLEVER BUT UNLUCKY

By G. W. CHISHOLM

Leicester City 1, Portsmouth 4

BIRMINGHAM, Saturday.

One side play fast and enterprising football; the other play cleverly, have no luck, miss a few scoring chances, and make fatal errors in defence. In other words, enterprising Portsmouth; clever, but luckless, Leicester City.

Portsmouth deserved to win, yet in many respects Leicester played with such skill that one felt they should have had some reward in their first F.A.Cup semi-final. Portsmouth will make their second appearance at Wembley because they have the attributes of a modern Cup-fighting side; strong in defence, constructive at half-back, and enterprise and speed in the forward line.

Deadly Weddle

But what a fight Leicester made! Within six minutes of the start came the first blow—a lucky goal to Portsmouth. John Smith took a free kick just outside the penalty area, and Rutherford made a desperate effort to head in. He managed it, and did not score, but the ball dropped at the feet of Weddle, who ran in at top speed, and it was more by luck than judgment that he dragged the ball into the net with him.

Then 22 minutes after the start Weddle scored again—a great goal this time—following a fine run by Worrall, who, up to that point, had been a menace to the Leicester defence.

Two goals down so early, yet Leicester actually played like a winning team. Smith, the cleverest right-half in the game, was behind most of the Leicester moves carried out with delightful skill by Adcock and Lochhead. Leicester could not fail, it seemed, but one by one the scoring chances were missed. Lochhead shot high; Chandler shot high.

After 37 minutes, however, the ball passed from Gardiner to Liddle, and back to Lochhead in yet another of Leicester's dazzling moves, and the inside left scored a brilliant goal.

Seven minutes after the interval a defensive mistake threw Leicester's last chance of saving the game away. Black tried to clear, but he dropped the ball at the feet of Weddle, and the Portsmouth centre-forward got his third goal.

Portsmouth's fourth goal came from a throw-in at the right corner flag. The ball swung over to Rutherford. Black hesitated, and Rutherford shot first time and scored—and that was the end of Leicester. They played hard for a time, and Chandler put through when off-side, but they fell away and in the later stages the game was very poor. Weddle was a great opportunist.

PORTSMOUTH.—Gilfillan; Mackie, Smith (W.), Nichol, Allen, Smith (A.); Worrall, Smith (J.), Weddle, Easson, and Rutherford.

LEICESTER CITY.—McLaren; Black, Wood; Smith (S.), Heywood, Grosvenor; Adcock, Gardiner, Chandler, Lochhead, and Liddle.

F.A. CUP SEMI-FINALS

	Attendance.	Receipts.
Manchester City v. Aston Villa	45,473	£4,350
*Leicester City v. Portsmouth	66,544	£5,078

* Record for the Birmingham ground.

The Sunday Times report of City's first FA Cup Semi-Final.

enjoyed the honour of leading City out on their most famous occasion to date; new full back Dai Jones was capped twice for Wales (and notched an own goal on behalf of West Brom in both home and away League fixtures!); winger Danny Liddle topped the scoring list; and George Dewis joined the club from Nuneaton Town. This last event drew little attention at the time, but Dewis would eventually prove a key figure in the development of the club over many years, both in his centre-forward role and in his backroom capacity as prime motivator of young City talent.

As the club celebrated its Golden Jubilee, it was a particularly poignant and tragic moment when, on the eve of the new season, one of its finest servants passed away. Peter Hodge, who had never spared himself in attempts either to push City into the front rank or to keep them there, was admitted to Perth Infirmary on July 30th suffering from an internal complaint, and died on August 18th. The blow to the club was tremendous. He was held in such esteem by his players that six of them - Adcock, Black, Chandler, Heywood, Lochhead and McLaren - acted as pall-bearers at his funeral.

His replacement was not appointed until October, when the board persuaded Arthur Lochhead to retire from the playing staff and take over the role of manager. Meanwhile, George Smith was promoted to the post of club secretary - a move which formally separated the two functions for the first time. Whoever took charge of team affairs, though, was on the proverbial hiding to nothing. The Cup run of the previous season had been the last gasp of City's ageing, ailing heroes, and had barely masked the side's deficiency as a top flight unit, while the loss of Hodge had torn the heart from the club. Relegation was written on the wall and, bravely as he tried, Lochhead could not smudge it out.

Amazingly, as veteran forces were shuffled and new faces tried (including close-season buy Tommy Mills, capped twice for Wales during the campaign, and young full-back Billy Frame, who soon recovered from the trauma of scoring an own-goal on his debut at White Hart Lane), City maintained hope of avoiding the drop for a considerable time. Indeed, cash was made available to Lochhead in February to recruit two forwards to the survival battle. But Tony Carroll (£2,200 from Clyde) and Gene O'Callaghan (£2,250 from Spurs) eventually proved unable to stem the tide. Their purchases also stretched the club's finances to the limit. There was no way City could afford the £4,000 asked by Sheffield Wednesday in March for Burgess, and the plan to build another double-decker stand on the Popular Side was abandoned. The directors settled instead for a cheaper scheme to roof the terracing.

In the end, City failed to win any of their last six games (they took just three points from the twelve available) and were relegated by a single point while Middlesbrough, one place above, escaped.

When the retain and transfer list was issued in May, Black and Chandler were to be given free transfers, whilst Adcock was listed for just £250. This time it really was the end of an era.

Channy's departure in 1935
*was marked by a special cartoon in the local press, filled with reminders of his playing
career with the club. City's loyal servant was presented with the original drawing.*

1935 - 36

During the summer of 1935, Arthur Chandler joined Notts County and Hugh Adcock moved on to Bristol Rovers for an eventual fee of £150. Adam Black, meanwhile, had chosen to retire from the first-class game.

Considering the fact that no money was available to spend on new players, Lochhead did well to guide his team to a final place of 6th in Division Two. The financial state of the club was causing great concern and, in October, the club's bankers, Barclays, refused to grant an overdraft of more than £1,000. The directors felt this limit unreasonable and hastily arranged with Martins Bank to take over the club's account, with an agreed overdraft limit of £5,000. This move at least allowed Lochhead to secure one newcomer during the season, Owen McNally from Distillery for £1,000.

Despite their troubles, the directors staunchly refused to sell off their few assets. Sep Smith was the subject of enquiries by Liverpool and Tottenham; Spurs were also interested in Fred Sharman, whilst Middlesbrough wanted to sign Sandy McLaren and Danny Liddle. The board knew as well as any the need to signal their ambitions for

a return to the top flight, and were willing to augment their own number if an injection of new capital resulted. Such was the club's parlous state, however, that all invitations to potential new directors met with rejection.

Very little more need be said about this particular campaign. Gene O'Callaghan was given the task of leading the team and did a reasonably effective job; Fred Sharman showed his versatility by regularly switching between the centre-half and centre-forward positions, and scored only one goal less than joint top-scorers Tony Carroll and 'Digger' Maw; Sep Smith won long overdue international recognition for England against Ireland; Dai Jones again won two Welsh caps during the season, so emulating his achievement of the previous two campaigns; and former favourite Ernie Hine induced a bout of nostalgia amongst City's small band of travelling fans by hitting a hat-trick for Barnsley in the drawn December fixture.

The Reserves were once again successful in the Leicestershire Senior Cup. This was their fourth victory in the past five seasons.

A picture taken on City's tour of Eastern Europe in 1937.
*On the train are Coach **Arthur Chandler**, **Dai Jones**, **Gene O'Callaghan** and Manager **Frank Womack**.*

The season of 1936/7 provided something of an oasis in the wilderness of the Thirties. It initially took shape as a hazy mirage, yet eventually proved sweetly refreshing. The trek began with the return of one old familiar face - Arthur Chandler had hung up his playing boots and returned to his spiritual home to act as coach. It continued, and changed course, with the departure of another, as Arthur Lochhead resigned as manager in October.

The board were quick to act to appoint a replacement. Frank Womack, a stalwart player at Birmingham, and more recently manager of Worcester City, Torquay United and Grimsby Town, was the man chosen to prompt City's revival. When he took over, City had collected a meagre six points from their first ten fixtures, and were contemplating the real possibility of a drop into Division Three for the first time in their history.

Womack, too, was quick to act. In November, he persuaded the board to increase their financial commitment and part with a club record fee of £7,500 to bring Jack Bowers to Filbert Street from Derby. Bowers' impact was truly amazing. In just 27 League outings he rattled in 33 goals, and if ever one man can be said to have won a team promotion, then Jack was that man. Of course, he did not perform miracles entirely without support. New skipper Sep Smith provided inspired generalship, whilst big Eric Stubbs, signed from Nottingham Forest a week before Bowers arrived, was the winger who gave Jack the splendid service he required to act as the scourge of Second Division defences.

So far behind the promotion race were City when Womack took over that it took until February for the club to climb into the top two. The impetus provided by Bowers can be judged by the fact he scored in each of his first six appearances, all victories, and registered 12 goals

in total during that spell. Indeed, he found the net in eleven of his first dozen games for City to spearhead the ascent.

City remained in second place from February onwards, and might well have finished there, which would have been creditable enough. But fellow promotion club Blackpool threw away their chance of the title with a 1-1 home draw against bottom club Doncaster Rovers in their final match, and City knew that a home win over Tottenham on May 1st would secure them their second championship shield. A fine 4-1 victory ensued; Bowers claimed a characteristic brace, then narrowly escaped the crowd which thronged the pitch at the end and briefly engulfed most of his team-mates.

The attendance on this joyful occasion strangely only numbered 28,000, but the Filbert Street record for a League game had been broken a few weeks previously, when 39,127 watched Bowers score the only goal to separate City and Aston Villa. A couple of weeks before that, the Filbert Street faithful had also seen one of only two games after Bowers' arrival that ended with a blank sheet. The goalless draw with Swansea might not have been worthy of note, but for the fact that the visitors had to field their veteran full-back Wilf Milne in goal throughout!

Although the rewards were great, the huge financial outlay to build the promotion team (inclusive of a further £2,000 expended on Sunderland's Bert Davis, who failed to fit in) was bound to leave its mark. Even so, the board still refused to submit to what they saw as gimmicky fund-raising requests. Consequently a suggestion that a special challenge tennis match between Fred Perry and Ellsworth Vines be staged at the ground during the summer was turned down flat.

*The full City squad pose for a commemorative photograph with the **Second Division Championship shield** at the end of the 1936/7 season.*

The Board of Directors in June 1937 with the Second Division Championship shield.
*Back : **G.Smith** (Secretary), **W.Needham, L.Burridge, W.Tompkins, F.Smith, F.Womack** (Manager).*
*Front : **A.Rice, W.Squires, E.Gregson** (Chairman), **A.Pudan**.*

1937 - 38

City's return to the top flight was greeted with great enthusiasm by the supporters, and in early September a new record League gate of 39,500 was accommodated at Filbert Street to witness a 1-1 draw with Arsenal. But it was soon evident to all but the most myopic that City found it hard to cope with their new elevated status.

Jack Bowers again led the line, but with much less success than during the promotion campaign. It was clear he needed support up front. In October, City offered £1,000 to Arsenal for Joe Hulme, but the figure did not match the Gunners' valuation. By November, however, Matt Moralee had been signed from Aston Villa. He had attracted City's attention the previous season while playing for Grimsby Town, but the Villains had acted more quickly on that occasion. Dewis, Billy Coutts and Peter Hodge's final signing, Muncie, were also tried in the forward line as City desperately tried to find the right balance.

In the end, an unbeaten run of eight games in February and March, only two of which were won, proved sufficient to lift City clear of relegation. They were brought down to earth by mid-April, though, when trounced 1-10 at Molineux, with Westcott and Dorsett each notching four goals against an experimental City line-up, and even City's lone reply was gifted by Wolves'

centre-half Stan Cullis! Ironically, three days later, the same two teams drew 1-1 at Filbert Street. A City defence which now regularly included Maurice Reeday also shipped hat-tricks from Birmingham's Jones, Manchester City's Doherty and Portsmouth's Beattie during the campaign; while future City signings Frank Soo (for Stoke) and Dave McCulloch (for Brentford) also exposed current frailties. Only left-half Percy Grosvenor ended the season as an ever-present as City finished 16th.

Once again, despite financial difficulties, the directors refused to part with their more valuable players. Young Dewis' potential had been noted by both Stockport County and Newcastle United, but all enquiries were rebuffed. West Bromwich Albion were keen enough to capture Bowers to offer Richardson in exchange, but the board would not entertain the suggestion.

By season's end, however, more finance had to be generated. A bank loan of £15,000 was eventually agreed, with the directors personally guaranteeing £10,000 of this figure. Unfortunately, most of the money was required to pay for the covering of the old Popular Side terrace, the plans for which had been drawn up as long ago as 1934. The work was eventually completed during the opening months of the subsequent season.

1938 - 39

Problems of common good taste, as well as of perspective, are automatically raised in attempting to cast City's struggles during this unfortunate season in too apocalyptic a light. That the club's hopes and mid-term prospects lay in ruins by the end of the campaign, and its very future once more looked bleak, are undeniable facts. But description of a relegation campaign could hardly command all the usual adjectival notations - tragic, disastrous, shattering - when football's tensions were at the time so overwhelmingly minimised by those afflicting the country and the culture as a whole.

The entire term was played out against the gathering threat of war, and under the looming shadow of pan-European fascism. At the end of September the Munich Agreement was signed by Chamberlain, Daladier, Hitler and Mussolini, and anxieties eased temporarily, but there was still little confidence that conflict could be averted.

Football was a valuable diversion for those who had little say in the power politics of the time, but who knew they would be in the front line if war indeed came. It was not, however, a particularly joyful diversion for those watching their football in Leicester.

City had been in no position to substantially alter their floundering team of the previous term. Tony Carroll had left for Luton, and in September young Mal Griffiths arrived from Arsenal to assume his place on the right wing, after the other newcomer, Arthur Smith, proved inadequate to the task. Despite Griffiths' evident promise,

and the sterling efforts of Sep Smith, City could not hit on a successful blend. George Dewis shouldered too much of the front-line responsibility, and Fred Sharman too often stood exposed at the heart of the defence. City tenuously held on to a mid-table placing in the early months, but confidence wilted, the goal supply dried up, and the slide into the relegation zone was rapid.

Sandy McLaren was lost for a spell after being injured in a 2-8 mauling at Leeds in which Gordon Hodgson claimed his five goals against three different goalkeepers (Sharman and Frame taking over in turn); while his specialist deputy, Joe Calvert, conceded four from Grimsby's Howe in a 1-6 defeat at Blundell Park. Fred Sharman finished the campaign with two penalties to his credit but, in hapless fashion, had by then already got on the scoresheet for each of Birmingham, Blackpool and Charlton with own goals.

This time there would be no upturn in fortunes, no dramatic finale. From early February onwards, only two victories were achieved, and City finished rock bottom. The depression was compounded before the final game with the resignation of manager Frank Womack. Even the Reserves' accomplishment in taking the Senior Cup for the fifth successive season was a minor consolation.

With the German army already mobilised, conscription beginning in Great Britain, and the club doomed to what looked likely to be a lengthy spell in Division Two, the prospect for City and their followers seemed almost as arid as it had for Fosse just prior to the First World War.

CITY AT WAR

1939 - 1946

The summer of 1939 was no time for optimism. Chamberlain's 'peace in our time' message looked increasingly open to ridicule, and the likelihood of war was becoming fearfully accepted. At Filbert Street little happened to relieve the gloom. Following Frank Womack's resignation, a number of the other backroom staff also departed. In June trainers Laurie Edwards and Walter McLean, and coach Arthur Chandler, each severed their associations; while director Arthur Needham also resigned, though in his case the reason was one of failing health.

Conscious of the club's ever-worsening financial state, the directors finally bowed to pressure and made Sep Smith available for transfer at an asking price of £8,000. But, before any firm offer was received, outside events intervened to shelve all such dealings.

On July 14th, Tom Bromilow - a former Liverpool player and Burnley and Crystal Palace manager - took over Womack's office. Two weeks later, Jim Metcalfe from Preston North End and Fred Rose from Oldham Athletic were appointed as first and second team trainers respectively. The new management team prepared their squad for the coming season with as much spirit as could be mustered under the circumstances, but everyone's thoughts were understandably focussed on events the other side of the Channel.

The first few days of the 1939/40 season coincided with some of the most momentous in history as world events rapidly overwhelmed the Football League programme. The Second Division campaign opened with a victory over Manchester City and a defeat at Birmingham. In the boardroom, arrangements were made to bid for Jimmy Cunliffe of Everton, and a benefit game for Billy Coutts was under discussion. Elsewhere, Poland had been invaded by the Germans, Great Britain and France had mobilised their forces, and evacuation schemes had been put into motion in England and Wales. On September 2nd City won at Upton Park, as military service for men between the ages of 18 and 41 was made compulsory, and the return journey from London was made in the blackout. The following day, war was declared.

The Football League, accused by many of being a year late in responding to the outbreak of the First World War, this time acted immediately to abandon their fixtures.

In fact, all forms of sport came to a halt as a universal ban on the assembly of crowds came into force. This ban only lasted a few days, and in the meantime the Football Association held talks with the Home Office to authorise the continuation of football on a regional basis, as had been done from 1915-1919. The difference this time was that football was to help boost public morale and cup competitions would be actively encouraged.

Elsewhere in Leicester, the Aylestone Road Cricket Ground was again loaned for war purposes. It was eventually used by the U.S. Army Pioneer Corps and the National Fire Service, but was so badly damaged that a new home for Leicestershire County Cricket Club was required on the resumption of first-class cricket in 1946, resulting in the return to Grace Road.

After a makeshift opening game to the season, Leicester Tigers played no more Rugby Union until 1945/6, although a Leicester Harlequins team was formed to play games for charity. Over £10,700 would eventually be raised by this team.

However, Leicester City decided to soldier on. The wages of both players and groundstaff were initially suspended, but despite that, the lack of income was now a serious problem. On September 13th, City played an Army XI in a friendly at Filbert Street, winning 7-2. This was one of the first fixtures to be played anywhere after the abandonment of the League programme. From then until late October, when Regional fare began, a series of further friendlies were undertaken.

When the new League got underway, Leicester found themselves in the Midland Division along with seven other clubs. It was not to prove a successful season, with the team finishing in the penultimate position. That first winter of the war was actually the coldest since 1894, and football suffered its share of problems. Postponements were frequent, with no football on four successive Saturdays during January and February due to snow and ice. However, as the censor decreed no weather information should appear in the press lest it should help the enemy, no advance warning of these postponements was published. Unsurprisingly, attendances plummeted as the season advanced, and things got worse following the introduction of rationing in January.

The guest player system, so necessary during the First World War, was reintroduced. The most notable effect

Football resumed again at Filbert Street in September 1939 with a series of friendlies after the League campaign had been abandoned.
The visiting Aston Villa team shown here clearly drew a sizeable crowd.

seen in Leicester in 1939/40 was the appearance of the legendary Tommy Lawton in three games during November and December. He scored five goals, yet never tasted victory. Of the regulars, Sep Smith, Dai Jones, Sandy McLaren and Jack Bowers were the main stalwarts, with Bowers heading the scorers' list, just ahead of Billy Coutts.

The first ever League War Cup began in April and City bowed out in the second round at the hands of the eventual winners, West Ham United. The final took place at Wembley during the week of the retreat from Dunkirk, and some survivors were admitted free of charge. Thus, that first wartime season drew to a close just as England faced her darkest hour, with an invasion appearing imminent.

Leicester City, too, was facing its own darkest hour. Off the field, the financial situation had become critical during the season. Three new directors, A.E.Pallett, L.L.Green and L.T.Shipman, had joined the board in November to provide an influx of capital, but a major reconstruction of the club's finances was proposed in January. The members of the board were each asked to either increase their own liability or to resign. Three of the long-serving directors, A.E.Pudan, W.H.Squires and E.Gregson, were all asked to step down in due course, whilst George Smith was suspended from his duties as club secretary, pending the deliberations of a Football Association commission which began an investigation into the club's books during April. Leslie Green was not cut out for such proceedings and also resigned his directorship only a few months after taking up the post.

On May 20th, the FA held an inquiry into the affairs of the club. They were primarily concerned with the payment of excessive bonuses and signing-on fees, plus the provision of irregular payments to amateur players over a lengthy period of time. The club was found guilty and fined £500 plus costs, and the former manager, Frank Womack, was suspended from football for twelve months. Five directors - W.A.Tompkins, W.H.Squires,

E.Gregson, A.E.Pudan and F.S.Smith - were all suspended *sine die*, whilst other suspensions were handed out to A.Needham and L.H.Burridge (three years each), A.Rice (two years), and W.S.G.Needham (one year). The newcomers, A.E.Pallett and L.T.Shipman, were of course, absolved from blame and were the only directors present at the subsequent board meeting on May 28th. George Smith was also cleared and invited to resume his duties. Eventually, a total of twelve current and former players would also be suspended for one year. Such was the impact and strain on the individual directors that several suffered serious illness shortly thereafter.

At one stage during the summer of 1940 talk was of liquidation, but a new Board of Directors was formed and the club set itself to begin the 1940/1 season under the shadow of the Battle of Britain, which had raged since July.

The season overall was probably the most arduous of the whole war, with play automatically suspended whenever the air-raid signals sounded. A sign of the times, which raised many a much-needed laugh around the terraces, was that the Football League, desperate to keep competitions running, allowed referees who wore spectacles to officiate at Regional matches.

Oddly enough, just as things seemed at their lowest ebb for the club, performances on the field picked up considerably. City competed this time in the South Regional League, and eventually attained 14th place among the 34 member clubs. For the one and only time, final positions were determined by goal average rather than points. One of the prime reasons for City's improvement could be directly attributed to the decision by Wolverhampton Wanderers not to compete that season. Consequently, all their players were loaned out to other clubs, and two of their most promising young forwards, Jimmy Mullen and Billy Wright (only later to revert to centre-half), played for City for much of the campaign.

Coincidentally, it was another Wright - Dennis - who made the headlines in November when City visited

Mansfield. He was the Stags' reserve goalkeeper, but played at outside-right for City, who had arrived with only ten men, and scored both goals in a 2-4 defeat. Generally, the City forward-line proved prolific marksmen throughout the season, though the defence suffered the occasional disaster. This was amply illustrated on Christmas Day when two (!) fixtures with Northampton Town were undertaken. At 10.45am City crashed 2-5 at the County Ground, but at 3.00pm at Filbert Street, instant revenge was extracted by 7-2.

The improvement in fortunes was not confined to League games, for the club also completed a most successful season in cup competitions. The Midland Cup was secured with a 2-0 win over Walsall at Filbert Street on May 3rd, with Mullen and Wright getting the goals, whilst, a week earlier, the club had been on the verge of a first ever appearance at Wembley, only to be foiled by Arsenal in a two-legged semi-final of the League War Cup.

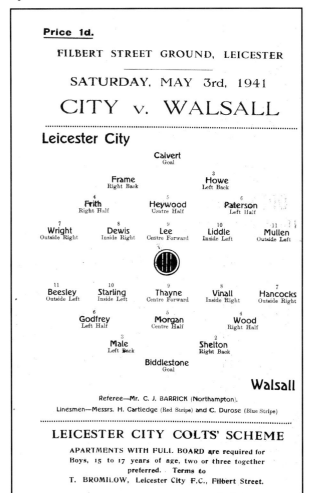

*City collected their first wartime trophy in May 1941, when Walsall were beaten in the **Midland Cup Final**.The programme, like all wartime home issues, was just a single sheet.*

Having returned from White Hart Lane (where Arsenal were wartime tenants) with only a single goal reverse, hopes were high for a second-leg comeback. But City also lost this game, by 1-2, and were denied their walk down Wembley Way. When the season ended, Billy Frame was the only ever-present, although several players managed over 30 appearances, whilst George Dewis proved the prince of strikers, collecting 24 goals from 30 games.

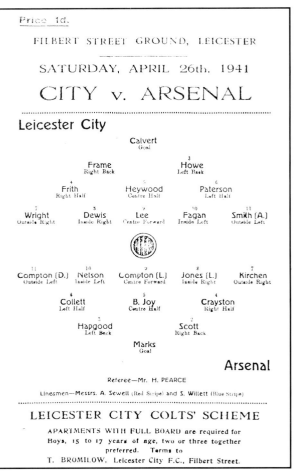

*City came close to a first ever trip to Wembley when they reached the **War Cup Semi-Final** in 1940/1, but a star-studded Arsenal team proved too strong.*

Off the field, times were almost as eventful. On November 14th, the night of the major blitz on Coventry, Filbert Street was hit by a German bomb. Damage was done primarily to the Main Stand, towards the Double Decker end, but affected the roof, seats, kitchen, toilets, gymnasium and boardroom, and a vain request to the FA for a loan left City facing an estimated repair bill for £15,000 alone. City were more successful in gaining the Football League's assistance, albeit only in resolving a contract dispute with Wolves over Arthur Smith, who was found to be registered for both clubs! In order to raise funds, the directors sanctioned a boxing tournament at Filbert Street on August 4th - a decision which reminded everyone how precarious was the state of the club's finances, given the stance previously taken against such ventures.

However, the outlook for the club and for Britain in general had improved considerably over the previous twelve months, and the 1941/2 season was greeted with cautious optimism. Owing to the breakaway of the London clubs, who wished to form their own Regional section, there was a restructuring of fixtures this season, with the championship split into two separate halves; the first running up to Christmas Day, and the second, incorporating the War Cup, occupying the remainder of the season.

Against a background of commodity shortages (new kit came under coupon legislation, petrol was not given priority for sporting purposes, and there was even a drop in the number of footballs being manufactured!), City exploited the absence of the metropolitan clubs from the South Regional League, and clinched the 14-club championship on Christmas Day with a 2-0 home win over Nottingham Forest. This climaxed a sequence of six successive victories and was enough to bring the title to Leicester by a margin of 0.1 of a point from West Bromwich Albion, who did not have a match on that final day. The criteria for deciding positions was one of average points, based on an assumed norm of 18 games per club.

Billy Wright started his career as a winger, and guested for City in the team that captured the Midland Cup in 1941. Later, he found fame as a centre-half and led Wolves to success in the 1949 FA Cup Final against City. He is pictured here after that 3-1 victory.

Thus, barely two weeks after the Japanese attack on Pearl Harbour, City had affirmed their comeback from the depths and, moreover, made their name without the illustrious guests of the previous season. Mullen and Wright had returned to Wolves, who themselves had resumed business with a new youth policy. Their team which visited Filbert Street on September 27th had an average age of 17, with the veteran of the side 19-year-old Derek Ashton! The policy was to prove the foundation of considerable postwar success for the Wolves, but did not pay immediate dividends.

The second half of the campaign saw City as a target for other clubs, and not a terribly durable one at that - they slid to 17th place of the 22 clubs who actually completed enough fixtures to qualify for the final table.

On an individual basis, Billy Frame was again an ever-present, a distinction he shared with Bert Howe, whilst youngster Gordon Jayes, Sep Smith and guest

Harry Barratt all played in 30 or more of the 35 fixtures. Dennis Cheney and Jayes were the chief marksmen, finishing with 15 and 14 goals respectively. The most notable guest to don the blue and white of the City during the season was Ted Drake of Arsenal, who appeared in the 1-2 defeat at Walsall on November 8th.

Things were much quieter behind the scenes by now, but another setback occurred on June 29th 1942 when a fire in the Main Stand caused extensive damage. Starting at the Double Decker end, it quickly spread to destroy the dressing rooms, gymnasium, trainers', kit and referee's rooms, as well as much of the upper seating. In addition, the boardroom and offices suffered water damage in the fire-fighting operation.

By the time the Football League's AGM came round, also in June, the changing face of the war was considered, and a committee established to discuss postwar arrangements. During the season a Victory Cup was purchased, though this seemed somewhat premature as the Allies' fortunes continued to fluctuate. At a League meeting in January 1943, the decision was made that a transitional season would be implemented once hostilities ended, prior to the normal peacetime formula being resumed.

The 1942/3 season, which covered roughly the period from the battle for El Alamein to the flight of the famous Dambusters, was a fairly indifferent one for City, who this time were placed in the Northern Section of the Regional League. The unavailability of many of the club stalwarts on a regular basis led to major problems of team selection, and a total of 58 players were used to complete the 38 fixtures, including the high number of 26 listed guests. Once again the campaign consisted of two separate championships. Final placings of 33rd out of 48 and 22nd out of 54 accurately indexed City's mediocrity over the season.

Two wartime records were established, however. On December 12th, as Wolves were humbled 5-0 at Filbert Street, Freddie Steele, a guest from Stoke City, became the first player to score four goals in a game, whilst, on January 2nd, City ran up a record victory of 9-0 over West Brom in a match which also counted as a qualifier for the League War Cup (North).

Sep Smith, Bert Howe and goalkeeper Alick Grant were the only players to top the 30 appearance mark and Freddie Steele, with 13, was the only marksman to reach double figures. Conscious of the need to raise outside income, the directors actually hired out the ground for a gymkhana on two occasions, as well as contacting American forces stationed in the area with a view to staging baseball at Filbert Street for the first time since 1897! Nothing came of this 'new' initiative, though.

The 1943/4 season was played out against a background of considerable optimism throughout the country as the tide of war began to turn significantly in the Allies' favour. Shortages at home were beginning to bite harder, and German air-raids actually intensified (the FA offices were hit by an incendiary bomb), but football attendances rose appreciably in tune with spirits.

City's season was again moderate; 28th position out of 50 was achieved in the first championship, whilst a respectable 14th slot of the 56 participants in the second brought the season to a satisfactory close. The highlights on the field were reserved for two of the clashes with Notts County. On October 30th, George Dewis and Arthur Smith hit four goals apiece as City triumphed 9-1 at Meadow Lane. Then on New Year's Day, it was the turn of Sep Smith and guest Norman Bowden to record hat-tricks in a 7-2 frolic at Filbert Street.

Once again, Billy Frame, Sep Smith and Alick Grant were the mainstays of the team. No-one emerged as a regular goalscorer, though, with Arsenal reserve Bowden leading the way with 11 goals from his 9 appearances.

As the season drew to a close, the Second Front invasion of Europe was imminent, and finally took place on June 6th. In the City boardroom D-Day was marked by the decision to adopt Middlesbrough Swifts as an official nursery club. This followed a recommendation by ex-City stalwart George Carr, and hopes were high that some of the talent emerging from that footballing hotbed of the North-East could be diverted to Filbert Street. Indeed, Don Revie soon arrived from that very source, but the promising theory was destined never to be tested during peacetime.

The success of the D-Day landings had raised expectations throughout the country of an early end to hostilities, and talk at the postponed AGMs of both the FA and League was of plans for the transitional season. In the meantime, though, the despatch of military personnel into Europe in the wake of the Second Front had led to the guest system again being overworked during the 1944/5 season. Leicester suffered as much as anyone and a total of 62 players, the highest of any season during World War Two, was used to complete the campaign. The disruption was particularly bad during the early part of the season, and a dismal final placing of 52nd in the first championship, with only two clubs faring worse, was no surprise. As things settled down after Christmas, a steady improvement was made and the club rose to 34th position of the 60 clubs in the second competition.

Much of the credit for this was due to the inclusion of Motherwell's Billy Leitch as a regular guest after Christmas. The Scottish centre-forward scored a dozen times at the rate of a goal per game, and also seemed to bring the best out of Sep Smith, who reached double figures in post-Christmas goals, having found the net only twice previously. Leitch's hat-trick was the highlight of the 8-3 thumping of Mansfield Town in January, and it was only after his departure that four of the final five fixtures were lost.

Throughout the season, Sep Smith and Billy Frame were yet again the stalwarts, with Frank Sheard also establishing himself as a regular defensive pivot. No-one else came near to matching the dozen goals of Leitch and Smith, but such facts paled into insignificance as the season closed with reports of Hitler's suicide and the final surrender of Germany.

Closer to home, the season's end was marked by the resignation of Tom Bromilow as manager. He had steered the club through an immensely difficult period, but his relationship with the board had deteriorated, and he felt it was no longer possible to continue. His successor was Tom Mather, a former boss at Stoke and Newcastle, and a man with a reputation as a talent-spotter. He had, in fact, signed Stanley Matthews for the Potteries club, and the Leicester board were hopeful he might unearth similar class in the East Midlands.

As he made plans for the transitional season of 1945/6, the world was rocked by the use of the atomic bombs on Hiroshima and Nagasaki. Within days Japan

BILLY FRAME

A stalwart during the war years,
he topped the City appearance charts with 221 outings.

had surrendered, and the Second World War came to an official end just two weeks into the footballing campaign.

The arrangements for the transitional season were slightly different to those during the previous few years. The old First and Second Division clubs were combined, then split into North and South Divisions, whilst the Third Divisions were split into four smaller sections. The popular League War Cup competitions were scrapped, but the FA Cup was reinstated, though ties were to be played on a two-leg basis at the request of the clubs to generate extra revenue.

Leicester City were placed in the League South and met with little success, ultimately finishing 20th of the 22 competitors. They also made an early Cup exit, losing on aggregate to Chelsea at the first hurdle. In October the club's official nursery, Middlesbrough Swifts, folded up due to lack of funds, and a potential source of fresh talent was lost.

The previous month, Mather had persuaded one of his discoveries from Stoke to make the move to Filbert Street. Wartime international Frank Soo was a highly-prized signing, but he was destined for only a short stay with City. On Christmas Eve he turned out for Port Vale without previously having obtained the board's permission and, following a heated dispute, was placed on the transfer list. The rift was never healed and, during the summer, Soo moved on to Luton Town.

Frank Soo - *signed from Stoke City, the wartime international was destined for only a short stay after a disagreement with the board.*

only one other, Danny Liddle with 116, reached three figures. Of the goalscorers, George Dewis earned pride of place with 62 goals in 81 games. Sep Smith managed to accumulate 48 goals over the period, his total boosted by 12 successful spot kicks. Two of City's managers had come and gone without selecting a side for an official League game.

Wartime football was hardly going to be mourned by City. The period of makeshift competition and major internal upheaval had, however, seen the club emerge on a sounder footing than that on which they entered it, and the prospect of a fresh start in Division Two, free of the stigma of the pre-war relegation debacle, was one to be relished.

Tom Mather himself never really settled at Leicester, and in mid-March handed in his resignation. He had occupied the managerial chair for a mere ten months. Before his departure, however, he had recognised City's need for an experienced general to marshal his young team. To this end he tried to persuade Wolves to part with Stan Cullis, but the Molineux club rejected the proposal.

Two days after Mather resigned, John Duncan, the man who had captained City in their halcyon days of the late 1920s, was appointed to take over the managerial reins. It was too late for him to change the club's fortunes for that season but his day would come.

Sep Smith and Billy Frame once more led the appearance charts as wartime football drew to a close, whilst Stan Mercer was the leading marksman with 10 goals. Crowds had returned to reasonable levels despite the 'artificial' nature of the competitive fare on offer, but the remarkable Filbert Street attendance of 32,904 attracted in May by a schoolboy match - albeit the first leg of the Final of the English Schools FA Trophy - indexed the potential peacetime drawing power of the game. (Incidentally, Leicester Boys - under the captaincy of future County Cricket skipper Maurice Hallam - overcame their Stockton counterparts with a 4-1 home win and a further 3-0 victory at Ayresome Park to bring this particular pot home for the first time).

Over the seven seasons covered by World War Two, City had played 273 competitive matches, including the three League games of 1939/40 and the two FA Cup ties of 1945/6, winning 96 and losing 122. Three players topped the 200 appearance mark - Billy Frame with 221, Sep Smith 215 and Bert Howe 211 - yet such were the outside demands on players' time during this period that

Sep Smith *lost many of his best playing years to the war. He made 215 appearances and scored 48 goals during the hostilities.*

PEACE AND PROGRESS

1946 - 47

The prospect of Leicester City's return to peacetime soccer and a genuine Football League programme remarkably resembled that which had faced the club at the end of the Great War. The team were once again in Division Two, were under new management, and the club had undergone a major financial and structural overhaul during the break occasioned by the hostilities.

Once again, the backbone of the City squad would be formed from two groups of players - the handful of mainly youthful discoveries who had staked their claim during the years of Regional football, and several hardy survivors from the pre-war era. Each of the players in the latter category had, of course, lost some seven seasons of their professional careers to the war, and some, like skipper Sep Smith, were now very much at the veteran stage.

Behind the scenes, as Johnny Duncan plotted his first campaign with the assistance of trainers George Ritchie and Bill McLean, there was one other significant change, with the appointment of Charles Maley as Club Secretary.

The fixture list for 1946/7 duplicated that originally drawn up for the abandoned season of 1939/40, but this time City did not get off to such a good start. In fact only five points were gleaned from the first eight fixtures, and Duncan was quick to ring the team changes, discarding, among others, his new centre-forward Dave McCulloch, who could not rediscover his pre-war scoring knack. But the team's form picked up in October to such an extent that only one defeat was suffered in the next ten outings, and a useful attacking partnership between Jack Lee and George Dewis began to emerge, materially assisted by the stylish promptings of Don Revie.

Eventually, a crop of niggling injuries disrupted the balance of the side, but the final League placing of ninth gave modest grounds for optimism. The twin effect of those injuries and of Duncan's search for an effective blend can best be seen from the fact that no player managed to turn out in more than 36 of the 42 League fixtures. Mal Griffiths topped the appearance charts, and was also the first City player capped after the war, when chosen on Wales' right wing against Ireland in April. Jack Lee led the scoring list with 18 League goals from only 24 games, though George Dewis supplemented his League tally of 16 with three Cup strikes.

Overall, the season was not quite the boom year that nostalgic myth would have it. The fixture list was severely disrupted by what was, to that date, the worst winter on record. The combination of this and a Government ban on midweek League games led to the season extending into June. Supporters' enthusiasm was understandably somewhat dimmed, and City's final home game with Fulham drew a gate of only 8,006 - which remained a postwar record low for a League match at Filbert Street for over 35 years.

City did, though, manage to stir their fans' interest with their FA Cup exploits. A fine away win over West Ham in Round Three was followed by a long-drawn-out affair with First Division Brentford, dogged by ice and snow, and it took a third-game victory at neutral Villa Park to bring the reward of a Fifth Round tie with Newcastle United. 50,309 witnessed City emerge from St.James' Park with a brave draw, but the Geordies triumphed in another icy spectacular at Leicester to end City's Wembley hopes.

Dave McCulloch
- pictured here in Brentford strip -
was soon discarded by Duncan when he failed
to reproduce his pre-war form.

Although some degree of stability had been achieved during Johnny Duncan's first season in charge, it was clear the team needed to be strengthened if a promotion bid was to be made. To this end, the club paid out a fee of £4,600 to Swansea Town in July to secure the services of the versatile Jack Haines.

The future England international did not settle in particularly well though, and by March was transferred to West Bromwich Albion in part exchange for Scottish playmaker Peter McKennan. City also expended £6,000 in cash to complete this deal so, although a value was never formally put on the transfer, it may legitimately be regarded as the equivalent of a club record.

The other transaction of significance during the season occurred in January, when no less than five City players moved to Watford on the same day - a deal thought to be unique in football history. Calvert, Eggleston, Osborne and Hartley all made a permanent switch to Vicarage Road, whilst Cheney was loaned until the end of the season. Hartley, incidentally, was an inside-forward who had only been on City's books for a month after signing from Chesterfield.

The club made further attempts to reinforce the senior squad, including enquiries for Joe Arnison of Rangers and Reg Lewis of Arsenal, but no actual bids were tabled. Another young player watched during the season was Danny Blanchflower of Glentoran, but again no action was taken, and City's loss would much later be Spurs' decided gain.

Trainers Chandler and McLean help injury victim **Johnny King** *off the pitch at Filbert Street.*

*Sep **Smith** leads out City for the FA Cup tie with Sheffield Wednesday, followed by **Walter Harrison** and **Jimmy Harrison**. City won 2-1.*

The season itself pretty closely mirrored the previous one. The team again finished ninth in Division Two, generally betraying elegant approach work with penalty-area profligacy, and again reached the Fifth Round of the FA Cup, this time tasting defeat at White Hart Lane after removing Bury and Sheffield Wednesday from the competition. A massive 69,049 gate saw three Spurs' goals in three minutes kill off City's plucky challenge after the score had stood at 2-2 with 64 minutes gone.

Injuries again took their toll, with Revie and Lee both sidelined for long periods, and once more no player came close to being ever-present. Lee, with 13 League goals and two more in the Cup, was the only scorer in double figures, but young Derek Hines burst onto the scene towards the end of the campaign, and notched six in nine games.

Indeed, it was from the less experienced members of Duncan's quietly reshaped squad that City drew most encouragement in this generally mediocre season. The Reserves demonstrated their promise by capturing the Combination Cup, beating Bournemouth & Boscombe Athletic 2-1 in the Filbert Street Final with goals from Sandy Scott (penalty) and Arthur Smith.

The site of Filbert Street itself was the subject of some boardroom discussion. There was then no prospect of purchasing the ground from the City Council and, as the lease was coming up for renewal, the directors took the interim opportunity to consider other sites for a ground the club might own. Possible moves to Enderby, Abbey Lane or Saffron Lane were, however, all rejected, and continuing tenancy of the club's traditional home confirmed.

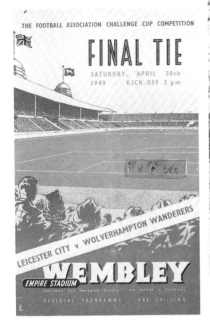

*Manager **John Duncan** and skipper **Norman Plummer** lead City out at Wembley for their first FA Cup Final, followed by **Gordon Bradley**, **Walter Harrison** and **Sandy Scott**.*

During the summer of 1948, the board decided that a club crest would henceforth be worn on the players' jerseys. The design chosen, representing the hunting traditions of the county, was that of a fox's head, surrounded by the letters 'LCFC'. Little could the directors have imagined that, within a year, City's unlikely trophy-hunting ambitions would lead to the new badge being worn with pride at Wembley.

Johnny Duncan meanwhile sifted his squad for another attempt at producing a promotion-worthy blend. A useful £14,750 fee was picked up from Bolton during the summer for Jimmy Hernon, and this meant enquiries for both Don Revie (from Notts County and Arsenal) and Jack Lee (from Nottingham Forest and Coventry City) could be dismissed. As the season got underway, the opening-day promise of a 6-2 slaughter of Leeds soon gave way to a worrying slide, so Duncan played the market again. Out went Peter McKennan (to Brentford for £7,000) to be replaced briefly by Scottish junior Tom Paterson. In, as the slither into the relegation zone became precipitate, came Third Lanark's inside-forward Jimmy Ayton (for £7,750), Arbroath's goalkeeper Ian McGraw and, in time for a New Year's Day debut, Leeds inside-left Ken Chisholm, for a record £11,000 outlay.

Second Division failings were becoming a severe embarrassment by the time the diversion of the FA Cup came around. Charlie Wayman had helped himself to five of Southampton's six against City, but a shot-shy forward line earned as much criticism as the occasionally rickety defence. The side was anything but settled; Sep Smith was coming to the end of an illustrious career, and he saw Norman Plummer take over both his centre-half position and the club captaincy; yet even the latter was uncertain of automatic selection.

As City lined up for their Third Round tie away to Birmingham City, the League table showed them in 19th place in Division Two, with only Grimsby Town, Nottingham Forest and Lincoln City below them. It took some time - three games and 330 minutes, in fact - for City to register a heartening giant-killing over their top-flight rivals, but the tonic effect was welcome.

A 5-3 thumping of fellow strugglers Lincoln City had lifted City to 17th place in the table when Preston North End came to Filbert Street in Round Four. The Lancastrians would eventually be relegated from Division One, and City had little trouble in building on an opening-minute penalty lead to complete another giant-killing act and reach Round Five for the third consecutive season.

This time fellow Second Division club Luton Town provided the opposition. The game, at Kenilworth Road, was among the most exciting cup-ties ever staged. After six minutes City scored the opener, four minutes later Luton led 2-1, by half-time City had nosed in front by 3-2, and at the end of 90 minutes the score stood at 3-3. An extra half-hour was to be played, and City quickly restored their lead, but by the mid-point of the extra period, Luton again held the advantage, by 5-4. As the game drifted into injury time, it looked as if this would be the final result, but Mal Griffiths sent over a last-ditch corner and Jack Lee rose to head home the equaliser. It was Lee's fourth goal of the game.

The replay, the following week, was no anti-climax. Luton netted in the first minute, but City stormed back to lead 4-1 shortly after half-time. The Hatters then staged a rally to reduce the arrears to 4-3 and keep the 38,822 crowd on tenterhooks before a late Griffiths goal ensured City's passage to the quarter-finals.

THE ROAD TO

*1: **Third Round v Birmingham City :** Revie and Lee pressurise the Blues goal in the first replay.*
*2: **Fourth Round v Preston North End:** Lee's second minute penalty fires City ahead. 3: **Fifth Round v Luton Town :** Lee's replay*
*spot kick makes it 4-1 early in the second half. 4: **Sixth Round v Brentford :** A bullet header from Lee puts City in front,*
*with Chisholm in support. 5: **Semi-Final v Portsmouth :** Revie nets City's first goal, as Lee and Chisholm look on.*

WEMBLEY 1949

1: City players introduced to the Duke of Gloucester before the kick-off are: Plummer, W.Harrison, King, Griffiths, Lee, J.Harrison, Chisholm and Adam. 2: Anxious moments for Bradley, Chisholm and Scott. 3: Griffiths evades the Wolves challenge, with Jimmy Harrison in support. 4: Griffiths goal puts City back into the game. 5: Bradley under pressure, with Jelly looking on. 6: Chisholm's 'equaliser' was ruled out by an offside decision.

City were back down in 18th place when they travelled to Griffin Park to meet Brentford in Round Six. The Londoners were only three places higher, however, and Leicester, boosted by a classic diving header from Lee, won comfortably by 2-0 to reach the semi-final for only the second time in their history.

Highbury was the venue for City's clash with Portsmouth, leaders and eventual champions of Division One. City had slipped again, down to 20th position in Division Two, and were frankly given next to no chance of extracting revenge for their defeat at this stage in 1934. What followed, though, is still regarded by many as City's finest hour.

The Leicester performance that afternoon was quite magnificent, with Don Revie the orchestrator as well as the scorer of two goals. This was no hit-and-run display; City simply outplayed their more illustrious opponents on the day, silenced the Pompey chimes, and ran out 3-1 winners to clinch their first-ever appearance in the FA Cup Final.

Fate, however, stepped in to deal the club two cruel blows before the trip to Wembley. Only a week after the Highbury success, City found themselves involved in a real rough-house of a battle against Grimsby at home. They scraped a point from the encounter, but suffered several injuries, including one to 'keeper Ian McGraw's hand which ruled him out of the Final, and eventually led to him losing a finger. Then Don Revie, the architect of the Cup run, suffered a serious nose injury and a near-fatal loss of blood, so was barred even from making the trip to Wembley, let alone playing.

City were still very much on the brink of relegation to the Third Division, with only three League games still to play, when they faced Wolves at Wembley with something of a makeshift line-up. The First Division outfit unsurprisingly dominated the first half and two goals from Jesse Pye looked to have the game sewn up before the interval. However, Johnny Duncan reorganised his forward-line during the break and, just two minutes into the second half, City struck back. Mal Griffiths was the man who scored, latching on to Bert Williams' parry of Chisholm's power-drive, and Wolves suddenly began to totter.

A newly-confident City continued to press for the equaliser, but in the 64th minute came the incident that effectively settled the game. Taking a long cross from Jim Harrison, Ken Chisholm netted from an acute angle for City, only to be ruled marginally offside. With the players still deflated by referee Mortimer's decision, Wolves broke away and, within 60 seconds, Sammy Smyth had scored to make it 1-3. So, the Cup was lost and City, with widespread praise for gallantry ringing in their ears, returned to their desperate relegation battle.

Four days after the Final, City gained an invaluable win at Bury, but within 24 hours, this advantage had been nullified by a crushing home defeat at the hands of West Bromwich Albion, who thereby sealed their own promotion. By this time, Lincoln already knew they would be relegated; it was a toss-up whether City or Nottingham Forest would accompany them into the Third.

Thus City came to their final match, against Cardiff City at Ninian Park, needing a point to ensure safety, assuming Forest would beat Bury in their final fixture. When news filtered through of Forest's duly accomplished victory, in a game with an earlier kick-off time,

City were clearly in deep trouble. They trailed to a 65th minute goal by Baker, yet were being urged on even by the Cardiff fans. Eventually, with only 13 minutes of the season remaining, Jack Lee's head came to the rescue, and his rather soft equaliser banished the spectre of the drop.

Recently, this match has been the subject of a suggestion (by Ken Chisholm) that the result was induced by collusion. (See Simon Inglis's 'Soccer In The Dock', Willow Books, 1985). However, such accusations are not that uncommon where vital games are concerned, and no evidence has been produced to adequately support the claim, which naturally has been refuted by all others concerned with either club. The final game was also notable in marking the last appearance of Sep Smith in a City shirt, almost 20 years after his debut. Later in May he took up a new position as club coach.

A postscript to this extraordinary season would note that the board, elated at the twin achievements of Cup glory and Second Division survival, definitively turned down the opportunity to purchase the Blackbird Road speedway and greyhound stadium, and once more committed the club to its Filbert Street base.

The Sports Mercury reports City's brave challenge. Note how a full league programme was played on the same day.

Charlie Adam's *1949 FA Cup Runners-Up medal. Front (left) and Reverse (right).*

City fans could well have been forgiven for looking back from the summer of 1949 in the firm belief they had recently seen enough dramatic action to last them a couple of years. Such sentiments would have been premonitory. The season of 1949/50 almost defined on-field mediocrity, and pretty much all the drama involved the swinging to and fro of the main doors at Filbert Street, as backroom and playing personnel came and went with near-bewildering rapidity.

JIMMY HARRISON

Jimmy Harrison, in a £12,000 deal with Aston Villa in July, was the first of the Cup Final eleven to depart, and when the League term started with a lacklustre performance at Hillsborough, Wembley skipper Norman Plummer also found himself out of favour, replaced by strongman Tom McArthur. Joint trainer Bill McLean was another to make a close season exit, and Jim Metcalfe assumed the role of head trainer. The rumour machine also rattled into action from Day One of the season, with allegations rife of dressing room dissension.

As if to give substance to the whispers, new captain Don Revie had a transfer request granted in September. A veritable flood of enquiries ensued, but Johnny Duncan held out for a part-exchange deal. By mid-October, with little sign of this materialising, little improvement in results and, indeed, little evidence of the side being otherwise substantially strengthened, the manager was asked to resign.

The City board, only briefly deflected by an inconclusive Football Association investigation into reports that the club had been party to Cup Final ticket profiteering (the appropriate evidential file of ticket applications had been accidentally destroyed!), set itself the dual task of progressing Revie's transfer and finding the club a new manager.

First a player-exchange deal with Arsenal foundered, then Revie himself turned down Manchester City after a £25,000 bid had been accepted. Eventually, Hull City stepped in to secure the services of the future England international for £20,000. At the same time, though, the board rejected outright Everton's overtures for Jack Lee.

Former Bury boss Norman Bullock was the man chosen to reinvigorate a struggling side, and he eased into the manager's chair at the end of November, by which time only four Second Division victories had accrued. Eire international goalkeeper Tommy Godwin arrived at Filbert Street only days before Duncan's departure, but there were to be six more senior purchases by new-broom Bullock before the end of the campaign.

One-time Pompey foe Bert Barlow joined the forward line, and Wrexham schoolteacher Ron Jackson inherited Sandy Scott's No.3 shirt. Blackburn wing-half Jimmy Baldwin buttressed the side midway through its face-saving improvement in March, and no less than three newcomers arrived on transfer deadline day - wingers Peter Small and Ian Wilson, and inside forward Jack Marsh; the latter in a part-exchange deal that also saw Ken Chisholm move on to Coventry. Chisholm had been agitating for a move since February, and had previously rebuffed both Sheffield Wednesday and Plymouth Argyle.

It was a much shuffled side which ended the season in a lowly 15th place. Only a decent spell in February and March had kept City out of the relegation zone, yet even that momentum had not been maintained to the end of the term. The defence had leaked badly, the forwards (apart from reliable Jack Lee) had rarely appeared incisive, and even the captaincy had passed from hand to hand, as Revie, Walter Harrison and the reinstated Plummer each took spells leading out the team. Almost inevitably, this year's FA Cup effort had ended in meek surrender at the initial hurdle, at Bramall Lane.

Bullock, having achieved the immediate, consolidatory stage of what he maintained would be a five-year struggle for promotion, was still far from happy with the resources at his disposal. May saw George Ritchie and Sep Smith sever their long associations with the City as they followed head trainer Metcalfe out of Filbert Street; veterans Billy Frame and George Dewis were given free transfers, and six more players with senior experience put on the list. June saw David Jones installed as new trainer.

But it was the transfer activity of July which would prove most important to the City story. Controversy was the immediate upshot when two deals were announced on the same day - popular centre-forward Jack Lee was sold to Derby for £16,000, and £14,000 of the fee invested in his little-heralded replacement from Fulham. It would not, however, take long for the new forward to stifle the initially heartfelt criticisms of this most shrewd bit of Bullock business: the City faithful would soon have a new hero in Arthur Rowley.

Making his City debut in a No.9 shirt, Arthur Rowley nabbed a late winner at Bury on the new season's opening day. But initial optimism that this was to be City's big year soon dissipated. After all five forwards got themselves on the scoresheet in the opening home game against QPR, the team went seven games without a win, and it was soon apparent that a mid-table slot would again represent the height of the season's Second Division ambitions.

Norman Bullock once more played the transfer market. Full-back 'Buller' Lever was tempted to Filbert Street from Cardiff City for a £15,000 fee, and was immediately installed as club captain. Wing-half Reg Halton rejoined his former Gigg Lane manager, and bold bids for Roy Pritchard from Wolves and for Stoke's ex-England skipper Neil Franklin only foundered on the unwillingness of the players to move after terms had been agreed with their clubs. In the latter case, Bullock was indeed ready to shell out a club record £20,000 fee.

A more crucial managerial intervention, however, turned out to be the recall of young centre-forward Derek Hines, and the shifting of Rowley to the inside-left position, a berth from which he would henceforth terrorise defences for well over a decade. 'The Gunner' scored the decisive goal at Hull past Don Revie, on emergency duty between the sticks after an injury to the Tigers' goalie; took up the mantle of responsibility for City's penalties; notched his first Filbert Street hat-trick against Bury; and was soon on his way to a seasonal tally of 28

goals - the best post-war League return from a City marksman, and a total which placed him second in the Division Two scoring chart, behind Cecil McCormack of Barnsley.

That Rowley was such a crowd-pleaser was just as well, for his predecessor Jack Lee was finally called up to lead the England line against Ireland in October, when mutterings of discontent about the former favourite's release were still barely muted. City's own international, Mal Griffiths, added two Welsh caps to his collection during this term, and at least thereby showed that 'unfashionable' City were not entirely out of the selectors' orbit.

City pulled themselves out of the early-season mire with a sequence of results between December and mid-March which saw only one defeat in ten fixtures, and eventually achieved a comfortable position of 14th. In the midst of this face-saving effort, champions-to-be Preston North End handed out a Third Round Cup drubbing at Filbert Street to quash hopes of knock-out glory, and the same side followed up with an Easter League double over City, yet managed, however, to attract over 37,000 spectators to the game at Leicester when the outcome was almost academic to the home side.

Bullock strengthened the ex-Bury contingent at Filbert Street with the acquisition, late in March, of inside-right Fred Worthington; but otherwise seemed quite happy with his playing resources as the basis for a renewed promotion push in the autumn.

City clung to the fringe of the promotion race throughout this winter as the forward combination of Hines and Rowley tormented opposing defences. By the end of the season, Rowley was again ranked second in the Division Two goalscorers' list - behind Sheffield Wednesday's Derek Dooley - but this time with a club record of 38 League goals. One sequence saw Rowley strike in seven consecutive games, collecting eleven credits, while the 'scorer's apprentice', Hines, himself amassed a 17-goal tally as City battled to maintain their promotion hopes.

In the end that target was missed by a mere four points, and City had to settle for 5th place in the table despite manager Bullock's tinkerings with his squad. Tom Dryburgh had now assumed Charlie Adam's left-flank position, and full-back Bill Webb, goalkeeper Adam Dickson and inside-forward Arthur Dixon were all given runs, but it was January before City made any significant splash in the transfer market, when centre-half Matt Gillies was persuaded to leave Bolton Wanderers to try his luck in the East Midlands. Upon his signing,

Gillies also took over the captaincy from Lever. By mid-March, with promotion still a possibility, the club parted with a sizeable fee to secure the signature of England 'B' full-back Stan Milburn from Chesterfield. Unfortunately, the final push did not ensure success, as three victories over the Easter weekend could not compensate for three desperately depressing defeats immediately prior to the holiday. In the first of these, City shipped five goals to the Sheffield United attack for the second time in the season - the Filbert Street meeting in November had produced the third 5-5 draw in the club's history.

The Third Round of the FA Cup proved to be an insurmountable hurdle for City for the third consecutive season - quite a let-down for a club that had recently tasted the atmosphere of a Wembley final. This time it was Coventry City who did the damage. Like Preston the previous year, they were eventually destined to leave the Second Division at the end of the season, but unlike the Lancastrians, their exit would signal the beginning of a period of obscurity in the lower Divisions. Against Leicester, however, they fielded a team including Jimmy

Harrison and Ken Chisholm, achieved a draw at Filbert Street, then handed City a 4-1 hiding in the replay, with both former City Cup heroes amongst their scorers.

The improvement in City's stature as credible promotion challengers was at least recognised at the season's end by the club's own directors, who arranged a four-game tour of Holland as the first post-war taste of continental football. Three wins and a draw resulted, and the experience was deemed extremely useful - while the fans back home sincerely hoped such 'away' form would be carried over to the next term's crack at securing a top-flight return.

1952 - 53

Arthur Chandler congratulates *Arthur Rowley* on breaking his club goalscoring record with 41 League and Cup strikes.

To continue to fuel City's promotion hopes, Bullock was again ready to plunge into the transfer market. An early enquiry for Denis Wilshaw was rejected by Wolves, but in October the club again paid out a record fee. This time the target was Derby's Johnny Morris, and the sum involved was £21,500. The international inside-forward's signing was, however, to prove the start of a stormy relationship.

By that time, City had already established themselves amongst the Division's front-runners. Four of the first five games were won, including two 6-goal romps against Fulham, and Rowley and Hines were once again the scourge of the penalty area, with 'The Gunner' claiming four and three goals from his previous club in the home and away fixtures. (In mitigation it should be noted Fulham had to move goalkeeper Ian Black to centre-forward midway through the first game - yet it was he who claimed their consolation goal!)

However, in late November, it was City who were handed a salutary lesson in football skills, when Sheffield United ran out winners at Bramall Lane by 7-2. Predictably, the Blades would go on to become Second Division champions, while City, despite scoring more goals and winning more points than in the previous season, again had to settle for 5th place - ten points adrift of promotion.

Rowley finally managed to finish the season as the Division's leading scorer, setting a new club record of 39 League goals and, indeed, topping the entire Football League list. Hines continued to provide support, this time with 14 goals, and so well noted had the pairing become

that Portsmouth actually made an enquiry during December as to whether they might be able to purchase both. Needless to say, Bullock firmly rejected the approach.

One oddity about the 89 League goals scored by Leicester this season was that no less than 85 of them came from the forward line. In addition, two of the other four were actually own-goals, so there was clearly no mistaking the roles of the various units in Bullock's squad!

For the fourth successive year, the FA Cup challenge ended in disaster. This time the Third Round visitors were a Notts County team well below City in the table and destined to finish 19th, but once more the story was a familiar one as the Magpies triumphed by 4-2. Thus City had still not tasted success in a cup-tie since their famous semi-final against Portsmouth in 1949. Arthur Rowley also collected both City's goals in this game, giving him an overall total of 41 for the season - again a new club record.

City's reserves, playing for the first time in the Second Division of the recently reorganised Football Combination, at least achieved the promotion target their seniors had missed, finishing as runners-up.

When Norman Bullock had taken over from John Duncan in 1949, he had stated that he could take the club back to Division One within five years provided he was given a free hand and enough money to buy the players he required. The directors had lived up to their part of the bargain admirably. Now Bullock had just one more season to go to justify his prophecy.

*Matt Gillies, the City skipper, receives the **Division Two Championship shield** from Arthur Oakley, Vice-President of the Football League.*

Draws at home to Derby County and Fulham, and an intervening 1-4 defeat in London at the hands of West Ham, hardly represented the opening to the season both players and supporters were looking for. If promotion was to be a realistic aim, the team simply could not afford to drop too far behind the leaders in the early weeks of the campaign. Bullock quickly roused his men, however, and convinced them their forward-line was the most feared in the Division. As if on cue, in September, his assessment was backed up by Arsenal, who enquired vainly whether City might part with Morris, Hines and Rowley - quite a compliment to a Second Division outfit!

The goals indeed began to flow regularly again from the forwards as City embarked on an unbeaten run covering 14 matches to establish themselves firmly in the promotion race, culminating in a 2-1 victory over Everton at Goodison Park, achieved despite the late loss of goalkeeper Johnny Anderson, that was ultimately to prove absolutely crucial. In late November, Lincoln City were crushed 9-2 at Filbert Street, Derek Hines netted no less than five times, and the fans began to believe in Bullock's powers of prophecy.

Then, at the turn of the year, came an alarming reversal in fortunes. The three League fixtures played during January were all lost, and a 1-7 thumping at Elland Road (featuring a hat-trick by City reject Ray Iggleden) threatened to dent confidence severely. That this essential element was quickly restored was in no small way due to a Third Round FA Cup victory over First Division Middlesbrough - City's first Cup win since 1949.

The team pulled themselves together with five successive League wins, and enjoyed an eight-game Cup run which only came to an end in a quarter-final second replay, when eventual finalists Preston North End triumphed at neutral Hillsborough.

As Easter approached, the promotion battle had settled into a three-horse race between City, Everton and Blackburn Rovers. Just as the supporters got ready to celebrate, City very nearly managed to throw everything away. A three-goal defeat at Blackburn on Good Friday and a draw with Notts County at Filbert Street the following day put the club's position in jeopardy, but the response was all that could be asked. On Easter Monday, City slammed Blackburn 4-0 in the return fixture (in front of a new record League crowd of 40,040) and, on the following Saturday, won 3-1 at Brentford in the final game. As Everton only drew 1-1 at Lincoln on Easter Monday, and left themselves needing two wins to draw level on points with City, the Second Division Championship shield returned to Filbert Street for the third time.

City triumphed on goal average from the Merseysiders with a final average of 1.62 as opposed to the Toffees' 1.59. Blackburn had finished just one point behind with a far superior goal average; anything less than victory in those last two matches meant City would have missed promotion altogether.

Manager Bullock had seen his 'five-year plan' come to fruition and had largely shown faith in the forces assembled over the previous four years. There had been no close-season signings, and the only additions to the first-team squad during the campaign had been those of left-half Eddie Russell from Middlesbrough, in November, and of Portsmouth's versatile former England international, Jack Froggatt, in March. The team's final total of 97 League goals was a new club record, and all five regular forwards reached double figures. Rowley, inevitably, led the way, though his total of 30 League goals was almost an anti-climax in the light of the previous two seasons' hauls; whilst Derek Hines again provided the main supporting role with 19.

Mal Griffiths, for Wales, and Johnny Anderson, for Scotland, both won international recognition, but there was still no sign of a call-up for Rowley. Perhaps the chance to display his talents in Division One would change things?

Norman Bullock was shrewd enough to know his squad needed further strengthening if the club's new status was to be consolidated. But the £15,000 expended on Froggatt had seriously depleted the club coffers, and interest in Brentford's Jimmy Bloomfield was thwarted when the player signed for Arsenal. Worryingly, Johnny Morris, who had never managed to form a good relationship with Bullock, was granted his request to be listed during the summer, but a lack of bids meant the promotion team was in fact the one which started the new campaign.

A home draw with Chelsea and a 3-2 win at The Valley gave brief cause for optimism, but four straight defeats followed, and the writing was well and truly on the wall by the end of October, when City had only two wins out of fifteen fixtures to their credit. Bullock attempted to introduce new faces - making enquiries for Bolton's Bell, Villa's Blanchflower, and the Newcastle pair of Hannah and Stokoe - but all foundered, and a series of injury problems led to the early blooding of several reserves.

The initial defeat at Cardiff was symptomatic of early-season problems piling up - City were down to nine men, including an injured goalkeeper, before conceding a late, decisive goal.

Willie Cunningham was signed from St.Mirren for £4,750 in November to bolster an ailing defence but, at the same time, a £15,000 bid for Burnley wing-half Les Shannon was firmly rebuffed. Eventually, in December, with Derek Hines sidelined through injury, City paid out a club record fee of £27,600 for Lincoln's free-scoring centre-forward Andy Graver. The new man netted on his debut at Stamford Bridge, but, in a 1-3 defeat, it was one of the goals at the other end which summed up City's plight - Stan Milburn and Jack Froggatt contrived to kick the ball simultaneously past Johnny Anderson and found themselves credited with a unique 'shared' own-goal!

The club's confidence in Bullock was eroding swiftly, and, at the end of the year, the directors asked him to resign once the season was over. As it transpired, an incident at a Whitley Bay hotel in February, following a defeat away to Newcastle, brought matters to a head somewhat prematurely. An emergency board meeting the next day resulted in a statement being issued that it was "impossible for the manager to conduct the affairs of the club or be able to control the playing staff."

*Heading practice in 1954 for **Matt Gillies**, **Mal Griffiths**, **Arthur Rowley**, **Derek Hines** and **Jack Froggatt**.*

Johnny Morris and *Derek Hines* put pressure on the Blackpool goal
during a 2-2 draw at Filbert Street on 30th October 1954.

Norman Bullock was given the opportunity of resigning immediately, and this he did. Johnny Morris, Bullock's main adversary, was himself suspended for 14 days for his part in the incidents at Whitley Bay.

Managerless City briefly rallied, but could find no consistency before the season's end. Attempts to avoid relegation failed, but eventually they had the right to consider themselves a shade unlucky, as the club's total of 35 points was the highest for a relegated club since 1937/8. Additionally, an extremely tight First Division table had seen second-placed Wolves only eight points clear of 17th-placed West Brom. A more settled City side, or perhaps one pulled together by a replacement manager, might well have saved itself.

Lack of support from the terraces and stands could certainly not be blamed for the fall from grace. Not only had a new (and definitive) Filbert Street record gate for a League game been established - 42,486 were attracted by the October visit of Arsenal - but the average home attendance for the season represented the highest-ever at 30,964.

The unhappy Andy Graver, who had failed to settle and had given way to a fit-again Hines, was the target for end-of-season enquiries from Sheffield Wednesday, Stoke City and Preston, but eventually rejoined Lincoln City for a record outgoing fee of £26,000.

The board got around to considering candidates for the vacant manager's post early in the close season. They enquired after Barnsley's Tim Ward, but then interviewed two more strong candidates - David Halliday and Joe Mercer. After some debate, the directors decided to entrust the former with the task of resurrecting City's fortunes and securing an early return to the top Division.

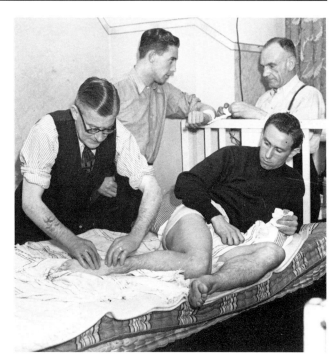

*Minor repairs in the treatment room.
Pictured are Bill McLean,* **Barrie Thomas***,* **Johnny King**
and Arthur Chandler

1955 - 56

The previous season, Halliday had guided Aberdeen to the Scottish League Championship, and his faith in Caledonian quality was manifestly strong as, during his first year at Filbert Street, he signed eleven players from north of the border, including no less than five from his former club. His most significant signing turned out to be Willie Gardiner, a centre-forward from Rangers, who actually achieved the barely credible feat of toppling Arthur Rowley from the head of the club's scoring list.

In fact, the gangling Gardiner finished the season as the leading goalscorer in Division Two, with 34 goals. Rowley was five behind his new partner in the League but, when FA Cup goals were accounted for (from a win over Luton and a draw and defeat against Stoke), the pair of them finished up with 35 apiece.

Mainly on the strength of this duo's spectacular efforts, City were able to remain on the fringe of the promotion race throughout the season. Jack Froggatt retained the captaincy he had taken over from Matt Gillies the previous term, Derek Hogg was now a left-flank regular, and defenders John Ogilvie and Pat Ward were other Halliday acquisitions to shine.

Consistency was, however, hardly the side's keynote. City reaped nine goals from their opening two wins, but within a fortnight had conceded thirteen in two successive away defeats! They went on to thrash then-leaders Swansea by 6-1, and promotion-winners Leeds by 5-2, yet soon surrendered at home to relegation-bound Hull. Ultimately it was a defeat at the hands of champions-elect Sheffield Wednesday on Easter Monday that dashed hopes of an immediate return to Division One, and City had to be content with 5th position, four points adrift of their target. Yet clearly Halliday had succeeded in reshaping his team in readiness for a major assault during the following campaign.

Two deals which did fall through, however, were an attempt to sign Billy Bingham from Sunderland, and a

Johnny Anderson - ever present this season.

player exchange transaction involving Derek Hines and West Ham's Harry Hooper. Halliday's transfer market proficiency apparently held less sway south of the border. Another proposal to hit the dust was put together by the City board for a League conference in March, when they were prepared to advocate a radical restructuring of the competition into, effectively, five sections. The same board were, however, unprepared to sanction another break with tradition by allowing a mooted boxing tournament to take place at Filbert Street during the summer.

1956 - 57

The close season of 1956 was marked primarily by a series of negotiations between the Football League and the television companies over conflicting bids to broadcast live the second-half of selected games over the coming season. ATV proposed to put 35 such matches on the small screen on Saturday evenings, while the BBC responded with an offer to cover the final 45 minutes of twelve games on Tuesday evenings. No agreement was reached - the fact that still relatively few clubs possessed floodlights had some bearing - and it was very much 'business as usual' when the new campaign kicked off in August.

For Leicester City, however, the season turned out to be something rather special. The Championship of Division Two was brought to Filbert Street for the fourth time and with it came no less than six new club records. Fresh benchmarks were set for most wins (25), most away wins (11), fewest defeats (6), most points (61), most goals (109), and for highest individual scoring. Arthur Rowley claimed 44 and again topped the marksmanship list for the entire Football League. Runner-up to him in the Division Two chart was a certain Brian Clough of Middlesbrough with 38.

*__Arthur Rowley__ in action against Nottingham Forest
during the record-breaking Second Division championship season when he hit 44 goals.*

With few newcomers to the senior squad (the right wing-berth was taken successively by Tommy McDonald and Billy Wright, while goalkeeper Dave MacLaren arrived from Dundee in January to replace the seriously injured Anderson), the team spirit in the City camp was superb throughout the campaign, and testament to this could be found in the fact that not only did the team never lose successive games, but also managed seven victories in matches when they had trailed at the interval. Their positive attitude shone through perhaps most brightly on March 30th, when City, as League leaders, travelled to second-placed Nottingham Forest to face one of their most demanding tests. Ian McNeill found the net within 10 seconds, City produced a masterly display to win 2-1, and their Trentside rivals effectively conceded the Championship.

The return passage to Division One was nominally clinched the following Saturday as West Ham were beaten 5-3, largely thanks to Rowley's fourth hat-trick of the campaign, and in the course of this game City reached their seasonal century of League goals for the first time. The Championship was formally sealed with a 5-1 win at Leyton Orient on Easter Monday and, despite an irrelevant hiccup in the return game, City closed their account with a seven-point margin over Forest.

For the second successive season Willie Cunningham had earned Irish caps while turning out regularly in City's reserves, but the nearest Arthur Rowley came to international honours was an appearance for the Football League against the Irish League at Newcastle.

As the promotion celebrations died down, work began on the installation of a floodlighting system at Filbert Street, and the City board sent out invitations to several famous European clubs in the hope of bringing the fans a series of notable floodlit friendlies in the future. Though the likes of Real Madrid, Juventus and AC Milan would not actually grace the Filbert Street turf during the following season, the directors' outlook was certainly a positive one as City stood on the threshold of a new era back in Division One.

*The new champions of Division Two are cheered off the field
despite the hiccup of a home defeat by Leyton Orient in their final match.*

Work may have proceeded apace on the new Filbert Street pylons, but David Halliday and his board were rather slower off the mark when applying reconstruction plans to City's playing resources. A degree of confidence in the Second Division record-breakers of the previous term was understandable, but the harsh lessons of the club's 1954/5 top flight misadventure might profitably have been heeded earlier.

City's combativeness for the challenge was in little doubt - Johnny Morris even contrived to get himself sent off in the pre-season public practice match! - but the cliche that Division One is a whole new ball game was rammed home emphatically in the campaign's early weeks. Six of the first seven fixtures ended in defeat, and only five victories accrued before Christmas. City were marked early as relegation favourites.

Halliday shuffled his playing pack ceaselessly, and then entered the market for reinforcements. 'Busby Babe' John Doherty arrived for £6,500, but was soon found to be carrying a long-term injury problem. Then, as veteran skipper Jack Froggatt moved on to Kettering for £6,000, in came Birmingham centre-half John Newman at twice the price, only to make his debut at the heart of a City defence which shipped seven Burnley goals.

Carefree defending of this sort was no longer wholly compensated for by the once brilliant attack. Rowley, Gardiner and Hines were all in partial or relative decline (even if each were the target of several new transfer bids), and only the consistent peak form of Derek Hogg kept City in the picture until their fortunes were boosted after the New Year by the emergence of Jimmy Walsh and the availability of Howard Riley. Then a private in the Royal Leicestershire Regiment, Riley became City's first Under-23 cap, while Willie Cunningham, who took over the captaincy after Froggatt's departure, added two further Irish international appearances to his record during this term.

Despite a distinct imbalance between such encouragements and severe embarrassments, Leicester kept in close enough contact with their similarly inconsistent partners in First Division distress, and were not about to give up their new status without a supreme struggle.

They certainly entertained a public which could afford to be almost blase about goals. In fact City claimed 91 successes over the season to set against the new record tally of 112 conceded. In seven matches City scored four or more goals, while they let in at least four on eleven occasions. Indeed, they achieved both feats simultaneously when meeting Manchester City at Filbert Street on February 22nd - running out 8-4 winners, with Walsh claiming four himself. A 4-1 away win at Tottenham in December was another seasonal highlight, though Spurs later removed City from the FA Cup at the initial hurdle for the second successive season, and threatened to hasten City's downward doom when winning at Filbert Street in the campaign's penultimate match.

Ultimately, only one escape route remained. Victory at St.Andrews on the final day could keep City up.

Halliday gambled on five team changes, introduced young Len Chalmers for a nerve-wracking debut, and saw Ian McNeill replace Rowley and poach the goal which beat Birmingham, lifted City to 18th place and condemned Sunderland to a first-ever relegation.

Relief was followed immediately by the realisation that genuine consolidation required reinvestment in the team. At various stages of the season, Halliday had made enquiries for Manchester United's Ronnie Cope and Freddie Goodwin, Derby's Jack Parry and Tottenham's Jim Iley, and had been frustrated each time. He had also despatched scouts to monitor the progress of a young Preston wing-half, but Gordon Milne's role in City's history would not be assumed until much later. Now, however, Halliday's dealings bore fruit.

In April, promising Northampton forward Ken Leek guested against Canto do Rio in the third of the season's international floodlit friendlies (the lights had been christened back in October, when 18,398 watched City beat Borussia Dortmund with a Gardiner goal), and signed days later for £5,750. Then, using most of the £20,000 received from the surprise sale of Derek Hogg to West Brom, Halliday captured wing-half Ken Keyworth from Rotherham, full-back Ian MacFarlane from Chelsea and winger Gordon Wills from Notts County. The manager however, had one major close-season shock still up his sleeve.

*Despite injuries, **Arthur Rowley** still managed 20 goals in 25 League appearances. He is challenged here by Burnley's Jimmy Adamson, but scored twice during the 5-3 home win in April.*

Arthur Rowley had rattled up a total of 265 goals in 321 appearances for City, and looked poised to overtake Arthur Chandler as the club's all-time record marksman, when David Halliday stunned Leicester supporters in June with the news that 'The Gunner' was to be allowed to move on to lowly Shrewsbury Town for a fee of £4,250. As a close-season controversy, there had been nothing to match this particular bombshell since 1950, when Jack Lee had departed and Rowley himself arrived.

Ken Leek donned Rowley's No.10 shirt in the season's curtain-raiser, and netted in a 2-0 home win over Everton that would actually prove to be the club's last opening-day victory for twelve seasons. It would also prove to be a false dawn for 1958, as City conceded ten goals in their next two fixtures to paint a more accurate picture of their immediate First Division prospects.

These soon swung from bad to worse, and four successive dismal defeats led to the resignation of David Halliday on November 4th. Two days later, coach Matt Gillies took over as acting manager, and eventually the former centre-half was confirmed in the full time position on January 28th.

Gillies had his own ideas of the kind of player needed to transform City into a solid First Division outfit, and behind-the-scenes activity intensified during the following months. Little of this resulted in actual deals, though the ambition of the man can be judged by the calibre of players for whom unsuccessful enquiries were made; Gordon Harris and John Connelly (Burnley), Geoff Strong (Arsenal), Peter McParland (Aston Villa), Tony Kay (Sheffield Wednesday) and Bobby Robson (West Brom).

By and large, though, City had to soldier on with their established squad. The first home game with Gillies in charge produced a 6-3 win over Aston Villa in which Derek Hines notched four goals, and a good spell bracketing Christmas relieved some of the gloom from Filbert Street. Twelve games without a win, however, left City squarely in the relegation zone, and Good Friday arrived with the club in 21st place and seemingly doomed.

A Houdini act was once more required and, remarkably, duly delivered. Of the nine remaining fixtures, four were won and three drawn. A 4-1 win on Trentside helped set up a grandstand finale, and 38,466 watched a tense home victory in the penultimate game against League runners-up Manchester United confirm the team's status for another year. Defeat in the last match at Maine Road hardly worried nineteenth-placed Leicester, but it still had a crucial bearing on the relegation issue, with Manchester City thereby saving themselves at Aston Villa's expense.

Leaving such dramatic escapology aside, the campaign had been illumined less by highlights than sidelights, one of which saw both FA Cup finalists progress to Wembley via Filbert Street. Luton Town had drawn there before despatching City in a Fourth Round replay, while Nottingham Forest had eliminated a troublesome Birmingham City at the third attempt on the neutral Leicester ground. Birmingham had also been the visitors in March when Filbert Street hosted its first-ever all-floodlit League game.

Perhaps ironically in view of the seniors' struggles, City's reserves captured the Football Combination title for the first (and only) time, pipping reigning champions Chelsea by a point. Clearly, the club's complement of up-and-coming talent - bolstered by Matt Gillies' end-of-season capture of promising young goalkeeper Gordon Banks - offered a substantial cause for renewed optimism.

Ken Leek
Made his debut in Rowley's No. 10 shirt.

Derek Hines
Netted four goals at home to Aston Villa.

THE CUPS THAT (ALMOST) CHEERED

1959 - 60

Matt Gillies made just one dent in the club record profit of £36,797 during the summer, securing forward Albert Cheesebrough from Burnley for £19,775, but otherwise contented himself with taking on former wartime colleague Bert Johnson as chief scout.

However, another poor start to the season soon had him chasing quality new blood, only to find on-field disappointments being matched by rebuffs off it. Offers were made for John White of Falkirk (£15,000 plus Walsh, or £10,000 plus Cunningham) and for Joe Baker of Hibernian (£30,000), but all were turned down. Enquiries for Brian Clough (Middlesbrough) and Billy Bingham (Luton) met with no encouragement, and scouting missions to watch Huddersfield's young Denis Law saw him turn in unimpressive displays on two separate occasions!

Early in September, Dave MacLaren was carried off after 30 minutes at the Hawthorns and a 0-5 scoreline resulted. This accident opened the way for Gordon Banks to make his debut in the following match and, not much more than a month later, he had established himself as first choice 'keeper. Also promoted from the reserves during September was a young, slim wing-half called Frank McLintock.

To talk of immediate impact from the new stars-to-be, however, would be to ignore the uncomfortable facts of First Division life. By December, City were once more in 21st place in the table. One result, though, seemed to turn their season around. Wolves were reigning champions, and the only top-flight club to have maintained an unbeaten home record, when City went to Molineux and

triumphed 3-0. A fine, steady revival from Leicester thereafter lifted them well up the table to an eventual 12th place; a significant factor was that more away points (17) had been secured by the club than ever before in a Division One campaign.

In the FA Cup too, City finally put together a noteworthy run. Negotiating a difficult away tie at Wrexham and eclipsing Fulham at Filbert Street, City met West Brom (with a certain Jock Wallace in goal) in the Fifth Round, and got through for the third time with a 2-1 scoreline, in a match clouded by the tragedy of the half-time death of referee Jack Husband. In the quarter-final game with Wolves however, the share out of the three goals went in the visitors' favour, with Len Chalmers heartbroken by his own-goal contribution. Wolves went on to win the Cup, but City completed the League double over them, ironically only a week after the Cup exit.

The Wolves Cup-tie also gave rise to one of the other ironies of the season. With tickets for the game much coveted items, the decision to sell them at the turnstiles on 27th February led to a crowd of 22,800 attending the reserves' Combination fixture with Bournemouth - on the same day that only 18,691 watched City's seniors take on Luton at Kenilworth Road!

On the representative front, Willie Cunningham won three more Irish caps to bring his tally to 23 gained whilst with City, making him then the club's most-capped player. Tony Knapp played for the Football League and was also a member of the full England party for their European tour during May, though he was fated never to win a full cap.

THE FOOTBALL ASSOCIATION CHALLENGE CUP COMPETITION

FINAL TIE
LEICESTER CITY
v
TOTTENHAM HOTSPUR

SATURDAY, MAY 6th, 1961   KICK-OFF 3 p.m.

EMPIRE STADIUM
WEMBLEY

OFFICIAL PROGRAMME   ONE SHILLING

*Manager **Matt Gillies** leads out the City team for the **1961 FA Cup Final** against Double-chasing Tottenham Hotspur at Wembley.*

Whatever the expectations of the City faithful - and even the committed optimists were not looking far beyond their favourites managing to avoid the annual relegation scare - none could have been quite prepared for the events of the new campaign.

Tottenham Hotspur grabbed all the early-season headlines with an opening sequence of 11 successive victories (the ninth coming at Filbert Street), and showed every sign of carrying all before them. City, meanwhile, with much the same line-up as in the previous campaign, recovered from an initial wobbly patch to settle comfortably into the middle of the table by the season's halfway stage.

Matt Gillies was again frustrated in early efforts to strengthen his team, as a £30,000 bid for Arsenal's David Herd was rejected, and he received no joy from enquiries for Terry Medwin (Spurs), Alan Gilzean (Dundee) or Pat Crerand (Celtic). Jimmy Walsh had taken over the captaincy from Len Chalmers, and had made his mark on the new Football League Cup competition, introduced in low-key fashion amid much hostility from the leading clubs (many of whom declined to enter). Walsh claimed the competition's opening goal on his way to a hat-trick in City's First Round victory over Mansfield Town, but the ignominy of a home defeat by Rotherham United (eventual finalists) at the next hurdle was City's back-handed reward.

Certainly, there was little evidence here (or in a second-half collapse at Fulham, when a Graham Leggat hat-trick sparked the Cottagers' four-goal reply to City's 2-0 lead) to suggest the imminent upturn in Leicester's

fortunes. But a Boxing Day win over Bolton sparked an unbeaten 13-game run into March, by which time City were well established in the upper reaches of the League table, and confirmed as Cup semi-finalists.

League form peaked with fine home wins over Everton and Newcastle, a magnificent 6-0 demolition of Manchester United, and a record-breaking 3-2 win at White Hart Lane (where Super Spurs were hitherto unbeaten), but City's most significant FA Cup run for 12 years was now getting into its stride.

Non-Leaguers Oxford United were City's Round Three victims at Filbert Street, but the Cup run hiccuped to a temporary halt three weeks later when a quagmire of a pitch forced the half-time abandonment of the home tie with Bristol City. A Richie Norman own goal was the first meaningful action when the tie was re-staged, but the Robins were then swept aside by a 20-minute whirlwind of five City goals.

It took a home replay to dispose of Birmingham City in Round Five, and extra-time in an Oakwell replay to overcome the plucky challenge of Third Division Barnsley, who had kept City scoreless for the first time since Christmas when drawing at Leicester. Ken Leek's late winner meant he had scored in each round to date.

A 0-1 League defeat at the Hawthorns (with George Heyes deputising for Banks) ended City's unbeaten run, but they entered the Cup semi-final at Elland Road as clear favourites to beat Second Division Sheffield United and reach Wembley for the second time. In the event, the game was a goalless anti-climax, with the most significant occurrence an injury to winger Gordon Wills that brought his season to a sadly premature close.

The replay, staged by Nottingham Forest, was a dour carbon copy, with both sides seemingly inhibited by fear of failure, but the third meeting, at St Andrews, possessed more than its fair share of drama. After just 11 minutes, Ian King saw his penalty saved after he stubbed his toe into the ground at the moment of impact. Then, after 24 minutes, Jimmy Walsh headed City into the lead (signalling the end of an overall sequence of 451 minutes' play without a goal by City since the Barnsley matchwinner). Ken Leek added a second just after half-time, but the Blades were given an opportunity to revive their hopes with a penalty after 65 minutes. Graham Shaw stepped up, pulled his shot wide, and City were effectively through to meet Double-chasing Spurs.

The team continued to impress in League performance after the semi-final marathon, and eventually finished sixth, their highest placing for 32 years. Banks and Riley were both honoured with England Under-23 appearances, and Ken Leek was capped by Wales. Two youngsters were drafted in towards the end of the campaign, and both made scoring debuts. Local discovery Graham Cross would go on to play a major role in the City story over the next 15 years, but Scottish junior Hugh McIlmoyle could hardly guess at the mark he would make almost immediately in City annals.

City's preparations for the Wembley showcase were outwardly unremarkable. Wills had been ruled out for weeks, but no new injury worries impinged on Gillies' plans to tackle Tottenham. Spurs already had the League title in the bag, but nagging away at their confidence, as they sought to become the first side this century to take the Double, was the memory of how City had mastered them at White Hart Lane, and especially of how Ken Leek had always given Maurice Norman a torrid time.

Then, only days before the match, came City's bombshell. Leading scorer Leek was dropped, and young McIlmoyle handed his place. Matt Gillies claimed it was a matter of current form. Since the semi-final Leek had played four League games and scored in three, while McIlmoyle's seven appearances (the extent of his senior experience) had netted him four goals. The public could not believe it. Every sort of rumour flew around Leicester, but the club stuck by Gillies' explanation, and has done ever since. (Only those directly concerned could possibly contradict, as the pages of the boardroom minute book which cover the pre-Cup Final meeting have been removed!)

When City strode out at Wembley though, there were no discernible ill-effects on their spirit from this rumpus. They settled to the game faster than Spurs, and it should be emphasised that McIlmoyle's deeper-lying style posed a considerable threat to a Tottenham defence probably better prepared to face the more conventional spearhead of Leek. It was however, the old Wembley hoodoo which had most bearing on the outcome as Len Chalmers came out of a first-half challenge by Les Allen with a crippling leg injury, and thereafter City were effectively reduced to 10 men, despite the full-back gallantly remaining on the field for pure nuisance value. McLintock was pulled back into defence, and Spurs cannily exploited their advantage by virtually running City's depleted forces off their feet. A tiring City conceded two late goals and the game, but were far from disgraced as the North Londoners celebrated their historic achievement.

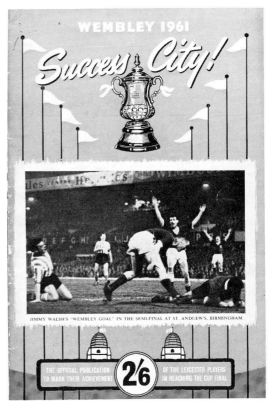

*A special **Souvenir Brochure** was produced to celebrate the club's second trip to Wembley.*

The Sports Mail *reflected on the injury to Len Chalmers and the shock dropping of Ken Leek.*

THE ROAD TO

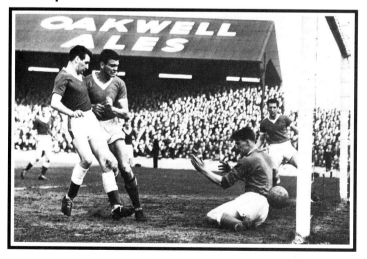

1: Third Round v Oxford United: Kyle challenges Jimmy Walsh. 2: Fourth Round v Bristol City: McLintock struggles through the mud in the abandoned game. 3: Fifth Round v Birmingham City: Riley's goal earns City a replay.
4: Sixth Round v Barnsley: Leek is in close attendance as Riley's goal clinches the replay victory.
5: Semi-Final v Sheffield United: Leek puts the Blades defence under pressure in the Nottingham replay.

WEMBLEY 1961

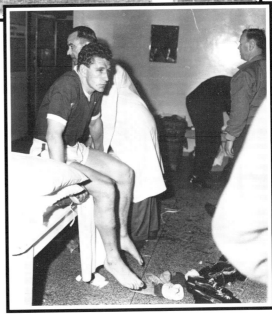

1: Skipper Walsh gives a pre-match interview. 2: Walsh pressurises Spurs' Mackay and goalkeeper Brown.
3: An early effort on goal from McIlmoyle with Cheesebrough in support. 4: Despair for Banks, McLintock, King
and Norman as Bobby Smith fires Spurs ahead. 5: A glum Len Chalmers reflects in the dressing-room
on what might have been.

Unsurprisingly, in view of the events of May, Ken Leek was a summer departure from Filbert Street, joining Newcastle United for £24,700. Also leaving City was another class performer, Tony Knapp, who had lost out to Ian King in a close contest for the No.5 shirt. Liverpool and Wolves were interested, and City proposed an exchange deal with the latter that would have involved Peter Broadbent, but Knapp eventually moved to Southampton for an initial fee of £25,000, which would rise by ten per cent after he had made 25 senior appearances. Otherwise, Matt Gillies' satisfaction with his squad seemed complete. The only incoming transfer during the summer heralded a frustrating City sojourn for Dunfermline's Scottish Cup hero David Thomson, while trialist winger John Mitten was the only first-team newcomer over the first half of the season.

A new experience awaited City this term - one they have never been able to enjoy since. A spin-off of Spurs' Double achievement was that beaten Cup Finalists City would compete as English representatives in the European Cup Winners Cup, while Spurs carried the banner in the premier competition. Comfortable victories both home and away over Irish Cup-holders Glenavon earned City a glamorous clash with Spanish stylists Atletico Madrid in Round Two, and a classic first leg at Filbert Street ended at 1-1 when Mendoza managed a last-minute reply to Ken Keyworth's opener. The second leg drew over 50,000 to watch a stubborn City exit to the eventual Cup winners -

*No programmes were produced for either of City's two away games in European competition. However, **Atletico Madrid** advertised the arrival of City with a spectacular poster.*

but not before Graham Cross had distinguished himself with a fine centre-half performance on his 18th birthday, and Gordon Banks had kept out the first of two Atletico penalties.

This night was one of the few proud memories City could retain from a generally anti-climatic season. The League challenge never got off the ground, and City were anchored around the middle of the table throughout the campaign, eventually finishing 14th. Two September defeats by Burnley were among the term's noteworthy events - the 0-2 setback at Turf Moor was sustained courtesy of own goals by both Colin Appleton and Ian King, while the 2-6 reverse at home had the Filbert Street fans granting a heartfelt standing ovation to the visitors for a quite breathtaking display. Burnley in fact returned to Leicester later in the season, to earn their trip to Wembley by overcoming Fulham in an FA Cup semi-final replay.

City's own domestic pot-hunting efforts both proved disastrous. In the League Cup, Fourth Division York City delivered a humiliating knockout, and the board later debated the wisdom of continuing to enter this competition, before concluding they would do so until it was discontinued. In the FA Cup, Leicester were ousted in a Third Round replay by Stoke City, losing 2-5, with two 'goals' disallowed for offside. Essentially, though, the tie hinged on a wondrous performance by the veteran Stanley Matthews, who gave Richie Norman the runaround of his career.

This latter Cup exit prompted Gillies into the transfer market to try and salvage something from the season. He had met a rebuff when enquiring about Airdrie's centre-forward Jim Storrie, but was then successful with two bids of £25,000 each - to be repaid in kind many times over - for Mansfield's rangy left-winger Mike Stringfellow and Hibernian's superbly skilful schemer David Gibson. Gibson was still on National Service, and his appearances for the rest of the term therefore restricted, while Stringfellow initially struggled to find his shooting boots, but soon there were glimpses of just what an exciting left-flank partnership this pair would forge.

There was also a glimpse of the effectiveness of another City hero-to-be this year. Derek Dougan claimed one of Aston Villa's goals in their 2-0 win at Filbert Street, and two more in their 8-3 crushing of City at Villa Park in April - the last occasion Leicester conceded so many goals. Gordon Banks was rarely so embarrassed, and his justifiably growing reputation was acknowledged by selection for the Football League. Scottish Under-23 honours for Frank McLintock completed City's representative haul this term.

Developments off the field were perhaps of most consequence. In March, the club agreed to purchase the freehold of the Filbert Street ground from the council for a sum of £30,500, and thereby secured their most valuable asset. Then, at the end of the season, long-serving club secretary Charles Maley retired. He was, unfortunately, not in the best of health and in fact passed away three years later.

*Manager **Matt Gillies** leads out the City team*
*for the **1963 FA Cup Final** against Manchester United at Wembley.*

Eddie Plumley was appointed club secretary in July, and was immediately involved in the formation of the Leicester City Development Association. A weekly pool and daily tote was to be run to fund ground improvements now the club had sole responsibility for such matters. Money was still available to Matt Gillies for team-strengthening, but he chose not to expend any during the summer, and was rewarded for such faith in his side as City made their best start to a First Division campaign since 1925/6, taking 18 points from the first 13 fixtures to lie in fifth place.

For once, Gillies was now in the enviable position of having to fend off enquiries for his players: from Wolves (McLintock), Arsenal and Newcastle (Banks), Preston and Bury (Cheesebrough) and Blackpool and Northampton (Riley). Indeed, during December, Arsenal manager Billy Wright was actually reported to the League for an illegal approach to Banks.

City's inventive tactical approach to their campaign (often involving an elegant interchange of roles between McLintock and Cross and essentially based on a counter-attacking style) was already being remarked upon by the national press as Christmas neared with City still up among the challengers. The League Cup had again proved an embarrassment, as City squandered a clear four-goal lead over Charlton at Filbert Street (when even Gordon Banks contributed an own goal), and lost the replay at The Valley; but League form was distinctly pleasing.

Boxing Day 1962 proved a particularly significant date. It heralded the beginning of the most severe winter this century which eventually threw fixture lists into chaos, though City's astute use of chemically-treated topsoil would generate enough warmth to break the icy Filbert Street surface and allow home fixtures to be completed. It was also the date on which Colin Appleton took over from Jimmy Walsh as captain, Leyton Orient were trounced 5-1 at Filbert Street, and a record-breaking run of 16 games undefeated, including 10 successive victories, got underway. City were about to earn their tag of 'Ice-Age Champs'.

No League games were played during January, but Grimsby and Ipswich were each dismissed in FA Cup-ties. Four straight League victories followed in February, then, on 2nd March, City completed a League double over Liverpool with a 2-0 triumph at Anfield - the first time the Merseysiders had failed to score in 55 successive home games. It was City's eighth consecutive victory. A Fifth Round Cup win at Leyton Orient and a League success against Blackburn took the sequence into double figures to set the scene for the visit of League leaders Tottenham.

Spurs themselves were unbeaten in League matches since 8th December, and stood just one place above City. A crowd of 41,622 witnessed high drama on the stroke of half-time as Jimmy Greaves netted only to find the referee's whistle had blown a split second earlier. The final scoreline was 2-2 and City continued their unbeaten

THE ROAD TO

1: Third Round v Grimsby Town: *Banks, Sjoberg and King combine to foil a Mariners attack.* **2: Fourth Round v Ipswich Town:**
Keyworth nets City's second goal. **3: Fifth Round v Leyton Orient:** *Gibson makes an airborne effort on goal at Brisbane Road.*
4: Sixth Round v Norwich City: *Keyworth congratulates scorer Stringfellow as City take the lead.*
5: Semi-Final v Liverpool: *Stringfellow jumps to net the decisive header at Hillsborough.*

WEMBLEY 1963

1: Denis Law turns on a sixpence to shoot United ahead. 2: Stringfellow's effort flashes across the United goal with Keyworth closing in. 3: Keyworth's spectacular diving header... and 4: goalkeeper Gaskell is beaten at last. 5: Late City pressure from Riley, Appleton, Norman, Sjoberg and Cross.

run - including a Sixth Round Cup victory in front of Norwich's all-time record crowd - to Monday, 8th April. On that night, following a 1-1 draw at Blackpool, the First Division table showed City in top position for the first time since September 1927.

	P	W	D	L	F	A	Pts
Leicester City	**34**	**19**	**10**	**5**	**68**	**35**	**48**
Tottenham Hotspur	33	20	7	6	92	45	47
Everton	33	18	9	6	66	36	45
Burnley	31	16	8	7	60	42	40
Wolverhampton W	32	15	8	9	74	51	38
Liverpool	31	14	8	9	57	40	36

The following Saturday, at Easter, the run ended at Upton Park and top place was lost. However, a draw at Old Trafford on Easter Monday was followed by a breath-taking return fixture the next day when the pinnacle was regained. Ken Keyworth notched a hat-trick in the space of six minutes, Denis Law claimed three for United (including a miraculous bicycle kick), and a Terry Heath goal split the two sides, 4-3 in City's favour.

City's fourth game in eight days, a home draw against Wolves, saw them once more toppled from premier position. A brief respite followed, before City travelled to Hillsborough to take on Liverpool in the FA Cup semi-final. Mike Stringfellow headed the decisive goal after 18 minutes in one of City's few attacks, and a magnificent rearguard action, with Banks outstanding, saw City safely through to Wembley for the third time. No-one could possibly have envisaged that this was to be City's last victory of the season.

Matt Gillies had made pre-deadline attempts to bolster his squad for the anticipated run-in towards the elusive League and Cup Double. An enquiry for Bradford's Kevin Hector was rebuffed, as were two bids for Motherwell's Bobby Roberts. This failure to reinforce would indeed prove costly, as City's League challenge petered out with four successive away defeats. A final First Division placing of fourth was a crushing disappointment, despite being the club's best performance since 1928/9!

City's hopes were nonetheless high that Cup glory was at hand. Opponents Manchester United had been involved in the relegation battle all season, and the credit balance from the Easter clashes was definitely in City's favour. Three new full internationals would be in City colours - Banks, McLintock and Gibson - whilst Appleton had represented the Football League and Cross had gained his first Under-23 cap. Surely, it would be a case of third time lucky for City?

Alas, on the big day, City's stars froze into something approaching dazed ineptitude, whilst United's talented individuals blossomed. Denis Law turned on a sixpence to shoot United ahead, Banks mishandled to allow David Herd to slot home a second, Ken Keyworth lifted City hopes with a superb diving header with just nine minutes remaining, but Banks erred again for Herd to seal United's victory by 3-1. City simply had not done themselves justice.

The bigger the stakes, the harder it became to swallow the disappointments. Certainly, Gillies had established the club amongst the elite. But would any tangible reward or trophy ever result?

The Sports Mail admitted that this time it was not one of City's better days.

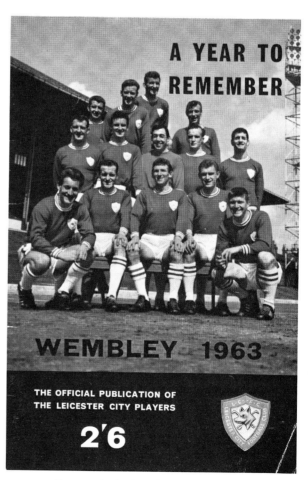

*Once again the feat of reaching Wembley was marked by the issue of a **Souvenir Brochure**.*

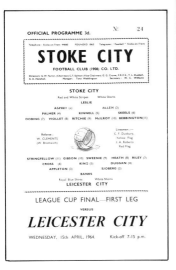

Colin Appleton collects the *1964 League Cup*
after City's 4-3 aggregate win over Stoke City.

An attempt to sign Bury centre-forward George Jones failed during the summer, so it was the familiar Cup Final eleven who lined up for the start of the new season - only the second time in the club's history, and the first since 1937, that exactly the same team selection had been made for both the final game of one season and the first of the next. (the third and most recent example of this phenomenon would occur in 1976).

Again, City flattered to deceive. A draw at the Hawthorns, a 3-0 home victory over Birmingham City and a spectacular 7-2 Filbert Street win against Arsenal (handicapped by the early loss of goalkeeper Jack McClelland) saw City head the first published tables of the season. But inconsistency dogged the side thereafter, nullifying the effect of five straight League wins around Christmas, and the respectability of 11th place was the final return from the League campaign.

Bargain signings Jimmy Goodfellow and Billy Hodgson flitted in and out of the team, and even the eventual capture of Bobby Roberts from Motherwell (at a club record fee of £41,000) did not pay immediate dividends. Additionally, City interest in Swindon's Don Rogers and Manchester City's Neil Young was quashed at the enquiry stage.

The FA Cup proved a huge disappointment, as a surprise 2-3 home defeat came at the hands of Leyton Orient in Round Three. Malcolm Musgrove, later to become City's coach, netted twice for the visitors.

Substantial consolation accrued, however, from the less vaunted Football League Cup.

A series of competent performances in the early rounds accounted for Aldershot, Tranmere, Gillingham and Norwich, and allowed first-team bloodings for youngsters Bob Newton, Max Dougan and Tom Sweenie. An extra-time winner from Howard Riley in the home replay against the Canaries set City up for a semi-final clash with West Ham, and a 4-3 thriller in the first leg at Filbert Street left the tie finely balanced. The second leg was a football connoisseur's delight, with City producing their performance of the season to triumph 2-0.

The similarly two-legged Final got underway with a 1-1 draw at Stoke City's Victoria Ground - David Gibson netting for Leicester - while the return at Filbert Street finally brought the club its first-ever major trophy. Mike Stringfellow's goal separated the teams at half-time, and Stoke also conceded further strikes from Gibson and Howard Riley as an intriguing contest finished 3-2 to City on the night, and 4-3 on aggregate. Skipper Colin Appleton was able to display the silverware the following week at his well-earned Testimonial game.

During the season, Richie Norman took his club record for consecutive appearances to 194 games before a pulled muscle ended the run; 16-year-old goalkeeper David Timson became City's youngest debutant to date; and the club's international trio of Banks, Gibson and McLintock all added to their tally of caps.

Mike Stringfellow scores City's first goal in the 3-2 second-leg win that clinched an aggregate 4-3 victory over Stoke City in the 1963/4 League Cup Final.

Davie Gibson nets City's second with a glancing header from a corner.

Howard Riley drives home City's third and winning goal.

Post match celebrations in the City dressing room with
***Bert Johnson, Richie Norman, Colin Appleton, Ian King, Matt Gillies, Tom Sweenie, Sid Needham** and **Eddie Plumley**.*

*Bobby Roberts shoots for goal but Peter Bonetti saves as **Graham Cross** looks on. The second-leg of the **1965 League Cup Final** ended 0-0 and Chelsea won the trophy 3-2 on aggregate.*

Hopes for another season of success were rocked early in the summer months of 1964. Several players were involved in contractual disputes and, by the opening day of the campaign, six senior players - Appleton, Banks, Cross, Gibson, McLintock and Roberts - had all still failed to reach agreement. Most of the negotiations were over improved terms, though Gibson had requested permission to run a licensed bar at Filbert Street on matchdays, an idea summarily rejected by the directors. In addition, Banks had been transfer-listed during June following an unauthorized outburst in the press. Eventually, most problems were settled, though not before Frank McLintock moved to Arsenal for a record incoming fee of £80,000 in early October - after City had rejected enquiries for him from both Wolves and Coventry.

Against this backdrop of turmoil, it was somewhat surprising that City did not taste defeat until their seventh game, but it was not long before they flagged badly. In contrast to their winter form of recent seasons, City embarked on a run of 13 League games without a win from November to February, and were grateful for their earlier points haul when defeat in each of the last three fixtures saw a drop to eighteenth spot. Gillies was unable to spend any of the McLintock cash, having no luck with enquiries for Colin Bell (Bury), Martin Chivers (Southampton) or Peter Knowles (Wolves).

There was, however, distinct relief from the League travails in two substantial Cup runs. The FA Cup produced an exciting, hard-fought slog to the last eight before eventual winners Liverpool triumphed by the only goal in an Anfield replay, while City also conjured a valiant attempt to retain the League Cup, which for the first time carried with it the incentive of a place in the Inter-Cities Fairs Cup for the winners.

Leicester made heavy weather of a couple of their early League Cup clashes as they disposed of Peterborough, Grimsby and Crystal Palace, but really startled their fans with an uncharacteristic local derby display against Second Division Coventry City in the Highfield Road quarter-final. Sky Blues skipper George Curtis netted an own goal and then departed with an injury; City 'keeper

Banks also went off injured, although only temporarily; full-back Richie Norman scored twice; and City eventually romped home by 8-1 (still the competition's record away win). Norman, who also scored in Round Three at Grimsby, thus notched three goals during this Cup run - significant, because he only scored two others in his entire City career, spanning some 365 matches in total!

Plymouth Argyle were toppled in the semi-final, by 4-2 on aggregate (City had also removed the Pilgrims from the FA Cup, skating to a 5-0 win on an icy Filbert Street), but Chelsea posed a sterner threat in the Final. Goals from Colin Appleton and Jimmy Goodfellow could not prevent a 2-3 reverse in the first leg at Stamford Bridge (where they still talk in awe of Eddie McCreadie's individualist goal that night), and constant one-way pressure could not unlock the well-drilled Chelsea defence at Filbert Street, where a 0-0 scoreline saw the trophy wrenched from City's grasp.

(Incidentally, a draw resulted in Filbert Street's other national Cup Final of this year: with Leicester Boys and Swansea Boys sharing the English Schools FA Trophy after a hearteningly skilful second-leg display had failed to separate the teams).

In total, City packed 58 senior competitive games - more than ever before - into their season, from the August day they faced newly-promoted Sunderland's 15-year-old 'keeper Derek Forster at Roker, to their dull-as-ditchwater April home defeat by Stoke. Even so, the passed-up opportunity to add two friendlies to this roster reflected rather badly on the City board.

In September, they rejected terms offered by the FA for a match against top Brazilian club Santos, featuring the incomparable Pele, and in January turned down a request by Arthur Rowley to stage a Testimonial game at Filbert Street. At the end of the season, Shrewsbury player-manager Rowley finally hung up his shooting boots, having registered a Football League record of 434 goals, 251 of them for City. The fans were left wondering if a forward of such character would ever don a City jersey again.

The cover of a City programme from 1965-66 for the First Division 'derby' against Northampton Town.

City fielded internationals from all four home countries:
Derek Dougan *(Northern Ireland),* **Gordon Banks** *(England),* **David Gibson** *(Scotland) and* **Peter Rodrigues** *(Wales).*

Character, in fact, was one of the words most often used to describe City's major summer signing. Derek Dougan cost £21,000 from Third Division Peterborough, and quickly grasped City's lifeline to put his colourful career back on the rails. The charismatic centre-forward soon became the fans' favourite, especially in harness with fellow-newcomer Jackie Sinclair, a £25,000 capture from Dunfermline.

Not all the auguries for the campaign ahead were good. An ill-fated pre-season friendly with Northampton saw Gordon Banks break a wrist, so George Heyes, an unheralded understudy for so long, began the season with a guaranteed place for several weeks.

An innovation in League football this term was the permitted use of a substitute to replace an injured player. Jimmy Goodfellow was City's first nominated No.12, and was called on to replace Graham Cross late in the opening fixture. This game, a 1-3 home reverse to Liverpool, signalled a shaky start to the campaign, which did not really pick up until Banks returned in late September, and Dougan and Sinclair developed an effective understanding with their new team-mates.

In fact, Matt Gillies made a club record bid of £50,000 to Chelsea in an attempt to add Barry Bridges to his forward line at this time, but the deal fell through. City's record fee was eventually adjusted upwards at the end of the year, when full-back Peter Rodrigues was signed from Cardiff for £42,500.

On the field, matters were rarely dull, and November pretty well encapsulated City's roller-coaster fortunes. They began the month with a 2-1 win at Goodison that would have been even better had not the referee's half-time whistle cancelled out a Sinclair scorcher. The following week Manchester United triumphed at Filbert Street, but the stark 0-5 scoreline hid the story of a superb game to which City had contributed marvellously. The Reds may have given City a lesson in the economy of finishing, but Leicester were still cheered off by their own fans after gaining 36 corner kicks without reward! They simply took out their frustrations on Newcastle a week later, waltzing to a 5-1 win at St.James' Park.

By Easter, City's fortunes had picked up considerably.

Two goals by Mike Stringfellow at Old Trafford exacted revenge for the November mauling and ended United's run of 41 home games without defeat. Days later, Tom Sweenie became City's first scoring substitute after replacing Stringfellow against Blackburn. Such efforts also helped lift City to sixth place, and briefly encouraged hopes of Fairs Cup qualification at the season's end.

Stutters over the final few fixtures, however, left them seventh in the chart. John Sjoberg contributed two own goals to West Brom's cause in a 1-5 defeat at the Hawthorns, while a week later Graham Cross netted all three goals in a 2-1 Filbert Street win over Nottingham Forest. The next game, at home to Cup winners-elect Everton, saw 16-year-old Peter Shilton keep a characteristic clean sheet on his debut, as the club's youngest senior player at that date.

For once, there was little to report on the Cup front. Manchester City closed City's interest in the League Cup at the first hurdle, and also shocked Filbert Street by shading a Fifth Round FA Cup replay after it appeared City's fine away form was going to carry them through their third awkward draw - they had already had to visit Birmingham twice to oust Villa and Blues.

Representative honours accumulated interestingly this term. All three newcomers - Dougan (Northern Ireland), Sinclair (Scotland) and Rodrigues (Wales) - won full caps, as did Banks for England, giving City the rare distinction of current internationals for all four home countries. There were also celebrations in the boardroom, especially for the Shipman family. Len was honoured by his election as President of the Football League, whilst son Terry became a fellow City director.

Another significant off-field development was the opening of licensed bars at the ground for the first time, and such was the financial success of this move that in April the directors decided to plan for the summer construction of the Fosse Bar at the Double Decker end of the Main Stand. It was somewhat ironic that in March, former club stalwart John Duncan had passed away. He was of course the first man to challenge openly the club's original principled objections that drink and football did not mix.

1966 - 67

The summer of 1966 was dominated by the World Cup finals. England's eventual victory at Wembley over West Germany was a source of much national pride, and a particular parochial slice of that pride attached to Leicester City, who had provided the faultless Gordon Banks for the winning team, and seen him hailed as successor to the legendary Lev Yashin as the world's premier goalkeeper. Football in general was to receive a terrific boost to its image and status from the events of July, but the question remained as to how much effect would be felt at Filbert Street.

There were no new faces in the City side as the season got underway with an unfortunate defeat at Anfield, and only a change in the team's strip (to all blue) impinged on the fairly pleasurable sense of deja vu which stretched almost to the end of the campaign. Sinclair hit a hat-trick in the first home fixture, a characteristically entertaining 5-4 win over West Ham, while Dougan subjected his former Villa comrades to a similar torment a few weeks later as City notched five without reply. Both regular goalscorers passed the 20-mark in League and Cup matches for the second season running, and it was perhaps no surprise that other aspects of the campaign seemed to mirror fairly accurately the events of the term before.

An eighth place finish resulted from the League challenge, and Manchester City again removed City from the FA Cup, this time at Maine Road in Round Three. This year City also set out on an alternative route to Wembley, where the League Cup Final was to be staged for the first time. However, after 5-0 victories over both Reading and Lincoln, they came a cropper at Loftus Road and went down 2-4 to an inspired Queens Park Rangers, who would eventually capture the trophy as the first Third Division club to appear in a Wembley final.

Sidelights to the seasonal flow came in September, when Denis Howell, the Government Minister with special responsibility for sport, officially opened the new Fosse Bar, and when manager Matt Gillies was appointed to the local magistrates' bench. Transfer activity was minimal around this time. Nothing arose from enquiries about Luton's Bruce Rioch or Sheffield United's Alan Birchenall, and when Sunderland's Nick Sharkey did arrive at Filbert Street in October for a small fee, he lost his place after one game to goalscoring debutant David Nish.

It was transfer activity, however, which prompted two major controversies that overshadowed all else (even a shameful outbreak of violent hooliganism at a Filbert Street 'friendly' against Rangers) in the final months of the season. Swiftly and unexpectedly, City parted with two of their genuine stars. In March, Derek Dougan was sold to Wolves for £50,000 to help seal their promotion effort, and then in April another £50,000 fee was accepted from Stoke City for Gordon Banks. 'The Doog' was a prolific scorer and immensely popular with the Filbert Street fans, while Banks had won a record 37 caps during his time with City, and was thought by many still to be approaching his peak.

The supporters found it hard to forgive Gillies or his directors over the Dougan sale, although there was a general realisation that a difficult decision had to be made over the goalkeeping dilemma, especially once the prodigiously talented Peter Shilton had made his ambitions plain. The sheer speed of the Banks move, however, caught out even Liverpool's legendary boss Bill Shankly, who rang to table a bid literally seconds after the 'keeper had signed for Stoke.

Neither the knowledge the club now had money in the bank, nor that it possessed a fine crop of youngsters, did much to placate the disgruntled supporters. The Reserves did, however, manage to draw 8,804 of them to Filbert Street for the second leg of the Football Combination Cup Final, and pulled back a deficit to draw 2-2 on aggregate with Spurs and share the trophy. Here, apparently, was long-term promise; but could either City or their fans find the patience to wait for its fulfilment?

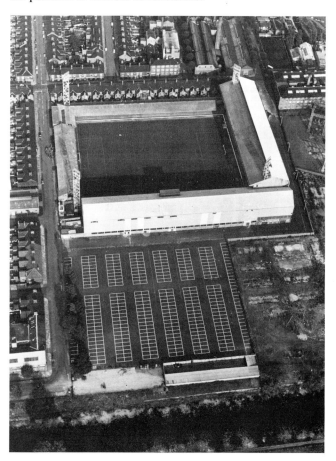

*An aerial view of **Filbert Street** in the mid-60's.*
Cover was now provided on all sides, but modern innovations
such as Executive Boxes had not yet been built. At that time
Season Ticket holders still entered via main gates as turnstiles
had not been installed in the Centre Stand.

1967 - 68

To the impartial eye, it looked as if City were letting the grass grow under their feet. Literally, in the sense that Filbert Street was wholly returfed this close season with a surface cut from the Belvoir Drive training ground; and metaphorically, in that nothing tangible by way of signings resulted from Matt Gillies' attempts at team-building. Enquiries were made for Jim McCalliog (Sheffield Wednesday), Ron Davies (Southampton), Mike Doyle (Manchester City), Fred Pickering (Everton), Alf Arrowsmith (Liverpool) and Maurice Setters (Stoke), but not a single deal developed.

The season opened with two defeats and, in what appeared a panic measure, centre-half John Sjoberg was switched to lead the attack in the third fixture, at Old Trafford. City did salvage their first point, but not before suffering a real scare. Peter Shilton was carried off injured, and Bobby Roberts had to don the 'keeper's jersey for the final eight minutes. The sale of Banks had rebounded on City in unexpected fashion, and Gillies had to persuade Forest reserve Brian Williamson to join the club on loan to cover Shilton's ensuing absence.

The manager suffered more disappointments when bids of £70,000 for Hull striker Chris Chilton and of £110,000 for Burnley's Andy Lochhead were each rejected, and was successful only in shoring up the defence with Willie Bell from Leeds. The team also experienced mixed fortunes. A fit-again Shilton actually scored a goal with a punt from his own area in a 5-1 victory over Southampton at The Dell (the club's sole win there, ever!), but Graham Cross suffered a broken leg in a friendly in Strasbourg.

Significant signings finally came in November. Much-travelled Frank Large arrived from Northampton in time to take part in a 0-6 hammering at Maine Road, and was joined a week later by Charlton winger Len Glover, who cost a record £80,000. Glover's impact with City was initially muted by injuries, but the enthusiastic Large was an almost instant hit. City were by now in a lowly League position, but gradually lifted themselves towards the relative comfort of a thirteenth place finish, mainly thanks to the overspill impetus from another memorable Cup run.

Manchester City again ended City's interest in the League Cup, and when the two teams were paired in the FA Cup for the third successive season, there was little optimism in the City camp. Leicester held out, however, at Maine Road, and brought their rivals back home for a scintillating classic of a Fourth Round replay. Two goals down inside the opening half-hour, City appeared to be heading for their customary exit, but a Large-inspired fightback on either side of half-time heralded a four-goal salvo, and City eventually won 4-3 with the Filbert Street crowd in raptures.

The regular 60's ritual of all-night queueing for tickets at Filbert Street preceded the Fifth Round trip to Rotherham, and a home replay win over the Millers further kindled Cup fever. The adventure ended though, at the quarter-final stage, with Everton pouncing on home defensive errors to produce a 1-3 scoreline.

Matt Gillies missed most of the New Year excitement, having been ordered in January to take a three-month rest from the game on medical grounds. His chief coach Bert Johnson stood in temporarily, and it was he who was responsible for first blooding another hero of the Manchester City tie, Rodney Fern. Brian Potts, Don Hutchins and Malcolm Manley also earned later promotions from the Combination ranks. Gillies would though return in the summer to continue his search for a more consistently successful City blend.

Frank Large *arrived from Northampton and was an almost instant hit as City revived to finish in 13th place in the table.*

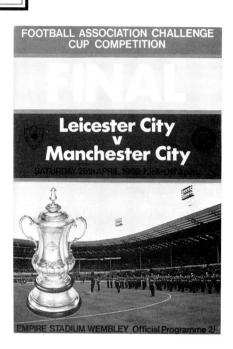

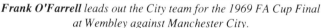

Frank O'Farrell leads out the City team for the 1969 FA Cup Final at Wembley against Manchester City.

This year it was clearly decided there should be no suggestions City had settled for second-best. Gillies got his board's backing to go out and break the British transfer record, and the target he returned with was Fulham's young forward star, Allan Clarke, in a deal valued at £150,000. City paid £110,000 in cash, but also had to let proven inspiration Frank Large move to Craven Cottage to make up the full fee. Even before hindsight could be applied, there were those who questioned the wisdom of such a deal. Ironically, the other main summer arrival at Filbert Street was Ray Shaw, a former manager of Clarke's at Walsall, and now City's chief scout. One man close to departure was Graham Cross. City accepted an £80,000 offer from Derby, but the player himself rejected the move.

Indeed, Cross lined up alongside Clarke for City's opener at Loftus Road, and the new man's debut goal gave City a share of the points. A glorious hat-trick from Clarke a few weeks later against Manchester City was another early highlight, but on the whole City's start to the campaign was disappointingly unimpressive, with goals proving hard to come by. Thoughts turned from expectancy of a title challenge to the reality of a relegation struggle. In October, Gillies tried to buy back Large for £20,000, but Fulham turned him down, so he switched to another long-time target, Burnley's Andy Lochhead, expending £80,000 on the centre-forward's experience.

By November, Derby returned with further enquiries for Cross, David Nish and Malcolm Manley, but City rebuffed their approach. It was clear to the public, however, that something was amiss at the club, with dressing-room morale and harmony at a low ebb. At a special meeting on November 28th involving the directors, three senior players and the manager, the following three points were resolved:

i) *The board expressed their confidence in the manager.*
ii) *The assistant manager (Bert Johnson) and the assistant coach (George Dewis) were to be relieved of their duties.*
iii) *Dewis was to be offered the post of A-team trainer.*

On November 29th, Gillies, who was not in agreement with these resolutions, tendered his resignation, with the announcement to be made officially at 4pm the next day. Ironically, earlier the same month, Gillies had celebrated becoming the first City manager to survive 10 years in the post. On that following day, City crashed 1-7 at Goodison to complete the miserable picture.

During December, Torquay's Frank O'Farrell was appointed manager. (The other shortlisted candidate, Allan Brown, met a double disappointment, being sacked by Luton as soon as news of his application was publicised.) By January, Malcolm Musgrove was employed as coach, so in fact, within a short space of time, all the key members of the club's backroom staff had changed. Secretary Eddie Plumley had left in October for Coventry, and had been replaced by John Smith, recently returned from Stateside football administration.

Bad weather during February led to a clutch of postponements and an unhealthy backlog of fixtures as City continued to battle against relegation. This fixture pile-up was exacerbated by another inexplicably good run in the FA Cup. Barnsley and Millwall had been

THE ROAD TO

1: Third Round v Barnsley: *Clarke's effort is blocked on the line in the tie at Oakwell.* **2: Fourth Round v Millwall:** *Glover's goal secures City's passage through.* **3: Fifth Round v Liverpool:** *Lochhead's bullet header gives City the edge at Anfield.*
4: *Peter Shilton's superb penalty save from Tommy Smith clinches a famous replay victory at Liverpool.*
5: Sixth Round v Mansfield Town: *Rodrigues, Clarke, Roberts and Sjoberg watch anxiously as the Stags attack.*
6: Semi-Final v West Bromwich Albion: *Fern and goalscorer Clarke are blocked here, but City won through at Hillsborough.*

WEMBLEY 1969

1: Nish, Gibson, Cross and Clarke are featured as Princess Anne meets the City team. 2: Shilton reacts smartly to thwart a Man.City attack supported by Cross. 3: 'Man of the Match' Clarke pressurises the Manchester defence. 4: Shilton, Woollett and Rodrigues are helpless to prevent Young's decisive goal. 5: Lochhead is foiled by Booth as City search for an equaliser.
6: Nish and Glover combine to halt a raid by Bell and Summerbee.

conquered during January, but a much-postponed Fifth Round tie with Liverpool could not take place until March. A goalless draw at Filbert Street took the teams to Anfield two days later, with struggling City marked as lambs for the slaughter. However, a bullet header from Andy Lochhead, combined with a superb Peter Shilton penalty save from Tommy Smith, inspired City to another famous Cup-tie victory. Five days later, Rodney Fern's far-post header saw off Mansfield at an overflowing Field Mill, and suddenly City were unlikely semi-finalists once more.

Hillsborough was again the venue, Cup-holders West Brom the opposition. Allan Clarke, appearing to take rather less interest in mundane League affairs, proved to be the man for the big occasion, snatching the only goal of the day with barely three minutes remaining. So City were in their fifth Cup Final of the decade, and this time their opponents would be none other than Manchester City - for the fourth successive year in the FA Cup.

There was hardly time for euphoria - not with eleven League fixtures still to play, and a crucial away encounter with fellow-strugglers Coventry City on the Tuesday. Indeed, this tense and controversial game proved most significant. City held their own comfortably until, with seven minutes to go, substitute Brian Greenhalgh was scythed down in the Coventry box and City were awarded a penalty. The ball was on the spot before the referee consulted his linesman, and mayhem ensued when he reversed the decision and gave the Sky Blues a free kick. A deflated Leicester team were left helpless as Coventry raced away to score immediately through Neil Martin at the other end.

Only two more points accrued from the next five games before, on April 26th, David Nish became the youngest captain to lead his Cup team out at Wembley. Despite City's spirited and sometimes elegant contribution to a decent footballing Final, Nish was destined to suffer the same fate as all Leicester skippers before him. Neil Young scored the only goal of the game after 23 minutes for the Mancunians, driving a low centre from Mike Summerbee high past Peter Shilton's despairing dive and, despite creating a couple of useful chances, City were vanquished at the last once again.

Following the Final, such was the imbalance in fixtures that Coventry, City's main relegation rivals, had completed their League programme, whilst Leicester still had five games to play in three weeks. At least City knew their target for survival - a further seven points.

A Clarke goal brought victory over Tottenham, but the same could not prevent defeat at Ipswich. Young debutant Ally Brown's two goals edged out Sunderland, and Graham Cross netted to salvage a draw against Everton in a bad-tempered home encounter. So City came to their final fixture requiring a victory to avoid relegation. Manchester United were the opposition, Old Trafford the venue, and the Reds were motivated by the fact this was Sir Matt Busby's final game as team manager. Skipper Nish gave City the lead in the opening minute, but three minutes later they were in arrears to an unfortunate own goal and a typical piece of George Best magic. Eventually City went down 2-3, and so ended the club's longest-ever spell in the top flight.

The attempt to climb back under O'Farrell's guidance would be witnessed by virtually a generation of fans who had never known City to be anything other than a First

Division outfit - quite a contrast to earlier days! One aspect of tradition, though, had been restored during this campaign, with the reversion to a playing strip once more featuring white shorts.

The Sports Mercury summed up City's disappointment at yet another Wembley defeat.

The achievement of reaching Wembley was once again marked by the issue of a special Souvenir Brochure.

TOUCHES OF CLASS

1969 - 70

The major transfer activity of the summer once more involved a British record fee for Allan Clarke, who had taken the 'Man of the Match' award from the Cup Final, but whose temperament was unlikely to be of much value to City in the Second Division. This time Leeds were the purchasers, at £165,000. Veteran full-back Billy Houghton was the only newcomer to Filbert Street, at the merest fraction of the Clarke fee.

The season itself started in early August, with its close scheduled for mid-April - a move designed to give the England team time to acclimatise to conditions in Mexico, where they would attempt to retain the World Cup in 1970. City seemed to like the early start, uncharacteristically opening with a victory over Birmingham that featured a spectacular overhead kick from Rodney Fern for the club's first Second Division goal in over 12 years. The side continued to prosper during the first half of the season, kept well up with the front-runners, and actually found the net in each of their opening 21 League fixtures - the best sequence in the entire competition.

Andy Lochhead initially hit a rich vein of goals, but was later jettisoned to Aston Villa for £30,000. Wolves winger John Farrington arrived for the same fee, but higher bids from O'Farrell for Watford's Stewart Scullion (£55,000) and Birmingham's Bob Latchford (£35,000) were unsuccessful. Reserve forwards Murray Brodie and David Tearse made contrasting breakthroughs; the former scored in his first two games, the latter was pressed into service as an emergency right-back at Blackburn. Kenny Sandercock, a youthful buy from Torquay, was a first-minute injury victim on his full debut, while Rodney Fern hit a hat-trick at Bolton - the first by a City player on opposition soil since the days of Arthur Rowley.

Minor off-field controversies adhered to the club as the promotion drive seemed to be going well, but rather more serious rows followed later in the term. In September the Football League objected to the design of a goalkeeping jersey worn and marketed by Peter Shilton, on the grounds that the collar fastening was potentially dangerous.

A few months on, disagreements were of a more local nature, as the 'Leicester Mercury' complained about Frank O'Farrell's policy of naming a 14-man squad on the Friday before a match, rather than the actual team line-up. A reduction of press coverage was at one stage threatened, but common sense eventually prevailed.

Back on the field, by Easter, Huddersfield looked clear favourites for promotion, with City sitting just behind Blackpool and vying strongly for the runners-up spot. The Seasiders' visit to Filbert Street on Easter Tuesday would prove vital. On the night the weather was diabolical, as torrential rain rendered the pitch a mudbath. A postponement looked likely, but the referee decided to make a start. Abandonment looked certain, however, especially when Fern's goalbound shot stuck in the cloying mud just inches short of the line, but incredibly proceedings were allowed to continue. The almost inevitable 0-0 scoreline was sufficient to cost City promotion.

There was one further controversy in store. The following Saturday, relegation-threatened Aston Villa visited Filbert Street. City won 1-0, but not before Pat McMahon's shot had clearly entered the City net, hit the rear stanchion and rebounded into play. The referee waved play on and an incensed Villa were doomed to Division Three. After the incident, the City directors resolved to alter the type of stanchion used for the following season.

City's distractions from the near-miss promotion bid included fair runs in both Cup competitions. Seven games were played in the League Cup, from which West Brom removed City at the quarter-final replay stage, having attracted a new record Filbert Street crowd for the competition 35,121 to the first game. A further five matches, all against First Division opposition, saw City to a Fifth Round home replay against Liverpool in the FA Cup. Two goals from Alun Evans spelled the end of City's Wembley hopes for the season, and Evans would prove to hold a Cup hoodoo over City some eight years later, in rather more embarrassing circumstances.

Another competition exercised the thoughts of O'Farrell by the season's end. Conscious of the ever-pressing need for Leicester to develop their own youngsters, he applied for the club's reserves to transfer to the Central League for 1970/1, but found that no vacancies then existed.

*Skipper **David Nish** celebrates the **Second Division Championship** in 1971.*
The old Championship shield had been destroyed by a fire at Coventry in March 1968.

Having just failed to point his men to promotion at the first attempt, O'Farrell looked once more to the transfer market as a means of stiffening City's renewed challenge. During the summer he had bids of £55,000 for Celtic's Tommy Gemmell and £40,000 for Sheffield United's John Tudor turned down, but prior to the opening day he expended £48,500 on Bristol City's tenacious midfielder Bobby Kellard, and continued to wheel and deal for the next few months as City recovered from the shock of an initial home defeat to get up amongst the divisional leaders.

Investments in youthful promise brought Joe Jopling and Malcolm Partridge to Filbert Street, but it was the bargain £35,000 purchase in October of Derby's wily and experienced Willie Carlin that proved the manager's masterstroke. David Gibson and Peter Rodrigues moved on with City's thanks for sterling service (the latter deposed by local discovery Steve Whitworth), and a now settled squad knuckled down to meet O'Farrell's aims. In fact, the soft-spoken Irishman's methods were at this time the subject of a television documentary series on goal-oriented business management techniques, and the City boss would, eventually, thoroughly justify such exemplary status.

Despite the loss of Partridge with a broken elbow during a goalless draw at St.Andrews, City ended November nicely tucked into the leading pack. But December and January brought only three points from six League games, and the last of these - a 1-4 home defeat by Birmingham sustained while Colin Mackleworth stood in for the injured Shilton - seemed to imply City were going backwards.

On the contrary, however, City thereafter conceded only five more goals all season as they put together a magnificent closing run of 17 unbeaten League games. The 1-0 victory at Swindon on March 13th, which took City to the top of the table, was a characteristic display of ultra-cool defending and breakaway incisiveness, while the crucial Easter Monday clash at Luton was a model illustration of City's belief in their own class, as an inspired Rodney Fern orchestrated the comeback after an own-goal reverse to secure a 3-1 win.

Another 1-0 away win, courtesy of top-scorer Ally Brown's strike at Bristol City on the night of April 27th, clinched both promotion and the championship, and David Nish was handed the trophy at Fratton Park four days later, following yet another victory on opposition soil. Particularly elated amongst the City squad was veteran defender John Sjoberg, for the silverware would be on show at Filbert Street a few weeks later when City met Derby in his Testimonial game.

Supplemented by the ever-competitive midfield guile of Carlin and Kellard, City's defence was the cornerstone of the championship success, setting new records for niggardliness with only 30 League goals conceded throughout the campaign (14 at home, 16 away). Peter Shilton managed to keep no less than 23 clean sheets - and his elevation to the full England international side during the season was fully vindicated.

Shilton had though been beaten once more during the course of the League season. Despite the introduction of differently designed goal stanchions at Filbert Street after the previous season's incident in the Villa game, the self-same thing occurred when Portsmouth were the visitors, and Jim Storrie's header rebounded back into play with the referee unaware it had entered the net.

In a season of high excitement, City even managed to generate some more in the Cup competitions. Bristol City removed them from the League Cup after extra-time in a Fourth Round replay at Ashton Gate, while FA Cup progress was stymied only in controversial fashion. Notts County and Torquay were dismissed in the early rounds, then a brave fight by Oxford was overcome in extra-time in a Manor Ground replay. Both clubs had requested a change of referee for this game, so poorly had he performed in the original tie, but the FA refused the plea.

The quarter-final brought Double-chasing Arsenal to Filbert Street and an excruciatingly tense goalless draw resulted. In the Highbury replay, Fern had an apparently perfect headed goal disallowed by Jim Finney, nominally for pushing, and the Gunners scraped a single-goal win on their way to joint Cup and League success.

Behind the Filbert Street scenes, there had been plenty of activity, too. Back in the summer, secretary John Smith had raised the subject of ground development, mentioning factors such as members' clubs, the presentation of other sports, more seating, and general modernisation. The board decided to consider the appointment of a Public Relations Officer to examine such possibilities. Mike Turner was approached, but felt he could not accept because of his moral committment to Leicestershire C.C.C., and the idea faded for a while. February was also a busy month for the club, with the introduction of decimalisation and the decision to order a giant inflatable 'balloon', or polysphere, to protect the pitch from severe weather. The initial investment of £5,000 in this structure, soon popularly dubbed 'the tent', would reap substantial rewards in future seasons.

1971 - 72

Preparations for First Division football took a radical change as early as June. Manager O'Farrell accepted a lucrative offer to take over the reins at Manchester United, and coach Malcolm Musgrove followed him. The City board wasted no time in finding a successor, and appointed Orient boss Jimmy Bloomfield to usher in a new era at the club.

Bloomfield had no truck with sentiment, and barely gave the promotion side a chance to prove itself at the higher level before setting about a comprehensive rebuilding job. Arsenal midfielder Jon Sammels was the first import, at £100,000, arriving in time to help City to a morale-boosting FA Charity Shield win over Liverpool at Filbert Street (achieved via that genuine collector's item, a Steve Whitworth goal).

Ally Brown netted the first goal of the entire Football League season, after just 45 seconds, as City brought home a point from Huddersfield, but only two wins had accrued by October, prompting Bloomfield to splash out again. This time his captures were forwards Keith Weller (Chelsea, £100,000) and Alan Birchenall (Crystal Palace, £45,450 plus Bobby Kellard), and City were soon on course for consolidation.

Bloomfield, however, also had to battle to hold on to his inherited talents. Peter Shilton attracted an enquiry from Everton, a £175,000 bid from Derby, and an Arsenal offer of an exchange deal. City asked for £150,000 plus Bob Wilson, but no move materialised. David Nish was the other prime target, with Manchester United expressing interest, while Derby suggested John Robson, John McGovern, Alan Durban or Frank Wignall as bait for a possible part-exchange.

Adapting to Bloomfield's attacking gospel took Leicester some time, but they were rarely in danger of the drop. Sheffield United, promoted behind City, were the early pacemakers, and retained top spot in September when Alan Woodward netted a last-minute goal direct from a corner to sink City 0-1 at Filbert Street. A fruitful January brought another home win over Liverpool,

though there was a mini-slump a month later as City got over the embarrassment of FA Cup defeat at home by Bloomfield's former charges, Orient. City were forced to blood young 'keeper Carl Jayes in this Fourth Round tie, and he was badly at fault with the visitors' clincher.

City eventually played the market again to secure Mark Wallington from Walsall as cover for Shilton, and let top-scorer Ally Brown move on to West Brom for £55,000. By the end of the term, a wholly respectable First Division position of twelfth was attained.

This sort of stylised artwork was briefly in fashion for leaflets and programmes during the early 70's. Featured here are
Peter Shilton, Rodney Fern and Len Glover.

A fair bit of publicity was also garnered during the campaign by the club's efforts in two other tourneys. In a football-themed television quiz show, 'Quizball', City's representatives reached the Final before bowing to a team from Dunfermline Athletic, while in the Daily Express 5-a-side tournament at Wembley, City disposed of Everton, Celtic and West Brom before confronting Southampton in the Final. They eventually lost on penalties, but Keith Weller ended the evening as the event's top scorer.

The board, too, were evincing a more progressive attitude than in the past. They agreed in principle to a major rock concert (to have headlined local band Family) being staged at Filbert Street, and to the building of squash courts at the stadium, but neither development actually took place. The directors also commissioned, for £100, a club history from Billy King, doyen of local sports journalists. Though this never materialised as a comprehensive publication, it was several times utilised in serialised, skeletal form in club programmes over the next decade.

1972 - 73

The summer of 1972 was nothing if not eventful. At Filbert Street new floodlighting, with double the power of the old system, was installed at a cost of £10,000, and a penning arrangement introduced onto the Spion Kop terraces, to facilitate crowd control and segregation. The Football League and FA joined forces in a vain attempt to fight off the imposition of VAT on sporting admission prices, and the League introduced its own 'penalty' system of points awarded for bookable offences leading to automatic suspensions for on-field sinners. The most evidently dramatic change for City however, was Bloomfield's decision to alter the team's strip to an all-white outfit - partly in imitation of the successful Leeds side of the era, and partly on the rather dubious grounds that the players looked bigger when so attired!

Midsummer and early season transfer traffic was again heavy. Fern moved to Luton for £45,000, and Frank Worthington belatedly signed from Huddersfield for six figures in August, after it had looked as if Liverpool's intervention might deny City a long-coveted acquisition. A week later David Nish moved to champions Derby for a British record fee of £250,000, and to fill his No.3 shirt Bloomfield expended approximately half that amount on Orient's Dennis Rofe.

Five games had been played without a victory when Liverpool visited Filbert Street, and went two goals up through John Toshack. But a remarkable Keith Weller hat-trick turned the tables, and even if the woodwork did deny Toshack an equaliser on the night, City's 3-2 win had them up and running. (Incidentally, Weller's achievement can best be put in context by pointing out that no other player would net a triple against Liverpool until Coventry's Terry Gibson managed the feat in December 1983).

Results generally though were poor, and when a 'flu epidemic led to the postponement of the fixture with Newcastle at the end of November, City actually sank to the bottom of the table. Talented as the team appeared on paper, goals were increasingly hard to come by. However the defence, ably marshalled by Manley and Cross, proved equally miserly, and eventually survival was assured with a final placement of sixteenth which looked deceptively comfortable.

Worthington (against West Brom) was City's second hat-trick scorer of the term, a Birchenall double brought down high-flying Leeds and, in the final game of the season, City's obdurate defence denied champions Liverpool an Anfield celebration victory. There was little to shout about in first-hurdle Cup defeats, although the supporters had cause once more to berate a referee for an absurd decision against Leicester at Highbury. John Farrington seemed to have added to City's opener with a fine 20-yard drive, but the effort was disallowed for an offside decision against Birchenall, standing way out on the wing, in no position to interfere with anything! For all City's classy entertainment value that day, a late George Armstrong equaliser meant a 2-2 scoreline, and Arsenal nicked the replay by the odd goal in three.

Two boardroom decisions this season would take effect from the next. In January agreement was made to revert to a blue and white playing kit (the change having been neither successful nor popular), and in February plans were put in hand to build a number of Executive Boxes at the Filbert Street end of the ground. These would replace the roof at that end and offer a close-up, elevated view of proceedings for City's wealthier business clientele. What was desperately needed though, was some on-field success to generate more income through the regular turnstiles.

Dennis Rofe - *signed from Orient to replace City skipper David Nish.*

Despite the disappointing outcome to the previous season, Bloomfield kept a low profile during the summer of 1973, and preferred to work on instilling confidence in the players already at his disposal rather than searching for replacements.

A few changes were, however, in the air. The League introduced a three-up, three-down system of promotion and relegation between the top divisions, hoping to diminish the number of effectively meaningless games towards the end of the term. City, in an attempt to encourage more youngsters to attend games, opened a Family Enclosure in front of the Main Stand, where safety from any hooligan element amongst the crowd could be assured. Also, to help generate more income, the idea of individual match sponsorship was introduced. The Audnel Group were the first company associated with this scheme, backing the initial home game against Liverpool.

This game brought City's third successive draw, and though they remained unbeaten in their first eight fixtures, five returns of only a single point prevented them challenging for top spot. That place was held by the formidable Leeds outfit who visited Filbert Street on October 13th. City actually led by two goals after 20 minutes, but had to settle for a 2-2 draw by the end. Leeds went on to compile a League record run of 29 unbeaten games from the start of the season, and never again came quite so close to defeat during the sequence.

The following week, City were onlookers at a major demonstration staged by Derby County fans in protest at the departure of manager Brian Clough. Whether such signs of discord prompted complacency or not, City went down 1-2 when the match got underway.

December saw the debut of Bloomfield's only significant signing of the season, Steve Earle. The former Fulham striker effectively replaced the veteran, injury-blighted Mike Stringfellow in the regular line-up, which now boasted a centre-back pairing of Graham Cross, in his Testimonial year, and young Malcolm Munro. The same month, the first effects of the strike-hit 'winter of discontent', with its attendant three-day working week, were felt in football, when the use of floodlights was banned. By January, permission was given for the first time for games to be staged on Sundays, though City themselves took no advantage.

Some often entrancing entertainment was served up by City, but still too many games resulted in a share of the points as they finished the season in a creditable ninth place. Worthington was again a hat-trick scorer in City's best win (5-0 over Ipswich), but triples were conceded in each game against Birmingham, to Bob Latchford at St.Andrews and to Kenny Burns at Filbert Street.

However, it was City's exploits in the FA Cup which this year once more captured the public's imagination. Steve Earle netted a late goal to defeat Tottenham in Round Three; Len Glover replied to Alan Mullery's 'Goal of the Season' volley at Fulham, and then helped clinch success in the replay, while the whole team turned on a breathtaking performance to trounce Luton 4-0 away in Round Five. This masterpiece of a match was climaxed by a superb individual goal by Keith Weller, and drew from no less than 'The Sunday Times' a heartfelt comparison between City's football and that of Brazil!

> IF YOU SAVOUR football as a pure game of entertainment, character and, of course, spectacular goals, you should share with me the hope that Leicester City reach Wembley next May. They simply ran amok at Luton with all the culture, imagination and ball skills we have long believed to be either things of the past or secrets guarded by men of darker skins from far off Brazil.
> Leicester's first goal after 18 minutes was of such quality and entertainment that if they do, as their manager predicted long ago, reach Wembley they can lift the status of football, even of the nation. It was that good: class and enterprise, understanding and confidence which raises the game to that of art form.

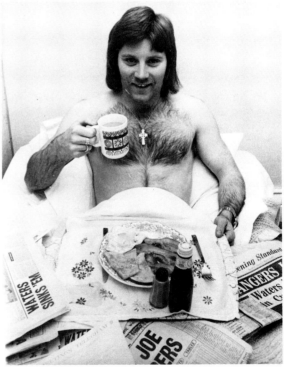

Joe Waters celebrates with breakfast in bed surrounded by newspaper headlines of his remarkable two-goal FA Cup debut.

So City came to the quarter-finals, drawn away to QPR and faced with an injury crisis. Alan Birchenall had been ruled out two weeks earlier and regular deputy Alan Woollett was also sidelined. Bloomfield decided to gamble on debutant midfielder Joe Waters, and the game turned into a fairy-tale come true as Waters notched both the goals which took City through to their sixth semi-final.

*Len Glover rams in City's equaliser in the 1974 FA Cup semi-final replay against Liverpool at Villa Park.
Rushing to congratulate him are Keith Weller and Steve Earle.*

The ensuing encounter with favourites Liverpool was a different matter. City only just survived the first goalless game at Old Trafford, when a late Kevin Keegan header struck a post and rebounded into Shilton's arms. They fell behind in the Villa Park replay, but equalised immediately through Glover, and for 15 minutes looked on the brink of another Wembley final. But a dazzling snap shot by Keegan turned the game, City wilted, and ultimately succumbed 1-3.

Still, Bloomfield's faith in City's quicksilver flair was being partially rewarded, and recognition of the high individual skill factor within the side came from England's caretaker manager, Joe Mercer, who called up both Weller and Worthington for their first caps during his short term in the post.

*Mike Stringfellow challenges Alec Lindsay and Ray Clemence during the semi-final replay,
but the veteran City man was unable to repeat his 1963 strike against the same opponents which took
Leicester to Wembley.*

The relative success of the previous season soon seemed a distant memory as the new campaign got underway. Bloomfield had again refrained from summer dealing, but found himself deep in a series of frustrating negotiations as City got off to a shaky start. Peter Shilton refused to sign a new contract, and Mark Wallington started the season in goal. A ding-dong affair that ended in a 4-3 win for City at St.Andrews, thanks to Dennis Rofe's last-minute solo run, gave deceptive hope that City were set for another carefree jaunt into the First Division's upper reaches.

It was not to be, and points were given away far too freely. Bloomfield moved in September for Ipswich iron-man Allan Hunter, but the player could not agree terms. He tempted Manchester United forward Brian Kidd, but when publicity broke about the projected deal, Arsenal nipped in with a better offer. Then, in November, Bloomfield sincerely believed he had got his man. A £160,000 deal was agreed with Liverpool for John Toshack, and the Welsh striker actually trained with City before the results of a club medical quashed the move. Indeed, the only transfer concluded that month involved Shilton, who once more emulated his mentor Gordon Banks by signing for Stoke, at a record fee for a goalkeeper of £325,000.

From early November to late February, City could not register a solitary League victory, and dressing-room discontent was all too apparent. Shortly before Christmas, Keith Weller had a transfer request turned down and, days later, refused to take the field for the second half of the home game against Ipswich. The Suffolk club won the match 1-0 to move to the top of Division One, whereas Weller was subsequently fined two weeks' wages and placed on the transfer list. Norwich manager John Bond launched a strong attack on the player through the media, and wrote to all First and Second Division club managers asking them to blacklist Weller. However, the player eventually settled his differences with the club, and such an incident never occurred again.

Shortly before this bombshell, City had got into a real mess with their goalkeeping resources. Wallington replaced the departed Shilton, but broke a bone in his hand for the second time in the season. Stoke's John Farmer arrived on loan, but was also injured, and Carl Jayes had to hold the position until Wallington returned in January to commence his record-breaking run of consecutive appearances.

City hit rock bottom on January 11th, when they were one of three clubs - Carlisle and Luton were the others - who found themselves five points adrift of Chelsea in 19th place. But Cup progress gave League form a little boost, and then two successful Bloomfield captures proved absolutely inspirational in helping City climb from the mire. Centre-back Jeff Blockley stiffened the rearguard, and striker Chris Garland galvanised a forward line that also now featured local lad Bob Lee as a regular. Garland's eight goals in ten games were the icing on the cake of a fine City recovery that lifted them eventually to

Len Glover trains under the famous air dome used to protect the Filbert Street pitch from the worst of the weather during the 1970's.
It covered 90,000 square feet, weighed 24 cwt and was 15 ft high in the middle.
It took two hours to lay out and inflate using four industrial electric fans.

sixteenth place.

Remarkably, City could laugh off a spectacular Weller own goal at Luton, and could honourably sit back and allow Derby to take away from Filbert Street the point they needed for the Championship in the penultimate game.

The Cup competitions this year provided further lashings of incident. Arsenal and Leicester just could not bear to be apart! City triumphed over the Gunners in a League Cup replay, but the roles were reversed after three nailbiting Fifth Round games in the FA Cup. Arsenal, incidentally, also took three points from the League meetings between the clubs.

The League Cup adventure ended mundanely at Middlesbrough (where earlier, the first attempt at a First Division meeting between the teams had been cut short after 24 minutes by a complete floodlight failure), but the Cup tie of the season for most people was in the Fourth Round of the premier competition. Drawn away to Isthmian League Leatherhead, City negotiated a switch of the venue to Filbert Street, and TV cameras were present to record their acute embarrassment at going 0-2 down to the minnows. Only a goal-line clearance kept the deficit within reason and reach until City fortunately regained form and stormed back with a three-goal reply.

On the year's individual front, Steve Whitworth was added to City's list of current internationals - providing further evidence that the team possessed the talent if only Bloomfield could mould them into a consistently effective unit - and long-serving Mike Stringfellow took a well deserved Testimonial game against Wolves.

1975 - 76

*Ten of City's opening 15 League games were drawn. Here **Mark Wallington** saves a penalty from Kevin Keegan in the 1-1 draw with Liverpool at Filbert Street in August 1975.*

The summer of 1975 was a famous one for Leicestershire. The County Cricket Club generated immense excitement and pride as they captured the Championship for the first time, although not quite everyone was as delighted as they might have been. City's directors decided to suspend Graham Cross for continuing to play cricket during July rather than report back for pre-season football training, and his subsequent dropping from the Anglo-Scottish Cup pipe-openers spelled the beginning of the end of a magnificent City career.

At Filbert Street, seating had been introduced on the old Popular Side terraces, which substantially reduced the ground capacity, while Bloomfield had supplemented his squad with the purchase of Steve Kember from Chelsea and Brian Alderson from Coventry.

The opening fixture, a topsy-turvy 3-3 draw at home to Birmingham, saw City finish - and indeed twice equalise - with only nine men, as Garland was sent off and Blockley carried off with a dislocated cartilage after the substitute had already been used. Such fortune was to prove a portent of things to come as City put together an unwanted run of fifteen games without a League victory - although as ten of these were draws, there was neither undue panic nor total surprise when Burnley were edged out by 3-2 at Filbert Street on November 8th.

Chris Garland heads the first goal of a spectacular hat-trick as City beat Sheffield United 3-0 in the FA Cup Third Round in January 1976.

Matters picked up healthily after this, though a further nine draws were interleaved in the seasonal record, which finally saw City finish a good seventh place in a tightly contested Division.

Most of the season's drama seemed to be saved for the month of March. On the 13th, a Stuart Boam own goal gave City a 1-0 win at Ayresome Park. A week later, Aston Villa's Chris Nicholl scored all four goals in a 2-2 draw at Filbert Street. Then, a week after that, Mark Wallington suffered a bad ankle injury trying to prevent the goal that gave Wolves a 2-1 lead, and while Keith Weller and Brian Alderson in turn assumed the green jersey, Frank Worthington claimed an unlikely but deserved equaliser to bring a useful point back from Molineux. Also during March, Graham Cross notched up his 600th senior game while on loan to Chesterfield.

The Cups this year provided only marginally less distraction than usual. In the League Cup, it took extra-time in a Filbert Street replay to separate City and Portsmouth, and Graham Taylor's Lincoln stretched the homesters too, before Burnley administered a Turf Moor knockout. A Chris Garland hat-trick saw off Sheffield United in the Third Round of the FA Cup, and Bob Lee's strike eliminated lowly Bury, but Manchester United shaded a 2-1 win in front of a Filbert Street full house. Gerry Daly claimed United's opener, but City were left smarting over two disallowed 'goals' at crucial stages of the tie.

Frustration, however, was now something of a state of mind at Leicester City as there was still no real sign of Bloomfield's side realising their much-vaunted potential in terms of a tangible trophy.

1976 - 77

The only summer additions to the City roster this year were new directors Bill Page and Colin McLeod, while their senior colleague Len Shipman was awarded the CBE in the Queen's birthday honours list. Jimmy Bloomfield seemed content to persevere with his existing squad and look, eventually, to some of the youthful talent at the club for new blood. A squad of City youngsters (including future first-teamers Tommy Williams, Winston White and Dean Smith) in fact represented the club at Wembley in August, playing in the final of the Pontins Six-A-Side tournament before the Charity Shield game, but lost out to Arsenal.

Their seniors made a sluggish start when the season proper began a week later, with six successive draws. In the last of these, at home to QPR, Dennis Rofe claimed his side's fourth goal of the campaign by floating a free-kick from his own half over an embarrassed Phil Parkes. In September, Frank Worthington publicly criticised the

team's style of play, and was fined a week's wages. Discontent was again rife, and a voluble 'Bloomfield Out' campaign flourished among some sections of the crowd, gaining in intensity when strikers Lee and Garland were both allowed to move on, despite the team's low scoring rate.

An air of unreality held sway for a while. After 13 games, City were fifth in the table, yet had only scored 13 goals. From this nominal high-point, a slide was ensured by characteristic inconsistency. Even a hitherto solid defence occasionally crumbled, as when Birmingham exploited their speed over a frozen Filbert Street pitch to register a 2-6 defeat on City (replete with another Kenny Burns hat-trick), and when Brian Kidd, once so nearly a City player, plundered four of Manchester City's five goals without reply at Maine Road.

Yet even with only one victory accruing from the final ten games, City still somehow managed to finish the term

*A memorable moment for City's popular and skilful centre-forward **Frank Worthington** as he slides the ball past Everton 'keeper Dai Davies to notch his 100th League goal during the 1-1 draw with the Merseysiders in September 1976.*

in eleventh place. In itself, this would be a pointer to a reasonable season, but sights had definitely been set higher, on European qualification at least, and the abiding spectre of City being comprehensively taken apart by West Brom at home was one that haunted the under-pressure manager as he looked back over a year which had also featured two first-hurdle Cup exits. Barely a week after the action stopped, Bloomfield resigned.

Radical rebuilding now forcibly rose to the top of the agenda, but at least it would take place at Filbert Street. Back in March, development plans for the Beaumont Leys area of Leicester had been published, and included specu-lative proposals for a 35,000-capacity, all-seater stadium, complete with synthetic pitch. The City board, however, soon firmly resolved not to consider a move.

***Keith Weller** salutes another goal.*
The City favourite scored twice
in this 4-1 win over Arsenal in October 1976.

***Frank Worthington**, another of City's stars of the 70's,*
challenges Arsenal's Jimmy Rimmer.
He later scored a penalty in the same 4-1 win.

THE YO-YO YEARS

1977 - 78

The major move the board did make however, was to appoint Bloomfield's successor. Frank McLintock, the former City favourite who had just completed his splendid playing career, was deemed the man to lift the club's fortunes, and the new boss' first additions to the staff (former QPR team-mate Eddie Kelly bolstering the midfield complement, and the experienced Ian MacFarlane returning to Filbert Street as coach) gave rise to renewed optimism.

High hopes soon lay in ruins. Three unbeaten League games had been negotiated when City tamely surrendered to Portsmouth in the League Cup, and then confidence and coherence utterly collapsed as McLintock set about a haphazard new-broom approach to restructuring his team. Thrust into the side in successive weeks were new signings Lammie Robertson, Alan Waddle, George Armstrong, David Webb and Geoff Salmons (plus youngster Tommy Williams), but none could effect a turnaround in City's rock-bottom form, which saw them lodged firmly in the relegation slot from October onwards. None did much for the fans' morale either, which was hit as much by the departure of folk hero Frank Worthington as by the series of disastrous results. There were few smiles when McLintock idly threatened to re-register himself as a player to bolster his spiritless squad.

December saw another transfer flurry as McLintock became desperate. While City could not match the wage demands of Liverpool's David Johnson, the board backed McLintock in gambling the club's record outlay of £250,000 on former Derby star Roger Davies, returning to English football from Bruges. Within weeks Davies would have a new partner in Billy Hughes, bought directly from the Baseball Ground. Almost all the new faces at Filbert Street were forwards or attacking midfielders, but City goals were by now like gold dust - precisely 11 were registered in 23 games by the turn of the year.

The FA Cup brought no relief from the pervading misery. A win at Hull only set up City for further humiliation at Third Division Walsall, where the veteran Alun Evans once more delivered the KO punch. Soon, relegation was a certainty in all but mathematical terms, and when that particular statistical guarantee was fulfilled,

*Record signing **Roger Davies** could do little to inspire City in their unsuccessful struggle against relegation. He finished joint top-scorer with a mere four goals.*

City fans were left to bet on just how many of the club's all-time 'worst' records would fall by the season's end.

They would have found few willing to take odds on McLintock's contract being renewed. The manager had anyway incurred the board's displeasure throughout his tenure for his continued refusal to move his home base from London (where he had business interests) to Leicester. This, combined with the team's poor showing led to McLintock's early exit. He resigned on April 5th with MacFarlane assuming caretaker duties for the campaign's finale.

A last-game 3-0 home victory over relegation companions Newcastle, saw City to a total of 26 in the 'goals for' column - a record low for a 42-game First Division season that would stand until Stoke City's even more shot-shy strugglers contrived a 24-goal haul during 1984/5. The same game also saw Davies and Salmons climb to the top of the City scoring charts - with four apiece! Club records to fall in this dire term included those for least wins (5), most defeats (25), most home defeats (10) and lowest points tally (22). Even Steve Whitworth's (then) record run of consecutive appearances came to end on number 198 during the season.

As if First Division rivalry had not already proved overwhelming enough, there was now even a renewed home-town challenge to the club's hold on its support, for the Tigers' exploits with the oval ball had this year taken them to their first Twickenham Cup Final.

1978 - 79

Tommy Williams scores in a spectacular 5-3 home win over Orient in February 1979.
The game was due to be screened on 'Match of the Day' but a landline failure meant viewers missed quite a treat!

City were now potentially a club in severe crisis. Rudderless, there was every chance they would find the Second Division seas as rocky as those of the First. Confidence in (or even amongst) their playing resources was in short supply. There was little spare cash available, as a fair amount had to be expended this summer on the stadium, to meet the new requirements of the Safety of Sports Grounds Act. The club's future literally hung on the board's ability to act decisively to stop the rot.

The decisive act in fact shocked the football world - for City somehow prised away from Ibrox one of the most successful managers of the decade, Jock Wallace. This formidable, charismatic figure - a disciplinarian and fitness fanatic - immediately stamped his inspirational mark on Filbert Street. New training regimes were instituted, both the backroom and playing staffs were cleared out, he embarked on an ambitious youth policy and, perhaps crucially, forged a warm, rousing rapport with the supporters.

Wallace's first season was, however, always going to be one of struggle, but at least it could now be faced with spirit under his motivational management. Bold team selections marked the campaign's early weeks. Young John O'Neill made an opening day debut at centre-back as City (in borrowed yellow shorts) battled to a draw at Turf Moor. Other juniors stepped up as the makeshift side contrived to keep its feet out of the relegation mire, supplemented by low-cost buys Martin Henderson, John Ridley and Bobby Smith.

The latter arrived from Hibernian over Christmas, and lined up on New Year's Day against Oldham alongside two other debutants - David Buchanan and Gary Lineker. While Smith and 16-year-old Buchanan claimed the winning goals and took the plaudits, the rather overawed

Lineker retreated to the reserves. His impact would be made (and sustained) in years to come.

Wallace's winning penchant for the unpredictable was now ready to be exposed to a wider audience. On a day when only three Third Round FA Cup ties went ahead, City's hot-air pitch cover allowed them to face First Division Norwich in front of the TV cameras, and the 3-0 success was marked equally by an individualist goal from Keith Weller (resplendent in white tights!) and an incredibly mature midfield display from yet another teenage apprentice, Andy Peake.

Such was the whirl of movement and incident at Leicester however, that by the time the much-postponed Fourth Round tie at Oldham was played (and lost, to an Alan Young hat-trick), Weller was playing in America, Peake was on England Youth duty, and the Latics' programme contained pen pictures for no less than twelve departed City players! Even the hitherto reliable polysphere had collapsed under heavy overnight snow, causing the postponement of an interim home fixture with Fulham.

The odd whiff of danger still attended some of City's remaining League fixtures as the inconsistencies of inexperience occasionally told, but this really was a season in which a final placing of 17th in Division Two could legitimately be regarded as a triumph. Further individual baptisms had brought mixed results (Neil Grewcock became another 16-year-old debut goalscorer; Lineker hit his first strike to win important points at Notts County; poor Everton Carr was sent off, and Alan Lee attacked on the pitch, during a farcical final game at Bramall Lane that also saw relegated Sheffield United awarded two laughable penalties). But there was no denying that City had been genuinely rejuvenated.

Long service to the club, though, still brought justifiable reward. Back at the start of the campaign, director Sid Needham (awarded an OBE the year previously) joined his colleague Len Shipman as one of only six Life Members of the FA in the country, while in mid-term another senior boardroom figure, Tom Bloor, retired to become the first-ever Life Member of the club itself. Steve Whitworth moved on in March, part-way through his well-earned Testimonial year, but he would nevertheless be allowed to stage a game (against Coventry) the following autumn. Finally, another ten-year club servant, secretary John Smith, took up an executive appointment at Luton, and was replaced by Alan Bennett.

1979 - 80

Larry May *bundles the ball over the line in City's final fixture at Orient. The goal clinched the club's sixth Second Division championship in 1980.*

The all-change ambience at Filbert Street remained as City prepared to face their second campaign in the lower Division. Top scorer Trevor Christie was allowed to move on as City made their first signing under the new Freedom of Contract arrangement for players - capturing the previous February's Cup scourge Alan Young for a record-equalling, tribunal-set fee of £250,000 after he had declined to re-sign for Oldham.

Other newcomers were defender Gregor Stevens and midfielders Ian Wilson and Pat Byrne. All four made their

bow as City commenced the season early, in First Round League Cup combat with Rotherham. Defeat home and away against Third Division opposition hardly augured well for the League campaign to follow, but it did not take long for the side to hit its stride. They were Divisional leaders when the initial League tables were published, after playing superbly to win 4-1 at Loftus Road, and thereafter never slipped below sixth position in a tight promotion race.

Young hit a useful early scoring seam, but the hapless

Stevens was quickly jettisoned. Valuable goals came from unexpected quarters (Dennis Rofe claimed two scorchers at Swansea; the returning Lineker shattered Sunderland with sheer pace; and young Derek Strickland started Wrexham's downfall in his first full game). Indeed, City scored in every game up until their 0-2 defeat at The Valley in mid-December (only their second setback away from home).

Handily placed as the New Year dawned, City received a blow that could have shattered their young side's confidence had Wallace ever allowed heads to drop. A hiding-to-nothing FA Cup draw against Isthmian League outsiders Harlow Town turned utterly nightmarish, as a late Filbert Street equaliser earned the minnows another shot at giant-killing glory, and accountant John Mackenzie enjoyed his fifteen minutes of fame with the only goal of the replay at the tiny Hammarskjold Road Sportcentre. It was the first time since 1914/15 that Leicester had fallen to non-League opposition in the Cup.

It therefore spoke volumes for City's character and resilience that, three games later, a 1-0 home win over Newcastle put them back on top of Division Two. Jitters did set in subsequently, as Chelsea, Sunderland and Birmingham joined the promotion fight in earnest, and captain Dennis Rofe actually moved to Chelsea, citing his belief that they were better bets to go up. Geoff Scott, from Stoke, assumed the No.3 shirt, and young winger Paul Edmunds made crucial contributions as City got back on course.

City held Sunderland at Roker, hiccupped badly at home to Preston, but then won each of the crunch home games against Chelsea and Birmingham. A foul on Edmunds at Wrexham left him with a broken wrist and ended his season, but from the free kick Eddie Kelly blasted an invaluable winner. Two games later, after a tense 2-1 home win over Charlton, City were all but assured of promotion, with Chelsea needing to make up a goal difference of eight to pip them. The mathematics proved irrelevant however, when Larry May's goal secured a final-day win at Brisbane Road. With Sunderland dropping a point on the same day, City were Champions once more.

John O'Neill, the supporters' Player of the Season, was capped for the first time by Northern Ireland during the campaign; but experienced Eddie Kelly, who had assumed the captaincy on Rofe's departure and done much to steady the side, surprisingly opted for a free transfer at the end of the term. Sadness had also tinged the final month of the promotion push, with City mourning the death of chief scout Ray Shaw; while boardroom changes earlier had seen the recruitment of new directors Bill Shooter and Tom Smeaton, and the shift to Life Member status of long-serving former club chairmen Len Shipman, Sid Needham and Alf Pallett.

Work had been put in hand to build a new, stylish function room at Filbert Street, to be known as the Belvoir Suite, for City's better-heeled clientele, but the vast majority of the supporters were wondering if Jock Wallace's young side, promoted earlier than anticipated, could survive their elevation in any style at all.

*The City players parade the 1980 **Second Division Championship** trophy at Filbert Street.*

*Celebrations everywhere after **Andy Peake** scored a spectacular long range goal against Liverpool in August 1980.*
On the front row of the crowd is former City star Mike Stringfellow, whilst showing their delight on the pitch are
***Jim Melrose, Bobby Smith, John O'Neill, Ian Wilson** and goalscorer **Andy Peake**.*

Characteristically, Jock Wallace stated his ambition for the new season was the capture of the First Division title. Also characteristically, his only close-season signing was a player of youthful promise rather than profound experience - though it did take another record-equalling £250,000 to bring Partick Thistle striker Jim Melrose to Leicester. It was no surprise either when Wallace threw yet another untried junior, left-back Billy Gibson, in at the deep end in the opening fixture.

City disappointed in their initial defeats by Ipswich and Everton, but showed just what they were capable of with a fine 2-0 win over Liverpool, cued by a spectacular long-range strike from Andy Peake. An Elland Road victory followed, but soon the 'goals against' column bulged, as successive 0-5 reverses at Manchester United and Nottingham Forest pointed to a campaign of scrabbling at the wrong end of the table.

More youngsters like Stewart Hamill, Kevin MacDonald and Paul Friar were introduced and, confident the conveyor belt of cost-free talent would continue to roll in the charge of recent appointee Dave Richardson, Wallace could take sporadic encouragement from City's performances against the 'bigger' clubs. But time ran out before his side could cohere around one style or system. Melrose finally hit the mark for the first time in a win at St.Andrews in December, while a cocky MacDonald calmly stepped up to slot home the winning spot-kick against Middlesborough in his first full game at Filbert

Street. Four early Southampton goals put paid to City at The Dell, but the fact City had 'drawn' the second half led them, half-seriously, to propose an alteration to the points system!

Another Cup embarrassment - this time at Exeter where Tony Kellow's hat-trick did the damage in a Fourth Round replay - could once more have been the prelude to collapse. In typically paradoxical fashion, it actually inspired City to complete the double over Liverpool with a 2-1 win at Anfield on the following Saturday - the Reds' first home defeat in 85 games. Manchester United, Spurs (further double victims) and Arsenal all fell to a semi-revived City - bolstered by February purchase Steve Lynex on the right wing - but the club's hopes of safety disappeared in a tempestuous match at Brighton on Easter Monday. Kevin MacDonald's header gave City the lead, but both he and Alan Young were sent off before Brighton turned the tables.

Two wins after this were of no real value to City, though Melrose's carefree hat-trick at Norwich sent the Canaries down as well. Paul Ramsey and Norman Leet were both given a place in the starting line-up for this game, but the biggest headlines of the second half of City's season had revolved around one player with a rather larger reputation than either of these could realistically aspire to.

In February, Wallace decided to gamble for high stakes, and opened negotiations to try to secure the services of Johan Cruyff, then 33 but formerly the world's top-rated individual player. By February 24th, Wallace had agreed terms for Cruyff to be paid on a match-by-match basis until the end of the season, giving the Dutchman between £4,000 and £5,000 per game, which Wallace was certain could be recouped from the bumper crowds he would attract. Then came a telephone call from Cruyff's agent with the news that Spanish club Levanthe had decided to 'exercise their option' on the player. It was claimed the Spaniards had offered a deal involving Cruyff pocketing 50% of the gate receipts for each match. By February 26th, the deal with Leicester had emphatically fallen through. Some cynics claimed the whole affair had been a publicity gimmick in the first place, but

Wallace had indeed been sincere in attempting to lure the best talent available to aid his youngsters in their relegation battle.

City certainly needed to maintain their crowd-pulling traditions somehow, for the ups and downs of the Wallace management period - and especially the lack of knock-out success - were set in contrast to the remarkable run enjoyed by the club's Welford Road near-neighbours. This year the Tigers returned from Twickenham for the fourth successive season, with a hat-trick of John Player Cup wins behind them, and it was not hard to envisage a subtle shift in the interests of the Leicester sporting public if City continued to fail to come up with the goods.

1981 - 82

This summer there were no major signings. Wallace had decided that the year's top-flight experience gained by most of his charges would stand them in good stead for an immediate return, and he also stuck by his choice of goalkeeper Mark Wallington as captain. His opening line-up was, however, notable for the inclusion of Gary Lineker in place of the injured Alan Young. Hitherto very much a fringe player in Wallace's squads, Lineker emerged this term as both a regular senior performer and leading goalscorer - a process he initiated with City's opening goal in the draw at Grimsby.

The capriciousness of a footballing career was however perhaps never better illustrated than by the fate which befell Stewart Hamill, who claimed the winning goal in each of City's next two games, yet never returned to first-team action again with Leicester. Each of these single-goal home wins was now worth three points - the Football League having introduced this amendment to encourage attacking play and maintain interest in the season for more teams for a greater length of time.

In City's case, promotion-oriented interest was indeed maintained until very late in the campaign. Early season form was unspectacular, and neither the arrival of comparative veteran Keith Robson nor the loan of Southampton's Trevor Hebberd did much to imbue the side with consistency. The return of Eddie Kelly was a more significant spark to improvement, but City had left themselves a lot to do if they were seriously to challenge the sides above them by the end of the year.

They had already ceded points to many of their rivals (notably experiencing an initial pointless return from QPR's new artificial pitch at Loftus Road), but revived strongly in February, March and April, by which time they had games in hand and a decent rhythm. Indeed, despite the odd setback, City were still in with a shout as, with three games to play, they faced two apparent home bankers against Grimsby and Shrewsbury. Nervily scrambling only a single point off this pair meant City had frittered away a genuine opportunity, though an eventual placing of eighth rather disguised just how frustratingly close they had come to an immediate return 'upstairs'.

Frustration was in fact the entire season's keynote, for the Cups brought their share too. In the League Cup, City actually got past the first hurdle for the first time since 1975, only to go down away to Aston Villa in a Third Round replay. In the FA Cup, however, City put together a fine exciting run, starting with a 3-1 demolition of First Division Southampton, and gathering pace with competent victories over Hereford and Watford, to set up a Filbert Street quarter-final clash with Shrewsbury.

Quite unexpectedly, this all-Second Division encounter turned out to be a story-book affair, complete with tortuous plot and heroes and villains. Larry May gave City an early lead, then Mark Wallington was badly injured in a clash with Town's Chic Bates. The severely hampered goalkeeper was powerless to prevent the visitors equalising and then taking the lead. As he inevitably limped out of the game, it seemed fate had struck City a cruel blow. But fate produced another twist on the stroke of half-time, this time in the shape of a bizarre Shrewsbury own goal to level things up. By the time the second period started, the crowd were frantic and the City team inspired. It mattered little that three goalkeepers were eventually used; stand-in Alan Young was himself injured in another clash with Bates, and Steve Lynex took over the green jersey for a spell before Young's head had cleared sufficiently for him to return. City simply swept the Shrews aside on a rush of adrenalin and passion, with substitute Jim Melrose netting twice and Gary Lineker once to clinch a 5-2 victory and a place in another Villa Park semi-final, this time against Cup-holders Tottenham Hotspur.

There was though, no fairy-tale ending for City. Ossie Ardiles prompted Spurs forward on his last appearance for the club for some time, only the day after the Falklands/Malvinas conflict had erupted, and Garth Crooks' opening strike in the second half was followed by a double dose of tragedy for City, as Tommy Williams broke his leg and Ian Wilson conceded an own goal. The better team on the day had won through to Wembley, but there was much post-match criticism of Jock Wallace's decision to play Alan Young from the start and leave the in-form Melrose on the bench.

Wallington had recovered in time for the semi-final

*The City v Shrewsbury FA Cup sixth round tie was an epic. Here **Larry May** celebrates giving City an early lead.*

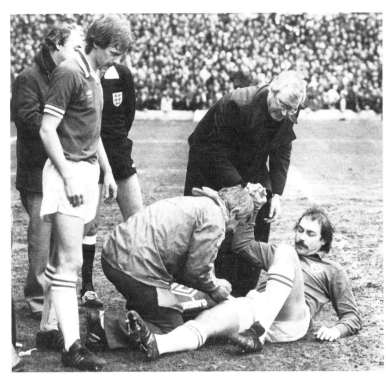

***Tommy Williams** and Manager **Jock Wallace** show concern as goalkeeper **Mark Wallington** receives running repairs from physio **John McVey**. The thigh injury was the result of a hefty challenge from Shrewsbury's Chic Bates.*

***Larry May**, partly hidden by **Steve Lynex** (No.7) and **Tommy Williams** (no.2) points out that **Alan Young** may need to go in goal. Other City players gathered round include **Andy Peake** and (right) **Gary Lineker** and **John O'Neill**.*

***Alan Young** collects the ball under pressure from the 'villain' of the day Chic Bates. The drama had a happy ending as City won a thrilling tie 5-2.*

disappointment, but the injury he received in the previous round at last broke his club record sequence of consecutive appearances on the 331 mark, allowing young Nicky Walker a six-game run in his stead.

As the season ended, the City board first celebrated director Bill Page's new status as Lord Mayor of Leicester, but then were soon pitched into acrimony. Manager Wallace abruptly resigned to take up a similar post with Motherwell. From the outside it looked a simple case of City's 'so near, so far away' season disheartening their boss. Initially the directors refused to accept Wallace's resignation, and accused the Scottish club of poaching. Eventually, there was little option but to allow him to leave, although as they searched for a successor, they vigorously pursued compensation claims from Motherwell for enticing Wallace to break his contract.

The search ended in August with the appointment of Gordon Milne from Coventry, a man who appeared the temperamental antithesis of Wallace, but who had developed a shrewd business sense at Highfield Road while keeping his charges in the top flight against the odds.

On surveying the Filbert Street scene, Milne immediately prioritised a drastic pruning of the playing staff at all levels. One player he would not dispose of though, was newcomer Alan Smith. The tall Brummie had been signed from Alvechurch by Wallace just days before his departure, and would soon forge a powerful striking partnership with Lineker.

Milne also had his own ideas about the playing style he wanted his team to adopt, and soon released Ian MacFarlane, replacing him with Gerry Summers as coach. City responded, in the early weeks of the season, with characteristic inconsistency, and Milne's acceptance by a wary Leicester public was not aided by his decision to exchange the popular Jim Melrose for his former Coventry striker Tom English. The manager was confident of pulling off another deal in September, but the prevarication of Ipswich's Mick Mills led City to withdraw their offer, and the player went to Southampton instead.

Certainly, there were few early omens that this might be another promotion-chasing campaign. Three of the opening four home fixtures were lost (though the exception saw both Lynex and Lineker claim hat-tricks against Carlisle), while a fine burst of winning League form in October (with Lineker bagging another treble at Derby) was bracketed by defeat in both legs of the Milk Cup tie against little Lincoln.

By the time the FA Cup came round, City were comfortably placed in the top half of the table, but the leading trio of QPR, Wolves and Fulham had started to pull well away from the pack. Third Round home defeat by First Division Notts County, who took an authoritative three-goal lead before City pulled two back in injury time as consolation, seemed to signal the end of City's glory-hunting for at least another year.

But an unlikely turning point was reached in February, initially marked by the arrival of cultured midfielder Gerry Daly, on loan from Coventry for the remainder of the season. It is a classic case of the benefit of hindsight to point to a routine home win over Shrewsbury as the moment City's climb took off in earnest, for the match itself attracted only 6,155 spectators, the lowest home League gate since the war.
A 5-0 walloping of high-flying Wolves followed and, with confidence growing, City embarked on a lengthy unbeaten run.

As City continued to make ground on the top three, so Fulham began to falter. The points gap closed inexorably until the vital head-to-head encounter came at Craven Cottage on April 23rd. Ian Wilson's goal clinched the points in a tension-filled atmosphere, and the balance looked to have been tipped in City's favour.

Still, however, it was neck and neck between the two clubs for the third promotion spot and, when it came to

Paul Ramsey nets City's second goal in a 2-1 win at Oldham.
City first moved into the promotion frame with only three fixtures remaining and this victory proved vital.

Happy scenes at Filbert Street after the final game of the season as (above)
Ian Wilson *leads the City celebrations.*
There were however, anxious moments during the 0-0 draw with Burnley
as can be seen from the faces (left)
of **Gerry Daly, Gerry Summers, John McVey** *and* **Gordon Milne***.*
Indeed, there was another anxious wait before a Football League enquiry confirmed
the club's promotion.

the final game of the season, City entertained an already relegation-doomed Burnley knowing a win would secure promotion, whilst Fulham travelled to Derby hoping to take advantage of any City slip.

On the day City could only manage a goalless draw. It was their 15th unbeaten game since February, but the supporters would have an anxious wait to find out whether it was to be enough. For there was drama indeed at the Baseball Ground where, late in the game, the crowd had literally spilled on to the running track and encroached over the touchlines. Conditions were clearly difficult and an incident involving a spectator and a Fulham player eventually led to the game being abandoned some 75 seconds before the 90 minute mark, with Fulham trailing 0-1.

The Football League held an enquiry, and City had a few worrying days before learning their fate. The League finally decided the Derby-Fulham result should stand, and it was Malcolm MacDonald, the Fulham manager, who was the first to telephone Filbert Street to congratulate City on their promotion - a fine gesture in the midst of his own disappointment.

Several individual landmarks peppered a campaign that was latterly notable for a remarkable degree of systematic teamwork. Mark Wallington, back to ever-present status, took a Testimonial game against Nottingham Forest in October; Gary Lineker broke the twenty-goal barrier for the first time to close with 26 League counters; Kevin MacDonald illustrated his confident versatility by filling in superbly at centre-back after Larry May was sidelined for much of the run-in, while young Robbie Jones came through his baptism of fire in the penultimate game at Oldham with the vital opening goal to his credit. One record set this term, however, was far from a source of pride - no less than five City players having been sent off.

Other significant developments during the season included the first-time sponsorship of the youth team, whose shirts now bore the brand-name legend of 'Fresha' on behalf of local bakery Squires & Kintons. In February came the appointment of the club's first-ever Vice President, Trevor Bennett, a local businessman who had over the years been a benefactor of both the Football Club and the County Cricket Club, where he would shortly take up a similar post.

There was, however, a further spectre at the promotion feast. The manner of City's challenge, coming from behind on the last lap, had generated significantly less spectator interest than usual, and the club actually showed a loss of over £300,000 on the season. All of Milne's business acumen, as well as his footballing brain, would be required to keep City in Division One this time.

1983 - 84

The summer of 1983 proved quite hectic in terms of Filbert Street comings and goings. George Dewis finally retired from his backroom duties at the age of 70; former player Alan Birchenall returned as Public Relations Officer; two more Vice Presidents arrived in Martin George and John Elsom; and Gordon Milne's transfer dealings landed West Brom 'keeper Mark Grew and Barnsley midfielder Ian Banks. Surprisingly, however, there was no contract deal for Gerry Daly, and Larry May was another to depart.

Sponsorship also made its mark during the summer. The Football League became the Canon League, and City adopted a new strip incorporating the name of brewers Ind Coope. The new look was further enhanced by the change of the club badge, with a copyrighted running fox logo replacing the former fox head and crossed riding crops design.

By kick-off day, Mark Wallington was still in contractual dispute, so Grew was given an early opportunity. He was also given plenty of practice, as the team patently failed to come to terms with the demands of top-level football. Old-boy Trevor Christie snatched a hat-trick against City in the opener, and six successive defeats represented the club's worst-ever start to a season, and labelled them early as relegation favourites.

Against this backdrop, the club was a hive of activity, but no substantial signings resulted, and the National Westminster Bank further thwarted Milne's team-strengthening ambitions by submitting a demand that the club reduce its £800,000 overdraft. Additionally, crowd trouble at the game with Tottenham confirmed the need to fence the main stand enclosure, again diverting slender financial resources.

City's first point came from a 2-2 home draw with Stoke on September 24th (a painful experience for Alan Smith, who had to retrieve three teeth from the pitch after they had been kicked out), but the first League win was delayed until the visit of Everton on October 29th. In the interim, Bob Hazell had been signed to bolster the central defence, Peter Eastoe came on loan to find his debut game against Southampton abandoned during a torrential downpour, and City had departed the Milk Cup following a penalty shoot-out at Chelsea. Two goals down from the home leg of this tie, City really regained their pride and shape in the 2-0 fightback at Stamford Bridge (the only game they would 'win' all season in their apparently jinxed new change colours of green and gold).

Form definitely picked up after this, though luck was still against City. When Manchester United visited in November, Lynex was the player to lose a tooth, but more seriously Eastoe broke his jaw, and was out of action for months (with City honorably agreeing to pay his wages until he was fit enough to conclude the loan period). City had their first taste of Sunday football during December, at Nottingham Forest and Sunderland and, during the same month, saw Smith collect his first hat-trick (against Wolves), while a last-minute Wallington penalty-save secured a point from Anfield.

There was now genuine substance to City's survival battle, and eventually relegation was formally avoided when Forest were beaten 2-1 at Filbert Street in May, with two games to spare. Home defeat by Sunderland in the final fixture kept the Wearsiders up too, and saw City finish in 15th place. A cumulative 50-goal haul from the striking trio of Lineker, Smith and Lynex was effectively City's salvation; the consistently prolific Lineker earned his first England call-up for a substitute appearance against Scotland, while young midfielder Paul Ramsey finished the season with three Irish caps to his name.

*Top scorer with 22 goals, **Gary Lineker** wheels away in triumph*
after netting the opener in a 3-0 win over Arsenal at Filbert Street in November.

*The changing face of **Filbert Street** can be seen from this aerial picture taken in 1984.*
Executive boxes have replaced the Filbert Street roof, and the Belvoir Suite has been built to link with the Main Stand.
The old Aylestone Road cricket ground, home of the Fosse in 1891 prior to the opening of Filbert Street, is in the top left hand corner.

1984 - 85

The prelude to the club's Centenary season, in which Milne hoped to consolidate City's top-flight acclimatisation, was unfortunately the sad news that one of Leicester's finest servants, Arthur Chandler, had died in hospital during the summer.

In June, the boardroom complement was strengthened by the elevation of John Elsom to director level, and backstage changes continued throughout the campaign, with Trevor Bennett becoming the club's first post-war President in October, and Ken Brigstock appointed Vice President in March.

The regular pre-season friendly fare - in which former Port Vale striker Mark Bright got to know his new colleagues, and Ian Wilson received his marching orders during a 2-2 draw at Ibrox - this year culminated in City's Centenary match. Aberdeen provided the tough Filbert Street opposition, drawing 1-1, but as much interest was generated by the pre-match entertainment, featuring a game between ex-City players of earlier eras, and the return to Leicester of numerous old favourites.

Competitive action brought the now customary stuttering start. Consistency was as elusive a quality as ever, as successive League games in October demonstrated. City crashed 0-5 at Hillsborough, then at home

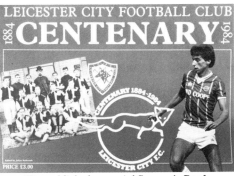

*City published a special **Souvenir Book**
to mark their Centenary.*

blasted Aston Villa 5-0. The month before, a single game, against Brentford in the Milk Cup, had also illustrated City's 'Jekyll & Hyde' act: two goals down with only nine minutes remaining, they contrived a blistering four-goal revival. However, a Third Round exit awaited at Luton.

This maddening mixture of the superb and the diabolical continued throughout the League calendar. City plundered four-goal returns from both North-Eastern citadels, Roker and St.James's, and hit Coventry for five on the occasion of the first Sunday game at Filbert Street (when David Rennie notched the club's 5,000th League goal). They managed another shock win at Anfield, but many other matches were best quietly forgotten, as City

City stars past and present gather together for the club's Centenary game against Aberdeen in 1984.
Back : J.Blockley, J.Sjoberg, E.Kelly, C.Jayes, J.Sammels, A.Clarke, G.Cross, G.Armstrong, J.Walsh,
J.Harrison, C.Appleton, K.MacDonald, M.Bright.
Second Row : H.Riley, B.Roberts (hidden), A.Tewley, T.Sweenie, K.Leek, P.Rodrigues, J.Waters, S.Whitworth, L.Glover, D.Nish, A.Woollett,
C.Walker, R.Norman, D.Hines, K.Chisholm, N.Plummer, A.Cheesebrough, K.Keyworth, G.Dewis.
Third Row : I.King, J.Goodfellow, F.McLintock, J.Anderson, A.Rowley, J.Ogilvie, M.Gillies, B.Johnson, E.Jelly, W.Coutts, G.Jayes, C.Adam.
Front : J.O'Neill, A.Peake, S.Lynex, G.Lineker, P.Ramsey, A.Smith, A.Birchenall, B.Smith, I.Andrews, I.Wilson, D.Rennie.

once more ended in 15th place.

The FA Cup this year prompted sensational head-lines of the wrong sort. In the Third Round, City were drawn away to Burton Albion, of the Northern Premier League, and the tie was switched to Derby's Baseball Ground.

City skated home by 6-1, but an incident occurred when the scores were level which eventually nullified the victory. Hundreds of Derby 'supporters' in the crowd had already clashed with their equally trouble-some Leicester counterparts when a missile was thrown from behind the Burton goal and struck 'keeper Paul Evans on the head, temporarily stunning him. An FA enquiry into the incident ruled the game should be replayed behind closed doors.

Originally scheduled again for Derby, the re-match was in fact switched to Coventry because of pitch conditions, and City duly won through by a single Ramsey goal, greeted with eerie silence from the virtually empty stands and terraces. Carlisle were ousted from the competition in the next round, but on a freezing winter night at The Den when City's finishing went badly awry, Third Division Millwall ended any thoughts of a Wembley march.

The season had also seen skipper Kevin MacDonald's transfer to Liverpool in November bring in a club record fee of £400,000; the emergence of Ian Andrews as goalkeeping successor to Mark Wallington (who would move to Derby in July); and the introduction of a partial Membership scheme for home supporters at Filbert Street, with the Main Stand being redesignated the Members' Stand in January.

Lineker, Smith and Lynex had combined to produce 59 goals this time; and Lineker's first full England game, against the Republic of Ireland in March, brought him his first international goal. New striker Bright had made little impact at senior level, but with the reserves claimed 28 goals in only 27 appearances as they romped away with the Second Division championship of the Central League - their

first season in the competition, having switched from the Football Combination at Milne's insistence.

However, events elsewhere as the season closed left a cloud hanging over the whole of English football. The Valley Parade fire and the Heysel Stadium disaster, with their attendant heavy death tolls, scarred the game's image badly, and caused City's Centenary campaign to end on the most sombre of notes.

The 1985 FA Cup Third Round replay against Burton Albion was (above) played behind closed doors at Coventry.

Gary Lineker and **Alan Smith**, *who later renewed their partnership with England, scored five goals between them in the void 6-1 tie with Burton at Derby's Baseball Ground.*

1985 - 86

Mark Bright had the unenviable task of replacing Lineker, but got off to the best possible start with two goals against Everton on the opening day. Here he blasts his first goal in City's 3-1 win.

A busy summer in the transfer market was dominated by one deal. Gary Lineker's contract was at an end, and in June he signed for Champions Everton. The fee was set by an independent tribunal at a club record of £800,000, plus a share of any future profits should the player be resold within two years. City had made Lineker a generous offer, but he felt the need to join a 'glamour' club if he was significantly to further his career. He had become only the sixth City player to complete a century of goals for the club and would clearly be a hard man to replace.

Mark Wallington and Andy Peake also departed during the close season, whilst new signings came in the shape of Ipswich defender Russell Osman and Motherwell midfielders Alister Mauchlen and Gary McAllister. Milne's dealings had brought an income in excess of £1.3 million in recent months, compared to an expenditure in the region of £0.5 million. The books were being balanced and the overdraft cut, but would the team be up to the task in hand, especially without its talismanic striker?

Fate conspired to send Everton to Filbert Street on the opening day of the season. Mark Bright assumed Lineker's position, then assured himself of the headlines as he netted twice in a 3-1 win over the Champions. This result soon, however, proved a false dawn. Only one of the next 13 games ended in victory, and there was a groundswell of public disquiet over Milne's management. In October, only 7,237 turned up to see City struggle to salvage a 2-2 draw with West Brom. It was bottom club Albion's first away point of the season, and City's lowest post-war First Division gate. Tony Sealy was by now augmenting the forward line, and young Simon Morgan had grasped the left-back slot, while Milne cast his net abroad for reinforcements. Danish forward Tommy Christensen arrived briefly on loan, then former England winger Laurie Cunningham settled in for a lengthier and rather more effective loan stint, albeit one bedevilled by injuries.

The Milk Cup brought no respite from League struggles. Derby, now languishing in Division Three, ousted City with some comfort at the first hurdle. The Filbert Street evening leg was followed by a night of rioting in the Highfields area of the city - its start being widely (but dubiously) ascribed to clashes between opposing football hooligans.

The League campaign continued to be an uphill struggle, punctuated by some excellent displays, such as a 3-0 home win over Manchester United in November and a 2-1 success at Everton, to complete a double, in December. There were, however, a rather greater number of shoddy performances, with results to match. City's FA Cup exit - humiliated by Third Division Bristol Rovers at Eastville - definitely fell into this category.

Right up until the season's final day, City looked fair bets for relegation and even the ultimate 2-0 home win over Newcastle proved to be a lifeline only because Ipswich lost at Sheffield Wednesday the same afternoon, leaving City safe in 19th place.

John O'Neill had by now taken his tally of Irish caps to 39, a record total for a City player; Alan Smith continued to find the net regularly, and Osman, McAllister and Mauchlen had all settled reasonably well. Yet a frankly poor campaign gave few grounds for optimism.

During May the directors held discussions with Swindon manager Lou Macari over a possible assistant manager's position at Filbert Street, but he rejected their overtures.

Ian Banks scores from a penalty to secure City's First Division future with a 2-0 win over Newcastle

That uncertainty was compounded for a while in June when Bryan Hamilton, the former Wigan boss, joined the Filbert Street payroll to share duties with Milne. The latter was redesignated as General Manager, whilst Hamilton assumed the title of Team Manager.

Other changes were in prospect for 1986/7. Canon had withdrawn from sponsorship of the Football League, eventually to be replaced by the Today newspaper; Ind Coope chose to display the 'John Bull' logo on City's shirts, to promote a particular brand of bitter; and the League introduced a play-off system for some promotion and relegation places, with the First Division due to be reduced to 21 clubs in 1987/8 and to 20 by 1988/9; the Second Division increasing in size accordingly.

Long-serving Tommy Williams moved on to Birmingham during the summer, but still was allowed to stage a hugely successful Testimonial game in the autumn, featuring City's current side against a team of former Filbert Street favourites which included both Frank Worthington and Gary Lineker. Lineker was by then a Barcelona player. He had flourished in the media glare at Goodison, his recent World Cup exploits in Mexico had made him a national hero, and City had received an unexpected windfall of £250,000 in July as their share of the deal between Everton and the Spaniards. This brought the local lad's club record fee up to £1,050,000, but only deepened the genuine sense of loss in Leicester. How City missed his talents now.

In fact, in a make-do spirit, City got off to their best start to a First Division season for some time, appearing briefly in the top half of the table for the first time since 1977. Central defender Steve Walsh had joined his former boss in the summer, and Hamilton soon made a club record outlay of £300,000 on Southampton's Steve Moran in an attempt to provide support for Alan Smith. Liverpool had once more been vanquished at Filbert Street, and away wins at both QPR and Manchester City were on the board when City's season started to fall apart.

A game at Charlton was thrown away following the dismissal of Walsh, and proved to be merely the first of 17 successive away defeats - a dismal record which proved too great a burden for sporadic home form to offset. The Cups brought equal misery: an Anfield exit from the newly-dubbed Littlewoods Challenge Cup, and a 2-5 thrashing on QPR's plastic in the premier competition.

By December, leading scorer Alan Smith, in the final year of his contract, had been reluctantly transfer-listed at £1 million. Chelsea were prepared to meet City's asking price, but Smith himself rejected the move. In March, though, Smith finally signed for Arsenal for £800,000, but was immediately loaned back to City until the end of the season. The same month, a below-form Steve Lynex was offloaded to West Brom; so City's once formidable striking trio were now definitively scattered.

Alan Smith scored here against Luton in the opening match of the season and finished as leading marksman with 20 League and Cup goals. He then departed for Arsenal as City returned to Division Two.

Youngsters and loan-spell triallists came and went as City fought on, but by the time they broke that horrendous away run with a goalless draw at Oxford on the season's final day, their fate - 20th place and automatic relegation - was sealed.

Early confidence, such as had seen Andrews and Morgan called up for England Under-21 duty, had dissipated entirely, and when next the consoling representative spotlight fell on Leicester, the result was a real mixed blessing. Both McAllister and Wilson starred for Scotland in a rare 'B' international, but the injury the former received kept him out of City's final three games when they still had a nominal chance of surviving the drop. At least Wilson went on to win full caps at season's end.

There was no way in which City's experiment with dual management could be regarded as a success; but neither was there much taste for assigning can-carrying duties to either boss on the immediate heels of the club's downfall. Gordon Milne, however, was missing day-to-day involvement with the players, and parted company with the club in May, leaving Hamilton in sole charge of their immediate Second Division future.

1987 - 88

Bryan Hamilton's forays into the summer transfer market brought three experienced heads to Leicester - goalkeeper Paul Cooper from Ipswich, midfielder Gary Ford from York, and the versatile Robbie James from QPR - plus one promising young striker in Nick Cusack from Alvechurch. He had, however, apparently been able to do little to repair morale over the break, and City suffered five deeply disheartening defeats in their initial six Second Division fixtures.

Worse still, on-field discipline was at a similarly low ebb. Steve Walsh was sent off on the opening day for breaking the jaw of Shrewsbury's goalscorer, David Geddis, and was eventually forced to miss eleven matches through suspension.

As metaphorical alarm bells sounded, Hamilton adopted a gambler's response. He snapped up Finnish international forward Jari Rantanen from IFK Gothenburg despite never having seen him in senior action, then broke the club transfer record to expend £350,000 on another central striker, Luton's Mike Newell. Prospects immediately looked brighter with three successive victories, but left-side impetus was then lost with Ian Wilson's move to Everton, and form dipped drastically again. Even the use

of two substitutes, allowed for the first time in League matches, could not help Hamilton effectively juggle his resources. New club sponsors Walkers Crisps must also have been puzzled by events as City slid down the Second Division chart.

Steve Moran moved on to Reading for £200,000 in November, ironically at the start of a record seven-game spell of scoreless performances from City. The loan system brought full-back David Langan and midfielder Kjetil Osvold briefly into the rather bleak picture, and then saw a sadly less than match-fit Kevin MacDonald fleetingly return.

The latter deal was sealed by coach and acting manager Peter Morris, for in early December the City board had decided to relieve Hamilton of his responsibilities. It was not long before they announced his permanent replacement, but David Pleat, the former Tottenham and Luton boss, left team matters in the hands of Morris over the Christmas period before assuming complete control.

Pleat's priority had to be a turnaround in League fortunes, for Oxford had supplied the killing blow in both major Cup competitions, and City were by now down amongst those scrabbling to avoid the drop to Division

*As City slid down the table former record signing **Steve Moran** (left) was sold to Reading but his New Year replacement*
***Nicky Cross** was part of the club's fine recovery under new manager David Pleat*
and is seen here scoring the winning goal against Manchester City in February 1988.

Three. The new manager's method was time-honoured, in the sense that it involved a rapid turnover of playing personnel, but it also hinged on a wonderfully effective tactical transformation of the side.

Out went Ford, James, Mark Venus and Kevin Jobling. In came Aberdeen winger Peter Weir, Walsall striker Nicky Cross, Grimsby utility man Phil Turner and, later, Burton Albion midfielder Paul Groves. And upwards and onwards went a City side that now also featured young left-footed striker Paul Reid on the right wing, Ali Mauchlen's battling qualities at right-back, and Paul Cooper as settled first-choice 'keeper. Alongside Weir, McAllister felt able to express creative skills which soon renewed covetous attention from the likes of Celtic and Spurs; while at the heart of the defence Steve Walsh now demonstrated genuine disciplined maturity.

Pleat's new-look team performed as well as any in the Division during the second half of the season and, scoring in each of their final 16 games, climbed to a comfortable 13th place. Spirits were restored, and their accurate passing game was too much for most rivals, as was seen to superb advantage when they stylishly eclipsed Middlesbrough in the final fixture, which the Ayresome side had needed to win to secure automatic promotion.

Sidelights on the season tended towards the ironic, and were probably appreciated most by supporters grateful to have had their faith rekindled. One involved City's eventual fate in their initial foray into the fledgling Full Members Cup (a competition they had shunned for two years, but which now carried attractive sponsorship from shoe firm Simod). Having brushed past Huddersfield and Charlton, City were ousted by Stoke on penalties. The grim jest here was that acknowledged spot-kick stopper Paul Cooper had already pulled off one such save during the game itself, but proved unable to get in the way of any in the ensuing shoot-out! A further irony was that neither of the two men who had been added this term to City's roster of full internationals - James and Rantanen - figured remotely in Pleat's plans; while one capped player who apparently did - QPR's versatile Israeli, David Pizanti - was denied a loan spell with City by the restrictive terms of his work permit.

The manager's plans themselves, of course, centred on mounting a realistic promotion bid next time out. Up the street at Welford Road, Tigers were celebrating their installation as inaugural winners of Rugby Union's Courage Championship, while Filbert Street regulars were busy convincing themselves that City had, under Pleat, cracked a championship code of their own. Optimism was back in fashion at Leicester.

1988 - 89

Those justifiably eternal optimists, the bookies, shared the view that City were not to be long for the Second Division - quoting the club as second favourites for promotion (behind Chelsea) before a ball was kicked in anger. There seemed little evidence - beyond the fact this term would see the longest-ever Second Division fixture list, involving 24 clubs - to contradict the opinion that 1988/9 would mark the end of City's fifth successive two-year spell at the lower level, following the down-up pattern of 1955-57, 1969-71, 1978-80 and 1981-83.

Certainly, the ins and outs of summer transfer dealing hardly suggested anything other than that City's resources were, overall, being augmented. The loss of the cultured and experienced Russell Osman was a blow, but appeared to be compensated for by the purchase of defenders Alan Paris, Tony Spearing and Steve Thompson. Jimmy Quinn, the previous season's overall divisional top scorer, arrived to challenge for a striker's role, while the outgoing Ian Andrews was replaced by top-class 'keeper Martin Hodge.

However, the script - which involved City either finishing among the automatically-promoted top two, or at least qualifying for the play-offs by virtue of a placing between third and sixth - proved surprisingly difficult to follow, and City's powers of improvisation rather failed them too. There were, to be fair, a few unforeseen casting blows. Thompson missed most of the pre-season build-up (and in fact soon moved on after being handed only an understudy's role); Hodge sustained a serious stomach injury only minutes into his debut; Quinn found difficulty interrupting the Cross/Newell partnership up front; and Peter Weir fell prey to homesickness. But it was too often the apparent collective on-field generosity of City's players which attracted some deservedly stinging appraisals from both the media and the terraces

At League level they developed an unfortunate knack of taking and then surrendering a hard-won lead (no less than thirteen times!); failed to put two consecutive wins together all season (a record matched only in the dismal 1977/8 relegation term); and could not even carry over into Second Division combat their fine Littlewoods Cup form (which saw them past the respective leaders of the top two divisions, Watford and Norwich, to honourable replay defeat against eventual winners Nottingham Forest). In too many games, it was left to a few isolated individuals to furnish the only real competitive spirit on show; and frustrations mounted on the back of those sporadic occasions when City's skills and Pleat's system genuinely gelled to produce a classy spectacle.

Watford took extra-time Simod Cup revenge for their Littlewoods pasting, and a disputed penalty removed City from the FA Cup at Maine Road (their fourth successive first-hurdle defeat in the senior knock-out competition), so there were few distractions from the League table, which showed City always out of reach of a top-six placing after the season's mid-point. In fact, 9th position in December proved the seasonal high-water mark, after a climb from 18th, the lowest point, in October. The final placing of 15th meant City had settled in the lower half of Division Two for a second successive season - a fate they had not known since 1951.

The only positive seasonal doubles came with the only two away wins, against relegated Birmingham and

Gary Mills arrived from Notts County in the Spring and is seen here in spectacular action during the home win over Walsall.

Walsall; while virtual repeats of the previous campaign's displays occurred in the home games with Swindon (a point-saving comeback from a 0-3 deficit) and Bournemouth (a totally frustrating single-goal Boxing Day defeat). The latter club were amongst four to put the home-and-away hoodoo on City (along with Ipswich, Barnsley and Oldham), and surrender at Dean Court was accompanied by a depressing illustration of just how unsuited Pleat's current squad were to the five-man-midfield formation he had favoured successfully at Tottenham.

Jimmy Quinn contrived to score both the winner for City against Bradford City at home, and for the Valley Paraders in the return fixture, following his transfer in March; while Gary McAllister persevered as penalty-taker until the last match, despite a less than 50% success rate. That said, twice as many spot-kicks were conceded throughout the term as were awarded to City.

A 4-0 trouncing of high-flying Blackburn represented the statistical high-point, while a battling 2-0 triumph over champions-elect Chelsea was the most satisfying result, delaying their promotion celebrations and bringing to an end a 27-match unbeaten run just short of the Divisional record. As befitted a term where inconsistency was virtually institutionalised, the latter win proved to be the only three-pointer of the final eight fixtures. The date of its achievement, however, proved one that will forever be edged in black in the game's calendar, for the Hillsborough disaster that day cast a pall of gloom over the nation, and once again football's more regular dramas were put into decidedly diminished perspective.

Throughout the season, Pleat always seemed to be on the verge of a major, morale-boosting signing, but his prey usually slipped away (as in the publicised cases of Bournemouth full-back Mark Newson and Spurs' £350,000-rated centre-back Chris Fairclough), or he was frustrated by fate (as when giant Romanian defender Gino Iorgolescu had his February trial period curtailed by an early training-ground injury); and even the manager's burst of deadline dealing was cut back by the refusal of out-of-favour Paul Ramsey to agree to an exchange with Walsall's Craig Shakespeare.

Though most of the term's newcomers settled to a senior niche of sorts, only Alan Paris (in a central defensive role) made major progressive strides, while City's best bit of business in regard to new blood turned out to be the belated introduction on loan of Forest youngster Gary Charles, who showed up many of his elders in both aptitude and attitude. Non-contract triallists to flit across the Filbert Street scene in the course of the campaign were, incidentally, a cosmopolitan bunch. In addition to the aforementioned Iorgolescu, three other internationals were briefly subjects of City scrutiny: the Nigerian Emeka Nwajiobi, the Moroccan Al Fadir, and the Northern Irishman Ian Stewart.

Senior friendly fare saw City beat Trinidad and Tobago's World Cup team (featuring a substitute named Philbert Jones); while the Reserves had to mount a fine grandstand finish to avoid relegation from the Central League's top flight, but won the County Challenge Cup. The youth team similarly won a knock-out pot, the Midland Purity Youth League Cup, while just missing out on their League title. Prospects Ian Baraclough and Paul Kitson each represented the League's Under-18 XI in Moscow, and the latter scored in a 2-1 win against their Soviet counterparts.

AFTERWORD

Two temptations immediately present themselves to your authors, at this point faced with the daunting task of neatly tying up the foregoing, narrative, and pointing towards its continuation. But we'll resist, to a large extent, the unproductive 'Whither City?' option (involving mere guesswork about short or long-term playing and trophy-hunting prospects), even as we recognise it as the very currency of committed, ever-optimistic fandom. We'll avoid too - in the wake of disasters, and in advance of potentially dangerous interventions from such hostile sources as Mrs Thatcher and ITV's Greg Dyke - apocalyptic speculations on the future of the game as a social, political or economic phenomenon.

Having declared early that this book is intended for the fans of Leicester City, we'll not insult readers by offering an interim summation of the 'lessons' of the foregoing history, either. Whether one has been hooked on Filbert Street fortunes for a lifetime or, say, merely the last three seasons, one will need no reminding that frustration comes with the territory, and that a thick skin is an essential pre-requisite for the committed. Whatever 'patterns' one tries to tease out of the progress of the club since 1884, one knows intuitively that in this context the only history likely to repeat itself (whether as tragedy or farce - or even, briefly, as joyous celebration) is one of intriguing inconsistency.

We hope our own affection for the game, the club, and the everyday rituals of attendance and amateur analysis, is evident within this text (and within later sections of the book): we are certain we share this particular set of passions with a vast body of folk who remain proud to call themselves supporters. Fair enough, we've carried our inquisitiveness about the club a little further than most have or would necessarily want to; and we've certainly indulged our opinions where interpretation (of the stated facts) has seemed appropriate. We hope we've not abused the privilege we've claimed for ourselves.

The point of trying to re-insert ourselves here within notions of collective support - as, if you like, two guys whose half time moans, memories, arguments and Ali Mauchlen jokes get quite naturally drowned in those of the Filbert Street faithful around us - is to pick up on the most heartening development around football of perhaps the last decade or so, which is the genuine attempt on behalf of fans themselves (ourselves included, in our way) to reclaim a voice in the game.

Whether this takes shape through the formal channels by which a body like the Football Supporters Association is attempting to negotiate a role within the decision-making infrastructure of football, or through the informal culture springing up rapidly around the allied 'fanzine' movement - there can be little doubt that the idea of communicating the invaluable wit and wisdom of the terraces beyond the boundaries of immediate, ephemeral earshot represents an avenue of genuine progress for the game.

The varied expressive qualities of irreverence, invective, irony and invention have not been part of our specific brief in here logging the activities of penalty-area, dressing-room and boardroom across 105 years; but we nonetheless recognise them as vital parts of the essential football experience. We hope also that they may become part of the necessary dialogue between football's 'professionals' and its 'punters' that will sustain the game in the future.

However City's fortunes may fluctuate in the 1990s, our true optimism is invested in the strengths of heart and humour that can only emanate from a community forged between club and crowd.

We sincerely hope that both may flourish.

STATISTICS
& RECORDS

The following section gives a match-by-match, season-by-season record incorporating details of fixtures, results, goalscorers and line-ups for all first-class matches, and also for selected other senior games. Competitions denoted as first-class are The FA Cup (excluding the Third Place Play Off of 1973/4), The Midland League, The Football League (excluding the three fixtures completed before the 1939/40 season was abandoned), The Football League Cup, The European Cup-Winners Cup, and The Full Members Cup. The other senior games to merit full details being given, but whose details are excluded from all individual career records contained herein, are the four fixtures excluded from the first-class records above, together with matches played in the following competitions — The Leicester-shire FA Senior Cup, The United Counties League, Regional Leagues in both World Wars, The Southern Professional Floodlit Cup, The FA Charity Shield, The Anglo-Italian Tournament, The Texaco Cup, and The Anglo-Scottish Tournament.

In recent years the following first-class competitions have been sponsored and known by a different name:

Football League:

1983/4—1985/6	: Canon League
1986/7	: Today League
1987/8—1988/9	: Barclays League

Football League Cup:

1982/3—1985/6	: Milk Cup
1986/7—1988/9	: Littlewoods Cup

Full Members Cup:

1987/8—1988/9	: Simod Cup

With regard to the opposition, we have attempted to utilise the title being used officially by any given club during any given season. Hence Small Heath later become Birmingham and subsequently Birmingham City. A full list of such name changes is given at the end of the supplementary table showing Leicester's complete record against all other clubs.

Wherever a neutral venue has been utilised for a fixture a note appears to that effect.

In the case of two fixtures the scoreline we record is at variance with that entered in Football League records. In both cases — 28 November 1896, at home to Walsall (where the League credit Fosse with a 4-1 win) and 26 April 1913, at Hull (recorded as a 1-2 defeat for City by the League) — we have minutely rechecked reports and result records in both local and national press and maintain our claim as to the greater accuracy of our own records. Consequently, the supplementary table denoting Leicester's season-by-season League record has been suitably adjusted.

Where genuine dispute has endured over the identity of a goalscorer, we have appended a note referring to alternative claims.

Though players did not wear numbered shirts until 1939, we have taken notice of the widespread tactical adherence to specialist positional play before this date, and have followed the practice of assigning numbers in the line-up grids as follows:

1-Goalkeeper; 2-Right-back; 3-Left-back; 4-Right-half; 5-Centre-half; 6-Left-half; 7-Outside-right; 8-Inside-right; 9-Centre-forward; 10-Inside-left; 11-Outside-left.

Due to the large number of players utilised during the World War seasons, the layout has been amended for these years, with goalscorers incorporated into the body of the line-up grids.

From 1965 onwards, substitutes are recorded only if they actually played for any part of the match in question, the number of the player withdrawn being marked by *. From 1986 onwards, we have recorded the number (12 or 14) the utilised substitute actually wore, and marked the number of the player(s) withdrawn with * when replaced by No.12, and with ^ when replaced by No.14.

The present structure of the FA Cup, with First and Second Division Football League clubs exempt until the Third Round Proper, was only settled on in 1925. The chart below lists equivalent rounds for competitions in which Leicester competed before 1925/6.

Present Round:				1	2	3	4	5	6	SF	F
1890/1 - 1895/6		Q1	Q2	Q3	Q4	1	2	3	SF	F
1896/7 - 1899/1900				Q3	Q4	Q5	1	2	3	SF	F
1900/1 - 1903/4			Q3	Q4	Q5	Int	1	2	3	SF	F
1904/5	Q3	Q4	Q5	Q6	Int	1	2	3	SF	F
1905/6			(Q4)	1	2	3	4	SF	F
1906/7 - 1913/14			(Q5)	1	2	3	4	SF	F
1914/15 - 1924/5			Q6	1	2	3	4	SF	F

(e.g. Fosse's achievement in reaching Round 2 in 1893/4 was the equivalent of reaching the modern Round 5).
Fosse's exemption status varied from season to season, the round of their entry being denoted in each seasonal table. City automatically entered the competition at Round 1 between 1919/20 and 1924/5.

Published attendance figures for individual games have been notoriously inaccurate over the years. The figures listed in the Football League records, only available from 1925/6 onwards, are often at variance with totals published in the press and, until recently, neither bore much resemblance to the actual number of spectators watching a particular game. Prior to World War Two, the figures recorded were often rounded and frequently assumed all season ticket holders were actually present. Consequently, we have ignored all such figures. To allow the reader to compare the relative levels of attendances in the modern era a figure for the average home League attendance is appended to the tables for post-World War Two years. This is rounded to the nearest 500 prior to 1960, but not rounded for subsequent seasons, as reporting accuracy has improved.

Details of attendance figures for individual fixtures of particular interest are referenced in the supplementary records section that follows the season-by-season tables, along with information on friendlies, reserve team records, sequences, transfer fees and various other notes that we hope will be of interest to the reader.

1890-91 F.A. CUP

DATE	OPPONENTS	V	F.T.	SCORERS	Walker	Rowson	Davis	Nuttall	Perry	Johnson J	Flint	Murdoch	Webb	Johnson E	Atter																			
Oct 4	Burton Wanderers	(Q1) H	0-4		1	2	3	4	5	6	7	8	9	10	11																			

Note: Played at Mill Lane

1

1) **LEICESTER FOSSE 1886-87**
Back: Hurndall,Hassell,W.Johnson,
W.Taylor *(umpire)*,H.Johnson,De Ville,Knight.
Middle: Smith,Ashmole,Gardner,West.
Front: J.Johnson,Bankart,E.Johnson.

2) **LEICESTER FOSSE 1888-89**

3) **LEICESTER FOSSE 1889-90**
Back: F.Gardner *(Secretary)*,Rowson,Walker,
Davis,W.Cooper *(umpire)*.
Middle: Squire,J.Johnson,Murdoch,Perry,Vickers.
Front: Bentley,Thompson,West,E.Johnson,Atter.

4) **LEICESTER FOSSE 1890-91** *(see opposite)*.

2

3

	APP's	GOALS
	FAC	FAC
Charlie Walker	1	
S.Rowson	1	
W.Davis	1	
Ernest Nuttall	1	
Dick Perry	1	
Jimmy Johnson	1	
J.Flint	1	
James Murdoch	1	
Harry Webb	1	
Teddy Johnson	1	
Jimmy Atter	1	

1891-92 MIDLAND LEAGUE
Final Position : 11th

DATE	OPPONENTS	V	F.T.	SCORERS	Old	Rowson	Bailey W H	Lord	Davis	Nuttall	Herrod	Webb	Bennett	Johnson	Atter J	Hufton	Vickers	Mouel	Wood	Owen	Walker	Perry	Gardner	Atter C	Harris	De Ville	Taylor	King	Lewis	Lisle	Atkins	Bailey H	Winter	Mabbott	Wilkins
Sep 12	Derby Junction	H	1-0	J.Atter	1	2	3	4	5	6	7	8	9	10	11																				
Oct 10	Grantham Rovers	H	3-1	Lord,Webb,J.Atter	1	2	3	4		6	7	8	9	10	11	5																			
17	Burton Wanderers	A	0-6		1	2	3	4	5	6	7	8		10	11	9																			
Nov 14	Loughborough	A	2-6	Mouel,J.Atter	1	2		4	3			8	9	10	11	5	6	7																	
28	Loughborough	H	1-2	Mouel	1	2		4		6		8	9	10	11	5		7	3																
Dec 5	Wednesbury Old Athletic	A	4-3	Hufton,Mouel,J.Atter,Webb	1			4		6		8	9	10	11	5		7	3	2															
19	Grantham Rovers	A	0-2		1	2	3	4		6		8	9	10	11	5		7																	
26	Doncaster Rovers	A	0-1				3	4					10	9	11	8				2		1	5	6	7										
Jan 2	Burton Wanderers	H	1-6	Bennett			3	4		6		9	8	10	11	5		7		2		1													
9	Rotherham Town	H	4-1	J.Atter 2,Mouel 2			3	4				9	8	10	11	5	6	7		2						1									
23	Long Eaton Rangers	A	1-5	Bennett			3	4				8	9	10	11	6		7		2						1	5								
30	Wednesbury Old Athletic	H	1-0	Johnson			3	4				9	8	10	11	6		7		2	5					1									
Feb 13	Gainsborough Trinity	H	0-3				3	4		6			8	10	11	5		7		2						1				9					
Mar 12	Derby Junction	A	0-0				3	4		6			10	9	11	8				2						1			5		7				
19	Gainsborough Trinity	A	0-1				3	4		6			8	10	11			7		2						1	5						9			
Apr 9	Long Eaton Rangers	H	0-0				3	4		6			10		11	8		7		2						1			5				9			
16	Rotherham Town	A	0-11				3	4		6				10		8		7		2						1	5						9			
19	Burslem Port Vale	H	1-3	H.Bailey			3	4		6				10		8		7		2	5					1							9	11		
28	Burslem Port Vale	A	0-4				3	4		6			9	10	11			7		2						1		5	8						
30	Doncaster Rovers	H	0-0				3	4		6				10	11			7		2						1		5						8	9

F.A. CUP

DATE	OPPONENTS	V	F.T.	SCORERS	Old	Rowson	Bailey W H	Lord	Davis	Nuttall	Herrod	Webb	Bennett	Johnson	Atter J	Hufton
Oct 3	Small Heath	(Q1) H	2-6	Nuttall,Herrod	1	2	3	4		6	7	8	9	10	11	5

Notes: 1) Sep 12, Oct 3, Oct 10 - played at Aylestone Road
2) Apr 16 - Fosse played with 10 men: A.Atkins failed to turn up.

LEICESTER FOSSE 1890-91
Back: Stubbs, W.Cooper *(Treasurer)*, Rowson, Walker, F.Gardner *(Secretary)*, Hillman.
Middle: Flint, Murdoch, J.Johnson, Davis, Nuttall.
Front: E.Johnson, Perry, Atter.
(No team photograph for 1891-92 available).

	APP's		GOALS	
	ML	FAC	ML	FAC
S.Old	7	1		
S.Rowson	6	1		
Harry Bailey	17	1		
Jack Lord	20	1		
W.Davis	3			
Ernest Nuttall	18	1		1
E.Herrod	7	1		1
Harry Webb	15	1	2	
A.Bennett	5	1	2	
Teddy Johnson	18	1	1	
Jimmy Atter	16	1	6	
S.Hufton	16	1	1	
A.Vickers	4			
E.Mouel	15		5	
A.Wood	2			
S.Owen	13			
Charlie Walker	2			
Dick Perry	5			
Frank Gardner	1			
C.Atter	1			
W.Harris	1			
T.De Ville	10			
Harry Taylor	3			
J.King	2			
R.Lewis	3			
C.Lisle	1			
A.Atkins	1			
Herbert Bailey	4		1	
R.Winter	1			
C.Mabbott	1			
E.Wilkins	1			

1892-93

MIDLAND LEAGUE
Final Position : 4th

DATE	OPPONENTS	V	F.T.	SCORERS	Thraves	Bailey	Taylor	Nuttall	Silvester	Lord	Lowe	Slack	Carter	Freeman	Dorrell	Owen	Webb	Thompson	Mabbott	Smith	Hardy	Frettingham	Atter	Stott	Priestman	Henrys	Worrall
Sep 17	Mansfield Town	A	1-4	Lowe	1	2	3	4	5	6	7	8	9	10	11												
26	Rotherham Town	A	1-6	Freeman	1		3	4		5	6	7	9	10	11	2	8										
Oct 1	Newark	H	7-1	Slack 3,Freeman 2,Silvester,Dorrell	1		3	4		5	6	7	9	10	11	2	8										
8	Kettering	A	4-0	Webb 3,Mabelstone (og)	1		3	4		5	6	7	9	10	11	2	8										
22	Derby Junction	H	4-0	Lowe,Dorrell,Freeman,Webb	1		3	4		5	6	7	9	10	11	2	8										
Nov 12	Loughborough	A	1-2	Slack	1		3	4		5	6	7	9	10	11	2	8										
26	Grantham Rovers	H	2-0	Mabbott,Slack	1		3	4		5	6	7	9	10	11			2	8								
Dec 17	Doncaster Rovers	A	1-0	Freeman	1		3	4	6	5	9	8		10	11		7			2							
24	Wednesbury Old Athletic	A	2-3	Hardy,Slack	1		3	4	6	5		9			11		8			2	7	10					
Jan 7	Doncaster Rovers	H	0-1		1		3	4	6	5	9	8			11		10			2	7						
14	Burton Wanderers	H	1-2	Hardy	1		3	4	6	5	9	8			11		10			2	7						
21	Gainsborough Trinity	A	2-1	Carter,Slack	1		3	4	6	5	9	8		10	11					2	7						
28	Grantham Rovers	A	2-1	Dorrell,Lowe	1		3	4	6	5	9	8		10	11					2	7						
Feb 4	Wednesbury Old Athletic	H	3-1	Lowe 2,Slack	1		3	4	6	5	9	8		10	11					2	7						
18	Gainsborough Trinity	H	2-1	Taylor,Lowe	1		3	4	6	5	10	9					7			2	8		11				
25	Burton Wanderers	H	0-3		1		3	4	6			5		10			7			2	8		11	9			
Mar 4	Rotherham Town	H	1-1	Lowe	1		3	4	6		5	9		10			7			2	8		11				
11	Long Eaton Rangers	A	1-2	Nuttall	1		3	4	6		5	9		10			7			2	8					11	
18	Loughborough	H	1-1	Dorrell	1		3	4	6		5	9		10			7			2	8		11				
Apr 1	Newark	A	3-3	Dorrell,Nuttall,Lowe	1		3	4	6		5	9		10			7			2			11		8		
3	Long Eaton Rangers	H	0-1		1		3	4	6		5			9		10	7			2			11		8		
8	Kettering	H	3-1	Dorrell 2,Slack	1		3	5	4			9				10	7		8	2			11		6		
22	Mansfield Town	H	5-1	Worrall,Lowe,Priestman 2,Slack	1		3	5	4		7	8			10					2			11		6	9	
27	Derby Junction	A	3-1	Webb 2,Dorrell	1		3			5		9				7	8			2			11	10	6		

F.A. CUP

DATE	OPPONENTS		V	F.T.	SCORERS	Thraves	Bailey	Taylor	Nuttall	Silvester	Lord	Lowe	Slack	Carter	Freeman	Dorrell	Owen	Webb
Oct 15	Rushden	(Q1)	H	7-0	Lowe,Webb 3,Dorrell 3 (1pen)	1		3	4		5	6	7	9	10	11	2	8
29	Notts Olympic	(Q 2)	A	3-3	Lowe,Freeman,Thompson (og)	1		3	4		5	6	7	9	10	11	2	8
Nov 5	Notts Olympic	(Q 2 rep)	H	7-0	Dorrell 4,Webb 2,Slack	1		3	4		5	6	7	9	10	11	2	8
19	Buxton	(Q 3)	H	1-2	Freeman	1		3		4	5	6	7	9	10	11	2	8

Note:1).Sep 17 - Lowe played in goal for the first 35 minutes, until Thraves turned up.
2).Oct 29 - abandoned during extra time, result at 90 minutes stood.

LEICESTER FOSSE 1892-93
Back: E.Marson *(Secretary)*, Carter,Lord,Bailey,Silvester,Smith *(Trainer)*.
Middle: Thraves,Lowe,Nuttall,Slack,Webb.
Front: Dorrell,Taylor.

	APP's		GOALS	
	ML	FAC	ML	FAC
Jimmy Thraves	24	4		
Harry Bailey	24	4		
Harry Taylor	24	3	1	
Ernest Nuttall	17	1	2	
Silvester	11	4	1	
Jack Lord	17	4		
W.Lowe	20	4	9	2
A.Slack	24	4	10	1
Carter	4		1	
Freeman	10	4	5	2
Billy Dorrell	24	4	8	7 (1p)
S.Owen	5	4		
Harry Webb	11	4	6	5
Arthur Thompson	1			
C.Mabbott	1		1	
George Smith	17			
W.Hardy	11		2	
G.Frettingham	1			
Jimmy Atter	8			
Stott	1			
J.Priestman	3		2	
Arthur Henrys	5			
Arthur Worrall	1		1	
Own Goals			1	1

1893-94 MIDLAND LEAGUE
Final Position : 2nd

DATE	OPPONENTS	V	F.T.	SCORERS	Thraves	Smith	Bailey W H	Seymour	Henrys	Lord	Hill	Miller	Worrall	Shaw	Dorrell	Rickus	Slack	Taylor	Edwards	Brown	Davis	Priestman	Bailey H	McArthur
Sep 9	Burton Wanderers	H	1-2	Worrall	1	2	3	4	5	6	7	8	9	10	11									
23	Long Eaton Rangers	H	3-0	Hill,Worrall,Henrys	1	2	3	4	5	6	7	8	9		11	10								
30	Gainsborough Trinity	A	0-0		1	2	3	4	5	6	7	9			11	8	10							
Oct 7	Loughborough	A	0-1		1	2	3	10	5	6	7	8	9		11			4						
21	Mansfield Town	H	4-0	Miller,Dorrell,Seymour,Edwards	1	2	3	4	5	6	7	9			11	10			8					
Nov 18	Doncaster Rovers	H	2-1	Brown,Dorrell	1	2	3	4	5	6	7	10			11				8	9				
Dec 2	Newark	H	3-0	Hill 2,Miller	1	2	3	4		6	7	10			11				8	9	5			
9	Mansfield Greenhalgh's	H	4-2	Dorrell,Brown 3	1		3	4		6	7	10			11			2	8	9	5			
23	Grantham Rovers	H	4-0	Miller 2,Brown 2	1	2	3	4	5	6	7	10			11				8	9				
Jan 6	Loughborough	H	4-0	Dorrell,Hill,Brown,Lord	1	2	3	4	5	6	7	10			11				8	9				
13	Gainsborough Trinity	H	3-1	Brown,Edwards,Hill	1	2	3	4	5	6	7	10			11				8	9				
20	Doncaster Rovers	A	2-1	Slack,Guild (og)	1	2	3	4	5	6	7	10			11		9		8					
Feb 3	Long Eaton Rangers	A	2-0	Miller,Fairbrother (og)	1		3	4	5	6	7	10			11			2	8	9				
24	Kettering	H	4-0	Brown,Hill,Miller,McDermott (og)	1	2	3	4	5	6	7	10			11				8	9				
Mar 3	Mansfield Greenhalgh's	A	3-0	Hill,Brown 2	1	2	3	4	5	6	7	10							8	9		11		
10	Burton Wanderers	A	1-2	Dorrell	1	2	3	4	5	6	7	10			11				8	9				
17	Newark	A	2-0	Dorrell 2	1	2	3	4	5	6	7	10			11					9		8		
24	Kettering	A	1-1	Brown	1	2	3	4	5	6	7	10			11					9		8		
Apr 4	Mansfield Town	A	3-0	Lord,Priestman,Brown	1	2	3	4	5	6	8	10			11					9		7		
28	Grantham Rovers	A	3-2	Miller,Brown,Dorrell	1	2	3	4		6	7	10			11			5		8				9

F.A. CUP

DATE	OPPONENTS		V	F.T.	SCORERS	Thraves	Smith	Bailey W H	Seymour	Henrys	Lord	Hill	Miller	Worrall	Shaw	Dorrell	Rickus	Slack	Taylor	Edwards	Brown	Davis	Priestman	Bailey H	McArthur
Nov 4	Mansfield Town	(Q2)	H	1-0	Dorrell	1	2	3	10	5	6	7	9			11			4	8					
25	Mansfield Greenhalghs	(Q3)	A	5-0	Brown,Hill,Lord,Miller,Haslam (og)	1	2	3	4	5	6	7	10			11				8	9				
Dec 16	Loughborough	(Q4)	A	1-0	Dorrell	1		2	6	5	4	7	10			11		3		8	9				
Jan 27	South Shore	(1)	H	2-1	Hill,Brown	1	2	3	4	5	6	7	10			11				8	9				
Feb 10	Derby County	(2)	H	0-0		1	2	3	4	5	6	7	10			11				8	9				
17	Derby County	(2 rep)	A	0-3		1	2	3	4	5	6	7	10			11				8	9				

Note:1).Nov 18 - abandoned after 50 minutes, when Doncaster walked off ; Midland League directed that result should stand.

2).Nov 25 - drawn away,but played at Filbert Street.

LEICESTER FOSSE 1893-94
(with various Committee members):*Back:* Unnamed,J.Hartopp,J.Lee,J.Curtis.
Middle: W.Jones,W.Cooper,W.Brown,Smith,Thraves,Bailey,Unnamed,Unnamed,Unnamed,Unnamed.
Front: C.Kilby,E.Marson *(Secretary)*,Hughes,Brown,McArthur,Henrys,Lord,F.Gardner.
On Ground: Hill,Unnamed,Miller,Dorrell.

	APP's		GOALS	
	ML	FAC	ML	FAC
Jimmy Thraves	20	6		
George Smith	18	5		
Harry Bailey	20	6		
Tom Seymour	20	6	1	
Arthur Henrys	18	6	1	
Jack Lord	19	6	2	1
John Hill	20	6	7	2
William Miller	20	6	7	1
Arthur Worrall	3		2	
Shaw	1			
Billy Dorrell	19	6	8	2
J.Rickus	3			
A.Slack	2		1	
Harry Taylor	3	1		
H.Edwards	12	6	2	
Jimmy Brown	14	6	14	2
W.Davis	2			
J.Priestman	4		1	
Herbert Bailey	1			
William McArthur	1			
Own Goals			3	1

1894-95 LEAGUE DIVISION TWO
Final Position : 4th

DATE	OPPONENTS	V	F.T.	SCORERS	Thraves	Smith	Bailey	Seymour	Brown	Henrys	Hill	Hughes	McArthur	Skea	Priestman	Whitelaw	Gallacher	Lord	Miller	Stirling	Gordon	McFarlane	Thompson
Sep 1	Grimsby Town	A	3-4	Skea 2,McArthur	1	2	3	4	5	6	7	8	9	10	11								
8	Rotherham Town	H	4-2	Skea 3,Gallacher	1		2	4	5	6	7	8	9	10		3	11						
15	Burton Wanderers	H	1-2	Skea	1		2	4		6	7	8	9	10		3	11	5					
22	Newton Heath	H	2-3	Skea,McArthur	1		2	4	5	6	7	8	9	10		3			11				
29	Newcastle United	A	0-2		1		2	4	5	6	7		8	9		3	11		10				
Oct 6	Notts County	A	0-3		1	2		4	5	6	7	8				3	11		9				
20	Newcastle United	H	4-4	McArthur,Henrys,Miller 2	1	2		4	5	6	7		8	10		3	11		9				
27	Newton Heath	A	2-2	Skea 2	1	2		4	5	6	7		8	10		3	11			9			
Nov 10	Darwen	H	2-1	Hill,McArthur	1	2		4			6	11	5	8	10		3			7	9		
17	Burton Swifts	H	2-2	Skea,Hackett (og)	1	2		4	5	6	7		8	10		3	11				9		
Dec 1	Notts County	H	5-1	Skea 3 (1pen),Gordon,McArthur	1	2		4		6	7		8	10		3	11				9		
8	Walsall Town Swifts	A	3-1	McArthur 2,Skea	1	2		4	6		7	5	8	10		3	11				9		
25	Bury	A	1-4	McArthur (Forsyth og)	1	2		4	5	6		7	8	10		3	11		9				
Jan 5	Walsall Town Swifts	H	9-1	McArthur,Gordon2,Brown,Skea2,Gallacher,Seymour	1	2	3	4	6		7	5	8	10			11				9		
7	Woolwich Arsenal	H	3-1	McArthur,Gordon,Hill	1	2		4	5	6	7		8	10		3	11				9		
12	Crewe Alexandra	A	2-2	Gallacher 2	1	2		4	5	6			8	10			11			7	9		3
15	Darwen	A	2-8	Skea,Gordon	1	2		4	5	6			8	10		3	11			7	9		
26	Rotherham Town	A	1-0	McArthur	1	2	3	4	5	6	7		8	10			11				9		
Feb 9	Burton Wanderers	A	1-1	Brown	1	2	3	4	7	6			5	10			11		8		9		
18	Crewe Alexandra	H	4-0	McArthur,Priestman,Stirling,Gordon	1		3		4	6			5	8	10	11	2			7	9		
23	Burslem Port Vale	A	1-1	Priestman	1	2	3		5	6	7		8	10	11	4					9		
Mar 2	Burton Swifts	A	5-0	Hughes,Skea 2,Gordon,McArthur	1	2	3	4	6			5	8	10	11	4					9		
4	Lincoln City	H	2-1	Skea,Gallacher	1	2	3	4	6			5	8	10	7		11				9		
9	Woolwich Arsenal	A	3-3	McArthur,Gordon,Skea	1	2	3	4	6			5	8	10	7		11				9		
16	Manchester City	H	3-1	Gordon,Hughes,McArthur	1	2	3	4	6			5	8	10	7		11				9		
23	Burslem Port Vale	H	2-1	Gordon,Skea	1		3		4	6			5	8	10	11	7				9	2	
30	Manchester City	A	1-1	Gordon	1	2	3	4	6		7	5	8	10			11				9		
Apr 6	Lincoln City	A	2-1	Gallacher,McArthur	1	2	3	4	6		7		8	10			11		9	5			
15	Grimsby Town	H	1-0	Skea	1	2	3	5			7		8	10			11	4	9	6			
20	Bury	H	1-0	Gordon	1	2	3	5			7		8	10			11	4	9	6			

F.A. CUP

DATE	OPPONENTS		V	F.T.	SCORERS	Thraves	Smith	Bailey	Seymour	Brown	Henrys	Hill	Hughes	McArthur	Skea	Priestman	Whitelaw	Gallacher	Lord	Miller	Stirling	Gordon	McFarlane	Thompson
Oct 13	Notts Olympic	(Q1)	A	13-0	Skea 3,Miller 4,McArthur 4,Hill 2	1	2	3	4		6	7	5	8	10			11		9				
Nov 3	Kimberley	(Q2)	H	7-2	Gordon 2,Gallacher,Skea 2,McArthur,Hill	1	2		4	5	6	7		8	10		3	11				9		
24	Rushden	(Q3)	A	3-2	Seymour,Gallacher,Skea (pen)	1	2		4	5	6	7		8	10		3	11				9		
Dec 15	Loughborough	(Q4)	H	1-1	Hill	1	2		4	5		7	6	8	10		3	11				9		
19	Loughborough	(Q4 rep)	A	2-2	Skea,Gallacher	1	2		4	5		7		8	10		3	11	6	9				
22	Loughborough	(Q4 rep 2)	H	3-0	Gallacher,Hill,Skea (pen)	1	2		4	5		7		8	10		3	11		9				
Feb 2	Bury	(1)	A	1-4	McArthur	1	2	3	4		6	7	5	8	10			11		9				

Notes: 1) .Oct 13 - drawn away but played at Filbert Street.
2) .Jan 5 - Brown generally credited with a goal from an indirect free-kick which deflected off an unnamed defender.
3) .Mar 9 - played at the Lyttleton Ground, Leyton.

No team photograph of Fosse for 1894-95 has yet come to light, but the County team of 1895 contained several past, present and future Fosse players.
LEICESTERSHIRE 1895
Back: Davis,Hogan,A.Lovell *(Chairman)*,Swift,Monteith.
Middle: G.Lee *(Treasurer)*,Cotterill,Atkins,Thompson,Dixon,J.Carpenter *(Secretary)*.
Front: Bull,Hibberd,Wood.

	APP's		GOALS	
	FL	FAC	FL	FAC
Jimmy Thraves	30	7		
George Smith	24	7		
Harry Bailey	19	2		
Tom Seymour	19	7	1	1
Jimmy Brown	27	5	2	
Arthur Henrys	26	5	1	
John Hill	20	7	2	5
Archie Hughes	18	3	2	
William McArthur	28	7	16	6
David Skea	30	7	23(1p)	8(2p)
J.Priestman	8		2	
Andrew Whitelaw	16	5		
Hugh Gallacher	25	7	6	4
Jack Lord	3	1		
William Miller	10	3	2	4
James Stirling	4		1	
Bob Gordon	21	4	12	2
Peter McFarlane	1			
Arthur Thompson	1			
Own Goals				2

1895-96

LEAGUE DIVISION TWO
Final Position : 8th

DATE	OPPONENTS	V	F.T.	SCORERS	Thraves	Baird	Davy	Brown	Walker	Henrys	Manson	McArthur	Trainer	Skea	Gallacher	Davies	Bailey	Atherton	Pickard	McWhirter	Bishop	Lynes	Lord	Dorrell	Thompson	Hibberd
Sep 7	Burton Swifts	H	2-1	Gallacher,Skea	1	2	3	4	5	6	7	8	9	10	11											
14	Manchester City	A	0-2		1	3	2	4	5	6	7	8	9	10	11											
21	Darwen	A	1-4	Skea	1	2	3	4	5	6	7	8		10	11	9										
28	Burton Wanderers	H	1-3	McArthur	1	2		4	5		7	9	8	10	11		3	6								
Oct 5	Loughborough	H	5-0	Brown,Skea,McArthur,Gallacher 2	1	2		4	5			8	9	10	11		3		7							
19	Burton Wanderers	A	0-0		1	2	4	7	5	6		8	9	10	11		3									
26	Darwen	H	2-3	Davies,Trainer	1	2		6	5	4		8	9			10	3				7	11				
Nov 9	Liverpool	A	1-3	Bishop	1		2	4	5	6		8	9	10			3				11	7				
16	Loughborough	A	4-1	Bishop,Davies 2,Lynes	1		2	4	5	6		8			10	9	3				7	11				
30	Liverpool	H	2-0	Davies,McArthur	1		2	4	5	6		8			10	9	3				7	11				
Dec 7	Woolwich Arsenal	A	1-1	Lynes	1		2	4	5	6		8			10	9	3				7	11				
21	Crewe Alexandra	H	4-1	Skea 2,McArthur,Stafford (og)	1		2	4	5			9	10	8			3				7	11	6			
Jan 1	Newcastle United	A	0-1		1		2	4	5			8	9	10	11		3				7		6			
4	Newton Heath	H	3-0	McArthur 2,Manson	1		2	4	5		8	9	10	11			3				7		6			
11	Notts County	H	2-1	Manson,Skea (pen)	1		2	4	5		8	9	10	11			3				7		6			
18	Rotherham Town	A	0-2		1		2	4	5	6	8		9	11	10		3				7					
25	Woolwich Arsenal	H	1-0	Lynes	1		2	4	5			8	10		11		3				7	9	6			
Feb 3	Newton Heath	A	0-2		1		2	4	5			8	10				3				7	11	9	6		
8	Notts County	A	2-1	McArthur,Manson	1		2	4	5		8	9	10	11			3				7		6			
15	Lincoln City	A	3-2	McWhirter,Manson,Boullemier (og)	1		2	4	5		8	9	10	11			3			7			6			
22	Crewe Alexandra	A	1-1	McArthur	1		2	4	5			8	9	10	11		3			7			6			
29	Lincoln City	H	1-3	Trainer	1		2	4	5			8	9	10	11		3			7			6			
Mar 7	Burslem Port Vale	A	1-1	Moss (og)	1		2	4	5			8	10	9	11		3			7			6			
21	Burslem Port Vale	H	5-0	Lord 2,Gallacher,Trainer,Dorrell	1	3	2	4	5			8	10		9					7			6	11		
28	Burton Swifts	A	2-0	McArthur,Gallacher	1	2	3	4	5			8	9		10					7			6	11		
Apr 3	Rotherham Town	H	8-0	Trainer 5,McArthur,Manson,Hobson (og)	1	3		7	5		8	9	10					2					6		4	
4	Manchester City	H	1-2	McArthur	1		2	4	5			8	9		10		3			7			6	11		
6	Grimsby Town	H	1-2	Dorrell	1		2	4	5			8	9		10		3			7			6	11		
7	Newcastle United	H	2-0	Trainer 2	1	3		4	8			9	10					2	5	7			6	11		
11	Grimsby Town	A	1-7	Manson	1		2	9	5		8		10	4			3			7			6	11		

F.A. CUP

DATE	OPPONENTS		V	F.T.	SCORERS	Thraves	Baird	Davy	Brown	Walker	Henrys	Manson	McArthur	Trainer	Skea	Gallacher	Davies	Bailey	Atherton	Pickard	McWhirter	Bishop	Lynes	Lord	Dorrell	Thompson	Hibberd
Oct 12	Hinckley Town	(Q1)	H	4-0	Trainer 2,Bishop,McArthur	1	2		4	5	6		8	9			10	3				7	11				
Nov 2	Hucknall St.Johns	(Q2)	H	3-1	Manson,Hibberd,Trainer	1		2	4	5		10		9				3				11	7	0			0
23	Kimberley	(Q3)	A	3-1	McArthur 2,Rowley (og)	1		2	4	5	6		8			10	9	3				7	11				
Dec 14	Kettering	(Q4)	H	1-2	Trainer	1		2	4	5	6		8	9		10		3				11	7				

Notes:1).Oct 26 - Trainer credited with second goal after a scramble also involving Davies.

2).Nov 2, Nov 9 - Lynes made his first two appearances under the pseudonym of "James".

LEICESTER FOSSE 1895-96
Back: Lee *(Secretary),*Baird,Atherton,Thompson,Strachan,Lord,Walker,Bailey,Newton*(Trainer).*
Middle: Hogan,Manson,Thraves,Davies,Pickard,Gallacher,Henrys.
Front: McArthur,Trainer,Skea,Brown.

	APP's		GOALS	
	FL	FAC	FL	FAC
Jimmy Thraves	30	4		
John Baird	13	1		
Harry Davy	22	3		
Jimmy Brown	29	4	1	
Jack Walker	30	4		
Arthur Henrys	11	3		
David Manson	23	1	6	1
William McArthur	27	3	11	3
Harry Trainer	17	3	10	4
David Skea	15		6(1p)	
Hugh Gallacher	22		5	
Richard Davies	7	3	4	
Harry Bailey	25	4		
James Atherton	2			
J.Pickard	1	1		
Peter McWhirter	17	1	1	
Matt Bishop	7	4	2	1
James Lynes	7	3	3	
Jack Lord	18	1	2	
Billy Dorrell	6		2	
Arthur Thompson	1			
John Hibberd		1		1
Own Goals			4	1

1896-97 LEAGUE DIVISION TWO
Final Position : 9th

DATE	OPPONENTS	V	F.T.	SCORERS	Thraves	Davy	Swift	Lord	Walker	Leighton	Dorrell	Freebairn	Lonie	Carnelly	McMillan	Brown	Manson	Bailey	Trainer	McDonald	Proudfoot	Bishop	Howes	Wood
Sep 5	Darwen	H	4-1	McMillan,Lonie,Walker,Freebairn	1	2	3	4	5	6	7	8	9	10	11									
12	Notts County	H	2-3	Manson 2	1	2	3		5	6	7		9	10	11	4	8							
19	Burton Swifts	A	1-2	Dorrell	1	2	3		5	6	7	8	9	10	11	4								
26	Loughborough	A	2-0	McMillan 2	1	2	3		5	6	11	7	9	8	10	4								
Oct 3	Blackpool	H	2-1	Dorrell,Carnelly	1	2	3		5	6	11	7	9	8	10	4								
17	Notts County	A	0-6		1		3		5	6		10	9	8	11	4		2	7					
24	Darwen	A	1-4	Lonie	1	2	3	6	5		7	10	9	8	11	4								
Nov 7	Lincoln City	H	4-1	McMillan 2,Carnelly,Freebairn	1	2	3	6	4		11	7		10	9	5			8					
14	Newcastle United	A	1-3	McMillan	1	2	3	6	4		11	7		10	9	5			8					
28	Walsall	H	4-2	Freebairn,Carnelly 2,McDonald	1	2	3	6	4		11	7		10	9	5			8					
Dec 5	Grimsby Town	H	4-2	McMillan 2,Dorrell,McDonald	1	2	3	6	4		11	7		10	9					8	5			
19	Burton Wanderers	A	1-2	McDonald	1	2	3	6	4		11	7		10	9					8	5			
25	Loughborough	H	4-2	McDonald,Dorrell,Freebairn 2	1	2	3		4	6	11	7		9					10	8	5			
28	Newton Heath	H	1-0	Dorrell	1	2	3	6	4		11	7		10		5				9	8			
Jan 9	Newcastle United	H	5-0	Trainer,McDonald 2,Carnelly,Dorrell	1		3			6	11	7		10		4		2	9	8	5			
16	Burton Wanderers	H	2-1	Brown,Trainer	1	2	3		4	6	10	7			5				9		8	11		
23	Grimsby Town	A	1-4	Dorrell	1	2	3			6	10	7	8		4				9		5	11		
Feb 6	Gainsborough Trinity	A	2-0	McMillan 2	1	2	3			6	11	7		10	8	4			9		5			
13	Woolwich Arsenal	H	6-3	Dorrell 2,Carnelly 2,Freebairn,Sinclair (og)	1	2	3			6	11	7		10	8	4			9		5			
20	Newton Heath	A	1-2	Carnelly	1	2	3			6	11	7		10	9	4			8		5			
27	Blackpool	A	0-3			2	3			6	11	7		9	4				10	8	5		1	
Mar 6	Burton Swifts	H	3-0	Carnelly,Dorrell,Freebairn		2	3	6			11	7		10	9	4				8	5		1	
13	Manchester City	A	0-4			2	3	6			7			10	11	4			9	8	5		1	
20	Walsall	A	1-1	Wood		2	3	6			7			10		4			9		5	11	1	8
27	Small Heath	H	0-1			2	3	6			11	7		10	9	4					5	11	1	8
Apr 10	Lincoln City	A	1-2	Freebairn		2	3	6			11	7		10	9	4				8	5		1	
12	Manchester City	H	3-3	McMillan,Carnelly,Ray (og)		2	3	6			11	7		10	9	4				8	5		1	
16	Small Heath	A	2-2	McDonald,Freebairn		2	3	6			11	7		10		4			9	8	5		1	
17	Woolwich Arsenal	A	1-2	Dorrell		2	3	6			11	7		10		4			9	8	5		1	
19	Gainsborough Trinity	H	0-0			2	3	6			11	7		10	9	4				8	5		1	

F.A. CUP

DATE	OPPONENTS		V	F.T.	SCORERS	Thraves	Davy	Swift	Lord	Walker	Leighton	Dorrell	Freebairn	Lonie	Carnelly	McMillan	Brown	Manson	Bailey	Trainer	McDonald	Proudfoot	Bishop	Howes	Wood
Nov 21	Bulwell United	(Q 3)	H	3-1	Freebairn 2,Lord	1	2	3	6	4		11	7		10	9	5			8					
Dec 12	Wellingborough Town	(Q 4)	A	3-2	McMillan,Dorrell,Freebairn	1	2	3	6	4		11	7		10	9	5				8				
Jan 2	Kettering	(Q 5)	A	1-2	Dorrell	1	2	3	6	4		11	8		10		7				9	5			

LEICESTER FOSSE 1896-97
Back: J.Jackson (Trainer),Lord,Davy,Bailey,Swift,Dorrell,H.Jackson (Secretary).
Middle: Brown,Lonie,Carnelly,Trainer,Thraves,Leighton,Walker.
Front: Freebairn,McMillan,Manson.

	APP's		GOALS	
	FL	FAC	FL	FAC
Jimmy Thraves	20	3		
Harry Davy	28	3		
George Swift	30	3		
Jack Lord	8	3		1
Jack Walker	24	3	1	
John Leighton	14			
Billy Dorrell	26	3	11	2
Willie Freebairn	30	3	9	3
Tom Lonie	7		2	
Albert Carnelly	28	3	10	
Johnny McMillan	22	2	11	1
Jimmy Brown	26	3	1	
David Manson	1		2	
Harry Bailey	2			
Harry Trainer	14	1	2	
David McDonald	16	2	7	
David Proudfoot	19	1		
Matt Bishop	3			
Arthur Howes	10			
Cecil Wood	2		1	
Own Goals				2

1897-98 LEAGUE DIVISION TWO
Final Position : 7th

DATE	OPPONENTS	V	F.T.	SCORERS	Howes	Walker	Swift	Jones	Proudfoot	Ball	Freebairn	McLeod	Smith	McMillan	Dorrell	King	Saer	Gillies	Rowell	Brown	Flanagan	Watkins	Eaton	Coulson	Keech
Sep 4	Luton Town	H	1-1	Freebairn	1	2	3	4	5	6	7	8	9	10	11										
11	Small Heath	A	1-2	Smith	1	2	3	4	5	6	7	8	9	10	11										
18	Grimsby Town	A	0-0			2	3	4	5	6	7	8	9			11	1	10							
Oct 2	Newton Heath	A	0-2			2	3			6	4	7	8	9		11	1	10							
9	Burnley	H	0-1			2	3	6	5	4		8	9		7	11	1	10							
16	Walsall	H	3-1	Smith 2,King		6	3	5		4	7	8	9	10		11	1	2							
23	Woolwich Arsenal	A	3-0	McMillan,McLeod,King		2	3	6		4	7	8	9	10		11	1			5					
Nov 6	Blackpool	H	4-1	Freebairn,McLeod 2,McMillan		2	3	6		4	7	8	9	10	11		1			5					
13	Loughborough	A	1-1	McLeod		2	3	6		4		8	9	10	11		1			5					
20	Newton Heath	H	1-1	McLeod		2	3	6		4		8	9	10	7	11	1			5					
27	Burton Swifts	A	3-2	Dorrell,Freebairn,McMillan		2	3	6		4	7	9		10	11		1			5	8				
Dec 4	Woolwich Arsenal	H	2-1	McLeod,Dorrell		2	3	6		4		9		10	7		1	11		5	8				
11	Manchester City	A	1-2	McMillan		2	3	6		4	7	9		10	11		1			5	8				
18	Darwen	A	2-1	McLeod,McMillan		2	3	6		4	7	9		10	11	8	1			5					
25	Loughborough	H	4-0	McMillan,Smith,McLeod,Freebairn		2	3	6		4	7	9	8	10	11		1			5					
Jan 8	Blackpool	A	1-2	Freebairn		2	3	6	5	4	7	9	8	10	11		1								
15	Burnley	A	0-4			2	3	6		4	7	9	8	10	11		1			5					
22	Newcastle United	A	2-4	McLeod,King		2	3	6		4	7	9		10	11	8	1			5					
Feb 5	Darwen	H	0-1			2	3	4				9			11	8	1	5	6	7	10				
12	Lincoln City	H	3-1	Coulson,McLeod,Dorrell		2	3	6		4		8		10	11	7	1			5				9	
26	Walsall	A	1-2	McLeod		2	3	6		4		8		10	11		1			5		7			9
Mar 5	Lincoln City	A	4-1	McLeod,McMillan,Dorrell,Keech		2	3	6		4		8		10	7	11	1			5					9
12	Burton Swifts	H	1-1	McMillan		2	3	6		4		8		10	7	11	1			5					9
19	Gainsborough Trinity	A	0-1			2	3	4				8	9	10	7	11	1		6	5					
26	Small Heath	H	2-0	McLeod,Keech		2	3	6		4		8		10	7	11	1			5					9
Apr 2	Manchester City	H	0-0			2	3	6		4		8		10	7	11	1			5					9
8	Luton Town	A	1-0	Dorrell		2		6		4		8		10	7	11	1	3		5					9
9	Newcastle United	H	1-1	Dorrell (pen)		2	3	6		4		8		10	7	11	1			5					9
11	Grimsby Town	H	1-0	McMillan		2	3	6		4				10	7	11	1			5			8		9
16	Gainsborough Trinity	H	3-1	Dorrell,Watkins,Keech		2	3	6		4		8		10	7		1			5		11			9

F.A. CUP

DATE	OPPONENTS	V	F.T.	SCORERS	Howes	Walker	Swift	Jones	Proudfoot	Ball	Freebairn	McLeod	Smith	McMillan	Dorrell	King	Saer	Gillies	Rowell	Brown	Flanagan	Watkins	Eaton	Coulson	Keech
Jan 29	Southampton (1)	A	1-2	McLeod		2	3	6		4	7	9		10	8	11	1			5					

BILLY DORRELL
Originally a star of Fosse's Midland League team, he moved to Aston Villa in 1894,
but returned to Fosse in 1896 to star once more in the League team until his retirement in 1899.
(No team photograph for 1897-98 available).

	APP's FL	APP's FAC	GOALS FL	GOALS FAC
Arthur Howes	2			
Jack Walker	29	1		
George Swift	30	1		
Dick Jones	28			
David Proudfoot	6	1		
Alf Ball	30	1		
Willie Freebairn	14	1	5	
Roddie McLeod	28	1	13	1
Harry Smith	15		4	
Johnny McMillan	26	1	9	
Billy Dorrell	26	1	7 (1p)	
Rab King	18	1	3	
Charlie Saer	28	1		
Alec Gillies	4			
Tom Rowell	5			
Jimmy Brown	22	1		
William Flanagan	4			
Alf Watkins	2		1	
Sam Eaton	3			
Henry Coulson	1	1		1
William Keech	9		3	

1898-99 LEAGUE DIVISION TWO
Final Position : 3rd

DATE	OPPONENTS	V	F.T.	SCORERS	Rowley	Walker	Swift	Ball	Brown	Jones	Galbraith	Dorrell	McMillan	King	Watkins	Beardsley	Parry	Keech	Howes	Eaton	Fulwood	Ballard	Thompson	Robinson	Goudie	Lyon	Wragg	Bradshaw	Bishop
Sep 3	Lincoln City	H	3-2	Watkins 2,King	1	2	3	4	5	6	7	8	9	10	11														
10	Woolwich Arsenal	A	0-4			2	3	4	5		7			10	8	11	1	6	9										
17	Luton Town	H	1-1	King		2	3	4	5	6	7			10	8	11	1		9										
24	Barnsley St Peters	A	4-3	Galbraith 2,Keech 2		2	3	4	5	6	7			10	8	11	1	9											
26	Walsall	A	1-1	Galbraith		2	3	4	5	6	7			10	8	11	1		9										
Oct 1	Darwen	A	0-3			2	3	4	5	6	7			10	8	11	1		9										
8	Gainsborough Trinity	H	1-0	Galbraith		2	3	4	5	6	7			10			1		9	8	11								
15	Manchester City	A	1-3	Eaton	5		3	4		6	7			10	9	11	1			8			2						
22	Glossop North End	H	4-2	King,Eaton,Watkins,Fulwood		2	3	4	5	6	7			9	11		1			8	10								
Nov 5	Burton Swifts	H	1-0	Watkins		2	3	4	5	6	7			9	10		1			8	11								
12	Burslem Port Vale	A	2-0	King,Galbraith		2	3	4	5	6	7		11	9	10		1			8									
26	Loughborough	A	3-0	Eaton,Fulwood,King		2	3	4	5	6	7			10	9		1			8	11								
Dec 3	Blackpool	H	4-0	Galbraith 2,King,Watkins		2	3	4	5	6	7			9	10		1			8	11								
17	Newton Heath	H	1-0	Fulwood			3	4		6	7			9	10		1			8	11	2	5						
24	New Brighton Tower	A	0-1			2	3	4		6	7			10	9		1			8	11		5						
26	Darwen	H	4-0	Eaton,Galbraith,McMillan,Watkins		2	3	4		6	7			10	9		1			8	11		5						
27	Loughborough	H	1-0	Ball		2		4		6	7			10	9		1			8	11	3	5						
31	Lincoln City	A	1-3	Robinson		2	3	4		6	7			10	9		1			8	11		5						
Jan 7	Woolwich Arsenal	H	2-1	King,Watkins		2	3	4		6	7			10	9	11	1			8			5						
14	Luton Town	A	6-1	King,Watkins,Galbraith 2,McMillan,Lyon		2	3	4		6	7			10	9	11						5	1	8					
21	Barnsley St Peters	H	3-1	Galbraith 2,King		2	3	4		6	7			10	9			1			11	5	8						
Feb 4	Gainsborough Trinity	A	0-4			2	3	4		6	7			10	9	11	1					5	8						
11	Manchester City	H	1-1	McMillan		2	3	4		6	7			10	9	11	1					5	8						
18	Glossop North End	A	3-1	King,Galbraith,Watkins		2	3	4		6	7			10	9	11	1					5	8						
25	Walsall	H	2-2	Watkins, Lyon		2	3	4		6	7			10	9	11	1					5	8						
Mar 4	Burton Swifts	A	1-1	McMillan		2	3	4		6	7			10	9	11	1					5	8						
11	Burslem Port Vale	H	1-1	McMillan		2	3	4		6	7			10	9	11	1					5	8						
18	Small Heath	A	3-0	Galbraith,Eaton,King		2	3	4		6	7			10	9	11	1			8			5						
31	Grimsby Town	A	0-1			2	3	4		6	7			10	9	11	1			8			5						
Apr 1	Blackpool	A	2-2	Galbraith,McMillan		2		4		6	7			10	9	11	1			8			5		3				
3	Grimsby Town	H	2-0	Watkins,Eaton		2		4		6				10	11	9	1			8			5		3	7			
15	Newton Heath	A	2-2	Bradshaw,McMillan			2	4		6				10	9	11	1			8			5		3	7			
22	New Brighton Tower	H	4-1	Galbraith,Bradshaw,Ball,King			3	4		6	7			10	9	11	1					2	5		8				
29	Small Heath	H	0-0				3	4		6	7				9		1			8		2	5				11	10	

F.A. CUP

DATE				SCORERS	Walker	Swift	Ball	Brown	Jones	Galbraith	King	Watkins	Beardsley	Parry	Keech	Howes	Eaton	Fulwood
Oct 29	Kimberley	(Q 3)	H	9-0	King 4,Watkins 2,Fulwood,Swift (pen),Brown (pen)	2	3	4	5	6	7	9	10	1				8	11
Nov 19	Rushden	(Q 4)	H	2-1	Galbraith,McMillan	2	3	4	5	6	7	11	9	10	1			8	
Dec 10	Kettering	(Q 5)	A	1-1	Fulwood	2	3	4	5	6	7	9	10	1				8	11
15	Kettering	(Q 5 rep)	H	1-2	Eaton	2	3	4	5	6	7	11	9	10		1		8	

Note: Apr 3 - Most reports credit Watkins with first goal, but some credit Eaton.

LEICESTER FOSSE 1898-99
Back: Ball,Galbraith,Watkins,Beardsley,Dorrell,R.Dunmore *(Trainer).*
Middle: G.Johnson *(Secretary)*, Brown,Eaton,Swift,Walker,McMillan.
Front: Jones,King.
Note: Both Watkins and Jones are wearing their Welsh international caps.

	APP's		GOALS	
	FL	FAC	FL	FAC
William Rowley	1			
Jack Walker	30	4		
George Swift	31	4		1 (1p)
Alf Ball	34	4	2	
Jimmy Brown	12	4		1 (1p)
Dick Jones	33	4		
Tommy Galbraith	32	4	16	1
Billy Dorrell	1			
Johnny McMillan	29	2	7	1
Rab King	30	4	12	4
Alf Watkins	29	4	11	2
Godfrey Beardsley	29	3		
Maurice Parry	1			
William Keech	6		2	
Arthur Howes	3	1		
Sam Eaton	19	4	6	1
Bennie Fulwood	11	2	3	2
Frank Ballard	2			
Arthur Thompson	2			
Walter Robinson	21		1	
Peter Goudie	1			
Herbert Lyon	8		2	
William Wragg	4			
Tom Bradshaw	4		2	
Matt Bishop	1			

1899-1900 LEAGUE DIVISION TWO
Final Position : 5th

DATE	OPPONENTS	V	F.T.	SCORERS	Beardsley	Wragg	Swift	Ball	Robinson	Jones	Galbraith	Bradshaw	Brown	McMillan	King	Eaton	Dainty	Bishop	Bailey	Allen	Lyon	Carter	Mercer	Wood
Sep 2	Woolwich Arsenal	A	2-0	King,Brown	1	2	3	4	5	6	7	8	9	10	11									
9	Barnsley	H	1-0	Wragg	1	2	3	4	5	6	7	8	9	10	11									
16	Burton Swifts	H	1-0	Ball	1	2	3	4	5	6	7		9	10	11	8								
23	Luton Town	A	0-0		1	2	3	4		6	7		10	9	8	5	11							
25	Walsall	A	2-1	Bradshaw,Brown		2	3	4		6	8	7	9	10	11		5		1					
30	Burslem Port Vale	H	2-0	Bradshaw,McMillan	1	2	3	4		6	8	7	9	10	11		5							
Oct 14	Middlesbrough	H	4-1	Brown,King 2,McMillan	1	2	3	4		6	8	7	9	10	11		5							
21	Chesterfield	A	0-0		1	2	3	4		6	8	7	9	10	11		5							
Nov 4	Bolton Wanderers	A	2-2	McMillan,Dainty	1	2	3	4		6	8	7	9	10	11		5							
11	Loughborough	A	2-0	Wragg,Brown	1	2	3	4		6	8	7	9	10	11		5							
25	Sheffield Wednesday	H	0-0		1	2	3	4		6	8	7	9	10	11		5							
Dec 2	Lincoln City	A	0-2		1	2	3	4		6	8	7	9	10	11		5							
16	New Brighton Tower	A	2-2	McMillan,Bradshaw	1	2	3	4		6	8	7		10	9		5			11				
23	Grimsby Town	H	3-0	McMillan 2,Mountain (og)	1	2	3	4		6	8	7		10	9		5			11				
25	Loughborough	H	5-0	Bradshaw,King 2,Galbraith,Allen	1	2	3	4		6	8	7		10	9		5			11				
27	Walsall	H	2-1	McMillan,King	1	2	3	4		6	8	7		10	9		5			11				
30	Woolwich Arsenal	H	0-0		1	2	3	4		6	8	7		10	9		5			11				
Jan 6	Barnsley	A	2-1	King,Dainty	1	2	3	4		6	8	7		10	9		5			11				
13	Burton Swifts	A	0-2		1	2	3	4		6	7			10	9		5	8		11				
20	Luton Town	H	2-2	Allen,McMillan	1	2	3	4	5	6	7	8		10	9					11				
Feb 3	Burslem Port Vale	A	2-0	Eaton 2		2	3	4		6	7			10	9	8	5			11	1			
17	Middlesbrough	A	1-0	Brown	1	2	3	4		6	7		9	10	8		5			11				
24	Chesterfield	H	2-2	McMillan,King	1	2	3	4		6			10	9	8		5			11			7	
Mar 3	Gainsborough Trinity	A	0-3		1	2	3	4		6			10	9	8		5			11			7	
10	Bolton Wanderers	H	0-0			2	3	4		6			9	10	8		5			11	1		7	
24	Newton Heath	H	2-0	King,Brown	1	2	3			6	7	8	9	10	11		5					4		
31	Sheffield Wednesday	A	0-2		1	2	3	4		6	8	7	9	10			5			11				
Apr 7	Lincoln City	H	2-0	Mercer,King	1	2	3	4		6	8		9	10	11		5						7	
13	Newton Heath	A	2-3	Mercer,Wragg	1	2	3	4		6			9	11	8		5				10		7	
14	Small Heath	A	1-4	Lyon	1	2	3	4		6			9	11	8		5				10		7	
16	Gainsborough Trinity	H	5-0	Wragg 2,Lyon,Dainty,King	1	5	3	2		4		8	9		11		6				10		7	
17	Small Heath	H	2-0	Bradshaw,Lyon	1	5	3	2		4		8	9	11	7		6				10			
21	New Brighton Tower	H	1-2	King	1	5	3	2		4		8	9	10	11		6						7	
28	Grimsby Town	A	1-6	King	1	5	3	2		4		8		10	11		6					9	7	

F.A. CUP

DATE	OPPONENTS		V	F.T.	SCORERS	Beardsley	Wragg	Swift	Ball	Robinson	Jones	Galbraith	Bradshaw	Brown	McMillan	King	Eaton	Dainty	Bishop	Bailey	Allen	Lyon	Carter	Mercer	Wood
Oct 28	Wellingborough	(Q 3)	H	3-1	McMillan,Bishop,Brown	1	2	3	4		6	8	7	9	10			5	11						
Nov 27	Burton Swifts	(Q 4)	A	3-1	Brown 2,Swift (pen)	1	2	3	4		6	8	7	9	10	11		5							
Dec 9	Hucknall Portland	(Q 5)	A	6-1	King,Bradshaw,McMillan 2,Lyon 2	1	2	3	4		6	7	8		10	11		5				9			
Jan 27	Sheffield United	(1)	A	0-1		1	2	3	4		6	7	8		10	9		5			11				

Notes: 1) Sep 25 - Bailey (goalkeeper) is the same player who played full-back 1894-97.
2) Nov 27 - drawn away, but played at Filbert Street.
3) Dec 9 - drawn away, but played at Filbert Street.
4) Dec 23 - Most reports credit McMillan with second goal, some credit King.
5) Mar 10 - Lyon (goalkeeper) is the same player who played as a forward during the season.
6) Apr 16 - Most reports credit Wragg with fourth goal, some credit Lyon.

COUNTY CRICKETERS.

MR. C. J. B. WOOD,
LEICESTERSHIRE.

CECIL WOOD
Made his final appearance for Fosse in March 1900. He had represented Leicestershire at both Football and Cricket, but it was as a County cricketer that he went on to make a significant sporting mark.
(No team photograph for 1899-1900 available).

	APP's		GOALS	
	FL	FAC	FL	FAC
Godfrey Beardsley	31	4		
William Wragg	34	4	5	
George Swift	34	4		1 (1p)
Alf Ball	11	1	1	
Walter Robinson	26	3		
Dick Jones	28	4		
Tommy Galbraith	30	2	1	
Tom Bradshaw	24	4	5	1
Tommy Brown	21	3	6	3
Johnny McMillan	29	4	9	3
Rab King	33	3	13	1
Sam Eaton	9		2	
Herbert Dainty	30	4	3	
Matt Bishop	2	2		1
Harry Bailey	1			
Harry Allen	13	1	2	
Herbert Lyon	7	1	3	2
Roger Carter	1			
John Mercer	9		2	
Cecil Wood	1			
Own Goals				1

1900-01 LEAGUE DIVISION TWO
Final Position : 11th

DATE	OPPONENTS	V	F.T.	SCORERS	Beardsley	Mills	Swift	Wragg	Foster	Jones	Brash	Kyle	Connachan	McMillan	Dunkley	Cochrane	Woolridge	Hamilton	Brown	Beadsworth	Daw	Robinson	Robertson	Langham	Henderson	Hammond	Allsop	Berry
Sep 1	Stockport County	H	2-2	McMillan, Connachan	1	2	3	4	5	6	7	8	9	10	11													
8	Small Heath	A	0-0		1	4	3		5	6	7	8	9	10		2	11											
15	Grimsby Town	H	4-0	McMillan 4 (1pen)	1	4	3			6	7	8	9	10	11	2	5											
22	Lincoln City	A	0-1		1	4	3			6	7	8	9	10	11	2	5											
29	Newton Heath	H	1-0	McMillan (pen)	1	4	3	6				10	8	7		2		5	9	11								
Oct 1	Burton Swifts	A	1-0	McMillan		4	3	6				10	8	7		2	11	5	9		1							
6	Glossop	A	1-3	Connachan	1	4	3	6				7	9	8	10	2	11	5										
13	Middlesbrough	H	1-0	Connachan	1		3	4	6		7	9	8	10	11	2		5										
20	Burnley	A	0-0		1		3	4	5			8	7	10	11	2	6	9										
27	Burslem Port Vale	H	0-0		1		3	4	5			8	7	10	11	2	6	9										
Nov 3	Woolwich Arsenal	A	1-2	Jones			3	9	4	6	7	8	10			2		5			1							
10	New Brighton Tower	A	0-0				3	6	4			7	8	9	11	2		5	10		1							
17	Burnley	H	1-1	Connachan			3	6	4			7	8	9	11	2		5	10		1							
24	Walsall	A	0-2				3	6	4			7	8	9	11	2		5	10		1							
Dec 1	Burton Swifts	H	5-2	Brash 4, Robertson			3				6	7	8	10	11	2		5			1	4	9					
15	Woolwich Arsenal	H	1-0	Kyle			3	4	6			8		10		2		5			1		9	7	11			
22	Blackpool	A	0-1				3	4	6			8		10		2		5			1		9	7	11			
25	Barnsley	H	2-0	Brash, Connachan			3	4	6	7			8	10		2		5			1		9		11			
29	Stockport County	A	1-3	Swift (pen)			3			6	7		8	10		2		5			1	4	9		11			
Jan 1	Barnsley	A	0-1			6	3	4			7	8		10		2		5	9		1				11			
5	Small Heath	H	1-1	Brown		6	3	4						10	11	2		5	9		1			7	8			
12	Grimsby Town	A	1-4	Brown		6	3	4						10	11	2			9		1	5		7	8			
19	Lincoln City	H	0-2				3	4	6			8		10	11	2		5	9		1			7				
Feb 16	Middlesbrough	A	1-2	Hammond			3	4				10				2		5			1	6		7	8	9	11	
21	Glossop	H	1-2	Kyle			3	4				10				2		5			1	6		7	8	9	11	
Mar 2	Burslem Port Vale	A	0-0				3	4	6			10				2		5			1			7	8	9	11	
9	Chesterfield	A	1-3	Allsop			3	4				10				2		5			1	6		7	8	9	11	
16	New Brighton Tower	H	1-1	Brown			3					10	7			2		5	9		1	6			8		11	4
20	Newton Heath	A	3-2	Swift, Connachan, Brown		2	3					10	7					5	9		1	6			8		11	4
23	Gainsborough Trinity	A	0-0			2	3					10	8					5	9		1	6		7			11	4
30	Walsall	H	5-0	Brown 3, Langham, Swift		2	3					10	8					5	9		1	6		7			11	4
Apr 5	Chesterfield	A	0-1			2	3		6			10	8						9		1	5		7			11	4
8	Gainsborough Trinity	H	1-0	Kyle		2	3		6			10	8						9		1	5		7			11	4
9	Blackpool	H	3-1	Brown 2, Langham		2	3		6			10	8						9		1	5		7			11	4

F.A. CUP

DATE	OPPONENTS	V	F.T.	SCORERS	Beardsley	Mills	Swift	Wragg	Foster	Jones	Brash	Kyle	Connachan	McMillan	Dunkley	Cochrane	Woolridge	Hamilton	Brown	Beadsworth	Daw	Robinson	Robertson	Langham	Henderson	Hammond	Allsop	Berry
Feb 9	Nottingham Forest (1)	A	1-5	Kyle			3		4	6		10			11	2		5	8		1			7		9		

GODFREY BEARDSLEY
A member of a famous sporting family of the period, he was undoubtedly one of the finest goalkeepers in the country during his spell with Fosse between 1898 and 1901.
(No team photograph for 1900-01 available).

	APP's		GOALS	
	FL	FAC	FL	FAC
Godfrey Beardsley	9			
Andy Mills	16			
George Swift	34	1	3 (1p)	
William Wragg	11			
James Foster	20	1		
Dick Jones	15	1	1	
Archie Brash	14		5	
Peter Kyle	31	1	3	1
James Connachan	29		6	
Johnny McMillan	16		7 (2p)	
Albert Dunkley	10	1		
Mick Cochrane	27	1		
John Woolridge	3			
John Hamilton	28	1		
Tommy Brown	15	1	9	
Arthur Beadsworth	4			
Teddy Daw	25	1		
Walter Robinson	13			
Hugh Robertson	5		1	
Billy Langham	14	1	2	
John Henderson	13			
Harry Hammond	4	1	1	
Tommy Allsop	11		1	
A. Berry	7			

1901-02 LEAGUE DIVISION TWO
Final Position : 14th

DATE	OPPONENTS	V	F.T.	SCORERS	Daw	Mills	Swift	Robinson	Dainty	Roulston	Webb	Richards	Brown	Marshall	King	Wilson	Gill	Allsopp	Berry	Burgess	Hackett	Stevenson	Benskin	Eaton	Collins	Atherley	Rosevear	Betts	Fletcher	Peers	Spriggs
Sep 7	Woolwich Arsenal	A	0-2		1	2	3	4	5	6	7	8	9	10	11																
14	Barnsley	H	2-0	Brown,King		2	3	4	5	6	7	8	9	10	11	1															
21	Burton United	H	4-0	Webb 2,Brown 2	1	2	3	4	5	6	7	8	9	10	11																
28	Preston North End	A	0-5		1	2	3	4	5	6	7	8	9	10	11																
Oct 5	Burnley	H	2-1	Richards,Brown		2	3	4	5	6	7	8	9	10	11	1															
12	Burslem Port Vale	A	0-3			2	3	4	5	6	7	8	9	10	11	1															
19	Chesterfield	H	3-0	Brown 3	1	2	3	4	5	6	7	8	9	10	11																
26	Gainsborough Trinity	A	3-3	Richards,Brown,Allsopp	1	2		4	5	6	7	8	9		10		3	11													
Nov 2	Middlesbrough	H	0-2		1	2	3	4	5	6	7	8	9		10			11													
9	Bristol City	A	1-2	Brown	1	2	3	4	5	6	7	8	9		10			11													
23	Stockport County	H	1-1	Burgess	1	2	3		5	6	7		9		10			11	4	8											
30	Newton Heath	H	3-2	Richards,Webb,Marshall	1	2	3	4	5	6	7	8	9	10	11																
Dec 7	Glossop	A	1-1	Marshall	1	2	3	4	5	6	7	8	9	10	11																
21	Lincoln City	A	0-2		1	2	3	4	5	6	7	8			10	9		11													
26	Doncaster Rovers	H	1-0	King	1	2	3		5	6	7	8			10	9		11	4												
28	West Bromwich Albion	H	0-3		1	2	3		5	6	7	8			10	9		11	4												
Jan 4	Woolwich Arsenal	H	2-1	King,Marshall	1	2	3	4	5	6	7	8			10	9		11													
6	West Bromwich Albion	A	0-1		1	2	3	4	5	6	7	8				9		11				10									
11	Barnsley	A	3-2	Marshall 2,King	1	2	3		5	6		8			10	9		11	4	7											
18	Burton United	A	0-2		1	2	3	4	5	6		8				9		11		7		10									
25	Burslem Port Vale	H	0-1		1	2	3	4		6	7	8				9		11				10	5								
Feb 1	Burnley	A	0-1		1	2	3	4	5	6	7	8				9		11				10									
15	Chesterfield	A	3-3	King,Richards 2	1		3	2	5	6	7	8				9		11	4			10									
22	Gainsborough Trinity	H	2-0	King,Stevenson	1	2	3	4	5	6	7	8				9		11				10									
Mar 1	Middlesbrough	A	0-5		1	3		2	5	6	7	8				9		11	4			10									
8	Bristol City	H	0-1		1	2			5	6	3	7	8			9		10	4			11									
15	Blackpool	H	1-0	Swift	1	2	3			6	5	10	7			9		11	4					8							
22	Stockport County	A	0-2		1	2	3			6	5					9		11	4		10			8							
28	Blackpool	A	0-4		1	2			3	6	7				10			11	4					8	5		9				
29	Newton Heath	A	0-2		1	2			3	6	7				10			11	4					8	5		9				
31	Preston North End	H	1-0	Eaton	1	2			3	4	7				10			11						8	5	6	9				
Apr 1	Glossop	H	1-1	Eaton	1	2			3	4	7				10			11						8	5	6	9				
12	Doncaster Rovers	A	1-2	Fletcher	1	2	3	4		6	7					9		11						8	5				10		
19	Lincoln City	H	3-1	Spriggs 2,Eaton		2	3	4		6	7				11	1								8					10	5	9

F.A. CUP

DATE	OPPONENTS	V	F.T.	SCORERS	Daw	Mills	Swift	Robinson	Dainty	Roulston	Webb	Richards	Brown	Marshall	King
Dec 14	Glossop	(Int) H	0-1		1	2	3	4	5	6	7	8	9	10	11

Notes: 1). Jan 4 - Most reports credit Marshall with second goal,some credit Swift.
2). Apr 19 - Most reports credit Spriggs with third goal,some credit Fletcher.

LEICESTER FOSSE 1901-02
Back: Brown (Trainer), Roulston,Dainty,Webb,Richards,W.Smith (Director).
Middle: Marshall,Mills,Swift,Daw,Gill,G.Johnson (Secretary).
Front: Robinson,Brown,King.

	APP's		GOALS	
	FL	FAC	FL	FAC
Teddy Daw	30	1		
Andy Mills	33	1		
George Swift	27	1	1	
Walter Robinson	33	1		
Herbert Dainty	23	1		
Arthur Roulston	34	1		
Charles Webb	32	1	3	
Charles Richards	25	1	5	
Tommy Brown	13	1	9	
Arthur Marshall	15	1	5	
Rab King	34	1	6	
W.Wilson	4			
Ernest Gill	1			
Tommy Allsopp	23		1	
A.Berry	11			
T.Burgess	3		1	
A.Hackett	2			
James Stevenson	7		1	
Ewart Benskin	1			
Sam Eaton	8		3	
Arthur Collins	5			
R.Atherley	1			
C.Rosevear	3			
Herbert Betts	2			
Tommy Fletcher	2		1	
Sam Peers	1			
F.Spriggs	1			2

1902-03 LEAGUE DIVISION TWO
Final Position : 15th

DATE	OPPONENTS	V	F.T.	SCORERS	Ling	Whitehead	Mills	Robinson	Peers	Roulston	Hadley	Belton	Lewis	Binney	Staples	Coles	Berry	Eaton	Hales	Pollock	Collins	Simpson	Brown	Wilson	Atterbury	Sharp	Benskin FS	Manship	Fletcher	Wild	Benskin WE	Stewart	Spriggs
Sep 6	Small Heath	H	1-3	Lewis	1	2	3	4	5	6	7	8	9	10	11																		
13	Chesterfield	A	0-5		1		3	4	5	6	7	8	9	10	11	2																	
20	Manchester City	A	1-3	Belton	1	2	3		5	6	7	10	9		11		4	8															
27	Burnley	H	2-1	Mills,Belton	1	2	3		5	6	7	10	9				4	8	11														
Oct 4	Preston North End	A	0-2		1	2	3		5	6	7	10	9		11			8		4													
11	Burslem Port Vale	H	2-0	Lewis,Mills (pen)	1	2	3			6	7	10	9		11					4	5												
18	Barnsley	A	2-1	Belton 2	1	2	3			6	7	10	9	8						4	5	11											
Nov 8	Bristol City	H	2-2	Belton,Mills (pen)	1	2	3			6	7	10		8						4	5	11	9										
22	Manchester United	H	1-1	Brown (pen)	1	2	3			6	7	10		8						4	5	11	9										
29	Stockport County	A	2-2	Simpson,Roulston		2	3	5		6	7	8			*		10			4		11	9	1									
Dec 6	Blackpool	H	2-1	Brown 2	1	2	3			6	7	10		8						4	5	11	9										
20	Doncaster Rovers	H	0-1		1	2	3			6	7	10		8						4	5	11	9										
25	Gainsborough Trinity	H	4-1	Brown 2,Belton,Simpson	1	2				6	7	10		8						4	5	11	9		3								
26	Burton United	A	3-2	Brown 2,Simpson	1	2				6	7	10		8						4	5	11	9		3								
27	Lincoln City	A	2-1	Simpson,Eaton	1	2				6		10		8			4	7			5	11	9		3								
Jan 3	Small Heath	A	3-4	Lewis,Simpson,Brown	1	4	2			6		10		8						7	5	11	9		3								
10	Chesterfield	H	0-2		1	2				6		10		8						4	5	11	9		3	7							
17	Manchester City	H	1-1	Pollock (pen)	1	2				6		10		8			7			4	5	11	9		3								
24	Burnley	A	3-1	Brown 2, F.S.Benskin	1	7	2	5	6									8		4		11	9		3		10						
31	Preston North End	H	1-1	Robinson	1	2				6	7	8					10			4	5	11	9		3								
Feb 7	Burslem Port Vale	A	0-2		1	2				6	7	8					10			4	5	11	9		3								
14	Barnsley	H	1-2	Brown	1	2	5			6	7	10		8						4		11	9		3								
21	Gainsborough Trinity	A	1-5	Brown	1	2				6	7	10		8						4	5	11	9		3								
28	Burton United	H	0-1		1	2				6	7			8						4	5	11	9		3			10					
Mar 7	Bristol City	A	1-6	Brown	1	2	5			6	7	10		8						4		11	9		3								
14	Glossop	H	3-2	Brown,Hadley,Belton	1	2				6	7	8			10	4					5	11	9		3								
21	Manchester United	A	1-5	Fletcher	1	3	2			6	7	8	9							4	5	11							10				
26	Stockport County	H	0-2		1	2				6	7	8	9							4	5	11			3				10				
Apr 4	Blackpool	A	0-2		1	2	5	9	6	7	8	10								4		11			3								
10	Glossop	A	2-1	Stewart,Belton	1	2				6	7	9		8						4		11			3						5	10	
11	Woolwich Arsenal	H	0-2		1	2				6	7	8								4	5	11	9		3					10			
13	Woolwich Arsenal	A	0-0		1	2				6	7	10		8						4	5	11	9		3						5		
14	Lincoln City	H	0-0		1	2				6	7	10		8						4	5	11	9		3								
18	Doncaster Rovers	A	0-0		1	2		11		6	7	10		8						4	5		9		3								

F.A. CUP

DATE	OPPONENTS		V	F.T.	SCORERS	Ling	Whitehead	Mills	Robinson	Peers	Roulston	Hadley	Belton	Lewis	Binney	Staples	Coles	Berry	Eaton	Hales	Pollock	Collins	Simpson	Brown	Wilson	Atterbury	Sharp	Benskin FS	Manship	Fletcher	Wild	Benskin WE	Stewart	Spriggs
Nov 1	Irthlingborough	(Q 3)	A	1-0	Belton	1		2	3	11	6		7	10					8		4	5						9						
15	Wellingborough	(Q 4)	A	1-4	Hadley	1		2	3	9	6		7	10	8						4	5	11											

Note: Nov 22 - Most reports credit penalty to Brown, one report credits Pollock.

LEICESTER FOSSE 1902-03
Back: Collins,Spriggs,Stark,Smith,Wilson,Staples,Atterbury,E.Benskin,A.Stewart(*Trainer*).
Middle: G.Johnson (*Secretary*), Whitehead,Belton,Mills,Lewis,Ling,Berry.
Front: Betts,Hadley,Eaton,Robinson,Peers,Roulston,Hales,F.S.Benskin.

	APP's		GOALS	
	FL	FAC	FL	FAC
Archie Ling	33	2		
Harry Whitehead	3			
Andy Mills	15	2	3 (2p)	
Walter Robinson	34	2	1	
Sam Peers	10	2		
Arthur Roulston	34	2	1	
Arthur Hadley	29	2	1	1
Tom Belton	29	2	8	1
W.Lewis	30	1	3	
John Binney	2			
John Staples	5			
Donald Coles	1			
A.Berry	4			
Sam Eaton	13	1	1	
A.Hales	1			
Bob Pollock	28	2	1 (1p)	
Arthur Collins	22	2		
Tom Simpson	27	1	5	
Tommy Brown	23		14 (1p)	
W.Wilson	1			
Sep Atterbury	21			
W.Sharp	1			
F.S.Benskin	1		1	
E.Manship	1			
Tommy Fletcher	2		1	
Arthur Wild	1			
Ewart Benskin	2			
Alick Stewart	1		1	
F.Spriggs		1		

1903-04 LEAGUE DIVISION TWO
Final Position : 18th

DATE	OPPONENTS	V	F.T.	SCORERS	Ling	Mountain	Robinson	Pollock	Bell	Collins	Hadley	Blessington	Evenson	Barlow	Peers	Berry	Harper	Belton	Lewis	Dilks	Gwynne	Warren	Benskin	Fletcher	Cheater	Coulson	Mounteney	Smith	West	Vickerstaffe	Simpson	Hougham
Sep 5	Barnsley	A	1-1	Peers	1	2	3	4	5	6	7	8	9	10	11																	
12	Lincoln City	H	2-2	Blessington,Pollock (pen)	1	2	3	4	5	6	7	8	9	10	11																	
19	Stockport County	A	0-2		1	2	3	4	5		7	8	9	10	11	6																
26	Chesterfield	H	0-0		1	2	3	4	5	6	7	8	9	10			11															
Oct 3	Bolton Wanderers	A	1-3	Barlow	1	2		4	5	6	7	8		10			11	9	3													
10	Burnley	H	0-0		1	2		4	5	6	7	8		10			11	9	3													
17	Preston North End	A	3-4	Pollock (pen),Blessington,Belton	1	2	9	4	5	6				10			11	7	3													
24	Grimsby Town	H	1-1	Hadley	1	2	6	4	5		7	8		10				9	3	11												
26	Woolwich Arsenal	A	0-8		1	2		4	5	6	7	8		10					3	11	9											
Nov 7	Blackpool	A	2-1	Barlow,Robinson	1	2	5	4		6	7	8	9		11			10	3													
21	Burton United	A	0-0		1	2	5	4		6	7	8	9		11			10	3													
Dec 12	Glossop	H	4-2	Belton 2,Blessington 2	1	2	5	4		6	7	8			11			10	3			9										
19	Bradford City	A	0-4		1	2	5	4		6	7	8			11			10	3			9										
25	Burslem Port Vale	H	1-1	Pollock	1	2	6	4	5		7	8			11			10	3			9										
26	Woolwich Arsenal	H	0-0		1	2	3	4	5		7	8			11			10				9	6									
Jan 2	Barnsley	H	2-0	Warren,Hadley	1	2	3	4	5		7	8						10				9	6	11								
9	Lincoln City	A	1-6	Blessington	1		3	4	5	2	7	8			11	6		10				9										
16	Stockport County	H	3-0	Collins,Warren,Belton	1		3	4	5		7	8			11			10				9	6	2								
23	Chesterfield	A	0-2		1		3	4	5			8	10					11				9	6	2	7							
30	Bolton Wanderers	H	2-2	Blessington,Pollock (pen)	1		3	4	5		7	8						11				9	6	2		10						
Feb 6	Burnley	A	1-2	Warren	1	2	3	4	5		7	8						10	11			9	6									
13	Preston North End	H	1-4	Blessington	1	2	3	4	5		7	8	10						11			9	6									
20	Grimsby Town	A	3-4	Warren 2,Evenson	1		3	4	5	6	7	8	10						11			9		2								
25	Bristol City	H	1-0	Evenson			3	4	5	6	7	8	10						11			9						1	2			
27	Burslem Port Vale	A	2-6	Evenson,Mullineux (og)			3	4	5		7	8	10				6		11			9						1	2			
Mar 5	Blackpool	H	5-1	Evenson 2,Collins,Hadley,Birket (og)		2	3	4	5	6	7	8	10		11							9						1				
12	Gainsborough Trinity	A	0-4		1	2	3	4	5	6	7	8	10		11							9										
19	Burton United	H	1-3	Evenson		2	3	4	5			8	10		11					7		9	6					1				
26	Bristol City	A	0-4				3	4	5	6		8	10		11							9						1	2	7		
Apr 2	Manchester United	H	0-1			2	3	4	5	6	7	8	10				11					9						1				
4	Gainsborough Trinity	H	2-2	Evenson 2		2		4	5	6	7	8	10				9											1		3	11	
9	Glossop	A	0-5			2	3	4	5	6	7	8	10				11					9						1				
16	Bradford City	H	1-2	Mounteney		2		4	5	6	7	8	10											3			9	1				11
30	Manchester United	A	2-5	Warren 2		2		4	5	6	7	8	10							3		9						1				11

F.A. CUP

DATE	OPPONENTS		V	F.T.	SCORERS	Ling	Mountain	Robinson	Pollock	Bell	Collins	Hadley	Blessington	Evenson	Barlow	Peers	Berry	Harper	Belton	Lewis	Dilks	Gwynne	Warren	Benskin	Fletcher	Cheater	Coulson	Mounteney	Smith	West	Vickerstaffe	Simpson	Hougham
Oct 31	Market Harborough	(Q 3)	A	10-0	Hadley 2,Evenson 3,Barlow,Belton 3,Blessington	1	2		4	5	6	7	8	9	10				11	3													
Nov 14	Wellingborough	(Q 4)	A	2-1	Pollock (pen),Belton	1	2	5	4		6	7	8	9	10				11	3													
28	Burton United	(Q 5)	A	1-1	Evenson	1	2	5	4		6	7	8	9	10			11		3													
Dec 3	Burton United	(Q 5 rep)	H	2-2	Pollock 2 (1pen)	1	2	5	4		6	7	8	9						3	11												
7	Burton United	(Q 5 rep 2)		0-2		1	2	5	4		6	7	8	9	10					3												11	

Notes: 1). Oct 31 - drawn away,played at Filbert Street.
2). Dec 7 - played at Derby.

LEICESTER FOSSE 1903-04

	APP's		GOALS	
	FL	FAC	FL	FAC
Archie Ling	24	5		
George Mountain	26	4		
Walter Robinson	28	5		
Bob Pollock	33	5	4(3p)	3 (2p)
John Bell	21	1		
Arthur Collins	32	5	2	
Arthur Hadley	30	5	3	2
Jimmy Blessington	34	5	7	1
Ike Evenson	19	5	8	1
John Barlow	22	5	2	1
Sam Peers	3		1	
A.Berry	2			
Billy Harper	4			
Tom Belton	20	3	4	4
George Lewis	10	5		
Tom Dilks	8	1		
Ernest Gwynne	1			
George Warren	21		7	
Ewart Benskin	8			
Tommy Fletcher	1			
J.Cheater	6			
Ernest Coulson	1			
Arthur Mounteney	2		1	
Walter Smith	10			
Alf West	3			
Ernest Vickerstaffe	1			
Frank Simpson	2	1		
H.Hougham	2			
Own Goals				2

1904-05 LEAGUE DIVISION TWO
Final Position : 14th

DATE	OPPONENTS	V	F.T.	SCORERS	Smith	Bennett	Oakes	Morgan	Bannister	Pollock	Durrant	Watkins	Brunton	Evenson	Allsopp	Robinson	Blessington	Mounteney	Sheffield	Perkins	Collins	Hubbard	Moran	Ling	Harper	Hyett	Lee	Hadley
Sep 3	Blackpool	A	0-0		1	2	3	4	5	6	7	8	9	10	11													
10	Doncaster Rovers	H	3-2	Evenson 2,Morgan (pen)	1	2	3	4	5	6	7	8	9	10	11													
17	Gainsborough Trinity	A	0-2		1	2		4	5	6	7	8	9	10	11		3											
24	Burton United	H	2-0	Mounteney,Bennett (pen)	1	2		6	5	4	7			10	11		3	8										9
Oct 1	Liverpool	A	0-4		1	2		4	5	6				10	11		3	8		7								9
8	Burslem Port Vale	H	3-0	Morgan,Evenson,Mounteney	1	2		4	5	6	7			10	11		3	8										9
15	Bristol City	A	0-3		1	2		4	5	6	7			10	11		3	8										9
22	Manchester United	H	0-3		1	2		4	5	6	7			10	11		3	8		7								9
Nov 5	Chesterfield	H	1-1	Mounteney	1	2		4	5	6	7	8	9		11		3	10										
19	Lincoln City	H	0-1			2		9	5	4	7						3	10		1	6			8	11			
Dec 3	Barnsley	A	1-2	Allsopp		2		9	5	4	7			10	11		3	8			6			1				
15	West Bromwich Albion	H	3-1	Collins,Mounteney,Morgan	1	2		9	5	4				10	11		3	8			6							
17	Burnley	A	0-2		1		2	4	5	6	7		9	10	11		3	8										
24	Grimsby Town	H	5-1	Allsopp,Mounteney 2,Morgan 2	1		2	9	5	4	7				11		3	8	10		6							
26	Glossop	H	0-2		1		2	9	5	4	7				11		3	8	10		6							
27	Bolton Wanderers	H	2-4	Durrant,Morgan	1	2		9	5	4	7			10	11		3	8			6							
31	Blackpool	H	3-1	Blessington 2,Mounteney	1	2		9	5		7				11	4	3	8			6							
Jan 7	Doncaster Rovers	A	0-3		1	2	3	9	5		7			10	11	4		8			6							
21	Burton United	A	3-0	Evenson 3	1	2		4		6	7			9		10		8			5	3						
28	Liverpool	H	0-3		1	2	3	4		6	7			10	11			8			5	9						
Feb 11	Bristol City	H	2-1	Durrant,Mounteney (pen)	1	2		9	5	4	7			10	11		3	8			6							
18	Manchester United	A	1-4	Durrant	1	2		9	5	4	7			10	11		3	8			6							
23	Gainsborough Trinity	H	1-1	Durrant	1	2		9	5	4	7			10	11		3	8			6							
Mar 4	Chesterfield	A	0-0		1	2		4	5		7			9	11	10	3	8			6							
11	Bradford City	H	1-2	Allsopp	1	2		4	5		7			9	11	10	3	8			6							
18	Lincoln City	A	1-5	Allsopp		2		4	5		7				11		3	8			6	9		1	10			
25	Bolton Wanderers	A	1-0	Collins	1	2		4	5		7				11	10	3	8			6	9						
Apr 1	Barnsley	H	2-0	Hubbard,Collins	1	2		4	5						11	10	3	8			6	9						7
3	Burslem Port Vale	A	3-1	Hubbard 2,Mounteney	1	2		4	5	6					11	10	3	8				9						7
8	West Bromwich Albion	A	0-2		1	2		4	5						11	10	3	8			6	9						7
15	Burnley	H	2-2	Mounteney,Hubbard	1		2	4	5						11	10	3	8			6	9						7
21	Glossop	A	0-0		1		2	4	5		7					10	3	8			6	9					11	
22	Grimsby Town	A	0-2		1		2	4	5		7				11	10	3	8			6	9						
24	Bradford City	A	0-0		1		2	4	5		7				11	10	3	8			6	9						

F.A. CUP

DATE	OPPONENTS		V	F.T.	SCORERS	Smith	Bennett	Oakes	Morgan	Bannister	Pollock	Durrant	Watkins	Brunton	Evenson	Allsopp	Robinson	Blessington	Mounteney	Sheffield	Perkins	Collins	Hubbard
Oct 29	Linby Church	(Q 3)	H	10-1	Mounteney 4,Bannister 2,Watkins 2,Durrant 2	1	2		4	5		7	8	9		11		3	10			6	
Nov 12	Gresley Rovers	(Q 4)	H	5-0	Morgan,Mounteney 2,Hubbard 2	1	2		9	5	4	7			10			3	8			6	11
26	Northampton	(Q 5)	A	2-2	Pollock (pen),Blessington	1	2		9	5	4	7			10	11		3	8			6	
Dec 1	Northampton	(Q 5 rep)	H	2-0	Morgan 2	1	2		9	5	4	7			10	11		3	8			6	
10	Southall	(Q 6)	A	4-0	Evenson 2,Durrant,Snarry (og)	1	2		9	5	4	7			10	11		3	8			6	
Jan 5	West Bromwich Albion	(Int)	A	5-2	Mounteney 3,Allsopp,Blessington	1	2		4	5		7		9	10	11		3	8			6	
Feb 4	Aston Villa	(1)	A	1-5	Mounteney (pen)	1	2			5	4	7		9	10	11		3	8			6	

LEICESTER FOSSE 1904-05
Back: J.Hartopp *(Committee)*,Mounteney,Bannister,Bennett,Morgan,Evenson,Collins.
Front: Blessington,Oakes,Pollock,Allsopp,Durrant,Brunton.
Note: This group was taken at the Manor House Hotel,Quorn.

	APP's		GOALS	
	FL	FAC	FL	FAC
Walter Smith	31	7		
Jack Bennett	27	7	1 (1p)	
W Oakes	11			
William Morgan	31	6	6 (1p)	3
Billy Bannister	28	7		2
Bob Pollock	32	6		1 (1p)
Jamie Durrant	27	7	4	3
Alf Watkins	4	1		2
Matt Brunton	5	1		
Ike Evenson	23	5	6	2
Tommy Allsopp	30	6	4	1
Walter Robinson	22	6		
Jimmy Blessington	28	6	2	2
Arthur Mounteney	28	4	10 (1p)	10 (1p)
Jack Sheffield	2			
George Perkins	1			
Arthur Collins	23	7	3	
Archibald Hubbard	10	1	4	2
Joe Moran	1			
Archie Ling	2			
Ernest Harper	1			
James Hyett	1			
Albert Lee	1			
Arthur Hadley	5			
Own Goals				1

1905-06 LEAGUE DIVISION TWO
Final Position : 7th

DATE	OPPONENTS	V	F.T.	SCORERS	Smith	Ashby	Oakes	Morgan	Bannister	Trueman	Durrant	Blessington	Cox	Moody	Hodgkinson	Pollock	Gould	Hubbard	Bradshaw	Bracey	Keogh	Turner	Hughes
Sep 2	Clapton Orient	H	2-1	Moody,Morgan	1	2	3	4	5	6	7	8	9	10	11								
16	Leeds City	H	0-1		1	2	3	4	5		7	8	9	10	11	6							
23	Burton United	A	0-0		1	2	3	4	5		7	8	9	10	11	6							
30	Chelsea	H	0-1		1	2	3	4	5		7	8		10	11	6		9					
Oct 2	Burnley	A	2-0	Hubbard,Durrant	1	2	3	4	5		7	8		10	11	6		9					
7	Gainsborough Trinity	A	1-0	Blessington	1	2	3	4	5		7	8		10	11	6		9					
14	Bristol City	H	1-2	Hubbard	1		2	4	5	6	7	8		10	11	3		9					
21	Manchester United	A	2-3	Hubbard,Pollock (pen)	1	2	3	4	5		7				11	6	10	9	8				
28	Glossop	H	2-1	Hubbard,Hodgkinson	1	2	3	4	5		7				11	6	10	9	8				
Nov 4	Stockport County	A	1-1	Blessington	1	2	3	4	5			8			11	6	10	9	7				
11	Blackpool	H	2-0	Hubbard 2	1	2	3	4	5		7				11	6	10	9	8				
18	Bradford City	A	3-3	Bradshaw 2,Durrant	1	2	3	4	5		7			10	11	6		9	8				
25	West Bromwich Albion	H	0-0		1	2	3	4	5		7			10	11	6		9	8				
Dec 2	Grimsby Town	A	1-1	Moody	1	2	3	4	5		7			10	11	6		9	8				
7	Hull City	H	1-2	Bannister (pen)	1	2	3	4	5					10	11	6		9	8	7			
9	Chesterfield	H	1-1	Bannister (pen)	1	2		4	5	6				10	11	3		9	8	7			
16	Lincoln City	H	3-1	Durrant,Moody,Hodgkinson	1	2		4	5	6	7	8		9	11	3		10					
23	Chesterfield	A	3-3	Durrant,Blessington 2	1	2	3	4	5		7	8		9	11	6		10					
25	Barnsley	H	1-0	Hodgkinson	1	2	3	4	5		7	8		9	11	6		10					
26	Burslem Port Vale	H	2-1	Moody 2	1	2	3	4	5		7	8		9	11	6		10					
30	Clapton Orient	A	2-0	Gould,Bannister (pen)	1	2	3	4	5		7	8		9	11	6	10						
Jan 6	Burnley	H	2-0	Hubbard,Morgan	1	2	3	4	5		7	8		9	11	6		10					
20	Leeds City	A	1-4	Morgan	1	2		4	5	6	7	8		9	11			10		3			
27	Burton United	H	1-1	Durrant	1	2	3	4	5	6	7	8		9	11			10					
Feb 5	Chelsea	A	3-3	Hodgkinson,Blessington,Hubbard	1	2	3	4	5		7	8		9	11	6		10					
10	Gainsborough Trinity	H	4-0	Hodgkinson,Hubbard,Durrant,Moody	1	2	3	4	5		7	8		9	11	6		10					
17	Bristol City	A	2-1	Bannister,Blessington	1	2	3	4	5		7	8		9	11	6		10					
24	Grimsby Town	H	2-2	Bannister,Hubbard	1	2		4	5	6	7	8		9	11	3		10					
Mar 3	Glossop	A	0-0		1	2		4	5	6		8		9	11	3		10		7			
10	Stockport County	H	2-0	Durrant,Hubbard	1	2		4	5	6	7	8		9	11	3		10					
17	Blackpool	A	1-0	Hubbard	1	2		4	5	6	7	8		9	11	3		10					
24	Bradford City	H	2-4	Durrant,Pollock	1	2		4	5	6	7	8			11	3		9				10	
29	Manchester United	H	2-5	Trueman 2	1	2		4	5	6	7	8		9	11	3		10					
31	West Bromwich Albion	A	0-3		1	2		4	5	6	7	8		9		3		10	11				
Apr 13	Burslem Port Vale	A	0-2		1	2	3	4	5	6	7	8		9				10	11				
14	Hull City	A	0-0		1	2	3		5	6	7	8		9				10	11		4		
16	Barnsley	A	0-0		1	2	3		5	6	7	8		9			4	10	11				
21	Lincoln City	A	1-3	Blessington	1	2	3		5	6	7	8		9			4	10	11				

F.A. CUP

DATE	OPPONENTS		V	F.T.	SCORERS	Smith	Ashby	Oakes	Morgan	Bannister	Trueman	Durrant	Blessington	Cox	Moody	Hodgkinson	Pollock	Gould	Hubbard	Bradshaw
Jan 13	Liverpool	(1)	A	1-2	Moody	1	2	3	4	5		7	8		9	11	6		10	

LEICESTER FOSSE 1905-06
Back: Morgan,Gould,Blessington,Smith,Moody,Trueman,Pollock,Thompson *(Trainer).*
Front: G.Johnson *(Secretary),*Bradshaw,Hubbard,Bannister,Oakes,Ashby,Hodgkinson.
On Ground: Durrant.

	APP's		GOALS	
	FL	FAC	FL	FAC
Walter Smith	38	1		
Harry Ashby	37	1		
W Oakes	28	1		
William Morgan	35	1	3	
Billy Bannister	38	1	5 (3p)	
Albert Trueman	17		2	
Jamie Durrant	34	1	8	
Jimmy Blessington	29	1	7	
William Cox	3			
Harry Moody	33	1	6	1
Albert Hodgkinson	33	1	5	
Bob Pollock	33	1	2 (1p)	
Willie Gould	6		1	
Archibald Hubbard	28		12	
Tom Bradshaw	15	1	2	
Fred Bracey	8			
George Keogh	1			
Billy Turner	1			
Bernard Hughes	1			

1906-07 LEAGUE DIVISION TWO
Final Position : 3rd

DATE	OPPONENTS	V	F.T.	SCORERS	Lewis	Ashby	Blackett	Leech	Bannister	Pollock	Durrant	Moody	Wilcox	Hubbard A	Middleton	Turner	Oakes	Shanks	Trueman	Norman	Blessington	Wesley	Hubbard S	King	Milnes
Sep 1	Burslem Port Vale	A	2-1	Middleton,Wilcox	1	2	3	4	5	6	7	8	9	10	11										
3	Grimsby Town	H	2-0	Middleton,Wilcox	1	2	3	4	5	6	7	8	9	10	11										
8	Burnley	H	2-0	Middleton,Moody	1	2	3	4	5	6	7	8	9	10	11										
15	Leeds City	A	1-1	Middleton	1	2	3	4	5	6	7	8	9	10	11										
22	Barnsley	H	2-1	Wilcox,Moody	1	2	3	4	5	6	7	8	9	10		11									
29	Chelsea	A	0-1		1	2	3	4	5	6	7	8	9	10		11									
Oct 6	Wolverhampton Wanderers	H	2-0	Durrant,Wilcox	1	2	3	4	5	6	7	8	9	10		11									
13	Clapton Orient	A	0-1		1	2		4	5	6	7	8	9		11		3	10							
20	Gainsborough Trinity	H	3-1	Moody,Leech,Wilcox	1	2	3	4	5	6	7	8	9		11			10							
27	Stockport County	A	0-1		1	2	3	4	5	6	7	8	9		11			10							
Nov 3	Hull City	H	3-0	Durrant,Shanks 2 (2 pen)	1	2	3	4	5	6	7	9	8		11			10							
10	Glossop	A	2-2	Pollock,Durrant	1	2	3	4	5	6	7	9	8	10		11									
17	Blackpool	H	5-1	Wilcox 2,Bannister,Shanks,A Hubbard	1	2	3	4	5		7	9	8	11				10	6						
24	Bradford City	A	1-3	Shanks	1	2	3	4	5			9	8	11				10	6	7					
Dec 1	West Bromwich Albion	H	3-0	Wilcox 2,Blessington	1	2	3	4	5	6	7		9		11			10			8				
8	Chesterfield	H	2-0	Shanks (pen),Wilcox	1	2	3	4	5	6	7		9		11			10			8				
15	Nottingham Forest	A	1-2	Middleton	1	2	3	4	5	6	7		9		11			10			8				
22	Lincoln City	H	3-0	Wilcox,Shanks,Norman	1	2		4	5	3		9	8		11			10	6	7					
25	Stockport County	H	1-0	Durrant	1	2		4	5	3	7	8	9		11			10	6						
26	Burton United	H	3-0	Moody,Middleton,Blessington	1	2		4	5	3	7	9			11			10	6		8				
29	Burslem Port Vale	H	4-1	Bannister 2,Moody,Durrant	1	2		4	5	3	7	9			11			10	6		8				
Jan 5	Burnley	A	0-5		1	2	3	4	5	6	7	9			11			10			8				
19	Leeds City	H	2-2	A Hubbard,Wilcox	1	2	3		5	4	7		9	10	11			8	6						
26	Barnsley	A	2-2	Durrant,Bannister (pen)	1	2	3		5	4	7	8		10	11				6			9			
Feb 2	Chelsea	H	1-1	Bannister (pen)	1	2	3	4	5	6	7	9	8	10	11										
9	Wolverhampton Wanderers	A	0-0		1	2	3	4	5		7		9	10	11				6		8				
16	Clapton Orient	H	2-1	Wilcox,Shanks	1	2	3	4	5	6	7	8	9			11		10							
23	Gainsborough Trinity	A	2-1	A Hubbard,Durrant	1	2	3	4	5	6	7		8	9	11			10							
Mar 9	Hull City	A	1-1	Shanks	1	2	3	4	5	6	7		8	9	11			10							
16	Glossop	H	2-2	Leech,A Hubbard	1		2	4	5	3	7		8	9	11			10	6						
23	Blackpool	A	0-1		1		2	4	5	3	7		8	9	11			10	6						
29	Burton United	A	1-0	Wilcox	1	2		4	5	3	7		8			11		10	6				9		
30	Bradford City	H	1-0	Durrant	1	2		4	5	3	7		8		11			10	6				9		
Apr 1	Grimsby Town	A	1-0	Bannister (pen)	1	2		4	5	3	7	9	8			11		10	6						
6	West Bromwich Albion	A	1-0	S Hubbard	1	2		4		3	7	8				11		10	6				9	5	
13	Chesterfield	A	1-2	Bannister	1	2		4	5	3	7	8				11		10	6				9		
20	Nottingham Forest	H	1-2	Middleton	1	2		4	5	3	7	8			11			10	6				9		
27	Lincoln City	A	2-2	S Hubbard,A Hubbard	1		3	4	5			7	8		11			10	6				9		2

F.A. CUP

DATE	OPPONENTS		V	F.T.	SCORERS	Lewis	Ashby	Blackett	Leech	Bannister	Pollock	Durrant	Moody	Wilcox	Hubbard A	Middleton	Turner	Oakes	Shanks	Trueman
Jan 12	Sunderland	(1)	A	1-4	Bannister	1	2	3		5	4	7		9	10	11			8	6

LEICESTER FOSSE 1906-07
Back: H.Thompson *(Trainer)*, Blessington,Oakes,Lewis,Pollock,Trueman,Leech.
Front: G.Johnson *(Secretary)*, Durrant,Moody,Bannister,Wilcox,Middleton,Blackett.
On Ground: Hubbard,Ashby.

	APP's		GOALS	
	FL	FAC	FL	FAC
Tal Lewis	38	1		
Harry Ashby	29	1		
Joe Blackett	33	1		
Billy Leech	36		2	
Billy Bannister	37	1	7 (3p)	1
Bob Pollock	34	1	1	
Jamie Durrant	35	1	8	
Harry Moody	21		5	
Harry Wilcox	35	1	14	
Archibald Hubbard	20	1	5	
Frank Middleton	27	1	7	
Bob Turner	9			
W Oakes	1			
Tommy Shanks	27	1	8 (3p)	
Albert Trueman	18	1		
Alf Norman	2		1	
Jimmy Blessington	7		2	
George Wesley	1			
Shirley Hubbard	6		2	
Teddy King	1			
Fred Milnes	1			

1907-08 LEAGUE DIVISION TWO
Final Position : 2nd

DATE	OPPONENTS	V	F.T.	SCORERS	Starbuck	Blackett	Thorpe	Leech	Bannister	Pollock	Durrant	Donnelly	Humphreys	Shanks	Middleton	Bailey	Hubbard S	Wilcox	Trueman	Mackie	Shinton	Blessington	Bracey	Turner R F	Hedley	Turner R W
Sep 7	Leeds City	H	2-2	Pollock (pen),Middleton	1	2	3	4	5	6	7	8	9	10	11											
9	Wolverhampton Wanderers	H	1-0	Humphreys		2	3	4	5	6	7	8	9		11	1	10									
14	Wolverhampton Wanderers	A	0-0			2	3	4	5	6	7		9	10	11	1		8								
21	Gainsborough Trinity	H	3-0	Humphreys 2,Wilcox		2	3	4	5	6	7		9	10	11	1		8								
28	Stockport County	A	1-2	Humphreys		2	3	4	5		7		9	10	11	1		8		6						
Oct 5	Glossop	H	3-1	Humphreys 2,Leech		2	3	4	5	6	7		9	10	11	1		8								
12	Grimsby Town	A	1-1	Bannister		2	3	4	5	6	7	10	9		11	1		8								
19	Blackpool	A	2-2	Humphreys,Pollock (pen)		2	3	4	5	6	7	10	9		11	1		8								
26	Stoke	H	1-0	Pollock		2	3	4	5	6	7	8			11	1		9	10							
Nov 2	West Bromwich Albion	A	1-1	Wilcox		2	3	4	5	6	7		9	10	11	1		8								
9	Bradford City	H	2-1	Humphreys,Donnelly		2	3	4	5	6		7	9	10	11	1		8								
16	Hull City	A	2-3	Humphreys,Donnelly		2		4	5	3		7	9	10	11	1		8		6						
23	Derby County	H	1-3	Donnelly			3	4	5	6	7	8	9		11	1	10			2						
30	Lincoln City	A	3-0	Shinton,Humphreys 2			3	4	5	6	7	8	9		11	1				2	10					
Dec 7	Fulham	H	2-3	Durrant,Donnelly		2	3	4	5	6	7		9		11	1					10					
14	Barnsley	A	3-1	Middleton 2,Hubbard				4			7	8		5	11	1	10			6	9					
21	Chesterfield	H	3-1	Humphreys 3		2	3	4			7			5	11	1	10			6	9	8				
25	Oldham Athletic	H	4-1	Hubbard,Humphreys 2,Shinton		2	3	4		6	7		9		11	1	10			5	8					
26	Clapton Orient	H	0-2			2	3	4		6			9		11	1	10			5	8		7			
28	Burnley	A	1-4	Humphreys	1	2	3	4	5	6			9				10				8		7	11		
Jan 4	Leeds City	A	0-0			2	3	4	5	6	7		9		11	1	10				8					
18	Gainsborough Trinity	A	1-1	Pollock (pen)			3	4	5	6	7		9			1	10			2	8			11		
25	Stockport County	H	2-1	Hubbard,Pollock (pen)			3	4	5	6	7		9		11	1	10			2	8					
Feb 8	Grimsby Town	H	1-1	Donnelly		2	3	4	5	6	7	8	9		11	1	10									
15	Blackpool	H	2-1	Humphreys 2			3	4	5	6	7		9			1	10			2	8			11		
22	Derby County	A	2-1	Shinton 2	1	2		4	5	6	7		9	10						3	8			11		
29	West Bromwich Albion	H	3-0	Donnelly,Shinton 2		2		4	5	6	7			10		1		9		3	8			11		
Mar 7	Bradford City	A	5-1	Shanks 2,Donnelly,Shinton,R F Turner		2		4	5	6	7			10		1		9		3	8			11		
14	Hull City	H	3-2	Donnelly,Hubbard,R F Turner		2		4	5	6	7			10		1		9		3	8			11		
24	Glossop	A	3-2	Donnelly 3			3	4	5	6	7			10		1		9		2	8			11		
28	Lincoln City	H	1-0	Shinton				4	5	3	7			10		1		9	6	2	8			11		
Apr 4	Fulham	A	1-5	Durrant				4	5	6	7	8		10		1	3	9		2				11		
11	Barnsley	H	4-0	Shinton,Hubbard,Bannister,Shanks				4	5	6	7			10		1	3	9		2	8			11		
18	Chesterfield	A	2-2	Shinton,Donnelly		2		4		6	7			5		1	3	9		2	8			11		10
20	Clapton Orient	A	1-0	Hubbard	1			4	5	6	7			10			3	9		2	8			11		
12	Oldham Athletic	A	1-1	Shanks	1	2		4	5	6	7			10			3	9			8			11		
25	Burnley	H	3-1	R F Turner 2,Hubbard		2		4	5	6	7			10		1	3	9			8			11		
27	Stoke	A	1-0	Shanks		2		4	5	6	7			10		1	3	9			8			11		

F.A. CUP

DATE	OPPONENTS		V	F.T.	SCORERS	Starbuck	Blackett	Thorpe	Leech	Bannister	Pollock	Durrant	Donnelly	Humphreys	Shanks	Middleton	Bailey	Hubbard S	Wilcox	Trueman	Mackie	Shinton
Jan 11	Blackburn Rovers	(1)	H	2-0	Humphreys,Pollock (pen)		2	3	4	5	6	7		9		11	1	10				8
Feb 1	Portsmouth	(2)	A	0-1			2	3	4	5	6	7	8	9		11	1	10				

LEICESTER FOSSE 1907-08
Back: J.Blessington (Manager), Ashby,Roberts,Davies,Starbuck,Mackie,Cummings,
Bracey,Blackett,H.Thompson (Trainer) .
Middle: G.Johnson (Secretary), Turner,Donnelly,Trueman,Humphreys,Bannister,Pollock,Thorpe,Bailey,Middleton.
Front: Shanks,Leech,Durrant,Hubbard,Shinton.

	APP's		GOALS	
	FL	FAC	FL	FAC
Jonty Starbuck	5			
Joe Blackett	27	2		
Harry Thorpe	26	2		
Billy Leech	38	2	1	
Billy Bannister	33	2	2	
Bob Pollock	35	2	5(4p)	1(1p)
Jamie Durrant	21	2	2	
Jimmy Donnelly	25	1	12	
Percy Humphreys	26	2	19	1
Tommy Shanks	20		5	
Frank Middleton	22	2	3	
Horace Bailey	33	2		
Shirley Hubbard	25	2	7	
Harry Wilcox	9		2	
Albert Trueman	8			
Bob Mackie	18			
Fred Shinton	24	1	10	
Jimmy Blessington	1			
Fred Bracey	2			
Bob Turner	16		4	
George Hedley	3			
Billy Turner	1			

1908-09 LEAGUE DIVISION ONE
Final Position : 20th

DATE		OPPONENTS	V	F.T.	SCORERS
Sep 1		Sheffield Wednesday	H	1-1	Donnelly
	5	Newcastle United	A	0-2	
	12	Bristol City	H	1-1	Shanks
	19	Preston North End	A	1-0	Hubbard
	26	Middlesbrough	H	1-1	Shanks (pen)
Oct 3		Manchester City	A	2-5	Walker,Hubbard
	10	Liverpool	H	3-2	Walker 2,R F Turner
	17	Bury	A	2-2	Shinton,Bannister
	24	Sheffield United	H	1-1	Durrant
	31	Aston Villa	A	1-1	Hubbard
Nov 7		Nottingham Forest	H	0-3	
	14	Sunderland	A	1-3	R F Turner
	21	Chelsea	H	5-2	Hubbard 2,Owen,R F Turner,Donnelly
	28	Blackburn Rovers	A	0-3	
Dec 5		Bradford City	H	1-4	Donnelly
	12	Manchester United	A	2-4	Hubbard,Donnelly
	19	Everton	H	0-2	
	25	Woolwich Arsenal	H	1-1	Owen
	26	Woolwich Arsenal	A	1-2	Pollock (pen)
Jan 1		Sheffield Wednesday	A	1-3	Owen
	2	Newcastle United	A	0-4	
	9	Bristol City	A	1-1	Shinton
	23	Preston North End	H	0-0	
	30	Middlesbrough	A	2-6	Walker,Hubbard
Feb 13		Liverpool	A	1-4	Walker
	20	Bury	H	2-5	Shanks,Walker
	27	Sheffield United	A	1-2	Walker
Mar 11		Manchester City	H	3-1	Shinton,Walker,Donnelly
	20	Sunderland	H	4-3	Walker,Shinton 2,Donnelly
	27	Aston Villa	H	4-2	Hedley (pen),Owen 2,Shinton
Apr 3		Blackburn Rovers	H	2-4	Donnelly,Shinton
	9	Notts County	A	3-2	Owen,Donnelly,Durrant
	10	Bradford City	A	1-4	Owen
	12	Notts County	H	0-2	
	17	Manchester United	H	3-2	R W Turner,West,Shinton
	21	Nottingham Forest	A	0-12	
	24	Everton	A	2-4	Donnelly 2
	29	Chelsea	A	0-1	

F.A. CUP

Jan 16	Watford	(1)	A	1-1	Shinton
20	Watford	(1 rep)	H	3-1	Donnelly,Walker,R F Turner
Feb 6	Derby County	(2)	H	0-2	

LEICESTER FOSSE 1908-09
Back: H.Thompson(Trainer),Gorman,Walker,Blessington,Bailey,Starbuck,Thorpe,Middleton,G.Johnson(Secretary).
Middle: Shinton,Shanks,Pollock,Turner,Bannister,Goldie,Blackett.
Front: Leech,Donnelly,Hedley,Randle,Mackie,Hubbard,Durrant.

	APP's		GOALS	
	FL	FAC	FL	FAC
Horace Bailey	20			
George Hedley	32	3	1(p)	
Joe Blackett	18			
Arthur Randle	32	2		
Billy Bannister	12		1	
Billy Goldie	30	1		
Jimmy Donnelly	29	1	10	1
Dave Walker	22	2	9	1
Shirley Hubbard	21	2	7	
Tommy Shanks	10	1	3(1p)	
Bob Turner	31	3	3	1
Billy Garraty	6			
James Gorman	3			
Jamie Durrant	23	2	2	
Bob Mackie	15	3		
Fred Shinton	16	2	8	1
Jonty Starbuck	18	3		
Bob Pollock	16	2	1(p)	
Teddy King	4			
Syd Owen	13	1	7	
Billy Leech	7	1		
Jimmy Blessington	1			
John Vincett	1			
Francis Webster	7	3		
Wally Smith	5	1		
Andy Aitken	13			
William Holding	2			
James West	6		1	
Billy Turner	5		1	

1909-10 LEAGUE DIVISION TWO
Final Position : 5th

DATE	OPPONENTS	V	F.T.	SCORERS
Sep 1	Wolverhampton Wanderers	H	2-1	Shinton, Threlfall
4	Manchester City	H	1-3	Shinton
11	Bradford Park Avenue	A	3-1	Shinton, Pudan (pen), Walker
18	Lincoln City	A	1-3	Pudan (pen)
25	Clapton Orient	H	4-0	Walker 2, Threlfall, Hind (og)
Oct 2	Blackpool	A	1-0	Shinton
9	Hull City	H	3-1	Donnelly, Hubbard 2
16	Derby County	A	1-0	Shinton
23	Stockport County	H	1-0	Donnelly
30	Glossop	A	0-1	
Nov 6	Birmingham	H	3-1	Shinton 2, King
13	West Bromwich Albion	A	2-1	Hubbard, Shinton
20	Oldham Athletic	H	3-0	Shinton 3
27	Barnsley	A	1-3	Hubbard
Dec 4	Fulham	H	2-3	Walker, Shinton
11	Burnley	A	2-5	Hubbard, Shinton
18	Leeds City	H	6-2	Pudan (pen), Hubbard, Shinton 3, Walker
25	Grimsby Town	H	3-1	Randle, Owen, Walker
27	Gainsborough Trinity	H	9-1	Shinton 3, Walker 4, Owen, Floyd (og)
28	Wolverhampton Wanderers	A	1-4	Hubbard
Jan 8	Manchester City	A	0-2	
22	Bradford Park Avenue	H	3-0	Pudan (pen), Shinton 2
29	Lincoln City	H	4-1	Lang 2, Shinton, Goldie
Feb 12	Blackpool	H	3-2	Shinton 2, Pudan (pen)
26	Derby County	H	6-0	Hubbard 2, Shinton 3, Pudan (pen)
Mar 12	Glossop	H	3-1	Shinton, Donnelly, Threlfall
19	Birmingham	A	1-2	Turner
25	Gainsborough Trinity	A	1-0	Turner
26	West Bromwich Albion	H	2-1	Walker, Shinton
28	Grimsby Town	A	0-0	
Apr 2	Oldham Athletic	A	1-2	Pudan
6	Stockport County	A	2-6	Simpson, Shinton
9	Barnsley	H	1-1	West
14	Hull City	A	1-2	Shinton
16	Fulham	A	0-2	
23	Burnley	H	1-1	Donnelly
25	Clapton Orient	A	0-3	
30	Leeds City	A	1-1	Shinton

Lineup grid (shirt numbers by player)

DATE	Bailey	Henry	Pudan	Randle	Aitken	Goldie	Donnelly	Shinton	Hubbard	Walker	Threlfall	Holding	Starbuck	Turner	West	Lang	Spriggs	Owen	Leech	King	Bannister	Currie	Simpson	Daw	Darby	Hanger
Sep 1	1	2	3	4	5	6	7	8	9	10	11															
Sep 4	1	2	3	4	5	6		8	9	10	11	7														
Sep 11		2	3	4	5	6		8	9	7			1	10	11											
Sep 18		2	3	4	5	6		8	9		11		1	10	7											
Sep 25		2	3	4	5	6		8	10	9	11		1	7												
Oct 2		2	3	4	5	6		8		10	11		1	7		9										
Oct 9		2	3	4	5	6	8	9	10		11		1	7												
Oct 16		2	3	4	5	6		8	9	10			1	7				11								
Oct 23		2	3	4	5	6	8	9	10				1	7				11								
Oct 30	1	2	3	4	5	6	7	8	9	10	11															
Nov 6	1	2	3		5		7	8	9	10	11								4	6						
Nov 13	1	2	3	4	5		7	8	9	10	11									6						
Nov 20	1	2	3	4	5		7	8	9	10	11									6						
Nov 27	1	2	3	4	5	6		8	9	10	11					7										
Dec 4	1	2	3	4	5	6		8	9	10						7	11									
Dec 11	1	2	3		5	6	7	8	9	10	11								4							
Dec 18	1	2	3	4	5	6	7	8	9	10	11															
Dec 25		2	3	4	5	6		8	9	10	7		1					11								
Dec 27		2	3	4	5	6		8	9	10	7		1					11								
Dec 28		2	3	4		6	7	8	9	10	11		1						5							
Jan 8		2	3			6		8	9	10	7		1					11	4	5						
Jan 22		2	3		5	6		8	9	10	7		1					11		4						
Jan 29		2	3		5	6		8	9	10	11		1	7						4						
Feb 12		2	3	4	5	6		8	9	10	7		1					11								
Feb 26		2	3	4	5	6		8	9	10	7		1					11								
Mar 12		2		4	3	6	8	9		10	7		1					11		5						
Mar 19		2		4	5	6	8	9			7	1	10					11					3			
Mar 25		2	3	4	5	6	8	9			11	1	10			7										
Mar 26	1	2	3	4	5	6	8	9		10	11					7										
Mar 28		2	3	4	5	6	8	9		10	11					7										
Apr 2	1	2	3	4		6		9		10	7							11		5			8			
Apr 6		2		4	5	6		9		10	7							11		3	8	1				
Apr 9	1	2		4	5	6		9		10					11	7				3	8					
Apr 14		2		4		6	7	9		10					11					5	3	8			1	
Apr 16		2		4	5	6		9		10					11	7				3	8			1		
Apr 23	1	2		4		6	7	9	10				11							3	8				5	
Apr 25		2		4		6	7	9	10				11							3	8		1		5	
Apr 30		2				6		8	9	10			11			7		4		3			1		5	

F.A. CUP

			V	F.T.	SCORERS	Henry	Pudan	Aitken	Goldie	Shinton	Hubbard	Walker	Threlfall	Starbuck	Owen	King	Randle
Jan 15	Birmingham	(1)	A	4-1	Hubbard 2, Shinton 2	2	3	5	6	9	8	10	7	1	11	4	
Feb 5	Bury	(2)	H	3-2	Threlfall 2, Owen	2	3	5	6	9	8	10	7	1	11	4	
Feb 19	Leyton	(3)	A	1-0	Threlfall	2	3	5	6	9	8	10	7	1	11		4
Mar 5	Newcastle United	(4)	A	0-3		2	3	5	6	9	8	10	7	1	11		4

LEICESTER FOSSE 1909-10
Inset : Starbuck, Bailey.
Back: Leech, Gorman, West, King.
Middle: Hurley (Assistant Trainer), Pudan, Shinton, Bannister, Currie, Goldie, Thompson (Trainer).
Front: Hubbard, Donnelly, Walker, Aitken, Randle, Turner, Threlfall, Henry.

	APP's		GOALS	
	FL	FAC	FL	FAC
Horace Bailey	15			
Billy Henry	38	4		
Dick Pudan	29	4	7(6p)	
Arthur Randle	32	2	1	
Andy Aitken	31	4		
Billy Goldie	35	4	1	
Jimmy Donnelly	20		4	
Fred Shinton	38	4	32	2
Shirley Hubbard	26	4	9	2
Dave Walker	29	4	11	
Fred Threlfall	27	4	3	3
William Holding	1			
Jonty Starbuck	18	4		
Billy Turner	7		2	
James West	4		1	
John Lang	17		2	
Frank Spriggs	1			
Syd Owen	13	4	2	1
Billy Leech	2			
Teddy King	11	2	1	
Billy Bannister	1			
Sam Currie	8			
Harry Simpson	7		1	
Teddy Daw	1			
Ernest Darby	4			
Percy Hanger	3			
Own Goals				2

1910-11 LEAGUE DIVISION TWO
Final Position : 15th

DATE	OPPONENTS	V	F.T.	SCORERS	Starbuck	Henry	Currie	Randle	King E	Goldie	Threlfall	Travers	Hall	Hubbard	Owen	Walker	Aitken	Messer	Leech	Osborn	Benfield	King G	Williamson	Butler	Grieve	Shinton	Watkin	Mearns	Haig	Hanger	Starkey	Burton	Harrison
Sep 3	Bolton Wanderers	H	5-0	Threlfall,Travers 2,Hall 2	1	2	3	4	5	6	7	8	9	10	11																		
10	Wolverhampton Wanderers	A	0-1		1	2	3	4	5	6	7	8	9	10	11																		
17	Chelsea	H	1-0	Hall	1	2	3	4	5	6	7	8	9		11	10																	
24	Clapton Orient	A	1-3	Aitken	1	2	3	4	5			11	8	9		10	6	7															
Oct 1	Blackpool	H	2-0	Hubbard,Owen	1	2	3	4	5	6	7	8	9	10	11																		
8	Glossop	A	0-1		1	2	3	4	5	6	7	8	9	10	11																		
15	Lincoln City	H	2-0	Walker,Owen	1	2	3		5	6	7		9	8	11	10		4															
22	Huddersfield Town	A	2-1	Owen,Hall	1	2	3	4	5	6	7		9		11	10				8													
29	Birmingham	A	2-0	Osborn,Threlfall	1	2	3	4	5	6	7		9		11	10				8													
Nov 5	West Bromwich Albion	A	1-5	Osborn	1	2	3	4	5	6	7		9		11	10				8													
12	Hull City	H	0-2		1	2	3	4		6			11		8	10			5		9	7											
19	Fulham	A	1-3	Osborn	1	2	3	4		6	11	7	9			10	5			8													
26	Bradford Park Avenue	H	2-0	Hall,Walker	1	2	3	4		6	11	7	9	8		10	5																
Dec 3	Burnley	A	1-2	Walker	1	2	3	4		6	7		9		11	10	5			8													
10	Gainsborough Trinity	H	1-0	E King	1	2		4	6		7	10			11	9	5			8	3												
17	Leeds City	A	3-2	Walker,Travers,Creichton (og)	1	2		4	6		7	10			11	9	5			8	3												
24	Stockport County	H	5-1	Walker,Travers 2,E King,Hubbard	1	2		4	5	6	7	8		10	9	11					3												
26	Derby County	A	0-3		1	2		4	5	6	7	8		10	9	11					3												
27	Barnsley	H	1-1	Threlfall (pen)	1	2		4	5	6	11	8			9	10					3			7									
31	Bolton Wanderers	A	2-6	Osborn,Hubbard	1	2	3	4			11				9	10				8	3			7									
Jan 7	Wolverhampton Wanderers	H	2-3	Grieve 2	1	2	3	4	6		7				11	10	5			8					9								
21	Chelsea	A	0-2		1	2		4	5	6	7		9		11	10		3		8													
28	Clapton Orient	H	2-1	Shinton,Walker	1	2	3	4	5		7				8	10					6				9	11							
Feb 11	Glossop	H	1-1	Watkin			3	4	5							2					6	9	11					1					
18	Lincoln City	A	0-2			2	3		6						10						5		8	7		6	10	9	11	1			
25	Huddersfield Town	H	2-1	Benfield 2		2	3								8			5	7		10			6	9			11	1			
Mar 4	Birmingham	A	0-1			2	3	4	5						7	10				8				6	9			1	11			
11	West Bromwich Albion	H	2-3	Randle,Walker		2	3	4							8	10								6	9			1	11			
18	Hull City	A	2-2	Currie (pen),Benfield		2	3	4	5						10	7				8					9			1	11	6		
25	Fulham	H	3-2	Shinton,Haig,Marvin (og)	1	2	3	4	6						10					8					9			1	11	5	7	
29	Blackpool	A	0-2			2	3	4	6						10					8					9			11	5	7	
Apr 1	Bradford Park Avenue	A	1-3	Shinton		2	3	6							10					8					9			1	11	5	7	
8	Burnley	H	1-1	Haig		2	3	4	6						10	5				8					9			1	11	5	7	4
14	Barnsley	H	1-1	Shinton		2	3	4	6						10	5				8					9			1	11		7	
15	Gainsborough Trinity	A	0-2			2	3	4	6						10					8					9			1	11	5	7	
17	Derby County	H	1-2			2	3	4	6						10					8					9				11		7	
22	Leeds City	H	2-1	Currie (pen),Hubbard		2	3		6						10					8					9			1	5	7	4	11
29	Stockport County	A	0-1			2	3	4							10		6			8					9	7	1	11	5		

F.A. CUP

DATE	OPPONENTS		V	F.T.	SCORERS	Starbuck	Henry	Currie	Randle	King E	Goldie	Threlfall	Travers	Hall	Hubbard	Owen	Walker	Aitken	Messer	Leech	Osborn	Benfield	King G	Williamson	Butler	Grieve	Shinton
Jan 14	Southampton	(1)	H	3-1	Walker,Osborn,Threlfall	1	2	3	4		6	7		9		11	10	5			8						
Feb 4	Middlesbrough	(2)	A	0-0		1	2	3	4			7		8	11	10	5									6	9
9	Middlesbrough	(2 rep)	H	1-2	Currie (pen)	1	2	3	4					8	11	10	5				7					6	9

LEICESTER FOSSE 1910-11
Back: Benfield,Hanger,Osborn,Messer,G.King.
Middle: Henry,Threlfall,Starbuck,Walker,Cameron,Hall,Currie.
Front: Randle,E.King,Goldie,Aitken,Travers,Hubbard,Owen.

	APP's		GOALS	
	FL	FAC	FL	FAC
Jonty Starbuck	24	3		
Billy Henry	37	3		
Sam Currie	32	3	2 (2p)	1(p)
Arthur Randle	35	3	1	
Teddy King	30		2	
Billy Goldie	17	1		
Fred Threlfall	23	2	3 (1p)	1
George Travers	12		5	
Jack Hall	15		5	
Shirley Hubbard	26	3	4	
Syd Owen	17	3	3	
Dave Walker	22	3	7	1
Andy Aitken	20	3	1	
Robert Messer	2			
Billy Leech	1			
Fred Osborn	12	1	4	1
Tommy Benfield	16	1	3	
George King	1			
Bill Williamson	2			
Richard Butler	7	2		
Bob Grieve	4		2	
Fred Shinton	14	2	5	
Frank Watkin	4		1	
Fred Mearns	14			
Paul Haig	12		2	
Percy Hanger	8			
A Starkey	8			
Horace Burton	2			
George Harrison	1			
Own Goals				2

1911-12 LEAGUE DIVISION TWO
Final Position : 10th

DATE	OPPONENTS	V	F.T.	SCORERS	Mearns	Henry	Currie	Butler	Hall	King E	Clark	Hubbard	Osborn	Rollinson	Bauchop	Benfield	Thompson	King W	Randle	Humphreys	Burton	Thorpe	Hanger	Allman	Harrison	Clay	Mills	Starbuck	Sparrow	McWhirter	Lightbody	Shepherd	Sharpley	Mitchell
Sep 2	Gainsborough Trinity	A	1-0	Osborn	1	2	3	4	5	6	7	8	9	10	11																			
4	Gainsborough Trinity	H	2-0	Hubbard,Rollinson	1	2	3	4	5	6	7	8	9	10	11																			
9	Grimsby Town	H	0-2		1	2	3	4	5	6	7	8	9	10	11																			
11	Burnley	A	0-3		1	2	3	4	5	6	7		9	10	11	8																		
16	Nottingham Forest	A	1-4	Hubbard	1	2		4	5	6		8		10	11	7	3	9																
23	Chelsea	H	2-0	W King,Bauchop	1	2			5	6		8		10	11	7	3	9		4														
30	Clapton Orient	A	1-4	W King	1	2	3		5	6		8		10	11	7		9		4														
Oct 7	Bristol City	H	2-0	Benfield,Humphreys	1	2	3		5	6		8		10	11	7			4	9														
14	Birmingham	A	0-4		1	2			5	6		8		10	11	7	3	9		4														
21	Huddersfield Town	H	0-2		1	2	3		5	6		8		10	11	7		9		4														
28	Blackpool	A	1-1	W King	1	2	3		5	6				10	11	7		8	4	9														
Nov 4	Glossop	H	1-0	Rollinson	1	2	3		5	6				10	11	7		8	4	9														
11	Hull City	A	1-4	Clark	1	2	3		5	6	7			10	11	8			4	9														
18	Barnsley	H	0-0		1	2	3	4		6				10		7			9				5	8	11									
25	Bradford Park Avenue	A	1-1	Humphreys	1			4		6		8				7	3		9				5	10	11	2								
Dec 2	Fulham	H	2-5	Benfield (pen),Allman	1			4		6		8				7	3		9				5	10	11	2								
9	Derby County	A	0-5		1		3	4	5	6		8		10		7			9						11	2								
16	Stockport County	H	1-1	Mills	1		3		5	6				10		7		4	9						11	2	8							
23	Leeds City	A	1-2	Allman	1		3			6				10	11	7					4		5	9		2	8							
25	Wolverhampton Wanderers	H	1-1	Allman	1		3			6				10	11	7					4		5	9		2	8							
26	Wolverhampton Wanderers	A	0-1									7	10		11			3		4	6		5	9		2	8	1						
Jan 6	Grimsby Town	A	0-4		1					6			4	10	11	7	3						5	9		2	8							
27	Chelsea	A	1-2	Osborn	1		3			6		10	8		11	7				4			5	9		2								
Feb 10	Bristol City	A	1-0	Sparrow			3			6		10	8			7				4			5		11	2			9	1				
17	Birmingham	H	5-2	Hubbard,Osborn 2(1pen),Sparrow 2			3			6		10	8			7				4			5		11	2			9	1				
24	Huddersfield Town	A	2-1	Harrison,Sparrow			3			6		10	8			7				4			5		11	2			9	1				
29	Nottingham Forest	H	1-1	Benfield			3			6		10	8			7				4			5		11	2			9	1				
Mar 2	Blackpool	H	4-0	Osborn 3 (1pen),E King			3			6			8			7			10	4			5		11	2			9	1				
9	Glossop	A	0-6				3	6					8			7			10	4			5		11	2			9	1				
16	Hull City	H	3-0	Benfield,Sparrow,Osborn			3			6			8			7				4			5		11	2			9	1				
23	Barnsley	A	0-0				3			6			8			7				4			5		11	2			9	1				
30	Bradford Park Avenue	H	3-0	Sparrow 3 (1pen)			3			6			8			7							5		11	2			9	1	4			
Apr 6	Fulham	A	1-4	Osborn			3			6			8			7							5		11	2			9	1				
8	Burnley	H	3-2	Sparrow 2,Benfield			3			6			8			7				4			5		11	2			9	1				
9	Clapton Orient	H	2-0	Harrison,W King	1			6				8				7	3	9	4						11	2	10				5			
13	Derby County	H	0-1		1			6				8				7	9	4					5		11	2								
20	Stockport County	A	3-2	Benfield,Mills,Osborn	1		3			6			9			7							5		11	2	8				4	10		
27	Leeds City	H	2-1	Sparrow,Harrison	1								10			7							5		11	2	8		9	4			3	6

F.A. CUP

DATE	OPPONENTS		V	F.T.	SCORERS	Mearns	Henry	Currie	Butler	Hall	King E	Clark	Hubbard	Osborn	Rollinson	Bauchop	Benfield	Thompson	King W	Randle	Humphreys	Burton	Thorpe	Hanger	Allman	Harrison	Clay	Mills	Starbuck	Sparrow
Jan 13	Croydon Common	(1)	A	2-2	Mills,Humphreys						6			10		11	7	3			4			5	9		2	8	1	
22	Croydon Common	(1rep)	H	6-1	Hubbard,Osborn,Humphreys 2,Hanger,Lee (og)			3			6		10	8		11	7				4			5	9		2		1	
Feb 3	Barnsley	(2)	A	0-1		1		3			6		10	8		11	7				9	4		5			2			

TEDDY KING

One of the club's finest servants. After joining Fosse in 1906, he went on to make more than 200 appearances for the first team, plus another 100 during World War One. When his playing days were over, he became City's Coach, a position he held until 1932.
(No team photograph for 1911-12 available).

	APP's		GOALS	
	FL	FAC	FL	FAC
Fred Mearns	26	1		
Billy Henry	14			
Sam Currie	29	2		
Richard Butler	19			
Ben Hall	14			
Teddy King	27	3	1	
William Clark	6		1	
Shirley Hubbard	26	3	3	1
Fred Osborn	21	2	10 (2p)	1
Frank Rollinson	17		2	
Willie Bauchop	18	3	1	
Tommy Benfield	34	3	6 (1p)	
Bob Thompson	8	1		
Willie King	7	1	4	
Arthur Randle	21	3		
Percy Humphreys	14	2	2	3
Horace Burton	2			
John Thorpe	2			
Percy Hanger	22	3		1
Messina Allman	7	3		
George Harrison	20		3	
Tommy Clay	24	3		
Billy Mills	8	1	2	1
Jonty Starbuck	12	2		
Harry Sparrow	12		11(1p)	
Douglas McWhirter	4			
Tom Lightbody	1			
James Shepherd	1			
William Sharpley	1			
J Mitchell	1			
Own Goals				1

1912-13 LEAGUE DIVISION TWO
Final Position : 15th

DATE	OPPONENTS	V	F.T.	SCORERS	Mearns	Clay	Currie	McWhirter	Hanger	King	Benfield	Noble	Sparrow	Osborn	Harrison	Randle	Thompson	Hubbard	Furr H	Burton	Furr W	Mills	Crews	Straughton	Proctor	Pudan	Lightbody	Douglas	Reynolds	Pepper	Harrold	Barnett
Sep 7	Nottingham Forest	H	3-1	Sparrow 2, Osborn (pen)	1	2	3	4	5	6	7	8	9	10	11																	
9	Lincoln City	A	0-3		1	2	3	4	5		7	8	9	10	11	6																
14	Bristol City	A	0-1		1		3	4	5	6	7	8	9	10	11		2															
21	Birmingham	H	1-2	Hubbard	1		3	4	5	6	7		9	8	11		2	10														
28	Huddersfield Town	A	0-3				3	4	5				9	8	11		2	10	1	6	7											
Oct 5	Leeds City	H	1-1	Harrison	1		3		5	6		7	9	10	11	4	2					8										
12	Grimsby Town	A	0-2		1		3	4		6	7		9	10	11		2					8	5									
19	Bury	H	3-0	Sparrow 2, Osborn	1	2	3	4	5	6	7		9	10	11							8										
26	Fulham	A	1-1	Osborn	1	2	3	4	5	6	7		9	10	11							8										
Nov 2	Barnsley	H	1-0	Sparrow	1	2	3	4	5	6	7		9	10	11							8										
4	Stockport County	A	2-1	Osborn, Sparrow	1	2		4	5	6	7		9	10	11			3				8										
9	Bradford Park Avenue	A	2-2	King, Mills	1	2	3	4	5	6	7		9	10	11							8										
16	Wolverhampton Wanderers	H	0-1		1	2	3	4	5	6	7			10	11							8		9								
23	Blackpool	A	1-2	Benfield	1	2	3	4	5	6	7			10	11							8		9								
30	Fulham	H	1-0	Osborn	1	2	3	4	5	6				10	11							7		9	8							
Dec 7	Preston North End	H	0-3		1	2	3	4	5	6			9	10	11							7			8							
14	Burnley	A	1-5	Osborn (pen)		2		4	5	6	7			10	11				1			8		9	3							
21	Hull City	H	3-2	Hubbard, Harrison, Straughton		2		4						10	11			8	1	6				9	3	5		7				
25	Clapton Orient	A	1-1	Straughton		2		4	5					10	11			8	1	6				9	3			7				
26	Glossop	H	1-4	Harrison		2		4	5						11				1	6		10		9	8	3		7				
28	Nottingham Forest	A	2-4	Sparrow 2		2		4	5		7		8	10	11				1	6				9	3							
Jan 4	Bristol City	H	3-1	Osborn, Benfield, Sparrow	1	2		4			7		9	10	11	5				6				8	3							
18	Birmingham	A	1-5	Proctor				4	5				9		11		2		1	6		10		8	3			7				
25	Huddersfield Town	H	0-0		1	2	3	4	5	6	7			10	11									9	8							
Feb 8	Leeds City	A	1-5	Harrison (pen)		2	3	4	5	6				10	11							9		8				7	1			
15	Grimsby Town	H	1-0	McWhirter	1		3	4		6					11		2	8				10	9					7			5	
22	Bury	A	2-2	Mills, Hubbard	1		3	4		6			9		11		2	8				10						7			5	
Mar 8	Barnsley	A	0-1		1		3	4		6			9		11		2	8				10						7			5	
15	Bradford Park Avenue	H	3-0	McWhirter, Osborn, Harrison (pen)	1		3	4		6			9	10	11		2					8						7			5	
21	Glossop	A	0-3		1		3			6	7		9	10	11		2				4	8									5	
22	Wolverhampton Wanderers	A	1-1	Sparrow	1		3		5	6	7		9	10	11		2				4	8										
24	Clapton Orient	H	1-0	Mills	1		3			6	7		9	10	11		2				4	8									5	
25	Lincoln City	H	1-0	Benfield	1		3				7		9	10	11		2			6		8					4				5	
29	Blackpool	H	5-1	Osborn 4, Sparrow	1		3	4					9	10	11		2			6		8						7			5	
Apr 5	Stockport County	H	4-1	Harrison (pen), Mills, Douglas, Osborn	1		3			6			9	10	11		2				4	8						7			5	
12	Preston North End	A	0-1		1		3	4					9	10	11		2			6		8						7			5	
19	Burnley	H	2-3	Osborn, Sparrow			3	4	5	6			9	10	11		2		1			8						7				
26	Hull City	A	0-2					4		6			9	10	11		2					8		3				7			5	1

F.A. CUP

DATE	OPPONENTS		V	F.T.	SCORERS	Mearns	Clay	Currie	McWhirter	Hanger	King	Benfield	Noble	Sparrow	Osborn	Harrison	Randle	Thompson	Hubbard	Furr H	Burton	Furr W	Mills	Crews	Straughton	Proctor
Jan 16	Norwich City	(1)	H	1-4	Proctor	1	2		4	5		7		9	10	11					6				8	3

	APP's		GOALS	
	FL	FAC	FL	FAC
Fred Mearns	28	1		
Tommy Clay	19	1		
Sam Currie	29			
Douglas McWhirter	31	1	2	
Percy Hanger	21			
Teddy King	31	1	1	
Tommy Benfield	20	1	3	
Robert Noble	4			
Harry Sparrow	27	1	12	
Fred Osborn	34	1	14 (2p)	
George Harrison	38	1	6 (3p)	
Arthur Randle	3			
Bob Thompson	19			
Shirley Hubbard	7		3	
Harold Furr	8			
Horace Burton	15	1		
Willie Furr	1			
Billy Mills	28		4	
Alex Crews	1			
James Straughton	10		2	
James Proctor	7	1	1	1
Dick Pudan	8	1		
Tom Lightbody	2			
George Douglas	13		1	
W Reynolds	1			
William Pepper	1			
Jimmy Harrold	11			
Charles Barnett	1			

LEICESTER FOSSE 1912-13
(Pictured v Preston North End on 7th December)
McWhirter, Hanger, Mills, Osborn, Clay, Currie, Sparrow, King, Harrison, Proctor, Mearns.

1913-14 LEAGUE DIVISION TWO
Final Position : 18th

DATE	OPPONENTS	V	F.T.	SCORERS	Brebner	Clay	Currie	McWhirter	Harrold	Burton	Douglas	Mills	Sparrow	Benfield	Waterall	King	Stoodley	Mortimer	Ridley	Bown	Russell	Walters	Straughton	Pudan	Pilkington	Berrington	Seed	Woodward	Whitfield
3	Nottingham Forest	A	3-1	Benfield,Waterall,Sparrow	1	2	3	4	5	6	7	8	9	10	11														
6	Woolwich Arsenal	A	1-2	Benfield	1	2	3	4	5	6	7	8	9	10	11														
11	Nottingham Forest	H	5-1	Mills 2,Sparrow,Benfield 2	1	2	3	4	5		7	8	9	10	11	6													
13	Grimsby Town	H	2-0	Benfield,Waterall	1	2	3	4	5		7	8	9	10	11	6													
20	Birmingham	A	0-1		1	2	3	4	5					10	7	6	8	9	11										
27	Bristol City	H	3-0	Mortimer 3	1	2	3	4	5		7			10	11	6	8	9											
4	Leeds City	A	1-2	Mortimer	1	2	3	4	5		7			10	11	6	8	9											
11	Clapton Orient	H	1-0	King	1	2	3	4	5		7			10	11	6	8	9											
18	Glossop	A	2-0	Waterall 2	1	2	3	4	5		7			10	11	6	8	9											
25	Stockport County	H	2-5	Benfield,Mortimer	1	2	3	4	5		7	8		10	11	6		9											
1	Bradford Park Avenue	A	2-3	Mills,Waterall	1	2	3	4	5		7	8		10	11	6		9											
8	Notts County	H	0-2			2	3	4	5		7	8		10	11	6		9			1								
15	Fulham	H	3-0	Harrold,Sparrow 2		2	3	4	5	6	7	8	9	10	11						1								
22	Wolverhampton Wanderers	A	1-2	Sparrow	1	2	3	4	5	6	7	8	9		11		10												
29	Hull City	H	0-4		1	2	3	4	5	6		8	9		11		10	7											
6	Barnsley	A	0-3		1	2	3	4		6		8	9		11	7	5	10		9									
13	Bury	H	0-0		1	2	3	4		6		8			7	11	5	10		9									
20	Huddersfield Town	A	2-1	Sparrow,King	1	2	3	4		6		9	8			5	10					7	11						
25	Blackpool	H	0-1		1	2	3	4	5	6		8	9				10					7	11						
26	Lincoln City	A	0-3		1	2	3	4	5	6				10	11		8					7	9						
27	Woolwich Arsenal	H	1-2	Mortimer		2	4	3		6			9			5	8	10		1		7	11						
3	Grimsby Town	A	0-3				3	5	4		7		9			6	8	10		1			11	2					
17	Birmingham	H	0-0				3	4		6	7			10		5	8	9		1				2	11				
24	Bristol City	A	0-1				5		3	11				4	10	6	8	9		1		7		2					
7	Leeds City	H	5-1	Walters 2,Waterall,Benfield 2		2			5	6	7			10	9	4	8			1		11				3			
14	Clapton Orient	A	0-1			2			5	6	7			10	9	4	8			1		11				3			
21	Glossop	H	1-3	Stoodley			3		5	6	7			10		4	8	9		1		11		2					
28	Stockport County	A	0-3				3		5	6						7	10			1		11		2			4	8	
7	Bradford Park Avenue	H	2-3	Mortimer,King			3		5	6	7			10	11	4	8	9		1				2					
14	Notts County	A	1-4	Stoodley			3		5	6	7			10	11	4	8	9		1				2					
21	Fulham	A	2-1	Benfield,Mortimer (pen)			3		5	6	7			10	11	4	8	9		1				2					
28	Wolverhampton Wanderers	H	2-3	Stoodley,King		2	4	5	3		7			10	11	6	8	9		1									
4	Hull City	A	0-0				3		5	6	7			10	11	4	8			1		9		2					
10	Blackpool	A	0-1				3		5	6	/			10	11	4	8			1		9		2					
11	Barnsley	H	0-2				3		5	6	7			10	11	4	8			1		9		2					
13	Lincoln City	H	2-0	Benfield 2			3		5	6	7			10		4	8			1		11		2					9
18	Bury	A	1-1	Whitfield			3		5	6	7			10		4	8			1		11		2					9
25	Huddersfield Town	H	0-1				3	5	2		7			10		4	8			1		11					6	9	

F.A. CUP

DATE	OPPONENTS		V	F.T.	SCORERS	Clay	Currie	McWhirter	Harrold	Burton	Douglas	Sparrow	Waterall	King	Stoodley	Mortimer	Bown
10	Tottenham Hotspur	(1)	H	5-5	Mortimer,Currie,Stoodley 3	2	3		5	6	7	9	11	4	8	10	1
15	Tottenham Hotspur	(1 rep)	A	0-2		2	3	4	5	6	7	9	11		8	10	1

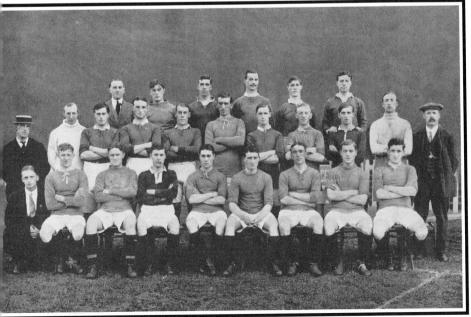

LEICESTER FOSSE 1913-14
Back: Barrett,Scoon,Woodward,Berrington,Straughton,Pudan.
Middle: Leech *(Trainer)*,Brebner,Russell,Webber,Burton,Harrold,Mortimer,Clay,Waterall,Bown, Thompson *(Assistant Trainer)*.
Front : Tillson,Ridley,Sparrow,Stoodley,Douglas,Mills,King,Benfield,Currie.

	APP's		GOALS	
	FL	FAC	FL	FAC
Ron Brebner	18			
Tommy Clay	20	2		
Sam Currie	37	2		1
Douglas McWhirter	23	1		
Jimmy Harrold	35	2	1	
Horace Burton	28	2		
George Douglas	30	2		
Billy Mills	12		3	
Harry Sparrow	9	2	6	
Tommy Benfield	36		11	
Tom Waterall	31	2	6	
Teddy King	29	1	4	
Claude Stoodley	25	2	3	3
Ernest Mortimer	22	2	8(1p)	1
Fred Ridley	1			
Herbert Bown	20	2		
William Russell	5			
Vic Walters	11		2	
James Straughton	5			
Dick Pudan	9			
Saville Pilkington	1			
W Berrington	2			
Angus Seed	3			
Maurice Woodward	2			
Norman Whitfield	4			1

1914-15 LEAGUE DIVISION TWO
Final Position : 19th

DATE	OPPONENTS	V	F.T.	SCORERS	Bown	Troughear	Currie	King	Harrold	Burton	Douglas	Sims	Simms	Hastie	Anderson	Mills	Thomson	Whitfield	Taylor	Wise	Barnett	Codd	Barron	Hogg	Legge	Barrett
Sep 2	Lincoln City	H	2-2	Simms 2	1	2	3	4	5	6	7	8	9	10	11											
5	Birmingham	H	1-0	Harrold (pen)	1	2	3	4	5	6	7			9	10	11	8									
12	Grimsby Town	A	0-1		1	2	3			5	6	7	9		10	11			4	8						
19	Huddersfield Town	H	1-2	Harrold	1		2	4	5		7	9				11	8	6	10	3						
21	Huddersfield Town	A	1-3	Whitfield	1		2	4	5	3	7		9			11		6	10		8					
26	Bristol City	A	0-1		1		2	4	5		7	9				11		6	10	3	8					
Oct 3	Bury	H	1-3	King	1		2	9	5	6	7				10	11		4	8	3						
10	Preston North End	A	0-1		1		2	4	5	3	7	9			10	11	8	6								
17	Nottingham Forest	H	3-1	Harrold,King,Anderson	1	2	3	4	5		7	9				11	8	6	10							
24	Blackpool	A	2-1	Sims,Thomson	1	2	3	7	5	4			9			11	8	6	10							
31	Barnsley	A	0-1		1	2	3		5		7	9		4		11	8	6	10							
Nov 7	Glossop	H	3-2	Sims,Whitfield 2	1	2	3	4	5		7	9				11	8	6	10							
14	Wolverhampton Wanderers	A	0-7		1	2	3	7	5	4		9				11	8	6	10							
21	Fulham	H	0-2			2	3	5		4	7	9	10			11	8	6			1					
28	Stockport County	A	0-3			2	3	5		4	7		10	11		8	6	9			1					
Dec 5	Hull City	H	1-1	King		2	3	4	5		7	9	10	11		8	6				1					
12	Leeds City	A	2-7	Mills,Douglas		2	3	9	5	4	7					11	8	6	10		1					
25	Arsenal	H	1-4	Mills	1	2	3	6		4	7		9	10	11	8	5									
26	Arsenal	A	0-6		1	2			5	4	7		3	10	9	8	6				11					
28	Derby County	H	0-6		1	2		9	5	4	10					8	6		3	7	11					
Jan 2	Birmingham	A	0-2					5	4	7			10	11	8	6		3	9	1		2				
16	Grimsby Town	H	2-0	Mills 2				9	5	4	7					10	6		3	8	1	11	2			
30	Clapton Orient	H	1-1	Mills				9	5	4	7					10	6		3	8	1	11	2			
Feb 6	Bury	A	1-3	King	1			9	5	4	7					10	6		3	8		11	2			
13	Preston North End	H	2-3	King,Burton				9	5	4	7					10	6		3	8	1	11	2			
20	Nottingham Forest	A	3-1	King,Harrold (pen),Douglas				9	5	4	7			8		10	6		3		1	11	2			
27	Blackpool	H	2-2	Mills,Hogg				9	5	4	7				11	10	6		3		1		2	8		
Mar 6	Barnsley	H	0-1					9		4	7		5			10	6		3	8	1	11	2			
13	Glossop	A	3-2	Mills 2,Wise			3		5	4	7				11	10	6			8	1		2		9	
20	Wolverhampton Wanderers	H	0-3				3		5	4	7				11	10	6			8	1		2		9	
25	Bristol City	H	1-3	Mills	1		2	6	5	4	7	9				8			3			11	10			
27	Fulham	A	0-1				3	8	5	4	7	9			11	10	6				1		2			
Apr 2	Lincoln City	A	3-2	King,Hastie,Simms			3	8	5	4	7		9	10		6				1		2			11	
3	Stockport County	H	5-4	Simms 2,King,Hogg,Harrold (pen)			2	8	5	4	7	9				6		3		1	11		10			
5	Derby County	A	0-1				3	8	5		7		9	4		6				1	11	2	10			
10	Hull City	A	1-2	Douglas	1		3	8		4	7	9	5			6					11	2	10			
17	Leeds City	H	5-1	Mills 2,Douglas,King 2			8			3	7	5	4		9	6					11	2	10			
24	Clapton Orient	A	0-2					5	3	7		8	4	11	9	6				1		2	10			

F.A. CUP

DATE	OPPONENTS	V	F.T.	SCORERS	Bown	Troughear	Currie	King	Harrold	Burton	Douglas	Sims	Simms	Hastie	Anderson	Mills	Thomson	Whitfield	Taylor	Wise	Barnett	Codd	Barron	Hogg	Legge	Barrett
Dec 19	Swansea Town	(Q 6) A	0-1		1	2	3	4		6	7		9	10	11	8	5									

LEICESTER FOSSE 1914-15
(Pictured v Wolverhampton Wanderers on 14th November. Players only are named.)
Back: Troughear,Burton,Harrold,Bown,Currie,Anderson.
Front : Mills,Sims,King,Whitfield,Thomson.

	APP's		GOALS	
	FL	FAC	FL	FAC
Herbert Bown	19	1		
Billy Troughear	15	1		
Sam Currie	26	1		
Teddy King	31	1	10	
Jimmy Harrold	32		5 (3p)	
Horace Burton	31	1	1	
George Douglas	36	1	4	
Stephen Sims	11		2	
Sam Simms	16	1	5	
George Hastie	17	1	1	
Andrew Anderson	25	1	1	
Billy Mills	29	1	11	
Bill Thomson	35	1	1	
Norman Whitfield	12		3	
A Taylor	14			
Harold Wise	11		1	
Charles Barnett	19			
T Codd	13			
Charles Barron	16			
Charles Hogg	7		2	
A Legge	2			
Alf Barrett	1			

1915-16 FOOTBALL LEAGUE MIDLAND SECTION — Final Position : 5th

DATE		OPPONENTS		FT	1	2	3	4	5	6	7	8	9	10	11
Sep	4	Bradford City	A	0-2	Barnett	Bettridge	Currie	Collins	King	Calderhead	Gibson	Hogg	E.Freeman	C.Freeman	Harrison
	11	Huddersfield Town	H	3-0	Smith	"	"	"	"	"	"	"1	"1	"	"1
	18	Grimsby Town	A	0-0	"	"	"	"	Hall	"	"	"	King	"	"
Oct	2	Derby County	A	1-1	"	"	Atterbury	"	King	"	Donaldson	Gibson 1	Hogg	"	"
	9	Sheffield Wednesday	H	3-1	"	"	"	"	"	Bailey	"	Mills	E.Freeman 2	"	"1p
	16	Bradford Park Avenue	A	2-1	"	"	"	"	"	Calderhead	Douglas	Gibson 1	Walker 1	Hogg	Cope
	23	Leeds City	H	4-0	"	"	"	"	"	Bailey	Donaldson	"1	"3	Benfield	E.Freeman
	30	Hull City	A	2-2	"	"	"	"	"	Calderhead	"	Hogg 1	"1	"	Bailey
Nov	6	Nottingham Forest	H	1-3	"	"	"	"	"	Bailey	"	Gibson 1	"	"	E.Freeman
	13	Barnsley	A	2-3	"	Collins	"	Calderhead	"2	"	"	"	"	"	Bailey
	20	Lincoln City	A	0-1	"	Pullen	"	Collins	Calderhead	Dunne	Lambert	"	"	Hogg	Bailey
	27	Sheffield United	H	2-5	"	Barron	"	Benfield	King	Bailey	Donaldson	"1	"	"1	E.Freeman
Dec	4	Bradford City	H	2-1	"	"	"	Lane	"1	"	Gibson	Benfield	E.Freeman 1	"	Edgley
	11	Huddersfield Town	A	1-2	"	"	"	Bailey	"	Leach	"	"1	"	"	"
	18	Grimsby Town	H	2-0	"	"	Currie	"	"	"	"	Walker	"1	Benfield	"1
	25	Notts County	A	2-1	"	Currie	Atterbury	Collins	Harrold	Lane	Benfield 1	King 1	Walker	Hogg	Bailey
	27	Notts County	H	2-1	"	"	"	"	King	Leach	"1	Lane	"1	"	E.Freeman
Jan	1	Derby County	H	2-0	"	"	"	"	"	"	"	Walker	Lane 1	E.Freeman 1	Edgley
	8	Sheffield Wednesday	A	1-3	"	"	"	"	"	"	Douglas	Gibson	E.Freeman 1	Benfield	"
	15	Bradford Park Avenue	H	2-1	"	"	"	"	"	"	Benfield	Hogg 1	Walker 1	E.Freeman	"
	22	Leeds City	A	0-1	"	"	"	"	"	"	Green	Fox	Bailey	Walker	"
	29	Hull City	H	4-0	"	"	"	"	"	"1	Benfield	Whitfield	Walker 3	E.Freeman	"
Feb	5	Nottingham Forest	A	0-1	Barnett	"	"	Bailey	Collins	"	Gibson	Benfield	"	"	"
	12	Barnsley	H	2-2	"	"	"	Collins	King 1	"	Benfield	Morrell	"1	"	"
	19	Lincoln City	H	1-1	Bown	"	"	"	"	"	"	Whitfield	"	"1p	"
Apr	25	Sheffield United	A	1-1	"	"	"	"	Hibbert	Gibson 1	Benfield	Parker	Walker	Sharp

FOOTBALL LEAGUE MIDLAND SECTION (Subsidiary Tournament - Southern Section) — Final Position: 3rd

DATE		OPPONENTS		FT	1	2	3	4	5	6	7	8	9	10	11
Mar	4	Notts County	H	0-0	Bown	Currie	Atterbury	Collins	King	Leach	Benfield	Bailey	Walker	E.Freeman	Edgley
	11	Derby County	A	5-2	Barnett	"	"1p	"	Bailey	"	"	Montgomery 1	"2	"	"
	18	Stoke	H	2-1	Smith	"	"	Bailey	Collins	"	"1	King 1	E.Freeman	Montgomery	"
	25	Nottingham Forest	A	0-4	"	"	"	Collins	King	"	"	Montgomery	Walker	E.Freeman	"
Apr	1	Chesterfield	A	1-3	"	"	"	"	"	"	"	Bailey 1	Parker	Walker	"
	8	Notts County	A	1-1	Bown	"	"1p	"	"	"	Gibson	Benfield	E.Freeman	"	"
	15	Derby County	H	3-2	"	"	"	"	"1	"	Benfield	E.Freeman	Parker 2	"	"
	22	Stoke	A	0-1	"	Waterfield	"	Bailey	Harrold	Webber	Goddard	Benfield	"	Currie	E.Freeman
	24	Chesterfield	H	2-2	"	Currie	"1p	Waterfield	King	Bailey	Collins	"1	"	Walker	"
	29	Nottingham Forest	H	1-3	Barnett	"	"	Collins	"1	Leach	Douglas	"	E.Freeman	"	Edgley

Note: 1) Apr 25, postponed from Feb 26.
   2) Mar 11, Haynes (og).

	GUEST CLUB	APPEARANCES		GOALS	
		FLM	FLM(2)	FLM	FLM(2)
Sep Atterbury	Plymouth Argyle	22	10		3 (3p)
T.Bailey	Gresley Rovers	13	6	1	
Charlie Barnett		3	2		
C.W.Barron		4			
Tommy Benfield		18	10	3	2
Walter Bettridge	Chelsea	9			
Herbert Bown		2	5		
David Calderhead	Chelsea	8			
Arthur Collins	Norwich City	22	9		
T.Cope		1			
Sam Currie		15	10		
Alec Donaldson	Bolton Wanderers	7			
George Douglas		2	1		
J.Dunne	Lincoln City	1			
Harold Edgley	Aston Villa	11	8	1	
Charles Freeman	Chelsea	5			
Ernest Freeman	Northampton Town	18	9	8 (1p)	
N.Fox	Leeds City	1			
R.Gibson	Birmingham	16	1	6	
Sid Goddard	Leicester Imperial		1		
W.J.Green	(ex-Burnley)	1			

	GUEST CLUB	APPEARANCES		GOALS	
		FLM	FLM(2)	FLM	FLM(2)
Ben Hall		1			
George Harrison	Everton	5		2 (1p)	
Jimmy Harrold		1	1		
H.C.Hibbert	Chesterfield	1			
C.Hogg		13		4	
Teddy King		24	8	5	3
J.W.Lambert	Belvoir S.S.	1			
H.Lane	Nottingham Forest	4		1	
Jimmy Leach	Aston Villa	11	8	1	
Billy Mills		1			
W.Montgomery	Bellis & Morcam		3		1
T.Morrell	Redditch	1			
P.Parker		1	4		2
H.Pullen	Queens Park Rangers	1			
G.Sharp	Chesterfield	1			
Walter Smith	Manchester City	21	3		
W.B.Walker	Birmingham	18	8	11	2
B.Waterfield	Leicester Imperial		2		
George Webber			1		
Norman Whitfield		2			
Own Goals					1

1916-17 FOOTBALL LEAGUE MIDLAND SECTION — Final Position :15th

DATE	OPPONENTS		FT	1	2	3	4	5	6	7	8	9	10	11
Sep 2	Leeds City	A	2-2	Bown	Currie	Atterbury	Collins	King	Leach	Hawden	Sturdy 1	Boyne	Parsonage 1	Edgley
9	Sheffield United	H	2-2	"	"	"	"	"	"	Benfield	Leigh	"	"1	"1
16	Bradford City	A	1-1	"	"	"	"	"	"	"1	"	"	"	"
23	Chesterfield	H	2-0	"	"	"	"	"1	"	Freeman	"1	"	"	"
30	Grimsby Town	H	0-0	"	"	"	Trueman	"	"	Collins	"	"	"	Freeman
Oct 7	Notts County	A	1-5	"	"	Cullen	Collins	"	"	Freeman	"1	"	"	Edgley
14	Rotherham County	H	3-1	"	"	Atterbury	Bailey	Collins	"	Broadley	Boyne	Freeman 1	"2	"
21	Huddersfield Town	A	1-4	"	"	"	"	"	"	Boyne	Joyce	"1	"	"
28	Lincoln City	H	1-1	"	"	"	"	"	"	Newman	Boyne 1	"	"	"
Nov 4	Sheffield Wednesday	A	0-3	"	"	"	"	King	"	Collins	"	Parsonage	Thurman	"
11	Bradford Park Avenue	H	0-2	"	"	"	Crutchley	"	"	S Goddard	"	Freeman	Parsonage	"
18	Birmingham	A	1-2	"	"	"	"	Collins	"	T.Day	King	Boyne	"1	"
25	Hull City	H	0-2	"	"	"	Collins	King	"	Southwell	Freeman	T.Day	"	"
Dec 2	Nottingham Forest	A	0-2	"	"	"	"	"	"	Boyne	Parsonage	C.Storer	Edgley	Timmins
9	Leeds City	H	1-4	"	"	"	"	"1	Bailey	Barratt	Bennett	"	Hubbard	Marriott
16	Sheffield United	A	0-1	"	"	"	Bailey	Benfield	Roulson	S.Smith	Boyne	"	"	"
25	Barnsley	H	1-2	"	"	"	Collins	Hall	Leach	Barratt	Parsonage	Hubbard	King 1	Webber
26	Barnsley	A	0-5	"	Stern	"	Bee	"	"	"	Botterill	"	Longlands	Currie
30	Chesterfield	A	0-2	"	Draycott	Currie	F.Smith	Collins	"	"	Sharp	C.Storer	Parsonage	Marriott
Jan 6	Grimsby Town	A	3-1	"	"	"	S.Storer	C.Storer	Atterbury	J.Goddard	Stainsby 1	Pykett	Padley 1	"
13	Notts County	H	0-1	"	"	"	F.Smith	"	Leach	S.Goddard	J.Goddard	King	Parsonage	Price
20	Rotherham County	A	0-1	"	"	"	"	"	"	Boyne	Brown	Whitworth	"	"
27	Huddersfield Town	H	2-0	"	"	"	S.Storer	"	Webber	S.Smith	King	Boyne 1	Price 1	Sharp
Feb 3	Lincoln City	A	1-3	"	Currie	Leach	Leyland	"	Dunne	Willmott	Nash	"	"	"1
10	Sheffield Wednesday	H	3-0	"	Draycott	Currie	S.Smith	"1	Leach	Benfield 2	"	"	"	"
17	Bradford Park Avenue	A	1-0	"	"	"	King	"	"	S.Smith 1	Fearnley	"	"	Clarke
24	Birmingham	H	1-1	"	"	"	"	"	"	Nash	"	"	"1	Sharp
Mar 3	Hull City	A	1-2	"1p	Day	"	"	"	"	Barrow	Willoughby	Pace	"	"
10	Nottingham Forest	H	1-1	"	Draycott	"	S.Storer	"	King	Starkey	Bird	Boyne	"1	"
Apr 10	Bradford City	H	0-2	"	Hampton	Walker	"	King	Hall	Swain	"	Cantrell	"	Brownlow

FOOTBALL LEAGUE MIDLAND SECTION (Subsidiary Tournament) — Final Position: 4th

Mar 24	Birmingham	A	1-5	Bown	Draycott	Hampton	King	C.Storer	Leach	Swain 1	Nash	Boyne	Price	Sharp
31	Nottingham Forest	A	0-1	"	"	Currie	"	"	"	Burton	Bird	"	"	Mullins
Apr 7	Notts County	H	2-1	"	"	"	S.Storer	King	Hall	Swain	"	Roberts 1	"1	Edwards
9	Notts County	A	3-2	"	Hampton	"	"	"	"	"	"1	"2	"	Brownlow
14	Birmingham	H	4-2	"	Draycott	"	Hall	"	Leach	"1	"	"1	"2	Mortimer
21	Nottingham Forest	H	2-1	"	"	"	"	"	"	"	"1	"	"1	Webber

Note: 1) Jan 6, Webster (og).
2) Apr 10, postponed from Dec 23.
3) Oct 28, 'A.Newman' is probably a pseudonym, the Football League records list 'T.Benfield'.

GUEST CLUB		APPEARANCES FLM	FLM(2)	GOALS FLM	FLM(2)
Sep Atterbury	Plymouth Argyle	18			
T.Bailey	Gresley Rovers	6			
J.Barratt	Nuneaton	4			
C.H.Barrow		1			
T.Bee		1			
Tommy Benfield		4		3	
F.Bennett	Queens Park Rangers	1			
Walter Bird		2	5		2
C.Botterill		1			
Herbert Bown		30	6	1(p)	
Reg Boyne		21	2	2	
F.Broadley		1			
A.Brown	Gresley Rovers	1			
T.Brownlow	Coalville	1	1		
J.H.Burton			1		
Jimmy Cantrell	Notts County	1			
W.Clarke		1			
Arthur Collins	Norwich City	16			
J.Crutchley		2			
P.H.Cullen	(ex- Chesterfield)	1			
Sam Currie		29	5		
T.Day		2			
- Day	Leics. Regiment	1			
George Draycott	Bradford City	9	5		
J.Dunne	Lincoln City	1			
Harold Edgley	Aston Villa	13		1	
N.Edwards			1		
E.Fearnley	Bradford City	1			
Ernest Freeman	Northampton Town	8		2	
J.W.Goddard		2			
Sid Goddard	Leicester Imperial	2			
Ben Hall		3	4		
G.Hampton		1	2		
H.Hawden		1			
Shirley Hubbard		4			
J.H.Joyce	Aston Villa	1			
Teddy King		21	6	3	

GUEST CLUB		APPEARANCES FLM	FLM(2)	GOALS FLM	FLM(2)
Jimmy Leach	Aston Villa	24	4		
Sid Leigh	Derby County	5		2	
A.Leyland		1			
J.Longlands		1			
E.Marriott	Pinxton	4			
Ernest Mortimer			1		
E.Mullins	Shirebrook		1		
H.Nash		3	1		
A.Newman		1			
Arthur Pace	Hull City	1			
George Padley	Worksop	1		1	
H.Parsonage		17		5	
Cliff Price	Coalville	10	6	3	4
B.Pykett	Notts County	1			
W.Tommy Roberts			4		4
J.Roulson	Birmingham	1			
G.Sharp	Chesterfield	7	1	1	
F.Smith	Whitwick Imperial	3			
S.Smith	Newhall	5		1	
J.Southwell		1			
Colin Stainsby		1		1	
A.E.Starkey		1			
J.Stern	Mexborough	1			
Charley Storer		14	2	1	
Sid Storer		4	2		
E.F.Sturdy	Leeds City	1		1	
A.Swain	Coalville	1	5		2
A.Thurman	Loughborough	1			
W.Timmins	Nottingham Forest	1			
Albert Trueman		1			
G.H.Walker	Notts County	1			
George Webber		2	1		
G.Whitworth	Rotherham County	1			
A.Willmott		1			
G.Willoughby		1			
Own Goals				1	

1917-18 FOOTBALL LEAGUE   MIDLAND SECTION   Final Position : 7th

DATE	OPPONENTS		FT	1	2	3	4	5	6	7	8	9	10	11
Sep 1	Notts County	A	1-2	Bown	Draycott	Currie	Hall	C.Storer	Leach	Moore	King	Roberts 1	Price	Donald
8	Notts County	H	1-0	"	"	"	King	"	"	Swain	Bird	"1	"	"
15	Huddersfield Town	A	2-1	"	"	"	"	"	"	"	"1	"	"1	"
22	Huddersfield Town	H	4-1	"	"	"	"	"	"	Benfield 1	"2	"	"1	"
29	Sheffield Wednesday	A	3-1	"	"	"	"1	"	"	Swain	"	"2	"	"
Oct 6	Sheffield Wednesday	H	1-2	"	"	"	"	"	"	Donaldson 1	"	"	"	"
13	Bradford City	H	2-0	"	"	"1p	"	"	"	"	"	"	"	"1
20	Bradford City	A	1-4	"	"	"	"	"	"	"	"1	"	"	"
27	Rotherham County	H	2-0	"	"	"	"	"	"	"	"	"1	"1	"
Nov 3	Rotherham County	A	2-4	"	"	"	"	Hall	"	Smelt	"	"1	"1	"
10	Lincoln City	H	4-0	"	"	"1	"	C.Storer	"	Donaldson	Benfield	"2	"	"
17	Lincoln City	A	1-1	"	"	"	S.Storer	"	"	King	Bird	"1	"	"
24	Grimsby Town	H	6-1	"	"	"	King 1	"	"	Donaldson 1	"1	"2	"1	"
Dec 1	Grimsby Town	A	1-1	"	"	"	Burton	Wale	"	Foreman	"1	C.Storer	"	Buckley
8	Hull City	A	1-3	"	Currie	C.Storer	King	Bird	"	Dalton	Donaldson	Roberts	"1	Donald
15	Hull City	H	3-1	"	Hall	Currie	"1	C.Storer	"	Donaldson	Bird	"	"2	"
22	Bradford Park Avenue	A	0-1	"	Draycott	Hall	"	"	"	Pollard	Fearnley	"	"	Murray
25	Birmingham	A	0-0	"	"	Currie	"	"	"	Donaldson	Millington	"	Turner	Donald
26	Birmingham	H	3-0	"	"	"	Hall	"	"	"1	King	"	Price 1	"1
29	Bradford Park Avenue	H	2-0	"	Hall	"	King	"	"	"	Osborn	"2	"	"
Jan 5	Nottingham Forest	H	2-0	"	Draycott	"	"1	"	"	"	"	"	"1	"
12	Nottingham Forest	A	0-2	"	"	Hall	Benfield	"	"	"	"	"	"	"
19	Leeds City	H	2-4	"	"	"	S.Storer	"	"	"1	King 1	Longlands	"	"
26	Leeds City	A	0-4	"	"	Gittins	Hall	"	"	Bowden	"	Chapman	"	Currie
Feb 2	Sheffield United	A	2-6	"	"	Currie	King	Brown	Hall	Barrett	Mills 1	C.Storer	"1	Donald
9	Sheffield United	H	1-2	"	"	"1p	Hall	C.Storer	Leach	Donaldson	Sarson	Goddard	"	"
16	Barnsley	A	0-1	"	Hall	"	Whiteman	"	"	Sarson	Tyler	Mortimer	"	"
23	Barnsley	H	5-1	"	Draycott	"	Hall	"1	"	Donaldson	Sarson 1	"	"3	"

FOOTBALL LEAGUE MIDLAND SECTION (Subsidiary Tournament)   Final Position: 12th

DATE	OPPONENTS		FT	1	2	3	4	5	6	7	8	9	10	11
Mar 16	Notts County	A	1-5	Bown	Draycott	Currie	King	C.Storer	Leach	Donaldson	Mortimer 1	Benfield	Price	Donald
23	Notts County	H	3-1	"	"	"1p	Hall	King	"	"	Bird	Mortimer 2	"	"
30	Nottingham Forest	H	1-0	"	"	"	"	C.Storer	"	Ellis	Sarson	"1	"	King
Apr 6	Nottingham Forest	A	0-2	"	"	"	"	"	"	Donaldson	King .	"	"	Donald
13	Birmingham	H	1-1	"	"	"	"	"	"	"	"	"1	"	"
20	Birmingham	A	0-1	"	"	"	"	"	"	E.Burton	"	"	Crowe	"

Note: Nov10, Jackson (og).

GUEST CLUB		APPEARANCES FLM	FLM(2)	GOALS FLM	FLM(2)
G.Barrett	Bradford Park Avenue	1			
Tommy Benfield		3	1	1	
Walter Bird		14	1	6	
V.H.Bowden	Balmoral	1			
Herbert Bown		28	6		
Tommy Brown	Bradford Park Avenue	1			
J.E.C.Buckley	(local army camp)	1			
E.Burton			1		
- Burton		1			
G.Chapman	Barnsley	1			
- Crowe			1		
Sam Currie		25	6	3 (2p)	1(p)
- Dalton		1			
David Donald	Derby County	25	5	2	
Alec Donaldson	Bolton Wanderers	16	4	4	
George Draycott	Bradford City	24	6		
A.Ellis			1		
E.Fearnley	Bradford City	1			
G.A.Foreman	(local army camp)	1			
Jack Gittins	Barnsley	1			
Sid Goddard	Leicester Imperial	1			
Ben Hall		13	5		

GUEST CLUB		APPEARANCES FLM	FLM(2)	GOALS FLM	FLM(2)
Teddy King		23	6	5	
Jimmy Leach	Aston Villa	27	6		
J.Longlands		1			
Charley Millington	Aston Villa	1			
Billy Mills		1		1	
A.Moore	Whitwick Imperial	1			
Ernest Mortimer		2	6		5
T.Murray		1			
G.Osborn		3			
S.Pollard		1			
Cliff Price	Coalville	27	5	14	
W.Tommy Roberts		21		13	
H.Sarson		3	1	1	
Jack Smelt	Rotherham County	1			
Charley Storer		27	5	1	
Sid Storer		2			
A.Swain	Coalville	3			
A.Turner	Notts County	1			
J.Tyler		1			
L.Wale	(local army camp)	1			
A.Whiteman	Barnsley	1			
Own Goals					1

1918-19 FOOTBALL LEAGUE MIDLAND SECTION   Final Position : 10th

DATE	OPPONENTS		FT	1	2	3	4	5	6	7	8	9	10	11
Sep 7	Rotherham County	H	4-1	Bown	Underwood	Currie	Parker	King	Leach	Donaldson	Mortimer	Roberts 2	Price 2	Donald
14	Rotherham County	A	3-0	"	"	"	Bailey	"	"	"	"	"3	"	"
21	Lincoln City	H	2-0	"	"	"1p	"	"	"	"	"	"	"1	"
28	Lincoln City	A	0-4	"	"	"	"	"	"	"	"	"	"1	"
Oct 5	Grimsby Town	H	5-3	"	"	"	"	"1	"	"	G.Davis 1	"2	"1	"
12	Grimsby Town	A	1-4	"	Currie	Lowe	"	"	"	S.Smith	Hubbard 1	Roach	Barber	Faulconer
19	Bradford City	A	0-2	"	Underwood	Currie	"	Storer	"	King	G.Davis	Hubbard	Price	Jordan
26	Bradford City	H	3-2	"	"	"	"	"	"	Donaldson	King 2	"	"	Donald
Nov 2	Sheffield Wednesday	A	2-0	"	"	"	"	"	King	"1	Hubbard 1	Vlamynck	"	"
9	Sheffield Wednesday	H	7-3	"	"	"	"	King 1	Hall	"	"1	"2	"1	"1
16	Huddersfield Town	A	0-2	"	"	"	"	"	"	"	"	"	"	"
23	Huddersfield Town	H	3-1	"	"	"	"	Storer	"	"	"	"1	"2	"
30	Notts County	A	0-1	"	"	"	G.Davis	"	"	"	Green	Mortimer	"	Dennis
Dec 7	Notts County	H	3-0	"	"	"	Storer	J.Harrold	Leach	"	King 1	Hubbard	"2	Donald
14	Barnsley	H	2-1	"	"	"1p	King	Storer	"	"	A.Davis 1	"	"	"
21	Barnsley	A	2-3	"	"	"	May	"	"	"	"1	"	King	Dennis 1
25	Birmingham	A	2-0	"	"	Pennington	King	"	"	"1	"	Roberts	Hubbard 1	"
26	Birmingham	H	0-4	"	"	"	"	"	"	"	Price	"	"	"
28	Bradford Park Avenue	H	1-2	"	"	Currie	"	"	"	Minney	A.Davis 1	Hubbard	Price	"
Jan 11	Nottingham Forest	A	1-1	"	"	"	"	"	"	Donaldson	"1	Hopkins	"	S.Harrold
18	Nottingham Forest	H	0-1	"	"	"	"	"	"	"	"	Leonard	"	"
25	Leeds City	A	2-4	"	T.Smith	"	"	"	"	"	Gibson 1	Kerrage 1	"	"
Feb 1	Leeds City	H	0-0	"	Peel	"	"	"	"	"	"	"	"	"
8	Sheffield United	H	2-1	"	Underwood	"	"	"	"	"	Price 1	Smart	Machin	Stanton 1
15	Sheffield United	A	0-1	Blackwell	G.Smith	"	Storer	J.Harrold	"	"	King	Stanton	Price	S.Harrold
22	Hull City	H	3-2	Bown	Mugglestone	G.Smith	"	"	"	"	"1	Nock 2	"	"
Mar 1	Hull City	A	2-5	"	G.Smith	Currie	King	Storer	"	Read	Brittain	"	"1	"1
8	Coventry City	H	2-2	"	"	"	Storer	J.Harrold	King 2	Donaldson	"	"	"	"
15	Coventry City	A	0-1	"	"	"	George	Storer	"	Norton	Phipps	"	Dobson	"
Apr 21	Bradford Park Avenue	A	1-2	"	Barron	"	King	J.Harrold	I.Smith	Armstrong	Richmond 1	"	Whitfield	"

FOOTBALL LEAGUE MIDLAND SECTION (Subsidiary Tournament)   Final Position: 2nd

DATE	OPPONENTS		FT	1	2	3	4	5	6	7	8	9	10	11
Mar 22	Notts County	H	5-1	Bown	G.Smith	Currie	Storer	J.Harrold	I.Smith	Norton	Richmond 2	Nock 1	Price 1	S.Harrold 1
29	Notts County	A	0-5	"	"	"	"	"	King	"	"	"	"	"
Apr 5	Nottingham Forest	A	2-0	"	"	"	King	"	I.Smith	"	Osborne 1	"1	Whitfield	"
12	Nottingham Forest	H	1-0	"	"	"	"	"	"	"	"	"1	"	"
19	Birmingham	A	0-3	"	Barron	"	"	"	"	"	Richmond	"	"	"
26	Birmingham	H	2-4	"	Watson	"1p	"	"	"	"	"1	"	"	"

Notes 1)   Nov 9, Stapleton (og)
2)   Apr 21, postponed from Jan 4.

GUEST CLUB		APPEARANCES FLM	FLM(2)	GOALS FLM	FLM(2)
A.Armstrong		1			
T.Bailey	Gresley Rovers	11			
J.Barber		1			
C.W.Barron		1	1		
E.Blackwell	Sheffield United	1			
Herbert Bown		29		6	
Harold Brittain	Chelsea	2			
Sam Currie		27	6	2 (2p)	1(p)
A.G.Davis	Birmingham	6		4	
George Davis	Asfordby	3		1	
G.T.Dennis		5		1	
H.Dobson	Coventry City	1			
David Donald	Derby County	12		1	
Alec Donaldson	Bolton Wanderers	24		2	
A.Faulconer		1			
W.George	Austin Motor Works	1			
R.Gibson	Birmingham	2	1		
- Green		1			
Ben Hall		4			
Jimmy Harrold		5	6		
Sid Harrold		10	6	1	1
L.G.Hopkins		1			
Shirley Hubbard		13		5	
G.Jordan	Overseal	1			
F.B.Kerrage	Nottingham Forest	2		1	
Teddy King		28	5	8	
Jimmy Leach	Aston Villa	22			
Harry Leonard	Derby County	1			
W.R.Lowe		1			

GUEST CLUB		APPEARANCES FLM	FLM(2)	GOALS FLM	FLM(2)
J.Machin		1			
R.May	Huddersfield Town	1			
H.Minney	Standard Engineering	1			
Ernest Mortimer		5			
E.Mugglestone	Coalville Swifts	1			
Jimmy Nock	Millwall	5	6	2	3
Joe Norton		1	6		
F.Osborne	Lincoln City		2		1
G.H.Parker		1			
A.Peel	("a northern club")	1			
Jesse Pennington	West Bromwich Albion	2			
C.H.Phipps	Belvoir S.S.	1			
Cliff Price	Coalville	25	2	11	1
William Read	(ex-Chelsea)	1			
Hugh Richmond	Kilmarnock	1	4	1	3
- Roach		1			
W.Tommy Roberts		7		7	
H.Smart		1			
G.R.Smith		5	4		
Ike Smith	Wednesbury	1	5		
S.Smith	Stanton	1			
T.Smith	Mansfield Town	1			
A.Stanton	Balmoral United	2		1	
Charley Storer		21	2		
J.Underwood		21			
Henri Vlamynck	(Belgian Army)	4		3	
J.Watson	Nottingham Works		1		
Norman Whitfield		1	4		
Own Goals					1

1919-20 LEAGUE DIVISION TWO
Final Position : 14th

DATE	OPPONENTS	V	F.T.	SCORERS	Bown	Barrett	Currie S	King E	Harrold J	Smith I	Douglas	Thornton	Richmond	Macauley	Harrold S	Thomson	Norton	Anstey	Jobey	Price	Essom	Bacon	Parker	Hubbard	Spittle	King H	Walker	Whitfield	Dorrell	Smith T	Paterson	Black	Currie W	Duffy
Aug 30	Wolverhampton Wanderers	H	1-2	Douglas	1	2	3	4	5	6	7	8	9	10	11																			
Sep 1	Tottenham Hotspur	A	0-4		1	2	3	4	5			8		10	11	6	9																	
6	Wolverhampton Wanderers	A	1-1	Richmond		2	3	4	5		7	8		10	11	6			1	9														
11	Tottenham Hotspur	H	2-4	Price 2		2	3	4	5		7				11	6			1	9	10													
13	Fulham	H	3-2	Price, Thomson, E King		2		8	5		7				11	6			1	9	10	3	4											
20	Fulham	A	0-5			2		8	5	6	7				11				4	1	10	3	9											
27	Coventry City	H	1-0	Douglas		2	3		5		7	8			11	6				1		4		9										
Oct 4	Coventry City	A	2-1	Hubbard, S Harrold		2	3		5		7	8			11	6				1		4	10	9										
11	Huddersfield Town	H	0-4			2	3		5		7	8			11	6				1		4	10	9										
18	Huddersfield Town	A	0-0		1	2	3				7				5	11	6		4					10	8	9								
25	Blackpool	H	2-3	Spittle, H King	1	2	3				7				5	11	6		4					10	8	9								
Nov 1	Blackpool	A	0-3		1	2	3	5			7					6	11		4					10	8	9								
8	West Ham United	H	0-0		1	2	3	6	5		7						11		4					10	8	9								
15	West Ham United	A	0-1		1	2	3	6	5		7						11		4					10	8	9								
22	South Shields	H	0-0		1	2	3	6	5		7					11			4				10		8	9								
29	South Shields	A	0-2		1	2	3	6						10		11	4	7		5					8	9								
Dec 6	Rotherham County	H	1-1	S Currie (pen)	1	2	3	6	5			8		10	11				4					9				7						
13	Rotherham County	A	0-1		1	2	3	6	5			8		10	11				4					9										
20	Stoke	H	3-1	S Harrold, Walker, Paterson	1	2	3	6	5					10	7				4								11			8	9			
25	Birmingham	H	1-0	Paterson	1	2	3	5						10		6	7		4								11			8	9			
26	Birmingham	A	1-0	Whitfield	1	2	3	5						10		6	7		4								11	9		8				
27	Stoke	A	0-3		1	2	3	5						10		6	7		4								11	9		8				
Jan 3	Grimsby Town	A	2-1	Macauley, Paterson	1	2	3	5						10		6			4								11			8	9			
17	Grimsby Town	H	2-0	Paterson, Macauley	1	2	3	5			7			10		6			4								11			8	9			
24	Hull City	H	3-2	Paterson (pen), Walker, Douglas	1	2		5			7			10		6			4								11	3		8	9			
Feb 7	Stockport County	H	0-2		1	2	3	5			7				11	6			4	10										8	9			
12	Hull City	A	1-5	Thornton	1		2	5			7	8			11	6			4									3	10		9			
14	Stockport County	A	2-0	Paterson, Walker	1	2					7					6			4							10	11			8	9	3	5	
28	Barnsley	A	1-0	Paterson	1	2	3	5			7			10		6			4								11			8	9			
Mar 4	Barnsley	H	0-0		1	2	3	5			7	10							4								11			8	9		6	
6	Nottingham Forest	A	0-0		1		3	5			7			10		6			4								11			8	9	2		
13	Nottingham Forest	H	0-0		1	2	3	5			7			10		6			4								11			8	9			
20	Lincoln City	A	3-0	S Currie (pen), Thornton, Whitfield	1	2	3	5			7	8				6			4							10	11	9						
27	Lincoln City	H	4-0	Paterson 3, Douglas	1	2	3	5			7	8				6			4							10	11				9			
Apr 3	Bury	A	0-1		1	2	3	5			7	8				6										10	11				9	4		
5	Bristol City	A	0-0		1	2	3	5			7	8		10		6											11				9	4		
6	Bristol City	H	2-1	Duffy, Paterson	1	2	3	5			7	8				6											11				9	4		10
10	Bury	H	0-5		1	2	3	5				8				6	7						9			11					4		10	
17	Port Vale	A	2-1	Douglas, Parker	1	2	3	5			7					6							9							8		4	11	10
24	Port Vale	H	0-1		1		3				7					6						4	9				10		8			2	5	11
26	Clapton Orient	A	0-3		1		3				7					6				10		4	9		8		11					2	5	
May 1	Clapton Orient	H	1-1	W. Currie	1	2	3				7	5				6				10					8		11					4	9	

F.A. CUP

DATE	OPPONENTS		V	F.T.	SCORERS	Bown	Barrett	Currie S	King E	Harrold J	Smith I	Douglas	Thornton	Richmond	Macauley	Harrold S	Thomson	Norton	Anstey	Jobey	Price	Essom	Bacon	Parker	Hubbard	Spittle	King H	Walker	Whitfield	Dorrell	Smith T	Paterson	Black	Currie W	Duffy
Jan 10	Newport County	(1)	A	0-0		1	2	3	5						10		6	7		4								11			8	9			
15	Newport County	(1 rep)	H	2-0	Walker, Paterson	1	2	3	5			7			10		6			4								11			8	9			
31	Manchester City	(2)	H	3-0	Douglas, Walker, T Smith	1	2	3	5			7			10		6			4								11			8	9			
Feb 21	Chelsea	(3)	A	0-3		1	2	3	5			7			10		6			4								11			8	9			

Note : Port Vale took over the Leeds City fixtures after Oct 14, when the latter were disbanded by order of the F.A. following alleged illegal practices.

LEICESTER CITY 1919-20
(Pictured v Birmingham on 26th December. Players only are named.)
Back : Barrett, Jobey, Bown, Harrold, S. Currie, Thomson.
Front : Norton, T. Smith, Whitfield, Macauley, Walker.

	APP's		GOALS	
	FL	FAC	FL	FAC
Herbert Bown	35	4		
Billy Barrett	38	4		
Sam Currie	38	4	2(2p)	
Teddy King	18		1	
Jimmy Harrold	30	4		
Ike Smith	2			
George Douglas	34	3	5	1
William Thornton	11		2	
Hugh Richmond	7		1	
James Macauley	19	4	2	
Sid Harrold	18		2	
Bill Thomson	34	4	1	
Joe Norton	11	1		
Brendel Anstey	7			
George Jobey	30	4		
Cliff Price	9		3	
Walter Essom	2			
Ernest Bacon	4			
John Parker	5		1	
Shirley Hubbard	3		1	
Billy Spittle	8		1	
Harry King	8		1	
Ernie Walker	27	4	3	2
Norman Whitfield	8		2	
Billy Dorrell	1			
Tom Smith	15	4		1
Jock Paterson	20	4	11(1p)	1
Adam Black	6			
Walter Currie	10		1	
Chris Duffy	4		1	

1920-21 LEAGUE DIVISION TWO
Final Position : 12th

DATE	OPPONENTS	V	F.T.	SCORERS	Bown	Clarke	Currie S.	Villiers	Harrold	Thomson	Douglas	Spittle	Paterson	Roxburgh A.	Walker	Black	King	Trotter	Pynegar	Tompkin	Barrett	Richmond	Currie W.	Smith	Roxburgh J.	Price	Graham	Hebden	
Aug 28	Clapton Orient	A	0-2		1	2	3	4	5	6	7	8	9	10	11														
Sep 2	Bury	H	4-0	Tompkin,Pynegar 2,Trotter	1	2			5	6	7	8				3	4	9	10	11									
4	Clapton Orient	H	2-1	Pynegar,Spittle	1	2			5	6	7	8				3	4	9	10	11									
8	Bury	A	0-4		1			4		6	7	8				3		9	10	11	2	5							
11	Leeds United	H	1-1	Pynegar	1				5	6	7		9			3		10	8	11	2		4						
18	Leeds United	A	1-3	Spittle	1		3		5	6	7	10					4	9	8	11	2								
25	Birmingham	H	3-0	Smith,Pynegar,Paterson	1		3		5	6	7		9					10	11	2				8					
Oct 2	Birmingham	A	0-5		1		3		5	6	7		9			2	4	10	11					8					
9	West Ham United	H	1-0	Tompkin	1		3		5	6		8	9			2	4			11					7	10			
16	West Ham United	A	1-0	Price	1		3		5	6		8				2	4			11				9	7	10			
23	Fulham	H	1-1	Smith	1		3		5	6		8				2	4			11				9	7	10			
30	Fulham	A	1-1	Price	1		3		5	6		8				2	4			11				9	7	10			
Nov 6	Cardiff City	H	2-0	Harrold,Paterson	1		3		5	6		8	9			2	4			11					7	10			
13	Cardiff City	A	0-2		1		3		5			7	8	9		2	4			11		6				10			
20	Notts County	A	1-1	Paterson	1		3		5			8	9			2	4			11		6			7	10			
27	Notts County	H	0-3		1		3		5	6		8	9			2	4			11					7	10			
Dec 4	Blackpool	A	0-2		1		3		5			8	9			2	4			11		6			7				
11	Blackpool	H	0-1		1		3		5				9	8		2	4	10		11		6			7				
18	Sheffield Wednesday	A	0-0		1		3		5	6			9			2	4			11				8	7	10			
25	Stoke	H	3-1	Paterson 3	1		3		5	6			9		11	2	4							8	7		10		
27	Stoke	A	1-1	Smith	1		3			6			9			2				11	5	4		8	7		10		
Jan 1	Sheffield Wednesday	H	2-1	Paterson 2	1		3		5	6			9			2	4			11				8	7		10		
15	Barnsley	A	1-2	Paterson	1				5			7	9			3	4		11	2		6		8			10		
22	Barnsley	H	2-0	King 2	1				5			7	9			3	4		11	2		6		8			10		
29	Bristol City	A	0-1		1				5			7	9			3	4		11	2		6		8			10		
Feb 5	Bristol City	H	0-0		1				5			7				3	4	9	11	2		6	10				8		
12	Nottingham Forest	A	2-1	Paterson 2	1							7	9			3	4	11			2	5	6	10			8		
19	Nottingham Forest	H	2-0	Paterson,Pynegar	1								9			3	4	11	8		2	5	6	10			7		
26	Rotherham County	A	1-1	Richmond	1		3		5				9					11	8		2	4	6				7	10	
Mar 5	Rotherham County	H	1-1	Paterson	1		3		5				9					11	8		2	4	6				7	10	
12	Port Vale	A	0-0		1		3		5			8	9					11			2	4	6				7	10	
19	Port Vale	H	0-0		1		3	4				8	9					11			2	5	6				7	10	
26	South Shields	H	2-0	J.Roxburgh,Paterson	1		3	6				4	8	9				11			2	5			7		10		
28	Coventry City	H	0-1		1		3	6	5			4	8	9				11			2				7		10		
29	Coventry City	A	0-1		1			6	5			4	9	10		3		11			2						8	7	
Apr 2	South Shields	A	3-4	Paterson 2,A.Roxburgh	1							4	9	8		3		11			2	5	6		7		10		
9	Hull City	H	0-0									4	9	8		3		11			2	5	6		7		10		1
16	Hull City	A	1-1	Trotter								4	9			3		11			2	5	6		7	10	8		1
28	Wolverhampton Wanderers	H	0-0						5							3		11	9		2	4	6		7	10	8		1
30	Wolverhampton Wanderers	A	0-3						5							3	9	11			2	4	6		7	10	8		1
May 2	Stockport County	H	0-0		1				5	6			9	10		3		11			2	4			7		8		
7	Stockport County	A	0-0		1				5	6			9	10		3		11			2	4			7		8		

F.A. CUP

DATE	OPPONENTS		V	F.T.	SCORERS	Bown	Harrold	Thomson	Paterson	Black	King	Tompkin	Barrett	Smith	Roxburgh J.	Graham
Jan 8	Burnley	(1)	H	3-7	Smith,J.Roxburgh,Paterson	1	5	6	9	3	4	11	2	8	7	10

Note : May 7 - played at Old Trafford

LEICESTER CITY 1920-21
(Pictured v Birmingham on 2nd October)
Back: Thomson,King,Bown,Harrold,S.Currie.
Front : Douglas,Smith,Paterson,Pynegar,Tompkin,Black.

	APP's		GOALS	
	FL	FAC	FL	FAC
Herbert Bown	38	1		
Bernard Clarke	3			
Sam Currie	24			
Henry Villiers	5			
Jimmy Harrold	33	1	1	
Bill Thomson	27	1		
George Douglas	14			
Billy Spittle	18		2	
Jock Paterson	32	1	16	1
Andrew Roxburgh	7		1	
Ernie Walker	2			
Adam Black	33	1		
Teddy King	24	1	2	
Alex Trotter	22		2	
Albert Pynegar	13		6	
Percy Tompkin	25	1	2	
Billy Barrett	24	1		
Hugh Richmond	16		1	
Walter Currie	21			
Tom Smith	21	1	3	1
John Roxburgh	22	1	1	1
Cliff Price	12		2	
Harry Graham	22	1		
George Hebden	4			

1921-22 LEAGUE DIVISION TWO
Final Position : 9th

DATE	OPPONENTS	V	F.T.	SCORERS	Bown	Barrett	Black	King E	Harrold	Thomson	Roxburgh J	Greatorex	Paterson	Graham	Trotter	Price	Currie S	Jones	Walker	Roxburgh A	Richmond	Smith	Pynegar	Tompkin	Currie W	Brooks	King J	Hebden	O'Brien	Waite
Aug 27	Bradford Park Avenue	A	1-0	Paterson	1	2	3	4	5	6	7	8	9	10	11															
29	Fulham	H	1-2	Greatorex	1	2	3	4	5	6	7	8	9	10	11															
Sep 3	Bradford Park Avenue	H	2-1	Greatorex,Trotter	1	2	3	4	5	6	7	8	9	10	11															
5	Fulham	A	0-0		1	2	3	4	5	6	7	8	9	10	11															
10	South Shields	H	1-0	E King	1	2	3	4	5	6	7	8	9	10	11															
17	South Shields	A	0-1		1	2	3	4	5	6	7	8	9	10	11															
24	Bristol City	H	4-1	Paterson 2,E King,J Roxburgh	1	2	3	4	5	6	7		9	8	11	10														
Oct 1	Bristol City	A	1-1	Trotter	1	2	3	4	5	6	7		9	8	11	10														
8	Nottingham Forest	H	2-2	Price 2	1	2	3	4	5	6	7		9	8	11	10														
15	Nottingham Forest	A	0-0		1	2		4	5	6	7		9	8	11	10	3													
22	Wolverhampton Wanderers	H	0-1		1	2		4	5	6	7		9	8	11	10	3													
29	Wolverhampton Wanderers	A	1-1	Price	1	2		4	5	6	7	8	9		11	10	3													
Nov 5	Barnsley	H	1-0	Paterson	1	2		4		6	7	8	9		11		3	5	10											
12	Barnsley	A	0-0		1	2		4	5	6	7	8	9		11		3		10											
19	Coventry City	A	0-0		1		2	4	5	6	7		9	8	11		3		10											
26	Coventry City	H	1-1	Smith	1	2		4	5	6	7				11		3		10	8		9								
Dec 3	Derby County	A	1-0	Smith	1	2		4	5	6			10	8			3					9	7	11						
10	Derby County	H	1-1	Pynegar	1	2		4	5	6			10	8			3					9	7	11						
17	Bury	A	1-0	Paterson	1	2			5	6	7		9	10	11		3	4				8								
24	Bury	H	0-0		1	2	3		5	6	7		9	10	11			4				8								
26	Blackpool	A	0-2		1	2		4	5	6	7		9		11		3					8	10							
27	Blackpool	H	1-0	Trotter	1	2			5	6	7		9		11			4	3			10	8							
31	West Ham United	A	0-1		1	2			5	6	7		9		11			4	3			10	8							
Jan 14	West Ham United	H	2-1	Paterson,Smith	1	2			5	6			9	8	11			4	3			10	7								
21	Clapton Orient	A	0-0		1	2			5	6			9	8	11			4	3			10	7								
Feb 4	Stoke	A	1-1	Pynegar (pen)	1	2			5	6			9	8	11			4	3			10	7								
9	Clapton Orient	H	1-0	Paterson	1	2			5	6			9	8	11			4	3			7		10							
11	Stoke	H	3-4	E King 2,J King	1		2	5		6			9	8	11			4	3			7		10							
20	Leeds United	A	0-3			2			5	6			9	8				4	3			10		11		7		1		
25	Leeds United	H	0-0			2			5	6			9	8	11			4	3			7		10				1		
Mar 4	Hull City	A	2-5	Pynegar (pen),A Roxburgh		2			5	6				8	11			4	3	9		10	7					1		
11	Hull City	H	0-1			2	3		5	6			9	8	11			4				7		10				1		
18	Notts County	H	3-0	Graham 2,Trotter		2	3			6			9	8	11			4				7		10				1	5	
Apr 1	Crystal Palace	H	2-0	J King 2		2	3		5	6			9	8	11			4				7					10	1		
8	Crystal Palace	A	0-1			2	3			6			9	8	11			4				7		10				1	5	
14	Port Vale	A	1-1	Trotter		2	3			6			9	8	11			4				7		10				1	5	
15	Rotherham County	H	1-0	Graham		2	3			6			9	8	11			4				7		10				1	5	
17	Port Vale	H	3-0	Trotter,Thomson,Graham		2	3		5	6			9	8	11			4				7		10				1	5	
22	Rotherham County	A	0-0			2	3		5	6			9	8	11			4				7		10				1		
26	Notts County	A	0-0		1	2	3		5	6			9	8	11			4				7		10						
29	Sheffield Wednesday	H	1-1	Trotter	1	2	3			6			9	8	11			4				7		10					5	
May 6	Sheffield Wednesday	A	0-1		1	2	3			6				8	11			4				7		10					5	9

F.A. CUP

DATE	OPPONENTS		V	F.T.	SCORERS	Bown	Barrett	Black	King E	Harrold	Thomson	Roxburgh J	Greatorex	Paterson	Graham	Trotter	Price	Currie S	Jones	Walker	Roxburgh A	Richmond	Smith	Pynegar	Tompkin	Currie W	Brooks	King J	Hebden	O'Brien	Waite
Jan 7	Clapton Orient	(1)	H	2-0	Pynegar (pen),Trotter	1	2			5	6	7		9		11			4	3			10	8								
28	Fulham	(2)	H	2-0	Graham,Paterson	1	2			5	6			9	8	11			4	3			10	7								
Feb 18	Arsenal	(3)	A	0-3		1	2			5	6			9	8	11			4	3			10	7								

LEICESTER CITY 1921-22
Back: D.Gardner (Trainer),H.Linney (Director), Walker,Paterson,W.Fox (Masseur),Black,Richmond,Bown,Harrold, Hebden,Price,E.Nixon (Assistant Trainer),A.Needham (Director),P.Hodge (Manager).
Middle : King,Spittle,Douglas,Thomson,Barrett,S.Currie,W.Currie,Clarke.
Front : Villiers,Trotter,Smith,A.Roxburgh,J.Roxburgh,Tompkin,Pynegar.

	APP's FL	APP's FAC	GOALS FL	GOALS FAC
Herbert Bown	31	3		
Billy Barrett	40	3		
Adam Black	23			
Teddy King	21		4	
Jimmy Harrold	36	3		
Bill Thomson	39	3	1	
John Roxburgh	20	1	1	
George Greatorex	11		2	
Jock Paterson	29	3	7	1
Harry Graham	31	2	4	1
Alex Trotter	38	3	7	1
Cliff Price	7		3	
Sam Currie	13			
Dennis Jones	23	3		
Ernie Walker	9	3		
Andrew Roxburgh	12		1	
Hugh Richmond	1			
Tom Smith	20	3	3	
Albert Pynegar	15	3	3(2p)	1(p)
Percy Tompkin	16			
Walter Currie	1			
Ernie Brooks	4			
Jack King	4		3	
George Hebden	11			
Mick O'Brien	6			
George Waite	1			

1922-23 LEAGUE DIVISION TWO
Final Position : 3rd

DATE	OPPONENTS	V	F.T.	SCORERS	Hebden	Barrett	Black	Thomson	Harrold	O'Brien	Roxburgh	Duncan J	Waite	Graham	Trotter	Duncan T	Walker	Jones	Tompkin	Smith	Pynegar	Price	Osborne	Watson	Middleton
Aug 26	Stockport County	A	5-4	J Duncan 2,Graham,Waite,Waterall (og)	1	2	3	4	5	6	7	8	9	10	11										
28	Rotherham County	H	3-0	Trotter,J Duncan,Waite	1	2	3	4	5	6		8	9	10	11	7									
Sep 2	Stockport County	H	2-0	Graham 2	1	2	3	4	5	6	7	8	9	10	11										
4	Rotherham County	A	0-0		1	2	3	4	5	6		8	9	10	11	7									
9	Clapton Orient	A	0-2		1	2	3	4	5	6	7	8	9	10	11										
16	Clapton Orient	H	2-0	J Duncan,Waite (pen)	1	2			6	5		7	8	9	10	11	3	4							
23	Crystal Palace	A	1-0	Jones	1	2			6	5		7	8	9	10	11	3	4							
30	Crystal Palace	H	3-0	Waite,J Duncan 2	1	2			6	5			8	9	10	7	3	4	11						
Oct 7	Bradford City	A	2-2	J Duncan,Waite	1	2			6	5			8	9	10	7	3	4	11						
14	Bradford City	H	2-0	J Duncan,T Duncan	1	2			6	5			8	9	10	7	3	4	11						
21	Leeds United	A	0-0		1	2			6	5			8	9	10	7	3	4	11						
28	Leeds United	H	2-1	Graham,J Duncan	1	2			6	5			8	9	10	7	3	4	11						
Nov 4	Hull City	H	0-1		1	2			6	5			8	9	10	7	3	4	11						
11	Hull City	A	3-1	J Duncan,Waite,T Duncan	1	2			6	5			8	9	10	7	3	4	11						
18	Southampton	H	2-1	T Duncan 2	1	2			6	5			8	9	10	7	3	4	11						
25	Southampton	A	0-0		1	2			6	5			8	9	10	7	3	4	11						
Dec 2	Sheffield Wednesday	H	3-1	J Duncan,Graham,T Duncan	1	2			6	5	3		8	9	10	7		4	11						
9	Sheffield Wednesday	A	1-2	Waite (pen)	1	2	3		6	5			8	9	10	7		4	11						
16	Derby County	A	0-2		1	2	3		6	5			8	9	10	7		4	11						
23	Derby County	H	0-1		1	2	3		6	5			8		10	9	7	4	11						
25	Blackpool	H	1-2	J Duncan	1	2	3		6	5	4		8	9	10	7			11						
26	Blackpool	A	2-1	Tompkin,J Duncan	1	2	3		6			5	8	9	10				11		7				
30	Barnsley	A	1-0	Waite	1	2			6			5	8	9	10		3	4	11		7				
Jan 6	Barnsley	H	2-2	Waite 2 (2 pen)	1	2			6			5	8	9	10		3	4	11		7				
20	Notts County	H	2-1	Waite 2 (1pen)	1	2			6	5		4	8	9	10		3		11		7				
27	Notts County	A	0-1		1	2			6	5		4	8	9	10		3		11		7				
Feb 10	West Ham United	A	2-2	J Duncan 2	1	2			6	5		4	8		7	10	3				9				
15	West Ham United	H	0-6		1	2			6	5		4	8		7	10	3				9				
17	South Shields	A	1-2	Pynegar	1	2			6			5	8		10	7	3	4	11		9				
26	South Shields	H	3-0	Pynegar 2,J Duncan	1	2			6			5	8		10	7	3	4			9	11			
Mar 3	Wolverhampton Wanderers	A	2-1	Pynegar,J Duncan	1	2			6			5	8		10	7	3	4			9	11			
10	Wolverhampton Wanderers	H	7-0	Pynegar 4 (1pen),J Duncan,Graham,O'Brien	1	2			6			5	8	10	11	7	3	4			9				
17	Coventry City	H	2-1	Pynegar,Smith	1	2			6			5	8		11	7	3	4		10	9				
24	Coventry City	A	1-1	Smith	1	2			6			5	8		11	7	3	4		10	9				
30	Fulham	A	0-2		1	2			6			5	8	10		7	3	4	11		9				
31	Port Vale	H	3-0	Pynegar 2,O'Brien	1	2			6			5	8	10		7	3	4	11		9				
Apr 2	Fulham	H	1-1	J Duncan	1	2			6			5	8	10		7		4	11		9	3			
7	Port Vale	A	0-0		1	2			6			5	8	10		7		4	11		9	3			
14	Manchester United	H	0-1		1	2			5			8		10		7		4	11		9	3	6		
21	Manchester United	A	2-0	J Duncan,Smith	1	2			5	6				10	11	7		4		8	9	3			
28	Bury	H	2-0	Smith 2	1	2			5	6				10	11	7		4		9		3			8
May 5	Bury	A	0-2		1	2			5					10	11	7		4		9		3	6		8

F.A. CUP

DATE	OPPONENTS		V	F.T.	SCORERS	Hebden	Barrett	Black	Thomson	Harrold	O'Brien	Roxburgh	Duncan J	Waite	Graham	Trotter	Duncan T	Walker	Jones	Tompkin	Smith	Pynegar
Jan 13	Fulham	(1)	H	4-0	J Duncan 2,Smith,Graham	1	2			6	5	4		8	9	10		3		11		7
Feb 3	Cardiff City	(2)	H	0-1		1	2			6	5	4		8	9	10		3		11		7

LEICESTER CITY 1922-23

Back: D.Gardner*(Trainer)*,W.Fox*(Masseur)*,O'Brien,Graham,E.King,T.Duncan,J.Duncan,Black,
E.Nixon*(Assistant Trainer)*,Hebden,Brown,Thomson.
Middle : Godderidge,Baron,Middleton,Newton,Harrold,Trotter,Barrett,Watson.
Front : J.Price,Smith,J.King,Adcock,Tompkin,Jones,F.Price,Pynegar.

	APP's		GOALS	
	FL	FAC	FL	FAC
George Hebden	42	2		
Billy Barrett	10			
Adam Black	42	2		
Bill Thomson	38	2		
Jimmy Harrold	29	2		
Mick O'Brien	24	2	2	
John Roxburgh	6			
John Duncan	41	2	20	2
George Waite	27	2	12 (5p)	
Harry Graham	39	2	6	1
Alex Trotter	15		1	
Tom Duncan	29		5	
Ernie Walker	25	2		
Dennis Jones	32		1	
Percy Tompkin	27	2	1	
Tom Smith	10	1	5	1
Albert Pynegar	14	1	11 (1p)	
Fred Price	2			
Reg Osborne	6			
Norman Watson	2			
Jack Middleton	2			
Own Goals				1

1923-24 LEAGUE DIVISION TWO
Final Position : 12th

DATE	OPPONENTS	V	F.T.	SCORERS	Hebden	Black	Osborne	Jones	O'Brien	Thomson	Adcock	Duncan J	Chandler	Graham	Tompkin	Smith	Trotter	Newton	King	Watson	Barrett	Duncan T	Pynegar	Davies	Walker	Carrigan	Middleton	Bamber	Price	Carr	Godderidge
Aug 25	Hull City	A	1-1	Graham	1	2	3	4	5	6	7	8	9	10	11																
27	Stoke	H	5-0	Chandler 2,Smith,O'Brien,Adcock	1	2	3	4	5	6	7	8	9			10	11														
Sep 1	Hull City	H	1-1	Chandler	1	2	3	4	5	6	7	8	9			10	11														
3	Stoke	A	0-1		1	2	3	4	5	6	7	8	9			10	11														
8	Leeds United	H	2-0	Chandler,Jones	1	2	3	4	5	6	7	8	9	10	11																
15	Leeds United	A	2-1	Chandler,J Duncan	1	2	3	4	5	6	7	8	9	10	11																
22	Port Vale	H	2-0	Chandler,J Duncan	1	2	3	4	5	6	7	8	9	10	11																
29	Port Vale	A	1-2	Graham	1	2	3	4	5	6	7	8	9	10	11																
Oct 6	Bradford City	H	0-1		1	2	3	4	5	6	7	8	9	10	11																
13	Bradford City	A	2-2	O'Brien,Chandler	1	2	3		5	6	7		9	8	11			4	10												
20	Barnsley	H	2-0	J Duncan,King	1	2	3		5		7	8	9		11			4	10	6											
27	Barnsley	A	1-3	J Duncan	1	2	3		5		7	8	9		11			4	10	6											
Nov 3	Manchester United	H	2-2	O'Brien,J Duncan	1		3		5	6		8		10			11	4			2	7	9								
10	Manchester United	A	0-3		1		3		5	6		8	9	10			11	4			2	7									
17	Bury	H	3-0	Chandler 2,Heap (og)	1		3		5	6		8	9	10			11	4			2	7									
Dec 1	South Shields	H	4-1	Graham,Chandler 3	1		3		5	6		8	9	10			11	4			2	7									
8	South Shields	A	2-1	J Duncan,Chandler			3		5	6		8	9	10			11	4			2	7				1					
15	Oldham Athletic	H	1-1	J Duncan			3		5	6		8	9	10			11	4			2	7				1					
22	Oldham Athletic	A	0-0		1		3		5	6		8	9	10			11	4			2	7									
25	Clapton Orient	A	0-1		1		3		5	6		8	9			10	11	4			2	7									
26	Clapton Orient	H	1-2	J Duncan	1		3		5	6		8	9			10	11	4			2	7									
29	Stockport County	H	1-1	T Duncan			3		5	6		8	9			10	11	4			2	7	1								
Jan 2	Bury	A	0-2		1					6			9	10	11			4			2	7		3	5	8					
5	Stockport County	A	1-3	Middleton	1		3			6	7		9	10	11			4			2					5	8				
19	Crystal Palace	A	3-4	Chandler,Middleton,Cracknell (og)	1		3			6	7		9	10	11			4			2					5	8				
26	Crystal Palace	H	1-0	Chandler	1		3		5	6	7		9	10	11			4			2						8				
Feb 9	Sheffield Wednesday	H	2-1	Chandler,J Duncan	1		3		5		7	8	9	10	11			4			2						6				
11	Sheffield Wednesday	A	1-2	Graham	1		3		5		7	8	9	10	11			4			2						6				
16	Coventry City	A	4-2	Chandler 3,J Duncan	1		3		5		7	8	9	10				4			2						6	11			
23	Coventry City	H	2-0	Chandler,Carr	1		3		5		7	8	9					4			2						6	11		10	
Mar 1	Bristol City	A	1-0	Carr	1		3				7	8	9				11	4			2					5	6			10	
8	Bristol City	H	5-1	Chandler,Carr,J Duncan 3	1		3		5		7	8	9		11			4			2						6			10	
15	Southampton	H	0-1		1		3		5		7	8	9					4			2					5	6			10	
22	Southampton	A	0-1		1		3		5		7	8	9					4			2						6			10	
29	Fulham	H	2-1	Adcock 2			3		5		7	8	9					4		6	2									10	1
Apr 5	Fulham	A	0-1				3		5		7		9		11			4		6	2						8			10	1
12	Blackpool	H	1-2	Chandler		2	3		5		7		9		11			4		6							8			10	1
19	Blackpool	A	1-3	O'Brien	1	2	3		5		7		9	8	11			4		6										10	
21	Nelson	A	1-1	Tompkin	1		3		5		7		9	8	11			4		6	2									10	
22	Nelson	H	3-1	Chandler 2,Adcock			3		5		7		9		11			4		6	2						8			10	1
26	Derby County	H	3-0	Carr 2,Middleton			3				7		9		11			4		6	2						8		5	10	1
May 3	Derby County	A	0-4				3				7		9		11			4		6	2						8		5	10	1

F.A. CUP

DATE	OPPONENTS		V	F.T.	SCORERS	Hebden	Black	Osborne	Jones	O'Brien	Thomson	Adcock	Duncan J	Chandler	Graham	Tompkin	Smith	Trotter	Newton	King	Watson	Barrett	Duncan T	Pynegar	Davies	Walker	Carrigan	Middleton	Bamber	Price	Carr	Godderidge
Jan 12	Sheffield Wednesday	(1)	A	1-4	Barrett (pen)	1	3				6		5	9	10	11			4			2	7					8				

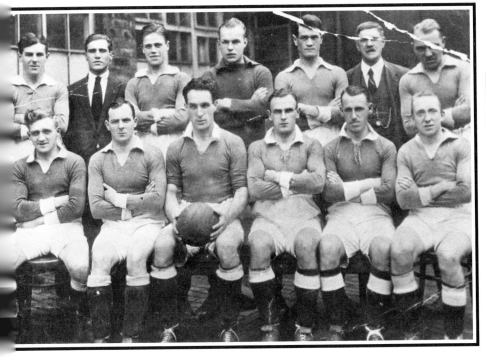

LEICESTER CITY 1923-24
Back: Jones,Smith,Black,Hebden,Osborne,D.Gardner *(Trainer)*,Thomson.
Front : Adcock,J.Duncan,O'Brien,Chandler,Graham,Tompkin.

	APP's		GOALS	
	FL	FAC	FL	FAC
George Hebden	33	1		
Adam Black	22	1		
Reg Osborne	33			
Dennis Jones	9		1	
Mick O'Brien	35		4	
Bill Thomson	24	1		
Hughie Adcock	30		4	
John Duncan	34	1	13	
Arthur Chandler	42	1	24	
Harry Graham	18	1	4	
Percy Tompkin	19		1	
Tom Smith	6		1	
Alex Trotter	21	1		
Billy Newton	30	1		
Jack King	3		1	
Norman Watson	7			
Billy Barrett	28	1		1(p)
Tom Duncan	12	1	1	
Albert Pynegar	2			
Ben Davies	3			
Ernie Walker	1			
Pat Carrigan	4			
Jack Middleton	9	1	3	
John Bamber	16			
Fred Price	2			
George Carr	13		5	
Albert Godderidge	6			
Own Goals				2

1924-25 LEAGUE DIVISION TWO
Final Position : 1st

DATE	OPPONENTS	V	F.T.	SCORERS	Godderidge	Hooper	Osborne	Bamber	Carrigan	Duncan	Adcock	Proctor	Chandler	Carr	Wadsworth	Middleton	Barrett	Black	Watson	Hebden	Newton	Sharp
Aug 30	Manchester United	A	0-1		1	2	3	4	5	6	7	8	9	10	11							
Sep 1	Chelsea	H	4-0	Adcock,Chandler,Carr 2	1	2	3	4	5	6	7	8	9	10	11							
6	Middlesbrough	H	0-0		1	2	3	4	5	6	7	10	9		11	8						
8	Chelsea	A	0-4		1			4	5	10	7	8	9		11		2	3	6			
13	Stoke	H	0-1					4	5	10	7	8	9		11		2	3		1		
15	Stockport County	A	2-0	Duncan,Barrett (pen)				6	5	8	7		9	10	11		2	3		1	4	
20	Coventry City	A	2-4	Carr,Chandler			3	6	5	8	7		9	10	11			2		1	4	
27	Oldham Athletic	H	3-0	Carrigan,Chandler,Duncan			3	6	5	8	7		9	10	11			2		1	4	
Oct 4	Sheffield Wednesday	A	4-1	Chandler,Wadsworth,Duncan 2			3	6	5	8	7		9	10	11			2		1	4	
11	Clapton Orient	H	4-2	Carr 2,Duncan 2			3	6	5	8	7		9	10	11			2		1	4	
18	Crystal Palace	A	2-0	Duncan,Chandler			3	6	5	8	7		9	10	11			2		1	4	
25	Barnsley	A	1-1	Chandler	1		3	6	5	8	7		9	10	11			2			4	
Nov 1	Wolverhampton Wanderers	H	2-0	Chandler,Duncan			3	6	5	8	7		9	10	11			2		1	4	
8	Fulham	A	2-2	Chandler,Bamber			3	6	5	8	7		9	10	11			2		1	4	
15	Portsmouth	H	4-0	Chandler,Carr,Duncan,Newton			3	6	5	8	7		9	10	11			2		1	4	
22	Hull City	A	1-2	Chandler			3	6	5	8	7		9	10	11			2		1	4	
29	Blackpool	H	0-2		1		3	6	5	8	7		9	10	11			2			4	
Dec 6	Derby County	A	3-0	Duncan,Carrigan,Chandler	1	3		6	5	8	7		9	10	11			2			4	
13	South Shields	H	1-1	Chandler	1	3		6	5	8	7		9	10	11			2			4	
20	Bradford City	A	1-1	Chandler	1	3		6	5	8	7		9	10	11			2	4			
25	Port Vale	H	7-0	Chandler,Duncan 6	1	3		6	5	8	7		9	10	11			2			4	
26	Port Vale	A	2-1	Chandler,Carr	1	3		6	5	8	7		9	10	11			2			4	
27	Manchester United	H	3-0	Chandler 2,Duncan	1	3		6	5	8	7		9	10	11			2			4	
Jan 3	Middlesbrough	A	5-1	Duncan 2,Chandler,Carr,Adcock	1	3		6	5	8	7		9	10	11			2			4	
17	Stoke	A	1-1	Adcock	1	3		6	5	8	7		9	10	11			2			4	
24	Coventry City	H	5-1	Sharp,Carr,Chandler 3	1	3		6	5		7		9	10	11			2			4	8
Feb 7	Sheffield Wednesday	H	6-1	Duncan 2,Black 2 (2 pen),Chandler 2	1	3		6		8	7		9	10	11			2	5		4	
14	Clapton Orient	A	1-0	Duncan	1	3		6	5	8	7		9	10	11			2			4	
28	Barnsley	H	6-0	Chandler 5,Duncan	1	3		6	5	8			9	10	11			2	7		4	
Mar 12	Crystal Palace	H	3-1	Carrigan,Black (pen),Duncan	1	3			5	8	7		9	10	11			2	6		4	
14	Fulham	H	4-0	Duncan 3,Adcock	1	3			5	8	7		9	10	11			2	6		4	
17	Oldham Athletic	A	1-0	Chandler	1	3			5		7		9	10	11			2	6		4	8
21	Portsmouth	A	1-1	Chandler	1	3		6	5	8	7		9	10	11			2			4	
28	Hull City	H	1-0	Carr	1	3		6	5	8	7		9	10	11			2			4	
30	Wolverhampton Wanderers	A	1-0	Chandler	1	3		6	5	8	7		9	10	11			2			4	
Apr 4	Blackpool	A	1-2	Duncan	1	3		6	5	8			9	10	11			2	7		4	
11	Derby County	H	0-0		1	3		6	5	8	7		9	10	11			2			4	
13	Southampton	A	0-0		1	3		6	5	8	7		9	10	11			2			4	
14	Southampton	H	0-0		1	3		6	5	8	7		9	10	11			2			4	
18	South Shields	A	1-1	Bamber	1		3	6		8	7		9	5	11			2	4		10	
25	Bradford City	H	1-0	Carr	1		3	6	5	8	7		9	10	11			2	4			
May 2	Stockport County	H	4-0	Duncan 2,Chandler,Carr	1	3		6	5	8	7		9	10	11			2			4	

F.A. CUP

DATE	OPPONENTS		V	F.T.	SCORERS	Godderidge	Hooper	Osborne	Bamber	Carrigan	Duncan	Adcock	Proctor	Chandler	Carr	Wadsworth	Middleton	Barrett	Black	Watson	Hebden	Newton	Sharp
Jan 10	Stoke	(1)	H	3-0	Duncan 2,Chandler	1	3		6	5	8	7		9	10	11			2			4	
31	Newcastle United	(2)	A	2-2	Chandler 2	1	3		6	5	8	7		9	10	11			2			4	
Feb 5	Newcastle United	(2 rep)	H	1-0	Carr	1	3		6	5	8	7		9	10	11			2			4	
21	Hull City	(3)	A	1-1	Duncan	1	3		6	5	8	7		9	10	11			2			4	
26	Hull City	(3 rep)	H	3-1	Chandler 3	1	3		6	5	8			9	10	11			2	7		4	
Mar 7	Cardiff City	(4)	A	1-2	Duncan	1	3		6	5	8	7		9	10	11			2			4	

LEICESTER CITY 1924-25
Back: E.King(Coach),Newton,Black,Carrigan,Godderidge,Hooper,Bamber,D.Gardner(Trainer).
Front : Adcock,Duncan,Chandler,Carr,Wadsworth.

	APP's		GOALS	
	FL	FAC	FL	FAC
Albert Godderidge	31	6		
Harry Hooper	26	6		
Reg Osborne	16			
John Bamber	39	6	2	
Pat Carrigan	40	6	3	
John Duncan	40	6	30	4
Hughie Adcock	40	5	4	
Norman Proctor	5			
Arthur Chandler	42	6	32	6
George Carr	40	6	12	1
Harold Wadsworth	42	6	1	
Jack Middleton	1			
Billy Barrett	3		1(p)	
Adam Black	39	6	3(3p)	
Norman Watson	10	1		
George Hebden	11			
Billy Newton	34	6	1	
Buchanan Sharp	3		1	

Date	Opponents	V	F.T.	Scorers	Godderidge	Black	Hooper	Newton	Watson	Bamber	Adcock	Duncan	Chandler	Carr	Wadsworth	Carrigan	Osborne	Jarvie	Sharp	Findlay	Brown	Lochhead	Campbell	Hine	Webb	Bell	Baxter
Aug 29	Liverpool	H	3-1	Chandler 2, Adcock	1	2	3	4	5	6	7	8	9	10	11												
31	Arsenal	A	2-2	Duncan 2 (1pen)	1	2	3	4	5	6	7	8	9	10	11												
Sep 5	Burnley	A	0-4		1	2	3	4		6	7	8	9	10	11	5											
7	Arsenal	H	0-1		1	2	3	4		6	7	8	9	10	11	5											
12	Leeds United	H	1-3	Chandler	1	2		4		6	7	8	9	10	11	5	3										
16	Manchester United	A	2-3	Chandler, Duncan (pen)		2		4	5	6	7	8	9		11		3					10	1				
19	Newcastle United	A	2-3	Bamber 2		2			5	6	7	8	9		11		3	4				10	1				
26	Bolton Wanderers	H	5-2	Chandler 2, Duncan 2, Wadsworth		2		4	5	6	7	8	9		11		3					10	1				
Oct 3	Notts County	A	2-2	Chandler 2		2		4	5	6	7	8	9		11		3					10	1				
10	Aston Villa	A	1-2	Duncan (pen)		2		4	5	6	7	8	9		11		3					10	1				
17	West Bromwich Albion	H	3-0	Chandler, Lochhead 2	1	2		4	5	6	7	8	9		11		3					10					
24	Birmingham	A	1-1	Chandler	1	2		4	5	6	7	8	9		11		3					10					
31	Tottenham Hotspur	H	5-3	Chandler 2, Sharp, Lochhead, Wadsworth	1	2		4	5	6	7		9		11		3		8			10					
Nov 7	Cardiff City	A	2-5	Chandler, Lochhead	1	2		4	5	6	7	8	9		11		3					10					
14	Sunderland	H	4-1	Duncan 2, Chandler, Lochhead		2		4	5	6	7	8	9		11		3					10	1				
21	Huddersfield Town	A	0-3			2		4	5	6	7	8	9		11		3					10	1				
28	Everton	H	1-1	Lochhead		2		4		6	7	8	9		11	5	3					10	1				
Dec 5	Manchester City	A	1-5	Chandler		2		4		6	7		9		11	5	3		8			10	1				
12	Bury	H	0-2			2	3	4		6	7		9		11	5			8			10	1				
19	Blackburn Rovers	A	0-0			2		4	5	6	7	8	9		11		3					10	1				
25	Sheffield United	A	4-2	Lochhead 2, Adcock, Duncan		2		4		6	7	8	9		11	5	3					10	1				
26	Sheffield United	H	2-2	Lochhead, Duncan		2		4		6	7	8	9		11	5	3					10	1				
28	Manchester United	H	1-3	Chandler		2		4		6	7	8	9		11	5	3					10	1				
Jan 2	Liverpool	A	3-0	Lochhead, Adcock, Chandler		2		4	5	6	7	8	9		11		3					10	1				
16	Burnley	H	3-2	Chandler, Hine 2		2		4	5	6	7		9		11		3					10	1	8			
23	Leeds United	A	0-1			2		4	5	6	7		9		11		3					10	1	8			
30	Everton	A	0-1			2		4	5	6	7				11		3	10				9	1	8			
Feb 6	Bolton Wanderers	A	2-2	Chandler, Bamber		2			5	6	7		9				3	4				10	1	8	11		
13	Notts County	H	1-0	Chandler		2			5	6	7		9		11		3	4				10	1	8			
20	Blackburn Rovers	H	2-1	Chandler, Duncan		2			5	6	7	10	9		11		3	4					1	8			
22	Newcastle United	H	3-2	Chandler, Lochhead, Duncan	1	2			5	6	7		9		11		3	4				10		8			
27	West Bromwich Albion	A	1-3	Hine		2		4	5	6	7		9				3					10	1	8		11	
Mar 6	Birmingham	H	1-0	Lochhead (pen)		2		4	5	6	7		9				3					10	1	8		11	
10	Aston Villa	A	2-2	Hine, Lochhead		2	3	4	5	6	7		9		11							10	1	8			
13	Tottenham Hotspur	A	3-1	Lochhead, Hine, Chandler		2		4	5	6	7		9		11		3					10	1	8			
20	Cardiff City	H	1-2	Chandler		2		4	5	6	7		9		11		3					10	1	8			
27	Sunderland	A	0-3			2	3	4	5	6	7		9									10	1	8		11	
Apr 2	West Ham United	A	1-1	Lochhead		2		4	5	6	7						3					10	1	9		11	
3	Huddersfield Town	H	2-0	Bell, Hine		2		4	5	6	7						3					10	1	9		11	
5	West Ham United	H	1-1	Chandler	1	2		4	5	6	7		9				3					10		8		11	
17	Manchester City	H	2-3	Hine, Chandler		2		4	5	6	7		9				3					10	1	8		11	
24	Bury	A	0-4			2		4	5	6	7	8	9				3					10	1	9		11	4

F.A. CUP

Date	Opponents		V	F.T.	Scorers	Godderidge	Black	Hooper	Newton	Watson	Bamber	Adcock	Duncan	Chandler	Carr	Wadsworth	Carrigan	Osborne	Jarvie	Sharp	Findlay	Brown	Lochhead	Campbell	Hine	Webb	Bell	Baxter
Jan 9	Notts County	(3)	A	0-2			2		4	5	6	7	8	9		11		3					10	1				

	APP's		GOALS	
	FL	FAC	FL	FAC
Albert Godderidge	11			
Adam Black	42	1		
Harry Hooper	7			
Billy Newton	23	1		
Norman Watson	36	1		
John Bamber	42	1	3	
Hughie Adcock	35	1	3	
John Duncan	34	1	12 (3p)	
Arthur Chandler	38	1	26	
George Carr	5			
Harold Wadsworth	38	1	2	
Pat Carrigan	6			
Reg Osborne	31	1		
John Jarvie	5			
Buchanan Sharp	9		1	
Billy Findlay	10			
Jack Brown	4			
Arthur Lochhead	32	1	15 (1p)	
Ken Campbell	26	1		
Ernie Hine	18		7	
Willie Webb	1			
William Bell	8	1		
James Baxter	1			

LEICESTER CITY 1925-26

Back : E.King *(Coach)*, Gibbs, Findlay, Tuckley, Brown, Jarvie, Hudson, Gouch, Webb, Allan, Baxter, W.Fox *(Masseur)*, E.Nixon *(Assistant Trainer)*.

Middle : C.Crossland *(Director)*, E.Gregson *(Director)*, L.Burridge *(Director)*, Watson, Heywood, Heathcock, Black, Godderidge, Hooper, Osborne, Waterston, Sharp, A.Pudan *(Director)*, W.Tompkins *(Director)*, A.Rice *(Director)*.

Front : A.Needham *(Director)*, P.Hodge *(Secretary)*, Chandler, Adcock, Newton, Duncan, J.Rice *(President)*, Bamber, Carrigan, Wadsworth, Carr, D.Gardner *(Trainer)*, W.Squires *(Chairman)*.

1926-27 LEAGUE DIVISION ONE
Final Position : 7th

Player columns: Campbell, Black, Osborne, Duncan, Watson, Bamber, Adcock, Hine, Chandler, Carr, Bell, Lochhead, Carrigan, Brown, Moyes, Bishop, Lane, Godderidge, Wadsworth, Heathcock, Findlay, McLaren

DATE	OPPONENTS	V	F.T.	SCORERS
Aug 28	West Ham United	A	3-3	Chandler 3
30	Birmingham	H	5-2	Bell,Lochhead,Chandler,Hine,Duncan
Sep 4	Sheffield Wednesday	H	5-3	Hine 3,Chandler,Bell
6	Tottenham Hotspur	A	2-2	Hine,Lochhead (pen)
11	Arsenal	A	2-2	Chandler,Lochhead (pen)
13	Tottenham Hotspur	H	2-2	Chandler,Bell
18	Everton	A	4-3	Chandler 2,Hine,Duncan
25	Blackburn Rovers	H	4-0	Lochhead,Hine,Duncan,Chandler
Oct 2	Huddersfield Town	A	3-5	Bamber 2,Chandler
9	Sunderland	H	2-1	Chandler 2
16	Leeds United	H	3-2	Carr 3
23	Liverpool	A	0-1	
30	Sheffield United	H	2-2	Lochhead 2 (1pen)
Nov 6	Derby County	A	1-4	Lane
13	Manchester United	H	2-3	Lane,Hine
20	Bolton Wanderers	A	0-2	
27	Aston Villa	H	5-1	Chandler 5
Dec 4	Cardiff City	A	1-0	Lochhead
11	Burnley	H	0-3	
18	Newcastle United	A	1-1	Chandler
25	West Bromwich Albion	H	5-0	Chandler 5
27	West Bromwich Albion	A	1-0	Lochhead
Jan 1	Birmingham	A	1-2	Cringan (og)
15	West Ham United	H	3-0	Adcock,Bishop,Hebden (og)
22	Sheffield Wednesday	A	2-2	Chandler,Hine
29	Sunderland	A	0-3	
Feb 5	Everton	H	6-2	Chandler,Wadsworth 2,Hine 2,Lochhead
10	Arsenal	H	2-1	Adcock,Bishop
12	Blackburn Rovers	A	1-2	Lochhead (pen)
19	Huddersfield Town	H	2-4	Wadsworth,Duncan
Mar 5	Leeds United	A	1-1	Bishop
12	Liverpool	H	3-2	Wadsworth,Hine,Chandler
19	Sheffield United	A	3-0	Hine,Heathcock 2
26	Derby County	H	1-1	Duncan
Apr 2	Manchester United	A	0-1	
7	Cardiff City	H	3-1	Hine 2,Chandler
9	Bolton Wanderers	H	0-1	
15	Bury	A	0-0	
16	Aston Villa	A	0-2	
18	Bury	H	1-1	Hine
30	Burnley	A	1-1	Lochhead
May 7	Newcastle United	H	2-1	Lochhead 2 (1pen)

F.A. CUP

Jan 8	Middlesbrough	(3) A	3-5	Duncan,Hine,Chandler

LEICESTER CITY 1926-27
Back : Baxter,Bamber,Brown,Godderidge,Campbell,Findlay,Gibbs,Webb.
Middle: W.Fox(Masseur),G.Smith(Assistant Secretary),Carrigan,Watson,Carr,Viner,Lochhead,
Osborne,Garner,Gouch,E.King (Coach).
Front : E.Nixon (Assistant Trainer),Gibson,Adcock,Hine,Chandler,Duncan,Bell,Bishop,
Heathcock,Hackett,D.Gardner (Trainer).

	APP's		GOALS	
	FL	FAC	FL	FAC
Ken Campbell	39	1		
Adam Black	23			
Reg Osborne	38	1		
John Duncan	42	1	5	1
Norman Watson	34	1		
John Bamber	16		2	
Hughie Adcock	42	1	2	
Ernie Hine	39	1	16	1
Arthur Chandler	34	1	28	1
George Carr	19		3	
William Bell	23		3	
Arthur Lochhead	29	1	13 (5p)	
Pat Carrigan	10	1		
Jack Brown	18			
David Moyes	3			
Sid Bishop	26	1	3	
Billy Lane	4		2	
Albert Godderidge	2			
Harold Wadsworth	18	1	4	
Bert Heathcock	1		2	
Billy Findlay	1			
Jim McLaren	1			
Own Goals			2	

1927-28 LEAGUE DIVISION ONE
Final Position : 3rd

DATE	OPPONENTS	V	F.T.	SCORERS	McLaren	Brown	Osborne	Duncan	Carrigan	Bishop	Adcock	Hine	Chandler	Lochhead	Bell	Black	Findlay	Watson	Carr	Barry	Baxter	Lane	Gibson	Campbell	Callachan	Russell
Aug 27	Aston Villa	A	3-0	Adcock,Bishop,Bell	1	2	3	4	5	6	7	8	9	10	11											
29	Sheffield United	H	3-1	Duncan,Hine,Adcock	1		3	4	5	6	7	8	9	10	11	2										
Sep 3	Sunderland	H	3-3	Lochhead 2,Chandler	1		3	4	5	6	7	8	9	10	11	2										
5	Sheffield United	A	1-1	Chandler	1		3	4	5	6	7	8	9	10	11	2										
10	Derby County	A	1-2	Chandler	1		3	4	5		7	8	9	10	11	2	6									
17	West Ham United	H	2-3	Chandler,Adcock	1		3			6	7	8	9	10	11	2					5					
22	Tottenham Hotspur	A	1-2	Hine	1		3	4		6	7	8	9	10	11	2					5					
24	Portsmouth	A	0-2		1		3	4		6	7	8	9	10		2				11	5					
Oct 1	Manchester United	H	1-0	Adcock	1		3			6	7	8	9	10		2		5	4	11						
8	Liverpool	H	1-1	Hine	1		3			6	7	8	9	10		2		5	4	11						
15	Arsenal	A	2-2	Adcock,Hine	1		3			6	7	8	9	10		2		5	4	11						
22	Blackburn Rovers	A	0-0		1		3			6	7	8	9	10		2		5	4	11						
29	Cardiff City	H	4-1	Lochhead,Hine 2,Chandler	1		3			6	7	8	9	10		2		5	4	11						
Nov 5	Everton	A	1-7	Chandler	1		3		5		7	8	9	10		2	6		4	11						
12	Bolton Wanderers	H	4-2	Lochhead 2,Hine,Chandler	1		3			6	7	8	9	10		2		5	4	11						
19	Sheffield Wednesday	A	2-1	Chandler,Hine	1		3				7	8	9	10		2	6	5	4	11						
26	Newcastle United	H	3-0	Chandler 2,Lochhead	1		3				7	8	9	10		2	6	5	4	11						
Dec 3	Birmingham	A	2-0	Lochhead,Hine	1		3				7	8	9	10		2	6	5	4	11						
10	Middlesbrough	H	3-3	Chandler 2,Lochhead	1		3				7	8	9	10		2	6	5	4	11						
17	Huddersfield Town	A	1-3	Chandler	1		3				7	8	9	10		2	6	5	4	11						
24	Tottenham Hotspur	H	6-1	Bishop,Chandler 3,Lochhead,Adcock	1		3			6	7	8	9	10		2		5	4	11						
26	Burnley	H	5-0	Adcock,Bishop,Lochhead 2,Hine	1		3			6	7	8	9	10		2		5	4	11						
27	Burnley	A	1-5	McCluggage (og)	1		3			6	7	8	9	10		2		5	4	11						
31	Aston Villa	H	3-0	Hine 2,Chandler	1		3			6	7	8	9	10		2		5	4	11						
Jan 2	Bury	A	1-2	Chandler	1		3			6	7	8	9	10		2		5	4	11						
7	Sunderland	A	2-2	Lochhead,Barry	1		3			6	7	8	9	10		2		5	4	11						
21	Derby County	H	4-0	Chandler 2,Lochhead,Adcock	1		3	4		6	7	8	9	10		2		5		11						
Feb 4	Portsmouth	H	6-2	Lochhead 2,Hine,Chandler 2,Barry	1		3	4		6	7	8	9	10		2		5		11						
11	Manchester United	A	2-5	Chandler,Duncan	1		3	4			7	8	9	10		2	6	5		11						
25	Arsenal	H	3-2	Bishop,Adcock,Duncan	1		3	4		6	7	8	9	10		2		5		11						
Mar 10	Cardiff City	A	0-3		1		3			6	7	8		10		2		5	4	11		9				
12	West Ham United	A	0-4		1		3			6	7	8	9			2		5	4	11			10			
17	Everton	H	1-0	Adcock	1		3	4		6	7	8	9	10		2		5		11						
24	Bolton Wanderers	A	3-3	Hine 2,Chandler	1		3	4		6	7	8	9	10		2		5		11						
31	Sheffield Wednesday	H	2-2	Hine,Chandler	1		3			6	7	8	9	10		2		5	4	11						
Apr 7	Newcastle United	A	5-1	Chandler 4,Hine						6	7	8	9	10		2		5	4	11				1	3	
9	Bury	H	2-2	Hine,Lochhead						6	7	8	9	10		2		5		11				1	3	
14	Birmingham	H	3-0	Barry,Chandler,Hine						6	7	8	9	10		2		5		11				1	3	4
21	Middlesbrough	A	1-1	Carr			3			6	7	8	9	10		2		5	4	11				1		
25	Liverpool	A	1-1	Chandler			3			6	7		9	10		2		5	4	11			8	1		
28	Huddersfield Town	H	1-2	Carr			3			6	7		9	10		2		5	4	11				1		
30	Blackburn Rovers	H	6-0	Hine,Chandler 3,Barry,Lochhead	1		3			6	7	8	9	10		2		5	4	11						

F.A. CUP

DATE	OPPONENTS		V	F.T.	SCORERS	McLaren	Osborne	Duncan	Bishop	Adcock	Hine	Chandler	Lochhead	Black	Carr	Barry
Jan 14	Hull City	(3)	A	1-0	Barry	1	3	5	6	7	8	9	10	2	4	11
28	Reading	(4)	A	1-0	Adcock	1	3	5	6	7	8	9	10	2	4	11
Feb 18	Tottenham Hotspur	(5)	H	0-3		1	3	5	6	7	8	9	10	2	4	11

LEICESTER CITY 1927-28
(Pictured v Birmingham on 3rd December)
Back : Carr,Black,McLaren,D.Gardner *(Trainer)*,Osborne,Lochhead.
Front : Baxter,Adcock,Hine,Chandler,Findlay,Barry.

	APP's FL	APP's FAC	GOALS FL	GOALS FAC
Jim McLaren	36	3		
Jack Brown	8			
Reg Osborne	32	3		
John Duncan	21	3	3	
Pat Carrigan	6			
Sid Bishop	23	3	4	
Hughie Adcock	42	3	10	1
Ernie Hine	41	3	20	
Arthur Chandler	41	3	34	
Arthur Lochhead	41	3	17	
William Bell	7		1	
Adam Black	41	3		
Billy Findlay	28			
Norman Watson	10			
George Carr	35	3	2	
Len Barry	34	3	4	1
James Baxter	3			
Billy Lane	1			
Tom Gibson	2			
Ken Campbell	6			
Harry Callachan	3			
Andy Russell	1			
Own Goals				1

1928-29 LEAGUE DIVISION ONE
Final Position : 2nd

DATE	OPPONENTS	V	F.T.	SCORERS	Campbell	Black	Brown	Findlay	Carr	Duncan	Adcock	Hine	Chandler	Lochhead	Barry	Osborne	Baxter	Gibson	McLaren	Watson	Ritchie	Carrigan	Bell	Langford	Lovatt
Aug 25	Manchester United	A	1-1	Hine	1	2	3	4	5	6	7	8	9	10	11										
27	Birmingham	H	5-3	Hine,Chandler 2,Lochhead 2	1	2	3	4	5	6	7	8	9	10	11										
Sep 1	Leeds United	H	4-4	Barry,Hine,Chandler 2	1	2	3	4	5	6	7	8	9	10	11										
8	Liverpool	A	3-6	Baxter,Chandler,Gibson	1	2		4	5		7	8	9		11		3	6	10						
10	Birmingham	A	0-1		1	2		4	5		7	8	9		11		3	6	10						
15	West Ham United	H	5-0	Barry,Chandler 2,Lochhead,Hine		2			5	4	7	8	9	10	11	3			1	6					
22	Newcastle United	A	0-1			2			6	4	7	8	9	10	11				1	5					
29	Burnley	H	1-1	Chandler		2			5	4	7	8	9	10	11	3			1						
Oct 6	Cardiff City	A	2-1	Carr,Hine		2		4	10		7	8	9		11	3			1	6	5				
13	Sheffield United	H	3-1	Chandler 2,Hine		2		4	10		7	8	9		11	3			1	6	5				
20	Portsmouth	H	10-0	Hine 3,Barry,Chandler 6		2	3	4	5		7	8	9	10	11				1	6					
27	Manchester City	A	3-2	Lochhead,Adcock,Hine		2	3	4	5		7	8	9	10	11				1	6					
Nov 3	Sheffield Wednesday	H	1-1	Hine		2	3	4	5		7	8	9	10	11				1	6					
10	Derby County	A	2-5	Hine,Lochhead		2	3	4	5		7	8	9	10	11				1	6					
17	Sunderland	H	1-0	Chandler		2	3	4	5	8	7		9	10	11				1	6					
24	Blackburn Rovers	A	1-1	Chandler		2	3	4	5		7	8	9	10					1	6	11				
Dec 1	Arsenal	H	1-1	Hine	1	2	3	4	5		7	8	9	10					6		11				
8	Everton	A	1-3	Chandler		2	3	4	5		7	8	9	10	11				1	6					
15	Huddersfield Town	H	4-1	Hine 2,Chandler 2		2	3	4	5		7	8	9	10	11				1	6					
22	Bolton Wanderers	A	0-5			2	3	4	5		7	8	9	10	11				1	6					
25	Bury	A	1-3	Chandler		2			5	4	7	8	9	10	11	3			1	6					
26	Bury	H	5-2	Hine 3,Adcock,Lochhead		2			5	4	7	8	9	10	11	3			1	6					
29	Manchester United	H	2-1	Hine 2		2	3		5		7	8	9	10	11		4		1	6					
Jan 5	Leeds United	A	3-4	Chandler,Lochhead,Hine		2	3		5		7	8	9	10	11		4		1	6					
19	Liverpool	H	2-0	Hine 2 (1pen)		2			5		7	8	9	10	11	3	4		1	6					
Feb 2	Newcastle United	H	1-1	Adcock			2		5		7	8	9		11	3	4		1	6	10				
9	Burnley	A	1-0	Chandler			2		5	4	7	8		9	11	3			1	6	10				
21	Cardiff City	H	2-0	Lovatt,Hine (pen)		2	3			4	7			10	11				1	6	5		9		
23	Sheffield United	A	4-1	Lochhead,Chandler 2,Hine		2				4			8	9	10	11		1	3	6	5		7		
Mar 4	West Ham United	A	1-2	Lovatt		2	3			4			8	9	10	11		1		6	5		7		
9	Manchester City	H	3-2	Hine 2,Lochhead		2	3		5	4	7	8	9	10	11				1	6					
16	Sheffield Wednesday	A	0-1			2	3		5	4	7	8	9	10	11				1	6					
23	Derby County	H	1-0	Hine		2	3		5	4	7	8	9	10	11				1	6					
30	Sunderland	A	2-1	Lochhead,Chandler		2	3	4	5	8	7		9	10	11				1	6					
Apr 1	Aston Villa	H	4-1	Adcock (pen),Lochhead,Duncan,Chandler		2	3		5	8	7		9	10	11				1	4	6				
2	Aston Villa	A	2-4	Chandler 2	1	2	3		5	8	7		9	10	11					4	6				
6	Blackburn Rovers	H	2-1	Chandler 2	1	2	3	4	5	8	7		9	10	11						6				
10	Portsmouth	A	0-0			2	3	4	5	8	7		9	10	11				1		6				
13	Arsenal	A	1-1	Chandler		2	3	4	5	8	7		9	10	11				1		6				
20	Everton	H	4-1	Chandler,Hine 2,Lochhead		2	3		5		7	8	9	10	11				1	4	6				
27	Huddersfield Town	A	1-1	Duncan		2	3		5	4	7	8	9	10	11				1		6				
May 4	Bolton Wanderers	H	6-1	Lochhead,Lovatt 3,Hine 2		2	3		5	4	7	8		10	11				1		6				9

F.A. CUP

					Campbell	Black	Brown	Findlay	Carr	Duncan	Adcock	Hine	Chandler	Lochhead	Barry	Osborne	Baxter	Gibson	McLaren	Watson	Ritchie
Jan 12	Lincoln City	(3) A	1-0	Lochhead		2	3		5		7	8	9	10	11		4		1	6	
26	Swansea Town	(4) H	1-0	Lochhead		2			5		7	8	9	10	11	3	4		1	6	
Feb 16	Bolton Wanderers	(5) H	1-2	Lochhead		2			5	4	7	8	9	10	11	3			1	6	

LEICESTER CITY 1928-29

Back : High,J.Smith,Brown,A.Smith,Campbell,G.Smith (Assistant Secretary),McLaren,Callachan,Wiggins,Carrigan.
Middle : W.Fox (Masseur),Chandler,Langford,Black,Osborne,Watson,
W.Orr(Manager),Garner,Carr,Raynor,Cairns,Bushell,D.Gardner (Trainer).
Front : E.Nixon (Assistant Trainer),Lochhead,Findlay,Hine,Duncan,Adcock,Lovatt,Barry,Bell,E.King (Coach).
On Ground: Wyness,Baxter.

	APP's		GOALS	
	FL	FAC	FL	FAC
Ken Campbell	8			
Adam Black	40	3		
Jack Brown	31	1		
Billy Findlay	19			
George Carr	39	3	1	
John Duncan	27	1	2	
Hughie Adcock	40	3	4 (1p)	
Ernie Hine	35	3	32 (2p)	
Arthur Chandler	40	3	34	
Arthur Lochhead	36	3	13	3
Len Barry	40	3	3	
Reg Osborne	12	2		
James Baxter	2		1	
Tom Gibson	2		1	
Jim McLaren	34	3		
Norman Watson	16	2		
George Ritchie	28	3		
Pat Carrigan	5			
William Bell	2			
Walter Langford	2			
Harry Lovatt	4		5	

1929-30 LEAGUE DIVISION ONE
Final Position : 8th

DATE	OPPONENTS	V	F.T.	SCORERS	McLaren	Black	Brown	Duncan	Carr	Ritchie	Adcock	Hine	Chandler	Smith	Barry	Wright	Carrigan	Langford	Watson	Lovatt	Lochhead	Findlay	Bushell	Woolliscroft	Harrison	Mandy	Bell	Osborne	Beby	Heywood
Aug 31	Huddersfield Town	A	2-3	Chandler 2	1	2	3	4	5	6	7	8	9	10	11															
Sep 2	Manchester United	H	4-1	Hine 2,Carr,Chandler		2	3	4	10	6	7	8	9		11	1	5													
7	Sheffield United	H	3-3	Chandler 3	1	2	3	4	10	6	7	8	9		11		5													
11	Manchester United	A	1-2	Barry		2	3	4	5	6	7	8	9		11	1		10												
14	Newcastle United	A	1-2	Hine		2	3	4	5	6	7	8	9		11	1			5											
21	Blackburn Rovers	H	1-1	Chandler	1	2	3	4	5	6	7	8	10		11					9										
28	Middlesbrough	A	2-0	Adcock,Chandler		2	3	4	5	6	7	8	9		11	1					10									
Oct 5	Liverpool	H	2-1	Lochhead,Hine		2	3	4	5	6	7	8	9		11	1					10									
12	West Ham United	A	2-1	Hine,Barry		2	3	4	5	6	7	8	9		11	1					10									
17	Birmingham	H	2-1	Chandler,Bushell		2	3	8	5	6			9		11	1					10		4	7						
19	Aston Villa	A	0-3			2	3	8	5	6			9		11	1					10		4	7						
26	Leeds United	H	2-2	Hine,Lochhead		2	3	4			7	8	9		11	1	5		6		10									
Nov 2	Sheffield Wednesday	A	0-4			2	3	4					9		11	1	5		6		10		7	8						
9	Portsmouth	H	0-5			2	3		5			7	8	9	11	1			6		10	4								
16	Sunderland	A	1-2	Hine	1	2	3	4	5	6	7	8			11			9	10											
23	Bolton Wanderers	H	5-2	Lovatt 3,Adcock,Duncan	1	2	3	4			6	7	8		11				10	5	9									
30	Everton	A	5-4	Langford 2,Lovatt,Barry,Adcock	1	2	3	4			6	7			11				10	5	9	8								
Dec 7	Derby County	H	0-0		1	2	3	4			6	7	8		11					9	10			5						
14	Manchester City	A	2-3	Chandler 2	1	2	3	4			6	7	8	9	11						10			5						
21	Burnley	H	4-3	Hine 2,Chandler,Duncan	1	2	3	4			6	7	8	9	11						10			5						
25	Grimsby Town	A	4-1	Hine 2,Chandler,Lochhead	1	2	3	4	5	6	7	8	9		11						10									
26	Grimsby Town	H	1-0	Chandler		2	3	4	5	6	7	8	9		11						10				1					
28	Huddersfield Town	H	1-2	Adcock		2	3	4	5	6	7	8	9								10				1	11				
Jan 4	Sheffield United	A	1-7	Lochhead		2	3	4			6	7	8	9	11						10			5	1					
18	Newcastle United	H	6-1	Chandler 3,Hine 2,Langford	1	2		4			6	7	8	9	11			10						5				3			
27	Blackburn Rovers	A	1-3	Adcock	1	2		4			6	7	8	9	11			10						5				3			
Feb 1	Middlesbrough	H	4-1	Chandler 2,Hine 2	1	2		4				7	8	9	11					6	10			5				3			
8	Liverpool	A	1-1	Lochhead	1	2		4				7	8	9	11					6	10			5				3			
15	Burnley	A	1-1	Chandler	1	2		4				7	8	9	11					6	10			5				3			
20	West Ham United	H	1-2	Lochhead	1	2		4				7	8	9	11					6	10			5				3			
22	Aston Villa	H	4-3	Chandler 3,Lochhead	1	2	3	4				7	8	9	11					6	10			5							
Mar 1	Leeds United	A	2-1	Hine 2	1	2	3	4				7	8	9	11					6	10			5							
8	Sheffield Wednesday	H	2-1	Hine,Chandler		2	3	4				7	8	9	11					6	10			5							
15	Portsmouth	A	0-3			2	3	4				7	8	9	11	1				6	10			5							
22	Sunderland	H	1-2	Chandler		2	3	4				7	8	9	11	1				6	10			5							
29	Bolton Wanderers	A	0-1		1	2	3	4				7	8	9	11					6	10			5							
Apr 5	Everton	H	5-4	Lochhead,Chandler 3,Barry	1	2	3	4				7	8	9	11					6	10			5							
12	Derby County	A	2-2	Chandler 2	1	2	3	4				7	8	9	11					6	10			5							
18	Arsenal	A	1-1	Chandler	1	2	3			4	7	8	9		11					6	10			5							
19	Manchester City	H	3-1	Duncan,Hine,Chandler		2	3	4				7	8	9	11	1				6	10			5							
21	Arsenal	H	6-6	Adcock 2,Lochhead 2,Hine,Barry		2	3	4				7	8	9	11	1				6	10			5							
May 3	Birmingham	A	0-3			2	3	4				7	8	9	11					6	10								1	5

F.A. CUP

DATE	OPPONENTS	V		F.T.	SCORERS	McLaren	Black	Brown	Duncan	Carr	Ritchie	Adcock	Hine	Chandler	Smith	Barry	Wright	Carrigan	Langford	Watson	Lovatt	Lochhead	Findlay	Bushell	Woolliscroft	Harrison
Jan 11	Sheffield United	(3)	A	1-2	Hine	1	2	3	4			6	7	8	9		11					10			5	

LEICESTER CITY 1929-30
(Pictured v Arsenal on 18th April)
Back : Watson,Carr,Lochhead,Brown,McLaren,Harrison,Black,D.Gardner *(Trainer)*.
Front : Adcock,Hine,Chandler,Ritchie,Barry.

	APP's		GOALS	
	FL	FAC	FL	FAC
Jim McLaren	23	1		
Adam Black	42	1		
Jack Brown	36	1		
John Duncan	40	1	3	
George Carr	16		1	
George Ritchie	24	1		
Hughie Adcock	39	1	7	
Ernie Hine	38	1	20	1
Arthur Chandler	38	1	32	
Sep Smith	1			
Len Barry	41	1	5	
Joe Wright	15			
Pat Carrigan	4			
Walter Langford	5		3	
Norman Watson	22			
Harry Lovatt	5		4	
Arthur Lochhead	33	1	10	
Billy Findlay	3			
William Bushell	3		1	
Arthur Woolliscroft	1			
Albert Harrison	21	1		
Aubrey Mandy	3			
William Bell	1			
Reg Osborne	6			
John Beby	1			
Roger Heywood	1			

1930-31
LEAGUE DIVISION ONE
Final Position : 16th

DATE	OPPONENTS	V	F.T.	SCORERS	McLaren	Black	Brown	Ritchie	Harrison	Watson	Adcock	Hine	Chandler	Lochhead	Barry	Beby	Osborne	Carr	Smith	Heywood	Bulling	Lovatt	Findlay	Richards	Dumbrell	Wiggins
Aug 30	Derby County	H	1-1	Ritchie	1	2	3	4	5	6	7	8	9	10	11											
Sep 1	Birmingham	H	2-1	Chandler,Hine		2	3	4	5	6	7	8	9	10	11	1										
6	Manchester City	A	2-0	Chandler,Cowan (og)		2	3	4	5	6	7	8	9	10	11	1										
8	Sheffield United	H	2-2	Adcock,Hine		2	3	4	5	6	7	8	9	10	11	1										
13	Portsmouth	H	3-1	Chandler,Lochhead 2		2	3	6	5	4	7	8	9	10	11	1										
20	Arsenal	A	1-4	Hine		2	3	6	5	4	7	8	9	10	11	1										
24	Sheffield United	A	2-0	Chandler,Lochhead	1	2	3	6	5	4	7	8	9	10	11											
27	Blackburn Rovers	H	3-1	Chandler,Adcock 2	1	2	3	6	5	4	7	8	9	10	11											
Oct 4	Blackpool	A	4-5	Lochhead,Hine 2,Harrison	1	2	3	6	5	4	7	8	9	10	11											
11	Leeds United	H	4-0	Hine 3(1pen),Chandler	1	2		6		4	7	8	9		11		3	5	10							
18	Huddersfield Town	A	1-4	Adcock	1	2		6		4	7	8	9		11		3	5	10							
25	Aston Villa	H	4-1	Smith,Hine 3	1	2		6	5	4	7	8	9		11		3		10							
Nov 1	Grimsby Town	A	2-8	Chandler,Watson	1	2		6	5	4	7	8	9	10	11		3									
8	Manchester United	H	5-4	Lochhead 2,Hine 2,Chandler		2		6		4	7	8	9	10	11	1	3	5								
15	Liverpool	A	1-3	Lochhead		2				4	7	8	9	10	11	1	3	5		6						
22	Sheffield Wednesday	H	2-5	Chandler 2		2				4	7	8	9	10	11	1	3	5		6						
29	West Ham United	A	0-2			2				4	7	8		10	11	1	3	5		6	9					
Dec 6	Middlesbrough	H	0-3			2	3			4	7	8	9		11	1		10	5	6						
13	Newcastle United	A	2-5	Ritchie,Lochhead		2	3	6			7	8	9	10	11	1		5					4			
20	Bolton Wanderers	H	2-1	Chandler 2		2	3	6			7	8	9	10	11	1		5					4			
25	Sunderland	A	5-2	Hine 3,Barry 2		2	3	6			7	8	9	10	11	1		5					4			
26	Sunderland	H	1-1	Hine		2	3	6			7	8	9	10	11	1		5					4			
27	Derby County	A	0-1			2	3	6			7	8	9	10	11	1		5					4			
Jan 3	Manchester City	H	3-2	Chandler,Hine 2(1pen)		2	3	6			7	8	9	10	11	1		5					4			
17	Portsmouth	A	1-2	Adcock		2		6		4	7	8	9			1	3	10	11	5						
Feb 5	Arsenal	H	2-7	Hine 2(1pen)		2		6			7	8	9	10		1	3			5			4	11		
7	Blackpool	H	6-0	Adcock,Chandler,Hine 4	1	2		6			7	8	9	10			3			5			4	11		
18	Leeds United	A	3-1	Hine 2,Adcock	1	2		6			7	8	9	10			3			5			4	11		
21	Huddersfield Town	H	1-2	Hine	1	2		6			7	8	9	10			3			5			4	11		
28	Aston Villa	A	2-4	Smith,Richards	1	2		6		4	7		9	10			3		8	5				11		
Mar 2	Blackburn Rovers	A	0-3		1			6		4	7		9	10			3		8	5				11	2	
7	Grimsby Town	H	0-1			2		6			7	8	9		11	1	3	10		5			4			
21	Liverpool	H	3-2	Hine 2(1pen),Adcock		2		6			7	8			11	1	3	10		5			4			9
25	Manchester United	A	0-0			2		6			7	8		10	11	1	3			5			4			9
28	Sheffield Wednesday	A	0-4			2		6			7	8	9		11	1	3	10		5			4			
Apr 4	West Ham United	H	1-1	Chandler	1	2	3	6			7	8	9	10	11					5			4			
6	Chelsea	A	0-1		1	2		6			7		9	10	11		3		8	5			4			
7	Chelsea	H	2-1	Chandler,Lochhead	1	2		6			7	8	9	10	11		3			5			4			
11	Middlesbrough	A	2-2	Barry,Lochhead	1	2		6			7		9	10	11		3		8	5			4			
18	Newcastle United	H	3-1	Chandler,Adcock,Lochhead	1	2		6			7	8	9	10	11		3			5			4			
25	Bolton Wanderers	A	1-4	Chandler	1	2				6	7	8	9	10	11		3			5			4			
May 2	Birmingham	A	1-2	Hine	1	2				6	7	8	9	10	11		3			5			4			

F.A. CUP

DATE	OPPONENTS	V	F.T.	SCORERS	McLaren	Black	Brown	Ritchie	Harrison	Watson	Adcock	Hine	Chandler	Lochhead	Barry	Beby	Osborne	Carr	Smith	Heywood	Bulling	Lovatt	Findlay	Richards	Dumbrell	Wiggins
Jan 10	Brighton & Hove Albion (3)	H	1-2	Lochhead		2	3	6			7	8	9	10	11	1		5					4			

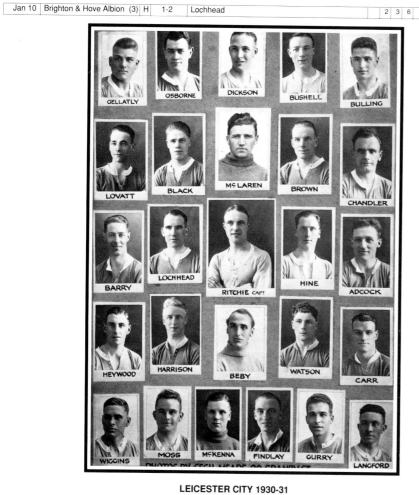

LEICESTER CITY 1930-31

	APP's		GOALS	
	FL	FAC	FL	FAC
Jim McLaren	20			
Adam Black	41	1		
Jack Brown	17	1		
George Ritchie	36	1	2	
Albert Harrison	11		1	
Norman Watson	23		1	
Hughie Adcock	42	1	9	
Ernie Hine	40	1	31 (4p)	
Arthur Chandler	37	1	18	
Arthur Lochhead	35	1	11	1
Len Barry	35	1	3	
John Beby	22	1		
Reg Osborne	22			
George Carr	11	1		
Sep Smith	11		2	
Roger Heywood	21			
Jim Bulling	4			
Harry Lovatt	1			
Billy Findlay	21	1		
Percy Richards	6		1	
George Dumbrell	4			
Joe Wiggins	2			
Own Goals				1

1931-32 LEAGUE DIVISION ONE
Final Position : 19th

DATE	OPPONENTS	V	F.T.	SCORERS	McLaren	Black	Osborne	Bulling	Heywood	Ritchie	Adcock	Hine	Smith	Lochhead	Barry	Wiggins	Findlay	Jackson	Watson	Calder	Chandler	Langford	Beby	Carr	Edwards	Dumbrell	Richards	Keeley	McKenna
Aug 29	Aston Villa	A	2-3	Smith 2	1	2	3	4	5	6	7	8	9	10	11														
31	Middlesbrough	H	2-2	Smith,Barry	1	2	3	4	5	6	7	8	9	10	11														
Sep 5	Manchester City	H	4-0	Hine,Smith 2,Ritchie	1	2	3	4	5	6	7	8	10		11	9													
7	Huddersfield Town	A	1-2	Hine (pen)	1	2	3	6	5		7	8	10		11	9	4												
12	Liverpool	H	2-1	Smith,Hine	1	2	3	6	5			8	10		11	9	4	7											
19	Grimsby Town	A	0-3		1	2	3	6	5			8	10		11		4		7	9									
26	Chelsea	H	1-0	Odell (og)	1	2	3		5		7	8	10	6	11		4				9								
Oct 3	West Ham United	A	4-1	Hine 2,Chandler 2	1	2	3		5		7	8	10	6	11		4				9								
10	Sheffield Wednesday	H	3-2	Hine 2,Barry	1	2	3		5		7	8		10	11		4		6		9								
15	Huddersfield Town	H	2-4	Chandler,Smith	1	2	3		5		7	8	10	11		4		6		9									
17	Derby County	A	1-1	Langford	1	2	3		5		7		8	11		4		6		9	10							
24	Arsenal	H	1-2	Barry	1	2	3		5		7	8		10	11		4		6		9								
31	Blackpool	A	3-2	Lochhead,Chandler 2	1	2	3		5	6	7	8		10	11		4				9								
Nov 7	Sheffield United	H	4-3	Lochhead 2,Chandler 2	1	2	3	4	5	6	7			10	11	8					9								
14	Birmingham	A	0-2		1	2	3		5	6	7	8		10	11		4				9								
21	Sunderland	H	5-0	Hine 2,Barry,Chandler,Osborne (pen)	1	2	3		5	6	7	8	10		11		4				9								
28	Everton	A	2-9	Hine,Barry	1	2	3		5	6	7	8		10	11		4				9								
Dec 5	West Bromwich Albion	H	2-3	Hine 2		2	3			6	7	8		10	11		4				9		1	5					
12	Blackburn Rovers	A	0-6		1	2	3		5	6	7		8	10	11						9				4				
25	Bolton Wanderers	A	0-1		1	2			5	4		8	10					7			9	6				3	11		
26	Bolton Wanderers	H	1-3	Hine	1	2			5	4		8	10					7			9	6				3	11		
Jan 2	Aston Villa	H	3-8	Smith,Hine (pen),Langford	1	2			5	4		8	10		11			7			9	6				3			
16	Manchester City	A	1-5	Hine	1	2	3		5	6	7	8	10		11		4				9								
27	Liverpool	A	3-3	Hine 2 (1pen),Adcock		2	3		5	6	7	8		10	11						9		1		4				
30	Grimsby Town	H	1-2	Richards		2		4	5	6	7	8		10							9		1			3	11		
Feb 4	Portsmouth	H	2-1	Smith 2		2			5	6	7	8	9	10			4						1			3	11		
6	Chelsea	A	0-1		1	2			5	6	7	8	10		11						9				4	3			
18	West Ham United	H	2-1	Chandler,Barry	1	2			5	6	7	8		10	11						9					3		4	
20	Sheffield Wednesday	A	1-3	Chandler	1	2			5	6	7	8	10		11						9					3		4	
27	Derby County	H	1-1	Smith	1	2			5	6	7		8	10	11				4		9					3			
Mar 5	Arsenal	A	1-2	Barry	1	2			5	6	7	8		10	11				4		9					3			
12	Blackpool	H	2-2	Barry,Hine (pen)	1	2			5	6	7	8		10	11				4		9					3			
19	Sheffield United	A	2-2	Chandler,Lochhead	1	2			5	6	7	8		10	11				4		9					3			
25	Newcastle United	A	2-3	Lochhead,Chandler	1	2			5	6	7	8		10	11				4		9					3			
26	Birmingham	H	3-1	Adcock,Lochhead 2		2			5	6	7	8		10	11				4		9					3		1	
29	Newcastle United	H	4-2	Ritchie,Hine 3		2	3		5	6	7	8		10	11				4		9		1						
Apr 2	Sunderland	A	1-4	Osborne (pen)		2	3		5	6	7	8		10	11				4		9		1						
9	Everton	H	0-1		1	2	3		5	6	7		10	8	11		4				9								
16	West Bromwich Albion	A	2-1	Lochhead,Hine	1	2	3		5	6	7	9	8	10	11											4			
23	Blackburn Rovers	H	1-0	Ritchie	1	2	3		5	6	7	8	9	10	11											4			
30	Portsmouth	A	1-0	Lochhead	1	2	3		5	6	7	8		10	11						9					4			
May 7	Middlesbrough	A	1-1	Barry	1	2	3		5	6	7	8		10	11						9					4			

F.A. CUP

DATE	OPPONENTS		V	F.T.	SCORERS	McLaren	Black	Osborne	Bulling	Heywood	Ritchie	Adcock	Hine	Smith	Lochhead	Barry	Wiggins	Findlay	Jackson	Watson	Calder	Chandler	Langford	Beby	Carr	Edwards	Dumbrell	Richards	Keeley	McKenna
Jan 9	Crook Town	(3)	A	7-0	Hine 5,Langford,Chandler	1	2			5	6	7	8			11		4				9	10				3			
23	Port Vale	(4)	A	2-1	Hine,Chandler	1	2	3		5	6	7	8		10	11		4				9								
Feb 13	Newcastle United	(5)	A	1-3	Lochhead	1	2			5	6	7	8		10	11		4				9					3			

Note : Jan 9th,drawn away, but switched to Filbert Street

LEICESTER CITY 1931-32
Back : Smith,Dumbrell,Black,Beby,D.Gardner*(Trainer)*, McLaren,Heywood,Watson,Osborne.
Front : Barry,Findlay,Chandler,Hine,Adcock,Lochhead,Carr,Richards.
On Ground : Wiggins,Langford.

	APP's		GOALS	
	FL	FAC	FL	FAC
Jim McLaren	35	3		
Adam Black	42	3		
Reg Osborne	28	1	2 (2p)	
Jim Bulling	8			
Roger Heywood	41	3		
George Ritchie	33	3	3	
Hughie Adcock	37	3	2	
Ernie Hine	36	3	22 (4p)	6
Sep Smith	22		11	
Arthur Lochhead	31	2	9	1
Len Barry	38	3	9	
Joe Wiggins	3			
Billy Findlay	18	3		
Billy Jackson	4			
Norman Watson	13			
John Calder	1			
Arthur Chandler	33	3	12	2
Walter Langford	4	1	2	1
John Beby	6			
George Carr	1			
Leslie Edwards	3			
George Dumbrell	18	2		
Percy Richards	4		1	
Ernest Keeley	2			
Jim McKenna	1			
Own Goals				1

1932-33 LEAGUE DIVISION ONE
Final Position : 19th

Date	Opponents	V	F.T.	Scorers	Calvert	Black	Osborne	Smith	Heywood	Ritchie	Adcock	Lowery	Paterson	Lochhead	Liddle	Chandler	McLaren J	Barry	Keeley	Dumbrell	Miles	Young	Gurry	Campbell	Maw	Langford	Wiggins	McLaren A	Wood
Aug 27	Sheffield United	H	1-1	Paterson	1	2	3	4	5	6	7	8	9	10	11														
29	Huddersfield Town	A	1-4	Chandler	1	2	3	4	5	6	7	8		10	11	9													
Sep 3	Wolverhampton Wanderers	A	1-1	Lowery		2	3	4	5	6	7	8		10		9	1	11											
5	Huddersfield Town	H	3-1	Ritchie,Lochhead 2		2	3	4	5	6	7	8		10		9	1	11											
10	Newcastle United	H	0-3			2	3	4	5	6	7	8	9	10			1	11											
17	Aston Villa	A	2-4	Paterson,Heywood		2	3	4	5	6	7	8	9	10			1	11											
24	Middlesbrough	H	1-1	Lochhead		2	3	4	5	6	7	8	9	10			1	11											
Oct 1	Bolton Wanderers	A	0-5		1	2	3	4	5	6	7	8		10	11	9													
8	Liverpool	H	1-2	Liddle	1	2	3	10	5	6	7	8			11	9		4											
15	Blackpool	A	1-2	Paterson	1	2		4	5	6	7	8	9	10	11				3										
22	Everton	H	2-2	Liddle,Miles	1	2		4	5	6				10	11	9			3	8	7								
29	Arsenal	A	2-8	Chandler,Ritchie	1	2		4	5	6		8				9			3		7	10							
Nov 5	Sheffield Wednesday	H	0-0			2		4	5	6		8			11	9	1			3	7	10							
12	Leeds United	A	1-1	Chandler		2			5	6		8		10	11	9	1			3	7	4							
19	Blackburn Rovers	H	1-1	Lochhead		2			5	6		8		10	11	9	1			3	7	4							
26	Derby County	A	2-3	Lochhead,Smith		2	3	8	5	6				10		9	1	11			7	4							
Dec 3	Manchester City	H	1-2	Chandler		2			5	6			9	10		8	1	11		3	7		4						
10	Sunderland	A	1-2	Smith		2		8	5	6				10		9	1	11		3	7		4						
17	Birmingham	H	2-2	Smith (pen),Campbell		2		8	5	6	7			10	11		1			3			4	9					
24	West Bromwich Albion	A	3-4	Lochhead,Campbell,Smith		2		8	5	6	7			10	11		1			3			4	9					
26	Portsmouth	A	1-2	Lochhead		2		8	5	6	7			10	11		1			3			4	9					
27	Portsmouth	H	2-1	Campbell,Smith (pen)		2		8	5	6	7			10	11		1			3			4	9					
31	Sheffield United	A	2-5	Liddle,Adcock		2		8	5	6	7			10	11		1			3			4	9					
Jan 7	Wolverhampton Wanderers	H	2-2	Campbell,Liddle		2			5	6	7				11		1			3			4	9	8	10			
21	Newcastle United	A	1-2	Campbell	1	2		10	5		7				11							4	6	9	8	3			
Feb 4	Middlesbrough	A	1-1	Barry		2	3	4	5	6	7			10			1	11						9	8				
9	Aston Villa	H	3-0	Maw 3		2	3	4	5	6	7			10			1	11						9	8				
11	Bolton Wanderers	H	2-0	Maw,Campbell		2	3	4	5		7			10			1	11					6	9	8				
18	Liverpool	A	2-1	Campbell,Heywood		2	3	4	5	6	7			10			1	11						9	8				
Mar 8	Everton	A	3-6	Maw,Campbell,Cresswell (og)		2	3	4	5	6	7			10				11						9	8			1	
11	Arsenal	H	1-1	Lochhead		2		4	5	6	7			10				11						9	8		3	1	
18	Sheffield Wednesday	A	1-4	Lochhead		2		4	5	6	7			10				11						9	8		3	1	
25	Leeds United	H	3-1	Paterson 2,Lochhead		2		4	5	6	7		9	10	11										8		3	1	
30	Blackpool	H	3-0	Paterson,Lochhead,Maw		2		4	5	6	7		9	10	11										8			1	3
Apr 1	Blackburn Rovers	A	1-1	Liddle		2		4	5	6	7		9	10	11										8			1	3
8	Derby County	H	4-0	Adcock,Paterson 2,Maw		2			5	6	7		9	10	11								4		8			1	3
14	Chelsea	A	1-4	Paterson		2		4	5	6	7		9	10	11										8			1	3
15	Manchester City	A	1-4	Cann (og)		2		4	5	6	7		9	10	11										8			1	3
18	Chelsea	H	1-1	Liddle		2			5	6	7			10	11								4	9	8			1	3
22	Sunderland	H	4-2	Maw 2,Lochhead,Black		2		4	5	6	7		9	10	11										8			1	3
29	Birmingham	A	4-0	Ritchie,Paterson,Maw 2		2		4	5	6	7		9	10	11										8			1	3
May 6	West Bromwich Albion	H	6-2	Liddle 2,Maw 3,Paterson		2		4	5	6	7		9	10	11										8			1	3

F.A. CUP

Date	Opponents		V	F.T.	Scorers	Calvert	Black	Osborne	Smith	Heywood	Ritchie	Adcock	Lowery	Paterson	Lochhead	Liddle	Chandler	McLaren J	Barry	Keeley	Dumbrell	Miles	Young	Gurry	Campbell	Maw	Langford	Wiggins	McLaren A	Wood
Jan 14	Everton	(3)	H	2-3	Campbell 2	1	2	3	10	5	6	7				11									9	8	4			

LEICESTER CITY 1932-33

	APP's		GOALS	
	FL	FAC	FL	FAC
Joe Calvert	8	1		
Adam Black	41	1	1	
Reg Osborne	16	1		
Sep Smith	37	1	5 (2p)	
Roger Heywood	41	1	2	
George Ritchie	40	1	3	
Hughie Adcock	35	1	2	
Ted Lowery	10		1	
Jim Paterson	19		11	
Arthur Lochhead	37		12	
Danny Liddle	27	1	8	
Arthur Chandler	13		4	
Jim McLaren	21			
Len Barry	15		1	
Ernest Keeley	2			
George Dumbrell	14			
Idris Miles	7		1	
Archie Young	5			
Jack Gurry	14			
John Campbell	14	1	8	2
Arthur Maw	18	1	14	
Walter Langford	2	1		
Joe Wiggins	4			
Sandy McLaren	13			
Sandy Wood	9			
Own Goals				2

1933-34 LEAGUE DIVISION ONE
Final Position : 17th

DATE	OPPONENTS	V	F.T.	SCORERS	McLaren	Black	Jones	Smith	Heywood	Ritchie	Adcock	Maw	Paterson	Lochhead	Liddle	Gurry	Chandler	Lowery	Dumbrell	Philp	Young	Campbell	Wood	Dewis	Grosvenor	Sharman	Gardiner
Aug 26	Aston Villa	A	3-2	Maw 2,Lochhead	1	2	3	4	5	6	7	8	9	10	11												
28	Sheffield United	H	4-0	Liddle 4	1	2	3	4	5	6	7			10	11	8	9										
Sep 2	Manchester City	H	0-0		1	2	3	4	5	6	7	8	9		11				10								
4	Sheffield United	A	1-2	Paterson	1	2	3	4	5		7	8	9		11				10	6							
9	Tottenham Hotspur	H	1-3	Paterson	1	2	3		5	6	7	8	9		11				10		4						
16	Liverpool	A	3-1	Adcock,Lochhead,Maw	1	2	3		5		7		9	10	11	4	8			6							
23	Chelsea	H	1-1	Liddle	1	2	3		5	6	7	8		10	11	4						9					
30	Sunderland	A	1-2	Campbell	1	2	3		5	6	7	8		10	11	4						9					
Oct 7	Portsmouth	H	2-1	Liddle,Campbell	1	2	3	4	5	6	7	8		10	11							9					
14	Huddersfield Town	A	1-5	Liddle	1	2	3	4	5	6	7			10	11	8						9					
21	Arsenal	A	0-2		1	2	3	4	5		7	8		10	11						6	9					
28	Everton	H	3-1	Maw,Adcock,Campbell	1	2	3	4	5		7	8		10	11						6	9					
Nov 4	Derby County	A	1-2	Campbell	1	2		4	5		7	8		10	11						6	9	3				
11	Blackburn Rovers	H	1-2	Chandler	1	2	3	4	5	6	7	10	8		11		9										
18	Newcastle United	A	1-1	Liddle	1	2	3	4	5	6	7	8	10		11		9										
25	Leeds United	H	2-2	Paterson 2	1	2	3	4	5	6	7	8	10		11		9										
Dec 2	Sheffield Wednesday	A	1-1	Chandler	1	2	3	4	5	6	7	8	10		11		9										
9	West Bromwich Albion	H	0-1		1	2	3	4	5	6	7	8	10		11								9				
23	Middlesbrough	H	1-2	Dewis	1	2	3	4	5	6	7	8	10		11								9				
25	Stoke City	A	1-2	Paterson	1	2	3	4	5	6	7	8	10		11								9				
26	Stoke City	H	3-1	Liddle,Adcock,Chandler	1	2			5	6	7		8	10	11	4	9						3				
30	Aston Villa	H	1-1	Liddle	1	2	3	4	5		7		9	10	11	8									6		
Jan 6	Manchester City	A	1-1	Maw	1	2	3	4	5		7	8	9	10	11										6		
20	Tottenham Hotspur	A	1-0	Lochhead	1	2		4	5		7	8		10	11		9						3		6		
Feb 1	Liverpool	H	1-0	Liddle	1	2		4			7	8		10	11		9						3		6	5	
10	Sunderland	H	0-0		1	2		4			7	8		10	11		9						3		6	5	
21	Portsmouth	A	5-3	Gardiner 4,Liddle	1	2		4	5		7	8			11	10							3		6		9
24	Huddersfield Town	H	1-0	Maw	1	2		4	5		7	8		10	11								3		6		9
Mar 8	Arsenal	H	4-1	Gardiner 3,Chandler	1	2		4	5		7		10		11		9						3		6		8
10	Everton	A	1-1	Gardiner	1	2		4	5		7		10		11		9						3		6		8
24	Blackburn Rovers	A	0-3		1	2		4	5	6	7	8		10	11								3				9
28	Birmingham	A	0-3		1		2	4		6	7	10	8		11								3			5	9
31	Newcastle United	H	3-2	Maw,Lochhead,Paterson	1		2	4		6	7	8		10	11								3			5	9
Apr 2	Wolverhampton Wanderers	A	1-1	Maw	1		2	4			7	8		10	11								3			5	9
3	Wolverhampton Wanderers	H	1-1	Maw	1		2	4			7	8		10	11								3			5	9
7	Leeds United	A	0-8		1		2	4			7	8		10	11								3			5	9
14	Sheffield Wednesday	H	2-0	Gardiner,Adcock	1	2	3	4	5	6	7	10	8		11												9
19	Derby County	H	2-0	Liddle,Gardiner	1	2	3	4	5	6	7	10	8		11												9
21	West Bromwich Albion	A	0-2		1	2	3	4	5	6	7	10	8		11												9
23	Chelsea	A	0-2		1	2	3	4	5	6	7	10		8	11												9
28	Birmingham	H	3-7	Chandler 2,Maw	1	2	3	4	5	6	7	8		10	11		9										
May 5	Middlesbrough	A	1-4	Maw	1	2	3	4	5	6	7	8		10	11												9

F.A. CUP

DATE	OPPONENTS		V	F.T.	SCORERS	McLaren	Black	Jones	Smith	Heywood	Ritchie	Adcock	Maw	Paterson	Lochhead	Liddle	Gurry	Chandler	Lowery	Dumbrell	Philp	Young	Campbell	Wood	Dewis	Grosvenor	Sharman	Gardiner
Jan 13	Lincoln City	(3)	H	3-0	Maw,Lochhead,Paterson	1	2	3	4	5		7	8	9	10	11										6		
27	Millwall	(4)	A	6-3	Smith,Chandler 2,Maw,Liddle,Lochhead	1	2		4	5		7	8		10	11		9						3		6		
Feb 17	Birmingham	(5)	A	2-1	Chandler 2	1	2		4	5		7	8		10	11		9						3		6		
Mar 3	Preston North End	(6)	A	1-0	Chandler	1	2		4	5		7	8		10	11		9						3		6		
17	Portsmouth	(sf)		1-4	Lochhead (at St.Andrews,Birmingham)	1	2		4	5		7			10	11		9						3		6		8

LEICESTER CITY 1933-34
Back : Maw,Miles,Lowery,Liddle,Adcock,Paterson,Wood,Frame,Eastwood.
Middle : L.Edwards *(Trainer)*,W.Fox *(Masseur)*,Young,Keeley,Sharman,Jones,McLaren, Heywood,Wiggins,Calvert,W.McLean *(Assistant Trainer)*,Smith.
Front : Chandler,Ritchie,Dutton,Dewis,Gurry,Black,Grosvenor,Udall,Grogan,Lochhead.

	APP's		GOALS	
	FL	FAC	FL	FAC
Sandy McLaren	42	5		
Adam Black	37	5		
Dai Jones	32	1		
Sep Smith	39	5		1
Roger Heywood	35	5		
George Ritchie	26			
Hughie Adcock	38	5	4	
Arthur Maw	36	4	11	2
Jim Paterson	24	1	6	1
Arthur Lochhead	25	5	4	3
Danny Liddle	42	5	13	1
Jack Gurry	8			
Arthur Chandler	12	4	6	5
Ted Lowery	4			
George Dumbrell	1			
John Philp	1			
Archie Young	4			
John Campbell	7		4	
Sandy Wood	15	4		
George Dewis	3		1	
Percy Grosvenor	9	5		
Fred Sharman	7			
Archie Gardiner	15	1	10	

1934-35 LEAGUE DIVISION ONE
Final Position : 21st

Date	Opponents	V	F.T.	Scorers	McLaren	Black	Jones	Smith	Heywood	Ritchie	Adcock	Maw	Gardiner	Coutts	Liddle	Paterson	Summers	Mills	Chandler	Lochhead	Sharman	Wood	Gurry	Frame	Muncie	Dewis	Gibson	Liggins	Grosvenor	Young	Clarke	Carroll	O'Callaghan
Aug 25	Wolverhampton Wanderers	H	1-1	Coutts	1	2	3	4	5	6	7	8	9	10	11																		
29	Everton	A	1-2	Gardiner	1	2	3	4	5	6		8	9	10	11	7																	
Sep 1	Chelsea	A	1-3	Summers	1	2	3	4	5	6		8	9	10	11		7																
3	Everton	H	5-2	Lochhead 2,Liddle,Chandler,Mills	1	2	3	4	5	6					11		7	8	9	10													
8	Aston Villa	H	5-0	Chandler 3,Liddle,Mills	1	2	3	4		6					11		7	8	9	10	5												
15	Derby County	A	1-1	Summers	1	2	3	4		6					11		7	8	9	10	5												
22	Manchester City	H	1-3	Mills	1	2	3	4		6					11		7	8	9	10	5												
29	Sunderland	H	0-2		1	2		8		6				10	11	7	9					5	3	4									
Oct 6	Tottenham Hotspur	A	2-2	Liddle,Maw	1		3	4		6	7	8			11		10	9			5			2									
13	Preston North End	H	0-0		1		3	4		6	7	8			11		10	9			5			2									
20	Middlesbrough	A	0-1		1		3	4		6		8			11		10	9			5			2	7								
27	Blackburn Rovers	H	0-1		1		3	4	5	6	7	8					10	9						2					11				
Nov 3	Birmingham	A	3-2	Liddle,Smith (pen),Booton (og)	1		3	4	5	6	7	8			11			10	9					2									
10	Stoke City	H	0-3		1		3	4	5	6		8			11	7		10	9					2									
17	Liverpool	A	1-5	Liddle	1	2	3	4	5	6	7	10			11			8	9														
24	Leeds United	H	1-0	Liggins	1	2	3	4		6		10			11		7	8			5							9					
Dec 1	West Bromwich Albion	A	1-4	Maw	1	2	3	4		6		10			11		7	8			5							9					
8	Sheffield Wednesday	H	0-1		1		3	4		6		10			11		7	8			5	2						9					
15	Arsenal	A	0-8		1		3	4				10			11		7	8			5	2						9	6				
22	Portsmouth	H	6-3	Mills,Maw,Chandler 2,Liddle,Salmond (og)	1	2		4			7	8			11			10	9		5	3							6				
25	Huddersfield Town	H	0-3		1	2		4			7	8			11			10	9		5	3							6				
26	Huddersfield Town	A	3-2	Muncie,Chandler 2	1			8		6	7				11				9		5	3			2					4		10	
29	Wolverhampton Wanderers	A	1-3	Chandler	1			8		6	7				11				9		5	3		2						4		10	
Jan 5	Chelsea	H	1-0	Liddle	1		3	4		6	7	8			11				9		5	2								10			
19	Aston Villa	A	0-5		1		3	4		6	7	8			11				9		5	2								10			
31	Derby County	H	0-1		1	2	3	4		6	7	8			11			10	9		5												
Feb 2	Manchester City	A	3-6	Muncie,Liddle,Smith (pen)	1	2		8	5	6					11				9					7	3					4		10	
9	Sunderland	A	0-2		1	2		4	5			8			11			10	9			3		7					6				
23	Preston North End	A	0-2		1			4	5			8			11			10	9			3		2					6			7	
Mar 2	Middlesbrough	H	3-1	Dewis 2,Maw	1				5	6		10			11							3		2	4	9						7	8
9	Blackburn Rovers	A	0-0		1			4	5	6		10			11							3		2		9						7	8
16	Birmingham	H	2-1	Dewis 2	1	2				6		10			11						5	3			4	9						7	8
23	Stoke City	A	0-3		1	2				6		10			11						5	3				9						7	8
28	Tottenham Hotspur	H	6-0	Liggins 2,Carroll,Liddle 2,Channell (og)	1	2				6		10			11						5	3						9	4			7	8
30	Liverpool	H	3-1	Liddle,Maw,O'Callaghan	1	2		4		6		10			11						5	3				9						7	8
Apr 6	Leeds United	A	2-0	Liggins,Liddle	1	2		4	5	6		10			11							3						9				7	8
13	West Bromwich Albion	A	0-0		1	2		4	5	6		10			11							3						9				7	8
19	Grimsby Town	A	1-3	Maw	1	2		4	5	6		10			11							3						9				7	8
20	Sheffield Wednesday	A	1-1	O'Callaghan	1			4	5			10			11							3		2		9			6			7	8
22	Grimsby Town	H	2-2	Liddle 2	1		3	4	5			10			11									2		9			6			7	8
27	Arsenal	H	3-5	Maw,Dewis,Ritchie	1		3	4	5	6		10			11									2		9						7	8
May 4	Portsmouth	A	1-1	O'Callaghan	1		3	4	5	6		10			11									2		9						7	8

F.A. CUP

Date	Opponents		V	F.T.	Scorers	McLaren	Black	Jones	Smith	Heywood	Ritchie	Adcock	Maw	Gardiner	Coutts	Liddle	Paterson	Summers	Mills	Chandler	Lochhead	Sharman	Wood	Gurry	Frame	Muncie	Dewis	Gibson	Liggins	Grosvenor	Young	Clarke	Carroll	O'Callaghan
Jan 12	Blackpool	(3)	H	2-1	Maw,Ritchie	1		3	4		6	7	8			11				9		5	2								10			
26	Arsenal	(4)	H	0-1		1	2	3	4		6	7	8			11			10	9		5												

LEICESTER CITY 1934-35
Back : Liggins,Sharman,McLaren,Gardiner,Dewis,Calvert,Heywood,Smith.
Middle: L.Edwards *(Trainer)*,W.Fox *(Masseur)*, Ritchie,Young,Grogan,Lochhead,Jones, Gurry,W.McLean *(Assistant Trainer)*.
Front : Adcock,Mills,Maw,Paterson,Frame,Clarke,Coutts,Liddle.
On Ground: Black,Grosvenor,Chandler,Summers,Wood,Muncie.

	APP's FL	APP's FAC	GOALS FL	GOALS FAC
Sandy McLaren	42	2		
Adam Black	14	1		
Dai Jones	32	2		
Sep Smith	38	2	2 (2p)	
Roger Heywood	21			
George Ritchie	35	2	1	1
Hughie Adcock	14	2		
Arthur Maw	33	2	7	1
Archie Gardiner	3		1	
Billy Coutts	6		1	
Danny Liddle	40	2	14	
Jim Paterson	5			
John Summers	11		2	
Tommy Mills	15	1	4	
Arthur Chandler	23	2	9	
Arthur Lochhead	4		2	
Fred Sharman	28	2		
Sandy Wood	21	1		
Jack Gurry	1			
Billy Frame	9			
William Muncie	5		2	
George Dewis	8		5	
George Gibson	2			
Jack Liggins	7		4	
Percy Grosvenor	14			
Archie Young	5	1		
Pat Clarke	1			
Tony Carroll	12		1	
Gene O'Callaghan	13		3	
Own Goals			3	

1935-36 LEAGUE DIVISION TWO
Final Position : 6th

DATE	OPPONENTS	V	F.T.	SCORERS	McLaren	Jones	Wood	Smith	Sharman	Ritchie	Carroll	O'Callaghan	Dewis	Maw	Liddle	Grosvenor	Heywood	Calvert	Frame	Mills	Coutts	Grogan	Liggins	Bedford	Muncie	McNally	Bruce
Aug 31	Sheffield United	A	2-1	O'Callaghan 2	1	2	3	4	5	6	7	8	9	10	11												
Sep 2	Swansea Town	A	0-2		1	2	3	4	5	6	7	8	9	10	11												
7	Southampton	H	1-1	Carroll	1	2	3	4	5		7	8	9	10	11	6											
9	Swansea Town	H	4-1	Carroll 3,Maw	1	2	3	4	9		7	8		10	11	6	5										
14	Norwich City	A	2-1	Sharman,Maw	1	2	3	4	9		7	8		10	11	6	5										
16	Bradford City	H	2-1	Sharman,Mills			3	4	9		7				11	6	5	1	2	8	10						
21	Nottingham Forest	H	2-1	O'Callaghan,Liddle			3	4	9		7	8		10	11	6	5	1	2								
28	Blackpool	A	5-3	Maw 2,O'Callaghan,Carroll,Liddle	1	3		4	9		7	8		10	11	6	5		2								
Oct 5	Doncaster Rovers	H	6-0	O'Callaghan 2,Sharman 3,Liddle	1	3		4	9		7	8		10	11	6	5		2								
12	Bury	A	0-3		1	3		4			7	8			11	6	5		2	10	9						
19	Newcastle United	A	1-3	Liggins	1	3					7	8		10	11	6	5		2				4	9			
26	Tottenham Hotspur	H	4-1	Carroll 2,Maw,Sharman	1	3		4	9		7	8		10	11	6	5		2								
Nov 2	Manchester United	A	1-0	Sharman	1	3		4	9		7	8		10	11	6	5		2								
9	Port Vale	H	2-0	Maw,Carroll	1	3		4	9		7	8		10	11	6	5		2								
16	Fulham	A	0-2		1	3		4	9		7	8		10	11	6	5		2								
23	Plymouth Argyle	H	2-0	Carroll,O'Callaghan	1	3		4	9		7	8		10	11	6	5		2								
30	Charlton Athletic	A	0-1		1	3		4	9		7	8		10	11	6	5		2								
Dec 7	Hull City	H	2-2	O'Callaghan,Carroll	1	3		4	9		7	8		10	11	6	5		2								
14	Barnsley	A	3-3	Maw,Sharman 2	1	3		4	9		7	8		10	11	6			2				5				
21	Burnley	H	2-0	Maw 2	1	3		4	9		7	8		10	11	6	5		2								
25	Bradford Park Avenue	H	5-0	Carroll,O'Callaghan,Sharman,Maw,Liddle	1	3		4	9		7	8		10	11	6	5		2								
28	Sheffield United	H	1-3	Maw	1	3		4	9		7	8		10	11	6	5		2								
Jan 1	Bradford Park Avenue	A	1-3	O'Callaghan	1	3		4	5	6		8		9	11				2		10				7		
4	Southampton	A	0-1		1	3		4	9			8		10	11	6			2					5	7		
18	Norwich City	H	1-1	Jones	1	3		4	5			8	9	10	11	6			2						7		
30	Nottingham Forest	A	1-0	Maw	1	3		4	5		7	8		10	11	6			2							9	
Feb 1	Blackpool	H	4-1	Liddle,McNally 2,Muncie	1	3		4	5			8		10	11	6			2						7	9	
8	Doncaster Rovers	A	0-1		1	3		4	5			8		10	11	6			2						7	9	
20	Bury	H	1-2	Ritchie	1	3		4	5	6		8		10	11				2						7	9	
29	Hull City	A	3-3	O'Callaghan,McNally 2	1	3		4	5	6		8		10	11				2						7	9	
Mar 7	Fulham	H	5-2	Maw,Smith (pen),Carroll,Muncie,McNally	1	3		4	5	6	7	8		10					2						11	9	
14	Port Vale	A	1-1	Carroll	1	3		4	5	6	7	8		10					2						11	9	
10	Newcastle United	H	1-0	Sharman	1	3		8	9	6				10	11	4	5		2						7		
21	Manchester United	H	1-1	Maw	1	3		8	9	6	7			10	11	4	5		2								
28	Plymouth Argyle	A	1-2	Sharman	1	3		8	9	6	7			10	11		5		2			4					
Apr 4	Charlton Athletic	H	4-1	Sharman,Carroll,Jones,Coutts	1	3			9	6	7	8			11	4	5		2		10						
10	West Ham United	A	2-3	Carroll,O'Callaghan	1	3		4	9	6	7	8		10	11		5		2								
11	Tottenham Hotspur	A	1-1	Sharman	1	3		4	9		7	8				6	5		2		10						
13	West Ham United	H	1-1	Dewis	1	3		4			7	8	9		11	6	5		2							10	
18	Barnsley	H	2-0	Muncie,Maw	1	3	2			6		8	9	7		4	5								11	10	
25	Burnley	A	2-2	Dewis,Ritchie	1	3				6		8	9			4	5		2						11	10	7
May 2	Bradford City	A	0-2		1	3				6		8	9		11	4	5		2		10				7		

F.A. CUP

DATE	OPPONENTS		V	F.T.	SCORERS	McLaren	Jones	Wood	Smith	Sharman	Ritchie	Carroll	O'Callaghan	Dewis	Maw	Liddle	Grosvenor	Heywood	Calvert	Frame	Mills	Coutts	Grogan	Liggins	Bedford	Muncie	McNally	Bruce
Jan 11	Brentford	(3)	H	1-0	Maw	1	3		4	5			8	9	10	11	6			2						7		
25	Watford	(4)	H	6-3	Maw 2,Dewis,Liddle 3	1	3		4	5		7	8	9	10	11	6			2								
Feb 15	Middlesbrough	(5)	A	1-2	McNally	1	3		4	5	6	7	8		10	11				2							9	

LEICESTER CITY 1935-36
Muncie,Liddle,McNally,O'Callaghan,Maw,Ritchie,Frame,Smith,Sharman,Jones,McLaren.

	APP's		GOALS	
	FL	FAC	FL	FAC
Sandy McLaren	40	3		
Dai Jones	41	3	2	
Sandy Wood	7			
Sep Smith	36	3	1(p)	
Fred Sharman	37	3	14	
George Ritchie	15	1	2	
Tony Carroll	31	2	15	
Gene O'Callaghan	36	3	12	
George Dewis	8	2	2	1
Arthur Maw	37	3	15	3
Danny Liddle	38	3	5	3
Percy Grosvenor	33	2		
Roger Heywood	28			
Joe Calvert	2			
Billy Frame	36	3		
Tommy Mills	2		1	
Billy Coutts	6		1	
John Grogan	2			
Jack Liggins	1		1	
George Bedford	2			
William Muncie	13	1	3	
Owen McNally	10	1	5	1
David Bruce	1			

1936-37 LEAGUE DIVISION TWO
Final Position : 1st

DATE	OPPONENTS	V	F.T.	SCORERS	McLaren	Frame	Jones	Smith	Heywood	Ritchie	Muncie	O'Callaghan	Dewis	Maw	Liddle	Calvert	Sharman	McNally	Coutts	Grosvenor	Grogan	Carroll	Bedford	Stubbs	Bowers	Davis
Aug 29	Blackpool	H	1-2	O'Callaghan	1	2	3	4	5	6	7	8	9	10	11											
31	Bradford Park Avenue	H	5-0	Muncie 2,Ritchie,O'Callaghan,McNally			3	4	5	6	7	8			11	1	2	9	10							
Sep 5	Blackburn Rovers	A	0-0				3	4	5	6	7	8			11	1	2	9	10							
9	Bradford Park Avenue	A	2-1	O'Callaghan,McNally			3	4	5	6	7	8			11	1	2	9	10							
12	Bury	H	0-3				3	4	5	6	7				11	1	2	9	10							
14	Tottenham Hotspur	A	2-4	O'Callaghan 2 (1pen)		2	3				7	8			11	1	5	9	10	6	4					
19	Plymouth Argyle	A	1-2	Gorman (og)	1	2	3				7	8	9	10	11		5			6	4					
26	West Ham United	A	1-4	O'Callaghan	1	2	3				7	8	9		11		5		10	6	4					
Oct 3	Norwich City	H	2-2	O'Callaghan 2	1	2	3	4			7	8			11		5	9	10	6						
10	Newcastle United	A	0-1		1	2	3	4			11	8	9	10			5			6			7			
17	Coventry City	H	1-0	Dewis	1	2	3	4			11	8	9	10			5			6			7			
24	Doncaster Rovers	A	0-0		1	2	3	4			11	8	9	10			5			6		7				
31	Fulham	H	2-0	Dewis,O'Callaghan	1	2	3	4				8	9		11		5		10	6		7				
Nov 7	Burnley	A	0-0		1	2	3	4				8	9		11		5			6		7		10		
14	Southampton	H	2-2	Liddle,Sharman	1	2	3	4							10		5			6		7		9	11	
21	Swansea Town	A	3-1	Muncie,Bowers,Liddle	1	2	3	4			7	8			10		5			6				11	9	
28	Bradford City	H	4-1	Bowers 2,Stubbs 2	1	2	3	4			7	8			10		5			6				11	9	
Dec 5	Aston Villa	A	3-1	Bowers 2,O'Callaghan	1	2	3	4				8	7		10		5			6				11	9	
12	Chesterfield	H	3-1	Bowers 2,Wass (og)	1	2	3	4							10		5		8	6				11	9	7
19	Nottingham Forest	A	3-0	Bowers 2 (1pen),O'Callaghan	1	2	3	4				8			10		5			6		7		11	9	
25	Barnsley	H	5-1	Bowers 3,Stubbs,Liddle	1	2	3	4				8			10		5			6		7		11	9	
26	Blackpool	A	2-6	O'Callaghan,Stubbs	1	2	3	4				8			10		5			6		7		11	9	
28	Barnsley	A	2-1	Grosvenor,Bowers	1	2	3	4				8		10			5			6				11	9	7
Jan 1	Sheffield United	A	1-3	Bowers (pen)	1	2	3	4				8					5	10		6				11	9	7
2	Blackburn Rovers	H	1-0	Bowers	1	2	3					8					5	10		6	4			11	9	7
9	Bury	A	1-0	Bowers	1	2	3	4	6			8			10		5					7		11	9	
23	Plymouth Argyle	H	3-2	Bowers,Stubbs,O'Callaghan	1	2	3	4	6			8			10		5					7		11	9	
Feb 4	West Ham United	H	2-2	O'Callaghan,Liddle	1	2	3		6			8			10		5				4			11	9	7
6	Norwich City	A	2-1	Sharman (pen),Liddle	1	2	3		6			8			10		5				4			11	9	7
13	Newcastle United	H	3-2	Liddle,Carroll,Stubbs	1	2	3		6			8			10		5				4	7		11	9	
25	Coventry City	A	2-0	Bowers 2	1	2	3					8			10		5			6	4			11	9	
27	Doncaster Rovers	H	7-1	Bowers 3,Carroll 2,O'Callaghan,Jacobson (og)	1	2	3					8			10		5			6	4	7		11	9	
Mar 6	Fulham	A	0-2		1	2	3					8			10		5			6	4	7		11	9	
13	Burnley	H	7-3	Liddle,Carroll 2,Bowers 4	1	2	3					8			10		5			6	4	7		11	9	
20	Southampton	A	1-1	Bowers	1	2	3	4				8			10		5			6		7		11	9	
27	Swansea Town	H	0-0		1	2	3	4				8			10		5			6		7		11	9	
29	Sheffield United	H	1-2	Liddle	1	2	3	4				8			10		5			6		7		11	9	
Apr 3	Bradford City	A	2-1	Liddle,Bowers	1	2	3	4						8	10		5			6				11	9	7
10	Aston Villa	H	1-0	Bowers	1	2	3	4						8	10		5			6				11	9	7
17	Chesterfield	A	5-2	Stubbs 2,Bowers,Maw,Smith	1	2	3	4						8	10		5			6		7		11	9	
24	Nottingham Forest	H	2-1	Bowers,Maw	1	2	3	4						8	10		5			6		7		11	9	
May 1	Tottenham Hotspur	H	4-1	Bowers 2,Maw,Carroll	1	2	3	4						8	10		5			6		7		11	9	

F.A. CUP

DATE	OPPONENTS		V	F.T.	SCORERS	McLaren	Frame	Jones	Smith	Heywood	Ritchie	Muncie	O'Callaghan	Dewis	Maw	Liddle	Calvert	Sharman	McNally	Coutts	Grosvenor	Grogan	Carroll	Bedford	Stubbs	Bowers	Davis
Jan 16	Bristol Rovers	(3)	A	5-2	Bowers 2,Carroll,O'Callaghan,Stubbs	1	2	3	4	6			8			10		5					7		11	9	
30	Exeter City	(4)	A	1-3	Liddle	1	2	3	4	6			8			10		5							11	9	7

Note : Feb 27, most reports credit Jacobson (og),some credit Carroll.

LEICESTER CITY 1936-37
Back : Smith,Frame,Grosvenor,Jones.
Middle : W.McLean *(Assistant Trainer)*, Sharman,McLaren,Bowers,L.Edwards *(Trainer)*.
Front : G.Smith *(Secretary)*, Carroll,Maw,O'Callaghan,Liddle,Stubbs,F.Womack *(Manager)*.

	APP's		GOALS	
	FL	FAC	FL	FAC
Sandy McLaren	37	2		
Billy Frame	38	2		
Dai Jones	42	2		
Sep Smith	31	2	1	
Roger Heywood	5			
George Ritchie	10	2	1	
William Muncie	14		3	
Gene O'Callaghan	34	2	15 (1p)	1
George Dewis	8		2	
Arthur Maw	9		3	
Danny Liddle	40	2	9	1
Joe Calvert	5			
Fred Sharman	41	2	2 (1p)	
Owen McNally	6		2	
Billy Coutts	11			
Percy Grosvenor	34		1	
John Grogan	10			
Tony Carroll	22	1	6	1
George Bedford	2			
Eric Stubbs	28	2	8	1
Jack Bowers	27	2	33 (2p)	2
Bert Davis	8	1		
Own Goals			3	

1937-38

LEAGUE DIVISION ONE
Final Position : 16th

DATE	OPPONENTS	V	F.T.	SCORERS	McLaren	Frame	Jones	Smith	Sharman	Grosvenor	Carroll	Maw	Bowers	Liddle	Stubbs	Grogan	Calvert	Reeday	O'Callaghan	Moralee	Dewis	Heywood	Woodvine	Coutts	Muncie	Tompkin
Aug 28	Derby County	H	0-0		1	2	3	4	5	6	7	8	9	10	11											
30	Sunderland	H	4-0	Stubbs,Liddle 2,Bowers	1	2	3		5	6	7	8	9	10	11	4										
Sep 4	Manchester City	A	0-3		1	2	3		5	6	7	8	9	10	11	4										
8	Sunderland	A	0-1		1	2	3		5	6	7	8	9	10	11	4										
11	Arsenal	H	1-1	Bowers			3		5	6	7	8	9	10	11	4	1	2								
15	Birmingham	A	1-4	Maw			3		5	6	7	8	9	10	11	4	1	2								
18	Blackpool	A	4-2	Bowers,Stubbs,Maw 2			3	4	5	6	7	8	9	10	11		1	2								
25	Brentford	H	0-1				3	4	5	6	7	8	9	10	11		1	2								
Oct 2	Bolton Wanderers	A	1-6	Tennant (og)	1		3	4	5	6	7	8	9		11			2	10							
9	Huddersfield Town	H	2-1	Carroll,Bowers	1		3	4	5	6	7	8	9	10	11			2								
16	West Bromwich Albion	H	4-1	Bowers 3,Liddle	1		3	4	5	6	7	8	9	10	11			2								
23	Liverpool	A	1-1	Stubbs	1		3		5	6	7	8	9	10	11	4		2								
30	Leeds United	H	2-4	Stubbs,Liddle	1		3	4	5	6	7	8	9	10	11			2								
Nov 6	Portsmouth	A	1-1	Bowers	1		3	8	5	6		10	9	11	7	4		2								
13	Preston North End	H	1-0	A.Beattie (og)	1		3	4	5	6	7		9	8	11			2		10						
20	Middlesbrough	A	2-4	Carroll,Liddle	1		3	4	5	6	7		9	8	11			2		10						
27	Chelsea	H	1-0	Liddle	1		3	4	5	6	7		9	10	11			2		8						
Dec 4	Grimsby Town	A	1-2	Smith (pen)	1		3	4	5	6	7		9	10	11			2		8						
11	Stoke City	H	2-0	Liddle,Smith (pen)	1		3	4	5	6	7		9	10	11			2		8						
18	Charlton Athletic	A	0-2		1		3	4	5	6	7		9	10	11			2		8						
25	Everton	H	3-1	Bowers,Moralee,Britton (og)	1		3	4	5	6	7	8	9		11			2		10						
27	Everton	A	0-3		1		3	4	5	6	7	8	9		11			2		10						
Jan 1	Derby County	A	1-0	Dewis	1	2		4	5	6			9	8	11			3		10	7					
15	Manchester City	H	1-4	Moralee	1		3		5	6			9	8	11	4		2		10	7					
29	Blackpool	H	0-1		1		3		5	6	7	8	9		11	4		2		10						
Feb 2	Arsenal	A	1-3	Smith (pen)	1		3	8	5	6	7		9		11	4		2		10						
5	Brentford	A	1-1	Muncie	1	2		4	5	6			9		11			3				8		7	10	
12	Bolton Wanderers	H	1-1	Bowers	1	2		4	5	6			9		11			3				8		7	10	
19	Huddersfield Town	A	0-0		1	2		4	5	6		8	9		11			3				10		7		
26	West Bromwich Albion	A	3-1	Moralee,Liddle,Smith (pen)		2		4	5	6		8	9		11		1	3		10				7		
Mar 5	Liverpool	H	2-2	Muncie 2		2		4	5	6		8	9		11		1	3		10				7		
9	Preston North End	A	0-0		1	2		4	5	6	7				11			3			8	9		10		
12	Leeds United	A	2-0	Dewis,Stubbs	1	2	3	4	5	6	7	8			11						9	10				
19	Portsmouth	H	3-3	Dewis 2,Coutts	1	2	3	4	5	6	7	8			11						9			10		
Apr 2	Middlesbrough	H	0-1		1	2	3	4	5	6	7	8			11						9	10				
9	Chelsea	A	1-4	Maw	1	2	3		5	6	7	8	9		11	4						10				
15	Wolverhampton Wanderers	A	1-10	Cullis (og)			3	4			7		9	10	11			2				8	5		6	
16	Grimsby Town	H	1-0	Smith (pen)	1	2		4	5	6	7		9					3				8		10	11	
18	Wolverhampton Wanderers	H	1-1	Coutts	1	2		4	5	6	7			10				3				9		8	11	
23	Stoke City	A	2-1	Dewis,Carroll		2			5	6	7			10		4	1	3			9			8	11	
30	Charlton Athletic	H	1-0	Liddle		2			5	6	7			10		4	1	3			9			8	11	
May 7	Birmingham	H	1-4	Liddle	1	2			5	6				10		4		3			9			8	11	7

F.A. CUP

DATE	OPPONENTS		V	F.T.	SCORERS	McLaren	Frame	Jones	Smith	Sharman	Grosvenor	Carroll	Maw	Bowers	Liddle	Stubbs	Grogan	Calvert	Reeday	O'Callaghan	Moralee	Dewis	Heywood	Woodvine	Coutts	Muncie	Tompkin
Jan 8	Mansfield Town	(3)	A	2-1	Liddle,Bowers	1	2		4	5	6			9	8	11			3		10	7					
22	Preston North End	(4)	A	0-2		1		3		5	6			9	8	11	4		2		10	7					

Note : Nov 13, most reports credit A.Beattie (og),some credit Bowers.

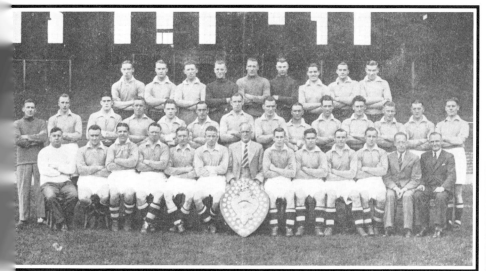

LEICESTER CITY 1937-38
Back : Norton,Bedford,Reeday,Calvert,Halliwell,McLaren,Grogan,Stubbs,Johnson.
Middle: W.McLean*(AssistantTrainer)*, C.Grosvenor,Gummer,Howe,Hay,Coutts,Heywood,Jones,
O'Callaghan,A.Smith,Bowers,Frame,P.Grosvenor,Sharman.
Front: L.Edwards *(Trainer)*,S.Smith,Muncie,Carroll,Hillard,Maw,F.Womack*(Manager)*, Priestley,Headley,Clarke,
Liddle,G.Smith*(Secretary)*, A.Chandler *(Coaching Staff)*.

	APP's		GOALS	
	FL	FAC	FL	FAC
Sandy McLaren	34	2		
Billy Frame	20	1		
Dai Jones	30	1		
Sep Smith	30	1	5 (5p)	
Fred Sharman	36	2		
Percy Grosvenor	42	2		
Tony Carroll	29		3	
Arthur Maw	25		4	
Jack Bowers	34	2	10	1
Danny Liddle	39	2	10	1
Eric Stubbs	25	2	5	
John Grogan	13	1		
Joe Calvert	8			
Maurice Reeday	34	2		
Gene O'Callaghan	1			
Matt Moralee	14	2	3	
George Dewis	16	2	5	
Roger Heywood	7			
Albert Woodvine	1			
Billy Coutts	13		2	
William Muncie	10		3	
Maurice Tompkin	1			
Own Goals				4

1938-39

LEAGUE DIVISION ONE
Final Position : 22nd

DATE	OPPONENTS	V	F.T.	SCORERS	McLaren	Frame	Reeday	Smith S	Sharman	Grosvenor	Smith A	Maw	Dewis	Moralee	Liddle	Baines	Bowers	Griffiths	Coutts	Calvert	Heywood	Stubbs	Jones	Grogan	Howe
Aug 27	Stoke City	H	2-2	Dewis 2	1	2	3	4	5	6	7	8	9	10	11										
29	Wolverhampton Wanderers	A	0-0		1	2	3	4	5	6	7	8	9	10	11										
Sep 3	Chelsea	A	0-3		1	2	3	4	5	6	7	8	9	10	11										
7	Birmingham	A	1-2	Moralee	1	2	3	4	5	6	7	8	9	10	11										
10	Preston North End	H	2-1	Dewis,S.Smith (pen)	1	2	3	4	5	6	7	8	9	10		11									
12	Birmingham	H	2-1	Bowers,Dewis	1	2	3	4	5	6	7	8	10		11		9								
17	Charlton Athletic	A	0-1		1	2	3	4	5	6	7		10		8	11	9								
24	Bolton Wanderers	H	0-0		1	2	3	4	5	6		8		10		11	9	7							
Oct 1	Leeds United	A	2-8	Baines,Bowers	1	2	3	4	5	6				10		11	9	7	8						
8	Liverpool	H	2-2	Griffiths,Dewis		2	3	4	5	6			9	10		11		7	8	1					
15	Sunderland	H	0-2			2	3	4	5	6			9	10		11		7	8	1					
22	Aston Villa	A	2-1	Dewis,Reeday (pen)		2	3		5	6		8	9	10				7		1	4	11			
29	Everton	H	3-0	Maw,Dewis,Griffiths		2	3		5	6		8	9	10				7		1	4	11			
Nov 5	Huddersfield Town	A	0-2			2	3		5	6		8	9	10				7		1	4	11			
12	Portsmouth	H	5-0	Stubbs,Griffiths,Maw 3		2	3		5	6		8	9	10				7		1	4	11			
19	Arsenal	A	0-0			2	3		5	6		8	9	10				7		1	4	11			
26	Brentford	H	1-1	Moralee		2	3		5	6		8	9	10				7		1	4	11			
Dec 3	Blackpool	A	1-1	Griffiths		2			5	6		8	9	10				7		1	4	11	3		
10	Derby County	H	2-3	Liddle 2		2			5	6		8	9	10	11			7		1	4		3		
17	Grimsby Town	A	1-6	Reeday (pen)		2	3		5	6		8	9	10				7		1	4	11			
24	Stoke City	A	0-1		1	2	3		5	6		8		10			9	7			4	11			
26	Manchester United	A	0-3		1	2	3		5	6		8		10	11		9	7			4				
27	Manchester United	H	1-1	Griffiths	1	2	3		5	6		8	9	10	11			7			4				
31	Chelsea	H	3-2	S.Smith 2,Liddle	1	2	3	8	5	6			9	10	11			7			4				
Jan 14	Preston North End	A	1-2	Bowers	1	2	3	8		6				10	11		9	7			4	5			
28	Bolton Wanderers	A	0-4		1	2	3	8	5		7		9	10				6			4	11			
Feb 4	Leeds United	H	2-0	Liddle,Dewis	1	2	3	8	5	6			9		11			7	10						
9	Charlton Athletic	H	1-5	S.Smith	1	2	3	4	5		9	8						7	10	6		11			
18	Sunderland	A	0-2		1		3		5	6		8	9	10	11			7			4		2		
25	Aston Villa	H	1-1	Bowers	1		3	8	5	6			9	10	11			7			4		2		
Mar 4	Liverpool	A	1-1	S.Smith	1		3	8	5	6			9		11			7	10		4		2		
8	Everton	A	0-4		1		3	8	5	6			9		11			7	10		4		2		
11	Huddersfield Town	H	0-1		1		3	8	5	6			9		11			7	10		4		2		
18	Portsmouth	A	1-0	Dewis	1		3	8	5	6			9	10				7			4	11	2		
25	Arsenal	H	0-2		1		3	8	5	6			9	10				7			4	11	2		
Apr 1	Brentford	A	0-2		1		3	8	5	6			9	10				7			4	11	2		
8	Blackpool	H	3-4	Bowers 2,Moralee	1		3		5	6	7	8		10			9				4	11	2		
10	Middlesbrough	A	2-3	Bowers 2	1		3	8		6		10					9	7	5			11	2	4	
11	Middlesbrough	H	5-3	Sharman 2 (2 pen),Dewis,Bowers,Jones	1		3		5	6		8		10			9	7			4	11	2		
15	Derby County	A	1-1	Liddle	1		3	8	5					10			9	7	6			11	2	4	
22	Grimsby Town	H	0-2		1		3	8	5					10			9	7	6			11	2	4	
May 4	Wolverhampton Wanderers	H	0-2		1		3	8	5					10			9	7				11	2	4	6

F.A. CUP

DATE	OPPONENTS		V	F.T.	SCORERS	McLaren	Frame	Reeday	Smith S	Sharman	Grosvenor	Smith A	Maw	Dewis	Moralee	Liddle	Baines	Bowers	Griffiths	Coutts	Calvert	Heywood	Stubbs	Jones	Grogan	Howe
Jan 7	Stoke City	(3)	H	1-1	Dewis	1	2	3	8		6			9	10	11			7			4	5			
11	Stoke City	(3 rep)	A	2-1	Dewis,Liddle	1	2	3	8		6			9	10	11			7			4	5			
21	Wolverhampton W.	(4)	A	1-5	Bowers	1	2	3	8	5	6			9	10	11			7			4				

APP's / GOALS

	FL	FAC	FL	FAC
	APP's		**GOALS**	
Sandy McLaren	31	3		
Billy Frame	28	3		
Maurice Reeday	40	3	2 (2p)	
Sep Smith	24	3	5 (1p)	
Fred Sharman	41	1	2 (2p)	
Percy Grosvenor	36	3		
Arthur H Smith	8			
Arthur Maw	21		4	
George Dewis	29	3	10	2
Matt Moralee	24	3	3	
Danny Liddle	29	3	5	1
Stan Baines	7		1	
Jack Bowers	18	1	9	1
Mal Griffiths	33	2	5	
Billy Coutts	12	2		
Joe Calvert	11			
Roger Heywood	28	3		
Eric Stubbs	21		1	
Dai Jones	16		1	
John Grogan	4			
Bert Howe	1			

LEICESTER CITY 1938-39
Back : Sharman,Oldham,Howe,Bedford,Dewis,Frame,Grogan,Moralee.
Middle : L.Edwards(Trainer),Norton,Hubbard,Gummer,McLaren,Stubbs,Calvert,Heywood,Jones, W.McLean (Assistant Trainer).
Front : Thompson,Woodvine,Osborne,Jayes,F.Womack(Manager),Baines,Coutts,Liddle,G.Smith(Secretary).
On Ground: A.H.Smith,Reeday,S.Smith,Bowers,Maw,Grosvenor.

1939-40 LEAGUE DIVISION TWO
Season abandoned

DATE	OPPONENTS	V	F.T.	SCORERS	McLaren	Jones	Reeday	Osborne	Sharman	Coutts	Smith A	Smith S	Bowers	Liddle	Stubbs	Heywood	Grosvenor	Griffiths	Dewis
Aug 26	Manchester City	H	4-3	A.Smith 2,Sharman (pen),Stubbs	1	2	3	4	5	6	7	8	9	10	11				
30	Birmingham	A	0-2		1	2	3		5		7	8	9	10	11	4	6		
Sep 2	West Ham United	A	2-0	Dewis,Griffiths	1	2	3		5	6			4	8	10	11		7	9

Note : Season abandoned, due to outbreak of Second World War
These matches are excluded from players' first class career records

LEICESTER CITY 1939-40
Back: A.H.Smith,Heywood,Sharman,
F.Rose *(Assistant Trainer)*, Bedford,Howe,Bowers.
Middle : Frame,Reeday,Calvert,S.Smith,Jones,
McLaren,Grosvenor,Stubbs.
Front : J.Metcalfe*(Trainer)*,Griffiths,Grogan,Woodvine,
T.Bromilow *(Manager)*,Osborne,Adam,
Forrest,G.Smith *(Secretary)*.
On Ground : Coutts,Dewis,Thompson,Liddle.

LEICESTER CITY 1939-40
This team photograph was taken on 23rd August 1939.
Within two weeks,World War Two had begun,and the League programme had been abandoned.

LEICESTER CITY 1941-42
Pictured v West Bromwich Albion on 13th September.
Back : Beard,Frith,Frame,Parker,Calvert,Howe,Mansfield,J.Butler *(Trainer)*.
Front : Barratt,S.Smith,Jayes,A.H.Smith,Adam,Paterson.

LEICESTER CITY 1945-46
Pictured v Aston Villa on 22nd April
Back : S.Smith,Frame,Grant,J.Butler *(Trainer)*,Jones,Towers.
Front : Griffiths,Revie,Pimbley,A.E.Smith,Woodvine,Grogan.

	APP's		GOALS	
	FL	FAC	FL	FAC
Sandy McLaren	3			
Dai Jones	3			
Maurice Reeday	3			
John Osborne	1			
Fred Sharman	3		1 (1p)	
Billy Coutts	2			
Arthur H Smith	2		2	
Sep Smith	3			
Jack Bowers	3			
Danny Liddle	3			
Eric Stubbs	3		1	
Roger Heywood	1			
Percy Grosvenor	1			
Mal Griffiths	1		1	
George Dewis	1		1	

1939-40 REGIONAL LEAGUE MIDLAND DIVISION Final Position : 7th

DATE	OPPONENTS		FT	1	2	3	4	5	6	7	8	9	10	11
Oct 21	Walsall	H	6-1	McLaren	Frame	Jones	S.Smith	Bedford	Coutts	King 1	Dewis	Bowers 3	Liddle	Barron 1
28	Luton Town	A	2-4	"	"	"	"	"	"	"	"1	"	"1	"1
Nov 4	Coventry City	H	4-2	"	"	"	"1	"	"	Thompson	"2	"1	"	"
11	West Bromwich Albion	A	0-1	"	"	"	"	"	"	Dewis	Jayes	"	Howe	Pritchard
18	Northampton Town	A	2-2	"	"	"	"	"	"	Thompson	Dewis	"2	Shell	"
25	Birmingham	H	1-3	"	Jones	Howe	"	"	"	"	Liddle	Lawton 1	Bowers	Barron
Dec 2	Wolverhampton Wanderers	A	0-5	"	Sharman	Jones	"	"	"	"	Jayes	Bowers	Eastham	Pritchard
9	Walsall	A	3-4	"	Frame	"	Sharman	"	Grosvenor	"	Eastham	Lawton 3	Bowers	"
16	Luton Town	H	3-3	"	Jones	Beattie	"	"	"	"	"	"1	"2	Barron
23	Coventry City	A	1-0	"	"	"	Grogan	Sharman	"	"	Dewis	"1p	Kinghorn
30	West Bromwich Albion	H	2-5	"	Frame	Jones	S.Smith	"	Coutts	Pritchard	Jayes 1	Bowers	Eastham	"1
Jan 6	Northampton Town	H	1-1	Calvert	"	Beattie	"1	"	Grosvenor	Thompson	Grogan	Jones	Bowers	Pritchard
13	Birmingham	A	3-3	"	"	"	Grogan	"	Howe	"	S.Smith 1	Bowers 1	Eastham	Barron
20	Wolverhampton Wanderers	H	1-2	"	"	Jones	"	"	Grosvenor	"	"	"	Jayes 1	Pritchard
Feb 24	Northampton Town	A	2-4	McLaren	"	"1	"	"	Howe	"1	"	"	Haycock	Ansell
Mar 2	Birmingham	H	2-1	"	"	"	"	"	"	"	"	Dewis 2	"	Pritchard
9	Wolverhampton Wanderers	A	1-5	"	"	"	"	"	"	Pritchard	"1	"	Iverson	Houghton
16	Walsall	A	2-3	"	"	"	"	"	"	"1	"1	"	Haycock	Houghton
23	Luton Town	H	1-2	"	"	Howe	"	"	Iverson	Thompson	"	"	"1	"
26	West Bromwich Albion	A	1-5	"	"	"	S.Smith 1	"	"	"	Jayes	Bowers	"	"
30	Coventry City	A	1-4	"	Jones	"	Grogan	"	"	"	S.Smith	Dewis 1	"	"
Apr 6	West Bromwich Albion	H	5-2	"	"	"	"	"	"	Sansome	"1	"3	"	"1
May 18	Luton Town	A	1-5	"	Frame	Jones	"	Heywood	"	Bowers 1	"	"	"	"
20	Birmingham	A	0-0	Queenborough	"	"	S.Smith	Bedford	Howe	Haycock	J.Smith	Bowers	Iverson	"
25	Wolverhampton Wanderers	H	3-1	"	"	"	"	"	"	Rochester	"2	"1	Jayes	"
30	Coventry City	H	1-3	McLaren	"	"	"	"	"	Sansome	"	"1	"	"
Jun 1	Walsall	H	0-0	"	"	Howe	"	"	Dewis	"	"	"	Haycock	"
8	Northampton Town	H	2-0	"	"	Jones	"	Sharman	Howe	"	"	"	Logan 1	"1

LEAGUE WAR CUP

DATE	OPPONENTS			FT	1	2	3	4	5	6	7	8	9	10	11
Apr 20	Clapton Orient	(1 leg 1)	H	5-2	McLaren	Frame	Jones	Grogan	Sharman	Iverson	Dewis 1	S.Smith 1	Bowers 1	Haycock 2	Houghton
27	Clapton Orient	(1 leg 2)	A	0-2	"	"	"	"	"	"	"	"	"	"	Barron
May 4	West Ham United	(2 leg 1)	H	1-1	"	"	"	Heywood	"	"	"	"1	"	"	Houghton
11	West Ham United	(2 leg 2)	A	0-3	"	"	"	Grogan	Heywood	"	Bowers	"	Sharman	Jayes	"

Note: 1) Oct 21, Williams (og).

2) Jan 13, Turner (og).

GUEST PLAYER	CLUB	SIGNING DATE	APPEARANCES RLM	APPEARANCES LWC	GOALS RLM	GOALS LWC
Tom Ansell			1			
William Barron	Northampton Town		6	1	1	
Andy Beattie	Preston North End		4			
George Bedford			13			
Jack Bowers			22	4	13 (1p)	1
Joe Calvert			3			
Billy Coutts			8			
George Dewis			14	3	9	1
Harry Eastham	Liverpool		6			
Billy Frame			22	4		
John Grogan			12	3		
Percy Grosvenor			5			
Fred Haycock	Aston Villa	8-4-40	10	3	1	2
Roger Heywood			1	2		
Eric Houghton	Aston Villa	8-4-40	12	3	2	
Bert Howe			16			
Bob Iverson	Aston Villa	8-4-40	7	4		
Gordon Jayes		8-5-39	7	1	2	

GUEST PLAYER	CLUB	SIGNING DATE	APPEARANCES RLM	APPEARANCES LWC	GOALS RLM	GOALS LWC
Dai Jones			24	4	1	
Bob King	Northampton Town		2		1	
Bill Kinghorn	Liverpool		2		1	
Tommy Lawton	Everton		3		5	
Danny Liddle			4		1	
S.Logan			1		1	
Sandy McLaren			23	4		
Jack Pritchard	Manchester City		10		1	
Arthur Queenborough		23-2-40	2			
Alan Rochester			1			
Fred Sansome		6-4-40	4			
Fred Sharman			17	4		
Frank Shell	Aston Villa		1			
John Smith		25-4-40	5		2	
Sep Smith			25	4	7	2
Tommy Thompson		23-8-39	15		1	
Own Goals					2	

1940-41 SOUTH REGIONAL LEAGUE

Final Position : 14th

DATE	OPPONENTS		FT	1	2	3	4	5	6	7	8	9	10	11
Aug 31	Coventry City	A	1-1	Calvert	Frame	Howe	S.Smith	Heywood	Thornhill	W.Wright	J.Smith	Bowers 1	L.Smith	Mullen
Sep 7	Coventry City	H	0-2	"	"	"	Towers	"	"	"	"	Dewis	"	"
14	Nottingham Forest	A	3-6	"	"	"	"	"	Grogan	"1	"	"2	"	"
21	Nottingham Forest	H	2-2	"	"	"	Sharman	"1p	Thornhill	"	"1	Steele	Liddle	"
28	Stoke City	H	1-0	"	"	Jones	"	"	Howe	"	"	Dewis	"1	"
Oct 5	Stoke City	A	3-3	"	"	Howe	"	"1p	Johnston	"	"	"1	"1	"
12	Luton Town	A	0-2	"	"	"	Towers	"	Wilson	Cunningham	"	"	Johnston	Liddle
19	Luton Town	H	4-0	"	"	"	Sharman	"	Johnston	W.Wright	"	Steele 1	Liddle 1	Mullen 2
26	Birmingham	H	2-1	"	"	"	Rochester	"	"	"	Jayes	"1	"1	"
Nov 2	Birmingham	A	2-1	"	"	"	"	"	Dewis	"1	"	"	"	"1
9	Mansfield Town	H	3-2	"	"	"	"	"	Liddle	"1	J.Smith	"2	Cheney	"
16	Mansfield Town	A	2-4	"	"	"	"	"	"	D.Wright 2	"	W.Wright	"	"
23	Walsall	A	0-5	"	"	Dewis	"	"	"	W.Wright	"	Steele	"	"
30	Walsall	H	1-1	"	"	Howe	"	"	"	"	Jayes	"1	A.Smith	"
Dec 7	Notts County	H	6-0	"	Harrison	"	Frame	"	"	"1	Rochester	Dewis 2	"	"3
14	West Bromwich Albion	H	4-3	"	"	"	"	"	"	"	"	"2	"1	"1
21	West Bromwich Albion	A	5-4	"	"	Springthorpe	"	"	"	"	"	"2	"	"3(1p)
25	Northampton Town	A	2-5	"	"	Howe	"	"	"	"	"	"2	"	"
25	Northampton Town	H	7-2	"	Frame	"	Rochester	"	"	"1	Dewis 1	Lee 1	"2	"2(1p)
28	Notts County	A	2-4	"	Harrison	"	Frame	"	"	"1	Rochester	Dewis 1	"	"
Jan 4	Stoke City MC1/1	H	6-2	"	Frame	"	Rochester	Frith	"	"2	Dewis 1	Lee	"2	"1
11	Stoke City MC1/2	A	5-3	"	"	"	Frith	Heywood	"	"	"1	"1	"1	"1
Feb 1	Nottingham Forest MC2	H	6-2	"	"	"2(2p)	"	"	"	"1	Lee 2	Dewis 1	"	"
8	Lincoln City MCsf/1	H	4-1	"	"	"	Rochester	"	"	"	Dewis 2	Sanderson 1	"1	"
Apr 12	Lincoln City MCsf/2	A	4-5	"	"	"	Grogan	Sheard	Paterson	Frost	Jayes 1	Lee 2	Liddle	W.Wright 1
14	Lincoln City	H	1-1	"	"	Wyles	Rochester	"	"	W.Wright	"	"	Burditt	Chapman 1
May 3	Walsall MC F	H	2-0	"	"	Howe	Frith	Heywood	"	"1	Dewis	"	Liddle	Mullen 1
10	Walsall	A	1-3	"	"	"	"	Sheard	Liddle	Frost	"	"1	Rochester	"
17	Tottenham Hotspur	H	1-2	Ward	"	"	"	Heywood	"	"	Jayes 1	"	"	Freer
24	Tottenham Hotspur	A	0-3	Calvert	"	"	"	"	Paterson	Sanderson	Burditt	Jayes	Witcomb	Adam
31	Northampton Town	H	3-2	"	"	"	"	"	"	"	Dewis 1	"	Liddle 2	"
Jun 2	Nottingham Forest	H	2-0	"	"	"	Sheard	"	"	"	A.Smith 1	Dewis 1	Burditt	Roome
7	Stoke City	H	2-1	"	"	"	Frith	Sheard	"	"	"1	"1	Liddle	Adam

LEAGUE WAR CUP

DATE	OPPONENTS		FT	1	2	3	4	5	6	7	8	9	10	11
Feb 15	Birmingham (1 leg 1)	H	3-3	Chesters	Frame	Howe	Frith	Heywood	Liddle	Jayes 1	Dewis	Lee 1	Cheney	Foster 1
22	Birmingham (1 leg 2)	H	3-2	Calvert	"	"	"	"	"1	Rochester	"1	"	A.Smith 1	Lyman
Mar 1	Nottingham Forest (2 leg 1)	A	2-0	Chesters	"	"	Towers	"	"	"	"1	"1	"1	"
8	Nottingham Forest (2 leg 2)	H	1-1	"	"	"	"	"	"	W.Wright	L.Smith	"1	"	"
15	Mansfield Town (3 leg 1)	H	2-2	"	Jones	"	Frame	"	"	"1	Dewis	"1	"	"
22	Mansfield Town (3 leg 2)	A	2-1	Calvert	Frame	"	Frith	Sheard	Rochester	"	"1	"	"	Liddle 1
29	Queens Park R. (4 leg 1)	A	1-2	"	"	"	"	Heywood	"	"	"1	"	"	"
Apr 5	Queens Park R. (4 leg 2)	H	6-1	"	"	"	"	"	Paterson	"	Jayes 2	"1	Burditt	A.Smith 3
19	Arsenal (sf leg 1)	A	0-1	"	"	"	"	"	"	"	Dewis	"	Liddle	Chapman
26	Arsenal (sf leg 2)	H	1-2	"	"	"	"	"	"	"	"	"1	Fagan	A.Smith

Note: 1) Dec 25, two fixtures played on the same day, kick offs 10.45am and 3.00pm.
2) Jan 11, Challinor (og).

3) Feb 15, Feb 22, both played at Filbert Street.
4) The six Midland Cup ties also counted towards the League table.

GUEST	SIGNING		APPEARANCES		GOALS	
CLUB	DATE		SRL	LWC	SRL	LWC
Charlie Adam			3			
Jack Bowers			1		1	
Ken Burditt	Notts County		3	1		
Joe Calvert			32	6		
Vernon Chapman		26-3-41	1	1	1	
Denis Cheney			3	1		
Arthur Chesters	Crystal Palace			4		
Edwin Cunningham	Bristol City		1			
George Dewis			22	8	20	4
Willie Fagan	Liverpool			1		
Walter Foster		12-2-41		1		1
Billy Frame			33	10		
Billy Freer		23-8-39	1			
William Frith	Coventry City		9	7		
Stan Frost		28-3-41	3			
John Grogan			2			
Jimmy Harrison			5			
Roger Heywood			28	9	2 (1p)	
Bert Howe			30	10	2 (2p)	
Gordon Jayes			8	2	3	2
Harry Johnston	Blackpool		4			
Dai Jones			1	1		
Jack Lee			9	10	7	6
Danny Liddle			27	8	6	2

GUEST	SIGNING		APPEARANCES		GOALS	
CLUB	DATE		SRL	LWC	SRL	LWC
Colin Lyman	Tottenham Hotspur			4		
Jimmy Mullen	Wolverhampton W.		25		15 (2p)	
George Paterson	Celtic	11-4-41	7	3		
Alan Rochester		15-11-40	17	4		
Robert Roome		20-12-40	1			
Don Sanderson		12-2-41	5		1	
Fred Sharman			4			
Frank Sheard			5	1		
Arthur E.Smith	Wolverhampton W.		13	8	9	5
John Smith			11		1	
Les Smith		cs-1940	3	1		
Sep Smith			1			
Terry Springthorpe	Wolverhampton W.		1			
Fred Steele	Stoke City		7		5	
Dennis Thornhill	Wolverhampton W.		3			
Bill Towers		26-3-40	3	2		
E.Ward			1			
Fred Wilson	Bournemouth & B.A.		1			
Doug Witcomb	West Brom. Albion		1			
Dennis Wright	Mansfield Town		1		2	
Billy Wright	Wolverhampton W.		26	7	11	1
Harold Wyles		26-8-39	1			
Own Goals					1	

Leicester players who guested for other clubs during the season:
Charlie Adam — **Queens Park Rangers**
Mal Griffiths — **Fulham**
Maurice Reeday — **Blackburn Rovers / Rochdale**

1941-42 FOOTBALL LEAGUE SOUTHERN SECTION — Final Position : 1st

DATE	OPPONENTS		FT	1	2	3	4	5	6	7	8	9	10	11
Aug 30	Norwich City	H	1-1	Calvert	Frame	Howe	Frith	Sheard	Mansfield	Barratt	Jayes 1	Lee	A.Smith	Adam
Sep 6	Norwich City	A	0-0	"	"	"	Rochester	"	"	"	"	"	"	"
13	West Bromwich Albion	A	1-4	Parker	"	"	Frith	Paterson	"	"	S.Smith 1	Jayes	"	"
20	West Bromwich Albion	H	3-2	"	"	"	S.Smith 1	Frith	Paterson	"	Jayes	Chapman	"	Cheney 2
27	Wolverhampton Wanderers	H	2-0	Morgan	"	"	"	"	"	"	"	"2	"	"
Oct 4	Wolverhampton Wanderers	A	0-0	"	"	"	"	"	L.Jones	"	A.Smith	Jayes	Iggleden	"
11	Luton Town	A	2-3	"	"	"	Frith	S.Smith	Liddle	"1	Jayes	Lee	"	"1
18	Luton Town	H	7-2	"	"	"	"	"	Paterson	"	A.Smith 2	Jayes 1	L.Smith 1	"3
25	Northampton Town	H	1-0	"	"	"	S.Smith	Frith	"	"	Iggleden	"1	"	"
Nov 1	Northampton Town	A	1-0	"	"	"	"	"	"	"1	Mulraney	"	A.Smith	"
8	Walsall	A	1-2	"	"	"	"	Sheard	Frith	"	Drake	"1	"	"
15	Walsall	H	6-0	Grant	"	"	"1	Frith	Paterson	"2	Jayes 1	Sanderson	"	"1
22	Nottingham Forest	H	3-0	Morgan	"	"	"	"	Mansfield	"	Rochester	"1	"1	"1
29	Nottingham Forest	A	1-0	Grant	"	"	"	"	Paterson	"	"	"1	"	"
Dec 6	Norwich City	H	6-1	Morgan	"	"	"1	"	"	"1	Jayes 1	"1	"	"2
20	Nottingham Forest	A	3-2	Grant	"	"	"	"	"	"	"1	"1	"	"1
25	Nottingham Forest	H	2-0	"	"	"1p	"	Sheard	Liddle	"	"1	"	"	"

FOOTBALL LEAGUE CHAMPIONSHIP — Final Position: 17th

DATE	OPPONENTS			FT	1	2	3	4	5	6	7	8	9	10	11
Dec 27	Chesterfield	WCQ	A	3-3	Calvert	Frame	Howe	S.Smith	Frith	Liddle	Barratt	Jayes	Dewis 3	A.Smith	Cheney
Jan 3	Chesterfield	WCQ	H	4-1	Grant	"	"	"	"	"	Frost	"1	"1	"1	"1
10	Luton Town	WCQ	H	3-0	Calvert	"	"	"	"	Paterson	"	"	Chapman 1	"1	Liddle 1
17	Luton Town	WCQ	A	2-2	Grant	"	"	"	"	"	"	Barratt	Jayes	"1	Cheney 1
Feb 14	West Brom. Albion	WCQ	A	2-3	Calvert	"	"	"	"	"	"1	"1	"	"	"
21	Norwich City	WCQ	H	1-1	"	"	"	Frith	Sheard	"	Barratt	S.Smith	"	"	Liddle 1
28	Norwich City	WCQ	A	3-6	Grant	"	"	S.Smith	"	Liddle	"	Jayes 1	Paterson 1	"1	Cheney
Mar 14	Sheffield Wednesday	WCQ	H	5-1	"	"	"	"1	Frith	Paterson	"1	"	Dewis 3	Buchan	Taylor
21	West Brom. Albion	WCQ	H	4-2	"	"	"	"1	Crawley	A.Smith	"	"1	Bowers	"2	Cheney
28	Northampton Town		A	1-1	Morgan	"	"	"	"	Liddle	"	"	Paterson	A.Smith	Taylor 1
Apr 4	Norwich City	WC 1/1	H	2-0	"	"	"1p	"	Frith	"	Rochester	"1	Crawley	"	Adam
6	Norwich City	WC 1/2	A	0-3	"	"	"	"	Crawley	Frith	Barratt	"	Sanderson	"	Cheney
11	Sheffield Wednesday		A	1-4	"	"	Wyles	"	Frith	Paterson	"	Lee	Howe	"	"1
18	Sheffield Wednesday		H	0-1	"	"	Howe	Harrison	Grogan	"	Sanderson	Jayes	Lee	Buchan	Bulger
May 16	Northampton Town		A	1-3	"	"	"	S.Smith	Frith	Wyles	Barratt	"1	D.Jones	Liddle	Hernon
23	Bristol City		H	5-1	"	"	"	"	Wyles	Barnes	"2	"	Cheney 1	"2	"
25	Northampton Town		H	1-4	Graham	"	"	"	"	Paterson	Cheney	"	Sanderson 1	"	"
30	Bristol City		A	1-3	Morgan	"	"	"	"	Barnes	Barratt	"1	"	Buchan	"

Note: 1) Nov 15, Shelton (og).

2) The eleven War Cup games also counted towards the League Championship table, but goals scored in extra time did not.

3) Apr 6, after extra time, score at 90 minutes 0-2

GUEST	SIGNING	APPEARANCES		GOALS	
	CLUB	DATE	FLS FLC	FLS	FLC
Charlie Adam			3 1		
William Barnes		1-5-42	2		
Harry Barratt	Coventry City		17 13	4	4
Jack Bowers			1		
William Buchan	Blackpool		4		2
Charles Bulger	Walsall		1		
Joe Calvert			2 4		
Vernon Chapman			2 1	2	1
Denis Cheney			14 10	11	4
Tom Crawley	Coventry City		4		
George Dewis			3	7	
Ted Drake	Arsenal		1		
Billy Frame			17 18		
William Frith	Coventry City		15 11		
Stan Frost			4		1
Dick Graham		2-12-41	1		
Alick Grant			4 5		
John Grogan			1		
Jimmy Harrison			1		
Jimmy Hernon			4		
Bert Howe			17 18	1 (p)	1 (p)

GUEST	SIGNING	APPEARANCES		GOALS	
	CLUB	DATE	FLS FLC	FLS	FLC
Ray Iggleden			3		
Gordon Jayes			15 17	8	6
Dai Jones			1		
Les J.Jones	Arsenal		1		
Jack Lee			3 2		
Danny Liddle			2 10		4
Reg Mansfield		11-12-40	4		
Bill Morgan	Coventry City		9 8		
Ambrose Mulraney	Ipswich Town		1		
Harry Parker		15-9-41	2		
George Paterson	Celtic		10 10	1	1
Alan Rochester			3 1		
Don Sanderson			6 4	4	1
Frank Sheard			4 2		
Arthur E.Smith			15 12	3	4
Les Smith	Brentford		2	1	
Sep Smith			15 17	4	2
George Taylor	Coventry City		2		1
Harold Wyles			5		
Own Goals				1	

Leicester players who guested for other clubs during the season:

Jack Bowers	Nottingham Forest
Billy Coutts	Nottingham Forest
George Dewis	Chesterfield
Dick Graham	Norwich City
Mal Griffiths	Bournemouth & B.A.
Dai Jones	Wrexham
William Muncie	Nottingham Forest
Don Sanderson	Luton Town
Eric Stubbs	Chester

1942-43 FOOTBALL LEAGUE NORTH

Final Position : 33rd

DATE	OPPONENTS		FT	1	2	3	4	5	6	7	8	9	10	11
Aug 29	Birmingham	H	0-1	Grant	Frame	Howe	S.Smith	Wyles	Liddle	Dunkley	Kirkaldie	Jayes	Buchan	Hernon
Sep 5	Birmingham	A	1-2	"	"	"	"	Sheard	"	Kirkaldie	R.Walton	Sanderson 1	Hernon	Cheney
12	West Bromwich Albion	A	2-3	"	"	"	"	Wyles	"	Hillard	Jayes 1	"	"1	"
19	West Bromwich Albion	H	0-0	"	"	"	"	"	Kendall	H.Walton	Gallagher	R.Walton	"	"
26	Coventry City	H	0-0	"	"	"	"	Sheard	Wyles	Cheney	Jayes	"	Gallagher	Hernon
Oct 3	Coventry City	A	1-5	"	"	"	"	"	"	Kirkaldie	J.Smith	Cheney	Hernon	Plummer 1
10	Notts County	H	1-3	"	Harrison	"	"	"	"	Barratt	Jayes	F.Steele 1	"	Hernon
17	Notts County	A	1-1	"	Wyles	"	"	Plummer	Paterson	"	J.Smith	"	Carver 1	Hernon
24	Mansfield Town	A	2-1	"	Snape	"	"	Wyles	Robertson	McAskill	Gardiner 1	Plummer 1	A.Smith	
31	Mansfield Town	H	5-2	"	Plummer	"	"	"	Hillard	Cheney 2	Hughes	F.Steele 2	"1	"
Nov 7	Derby County	H	2-3	"	Snape	"	"2(1p)	Sheard	"	Hughes	Jayes	Plummer	F.Steele	"
14	Derby County	A	3-5	Bradley	"	"	"	Bedford	"	Dunkley 1	Hughes 1	"	A.Smith 1	E.Steele
21	Nottingham Forest	H	2-1	Grant	Frame	"	"	Snape	Plummer	"	Barratt	F.Steele 1	"	"1
28	Nottingham Forest	A	1-1	"	R.Walton	"	"	Gemmell	Snape	McAskill	F.Steele	Chapman	Hernon 1	Flint
Dec 5	Wolverhampton Wanderers	A	2-0	"	"	"	"	"	"	Chapman	Barratt	F.Steele 2	A.Smith	Plummer
12	Wolverhampton Wanderers	H	5-0	"	"	"	"	"	Plummer	Thompson	"1	"4	Hernon	Flint
19	Aston Villa	A	2-4	Bradley	"	"	"1	"	"	"	Betteridge	"1	"	E.Steele
25	Aston Villa	H	2-5	Grant	"	"	"	"	"	Barratt 1	Gardiner	Chapman 1	A.Smith	Hernon

FOOTBALL LEAGUE NORTH (Second Competition)

Final Position: 22nd

DATE	OPPONENTS			FT	1	2	3	4	5	6	7	8	9	10	11
Dec 26	West Brom. Albion	LNCQ	A	1-5	Grant	R.Walton	Howe	S.Smith	Plummer	Hernon	Gemmell	Barratt	Chapman 1	A.Smith	Flint
Jan 2	West Brom. Albion	LNCQ	H	9-0	"	"	"1p	"	Gemmell	Plummer	Barratt 2	Dewis 1	F.Steele 2	Cheney 3	E.Steele
9	Birmingham	LNCQ	A	0-5	"	"	"	"	"	"	Hernon	"	"	Sanderson	Liddle
16	Birmingham	LNCQ	H	2-1	"	"	"	"	"	"	Frost	Barratt 1	Sanderson	A.Smith	E.Steele
23	Nottingham Forest	LNCQ	H	5-0	"	"	"	"1	"	Wyles	Dunkley 1	"	Plummer 3	Liddle	Frost
30	Nottingham Forest	LNCQ	A	0-4	"	"	"	"	"	"	Barratt	A.Smith	"	Jayes	Cheney
Feb 6	Coventry City	LNCQ	H	0-2	Bradley	"	Gemmell	"	Sharman	Howe	Rochester	Barratt	"	A.Smith	Flint
13	Coventry City	LNCQ	A	3-1	Grant	"	"	"1	"	Hamilton	Barratt 1	Dewis 1	"	Johnston	Liddle
20	Northampton Town	LNCQ	A	3-2	"	"	"	"1p	"	"	Hughes	Barratt	"1	"1	Cheney
27	Northampton Town	LNCQ	H	4-2	"	"	"	"1p	"	"	"	"2	Dewis	"1	Liddle
Mar 6	Nottingham Forest	LNC 1/1	A	1-0	King	"	Howe	"	"	"	Pritchard	Jayes	"1	"	Liddle
13	Nottingham Forest	LNC 1/2	H	0-2	"	"	Gemmell	"	"	Howe	Dunkley	"	Plummer	"	"1
20	Derby County		A	2-3	"	"	Howe	"	"	Jones	McCormick	Hughes	Harrison 1	Lewis	"1
27	Derby County		H	3-1	"	"	Gemmell	"1	"	"	Hughes	Phillips	"1	McCormick	Howe 1
Apr 3	Northampton Town		H	3-0	Grant	"	"	"	"	Kendall	"	Dewis 1	"1	Phillips 1	"
10	Northampton Town		A	2-2	"	"	Howe	"	"	"	Dunkley	Phillips	"	Johnston 1	Rutherford 1
17	Coventry City		H	1-3	"	"	"	"1p	"	"	McCormick	"	"	"	"
24	Coventry City		A	0-0	"	Sharman	"	"	Gemmell	"	Hughes	"	R.Walton	"	Hernon
26	Stoke City		H	1-2	"	R.Walton	Wyles	Johnston	"	Howe	"	"	Sharman	Browne	Liddle 1
May 1	Stoke City		A	0-3	"	"	Gemmell	S.Smith	Burditt	Johnston	Birks	Staples	Harrison	Dunkley	Longland

Note: 1) Nov 21, played at Coalville.

2) Mar 13, after extra time, score at 90 minutes 0-1

3) The twelve League North Cup ties also counted towards the League North table, but goals scored in extra time did not.

GUEST	CLUB	SIGNING DATE	APPEARANCES FL	FL(2)	GOALS FL	FL(2)
Harry Barratt	Coventry City		6	9	2	6
George Bedford	Northampton Town		1			
Mick Betteridge		15-12-42	1			
W.J.Birks	Port Vale			1		
Gordon Bradley			2	1		
J.H.Browne	Aston Villa			1		
William Buchan	Blackpool		1			
Ken Burditt	Notts County			1		
W.Carver	Arbroath		1		1	
Vernon Chapman			3	1	1	1
Denis Cheney			6	3	2	3
George Dewis				6		4
Maurice Dunkley	Manchester City		3	4	1	1
Ken Flint	Bedford Town	20-11-42	2	2		
Billy Frame			7			
Stan Frost				2		1
Pat Gallagher	Stoke City		2			
C.Gardiner	Montrose		2		1	
Jim Gemmell	Bury		5	16		
Alick Grant			16	15		
William Hamilton	Preston North End			4		
Jimmy Harrison			1	6		3
Jimmy Hernon			15	3	2	
Jock Hillard	Northampton Town	3-11-42	4			
Bert Howe			18	16		2 (1p)
Tom Hughes		30-10-42	3	7	1	
Gordon Jayes			5	3	1	
Tom Johnston	Northampton Town	13-3-43		10		3
Leslie O.Jones		29-3-43		2		

GUEST	CLUB	SIGNING DATE	APPEARANCES FL	FL(2)	GOALS FL	FL(2)
John Kendall		17-1-42	1	4		
Sid King		9-3-43		4		
Jack Kirkaldie	Doncaster Rovers		3			
John Lewis	Crystal Palace			1		
Danny Liddle			3	8		2
E.Longland	Stoke City			1		
A.McAskill	Third Lanark		2			
Jim McCormick	Tottenham Hotspur			3		
George Paterson	Celtic		1			
Russell Phillips		29-3-43		6		1
Norman Plummer			12	10	2	4
Jack Pritchard	Manchester City			1		
James Robertson	Bradford City		1			
Alan Rochester				1		
Bill Rutherford		9-4-43		2		1
Don Sanderson			2	2	1	
Fred Sharman				13		
Frank Sheard			5			
Arthur E.Smith			6	4	2	
John Smith			2			
Sep Smith			18	19	3 (1p)	6 (3p)
John Snape	Coventry City		6			
Len Staples		8-6-42		1		
Eddie Steele	Crystal Palace		3	2	1	
Fred Steele	Stoke City		9	2	11	2
Tommy Thompson			2			
Harry Walton		21-9-42	1			
Dick Walton		8-6-42	8	20		
Harold Wyles			9	3		

Leicester players who guested for other clubs during the season:

Jack Bowers	Notts County	Mal Griffiths	Bournemouth & B.A. / Southampton
Gordon Bradley	Sheffield United / Grimsby Town	Dai Jones	Notts County
Dick Graham	Southport	Danny Liddle	Notts County
Alick Grant	Nottingham Forest	Fred Sharman	Notts County

1943-44 FOOTBALL LEAGUE NORTH

Final Position : 28th

DATE	OPPONENTS		FT	1	2	3	4	5	6	7	8	9	10	11
Aug 28	Mansfield Town	H	4-1	A.Grant	Frame	Howe	S.Smith	Sharman	Liddle	McNeil	Phillips 3	Dewis 1	Dickie	Bulger
Sep 4	Mansfield Town	A	0-0	"	"	"	"	"	"	Staples	"	Steward	"	"
11	Birmingham	A	0-3	"	"	"	"	"	"	Frost	"	Chapman	North	"
18	Birmingham	H	2-2	"	"	"	"1	Gemmell	"	Cronin	"	"	Dickie	"1
25	Coventry City	A	1-0	"	"	"	"	"	"	"	Dickie 1	Bulger	Lycett	Roberts
Oct 2	Coventry City	H	1-0	"	"	"	"	"	"	"	Dewis	"	"	L.O.Jones
9	West Bromwich Albion	H	0-3	"	"	"	"	"	"	"	Dickie	Phillips	"	Campbell
16	West Bromwich Albion	A	2-2	"	"	Becci	Sheard	"	"	Campbell 1	S.Smith	Bowden	"1	Hillard
23	Notts County	H	5-0	"	"	"	S.Smith	"	"	Cronin	Dickie	"2	"1	Campbell 1
30	Notts County	A	9-1	"	"	"	"	"	"	"	"	Dewis 4	A.Smith 4	"1
Nov 6	Derby County	H	0-1	"	"	"	"	"	"	"	A.Smith	Phillips	Dickie	"
13	Derby County	A	2-3	"	"	Howe	"	"	Dickie	Little	Phillips	Sutton	Lycett	Alsop 1
20	Nottingham Forest	A	0-1	"	"	"	"	"	Phillips	"	Dickie	Dewis	Cheney	Bulger
27	Nottingham Forest	H	3-3	"	"	Gemmell	Dickie	S.Smith	Liddle	Campbell	Staples 1	Bowden 2	"	Alsop
Dec 4	Wolverhampton Wanderers	H	1-0	"	"	Becci	S.Smith	Gemmell	Dickie	Hillard	"	"1	Lycett	Campbell
11	Wolverhampton Wanderers	A	1-4	"	"	Harrison	"	"	Liddle	Cronin	"	Alsop 1	Dickie	"
18	Aston Villa	H	1-3	Major	"	Becci	Sheard	"	Dickie	Campbell 1	Lycett	Bowden	Dimond	Alsop
25	Aston Villa	A	1-3	"	"	"	S.Smith	Sheard	Plummer	"	"1	R.Grant	"	"

FOOTBALL LEAGUE NORTH (Second Competition)

Final Position:14th

DATE	OPPONENTS			FT	1	2	3	4	5	6	7	8	9	10	11
Dec 26	Notts County	LNCQ	A	2-1	A.Grant	Frame	Becci	Sheard	Gemmell	Liddle	Goffin	S.Smith	Bowden 2	Lycett	Campbell
Jan 1	Notts County	LNCQ	H	7-2	"	"	Sharman	"	"	"	"	"3(1p)	"3	"	"1
8	Derby County	LNCQ	A	1-0	"	"	"	"	"	Dickie	Alsop	"	"1	Campbell	Goffin
15	Derby County	LNCQ	H	1-0	"	"	"	"	"	"	Goffin	"	"	Lycett	Campbell 1
22	Mansfield Town	LNCQ	H	5-2	Major	"	"	"	"	Liddle	Cronin 1	"2	Alsop 1	Dickie	"1
29	Mansfield Town	LNCQ	A	1-1	A.Grant	"	Howe	"	Sharman	"	"	"	Knott 1	"	"
Feb 5	Sheffield Wednesday	LNCQ	H	1-1	"	"	"	"	"	"	Morton	"	"	Campbell	Alsop
12	Sheffield Wednesday	LNCQ	A	3-0	"	"	"	"	Gemmell	Dickie	Knott 2	"	Dewis 1	Jayes	Campbell
19	Nottingham Forest	LNCQ	A	0-1	"	"	Davidson	"	"	Howe	Cronin	"	Knott	Liddle	Little
26	Nottingham Forest	LNCQ	H	1-1	"	"	Howe	King	"	Sheard	Little	"	"	L.J.Jones 1	Campbell
Mar 4	Birmingham	LNC1/1	A	1-3	"	"	"	Sheard	"	L.J.Jones 1	"	"	Rickards	Knott	"
11	Birmingham	LNC1/2	H	2-1	"	"	"1p	S.Smith	"	Dickie	"	A.Smith	Sheard	L.J.Jones	Muncie 1
18	Stoke City	MC1/1	A	5-2	Bradley	"	"	"	"	"	"1	"1	Knott 3	"	Crossland
25	Stoke City	MC1/2	H	2-2	"	"	"	Sparrow	"	Sheard	King	S.Smith	Dewis 2	Dickie	Hillard
Apr 1	Northampton Town	MC2/1	A	0-2	A.Grant	"	"	S.Smith	"	"	Little	Dewis	Knott	"	Campbell
8	Northampton Town	MC2/2	A	1-3	"	"	Reeday	"	Sheard	Howe	Frost	Little	Walton	Liddle	Wattie 1
10	Wolverhampton Wanderers		A	1-4	"	Sparrow	Wyles	King	Sharman	"	Little	Phillips	Sheard 1p	Kilshaw	"
15	Coventry City		H	1-1	"	Frame	Walton	"	Gemmell	Sheard	"	"1	Sharman	Dickie	"
22	Coventry City		A	2-6	"	"	"	"	Sharman	Lycett	Hillard	"	Sanderson 2	Middleton	Campbell
29	Derby County		A	2-0	"	"	Sharman	"	Gemmell	Dickie	Campbell	S.Smith	Sheard 1	Windle 1	Bulger
May 6	Derby County		H	1-0	"	"	Howe	"	"	Kendall	"	"	"	Dickie	"

Note: 1) Oct 23, Marshall (og)
2) Nov 13, Vose (og)
3) Feb 5, Russell (og)
4) May 6, Leuty (og)
5) The twelve League North Cup ties and four Midland Cup ties also counted towards the League North table, but goals scored in extra time did not.
6) Mar 11, after extra time, score at 90 minutes 2-0.

	GUEST CLUB	SIGNING DATE	APPEARANCES FLN	FLN (2)	GOALS FLN	FLN (2)
Gilbert Alsop	Walsall		5	3	2	1
Attilio Becci	Arbroath		7	1		
Norman Bowden	Arsenal		5	4	5	6
Gordon Bradley				2		
Charles Bulger	Walsall		7	2	1	
Jim Campbell			10	14	4	3
George Chapman		9-9-43	2			
Denis Cheney			2			
David Cronin		14-5-41	8	3	1	1
Ben Crossland	Burnley			1		
David Davidson	Bradford Park Ave.			1		
George Dewis			4	3	5	3
Percy Dickie	Blackburn Rovers		14	12	1	
Stuart Dimond	Manchester United		2			
Billy Frame			18	20		
Stan Frost			1	1		
Jim Gemmell	Bury		14	16		
Billy Goffin	Aston Villa			4		
Alick Grant			16	18		
Ron Grant			1			
Jimmy Harrison			1			
Jock Hillard			2	2		
Bert Howe			9	13		1 (p)
Gordon Jayes				1		
Les J.Jones	Arsenal			4		2
Leslie O.Jones			1			
John Kendall				1		
Fred Kilshaw				1		
Johnny King				7		

	GUEST CLUB	SIGNING DATE	APPEARANCES FLN	FLN (2)	GOALS FLN	FLN (2)
Herbert Knott	Hull City			8		6
Danny Liddle			13	7		
George Little	Doncaster Rovers		2	9		1
Tim Lycett		10-8-43	9	4	3	
W.McNeil	Hamilton Academ.		1			
Les Major			2	1		
William Middleton				1		
Alex Morton		2-2-44		1		
William Muncie				1		1
Tommy North		2-7-43	1			
Russell Phillips			8	3	3	1
Norman Plummer			1			
Maurice Reeday				1		
Charlie Rickards	Mansfield Town			1		
Gordon Roberts	Wolverhampton W.		1			
Don Sanderson				1		2
Fred Sharman			3	10		
Frank Sheard			3	19		2 (1p)
Arthur E.Smith			2	2	4	1
Sep Smith			17	18	1	5 (1p)
Terry Sparrow		7-3-44		2		
Len Staples			4	1		
- Steward			1			
A.Sutton	Third Lanark		1			
Dick Walton				3		
J.H.Wattie	Dundee United			3		1
Eric Windle	Derby County		1		1	
Harold Wyles				1		
Own Goals					2	2

Leicester players who guested for other clubs during the season:

Gordon Bradley	Lincoln City / Notts County	Dai Jones	Notts County / West Ham United
George Dewis	Leeds United	Les Major	Notts County
Dick Graham	Notts County	Maurice Reeday	Burnley
Mal Griffiths	Bournemouth & B.A.	John Smith	Southampton
John Grogan	Crystal Palace	Dick Walton	Middlesbrough / Chester
Jimmy Harrison	Reading		

1944-45 FOOTBALL LEAGUE NORTH

Final Position : 52nd

DATE	OPPONENTS		FT	1	2	3	4	5	6	7	8	9	10	11
Aug 26	Wolverhampton Wanderers	H	2-2	Grant	Frame	Howe	King	Gemmell	Dickie	Revie	S.Smith	Dewis 2	L.J.Jones	Campbell
Sep 2	Wolverhampton Wanderers	A	0-4	"	"	Harrison	"	"	Sheard	"	"	"	Dickie	"
9	Walsall	H	2-3	"	"	Cobley	S.Smith	Sheard	Dickie	T.Jones	King	Phillips 2	L.J.Jones	Smart
16	Walsall	A	1-0	"	"	"	"	"	Paterson	"	"	Mercer 1	Woodvine	Campbell
23	Birmingham	H	0-1	"	"	Howe	"	"	Dickie	"	A.Smith	Rickards	L.J.Jones	Woodvine
30	Birmingham	A	3-3	"	"	"	King	"	L.J.Jones	"	Rickards 1	Mercer 2	S.Smith	Campbell
Oct 7	West Bromwich Albion	A	1-1	Major	"	"	"	"	"	"	Dewis	"	"1	"
14	West Bromwich Albion	H	0-2	"	"	"	"	"	"	Campbell	Brown	Rickards	"	Woodvine
21	Port Vale	H	4-1	"	"	Cobley	"	"	"	"1	Rickards 3 (1p)	Bowden	"	Douglas
28	Port Vale	A	1-2	"	"	Howe	"	"	"	"	"1	"	"	"
Nov 4	Coventry City	H	2-1	"	"	"	"	"	"	"1	"	Chapman	"1	Muncie
11	Coventry City	A	1-3	"	"	"	"	"	"	"	"	Kelly 1	"	Dickie
18	Northampton Town	A	1-3	"	"	"	Grogan	"	"	Dunkley 1	"	"	"	Long
25	Northampton Town	H	2-2	"	"	Hubble	King	"	"	Kelly	"1	Bowden 1	"	Dunkley
Dec 2	Aston Villa	H	0-3	"	"	Howe	S.Smith	"	King	Dunkley	"	Mercer	L.J.Jones	Hubble
9	Aston Villa	A	0-5	"	"	Hubble	"	"	"	A.Smith	Stephan	Kelly	Iddon	Chapman
16	Stoke City	A	2-5	"	"	Howe	Towers	Morby	Sheard	Dunkley	S.Smith	Sanderson	"1	Cheney 1
23	Stoke City	H	1-5	Bradley	"	"	"	S.Smith	"	"	Rickards 1	"	"	Buckby

FOOTBALL LEAGUE NORTH (Second Competition)

Final Position: 34th

DATE	OPPONENTS			FT	1	2	3	4	5	6	7	8	9	10	11
Dec 30	Nottingham Forest	LNCQ	A	0-0	Major	Frame	Howe	S.Smith	Sheard	King	Dunkley	Rickards	Wyles	Riley	Campbell
Jan 6	Mansfield Town	LNCQ	A	2-2	Grant	"	"	Kilshaw 1	Wyles	Lindley	"	S.Smith 1p	Dewis	"	Liddle
13	Mansfield Town	LNCQ	H	8-3	Major	"	"	King	Sheard	Towers	"1	"2	Leitch 3	Iddon	"2
20	Chesterfield	LNCQ	A	0-1	"	"	"	Towers	"	Lindley	Campbell	"	Wyles	"	"
27	Chesterfield	LNCQ	H	2-2	"	"	"	"	"	Wyles	Kilshaw	"1p	Leitch 1	"	"
Feb 3	Notts County	LNCQ	A	4-1	"	"	"	R.Jones	"	Towers	Buckby	"1	"2	Stephan 1	"
10	Notts County	LNCQ	H	4-1	"	"	"	Towers	"	R.Jones	Bowden 1	"1	"1	"	"1
17	Derby County	LNCQ	H	2-2	"	"	"	Kilshaw	"	Towers	Dunkley	Bowden	"2	"	"
24	Derby County	LNCQ	A	0-3	"	"	"	S.Smith	"	"	C.Smith	Mercer	"	Bowden	"
Mar 3	Nottingham Forest	LNCQ	H	1-1	"	"	"	"	"	"	Dunkley	Tapping	"1	Iddon	"
10	Wolverhampton Wanderers		A	2-3	"	Hanford	"	Tapping	Leitch	Riley	Cronin 1	S.Smith	Bowden	"	"
17	Coventry City		H	2-2	"	Frame	Hanford	Sheard	Plummer	"	"	"	"1	Thompson	Douglas 1
24	Derby County	LNC1/1	H	2-1	"	McCall	Howe	Elliott	Sheard	Baxter	Bowden	"1	Leitch	Iddon	Clare
31	Derby County	LNC1/2	A	0-2	"	"	"	Baxter	"	Elliott	Cronin	"	"	Bowden	Cheney
Apr 2	Sheffield Wednesday		H	2-1	Graham	Frame	"	Kilshaw	"	Wyles	"	Tapping 1	Bowden	Cheney 1	Liddle
7	Aston Villa		H	2-0	"	"	"	Tapping 1	"	Towers	Frost	S.Smith	Leitch 1	Bowden	Morrison
14	Aston Villa		A	2-7	Major	"	"	"	"	"	Cronin	"1p	"1	Thompson	"
21	West Brom. Albion	MC1/1	A	0-1	Graham	"	"	King	"	"	"	"	Mercer	"	Liddle
28	West Brom. Albion	MC1/2	H	3-0	"	"	"	Tapping	"	"	Dunkley	"2	Dewis 1	Iddon	"
May 5	Derby County	MC2/1	A	1-3	"	"	"	"	"	"	"	"	"1	Bowden	Johnston
12	Derby County	MC2/2	H	1-2	"	"	"	Kilshaw	"	Elliott	"	"	"1	Bowden	"

Notes: 1) Mar 10, Ashton (og)

2) The twelve League North Cup ties and four Midland Cup ties also counted towards the League North table.

GUEST	SIGNING	APPEARANCES		GOALS	
CLUB	DATE	FLN	FLN (2)	FLN	FLN (2)
Bill Baxter	Nottingham Forest		2		
Norman Bowden	Arsenal	3	10	1	2
Gordon Bradley		1			
Robert Brown	Charlton Athletic	1			
Maurice Buckby	12-12-44	1	1		
Jim Campbell		10	2	2	
Vernon Chapman		2			
Denis Cheney		1	2	1	1
Joe Clare	Lincoln City		1		
William Cobley	Aston Villa	3			
David Cronin			6		1
George Dewis		3	4	2	3
Percy Dickie	Blackburn Rovers	5			
David Douglas	21-10-44	2	1		1
Maurice Dunkley	Manchester City	5	8	1	1
Bernard Elliott	Nottingham Forest		3		
Billy Frame		18	18		
Stan Frost			1		
Jim Gemmell	Bury	2			
Dick Graham			6		
Alick Grant		6	1		
John Grogan		1			
Norman Hanford	9-8-44		2		
Jimmy Harrison		1			
Bert Howe		12	20		
Len Hubble	Newcastle United	3			
Harry Iddon	Preston North End	3	8	1	1
Tom Johnston	Nottingham Forest		2		
Les J.Jones	Arsenal	13			
Ralph Jones	16-5-44		2		
Tommy Jones	Derby County	5			
Don Kelly	8-11-44	4		1	

GUEST	SIGNING	APPEARANCES		GOALS	
CLUB	DATE	FLN	FLN (2)	FLN	FLN (2)
Fred Kilshaw			5		1
Johnny King		14	3		
W.Leitch	Motherwell		12		12
Danny Liddle			13		3
Maurice Lindley	Everton		2		
Danny Long		1			
Bob McCall	Nottingham Forest		2		
Les Major		11	14		
Stan Mercer	19-7-44	4	2	3	
John Morby	Aston Villa	1			
Angus Morrison	Derby County		2		
William Muncie		1			
George Paterson	Glasgow Celtic	1			
Russell Phillips		1		2	
Norman Plummer			1		
Don Revie		2			
Charlie Rickards	Mansfield Town	11	1	7 (1p)	
Richard Riley	5-1-45		4		
Don Sanderson		2			
Frank Sheard		17	19		
- Smart	Dundee	1			
Arthur E.Smith		2			
Charles Smith	Aberdeen		1		
Sep Smith		18	19	2	10 (3p)
Harry Stephan	Blackburn Rovers	1	3		1
Fred Tapping	Blackpool		7		2
Ron Thompson	Sheffield W.		3		
Bill Towers		2	13		
Albert Woodvine		3			
Harold Wyles			5		
Own Goals					1

Leicester players who guested for other clubs during the season:

George Dewis	Sheffield United	John Grogan	Luton Town / Swansea Town / Grimsby Town	Maurice Reeday	Accrington Stanley
David Douglas	Wrexham	Dai Jones	West Ham United	Arthur H.Smith	Walsall
Dick Graham	Crewe Alexandra	Danny Liddle	Mansfield Town	
Alick Grant	Derby County	Tim Lycett	Walsall	

1945-46 FOOTBALL LEAGUE SOUTH

Final Position : 20th

DATE	OPPONENTS		FT	1	2	3	4	5	6	7	8	9	10	11
Aug 25	Charlton Athletic	H	2-3	D.Graham	Frame	Jones	S.Smith	Sheard	Howe	Cronin 1	Revie	Mercer 1	Riley	Liddle
Sep 1	Charlton Athletic	A	1-2	"	"	"	J.Graham	Grogan	Towers	Attwood	"	"1	Hernon	"
6	Brentford	A	2-1	"	"	"	S.Smith	"	Russell	Sinclair	"	"1	Liddle 1	Anderson
8	Fulham	A	1-1	"	"	"	"	"	Robinson	Revie	McInally	"1	"	"
12	Tottenham Hotspur	A	2-6	"	"	"1	"1p	"	"	"	"	Bowden	"	"
15	Fulham	H	0-1	"	"	"	"	"	Towers	Anderson	Revie	Small	"	Aldecoa
22	Plymouth Argyle	A	3-2	"	"	"	"	Howe	"	Campbell 1	"	Mercer 1	Aldecoa	Stubbs
29	Plymouth Argyle	H	2-2	"	"	"	"	"	Soo	Revie 1	A.Smith 1	"	Liddle	Aldecoa
Oct 6	Portsmouth	A	0-2	"	Jones	Howe	"	Davies	"	Campbell	Revie	"	A.Smith	Liddle
13	Portsmouth	H	3-2	"	Frame	"	"1p	"	"1	"	"	"	"1	Aldecoa
20	Nottingham Forest	H	0-0	Calvert	"	"	"	Sheard	Towers	"	"	"	Middleton	Poulton
27	Nottingham Forest	A	1-1	"	"	"	"	"	Soo 1	Anderson	"	Dewis	Towers	Liddle
Nov 3	Newport County	A	0-2	D.Graham	"	"	"	E.Smith	Pearce	Campbell	King	Mercer	"	"
10	Newport County	H	2-0	Grant	"	"	"	"	Soo	"	Towers	"	Lycett	"2
17	Wolverhampton Wanderers	H	1-2	"	"	"	"	"	"	"	Revie	Jones	"1	"
24	Wolverhampton Wanderers	A	0-3	"	"	"	"	"	"	Dewis	Grogan	Mercer	"	Johnson
Dec 1	West Ham United	A	2-2	"	"	"	Grogan	"	Towers	Revie 1	S.Smith	"1	"	Liddle
8	West Ham United	H	4-1	"	"	"	S.Smith	"	Soo	"	King 1	"1	Towers 2	"
15	West Bromwich Albion	H	1-3	"	"	"	Osborne	"	"	"	"	"1	"	Aldecoa
22	West Bromwich Albion	A	2-3	"	"	Watts	S.Smith	Sheard	"1	Campbell	Dewis	"	Pimbley 1	Weatherston
25	Birmingham	A	2-6	Calvert	"	Howe	"	Grogan	"	Revie	Hernon	Dewis 2	"	Liddle
26	Birmingham	H	0-1	"	"	Jones	"	"	Towers	"	"	"	Osborne	Weatherston
29	Tottenham Hotspur	H	4-0	"	"	"	Osborne	Sheard	"	"1	S.Smith 2	Mercer 1	Soo	Adam
Jan 12	Chelsea	H	1-7	"	Watts	Howe	S.Smith	"	Grogan	Mercer	A.Smith	Sutton	Chisholm	Foster 1
19	Chelsea	A	0-4	Grant	Frame	"	Osborne	"	Towers	King	S.Smith	Mercer	A.Smith	"
26	Arsenal	H	4-5	"	"	Jones	S.Smith	"	"	Revie	Chisholm 1	"1	"	"2
Feb 2	Millwall	H	2-6	"	"	"	"	"	"	"	Harrison 1	Lee	Osborne 1	Weatherston
9	Southampton	H	1-2	Calvert	"	Howe	Osborne	E.Smith	"	"	S.Smith 1p	Dewis	Chisholm	Letters
16	Southampton	A	1-3	"	"	"	S.Smith	"	King	"	Iggleden	"	Pimbley 1	Foster
23	Derby County	H	1-1	"	"	"	"	"	Soo	"	"	Mercer	"1	"
Mar 9	Swansea Town	A	3-4	"	"	"	"	"	King	Campbell 1	Revie 1	Cutting	"1	"
16	Swansea Town	H	0-2	"	"	"	"	"	"	"	"	Pimbley	Iggleden	"
23	Coventry City	H	1-3	"	Ashton	"	"	"	"	Griffiths	Osborne	Dewis	Harrison	"1
30	Coventry City	A	1-0	"	Jones	"	Osborne	Grogan	"	"1	S.Smith	"	Towers	"
Apr 6	Luton Town	A	1-2	Grant	"	"	"	"	"	"	"	"	"	Cutting
10	Derby County	A	1-4	"	"	"	"	"	Soo	"	Revie	Lee	King 1	Lycett
13	Luton Town	H	0-2	"	Frame	"	S.Smith	"	Towers	"	A.Smith	Osborne	"	Lycett
15	Millwall	A	2-2	"	"	"	"1p	"	"	Revie	King	Griffiths	A.Smith 1	Cutting
20	Arsenal	A	2-1	Calvert	"	"	"	"	"	"	"	"1	"1	Liddle
22	Aston Villa	A	0-3	Grant	"	Jones	"	"	"	Griffiths	Revie	Pimbley	"	Woodvine
23	Aston Villa	H	0-1	"	"	"	Osborne	"	"	Revie	S.Smith	King	"	Pimbley
May 4	Brentford	H	1-3	Calvert	Jones	Howe	S.Smith	"	"	Griffiths	Edwards	Heathcote 1	"	Goffin

F.A.CUP

DATE	OPPONENTS			FT	1	2	3	4	5	6	7	8	9	10	11
Jan 5	Chelsea	(3 leg 1)	A	1-1	Calvert	Jones	Howe	Osborne	Sheard	Towers	Campbell	S.Smith	Mercer	Soo	Adam 1
10	Chelsea	(3 leg 2)	H	0-2	"	Frame	"	"	"	"	Adam	"	"	"	Liddle

Note: The F.A.Cup recommenced one year ahead of the normal Football League, but the two F.A.Cup ties did not count towards the League South table.

	GUEST CLUB	SIGNING DATE	APPEARANCES FLS	APPEARANCES FAC	GOALS FLS	GOALS FAC
Charlie Adam			1	2		1
Emilio Aldecoa	Wolverhampton W.		4	1		
Robert Anderson			5			
Derek Ashton	Wolverhampton W.		1			
Arthur Attwood	Bristol Rovers	4-9-45	1			
Norman Bowden	Arsenal		1			
Joe Calvert			15	2		
Jim Campbell			10	1	2	
Ken Chisholm	Queens Park		3		1	
David Cronin			1		1	
Fred Cutting		23-1-46	3			
Robert Davies	Nottingham Forest		2			
George Dewis			10		3	
George Edwards	Aston Villa		1			
Walter Foster		5-12-45	9		4	
Billy Frame			35	1		
Billy Goffin	Aston Villa		1			
Dick Graham			11			
Jim Graham		4-9-45	1			
Alick Grant			16			
Mal Griffiths			10		2	
John Grogan			19			
Walter Harrison			2		1	
Wilf Heathcote	Queens Park R.		1		1	
Jimmy Hernon			3			
Bert Howe			30	2		
Ray Iggleden			3			
John Johnson	West Brom. Albion		1			
Dai Jones			20	1	1	

	GUEST CLUB	SIGNING DATE	APPEARANCES FLS	APPEARANCES FAC	GOALS FLS	GOALS FAC
Johnny King			16		2	
Jack Lee			2			
W.J.Letters	Rangers		1			
Danny Liddle			17	1	3	
Tim Lycett			6		1	
J.McInally	Motherwell		2			
Stan Mercer			21	2	10	
William Middleton		10-7-45	1			
John Osborne			12	2	1	
George Pearce	Walsall		1			
Doug Pimbley		7-12-45	8		4	
Wallace Poulton	Stoke City		1			
Don Revie			31		4	
Richard Riley			1			
Peter Robinson	Manchester City		2			
Robert Russell	Chelsea		1			
Frank Sheard			9	2		
Tom Sinclair	Bolton Wanderers		1			
Sam Small	West Ham United		1			
Arthur E.Smith			10		4	
Eric Smith			13			
Sep Smith			39	2	6 (4p)	
Frank Soo			14	2	3	
Eric Stubbs			1			
Len Sutton			1			
Bill Towers			24	2	2	
Ray Watts		27-4-45	2			
Andy Weatherston		19-12-45	3			
Albert Woodvine			1			

Leicester players who guested for other clubs during the season:

Jim Campbell	Reading
Alick Grant	Mansfield Town / Notts County / Nottingham Forest
Stan Mercer	Arsenal / Accrington Stanley
Doug Pimbley	Nottingham Forest
Frank Soo	Port Vale / Burnley / Crewe Alexandra / Millwall
Albert Woodvine	Tranmere Rovers

1946-47 LEAGUE DIVISION TWO
Final Position : 9th
Ave. Home League Att: 24,000

DATE	OPPONENTS	V	F.T.	SCORERS	Grant	Frame	Jones	Smith S	Smith E	Eggleston	Griffiths	Revie	McCulloch	King	Adam	Towers	Dewis	Calvert	Howe	Anderson	Harrison W	Dawson	Grogan	Harrison J	Lee	Iggleden	Mercer	Bradley	Smith A	Chapman	McArthur	Garvey	Jelly	Hernon
Aug 31	Manchester City	H	0-3		1	2	3	4	5	6	7	8	9	10	11																			
Sep 4	Birmingham City	A	0-4		1	2	3	4	5		7		9	10	11	6	8																	
7	West Ham United	A	2-0	Jones,Anderson			2		5	6	7	8		10			9	1	3	11	4													
12	Birmingham City	H	2-1	King,S Smith (pen)			2	6	5			8		10			9	1	3	7	4	11												
14	Sheffield Wednesday	H	3-5	McCulloch 2,Adam			2	6	5			8	9	10	11			1	3	7	4													
19	Chesterfield	H	0-1				2	4			7		9	10	11	6		1	3	8			5											
21	Fulham	A	2-4	Adam,J Harrison			2	8						10	11	6		1	3	7	4		5	9										
28	Bury	H	0-0				2			8				10	11	6	9	1	3	7	4		5											
Oct 5	Luton Town	A	2-1	Lee 2			2			6	7				11		8	1	3		4		5	9	10									
12	Plymouth Argyle	H	4-1	Lee,Dewis 2,Revie			2	4		6	7	8			11		10	1	3				5	9										
19	Coventry City	H	1-0	Adam			2	4		6	7	8			11		10	1	3				5	9										
26	Nottingham Forest	A	0-2				2	4		6	7	8					10	1	3	11			5	9										
Nov 2	Southampton	H	2-0	Dewis 2			2	5		6	7	8					10	1	3	11	4			9										
9	Newport County	A	3-2	Lee 2,Dewis			2	5		6	7	8					10	1	3	11	4			9										
16	Barnsley	H	6-0	Eggleston 2,Lee 2,Dewis,Pallister (og)			2	5		6	7	8					10	1	3	11	4			9										
23	Burnley	A	0-0				2	5		6	7			8	11		10	1	3		4					9								
30	Tottenham Hotspur	H	1-1	Dewis			2	5		6	7			10	11		9	1	3		4													
Dec 7	Swansea Town	A	4-3	Lee 3,Dewis			2	5		6	7	8			11		10	1	3		4			9										
14	Newcastle United	H	2-4	Lee 2			2	5		6	7	8			11		10	1	3		4			9										
21	West Bromwich Albion	A	2-4	Lee,Dewis			2	5		6	7			8	11		10		3		4			9			1							
25	Bradford Park Avenue	A	2-1	S Smith (pen),Griffiths				5		6	7			8	11		10		3		4		2	9			1							
26	Bradford Park Avenue	H	2-1	Griffiths 2			2	5			7			8	11		10		3		4		4	6	9									
28	Manchester City	A	0-1					5			7	8		6	11		10	1	3		4		2	9										
Jan 4	West Ham United	H	4-0	Lee 2,Dewis,Griffiths			2				7	8		6	11		10	1	3		4		5	9										
18	Sheffield Wednesday	A	3-1	Dewis 2,Revie (pen)			2				7	8		6	11		10		3		4		5	9		1								
Feb 1	Bury	A	3-2	Dewis,Griffiths,Revie		2				6	7	8		10	11		9				4		5	3			1							
15	Plymouth Argyle	A	0-4				2	4		6	7	8					9	1		11			5	3				10						
Mar 1	Nottingham Forest	H	1-1	Revie (pen)		2				6	7	8		10					3	11	4		5	9			1							
15	Newport County	H	3-0	King 2,Griffiths		2		4		6	7	8		10	11		9	1	3				5											
22	Barnsley	A	0-1			2		9		6	7	8		10	11			1	3		4		5											
Apr 4	Millwall	A	0-1				2	4		6	7			10	11		8	1					5	3	9									
5	Tottenham Hotspur	A	1-2	A Smith	2	3	4		6	7	8			11		9	1						5					10						
8	Millwall	H	5-0	Dewis 3,Griffiths 2	2	3	5		6	7	8			11		9	1			4								10						
12	Swansea Town	H	0-1		2	3	5		6		8			11		9				4							1	10	/					
19	Newcastle United	A	1-1	Corbett (og)	2	3	5		6	7	8			11			1			4				9	10								
26	West Bromwich Albion	H	1-1	Revie	2	3	5		6	7	8			11	10		1			4				9									
May 3	Luton Town	H	2-1	Adam,Revie	2	3	5		6	7	8			11	10		1			4				9									
10	Coventry City	A	1-2	Lee	2	3	5		6	7	8			11	10		1			4				9									
17	Chesterfield	A	0-2		2	3	4		6	7	8			11			1							9	10				5				
24	Burnley	H	1-4	Lee	2		5			7	8			11			1			4			3	9				10		6			
26	Southampton	A	1-1	Lee			4			8				11	10			7					3	9		1		5	6	2			
Jun 7	Fulham	H	2-0	Adam,Revie			4			7	8			11			3							9		1		5	6	2	10		

F.A. CUP

DATE	OPPONENTS		V	F.T.	SCORERS	Frame	Jones	Smith S	Griffiths	Revie	King	Adam	Dewis	Calvert	Anderson	Harrison W	Dawson	Grogan	Lee	Iggleden	Smith A	Chapman
Jan 11	West Ham United	(3)	A	2-1	Adam,Dewis	2			7	8	6	11	10	1	3	4	5		9			
25	Brentford	(4)	A	0-0		2			7	8	6	11	9	1		4	5	3			10	
30	Brentford	(4rep)	H	0-0		2			7	8	6	11	9	1		4	5	3			10	
Feb 3	Brentford	(4rep 2)		4-1	Griffiths,A Smith 2,Dewis	2			7	8	6	11	9	1		4	5	3			10	
8	Newcastle United	(5)	A	1-1	Dewis	2			7	8	6	11	9	1		4	5	3			10	
20	Newcastle United	(5rep)	H	1-2	S Smith (pen)		2	5	7	8	6	11	9			4		3			1	10

Notes : 1) The fixture list used for 1946-47 was identical to that designed for 1939-40.
2) Feb 3; played at Villa Park,Birmingham.

LEICESTER CITY 1946-47
Pictured v Birmingham City on 4th September .
Back : G.Ritchie *(Trainer)*,S.Smith,Frame,Grant,Jones,W.McLean *(AssistantTrainer)*,Towers,Iggleden.
Front : Griffiths,Dewis,McCulloch,King,Adam,E.Smith.

	APP's		GOALS	
	FL	FAC	FL	FAC
Alick Grant	2			
Billy Frame	15	4		
Dai Jones	33	2	1	
Sep Smith	35	1	2 (2p)	1 (p)
Eric Smith	5			
Tom Eggleston	30		2	
Mal Griffiths	36	6	8	1
Don Revie	32	6	7 (2p)	
Dave McCulloch	4		2	
Johnny King	21	6	3	
Charlie Adam	34	6	5	1
Bill Towers	4			
George Dewis	32	6	16	3
Joe Calvert	32	5		
Bert Howe	27	1		
Robert Anderson	13		1	
Walter Harrison	28	6		
Jim Dawson	1			
John Grogan	17	5		
Jimmy Harrison	10	5	1	
Jack Lee	24	1	18	
Ray Iggleden	3			
Stan Mercer	1			
Gordon Bradley	8	1		
Arthur E Smith	5	5	1	2
Vernon Chapman	1			
Tom McArthur	3			
Jim Garvey	3			
Ted Jelly	2			
Jimmy Hernon	1			
Own Goals			2	

1947-48 LEAGUE DIVISION TWO
Final Position : 9th
Ave. Home League Att: 27,000

DATE	OPPONENTS	V	F.T.	SCORERS	Calvert	Frame	Harrison J	Harrison W	Smith S	Haines	Griffiths	Revie	Lee	Hernon	Adam	Major	Eggleston	Cheney	McArthur	King	Dewis	Smith A	Bradley	Jelly	Iggleden	Plummer	Anderson	Scott	Garvey	McKennan	McGregor	Hines	Barratt
Aug 23	Leeds United	A	1-3	Griffiths	1	2	3	4	5	6	7	8	9	10	11																		
25	Plymouth Argyle	H	2-1	Lee 2		2	3	4	5	10	7	8	9		11	1	6																
30	Fulham	H	0-2			2	3	4	5	10	7	8	9			1	6		11														
Sep 3	Plymouth Argyle	A	0-0			2	3	4		10	7	8	9			1	6		11														
6	Coventry City	A	1-0	Griffiths		2	3	4			7	8	9	10	11	1						5	6										
8	Luton Town	H	3-2	Griffiths,Haines 2		2	3	4		9	7	8		10	11	1						5	6										
13	Newcastle United	H	2-2	Griffiths,Revie		2	3	4		9	7	8		10	11	1						5	6										
17	Luton Town	A	1-2	Dewis		2	3	4			7	8		10	11	1					9	5	6										
20	Birmingham City	A	0-1			2	3	4			7		9	10	11	1					8	5	6										
27	West Bromwich Albion	A	1-1	Revie (pen)		2	3	4	5		7	8	9		11	1				6	10												
Oct 4	Barnsley	A	0-2			2	3	4	5		7	8		10	11	1				6		9											
11	Nottingham Forest	H	3-1	Dewis,Lee 2		2	3	4	5		7		9		11	1				6	10	8											
18	Bradford Park Avenue	A	2-0	Griffiths,Stephen (og)		2	3	4	5		7	8	9		11	1				6		10											
25	Cardiff City	H	2-1	Lee 2		2	3		5	4	7	8	9		11	1				6		10											
Nov 1	Sheffield Wednesday	A	1-1	A Smith		2	3	4	5		7	8	9		11	1				6		10											
8	Tottenham Hotspur	H	0-3			2	3	4	5		7	8	9		11	1				6		10											
15	Millwall	A	4-0	Hernon,Lee 2,A Smith	1	2	3	4	5		7		9	10	11					6		8											
22	Chesterfield	H	1-2	Adam	1	2	3	4	5		7		9	10	11					6		8											
29	West Ham United	A	1-1	Adam	1	2	3	4	5		7		9	10	11					6		8											
Dec 6	Bury	H	2-1	Dewis,Adam	1	2	3	4	5		7	8			11					6	10												
13	Southampton	A	1-3	Adam	1	2	3	4	5		9	7			11					6	10												
20	Leeds United	H	2-0	Griffiths,Lee			3	4	5		7		9	8	11					6			10	1	2								
25	Brentford	A	2-2	Hernon 2			3	4	5		7			8				6		10				1	2	11	9						
27	Brentford	H	1-2	W Harrison			3	4			7			8			6	5						1	2	10	9	11					
Jan 3	Fulham	A	1-3	Lee		2							9	8	11					6				1	8	5		3					
17	Coventry City	H	2-2	Lee 2			2		4	5	8	7	9	10						6				1				3					
31	Newcastle United	A	0-2			2	3	4	5		7		9	8	11					6				1			10						
Feb 14	West Bromwich Albion	A	3-1	Lee,Haines,Griffiths		2		4	5	8	7		9		11					6	10			1				3					
28	Nottingham Forest	A	0-1			2		4	5	8	7		9	10	11					6				1				3					
Mar 6	Bradford Park Avenue	H	2-0	Hernon,King		2	3	4	5		7		9	8						6				1					10				
13	Cardiff City	A	0-3			2	3	4	5		7			10					11	6	9		1						8			
20	Sheffield Wednesday	H	2-3	Dewis,Hernon (pen)		2	3	4	5		7			10						6	9		1	11					8			
26	Doncaster Rovers	A	1-1	McKennan		2	3	4	5		7			10						6		8	1	11					9			
27	Tottenham Hotspur	A	0-0				3	4						11			5	6		10	1					7			8	2	9	
29	Doncaster Rovers	H	3-2	Hines 2,McKennan		2	3	7	4					10						6			1		5	11				8		9	
Apr 3	Millwall	H	3-0	Hines,Anderson,Hernon		2		7	4					10						6			1	11	5		3			8		9	
5	Barnsley	H	4-1	W Harrison,Iggleden 2,Hernon		2		4						10	11					6			1	7	5		3			8		9	
10	Chesterfield	A	3-2	Hines 2,McKennan		2	3	4						10	11					6			1	5	7					8		9	
17	West Ham United	H	1-3	McKennan (pen)		2	3	4			7			10	11					6			1							8		9	5
19	Birmingham City	H	0-0			2	3	4						10	11					6			1	7						8		9	5
24	Bury	A	2-0	S Smith,Hines		2	3	8	4		7			10	11					6			1									9	5
28	Southampton	H	0-0			2	3	4			7	8								6			1	5	11				10		9	

F.A. CUP

DATE	OPPONENTS		V	F.T.	SCORERS	Calvert	Frame	Harrison J	Harrison W	Smith S	Haines	Griffiths	Revie	Lee	Hernon	Adam	Major	Eggleston	Cheney	McArthur	King	Dewis	Smith A	Bradley	Jelly	Iggleden	Plummer	Anderson	Scott	Garvey	McKennan	McGregor	Hines	Barratt
Jan 10	Bury	(3)	H	1-0	Lee		2		4	5	8	7		9	10	11					6			1					3					
24	Sheffield Wednesday	(4)	H	2-1	W Harrison,Haines		2	3	4	5	8	7		9	10	11					6			1										
Feb 7	Tottenham Hotspur	(5)	A	2-5	W Harrison,Lee		2		4	5	8	7		9	10	11								1					3	6				

LEICESTER CITY 1947-48
Back: G.Ritchie *(Trainer)*,McArthur,Eggleston,Grogan,Calvert,Dewis,W.Harrison,Jones,
W.McLean *(Assistant Trainer)*.
Middle : Griffiths,Frame,Adam,J.Duncan *(Manager)*, Smith,Anderson,Lee.
Front : Jelly,King,J.Harrison Revie,Hernon,Haines.

	APP's		GOALS	
	FL	FAC	FL	FAC
Joe Calvert	6			
Billy Frame	37	3		
Jimmy Harrison	37	1		
Walter Harrison	35	3	2	2
Sep Smith	34	3	1	
Jack Haines	12	3	3	1
Mal Griffiths	36	3	7	
Don Revie	15		2 (1p)	
Jack Lee	22	3	13	2
Jimmy Hernon	30	3	7 (1p)	
Charlie Adam	32	3	4	
Les Major	15			
Tom Eggleston	4			
Dennis Cheney	1			
Tom McArthur	8			
Johnny King	38	2	1	
George Dewis	10		4	
Arthur E Smith	12		2	
Gordon Bradley	21	3		
Ted Jelly	3			
Ray Iggleden	8		2	
Norman Plummer	8			
Robert Anderson	6		1	
Sandy Scott	6	2		
Jim Garvey	2	1		
Peter McKennan	11		4 (1p)	
Bill McGregor	1			
Derek Hines	9		6	
Alf Barratt	3			
Own Goals				1

1948-49 LEAGUE DIVISION TWO
Final Position : 19th
Ave. Home League Att: 30,000

DATE	OPPONENTS	V	F.T.	SCORERS	Bradley	Frame	Harrison J	Harrison W	Smith	Garvey	Griffiths	McKennan	Lee	Revie	Adam	Plummer	Major	Hines	Johnston	Paterson	Dewis	Cheney	Dawson	King	Ayton	McArthur	Edwards	McGraw	Jelly	Chisholm	Scott	Moran	Anderson	Barratt
Aug 21	Leeds United	H	6-2	Revie 2,Lee 2,McKennan 2	1	2	3	4	5	6	7	8	9	10	11																			
26	Queens Park Rangers	A	1-4	Jefferson (og)	1	2	3	4	5	6	7	8	9	10	11																			
28	Coventry City	A	2-1	Revie,Griffiths	1	2	3	4	5	6	7	8	9	10	11																			
30	Queens Park Rangers	H	2-3	Lee 2	1	2	3	4		6	7	8	9	10	11	5																		
Sep 4	Sheffield Wednesday	H	2-2	McKennan,Revie	1	2	3	7	4	6	11	8	9	10		5																		
6	Brentford	H	0-0			2	3	4		6	7	8	9	10	11	5	1																	
11	Lincoln City	A	0-2			2	3	4	5	6	7	8		10	11		1	9															
15	Brentford	A	2-1	Revie (pen),Paterson		2	3	4			7			10		5	1		6	8	9	11												
18	Chesterfield	H	2-2	Revie (pen),Hines		2	3	4			7			10		5	1	9	6	8						11								
25	West Bromwich Albion	A	1-2	Revie	1	2	3	4			7		11	10		5		9	6	8														
Oct 2	Bury	H	3-2	Adam,Lee,Hart (og)	1	2	3	4			7		9		8	11	5		6				10											
9	Luton Town	A	1-1	W Harrison	1	2	3	4			7		9		8	11	5		6				10											
16	Bradford Park Avenue	H	2-2	Adam,Lee	1	2	3	4			7		9		8	11	5		6				10											
23	Southampton	A	0-6		1	2	3	4	8		7		9	10	11	5			6															
30	Barnsley	H	1-1	Lee	1	2	3	4			7		9	8	11	5			6				10											
Nov 6	Grimsby Town	A	0-1		1	2	3	4			7		9	8	11	5			6				10											
13	Nottingham Forest	H	4-2	Lee,Revie 3 (1pen)	1	2	3	4			7		9	8	11				6				10	5										
20	Fulham	A	0-1		1	2	3	4			7		9	8	11	5			6				10											
27	Plymouth Argyle	H	1-1	Ayton	1	2	3	4	5		7			8	11			9	6				10											
Dec 4	Blackburn Rovers	A	0-2		1	2	3		5	4	7		10	8	11			9	6															
11	Cardiff City	H	2-2	Revie (pen),Lee		2	3		5		7		9	10	11	1			6	8			4											
18	Leeds United	A	1-3	Edwards		2	3		5		7		9	10		1			6	8			4			11								
25	Tottenham Hotspur	H	1-2	Paterson		2	3	4			7		9	10	11	5				8			6		1									
27	Tottenham Hotspur	A	1-1	Griffiths		2	3	4			7		10		11	5	9	6		8					1									
Jan 1	Coventry City	H	3-1	Revie,Lee,Barrett (og)			3	4			7		9	8	11	5			6										1	2	10			
22	Lincoln City	H	5-3	Revie,Lee 3,Chisholm			3	4			7		9	8	11	5			6										1	2	10			
Feb 5	Chesterfield	A	1-1	Lee		2		4			7		9	8	11	5			6										1		10	3		
Mar 5	Luton Town	H	1-1	Hall (og)	1			4			7		9					8						11	6	5				2	10	3		
12	Bradford Park Avenue	A	3-3	Revie 2,Lee				4			7		9	8				11							6	5			1	2	10	3		
19	Southampton	H	1-3	Lee				4			7		9	8	11	5		6											1	2	10	3		
Apr 2	Grimsby Town	H	1-1	Chisholm							7		9	4	11	5			6										1	2	10	3	8	
6	Barnsley	A	1-3	Chisholm			3	4		6			9	8		5			7											2	10	11		1
9	Nottingham Forest	A	1-2	Gager (og)	1		3	4			7		9	8					6						5					2	10	11		
11	Sheffield Wednesday	A	1-0	Lee	1		3	4			7		9	8				10	6						5					2	11			
15	West Ham United	A	1-4	Griffiths	1	2	3	4		10	7		9	8		5			6												11			
16	Fulham	H	0-3		1		3	6			7		9	8		5			4						11						10			2
18	West Ham United	H	1-1	Lee			3				7		9	8			1	6							4	5	11			2	10			
21	Blackburn Rovers	H	3-1	Lee,Griffiths,Revie				4			7		9	8	11	1									6	5				2	10	3		
23	Plymouth Argyle	A	1-1	Chisholm			9	4			7		8		11	5	1	6												2	10	3		
May 4	Bury	A	2-1	Lee,Griffiths				4			7		9		11	5	1	6							8					2	10	3		
5	West Bromwich Albion	H	0-3					4			7		9		11	5	1	6							8					2	10	3		
7	Cardiff City	A	1-1	Lee	1	2	3		4	10	7		9		11				8						6	5				2				

F.A. CUP

DATE	OPPONENTS		V	F.T.	SCORERS	Bradley	Frame	Harrison J	Harrison W	Smith	Garvey	Griffiths	McKennan	Lee	Revie	Adam	Plummer	Major	Hines	Johnston	Paterson	Dewis	Cheney	Dawson	King	Ayton	McArthur	Edwards	McGraw	Jelly	Chisholm	Scott	Moran	Anderson	Barratt
Jan 8	Birmingham City	(3)	A	1-1	Revie (pen)			3	4			7		9	8	11	5			6										1	2	10			
15	Birmingham City	(3 rep)	H	1-1	Griffiths			3	4			7		9	8	11	5			6										1	2	10			
17	Birmingham City	(3 rep 2)	A	2-1	J Harrison,Revie			3	4			7		9	8	10	5			6										1	2	11			
29	Preston North End	(4)	H	2-0	Lee (pen),Griffiths			3	4			7		9	8	11	5			6										1	2	10			
Feb 12	Luton Town	(5)	A	5-5	Lee 4,Griffiths		2		4			7		9	8	11	5			6										1		10	3		
19	Luton Town	(5 rep)	H	5-3	Lee 2 (1pen),Griffiths 2,Chisholm				4			7		9	8	11	5			6										1	2	10	3		
26	Brentford	(6)	A	2-0	Lee,Griffiths				4			7		9	8	11	5			6										1	2	10	3		
Mar 26	Portsmouth	(sf)		3-1	Revie 2,Chisholm *(at Highbury)*				4			7		9	8	11	5			6										1	2	10	3		
Apr 30	Wolverhampton W	(F)		1-3	Griffiths *(at Wembley)*	1		9	4			7		8		11	5			6											2	10	3		

LEICESTER CITY 1948-49

Back : Siddon (*Assistant Secretary*),Barratt,Iggleden,Revie,Paterson,Garvey,Johnston,Cheney, A.Chandler (*Training Staff*). *Middle :* G.Ritchie (*Trainer*),Plummer,Scott,J.Harrison, Major,Churchill,Bradley,Dewis,W.Harrison,Jelly,W.McLean (*Assistant Trainer*). *Front :* J.Duncan (*Manager*),Griffiths,Frame,McArthur,Adam,S.Smith,Lee,McKennan,C.Maley (*Secretary*). *On Ground :* Staples,Moran,McGregor.

	APP's		GOALS	
	FL	FAC	FL	FAC
Gordon Bradley	22	1		
Billy Frame	27	1		
Jimmy Harrison	34	5		1
Walter Harrison	36	9	1	
Sep Smith	12			
Jim Garvey	10			
Mal Griffiths	41	9	5	7
Peter McKennan	7		3	
Jack Lee	38	9	21	8 (2p)
Don Revie	36	8	16 (4p)	4 (1p)
Charlie Adam	29	9	2	
Norman Plummer	26	9		
Les Major	11			
Derek Hines	6		1	
Jim Johnston	16			
Tom Paterson	11		2	
George Dewis	1			
Dennis Cheney	1			
Jim Dawson	4			
Johnny King	25	9		
Jimmy Ayton	5		1	
Tom McArthur	8			
Walter Edwards	3		1	
Ian McGraw	8	8		
Ted Jelly	14	8		
Ken Chisholm	17	6	4	2
Sandy Scott	11	8		
Eddie Moran	1			
Johnny Anderson	1			
Alf Barratt	1			
Own Goals			5	

1949-50 — LEAGUE DIVISION TWO
Final Position : 15th
Ave. Home League Att: 29,000

LEICESTER CITY 1949-50 — Results & Line-ups

DATE	OPPONENTS	V	F.T.	SCORERS	Bradley	Jelly	Scott	Harrison	McArthur	King	Griffiths	Revie	Lee	Chisholm	Adam	Kirkman	McGregor	Ayton	Moran	Frame	Corbett	Johnston	Hines	Plummer	Paterson	Godwin	Dewis	Barlow	Jackson	Baldwin	Small	Marsh	Wilson	Anderson
Aug 20	Sheffield Wednesday	A	1-3	Adam	1	2	3	4	5	6	7	8	9	10	11																			
24	Bradford Park Avenue	A	2-2	Griffiths,Chisholm	1	2	3	4	5	6	7	8	9	10	11																			
27	Hull City	H	1-2	Lee	1	2		4	5	6	7	8	9	10	11		3																	
29	Bradford Park Avenue	H	4-1	Lee 3,Chisholm	1	2	3	4	5	6	7	8	9	10	11																			
Sep 3	Brentford	A	1-0	Chisholm	1	2	3	4	5	6	7	8	9	10	11																			
10	Blackburn Rovers	H	3-3	Chisholm 2,Griffiths	1	2	3	4	5	6	7	8	9	10	11																			
12	Chesterfield	A	0-1		1		3	4	5	6	7	8	9	10	11			2																
17	Cardiff City	A	4-2	Chisholm 2,Lee,Griffiths	1				5	6	7	4	9	10	11		3	2	8															
19	Chesterfield	H	0-1		1				5	6	7	4	9	10	11		3	2		8														
24	Tottenham Hotspur	H	1-2	Adam	1			4	5	6	7	8	9	10	11		3					2												
Oct 1	Bury	A	0-3		1			4			7	8	9	10	11		3					2	5	6										
8	Luton Town	A	0-1		1	2	3	4			7	8		10	11								5	6	9									
15	Barnsley	H	2-2	Scott,Chisholm	1	2	3	7		6		8	9	10									5					4	11					
22	West Ham United	A	2-2	Lee,Chisholm	1	2	3	8		6	7		9	10	11									5				4						
29	Sheffield United	H	1-1	Plummer	1	2	3	8		6	7		9	10	11									5				4						
Nov 5	Grimsby Town	A	1-2	Lee	1	2	3	8		6	7		9	10	11									5				4						
12	Queens Park Rangers	H	3-2	Lee 2,Chisholm	1	2	3	8			7		9	10	11									5	6			4						
19	Preston North End	A	1-2	Lee	1	2	3	4			7		9	10	11									5	6			8						
26	Swansea Town	H	0-0				3	4			7	8	9	10	11					2				5	6	1								
Dec 3	Leeds United	A	1-1	Adam			3	4			7	8	9	10	11					2				5	6	1								
10	Southampton	H	2-2	Griffiths,Lee			3	4			7	8	9		11					2				5	6	1		10						
17	Sheffield Wednesday	H	2-2	Lee 2			3	4		10	7		9		11					2				5	6	1			8					
24	Hull City	A	0-4			2		4		10	7		9		11									5	6	1		8	3					
26	Coventry City	H	1-0	Adam (pen)				4		10	7		9		11					2				5	6	1		8	3					
27	Coventry City	A	2-1	Adam,Paterson						4	7		9	10						2				5	6	1	11	8	3					
31	Brentford	H	1-1	Paterson						4	7		9	10	11					2				5	6	1		8	3					
Jan 14	Blackburn Rovers	A	0-3						5	4	7			10	11					2				6	9	1		8	3					
21	Cardiff City	H	1-0	Chisholm					4	5	6	7		10	11	2									9	1		8	3					
Feb 4	Tottenham Hotspur	A	2-0	Adam (pen),Barlow		2		4		6	7		9	10										5	11	1		8	3					
11	Plymouth Argyle	H	0-0			2		4		6	7		9	10										5	11	1		8	3					
18	Bury	H	0-2			2		4		6	7		9	10									10	5		1		8	3					
25	Luton Town	H	3-2	Chisholm 2,Lee		2				6	7		9	10	11									5		1		8	3	4				
Mar 4	Barnsley	A	2-2	Barlow 2		2				6	7		9	10	11									5		1		8	3	4				
11	West Ham United	H	2-1	Lee 2		2				6	7		9	10	11									5		1		8	3	4				
18	Sheffield United	A	2-2	Jelly,Lee (pen)		2				6			9									4		5		1		8	3			7	10	11
25	Grimsby Town	H	1-0	Lee		2				9							3							6		1		8		4		7	10	11
Apr 1	Swansea Town	A	0-0			2				9							3							6		1		8		4		7	10	11
8	Leeds United	H	1-1	Lee		2				9							3							6		1		8		4		7	10	11
10	Plymouth Argyle	A	1-2	Lee		2				9					11	3								6		1		8		4		7	10	
15	Queens Park Rangers	A	0-2			2				9					11	3								6		1		8		4		7	10	
22	Preston North End	H	1-0	Barlow		2				6	7		9		11	3								5				8		4			10	1
29	Southampton	A	3-5	Lee 2,Barlow		2				6	7		9		11	3								5				8		4			10	1

F.A. CUP

DATE	OPPONENTS		V	F.T.	SCORERS	Scott	King	Griffiths	Lee	Chisholm	Adam	Frame	Corbett	Johnston	Godwin	Barlow	Jackson
Jan 7	Sheffield United	(3)	A	1-3	Adam	3	4	7	9	10	11	2	5	6	1	8	

LEICESTER CITY 1949-50
Back : A.Chandler *(Assistant Trainer)*, Richardson, Edwards, Plummer,
G.Ritchie *(Assistant Trainer)*, Dewis, Barratt, Scott, Smith.
Middle : Garvey, Kirkman, Frame, Bradley, McArthur, McGraw, Jelly, Corbett, McGregor.
Front : J.Metcalfe *(Trainer)*, Griffiths, Harrison, Revie, Ayton, Chisholm, Lee, Adam, J.Duncan *(Manager)*.
On Ground : Johnston, Paterson, King, Moran.

	APP's		GOALS	
	FL	FAC	FL	FAC
Gordon Bradley	18			
Ted Jelly	31	1	1	
Sandy Scott	14		1	
Walter Harrison	24			
Tom McArthur	12			
Johnny King	35	1		
Mal Griffiths	35	1	4	
Don Revie	13			
Jack Lee	39	1	22 (1p)	
Ken Chisholm	25	1	13	
Charlie Adam	37	1	6 (2p)	1
Norman Kirkman	12			
Bill McGregor	4			
Jimmy Ayton	1			
Eddie Moran	1			
Billy Frame	10	1		
Bill Corbett	16	1		
Jim Johnston	19	1		
Derek Hines	4			
Norman Plummer	19		1	
Tom Paterson	6		2	
Tom Godwin	22	1		
George Dewis	1			
Bert Barlow	21	1	5	
Ron Jackson	13			
Jimmy Baldwin	10			
Peter Small	6			
Jack Marsh	8			
Ian Wilson	4			
Johnny Anderson	2			

1950-51
LEAGUE DIVISION TWO
Final Position : 14th
Ave. Home League Att: 25,000

DATE	OPPONENTS	V	F.T.	SCORERS	Godwin	Jelly	Jackson	Baldwin	Plummer	King	Griffiths	Barlow	Rowley	Marsh	Wilson	Harrison	McGraw	McArthur	Small	Dryburgh	Lever	Ayton	Hines	Halton	Adam	Moran	Anderson	McGregor	Crawford	Dunne	Worthington
Aug 19	Bury	A	3-2	Marsh 2,Rowley	1	2	3	4	5	6	7	8	9	10	11																
23	Birmingham City	A	0-2		1	2	3	4	5	6	7	8	9	10	11																
26	Queens Park Rangers	H	6-2	Marsh 2,Griffiths,Rowley,Barlow,Wilson	1	2	3	4	5	6	7	8	9	10	11																
28	Birmingham City	H	1-3	Rowley	1	2	3	4	5	6	7		9	10	11	8															
Sep 2	Chesterfield	A	0-1			2	3	4		6	7	8	9	10	11		1	5													
4	Notts County	H	1-1	Barlow		2	3	4		6		8	9	10			1	5		7	11										
9	Sheffield United	H	2-2	Wilson,Barlow			3	4		6		8	9		11		1	5		7	2	10									
16	Manchester City	H	1-2	Rowley			3	4		6		8	9		11		1	5		7	2	10									
23	Coventry City	A	1-2	Rowley (pen)			3	4		6		8	9	10	11		1	5		7	2										
30	Cardiff City	H	1-1	Hines	1		3	4			7	8		10				5		11	2		9	6							
Oct 7	Hull City	A	3-1	Hines,Rowley 2	1		3	4			7	8	10					5		11	2		9	6							
14	Doncaster Rovers	H	2-0	Rowley,Hines	1		3	4			7	8	10					5		11	2		9	6							
21	West Ham United	A	0-0		1		3	4			7	8	10					5		11	2		9	6							
28	Swansea Town	H	2-3	Griffiths,Dryburgh	1		3	4			7	8	10					5		11	2		9	6							
Nov 4	Luton Town	A	2-0	Adam,Hines	1		3	4			7	8	10					5			2		9	6	11						
11	Leeds United	H	1-5	Rowley	1		3				7	8	10			4		5			2		9	6	11						
18	Brentford	A	0-0		1		3	4			7		10					5			2		9	6	11	8					
25	Blackburn Rovers	H	2-0	Rowley (pen),Moran	1		3	4			7		10					5			2		9	6	11	8					
Dec 2	Southampton	A	2-2	Adam,Rowley	1		3	4			7		10					5			2		9	6	11	8					
9	Barnsley	H	1-2	Rowley (pen)	1		3	4			7		10					5			2		9	6	11	8					
16	Bury	H	4-0	Rowley 3,Hines	1		3	4			7		10					5			2		9	6	11	8					
23	Queens Park Rangers	A	0-3		1		3	4			7		10					5			2		9	6	11	8					
25	Grimsby Town	A	2-0	Rowley,Hines			3	4				8	10					5		7	2		9	6	11		1				
26	Grimsby Town	H	0-0				3	4					10					5		7			9	6	11		1	2	8		
30	Chesterfield	H	1-0	Griffiths			3	4			7	8	10					5					9	6	11		1	2			
Jan 13	Sheffield United	A	1-2	Rowley			3	8		4	7		10					5			2		9	6	11		1				
20	Manchester City	A	1-1	Rowley			3	8		4	7		9					5			2			6	11		1	10			
Feb 3	Coventry City	H	3-0	Griffiths,Hines,Rowley			3	8		4	7		10					5			2		9	6	11		1				
17	Cardiff City	A	2-2	Rowley (pen),Hines			3	8		4	7		10				1	5			2		9		11				6		
24	Hull City	H	4-0	Rowley,Hines,Griffiths,Adam			3	8		4	7		10					5			2		9	6	11		1				
Mar 3	Doncaster Rovers	A	2-2	Adam,Rowley (pen)			3	8		4	7		10					5			2		9	6	11		1				
10	West Ham United	H	1-0	Hines			3	8		4	7		10					5			2		9	6	11		1				
17	Swansea Town	A	1-2	Baldwin			3	8		4	7		10					5			2		9	6	11		1				
24	Luton Town	H	3-1	Hines,Rowley 2			3	8		4	7		10					5			2		9	6	11		1				
26	Preston North End	A	2-3	Adam,Rowley (pen)			3	8		4	7		10					5			2		9	6	11		1				
27	Preston North End	H	2-3	Rowley 2			3	8		4	7		10					5			2		9	6	11		1				
31	Leeds United	A	1-2	Hines			3			4	7		10					5			2		9	6	11		1				8
Apr 7	Brentford	H	1-2	Halton (pen)	1		3			4	7		10					5			2		9	6	11						8
14	Blackburn Rovers	A	0-1		1		3	10		4	7							5		11	2		9	6							8
21	Southampton	H	3-1	Baldwin,Dryburgh 2	1		3	4			7							5		11	2		9	6	10			3			8
28	Barnsley	A	0-0		1		3	4					10					5		7	2		9	6	11						8
May 5	Notts County	A	3-2	Hines,Rowley,Barlow	1		3	4			7	8	10					5			2		9	6	11						

F.A. CUP

DATE	OPPONENTS		V	F.T.	SCORERS	Godwin	Jelly	Jackson	Baldwin	Plummer	King	Griffiths	Barlow	Rowley	Marsh	Wilson	Harrison	McGraw	McArthur	Small	Dryburgh	Lever	Ayton	Hines	Halton	Adam	Moran	Anderson	McGregor	Crawford	Dunne	Worthington
Jan 6	Preston North End	(3)	H	0-3				3	4			7	8	10					5					9	6	11		1	2			

LEICESTER CITY 1950-51
(Pictured at a friendly v Reading on 10th February.)
Back : Griffiths,McArthur,Godwin,Halton,Jackson.
Front : Hines,King,Baldwin,Lever,Rowley,Adam.

	APP's		GOALS	
	FL	FAC	FL	FAC
Tom Godwin	22			
Ted Jelly	6			
Ron Jackson	41	1		
Jimmy Baldwin	31		2	
Norman Plummer	4			
Johnny King	31			
Mal Griffiths	34	1	5	
Bert Barlow	19	1	4	
Arthur Rowley	39	1	28 (6p)	
Jack Marsh	6		4	
Ian Wilson	8		2	
Walter Harrison	2			
Ian McGraw	5			
Tom McArthur	38	1		
Peter Small	7			
Tom Dryburgh	10		3	
Arthur Lever	34			
Jimmy Ayton	2			
Derek Hines	33	1	13	
Reg Halton	32	1	1 (p)	
Charlie Adam	26	1	5	
Eddie Moran	6		1	
Johnny Anderson	15	1		
Bill McGregor	3	1		
Jimmy Crawford	2			
Tommy Dunne	1			
Fred Worthington	5			

1951-52 LEAGUE DIVISION TWO

Final Position : 5th

Ave. Home League Att: 26,000

DATE	OPPONENTS	V	F.T.	SCORERS	Anderson	Lever	Jackson	Baldwin	McArthur	Halton	Griffiths	Barlow	Hines	Rowley	Dryburgh	Worthington	Webb	Plummer	Small	Dixon	Godwin	Dickson	King	Dunne	Gillies	McGregor	Milburn	Littler
Aug 18	Cardiff City	A	0-4		1	2	3	4	5	6	7	8	9	10	11													
20	Sheffield Wednesday	H	3-1	Rowley 2,Hines	1	2	3	4	5	6	7	8	9	10	11													
25	Birmingham City	H	4-0	Worthington,Rowley 3	1	2	3	4	5	6	7		9	10	11	8												
27	Sheffield Wednesday	A	0-1		1	2		4	5	6	7		9	10	11	8	3											
Sep 1	Luton Town	H	3-3	Dryburgh,Hines 2	1	2		4		6			9	10	11	8	3	5	7									
3	Southampton	H	3-0	Dryburgh,Hines 2	1	2		4	5	6			9	10	11	8	3		7									
8	Nottingham Forest	A	2-2	Dryburgh,Small	1	2		4	5	6			9	10	11	8	3		7									
15	Brentford	H	1-1	Halton	1	2		4	5	6			9	10	11	8	3		7									
22	Doncaster Rovers	A	2-2	Dryburgh,Rowley	1	2		4	5	6			9	10	11	8	3		7									
29	Everton	H	1-2	Rowley	1	2		4	5	6			9	10	11	8	3		7									
Oct 6	Bury	H	1-1	Hines	1	2		4	5	6	7		9	10	11		3			8								
13	Swansea Town	A	0-1			2		4		6	7		9	10	11		3	5		8	1							
20	Coventry City	H	3-1	Griffiths,Hines,Rowley	1	2		4		6	7		9	10	11		3	5		8								
27	West Ham United	A	3-2	Rowley,Hines 2		2		4		6	7		9	10	11		3	5		8	1							
Nov 3	Sheffield United	H	5-5	Rowley 2,Hines,Dryburgh,Griffiths	1	2		4		6	7		9	10	11		3	5		8								
10	Barnsley	A	3-3	Dryburgh,Rowley 2	1	2		4		6	7		9	10	11		3	5		8								
17	Hull City	H	1-0	Rowley	1	2		4		6	7		9	10	11	8	3						6					
24	Blackburn Rovers	A	1-2	Rowley	1	2	3	4	5		7		9	10	11	8							6					
Dec 1	Queens Park Rangers	H	4-0	Rowley 3,Dryburgh	1	2	3		5	6	7		9	10	11	8								4				
8	Notts County	A	3-2	Worthington,Hines,Halton (pen)	1	2	3		5	6	7		9	10	11	8								4				
15	Cardiff City	H	3-0	Rowley,Hines,Worthington	1	2	3		5	6	7		9	10	11	8								4				
22	Birmingham City	A	0-2		1	2	3		5	6	7		9	10	11	8								4				
25	Leeds United	H	1-2	Hines	1	2	3		5	6	7		9	10	11	8								4				
26	Leeds United	A	1-2	Hines	1	2	3		5	6	7		9	10	11	8						4						
29	Luton Town	A	2-1	Dryburgh 2	1	2	3	4	5		7		9	10	11	8							6					
Jan 5	Nottingham Forest	H	3-1	Rowley,Griffiths 2		2	3	4	5	6	7		9	10	11	8					1							
19	Brentford	A	3-1	Rowley 3	1	2	3	4	5		7		9	10	11	8							6					
26	Doncaster Rovers	H	2-1	Rowley 2	1	2	3	4			7		9	10	11	8							6		5			
Feb 9	Everton	A	0-2		1	2	3	4			7		9	10	11	8							6		5			
16	Bury	A	4-1	Hines 2,Rowley 2	1	2	3	4			7		9	10	11	8							6		5			
23	Southampton	A	0-2		1	2	3	4	5		7		9	10	11	8							6					
Mar 1	Swansea Town	H	1-1	Hines	1	2	3	4			7		9	10	11	8							6		5			
8	Coventry City	A	3-1	Rowley 2 (1pen),Dryburgh		2	3	4			7		9	10	11	8				1			6		5			
15	West Ham United	H	3-1	Griffiths,Rowley 2	1		3	4			7		9	10	11	8							6		5	2		
22	Sheffield United	A	0-5		1		3	4			7		9	10	11	8							6		5		2	
29	Barnsley	H	1-2	Rowley	1		3	4		6	7		9	10	11							8			5		2	
Apr 5	Hull City	A	1-3	Rowley	1		3	4			7		9	10	11	8							6		5		2	
12	Blackburn Rovers	H	2-1	Rowley 2 (1pen)	1		3	4			7		9	10	11	8							6		5		2	
14	Rotherham United	A	2-0	Dryburgh,Rowley	1		3	4		6	7			10	11	8		9							5		2	
15	Rotherham United	H	2-0	Rowley 2	1		3	4		6	7			10	11	8		9							5		2	
19	Queens Park Rangers	A	0-1		1			4		6	7			10	11	8	3	9							5		2	
26	Notts County	H	1-1	Littler	1			4		6	7		11	10			3					8			5		2	9

F.A. CUP

DATE	OPPONENTS		V	F.T.	SCORERS	Anderson	Lever	Jackson	Baldwin	McArthur	Halton	Griffiths	Barlow	Hines	Rowley	Dryburgh	Worthington	Webb	Plummer	Small	Dixon	Godwin	Dickson	King	Dunne	Gillies	McGregor	Milburn	Littler
Jan 12	Coventry City	(3)	H	1-1	Griffiths	1	2	3	4	5	6	7		9	10	11	8												
14	Coventry City	(3 rep)	A	1-4	Dryburgh	1	2	3			5	7		9	10	11	8							6	4				

LEICESTER CITY 1951-52

Back : D.Jones *(Trainer)*,Dewis,Griffiths,Dickson,McGraw,Godwin,Plummer,Smith,A.Chandler *(Assistant Trainer)*.
Middle : Baldwin,Littler,Unnamed,Rowley,McArthur,Lever,Dunne,Warner,Halton.
Front : C.Maley *(Secretary)*,Jackson,Small,Barlow,Worthington,McGregor,Crawford, Wilson, N.Bullock *(Manager)*.
On Ground : King,Unnamed,Webb,Dryburgh.

	APP's FL	APP's FAC	APP's FLC	GOALS FL	GOALS FAC	GOALS FLC
Johnny Anderson	38	2				
Arthur Lever	33	2				
Ron Jackson	26	2				
Jimmy Baldwin	36	1				
Tom McArthur	18	1				
Reg Halton	32	2		2 (1p)		
Mal Griffiths	36	2		5	1	
Bert Barlow	2					
Derek Hines	39	2		17		
Arthur Rowley	42	2		38 (2p)		
Tom Dryburgh	41	2		11	1	
Fred Worthington	32	2		3		
Bill Webb	16					
Norman Plummer	9					
Peter Small	6			1		
Arthur Dixon	8					
Tom Godwin	1					
Adam Dickson	3					
Johnny King	15	1				
Tommy Dunne	5	1				
Matt Gillies	14					
Bill McGregor	1					
Stan Milburn	8					
Eric Littler	1			1		

1952-53 LEAGUE DIVISION TWO
Final Position : 5th
Ave. Home League Att: 24,500

DATE	OPPONENTS	V	F.T.	SCORERS
Aug 23	Notts County	H	3-0	Hines,Griffiths,Rowley
25	Fulham	H	6-1	Rowley 4 (1pen),Worthington,Griffiths
30	Southampton	A	2-5	Dryburgh,Elliott (og)
Sep 3	Fulham	A	6-4	Rowley 3,King,Dryburgh 2
6	Bury	H	3-2	Griffiths,Worthington,Hines
8	West Ham United	H	0-0	
13	Birmingham City	A	1-3	Rowley
15	West Ham United	A	1-4	Rowley (pen)
20	Luton Town	H	1-1	Rowley
27	Leeds United	A	1-0	Hines
Oct 4	Plymouth Argyle	H	2-0	Rowley,Hines
11	Nottingham Forest	A	3-1	Dryburgh,Hines,Rowley
18	Everton	H	4-2	Dryburgh, Morris 2,Rowley
25	Brentford	A	2-4	Baldwin,Griffiths
Nov 1	Doncaster Rovers	H	4-2	Dryburgh,Hines 2,Rowley
8	Swansea Town	A	1-1	Morris
15	Huddersfield Town	H	2-1	Rowley,Quested (og)
22	Sheffield United	A	2-7	Rowley,Hines
29	Barnsley	H	2-2	Dryburgh,Rowley (pen)
Dec 6	Lincoln City	A	2-3	Hines,Rowley
13	Hull City	H	5-0	Hines,Rowley 3,Dryburgh
20	Notts County	A	2-2	Rowley 2
25	Blackburn Rovers	A	0-2	
27	Blackburn Rovers	H	2-1	Griffiths,Hines
Jan 3	Southampton	H	4-1	Dryburgh,Griffiths,Rowley (pen),Crawford
17	Bury	A	4-1	Griffiths,Crawford,Rowley,Hines
24	Birmingham City	H	3-4	Hines,Rowley (pen),Griffiths
Feb 7	Luton Town	A	0-2	
14	Leeds United	H	3-3	Morris,Rowley 2
21	Plymouth Argyle	A	1-2	Worthington
28	Nottingham Forest	H	1-1	Hogg
Mar 7	Everton	A	2-2	Worthington,Dryburgh
14	Brentford	H	2-3	Rowley 2 (1pen)
21	Doncaster Rovers	A	0-0	
28	Swansea Town	H	2-1	Dryburgh,Morris
Apr 4	Huddersfield Town	A	0-1	
6	Rotherham United	A	0-0	
7	Rotherham United	H	3-2	Hines,Rowley 2
11	Sheffield United	H	0-0	
16	Hull City	A	1-1	Rowley
18	Barnsley	A	3-0	Small,Rowley 2 (1pen)
25	Lincoln City	H	3-2	Rowley 3 (2pen)

F.A. CUP

Jan 10	Notts County	(3) H	2-4	Rowley 2 (1pen)

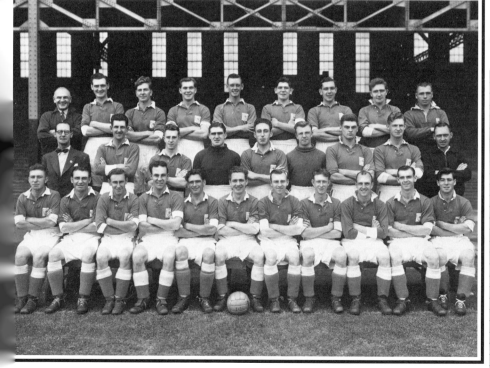

LEICESTER CITY 1952-53

Back : A.Chandler(*Assistant Trainer*), Gillies,Lever,Livie,Rushworth,Smith,Rowley,Littler,G.Dewis(*Third Team Coach*).
Middle : N.Bullock(*Manager*),Halton,Milburn,Anderson,Dunne,Dickson,Warner,McArthur,D.Jones (*Trainer*).
Front : Burbeck,Griffiths,King,McGregor,Small,Worthington,Dixon,Crawford,Baldwin,Dryburgh,Lockwood.

	APP's			GOALS		
	FL	FAC	FLC	FL	FAC	FLC
Johnny Anderson	36					
Arthur Lever	29	1				
Stan Milburn	39	1				
Jimmy Baldwin	38	1		1		
Matt Gillies	34	1				
Johnny King	31	1		1		
Mal Griffiths	32	1		8		
Fred Worthington	13			4		
Derek Hines	38	1		14		
Arthur Rowley	41	1		39 (9 p)	2 (1p)	
Tom Dryburgh	35	1		11		
Eric Littler	1					
Peter Small	9			1		
Ron Burbeck	1					
Arthur Dixon	3					
Johnny Morris	20			5		
Bill Webb	11					
Reg Warner	4					
Tom McArthur	9					
Adam Dickson	6	1				
Jimmy Crawford	7	1		2		
Derek Hogg	8			1		
Ron Jackson	8					
Tommy Dunne	8					
Gordon Fincham	1					
Own Goals					2	

1953-54
LEAGUE DIVISION TWO
Final Position : 1st
Ave. Home League Att: 28,000

DATE	OPPONENTS	V	F.T.	SCORERS	Anderson	Lever	Jackson	Baldwin	Gillies	Dunne	Griffiths	Morris	Hines	Rowley	Dryburgh	Warner	Small	Webb	Hogg	Crawford	Russell	Milburn	McArthur	Littler	Fincham	Froggatt	Worthington
Aug 19	Derby County	H	2-2	Rowley,Hines	1	2	3	4	5	6	7	8	9	10	11												
22	West Ham United	A	1-4	Rowley (pen)	1	2	3	4	5	6	7	8	9	10	11												
24	Fulham	H	2-2	Morris 2	1	2	3	4	5	6	7	8	9	10	11												
29	Leeds United	H	5-0	Rowley 2,Hines 3	1	2	3		5	6	7	8	9	10		4	11										
Sep 2	Fulham	A	1-1	Hines	1	2	3		5	6	7	8	9	10		4	11										
5	Birmingham City	A	2-1	Rowley,Hines	1	2	3				7	8	9	10		4		11									
7	Stoke City	H	4-0	Griffiths 3,Rowley	1	2	3	4	5	6	7	8	9	10			11										
12	Nottingham Forest	H	1-0	Small	1	2	3	4	5	6	7	8	9	10			11										
14	Stoke City	A	2-2	Small 2	1	2	3	4	5	6	7	8	9	10			11										
19	Luton Town	A	2-2	Griffiths,Rowley (pen)	1	2	3	4	5	6	7	8	9	10			11										
26	Plymouth Argyle	H	4-2	Griffiths,Small 2,Rowley	1	2	3	4	5	6	7	8	9	10			11										
Oct 3	Swansea Town	A	0-0		1	2	3	4	5	6	7	8	9	10			11										
10	Doncaster Rovers	H	2-0	Small,Rowley	1	2	3	4	5	6	7	8	9	10			11										
17	Bury	A	5-2	Rowley,Morris 2,Small,Hines	1	2	3	4	5	6		8	9	10			11		7								
24	Oldham Athletic	H	1-0	Rowley	1	2	3	4	5	6		8	9	10			11			7							
31	Everton	A	2-1	Morris,Hines	1	2	3	4	5	6	7	8	9	10			11										
Nov 7	Hull City	H	1-3	Morris	1	2	3	4	5	6	7	8	9	10			11										
14	Notts County	A	1-1	Small	1	2	3	4	5		7	8	9	10			11				6						
21	Lincoln City	H	9-2	Hines 5,Morris,Griffiths,Rowley 2 (1pen)	1	2	3	4	5		7	8	9	10			11				6						
28	Bristol Rovers	A	0-3		1	2	3	4	5		7	8	9	10			11				6						
Dec 5	Brentford	H	6-0	Rowley 2,Morris,Dryburgh,Small,Baldwin	1		3	4	5		7	8		10	11		9				6	2					
12	Derby County	A	1-2	Rowley (pen)	1		3	4	5		7	8	9	10			11				6	2					
19	West Ham United	H	2-1	Rowley,Russell	1	2	3	4	5		7	8	9	10			11				6						
25	Rotherham United	H	4-1	Rowley 3,Hines	1		3	4	5		7	8	9	10			11				6	2					
26	Rotherham United	A	1-1	Griffiths	1		3	4	5		7	8	9	10	11						6	2					
Jan 2	Leeds United	A	1-7	Griffiths	1		3	4			7	8		10			11				6	2	5	9			
16	Birmingham City	H	3-4	Hines 2,Rowley	1	2	3			6	7	8	9	10							4		5				
23	Nottingham Forest	A	1-3	Rowley	1	2	3				7	8	9	10			11				6		5				
Feb 6	Luton Town	H	2-1	Rowley (pen),Small	1		3	4	5		7	8	9	10			11				6	2					
13	Plymouth Argyle	A	3-0	Hines,Small,Rowley	1		3	4	5		7	8	9	10			11				6	2					
23	Swansea Town	H	4-1	Rowley,Morris 2,Dryburgh	1		3	4	5	6	7	8	9	10	11							2					
27	Doncaster Rovers	A	2-0	Littler,Dryburgh	1		3	4	5		7	8		10	11						6	2		9			
Mar 6	Bury	H	2-0	Rowley,Dryburgh	1		3	4	5		7	8		10	11						6	2			9		
20	Everton	H	2-2	Hines,Small	1		3		5	4		8	9	10		7					6	2				11	
27	Lincoln City	A	1-3	Rowley	1		3	4	5		7			10		11					6	2			9		8
Apr 3	Bristol Rovers	H	1-0	Froggatt	1		3	4	5			8	9	10		7					6	2				11	
6	Oldham Athletic	A	2-0	Small,Hines	1		3	4	5			8	9	10		7					6	2				11	
10	Hull City	H	3-0	Rowley,Griffiths,Froggatt	1		3	4	5		7		9	10			8				6	2				11	
16	Blackburn Rovers	A	0-3		1		3	4	5		7		9	10			8				6	2				11	
17	Notts County	H	2-2	Small,Griffiths	1		3	4	5		7	8		10	11		9				6	2					
19	Blackburn Rovers	H	4-0	Rowley 2,Morris 2	1		3	4	5		7	8	9	10			11				6	2					
24	Brentford	A	3-1	Griffiths,Morris,Home (og)	1		3	4	5		7	8	9	10			11				6	2					

F.A. CUP

DATE	OPPONENTS		V	F.T.	SCORERS	Anderson	Lever	Jackson	Baldwin	Gillies	Dunne	Griffiths	Morris	Hines	Rowley	Dryburgh	Warner	Small	Webb	Hogg	Crawford	Russell	Milburn	McArthur	Littler	Fincham	Froggatt	Worthington
Jan 9	Middlesbrough	(3)	A	0-0		1	2	3	6			7	8		10			11				4			9	5		
14	Middlesbrough	(3 rep)	H	3-2	Rowley 3	1	2	3	6			7	8	9	10		5	11				4						
30	Stoke City	(4)	A	0-0		1		3	4	5		7	8	9	10			11				6	2					
Feb 2	Stoke City	(4 rep)	H	3-1	Morris,Small 2	1		3	4	5		7	8	9	10			11				6	2					
20	Norwich City	(5)	A	2-1	Rowley (pen),Small	1		3	4	5		7	8	9	10			11				6	2					
Mar 13	Preston North End	(6)	H	1-1	Jackson	1		3	4	5		7	8	9	10			11				6	2					
17	Preston North End	(6 rep)	A	2-2	Small,Rowley	1		3	4	5		7	8	9	10			11				6	2					
22	Preston North End	(6 rep2)		1-3	Rowley	1		3	4	5		7	8	9	10	11						6	2					

Note : Mar 22,played at Hillsborough,Sheffield

LEICESTER CITY 1953-54
Back : Baldwin,Jackson,Milburn,D.Jones *(Trainer)*, Dickson,Russell,Hines,Froggatt.
Front : C.Maley *(Secretary)*, Griffiths,Morris,Gillies,Rowley,Small,N.Bullock *(Manager)*.

	APP's FL	APP's FAC	GOALS FL	GOALS FAC
Johnny Anderson	42	8		
Arthur Lever	23	2		
Ron Jackson	42	8		1
Jimmy Baldwin	38	8	1	
Matt Gillies	39	6		
Tommy Dunne	19			
Mal Griffiths	37	8	11	
Johnny Morris	39	8	13	1
Derek Hines	36	7	19	
Arthur Rowley	42	8	30 (5p)	6 (1p)
Tom Dryburgh	9	1	4	
Reg Warner	3	1		
Peter Small	34	7	14	4
Bill Webb	1			
Derek Hogg	1			
Jimmy Crawford	1			
Eddie Russell	24	8	1	
Stan Milburn	19	6		
Tom McArthur	1			
Eric Littler	2	1	1	
Gordon Fincham	2	1		
Jack Froggatt	7		2	
Fred Worthington	1			
Own Goals				1

1954-55 — LEAGUE DIVISION ONE
Final Position : 21st
Ave. Home League Att: 31,000

Player columns (left to right): Anderson, Milburn, Jackson, Baldwin, Gillies, Russell, Griffiths, Morris, Hines, Rowley, Froggatt, Dickson, King, Small, Appleton, Jakeman, Hogg, Richardson, Webb, Worthington, Cunningham, Littler, Graver, Thomas, Fincham, Dunne

DATE	OPPONENTS	V	F.T.	SCORERS
Aug 21	Chelsea	H	1-1	Griffiths
26	Charlton Athletic	A	3-2	Froggatt, Hines, Rowley
28	Cardiff City	A	1-2	Froggatt
30	Charlton Athletic	H	0-1	
Sep 4	Manchester City	H	0-2	
6	Burnley	A	1-3	Rowley
11	Everton	A	2-2	Rowley, Froggatt
13	Burnley	H	2-2	Rowley, Hines
18	Newcastle United	H	3-2	Morris, Froggatt, Griffiths
25	West Bromwich Albion	A	4-6	Hines, Rowley, Griffiths, Morris
Oct 2	Arsenal	H	3-3	Rowley 2 (1 pen), Hines
9	Bolton Wanderers	A	1-4	Rowley
16	Huddersfield Town	H	1-3	Rowley
23	Portsmouth	A	1-2	Dickinson (og)
30	Blackpool	H	2-2	Rowley, Hines
Nov 6	Aston Villa	A	5-2	Worthington 2, Rowley, Griffiths, Hines
13	Sunderland	H	1-1	Rowley (pen)
20	Tottenham Hotspur	A	1-5	Rowley
27	Sheffield Wednesday	H	4-3	Russell 2, Morris, Rowley
Dec 4	Manchester United	A	1-3	Hines
11	Wolverhampton Wanderers	H	1-2	Rowley
18	Chelsea	A	1-3	Graver
25	Sheffield United	A	1-1	Graver
27	Sheffield United	H	0-1	
Jan 1	Cardiff City	H	2-1	Hogg, Morris
15	Manchester City	A	2-2	Morris, Griffiths
Feb 5	Newcastle United	A	0-2	
12	West Bromwich Albion	H	6-3	Rowley 3, Griffiths, Hogg, Graver
19	Arsenal	A	1-1	Rowley
Mar 5	Wolverhampton Wanderers	A	0-5	
12	Portsmouth	H	4-0	Rowley 2, Hines, Hogg
19	Blackpool	A	0-2	
26	Aston Villa	H	4-2	Hines, Froggatt, Hogg, Rowley (pen)
Apr 2	Sunderland	A	1-1	Hines
8	Preston North End	A	4-2	Rowley, Morris 2, Walton (og)
9	Manchester United	H	1-0	Froggatt
11	Preston North End	H	0-1	
16	Sheffield Wednesday	A	0-1	
20	Everton	H	2-2	Hogg, Froggatt
23	Tottenham Hotspur	H	2-0	Hines, Hogg
30	Huddersfield Town	A	1-3	Morris
May 4	Bolton Wanderers	H	4-0	Thomas 3, Hogg

F.A. CUP

DATE	OPPONENTS		V	F.T.	SCORERS
Jan 8	Rotherham United	(3)	A	0-1	

LEICESTER CITY 1954-55
Back : F.King *(Training Staff)*, Baldwin, Small, Reed, Dunne, Jayes, Heath, Morris, Froggatt, Hogg, G.Dewis *(Training Staff)*.
Middle : Gillies, Littler, Warner, Rowley, Dickson, Anderson, Russell, Hines, Knapp, Richardson.
Front : C.Maley *(Secretary)*, Jackson, Milburn, Worthington, N.Bullock *(Manager)*,
Webb, Jakeman, Griffiths, D.Jones *(Trainer)*.
On Ground : Wilson, Thomas, Jenkins, King.

	APP's		GOALS	
	FL	FAC	FL	FAC
Johnny Anderson	35	1		
Stan Milburn	34	1		
Ron Jackson	31	1		
Jimmy Baldwin	24			
Matt Gillies	16	1		
Eddie Russell	30	1	2	
Mal Griffiths	36		6	
Johnny Morris	37	1	8	
Derek Hines	32		11	
Arthur Rowley	36	1	23 (3p)	
Jack Froggatt	41	1	7	
Adam Dickson	7			
Johnny King	1			
Peter Small	3			
Colin Appleton	4			
Les Jakeman	1			
Derek Hogg	36	1	7	
Dave Richardson	2			
Bill Webb	3	1		
Fred Worthington	4		2	
Willie Cunningham	16			
Eric Littler	1			
Andy Graver	11	1	3	
Barrie Thomas	5		3	
Gordon Fincham	14			
Jimmy Dunne	2			
Own Goals				2

1955-56

LEAGUE DIVISION TWO
Final Position : 5th
Ave. Home League Att: 27,500

DATE	OPPONENTS	V	F.T.	SCORERS
Aug 20	Hull City	A	4-2	Morris,Rowley 2,Hines
22	Nottingham Forest	H	5-2	Morris,Hogg 2,Hines 2
27	Blackburn Rovers	H	0-2	
31	Nottingham Forest	A	0-2	
Sep 3	Lincoln City	A	1-7	Hines
5	Doncaster Rovers	A	2-6	Rowley,Gardiner
10	Barnsley	H	0-0	
12	Sheffield Wednesday	A	1-1	Rowley
17	Liverpool	H	3-1	Hogg,Gardiner 2
24	Plymouth Argyle	A	1-0	Rowley
Oct 1	Stoke City	H	3-1	Hogg, Gardiner,Rowley
8	Middlesbrough	A	3-4	Rowley,Gardiner 2
15	Bristol City	H	2-2	Rowley 2 (1 pen)
22	Fulham	A	2-3	Rowley 2
29	Port Vale	H	4-1	Gardiner 4
Nov 5	Rotherham United	A	1-3	Rowley
12	Swansea Town	H	6-1	Griffiths,Morris,Gardiner 3,Rowley
19	Notts County	A	1-1	Rowley
26	Leeds United	H	5-2	Rowley 2 (1pen),Gardiner 3
Dec 3	West Ham United	A	3-1	Rowley,Froggatt,Gardiner
10	Bury	H	5-0	Gardiner 2,Hogg,Rowley,Froggatt
17	Hull City	H	1-2	Gardiner
24	Blackburn Rovers	A	3-2	Morris,Rowley 2 (1pen)
26	Bristol Rovers	A	1-2	Morris
27	Bristol Rovers	H	4-2	Froggatt,Gardiner 2,Rowley
31	Lincoln City	H	4-0	Gardiner 2,Rowley 2 (1pen)
Jan 14	Barnsley	A	1-0	Gardiner
21	Liverpool	A	1-3	Rowley
Feb 4	Plymouth Argyle	H	5-1	Froggatt,Riley 2,Rowley 2
11	Stoke City	A	0-2	
18	Notts County	H	4-0	Hogg,Gardiner 2,Rowley
25	Bristol City	A	1-1	Riley
Mar 3	Fulham	H	2-1	Froggatt 2
10	Bury	A	1-3	Rowley
17	Rotherham United	H	3-1	Hogg,Rowley (pen),Gardiner
24	Swansea Town	A	1-6	Froggatt
31	Middlesbrough	H	1-1	Gardiner
Apr 2	Sheffield Wednesday	H	1-2	Gardiner
7	Leeds United	A	0-4	
14	West Ham United	H	2-1	Griffiths,Gardiner
21	Port Vale	A	3-2	Froggatt,Gardiner 2
28	Doncaster Rovers	H	3-0	McNeill,Gardiner,Hogg

F.A. CUP

Jan 11	Luton Town	(3)	A	4-0	Gardiner, Rowley 3
28	Stoke City	(4)	H	3-3	Rowley 2 (1pen),Griffiths
30	Stoke City	(4 rep)	A	1-2	Rowley

LEICESTER CITY 1955-56

Back : F.King *(Training Staff)*, Appleton,Reed,Beeby,Fincham,Burbeck,Cunningham,A.Chandler *(Training Staff)*.
Middle : G.Dewis *(Training Staff)*, Gillies,Jayes,Dunne,Torrance,Anderson,Graney,Webb,Knapp, Heath,D.Jones *(Trainer)*.
Front : C.Maley *(Secretary)*,Baldwin,Milburn,Thomas,Morris,Froggatt,Griffiths,Rowley,Hogg, Russell,D.Halliday *(Manager)*.

	APP's		GOALS	
	FL	FAC	FL	FAC
Johnny Anderson	42	3		
Stan Milburn	12			
Willie Cunningham	34	3		
Jimmy Baldwin	3			
Jack Froggatt	42	3	8	
Eddie Russell	16	2		
Mal Griffiths	17	3	2	1
Johnny Morris	39	3	5	
Derek Hines	17	1	4	
Arthur Rowley	36	3	29 (5p)	6 (1p)
Derek Hogg	42	3	8	
Howard Riley	11		3	
Brian Jayes	3			
Barrie Thomas	2			
Jimmy Dunne	2			
Oliver Beeby	1			
Bill Webb	13	1		
Gordon Fincham	32	3		
Colin Appleton	1			
Willie Gardiner	33	2	34	1
Billy Wright	2			
Pat Ward	27	1		
John Ogilvie	24	2		
Tony Knapp	4			
Ian McNeill	5		1	
Ron Burbeck	2			

1956-57 LEAGUE DIVISION TWO
Final Position : 1st
Ave. Home League Att: 30,500

DATE	OPPONENTS	V	F.T.	SCORERS	Anderson	Milburn	Ogilvie	Morris	Froggatt	Ward	McDonald	McNeill	Gardiner	Rowley	Hogg	Webb	Hines	Appleton	Wright	Sinclair	Maclaren	Walsh	Moran	Cunningham
Aug 18	Doncaster Rovers	H	3-1	McDonald 2,Hogg	1	2	3	4	5	6	7	8	9	10	11									
20	Huddersfield Town	A	2-1	McNeill,Rowley	1	2	3	4	5	6	7	8	9	10	11									
25	Stoke City	A	1-3	Rowley	1	2	3	4	5	6	7	8	9	10	11									
29	Huddersfield Town	H	2-2	Rowley,Gardiner	1	2	3	4	5	6	7	8	9	10	11									
Sep 1	Middlesbrough	H	1-1	Gardiner	1	2	3	4	5	6	7	8	9	10	11									
8	Sheffield United	A	1-1	Rowley	1	2	3	4	5	6	7	8	9	10	11									
12	Bury	H	3-0	Rowley 3	1	2	3	4	5	6	7	8	9	10	11									
15	Bristol Rovers	A	2-1	Rowley,McDonald	1	2	3	4	5	6	7	8	9	10	11									
17	Bury	A	5-4	McNeill 2,Gardiner,Rowley,Milburn	1	2		4	5	6	7	8	9	10	11	3								
22	Notts County	H	6-3	Rowley 3,McDonald,Gardiner,McNeill	1	2	3	4	5	6	7	8	9	10	11									
29	Liverpool	A	0-2		1	2	3	4	5	6	7	8	9	10	11									
Oct 6	Barnsley	H	5-2	McNeill 2,Rowley 2,Hines	1	2	3	4	5	6	7	8		10	11		9							
13	Port Vale	A	3-2	Hogg,Rowley 2	1	2	3	4	5	6	7	8		10	11		9							
20	Blackburn Rovers	H	6-0	Rowley 3 (1pen),Hogg,McNeill,Hines	1	2	3	4	5	6	7	8		10	11		9							
27	Lincoln City	A	3-2	McNeill,Rowley	1	2	3	4	5	6	7	8		10	11		9							
Nov 3	Swansea Town	H	1-1	Rowley	1	2	3	4	5	6	7	8		10	11		9							
10	Fulham	A	2-2	Rowley,Hogg	1	2	3	4	5		7	8		10	11		9	6						
17	Nottingham Forest	H	0-0		1	2	3	4	5		7	8	9	10	11			6						
24	West Ham United	A	1-2	Rowley	1	2	3	4	5	6	7	8	9	10	11									
Dec 1	Rotherham United	H	5-2	Hines 2,McNeill 2,Rowley	1	2	3	4	5	6	7	8		10	11		9							
8	Bristol City	A	2-0	McNeill 2	1	2	3	4	5	6	7	8		10	11		9							
15	Doncaster Rovers	A	2-0	Rowley,Graham (og)	1	2	3	4	5	6	7	8		10	11		9							
22	Stoke City	H	3-2	McNeill,Hines,Rowley	1	2	3	4	5		7	8		10	11		9	6						
25	Grimsby Town	A	2-2	Rowley,Hines	1	2	3	4	5		7	8		10			9	6	11					
29	Middlesbrough	A	3-1	Wright,Appleton,Rowley	1	2	3	4	5		7	8		10			9	6	11					
Jan 12	Sheffield United	H	5-0	Hines,McNeill,Wright,Rowley 2	1	2	3	4	5		7	8		10			9	6	11					
19	Bristol Rovers	H	7-2	McDonald 2,Rowley 2 (1pen),Wright 2,Hines	1	2	3	4	5		7	8		10			9	6	11					
26	Grimsby Town	H	4-3	Wright,Hines,Rowley,McNeill		2	3	4	5		7	8		10			9	6	11	1				
Feb 2	Notts County	A	0-0			2	3	4	5		7	8		10			9	6	11	1				
9	Liverpool	H	3-2	Hines,Rowley 2 (1pen)		2	3	4	5			8		10	7		9	6	11	1				
23	Port Vale	H	2-1	McDonald,Rowley		2	3	4	5		7	8		10	11		9	6		1				
27	Barnsley	A	0-2			2	3	4	5		7	8		10	11		9	6		1				
Mar 2	Blackburn Rovers	A	1-1	Hines		2	3	4	5			8		10	11		9	6	7	1				
9	Lincoln City	H	4-3	Rowley 2 (1pen),Wright,Neal (og)		2	3	4	5			8		10	11		9	6	7	1				
16	Swansea Town	A	3-2	Hines,McNeill,Rowley (pen)		2	3	4	5	6		8		10	11		9		7	1				
23	Fulham	H	1-3	Rowley		2	3	4	5					10	11		9	6	7	1		8		
30	Nottingham Forest	A	2-1	McNeill,Hines		2	3	4	5	6		8		10	11		9		7	1				
Apr 6	West Ham United	H	5-3	Rowley 3,Wright 2		2	3	4	5	6		8		10	11		9		7	1				
13	Rotherham United	A	1-1	Morris		2	3	4	5	6		8		10	11		9		7	1				
19	Leyton Orient	A	5-1	Wright,Moran,Rowley,Hogg,Facey (og)		2		4	5	6				10	11	3	9		7	1			8	
20	Bristol City	H	1-1	Hines		2		4	5	6				10	11	3	9		7	1			8	
22	Leyton Orient	H	1-4	Wright		2		4	5	6				10	11		9		7	1			8	3

F.A. CUP

DATE	OPPONENTS	V	F.T.	SCORERS	Anderson	Milburn	Ogilvie	Morris	Froggatt	Ward	McDonald	McNeill	Gardiner	Rowley	Hogg	Webb	Hines	Appleton	Wright	Sinclair	Maclaren	Walsh	Moran	Cunningham
Jan 5	Tottenham Hotspur	(3) A	0-2		1	2	3	4	5		7	8		10			9	6	11					

LEICESTER CITY 1956-57
Back : A.Dowdells *(Trainer)*, Ward,Ogilvie,Anderson,Gardiner,Maclaren,Appleton,Milburn,Froggatt.
Front : W.Wileman *(Director)*, McDonald,McNeill,Hines,Rowley,Hogg,D.Halliday *(Manager)*.
On Ground : Morris,Wright.

	APP's		GOALS	
	FL	FAC	FL	FAC
Johnny Anderson	27	1		
Stan Milburn	42	1	1	
John Ogilvie	38	1		
Johnny Morris	42	1	1	
Jack Froggatt	42	1		
Pat Ward	27			
Tommy McDonald	31	1	7	
Ian McNeill	38	1	18	
Willie Gardiner	13		4	
Arthur Rowley	42	1	44 (5p)	
Derek Hogg	36		5	
Bill Webb	3			
Derek Hines	29	1	14	
Colin Appleton	15	1	1	
Billy Wright	17	1	10	
Harvey Sinclair	1			
Dave Maclaren	14			
Jimmy Walsh	1			
Jimmy Moran	3		1	
Willie Cunningham	1			
Own Goals			3	

1957-58

LEAGUE DIVISION ONE
Final Position : 18th
Ave. Home League Att: 31,500

DATE	OPPONENTS	V	F.T.	SCORERS
Aug 24	Manchester United	H	0-3	
28	Sunderland	H	4-1	McNeill 3,O'Neil
31	Leeds United	A	1-2	Rowley
Sep 4	Sunderland	A	2-3	McDonald,Hines
7	Bolton Wanderers	H	2-3	Rowley (pen),O'Neil
11	Sheffield Wednesday	A	1-2	Rowley
14	Arsenal	A	1-3	Froggatt
18	Sheffield Wednesday	H	4-1	Gardiner 2,Rowley 2
21	Wolverhampton Wanderers	H	2-3	Russell,McNeill
28	Aston Villa	A	1-5	Morris
Oct 5	Everton	H	2-2	Gardiner,Hogg
12	Manchester City	A	3-4	Rowley 2 (1pen),McDonald
19	Nottingham Forest	H	3-1	McDonald,Gardiner,Whare (og)
26	Portsmouth	A	0-2	
Nov 2	Newcastle United	H	2-1	Gardiner,Russell
9	Burnley	A	3-7	Doherty 2,Hogg
16	Preston North End	H	1-3	McDonald
23	Chelsea	A	0-4	
30	West Bromwich Albion	H	3-3	Rowley 2,Doherty
Dec 7	Tottenham Hotspur	A	4-1	Doherty 2,McDonald,Rowley
14	Birmingham City	H	2-2	Rowley 2
21	Manchester United	A	0-4	
25	Blackpool	A	1-5	Gardiner
26	Blackpool	H	2-1	Walsh,Gardiner
28	Leeds United	H	3-0	Rowley 2 (1pen),Walsh
Jan 11	Bolton Wanderers	A	3-2	Walsh,Cunningham,Higgins (og)
18	Arsenal	H	0-1	
Feb 1	Wolverhampton Wanderers	A	1-5	Walsh
8	Aston Villa	H	6-1	Walker,Hogg 2,Riley 2,Lynn (og)
15	Everton	A	2-2	Walsh 2
22	Manchester City	H	8-4	Walsh 4,Riley 2 (1pen),Hines,Hogg
Mar 1	Nottingham Forest	A	1-3	Walsh
8	Portsmouth	H	2-2	Hines,Cunningham (pen)
15	Newcastle United	A	3-5	Walsh,Riley,McNeill
22	Chelsea	H	3-2	Hines 2,Cunningham (pen)
29	Preston North End	A	1-4	Rowley
Apr 5	Burnley	H	5-3	Rowley 2,Walsh,Riley 2
7	Luton Town	A	1-2	Hines
8	Luton Town	H	4-1	Rowley 2,Hines,Gardiner
12	West Bromwich Albion	A	2-6	Rowley,Gardiner
19	Tottenham Hotspur	H	1-3	Gardiner
26	Birmingham City	A	1-0	McNeill

F.A. CUP

DATE	OPPONENTS		V	F.T.	SCORERS
Jan 4	Tottenham Hotspur	(3)	A	0-4	

LEICESTER CITY 1957-58

Back : Currie,King,Hines,Gardiner,Froggatt,Ward,Fincham,Appleton,Chalmers,Ogilvie.
Middle : F.King *(AssistantTrainer),*Walsh,Gammie,O'Neil,Maclaren,Anderson,Rowley, Knapp,Cunningham,Russell,M.Gillies *(Coach).*
Front : A.Dowdells*(Trainer),*McDonald,W.Wright,Moran,McNeill,Hogg,Milburn,Calder,D.Halliday *(Manager).*
On Ground : Baillie,B.Wright.

	APP's FL	APP's FAC	GOALS FL	GOALS FAC
Dave Maclaren	24	1		
Stan Milburn	19	1		
John Ogilvie	15			
Johnny Morris	29	1	1	
Jack Froggatt	11		1	
Joe O'Neil	5		2	
Tommy McDonald	22		5	
Ian McNeill	17		6	
Derek Hines	23	1	7	
Arthur Rowley	25	1	20 (3p)	
Derek Hogg	38		5	
Willie Gardiner	23		10	
Eddie Russell	20		2	
Billy Wright	8	1		
Willie Cunningham	28		3 (2p)	
Ian King	23	1		
Jimmy Walsh	19	1	13	
Johnny Anderson	18			
Pat Ward	3			
Gordon Fincham	1			
Colin Appleton	2			
John Doherty	12		5	
Don Walker	28	1	1	
Tony Knapp	1			
Howard Riley	16	1	7 (1p)	
John Newman	10			
Joe Baillie	21	1		
Len Chalmers	1			
Own Goals				3

1958-59

LEAGUE DIVISION ONE
Final Position : 19th
Ave. Home League Att: 28,000

DATE	OPPONENTS	V	F.T.	SCORERS	Maclaren	Cunningham	Baillie	Newman	King	Keyworth	Riley	Walsh	Hines	Leek	Calder	Knapp	McDonald	Kelly	Wills	McNeill	MacFarlane	Anderson	Chalmers	Appleton	Walker	Lornie	Ogilvie	Stephenson
Aug 23	Everton	H	2-0	Leek,Riley	1	2	3	4	5	6	7	8	9	10	11													
25	Blackburn Rovers	A	0-5		1	2	3	4	5	6	7	8	9	10	11													
30	Arsenal	A	1-5	Leek	1	2	3	4		6			9	10		5	7	8		11								
Sep 3	Blackburn Rovers	H	1-1	Walsh	1	2	3	4		6			9			5	7	8		11	10							
6	Manchester City	H	3-1	McDonald,Kelly,Walsh	1	2	3	4		6			9			5	7	8		11	10							
13	Leeds United	A	1-1	McDonald	1	2	3	4		6			9			5	7	8		11	10							
17	Preston North End	H	2-2	Kelly,Walsh	1	2	3	4		6			9			5	7	8		11	10							
20	West Bromwich Albion	H	2-2	Walsh,Newman	1	2	3	4		6			9			5	7	8		11	10							
22	Preston North End	A	1-3	Walsh	1	2	3	4		6			9	10	11	5	7			8								
27	Birmingham City	A	2-4	Kelly 2	1	2	3	4		6			9			5	7	8		11	10							
Oct 4	Luton Town	H	3-1	McNeill,Walsh,Kelly	1		3	4		6			9			5	7	8		11	10	2						
11	Newcastle United	A	1-3	Kelly (pen)	1		3	4	5	6			9	10		2	7	8		11								
18	Tottenham Hotspur	H	3-4	Kelly,Walsh 2	1		3	4	5	6		8	9			2	7	10		11								
25	Chelsea	A	2-5	Kelly,Walsh			3	4	5	6		8	9			2	7	10		11	1							
Nov 1	Blackpool	H	0-3		1	5	3	4			7		9			2		8		11	10		6					
8	Portsmouth	A	1-4	Hines	1	5	3	4		6		10	9		11	2	7	8										
15	Aston Villa	H	6-3	Hines 4,Walsh,Kelly	1	2	3	4	5	6		10	9		11		7	8										
22	West Ham United	A	3-0	Kelly,Keyworth,Hines	1	2	3	4	5	6		10	9		11		7	8										
29	Nottingham Forest	H	0-3		1	2	3	4	5	6		10	9		11		7				8							
Dec 6	Manchester United	A	1-4	Kelly	1	2	3	4	5	6	7	10	9		11		8											
13	Wolverhampton Wanderers	H	1-0	Walsh	1	2	3	4	5	6		10	9		11		7	8										
20	Everton	A	1-0	Hines	1	2	3	4	5	6	7	10	9		11		8											
26	Burnley	H	1-1	Leek	1	2	3	4	5	6	7	10	9		11		8											
27	Burnley	A	3-3	Riley 2,Leek	1	2	3	4	5		7		9		11					8			6	10				
Jan 3	Arsenal	H	2-3	Walsh,Kelly	1	2	3	4	5	6	7	10	9				8			11								
31	Leeds United	H	0-1		1	2	3	4	5	6	7	10	9		11		8											
Feb 7	West Bromwich Albion	A	2-2	Lornie,Riley	1	2	3	4	5		7	8								11			6	10		9		
21	Luton Town	A	3-4	Leek,Newman,Lornie	1	2	3	4	5		7	8								11			6	10		9		
28	Newcastle United	H	0-1			2	3	4	5			10			11		7	8					6		1	9		
Mar 7	Tottenham Hotspur	A	0-6			2	3	4	5	6	7		9	10						11				8	1			
14	Chelsea	H	0-3			2		4	5	6							7	10		11				9	1		3	8
18	Birmingham City	H	2-4	Walsh 2		2		4	5	6		9					7	8		11				10	1		3	
21	Blackpool	A	1-2	Kelly				4	5			9		10			7	8		11			2	6	1		3	
27	Bolton Wanderers	A	3-3	Wills,Leek,Ogilvie (pen)	1			4		6		9		10		5	7		11				2				3	8
28	Portsmouth	H	3-1	Walsh,Ogilvie (pen),Leek	1			4		6		9		10		5	7		11				2				3	8
30	Bolton Wanderers	H	0-0		1		3	4				9		10		5	7		11				2	6				8
Apr 4	Aston Villa	A	2-1	Walsh 2	1		3	4				9		10		5	7		11				2	6				8
11	West Ham United	H	1-1	McDonald	1		3	4				9		10		5	7		11				2	6				8
18	Nottingham Forest	A	4-1	Walsh,Keyworth,McDonald,Whare (og)	1		3	4		8		9		10		5	7		11				2	6				
22	Wolverhampton Wanderers	A	0-3		1		3	4		8		9		10		5	7		11				2	6				
25	Manchester United	H	2-1	Walsh,Wills	1		3	4		8		9		10		5			11				2	6			7	
29	Manchester City	A	1-3	Walsh	1		3	4		6		9		10		5	7		11				2					8

F.A. CUP

DATE	OPPONENTS		V	F.T.	SCORERS	Maclaren	Cunningham	Baillie	Newman	King	Keyworth	Riley	Walsh	Hines	Leek	Calder	Knapp	McDonald	Kelly	Wills	McNeill	MacFarlane	Anderson	Chalmers	Appleton	Walker	Lornie	Ogilvie	Stephenson
Jan 10	Lincoln City	(3)	H	1-1	Kelly	1	2	3	4	5	6	7		9		11		8					10						
14	Lincoln City	(3 rep)	A	2-0	Kelly,Hines	1	2	3	4	5	6	7		9		11		8			10								
24	Luton Town	(4)	H	1-1	McNeill	1	2	3	4	5	6	7		9		11		8			10								
28	Luton Town	(4 rep)	A	1-4	Leek	1	2	3	4	5	6	7	8	9		11					10								

	APP's		GOALS	
	FL	FAC	FL	FAC
Dave Maclaren	37	4		
Willie Cunningham	28	4		
Joe Baillie	37	4		
John Newman	42	4	2	
Ian King	22	4		
Ken Keyworth	32	4	2	
Howard Riley	13	4	4	
Jimmy Walsh	38	1	20	
Derek Hines	16	4	7	1
Ken Leek	31	4	7	1
Bill Calder	3			
Tony Knapp	23			
Tommy McDonald	29		4	
Bernard Kelly	24	3	13 (1p)	2
Gordon Wills	22		2	
Ian McNeill	12	3	1	1
Ian MacFarlane	1			
Johnny Anderson	5			
Len Chalmers	11			
Colin Appleton	12			
Don Walker	4	1		
Jack Lornie	5		2	
John Ogilvie	5		2 (2p)	
Roy Stephenson	10			
Own Goals				1

LEICESTER CITY 1958-59
Back : Newman,Chalmers,Gardiner,Maclaren,Anderson,King,Keyworth,Baillie.
Middle : A.Dowdells (Trainer),MacFarlane,Walker,Cunningham,Kelly,Wills,D.Halliday (Manager).
Front : Walsh,McDonald,McNeill,Hines,Leek.

1959-60

LEAGUE DIVISION ONE
Final Position : 12th
Ave. Home League Att: 25,389

DATE	OPPONENTS	V	F.T.	SCORERS	Maclaren	Chalmers	Baillie	Newman	Knapp	Appleton	Riley	Cheesebrough	Hines	Leek	Wills	Cunningham	Stephenson	McDonald	Banks	McLintock	Keyworth	White	Walsh	King	Lornie	Norman
Aug 22	West Ham United	A	0-3		1	2	3	4	5	6	7	8	9	10	11											
26	Leeds United	H	3-2	Hines 2,Cheesebrough	1	2	3	4	5	6	7	8	9	10	11											
29	Chelsea	H	3-1	Cheesebrough,Cunningham,Leek	1	2		4	5	6	7	8	9	10	11	3										
Sep 2	Leeds United	A	1-1	Leek	1	2	3	4	5	6		8	9	10	11		7									
5	West Bromwich Albion	A	0-5		1	2	3	4	5	6		8	9	10	11		7									
9	Blackpool	H	1-1	Leek		2	3	4	5	6		8	9	10	11	7		1								
12	Newcastle United	H	0-2			2	3	4	5	6		8	9	10	11			7	1							
14	Blackpool	A	3-3	Wills 2,McDonald	1	2	3			5	6		10	9		11		7		4	8					
19	Birmingham City	A	4-3	Riley,Keyworth 2,Cheesebrough	1	2	3			5	6	7	10	9		11				4	8					
26	Tottenham Hotspur	H	1-1	McDonald	1	2	3	5		6			10	9		11		7		4	8					
Oct 3	Manchester United	A	1-4	Hines	1	2	3			5	6		10	9		11		7		4	8					
10	Blackburn Rovers	H	2-3	Cheesebrough 2	1	2	3			5	6		10	9		11		7		4	8					
17	Manchester City	A	2-3	McDonald 2		2	3			5	6		10		9	11		7	1	4	8					
24	Arsenal	H	2-2	Wills,McDonald		2	3			5	6		10		9	11		7	1	4	8					
31	Everton	A	1-6	McDonald		2	3	4		5	6		10		9	11		7	1		8					
Nov 7	Sheffield Wednesday	H	2-0	McDonald,Keyworth		2	3			5	6		10			11		7	1	8	4	9				
14	Nottingham Forest	A	0-1			2	3			5	6	7	10			11			1	8	4	9				
21	Fulham	H	0-1			2				3	6		10			11		7	1	8	4	9	5			
28	Bolton Wanderers	A	1-3	Cheesebrough		2				3	6		8		10	11		7	1	9	4		5			
Dec 5	Luton Town	H	3-3	Appleton,Wills,McDonald		2	3				6		8		10	11		7	1	9	4		5			
12	Wolverhampton Wanderers	A	3-0	McDonald,Leek,Cheesebrough		2				5	6		8		10	11	3	7	1	9	4					
19	West Ham United	H	2-1	White,Cheesebrough		2				5	6		8		10	11	3	7	1	9	4					
26	Preston North End	H	2-2	Chalmers (pen),Leek		2				5	6		8		10	11	3	7	1	9	4					
28	Preston North End	A	1-1	Cheesebrough		2				5	6		8			11	3	7	1		4	10	9			
Jan 2	Chelsea	A	2-2	Leek 2		2				5	6		8		9	11	3	7	1		4	10				
16	West Bromwich Albion	H	0-1			2				5	6		8		9	11	3	7	1		4	10				
23	Newcastle United	A	2-0	Walsh,McDonald		2				5	6		8		9	11		7	1		4	10		3		
Feb 6	Birmingham City	H	1-3	McDonald		2				5	6		8		9	11	3	7	1		4	10				
13	Tottenham Hotspur	A	2-1	Walsh 2						5	6		8		9	11	2	7	1		4	10		3		
24	Manchester United	H	3-1	McLintock,Cheesebrough,Wills		2				5	6		8		9	11	3	7	1	4		10				
27	Luton Town	A	0-2			2					6		8		9	11	3	7	1	4		10	5			
Mar 5	Manchester City	H	5-0	Wills 2,Cheesebrough,Leek 2		2				5	6		8		9	11	3	7	1	4		10				
15	Arsenal	A	1-1	Wills		2				5	6		8		9	11	3	7	1	4		10				
19	Wolverhampton Wanderers	H	2-1	Walsh,Cheesebrough		2				5	6		8		9	11	3	7	1	4		10				
Apr 2	Nottingham Forest	H	0-1			2				5	10					11	3	7	1	4	9	6	8			
6	Sheffield Wednesday	A	2-2	Cheesebrough,Wills		2				5	6		8		9	11		7	1	4		10				
9	Fulham	A	1-1	Bentley (og)		2				5	6		8		9	11	3		1	4		10		3		
15	Burnley	A	0-1			2				5	6	7	8		9	11	3		1	4		10				
16	Everton	H	3-3	Chalmers (pen),Cheesebrough,McLintock		2				5	6		8		9	11	3	7	1	4		10				
18	Burnley	H	2-1	Wills,Cheesebrough						5	6	7	8			11	2		1		9	4	10		3	
23	Blackburn Rovers	A	1-0	Wills						5	6	7	8			11	2		1		9	4	10		3	
30	Bolton Wanderers	H	1-2	Riley		2				5	6	7	8			11			1		9	4	10		3	

F.A. CUP

DATE	OPPONENTS		V	F.T.	SCORERS	Maclaren	Chalmers	Baillie	Newman	Knapp	Appleton	Riley	Cheesebrough	Hines	Leek	Wills	Cunningham	Stephenson	McDonald	Banks	McLintock	Keyworth	White	Walsh	King	Lornie	Norman
Jan 9	Wrexham	(3)	A	2-1	Cheesebrough,Leek		2				5	6		8		9	11	3	7	1		4	10				
30	Fulham	(4)	H	2-1	McDonald,Wills		2				5	6		8		9	11	3	7	1		4	10				
Feb 20	West Bromwich Albion	(5)	H	2-1	Walsh,Cheesebrough		2				5	6		8		9	11	3	7	1		4	10				
Mar 12	Wolverhampton W.	(6)	H	1-2	McDonald		2				5	6		8		9	11	3	7	1	4		10				

Note: Apr 9, most reports credit Bentley (og), some credit Cheesebrough

LEICESTER CITY 1959-60
Back: Hines,Leek,Ogilvie,Maclaren,King,Chalmers,Appleton,Keyworth.
Front : A.Dowdells *(Trainer)*,Baillie,Cheesebrough,Newman,Walsh,Stephenson,Wills,M.Gillies *(Manager)*.
On Ground : McDonald,Cunningham.

	APP's		GOALS	
	FL	FAC	FL	FAC
Dave Maclaren	10			
Len Chalmers	39	4	2 (2p)	
Joe Baillie	17			
John Newman	9			
Tony Knapp	39	4		
Colin Appleton	42	4	1	
Howard Riley	9		2	
Albert Cheesebrough	41	4	15	2
Derek Hines	12		3	
Ken Leek	32	4	9	1
Gordon Wills	39	4	11	1
Willie Cunningham	20	4	1	
Roy Stephenson	2			
Tommy McDonald	31	4	11	2
Gordon Banks	32	4		
Frank McLintock	17	1	2	
Ken Keyworth	20		3	
Ian White	18	3	1	
Jimmy Walsh	22	4	4	1
Ian King	4			
Jack Lornie	1			
Richie Norman	6			
Own Goals			1	

1960-61
LEAGUE DIVISION ONE
Final Position : 6th
Ave. Home League Att: 24,041

DATE	OPPONENTS	V	F.T.	SCORERS	Banks	Chalmers	Norman	White	Knapp	Appleton	Meek	Cheesebrough	Hines	Walsh	Wills	McLintock	Riley	Leek	King	Slack	Lornie	Sjoberg	Keyworth	Heyes	McIlmoyle	Cross
Aug 20	Blackpool	H	1-1	Appleton	1	2	3	4	5	6	7	8	9	10	11											
24	Chelsea	A	3-1	Wills 2,Walsh	1	2	3	4	5	6	7	8	9	10	11											
27	Everton	A	1-3	Cheesebrough	1	2	3	4	5	6	7	8	9	10	11											
31	Chelsea	H	1-3	Walsh	1	2	3	4	5	6	7	8	9	10	11											
Sep 3	Blackburn Rovers	H	2-4	Walsh,Wills	1	2	3		5	6		8		10	11	4	7	9								
7	Wolverhampton Wanderers	A	2-3	Wills,Leek	1	2	3		5	6		8		10	11	4	7	9								
10	Manchester United	A	1-1	Walsh	1		3		5	6		10			8	11	4	7	9		2					
14	Wolverhampton Wanderers	H	2-0	Walsh,King (pen)	1		3		5	6		10			8	11	4	7	9		2					
17	Tottenham Hotspur	H	1-2	Riley	1		3		5	6		10			8	11	4	7	9		2					
24	Newcastle United	A	3-1	Leek 2,Cheesebrough	1		3		5	6		10			8	11	4	7	9		2					
Oct 1	Aston Villa	A	3-1	Walsh 2,Wills	1		3		5	6		10			8	11	4	7	9		2					
8	Arsenal	H	2-1	Leek 2	1		3		5	6		10			8	11	4	7	9		2					
15	Manchester City	A	1-3	Leek	1		3		5	6		10			8	11	4	7	9		2					
22	West Bromwich Albion	H	2-2	Lornie,Cheesebrough	1		3		5	6		10			8	11	4	7		2	9					
28	Cardiff City	A	1-2	Walsh	1		3			6		10			8	11	4	7	9	2		5				
Nov 4	Preston North End	H	5-2	Leek 2,Walsh,Cheesebrough,Riley	1	2	3		5	6		10			8	11	4	7	9							
12	Fulham	A	2-4	King (pen),Cheesebrough	1		3		5	6		8			11	4	7	10	2	9						
19	Sheffield Wednesday	H	2-1	Walsh,Wills	1	2	3			6		10			8	11	4	7	9	5						
26	Birmingham City	A	2-0	Leek,Wills	1	2	3			6		10			8	11	4	7	9	5						
Dec 3	Nottingham Forest	H	1-1	Cheesebrough	1	2	3			6		10			8	11	4	7	9	5						
10	Burnley	A	2-3	Wills,Leek	1	2	3			6		10			8	11	4	7	9	5						
17	Blackpool	A	1-5	Walsh	1	2	3			6		10			8	11	4	7	9	5						
24	Bolton Wanderers	A	0-2		1	2	3			6	11	10			8		4	7	9	5						
26	Bolton Wanderers	H	2-0	Wills,Keyworth	1	2	3			6					8	11	4	7	9	5			10			
31	Everton	H	4-1	Riley,Walsh,Leek 2	1	2	3			6					8	11	4	7	9	5			10			
Jan 14	Blackburn Rovers	A	1-1	Leek	1	2	3			6					8	11	4	7	9	5			10			
21	Manchester United	H	6-0	Walsh 2,Keyworth 2,Wills,Riley (pen)	1	2	3			6					8	11	4	7	9	5			10			
Feb 4	Tottenham Hotspur	A	3-2	Leek,Walsh 2	1	2	3			6					8	11	4	7	9	5			10			
11	Newcastle United	H	5-3	King 2 (2pen),Cheesebrough,Leek,Dalton (og)	1	2	3			6				11	8		4	7	9	5			10			
25	Arsenal	A	3-1	Keyworth 2,Appleton	1	2	3	4	5	6	11	8					7	9					10			
Mar 11	West Bromwich Albion	A	0-1			2	3	6				10			8	11	4	7	9	5			1			
25	Preston North End	A	0-0		1		3	4	5	6	11	8	9				7				2	10				
31	West Ham United	A	0-1		1		3			6	11	8			4		7	9	5		2	10				
Apr 1	Burnley	H	2-2	Leek,Walsh	1		3			6		11			8		4	7	9	5		2	10			
3	West Ham United	H	5-1	Cheesebrough 3,Riley,McIlmoyle	1		3	4	5		11	10			8	6	7					2			9	
8	Sheffield Wednesday	A	2-2	Walsh,McLintock	1	2	3			6	11	10			8	4	7			5					9	
10	Cardiff City	H	3-0	Walsh 2,McIlmoyle	1	2	3			6	11				8	4	7			5			10		9	
15	Fulham	H	1-2	Walsh	1	2	3			6	11				8	4	7			5			10		9	
19	Aston Villa	H	3-1	McIlmoyle 2,Keyworth	1	2	3	4		6	7	11			8					5			10		9	
22	Nottingham Forest	A	2-2	Cheesebrough,Leek	1	2	3	4			11				8		7	9	5				10			
26	Manchester City	H	1-2	Walsh	1	2	3			6	11				8	4	7			5			10		9	
29	Birmingham City	H	3-2	Cross,Riley,Leek		2	3			6	11					McL	4	7	10	5				1	9	8

F.A. CUP

Date	Opponent		V	F.T.	SCORERS	Banks	Chalmers	Norman	White	Knapp	Appleton	Meek	Cheesebrough	Hines	Walsh	Wills	McLintock	Riley	Leek	King	Slack	Lornie	Sjoberg	Keyworth	Heyes	McIlmoyle	Cross
Jan 7	Oxford United	(3)	H	3-1	Walsh,Leek,Riley	1	2	3			6					8	11	4	7	9	5			10			
31	Bristol City	(4)	H	5-1	Wills,Leek 2,Walsh 2	1	2	3			6					8	11	4	7	9	5			10			
Feb 18	Birmingham City	(5)	A	1-1	Riley	1	2	3			6				11	8		4	7	9	5			10			
22	Birmingham City	(5 rep)	H	2-1	Leek 2	1	2	3			6				11	8		4	7	9	5			10			
Mar 4	Barnsley	(6)	H	0-0		1	2	3			6					8	11	4	7	9	5			10			
8	Barnsley	(6 rep)	A	2-1	Riley,Leek	1	2	3			6					8	11	4	7	9	5			10			
18	Sheffield United	(sf)		0-0	(at Elland Road, Leeds)	1	2	3			6					8	11	4	7	9	5			10			
23	Sheffield United	(sf rep)		0-0	(at City Ground, Nottingham)	1	2	3			6				11	8		4	7	9	5			10			
27	Sheffield United	(sf rep 2)		2-0	Walsh,Leek (at St Andrews, Birmingham)	1	2	3			6				11	8		4	7	9	5			10			
May 6	Tottenham Hotspur	(F)		0-2	(at Wembley)	1	2	3			6				11	8		4	7		5			10	9		

F.L. CUP

Date	Opponent		V	F.T.	SCORERS	Banks	Chalmers	Norman	White	Knapp	Appleton	Meek	Cheesebrough	Hines	Walsh	Wills	McLintock	Riley	Leek	King	Slack	Lornie	Sjoberg	Keyworth	Heyes	McIlmoyle	Cross
Oct 12	Mansfield Town	(1)	H	4-0	Cheesebrough,Walsh 3			3		5	6		10			8	11	4	7	9	2	1					
26	Rotherham United	(2)	H	1-2	King (pen)	1		3		5	6		10			8	11	4	7		2	9					

LEICESTER CITY 1960-61
Back : Knapp,King,Heyes,Keyworth,Banks,Chalmers,Hines.
Front : A. Dowdells *(Trainer)*,Appleton,Riley,Cheesebrough,Leek,Walsh,Wills,M.Gillies *(Manager)*.
On Ground : White,Norman.

	APP's			GOALS		
	FL	FAC	FLC	FL	FAC	FLC
Gordon Banks	40	10	1			
Len Chalmers	28	10				
Richie Norman	42	10	2			
Ian White	10					
Tony Knapp	19		2			
Colin Appleton	40	10	2	2		
George Meek	13					
Albert Cheesebrough	35	5	2	11		1
Derek Hines	5					
Jimmy Walsh	37	10	2	22	4	3
Gordon Wills	28	5	2	10	1	
Frank McLintock	34	10	2	1		
Howard Riley	37	10	2	6 (1p)	3	
Ken Leek	30	9	1	18	7	
Ian King	32	10	2	4 (4p)		1 (p)
Rodney Slack		1				
Jack Lornie	2	1		1		
John Sjoberg	5					
Ken Keyworth	15	10		6		
George Heyes	2					
Hugh McIlmoyle	7	1		4		
Graham Cross	1			1		
Own Goals				1		

1961-62

LEAGUE DIVISION ONE
Final Position : 14th
Ave. Home League Att: 19,459

DATE	OPPONENTS	V	F.T.	SCORERS	Banks	Chalmers	Norman	White	King	Appleton	Riley	Walsh	McIlmoyle	Keyworth	Wills	Cheesebrough	Cross	McLintock	Mitten	Heyes	Stringfellow	Gibson	Sjoberg	Thomson
Aug 19	Manchester City	A	1-3	Wills	1	2	3	4	5	6	7	8		9	10	11								
23	Arsenal	H	0-1		1	2	3	4	5	6	7	8		9	10	11								
26	West Bromwich Albion	H	1-0	Riley	1	2	3	4	5	6	7	8		9	11	10								
29	Arsenal	A	4-4	Walsh,Cheesebrough 2,Keyworth	1	2	3	4	5	6	7	8		9	11	10								
Sep 2	Birmingham City	A	5-1	Keyworth 2,Wills 2,Walsh	1	2	3	4	5	6	7	8		9	11	10								
5	Burnley	A	0-2		1	2	3	4	5	6	7	8	10	9	11									
9	Everton	H	2-0	Wills,Walsh	1	2	3	4	5	6	7	8	10	9	11									
16	Fulham	A	1-2	Keyworth	1	2	3	4	5	6	7	8		9	11	10								
20	Burnley	H	2-6	Walsh 2	1	2	3	4	5	6	7	8		9	11			10						
23	Sheffield Wednesday	H	1-0	Riley (pen)	1	2	3	4	5	6	7	8		9	11			10						
30	West Ham United	A	1-4	McLintock	1	2	3		5	6	7		9	8	10			4	11					
Oct 7	Sheffield United	H	4-1	Riley,Walsh,Wills,Chalmers	1	2	3		5	6	7	8		9	10			4	11					
14	Chelsea	A	3-1	Wills,McLintock 2	1	2	3	6	5	10	7		9	8	11			4						
21	Blackpool	H	0-2		1	2	3	6	5	10	7		9	8	11			4						
28	Blackburn Rovers	H	1-2	Keyworth	1	2	3	6	5	10	7			8	9			4	11					
Nov 4	Wolverhampton Wanderers	H	3-0	Riley (pen),Wills,Appleton	1	2	3	6	5	10	7			8	9			4	11					
11	Manchester United	A	2-2	McLintock,Appleton	1	2	3	6	5	10	7			8	9			4	11					
18	Cardiff City	H	3-0	Appleton,Keyworth,McIlmoyle	1	2	3	4	5	10			9	8	7		6		11					
25	Tottenham Hotspur	A	2-1	Keyworth,Appleton		2	3		5	10	7		9	6		8		4	11	1				
Dec 2	Aston Villa	H	0-2		1	2	3		5	10	7		9	6		8		4	11					
9	Nottingham Forest	A	0-0		1	2	3		5	10		8	9	6	7			4	11					
16	Manchester City	H	2-0	Cheesebrough,Walsh	1	2	3		5	10		8	9	6		7		4	11					
23	West Bromwich Albion	A	0-2		1	2	3		5	10		8	9	6		7		4	11					
26	Ipswich Town	A	0-1		1	2	3		5	10	7	8		6		9		4	11					
Jan 13	Birmingham City	H	1-2	Cheesebrough	1	2	3		5	6	7	8		9	11	10		4						
20	Everton	A	2-3	Walsh,Riley (pen)	1	2	3		5	6	7	8		9		10		4			11			
Feb 3	Fulham	H	4-1	Walsh 2,Keyworth,Riley (pen)	1	2	3		5	6	7	8		9				4			11	10		
10	Sheffield Wednesday	A	2-1	Walsh,Johnson (og)	1	2	3		5	6	7	8		9				4			11	10		
17	West Ham United	H	2-2	Keyworth 2	1	2	3	4	5	6	7	8		9							11	10		
24	Sheffield United	A	1-3	Keyworth	1	2	3		5	6	7	8		9				4			11	10		
Mar 10	Blackpool	A	1-2	Cheesebrough	1	2	3		5	6	7	8		9		10		4			11			
17	Blackburn Rovers	H	2-0	Keyworth,Cheesebrough	1	2	3		5	6	7	10		9		8		4			11			
24	Wolverhampton Wanderers	A	1-1	Gibson	1	2	3		5	6	7	8		9				4			11	10		
28	Ipswich Town	H	0-2		1	2	3		5	6	7	9		10		8		4			11			
Apr 4	Manchester United	H	4-3	Cheesebrough 2,Keyworth 2	1	2	3		5	6	7	9		8		10		4			11			
7	Cardiff City	A	4-0	Cheesebrough 2,Keyworth,King	1	2	3		5	6	7	9		8		10		4			11			
11	Chelsea	H	2-0	Cheesebrough,Norman	1	2	3		5	6	7	9		8		10		4			11			
21	Aston Villa	A	3-8	Walsh 2,Riley (pen)	1	2	3		5	6	7	9		8	11	10								
23	Bolton Wanderers	A	0-1		1	2	3		5	6	7	9		8	11	10								
24	Bolton Wanderers	H	1-1	Walsh	1	2	3	4		6	7	10			11	9			8				5	
28	Nottingham Forest	H	2-1	McLintock 2	1	7	3	4	5	6		10			11	9		8					2	
30	Tottenham Hotspur	H	2-3	Cross,Thomson	1	2	3			6		8			11	7	9	4				5		10

F.A. CUP

DATE	OPPONENTS		V	F.T.	SCORERS	Banks	Chalmers	Norman	White	King	Appleton	Riley	Walsh	McIlmoyle	Keyworth	Wills	Cheesebrough	Cross	McLintock	Mitten
Jan 10	Stoke City	(3)	H	1-1	Riley	1	2	3		5	10	7	8		6		9		4	11
15	Stoke City	(3 rep)	A	2-5	Riley (pen),Keyworth	1	2	3		5	6	7	8		9	11	10		4	

F.L. CUP

DATE	OPPONENTS		V	F.T.	SCORERS	Banks	Chalmers	Norman	White	King	Appleton	Riley	Walsh	McIlmoyle	Keyworth	Wills	Cheesebrough	Cross	McLintock	Mitten
Oct 9	York City	(2)	A	1-2	Mitten	1	2	3		5	6	7	8		9	10			4	11

E.C.W. CUP

DATE	OPPONENTS		V	F.T.	SCORERS	Banks	Chalmers	Norman	White	King	Appleton	Riley	Walsh	McIlmoyle	Keyworth	Wills	Cheesebrough	Cross	McLintock	Mitten
Sep 13	Glenavon	(1leg1)	A	4-1	Walsh 2,Appleton,Keyworth	1	2	3	4	5	6	7	8		9	11	10			
27	Glenavon	(1leg2)	H	3-1	Wills,Keyworth,McIlmoyle	1	2	3	4	5	6	7		9	10	11	8			
Oct 25	Atletico Madrid	(2leg1)	H	1-1	Keyworth	1	2	3	6	5	10	7		8	9				4	11
Nov 15	Atletico Madrid	(2leg2)	A	0-2		1	4	3	6	2	10	7		8	9			5		11

LEICESTER CITY 1961-62

Back: G.Dewis *(Third Team Coach)*, Walker,Tewley,Elliot,Hopewell,A.Chandler *(Training Staff)*, Johnston,R.Riley, Gamble,Heath,B.Johnson *(Chief Scout)*. *Middle :* McIlmoyle,McLintock,Hines,Banks,Heyes,King,Sjoberg,Knapp. *Front :* A.Dowdells *(Trainer)*, Norman,Appleton,H.Riley,Walsh,M.Gillies *(Manager)*, Keyworth, Wills,Chalmers,D.Jones *(Assistant Trainer)*. *On Ground :* White,Knowles,Cheesebrough.

	APP's				GOALS			
	FL	FAC	FLC	ECWC	FL	FAC	FLC	ECWC
Gordon Banks	41	2	1	4				
Len Chalmers	42	2	1	4	1			
Richie Norman	42	2	1	4	1			
Ian White	19			4				
Ian King	40	2	1	4	1			
Colin Appleton	42	2	1	4	4			1
Howard Riley	36	2	1	4	7 (5p)	2 (1p)		
Jimmy Walsh	33	2	1	4	14			2
Hugh McIlmoyle	13		1	1	1			1
Ken Keyworth	39	2	1	4	15	1		3
Gordon Wills	22	1	1	4	7			
Albert Cheesebrough	23	2		1	11			
Graham Cross	6			2	1			
Frank McLintock	30	2	1	1	6			
John Mitten	12	1	1	2			1	
George Heyes	1							
Mike Stringfellow	12							
David Gibson	5				1			
John Sjoberg	3							
David Thomson	1				1			
Own Goals					1			

1962-63

LEAGUE DIVISION ONE
Final Position : 4th
Ave. Home League Att: 25,729

DATE	OPPONENTS	V	F.T.	SCORERS	Banks	Chalmers	Norman	McLintock	King	Appleton	Riley	Walsh	Keyworth	Gibson	Stringfellow	Cheesebrough	Cross	Sjoberg	Heath	Heyes	McDerment
Aug 18	Fulham	A	1-2	Stringfellow	1	2	3	4	5	6	7	8	9	10	11						
22	Sheffield Wednesday	H	3-3	Walsh,Stringfellow,Riley	1	2	3	4	5	6	7	8	9	10	11						
25	Nottingham Forest	H	2-1	Stringfellow 2	1	2	3	4	5	6		8	9	10	11	7					
29	Sheffield Wednesday	A	3-0	Stringfellow 2,Walsh	1	2	3	4	5	6		8		10	11	7	9				
Sep 1	Bolton Wanderers	H	4-1	Walsh 2,Cross,Gibson	1	2	3	4	5	6		8		10	11	7	9				
4	Burnley	A	1-1	Gibson	1	2	3	4	5	6		8		10	11	7	9				
8	Everton	A	2-3	Walsh,Riley	1	2	3	4	5	6	7	8		10		11	9				
15	West Bromwich Albion	H	1-0	Cross	1	2	3	4	5	6	7	8		10		11	9				
19	Burnley	H	3-3	Keyworth,McLintock,Riley	1	2	3	4	5	6	7	8	9	10		11					
22	Arsenal	A	1-1	Keyworth	1	2	3	4	5	6	7	8	9	10		11					
29	Birmingham City	H	3-0	Keyworth,Cheesebrough,Foster (og)	1	2	3	4	5	6	7	8	9	10		11					
Oct 6	Ipswich Town	A	1-0	McLintock	1	2	3	10	5	6	7	8	9			11	4				
13	Liverpool	H	3-0	Gibson,Cheesebrough,Cross	1	2	3	8	5	6	7		9	10		11	4				
20	Blackburn Rovers	A	0-2		1	2	3	8	5	6	7		9	10		11	4				
27	Sheffield United	H	3-1	Keyworth 2,Cross	1		3	10	5	6		8	9		11	7	4	2			
Nov 3	Tottenham Hotspur	A	0-4		1	2	3	4	5	6		8	9	10	11	7					
10	West Ham United	H	2-0	Stringfellow,McLintock	1	2	3	4	5	6			9	10	11	7		8			
17	Manchester City	A	1-1	Keyworth	1	2	3	4	5	6			9	10	11	7					
24	Blackpool	H	0-0		1	2	3	4	5	6		8	9	10	11	7					
Dec 1	Wolverhampton Wanderers	A	3-1	Gibson 2,Flowers (og)	1	2	3	4	5	6	7	8	9	10		11					
8	Aston Villa	H	3-3	Gibson 2,Stringfellow	1	2	3	4	5	6	7	8	9	10	11						
15	Fulham	H	2-3	Walsh,Stringfellow	1	2	3	4	5	6	7	8	9	10	11						
26	Leyton Orient	H	5-1	Keyworth 2,Cheesebrough,Appleton,Charlton (og)	1		3	4	5	6			9	8	11	7	10	2			
Feb 9	Arsenal	H	2-0	Keyworth 2	1		3	4	5	6	7		9	10	11		8	2			
12	Everton	H	3-1	Keyworth,Stringfellow,Cross	1		3	4	5	6	7		9	10	11		8	2			
19	Nottingham Forest	A	2-0	Keyworth 2	1		3	4	5	6	7		9	10	11		8	2			
23	Ipswich Town	H	3-0	Gibson,Stringfellow,Riley	1		3	4	5	6	7		9	10	11		8	2			
Mar 2	Liverpool	A	2-0	Keyworth.Gibson	1		3	4	5	6	7		9	10	11		8	2			
9	Blackburn Rovers	H	2-0	Riley,Stringfellow	1		3	4	5	6	7		9	10	11		8	2			
23	Tottenham Hotspur	H	2-2	Stringfellow,Keyworth	1		3	4	5	6	7		9	10	11		8	2			
26	Sheffield United	A	0-0		1		3	4	5		7	9		10	11	8	6	2			
Apr 3	Leyton Orient	A	2-0	Stringfellow 2	1	2	3	4	5	6	7		9		11	8			10		
6	Manchester City	H	2-0	Stringfellow 2			3	4	5	6	7		9	10	11	8	2	1			
8	Blackpool	A	1-1	Keyworth	1	2	3	4		6	7		9	10	11	8	5				
13	West Ham United	A	0-2		1		3	4	5	6	7		9	10	11		8	2			
15	Manchester United	A	2-2	Cross,Norman	1		3	4	5	6	7		9	10		8	11	2			
16	Manchester United	H	4-3	Heath,Keyworth 3	1		3	10	5	6	7		9	11		4	2		8		
20	Wolverhampton Wanderers	H	1-1	Keyworth	1		3	10	5	6	7		9	11		4	2		8		
May 4	West Bromwich Albion	A	1-2	Cross	1		3	4	5	6	7		9	10	11		8	2			
11	Bolton Wanderers	A	0-2				3	4	5	6	7	9		10	11	8	2	1			
15	Aston Villa	A	1-3	Keyworth			3	4		6	7	10	9		11	8	2	1	5		
18	Birmingham City	A	2-3	Heath,McLintock			3	4			7	10	9		11	6	2	8	1	5	

F.A. CUP

DATE	OPPONENTS		V	F.T.	SCORERS	Banks	Chalmers	Norman	McLintock	King	Appleton	Riley	Walsh	Keyworth	Gibson	Stringfellow	Cheesebrough	Cross	Sjoberg
Jan 8	Grimsby Town	(3)	A	3-1	Gibson 2,Keyworth	1		3	4	5	6	7		9	8	11		10	2
30	Ipswich Town	(4)	H	3-1	Cross,Keyworth 2	1		3	4	5	6	7		9	10	11		8	2
Mar 16	Leyton Orient	(5)	A	1-0	Keyworth	1		3	4	5	6	7		9	10	11		8	2
30	Norwich City	(6)	A	2-0	Stringfellow,Gibson	1		3	4	5	6	7		9	10	11		8	2
Apr 27	Liverpool	(sf)		1-0	Stringfellow (at Hillsborough, Sheffield)	1		3	4	5	6	7		9	10	11		8	2
May 25	Manchester United	(F)		1-3	Keyworth (at Wembley)	1		3	4	5	6	7		9	10	11		8	2

F.L. CUP

DATE	OPPONENTS		V	F.T.	SCORERS	Banks	Chalmers	Norman	McLintock	King	Appleton	Riley	Walsh	Keyworth	Gibson	Stringfellow	Cheesebrough	Cross
Sep 26	Charlton Athletic	(2)	H	4-4	Gibson,Walsh 2,Riley	1	2	3	4	5	6	7	8		10		11	9
Oct 2	Charlton Athletic	(2rep)	A	1-2	Keyworth	1	2	3	4	5	6	7		8	10		11	9

LEICESTER CITY 1962-63
Back : Keyworth,Norman,Cross,Banks,McLintock.
Front : King,Appleton,Gibson,Riley,Stringfellow.
On Ground : Sjoberg.

	APP's			GOALS		
	FL	FAC	FLC	FL	FAC	FLC
Gordon Banks	38	6	2			
Len Chalmers	23		2			
Richie Norman	42	6	2	1		
Frank McLintock	42	6	2	4		
Ian King	39	6	2			
Colin Appleton	40	6	2	1		
Howard Riley	32	6	2	5		
Jimmy Walsh	26		1	6		2
Ken Keyworth	32	6	1	21	5	1
David Gibson	36	6	2	9	3	1
Mike Stringfellow	29	6		17	2	
Albert Cheesebrough	23		2	3		
Graham Cross	29	6	2	7	1	
John Sjoberg	20	6				
Terry Heath	5			2		
George Heyes	4					
Bill McDerment	2					
Own Goals				3		

1963-64

LEAGUE DIVISION ONE
Final Position : 11th
Ave. Home League Att: 24,135

DATE	OPPONENTS	V	F.T.	SCORERS	Banks	Sjoberg	Norman	McLintock	King	Appleton	Riley	Cross	Keyworth	Gibson	Stringfellow	Goodfellow	Heyes	Hodgson	Roberts	McDerment	Newton	Chalmers	Dougan	Sweenie	Heath	Timson	Walker
Aug 24	West Bromwich Albion	A	1-1	Keyworth	1	2	3	4	5	6	7	8	9	10	11												
28	Birmingham City	H	3-0	Riley,Keyworth,Stringfellow	1	2	3	4	5	6	7	8	9	10	11												
31	Arsenal	H	7-2	Riley,Keyworth 2,Gibson 2,Stringfellow,McLintock	1	2	3	4	5	6	7	8	9	10	11												
Sep 4	Birmingham City	A	0-2		1	2	3	4	5	6	7	8	9	10	11												
7	Stoke City	A	3-3	Appleton,Cross 2	1	2	3	4	5	6	7	8	9		11	10											
11	Sheffield Wednesday	H	2-0	Keyworth,Stringfellow	1	2	3	4	5	6	7	8	9	10	11												
14	Bolton Wanderers	A	0-0			2	3	4	5	6	7	8	9		11		1	10									
21	Fulham	H	0-1		1	2	3	4	5		7	8	9	10	11			6									
28	Manchester United	A	1-3	Gibson	1	2	3	4	5		7	8	9	10			11	6									
Oct 2	Sheffield Wednesday	A	2-1	Cross,Stringfellow	1		3	4	5	6		9		10	11			7	8			2					
5	Burnley	H	0-0		1		3	4	5	6	7		9	10	11							2					
8	Nottingham Forest	A	0-2		1		3	4	5	6	7		9	10	11			8				2					
14	Wolverhampton Wanderers	H	0-1		1		3	4	5	6	7	8	9	10	11							2					
19	Tottenham Hotspur	A	1-1	McLintock	1		3	4	5	6	7	8	9	10	11							2					
26	Blackburn Rovers	H	4-3	Gibson,McLintock 2,Keyworth	1		3	4	5	6	7	8	9	10	11							2					
Nov 2	Liverpool	A	1-0	Keyworth	1		3	4	5	6	7	8	9	10	11							2					
9	Sheffield United	H	0-1		1		3	4	5	6	7	8	9	10	11							2					
16	West Ham United	A	2-2	Stringfellow,Keyworth	1		3	4	5	6	7	8	9	10	11							2					
23	Chelsea	H	2-4	Stringfellow,Cross	1		3	4	5	6	7	8	9		11					10		2					
30	Blackpool	A	3-3	Chalmers (pen),Sweenie 2	1		3	6	5		7					8	11	9	4			2		10			
Dec 7	Aston Villa	H	0-0		1		3	4	5	6		8				7	11	9				2		10			
14	West Bromwich Albion	A	0-2		1		3	4	5	6		9		10	11	7						2	8				
21	Arsenal	A	1-0	McLintock	1	2	3	4	5	6	7	8	9	10	11												
26	Everton	H	2-0	Keyworth 2	1		3	4	5	6	7	8	9	10	11							2					
28	Everton	A	3-0	Stringfellow,Roberts 2	1		3	4	5	6	7	8		10	11				9			2					
Jan 11	Stoke City	H	2-1	Gibson,Stringfellow	1		3		5	6	7	4		10	11		8	9				2					
18	Bolton Wanderers	H	1-0	Gibson	1	2	3		5	6	7	4		10	11			8									
Feb 1	Fulham	A	1-2	Cross	1	2	3		5	6	7	4	9	10	11			8									
8	Manchester United	H	3-2	Stringfellow,Hodgson 2	1	2	3		5	6		4	9	10	11			7	8								
22	Wolverhampton Wanderers	A	2-1	Gibson,King (pen)	1	2	3	4	5	6		8	9	10	11			7									
29	Nottingham Forest	H	1-1	Hodgson	1	2	3	4	5	6		8	9	10	11			7									
Mar 7	Blackburn Rovers	A	2-5	Hodgson,Stringfellow		2		4	5		3		6	9	10	11	1	7	8								
10	Burnley	A	0-2			2		4	5		3		6	9	10	11	1	7	8								
18	West Ham United	H	2-2	Gibson,Keyworth		2		4	5		3		6	9	10	11	1	7							8		
21	Sheffield United	A	1-0	McLintock		2		4	5		3		6		10	11	1	7						9	8		
28	Liverpool	H	0-2		1		3	4	5	2		6			10	11		7	9						8		
30	Ipswich Town	A	1-1	Goodfellow	1	2	3	4					6	10		7	11	9				5					
31	Ipswich Town	H	2-1	Stringfellow,Keyworth	1	2	3	4		6	7		9	10	11			8				5					
Apr 6	Chelsea	A	0-1		1	2			5	3	7		9	10	11				4			6	8				
11	Blackpool	H	2-3	Stringfellow,Appleton (pen)		2		9	5	3	7	8		10	11				4			6			1		
18	Aston Villa	A	3-1	Riley,Sweenie,Gibson	1	2			5		7	6		10	11			8				4	9	3			
25	Tottenham Hotspur	H	0-1		1	2	3		5	6	7	4	9	8	11							10					

F.A. CUP

DATE	OPPONENTS		V	F.T.	SCORERS	Banks	Sjoberg	Norman	McLintock	King	Appleton	Riley	Cross	Keyworth	Gibson	Stringfellow	Goodfellow	Heyes	Hodgson	Roberts	McDerment	Newton	Chalmers
Jan 4	Leyton Orient	(3)	H	2-3	Cross,Keyworth	1		3	4	5	6	7	8	9	10	11							2

F.L. CUP

DATE	OPPONENTS		V	F.T.	SCORERS	Banks	Sjoberg	Norman	McLintock	King	Appleton	Riley	Cross	Keyworth	Gibson	Stringfellow	Goodfellow	Heyes	Hodgson	Roberts	McDerment	Newton	Chalmers	Dougan	Sweenie
Sep 25	Aldershot	(2)	H	2-0	Newton,Keyworth	1	2	3	4	5			7	8	9	10					6	11			
Oct 16	Tranmere Rovers	(3)	A	2-1	Hodgson,Roberts	1		3		5	6			9	10	11			7	8	4		2		
Nov 27	Gillingham	(4)	H	3-1	Keyworth,McLintock,Hodgson	1		3	6	5				8			7		11	4			2	9	10
Dec 18	Norwich City	(5)	H	1-1	Riley			3	4	5	6	7	8	9	10	11		1					2		
Jan 15	Norwich City	(5 rep)	H	2-1	Hodgson,Riley	1	2	3		5	6	7	4		10	11		8	9						
Feb 5	West Ham United	(sf leg 1)	H	4-3	Keyworth,Roberts,Stringfellow,McLintock	1	2	3	4	5	6			9	10	11			7	8					
Mar 23	West Ham United	(sf leg 2)	A	2-0	McLintock,Roberts	1	2	3	4	5	6			8		10	11		7	9					
Apr 15	Stoke City	(F leg 1)	A	1-1	Gibson	1	2			5	3	7	4		10	11							6	8	
22	Stoke City	(F leg 2)	H	3-2	Stringfellow,Gibson,Riley	1	2	3		5	6	7	4	9	8	11							10		

LEICESTER CITY 1963-64
Back : Mitchellson,Nicholls,Tuckwood,Newton,McCaffrey,Balmer,A.Chandler*(Training Staff)*, Muggleton,McLintock,McDerment,Gamble,Chalmers.
Middle : Appleton,Norman,King,Sjoberg,Heyes,Banks,Timson,Smith,Cross,Dougan.
Front : E.Plumley *(Secretary)*, Walsh,H.Riley,Tewley,M.Gillies *(Manager)*, Stringfellow,Heath, Keyworth,A.Dowdells *(Trainer)*. *On Ground :* Walker,Loughlan,R.Riley,Gibson,Woollett,Goodfellow,Marshall.

	APP's			GOALS		
	FL	FAC	FLC	FL	FAC	FLC
Gordon Banks	36	1	8			
John Sjoberg	25		6			
Richie Norman	35	1	8			
Frank McLintock	35	1	5	6		3
Ian King	40	1	9	1 (p)		
Colin Appleton	38	1	7	2 (1p)		
Howard Riley	30	1	5	3		3
Graham Cross	39	1	6	5	1	
Ken Keyworth	30	1	7	12	1	3
David Gibson	37	1	8	9		2
Mike Stringfellow	38	1	7	12		2
Jimmy Goodfellow	5		1	1		
George Heyes	5		1			
Billy Hodgson	16		5	4		3
Bobby Roberts	17		4	2		3
Bill McDerment	3		3			
Bob Newton			1			1
Len Chalmers	16	1	3	1 (p)		
Max Dougan	5		2			
Tom Sweenie	7		2	3		
Terry Heath	3		1			
David Timson	1					
Clive Walker	1					

1964-65 LEAGUE DIVISION ONE
Final Position : 18th
Ave. Home League Att: 19,938

Player columns (left→right): Banks, Cross, Norman, McLintock, King, Appleton, Riley, Sweenie, Keyworth, Gibson, Stringfellow, Sjoberg, Chalmers, Roberts, Svarc, Hodgson, Goodfellow, Heyes, McDerment, Newton, Walker, Matthews.

DATE	OPPONENTS	V	F.T.	SCORERS	Bank	Cros	Norm	McLi	King	Appl	Rile	Swee	Keyw	Gibs	Stri	Sjob	Chal	Robe	Svar	Hodg	Good	Heye	McDe	Newt	Walk	Matt
Aug 22	Sunderland	A	3-3	Stringfellow,Sweenie,Keyworth	1	2	3	4	5	6	7	8	9	10	11											
26	Wolverhampton Wanderers	H	3-2	McLintock,Keyworth,Appleton (pen)	1		3	4	5	6	7	8	9	10	11	2										
29	Manchester United	H	2-2	Keyworth,Appleton	1	3		4	5	6	7	8	9	10	11	2										
Sep 2	Wolverhampton Wanderers	A	1-1	McLintock	1		3	4		6	7	8	9	10	11	5	2									
5	Chelsea	H	1-1	Appleton	1		3	4	5	6	7	8	9	10	11	2										
9	Liverpool	H	2-0	McLintock,Keyworth	1		3	4	5	6	7	8	9	10	11	2										
12	Leeds United	A	2-3	Riley,Sweenie	1	8	3	4		6	7		9	10	11	2										
19	Arsenal	H	2-3	McLintock 2	1	8	3	4	5	6	7	11	9	10		2										
26	Blackburn Rovers	A	1-3	Gibson	1		3	4	5	6		8	9	10	11	2		7								
30	West Bromwich Albion	H	4-2	Appleton (pen),Hodgson,McLintock,Svarc	1		3	4	5	6				10	11	2		8	9	7						
Oct 5	Blackpool	H	3-2	Goodfellow,Stringfellow,Roberts	1	10	3			5	6				11	2		4	9	7	8					
10	Fulham	A	2-5	Roberts 2	1	10	3			5	6				11	2		4	9	7	8					
13	Liverpool	H	1-0	Stringfellow	1		3			5	6		10		11	2		4	9	7	8					
17	Nottingham Forest	H	3-2	Hodgson,Appleton (pen),Stringfellow	1	8	3			5	6				11	2		4	9	7	10					
24	Stoke City	A	3-3	Goodfellow 2,Roberts		8	3		5					10	11			2		6	7	9	1	4		
31	Tottenham Hotspur	H	4-2	Cross,Gibson,Stringfellow,Goodfellow	1	8	3		5	6				10	11	2		4		7	9					
Nov 7	Burnley	A	1-2	Roberts	1	8	3		5					10	11	2		4		7	9	6				
14	Sheffield United	H	0-2		1	6	3		5			8	10	11	2		4		7	9						
21	Everton	A	2-2	Goodfellow,Sjoberg	1	6	3		5			8		10	11	2		4		7	9					
28	Birmingham City	H	4-4	Gibson,Goodfellow,Hodgson,Roberts	1	6	3		5			8		10	11	2		4		7	9					
Dec 5	West Ham United	A	0-0		1	8	3		5					10	11	2		4		7	9	6				
12	Sunderland	H	0-1		1	8	3		5				10		11	2		4		7	9	6				
26	Sheffield Wednesday	H	2-2	Roberts 2	1	8	3		5		7			10	11		2	4			9	6				
28	Sheffield Wednesday	A	0-0		1	8	3							10	11	5	2	4		7	9	6				
Jan 2	Chelsea	A	1-4	Stringfellow	1	8	3		5					10	11		2	4		7	9	6				
16	Leeds United	H	2-2	Cross,Stringfellow	1	9	3			6				10	11	5	2	8			7		4			
23	Arsenal	A	3-4	Appleton (pen),Stringfellow,McDerment	1	9	3			6				10	11	5	2	8			7		4			
Feb 6	Blackburn Rovers	H	2-3	Hodgson,Gibson	1	8	3			6				10		5	2	4		7	9					11
13	Blackpool	H	1-1	Goodfellow	1	8	3		5	6				10	11		2	4		7	9					
24	Fulham	H	5-1	Gibson,Goodfellow 3,Appleton (pen)	1	8	3		5	6				10	11		2	4		7	9					
27	Nottingham Forest	A	1-2	Cross	1	8	3			6				10	11	5	2	4		7	9					
Mar 13	West Bromwich Albion	A	0-6		1	8	3		5					10			2	4		7	9		6	11		
20	Burnley	H	0-2				3		5	6		8		10	11	2	4			7	9	1				
26	Sheffield United	H	2-0	Sweenie,Hodgson	1	9	3			6			10		8	11	5			7			4			2
Apr 3	Everton	H	2-1	Stringfellow,Appleton (pen)	1	9	3			6			10		8	11	5			4	7					2
10	Birmingham City	A	0-2			8	3						10			11	5		4	7	9	1	6			2
12	Manchester United	A	0-1		1	6	3						10		8	11	5		4	7	9					2
17	West Ham United	H	1-0	Gibson	1	4	3			6		8	10		5		9			7	11					2
19	Aston Villa	H	1-1	Hodgson	1	4	3		5	6								9		8	10				2	7
20	Aston Villa	A	0-1		1	4	3		5	6			10		8	11				7	9				2	
24	Tottenham Hotspur	A	2-6	Stringfellow,Goodfellow	1	4	3		5	6			10		8	11				7	9				2	
26	Stoke City	H	0-1			4	3		5	6			10		8	11			9			1		2	7	

F.A. CUP

DATE	OPPONENTS		V	F.T.	SCORERS	Bank	Cros	Norm	McLi	King	Appl	Rile	Swee	Keyw	Gibs	Stri	Sjob	Chal	Robe	Svar	Hodg	Good	Heye
Jan 9	Blackburn Rovers	(3)	H	2-2	Stringfellow,Roberts	1		3			6				10	11	5	2	8			7	9	4
14	Blackburn Rovers	(3 rep)	A	2-1	Roberts,Cross	1	9	3			6				10	11	5	2	8			7		4
30	Plymouth Argyle	(4)	H	5-0	Stringfellow,Goodfellow 2,Gibson,Roberts	1	8	3			6				10	11	5	2	4			7	9
Feb 20	Middlesbrough	(5)	A	3-0	Cross 2,Gibson	1	8	3		5	6				10	11		2	4			7	9
Mar 6	Liverpool	(6)	H	0-0		1	8	3		5	6				10	11	2		4			7	9
10	Liverpool	(6 rep)	A	0-1		1	8	3		5	6				10	11	2		4			7	9

F.L. CUP

DATE	OPPONENTS		V	F.T.	SCORERS
Sep 23	Peterborough United	(2)	H	0-0	
Oct 8	Peterborough United	(2 rep)	A	2-0	Appleton (pen),Goodfellow
19	Grimsby Town	(3)	A	5-0	Norman,Cross,Gibson,Stringfellow,Sjoberg
Nov 4	Crystal Palace	(4)	H	0-0	
11	Crystal Palace	(4 rep)	A	2-1	Goodfellow 2 (Curtis og)
Dec 1	Coventry City	(5)	H	8-1	Stringfellow 2,Hodgson 2,Gibson,Norman 2,
Jan 20	Plymouth Argyle	(sf leg 1)	A	3-2	Roberts,Gibson,Williams (og)
Feb 10	Plymouth Argyle	(sf leg 2)	H	1-0	Sjoberg
Mar 15	Chelsea	(F leg 1)	A	2-3	Appleton,Goodfellow
Apr 5	Chelsea	(F leg 2)	H	0-0	

LEICESTER CITY 1964-65
Back : King,Cross,Sjoberg,Heyes,Banks,Chalmers,Stringfellow,Appleton.
Front : Hodgson,Roberts,Goodfellow,Norman,Gibson.
On Ground : McDerment,Sweenie.

	APP's			GOALS		
	FL	FAC	FLC	FL	FAC	FLC
Gordon Banks	38	6	9			
Graham Cross	35	5	9	3	3	1
Richie Norman	40	6	10			3
Frank McLintock	10		1	6		
Ian King	31		7			
Colin Appleton	29	6	7	8 (6p)		2(1p)
Howard Riley	9		1	1		
Tom Sweenie	22		2	3		
Ken Keyworth	9		2	4		
David Gibson	35	6	9	6	2	3
Mike Stringfellow	38	6	8	10	2	3
John Sjoberg	37	6	10	1		2
Len Chalmers	7	3	3			
Bobby Roberts	27	6	9	8	3	1
Bobby Svarc	7		2	1		
Billy Hodgson	30	5	8	6		2
Jimmy Goodfellow	29	6	9	11	2	4
George Heyes	4		1			
Bill McDerment	12	2	2	1		
Bob Newton	2					
Clive Walker	9		1			
Paul Matthews	2					
Own Goals						2

1965-66

LEAGUE DIVISION ONE
Final Position : 7th
Ave. Home League Att: 22,285

Player columns (left to right): Heyes, Walker, Norman, Roberts, Sjoberg, Cross, Sinclair, Gibson, Dougan D, Sweenie, Stringfellow, Goodfellow, Chalmers, King, Clarke, Banks, Appleton, Riley, McDerment, Matthews, Dougan M, Rodrigues, Shilton

DATE	OPPONENTS	V	F.T.	SCORERS
Aug 21	Liverpool	H	1-3	Sinclair
25	Tottenham Hotspur	A	2-4	Stringfellow,Sweenie
28	Aston Villa	A	2-2	Sjoberg,Sinclair
Sep 1	Tottenham Hotspur	H	2-2	Gibson 2
4	Sunderland	H	4-1	Stringfellow,D.Dougan,Gibson,Sinclair
6	Blackpool	A	0-4	
11	West Ham United	A	5-2	D.Dougan 2,Sinclair 2,Goodfellow
14	Blackpool	H	0-3	
18	Leeds United	H	3-3	D.Dougan 2,Goodfellow
25	Sheffield United	A	2-2	Goodfellow,Sinclair
Oct 2	Northampton Town	H	1-1	Goodfellow
9	Stoke City	A	0-1	
16	Burnley	H	0-1	
23	Chelsea	A	2-0	Sjoberg,D.Dougan
30	Arsenal	H	3-1	Cross,D.Dougan,Goodfellow
Nov 6	Everton	A	2-1	Goodfellow,Sinclair
13	Manchester United	H	0-5	
20	Newcastle United	A	5-1	Goodfellow,Sinclair 2, D.Dougan,Stringfellow
27	West Bromwich Albion	H	2-1	Goodfellow,D.Dougan
Dec 4	Nottingham Forest	A	0-2	
11	Sheffield Wednesday	H	4-1	Stringfellow 2,D.Dougan,Sinclair
18	Burnley	A	2-4	Gibson,Sinclair
28	Fulham		5-0	Sinclair 2,Gibson,Roberts,Stringfellow
Jan 1	Stoke City	H	1-0	D.Dougan
8	Sheffield Wednesday	A	2-1	Stringfellow,Goodfellow
29	Liverpool	A	0-1	
Feb 5	Aston Villa	H	2-1	Cross,Roberts
19	Sunderland	H	3-0	Sinclair 2,D.Dougan
Mar 12	Leeds United	A	2-3	Sinclair (pen),Stringfellow
19	Sheffield United	H	1-0	Stringfellow
21	Chelsea	H	1-1	D.Dougan
26	Northampton Town	A	2-2	Stringfellow,Sinclair
Apr 8	Blackburn Rovers	A	2-0	Matthews,D.Dougan
9	Manchester United	A	2-1	Stringfellow 2
12	Blackburn Rovers	H	2-0	Sweenie,Sinclair
16	Newcastle United	H	1-2	Sweenie
18	Fulham	A	4-0	D.Dougan 2,Sinclair 2
22	West Bromwich Albion	A	1-5	D.Dougan
30	Nottingham Forest	H	2-1	Cross 2
May 4	Everton	H	3-0	Sinclair (pen),D.Dougan,Matthews
7	Arsenal	A	0-1	
9	West Ham United	H	2-1	Sinclair,D.Dougan

F.A. CUP

Jan 22	Aston Villa	(3)	A	2-1	D.Dougan,Stringfellow
Feb 12	Birmingham City	(4)	A	2-1	Sinclair,Goodfellow
Mar 5	Manchester City	(5)	A	2-2	Sinclair,Stringfellow
9	Manchester City	(5 rep)	H	0-1	

F.L.CUP

Sep 22	Manchester City	(2)	A	1-3	Roberts (pen)

LEICESTER CITY 1965-66
Back : Roberts,Sjoberg,King,D.Dougan,Heyes,Banks,Cross,Norman,Stringfellow,Chalmers,Appleton.
Front : Gibson,Sinclair,Sweenie,G.Dewis *(Assistant Trainer)*, B.Johnson *(Coach)*, M.Gillies *(Manager)*,
D.Sharp *(Chairman)*,E.Plumley *(Secretary)*, D.Jones *(Trainer)*, Matthews,Walker,Goodfellow.

	APP's			GOALS		
	FL	FAC	FLC	FL	FAC	FLC
George Heyes	9					
Clive Walker	7					
Richie Norman	40	4	1			
Bobby Roberts	41	4	1	2		1(p)
John Sjoberg	38	3	1	2		
Graham Cross	38	4	1	4		
Jackie Sinclair	42	4	1	22 (2p)	2	
David Gibson	42	4	1	5		
Derek Dougan	37	4		19	1	
Tom Sweenie	10/1			3		
Mike Stringfellow	34	4		12	2	
Jimmy Goodfellow	30/1	3	1	9	1	
Len Chalmers	4					
Ian King	13		1			
Malcolm Clarke	-/1					
Gordon Banks	32	4	1			
Colin Appleton	12	2	1			
Howard Riley			1			
Bill McDerment	2/2					
Paul Matthews	11			2		
Max Dougan	2					
Peter Rodrigues	17	4				
Peter Shilton	1					

1966-67

LEAGUE DIVISION ONE
Final Position : 8th
Ave. Home League Att: 24,435

DATE	OPPONENTS	V	F.T.	SCORERS	Banks	Rodrigues	Norman	Roberts	Sjoberg	Cross	Sinclair	Goodfellow	Dougan D	Gibson	Stringfellow	Matthews	Dougan M	Sweenie	Shilton	Sharkey	Nish	McDerment	Woollett	Timson	Tewley
Aug 20	Liverpool	A	2-3	D.Dougan 2	1	2	3	4	5	6	7	8	9	10	11										
22	Blackpool	A	1-1	Goodfellow	1	2	3	4	5	6		8	9	10	11	7									
27	West Ham United	H	5-4	D.Dougan, Sinclair 3, Goodfellow	1	2	3	4	5	6	7	8	9	10	11										
31	Blackpool	H	3-0	D.Dougan 2, Roberts	1	2	3	4	5	6	7	8	9	10	11										
Sep 3	Sheffield Wednesday	A	1-1	D.Dougan	1	2	3	4	5	6	7	8	9	10	11										
7	Chelsea	A	2-2	D.Dougan, Gibson	1	2	3	4	5	6	10	8	9	7	11										
10	Southampton	H	1-1	Sinclair (pen)	1	2	3	4	5	6	7	8	9	10	11										
17	Sunderland	A	3-2	D.Dougan, Roberts, Rodrigues	1	2	3	4	5	6	7	8	9	10	11										
24	Aston Villa	H	5-0	Goodfellow, D.Dougan 3, Sinclair	1	2	3	4	5	6	7	8	9	10	11										
Oct 1	Arsenal	A	4-2	Sinclair, Stringfellow, Goodfellow, Simpson (og)	1	2	3	4	5	6	7	8	9	10	11										
8	Nottingham Forest	H	3-0	Gibson, Goodfellow, Stringfellow	1	2	3	4	5	6	7	8	9	10	11										
15	Burnley	A	2-5	Sinclair, D.Dougan	1		3	6	5	2	7	8	9	10	11	4									
29	Everton	A	0-2		1	2	3	4	5	6	7	8	9		11		10								
Nov 5	Burnley	H	5-1	Rodrigues, Sinclair 2, Gibson, Stringfellow	1	2	3	4	5	6	7	8	9	10	11										
12	Leeds United	A	1-3	D.Dougan	1	2	3	4	5	6	7	8	9	10	11										
19	West Bromwich Albion	H	2-1	Stringfellow, D.Dougan			3	4	5	6	7	8	9	10	11	2	1								
26	Sheffield United	H	1-0	Sinclair	1	2	3	4	5	6	7	8	9	10	11										
30	Manchester United	H	1-2	Gibson	1	2	3	4	5	6	7		9	10	11				8						
Dec 3	Stoke City	H	4-2	Rodrigues, D.Dougan, Nish, Sinclair	1	2	3	4	5	6	7		9	10	11	12		8*							
10	Tottenham Hotspur	A	0-2		1	2	3	4	5	6	7		9	10	11			8							
26	Fulham	H	0-2		1	2	3	4	5	6	7		9	10	11			8							
27	Fulham	A	2-4	Sinclair, Gibson	1	2	3	4	5	6	7		9	10	11	8									
31	West Ham United	A	1-0	Sinclair	1	2	3	4	5		7		9	10	11			8			6				
Jan 7	Sheffield Wednesday	H	0-1		1	2	3	4	5	6	7		9	10	11			8							
14	Southampton	A	4-4	Sweenie 2, Gibson, Roberts	1	2	3	4	5	6	7		9	10	11			8							
18	Liverpool	H	2-1	Stringfellow, Cross	1	2	3	4	5	6	7		9	10	11			8							
21	Sunderland	H	1-2	Sinclair (pen)	1	2	3	4	5	6	7		9	10	11			8							
Feb 4	Aston Villa	A	1-0	Roberts	1	2	3	4		5	7		9	10	11			8			6				
11	Arsenal	H	2-1	Stringfellow, D.Dougan	1	2	3	4	5	6	7		9	10	11			8							
25	Nottingham Forest	A	0-1		1	2	3	4		5	7		9	10	11	12	8*				6				
Mar 4	Everton	H	2-2	Roberts, Sinclair (pen)	1	2	3	4		5	7	8	9	10	11						6				
18	Manchester United	A	2-5	Sinclair 2	1	2	3	4		5	11	8		10	9	7					6				
24	Manchester City	A	3-1	Sinclair 2 (2 pen), Stringfellow	1	2	3	4		5	11	8		10	9	7					6				
25	Tottenham Hotspur	H	0-1		1	2	3	4		5	11	8			9	7					6	10			
28	Manchester City	H	2-1	Sinclair 2	1	2	3	4		5	7	8		10	9		11				6				
Apr 1	Newcastle United	A	0-1		1	2	3	4		5	7	8		10	9		11				6				
10	Leeds United	A	0-0		1	2	3	4		5	11	8		10	9	7					6				
15	West Bromwich Albion	A	0-1			2	3	4		5	11	8		10	9	7			1		6*	12			
22	Sheffield United	H	2-2	Stringfellow, Roberts		2	3	4		5	11	8		10	9	7*			1		6	12			
29	Stoke City	A	1-3	Stringfellow		2	3	4		5	11	7		10	9			8	1		6				
May 6	Newcastle United	H	4-2	Stringfellow, Sharkey 2, McNamee (og)		2	3	4		5	11*	7		10	9					8	6			1	12
9	Chelsea	H	3-2	Sharkey 2, Roberts		2	3	4		5	11	7		10	9					8	6			1	

F.A. CUP

DATE	OPPONENTS		V	F.T.	SCORERS	Banks	Rodrigues	Norman	Roberts	Sjoberg	Cross	Sinclair	Goodfellow	Dougan D	Gibson	Stringfellow	Matthews	Dougan M	Sweenie
Jan 28	Manchester City	(3)	A	1-2	Sweenie	1	2	3	4	5	6	7		9	10	11			8

F.L.CUP

DATE	OPPONENTS		V	F.T.	SCORERS	Banks	Rodrigues	Norman	Roberts	Sjoberg	Cross	Sinclair	Goodfellow	Dougan D	Gibson	Stringfellow	Matthews
Sep 14	Reading	(2)	H	5-0	Stringfellow, Roberts, Goodfellow, D.Dougan 2	1	2	3	4	5	6	7	8	9	10	11	
Oct 5	Lincoln City	(3)	H	5-0	Goodfellow 2, D.Dougan, Sinclair (pen), Gibson	1	2	3	4	5	6	7	8	9	10	11	
25	Queens Park Rangers	(4)	A	2-4	D.Dougan 2	1	2	3	4	5	6	7	8	9	10*	11	12

LEICESTER CITY 1966-67
Back : Cross, Nish, Stringfellow, D.Dougan, Norman, Rodrigues, Matthews.
Middle : Sinclair, Roberts, Banks, Sjoberg, Shilton, Bebbington, Goodfellow.
Front : G.Dewis *(Assistant Trainer)*, B.Johnson *(Coach)*, M.Gillies *(Manager)*, D.Sharp *(Chairman)*,
E.Plumley *(Secretary)*, D.Jones *(Trainer)*.
On Ground : Gibson, Tewley, Sweenie.

	APP's			GOALS		
	FL	FAC	FLC	FL	FAC	FLC
Gordon Banks	36	1	3			
Peter Rodrigues	40	1	3	3		
Richie Norman	42	1	3			
Bobby Roberts	42	1	3	7		1
John Sjoberg	28	1	3			
Graham Cross	41	1	3	1		
Jackie Sinclair	41	1	3	21(5p)		1(p)
Jimmy Goodfellow	29		3	5		3
Derek Dougan	31	1	3	16		5
David Gibson	40	1	3	6		1
Mike Stringfellow	42	1	3	10		1
Paul Matthews	8/2		-/1			
Max Dougan	2					
Tom Sweenie	11	1		2	1	
Peter Shilton	4					
Nick Sharkey	3			4		
David Nish	18			1		
Bill McDerment	1/1					
Alan Woollett	1/1					
David Timson	2					
Alan Tewley	-/1					
Own Goals				2		

1967-68 LEAGUE DIVISION ONE
Final Position : 13th
Ave. Home League Att: 24,555

DATE	OPPONENTS	V	F.T.	SCORERS	Shilton	Rodrigues	Norman	Roberts	Sjoberg	Cross	Sinclair	Nish	Stringfellow	Gibson	Sharkey	Goodfellow	Woollett	Tewley	Williamson	Bell	Svarc	Large	Glover	Fern	Mackleworth	Potts	Hutchins	Manley
Aug 19	Tottenham Hotspur	H	2-3	Sharkey,Gibson	1	2	3	4	5	6	7	8	9	10	11													
23	Sheffield Wednesday	A	1-2	Sjoberg	1	2	3	4	5	6	7	8	9	10	11*	12												
26	Manchester United	A	1-1	Stringfellow	1*	2	3	4	9	6	7	8	11	10			5	12										
30	Sheffield Wednesday	H	3-0	Sinclair,Stringfellow,Sjoberg		2	3	4	9	6	7	8	11	10			5		1									
Sep 2	Sunderland	H	0-2			2	3	4			6	7	8	11	10	9		5		1								
6	Stoke City	A	2-3	Sinclair,Sjoberg		2	3	4	9	6	7	8	11	10			5		1									
9	Wolverhampton Wanderers	A	3-1	Nish,Sinclair,Stringfellow		2	3	4	9	6	7	8	11	10			5		1									
16	Fulham	H	1-2	Roberts	1	2	3	4	9	6	7	8	11	10			5											
23	Leeds United	A	2-3	Gibson,Nish		2	3	4	5		7	8	11	10		9	6		1									
30	Everton	H	0-2			2		4	5	6	7	8	11	10		9			1	3								
Oct 7	Liverpool	H	2-1	Stringfellow 2	1	2		4	5	6	7	8	11	10		9				3								
14	Southampton	A	5-1	Stringfellow 2,Tewley,Sinclair,Shilton	1	2	3	4	5		7	8	9	10*			12	11		6								
25	Chelsea	H	2-2	Roberts 2	1	2	3	4	5		7	8	11	10						6	9							
28	West Bromwich Albion	A	0-0		1	2	3	4	5		7	8	11	10						6	9							
Nov 4	Newcastle United	H	2-2	Sinclair,Stringfellow	1	2	3	4	5		7	8	9	10				11		6								
11	Manchester City	A	0-6		1	2	3	4			7	8	11	10			5			6		9						
18	Arsenal	H	2-2	Large,Sinclair (pen)	1	2		4*	5		7	6	9	10			12			3		8	11					
25	Sheffield United	A	0-0		1	2			5		7	6		10			4			3	9	8	11					
Dec 2	Coventry City	H	0-0		1	2		4	5		7	6	9	10				11		3		8						
16	Tottenham Hotspur	A	1-0	Tewley	1	2		4	5			6	9	10				7		3		8	11					
23	Manchester United	H	2-2	Sjoberg,Tewley	1	2		4	5			6	9	10				7		3		8	11					
26	West Ham United	A	2-4	Large,Sinclair	1	2		4	5	11	6		9	10				7		3		8						
30	West Ham United	H	2-4	Svarc,Large	1	2		4	5			6		10*			12	7		3	9	8	11					
Jan 6	Sunderland	A	2-0	Large 2	1	2		4	5	10		6	9	7						3		8	11					
13	Wolverhampton Wanderers	H	3-1	Glover,Gibson,Large	1	2		4	5	10		6	9	7						3		8	11					
20	Fulham	A	1-0	Stringfellow	1	2		4	5	10		6	9	7			12			3		8	11*					
Feb 3	Leeds United	H	2-2	Stringfellow,Large	1	2		4	5	10		6	11	7						3		8		9				
24	Liverpool	A	1-3	Fern	1	2		4	5	6		9	10	11						3		8		7				
Mar 2	Sheffield United	H	3-1	Large,Fern,Nish (pen)	1			4	5	6		10	9	11			2			3		8		7				
16	Chelsea	A	1-4	Sjoberg				4	5	6		10		11			2			3		8	7	9	1			
19	Nottingham Forest	A	1-2	Tewley	1			4	5	6		10		11			2	7		3		8		9				
23	West Bromwich Albion	A	2-3	Nish,Tewley	1			4	5	6		10		11			2	7		3		8		9				
Apr 3	Newcastle United	A	0-0		1	2*		4	5	6		8	11	10						3		9		7	12			
6	Manchester City	H	1-0	Stringfellow	1	2		4	5	6		8	11	10				7		3		9						
9	Everton	A	1-2	Nish (pen)	1	2		4	5	6		8	11	10			7*			3		9	12					
13	Arsenal	A	1-2	Nish	1	2		4	5	6		8	11	10*			12	7		3		9						
15	Burnley	A	1-1	Rodrigues (pen)	1	2		4	5	6		8	9				10			3			7		11			
16	Burnley	H	0-2		1	2		4	5	6		8	11	10			12			3		9		7*				
20	Southampton	H	4-1	Nish,Roberts,Gibson,Stringfellow	1			8	5	2		4	11	10						3		9		7			6	
27	Coventry City	A	1-0	Stringfellow	1			8	5	2		4	11	10						3		9		7			6	
May 4	Nottingham Forest	H	4-2	Fern 2,Roberts 2	1			8	5	2		4	11	10						3		9		7			6	
11	Stoke City	H	0-0		1			8	5	2		4*	11	10						3		9	12	7			6	

F.A. CUP

DATE	OPPONENTS		V	F.T.	SCORERS	Shilton	Rodrigues	Norman	Roberts	Sjoberg	Cross	Sinclair	Nish	Stringfellow	Gibson	Sharkey	Goodfellow	Woollett	Tewley	Williamson	Bell	Svarc	Large	Glover	Fern	Mackleworth	Potts	Hutchins	Manley
Jan 27	Barrow	(3)	A	2-1	Sjoberg,Arrowsmith (og)	1	2		4	5	10		6	9	7						3	11	8						
Feb 17	Manchester City	(4)	A	0-0		1	2		4	5	6		8	10							3		9	11	7				
19	Manchester City	(4 rep)	H	4-3	Fern,Large 2,Nish	1	2		4	5	10		6	9	11						3		8		7				
Mar 9	Rotherham United	(5)	A	1-1	Nish (pen)		2		4	5	6		10	9	11						3		8		7	1			
13	Rotherham United	(5 rep)	H	2-0	Large,Stringfellow		2*		4	5	6		10	9	11						3		8	12	7	1			
30	Everton	(6)	H	1-3	Nish	1			4	5	6		10	9	11			2			3		8		7				

F.L.CUP

DATE	OPPONENTS		V	F.T.	SCORERS	Shilton	Rodrigues	Norman	Roberts	Sjoberg	Cross	Sinclair	Nish	Stringfellow	Gibson	Sharkey	Goodfellow	Woollett	Tewley	Williamson	Bell	Svarc	Large	Glover	Fern	Mackleworth	Potts	Hutchins	Manley
Sep 13	Manchester City	(2)	A	0-4			2	3	4	9	6	7	8	11	10			5		1									

LEICESTER CITY 1967-68
Back : Glover,Cross,Large,Stringfellow,Shilton,Rodrigues,Woollett,Nish,Bell.
Front : Sjoberg,Sinclair,Svarc,Roberts,Tewley,Gibson,Norman.

	APP's			GOALS		
	FL	FAC	FLC	FL	FAC	FLC
Peter Shilton	35	4		1		
Peter Rodrigues	34	5	1	1(p)		
Richie Norman	14		1			
Bobby Roberts	41	6	1	6		
John Sjoberg	40	6	1	5	1	
Graham Cross	29	6	1			
Jackie Sinclair	20		1	7(1p)		
David Nish	42	6	1	7(2p)	3(1p)	
Mike Stringfellow	37	6	1	13	1	
David Gibson	41	5	1	4		
Nick Sharkey	3			1		
Jimmy Goodfellow	3/1					
Alan Woollett	14/6	1	1			
Alan Tewley	12/1			5		
Brian Williamson	6		1			
Willie Bell	33	6				
Bobby Svarc	4	1		1		
Frank Large	26	6		8	3	
Len Glover	9/1	1/1		1		
Rodney Fern	13/1	5		4	1	
Colin Mackleworth	1	2				
Brian Potts	-/1					
Don Hutchins	1					
Malcolm Manley	4					
Own Goals					1	

1968-69 LEAGUE DIVISION ONE
Final Position : 21st
Ave. Home League Att: 28,445

DATE	OPPONENTS	V	F.T.	SCORERS
Aug 10	Queens Park Rangers	A	1-1	Clarke
13	Arsenal	A	0-3	
17	Ipswich Town	H	1-3	Nish (pen)
21	Manchester City	H	3-0	Clarke 3
24	Stoke City	A	0-1	
28	Wolverhampton Wanderers	A	0-1	
31	Southampton	H	3-1	Clarke,Manley,Mackay
Sep 7	Sunderland	A	0-2	
14	Leeds United	H	1-1	Gibson
21	Liverpool	A	0-4	
28	Coventry City	H	1-1	Fern
Oct 5	Tottenham Hotspur	A	2-3	Clarke,Glover
9	Wolverhampton Wanderers	H	2-0	Stringfellow,Fern
12	West Bromwich Albion	H	0-2	
19	Chelsea	A	0-3	
26	Burnley	H	0-2	
Nov 2	Newcastle United	A	0-0	
9	Nottingham Forest	H	2-2	Glover,Lochhead
16	West Ham United	A	0-4	
23	Sheffield Wednesday	H	1-1	Clarke
30	Everton	A	1-7	Fern
Dec 7	Manchester United	H	2-1	Nish (pen),Fern
14	West Bromwich Albion	A	1-1	Lochhead
21	Chelsea	H	1-4	Stringfellow
28	Burnley	A	1-2	Clarke
Jan 11	Newcastle United	H	2-1	Fern,Clarke
18	Nottingham Forest	A	0-0	
Feb 1	West Ham United	H	1-1	Clarke
Mar 12	Queens Park Rangers	H	2-0	Lochhead 2
15	Stoke City	H	0-0	
22	Southampton	A	0-1	
Apr 1	Coventry City	A	0-1	
4	Manchester City	A	0-2	
8	Arsenal	H	0-0	
12	Liverpool	H	1-2	Rodrigues
14	Sheffield Wednesday	A	3-1	Lochhead 2,Branfoot (og)
19	Leeds United	A	0-2	
29	Tottenham Hotspur	H	1-0	Clarke
May 3	Ipswich Town	A	1-2	Clarke
5	Sunderland	H	2-1	Brown 2
14	Everton	H	1-1	Cross
17	Manchester United	A	2-3	Nish,Fern

F.A. CUP

DATE	OPPONENTS		V	F.T.	SCORERS	
Jan 4	Barnsley	(3)	A	1-1	Glover	
8	Barnsley	(3 rep)	H	2-1	Fern,Glover	
25	Millwall	(4)	A	1-0	Glover	
Mar 1	Liverpool	(5)	H	0-0		
3	Liverpool	(5 rep)	A	1-0	Lochhead	
8	Mansfield Town	(6)	A	1-0	Fern	
29	West Bromwich Albion	(sf)		1-0	Clarke	(at Hillsborough,Sheffield)
Apr 26	Manchester City	(F)		0-1		(at Wembley)

F.L.CUP

DATE	OPPONENTS		V	F.T.	SCORERS
Sep 4	Darlington	(2)	A	2-1	Clarke 2
24	Carlisle United	(3)	A	3-0	Clarke,Fern,Stringfellow
Oct 16	Burnley	(4)	A	0-4	

LEICESTER CITY 1968-69
Back : M.Musgrove *(Coach),* Lochhead,Woollett,Fern,Mackay,Shilton,Clarke,Stringfellow.
Front : Roberts,Sjoberg,Rodrigues,Cross,F.O'Farrell *(Manager),* Nish,Glover,Manley,Gibson.

	APP's			GOALS		
	FL	FAC	FLC	FL	FAC	FLC
Peter Shilton	42	8	3			
Alan Woollett	32/1	4	3			
Willie Bell	16		2			
David Nish	40	8	3	3(2p)		
John Sjoberg	23/1	7	2			
Malcolm Manley	28	-/3	2	1		
David Gibson	29/3	6	3	1		
Allan Clarke	36	8	2	12	1	3
Mike Stringfellow	22		2	2		1
Graham Cross	37	8	2	1		
Len Glover	27	8	2	2	3	
Rodney Fern	29/6	7/1	2	6	2	1
Bobby Mackay	6/1	1	-/1	1		
Bobby Roberts	25/3	8	1/1			
Alan Tewley	3/1		1			
Bobby Svarc	2		2			
Brian Potts	9		1			
Andy Lochhead	24/1	8		6	1	
Don Hutchins	3					
Peter Rodrigues	18	7		1		
Paul Matthews	7/1					
Brian Greenhalgh	2/2					
Ally Brown	2			2		
Own Goals				1		

1969-70

LEAGUE DIVISION TWO
Final Position : 3rd
Ave. Home League Att: 25,104

DATE	OPPONENTS	V	F.T.	SCORERS
Aug 9	Birmingham City	H	3-1	Fern,Manley,Lochhead
16	Middlesbrough	A	1-2	Lochhead
20	Bolton Wanderers	H	2-2	Cross,Lochhead
23	Norwich City	H	3-0	Sjoberg,Lochhead,Forbes (og)
27	Aston Villa	A	1-0	Glover
30	Millwall	A	1-0	A.Brown
Sep 6	Portsmouth	H	2-1	Lochhead 2
13	Cardiff City	A	1-1	Carver (og)
17	Carlisle United	H	1-2	Rodrigues
20	Huddersfield Town	H	1-0	A.Brown
27	Swindon Town	A	1-1	Glover
Oct 4	Watford	H	3-1	Glover,Nish (pen),Brodie
8	Middlesbrough	H	2-1	Brodie,Cross
11	Preston North End	A	1-2	A.Brown
18	Bristol City	H	2-0	Fern,Glover
25	Blackburn Rovers	A	1-3	Fern
Nov 1	Oxford United	H	2-1	Glover,Matthews
8	Blackpool	A	1-1	Matthews
12	Bolton Wanderers	A	3-2	Fern 3
15	Charlton Athletic	H	2-2	Fern,Nish (pen)
22	Queens Park Rangers	A	1-1	Stringfellow
Dec 6	Sheffield United	A	0-1	
13	Cardiff City	H	1-2	Fern
17	Hull City	H	2-2	Nish,Fern
20	Portsmouth	A	3-2	Farrington,Fern 2
26	Norwich City	A	0-3	
27	Millwall	H	1-1	Tearse
Jan 17	Swindon Town	H	0-2	
31	Watford	A	1-2	Glover
Feb 14	Birmingham City	A	1-0	Farrington
25	Preston North End	H	3-0	Farrington, A.Brown,Glover
28	Bristol City	A	0-0	
Mar 10	Huddersfield Town	A	1-1	Fern
14	Hull City	A	1-4	Sjoberg
17	Blackburn Rovers	H	2-1	Farrington,Fern
21	Sheffield United	H	2-1	Glover,Fern
27	Oxford United	A	1-0	Roberts
28	Charlton Athletic	A	5-0	Matthews,Fern 2,Glover, A.Brown
31	Blackpool	H	0-0	
Apr 4	Aston Villa	H	1-0	A.Brown
14	Carlisle United	A	2-2	Fern, A.Brown
18	Queens Park Rangers	H	2-1	Nish, A.Brown

F.A. CUP

DATE	OPPONENTS		V	F.T.	SCORERS
Jan 3	Sunderland	(3)	H	1-0	Roberts
24	Southampton	(4)	A	1-1	Farrington
28	Southampton	(4 rep)	H	4-2	Lochhead 2,Farrington,Nish (pen)
Feb 7	Liverpool	(5)	A	0-0	
11	Liverpool	(5 rep)	H	0-2	

F.L.CUP

DATE	OPPONENTS		V	F.T.	SCORERS
Sep 2	Bristol City	(2)	A	0-0	
10	Bristol City	(2 rep)	H	0-0	
15	Bristol City	(2 rep 2)	H	3-1	Lochhead 3
24	Bournemouth & B.A.	(3)	A	2-0	Manley,Fern
Oct 15	Sheffield United	(4)	H	2-0	A.Brown,Lochhead
29	West Bromwich Albion	(5)	H	0-0	
Nov 5	West Brom. Albion	(5 rep)	A	1-2	Cross

LEICESTER CITY 1969-70
Back : Beaton,Tearse,Brodie,Burt,Mackleworth,Harrison,Whitworth,G.Brown,Tewley.
Middle : A.Brown,Woollett,Cross,Lochhead,Shilton,Sjoberg,Stringfellow,Fern,McLeod.
Seated : Roberts,Glover,Gibson,Nish,Houghton,Manley,Matthews,Mackay.
Front : Ralston,Bowerbank,Watts,Russell,Munro,Waters,Vickers.

	APP's			GOALS		
	FL	FAC	FLC	FL	FAC	FLC
Peter Shilton	39	5	7			
Peter Rodrigues	29/1	1/1	6	1		
Billy Houghton	6/1		3			
David Nish	42	5	7	4(2p)	1(p)	
John Sjoberg	39	5	6	2		
Graham Cross	42	5	6	2		
Len Glover	37	4	6	9		
Rodney Fern	39/1	5	5	17		
Andy Lochhead	16/3	4/1	6	6	2	
David Gibson	9/3		3			
Malcolm Manley	9/2		2	1		
Bobby Roberts	31/2	5	2	1	1	
Alan Woollett	27	5	3			
Ally Brown	26/5		6	8		
Derek Harrison		1				
Bobby Mackay		1				
Alan Tewley			-/1			
Paul Matthews	24	4	5	3		
Murray Brodie	3			2		
David Tearse	5/1	1/2	-/1	1		
John Farrington	16	5	2	4	2	
Mike Stringfellow	7/1	1	-/1	1		
Ken Sandercock	5/5					
Colin Mackleworth	3					
Graham Brown	-/1					
Own Goals					2	

1970-71 LEAGUE DIVISION TWO
Final Position : 1st
Ave. Home League Att: 25,869

DATE	OPPONENTS	V	F.T.	SCORERS	Shilton	Rodrigues	Woollett	Nish	Sjoberg	Cross	Farrington	Fern	Brown	Kellard	Glover	Stringfellow	Matthews	Whitworth	Manley	Partridge	Harrison	Jopling	Carlin	Tearse	Mackleworth
Aug 15	Cardiff City	H	0-1		1	2	3	4	5	6	7	8*	9	10	11	12									
22	Queens Park Rangers	A	3-1	Kellard,Brown,Farrington	1	2	3		5	6	7	8	10*	4	11	9	12								
29	Carlisle United	H	2-2	Nish,Glover	1	2	3		5	6	7	8	10	4	11	9									
Sep 2	Bristol City	H	4-0	Farrington,Kellard,Brown,Nish (pen)	1		3		5	6	7	12	10	4	11	9*	8	2							
5	Oxford United	A	0-1		1		3		5	6	7	10*		4	11	9	8	2	12						
12	Luton Town	H	1-0	Brown	1		3		5	6	7	8	9	4	11		10	2							
19	Charlton Athletic	A	1-0	Partridge	1		3		5	6	7		9	10	11			2	4	8					
26	Portsmouth	H	2-0	Glover,Farrington	1		3		5	6	7		9	10	11			2	4	8					
30	Middlesbrough	H	3-2	Brown 2,Kellard	1		3		5	6	7		9	10	11			2	4	8					
Oct 3	Blackburn Rovers	A	2-0	Partridge,Nish (pen)	1		3		5	6	7		9	10	11			2	4	8					
10	Sunderland	H	1-0	Glover	1				5	6	7		9	10	11			2	4	8		3			
17	Cardiff City	A	2-2	Farrington,Sjoberg	1	3*			5	6	7	12	9	10	11			2	4	8					
20	Birmingham City	A	0-0		1		3		5	6	7		9	4	11			2	12	8*			10		
24	Sheffield Wednesday	A	3-0	Brown,Nish 2 (1pen)	1		3		5	6	7		9	4	11			2		8			10		
31	Bolton Wanderers	H	1-0	Kellard	1		3		5	6	7		9	4	11			2		8			10		
Nov 7	Watford	A	1-0	Nish (pen)	1		3		5	6	7		9	10	11			2	4				8		
14	Swindon Town	H	3-1	Brown,Jones (og),Harland (og)	1		3		5	6	7		9	4	11			2	12	8*			10		
21	Norwich City	A	2-2	Manley,Farrington	1		3		5	6	7	12	9	10	11*			2	4				8		
28	Orient	H	4-0	Manley,Brown 2,Kellard	1		3		5	6	7		9	8	11			2	4				10		
Dec 5	Hull City	A	0-3		1		3		5	6	7	12	9	8	11*			2	4				10		
12	Millwall	H	2-1	Kellard,Fern	1		3		5	6	7	8		4	11	9*		2	12				10		
19	Queens Park Rangers	H	0-0		1		3		5	6	7	8		4	11	9		2					10		
26	Sheffield United	A	1-2	Farrington	1		3		5	6	7		9	4	11			2		8			10		
Jan 9	Middlesbrough	A	0-1				3		5	6	7		9	4	11	12	2			8			10*	1	
16	Birmingham City	H	1-4	Sjoberg			3		5	6	7	9				11	2	4		8			10	1	
Feb 6	Hull City	H	0-0		1		3		5	6	7	9			4			2		8			10		
20	Norwich City	H	2-1	Fern,Partridge	1		3	5*		6	7	9	8	4			2	11	12				10		
27	Bolton Wanderers	A	3-0	Brown,Sjoberg 2	1		3		5	6	7	9	8	4	11			2	12				10*		
Mar 1	Millwall	A	0-0		1		3		5	6	7	9	8	4	11			2					10		
10	Sheffield Wednesday	H	1-0	Brown	1		3		5	6	7	9	8	4				2					10		
13	Swindon Town	A	1-0	Kellard	1	11	3		5	6	7	9	8	4				2					10		
20	Watford	H	1-1	Nish	1	5	3			6	7	9	8	4*	11			2	12				10		
27	Oxford United	H	0-0		1	12	3		5	6	7		9*		11			2	4				10		8
29	Orient	A	1-0	Glover	1	3	7		5	6			9	8	4	11		2					10		
Apr 3	Carlisle United	A	1-0	Brown	1	3	7		5	6			9	8	4	11		2					10		
10	Sheffield United	H	0-0		1	3	7		5	6			9	8	4	11*		2					10		
12	Luton Town	A	3-1	Manley,Farrington,Brown	1		3		5	6	7	9	8			12		2	4*	11			10		
13	Blackburn Rovers	H	1-1	Carlin	1		3		5	6	7	9	8	4				2	11				10		
17	Sunderland	A	0-0		1		3		5	6		9*	8	4		12		2	11		7		10		
24	Charlton Athletic	H	1-0	Went (og)	1		3		5	6		9	8	4		12		2	11		7*		10		
27	Bristol City	H	1-0	Brown	1		3	5*		6	7	9	8	4		12		2	11				10		
May 1	Portsmouth	A	2-1	Farrington,Brown	1		3			6	7	9	8	4	11			2	5	12			10*		

F.A. CUP

DATE	OPPONENTS		V	F.T.	SCORERS	Shilton	Woollett	Sjoberg	Cross	Farrington	Fern	Brown	Kellard	Glover	Whitworth	Partridge	Manley	Carlin	Tearse
Jan 2	Notts County	(3)	H	2-0	Brown,Partridge		3	5	6	7		9	4	11	2	8		10	1
25	Torquay United	(4)	H	3-0	Glover,Partridge,Cross	1	3	5	6	7	9	12	4	11	2	8		10*	
Feb 13	Oxford United	(5)	H	1-1	Partridge	1	3	5	6	7	9	12	4	11*	2	8		10	
17	Oxford United	(5 rep)	A	3-1	Brown,Fern 2	1	3	5	6	7	9	8	4	11	2			10	
Mar 6	Arsenal	(6)	H	0-0		1	3	5	6	7	9	8	4	11	2			10	
15	Arsenal	(6 rep)	A	0-1		1	3	5	6	7	9	8*	4	11	2		12	10	

F.L. CUP

DATE	OPPONENTS		V	F.T.	SCORERS	Shilton	Rodrigues	Woollett	Sjoberg	Cross	Farrington	Fern	Brown	Kellard	Glover	Stringfellow	Matthews	Whitworth	Partridge
Sep 9	Southampton	(2)	H	3-2	Farrington,Glover,Fern	1	12	3*	5	6	7	8	9	10	11		2	4	
Oct 7	Bolton Wanderers	(3)	A	1-1	Farrington	1	4	3*		6	7	8	9	10	11	12	2		5
12	Bolton Wanderers	(3 rep)	H	1-0	Sjoberg	1	3		5	6	7	8	9	10		11	2	4	
28	Bristol City	(4)	H	2-2	Farrington,Nish (pen)	1		3	5	6	7		8	10	11	9	2	4	
Nov 3	Bristol City	(4 rep)	A	1-2	Nish (pen)	1		3	5	6	7	8	12	10	11	9*	2	4	

LEICESTER CITY 1970-71
Back : Fern,Woollett,Manley,Jopling,Partridge,Shilton,Stringfellow,Cross,Sjoberg,Brown.
Front : Rodrigues,Whitworth,Glover,Nish,Farrington,Kellard,Matthews.

	APP's			GOALS		
	FL	FAC	FLC	FL	FAC	FLC
Peter Shilton	40	5	5			
Peter Rodrigues	1		1/1			
Alan Woollett	9/1		1			
David Nish	40	6	4	7(4p)		2(2p)
John Sjoberg	40	6	4	4		1
Graham Cross	42	6	5		1	
John Farrington	37	6	5	8		3
Rodney Fern	23/4	5	4	2	2	1
Ally Brown	38	4/2	4/1	15	2	
Bobby Kellard	39	6	5	7		
Len Glover	33	6	4	4	1	1
Mike Stringfellow	7/5		2			
Paul Matthews	4/2		1/1			
Steve Whitworth	39	6	5			
Malcolm Manley	20/4		4	3		
Malcolm Partridge	15/5	3/1		3	3	
Derek Harrison		1				
Joe Jopling	1					
Willie Carlin	30	6		1		
David Tearse	2					
Colin Mackleworth	2	1				
Own Goals				3		

1971-72

LEAGUE DIVISION ONE
Final Position : 12th
Ave. Home League Att: 28,557

DATE	OPPONENTS	V	F.T.	SCORERS	Shilton	Whitworth	Nish	Kellard	Sjoberg	Cross	Farrington	Brown	Fern	Sammels	Glover	Carlin	Manley	Woollett	Partridge	Matthews	Munro	Weller	Birchenall	Tomlin	Jayes	Wallington	Lee
Aug 14	Huddersfield Town	A	2-2	Brown, Nish	1	2	3	4	5	6	7	8	9	10	11												
18	Nottingham Forest	H	2-1	Brown, O'Kane (og)	1	2	3	4	5	6	7	8	9	10	11												
21	Derby County	H	0-2		1	2	3	4	5	6	7	8	9	10	11												
25	Stoke City	A	1-3	Brown	1	2	3	4	5	6	7	8	9	10	11												
28	Liverpool	A	2-3	Fern, Farrington	1	2	3	4	5	6	7	8	9	10	11												
Sep 1	Southampton	H	0-1		1	2	3	4	5*	6	7	8	9	10	11	12											
4	Manchester City	H	0-0		1	2	3	4		6	7		9	10	11	5	8										
11	Ipswich Town	A	2-1	Sammels, Kellard	1	2	3*	4	5	6		8	9	10	11			12			7						
18	Sheffield United	H	0-1		1	2	3	8	5	6		9	7	10	11			4									
25	Arsenal	A	0-3		1	2	3		5	6	7	8	9	10	11*		4	12									
Oct 2	Crystal Palace	H	0-0		1	2	3		5	4	7		9*	12	10		6					8	11				
9	West Ham United	A	1-1	Cross	1	2	3		5	4		12	9	10	7		6*					8	11				
16	Huddersfield Town	H	2-0	Sammels, Weller	1	2	3		5	4		6	8	10	11							7	9				
23	West Bromwich Albion	A	1-0	Weller	1	2	3		5	4		6	8	10	11							7	9				
30	Chelsea	H	1-1	Birchenall	1	2	3		5	4		6	8	10	11*		12					7	9				
Nov 6	Leeds United	A	1-2	Brown	1	2	3		5	4		6	8	10	11*		12					7	9				
13	Newcastle United	H	3-0	Brown, Sammels, Fern	1	2	3		5	4		6	8	10	11							7	9				
20	Manchester United	A	2-3	Birchenall, Glover	1	2	3		5	4		6	8	10	11							7	9				
27	Everton	H	0-0		1	2	3		5	4		6	8	10	11							7	9				
Dec 4	Coventry City	A	1-1	Brown	1	2	3		5	4		6	8	10	11							7	9				
11	Tottenham Hotspur	H	0-1		1	2	3		5	4		6	8	10	11							7	9				
18	Manchester City	A	1-1	Weller	1	2	3		5	4		6	10	8	11							7	9				
27	Wolverhampton Wanderers	H	1-2	Sammels	1	2	3		5	4		6	8	10	11*		12					7	9				
Jan 1	Sheffield United	A	1-1	Sjoberg	1	2	3		5	4		6	8	10	11							7	9				
8	Liverpool	H	1-0	Brown	1	2	3			4		8	6	10	11		5					7	9				
22	Nottingham Forest	A	2-1	Weller, Birchenall	1	2	3		5	4		8	6*	10	11		12					7	9				
29	Stoke City	H	2-1	Glover, Farrington	1	2	3			4		8	6	10	11		5					7	9*				
Feb 12	West Bromwich Albion	H	0-1		1	2	3		5	4*		8	6	10	11		12					7	9				
19	Chelsea	A	1-2	Glover	1	2	3			4		12	8*	10	11		5	6				7	9				
Mar 4	Newcastle United	A	0-2		1	2	3			4*	8	12	9	6	11		5					7	10				
11	West Ham United	H	2-0	Nish 2		2	3		5	4	7*	6	8		11		12					9	10			1	
18	Derby County	A	0-3			2	3			4	7*		8		11		5	6				9	10	12		1	
22	Leeds United	H	0-0		1	2	3			4			8		11		5	6				7	9	10			
25	Ipswich Town	H	1-0	Tomlin	1	2	3			4			8		11		5	6				7	9	10			
Apr 1	Wolverhampton Wanderers	A	1-0	Shaw (og)	1	2	3			4		12	8		11		5	6				7	9*	10			
3	Crystal Palace	A	1-1	Fern		2	3			4			9		11		5	6	8	12		7	10*			1	
4	Arsenal	H	0-0			2	3			6			8		11		5	4				7	9	10		1	
8	Manchester United	H	2-0	Weller, Birchenall	1	2	3			6		12	8		11		5	4				7	9	10*			
11	Southampton	A	0-1		1	2	3			6		12	8		11		5	4				7*	9	10			
15	Everton	A	0-0		1	2	3			4			8	9	11*		5	6				7	12	10			
22	Coventry City	H	1-0	Glover	1	2	3*			6		12	8		11		5	4				7	9	10			
29	Tottenham Hotspur	A	3-4	Glover, Sammels (pen), Partridge		2	3			4			8		11		5	6	10			7	9			1	

F.A. CUP

DATE	OPPONENTS		V	F.T.	SCORERS	Shilton	Whitworth	Nish	Kellard	Sjoberg	Cross	Farrington	Brown	Fern	Sammels	Glover	Carlin	Manley	Woollett	Partridge	Matthews	Munro	Weller	Birchenall	Tomlin	Jayes	Wallington	Lee
Jan 15	Wolverhampton W.	(3)	A	1-1	Farrington	1	2	3		5	4		8	6	10	11							7	9				
19	Wolverhampton W.	(3 rep)	H	2-0	Farrington, Glover	1	2	3		5	4		8	6	10	11							7	9				
Feb 5	Orient	(4)	H	0-2			2	3		5	4		8	6*	10	11			12				7	9		1		

F.L. CUP

DATE	OPPONENTS		V	F.T.	SCORERS	Shilton	Whitworth	Nish	Kellard	Sjoberg	Cross	Farrington	Brown	Fern	Sammels	Glover	Carlin	Manley	Woollett	Partridge	Matthews	Munro	Weller	Birchenall	Tomlin	Jayes	Wallington	Lee
Sep 7	Charlton Athletic	(2)	A	1-3	Partridge	1	2	3	4		6	7		8	10				5	11*	9	12						

LEICESTER CITY 1971-72
Back : D.Coates (*Trainer*), Whitworth, Sjoberg, Jopling, Partridge, Shilton, Stringfellow, Brown, Cross, Sammels, Manley, G.Preston (*Physiotherapist*).
Front : Carlin, Woollett, Farrington, Nish, L.Shipman (*Chairman*), J.Bloomfield (*Manager*), J.Smith (*Secretary*), Glover, Fern, Matthews, Kellard.

	APP's			GOALS		
	FL	FAC	FLC	FL	FAC	FLC
Peter Shilton	37	2	1			
Steve Whitworth	42	3	1			
David Nish	42	3	1	3		
Bobby Kellard	9		1	1		
John Sjoberg	26	3		1		
Graham Cross	39	3	1	1		
John Farrington	15/1	3	1	2	2	
Ally Brown	27/3	3		7		
Rodney Fern	29/7		1	3		
Jon Sammels	40	3	1	5(1p)		
Len Glover	35/2	3		5	1	
Willie Carlin	1					
Malcolm Manley	23/3	-/1	1			
Alan Woollett	13		1			
Malcolm Partridge	8/2		1	1		1
Paul Matthews			-/1			
Malcolm Munro	1/1					
Keith Weller	32	3		5		
Alan Birchenall	29	3		4		
David Tomlin	9/1			1		
Carl Jayes		1				
Mark Wallington	5					
Bob Lee	-/1					
Own Goals				2		

1972-73 LEAGUE DIVISION ONE
Final Position : 16th
Ave. Home League Att: 22,706

DATE	OPPONENTS	V	F.T.	SCORERS	Shilton	Whitworth	Nish	Woollett	Sjoberg	Manley	Farrington	Sammels	Weller	Birchenall	Glover	Partridge	Cross	Stringfellow	Worthington	Rofe	Munro	Wallington	Tomlin	Jopling	Lee
Aug 12	Arsenal	H	0-1		1	2	3	4*	5	6	7	8	9	10	11	12									
16	Chelsea	H	1-1	Farrington	1	2	3	4		5	7	8	9	10*	11	12	6								
19	West Ham United	A	2-5	Stringfellow,Glover	1	2	3	4	5		7	8	9		11			6	10						
23	Manchester United	A	1-1	Worthington	1	2	3	5			7	6	9	10			4	11	8						
26	Coventry City	H	0-0		1	2		5			6	8	7	10	11		4		9	3					
30	Liverpool	H	3-2	Weller 3	1	2		5			7	6	9		11		4	10	8	3					
Sep 2	Manchester City	A	0-1		1	2		5		11	7	6	9			12	4	10	8	3*					
9	Everton	H	1-2	Sammels	1	2		5			7	6	9		11	12	4	10*	8	3					
16	Leeds United	A	1-3	Glover	1	2		4			7	6	9	10	11		5		8	3					
23	Wolverhampton Wanderers	H	1-1	Farrington	1	2		5			7	4	9	8	11		6		10	3					
30	Ipswich Town	A	2-0	Glover,Worthington	1	2		5			7	4	9	8	11		6		10	3					
Oct 7	Southampton	H	1-0	Sammels (pen)	1	2		5			7*	4	9	8	11		6	12	10	3					
14	Derby County	A	1-2	Weller	1	2		5			7	4	9	8*	11		6	12	10	3					
21	Norwich City	H	1-2	Weller	1	2			6	5	7	4	9	8	11				10	3					
28	Stoke City	A	0-1		1	2		3		12	7	4		8	11	9*	5		10		6				
Nov 4	Manchester United	H	2-2	Sammels,Farrington	1	2					7	4	9	8	11		6		10	3	5				
11	Chelsea	A	1-1	Sammels	1			2	5		7	4	9	8	11		6		10	3					
18	Tottenham Hotspur	H	0-1			2		4	5*	12	7	8		10	11		6		9	3		1			
Dec 2	West Bromwich Albion	H	3-1	Worthington 3	1	2		4			5	7	8*		10	11	6		9	3			12		
9	Birmingham City	A	1-1	Cross	1	2					5	7	8	4	10	11	6		9	3					
16	Sheffield United	A	0-2		1	2					5	7	4*		9	8	11	6		10	3		12		
23	Crystal Palace	H	2-1	Worthington (pen),Birchenall	1	2		4*			6	7		9	8	11	5		10	3			12		
26	Wolverhampton Wanderers	A	0-2		1	2		4*			5	7		9	8	11			10	3			12	6	
30	West Ham United	H	2-1	Farrington,Worthington	1	2		4			5	7		9	8	11			10	3			6		
Jan 1	Newcastle United	A	2-2	Birchenall,Worthington	1	2		4			5*	7		9	8	11	6	12	10	3					
6	Coventry City	A	2-3	Worthington,Weller	1	2		4				7		9	6	11	5	8*	10	3			12		
20	Manchester City	H	1-1	Worthington	1	2		4			5	7		9		11	6	8	10	3					
27	Everton	A	1-0	Wright (og)	1	2		4			5	7		9	8	11	6		10	3					
Feb 10	Leeds United	H	2-0	Birchenall 2	1	2		4			5	7		9	8	11	6		10	3					
17	Arsenal	A	0-1		1	2		4*			5	7	12	9	8	11	6		10	3					
24	Sheffield United	H	0-0		1	2		4			5	7		8	9	11	6		10	3					
Mar 3	Southampton	A	0-0		1	2		4			5		7	9	8	11	6		10	3					
10	Derby County	H	0-0		1	2					5	7	4	9	8	11	6		10	3					
17	Norwich City	A	1-1	Glover	1	2					5	7	4	9	8	11	6		10	3					
24	Stoke City	H	2-0	Tomlin,Birchenall	1	2					5	7	4	9	8	11*	6		10	3			12		
31	Newcastle United	H	0-0		1	2					5	7	4	9	8		6		10	3			11		
Apr 7	West Bromwich Albion	A	0-1		1	2		12			6	7	4	9	8		5		10	3			11*		
14	Birmingham City	H	0-1		1	2		12			5	7*	4	9	8	11	6		10	3					
20	Crystal Palace	A	1-0	Weller	1	2		4			5	7		9	8	11	6		10	3					
21	Tottenham Hotspur	A	1-1	Weller	1	2		4			5		7	9	8	11*	6	12	10	3					
24	Ipswich Town	H	1-1	Cross	1	2		4						9		11	6	12	10	3	5		7	8*	
28	Liverpool	A	0-0		1	2					5		7	9	8	11	6	4	10	3					

F.A. CUP

DATE	OPPONENTS		V	F.T.	SCORERS	Shilton	Whitworth	Nish	Woollett	Sjoberg	Manley	Farrington	Sammels	Weller	Birchenall	Glover	Partridge	Cross	Stringfellow	Worthington	Rofe	Munro	Wallington	Tomlin	Jopling	Lee
Jan 13	Arsenal	(3)	A	2-2	Worthington,Farrington	1	2		4	5		7		9	8	11		6		10	3					
17	Arsenal	(3 rep)	H	1-2	Farrington	1	2		4			5	7		9	8*	11	6		10	3			12		

F.L.CUP

DATE	OPPONENTS		V	F.T.	SCORERS	Shilton	Whitworth	Nish	Woollett	Sjoberg	Manley	Farrington	Sammels	Weller	Birchenall	Glover	Partridge	Cross	Stringfellow	Worthington	Rofe	Munro	Wallington	Tomlin	Jopling	Lee
Sep 6	Norwich City	(2)	A	1-2	Sammels	1	2		4	3	5*	11	8	7			12	6	10	9						

LEICESTER CITY 1972-73
Back : Woollett,Sjoberg,Yates,Stringfellow,Jopling,Munro,Manley,Matthews.
Middle : D.Coates *(Coach)*, Partridge,Birchenall,Jayes,Shilton,Wallington,Cross,G.Preston *(Physiotherapist)*,
G.Dewis *(Coach)*, J.Smith *(Secretary)*.
Front : Whitworth,Tomlin,Sammels,L.Shipman *(Chairman)*, Weller,J.Bloomfield *(Manager)*, Glover,Farrington,Nish.

	APP's			GOALS		
	FL	FAC	FLC	FL	FAC	FLC
Peter Shilton	41	2	1			
Steve Whitworth	41	2	1			
David Nish	4					
Alan Woollett	27/2	2	1			
John Sjoberg	10	1	1			
Malcolm Manley	25/2	1	1			
John Farrington	38	2	1	4	2	
Jon Sammels	30/1		1	4 (1p)		1
Keith Weller	39	2	1	8		
Alan Birchenall	36	2		5		
Len Glover	38	2		4		
Malcolm Partridge	1/4		-/1			
Graham Cross	38	2	1	2		
Mike Stringfellow	8/5		1	1		
Frank Worthington	39	2	1	10 (1p)	1	
Dennis Rofe	37	2				
Malcolm Munro	3					
Mark Wallington	1					
David Tomlin	4/6	-/1		1		
Joe Jopling	1					
Bob Lee	1					
Own Goals					1	

1973-74 LEAGUE DIVISION ONE
Final Position : 9th
Ave. Home League Att: 24,825

DATE	OPPONENTS	V	F.T.	SCORERS
Aug 25	Ipswich Town	A	1-1	Sammels
28	Everton	A	1-1	Weller
Sep 1	Liverpool	H	1-1	Birchenall
5	Manchester United	H	1-0	Worthington
8	Arsenal	A	2-0	Glover,Stringfellow
12	Manchester United	A	2-1	Weller,Stringfellow
15	Manchester City	H	1-1	Weller
22	West Ham United	A	1-1	Worthington
29	Coventry City	H	0-2	
Oct 6	Sheffield United	A	1-1	Weller
13	Leeds United	H	2-2	Worthington,Birchenall
20	Derby County	A	1-2	Worthington
27	Southampton	H	0-1	
Nov 3	Norwich City	A	0-1	
10	Newcastle United	H	1-0	Weller
17	Burnley	H	2-0	Glover,Stringfellow
24	Birmingham City	A	0-3	
Dec 1	Tottenham Hotspur	H	3-0	Glover 2,Earle
8	Chelsea	A	2-3	Worthington,Earle
15	Queens Park Rangers	H	2-0	Worthington,Glover
22	Coventry City	A	2-1	Glover,Worthington
26	Wolverhampton Wanderers	H	2-2	Worthington 2 (1pen)
29	Arsenal	H	2-0	Worthington,Earle
Jan 1	Liverpool	A	1-1	Weller
12	Manchester City	A	0-2	
19	Ipswich Town	H	5-0	Worthington 3 (2 pen),Munro,Beattie (og)
Feb 2	Queens Park Rangers	A	0-0	
9	West Ham United	A	0-1	
23	Sheffield United	H	1-1	Worthington
26	Leeds United	A	1-1	Weller
Mar 2	Everton	H	2-1	Worthington,Earle
16	Derby County	H	0-1	
18	Southampton	A	0-1	
23	Newcastle United	A	1-1	Waters
Apr 6	Birmingham City	H	3-3	Cross,Glover 2
13	Burnley	A	0-0	
15	Stoke City	A	0-1	
16	Stoke City	H	1-1	Worthington
20	Chelsea	H	3-0	Worthington 2,Glover
23	Wolverhampton Wanderers	A	0-1	
27	Tottenham Hotspur	A	0-1	
29	Norwich City	H	3-0	Worthington 2,Earle

F.A. CUP

DATE	OPPONENTS		V	F.T.	SCORERS	
Jan 5	Tottenham Hotspur	(3)	H	1-0	Earle	
26	Fulham	(4)	A	1-1	Glover	
30	Fulham	(4 rep)	H	2-1	Glover,Worthington	
Feb 16	Luton Town	(5)	A	4-0	Earle 2,Worthington,Weller	
Mar 9	Queens Park Rangers	(6)	A	2-0	Waters 2	
30	Liverpool	(sf)		0-0		(at Old Trafford,Manchester)
Apr 3	Liverpool	(sf rep)		1-3	Glover	(at Villa Park,Birmingham)

F.L.CUP

DATE	OPPONENTS		V	F.T.	SCORERS
Oct 8	Hull City	(2)	H	3-3	Weller 2,Worthington
31	Hull City	(2 rep)	A	2-3	Stringfellow,Worthington

LEICESTER CITY 1973-74

Back : Rofe,Woollett,Kruse,Lee,Jopling,Yates,Tomlin,Farrington.
Middle : G.Preston (Physiotherapist), Manley,Stringfellow,Jayes,Shilton,Wallington, Birchenall,Munro,D.Coates (Coach).
Front : Whitworth,Cross,Partridge,J.Bloomfield (Manager), Weller,Worthington,Sammels

	APP's			GOALS		
	FL	FAC	FLC	FL	FAC	FLC
Peter Shilton	42	7	2			
Steve Whitworth	41	7	1			
Dennis Rofe	42	7	2			
Mike Stringfellow	17/6	1/1	2	3		1
Malcolm Munro	39	7	2	1		
Graham Cross	40	7	1	1		
Keith Weller	42	7	2	7	1	2
Jon Sammels	41	7	2	1		
Frank Worthington	42	7	2	20(3p)	2	2
Alan Birchenall	33	4	2	2		
Len Glover	36	6	2	9	3	
John Farrington	1/2		-/2			
Malcolm Partridge	1					
Malcolm Manley		1				
Alan Woollett	6/2		1			
Joe Jopling	-/1					
Steve Earle	25	7		5	3	
David Tomlin	4	1				
Joe Waters	8	2		1	2	
Steve Yates	-/2					
Pat Kruse	2					
Own Goals				1		

1974-75

LEAGUE DIVISION ONE
Final Position : 18th
Ave. Home League Att: 23,765

Date	Opponents	V	F.T.	Scorers	Wallington	Whitworth	Rofe	Sammels	Munro	Cross	Weller	Earle	Worthington	Birchenall	Glover	Waters	Woollett	Shilton	Partridge	Yates	Stringfellow	Jayes	Farmer	Lee	Tomlin	Blockley	Garland
Aug 17	Arsenal	H	0-1		1	2	3	4	5	6	7	8	9	10	11												
20	Birmingham City	A	4-3	Weller,Worthington 2,Rofe	1	2	3	4	5	6	7	8	9	10	11												
24	Liverpool	A	1-2	Weller	1	2	3	4	5	6	7	8	9	10	11												
27	Birmingham City	H	1-1	Worthington	1	2	3	4	5	6	7	8	9	10	11												
31	Carlisle United	H	1-1	Worthington (pen)	1	2	3	4	5	6	7	8*	9	10	11	12											
Sep 7	Wolverhampton Wanderers	A	1-1	Glover	1	2	3	4	5		7	8	9	10	11		6										
14	Queens Park Rangers	H	3-1	Worthington 2,Glover	1	2	3	4	5		7	8	9	10	11		6										
21	West Ham United	A	2-6	Worthington 2 (1pen)	1	2	3	4	5	12	7	8	9	10*	11		6										
28	Coventry City	H	0-1			2	3	4	5	6	7	8	9		11		10	1									
Oct 5	Luton Town	H	0-0			2	3	4	5	12	7	8	9		11		10	1	6*								
12	Derby County	A	0-1			2		4	5	6	7	8	9	10	11			1		3							
19	Sheffield United	H	3-0	Worthington 2,Glover		2			5	6	7	8	9	10	11			1		3							
26	Newcastle United	A	1-0	Earle		2	3*	8	5	6	7	4	9	10	11			1			12						
Nov 2	Burnley	H	1-0	Sammels	1	2		8	5	6	7	4	9	10	11						3						
9	Chelsea	A	0-0		1	2	3*	8	5	6	7	4	9	10	11						12						
16	Tottenham Hotspur	H	1-2	Earle	1	2		8	5	6	7	4	9	10	11						3*	12					
23	Manchester City	A	1-4	Birchenall	1	2		8	5	6*	7	4	9	10	11	12					3						
30	Stoke City	A	0-1			2		8	5	6	7	4	9	10	11						3	1					
Dec 7	Everton	H	0-2			2		8	5	6	7	4*	9	10	11						3	12	1				
10	Middlesbrough	A	0-3			2		8	5	6	7	4	9	10	11						3	1					
14	Arsenal	A	0-0			2		8	5	6	7	4	9	10	11						3	1					
20	Ipswich Town	H	0-1			2		8	5	6	7*	4	9	10	11						3	1		12			
26	Queens Park Rangers	A	2-4	Lee 2		2		8	5	6		4	9	10	11						3	1		7			
28	Leeds United	H	0-2			2		8	5	6		4	9	10	11						3		1	7			
Jan 11	Everton	A	0-3		1	2		8	5	6	7	4	9	10	11						3						
18	Stoke City	H	1-1	Glover	1	2	3	8	5	6	7	4	9	10	11												
Feb 1	Chelsea	H	1-1	Weller	1	2	3	8		6	7	4	9	10	11											5	
8	Burnley	A	0-2		1	2	3	8		6	7		9	10	11									4		5	
22	Tottenham Hotspur	A	3-0	Stringfellow,Worthington,Sammels	1	2	3	8		6	7		9	10							11			4		5	
Mar 1	Carlisle United	A	1-0	Worthington	1	2	3	8		6	7		9	10	11									4		5	
8	Manchester City	H	1-0	Lee	1	2	3	8		6	7	11*	9	10	12									4		5	
15	Coventry City	A	2-2	Worthington,Lee	1	2	3	8		6	7		9	10										4		5	11
18	Liverpool	H	1-1	Worthington	1	2	3	8		6*	7		9	10	12									4		5	11
22	Wolverhampton Wanderers	H	3-2	Garland 3	1	2	3	8		6	7		9	10										4		5	11
29	Ipswich Town	A	1-2	Worthington	1	2	3	8		6	7		9	10*	12									4		5	11
31	Leeds United	A	2-2	Lee,Garland	1	2	3	8		6	7		9	10										4		5	11* 12
Apr 1	West Ham United	H	3-0	Worthington (pen),Garland 2	1	2	3	8		6	7		9*	10	12									4		5	11
5	Newcastle United	H	4-0	Garland 2,Lee,Worthington	1	2	3	8		6	7		9	10										4		5	11
9	Middlesbrough	H	1-0	Worthington	1	2	3	8		6	7		9	10*	12									4		5	11
12	Luton Town	A	0-3		1	2	3	8		6*	7	12	9	10										4		5	11
19	Derby County	H	0-0		1	2	3	8		6	7		9	10	12									4		5	11*
26	Sheffield United	A	0-4		1	2	3	8		6	7	11*	9	10	12									4		5	

F.A. CUP

Date	Opponents		V	F.T.	Scorers	Wallington	Whitworth	Rofe	Sammels	Munro	Cross	Weller	Earle	Worthington	Birchenall	Glover	Waters	Woollett	Shilton	Partridge	Yates	Stringfellow	Jayes	Farmer	Lee	Tomlin	Blockley	Garland
Jan 4	Oxford United	(3)	H	3-1	Worthington,Earle 2	1	2		8	5	6	7	4	9	10	11*						3			12			
25	Leatherhead	(4)	A	3-2	Sammels,Earle,Weller	1	2	3	8	5	6	7	4	9	10	11												
Feb 15	Arsenal	(5)	A	0-0		1	2	3	8		6	7	4	9	10	11											5	
19	Arsenal	(5 rep)	H	1-1	Birchenall	1	2	3	8		6	7	4*	9	10	11						12					5	
24	Arsenal	(5 rep 2)	H	0-1		1	2	3	8		6	7	4*	9	10										12		5	

F.L.CUP

Date	Opponents		V	F.T.	Scorers	Wallington	Whitworth	Rofe	Sammels	Munro	Cross	Weller	Earle	Worthington	Birchenall	Glover	Waters	Woollett	Shilton	Partridge	Yates	Stringfellow	Jayes	Farmer	Lee	Tomlin	Blockley	Garland
Sep 10	Arsenal	(2)	A	1-1	Birchenall	1	2	3	4	5	6	7	8	9	10	11												
18	Arsenal	(2 rep)	H	2-1	Munro,Glover	1	2	3	4	5		7	8	9	10	11		6										
Oct 8	Middlesbrough	(3)	A	0-1			2	3*	4	5	6	7	8	9		11		10	1	12								

Note: Jan 25,drawn away,but switched to Filbert Street.

LEICESTER CITY 1974-75
Back : Rofe,Woollett,Kruse,Jayes,Yates,Tomlin,Earle,Waters.
Middle : D.Coates (Coach), Stringfellow,Lee,Wallington,Shilton,Partridge,Munro,G.Preston (Physiotherapist).
Front : Glover,Cross,Whitworth,J.Smith(Secretary), J.Bloomfield(Manager),
Weller,Worthington,Birchenall,Sammels.

	APP's			GOALS		
	FL	FAC	FLC	FL	FAC	FLC
Mark Wallington	30	5	2			
Steve Whitworth	42	5	3			
Dennis Rofe	29	4	3	1		
Jon Sammels	41	5	3	2	1	
Malcolm Munro	26	2	3			1
Graham Cross	38/2	5	2			
Keith Weller	40	5	3	3	1	
Steve Earle	28/1	5	3	2	3	
Frank Worthington	42	5	3	18(3p)	1	
Alan Birchenall	40	5	2	1	1	1
Len Glover	30/2	5	3	4		1
Joe Waters	3/2		1			
Alan Woollett	7/2		1			
Peter Shilton	5		1			
Malcolm Partridge			-/1			
Steve Yates	11/2	1				
Mike Stringfellow	1/6	-/1		1		
Carl Jayes	5					
John Farmer	2					
Bob Lee	16/1	-/1		6		
David Tomlin		-/1				
Jeff Blockley	16	3				
Chris Garland	10			8		

1975-76

LEAGUE DIVISION ONE
Final Position : 7th
Ave. Home League Att: 22,049

DATE	OPPONENTS	V	F.T.	SCORERS	Wallington	Whitworth	Rofe	Sammels	Blockley	Birchenall	Kember	Alderson	Lee	Garland	Tomlin	Earle	Sims	Cross	Weller	Worthington	Woollett	Yates	Glover
Aug 16	Birmingham City	H	3-3	Sammels (pen),Alderson,Roberts (og)	1	2	3	4	5	6	7	8	9	10	11*	12							
20	Manchester City	A	1-1	Lee	1	2	3	10		6	4	7	9			11	8	5*	12				
23	Newcastle United	A	0-3		1	2	3	10		6	4	7	9			8*		5	12	11			
27	Stoke City	H	1-1	Garland	1	2	3	10		6	4		8	11			5		7	9			
30	Liverpool	H	1-1	Weller	1	2	3	10		6	4	12	8*	11			5		7	9			
Sep 6	Arsenal	A	1-1	Sammels	1	2	3	10			4	8	12	11			5*		7	9			
13	West Ham United	H	3-3	Worthington,Sammels 2	1	2	3	10			4	8	11				5		7	9	6		
20	Norwich City	A	0-2		1	2	3	8			4	12	10*	11			5		7	9	6		
23	Queens Park Rangers	A	0-1		1	2	3	8			4		10	11			5		7	9	6		
27	Coventry City	H	0-3		1	2	3	8		6	4	11		10			5		7	9			
Oct 4	Manchester United	A	0-0		1	2	3	10			4	8		11			5		7	9	6		
11	Middlesbrough	H	0-0		1	2	3	10			4	8*	12	11			5		7	9	6		
18	Ipswich Town	A	1-1	Lee	1	2	3	8	5		4	10	11						7	9	6		
25	Tottenham Hotspur	H	2-3	Weller 2	1	2	3	10	5		4*	8	11	12					7	9	6		
Nov 1	Everton	A	1-1	Lee	1	2	3	8	5		4	10	11	9					7		6		
8	Burnley	H	3-2	Weller,Kember,Garland	1	2	3	8	5		4	10*	9	11					7	12	6		
15	Sheffield United	A	2-1	Alderson,Rofe	1	2	3	8	5		4	10	12	9*					7	11	6		
22	Ipswich Town	H	0-0		1	2	3	8	5		4		10						7	11	6		
29	Aston Villa	A	1-1	Worthington	1	2	3	10	5		4	8		11					7	9	6		
Dec 6	Wolverhampton Wanderers	H	2-0	Weller,Worthington	1	2	3	8*	5		4	10	12	11					7	9	6		
13	Newcastle United	H	1-0	Weller	1	2	3		5		4	10	8	9*					7	11	6		
20	Birmingham City	A	1-2	Lee	1	2	3		5	12	4	10	11			8			7	9	6		
26	Derby County	H	2-1	Lee,Worthington	1	2	3		5		4	10	8	9					7	11	6		
27	Leeds United	A	0-4		1	2	3	4	5			8	10	9					7	11	6		
Jan 10	West Ham United	A	1-1	Lee	1	2	3	12	5		4	8	10	9*					7	11	6		
17	Arsenal	H	2-1	Alderson,Lee	1	2	3		5		4	10	8	9					7	11	6		
31	Manchester City	H	1-0	Lee	1	2	3		5		4	8	10	9					7	11	6		
Feb 7	Stoke City	A	2-1	Worthington,Lee	1	2	3	8	5		4	10	7	9						11	6		
17	Burnley	A	0-1		1	2	3	10	5		4		8	11					7	9	6		
21	Sheffield United	H	1-1	Blockley	1	2	3		5		4	10	8	11					7	9	6		
25	Queens Park Rangers	H	0-1		1	2	3	12	5		4	10	8	11*					7	9	6		
28	Tottenham Hotspur	A	1-1	Kember	1	2	3	11	5		4	10	8						7	9	6		
Mar 6	Everton	H	1-0	Worthington	1	2	3		5		4	10*	8						7	11	6	12	
13	Middlesbrough	A	1-0	Boam (og)	1	2	3	10	5		4		8	9					7	11	6		
20	Aston Villa	H	2-2	Nicholl 2 (2og)	1	2	3	8	5		4	10	9						7	11	6		
27	Wolverhampton Wanderers	A	2-2	Sammels (pen),Worthington	1*	2	3	8	5		4	10	9	12					7	11	6		
Apr 3	Coventry City	A	2-0	Weller,Lee	1	2	3	8	5		4	10	9						7	11	6		
6	Liverpool	A	0-1		1	2	3	11	5		4	10	8						7	9	6		
10	Norwich City	H	0-0		1	2	3	11	5		4	10*	8						7	9	6	12	
17	Derby County	A	2-2	Alderson,Garland	1	2	3		5		4	8	9	10					7	11	6		
20	Leeds United	H	2-1	Worthington 2	1	2	3		5		4	10	8	11					7	9	6		
24	Manchester United	H	2-1	Lee,Garland	1	2	3		5		4	10	8	11					7	9	6		

F.A. CUP

DATE	OPPONENTS		V	F.T.	SCORERS	Wallington	Whitworth	Rofe	Sammels	Blockley	Birchenall	Kember	Alderson	Lee	Garland	Tomlin	Earle	Sims	Cross	Weller	Worthington	Woollett
Jan 3	Sheffield United	(3)	H	3-0	Garland 3	1	2	3		5		4	10	8	9					7	11	6
24	Bury	(4)	H	1-0	Lee	1	2	3		5		4	8	10	9					7	11	6
Feb 14	Manchester United	(5)	H	1-2	Lee	1	2	3	12	5		4	10*	8	9					7	11	6

F.L.CUP

DATE	OPPONENTS		V	F.T.	SCORERS	Wallington	Whitworth	Rofe	Sammels	Blockley	Birchenall	Kember	Alderson	Lee	Garland	Tomlin	Earle	Sims	Cross	Weller	Worthington	Woollett
Sep 9	Portsmouth	(2)	A	1-1	Garland	1	2	3	10			4		8	11			5		7	9	6
17	Portsmouth	(2 rep)	H	1-0	Sammels	1	2		10		6	4	12	8	11	9*		5		7		3
Oct 8	Lincoln City	(3)	H	2-1	Weller,Sammels (pen)	1	2	3	10			4	8		11			5		7	9	6
Nov 11	Burnley	(4)	A	0-2		1	2	3*		8	5	4	10	11	9					7	12	6

LEICESTER CITY 1975-76
Back : Waters,Kember,Rofe,M.Everitt *(Coach)*, Earle,Wilcox,Alderson.
Middle : D.Coates *(Coach)*, Tomlin,Sims,Wallington,Lee,Jayes,Yates,Woollett,G.Preston *(Physiotherapist)*.
Front : Glover,Whitworth,Worthington,J.Smith*(Secretary)*,J.Bloomfield*(Manager)*, Sammels,
Blockley,Birchenall,Weller,Garland.

	APP's			GOALS		
	FL	FAC	FLC	FL	FAC	FL
Mark Wallington	42	3	4			
Steve Whitworth	42	3	4			
Dennis Rofe	42	3	3	1		
Jon Sammels	31/2	-/1	4	5(2p)		2(
Jeff Blockley	31	3	1	1		
Alan Birchenall	7/1		1			
Steve Kember	41	3	4	2		
Brian Alderson	37/2	3	2/1	4		
Bob Lee	34/4	3	3	11	2	
Chris Garland	28/2	3	4	4	3	
David Tomlin	2		1			
Steve Earle	3/1					
Steve Sims	10		3			
Graham Cross	1/1					
Keith Weller	38/1	3	4	7		
Frank Worthington	38/1	3	2/1	9		
Alan Woollett	35	3	3			
Steve Yates			1			
Len Glover	-/2					
Own Goals				4		

1976-77

LEAGUE DIVISION ONE
Final Position : 11th
Ave. Home League Att: 18,806

DATE	OPPONENTS	V	F.T.	SCORERS	Wallington	Whitworth	Rofe	Kember	Blockley	Woollett	Weller	Alderson	Worthington	Lee	Garland	Birchenall	Earle	Sammels	Sims	Yates	White	May	Bicknell	Welsh
Aug 21	Manchester City	H	2-2	Alderson,Garland	1	2	3	4	5	6	7	8	9	10	11									
24	Sunderland	A	0-0		1	2	3	4	5	6	7	8	9	10	11									
28	West Ham United	A	0-0		1	2	3	4*	5	6	7	8	9	10	11	12								
Sep 4	Everton	H	1-1	Worthington	1	2	3	4	5	6	7	8	9	11	10									
11	Ipswich Town	A	0-0		1	2	3	4	5	6	7	8*	9	12	11	10								
18	Queens Park Rangers	H	2-2	Rofe,Garland	1	2	3	4	5	6	7		9	12	11	10*	8							
25	Aston Villa	A	0-2		1	2	3	4	5	6	7		9	11			8	10						
29	Stoke City	H	1-0	Worthington	1	2	3	4	5	6	7		9		11		8*	12	10					
Oct 2	Coventry City	A	1-1	Worthington	1	2	3	4	5	6	7		9		11	10*	12	8						
16	Bristol City	A	1-0	Worthington	1	2	3	4		6	7	8	9		11									
23	Arsenal	H	4-1	Weller 2,Earle,Worthington (pen)	1	2	3	4		6	7	10	9				11	8	5					
27	Liverpool	H	0-1		1	2	3	4		6	7	10*	9	12			11	8	5					
30	Middlesbrough	A	1-0	Worthington	1	2	3	4		6	7	8	9		11*		12	10	5					
Nov 6	Norwich City	H	1-1	Worthington	1	2	3	4		6	7	10	9		11			8	5					
9	Liverpool	A	1-5	Worthington	1	2	3	4		6	7	10	9		11			8	5					
20	Manchester United	H	1-1	Garland	1	2	3	4*		6	7	8	9		11		12	10	5					
27	Leeds United	A	2-2	Worthington,Earle	1	2	3	4	5		7	8	9				11	10	6					
Dec 4	Birmingham City	H	2-6	Kember,Worthington (pen)	1	2	3	4	5		7	10	9			12	11*	8	6					
11	West Bromwich Albion	A	2-2	Weller,Sims	1	2	3	4	5		7*	8	9			12	11	10	6					
18	Tottenham Hotspur	H	2-1	Blockley,Earle	1	2	3	4	5		7	10	9				11	8	6					
27	Derby County	A	0-1		1	2	3	4	5		7	10	9				11	8	6					
Jan 1	Norwich City	A	2-3	Sammels,Earle	1	2	3	4	5		7	10	9				11	8	6					
15	Sunderland	H	2-0	Alderson,Earle	1	2	3	4	5		7	10*	9			12	11	8	6					
22	Manchester City	A	0-5		1	2	3	4	5		7		9	10			11	8	6					
Feb 5	West Ham United	H	2-0	Worthington,Weller	1	2	3	4	5		7	10*	9			12	11	8	6					
12	Everton	A	2-1	Earle,Alderson	1	2	3	4	5		7		9	10			11	8	6					
19	Ipswich Town	H	1-0	Earle	1	2	3	4		5	7	10	9				11	8	6					
26	Queens Park Rangers	A	2-3	Earle,Sammels	1	2	3	4	5		7	10	9				11	8	6					
Mar 5	Aston Villa	H	1-1	Sammels (pen)	1	2	3	4	5		7	10	9				11	8	6					
12	Coventry City	H	3-1	Alderson,Earle,Worthington	1	2	3	4		6	7	8	9	10	11				5					
15	Middlesbrough	H	3-3	Worthington,Kember,Earle	1	2	3	4		5	7*	10	9	12			11	8	6					
19	Stoke City	A	1-0	Worthington	1	2	3	4*		5		10	9	8			11		6	12	7			
26	Bristol City	H	0-0		1	2	3*	4		5		10	9	7			11	8	6		12			
Apr 2	Arsenal	A	0-3		1	2	3	4		5		10	9	7			11	8	6					
9	Newcastle United	A	0-0		1	2	3	4		6		10	9				8	5		7	11			
12	Derby County	H	1-1	Alderson	1	2	3	4	5		7		9	10			8	6			11			
16	Manchester United	A	1-1	Earle	1	2	3	4		6	7		9	10			8	5			11			
30	Birmingham City	A	1-1	Earle	1	2	3	4		6	7		9	10			8	5			11			
May 4	Newcastle United	H	1-0	Earle	1	2	3	4		6	7		9	10			8	5			11			
7	West Bromwich Albion	H	0-5		1	2	3	4*		6	7		9	10			8	5	12		11			
14	Tottenham Hotspur	A	0-2		1	2	3			6	11		9	10			8	5		7			4	
16	Leeds United	H	0-1		1	2	3			6	7		9	10			8	5	11*				4	12

F.A. CUP

DATE	OPPONENTS		V	F.T.	SCORERS	Wallington	Whitworth	Rofe	Kember	Blockley	Woollett	Weller	Alderson	Worthington	Lee	Garland	Birchenall	Earle	Sammels	Sims
Jan 8	Aston Villa	(3)	H	0-1		1	2	3	4	5		7	10	9				11	8	6

F.L.CUP

DATE	OPPONENTS		V	F.T.	SCORERS	Wallington	Whitworth	Rofe	Kember	Blockley	Woollett	Weller	Alderson	Worthington	Lee	Garland	Birchenall
Sep 1	Wrexham	(2)	A	0-1		1	2	3	4	5	6		8	9	7	11	10

LEICESTER CITY 1976-77
Back : Kember,Rofe,Earle,Yates,Tomlin,Alderson.
Middle : M.Everitt *(Coach)*,Sims,Wallington,Lee,Jayes,Woollett,G.Preston *(Physiotherapist)*.
Front : Garland,Whitworth,Worthington,Blockley,J.Bloomfield *(Manager)*, Sammels,Birchenall,Weller.

	APP's			GOALS		
	FL	FAC	FLC	FL	FAC	FLC
Mark Wallington	42	1	1			
Steve Whitworth	42	1	1			
Dennis Rofe	42	1	1	1		
Steve Kember	40	1	1	2		
Jeff Blockley	21	1	1			
Alan Woollett	30		1			
Keith Weller	30	1		4		
Brian Alderson	37	1	1	5		
Frank Worthington	41	1	1	14 (2p)		
Bob Lee	4/2		1			
Chris Garland	14/1		1	3		
Alan Birchenall	11/6		1			
Steve Earle	29/4	1		13		
Jon Sammels	34	1		3 (1p)		
Steve Sims	32		1	1		
Steve Yates	1/3					
Winston White	4					
Larry May	1					
Steve Bicknell	6/1					
Peter Welsh	1					

1977-78 LEAGUE DIVISION ONE
Final Position : 22nd
Ave. Home League Att: 17,768

DATE	OPPONENTS	V	F.T.	SCORERS
Aug 20	Manchester City	A	0-0	
24	West Ham United	H	1-0	Kember
27	Bristol City	H	0-0	
Sep 3	Queens Park Rangers	A	0-3	
10	Everton	H	1-5	Sims
17	Arsenal	A	1-2	Worthington
24	Nottingham Forest	H	0-3	
Oct 1	Wolverhampton Wanderers	A	0-3	
5	Chelsea	A	0-0	
8	Aston Villa	H	0-2	
15	Coventry City	H	1-2	Sammels (pen)
22	Norwich City	A	0-2	
29	Leeds United	H	0-0	
Nov 5	West Bromwich Albion	A	0-2	
12	Ipswich Town	H	2-1	Williams, Salmons
19	Birmingham City	A	1-1	Waddle
26	Liverpool	H	0-4	
Dec 3	Newcastle United	A	0-2	
10	Derby County	H	1-1	Kelly
17	Ipswich Town	A	0-1	
26	Middlesbrough	H	0-0	
27	Manchester United	A	1-3	Goodwin
31	West Ham United	A	2-3	Kember, Sims
Jan 2	Manchester City	H	0-1	
14	Bristol City	A	0-0	
21	Queens Park Rangers	H	0-0	
Feb 4	Everton	A	0-2	
11	Arsenal	H	1-1	Williams
25	Wolverhampton Wanderers	H	1-0	Goodwin
Mar 4	Aston Villa	A	0-0	
11	Coventry City	A	0-1	
14	Nottingham Forest	A	0-1	
18	Norwich City	H	2-2	Williams, Davies
25	Manchester United	H	2-3	Smith, Salmons
27	Middlesbrough	A	1-0	Hughes
28	Leeds United	A	1-5	Davies (pen)
Apr 1	West Bromwich Albion	H	0-1	
8	Liverpool	A	2-3	Hughes (pen), White
15	Birmingham City	H	1-4	Salmons
22	Derby County	A	1-4	Davies
26	Chelsea	H	0-2	
29	Newcastle United	H	3-0	Goodwin, Davies, Salmons

F.A. CUP

DATE	OPPONENTS		V	F.T.	SCORERS
Jan 7	Hull City	(3)	A	1-0	Armstrong
28	Walsall	(4)	A	0-1	

F.L.CUP

DATE	OPPONENTS		V	F.T.	SCORERS
Aug 30	Portsmouth	(2)	A	0-2	

LEICESTER CITY 1977-78
Back : Alderson, Bicknell, Earle, Williams, Kelly, Kember, White.
Middle : I.MacFarlane (*Assistant Manager*), Welsh, Wallington, Sims, May, Jayes, Yates, J.Peacock (*Physiotherapist*).
Front : Sammels, Worthington, Blockley, J.Smith (*Secretary*), F.McLintock (*Manager*), Rofe, Whitworth, Weller, Woollett.

	APP's			GOALS		
	FL	FAC	FLC	FL	FAC	FLC
Mark Wallington	42	2	1			
Steve Whitworth	34/1		1			
Dennis Rofe	33	2	1			
Eddie Kelly	24	2	1	1		
Steve Sims	28/1	2	1	2		
Alan Woollett	12		1			
Brian Alderson	13/1					
Steve Kember	26/1	1	1	2		
Frank Worthington	7		1	1		
Jon Sammels	19/2	1	1	1(1p)		
Steve Earle	6/2					
Jeff Blockley	7/1		-/1			
Keith Weller	23/1	2	1			
Larry May	3/2					
Dean Smith	8/2			1		
Lammie Robertson	6/1					
Alan Waddle	11			1		
George Armstrong	11/1	1			1	
Dave Webb	29/1	2				
Tommy Williams	31/1	2		3		
Geoff Salmons	25/1	2		4		
Winston White	5/1			1		
Roger Davies	14/4	2		4(1p)		
Mark Goodwin	14			3		
Kevin Farmer	1					
Billy Hughes	18	1		2(1p)		
Nev Hamilton	4					
Trevor Christie	5					
Derek Dawkins	3					

1978-79 LEAGUE DIVISION TWO
Final Position : 17th
Ave. Home League Att: 14,187

Player columns (left to right): Wallington, Whitworth, Rofe, Kelly, O'Neill, Webb, Armstrong, Williams, Davies, Hughes, Christie, Goodwin, Kember, May, Sims, Weller, Duffy, White, Welsh, Henderson, Ridley, Reed, Lineker, Buchanan, Smith, Peake, Grewcock, Carr, Lee

DATE	OPPONENTS	V	F.T.	SCORERS
Aug 19	Burnley	A	2-2	Hughes (pen),Christie
23	Sheffield United	H	0-1	
26	Cambridge United	H	1-1	Christie
Sep 2	Wrexham	A	0-0	
9	Notts County	H	0-1	
16	Blackburn Rovers	A	1-1	Weller
23	Brighton & Hove Albion	H	4-1	Christie,Hughes 2 (1pen),Weller
30	Orient	A	1-0	Christie
Oct 7	Newcastle United	A	0-1	
14	Charlton Athletic	H	0-3	
21	Cardiff City	A	0-1	
28	Bristol Rovers	H	0-0	
Nov 4	Luton Town	A	1-0	Christie
11	Burnley	H	2-1	Weller,Christie
18	Cambridge United	A	1-1	Henderson
22	Wrexham	H	1-1	Christie
25	West Ham United	H	1-2	Christie
Dec 2	Stoke City	A	0-0	
16	Crystal Palace	A	1-3	May
23	Preston North End	H	1-1	Davies
26	Sunderland	A	1-1	Henderson
Jan 1	Oldham Athletic	H	2-0	Buchanan,Smith
20	Blackburn Rovers	H	1-1	May
Feb 3	Brighton & Hove Albion	A	1-3	Davies
10	Orient	H	5-3	Smith,Buchanan,May,Williams,Goodwin
17	Newcastle United	H	2-1	Peake,Buchanan
24	Charlton Athletic	A	0-1	
Mar 3	Cardiff City	H	1-2	Grewcock
10	Bristol Rovers	A	1-1	Smith (pen)
21	Fulham	H	1-0	Buchanan
28	Luton Town	H	3-0	May,Smith,Williams
31	West Ham United	A	1-1	Henderson
Apr 4	Millwall	A	0-2	
7	Stoke City	H	1-1	Buchanan
14	Sunderland	H	1-2	Henderson
16	Oldham Athletic	A	1-2	Smith
17	Preston North End	A	0-4	
20	Crystal Palace	H	1-1	Smith
24	Notts County	A	1-0	Lineker
28	Fulham	A	0-3	
May 5	Millwall	H	0-0	
8	Sheffield United	A	2-2	Peake,Duffy

F.A. CUP

Jan 6	Norwich City	(3) H	3-0	May,Weller,Henderson
Feb 26	Oldham Athletic	(4) A	1-3	Henderson

F.L.CUP

Aug 30	Derby County	(2) H	0-1	

LEICESTER CITY 1978-79
Back : Christie,Davies,Wallington,May,Rafter,Sims,Farmer.
Middle : J.Wallace (Manager), Kelly,Webb,Salmons,Dawkins,Hughes,Whitworth,Williams,
I.MacFarlane (Assistant Manager).
Front : Armstrong,Hamilton,Rofe,White,Convey,Reed,Goodwin.

	APP's			GOALS		
	FL	FAC	FLC	FL	FAC	FLC
Mark Wallington	42	2	1			
Steve Whitworth	29	2	1			
Dennis Rofe	39	2	1			
Eddie Kelly	27	-/1	1			
John O'Neill	23	2				
Dave Webb	3					
George Armstrong	3		1			
Tommy Williams	32/3	2	1	2		
Roger Davies	8		-/1	2		
Billy Hughes	18/1		1	3 (2p)		
Trevor Christie	23/3		1	8		
Mark Goodwin	23/5	2	1	1		
Steve Kember	8/1					
Larry May	36	2	1	4	1	
Steve Sims	8		1			
Keith Weller	16	1		3	1	
Mick Duffy	7/4			1		
Winston White	1/1					
Peter Welsh	4/2					
Martin Henderson	31/2	2		4	2	
John Ridley	17/7	2				
Kevin Reed	-/1					
Gary Lineker	7			1		
Dave Buchanan	17/2	2		5		
Bobby Smith	17	1		6 (1p)		
Andy Peake	17/1	1		2		
Neil Grewcock	1			1		
Everton Carr	2/1					
Alan Lee	3					

1979-80

LEAGUE DIVISION TWO
Final Position : 1st
Ave. Home League Att: 18,636

DATE	OPPONENTS	V	F.T.	SCORERS	Wallington	Williams	Carr	Stevens	May	Wilson	Byrne	Kelly	Young	Henderson	Smith	Rofe	Peake	Goodwin	Lee	O'Neill	Strickland	Welsh	Lineker	Duffy	Buchanan	Scott	Edmunds
Aug 18	Watford	H	2-0	Young 2	1	2		4	5	6	7	8*	9	10	11	3	12										
21	Cambridge United	A	1-1	Young	1	2		4	5	6*	7		9	10		3	8	12	11								
25	Queens Park Rangers	A	4-1	Peake 2,May,Goodwin	1	2		4	5		7	6	9	10		3	8	12	11*								
Sep 1	Luton Town	H	1-3	May	1	2		4	5		7	6	10	9		3	8	12	11*								
8	Notts County	H	1-0	Young	1	2			5		7	10	9	8	11	3*	4	12		6							
15	Newcastle United	A	2-3	Smith 2 (1pen)	1	2			5		7	10	9	8*	11	3	4	12		6							
22	Fulham	H	3-3	Young 2,Smith	1				5		7*	10	9	8	11	3	4	2		6	12						
29	Swansea City	A	2-0	Rofe 2	1	2			5		7	10	9	8*	11	3	4	12		6							
Oct 6	Shrewsbury Town	A	2-2	Goodwin,Byrne	1	2			5	10	7		9		11	3	6	8		4							
10	Cambridge United	H	2-1	Young,Wilson	1	2			5	10	7		9	12	11	3	4	8*		6							
13	West Ham United	H	1-2	Williams	1	2			5	10	7*		9	8	11	3	4						6	12			
20	Oldham Athletic	A	1-1	Young	1	2			5	8*	7		9	11		3	6						4	12			
27	Sunderland	H	2-1	Lineker 2	1	2			5			10	9	8	11	3	4						6	7			
Nov 3	Watford	A	3-1	Smith 2 (1pen),Peake	1	2			5			10	9*	8	11	3	4						6	7	12		
10	Burnley	H	1-1	Young	1	2		4				8*	9	11	10	3	6	12	5				7				
17	Preston North End	A	1-1	Lineker	1	2			5	12		8*	9	11	10	3	6		4				7				
24	Wrexham	H	2-0	Strickland,Henderson	1	2		4		12		8	9*	11		3				5	6		7				
Dec 1	Birmingham City	A	2-1	Smith,Henderson	1	2			5			4	9	8	11	3				6	10*	12	7				
8	Orient	H	2-2	Henderson,Goodwin	1	2			5	10*			9	8	11	3		12		6			4	7			
15	Charlton Athletic	A	0-2		1	2			5			10	9	8	11	3	4			6			7				
21	Cardiff City	H	0-0		1	2			5			10	9	8	11	3	4*	12		6			7				
26	Chelsea	A	0-1		1	2			5	12	7*	10	9	8	11	3	4			6							
29	Queens Park Rangers	H	2-0	Rofe,Henderson	1	2			5	12	7	10	9	8	11*	3	4			6							
Jan 1	Bristol Rovers	H	3-0	Smith 2,Goodwin	1	2			5		7	10	9	8	11	3	4			6							
12	Luton Town	A	0-0		1	2			5		7	10*	9	8	11		4			6	12	3					
19	Notts County	A	1-0	Strickland	1				5	10		4	9		11		2			6	8*	3	7	12			
Feb 2	Newcastle United	H	1-0	Smith (pen)	1	2			5	10		4	9	8*	11	3				6	12		7				
9	Fulham	H	0-0		1	2			5	10		4	9	8	11	3				6	12		7*				
20	Swansea City	H	1-1	Henderson	1	2			5	10		4	9	8	11					6	7*		12	3			
23	West Ham United	A	1-3	Young	1	2			5			4	9	8	11	10	7			6			3				
Mar 1	Oldham Athletic	H	0-1		1	2			5	12		8	9	10	11		7	4*		6			3				
8	Sunderland	A	0-0		1	2			5			10	9*	11			4	12		6			8			3	7
15	Shrewsbury Town	H	2-0	Young,Edmunds	1	2			5			10	9*	11			4	8		6			12			3	7
22	Burnley	A	2-1	Edmunds,Young	1	2			5			8	9	10			4	7		6						3	11
29	Preston North End	H	1-2	Kelly	1	2			5	12		10*	9	11			4	8		6						3	7
Apr 5	Chelsea	H	1-0	May	1	2			5	11		10	9			3	4*	12		6			8			7	
8	Cardiff City	A	1-0	Smith	1	2			5	11		4	9			3		8		6			10			7	
12	Birmingham City	H	2-1	Wilson,Young	1	2			5	10	7	4	9*	12	11			8		6						3	
19	Wrexham	A	1-0	Kelly	1	2			5	10	12	4	9		11			8		6						3	7*
23	Bristol Rovers	A	1-1	Smith	1	2			5	10	7*	4	9	12	11			8		6						3	
26	Charlton Athletic	H	2-1	Young,Smith	1	2			5	10	12	4	9		11			8		6			3			7*	
May 3	Orient	A	1-0	May	1	2			5	10	7	4	9	12	11			8*		6						3	

F.A. CUP

					Wallington	Williams	Carr	Stevens	May	Wilson	Byrne	Kelly	Young	Henderson	Smith	Rofe	Peake	Goodwin	Lee	O'Neill	Strickland	Welsh	Lineker	Duffy	Buchanan	Scott	Edmunds
Jan 5	Harlow Town (3)	H	1-1	Henderson	1	2			5		7	10	9	8	11	3	4			6							
8	Harlow Town (3 rep)	A	0-1		1	2			5			10	9	8	11	3	4			6			7				

F.L. CUP

					Wallington	Williams	Carr	Stevens	May	Wilson	Byrne	Kelly	Young	Henderson	Smith	Rofe	Peake	Goodwin	Lee	O'Neill	Strickland	Welsh	Lineker	Duffy	Buchanan	Scott	Edmunds
Aug 11	Rotherham United (1 leg 1)	H	1-2	Young	1	2	3	4	5	6	7	8	9	10	11												
14	Rotherham United (1 leg 2)	A	0-3		1	2		4	5	6	7	8	9	10	11	3											

LEICESTER CITY 1979-80

Back : Edmunds,Hughes,Lee,Stevens,O'Neill,Byrne,Grewcock,Buchanan.
Middle : I.MacFarlane *(Assistant Manager)*, Welsh,May,Ridley,Humphries,Wallington,Henderson, Young,Williams,J.Wallace *(Manager)*.
Front : Lineker,Duffy,Smith,Kelly,Rofe,Peake,Goodwin,Wilson.

	APP's			GOALS		
	FL	FAC	FLC	FL	FAC	FLC
Mark Wallington	42	2	2			
Tommy Williams	40	2	2	1		
Everton Carr			1			
Gregor Stevens	4		2			
Larry May	42	2	2	4		
Ian Wilson	18/6		2	2		
Pat Byrne	21/2	1	2	1		
Eddie Kelly	34	2	2	2		
Alan Young	42	2	2	14		
Martin Henderson	32/4	2	2	5	1	
Bobby Smith	35	2	2	12 (3p)		
Dennis Rofe	26	2	1	3		
Andy Peake	24/1			3		
Mark Goodwin	19/11	2		4		
Alan Lee	3					
John O'Neill	33	2				
Derek Strickland	4/3			2		
Peter Welsh	9/2					
Gary Lineker	16/3	1		3		
Mick Duffy	-/1					
Dave Buchanan	-/2					
Geoff Scott	11					
Paul Edmunds	7			2		

1980-81

LEAGUE DIVISION ONE
Final Position : 21st
Ave. Home League Att: 19,476

DATE	OPPONENTS	V	F.T.	SCORERS	Wallington	Williams	Gibson	Peake	May	O'Neill	Edmunds	Melrose	Young	Wilson	Smith	Henderson	Goodwin	Carr	Grewcock	Welsh	Scott	Buchanan	Lineker	Byrne	Hamill	MacDonald	Friar	Lynex	Ramsey	Leet
Aug 16	Ipswich Town	H	0-1		1	2	3	4	5	6	7*	8	9	10	11	12														
19	Everton	A	0-1		1	2	3	4	5	6		8	9	10	11	7														
23	Liverpool	H	2-0	Peake,Henderson	1	2	3	4	5	6		8*	9	10	11	12	7													
30	Leeds United	A	2-1	O'Neill,Henderson	1	2	3	4	5	6		8*	9	10		11	7	12												
Sep 6	Sunderland	H	0-1		1	2	3		5	6		12	9	10	8	11	4		7*											
13	Manchester United	A	0-5		1	2	3		5	6		12	9	10	11	8	4		7*											
20	Nottingham Forest	A	0-5		1	2	3		5	6*			9	10	8		4		7	12										
27	Tottenham Hotspur	H	2-1	Smith,Buchanan	1	4	3		5				9	10	8	7		2*				12	6	11						
Oct 4	Arsenal	A	0-1		1	4	3		5				9	10	8	7		2					6	11						
8	Stoke City	H	1-1	Wilson	1	2	3		5			12	10	11	9	4						6	8*	7						
11	Coventry City	H	1-3	Lineker	1	2	3		5			12	10	11	9	4						6	8*	7						
18	Crystal Palace	A	1-2	Young	1	2			5			12	9	10	11	8	7*	3				6	4							
21	Middlesbrough	A	0-1		1	2			5			7	9	10	11	8		2				6								
25	Wolverhampton Wanderers	H	2-0	Henderson,Young	1	4	3		5			7	9	10	11	8*		2				6	12							
Nov 1	Aston Villa	A	0-2		1	4	3		5			7	9	10	11	8		2				6								
8	Manchester City	H	1-1	Young	1	11		4	5	6			9	10		12		2				3		8		7*				
12	Everton	H	0-1		1	11		4	5	6			9	10		12		2				3		8		7*				
15	Ipswich Town	H	1-3	Williams	1	11		4	5	6			9	10		12		2				3		8*		7				
22	West Bromwich Albion	A	1-3	Lineker	1	11		4	5	6			9	10		12		2*				3		8		7				
29	Norwich City	H	1-2	Young	1	2	3	4		6		8	9	10	11						5					7*	12			
Dec 6	Birmingham City	A	2-1	Melrose 2	1	2	3	4		6		8	9*	10						12	5					7	11			
13	Middlesbrough	H	1-0	MacDonald (pen)	1	2	3	4				8		10			12				5	9				7*	11			
20	Stoke City	A	0-1		1	2	3	4		6		8		10			12				5					7*	11			
26	Brighton & Hove Albion	H	0-1		1	2	3	4		6		8	9	10		7*				12	5						11			
27	Southampton	A	0-4		1	2		4		6		8	9	10		7				3	5						11			
Jan 10	West Bromwich Albion	H	0-2		1	2	3	4*		6			9		10		12				5	8	7				11			
17	Leeds United	H	0-1		1	4		7*		6		12		10	11	9	2				5	8				3				
31	Liverpool	A	2-1	Byrne,Melrose	1	2		4	5	6		8	9	10		12							7*	11		3				
Feb 7	Manchester United	H	1-0	Melrose	1	2		4	5	6		8	9	10		12							7	11*		3				
14	Sunderland	A	0-1		1	2		4*	5			8	9	10									7			12	3	11		
21	Tottenham Hotspur	A	2-1	Lynex,Byrne	1	2		4	5	6		8*	9	10									12	11			3	7		
28	Nottingham Forest	H	1-1	Lynex	1	2		4	5	6		8	9	10									12	11			3	7*		
Mar 7	Arsenal	H	1-0	Williams	1	2		4	5	6		8*	9	10									7	11			3		12	
14	Coventry City	A	1-4	Young	1	2		4	5	6		8	9	10										11			3	7		
21	Crystal Palace	H	1-1	O'Neill	1	2			5	6		8	9	10*	12							4		11			3	7		
28	Wolverhampton Wanderers	A	1-0	Melrose	1	2			5	6*		8	9	10	12							4		11			3	7		
31	Manchester City	A	3-3	Williams,Young,Melrose	1	2			5			8	9	10					11	6		4*		12			3	7		
Apr 4	Aston Villa	H	2-4	Lynex 2 (1pen)	1	2			5			8	9	10					11	6		4					3	7		
18	Southampton	H	2-2	Young,Lynex (pen)	1	2			5	6		8*	9	10	11							4				12	3	7		
20	Brighton & Hove Albion	A	1-2	MacDonald	1	2			5	6		8	9	10						11*		12				4	3	7		
25	Birmingham City	H	1-0	Williams	1	2		4	5	6		8*		10		11						9					3	7	12	
May 2	Norwich City	A	3-2	Melrose 3	1	2			5	6		8	9	10		12										11		7	4	3*

F.A. CUP

DATE	OPPONENTS		V	F.T.	SCORERS	Wallington	Williams	Gibson	Peake	May	O'Neill	Edmunds	Melrose	Young	Wilson	Smith	Henderson	Goodwin	Carr	Grewcock	Welsh	Scott	Buchanan	Lineker	Byrne	Hamill	MacDonald	Friar	Lynex	Ramsey	Leet
Jan 3	Cardiff City	(3)	H	3-0	Lineker,Buchanan,Melrose	1	2	3	4		6		12	9	10							5	8*	7			11				
24	Exeter City	(4)	H	1-1	Henderson	1	2			5	6		7*	9	10	11	8					3	12	4							
28	Exeter City	(4rep)	A	1-3	Melrose	1	2		4*	5	6		8	9	10		12										7	11	3		

F.L.CUP

DATE	OPPONENTS		V	F.T.	SCORERS	Wallington	Williams	Gibson	Peake	May	O'Neill	Edmunds	Melrose	Young	Wilson	Smith	Henderson	Goodwin	Carr	Grewcock	Welsh	Scott	Buchanan	Lineker	Byrne	Hamill	MacDonald	Friar	Lynex	Ramsey	Leet
Aug 26	West Brom.Albion	(2 leg 1)	A	0-1		1		3	4	5	6		8	9	10	11*	12	7	2												
Sep 3	West Brom.Albion	(2 leg 2)	H	0-1		1	2	3	4*	5	6		8	9	10		11	7			12										

	APP's			GOALS		
	FL	FAC	FLC	FL	FAC	FLC
Mark Wallington	42	3	2			
Tommy Williams	42	3	1	4		
Willie Gibson	20	1	2			
Andy Peake	24	2	2	1		
Larry May	34	2	2			
John O'Neill	32	3	2	2		
Paul Edmunds	1					
Jim Melrose	28/4	2/1	2	9	2	
Alan Young	36/2	3	2	7		
Ian Wilson	40	3	2	1		
Bobby Smith	17/2	1	1	1		
Martin Henderson	16/6	1	1/1	3	1	
Mark Goodwin	13/6	-/1	2			
Everton Carr	9		1			
Neil Grewcock	6/1		-/1			
Peter Welsh	3/4					
Geoff Scott	21	2				
Dave Buchanan	6/1	1/1		1	1	
Gary Lineker	9	1		2	1	
Pat Byrne	10/3	2		2		
Stewart Hamill	8					
Kevin MacDonald	16/4	2		2 (1p)		
Paul Friar	15	1				
Steve Lynex	12			5 (2p)		
Paul Ramsey	1/2					
Norman Leet	1					

LEICESTER CITY 1980-81

Back : I.MacFarlane (*Assistant Manager*), Grewcock,Gibson,Welsh,May,Young,Wallington,Humphries,
Henderson,O'Neill,Scott,MacDonald,Lineker,J.Wallace (*Manager*).
Front : Strickland,Byrne,Buchanan,Peake,Lee,Williams,Melrose,Carr,Smith,Wilson,Goodwin,Edmunds.

1981-82

LEAGUE DIVISION TWO
Final Position : 8th
Ave. Home League Att: 14,183

DATE	OPPONENTS	V	F.T.	SCORERS	Wallington	Williams	Gibson	Peake	May	O'Neill	Lynex	Melrose	Lineker	Wilson	MacDonald	Smith	Hamill	Young	Robson	Ramsey	Leet	Scott	Welsh
Aug 29	Grimsby Town	A	2-2	Lineker,Melrose	1	2	3	4*	5	6	7	8	9	10	11	12							
Sep 5	Wrexham	H	1-0	Hamill	1	2	3	4	5	6	7	8*	9	10	12		11						
8	Barnsley	H	1-0	Hamill	1	2	3	4	5	6	7	8	9	10			11						
12	Derby County	A	1-3	Melrose	1	2	3	4	5	6	7	8	12	10				9*	11				
19	Luton Town	H	1-2	Lynex (pen)	1	2	3	4	5	6	7	8	9	10					11				
22	Rotherham United	A	1-1	May	1	2	3	4	5	6	7	8		10				9	11				
26	Blackburn Rovers	A	1-1	May,Melrose	1	2	3		5	6	7	8						9		4			
Oct 3	Crystal Palace	H	1-1	Lineker	1	2			5	6	7	8	12	10*	11			9		4			
10	Bolton Wanderers	A	3-0	Melrose 2,Young	1	2				6	12	8	7		11			9	10	4*	3	5	
16	Chelsea	H	1-1	Melrose	1	2				6		8	7		10			9	11	4	3	5	
24	Queens Park Rangers	A	0-2		1	2				6	12	8	7		10			9*	11	4	3	5	
31	Sheffield Wednesday	H	0-0		1	2				6		7	8	9	10	4			11		3	5	
Nov 7	Charlton Athletic	A	4-1	Melrose,Lynex (pen),Lineker 2	1	2				6	7	8	9	10	4				11*		3	5	12
14	Orient	H	0-1		1	2				6	7	8*	9	10	4	11					3	5	12
21	Cardiff City	A	1-3	Welsh	1	2		4		6	7		9	10	11	8					5	3	
28	Cambridge United	H	4-1	Lynex,Hebberd,Peake,Lineker	1	2		4	5	6	7		9	10	11*	12		3					8
Dec 5	Norwich City	A	0-0		1	2		4	5	6	7		9	10				3			8	11	
12	Watford	H	1-1	Lineker	1	2		4	5	6	7		9	10				3			8	11	
28	Oldham Athletic	A	1-1	Lynex	1	2			5	6	7		8	10				9			11	4	
Jan 30	Luton Town	A	1-2	Lineker	1	2		4	5	6	7	12	8	10				9	11*			3	
Feb 6	Derby County	H	2-1	Lynex (pen),Lineker	1	2		4	5	6	7	12	8	10				9			11*	3	
20	Blackburn Rovers	H	1-0	Peake	1	2		4	5	6	7*	12	8	10				9			11	3	
27	Bolton Wanderers	A	1-0	Lynex (pen)	1	2		4	5	6	7	12	8	10				9*			11	3	
Mar 2	Newcastle United	H	3-0	Young,Lineker 2	1	2		4	5	6	7	12	8	10				9			11*	3	
9	Chelsea	A	1-4	Lynex		2		4	5	6	7	12	8	10*				9			11	3	1
13	Queens Park Rangers	H	3-2	Lynex (pen),Young,Melrose		2		4	5	6	7	12	8	10				9*			11	3	1
17	Rotherham United	H	1-0	Melrose		2		4	5	6	7*	9	8	10	11				12			3	1
20	Sheffield Wednesday	A	0-2			2		4	5	6	7*	9	8	10	11			9				3	1
23	Crystal Palace	A	2-0	Lynex,Lineker		2		4	5		7*	12	8	10	11			9		6		3	1
27	Charlton Athletic	H	3-1	Young 2,MacDonald		2		4	5	6*	7	12	8	10	11			9				3	1
30	Shrewsbury Town	A	1-1	Lineker	1	2		4	5	6	7	12	8	10				9*			11	3	
Apr 10	Newcastle United	A	0-0		1			4	5	6	7	9*	8	10	11				3		12	2	
13	Oldham Athletic	H	2-1	Melrose,Lineker	1			4	5	6	7	9*	8	10	11				3		12	2	
17	Cardiff City	H	3-1	Lineker 2,Lynex	1				5	6	7		8	10*	11			9	4	3	12	2	
20	Wrexham	A	0-0		1				5	6	9		8	10*	4				7	3	12	11	2
24	Cambridge United	A	2-1	Lineker,Welsh	1			4	5	6	7	9	8						3		10	11	2
May 1	Norwich City	H	1-4	May	1			4	5	6	7	9	8						3		10	11	2
4	Barnsley	A	2-0	Welsh,Lineker	1			4	5	6	7	9	8		11				10		12	2*	3
8	Watford	A	1-3	Melrose	1			4	5	6	2	7	8*		11			9	10		12		3
12	Grimsby Town	H	1-2	Welsh (pen)	1			4	5	6	12	7	8	10*	11			9			2		3
15	Shrewsbury Town	H	0-0		1			4	5	6	12	7*	8	10	11			9			2		3
18	Orient	A	0-3		1			4		6	7	8		10*	11			9		5	2		3

F.A. CUP

DATE	OPPONENTS		V	F.T.	SCORERS	Wallington	Williams	Gibson	Peake	May	O'Neill	Lynex	Melrose	Lineker	Wilson	MacDonald	Smith	Hamill	Young	Robson	Ramsey	Leet	Scott	Welsh
Jan 2	Southampton	(3)	H	3-1	Young 2,Lineker	1	2		4	5	6	7	12	8	10				9*				11	3
23	Hereford United	(4)	A	1-0	May	1	2		4	5	6	7	12	8	10				9	11*				3
Feb 13	Watford	(5)	H	2-0	O'Neill,Terry (og)	1	2		4	5	6	7*	12	8	10				9				11	3
Mar 6	Shrewsbury Town	(6)	H	5-2	May,Melrose 2,Lineker,Cross (og)	1*	2		4	5	6	7	12	8	10				9				11	3
Apr 3	Tottenham Hotspur	(sf)		0-2	*(at Villa Park,Birmingham)*	1	2		4	5	6	7	12	8	10				9*				11	3

F.L. CUP

DATE	OPPONENTS		V	F.T.	SCORERS	Wallington	Williams	Gibson	Peake	May	O'Neill	Lynex	Melrose	Lineker	Wilson	MacDonald	Smith	Hamill	Young	Robson	Ramsey	Leet	Scott	Welsh
Oct 6	Preston North End (2 leg 1)		A	0-1		1	2	3		5	6	7	8			11	10		9		4			
28	Preston North End (2 leg 2)		H	4-0	Robson,Lynex,Melrose,O'Riordan (og)	1	2		12		6	7	8	9	10*	4				11		3	5	
Nov 11	Aston Villa	(3)	H	0-0		1	2				6	7	8	9	10	4	11					3	5	
25	Aston Villa	(3 rep)	A	0-2		1	2		4		6	7	8	9	10	11	12					3*	5	

LEICESTER CITY 1981-82

Back : Lineker,Peake,Williams,O'Neill,MacDonald,Henderson,Gibson.
Middle : Ramsey,Scott,Young,May,Walker,Wallington,Leet,Welsh,Hamill.
Front : I.MacFarlane *(Assistant Manager)*, Grewcock,Buchanan,Lynex,Melrose,Wilson, Smith,Friar,J.Wallace *(Manager)*.

	APP's			GOALS		
	FL	FAC	FLC	FL	FAC	FLC
Mark Wallington	36	5	4			
Tommy Williams	31	5	4			
Willie Gibson	8		1			
Andy Peake	31	5	1/1	2		
Larry May	34	5	1	3	2	
John O'Neill	41	5	4		1	
Steve Lynex	37/4	5	4	10 (5p)		1
Jim Melrose	24/11	-/5	4	11	2	1
Gary Lineker	37/2	5	3	17	2	
Ian Wilson	35	5	3			
Kevin MacDonald	24/1		4	1		
Bobby Smith	2/2		2/1			
Stewart Hamill	2			2		
Alan Young	24	5	1	5	2	
Keith Robson	8	1	1			1
Paul Ramsey	10		1			
Norman Leet	17		3			
Geoff Scott	7		3			
Peter Welsh	7/9			4 (1p)		
Trevor Hebberd	4			1		
Eddie Kelly	14	4				
Paul Friar	23	5				
Nicky Walker	6					
Dave Buchanan	-/1					
Own Goals					2	1

1982-83

LEAGUE DIVISION TWO
Final Position : 3rd
Ave. Home League Att: 12,819

DATE	OPPONENTS	V	F.T.	SCORERS
Aug 28	Charlton Athletic	H	1-2	R.Smith
31	Rotherham United	A	3-1	Melrose,A.Smith,Lineker
Sep 4	Chelsea	A	1-1	Lineker
8	Leeds United	H	0-1	
11	Carlisle United	H	6-0	Lynex 3 (2 pen),Lineker 3 (1pen)
18	Blackburn Rovers	A	1-3	A.Smith
25	Queens Park Rangers	H	0-1	
Oct 2	Shrewsbury Town	A	2-0	MacDonald,O'Neill
9	Grimsby Town	H	2-0	Lynex,Lineker
16	Wolverhampton Wanderers	A	3-0	Wilson,Lineker,English
23	Derby County	A	4-0	Lineker 3,A.Smith
30	Sheffield Wednesday	H	0-2	
Nov 6	Cambridge United	A	1-3	Lineker
13	Newcastle United	H	2-2	English,Lineker
20	Crystal Palace	H	0-1	
27	Bolton Wanderers	A	1-3	Wilson
Dec 4	Fulham	H	2-0	Buchanan,Lineker
11	Burnley	A	4-2	Lineker,Lynex (pen),A.Smith 2
18	Oldham Athletic	H	2-1	MacDonald (pen),A.Smith
27	Middlesbrough	A	1-1	Lineker
28	Barnsley	H	1-0	A.Smith
Jan 1	Crystal Palace	A	0-1	
3	Chelsea	H	3-0	Lineker 2,A.Smith
15	Charlton Athletic	A	1-2	Wilson
22	Blackburn Rovers	H	0-1	
Feb 5	Carlisle United	A	1-0	MacDonald
19	Grimsby Town	A	0-2	
22	Shrewsbury Town	H	3-2	Lineker 2,Wilson
26	Wolverhampton Wanderers	H	5-0	Lynex 2,A.Smith,Lineker,Daly
Mar 5	Derby County	H	1-1	Lynex
19	Cambridge United	H	4-0	A.Smith 2,Lynex (pen),Wilson
22	Sheffield Wednesday	A	2-2	MacDonald,A.Smith
26	Newcastle United	A	2-2	Lineker 2
Apr 2	Barnsley	A	2-1	Wilson,English
5	Middlesbrough	H	1-0	O'Neill
9	Queens Park Rangers	A	2-2	Lineker 2
16	Rotherham United	H	3-1	Wilson,Lineker 2
23	Fulham	A	1-0	Wilson
30	Bolton Wanderers	H	0-0	
May 2	Leeds United	A	2-2	A.Smith,May
7	Oldham Athletic	A	2-1	Jones,Ramsey
14	Burnley	H	0-0	

F.A. CUP

DATE	OPPONENTS		V	F.T.	SCORERS
Jan 8	Notts County	(3)	H	2-3	A.Smith,Wilson

F.L.CUP

DATE	OPPONENTS		V	F.T.	SCORERS
Oct 6	Lincoln City	(2 leg 1)	A	0-2	
27	Lincoln City	(2 leg 2)	H	0-1	

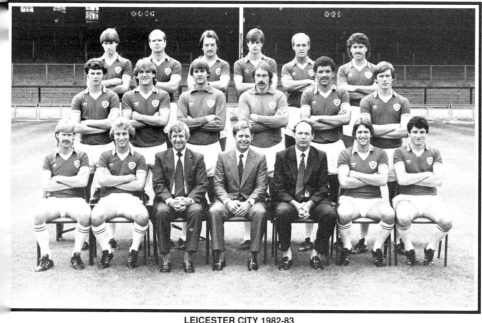

LEICESTER CITY 1982-83
Back : Friar,Kelly,Lynex,Melrose,Wilson,Smith.
Middle : MacDonald,Young,Walker,Wallington,May,O'Neill.
Front : Williams,Peake, J.McVey *(Physiotherapist),* G.Milne *(Manager),*
I.MacFarlane *(Assistant Manager),* Lineker,Ramsey.

	APP's			GOALS		
	FL	FAC	FLC	FL	FAC	FLC
Mark Wallington	42	1	2			
Paul Ramsey	40	1	2	1		
Paul Friar	18/2			1		
Kevin MacDonald	42	1	2	4(1p)		
Larry May	30/5	1	2	1		
John O'Neill	41	1	2	2		
Steve Lynex	34/4	1	2	9(4p)		
Gary Lineker	39/1	1	2	26(1p)		
Alan Smith	35/4	1	1	13	1	
Jim Melrose	5			1		
Bobby Smith	26			1		
Eddie Kelly	20		1			
Tom English	25/3	1	2	3		
Ian Wilson	36	1	2	8	1	
Jimmy Holmes	2					
Dave Buchanan	1/3	1		1		
Norman Leet	1					
Tommy Williams	4					
Paul Brown		1				
Keith Robson	-/1	-/1				
Gerry Daly	17			1		
Andy Peake	2/2					
Robert Jones	2		1			

1983-84

LEAGUE DIVISION ONE
Final Position : 15th
Ave. Home League Att: 14,923

DATE	OPPONENTS	V	F.T.	SCORERS
Aug 27	Notts County	H	0-4	
31	Luton Town	H	0-3	
Sep 3	West Bromwich Albion	A	0-1	
6	West Ham United	A	1-3	Lineker
10	Tottenham Hotspur	H	0-3	
17	Coventry City	A	1-2	Lineker
24	Stoke City	H	2-2	Jones,Lineker
Oct 1	Birmingham City	A	1-2	Lineker
19	Norwich City	A	1-3	Eastoe
22	Ipswich Town	A	0-0	
29	Everton	H	2-0	A.Smith,Ramsey
Nov 5	Watford	A	3-3	Lynex 2 (1pen),Banks
12	Manchester United	H	1-1	Lynex
19	Aston Villa	A	1-3	Lynex (pen)
26	Arsenal	H	3-0	Lineker,Lynex,A.Smith
30	Southampton	H	2-1	A.Smith,Lineker
Dec 4	Nottingham Forest	A	2-3	Jones,A.Smith
10	Wolverhampton Wanderers	H	5-1	Lineker,A.Smith 3,Lynex
18	Sunderland	A	1-1	Hazell
26	Queens Park Rangers	H	2-1	Lineker,Lynex
27	Liverpool	A	2-2	A.Smith,Banks
31	West Bromwich Albion	H	1-1	Lynex (pen)
Jan 2	Stoke City	A	1-0	A.Smith
14	Notts County	A	5-2	MacDonald,Lineker 3,Peake
21	Coventry City	H	1-1	Lineker
Feb 4	Birmingham City	H	2-3	A.Smith 2
11	Tottenham Hotspur	A	2-3	Lineker 2
25	Ipswich Town	H	2-0	A.Smith,O'Neill
Mar 3	Watford	H	4-1	Peake 2,Lineker,A.Smith
10	Manchester United	A	0-2	
17	West Ham United	H	4-1	Hazell,Lynex 2 (2 pen),Lineker
20	Everton	A	1-1	Lineker
24	Luton Town	A	0-0	
31	Norwich City	H	2-1	A.Smith 2
Apr 7	Southampton	A	2-2	Lineker 2
14	Aston Villa	H	2-0	O'Neill,Banks
18	Liverpool	H	3-3	Peake,Lynex,Lineker
21	Queens Park Rangers	A	0-2	
28	Arsenal	A	1-2	Lineker
May 5	Nottingham Forest	H	2-1	Lynex,Lineker
7	Wolverhampton Wanderers	A	0-1	
12	Sunderland	H	0-2	

F.A. CUP

DATE	OPPONENTS		V	F.T.	SCORERS
Jan 7	Crystal Palace	(3)	A	0-1	

F.L.CUP

DATE	OPPONENTS		V	F.T.	SCORERS
Oct 5	Chelsea	(2 leg 1)	H	0-2	
25	Chelsea	(2 leg 2)	A	2-0	A.Smith,English

Note : Oct 25, lost 3-4 on penalties ,English,Hazell,Eastoe scored for Leicester.

LEICESTER CITY 1983-84
Back : Williams,Ramsey,Forster,Grew,Andrews,Wallington,O'Neill,Robson,English.
Middle : D.Richardson *(Youth Team Coach)*, Hutchinson,Kelly,MacDonald,A.Smith,May,Banks,
Rennie,Cliff,J.McVey *(Physiotherapist)*.
Front : Lynex,Peake,Lineker,G.Milne *(Manager)*, G.Summers *(Coach)*, R.Smith,Wilson,Jones.

	APP's			GOALS		
	FL	FAC	FLC	FL	FAC	FL
Mark Grew	5					
Paul Ramsey	33		2	1		
Bobby Smith	35/1	1	1			
Kevin MacDonald	38	1	2	1		
Ian Banks	22/4	1	1	3		
John O'Neill	31	1	1	2		
Steve Lynex	40	1	2	12 (5p)		
Gary Lineker	38/1	1	1	22		
Alan Smith	39/1	1	1/1	15		
Robert Jones	6/2		1	2		
Ian Wilson	41	1	2			
Andy Peake	22/2	1		4		
David Rennie	15		1			
Tom English	4/12	-/1	-/1			
Mark Wallington	35	1	2			
Tommy Williams	21/1		2			
Bob Hazell	27	1	2	2		
Peter Eastoe	5		1	1		
Andy Feeley	2/1					
Ian Andrews	2					
Robert Kelly	1					

1984-85 LEAGUE DIVISION ONE
Final Position : 15th
Ave. Home League Att: 14,530

DATE	OPPONENTS	V	F.T.	SCORERS	Wallington	Feeley	Smith R	Banks	Rennie	O'Neill	Lynex	Lineker	Smith A	Ramsey	Bright	MacDonald	Hazell	Peake	Wilson	Andrews	Williams	Eastoe	Jones
Aug 25	Newcastle United	H	2-3	Lineker 2	1	2	3	4	5	6	7	8	9	10	11								
27	Tottenham Hotspur	A	2-2	A.Smith,Banks	1	2	3	12		6	7	8	9	10*			4	5			11		
Sep 1	Coventry City	A	0-2		1	2	3	12		6	7	8	9	10			4*	5			11		
5	Watford	H	1-1	Lineker	1		3			6	7	8	9	10*	12	2	4	5			11		
8	Ipswich Town	H	2-1	Lineker,Lynex	1	2				6	7	8	9*	10	12	3	4	5			11		
15	Stoke City	A	2-2	Lineker,Lynex (pen)	1	2				6	7	8	9	10		3	4	5			11		
22	West Bromwich Albion	H	2-1	Lynex 2 (1pen)	1	2				6	7	8	9	10	12	3*	4	5			11		
29	Chelsea	A	0-3		1		3	10*		6	7	8		2	9		4	5			11	12	
Oct 6	West Ham United	A	1-3	Lynex	1		3			6	7	8	9	2	12		4	5			11*	10	
13	Arsenal	H	1-4	Anderson (og)	1	2				6	7	8	9	10	12	3	4*	5			11		
20	Sheffield Wednesday	A	0-5		1	2				6	7	8*	9	10	12	3	4	5			11		
27	Aston Villa	H	5-0	Lineker 3,Lynex (pen),Eastoe		2		12		6	7	8		10*			4		3	1	5	9	11
Nov 3	Everton	A	0-3			2				6	7	8		10			4	5	3	1		9	11
10	Manchester United	H	2-3	Banks,Lineker		2		11		6	7	8	12	10			4*	5	3	1		9	
17	Norwich City	H	2-0	Banks,Lynex (pen)		2		4	11	6	7	8	12	10				5	3	1		9*	
25	Nottingham Forest	A	1-2	Banks		2		4	11	6	7	8	12	10				5*	3	1		9	
Dec 1	Queens Park Rangers	H	4-0	Lineker,A.Smith,Lynex,Banks		2		4	11	6	7	8	9	10					3	1	5		
8	Sunderland	A	4-0	A.Smith 2,Lineker,Lynex		2		4	11	6	7	8	9	10					3	1	5		
15	Luton Town	H	2-2	Lynex, A.Smith		2		4	11	6	7		9	10					3	1	5	8	
23	Coventry City	H	5-1	Lynex (pen),Rennie,Lineker 2, A.Smith		2		4	11	6	7	8	9						3	1	5		
26	Liverpool	A	2-1	A.Smith,Lineker		2		4	11	6	7	8	9						3	1	5		
29	Watford	A	1-4	O'Neill		2		4	11	6	7	8	9	10					3	1	5		
Jan 1	Southampton	H	1-2	Banks		2		4	11	6	7	8	9	10					3	1	5		
12	Stoke City	H	0-0			2		4	11	6	7	8	9	10					3	1	5		
Feb 2	Chelsea	H	1-1	Lineker		2		11		6	7	8	9	10				4	3	1	5		
23	Everton	H	1-2	Lynex		2		11		6	7	8	9*	10	12			4	3	1	5		
Mar 2	Aston Villa	A	1-0	A.Smith		2		11		6	7	8	9	10				4	3	1	5		
9	Sheffield Wednesday	H	3-1	Lineker,O'Neill, A.Smith		2		11		6	7	8	9	10*	12			4	3	1	5		
16	Arsenal	A	0-2			2		11		6	7	8	9	10	12			4*	3	1	5		
20	Newcastle United	A	4-1	Banks 2,Lineker, A.Smith		2	4	11		6	7	8	9	10					3	1	5		
23	West Ham United	H	1-0	Lineker		2*	4	11		6	7	8	9	10	12				3	1	5		
30	West Bromwich Albion	A	0-2			2*	4	11		6	7	8	9	10	12				3	1	5		
Apr 3	Manchester United	A	1-2	Lineker		2	4	11		6	7	8	9	10					3	1	5		
6	Liverpool	H	0-1			2	4	11*		6	7	8	9	10	12				3	1	5		
9	Southampton	A	1-3	Lynex (pen)		2	4	11		6	7	8	9	10					3	1	5		
13	Tottenham Hotspur	H	1-2	Peake		2	4			6	7	8	9*	10	12			11	3	1	5		
20	Norwich City	A	3-1	A.Smith 2,Banks		2	4	11		6	7	8	9			10			3	1	5		
23	Ipswich Town	A	0-2			2	4	11		6	7	8	9	12		10*			3	1	5		
27	Nottingham Forest	H	1-0	Lineker		2	4	11		6	7	8	9	10					3	1	5		
May 4	Queens Park Rangers	A	3-4	Lineker 2,Wilson			4	11		6	7	8	9	2		10			3	1	5		
6	Sunderland	H	2-0	Lineker 2		2		11		6	7	8	9	10				4	3	1	5		
11	Luton Town	A	0-4			2*		11		6	7	8	9	10	12			4	3	1	5		

F.A. CUP

DATE	OPPONENTS		V	F.T.	SCORERS	Wallington	Feeley	Smith R	Banks	Rennie	O'Neill	Lynex	Lineker	Smith A	Ramsey	Bright	MacDonald	Hazell	Peake	Wilson	Andrews	Williams
Jan 5	Burton Albion	(3)	A	6-1	Lineker 3, A.Smith 2,Lynex		2	4	11		6	7	8	9	10					3	1	5
16	Burton Albion	(3 rep)		1-0	Ramsey		2	4	11		6	7	8	9	10					3	1	5
26	Carlisle United	(4)	H	1-0	R.Smith		2	4	11		6	7	8	9	10					3	1	5
Feb 19	Millwall	(5)	A	0-2			2	4	11		6	7	8	9	10					3	1	5

F.L.CUP

DATE	OPPONENTS		V	F.T.	SCORERS	Wallington	Feeley	Smith R	Banks	Rennie	O'Neill	Lynex	Lineker	Smith A	Ramsey	Bright	MacDonald	Hazell	Peake	Wilson	Andrews	Williams	Eastoe	Jones
Sep 26	Brentford	(2 leg 1)	H	4-2	O'Neill,Banks,Lynex,Lineker	1		3	10		6	7	8		2	9	4		5			11		
Oct 9	Brentford	(2 leg 2)	A	2-0	Ramsey, A.Smith	1	4	3			6	7*	8	9	2	12			5			11		10
30	Luton Town	(3)	A	1-3	Lineker		2		12		6	7	8	9	10			4		3	1	5	11*	

Notes: 1) Jan 5, drawn away, but played at Baseball Ground, Derby. Subsequently ordered by the F.A. to be replayed behind closed doors.
2) Jan 16, originally scheduled for Derby, but switched to Highfield Road, Coventry by order of the F.A.

	APP's			GOALS		
	FL	FAC	FLC	FL	FAC	FLC
Mark Wallington	11		2			
Andy Feeley	35	4	2			
Bobby Smith	30	4	2		1	
Ian Banks	30/3	4	1/1	9		1
David Rennie	3			1		
John O'Neill	42	4	3	2		1
Steve Lynex	42	4	3	13(6p)	1	1
Gary Lineker	41	4	3	24	3	2
Alan Smith	36/3	4	2	12	2	1
Paul Ramsey	38/1	4	3		1	1
Mark Bright	2/14		1/1			
Kevin MacDonald	13		2			
Bob Hazell	14		2			
Andy Peake	21		2	1		
Ian Wilson	38/1	4	2	1		
Ian Andrews	31	4	1			
Tommy Williams	27	4	1			
Peter Eastoe	6			1		
Robert Jones	2		1			
Own Goals				1		

LEICESTER CITY 1984-85
Back : Kelly, Feeley, Peake, Hazell, A.Smith, O'Neill, Bright, Williams.
Middle : D.Richardson (Youth Team Manager), Banks, Ramsey, MacDonald, Wallington, Andrews, Rennie, Lineker, Jones. J.McVey (Physiotherapist).
Front : Burnside, Lynex, G.Summers (Coach), G.Milne (Manager), R.Smith, Wilson.

1985-86

LEAGUE DIVISION ONE
Final Position : 19th
Ave. Home League Att: 11,792

DATE	OPPONENTS	V	F.T.	SCORERS	Andrews	Ramsey	Smith R	Kelly	Osman	O'Neill	Lynex	Bright	Smith A	Wilson	Banks	Mauchlen	Williams	Jones	Feeley	Sealy	Rennie	McAllister	Morgan	Roberts	Christensen	Cunningham	Venus
Aug 17	Everton	H	3-1	R.Smith,Bright 2	1	2	3	4	5	6	7	8	9	10	11												
21	Manchester City	A	1-1	Wilson	1	2	3	4	5	6	7	8	9	10	11												
24	Oxford United	A	0-5		1	2	3	4	5	6	7	8	9*	10	11	12											
28	Chelsea	H	0-0		1	4	3		5	6	7	8	9	10	11		2										
31	Arsenal	A	0-1		1	4		11	5	6	7	8	9*	10	12	3	2										
Sep 4	Watford	H	2-2	Ramsey,Bright	1	4			5	6	7	8	9*	3	12	10	2	11									
8	Nottingham Forest	H	0-3		1	4			5	6	7	8	12	3	11	10	2	9*									
14	West Ham United	A	0-3		1	4*	3	7	5	6		8	9		11	10	2	12									
21	Birmingham City	A	1-2	Sealy	1	4		11	5*	6		8	9		12	10	2		3	7							
28	Ipswich Town	H	1-0	A.Smith	1	2				6	7		9	12	11	10			5	8*	3	4					
Oct 2	Oxford United	H	4-4	A.Smith,Wilson,McAllister,Lynex (pen)	1	2				6	7	8	9	12	11	10			5			4	3*				
6	Coventry City	A	0-3		1	10			5	6	7	8	9		11				2			4	3				
12	West Bromwich Albion	H	2-2	A.Smith,Lynex (pen)	1				5	6	7	8	9		11	10			2			4	3				
19	Sheffield Wednesday	H	2-3	Lynex, A.Smith	1				5	6	7	8	9	12	11	10*			2			4	3				
26	Tottenham Hotspur	A	3-1	A.Smith,Lynex (pen),Bright	1				5	6	7	8	9		11	10			2			4	3				
Nov 2	Liverpool	A	0-1		1				5	6	7	8	9		11	10			2			4	3				
9	Southampton	H	2-2	A.Smith,Lynex (pen)	1				5	6	7	8*	9		11	10			2			4	3			12	
16	Queens Park Rangers	A	0-2		1				5	6		8	9	12	11	10			2			4	3			7*	
23	Manchester United	H	3-0	McAllister, A.Smith 2	1				5	6	7		9		11	10			2			4	3			8	
30	Newcastle United	A	1-2	A.Smith	1				5	6	7		9		11	10			2			4	3			8	
Dec 7	Manchester City	H	1-1	A.Smith	1				5	6	7		9		11	10			2			4	3			8	
14	Everton	A	2-1	McAllister (pen), A.Smith	1				5	6	7	12	9		11	10			2			4	3			8*	
26	Aston Villa	H	3-1	A.Smith 2,Bright	1				5	6	7	12	9		11	10			2			4	3			8*	
28	Watford	A	1-2	A.Smith	1				5	6	7	8	9		11	10			2			4	3				
Jan 1	Luton Town	A	1-3	Bright	1	11			5	6	12	8	9		7	10			2			4*	3				
11	West Ham United	H	0-1		1	12			5	6	7	8*	9		11	10			2			4	3				
18	Arsenal	H	2-2	Banks,Sealy	1	8			5	6	7		9		11	10*			2	12		4	3				
Feb 1	Chelsea	A	2-2	Mauchlen,Lynex (pen)	1				5	6	7		9	4	11	10			2	8			3				
Mar 8	Coventry City	H	2-1	McAllister, A.Smith	1				5	6	7		9	11*		10			2	8		4	3			12	
12	Birmingham City	H	4-2	McAllister,Sealy, A.Smith,Lynex (pen)	1				5	6	7		9			10			2	8		4	3			11	
15	West Bromwich Albion	A	2-2	Sealy 2	1				5	6	7		9			10			2	8		4	3			11	
18	Sheffield Wednesday	A	0-1		1				5	6	7		9	11		10			2	8		4	3				
22	Nottingham Forest	A	3-4	A.Smith 2,Sealy	1				5	6	7*		9	12		10			2	8		4	3			11	
29	Luton Town	H	0-0		1				5	6	7		9	12		10			2	8		4	3			11*	
31	Aston Villa	A	0-1		1	12			5	6	7		9			10			2	8		4	3			11*	
Apr 5	Tottenham Hotspur	H	1-4	Lynex (pen)	1				5	6	7		9	11		10			2	8		4	3				
8	Ipswich Town	A	2-0	McAllister, A.Smith	1	2			5	6	7		9	11		10				8		4	3				
12	Southampton	A	0-0		1	2			5	6	7		9	11		10				8		4	3				
14	Queens Park Rangers	H	1-4	McAllister (pen)	1	3			5	6	7		9	11		10				8		4	2*			12	
26	Manchester United	A	0-4		1	7*	3		5	6	12			11		10			2	8		4				9	
30	Liverpool	H	0-2		1	3	11		5	6			9	12		10			2	8		4*				7	
May 3	Newcastle United	H	2-0	Mauchlen,Banks (pen)	1	3	4		5	6			9	12	11	10			2	8*						7	

F.A. CUP

DATE	OPPONENTS		V	F.T.	SCORERS	Andrews	Ramsey	Smith R	Kelly	Osman	O'Neill	Lynex	Bright	Smith A	Wilson	Banks	Mauchlen	Williams	Jones	Feeley	Sealy	Rennie	McAllister	Morgan	Roberts	Christensen	Cunningham	Venus
Jan 4	Bristol Rovers	(3)	A	1-3	McAllister (pen)	1	11			5	6		8	9		7	10			2			4	3				

F.L. CUP

DATE	OPPONENTS		V	F.T.	SCORERS	Andrews	Ramsey	Smith R	Kelly	Osman	O'Neill	Lynex	Bright	Smith A	Wilson	Banks	Mauchlen	Williams	Jones	Feeley	Sealy	Rennie	McAllister	Morgan	Roberts	Christensen	Cunningham	Venus
Sep 25	Derby County	(2 leg 1)	A	0-2		1	4		12			7	9		3	11*	10	5		2	8	6						
Oct 9	Derby County	(2 leg 2)	H	1-1	Wilson	1	10*			5	6	7	8	9	11					2	12		4	3				

Note: Leicester City did not enter the Full Members' Cup.

LEICESTER CITY 1985-86
Back : Feeley,Peake,Hazell,O'Neill,Bright,Williams.
Middle : Kelly,Banks,Rennie,Andrews,A.Smith,Osman,Jones.
Front : D.Richardson *(Youth Team Manager)*, Lynex,Ramsey,G.Summers *(Coach)*,
G.Milne *(Manager)*, R.Smith,Wilson,J.McVey *(Physiotherapist)*.

	APP's			GOALS		
	FL	FAC	FLC	FL	FAC	FLC
Ian Andrews	39	1	2			
Paul Ramsey	13		2	1		
Bobby Smith	13/1	1		1		
Robert Kelly	8/1		-/1			
Russell Osman	40	1	1			
John O'Neill	41	1	1			
Steve Lynex	28/2		2	8 (7p)		
Mark Bright	22/2	1	2	6		
Alan Smith	38/2	1	1	19		
Ian Wilson	24/1		2	2		
Ian Banks	24/7	1	1	2 (1p)		
Ali Mauchlen	35/2	1	1	2		
Tommy Williams	8		1			
Robert Jones	2/1					
Andy Feeley	26	1	2			
Tony Sealy	19/2		1/1	6		
David Rennie	3		1			
Gary McAllister	31	1	1	7(2p)	1(p)	
Simon Morgan	30	1	1			
Jerry Roberts	3					
Tommy Christensen	1/1					
Laurie Cunningham	13/2					
Mark Venus	1					

1986-87

LEAGUE DIVISION ONE
Final Position : 20th
Ave. Home League Att: 11,697

DATE	OPPONENTS	V	F.T.	SCORERS	Andrews	Ramsey	Venus	Osman	Walsh	McAllister	Lynex	Bright	Smith	Wilson	Banks	Sealy	Kelly	Morgan	Moran	Feeley	Mauchlen	Bunce	O'Neill	Alleyne	Horner	D'Avray	Reid	Wilkinson	Jobling	Buckley	Russell
Aug 23	Luton Town	H	1-1	Smith	1	2	3	4	5	6*	7	8	9	10	11	12															
30	Wimbledon	A	0-1		1	2	3	4	5	6		8	9		11*	12	7	10													
Sep 3	Liverpool	H	2-1	McAllister,Osman	1	2	3	4	5	6	12		9	10		8	7*	11													
6	Manchester United	H	1-1	Kelly	1	2	3	4	5	6			9	10	12	8	7	11													
13	Sheffield Wednesday	A	2-2	McAllister,Moran	1	2	3	4	5	6			9	10		12	7*	11	8												
17	Norwich City	A	1-2	Smith	1	2	3	4	5	6			9	10		12	7*	11	8												
20	Tottenham Hotspur	H	1-2	Morgan	1	7	3	4	5	6			9	10			12	11	8	2*											
27	Queens Park Rangers	A	1-0	Smith	1		3	4	5	6			9	10		12		11	8*	2	7										
Oct 4	Manchester City	A	2-1	Sealy,Smith	1		3	4	5	6	11		9	10		12		2	8*		7										
11	Nottingham Forest	H	3-1	Smith,McAllister 2 (1pen)	1		3	4	5	6			9	10		12		2	8*		7	11									
18	Charlton Athletic	A	0-2		1		3	4	5	6			9	10		8	12	2			7	11*									
25	Southampton	H	2-3	Osman,McAllister	1		3	4	5	6			9	10		12		2	8*		7	11									
Nov 1	Aston Villa	A	0-2		1		3	4		6			9	10		12		2	8		7	11*	5								
8	Newcastle United	H	1-1	Smith	1		3	4*		6			9	10		11	12	2	8		7		5								
15	Everton	H	0-2		1		3		5	6			9	10		11	12	2	8*		7		4								
22	Watford	A	1-5	Smith	1		3		5	6			9	10		11	12	2	8			7*	4								
29	Chelsea	H	2-2	McAllister (pen),O'Neill	1		3		5	6			9	10		11		2		8	7		4								
Dec 6	Coventry City	A	0-1		1		3	4	5*	6			9	10		11		2	12	8	7										
14	Oxford United	H	2-0	Smith,Wilson	1		3	4		6			9	10		11		2	12	8*	7		5								
20	Manchester United	A	0-2		1	3*		4		6			9	10			12	2	11	8	7		5								
26	Arsenal	H	1-1	Moran	1		3	4		6			9	10*			11	2	8	12	7		5								
28	Everton	A	1-5	Moran	1	4	3			6			9				11	2	8	10	7*	12	5								
Jan 1	West Ham United	A	1-4	Moran	1	10	3			6	7		9			11*		2	8	4			5	12							
3	Sheffield Wednesday	H	6-1	Ramsey,Smith 2,Moran 3	1	10	3			6	7		9				4	8	2				5*	11	12						
24	Luton Town	A	0-1		1	10*	3		5	6	12		9				7	8	2	11			4								
Feb 7	Wimbledon	H	3-1	Smith,Ramsey 2	1	10	11*		5	6	7		9	12			3	8			2		4								
14	Liverpool	A	3-4	Smith 2,Johnston (og)	1	10	3		5	6			9	11			2				7		4			8					
21	Norwich City	H	0-2		1	10	3*		5	6			9	11			2				7		4		12	8					
25	Tottenham Hotspur	A	0-5		1	10	3			6	12		9	11			2				7		4	5*	8						
Mar 7	Southampton	A	0-4		1	10		5		6			9	11			2			3	7		4	12		8*					
14	Charlton Athletic	H	1-0	Smith	1	2		4		6	7		9	11			3	8*			10		5			12					
22	Nottingham Forest	A	1-2	Mauchlen	1	2	12	4		6	7		9	11			3	8*			10		5			7					
25	Queens Park Rangers	H	4-1	McAllister 2 (1pen),Ramsey,McDonald (og)	1	10	3	4		6			9	11			2				7		5		8						
28	Manchester City	H	4-0	Morgan,Smith,McAllister,Ramsey	1	10	3	4		6			9	11			2	7*			5				8	12					
Apr 4	Newcastle United	A	0-2		1	10	3	4		6			9	11			2				5						7*	12			
11	Aston Villa	H	1-1	Moran	1	10	3	4		6			9	11			2	8			5						7*		12		
18	West Ham United	H	2-0	Smith,O'Neill	1	10	3	4		6			9	11			2			8	5								12	7*	
20	Arsenal	A	1-4	Osman	1	10	3	4	12	6			9	11			2			8	5						7*				
25	Watford	H	1-2	Moran	1	10	3	4		6			9	11			2	12		7*	5									8	
May 2	Chelsea	A	1-3	Smith	1	10	3	4					9	11			2	8		6	5								12	7*	
4	Coventry City	H	1-1	Ramsey	1	10	3	4					9	11			2	8		6	5								12	7*	
9	Oxford United	A	0-0		1	10	3	4					9	11			2	8		6	5								12	7*	

F.A. CUP

					Andrews	Ramsey	Venus	Osman	Walsh	McAllister	Lynex	Bright	Smith	Wilson	Banks	Sealy	Kelly	Morgan	Moran	Feeley	Mauchlen	Bunce	O'Neill	Alleyne	Horner	D'Avray	Reid	Wilkinson	Jobling	Buckley	Russell
Jan 10	Queens Park Rangers	(3) A	2-5	Smith,McAllister (pen)	1	10	3		5	6	7^		9	11*				4	8	2	12				14						

F.L.CUP

					Andrews	Ramsey	Venus	Osman	Walsh	McAllister	Lynex	Bright	Smith	Wilson	Banks	Sealy	Kelly	Morgan	Moran	Feeley	Mauchlen	Bunce	O'Neill	Alleyne	Horner	D'Avray	Reid	Wilkinson	Jobling	Buckley	Russell
Sep 23	Swansea City	(2 leg 1) A	2-0	McAllister,Smith	1	2	3	4	5	6			9	10			7	11	8												
Oct 8	Swansea City	(2 leg 2) H	4-2	Morgan,Smith,Moran 2	1		3	4	5	6	11		9*	10		12		2	8		7											
29	Liverpool	(3) A	1-4	Moran	1		3	4	5	6^	14		9	10		11*	12	2	8		7											

Note: Leicester City did not enter the Full Members' Cup.

LEICESTER CITY 1986-87
Back : Reid,Feeley,Banks,Andrews,Roberts,O'Neill,Kelly,Jobling.
Middle : D.Richardson *(Youth Team Manager)*, Ramsey,Morgan,Venus,Horner,A.Smith,Walsh,McAllister,
Bright,Osman,J.McVey *(Physiotherapist)*.
Front : Mauchlen,Lynex,Bunce,G.Milne *(General Manager)*, B.Hamilton *(Manager)*, Wilson,R.Smith,Sealy.

	APP's			GOALS		
	FL	FAC	FLC	FL	FAC	FLC
Ian Andrews	42	1	3			
Paul Ramsey	29	1	1	6		
Mark Venus	38/1	1	3			
Russell Osman	31		3	3		
Steve Walsh	20/1	1	3			
Gary McAllister	39	1	3	9 (3p)	1(p)	1
Steve Lynex	7/3	1	1/1			
Mark Bright	2					
Alan Smith	42	1	3	17	1	2
Ian Wilson	36/1	1	3	1		
Ian Banks	2/1					
Tony Sealy	9/9		1/1	1		
Robert Kelly	8/6		1/1	1		
Simon Morgan	41	1	3	2		1
Steve Moran	24/3	1	3	9		3
Andy Feeley	11/1	1				
Ali Mauchlen	30	-/1	2	1		
Paul Bunce	5/1					
John O'Neill	29			2		
Robert Alleyne	1/2					
Phil Horner	1/2	-/1				
Mich D'Avray	3					
Paul Reid	5/1					
Steve Wilkinson	-/1					
Kevin Jobling	1/2					
John Buckley	1/4					
Martin Russell	5					
Own Goals					2	

1987-88 LEAGUE DIVISION TWO
Final Position : 13th
Ave. Home League Att: 10,157

DATE	OPPONENTS	V	F.T.	SCORERS	Andrews	Morgan	James	Osman	Walsh	Wilson	Ford	McAllister	Cusack	Ramsey	Russell	Venus	Moran	Wilkinson	Horner	Reid	Cooper	Mauchlen	Rantanen	Newell	Brien	Langan	Jobling	Osvold	MacDonald	Weir	Prindiville	Cross	Turner	Brown	Groves
Aug 15	Shrewsbury Town	H	0-1		1	2	3	4	5	6	7	8^	9	10	11*	12	14																		
19	Leeds United	A	0-1		1	12	2	4	5	11	7	10	9^	6			3	8*	14																
29	Millwall	H	1-0	Moran	1	12	2	4		11	7	10		6			3*	8			5	9													
31	Stoke City	A	1-2	McAllister	1	12	2	4		11	7	10		6*	14		3	8			5	9^													
Sep 5	Aston Villa	H	0-2		1	2	9	4	5	11	7	10*		6	14		3^	8	12																
12	Crystal Palace	A	1-2	McAllister	12	2*		4	5	11	14	10		6*			3	8			1	7	9												
16	Oldham Athletic	H	4-1	Newell,Rantanen,Ford,Wilson		2	3	4	5	11	7	12		6				14			1	10*	9^	8											
19	Plymouth Argyle	H	4-0	Wilson,Ford,Newell,Rantanen		2	3	4	5	11*	7	12		6				14			1	10	9^	8											
26	Bournemouth	A	3-2	Newell,Osman,Mauchlen		2	3	4			7			6	11*	12	14			5	1	10	9^	8											
30	Ipswich Town	H	1-1	Moran		2	3	4			7			6					11	5*	1	10	9	8	12										
Oct 3	Manchester City	A	2-4	Newell,Rantanen		2^	3	4			7			6					11	12	1	10	9*	8	5										
10	Barnsley	H	0-0		12	3*		4	5		7	14		6				9	11		1	10		8	2^										
17	Sheffield United	A	1-2	McAllister	12	3^		4	5		7			6				9	11		1	10		8	2*										
21	West Bromwich Albion	H	3-0	Walsh,Moran 2		2	3*	4	5		7			6				9	11		1	10		8	12										
24	Hull City	A	2-2	McAllister,Walsh			3	4	5		7	14		6				9^	11		1	10		8	2										
31	Blackburn Rovers	H	1-2	Moran	12		3	4	5		7			6^				9	11*		1	10		8	2	14									
Nov 7	Swindon Town	H	3-2	Ramsey,Walsh,Venus			3	4	5	11	7	12		6							1	10*	9	8	2										
14	Birmingham City	A	2-2	Walsh,Cusack		3		4	5	11	7	14	10	6							1	12	9*	8^	2										
21	Bradford City	H	0-2			3*		4	5	11	7	14	10	6							1	12	9^	8	2										
28	Huddersfield Town	A	0-1			3*	12	4		11	7	9^	10	6							1	2	14	8	5										
Dec 5	Middlesbrough	H	0-0				2	4		10	7	9		3							1	12	14	8^	5				6	11*					
12	Oldham Athletic	A	0-2				2	4		10	7	9^		3				14			1	6		8	5				12	11*					
26	Bournemouth	H	0-1		1		4	2		11*	7	14	10^	3								6	9		5				12	8					
28	Plymouth Argyle	A	0-4		1		4	12		7^	10	14	2	3								8		9	5				11	6*					
Jan 1	Millwall	A	0-1		1		2				7			10			3	8	4	12		6		9	5					11*					
2	Crystal Palace	H	4-4	Brien,McAllister (pen),Reid,Wilkinson	1	12	2*				7			10			3	8	4	11^		14	9	5	6										
16	Shrewsbury Town	A	0-0		1		2		4		7	12	6				3	8*					9	5	10^				11	14					
30	Reading	A	2-1	Osman,Walsh	1	2		4	5		7		6				3					10					14		11^			8			
Feb 6	Aston Villa	A	1-2	Newell	1	2		4	5		7		6									10	3*	9	12				11		8			
13	Leeds United	H	3-2	McAllister 2 (1pen),Cross		3		4	5^		7	12	6									10*	1	2	9	14			11		8			
20	Ipswich Town	A	2-0	Reid,Newell		3		4	5		7		6									10	1	2	9				11		8			
27	Manchester City	H	1-0	Cross		3		4	5		7		6									10	1	2	9				11		8			
Mar 5	Sheffield United	H	1-0	Cross		3		4	5		7		6									10	1	2	9				11		8			
12	Barnsley	A	1-1	Walsh		3		4	5		7	12	6									10	1	2	9				11		8*			
16	Stoke City	H	1-1	Mauchlen		3		4	5		7		6									10	1	2	9				11		8			
19	Blackburn Rovers	A	3-3	Reid 2,Newell		3		4	5		7		6									10	1	2^	9				11		8	14		
26	Hull City	H	2-1	Newell,Weir (pen)		3^		4	5		7		6									10	1	2	9				11		8	14		
Apr 2	Swindon Town	A	2-3	Osman,McAllister		3*		4	5		7	12	6									10	1	2					11		8	9		
5	Birmingham City	H	2-0	Osman 2		3		4	5		7		6									10	1	2	9				11		8			
9	West Bromwich Albion	A	1-1	Cross		3		4	5				6									10	1	2	9				11		8	7		
23	Reading	H	1-0	Walsh		3		4^	5				6	14								10	1	2	9				11		8	7		
30	Bradford City	A	1-4	Reid		3			5		7	12	6									10	1	2	9*				11		8			
May 2	Huddersfield Town	H	3-0	Cross 2,Groves		3*			5		7		6									10	1	2	9				11^		8	14	4	
7	Middlesbrough	A	2-1	Weir,McAllister		3		4	5		7		6									10	1	2	9				11		8	12	4	14

F.A.CUP

DATE	OPPONENTS		V	F.T.	SCORERS	Andrews	Morgan	James	Osman	Walsh	Wilson	Ford	McAllister	Cusack	Ramsey	Russell	Venus	Moran	Wilkinson	Horner	Reid	Cooper	Mauchlen	Rantanen	Newell	Brien	Langan
Jan 9	Oxford United	(3)	A	0-2		1	2^		4			7	12	10				3		8			11		6		9 5* 14

F.L.CUP

DATE	OPPONENTS		V	F.T.	SCORERS	Morgan	James	Osman	Walsh	Ford	McAllister	Cusack	Ramsey	Russell	Moran	Horner	Reid	Cooper	Mauchlen	Rantanen	Newell	Brien
Sep 23	Scunthorpe United (2 leg 1)	H	2-1	McAllister,Newell	2	3	4		7*	12		6	11		14		5^	1	10	9	8
Oct 6	Scunthorpe United (2 leg 2)	A	2-1	Reid,Rantanen		3	4	5		7		6				14		11	1	10	9^ 8 2
28	Oxford United (3)	A	0-0			2	3	4	5	7		6			9			11	1	10	8
Nov 4	Oxford United (3 rep)	H	2-3	Newell 2		2	3	4	5	12	7		6		9^			11*	1	10	14 8

F.M.CUP

DATE	OPPONENTS		V	F.T.	SCORERS	Andrews	Morgan	James	Osman	Walsh	Ford	McAllister	Cusack	Ramsey	Russell	Venus	Moran	Reid	Cooper	Mauchlen	Rantanen	Newell	Brien	Langan	Jobling	Osvold	Cross	Turner
Nov 10	Huddersfield Town	(1)	H	1-0	Ford	3		4	5		7	6				11	12		1		9*	8	2			10		
Dec 1	Charlton Athletic	(2)	A	2-1	Jobling 2		2^	4			10	7	9	12		3		11*	1		14	8	5		6			
Jan 19	Stoke City	(3)	H	0-0		2			5		10	12	6			14			1	8*	9	4	7^				11	3

Note: Jan 19, lost 3-5 on penalties. McAllister,Weir,Venus scored for Leicester

LEICESTER CITY 1987-88

Back : Garwood,Williams,Russell,Andrews,Cooper,Muggleton,Alleyne,Prindiville,Reid.
Middle : Morgan,Horner,Ramsey,Walsh,McAllister,Cusack,Brien,Wilkinson.
Front : A.Davies *(Kit Manager),* Venus,Ford,Moran,James,B.Hamilton *(Manager),* Osman,P.Morris *(Coach),* Jobling,Mauchlen,Wilson,J.McVey *(Physiotherapist).*

MIKE NEWELL
City's record signing in action against Leeds United at Filbert Street,
taking on ex-City defender David Rennie.

	APP's				GOALS		
	FL	FAC	FLC	FMC	FL	FLC	FMC
Ian Andrews	12	1					
Simon Morgan	32/8	1	3	2			
Robbie James	21/2		4	1			
Russell Osman	37	1	4	2	5		
Steve Walsh	32		3	2	7		
Ian Wilson	8				2		
Gary Ford	15/1		1/1	2	2		1
Gary McAllister	40/2	1	3/1	3	9 (2p)	1	
Nick Cusack	5/11	-/1		1/1	1		
Paul Ramsey	41/1	1	4	1/1	1		
Martin Russell	2/3		1				
Mark Venus	19/2	1		2/1	1		
Steve Moran	11/5		2/2	-/1	5		
Steve Wilkinson	3/2	1			1		
Phil Horner	6/1		1				
Paul Reid	23/3	1	3	1	5	1	
Paul Cooper	32		4	3			
Ali Mauchlen	33/3	1	4		2		
Jari Rantanen	10/3		2/1	2/1	3	1	
Mike Newell	36	1	4	3	8	3	
Tony Brien	11/4	1	1	3	1		
Dave Langan	5						
Kevin Jobling	3/3	-/1		3			2
Kjetil Osvold	3/1						
Kevin MacDonald	3						
Peter Weir	18			1	2 (1p)		
Steve Prindiville	-/1			1			
Nicky Cross	17				6		
Phil Turner	4/4						
Grant Brown	2						
Paul Groves	-/1					1	

1988-89
LEAGUE DIVISION TWO
Final Position : 15th
Ave. Home League Att: 10,701

DATE	OPPONENTS	V	F.T.	SCORERS	Hodge	Mauchlen	Spearing	Ramsey	Walsh	Brown	Reid	Cross	Newell	McAllister	Turner	Quinn	Cooper	Paris	Weir	Morgan	Russell	Williams	Groves	Brien	Muggleton	Mills	Kennedy	Charles	North	Eccles	Puttnam	Wilkinson
Aug 27	West Bromwich Albion	H	1-1	Mauchlen	1	2	3	4	5	6	7*	8	9	10	11	12																
29	Portsmouth	A	0-3			2	3	4^	5		14	8*	9	10	7	12	1	6	11													
Sep 3	Birmingham City	A	3-2	Newell,Cross,Quinn		2	3	4	5	6	7	8*	9	10	11		1		12													
10	Ipswich Town	H	0-1			2*	3	4	5	6	7^	8	9	10	12	11	1		14													
17	Oxford United	A	1-1	Cross		2	3	4	5	6	12	8*	9	10	11		1		7													
21	Plymouth Argyle	H	1-0	Newell		2^	3	4	5	6		8	9	10	11		1		7	14												
24	Watford	H	2-2	Walsh,Reid		2		4	5	6	7	8	9	10			1		11	3												
Oct 1	Chelsea	A	1-2	Quinn		2		4	5	6	7	8	9	10	14		1			3	11^											
4	Hull City	A	2-2	McAllister,Williams				4	5		7	8	9	10		6	1	2		3		11										
8	Brighton & Hove Albion	H	1-0	Quinn				4	5	6	7	8	9	10		14	1	2^		3		11*	12									
15	Stoke City	H	2-0	Newell 2					5	6	7	8	9	10			1	2	11*	3		12	4									
22	Leeds United	A	1-1	Quinn			3		5	6	7	8	9	10		14	1	2	11*			12	4^									
26	Swindon Town	H	3-3	McAllister 2 (1pen), King (og)			3		5	6*	7	8	9	10		4	1	2	11			12										
29	Shrewsbury Town	A	0-3				3*	4	5		7	8	9	10		14	1	2	11^		6	12										
Nov 5	Manchester City	H	0-0				3	4	5		7	8	9	10	14		1	2			6	11^										
12	Walsall	A	1-0	Newell			3	4	5		7	8	9	10	14		1	2			6	11^										
19	Crystal Palace	A	2-4	Newell,McAllister			3	4			7	8	9	10	11		1	2			6			5								
26	Bradford City	H	1-0	Quinn			3	4	5		7		9	10	11		1	2			6	8										
Dec 3	Oldham Athletic	A	1-1	Quinn				4			7		9	10	3	11	1	2			6	8		5								
10	Sunderland	H	3-1	Newell,Cross,Reid				4^			7	12	9	10	3	11	1	2			6*	8	14	5								
17	Barnsley	A	0-3				3				7	8	9	10	4*	12	1	2			6	14	11	5*								
26	Bournemouth	H	0-1				3	4*	5		7	14	9	10	12	11	1	2			6	8^										
31	Blackburn Rovers	H	4-0	Turner,Cross,Newell,McAllister		2^	3	4	5*		7	8	9	10	11	14	1				6	12										
Jan 2	Ipswich Town	A	0-2			2	3	4^			7	8	9	10	11	14	1		5		6*	12										
14	Portsmouth	H	2-1	Turner,Reid		2	3	4			7	8		10	11	9	1			5	6											
21	West Bromwich Albion	A	1-1	Reid		2	3	4*			7^	8	9	10	11	14				5	6	12			1							
Feb 4	Hull City	H	0-2			2	3	4			7	8	9	10	11					5	6	8			1							
11	Brighton & Hove Albion	A	1-1	McAllister			3	4	5		7		9	10	11	14		2			6	8^			1							
18	Leeds United	H	1-2	Cross	1	2	3	4	5		7	8	9	10*	11	14					6	12			1							
25	Stoke City	A	2-2	Reid,Walsh	1	2	3	4*	5		7	8	9	10	11^	14					6	12			1							
28	Swindon Town	A	1-2	Newell	1	2	3		5		7	8	9	10	11	14					6		4^									
Mar 4	Walsall	H	1-0	Cross	1	2*	3	4	5		7	8	9	10							6	12					11					
11	Manchester City	A	2-4	McAllister,Newell	1	2	3^	4	5		7	8	9	10		14					6						11					
15	Shrewsbury Town	H	1-1	McAllister	1	2	3	4	5		7^	8	9	10		14					6						11					
18	Plymouth Argyle	A	1-1	Cross	1	2	3		5		7	8	9	10							6					4	11					
25	Birmingham City	H	2-0	Mauchlen 2	1	2			5		7	8*	9	10						3	6*					4	11	12	14			
27	Bournemouth	A	1-2	McAllister	1	8			5		7	12	9	10						3*	6					4^	11	2	14			
Apr 1	Oxford United	H	1-0	McAllister	1	2			5		7	8*	9	10							6					4	11	3	14			
8	Blackburn Rovers	A	0-0		1		3	4*			7	8	9	10							6	14				2	11	12	5^			
11	Barnsley	H	0-1		1		3	4			7	8*	9	10							6					5	11	2*	14	12		
15	Chelsea	H	2-0	Reid,Cross	1	2	3				7	8	9	10							6					5	11	4				
22	Watford	A	1-2	Newell	1	2	3				7	8^	9	10							6					5	11	4*	12	14		
29	Bradford City	A	1-2	Paris	1	2	3				7	8	9	10							6					5	11	4				
May 1	Oldham Athletic	H	1-2	Newell	1	2	3				7	8*	9	10							6					5	11*	4	12	14		
6	Crystal Palace	H	2-2	North,Cross	1		3	4^			7	12	9	10							6					5	14	2	8*		11	
13	Sunderland	A	2-2	McAllister,Newell (pen)	1		3	4		6	7		9	10												5		2	8		11^	14

F.A.CUP

DATE	OPPONENTS		V	F.T.	SCORERS	Hodge	Mauchlen	Spearing	Ramsey	Walsh	Brown	Reid	Cross	Newell	McAllister	Turner	Quinn	Cooper	Paris	Weir	Morgan	Russell	Williams
Jan 7	Manchester City	(3)	A	0-1			2	3	4*			7	8	9	10	11^	14	1		5		6	12

F.L.CUP

DATE	OPPONENTS		V	F.T.	SCORERS	Mauchlen	Spearing	Ramsey	Walsh	Brown	Reid	Cross	Newell	McAllister	Turner	Quinn	Cooper	Paris	Weir	Morgan	Russell	Williams	Groves	Brien
Sep 28	Watford	(2 leg 1) H		4-1	Reid,Walsh,Cross,McAllister (pen)	2		4*	5	6	7	8	9	10	14		1	12	11^	3				
Oct 11	Watford	(2 leg 2) A		2-2	Mauchlen,Newell			4	5	6	7	8	9	10			1	2		3		11		
Nov 2	Norwich City	(3) H		2-0	Newell,Reid		3	4	5		7	8	9	10			1	2			6	11		
30	Nottingham Forest	(4) H		0-0			3	4	5		7*	12	9	10	14	11	1	2			6	8^		
Dec 14	Nottingham Forest	(4 rep) A		1-2	Groves			4^			7	14	9	10	3	11	1	2			6	12	8	5*

F.M.CUP

DATE	OPPONENTS		V	F.T.	SCORERS	Spearing	Ramsey	Walsh	Reid	Cross	Newell	McAllister	Turner	Cooper	Paris	Weir	Russell	Williams
Nov 8	Watford	(1)	A	0-2		3	4	5*	7	8^	9	10	14	1	2	11	6	12

Note: May 6; goal credited to Cross, some reports credit Suckling (og).

GARY CHARLES

MICK KENNEDY

DAVE PUTTNAM

LEICESTER CITY 1988-89
Back : Turner,Brien,Weir,Paris,Morgan,Groves,Russell.
Middle : C.Lea *(Coach)*, R.Roberts *(Coach)*, Thompson,Rantanen,Muggleton,Walsh,Cooper,Quinn,Newell,G.Lee *(Coach)*, J.McVey *(Physiotherapist)*.
Front : Cross,McAllister,Ramsey,D.Pleat *(Manager)*, Mauchlen,Spearing,Reid.

	APP's				GOALS	
	FL	FAC	FLC	FMC	FL	FLC
Martin Hodge	19					
Ali Mauchlen	38	1	5	1	3	1
Tony Spearing	36	1	2	1		
Paul Ramsey	22	1	1			
Steve Walsh	30		4	1	2	1
Grant Brown	12		2			
Paul Reid	43/2	1	5	1	6	2
Nicky Cross	37/4	1	3/2	1	9	1
Mike Newell	45	1	5	1	13(1p)	2
Gary McAllister	46	1	5	1	11(1p)	1(p)
Phil Turner	14/2	1	1/1		2	
Jimmy Quinn	13/18	-/1	2/1	-/1	6	
Paul Cooper	24	1	5	1		
Alan Paris	37	1	4/1	1	1	
Peter Weir	8/2		1			
Simon Morgan	30/2	1	5	1		
Martin Russell	6/4		2/1	1		
Darren Williams	4/2		2		1	
Paul Groves	7/8	-/1	1	-/1		1
Tony Brien	1					
Carl Muggleton	3					
Gary Mills	13					
Mick Kennedy	9					
Gary Charles	5/3					
Marc North	1/7				1	
Peter Eccles	1					
Dave Puttnam	2/1					
Steve Wilkinson	-/1					
Own Goals					1	

GARY MILLS

MARC NORTH

THE
LEAGUE RECORD 1891-1989
LEICESTER FOSSE/CITY'S COMPLETE MIDLAND AND FOOTBALL LEAGUE RECORD
SEASON BY SEASON

MIDLAND LEAGUE

SEASON	P	HOME W	D	L	F	A	AWAY W	D	L	F	A	OVERALL W	D	L	F	A	Pts	Pos
1891-92	20	4	2	4	12	16	1	1	8	7	39	5	3	12	19	55	13	11
1892-93	24	7	2	3	29	11	5	1	6	21	26	12	3	9	50	37	27	4
1893-94	20	9	0	1	32	6	6	2	2	17	7	15	2	3	49	13	32	2

FOOTBALL LEAGUE

SEASON	P	HOME W	D	L	F	A	AWAY W	D	L	F	A	OVERALL W	D	L	F	A	Pts	Pos
DIVISION TWO																		
1894-95	30	11	2	2	45	20	4	6	5	27	33	15	8	7	72	53	38	4
1895-96	30	10	0	5	40	16	4	4	7	17	28	14	4	12	57	44	32	8
1896-97	30	11	2	2	44	20	2	2	11	15	37	13	4	13	59	57	30	9
1897-98	30	8	5	2	26	11	5	2	8	20	24	13	7	10	46	35	33	7
1898-99	34	12	5	0	35	12	6	4	7	29	30	18	9	7	64	42	45	3
1899-1900	34	11	5	1	34	8	6	4	7	19	28	17	9	8	53	36	43	5
1900-01	34	9	5	3	30	15	2	5	10	9	22	11	10	13	39	37	32	11
1901-02	34	11	2	4	26	14	1	3	13	12	42	12	5	17	38	56	29	14
1902-03	34	5	5	7	20	23	5	3	9	21	42	10	8	16	41	65	28	15
1903-04	34	5	8	4	26	21	1	2	14	16	61	6	10	18	42	82	22	18
1904-05	34	8	3	6	30	25	3	4	10	10	30	11	7	16	40	55	29	14
1905-06	38	10	3	6	30	21	5	9	5	23	27	15	12	11	53	48	42	7
1906-07	38	15	3	1	44	12	5	5	9	18	27	20	8	10	62	39	48	3
1907-08	38	14	2	3	41	20	7	8	4	31	27	21	10	7	72	47	52	2
DIVISION ONE																		
1908-09	38	6	6	7	32	41	2	3	14	22	61	8	9	21	54	102	25	20
DIVISION TWO																		
1909-10	38	15	2	2	60	20	5	2	12	19	38	20	4	14	79	58	44	5
1910-11	38	12	3	4	37	19	2	2	15	15	43	14	5	19	52	62	33	15
1911-12	38	11	4	4	34	18	4	3	12	15	48	15	7	16	49	66	37	10
1912-13	38	12	2	5	34	20	1	5	13	15	45	13	7	18	49	65	33	15
1913-14	38	7	2	10	29	28	4	2	13	16	33	11	4	23	45	61	26	18
1914-15	38	6	4	9	31	41	4	0	15	16	47	10	4	24	47	88	24	19
1915-1919				Competition suspended owing to First World War														
1919-20	42	8	6	7	26	29	7	4	10	15	32	15	10	17	41	61	40	14
1920-21	42	10	8	3	26	11	2	8	11	13	35	12	16	14	39	46	40	12
1921-22	42	11	6	4	30	16	3	11	7	9	18	14	17	11	39	34	45	9
1922-23	42	14	2	5	42	19	7	7	7	23	25	21	9	12	65	44	51	3
1923-24	42	13	4	4	43	16	4	4	13	21	38	17	8	17	64	54	42	12
1924-25	42	15	4	2	58	9	9	7	5	32	23	24	11	7	90	32	59	1
DIVISION ONE																		
1925-26	42	11	3	7	42	32	3	7	11	28	48	14	10	18	70	80	38	17
1926-27	42	13	4	4	58	33	4	8	9	27	37	17	12	13	85	70	46	7
1927-28	42	14	5	2	66	25	4	7	10	30	47	18	12	12	96	72	48	3
1928-29	42	16	5	0	67	22	5	4	12	29	45	21	9	12	96	67	51	2
1929-30	42	12	5	4	57	42	5	4	12	29	48	17	9	16	86	90	43	8
1930-31	42	12	4	5	50	38	4	2	15	30	57	16	6	20	80	95	38	16
1931-32	42	11	3	7	46	39	4	4	13	28	55	15	7	20	74	94	37	19
1932-33	42	9	9	3	43	25	2	4	15	32	64	11	13	18	75	89	35	19
1933-34	42	10	6	5	36	26	4	5	12	23	48	14	11	17	59	74	39	17
1934-35	42	9	4	8	39	30	3	5	13	22	56	12	9	21	61	86	33	21
DIVISION TWO																		
1935-36	42	14	5	2	53	19	5	5	11	26	38	19	10	13	79	57	48	6
1936-37	42	14	4	3	56	26	10	4	7	33	31	24	8	10	89	57	56	1
DIVISION ONE																		
1937-38	42	9	6	6	31	26	5	5	11	23	49	14	11	17	54	75	39	16
1938-39	42	7	6	8	35	35	2	5	14	13	47	9	11	22	48	82	29	22
1939-1946				Competition suspended owing to Second World War														

SEASON	P	HOME						AWAY						OVERALL						Pts	Pos
		W	D	L	F	A		W	D	L	F	A		W	D	L	F	A			
DIVISION TWO																					
1946-47	42	11	4	6	42	25		7	3	11	27	39		18	7	17	69	64		43	9
1947-48	42	10	5	6	36	29		6	6	9	24	28		16	11	15	60	57		43	9
1948-49	42	6	10	5	41	38		4	6	11	21	41		10	16	16	62	79		36	19
1949-50	42	8	9	4	30	25		4	6	11	25	40		12	15	15	55	65		39	15
1950-51	42	10	4	7	42	28		5	7	9	26	30		15	11	16	68	58		41	14
1951-52	42	12	6	3	48	24		7	3	11	30	40		19	9	14	78	64		47	5
1952-53	42	13	6	2	55	29		5	6	10	34	45		18	12	12	89	74		48	5
1953-54	42	15	4	2	63	23		8	6	7	34	37		23	10	9	97	60		56	1
DIVISION ONE																					
1954-55	42	9	6	6	43	32		3	5	13	31	54		12	11	19	74	86		35	21
DIVISION TWO																					
1955-56	42	15	3	3	63	23		6	3	12	31	55		21	6	15	94	78		48	5
1956-57	42	14	5	2	68	36		11	6	4	41	31		25	11	6	109	67		61	1
DIVISION ONE																					
1957-58	42	11	4	6	59	41		3	1	17	32	71		14	5	23	91	112		33	18
1958-59	42	7	6	8	34	36		4	4	13	33	62		11	10	21	67	98		32	19
1959-60	42	8	6	7	38	32		5	7	9	28	43		13	13	16	66	75		39	12
1960-61	42	12	4	5	54	31		6	5	10	33	39		18	9	15	87	70		45	6
1961-62	42	12	2	7	38	27		5	4	12	34	44		17	6	19	72	71		40	14
1962-63	42	14	6	1	53	23		6	6	9	26	30		20	12	10	79	53		52	4
1963-64	42	9	4	8	33	27		7	7	7	28	31		16	11	15	61	58		43	11
1964-65	42	9	6	6	43	36		2	7	12	26	49		11	13	18	69	85		35	18
1965-66	42	12	4	5	40	28		9	3	9	40	37		21	7	14	80	65		49	7
1966-67	42	12	4	5	47	28		6	4	11	31	43		18	8	16	78	71		44	8
1967-68	42	7	7	7	37	34		6	5	10	27	35		13	12	17	64	69		38	13
1968-69	42	8	8	5	27	24		1	4	16	12	44		9	12	21	39	68		30	21
DIVISION TWO																					
1969-70	42	12	6	3	37	22		7	7	7	27	28		19	13	10	64	50		51	3
1970-71	42	12	7	2	30	14		11	6	4	27	16		23	13	6	57	30		59	1
DIVISION ONE																					
1971-72	42	9	6	6	18	11		4	7	10	23	35		13	13	16	41	46		39	12
1972-73	42	7	9	5	23	18		3	8	10	17	28		10	17	15	40	46		37	16
1973-74	42	10	7	4	35	17		3	9	9	16	24		13	16	13	51	41		42	9
1974-75	42	8	7	6	25	17		4	5	12	21	43		12	12	18	46	60		36	18
1975-76	42	9	9	3	29	24		4	10	7	19	27		13	19	10	48	51		45	7
1976-77	42	8	9	4	30	28		4	9	8	17	32		12	18	12	47	60		42	11
1977-78	42	4	7	10	16	32		1	5	15	10	38		5	12	25	26	70		22	22
DIVISION TWO																					
1978-79	42	7	8	6	28	23		3	9	9	15	29		10	17	15	43	52		37	17
1979-80	42	12	5	4	32	19		9	8	4	26	19		21	13	8	58	38		55	1
DIVISION ONE																					
1980-81	42	7	5	9	20	23		6	1	14	20	44		13	6	23	40	67		32	21
DIVISION TWO																					
1981-82	42	12	5	4	31	19		6	7	8	25	29		18	12	12	56	48		66	8
1982-83	42	11	4	6	36	15		9	6	6	36	29		20	10	12	72	44		70	3
DIVISION ONE																					
1983-84	42	11	5	5	40	30		2	7	12	25	38		13	12	17	65	68		51	15
1984-85	42	10	4	7	39	25		5	2	14	26	48		15	6	21	65	73		51	15
1985-86	42	7	8	6	35	35		3	4	14	19	41		10	12	20	54	76		42	19
1986-87	42	9	7	5	39	24		2	2	17	15	52		11	9	22	54	76		42	20
DIVISION TWO																					
1987-88	44	12	5	5	35	20		4	6	12	27	41		16	11	17	62	61		59	13
1988-89	46	11	6	6	31	20		2	10	11	25	43		13	16	17	56	63		55	15
TOTALS																					
Midland League	64	20	4	8	73	33		12	4	16	45	72		32	8	24	118	105			
Division One	1592	368	216	212	1497	1097		151	194	451	945	1694		519	410	663	2442	2791			
Division Two	1798	505	208	186	1778	961		237	236	426	1036	1572		742	444	612	2814	2533			

Notes : 1896-97: Official League table incorrect - 28 November 1896 : Walsall (H) 4-2 not 4-1 as recorded in Football League records
1912-13: Official League table incorrect - 26 April 1913 : Hull City (A) 0-2 not 1-2 as recorded in Football League records.

THE
FOOTBALL LEAGUE RECORD 1894-1989
LEICESTER FOSSE/CITY'S COMPLETE RECORD AGAINST OTHER LEAGUE CLUBS

Leicester Fosse/City have met 87 other clubs in Football League fixtures. Of the League's members in 1988/89, the following list represents the clubs which Leicester have never met in either League or Cup competition: *Chester City, Colchester United, Halifax Town, Hartlepool United, Rochdale, Scarborough, Southend United* and *Wigan Athletic.*

Of the former members of the Football League, the following fall into the same category: *Aberdare Athletic, Accrington, Accrington Stanley, Ashington, Bootle, Durham City, Merthyr Tydfil, Middlesbrough Ironopolis, New Brighton, Northwich Victoria, Stalybridge Celtic, Thames, Wigan Borough* and *Workington.*

The following is a list of Football League clubs that have met Leicester in Cup ties, but never in League fixtures: *Aldershot, Barrow (ex-League), Darlington, Exeter City, Gillingham, Hereford United, Mansfield Town, Peterborough United, Scunthorpe United, Torquay United, Tranmere Rovers* and *York City.*

The only clubs to have met Leicester in Division One, Division Two, F.A.Cup, Football League Cup, and Full Members Cup are *Stoke City and Watford.*

The following have met Leicester in all except the Full Members Cup: *Arsenal, Aston Villa, Bolton Wanderers, Brentford, Bristol City, Burnley, Carlisle United, Chelsea, Coventry City, Crystal Palace, Derby County, Grimsby Town, Liverpool, Luton Town, Manchester City, Middlesbrough, Norwich City, Nottingham Forest, Oxford United, Portsmouth, Preston North End, Queens Park Rangers, Sheffield United, Southampton, West Bromwich Albion,* and *West Ham United.*

OPPONENTS	FIRST MEET	P	HOME					AWAY					OVERALL				
			W	D	L	F	A	W	D	L	F	A	W	D	L	F	A
Arsenal	1894-95	100	20	15	15	88	78	6	15	29	53	115	26	30	44	141	193
Aston Villa	1908-09	66	19	8	6	86	47	11	5	17	48	69	30	13	23	134	116
Barnsley	1898-99	74	21	10	6	67	25	12	12	13	45	51	33	22	19	112	76
Birmingham City	1896-97	108	28	10	16	112	91	15	8	31	66	103	43	18	47	178	194
Blackburn Rovers	1908-09	70	20	6	9	73	40	4	12	19	27	68	24	18	28	100	108
Blackpool	1896-97	84	22	7	13	87	52	8	11	23	51	89	30	18	36	138	141
Bolton Wanderers	1899-1900	52	13	8	5	54	28	5	5	16	31	66	18	13	21	85	94
Bournemouth	1987-88	4	0	0	2	0	2	1	0	1	4	4	1	0	3	4	6
Bradford City	1903-04	26	7	0	6	18	18	2	5	6	19	29	9	5	12	37	47
Bradford Park Avenue	1909-10	24	10	1	1	35	8	5	4	3	22	20	15	5	4	57	28
Brentford	1937-38	18	1	4	4	13	11	4	3	2	14	12	5	7	6	27	23
Brighton & Hove Albion	1978-79	6	2	0	1	5	2	0	1	2	3	6	2	1	3	8	8
Bristol City	1901-02	40	10	7	3	36	17	6	6	8	13	23	16	13	11	49	40
Bristol Rovers	1953-54	10	4	1	0	15	4	1	2	2	5	8	5	3	2	20	12
Burnley	1897-98	80	18	13	9	75	60	5	11	24	42	91	23	24	33	117	151
Burton Swifts	1894-95	14	5	2	0	15	6	4	1	2	13	7	9	3	2	28	13
Burton United	1901-02	12	3	1	2	11	5	3	2	1	7	4	6	3	3	18	9
Burton Wanderers	1894-95	6	1	0	2	4	6	0	2	1	2	3	1	2	3	6	9
Bury	1894-95	52	13	6	7	48	33	10	4	12	40	52	23	10	19	88	85
Cambridge United	1978-79	8	3	1	0	11	3	1	2	1	5	6	4	3	1	16	9
Cardiff City	1920-21	36	11	3	4	34	15	5	4	9	23	34	16	7	13	57	49
Carlisle United	1969-70	8	1	2	1	10	5	3	1	0	5	2	4	3	1	15	7
Charlton Athletic	1935-36	22	6	1	4	16	16	4	0	7	14	14	10	1	11	30	30
Chelsea	1905-06	74	17	14	6	59	42	3	8	26	34	83	20	22	32	93	125
Chesterfield	1899-1900	30	5	5	5	20	17	2	6	7	18	27	7	11	12	38	44
Coventry City	1919-20	54	14	7	6	41	25	10	5	12	34	38	24	12	18	75	63
Crewe Alexandra	1894-95	4	2	0	0	8	1	0	2	0	3	3	2	2	0	11	4
Crystal Palace	1921-22	24	5	6	1	20	12	4	1	7	15	18	9	7	8	35	30
Darwen	1894-95	10	3	0	2	12	6	1	0	4	6	20	4	0	6	18	26
Derby County	1907-08	60	8	13	9	37	31	6	5	19	31	58	14	18	28	68	89
Doncaster Rovers	1901-02	24	11	0	1	36	10	2	6	4	12	17	13	6	5	48	27
Everton	1908-09	80	20	10	10	80	55	9	9	22	53	104	29	19	32	133	159
Fulham	1907-08	68	16	4	14	69	52	5	8	21	39	73	21	12	35	108	125
Gainsborough Trinity	1896-97	30	12	3	0	41	7	5	3	7	12	26	17	6	7	53	33
Glossop	1898-99	30	8	3	4	30	26	5	4	6	17	28	13	7	10	47	54
Grimsby Town	1894-95	60	19	5	6	51	23	4	6	20	31	77	23	11	26	82	100
Huddersfield Town	1910-11	48	9	3	12	33	38	5	5	14	27	52	14	8	26	60	90
Hull City	1905-06	52	11	6	9	41	33	4	10	12	37	56	15	16	21	78	89
Ipswich Town	1961-62	34	9	3	5	22	13	5	5	7	15	17	14	8	12	37	30
Leeds City	1905-06	18	5	3	1	25	12	1	3	5	11	24	6	6	6	36	36
Leeds United	1920-21	82	16	15	10	77	58	7	11	23	49	96	23	26	33	126	154
Lincoln City	1894-95	50	19	3	3	67	28	8	1	16	35	61	27	4	19	102	89

OPPONENTS	FIRST MEET	P	HOME					AWAY					OVERALL				
			W	D	L	F	A	W	D	L	F	A	W	D	L	F	A
Liverpool	1895-96	72	20	7	9	61	49	8	8	20	46	75	28	15	29	107	124
Loughborough	1895-96	10	5	0	0	19	2	4	1	0	12	2	9	1	0	31	4
Luton Town	1897-98	46	9	11	3	41	32	7	5	11	27	33	16	16	14	68	65
Manchester City	1894-95	82	18	12	11	72	51	4	10	27	48	108	22	22	38	120	159
Manchester United	1894-95	96	25	11	12	90	72	5	11	32	51	115	30	22	44	141	187
Middlesbrough	1899-1900	50	10	11	4	38	29	8	5	12	34	45	18	16	16	72	74
Millwall	1946-47	12	4	2	0	12	2	2	1	3	5	4	6	3	3	17	6
Nelson	1923-24	2	1	0	0	3	1	0	1	0	1	1	1	1	0	4	2
New Brighton Tower	1898-99	6	1	1	1	6	4	0	2	1	2	3	1	3	2	8	7
Newcastle United	1894-95	82	26	8	7	90	53	6	10	25	47	72	32	18	32	137	125
Newport County	1946-47	2	1	0	0	3	0	1	0	0	3	2	2	0	0	6	2
Northampton Town	1965-66	2	0	1	0	1	1	0	1	0	2	2	0	2	0	3	3
Norwich City	1935-36	28	5	5	4	21	18	4	3	7	17	24	9	8	11	38	42
Nottingham Forest	1906-07	76	22	10	6	71	47	10	6	22	45	73	32	16	28	116	120
Notts County	1894-95	36	9	3	6	33	25	7	7	4	26	30	16	10	10	59	55
Oldham Athletic	1907-08	22	8	1	2	23	8	3	5	3	11	11	11	6	5	34	19
Orient	1905-06	42	14	3	4	43	23	8	2	11	17	27	22	5	15	60	50
Oxford United	1969-70	10	3	2	0	9	5	1	2	2	2	7	4	4	2	11	12
Plymouth Argyle	1935-36	22	9	2	0	28	8	2	3	6	10	18	11	5	6	38	26
Portsmouth	1924-25	34	14	2	1	58	22	5	3	9	19	30	19	5	10	77	52
Port Vale	1894-95	40	14	4	2	45	9	8	7	5	26	27	22	11	7	71	36
Preston North End	1901-02	38	6	6	7	26	28	2	4	13	17	39	8	10	20	43	67
Queens Park Rangers	1948-49	38	12	3	4	42	21	3	4	12	20	37	15	7	16	62	58
Reading	1987-88	2	1	0	0	1	0	1	0	0	2	1	2	0	0	3	1
Rotherham County	1919-20	8	2	2	0	6	2	0	3	1	1	2	2	5	1	7	4
Rotherham Town	1894-95	4	2	0	0	12	2	1	0	1	1	2	3	0	1	13	4
Rotherham United	1951-52	14	7	0	0	21	7	2	4	1	9	7	9	4	1	30	14
Sheffield United	1908-09	68	12	15	7	61	43	9	11	14	46	65	21	26	21	107	108
Sheffield Wednesday	1899-1900	80	20	12	8	85	56	10	12	18	48	65	30	24	26	133	121
Shrewsbury Town	1979-80	10	2	2	1	6	4	1	3	1	5	6	3	5	2	11	10
Southampton	1922-23	46	9	8	6	38	27	1	9	13	22	48	10	17	19	60	75
South Shields	1919-20	12	4	2	0	11	2	1	1	4	7	11	5	3	4	18	13
Stockport County	1900-01	36	10	5	3	36	21	5	3	10	22	36	15	8	13	58	57
Stoke City	1907-08	62	16	11	4	54	29	5	9	17	29	49	21	20	21	83	78
Sunderland	1908-09	56	15	4	9	52	33	6	9	13	36	45	21	13	22	88	78
Swansea City	1935-36	22	4	5	2	21	11	4	3	4	15	18	8	8	6	36	29
Swindon Town	1969-70	8	2	1	1	9	8	1	1	2	5	6	3	2	3	14	14
Tottenham Hotspur	1919-20	72	11	5	20	67	67	11	9	16	53	76	22	14	36	120	143
Walsall	1894-95	14	6	1	0	26	7	3	2	2	9	8	9	3	2	35	15
Watford	1969-70	18	3	5	1	17	11	2	1	6	13	22	5	6	7	30	33
West Bromwich Albion	1901-02	80	17	10	13	72	57	7	9	24	42	88	24	19	37	114	145
West Ham United	1919-20	94	26	12	9	89	57	9	13	25	60	101	35	25	34	149	158
Wimbledon	1986-87	2	1	0	0	3	1	0	0	1	0	1	1	0	1	3	2
Wolverhampton Wanderers	1906-07	76	18	9	11	67	41	9	11	18	36	70	27	20	29	103	111
Wrexham	1978-79	6	2	1	0	4	1	1	2	0	1	0	3	3	0	5	1
TOTAL		3390	873	424	398	3275	2058	388	430	877	1981	3266	1261	854	1275	5256	5324

Notes:

1) Accrington and Accrington Stanley were separate clubs.

2) Arsenal incorporates games played against Woolwich Arsenal.

3) Barnsley incorporates games played against Barnsley St Peters.

4) Birmingham City incorporates games played against Small Heath and Birmingham.

5) Bournemouth formerly met Leicester in the League Cup when known as Bournemouth and Boscombe Athletic.

6) Burton Swifts and Burton Wanderers amalgamated to form Burton United in 1901.

7) Glossop incorporates games played against Glossop North End.

8) Leeds City and Leeds United were separate clubs.

9) Manchester United incorporates games played against Newton Heath.

10) New Brighton Tower and New Brighton were separate clubs.

11) Orient incorporates games against Clapton Orient and Leyton Orient;the club have reverted to the name of Leyton Orient since the last meeting.

12) Port Vale incorporates games played against Burslem Port Vale.

13) Rotherham County and Rotherham Town amalgamated to form Rotherham United in 1925.

14) South Shields later became known as Gateshead.

15) Stoke City incorporates games played against Stoke.

16) Swansea City incorporates games played against Swansea Town.

17) Walsall incorporates games played against Walsall Town Swifts.

THE
FINAL WARTIME RECORD

Leicester Fosse, during the First World War, and Leicester City, during the Second World War, took part in a variety of Official Football League competitions, the season often being split into separate competitions part-way through the campaign.

FIRST WORLD WAR

SEASON	COMPETITION		P	HOME					AWAY					OVERALL					Pts	Pos
				W	D	L	F	A	W	D	L	F	A	W	D	L	F	A		
1915-16	Midland	(1)	26	9	2	2	30	15	2	4	7	12	19	11	6	9	42	34	28	5/14
	Midland	(2)	10	2	2	1	8	8	1	1	3	7	11	3	3	4	15	19	9	3/6
1916-17	Midland	(1)	30	4	5	6	17	19	2	2	11	12	34	6	7	17	29	53	19	15/16
	Midland	(2)	6	3	0	0	8	4	1	0	2	4	8	4	0	2	12	12	8	4/16
1917-18	Midland	(1)	28	11	0	3	38	12	2	3	9	14	31	13	3	12	52	43	29	7/15
	Midland	(2)	6	2	1	0	5	2	0	0	3	1	8	2	1	3	6	10	5	12/16
1918-19	Midland	(1)	30	10	2	3	37	23	3	1	11	16	30	13	3	14	53	53	29	10/16
	Midland	(2)	6	2	0	1	8	5	1	0	2	2	8	3	0	3	10	13	6	2/4

SECOND WORLD WAR

SEASON	COMPETITION		P	HOME					AWAY					OVERALL					Pts	Pos
				W	D	L	F	A	W	D	L	F	A	W	D	L	F	A		
1939-40	Midland		28	6	3	5	32	26	1	3	10	19	45	7	6	15	51	71	20	7/8
1940-41	South		33	14	3	2	57	24	3	2	9	30	49	17	5	11	87	73	-	14/34
1941-42	South	(1)	17	8	1	0	31	6	3	2	3	9	11	11	3	3	40	17	26.40	1/13
	National	(2)	18	6	1	2	25	11	0	3	6	14	27	6	4	8	39	38	20.44	17/22
1942-43	North	(1)	18	3	2	4	17	15	2	2	5	15	22	5	4	9	32	37	14	33/48
	North	(2)	20	6	0	4	28	12	3	2	5	12	25	9	2	9	40	37	20	22/54
1943-44	North	(1)	18	4	2	3	17	13	2	2	5	16	17	6	4	8	33	30	16	28/50
	North	(2)	21	5	4	1	21	11	5	1	5	19	21	10	5	6	40	32	25	14/56
1944-45	North	(1)	18	2	2	5	13	20	1	2	6	10	26	3	4	11	23	46	10	52/54
	North	(2)	21	6	4	1	29	15	1	2	7	11	23	7	6	8	40	38	20	34/60
1945-46	South		42	4	3	14	30	47	4	4	13	27	54	8	7	27	57	101	23	20/22

Notes : 1940-41 : Competition decided on goal average rather than points
1941-42 : In both competitions, Points were calculated on the basis of all teams playing a standard number of matches.

Skipper Sep Smith receives the 1941-42 Regional League South Championship Trophy
from Arthur Oakley, Vice-President of the Football League.
Pictured from left to right are: Arthur Oakley, Tom Bromilow, W.Taylor, Sep Smith, Alf Pallett, Eddie McLachlan and Frank Sheard.

NON - FIRST CLASS COMPETITIVE MATCHES

LEICESTERSHIRE F.A. SENIOR CUP 1887-88

DATE	OPPONENTS		FT	1	2	3	4	5	6	7	8	9	10	11
Oct 29	St.Saviours	(1) B	4-2	A.West	T.DeVille	T.S.Ashmole	G.S.Bankart 1	T.Poyner	F.Gardner	H.James 1	A.Hassell 1	G.A.Knight 1	H.Wright	E.A.Johnson
Nov 26	St.Saviours	(1) B	5-0	T.DeVille	W.Johnson	S.Sudbury	F.Gardner	Frost	T.S.Ashmole	"1	C.Bentley 2	E.Thompson 2	G.A.Knight	"
Dec 24	Shepshed	(2) A	3-3	A.West	"	"	T.Poyner	T.S.Ashmole	J.Staines	"	E.Thompson 2	G.A.Knight 1	E.A.Johnson 1	F.Gardner
Jan 21	Shepshed	(2 rep) A	2-2	"	"	J.Staines	T.S.Ashmole	T.Poyner	H.Wright	"	A.Foster	E.Thompson 1	G.A.Knight	E.A.Johnson
28	Shepshed	(2 rep 2)	1-2	"	"	T.S.Ashmole	S.Sudbury	"	"	"	"	"	"1	"

Notes: B = Belgrave Road; Oct 29, declared void due to poor light; Jan 21, scorers not listed; Jan 28, at Loughborough.

LEICESTERSHIRE F.A. SENIOR CUP 1888-89

Nov 10	Syston Wreake Valley	(1) V	12-1	T.DeVille	G.Gardner	S.Sudbury	J.Johnson	W.Johnson	T.Poyner	S.Glover 1	C.Bentley	H.Webb 6	G.A.Knight 4	E.A.Johnson 1
Feb 23	Loughborough	(3) A	0-2	J.Radford	"	H.Simpson	"	J.Timson	S.Sudbury	Rippon	Brady	"	"	"

Notes: V = Victoria Park; Fosse received a bye in Round 2

LEICESTERSHIRE F.A. SENIOR CUP 1889-90

Dec 14	Leicester Teachers	(2) M	2-0	C.J.Walker	S.Simmonds	W.Davis	J.Johnson	R.Perry	A.Vickers	C.Bentley	J.Murdoch	H.Webb 1	J.Parr	E.A.Johnson 1
Mar 1	Loughborough	(sf)	4-0	"	S.Rowson	"	"	"	"	"	"1	"2	E.A.Johnson 1	J.Eggleton
29	Coalville Town	(F)	1-1	"	"	"	"	"	"	"	"	"1	C.Squire	E.A.Johnson
Apr 12	Coalville Town	(F rep)	4-0	"	"1	"	"	J.Murdoch 1	"	F.Gardner 1	C.Bentley	E.Thompson 1	E.A.Johnson 1	A.West

Notes: M = Mill Lane; Fosse received a bye in Round 1; Mar 1, at Coalville; Mar 29, at Loughborough; Apr 12, at Loughborough.

LEICESTERSHIRE F.A. SENIOR CUP 1890-91

Jan 24	Melton Rovers	(1) M	10-0	C.J.Walker	S.Rowson	W.Davis 1	J.Johnson	R.Perry	E.A.Nuttall	J.Flint 1	J.Murdoch 2	H.Webb 2	E.A.Johnson 2	J.Atter 2
Feb 21	Leicester Teachers	(sf)	3-1	"	"	"	"	"	F.Gardner	"	"	"1	"	"2
Mar 21	Gresley Rovers	(F)	2-0	"	"	"	"	"	E.A.Nuttall	"	"	"1	"1	"

Notes: M = Mill Lane; Feb 21, at Coalville; Mar 21, at Loughborough.

UNITED COUNTIES LEAGUE 1894-95

Feb 16	Derby County	A	2-2	Thraves	Whitelaw	Bailey	Seymour	Hughes	Henrys	Brown	McArthur 1	Gordon 1	Skea	Priestman
Mar 14	Notts County	A	2-0	"	Bailey	Thompson	Lord	"	"	Stirling	Milliken	Miller	"2	Hill
25	Sheffield United	A	2-3	"	"	Whitelaw	Brown 1	"	"	Hill	Miller	Gordon 1	Milliken	Stirling
Apr 1	Derby County	H	1-4	"	Smith	Bailey	Lord	"	"	McArthur	"	Miller	"1	Gallacher
4	Nottingham Forest	A	0-3	Chappell	"	"	"	Brown	"	Priestman	Milliken	Miller	Skea	"
13	Notts County	H	2-1	"	Thompson	McFarlane 1	Miller	Seymour	Lord	Stirling	Pickard	Milliken	Narraway 1	Priestman
22	Nottingham Forest	H	1-1	"	"	"	Davis	McAlpin	Whitelaw	Tyler	Stirling 1	"	"	"

SOUTHERN PROFESSIONAL FLOODLIT CUP 1959-60

Oct 21	Charlton Athletic	(1) H	4-0	Slack	Chalmers	Baillie	McLintock 1	Knapp	Appleton 1	Riley 1	Keyworth	Leek	Cheesebrough 1	Wills
Nov 23	Arsenal	(2) A	2-4	Banks	"	Norman	White	Cunningham	"	"	Stephenson	Walsh 1	Leek	"1

F.A.CHARITY SHIELD 1971-72

Aug 7	Liverpool	H	1-0	Shilton	Whitworth 1	Nish	Kellard	Sjoberg	Cross	Farrington	Brown	Fern	Sammels	Glover *
														(Manley)

ANGLO - ITALIAN TOURNAMENT 1971-72

Jun 1	Cagliari	A	0-1	Wallington	Whitworth *	Nish	Cross	Sjoberg *	Manley	Partridge	Sammels	Weller	Birchenall	Glover
					(Farrington)			(Fern)						
Jun 4	Atalanta	A	3-5	"	Whitworth	"	"	Sjoberg	"	"	"2	"1	"	"
Jun 7	Cagliari	H	2-1	"	"	"1*	"	Manley	Sammels	Farrington	Weller 1	Birchenall	Partridge *	"
						(Sjoberg)							(Fern)	
Jun 10	Atalanta	H	6-0	Shilton	Woollett	Yates	"	"	Nish 1	Tomlin	"2	Partridge	Sammels 1	"1*
														(Farrington)1

Notes: Jun 4, substitutes Farrington and Fern both played, but players withdrawn not noted; Jun 10, substitute Sjoberg also played, but player withdrawn not noted.

TEXACO CUP 1972-73

Sep 13	Dundee United	(1 leg 1) H	1-1	Shilton	Whitworth	Rofe	Woollett	Cross	Sammels	Farrington	Worthington	Weller 1	Tomlin	Manley
27	Dundee United	(1 leg 2) A	2-2	"	"	"	"	"	Birchenall	"	Stringfellow *	"	Worthington 1	Glover 1
											(Partridge)			
Oct 24	Norwich City	(2 leg 1) H	2-0	"	"	Sammels	Munro	Woollett	"1	Birchenall	"*	"1	"	
											(Partridge)			
Nov 8	Norwich City	(2 leg 2) A	0-2	Wallington	"	"	"	"	"	"	Manley *	"	"	
											(Jopling)			

Notes: Sep 27, won 3-0 on penalties; Nov 8, lost 3-4 on penalties.

TEXACO CUP 1973-74

Sep 19	Ayr United	(1 leg 1) A	1-1	Shilton	Whitworth	Manley	Stringfellow *	Munro	Cross	Weller	Sammels	Worthington	Birchenall	Glover
							(Partridge)							
Oct 3	Ayr United	(1 leg 2) H	2-0	"	"	Yates	Stringfellow 1	"	"	"	"	"	"1	"
24	Dundee United	(2 leg 1) H	1-1	"	"*	Rofe	"	"	Woollett	"	"	"1p	"	"
					(Farrington)									
Nov 7	Dundee United	(2 leg 2) A	0-1	"	Whitworth	"	Farrington *	"	Manley	"	"	"	"	"
							(Stringfellow)							

Note: Sep 19, McAnespie (og).

F.A. CUP THIRD PLACE PLAY OFF 1973-74

May 9	Burnley	H	0-1	Wallington	Woollett	Rofe	Earle	Munro	Cross	Tomlin	Sammels	Stringfellow	Kilkelly	Glover *
														(Lee)

ANGLO - SCOTTISH TOURNAMENT 1975-76

Aug 2	Hull City	A	1-1	Wallington	Whitworth	Rofe	Sammels 1	Blockley	Birchenall	Alderson	Kember	Lee	Worthington	Garland
6	Mansfield Town	A	0-2	"	"	"	"	"	"	Kember	Glover	Worthington	Garland	Alderson
9	West Bromwich Albion	H	2-1	"	"	"	Kember	"	"	Alderson	Garland	"	Sammels	Lee 2

FRIENDLIES

Below is a list of friendlies played by Fosse/City since 1884. Over the years there have been frequent instances where the club has fielded a team containing a mixture of first team players and reserves. In such cases we have exercised our judgement as well as we are able, so that only friendlies classed as 'first team' are included. Matches played behind closed doors are excluded.

FOSSE IN PRE-LEAGUE DAYS.

(Key to venues: V=Victoria Park; R=Racecourse; B=Belgrave Road; M=Mill Lane; A=away).
(NB: Especially in the case of the initial three venues, it is sometimes impossible to gather whether a given game was officially a 'home' or 'away' fixture. A cumulative record for season 1884/5 shows Fosse additionally having played two untraced games: a 0-0 draw and a 0-2 defeat. Where no scoreline is appended to a fixture, we know only that the said fixture was arranged: either the game was cancelled or, more likely, simply not reported. A summary of results for the first decade, produced in the 1893 club history is sometimes at odds with the total of individual match reports unearthed in the local press).

01.11.84 Syston Fosse 5-0
(at Fosse Road)
08.11.84 Wyggeston Boys School (V) 1-1
15.11.84 Mill Hill House (R) 1-2
22.11.84 Syston St Peters (A) 2-1
(12-a-side)
29.11.84 Mill Hill House (R) 0-0
03.01.85 Melbourne Hall (V) 2-0
10.01.85 Syston Fosse (A) 1-0
(abandoned: rain)
24.01.85 St Mary's (R) 1-0
31.01.85 Mill Hill House (R) 1-1
07.02.85 Syston St Peters (R) 2-0
(12-a-side)
07.03.85 Wyggeston Boys School (V) 0-1
14.03.85 Mill Hill House (V) 2-0
21.03.85 St Mary's (V) 1-0

03.10.85 Trinity Band of Hope (V) 6-0
17.10.85 Wyggeston Boys School (V) 4-1
24.10.85 Harborough (2nd Team) (V) 1-1
07.11.85 Mill Hill House (V) 0-1
14.11.85 Belgrave (A) 3-0
21.11.85 St Mary's (V) 3-0
30.01.86 Mill Hill House (V) 3-0
06.02.86 Wyggeston Boys School (V) 1-0
13.02.86 Syston Wreake Valley (A) 2-1
20.02.86 Belgrave (V) 1-0
17.04.86 Leicester Town (V) 2-0

16.10.86 Leicester Association (V) 2-1
23.10.86 Barwell (A) 1-1
30.10.86 Leicester Wanderers (V) 0-2
06.11.86 Coalville (A) 0-0
(abandoned: Coalville walk-off)
13.11.86 Wyggeston School
　　Past & Present (V) 5-0
20.11.86 Belgrave (A) 2-0
27.11.86 Leicester Association (V) 0-1
04.12.86 St Mark's (V) 2-2
11.12.86 Leicester Wanderers (V) 3-0
22.01.87 Coalville (V) 3-0
29.01.87 Wigston (V) 6-0
05.02.87 Loughborough (A) 1-4
12.02.87 Belgrave (V) 5-0
19.02.87 Barwell (V) 2-0
26.02.87 Notts St Saviours (A) 1-1
05.03.87 Market Harborough (V) 0-1
19.03.87 Wyggeston School
　　Past & Present (V) 9-0
26.03.87 Loughborough (V) 3-0
09.04.87 Mill Hill House Past & Present (V) 1-0

01.10.87 Market Harborough (V) 4-0
08.10.87 Mill Hill House (V) 2-0
15.10.87 Wellingborough (A) 0-3
22.10.87 Notts County Reserves (B) 0-5
05.11.87 Burton Swifts (B) 0-4
12.11.87 Kettering (B) 2-4
19.11.87 Market Harborough (A) 2-2
03.12.87 Leicester Wanderers (B) 1-0
15.12.87 Leicester Banks (V) 4-6
26.12.87 Leicester Association (B)

07.01.88 Notts County Reserves (A) 0-1
14.01.88 Mill Hill House (B) 0-2
26.01.88 Thursday Half-Holiday XI (V)
04.02.88 Leicester Association (V)
11.02.88 Kettering (A) 0-3
03.03.88 Burton Swifts (A)
10.03.88 Leicester Association (V) 2-0
15.03.88 Leicester Banks (V)
17.03.88 Loughborough (B)
24.03.88 Mill Hill House Past & Present (V)
31.03.88 Leicester Wanderers (V) 1-1
07.04.88 Rushden (B)
21.04.88 Coalville Town (A) 3-1
05.05.88 Coalville Town (A) 1-5

15.09.88 Long Eaton Midland (A) 1-4
22.09.88 Nottingham Forest Reserves (V) 0-3
29.09.88 Loughborough (A) 0-4
06.10.88 Leicester Teachers (V) 5-0
13.10.88 Coalville Town (V) 4-0
20.10.88 Shepshed (A) 2-2
27.10.88 Market Harborough (A) 6-0
03.11.88 Kettering (A) 2-1
17.11.88 Loughborough (A) 1-3
24.11.88 Nottingham Forest Reserves (A) 1-2
01.12.88 Kettering (V) 0-1
08.12.88 Mill Hill House (A) 3-0
15.12.88 Wellingborough (V) 0-0
22.12.88 Beeston St John's (V)
29.12.88 Notts County Reserves (A)
05.01.89 Market Harborough (V)
12.01.89 Bulwell United (V) 0-0
19.01.89 Sawley Rangers (A) 3-1
26.01.89 Long Eaton Midland (V) 2-3
02.02.89 Notts County Reserves (V) 1-2
09.02.89 Wellingborough (A)
16.02.89 Notts St Johns (A) 2-2
02.03.89 Sawley Rangers (V)
09.03.89 Leicester Teachers (V) 2-1
16.03.89 Wellingborough (A) 8-2
23.03.89 Shepshed (V) 3-2
30.03.89 Leicester Teachers (V) 2-0
06.04.89 Bulwell United (A)
13.04.89 Mill Hill House (A) 3-2
(Leics Children's Hospital Fund)
20.04.89 Coalville Town (A) 1-0

28.09.89 Bulwell United (A) 0-3
05.10.89 Mill Hill House (M) 3-1
12.10.89 Grantham (A) 0-2
19.10.89 Notts Mapperley (M) 0-2
26.10.89 Leicester Teachers (M) 6-2
02.11.89 Coalville Town (A) 3-1
09.11.89 Market Harborough (M) 9-0
16.11.89 Long Eaton Midland (A) 0-2
23.11.89 Nottingham Forest Reserves (M) 0-1
30.11.89 Shepshed (M) 6-1
(Kettering Charity Cup Rd 1)
21.12.89 Grantham Rovers (A) 0-3
26.12.89 Stafford Rangers (A) 1-2
11.01.90 Notts County Reserves (M) 1-2
18.01.90 Kettering (A) 2-4
25.01.90 Beeston St Johns (A)

01.02.90 Beeston St Johns (M) 4-0
08.02.90 Kettering (A) 1-3
(Kettering Charity Cup Rd 3)
15.02.90 Leicester Wanderers (M)
22.02.90 Kettering (M) 2-2
(Kettering Charity Cup Rd 3)
08.03.90 Bulwell United (M) 5-0
15.03.90 Coalville Town (M) 1-1
04.04.90 Gresley Rovers (A)
05.04.90 Notts County Reserves (M) 2-3
08.04.90 Sheffield Montrose (M) 2-0

(NB: Kettering Charity Cup 1889/90: Fosse received bye in Rd 2; protested the result in Rd 3 over the state of Kettering's ground and gained a replay; but we have no record of a further replay after the 2-2 draw, and presume Fosse withdrew).

06.09.90 Boston Town (A) 7-4
13.09.90 Singers (Coventry) (M) 5-3
20.09.90 Northampton (M) 10-0
27.09.90 Notts Mapperley (M) 3-0
11.10.90 Long Eaton Rangers Reserves (M) 3-2
18.10.90 Burton Casuals (A) 0-1
25.10.90 Wellingborough Grammar
　　School (M) 4-1
01.11.90 Beeston St Johns (M) 4-0
08.11.90 Notts County Rovers (A) 4-3
15.11.90 Aston Villa Reserves (M) 2-3
24.11.90 Finedon (A) 0-1
(Kettering Charity Cup Rd 1)
29.11.90 Singers (Coventry) (A)
06.12.90 Derby County Wanderers (M) 3-1
13.12.90 Loughborough (M) 1-1
20.12.90 Beeston St Johns (A)
26.12.90 Stafford Rangers (A) 1-1
27.12.90 London Casuals (M) 1-0
29.12.90 Loughborough (B) 1-1
(Charity Match)
03.01.91 Kettering Town (A)
31.01.91 Leicester Teachers (M) 8-0
07.02.91 Loughborough (A) 1-3
14.02.91 Stafford Rangers (M) 0-2
28.02.91 Notts County Rovers (M) 3-3
07.03.91 Grantham Rovers (A) 2-3
14.03.91 Nottingham Forest Reserves (M) 2-3
28.03.91 Notts Olympic (M) 5-0
30.03.91 Burton Wanderers (M) 2-2
31.03.91 Nottingham Forest Reserves (M) 1-0
04.04.91 Sheffield Attercliffe (M) 2-3
11.04.91 Long Eaton Rangers (A) 3-0
11.04.91 Kettering Town (M) 3-2
(Mixed team. Two fixtures on same day)
13.04.91 Leicester Teachers/YMCA Select
(YMCA Benefit) (M) 2-1
18.04.91 Stafford Rangers (M) 1-0
25.04.91 Burton Alma (M) 5-1
27.04.91 Notts County (M) 2-2

FOSSE AS A MIDLAND LEAGUE/FOOTBALL LEAGUE CLUB.

(NB : Apart from the first five friendly fixtures marked (H*) below, which were played at the Aylestone Road Cricket Ground, all home fixtures hereafter took place at Filbert Street).

05.09.91 Stafford Rangers (A) 0-1
07.09.91 Derby County (H*) 1-3
14.09.91 Notts County (H*) 3-4
19.09.91 Stafford Rangers (H*) 5-2
26.09.91 Singers (H*) 4-1
24.10.91 Notts Olympic (H*) 6-1
31.10.91 Kettering (A) 2-0
07.11.91 Nottingham Forest 'A' (H) 1-1
21.11.91 Wellingborough (H) 6-1
    (Kettering Charity Cup Rd 1)
12.12.91 Kettering (A) 0-5
    (Kettering Charity Cup Rd 2)
28.12.91 Notts County Rovers (H) 0-0
16.01.92 Loughborough (A) 1-4
20.02.92 Singers (A) 1-3
27.02.92 Wolverhampton Wanderers
    Reserves (H) 1-3
05.03.92 Kettering (H) 2-2
26.03.92 Leicestershire XI (H) 4-1
    (Children's Hospital Charity)
31.03.92 Notts St Johns (H) 3-2
07.04.92 Notts Waverley (H) 5-1
18.04.92 Ilford (H) 1-2
23.04.92 Loughborough (H) 1-2
25.04.92 Bolton Wanderers (H) 0-2

03.09.92 Singers (H) 10-1
10.09.92 Rudge's (Coventry) (H) 5-3
21.09.92 Mansfield Greenhalgh's (A) 0-0
24.09.92 Finedon (H) 6-0
03.12.92 Derby Town (H) 1-1
    (abandoned 83 mins)
10.12.92 Royal Scots (H) 2-0
26.12.92 Casuals (H) 4-1
27.12.92 Stafford Rangers (H) 1-0
31.12.92 Oswaldtwistle Rovers (H) 5-1
11.02.93 Notts County Rovers (H) 7-2
04.04.93 Stoke Swifts (H) 2-2
05.04.93 Loughborough (A) 1-4
15.04.93 Nottingham Forest (H) 1-5
24.04.93 Burton Swifts (H) 0-1
29.04.93 Loughborough (H) 5-1

02.09.93 Gainsborough Trinity (H) 5-0
04.09.93 West Bromwich Albion (H) 3-0
16.09.93 Sheffield United (H) 4-1
25.09.93 Notts County (H) 1-2
09.10.93 Accrington (H) 1-0
14.10.93 Northwich Victoria (H) 5-1
28.10.93 Heanor Town (H) 3-1
11.11.93 Burslem Port Vale (H) 5-0
26.12.93 Casuals (H) 6-0
    (Bailey Benefit)
27.12.93 Corinthians (H) 0-1
30.12.93 Kettering (H) 8-0
    (Kettering Charity Cup sf)
26.03.94 Newcastle United (H) 2-0
27.03.94 Stockport County (H) 2-0
28.03.94 Rangers (H) 1-2
31.03.94 Loughborough (A) 1-1
02.04.94 Aston Villa (A) 1-5
    (Bass Charity Cup Rd 1)
07.04.94 Wolverton L&NWR (at Kettering) 3-1
    (Kettering Charity Cup F)
14.04.94 Loughborough (H) 6-0
21.04.94 Rotherham Town (H) 2-0
30.04.94 Wolverhampton Wanderers (H) 0-2

03.09.94 Derby County (H) 3-2
10.09.94 Preston North End (H) 3-1
17.09.94 Sunderland (H) 0-3
24.09.94 Sheffield Wednesday (H) 5-3
29.10.94 Rushden (H) 4-1

24.12.94 Casuals (H) 3-2
26.12.94 Corinthians (H) 1-2
19.01.95 Kings Own Scottish Borderers (H) 11-0
11.02.95 Kettering (H) 6-1
    (Kettering Charity Cup Rd 1)
11.03.95 Loughborough (at Kettering) 3-1
    (Kettering Charity Cup sf)
27.03.95 Aston Villa (at Burton Swifts) 2-1
    (Bass Charity Cup sf)
08.04.95 Burton Wanderers (at Kettering) 0-1
    (Kettering Charity Cup F)
12.04.95 Rotherham Town (H) 1-0
16.04.95 Rangers (H) 1-2
24.04.95 Burton Wanderers (at Burton Swifts) 1-2
    (Bass Charity Cup F)
25.04.95 Everton (H) 0-5

02.09.95 Nottingham Forest (H) 0-1
16.09.95 Millwall Athletic (H) 4-1
23.09.95 Millwall Athletic (A) 1-4
31.10.95 Nottingham Forest (A) 2-5
25.12.95 Cliftonville Athletic (H) 4-1
26.12.95 Corinthians (H) 1-2
28.12.95 Casuals (H) 6-5
    (largely Fosse reserve team)
02.01.96 Middlesbrough (A) 3-2
13.01.96 Walsall (A) 0-3
    (Wellingborough Charity Cup Rd 1)
15.01.96 Burton Wanderers (A) 0-1
    (Kettering Charity Cup Rd 1)
20.01.96 Burton Swifts (A) 1-2
    (Birmingham Charity Cup Rd 1)
01.02.96 Fairfield (H) 3-3
18.02.96 Loughborough (H) 2-2
14.03.96 Small Heath (H) 3-2
16.03.96 Wellingborough (A) 0-1
18.03.96 Loughborough (A) 0-0
25.03.96 Burton Wanderers (A) 0-1
    (Bass Charity Cup sf)
18.04.96 Preston North End (H) 0-4
25.04.96 Stoke (H) 1-3

01.09.96 Luton Town (H) 2-0
    (Thraves Benefit)
21.09.96 Aston Villa (H) 2-3
05.10.96 Luton Town (A) 0-2
10.10.96 Kettering (H) 5-2
15.10.96 Loughborough (H) 4-2
31.10.96 Grantham Rovers (H) 2-0
    (Rushden Charity Cup Rd 1)
07.12.96 Walsall (A) 3-8
    (Birmingham Charity Cup Rd 1)
26.12.96 Corinthians (H) 3-3
30.01.97 Reading (A) 3-4
04.02.97 Burton Wanderers (H) 2-2
    (Kettering Charity Cup Rd 1)
08.02.97 Burton Wanderers (A) 0-0
    (Kettering Charity Cup Rd 1 rep)
15.02.97 Burton Wanderers (at Kettering) 2-1
    (Kettering Charity Cup Rd 1 rep 2)
09.03.97 Wellingborough (at Rushden) 5-1
    (Rushden Charity Cup sf)
11.03.97 Luton Town (at Kettering) 0-3
    (Kettering Charity Cup sf)
31.03.97 Loughborough (A) 0-0
03.04.97 Nottingham Forest (H) 3-0
    (Burford Charity Cup sf)
20.04.97 Rangers (H) 1-1
24.04.97 Sheffield Wednesday (H) 1-0
28.04.97 Notts County (at Nottingham Forest) 2-0
    (Burford Charity Cup F)
29.04.97 Rushden (A) 4-0
    (Rushden Charity Cup F)

01.09.97 Glossop North End (H) 5-0
09.09.97 Derby County (H) 3-1
13.09.97 Bolton Wanderers (H) 5-1
    (Lord Benefit)
20.09.97 Nottingham Forest (H) 4-0
25.09.97 Long Eaton Rangers (H) 4-2
27.09.97 West Bromwich Albion (H) 4-1
11.10.97 Rushden (A) 1-0
    (Rushden Charity Cup sf)
30.10.97 Luton Town (H) 5-2
01.11.97 Wellingborough (at Rushden) 0-1
    (Rushden Charity Cup F)
27.12.97 Everton (H) 1-1
28.12.97 Corinthians (H) 1-2
01.01.98 Millwall Athletic (A) 2-3
17.01.98 Wolverhampton Wanderers (H) 1-3
    (Birmingham Charity Cup Rd 2)
24.02.98 Loughborough (H) 4-0
12.04.98 Burslem Port Vale (H) 1-2
13.04.98 Burton Wanderers (A) 1-1
    (Bass Charity Cup sf)
20.04.98 Burton Wanderers (A) 0-1
    (Bass Charity Cup sf rep)
23.04.98 Aston Villa (H) 2-1
25.04.98 Notts County (H) 2-1
    (Burford Charity Cup sf)
28.04.98 Nottingham Forest (A) 0-1
    (Burford Charity Cup F)

05.09.98 Southampton (H) 1-0
    (Brown Benefit)
14.09.98 Southampton (A) 0-1
19.12.98 Burslem Port Vale (A) 0-5
    (Birmingham Charity Cup Rd 1)
28.12.98 Corinthians (H) 2-2
    (Dorrell Benefit)
14.02.99 Brighton United (H) 6-4
25.03.99 Loughborough (H) 1-2
06.04.99 Nottingham Forest (H) 1-1
    (Bass Charity Cup sf)
08.04.99 Leicestershire Senior League (H) 1-1
17.04.99 Nottingham Forest (at Burton) 1-7
    (Bass Charity Cup sf rep)

04.09.99 Nottingham Forest (H) 1-4
07.10.99 Kaffirs (H) 7-3
19.10.99 Everton (H) 1-4
    (Walker Benefit)
06.11.99 Orson Wright & Sons (H) 2-0
26.12.99 Corinthians (H) 1-7
15.01.00 Aston Villa (H) 2-3
    (Birmingham Charity Cup Rd 1)
10.02.00 Stoke (H) 2-2
17.03.00 West Bromwich Albion (H) 3-1

03.09.00 Chesterfield (H) 0-1
    (Bass Charity Vase sf)
11.10.00 Wolverhampton Wanderers (H) 1-0
    (Swift Benefit)
08.12.00 Hinckley (A) 3-2
24.12.00 Notts County (H) 3-4
    (McMillan Benefit)
26.12.00 Corinthians (H) 2-1
23.02.01 Bristol City (A) 0-1
04.03.01 Northampton Town (A) 6-1
06.04.01 Scottish Amateurs (H) 3-2
13.04.01 Brighton & Hove Rangers (A) 0-0
20.04.01 Lincoln City (A) 1-2
    (Gibson Benefit)

02.09.01 Stourbridge (H) 3-0
16.09.01 Wellingborough (H) 4-0

25.09.01 Chesterfield (A) 2-3
(Bass Charity Vase sf)
01.10.01 Grimsby Town (A) 0-1
08.02.02 Brentford (A) 1-1
23.04.02 Ripley (A) 3-1

25.10.02 Clapton (A) 1-1
13.12.02 Queens Park Rangers (A) 3-2
24.03.03 Brighton & Hove Albion (A) 4-5
25.04.03 Reading (H) 1-0
27.04.03 Hinckley (A) 1-4

01.09.03 Kettering (H) 1-1
02.09.03 Reading (A) 1-4
14.09.03 Notts County (A) 0-2
28.12.03 Clapton (H) 1-1
(Robinson Benefit)
21.03.04 Hinckley (A) 6-1
01.04.04 Watford (A) 1-2
23.04.04 Northern Nomads
(at Goodison Park) 3-0

05.09.04 Northampton Town (H) 2-1
12.09.04 Luton Town (A) 2-2
19.09.04 Hull City (A) 0-2
25.02.05 Leeds City (A) 5-1
25.04.05 Nottingham Forest (H) 1-2
29.04.05 Clapton (H) 1-1

03.02.06 West Ham United (A) 0-2
12.03.06 Fulham (A) 2-6

07.04.06 Sheffield United (H) 2-0
17.04.06 Notts County (H) 1-1
23.04.06 Norwich City (A) 3-3
28.04.06 Coventry City (A) 3-1

15.10.06 Luton Town (A) 1-1
28.02.07 Luton Town (H) 1-0
02.03.07 Stockport County (H) 4-0

16.09.07 Luton Town (A) 1-5
23.09.07 Notts County (H) 6-3
30.09.07 Burton United (A) 2-1
29.04.08 Measham & District (A) 1-2
(Lawden Colliery Disaster Fund)

05.10.08 Blackburn Rovers (at Burton) 1-3
12.10.08 Northampton Town (A) 0-2
(Murrell Benefit)
26.04.09 Coventry City (A) 2-0
(Bass Charity Vase F)

01.01.10 Portsmouth (A) 1-2

25.10.10 Grimsby Town (A) 1-3

30.12.11 Barrow (A) 1-4
12.02.12 Merthyr Tydfil (A) 4-0
06.03.12 Croydon Common (A) 2-3
04.05.12 Leicestershire XI (H) 3-3
(Titanic Disaster Fund)

16.09.12 Swansea Town (A) 0-1
01.02.13 Gillingham (A) 2-0
01.03.13 Barrow (A) 1-3
18.06.13 Orgryte/Kamraterna Combined XI
(at Gothenburg) 3-2
20.06.13 Stockholm Select XI (A) 4-0
22.06.13 Swedish International Federation
(at Rosunda) 4-2
24.06.13 Gefle IF (A) 5-1
27.06.13 Swedish International Federation
(at Rosunda) 4-2

31.01.14 Northampton Town (A) 1-5

28.09.14 Swansea Town (A) 0-3
29.09.14 Llanelly (A) 1-2

25.09.15 Luton Town (A) 2-3
16.05.16 Birmingham (A) 3-6

17.03.17 Coalville Swifts (A) 2-2
(VAD Nursing Association Benefit Fund)
28.04.17 Coalville Swifts (A) 1-2
(Disabled Soldiers/Sailors Benefit)

01.04.18 Coventry City (H) 8-3

09.11.18 Coventry City (A) 2-0
28.04.19 British Expeditionary Force
(France) XI (H) 1-1

LEICESTER CITY

02.10.19 Select XI (H) 7-2
(Mills Benefit)
22.04.20 Nuneaton Town (A) 3-1

27.04.22 Northampton Town (A) 1-0
(Northampton Hospital Cup)
04.05.22 Northampton Town (H) 1-1
(Leicester Royal Infirmary Benefit)

01.10.23 Raith Rovers (A) 1-5

30.04.25 Airdrieonians (H) 3-1
(Leicestershire CCC Benefit)
04.05.25 Port Vale (A) 5-3
(Stoke Royal Infirmary Benefit)

15.03.26 Southampton (A) 0-2
(Allen/Shelley Benefit)
08.04.26 Hull City (A) 2-1
(Hull Hospital Cup)
10.04.26 Kettering Town (A) 3-1
20.04.26 Airdrieonians (H) 2-0
(Hodge Benefit)
26.04.26 Norwich City (A) 2-1
(Norfolk & Norwich Hospital Cup)
01.05.26 Torquay United (A) 2-0

26.02.27 Plymouth Argyle (A) 4-2
02.05.27 Norwich City (A) 4-1
(Norfolk & Norwich Hospital Cup)

03.03.28 St Mirren (H) 4-1
11.04.28 Scottish League XI (H) 7-2
(Leicestershire CCC Benefit)
03.05.28 Grimsby Town (A) 5-4
(Grimsby Hospital Cup)

22.04.29 Birmingham (at Loughborough) 5-2
(Hospital Benefit)
29.04.29 Northampton Town (A) 1-3
(Northants CCC Benefit)
06.05.29 Grimsby Town (A) 2-1
(Grimsby Hospital Cup)

30.04.30 Grimsby Town (A) 2-1
(Grimsby Hospital Cup)
10.05.30 Blackpool (A) 3-2
(Blackpool Hospital Cup)

24.01.31 Bournemouth & Boscombe
Athletic (A) 3-3
14.03.31 Aberdeen (A) 2-2
09.05.31 Blackpool (A) 3-2
(Blackpool Hospital Cup)

02.05.32 Northampton Town (A) 3-4
05.05.32 Crook Town (A) 6-4

19.09.32 Bristol Rovers (A) 3-1
27.09.32 Grimsby Town (at Spalding) 7-2
(Nursing Cup)
28.01.33 Rapid Vienna (H) 1-3

18.09.33 Yeovil & Petters United (A) 1-0
20.09.33 Exeter City (A) 2-3
16.04.34 St Johnstone (H) 2-1
26.04.34 Doncaster Rovers (A) 2-1
01.05.34 Shelbourne (A) 3-2
02.05.34 Linfield (A) 1-1

20.09.34 Tunbridge Wells Rangers (A) 4-1
15.04.35 Clapton Orient (A) 2-2

06.05.35 Coventry City (A) 3-3

30.04.36 Central Amateur League XI
(at Loughborough) 5-1

18.11.36 Cheltenham Town (A) 3-1
14.04.37 Coalville & District (A) 2-1
(Bradshaw Test)
26.04.37 Chesterfield (A) 4-2
(Hamilton Test)
04.05.37 Grimsby Town (A) 2-5
(Grimsby Hospital Cup)
12.05.37 Venus Bucharest (A) 0-2
13.05.37 Ripensia Bucharest (A) 1-2
16.05.37 Hungaria Budapest (A) 3-4

17.05.37 BSK Belgrade (A) 0-3
23.05.37 Bratislava (A) 1-3

20.08.38 Derby County (H) 4-2
(FL Jubilee Benevolent Fund)
20.04.39 Rushden (A) 5-2
(Rushden Charity Cup)
27.04.39 Stamford Town (A) 6-0
(Hospital Cup)

19.08.39 Derby County (A) 6-4
(FL Jubilee Benevolent Fund)
13.09.39 Army XI (H) 7-2
16.09.39 Aston Villa (H) 3-0
23.09.39 Birmingham (H) 6-4
30.09.39 Coventry City (A) 3-3
07.10.39 Sheffield United (H) 2-2
14.10.39 Port Vale (H) 2-2
26.12.39 Nottingham Forest (A) 1-3
01.01.40 Chesterfield (A) 2-7
25.03.40 Sheffield Wednesday (H) 5-2
13.04.40 Chelmsford City (A) 0-1

13.12.41 Czech Army XI (H) 8-1
25.04.42 Crystal Palace (A) 3-1
02.05.42 Birmingham (at Villa Park) 3-0
09.05.42 Birmingham (H) 4-2

19.05.45 Crystal Palace (H) 0-1
26.05.45 Crystal Palace (A) 4-1

02.03.46 Preston North End (A) 3-2
11.05.46 Notts County (A) 0-5

29.03.47 Arsenal (A) 1-3

22.04.48 Moira & District (A) 4-3
30.04.48 St Mirren (A) 0-3

05.09.49 Linfield (A) 5-1
28.01.50 Luton Town (A) 1-4
01.05.50 Exeter City (A) 0-1
(Gallagher Test)
03.05.50 Notts County (H) 3-0
(S.Smith Test)

27.01.51 Sheffield Wednesday (H) 1-0
10.02.51 Reading (A) 2-2
03.05.51 Derby County (H) 4-3
(Frame Test)
14.05.51 FK Austria (H) 1-2
(Festival of Britain)

05.03.52 Cheltenham Town (A) 3-1
21.04.52 Torquay United (A) 6-2
(Towers Test)
28.04.52 Portsmouth (H) 4-1
(Bradshaw Test)
07.05.52 Wisbech Town (A) 5-0
(Horace Racey Charity Cup)
13.05.52 North Holland XI (at Groningen) 1-1
17.05.52 East Holland XI (at Nijmegen) 4-1
21.05.52 Utrecht (A) 3-1
24.05.52 PSV Eindhoven (A) 3-2

31.01.53 Charlton Athletic (H) 4-3
22.04.53 Mansfield Town (A) 2-3
(Grogan/Carter Test)
29.04.53 Wolverhampton Wanderers (H) 1-2
(McGraw Test)
04.05.53 Wisbech Town (A) 2-1
(Horace Racey Charity Cup)

30.11.53 Weymouth (A) 3-1

29.01.55 Lincoln City (A) 4-3
11.05.55 Shelbourne (A) 2-1
(Fitzpatrick Test)
13.05.55 Cork Athletic (A) 4-1

26.09.55 Penzance (A) 6-2
02.05.56 Tommy Lawton's XI (at Kettering) 3-3
(Johnson/Waddell Test)
12.05.56 St Mirren (A) 3-1
(Paisley Charity Cup)
14.05.56 Inverness Select XI (A) 2-0

16.02.57 Hibernian (A) 3-2
25.04.57 International XI (H) 2-6
(Griffiths Test)
29.04.57 Hibernian (H) 1-4
02.05.57 Chelsea (A) 1-2
(Armstrong Test)

23.09.57 Aberdeen (A) 1-1
23.10.57 Borussia Dortmund (H) 1-0
(Floodlight Inauguration)
14.11.57 BSK Belgrade (H) 3-2
25.01.58 Peterborough United (A) 1-2
27.01.58 Walsall (A) 3-1
28.04.58 Canto do Rio (H) 1-0
30.04.58 Kettering Town (A) 2-4
(Toseland Test)
05.05.58 Norwich City (A) 2-3
(Norfolk Hospital Cup)
21.05.58 TUS Neuendorf (A) 1-1

10.08.58 Borussia Dortmund (A) 1-2
29.10.58 Borussia Dortmund (H) 2-2
26.11.58 Raith Rovers (H) 3-3
01.05.59 Shrewsbury Town (A) 2-2

26.10.59 Corby Town (A) 5-0
28.03.60 Hibernian (H) 0-1
02.05.60 Loughborough Brush (A) 6-0
(Hodges Test)

26.09.60 Dunfermline Athletic (A) 2-3
14.11.60 Peterborough United (A) 2-2
21.05.61 Southern Rhodesia (at Salisbury) 2-0
25.05.61 Southern Rhodesia (at Bulawayo) 4-3
27.05.61 Durban City (A) 2-0
31.05.61 Natal (at Pietermaritzburg) 6-0
03.06.61 Combined Transvaal XI
(at Johannesburg) 1-1

05.08.61 St Mirren (A) 1-3
(Paisley Charity Cup)
12.08.61 Walsall (A) 0-1
13.12.61 Arthur Chandler's XI (H) 8-3
(Chandler Test)
27.01.62 Rotherham United (A) 1-1
19.03.62 Oxford United (A) 2-5
(Love/Denial Benefit)
31.03.62 Partick Thistle (H) 2-1
09.05.62 Gibraltar (A) 5-0
12.05.62 Malaga (A) 1-0

11.08.62 Leeds United (A) 4-2
13.08.62 Leeds United (H) 2-2
23.01.63 Peterborough United (A) 2-1

13.08.63 GVAV Groningen (A) 3-2
15.08.63 Blau Wit (A) 3-0
19.08.63 Grimsby Town (A) 1-1
24.01.64 Coventry City (A) 1-0
08.04.64 Poole Town (A) 2-1
(Rickaby Test)
29.04.64 All Star XI (H) 7-3
(Appleton Test)
10.05.64 Ingoldstadt (A) 2-2
13.05.64 Lustenau (A) 0-1
15.05.64 LASK Linz (A) 1-2
18.05.64 Innsbruck (A) 5-2

15.08.64 Shrewsbury Town (A) 4-1
17.08.64 Peterborough United (A) 3-2
26.10.64 Hannover '96 (H) 5-1
11.05.65 GVAV Groningen (A) 1-1
15.05.65 Dresden Select (A) 2-2
18.05.65 Hannover '96 (A) 1-0

06.08.65 Shamrock Rovers (A) 5-2
09.08.65 Cork Hibernian (A) 6-3
12.08.65 Limerick (A) 6-1
16.08.65 Northampton Town (H) 6-1
25.10.65 Nuneaton Borough (A) 1-3
02.05.66 Scotland XI (H) 1-1
(Dowdells Test)

06.08.66 Borussia Munchengladbach (A) 3-0
10.08.66 Gottingen (A) 4-1
13.08.66 Werder Bremen (A) 3-1
21.09.66 PSV Eindhoven (A) 3-1
12.10.66 Oxford United (A) 3-1
16.02.67 Crystal Palace (A) 1-1
18.02.67 Rangers (H) 1-0
10.03.67 Derby County (A) 2-1
18.04.67 Borussia Dortmund (H) 6-0

01.05.67 Werder Bremen (H) 2-2
20.05.67 Southampton (at Kuala Lumpur) 3-1
25.05.67 Asian All Stars (at Penang) 7-0
30.05.67 Asian All Stars (at Kuala Lumpur) 3-0
03.06.67 Asian All Stars (at Singapore) 3-0
05.06.67 Southampton (at Singapore) 2-2

05.08.67 Kaiserslautern (A) 0-1
10.08.67 Eintracht Braunschweig (A) 2-1
11.08.67 VFB Stuttgart (A) 1-0
11.10.67 Racing Club de Strasbourg (A) 1-2
22.05.68 Zambian Combined FA XI (at Kitwe) 6-1
25.05.68 Zambian International XI (at Lusaka) 1-0
26.05.68 Zambian International XI (at Ndola) 2-0
29.05.68 English Coaches XI (at Mufilira) 4-1
02.06.68 Zambian International XI (at Lusaka) 3-2
03.06.68 Zambian Combined FA XI
(at Livingstone) 5-1

02.08.68 Schalke '04 (A) 1-2
05.08.68 Walsall (A) 0-1
17.12.68 Borussia Dortmund (A) 0-2
24.05.69 Gibraltar XI (A) 4-3

26.07.69 Scunthorpe United (A) 4-0
29.07.69 Rotherham United (A) 1-2
02.08.69 Portsmouth (A) 2-2
02.03.70 Plymouth Argyle XI (A) 4-3
(Corbett Test)

01.08.70 Rotherham United (A) 0-1
04.08.70 Notts County (A) 2-1
07.08.70 Eintracht Braunschweig (H) 2-0
09.08.70 ADO (Den Haag) (A) 0-3
18.11.70 Moscow Dynamo (H) 2-0
03.05.71 Vejle Boldklub (A) 0-3
04.05.71 Skive (A) 1-0
07.05.71 Fredrikshavn (A) 6-1
11.05.71 Landskrona (A) 2-0
25.05.71 Derby County (H) 1-0
(Sjoberg Test)

04.08.71 Coventry City (at Nuneaton) 0-0
26.10.71 Peterborough United (A) 2-5
(Wright/Conmy Test)
26.04.72 Hannover '96 (H) 5-1
09.05.72 Olympiakos (A) 1-2

29.07.72 Bristol City (A) 1-5
01.08.72 Port Vale (A) 0-1
05.08.72 FC Groningen (H) 2-2
07.08.72 Walsall (A) 0-0
(Baker Test)
10.04.73 Bournemouth (A) 1-2
(Green Test)
09.05.73 PAOK Thessalonikis (A) 2-2
26.05.73 Ipswich Town (at Barbados) 3-2
29.05.73 Barbados XI (A) 1-0
31.05.73 Ipswich Town (at Barbados) 1-1

29.07.73 GAIS Gothenburg (A) 5-2
(Sir Stanley Rous Cup)
01.08.73 Wolverhampton Wanderers
(at Gothenburg) 0-1
(Sir Stanley Rous Cup)
11.08.73 Notts County (A) 2-1
18.08.73 Aston Villa (A) 1-0
03.05.74 Oxford United (A) 1-2
(Fish Test)
06.05.74 Derby County (H) 2-2
(Cross Test)
13.05.74 Nottingham Forest (A) 1-1
(Winfield Test)
15.05.74 Corby Town (A) 0-3

27.07.74 Hannover SV (A) 2-0
01.08.74 FC Groningen (A) 1-3
04.08.74 VVV Venlo (A) 3-1
10.08.74 Nottingham Forest (A) 3-1

30.04.75 Wolverhampton Wanderers (H) 2-2
(Stringfellow Test)
05.05.75 Bristol City XI (A) 4-2
(Morgan Test)
09.05.75 Exeter City (A) 1-1
(Banks Test)

17.07.75 Trollhatton (A) 1-2
20.07.75 Orgryte (A) 3-0
23.07.75 IFK Gothenburg (A) 2-1
(Sir Stanley Rous Cup)
26.07.75 Varberg (A) 4-1
(Barometern Cup)
28.07.75 Skovde (A) 4-0
(Barometern Cup)
28.10.75 Fulham (A) 2-2
(Earle Test)
12.04.76 Northampton Town (A) 1-1
(Clarke Test)
26.04.76 Peterborough United (A) 2-3
(Robson Test)
27.04.76 Portsmouth (A) 1-3
(Manley Test)
13.05.76 Mjondalen (A) 5-0
17.05.76 Odd (A) 4-1
19.05.76 Molde (A) 3-1
23.05.76 Ski (A) 2-1

26.07.76 Jonkoping (A) 4-2
28.07.76 Kalmar (A) 0-1
01.08.76 Halmstads BK (A) 0-0
05.08.76 CSKA Sofia (at Valencia) 0-1
06.08.76 Levanthe (A) 2-1
14.08.76 Charlton Athletic (A) 3-1
07.03.77 Kuwait (A) 2-1
19.04.77 SK Brann (A) 1-1
25.04.77 Sheffield Wednesday (A) 3-2
(Prendergast Test)
10.05.77 Chelsea (H) 3-0
(Woollett Test)
18.05.77 Kettering Town (A) 2-1
(Ashby Test)
20.05.77 Southend United (A) 3-3
(Rowley Test)

01.08.77 Walsall (A) 1-1
08.08.77 Gallivare (A) 3-0
10.08.77 Tottenham Hotspur
(at Umea, Sweden) 1-2 (Nolia Cup)
13.08.77 Royal Union Bruxelles
(at Umea, Sweden) 2-1 (Nolia Cup)
12.09.77 Nottingham Forest (A) 0-0
(O'Kane Test)

06.08.78 Den Haag (A) 4-0
08.08.78 Amsterdam (A) 1-1
11.08.78 Heerenveen (A) 2-2
12.08.78 Volendam (A) 2-0

17.07.79 Vastra Nylland (A) 7-1
19.07.79 IFK Grankulla (A) 1-0
22.07.79 Lysekil SF (A) 6-1
24.07.79 GFF (A) 4-1
26.07.79 OSK (A) 3-2
30.07.79 Halverstorp (A) 13-1
01.08.79 Halmar (A) 3-0
02.08.79 Rydboholm (A) 2-0
05.09.79 Aberdeen (A) 1-1
17.09.79 Elgin City (A) 1-1
01.10.79 Hinckley Athletic (A) 1-0
(Floodlight Inauguration)
22.10.79 Tulsa Roughnecks (H) 1-1
06.11.79 Coventry City (H) 3-1
(Whitworth Test)
10.12.79 Hibernian (A) 2-3
15.01.80 Hibernian (H) 0-2
16.02.80 Kilmarnock (A) 1-1
16.05.80 Nottingham Forest (A) 0-0
(Robertson Test)

02.08.80 Hertha Berlin (A) 1-1
05.08.80 Karlsruhe (A) 0-1
06.08.80 Asberg (A) 5-0
09.08.80 Haarlem (A) 1-0
11.08.80 Hertha Berlin (H) 2-1
03.11.80 Haarlem (H) 3-2
24.11.80 Australia (H) 1-2
11.02.81 Red Star Belgrade (H) 3-0
07.04.81 Saarbrucken (A) 2-1

09.08.81 Hallevadsholm (A) 2-0
10.08.81 Laxarby (A) 7-2
15.08.81 Gunnilse (A) 3-0
19.08.81 Skoglunds (A) 0-1
20.08.81 Oddevold (A) 2-1
25.08.81 Saarbrucken (H) 4-0
12.10.81 Berwick Rangers (A) 0-1
(Centenary Match)
20.10.81 Desborough (A) 6-1
(Floodlight Inauguration)
19.01.82 Bideford (A) 5-0

13.08.82 Bideford (A) 2-0
16.08.82 Exeter City (A) 1-1
18.08.82 Plymouth Argyle (A) 3-2
20.08.82 Swansea City (A) 2-2
23.08.82 Notts County (H) 2-1
20.10.82 Nottingham Forest (H) 0-2
(Wallington Test)
08.03.83 Buckingham Town (A) 5-1
28.03.83 Inverness Caledonian (A) 4-0
16.05.83 Wolverhampton Wanderers (A) 1-3
(Palmer Test)

13.08.83 Heart of Midlothian (A) 3-2
15.08.83 St Johnstone (A) 2-1
19.08.83 Barnsley (A) 0-2

06.08.84 Telford United (A) 1-0
08.08.84 Rangers (A) 2-2
13.08.84 Aberdeen (H) 1-1
(Centenary Match)
18.08.84 Go Ahead Eagles (A) 4-1
20.08.84 PEC Zwolle (A) 3-2
03.10.84 Wycombe Wanderers (A) 0-0
(Centenary Match)
05.11.84 New Zealand (H) 4-1
13.11.84 Shepshed Charterhouse (A) 3-0

28.07.85 Newcastle United
(at Douglas, Isle of Man) 3-2

31.07.85 Wigan Athletic
(at Peel, Isle of Man) 0-2
02.08.85 Blackburn Rovers
(at Castletown, Isle of Man) 1-2
05.08.85 Sheffield United (A) 2-0
10.08.85 Grimsby Town (A) 2-1
30.10.85 Hinckley Athletic (A) 1-1
14.02.86 Combined Services (in Cyprus) 8-1
02.03.86 Dundee United (A) 1-0
06.05.86 Burton Albion (A) 0-1
(Warnock Test)

29.07.86 Vastervik (A) 3-2
30.07.86 Eskilstuna (A) 4-0
02.08.86 Skarblacka (A) 4-0
04.08.86 Boo (A) 7-0
06.08.86 Trosa (A) 8-1
09.08.86 Gloucester City (A) 6-1
13.08.86 VFB Lubeck (A) 2-0
15.08.86 TSV Auetal (A) 12-0
16.08.86 Hamburg Select XI (A) 10-0
30.09.86 Shepshed Charterhouse (H) 6-0
(County FA Centenary)
17.11.86 Al Itifaq (A) 2-1
01.12.86 Leicester City Past XI (H) 1-0
(Williams Test)
17.02.87 Iraq (at Doha, Qatar) 2-3
02.03.87 Valencia (A) 1-0

23.07.87 Laholm (A) 5-1
24.07.87 Solves (A) 2-0
26.07.87 Glimakra (A) 10-0
28.07.87 Tomelilla (A) 3-0
29.07.87 Farjestaden (A) 0-2
02.08.87 Kavlinge (A) 4-0
07.08.87 Mansfield Town (A) 1-1
09.08.87 Derry City (A) 5-0
15.04.88 Peterborough United (A) 1-2
(Harvey Test)
27.04.88 Burton Albion (A) 5-0
(Floodlight Inauguration)

04.08.88 Ayr United (A) 4-2
07.08.88 St Johnstone (A) 2-1
10.08.88 Kettering Town (A) 2-0
(Thacker Benefit)
15.08.88 Lincoln City (A) 4-1
19.08.88 Arsenal (H) 1-4
22.08.88 Cambridge United (A) 1-1
23.01.89 Spalding United (A) 4-2
24.04.89 Trinidad & Tobago (at Mucurapo) 2-0

Gary Lineker and **Frank Worthington** *prepare to line up with a Leicester City Past XI for Tommy Williams' Testimonial match in December 1986.*

ABANDONED MATCHES

date	competition	opposition (venue)	time	reason	score at time	(score in rematch)
30.12.94	Div 2	Darwen (A)	2 mins	gale	0-0	(2-8)
28.12.95	Div 2	Newton Heath (A)	65 mins	fog	0-2	(0-2)
16.11.01	Div 2	Blackpool (H)	67 mins	fog	1-0	(1-0)
05.12.03	Div 2	Manchester United (A)	78 mins	fog	2-1	(2-5)
09.09.05	Div 2	Burnley (A)	79 mins	waterlogged	0-1	(2-0)
11.01.13	FAC Rd.1	Norwich City (H)	65 mins	snow	0-0	(1-4)
19.12.31	Div 1	Portsmouth (H)	63 mins	fog	1-0	(2-1)
16.12.33	Div 1	Birmingham (A)	65 mins	fog	2-1	(0-3)
03.02.34	Div 1	Chelsea (A)	78 mins	fog	1-1	(0-2)
22.02.36	Div 2	Newcastle United (H)	80 mins	snow	2-1	(1-0)
28.01.61	FAC Rd.4	Bristol City (H)	45 mins	waterlogged	0-0	(5-1)
09.12.67	Div 1	Nottingham Forest (A)	51 mins	ice/frost	1-0	(1-2)
24.09.74	Div 1	Middlesbrough (A)	24 mins	floodlight failure	0-1	(0-3)
15.10.83	Div 1	Southampton (H)	22 mins	waterlogged	0-0	(2-1)

Tommy Williams, Steve Lynex and ex-City defender Dennis Rofe are amongst the bedraggled battlers as the elements engulf the home game against Southampton in October 1983.

Additionally, Fosse experienced two examples of drawn FA Cup games being abandoned during extra time because of bad light; though the 90-minute score was allowed to stand in both cases:

29.10.92 FAC QR2 Notts Olympic (H) 3-3
03.12.03 FAC QR5r Burton United (H) 2-2

Only one Midland League fixture was abandoned, on 18.11.93, when the Doncaster Rovers team left the field in protest at the conditions (a snowstorm) after 50 minutes, and conceded the points. The 2-1 scoreline to Fosse was entered into League records.

A friendly game at home to Derby Town on 3.12.92 was abandoned after 83 minutes with the score at 1-1 when opposition player Storer refused to leave the field when sent off by the referee for fighting.

A wartime League game at Nottingham Forest on 20.11.43 was abandoned ten minutes from time with City 0-1 down. The result stood, while reporting restrictions then in force meant that no reason for the abandonment could be published.

VOID GAMES : Fosse twice completed Midland League fixtures which were later declared void by the League authorities and ordered to be replayed.

On 2.4.1892, Fosse went down 0-2 away to Burslem Port Vale. They had played throughout with only ten men (Owen having missed his train), but a more crucial absentee had been the referee. A spectator had assumed whistling duties, and Fosse's later protests over his partiality were upheld. Ironically, a full-strength Fosse lost the rematch by 0-4.

On 25.3.1893, Fosse beat Derby Junction at Walnut Street by 6-0. However, Fosse had already met these opponents at home earlier in the campaign, and despite the Derby club's willingness to cede their scheduled home advantage on this occasion, the Midland League were not in agreement with this breach of their rules. The ordered rematch brought a 3-1 away win for Fosse.

AGE

YOUNGEST: There have been four 16-year-old League debutants for Leicester City since WW2: **David Timson** at 16 years, 231 days on 11.4.64; **Peter Shilton** at 16 years, 228 days on 4.5.66; **David Buchanan** at 16 years 192 days on 1.1.79 (the current club record); and **Neil Grewcock** at 16 years 311 days on 3.3.79. Both Buchanan and Grewcock scored on their debuts, while Shilton kept a clean sheet.

It is virtually certain that no player of such tender years played for either Fosse or City at senior level prior to WW2, though **Gordon Jayes** did make his debut in wartime regional football at the age of 16 years, 116 days. Jayes had previously played (and scored) in City's second Public Practice match prior to the 1938/9 season, when still aged only 14.

OLDEST: As we have been unable to research accurate birthdates for many early players, we can make no categorical statement regarding the oldest player to turn out for the club. However, the strongest candidate since WW1 is goalkeeper **Joe Calvert**, who was over 40 years, 10 months old when making his final City appearance in December 1947.

APPEARANCES

Adam Black holds the club record for League appearances; **Graham Cross** for overall senior appearances, and for most appearances in both major Cup competitions.
(Black: 528 Lge; 29 FAC. Cross: 495+3 Lge; 59 FAC; 40 LC.)

Mark Wallington holds the club record for the most consecutive appearances. From 4.1.75 to 6.3.82 he played in every one of 294 League games, 22 FA Cup ties and 15 League Cup matches: a total of 331 appearances before injury brought his run to an end. Some statisticians might contend that three additional appearances during this sequence, in Anglo-Scottish Cup matches, could legitimately extend the total figure to 334.

Graham Cross played in 52 consecutive FA Cup ties for City from 14.1.65 to 24.2.75; while the club record of 21 consecutive League Cup appearances is shared by **John Sjoberg** (15.1.64 to 4.9.68) and **Mark Wallington** (9.9.75 to 9.10.84).

Richie Norman made the most senior competitive appearances by a City player in a single season when turning out in 40 League games, 6 FA Cup ties and 10 League Cup matches in 1964/5; (i.e. in 56 out of 58 possible games).

Sep Smith holds the club record for the lengthiest first team career: his League debut coming on 31.8.29 and his final appearance being made on 7.5.49.

ARTIFICIAL PITCHES

Since Queens Park Rangers became the first League club (in 1981) to tear up their conventional grass playing area and replace it with an artificial Omniturf surface - to be followed later by Luton Town, Oldham Athletic and Preston North End - City have played a total of 11 League and Cup games on such pitches, with fairly atrocious results. As the following record shows, City have won once, drawn twice, and lost eight of their games on 'plastic' pitches; scoring 10 and conceding 24 goals:

1981/2: QPR 0-2 (Div 2); 1982/3: QPR 2-2 (Div 2); 1983/4: QPR 0-2 (Div 1); 1984/5: QPR 3-4 (Div 1); 1985/6: Luton 1-3, QPR 0-2 (both Div 1); 1986/7: Luton 0-1, QPR 1-0 (both Div 1), QPR 2-5 (FA Cup); 1987/8: Oldham 0-2 (Div 2); 1988/9: Oldham 1-1 (Div 2).

ATTENDANCES

The Filbert Street attendance record was set on 18.2.28, when Tottenham Hotspur were the visitors in the FA Cup Fifth Round, and the gate numbered 47,298.

The record gate for a League game was set on 2.10.54, when a Division One match against Arsenal attracted 42,486. The highest gate to watch a Division Two game at Leicester did so on 17.11.56, when Nottingham Forest drew 40,830; while for a League Cup tie the Filbert Street record stands at 35,121, attracted by a Fifth Round meeting with West Bromwich Albion on 29.10.69. The highest gate drawn to a Filbert Street friendly is believed to have been the 24,408 registered for the visit of Rangers on 18.2.67; though an approximate figure of 24,000 was also noted for John Sjoberg's Testimonial game against Derby County on 25.5.71.

Between the wars, and until the ground record was set, the progressive rise in highest attendance figures was marked thus:

31.01.20	v. Manchester City	FAC 2	23,109
08.01.21	v. Burnley	FAC 1	29,149
28.01.22	v. Fulham	FAC 2	30,022
03.02.23	v. Cardiff City	FAC 2	35,728
05.02.25	v. Newcastle United	FAC 2r	37,434
10.10.25	v. Aston Villa	Div 1	37,483

For many years after WW2, the Filbert Street capacity was regarded as being 42,000. Between 1954 and 1972, this figure was reached, or severely tested by crowds of over 40,000, on seventeen occasions — for eight FA Cup ties involving City, five home First Division games and three in the Second Division, and one Cup replay between Arsenal and Derby County.

The capacity was lowered in 1975 to 34,000; a figure afterwards reached only once (14.2.76 v.Manchester United, FA Cup Round Five). Indeed, there have been only two other crowds of over 30,000 since then: for City's final Division One game of the same season against the same opposition, Manchester United, on 24.4.76; and for the 4th replay of the FA Cup Round Three tie between Arsenal and Sheffield Wednesday on 22.1.79.

Subsequently, the ground capacity has been lowered again in stages commensurate with changes to the stadium layout and more stringent safety requirements. It now stands at around 31,000; though the effects of crowd segregation and membership schemes mean that the figure is most unlikely to be reached.

The record for the smallest gate for a Filbert Street senior game can never be reliably established due to the lack of official records for the Fosse period, when some abysmal gates were certainly experienced. The smallest home gate for a League game since WW2 was recorded on 22.2.83, when Shrewsbury Town visited in the Second Division and attracted 6,155.

The lowest First Division attendance is that of 7,237 drawn

to view West Bromwich Albion on 12.10.85; the smallest home FA Cup crowd since WW1, comprised the 14,635 who saw City overcome Carlisle United in Round Four on 26.1.85; the least number of people present at a home League Cup tie, 6,244, gathered for the clash with Rotherham United on 26.10.60; while the Full Members (Simod) Cup tie with Huddersfield Town on 10.11.87 was watched by only 3,440. There were only 1,840 present when Brighton & Hove Albion met Oldham Athletic in a League Cup Second Round Second Replay at Filbert Street in 1977.

Only one other League ground still attributes its record attendance to a game in which Leicester City were the visitors: Norwich City's Carrow Road, where the record gate of 43,984 was established by the FA Cup Sixth Round tie of 30.3.63.

Discounting the Wembley crowds for City's FA Cup Finals, the highest attendance the club has played before away from home was that of 69,049 at White Hart Lane for the Fifth Round FA Cup tie against Tottenham Hotspur on 7.2.48. Two seasons later at the same venue, 60,595 attended the Second Division game between the two clubs on 4.2.50: the largest crowd City have played a League game before.

Again it is far from certain what constitutes the lowest attendance City have attracted for a competitive game away from home. The reputed record of only 13 paying customers at the Stockport County v.City game on 7.5.21 is explained and qualified in the text on 1920/1. Since WW2, however, the smallest figure for a League game was that of 2,107 registered at Brisbane Road for the Orient v.City game of 18.5.82. A pitiful gathering of only 1,327 attended the Full Members (Simod) Cup tie between Charlton Athletic and City at Selhurst Park on 1.12.87. (There was, of course, an official attendance figure of nil for the FA Cup Third Round tie against Burton Albion on 16.1.85, replayed by order behind closed doors at Highfield Road, Coventry).

CHAMPIONSHIPS & PROMOTIONS

Though Leicester have never won the First Division championship, they share with Manchester City the record number of Second Division championship wins - six. In having been promoted to the First Division on eight occasions in total, City lag behind only Birmingham City and Manchester City (who've each performed the feat nine times) in the record books.

COSMOPOLITANISM

Ever since the rise and legalisation of professionalism, English clubs have relied heavily on players from other corners of the British Isles, and to a lesser extent on imports from further afield. Neither Fosse nor City have bucked this general trend; and a note on the last occasion the club both started and finished a game with a wholly English-born team might indicate why. In their First Division fixture away to Manchester City on 22.1.77, City fielded the following line-up:

Wallington, Whitworth, Rofe, Kember, Blockley, Sims, Weller, Sammels, Worthington, Birchenall, Earle.

All but Whitworth and Sims had cost substantial transfer fees; all but Earle would complete their careers with England

recognition up to at least Under-23 or Under-21 level. Leicester lost 0-5!

CRICKETERS

There can be few Football League clubs who have included in their senior line-ups so many of the old breed of versatile footballer/cricketers as have Leicester over the years. Those who have played for Fosse or City and in first-class cricket are:

Tommy Allsopp, Jimmy Atter, Harry Bailey, Ewart Benskin, Graham Cross, Ernest Gill, Teddy King, Jack Lee, John Mitten, Arthur Mounteney, Fred Osborn, Maurice Tompkin, Robert Turner, Harry Whitehead, and Cecil Wood (all for Leicestershire); Fred Bracey and Tom Fletcher (Derbyshire); Tal Lewis (Somerset); Jim Harrold (Essex); Tom Simpson (Nottinghamshire) and John Vincett (Sussex & Surrey). Additionally, Archie Ling played Minor Counties cricket for Cambridgeshire; while City trainer David Jones was a former Notts cricketer. Tom Jayes and Albert Matthews are among several County players to have turned out for Fosse or City Reserves.

COUNTY CRICKETERS.

W. E. BENSKIN,
LEICESTERSHIRE.

Incidentally, Leicestershire CCC have also included at county level several other all-round sportsmen of this type, including Chris Balderstone (Huddersfield, Carlisle, Doncaster), Les Berry (Sheffield Wednesday, Bristol Rovers, Swindon), Walter Cornock (Rochdale), Ted Glennon (Grimsby, Sheffield Wednesday, Rotherham County), Aubrey Sharp (Halifax), Jeff Tolchard (Torquay, Exeter), George Watson (Charlton) and Willie Watson (Huddersfield, Sunderland, Halifax, England).

DISCIPLINE

Almost hand in hand with City's reputation down the years as a 'footballing' side has gone an assessment of them as a 'fair' one: at no stage have they had to carry the 'cloggers' tag which still adheres to quite a few clubs whatever their turnover in personnel. Obviously though, cautions, bookings and dismissals have accrued against the club's players since League and Cup football commenced: what is perhaps most noteworthy about a full list of Fossils and City men sent off in the course of senior football is that a record of only 14 such instances from 1894 to 1979 has been augmented by no less than 26 further dismissals in the course of the last decade.

The first of a total of seven Fossils to receive his marching orders was Willie Freebairn, in the Second Division game at Lincoln on 10.4.97. The first and only Leicester player to be sent off in an FA Cup tie was George Mountain, in the second replay of a Qualifying Round tie against Burton United on 7.12.03. The first Fossil to take an early bath at Filbert Street was David Walker, on 28.1.11, when Clapton Orient were the visitors.

Teddy King was the first villain for the reconstructed City, being dismissed from the Craven Cottage pitch on 20.9.19. Johnny Morris, sent off while playing for the Blues v. Whites in the then-annual pre-season public practice match on 17.8.57, was widely deemed to be the only player anywhere so disgraced in such a game. Frank McLintock (in Innsbruck in 1964) and Ian Wilson, exiting the Ibrox pitch early during a 1984 clash with Rangers, are among the very few other City men to have been sent off in 'friendly' fixtures.

Wilson is also one of eight City players of recent years - Larry May, Kevin MacDonald, Eddie Kelly, Steve Lynex, Andy Peake, Steve Walsh and Mike Newell are the others - to have been dismissed twice while on the club's books. There have been only two occasions of two Leicester players being sent off in the same game: Bob Pollock and Ike Evenson at Bolton on 25.3.05, and Alan Young and Kevin MacDonald at Brighton on 20.4.81.

Though the Fosse directorate imposed fairly draconian suspensions on several players declared guilty of breaching internal disciplinary regulations, and several City players received lengthy bans after the FA Commission on the club's financial dealings reported during WW2, the longest disciplinary suspension imposed on a Leicester player in modern times was served by Steve Walsh during 1987/8. Following his dismissal on the season's opening day, the cumulative upshot of an automatic 'sentence' and that imposed after a later hearing was an eleven-game ban.

EVER-PRESENTS

Fosse and City have had 70 players who have completed at least one season as an ever-present (ie. played in every League game) since Jack Lord achieved the feat in the initial Midland League campaign of 1891/2. Mark Wallington did so on seven occasions (1975/6-1980/1 inclusive, plus 1982/3), while Jimmy Thraves, George Swift, Adam Black, Richie Norman and Steve Whitworth each did so four times, and Hugh Adcock, Arthur Rowley, David Nish and Dennis Rofe three times each.

There were five ever-presents in the second Midland League campaign (1892/3 - Bailey, Dorrell, Slack, Taylor, Thraves), and four in season 1973/4 (Shilton, Rofe, Weller and Worthington). There were no ever-present players at all over the course of 29 separate League seasons. Gary McAllister became at the end of 1988/9 the club's first 46-game ever-present.

FAMILIARITY

Leicester's most familiar opponents at a competitive level over the years have been those now known as Birmingham City and Arsenal.

Since Fosse first met Small Heath in the FA Cup Qualifying competition in 1891/2 there have been a total of 108 meetings in

the League and 9 in the FA Cup. Additionally, City met Birmingham in one game of the abandoned 1939/40 League season.

Since Fosse came up against Woolwich Arsenal during their initial Second Division season of 1894/5, the clubs have faced each other 100 times in the League, in 9 FA Cup ties, and 2 League Cup matches. Additionally, City and Arsenal met once in the Southern Professional Floodlit Cup in 1959/60.

Arsenal are also the team City have met the most times in one season: the clubs faced each other seven times in 1974/5 (twice in the First Division, three times in the FA Cup, and twice in the League Cup).

FILBERT STREET AS A NEUTRAL VENUE

Some of the more important or prestigious games to have been held on the ground of Leicester Fosse/City:

International & Representative Matches:
14.11.1921 Amateur
England 4 Ireland 1
18.12.1926 Amateur
England 1 Scotland 4
19.03.1927 Inter-League
Football League 2 Scottish League 2
19.02.1938 Amateur
England 1 Ireland 1
20.01.1951 Amateur
England 4 Wales 1
14.10.1970 Under-23
England 3 West Germany 1
20.11.1979 Under-21
England 5 Bulgaria 0

Football League:
27.04.1895 Test Match
Derby County 2 Notts County 1
04.02.1899 Division 2
Loughborough 1 Blackpool 3
02.09.1899 Division 2
Loughborough 2 Bolton Wanderers 3

F.A.Cup:
26.10.1903 Q Rd.2 rep 2
Burton United 5 Hinckley 1

18.01.1926 Rd.3 rep 2
Derby County 2 Portsmouth 0
24.03.1928 Semi-final
Arsenal 0 Blackburn Rovers 1
23.02.1959 Rd.5 rep 2
Birmingham City 0 Nottingham Forest 5
09.04.1962 Semi-final rep
Burnley 2 Fulham 1
13.03.1972 Rd.5 rep 2
Arsenal 1 Derby County 0
29.01.1973 Rd.3 rep 2
Nottingham Forest 1 West Bromwich Albion 3
13.01.1975 Rd.3 rep 2
Fulham 1 Hull City 0
25.03.1975 Rd.5 rep 2
Ipswich Town 0 Leeds United 0
27.03.1975 Rd.5 rep 3
Ipswich Town 3 Leeds United 2
16.01.1978 Rd.3 rep 2
Grimsby Town 1 Southampton 4
15.01.1979 Rd.3 rep 2
Arsenal 2 Sheffield Wednesday 2
17.01.1979 Rd.3 rep 3
Arsenal 3 Sheffield Wednesday 3
22.01.1979 Rd.3 rep 4
Arsenal 2 Sheffield Wednesday 0

Football League Cup:
20.09.1977 Rd.2 rep 2
Brighton & Hove Albion 1 Oldham Athletic 2
27.10.1987 Rd.3
Luton Town 3 Coventry City 1

F.A. Amateur Cup:
28.03.1896 Final
Bishop Auckland 1 Royal Artillery (Portsmouth) 0
31.03.1900 Final
Bishop Auckland 5 Lowestoft Town 1
05.03.1932 Semi-final
Marine 2 Yorkshire Amateurs 1

F.A. Trophy:
03.04.1971 Semi-final
Hereford United 0 Hillingdon Borough 2

FLOODLIGHTS

The official turning on of the Filbert Street floodlights was celebrated by a friendly on 23.10.57 against Borussia Dortmund. The lights were used for the first time for a League game less than a month later, on 16.11.57, when a First Division encounter with Preston North End was floodlit throughout to combat poor visibility, despite a 3.00pm kick-off. The first evening kick-off scheduled specifically to exploit City's possession of lights was a Division One game on 18.3.59 against Birmingham City.

Leicester Fosse played only one game under lights; a friendly against Blackburn Rovers at the Peel Croft ground, Burton-on-Trent, on 5.10.08 (see text for 1908/9).

FOOTBALLER OF THE YEAR

The Footballer of the Year award was instigated by the Football Writers' Association in 1947/8, and was supplemented in 1974 by a Player of the Year award announced by the Professional Footballers' Association.

No player has won either award while on the books of Leicester City, but several former stars have been so honoured after moving on: Don Revie (Manchester City, 1955), Frank McLintock (Arsenal, 1971), Gordon Banks (Stoke City, 1972), Peter Shilton (Nottingham Forest, 1978, PFA), and Gary Lineker (Everton, 1986, both awards). Steve Moran won the PFA's Young Player of the Year award in 1982, prior to joining Leicester.

GOALSCORING

CLUB RECORDS:
Wins:
League Div. One:
10-0 Portsmouth (H) 20.10.29
League Div. Two:
9-1 Walsall Town Swifts (H) 05.01.95
9-1 Gainsborough Trinity (H) 27.12.09
9-2 Lincoln City (H) 21.11.53
FA Cup Qualifying:
13-0 Notts Olympic (H) 13.10.94
FA Cup Proper:
7-0 Crook Town (H) 09.01.32
Football League Cup:
8-1 Coventry City (A) 01.12.64
Midland League:
7-1 Newark (H) 01.10.92

Defeats:
League Div. One:
0-12 Nottingham Forest (A) 21.04.09
1-10 Wolverhampton Wanderers (A) 15.04.38
League Div. Two:
0-8 Woolwich Arsenal (A) 26.10.03
2-8 Darwen (A) 15.01.95
FA Cup Qualifying:
2-6 Small Heath (H) 03.10.91
FA Cup Proper:
3-7 Burnley (H) 08.01.21
Football League Cup:
0-4 Manchester City (A) 13.09.67
0-4 Burnley (A) 16.10.68
Midland League:
0-11 Rotherham Town (A) 16.04.92

Draws:
League Div. One:
6-6 Arsenal (H) 21.04.30
League Div. Two:
5-5 Sheffield United (H) 03.11.51
FA Cup:
5-5 Tottenham Hotspur (H) 10.01.14
5-5 Luton Town (A) 12.02.49
Football League Cup:
4-4 Charlton Athletic (H) 26.09.62

Highest Seasonal H/A Aggregate:
19 goals

City/West Bromwich Albion	1954/5	(H) 6-3	(A) 4-6
City/Manchester City	1957/8	(H) 8-4	(A) 4-3

INDIVIDUAL RECORDS:

City Career Goals:

Arthur Chandler	259 Lge;	14 FAC	(273)
Arthur Rowley	251 Lge;	14 FAC	(265)

FA Cup:
14 goals
Arthur Chandler, Arthur Rowley

League Cup:
8 goals
Mike Stringfellow

Goals in Season:
Arthur Rowley   1956/7   44 (all Lge)

Goals in Game:
John Duncan   6 v Port Vale (H)   25.12.24
Arthur Chandler 6 v Portsmouth (H) 20.10.28

Goals on Debut:
Archie Gardiner 4 v Portsmouth (A) 21.02.34

Goals Against:
Tom McCairns   6 for Grimsby Town 11.04.96

INTERNATIONAL & REPRESENTATIVE HONOURS

These records relate only to caps and representative honours won whilst the player concerned was on the books of Leicester Fosse or City. Some of the players mentioned won additional honours at other junctures of their careers (usually mentioned in their entries in the Players' Who's Who), and the latter source also refers where appropriate to the numerous players honoured only before joining or after leaving Leicester.

FULL INTERNATIONALS

ENGLAND

H.Adcock: 1928/9 v.France, Belgium, Spain; 1929/30 v.N.Ireland, Wales (1 goal). *(Total: 5 caps; 1 goal)*
H.P.Bailey: 1907/8 v.Wales, Austria (twice), Hungary, Bohemia. *(Total: 5 caps)*
G.Banks: 1962/3 v.Scotland, Brazil, Czechoslovakia, E.Germany; 1963/4 v. Wales, Rest of the World, N.Ireland, Scotland, Uruguay, Portugal (twice), USA, Argentina; 1964/5 v.N.Ireland, Scotland, Hungary, Yugoslavia, W.Germany, Sweden; 1965/6 v.N.Ireland, Spain, Poland (twice), W.Germany (twice), Scotland, Yugoslavia, Finland, Uruguay, Mexico, France, Argentina, Portugal; 1966/7 v.N.Ireland, Czechoslovakia, Wales, Scotland. *(Total: 37 caps)*
L.J.Barry: 1927/8 v.France, Belgium; 1928/9 v.France, Belgium, Spain. *(Total: 5 caps)*
S.M.Bishop: 1926/7 v. Scotland, Belgium, Luxembourg (1 goal), France. *(Total: 4 caps; 1 goal)*
E.W.Hine: 1928/9 v.N.Ireland, Wales (1 goal); 1929/30 v.N.Ireland (1 goal), Wales; 1931/2 v.N.Ireland (1 goal), Wales (1 goal). *(Total: 6 caps; 4 goals)*
G.W.Lineker: 1983/4 v.Scotland (sub); 1984/5 v.Rep.Ireland (1 goal), Rumania (sub), Scotland (sub), Italy (sub), W.Germany, USA (2 goals). *(Total: 7 caps; 3 goals)*
R.Osborne: 1927/8 v.Wales. *(Total: 1 cap)*
P.L.Shilton: 1970/1 v.E.Germany, Wales; 1971/2 v.Switzerland, N.Ireland; 1972/3 v.Yugoslavia, Scotland (twice), N.Ireland, Wales, Czechoslovakia, Poland, USSR, Italy; 1973/4 v.Austria, Poland, Italy, Wales, N.Ireland, Scotland, Argentina. *(Total: 20 caps)*
S.C.Smith: 1935/6 v.N.Ireland. *(Total: 1 cap)*
K.Weller: 1973/4 v.Wales, N.Ireland (1 goal), Scotland, Argentina. *(Total: 4 caps; 1 goal)*

S.Whitworth: 1974/5 v.W.Germany, Cyprus, N.Ireland, Wales, Scotland; 1975/6 v.Switzerland, Portugal. *(Total: 7 caps)*
F.S.Worthington: 1973/4 v.N.Ireland (sub), Scotland, Argentina (1 goal), E.Germany, Bulgaria (1 goal), Yugoslavia; 1974/5 v.Czechoslovakia, Portugal (sub). *(Total: 8 caps; 2 goals)*

FINLAND
J.J.Rantanen: 1987/8 v.Czechoslovakia (twice), Sweden, Columbia (1 goal); 1988/9 v.USSR, W.Germany, Wales (sub), Egypt (1+1 sub). *(Total: 9 caps; 1 goal)*

IRELAND
M.Cochrane: 1900/1 v.Scotland. *(Total: 1 cap)*
M.T.O'Brien: 1921/2 v.Scotland, Wales; 1923/4 v.Scotland, Wales. *(Total: 4 caps)*

NORTHERN IRELAND
W.E.Cunningham: 1955/6 v.Scotland, England, Wales; 1956/7 v.England, Scotland, Portugal (twice), Wales, Italy; 1957/8 v.Scotland, Italy, Wales, Czechoslovakia (twice), Argentina, W.Germany, France; 1958/9 v.England, Scotland, Wales; 1959/60 v.Scotland, England, Wales. *(Total: 23 caps)*
A.D.Dougan: 1965/6 v.Scotland (1 goal), England, Albania, Wales, W.Germany, Mexico; 1966/7 v.England, Scotland. *(Total: 8 caps; 1 goal)*
J.P.O'Neill: 1979/80 v.Israel, Scotland, England, Wales, Australia (three times); 1980/1 v.Portugal (twice), Scotland (twice), Sweden; 1981/2 v. Scotland (twice), Israel, England, France (1+1 sub); 1982/3 v.Austria, W.Germany, Albania (twice), Turkey, Scotland; 1983/4 v.Scotland (sub); 1984/5 v.Israel, Finland (1 goal), England, Spain, Turkey; 1985/6 v.Turkey, Rumania, England, France, Denmark, Morocco, Algeria, Spain, Brazil. *(Total: 39 caps; 1 goal)*
J.M.Quinn: 1988/9 v.Rep.Ireland, Hungary (sub), Spain (1+1 sub). *(Total: 4 caps)*
P.C.Ramsey: 1983/4 v.Austria, W.Germany, Scotland; 1984/5 v.Israel, England, Spain, Turkey; 1985/6 v.Turkey, Morocco; 1986/7 v.Israel, England, Yugoslavia (sub); 1987/8 v.Yugoslavia; 1988/9 v.Spain. *(Total: 14 caps)*

REPUBLIC OF IRELAND
T.F.Godwin: 1949/50 v.Finland, Sweden, Belgium; 1950/1 v.Norway. *(Total: 4 caps)*

SCOTLAND
A.Aitken: 1909/10 v.England; 1910/11 v.Ireland, England. *(Total: 3 caps)*
J.Anderson: 1953/4 v.Finland. *(Total: 1 cap)*
J.Duncan: 1925/6 v.Wales (1 goal). *(Total: 1 cap; 1 goal)*
D.W.Gibson: 1962/3 v.Austria, Norway, Rep.Ireland, Spain (1 goal); 1963/4 v.N.Ireland; 1964/5 v.Wales (1 goal), Finland (1 goal). *(Total: 7 caps; 3 goals)*
F.McLintock: 1962/3 v.Norway (sub), Rep.Ireland, Spain (1 goal). *(Total: 3 caps; 1 goal)*
J.Paterson: 1919/20 v.England. *(Total: 1 cap)*
J.E.W.Sinclair: 1965/6 v.Portugal. *(Total: 1 cap)*
I.W.Wilson: 1986/7 v.England, Brazil. *(Total: 2 caps)*

WALES
M.W.Griffiths: 1946/7 v.N.Ireland; 1948/9 v.Portugal, Belgium; 1949/50 v.England (1 goal), Scotland, Belgium;

*City's most-capped player, **John O'Neill**, celebrates with his club and country's physiotherapist, **John McVey**, after Northern Ireland had qualified for the 1986 World Cup Finals by gaining a point at Wembley in November 1985.*

1950/1 v.England, N.Ireland, Portugal (1 goal), Switzerland; 1953/4 v.Austria. *(Total: 11 caps; 2 goals)*
R.M.James: 1987/8 v.Denmark (twice). *(Total: 2 caps)*
D.O.Jones: 1933/4 v.N.Ireland, England; 1934/5 v England, Scotland; 1935/6 v.England, N.Ireland; 1936/7 v.N.Ireland. *(Total: 7 caps)*
R.S.Jones: 1897/8 v.Scotland. *(Total: 1 cap)*
K.Leek: 1960/1 v.Scotland, England (1 goal), N.Ireland (1 goal), Spain (twice), Hungary. *(Total: 6 caps; 2 goals)*
A.R.Lever: 1952/3 v.Scotland. *(Total: 1 cap)*
T.J.Mills: 1934/5 v.England, Scotland. *(Total: 2 caps)*
P.J.Rodrigues: 1965/6 v.N.Ireland, Brazil (twice), Chile; 1966/7 v. Scotland; 1967/8 v.England, Scotland, N.Ireland; 1968/9 v.E.Germany, England, N.Ireland, Rest of UK; 1969/70 v.E.Germany, England, Scotland, N.Ireland.*(Total: 16 caps)*
A.E.Watkins: 1897/8 v.Scotland, England. *(Total: 2 caps)*

UNOFFICIAL INTERNATIONALS

England Jubilee International:
S.C.Smith: 1935/6 v.Scotland (sub).

England Victory International:
F.Soo: 1945/6 v.Wales.

F.A. XI 'Test Matches':
A.C.H.Chandler: 1929 v.South Africa (3 games; 6 goals). *(Chandler played in 16 of the 17 games the touring side played in S.A., scoring in every one, and totalling 33 goals. **R.Osborne** also took part in the tour, but played in no 'Test Matches').*

'B' INTERNATIONALS

ENGLAND
W.E.Harrison: 1948/9 v.Finland, Holland.
G.A.Rowley: 1955/6 v.Switzerland (1 goal).
S.F.Sims: 1977/8 v.Malaysia.

SCOTLAND
J.Anderson: 1953/4 v.England.
G.McAllister: 1986/7 v.France (1 goal).
I.W.Wilson: 1986/7 v.France.

UNDER-23 INTERNATIONALS

ENGLAND
G.Banks: 1960/1 v.Wales, Scotland.
A.J.Clarke: 1968/9 v.Portugal.
G.F.Cross: 1962/3 v.Yugoslavia (twice; 1 goal), Rumania; 1963/4 v.Wales, W.Germany, Scotland, France, Hungary, Israel, Turkey; 1965/6 v.Turkey.
D.J.Nish: 1968/9 v.Portugal (1+1 sub), Belgium; 1969/70 v.Wales, USSR, Scotland, Bulgaria (1 goal); 1970/1 v.Sweden, Wales, Scotland.
H.Riley: 1957/8 v.Wales; 1960/1 v.Wales.
D.Rofe: 1972/3 v.Czechoslovakia (sub).
P.L.Shilton: 1968/9 v.Wales, Holland (twice), Portugal (twice); 1969/70 v. Wales, Bulgaria, Scotland; 1970/1 v.W.Germany; 1971/2 v.Switzerland, E.Germany, Poland, USSR.
F.M.Wallington: 1975/6 v.Hungary (twice).
S.Whitworth: 1971/2 v.Switzerland, Wales; 1973/4 v.Yugoslavia, France; 1974/5 v.Scotland (twice; 1 goal), Wales.

NORTHERN IRELAND
G.McCaffrey: 1962/3 v.Wales.

SCOTLAND
F.McLintock: 1961/2 v.England.

UNDER-21 INTERNATIONALS

ENGLAND
I.E.Andrews: 1986/7 v.Sweden.
S.C.Morgan: 1986/7 v.Sweden, Yugoslavia.
A.M.Peake: 1981/2 v.Poland.
S.F.Sims: 1976/7 v.Wales, Scotland, Finland, Norway; 1977/8 v.Norway, Finland (1 goal), Italy (twice), Yugoslavia (twice).

NORTHERN IRELAND
J.P.O'Neill: 1977/8 v.Rep.Ireland.

REPUBLIC OF IRELAND
M.C.Russell: 1986/7 v.Belgium.

YOUTH INTERNATIONALS

ENGLAND: I.E.Andrews, O.Beeby, D.Buchanan, R.T.Burbeck, M.Capewell, G.F.Cross, D.J.Hines, P.M.Horner, M.G.Munro, D.J.Nish, M.Oakes, J.Pawley, A.M.Peake, H.Riley, J.Roberts, P.L.Shilton, B.E.Thomas, R.O.Warner, S.Whitworth, R.J.Wilcox, B.R.Wright.
NORTHERN IRELAND: S.Convey.
REPUBLIC OF IRELAND: A.J.Brien, G.Fitzpatrick, R.A.Kelly, T.F.Kilkelly, J.J.W.Waters, A.Welldrick.
SCOTLAND: A.Brown, P.Crawford, J.P.Friar, D.Rennie, J.N.Walker.
WALES: R.Jones.
FOOTBALL LEAGUE U-18: I.Baraclough, P.Kitson.

AMATEUR INTERNATIONALS

UNITED KINGDOM (Olympic Games)
H.P.Bailey: 1908 v.Sweden, Holland, Denmark (Final).

The 1982/3 season saw Youth internationals from four countries on City's books:
Robert Jones *(Wales),* **Ian Andrews** *(England),* **David Rennie** *(Scotland) and* **Robert Kelly** *(Republic of Ireland).*

D.McWhirter: 1912 v.Denmark (Final).

ENGLAND
H.P.Bailey: 1907/8 v.Wales, France, Holland;
1908/9 v.Germany.
R.G.Brebner: 1913/14 v.Ireland, Holland.
G.H.Douglas: 1912/13 v.Germany (2 goals), Holland.
J.G.W.Harrold: 1912/13 v.France.
D.McWhirter: 1912/13 v.Ireland, Germany, Holland.
A.S.Owen: 1909/10 v.Sweden (3 goals), Ireland (1 goal), Holland (1 goal), Belgium (1 goal); 1910/11 v.Ireland.

FOOTBALL LEAGUE

H.Adcock: 1929/30 v.Scottish League.
C.H.Appleton: 1962/3 v.Irish League.
G.Banks: 1961/2 v.Irish League; 1962/3 v.Irish League;
1963/4 v.Italian League (sub); 1965/6 v.League of Ireland.
S.M.Bishop: 1927/8 v.Scottish League.
A.C.H.Chandler: 1926/7 v.Scottish League.
E.W.Hine: 1926/7 v.Irish League; 1928/9 v.Scottish League
(1 goal); 1929/30 v.Irish League (1 goal), Scottish League.
D.Hogg: 1955/6 v.Scottish League.
A.Knapp: 1959/60 v.Scottish League.
D.J.Nish: 1970/1 v.Irish League; 1971/2 v.League of Ireland, Scottish League.
G.A.Rowley: 1956/7 v.Irish League.
P.L.Shilton: 1970/1 v.Irish League; 1972/3 v.Scottish League.
S.C.Smith: 1935/6 v.Scottish League.
K.Weller: 1972/3 v.Scottish League.
F.S.Worthington: 1972/3 v.Scottish League.

INTERNATIONAL TRIALS & MINOR REPRESENTATIVE HONOURS

ENGLAND
H.Adcock: 1929/30 England v.The Rest.
G.Banks: 1960/1 England Under-23 v.Vejle Boldklub; 1963/4
England v.Young England; 1964/5 England v.Young England.
S.M.Bishop: 1927/8 England v.The Rest (twice).
R.G.Brebner: 1913/14 Amateurs v.Professionals
(FA Charity Shield).
A.C.H.Chandler: 1924/5 North v.South (1 goal); 1926/7
The Rest v.England (1 goal);
1928/9 The Rest v.England (1 goal);
1929/30 Professionals v.Amateurs (FA Charity Shield) (1 goal).
G.F.Cross: 1963/4 Young England v.England;
1965/6 Young England v.England.

E.W.Hine: 1927/8 The Rest v.England (1 goal);
1928/9 England v.The Rest (twice; 1 goal);
1929/30 England v.The Rest.
D.J.Hines: 1953/4 Young England v.England (1 goal);
1954/5 Young England v.England.
R.Osborne: 1927/8 England v.The Rest (twice).
A.S.Owen: 1909/10 Whites v.Stripes (1 goal).
S.C.Smith: 1935/6 Possibles v.Probables.

SCOTLAND
A.Aitken: 1909/10 Anglo Scots v.Home Scots.
A.H.Black: 1922/3 Anglo Scots v.Home Scots.
J.Duncan: 1927/8 Anglo Scots v.Home Scots.
W.A.Henry: 1910/11 Anglo Scots v.Home Scots.
A.W.Lochhead: 1927/8 Anglo Scots v.Home Scots.
F.McLintock: 1961/2 Scotland v.Scottish League;
1963/4 Scotland v.Scottish League.
J.Paterson: 1919/20 Anglo Scots v.Home Scots (1 goal).

WALES
A.Mills: 1902/3 Whites v.Stripes.

OWN GOALS

6.10.34: Billy Frame became the first (and to date only) City player to net an own goal on his League debut, when scoring for Tottenham Hotspur in a 2-2 draw at White Hart Lane.

18.12.54: During City's defeat by Chelsea at Stamford Bridge, Leicester defenders Stan Milburn and Jack Froggatt simultaneously contrived to kick the ball into their own net while attempting a clearance, and were credited with a unique joint own goal.

30.4.66: Graham Cross put Nottingham Forest ahead with an own goal at Filbert Street, but then completed a rare 'hat-trick' by scoring twice for City.

20.3.76: Aston Villa defender Chris Nicholl netted all four goals in a 2-2 draw at Filbert Street. (The club initially credited Brian Alderson with the first City goal, but their records were later amended.)

3.1.77: Former City defender Pat Kruse, then playing for Torquay United, registered the fastest own goal on record, putting Cambridge United ahead after only six seconds.

PENALTIES

City's leading penalty-kick scorers are: Arthur Rowley 41 (38 Lge, 3 FAC); Steve Lynex 23 (all Lge); Sep Smith 14 (13 Lge, 1 FAC); David Nish 14 (10 Lge, 2 FAC, 2 LC). Next on the list comes Fosse's spot-kick expert Bob Pollock with 11 (10 Lge, 1 FAC).

City registered their highest number of successful penalties in 1985/6: scoring 10 in the League and 1 in the FA Cup. (There were also 4 penalties missed or saved during this campaign).

Only once have City netted three penalties in one game: on 11.9.82 at home to Carlisle United, when Steve Lynex claimed two and gave Gary Lineker the third for his hat-trick.

City Reserves were awarded no less than four penalties in their Combination Cup game with Ipswich during 1947/8: Ray Iggleden scored one and missed one, Alex Scott scored one, and Derek Hines missed one.

City conceded a penalty to Liverpool after only 19 seconds of the game at Anfield on 24.8.74, and duly went behind to an Alec Lindsay spot-kick. This is often quoted as a League record for the fastest goal so scored.

City first experienced the innovation of drawn knock-out ties being decided by a penalty shoot-out during their Texaco Cup games of 1972/3; so beating Dundee United but so being eliminated in the next round by Norwich City. In first-class competitive games, City were eliminated in such a manner from the League (Milk) Cup by Chelsea at Stamford Bridge on 25.10.83, and from the Full Members (Simod) Cup by Stoke City at Filbert Street on 19.1.88.

RESERVES

*For many years after the club's formation, the reserve XI was known as Leicester Fosse Rovers. This **1892/3** line-up represents the era before the Fosse Rovers entered League competition.*
*Back: **Brown, Bates, Lisle, Buswell, Davis, Cornell, Machin** (Trainer). Front: **DeVille, Gardner, Tomlinson, Mouel.** On Ground: **Carter, Vickers.***

FOSSE & CITY RESERVES: THE SEASONAL RECORD

	P	W	D	L	F:A	Pts	Position
Leicestershire & Northamptonshire League							
1894/5	20	17	1	2	75:20	35	Champions
1895/6	16	11	3	2	45:14	25	Champions
Leicestershire Senior League							
1896/7	20	14	1	5	63:18	27●	2nd/11
United Counties League							
1897/8	14	5	2	7	30:29	12	5th/8
Midland League							
1898/9	26	9	2	15	34:58	20	12th/14
1899/00	24	3	3	18	34:74	9	13th/13
1900/1	26	11	1	14	60:64	23	9th/14
1901/2	28	7	5	16	38:70	19	13th/15
1902/3	32	6	4	22	30:87	16	17th/17
Leicestershire Senior League							
1903/4	16	11	2	3	41:21	24	2nd/9
1904/5	20	14	2	4	75:27	30	Champions
1905/6	20	14	2	4	43:21	30	Champions
1906/7	22	19	2	1	101:25	40	Champions
Midland League							
1907/8	38	17	5	16	72:70	39	8th/20
1908/9	38	13	7	18	87:70	33	13th/20
1909/10	42	13	10	19	76:93	36	18th/22
1910/1	38	11	7	20	62:100	29	18th/20
1911/2	36	17	8	11	90:54	42	4th/19
Central Alliance							
1912/3	32	19	5	8	76:38	43	4th/17
1913/4♦	30	17	4	9	74:43	36●	5th/16
1914/5	30	8	7	15	44:45	21●	15th/16
South Eastern League							
1913/4♦	40	8	10	22	56:86	26	19th/21
Central Alliance							
1919/20	30	13	11	6	66:46	37	4th/16
1920/1	34	28	1	5	132:29	57	Champions
1921/2	34	27	4	3	132:19	58	Champions
1922/3	32	24	4	4	107:34	52	Champions
Southern League (Eastern Section)							
1923/4	30	19	3	8	72:30	41	2nd/16
1924/5 ♦	32	15	7	10	61:45	37	7th/17
1925/6 ♦	34	23	2	9	105:60	48	2nd/18
1926/7 ♦	32	12	5	15	94:72	29	11th/17
East Midlands League							
1924/5 ♦	18	7	4	7	37:25	18	—/10
1925/6 ♦	14	10	0	4	41:16	20	2nd/8

		P	W	D	L	F:A	Pts	Position
London Combination								
1926/7♦		42	28	5	9	121:61	61	2nd/22
1927/8		42	19	8	15	89:70	46	8th/22
1928/9		42	24	4	14	109:76	52	3rd/22
1929/30		42	20	5	17	111:99	45	8th/22
1930/1	Div.1	42	21	3	18	102:84	45	8th/22
1931/2	Div.1	42	16	9	17	109:103	41	11th/22
1932/3	Div.1	46	18	11	17	101:103	47	8th/24
1933/4		46	18	9	19	91:77	45	12th/24
1934/5		46	25	7	14	88:60	57	4th/24
1935/6		46	17	6	23	79:98	40	18th/24
1936/7		46	17	6	23	69:92	40	16th/24
1937/8		46	17	10	19	79:78	44	13th/24
Football Combination								
1946/7	Sect. B	30	14	5	11	69:54	33	7th/16
1947/8	Sect. B	30	15	5	10	53:33	35	6th/16
1948/9	Sect. B	30	11	5	14	40:40	27	11th/16
1949/50	Sect. A	30	10	10	10	42:37	30	8th/16
1950/1	Sect. A	30	11	6	13	54:57	28	11th/16
1951/2	Sect. A	30	10	7	13	60:64	27	10th/16
1952/3	Div.2	30	20	5	5	86:40	45	2nd/16
1953/4	Div.1	30	15	4	11	76:63	34	8th/16
1954/5	Div.1	30	15	2	13	61:56	32	7th/16
1955/6		42	17	12	13	103:88	46	10th/32
1956/7		42	23	6	13	116:66	52	8th/32
1957/8		42	23	7	12	108:63	53	4th/32
1958/9	Div.1	34	23	5	6	77:41	51	Champions
1959/60	Div.1	34	12	6	16	59:58	30	12th/18
1960/1	Div.1	34	12	3	19	55:83	27	15th/18
1961/2	Sat.Sect.	34	17	5	12	71:63	39	5th/18
1962/3	Sat.Sect.	34	9	8	17	66:91	26	15th/18
1963/4	Div.1	34	18	7	9	84:65	43	3rd/18
1964/5	Div.1	34	11	5	18	60:73	27	15th/18
1965/6	Div.1	34	17	6	11	61:53	40	7th/18
1966/7	Div.1	32	13	8	11	61:45	34	7th/17
1967/8	Div.1	28	10	7	11	47:47	27	9th/15
1968/9		25	9	6	10	35:37	24	11th/26
1969/70		25	13	4	8	51:34	30	8th/26
1970/1		42	16	11	15	53:51	43	12th/22
1971/2		40	18	11	11	71:50	47	5th/21
1972/3		40	12	10	18	45:55	34	14th/21
1973/4		42	20	12	10	56:33	52	4th/22
1974/5		40	14	12	14	54:48	40	10th/21
1975/6		42	13	10	19	56:55	36	16th/22
1976/7		42	14	14	14	71:57	42	12th/22
1977/8		42	24	6	12	74:50	54	5th/22
1978/9		42	8	11	23	47:72	27	19th/22
1979/80		42	17	7	18	66:65	41	12th/22
1980/1		42	18	9	15	71:58	45	10th/22
1981/2		38	10	10	18	47:64	30	15th/20
1982/3		42	11	12	19	65:84	34	18th/22
1983/4		42	18	9	15	96:63	45	11th/22
Central League								
1984/5	Div.2	34	27	6	1	81:20	87	Champions
1985/6	Div.1	34	12	10	12	60:58	46	11th/18
1986/7	Div.1	34	10	7	17	48:65	37	13th/18
1987/8	Div.1	34	14	3	17	61:55	45	12th/18
1988/9	Div.1	34	13	6	15	65:63	45	10th/18

(♦In seasons 1913/14 and 1924/5 - 1926/7 inclusive the club fielded Reserve sides in two League competitions)
(●In seasons 1896/7, 1913/14 and 1914/15 the Reserves had two points deducted from their seasonal total by the respective League authorities, for breaches of rule.}

For a number of postwar seasons, the Combination fare was augmented by a Cup competition, usually run on a group basis prior to its knockout stage. City Reserves won the Football Combination Cup outright in 1947/8, and shared the trophy with Spurs Reserves in 1966/7; they were beaten semi-finalists in 1948/9 and 1953/4.

Combination Cup Final details:
24.04.48 v.Bournemouth & Boscombe Athletic Reserves (Filbert St) 2-1 (Scott, A.Smith)
> Major, McGregor, Scott, Staples, McArthur, Revie, Dawson, A.Smith, Dewis, Iggleden, Anderson.

*Skipper **Tom McArthur** receives the 1948 Combination Cup from Mr J.E.Carter of Reading. **Les Major** and **Bill McGregor** look on.*

29.03.67 (First Leg) v.Tottenham Hotspur Reserves (White Hart Lane) 1-2 (Svarc)
> Shilton, Potts, Bebbington, Woollett, McDerment, Nish, Matthews, Mackay, Svarc, Sweenie, Tewley.

04.04.67 (Second Leg) v.Tottenham Hotspur Reserves (Filbert St) 1-0 (Sweenie)
> Unchanged team. Sub: Fern (for Sweenie).

Other Reserve Honours:
Leicestershire & Rutland Senior Cup
(Won by Leicester Fosse first XI in 1889/90, 1890/1).
Won by Fosse/City Reserves in 1894/5, 1895/6, 1907/8, 1908/9, 1911/2, 1913/4, 1918/9, 1919/20, 1920/1, 1923/4, 1924/5, 1925/6, 1926/7, 1929/30, 1930/1, 1931/2, 1932/3, 1934/5, 1935/6, 1936/7, 1937/8, 1938/9, 1945/6, 1949/50.

Leicestershire FA Challenge Cup
Won by City Reserves in 1950/1, 1951/2, 1952/3, 1953/4, 1954/5, 1955/6, 1956/7, 1982/3, 1988/9.

Bass Charity Vase
Only intermittently competed for by Leicester, this magnificent trophy was won by Fosse's first XI in 1909. The Burton-based competition underwent mixed fortunes in terms of the calibre of teams attracted over the next 60 or so years, but settled to become a pre-season invitational tournament in the '70s, and was won by City Reserves in 1977, 1978, 1979 and 1982.

During their Midland League and Central Alliance days, the club's Reserve team met several sides against whom their seniors would later compete as equals. Fosse and/or City Reserves therefore appear as opponents in the cumulative senior playing records of the following League clubs (seasons or years of meetings in brackets): Chesterfield (1898/9; 1909-1912); Doncaster Rovers (1898-1901; 1907-1912); Grimsby Town (1910/11); Huddersfield Town (1909/10); Lincoln City (1908/9); Mansfield Town (1912-15; 1919-23); Northampton Town (1899-1901) & Walsall (1901-1903). Additionally, Fosse Reserves met both Rotherham Town and Rotherham County (later to amalgamate as Rotherham United) betwen 1907-1912.

YOUTH AND JUNIOR TEAMS

In the final season before World War 2, a City third team played in the Midland Midweek League. After the war, City's Colts had a season (1947/8) in the United Counties League; one (1948/9) in the Birmingham League; and then switched to the Leicestershire Senior League, winning the Championship in 1954/5, 1956/7 and 1957/8. From 1958 to 1961, City ran both an 'A' and 'B' team: the latter carrying on the Leicestershire Senior League fixtures. The 'A' team came 2nd in the Second Division of the Birmingham & District League in 1958/9, and played the following season in the First Division of that League. Subsequently, City's 'thirds' have competed with much success in essentially specialist youth leagues, being founder members of the Midland Intermediate League, and alternating between this set-up and the Midland Youth League, plus their associated Cup competitions.

The City record in the major national competition, the FA Youth Cup, has not been, however, terribly auspicious in the years since its 1952/3 inauguration. No progress beyond the Fourth Round was made until 1982/3, when Luton overcame City in a Kenilworth Road quarter-final by 0-2; but City did reach the semi-finals in 1986/7 with a run that took them past the challenges of Shrewsbury Town, Manchester United, Sheffield United and Chelsea to face Charlton Athletic in a two-legged tie. A 0-4 deficit from the Selhurst Park leg proved too much to make up, however, and City's 2-1 Filbert Street win was not enough to win them a Final place against Coventry City.

SEASONAL RECORDS

All records relate to season of 42 games or more; and differ for shorter Fosse seasons only where marked * and appropriately annotated.

Most Wins: 25 (1956/7)
Most Home Wins: 16 (1928/9)
Most Away Wins: 11 (1956/7; 1970/1)

Most Defeats: 25 (1977/8)
Most Home Defeats: 10 (1977/8)
Most Away Defeats: 17 (1957/8; 1986/7)

Most Draws: 19 (1975/6)
Most Home Draws: 10 (1948/9)
Most Away Draws: 11 (1921/2)

Least Wins: 5 (1977/8)
Least Home Wins: 4 (1977/8)
Least Away Wins: 1 (1968/9; 1977/8)

Least Defeats: 6 (1956/7; 1970/1)
Least Home Defeats: 0 (1928/9)
Least Away Defeats: 4 (1956/7; 1970/1)

Least Draws: 5 (1957/8) *
Least Home Draws: 2 (1922/3; 1961/2) *
Least Away Draws: 1 (1957/8; 1980/1) *

Most Goals: 109 (1956/7)
Most Home Goals: 68 (1956/7)
Most Away Goals: 41 (1956/7)

Most Goals Conceded: 112 (1957/8)
Most Home Goals Conceded: 41 (1957/8)
Most Away Goals Conceded: 71 (1957/8)

Least Goals: 26 (1977/8)
Least Home Goals: 16 (1977/8)
Least Away Goals: 9 (1921/2)

City's 'Fresha' Youth squad: FA Youth Cup semi-finalists in 1986/7.
*Back: **Toone, Brown, Loughlan, D.Williams, Wilkinson, Walton, Muggleton, Gayle, Milne, Alleyne, Brien, Flanagan.***
*Front: **Bridge, Garwood, Kimberley, Prindiville, Ling, D.Richardson** (Coach), **Jobling, Reid, Torrance, P.Williams.***

Least Goals Conceded: 30 (1970/1)
Least Home Goals Conceded: 14 (1970/1) *
Least Away Goals Conceded: 16 (1970/1)

Best Positive Goal Difference: 58 (1924/5)
Worst Negative Goal Difference: 44 (1977/8) *

Most Points (2 per win): 61 (1956/7)
Most Points (3 per win): 70 (1982/3)
Least Points (2 per win): 22 (1977/8)
Least Points (3 per win): 42 (1986/7)

Most Clean Sheets: 23 (1970/1)
Least Clean Sheets: 2 (1948/9; 1957/8)

Most Players Used: 31 (1987/8)
Least Players Used: 17 (1962/3)

Most Players on Scoresheet: 18 (1919/20; 1987/8)
Least Players on Scoresheet: 8 (1951/2)

* Fosse achieved only 4 draws in each of 1895/6, 1896/7, 1909/10, 1913/14 and 1914/15; they had no home draws in 1895/6; and no away draws in 1914/15. They conceded only eight goals at home in 1899/1900; and had a negative goal difference of 48 in 1908/9.

SEQUENCES

These records relate to consecutive League games only.

Most Consecutive Wins: 7
(15.2.08-28.3.08; 24.1.25-17.3.25; 26.12.62-9.3.63)
Most Consecutive Defeats: 7 (28.11.31-16.1.32)
Most Consecutive Draws: 6 (21.4.73-1.9.73; 21.8.76-18.9.76)

Most Consecutive Games Unbeaten: 19 (6.2.71-19.8.71)
Most Consecutive Games without a Win: 18 (12.4.75-1.11.75)

Most Consecutive Games without Conceding a Goal: 7
(14.2.20-27.3.20)
Most Consecutive Games without Scoring a Goal: 7
(21.11.87-1.1.88)
Most Consecutive Goalless Draws: 3
(13.4.03-18.4.03; 4.3.20-13.3.20; 11.4.25-14.4.25;
24.2.73-10.3.73)

Most Consecutive Home Wins: 13 (3.9.06-29.12.06)
Most Consecutive Home Defeats: 4
(21.2.14-11.4.14; 25.3.78-26.4.78)
Most Consecutive Home Draws: 5
(14.4.03-24.11.03; 19.4.75-13.9.75)

Most Consecutive Away Wins: 4 (13.3.71-12.4.71)
Most Consecutive Away Defeats: 15 (18.10.86-2.5.87)
Most Consecutive Away Draws: 5 (1.10.21-19.11.21)

Most Consecutive Home Games Unbeaten: 40
(12.2.98-17.4.1900)
Most Consecutive Home Games without a Win: 8
(19.4.75-25.10.75)

Most Consecutive Away Games Unbeaten: 10
(27.2.71-14.8.71)
Most Consecutive Away Games without a Win: 22
(2.4.77-14.3.78)

SUBSTITUTES

The use of substitutes for competitive matches was first sanctioned by the Football League for season 1965/6, when one substitute per team could be used in the event of injury only. A similar rule was introduced in both the FA Cup and League Cup competitions the following season, and then was amended for all three competitions from 1967/8, when the use of one No.12 per team was allowed for any reason. For 1986/7, the use of two subs was permitted in Cup competitions only, but, since the beginning of 1987/8, two subs have been allowed in League games as well.

City's first substitute was Jimmy Goodfellow, who replaced Graham Cross against Liverpool at Filbert Street on the first day the new rule operated, 21.8.65.

The first game in which City utilised two substitutes was the League Cup tie at Liverpool on 29.10.86, when Steve Lynex replaced Gary McAllister to become the first No.14 to appear for the club.

Under the current two subs quota, City have yet to substitute a substitute.

The first City substitute to score a goal was Tom Sweenie, who netted in the home game against Blackburn Rovers on 12.4.66 after replacing Mike Stringfellow.

During the period to 1987 when only one sub was allowed, Mike Stringfellow was City's most-used No.12, with 26 such appearances in League and Cups. Mark Goodwin (23), Jim Melrose (21) and Rodney Fern (20) followed. Since the two-sub ruling has applied, Jimmy Quinn amassed 21 such appearances in less than a full season during 1988/9.

Jim Melrose scored 4 goals as a substitute (3 of them in FA Cup ties), and Ian Banks and Jimmy Quinn 3 each, all in League games. Ian Banks and Jon Sammels are the only City players to have scored penalties after coming on as subs. Paul Groves is the only City player to date to have scored on his debut as a sub.

For three players - Malcolm Clarke, Graham Brown and Kevin Reed - a single substitute appearance constituted their entire senior City career.

SUNDAY FOOTBALL

City's first experience of League matches scheduled for a Sunday kick-off came during 1983/4, with the First Division clashes at Nottingham Forest (4.12.83) and Sunderland (18.12.83). The first home game to take place on a Sunday was against Coventry City on 23.12.84.

TRANSFERS

PROGRESSIVE RISES IN RECORD FEES

Fees Paid   **(£)**

June	1923	A.C.H.Chandler	Queens Park Rangers	3,000	
Oct	1925	A.W.Lochhead	Manchester United	3,300	
Sept	1927	L.J.Barry	Notts County	3,450	
Nov	1936	J.W.A.Bowers	Derby County	7,500	
Mar	1948	P.S.McKennan	West Bromwich Albion	'record'	(a)
Oct	1948	J.Ayton	Third Lanark	7,750	
Jan	1949	K.M.Chisholm	Leeds United	11,000	+ H.Iggleden
July	1950	G.A.Rowley	Fulham	14,000	
Sept	1950	A.R.Lever	Cardiff City	15,000	
Oct	1952	J.Morris	Derby County	21,500	
Dec	1954	A.M.Graver	Lincoln City	27,600	(b)
Sept	1963	R.Roberts	Motherwell	41,000	
Dec	1965	P.J.Rodrigues	Cardiff City	42,500	
Nov	1967	L.Glover	Charlton Athletic	80,000	
June	1968	A.J.Clarke	Fulham	150,000	(c)
Dec	1977	R.Davies	Bruges	250,000	
July	1979	A.F.Young	Oldham Athletic	250,000	
July	1980	J.M.Melrose	Partick Thistle	250,000	
Sept	1986	S.J.Moran	Southampton	300,000	
Sept	1987	M.C.Newell	Luton Town	350,000	

Notes:
(a) McKennan fee consisted of £6,000 + J.T.W.Haines - total value undisclosed;
(b) Graver fee consisted of £27,000 + J.E.Littler;
(c) Clarke fee consisted of £110,000 + F.Large.

BOBBY ROBERTS

Fees Received   **(£)**

Mar	1922	J.Paterson	Sunderland	3,790	
June	1928	S.M.Bishop	Chelsea	3,800	
May	1932	E.W.Hine	Huddersfield Town	4,000	
June	1948	A.E.Smith	West Bromwich Albion	5,000	
Sept	1948	J.Hernon	Bolton Wanderers	14,750	
Nov	1949	D.G.Revie	Hull City	20,000	
June	1955	A.M.Graver	Lincoln City	26,000	
Aug	1961	A.Knapp	Southampton	27,500	(a)
Oct	1964	F.McLintock	Arsenal	80,000	
June	1969	A.J.Clarke	Leeds United	165,000	
Sept	1972	D.J.Nish	Derby County	250,000	
Nov	1974	P.L.Shilton	Stoke City	325,000	
Nov	1984	K.D.MacDonald	Liverpool	400,000	
June	1985	G.W.Lineker	Everton	1,050,000	(b)

Notes:
(a) Knapp fee consisted of £25,000 + £2,500 for first 25 apps;
(b) Lineker fee consisted of £800,000 + £250,000 as share of subsequent move to Barcelona.

Despite press speculation to the contrary, it has been confirmed on the Club's authority that no new transfer records - outgoing or incoming - were established by the June 1989 deal which saw Mike Newell depart for Everton and Wayne Clarke arrive from that source. A cash adjustment of £600,000 in Leicester's favour was arrived at by official valuations of £850,000 for Newell and £250,000 for Clarke.

KEVIN MacDONALD

*Introductions of a different kind as (above) Leicester City meet **King George V** before an FA Cup Third Round tie at Chelsea in February 1920. City players from the left are:*
Billy Thomson, Jimmy Harrold, Tom Smith, Sam Currie, Billy Barrett, Herbert Bown *and* **George Jobey***.*
*(Below); Star goalkeeper **Gordon Banks** hands teenager **Peter Shilton** a tip on how to win an England cap or two.*

WHO's WHO

THE PLAYERS

Leicester Fosse/City players - 730 of them - qualify for inclusion in the main section of this Who's Who by virtue of at least one active appearance for the club in a senior competitive match.

Where all relevant details are known to us, each entry is keyed as per this example:

SURNAME, FORENAME(S). ————— **AITKEN, ANDREW**

(A parenthesised forename refers to a non-registered name by which the player was nonetheless best known.)

Birthplace, birthdate.
Place and date of death.

Senior playing career - clubs and signing or transfer dates.
(Where a loan transfer was later made permanent, only the earlier date is shown.
Other loan or trial spells are parenthesised).
(Abbreviations: cs = close season; app = apprentice;
pro = professional; am = amateur; jnr = junior.)

Leicester Fosse/City debut details.

Career biography. —————

b. Ayr, 27.4.1877.
d. Ponteland, Northumberland, 15.2.1955.
Ayr Thistle/Ayr Parkhouse/Kilmarnock/
July 1895:Newcastle United/
Nov 1906:Middlesbrough (p/mgr)/
Feb 1909:FOSSE/Apr 1911:Dundee/
cs 1912:Kilmarnock/
cs 1913:Gateshead Town (p/mgr).
debut: 13.2.09 v.Liverpool (A).

Already a vastly-experienced international wing-half/centre-half when signed by Fosse late in their sole First Division campaign, Andy was then handed the position of player-manager in April 1909, and went on to skipper Scotland as he added three caps to his previous tally of eleven. Nicknamed 'Daddler' during his years on Tyneside, he had been part of Newcastle's 1898 promotion side, had won a Championship medal in 1905 and FA Cup runners-up medals in 1905 and 1906, and had captained that side in many of his 300-plus games; while during his Ayresome spell he had directed the play of such greats as Steve Bloomer and Alf Common. A classily creative defender even as a veteran, Andy led Fosse to 5th and 15th positions in his two full Second Division seasons at the helm, then moved back to Scotland before closing his active career with another player-manager stint in the North Eastern League. He then became a publican, and later acted as a Northern scout for Arsenal.

Leicester Fosse/City appearances and goals in senior competitive matches.
Apps: 64 Lge, 7 FAC.
Goals: 1 Lge.

Lge = Football League;
FAC = Football Association Cup;
LC = Football League Cup; *FMC* = Full Members Cup; *ECWC* = European Cup Winners Cup;
ML = Midland League.
(Note: League appearances for the abandoned 1939/40 season are omitted.)
(Where appearance totals incorporate a 'plus' (+) sign, the following figure represents appearances as playing substitute.)

OTHER PLAYERS

Two appendices give briefer profiles of those Fosse players who made appearances in the Midland League only (between 1891 and 1894), and of those Fosse and City reserve players who enjoyed senior football careers elsewhere.

THE BACKROOM STAFF

Profiles and career details of the men who have managed, trained, coached and administered on behalf of Leicester Fosse and City, 1884-1989.

ADAM, CHARLES
b. Glasgow, 22.3.1919.
Strathclyde/Sept 1938:CITY/
July 1952:Mansfield Town/
cs 1955:Corby Town.
debut (postwar): 5.1.46
v.Chelsea (A) FAC (1 goal).

It's harder than usual to resist applying epithets like 'flying' and 'constructive' to this particular City winger, for Charlie not only earned them on the field in the postwar years, but had in fact served throughout the WW2 period in the Building Trades Flying Squad, constantly on the move helping repair blitz damage. He had still to make his senior City debut when hostilities commenced, but managed the odd game for City, QPR and Leeds United in regional competitions, and then claimed City's first 'official' postwar goal when the FA Cup competition was resumed in 1945/6. Charlie thereafter became a regular for five seasons in the No.11 shirt, with a 1949 Wembley appearance the highlight, before lending his experience to the Stags for a further 94 League games (7 goals). Later he spent some 16 years as coach to the County Youth team - during which spell the FA County Youth Cup came to Leicestershire for the only time - and was also, briefly, a senior City scout.
Apps: 158 Lge; 22 FAC.
Goals: 22 Lge; 3 FAC.

HUGHIE ADCOCK

ADCOCK, HUGH
b. Coalville, 10.4.1903.
d. Coalville, 16.10.1975.
Coalville Town/
Apr 1921:Loughborough Corinthians/
Feb 1923:CITY/
July 1935:Bristol Rovers/
Sept 1936:Folkestone/
Ibstock Penistone Rovers.
debut: 25.8.23 v.Hull City (A).

Capped five times for England and once for the Football League in 1929 and 1930, after his direct right-wing play had helped City to runners-up spot in the First Division, Hughie was a fine clubman whose twelve-year service encompassed City's halcyon days as a major force in League football. His partnerships with inside men Johnny Duncan and Ernie Hine were especially fruitful, and his supply to Arthur Chandler immaculate, while his tearaway individualism brought him a fair personal tally of hard-struck goals. Hughie gained a Division Two championship medal in 1924/5, and was still exhibiting undiminished footballing enthusiasm over twenty years later, acting as trainer to Leicestershire Senior League outfits Whitwick Colliery and Coalville Town.
Apps: 434 Lge; 26 FAC.
Goals: 51 Lge; 1 FAC.

AITKEN, ANDREW
b. Ayr, 27.4.1877.
d. Ponteland, Northumberland, 15.2.1955.
Ayr Thistle/Ayr Parkhouse/Kilmarnock/
July 1895:Newcastle United/
Nov 1906:Middlesbrough (p/mgr)/
Feb 1909:FOSSE/Apr 1911:Dundee/
cs 1912:Kilmarnock/
cs 1913:Gateshead Town (p/mgr).
debut: 13.2.09 v.Liverpool (A).

Already a vastly-experienced international wing-half/centre-half when signed by Fosse late in their sole First Division campaign, Andy was then handed the position of player-manager in April 1909, and went on to skipper Scotland as he added three caps to his previous tally of eleven. Nicknamed 'Daddler' during his years on Tyneside, he had been part of Newcastle's 1898 promotion side, had won a Championship medal in 1905 and FA Cup runners-up medals in 1905 and 1906, and had captained that side in many of his 300-plus games; while during his Ayresome spell he had directed the play of such greats as Steve Bloomer and Alf Common. A classily creative defender even as a veteran, Andy led Fosse to 5th and 15th positions in his two full Second Division seasons at the helm, then moved back to Scotland before closing his active career with another player-manager stint in the North Eastern League. He then became a publican, and later acted as a Northern scout for Arsenal.
Apps: 64 Lge, 7 FAC.
Goals: 1 Lge.

ALDERSON, BRIAN RODERICK
b. Dundee, 5.5.1950.
Lochee Harp/July 1970:Coventry City/
July 1975:CITY/
Mar 1978:New England Tea Men/
Mar 1980:Atlanta Chiefs.
debut: 16.8.75 v.Birmingham City (H) (1 goal).

A small but stocky utility forward discovered by Coventry in Scottish junior football, Brian gained one Under-23 cap while at Highfield Road, and cost City a six-figure transfer fee. In two seasons as a Filbert Street regular, however, he failed to reproduce his previously prolific scoring form, and looked uncomfort-

able when played wide on the right. He eventually faded from the scene during the disastrous 1977/8 season, joining a nine-man transfer and loan exodus to the NASL.
Apps: 87+3 Lge; 4 FAC; 4+1 LC.
Goals: 9 Lge.

ALLEN, HENRY
b. Spondon.
d. Bulawayo, Sept 1939.
Alvaston/Oct 1898:Derby County/
Dec 1899:FOSSE/
May 1900:Derby County/
1900:Alvaston & Boulton.
debut: 16.12.99 v.New Brighton Tower (A).

A 'dainty' outside-left who picked up an FA Cup runners-up medal in his first season at Derby, Harry then surprisingly found himself surplus to the Rams' requirements after only two more appearances in their League side. With Fosse he briefly took the left-flank position from Rab King, but failed to make sufficient impact. He was reported to be applying to the FA for reinstatement as an amateur when returning to Derbyshire in April 1900; shortly thereafter emigrated to Rhodesia to help plan that country's railway system; and was much later heard of in a senior footballing context as vice-president of the Bulawayo FA.
Apps: 13 Lge; 1 FAC.
Goals: 2 Lge.

ALLEYNE, ROBERT ANTHONY
b. Dudley, 27.9.68.
app/pro Sept 1986:CITY/
(Oct 1987-loan-Wrexham)/
Mar 1988:Chesterfield.
debut: 1.1.87 (sub) v.West Ham United (A).

Plucked directly from the youth team ranks to warm the City bench during an injury crisis, Robert got his initial taste of League action without so much as a full reserve game to his credit, and two days later was contributing as a left-sided attacker to one of the relegation season's few highlights - the 6-1 drubbing of Sheffield Wednesday. He materially helped City to the semi-finals of the FA Youth Cup in 1987, then grabbed a chance to add more early experience to his promise with a first-team run at the Racecourse, marked by two goals in ten games. Robert moved on to Saltergate when David Pleat started his initial pruning of the City playing staff.
Apps: 1+2 Lge.

ALLMAN, MESSINA WILSON
b. Burslem, 1883.
1903:Burslem Port Vale/cs 1905:Reading/
May 1907:Portsmouth/
Nov 1907: Plymouth Argyle/
July 1908:Liverpool/cs 1909:Ton Pentre/
Nov 1911:FOSSE/
June 1912:Croydon Common.
debut: 18.11.11 v.Barnsley (H).

A well-travelled inside/centre-forward who failed to spark a goal-shy Fosse to a single win during his brief first-team tenure, which ended when he was one of six Fossils to leave the field early during the notorious weatherbeaten

game at Grimsby in January 1912. Before turning professional with his home-town club, Messina had followed a typical Potteries trade as an earthenware painter.
Apps: 7 Lge.
Goals: 3 Lge.

ALLSOPP, THOMAS CHARLESWORTH
b. Leicester, 18.12.1880.
d. Norwich, 7.3.1919.
Aug 1899:FOSSE/cs 1902:Luton Town/
May 1904:FOSSE/
cs 1905:Brighton & Hove Albion/
May 1907:Norwich City.
debut: 16.2.01 v.Middlesbrough (A).

One of several Fosse players to put in two stints with the club, Tommy was a speedy outside-left who also totted up over 200 appearances for his three (then) Southern League clubs, and was a useful cricketing all-rounder for both Leicestershire (1903-5) and Norfolk (1907-12). His goal aided Norwich's celebrated giant-killing of Cup-holders Sheffield Wednesday in 1908, and he was a regular penalty-taker for that club. Tommy survived Army service as a Labour Battalion sergeant in France in WW1, but succumbed to influenza on the ship home and died shortly afterwards while working as a Norwich licensee.
Apps: 64 Lge; 6 FAC.
Goals: 6 Lge; 1 FAC.

ANDERSON, ANDREW L.
b. Glasgow.
Ashfield/St.Mirren/
May 1908:Newcastle United/
May 1912:Third Lanark/July 1914:FOSSE.
debut: 2.9.14 v.Lincoln City (H).

Andrew's second spell in English football, as Fosse's regular outside-left during the dire final pre-war League season, was a sharp contrast to his first. His efforts in helping St.Mirren to the 1908 Scottish Cup final had originally earned him a £350 transfer to Tyneside, a supporting role in Newcastle's 1909 Championship win, and an international trial; but at Filbert Street his left-wing partnership with fellow Glaswegian Hastie unfortunately failed either to click or to lift Fosse out of the re-election zone.
Apps: 25 Lge; 1 FAC.
Goals: 1 Lge.

ANDERSON, JOHN
b. Barrhead, 8.12.1929.
St.Charles (Paisley)/Arthurlie/
Dec 1948:CITY/
July 1960:Peterborough United/
cs 1961:Nuneaton Borough/
Bedworth Town.
debut: 6.4.49 v.Barnsley (A).

On the short side for a goalkeeper, John nonetheless possessed sharp reflexes and a good sense of anticipatory positioning. Intermittent first team appearances marked his early years at Filbert Street, but he became a regular between the City sticks in 1951/2, and was ever-present in the Division Two championship season of 1954, at the close of which he

won a Scotland 'B' cap and then made his single full international appearance against Finland. Injury sidelined John for the run-in to the 1957 championship, and he subsequently had to battle with Dave MacLaren for the senior jersey. He suffered even worse luck with Posh when, finding himself permanent reserve during their record-breaking initial season in the League, he played in only a single League Cup defeat.
Apps: 261 Lge; 16 FAC.

ANDERSON, ROBERT
b. Newton Mearns, Ayrshire, 11.8.1928.
Mearns Amateurs/am Aug 1944/
pro Jan 1946:CITY/cs 1949:Coalville Town/
Sept 1951:Third Lanark/Nov 1951:Kilmarnock/
July 1953:Hamilton Academicals/
Feb 1954:Forres Mechanics.
debut (postwar): 7.9.46
v.West Ham United (A) (1 goal).

Having made a handful of appearances as a teenager in the final wartime season of regional football, this nippy Scottish winger then found himself cast in the role of permanent understudy to both Mal Griffiths and Charlie Adam when peaceful combat resumed.
Apps: 19 Lge.
Goals: 2 Lge.

IAN ANDREWS

ANDREWS, IAN EDMUND
b. Nottingham, 1.12.1964.
app 1980:Mansfield Town/
Sept 1981:CITY/
(Jan 1984-loan-Middlesbrough)/
(Jan 1984-loan-Swindon Town)/
July 1988:Celtic/
(Dec 1988-loan-Leeds United).
debut: 7.5.84
v.Wolverhampton Wanderers (A).

Originally signed on associate schoolboy forms by Nottingham Forest, but allowed to start his apprenticeship at Mansfield, goalkeeper Ian was snapped up by an alert Dave Richardson and groomed as a potential successor to Mark Wallington. Soon winning England Youth caps, he made prodigious progress to the fringe of the

first team, and made an unexpected League bow while on emergency loan to Swindon, only a week after commencing a similar spell at Ayresome. His agility and confidence seemed to mark him as a worthy heir to City's fine goalkeeping tradition, and following Wallington's departure, Ian's deserving candidacy for Under-21 honours was loudly canvassed. He was finally capped at that level as an over-age player in the early months of the 1986/7 season, when showing inspired First Division form. But, as City gradually slid into the danger zone, Ian's own confidence dipped alarmingly, and his comparative lack of experience began to cost the team dearly, with his sense of positioning in particular, coming under rigorous critical scrutiny. Subsequently, he lost his first-team place to Paul Cooper, but became a prime transfer target for several clubs before City accepted £300,000 from Celtic to allow him to contest the No.1 spot at Parkhead with Irish international (and one-time City triallist) Pat Bonner.
Apps: 126 Lge; 7 FAC; 6 LC.

ANSTEY, BRENDEL
b. Bristol, 1887.
d. Wednesbury, Dec 1933.
Bristol Rovers/Feb 1911:Aston Villa/
Sept 1919:CITY/cs 1920:Mid-Rhondda.
debut: 6.9.19
v.Wolverhampton Wanderers (A).

A patient understudy to international 'keeper Sam Hardy for much of his lengthy stay at Villa Park (where he totted up 45 pre-war League appearances), Brendel briefly usurped Herbert Bown's place between the Filbert Street sticks in the early part of 1919/20, but failed to satisfy Peter Hodge's exacting team-building requirements, and soon dropped down to Southern League level.
Apps: 7 Lge.

APPLETON, COLIN HARRY
b. Scarborough, 7.3.1936.
1951:Scarborough/Mar 1954:CITY/
May 1966:Charlton Athletic/
July 1967:Barrow (p/mgr)/
cs 1969:Scarborough (p/mgr).
debut: 4.9.54 v.Manchester City (H).

Recommended to City by former stalwart Reg Halton (then managing Scarborough), Colin made a rapid first team breakthrough, but found his progress in the late 50s hampered both by a stint of National Service and by the competition of successive senior left-halves Eddie Russell, Pat Ward, Don Walker and Ken Keyworth. From the start of 1959/60, though, Colin missed only eight League games over five seasons, having his coolly forceful defensive half-back play recognised with a Football League representative honour in 1962. He made two trips with City to Wembley, skippering the side on the second occasion, and was also, as captain, the first Leicester player to get his hands on a national knockout trophy when the club won the League Cup in 1964. The same year he took a deserved testimonial game, with City facing an All Star XI. A first-leg Final scorer in City's unsuccessful attempt to retain

COLIN APPLETON

the League Cup in 1965, Colin moved on a year later, and soon turned his experience to coaching and management. He was finally a Wembley winner with Scarborough in the 1973 FA Challenge Trophy Final (as full-back), and later led his team out there twice more in the same competition: indeed he was granted a second testimonial game by a grateful Scarborough in 1982. Briefly a coach at Grimsby, Colin subsequently managed Hull, Swansea, Exeter and little Bridlington Town. He was re-appointed as Hull manager in May 1989. His younger brother David was also on City's books in the early 60's.
Apps: 277 Lge; 27 FAC; 20 LC; 4 ECWC.
Goals: 19 Lge; 2 LC; 1 ECWC.

ARMSTRONG, GEORGE
b. Hebburn, 9.8.1944.
Hawthorn Leslie/Aug 1961:Arsenal/
Sept 1977:CITY/
(cs 1978-loan-Philadelphia Fury)/
Sept 1978:Stockport County.
debut: 24.9.77 v.Nottingham Forest (H).

Widely honoured with Arsenal (a League and Cup double medallist in 1971, a Fairs Cup winner in 1970, and with runners-up medals from a further FA Cup and two League Cup Finals), this little Geordie terrier - a rare perpetual-motion winger - was unfortunately past his peak when Frank McLintock laid out £15,000 to bring him to City. The pace that had seen him through over 600 games at Highbury (exactly 500 in the League), and had earned him five England Under-23 caps, was largely gone, and even his renowned spirit waned a little in City's abysmal relegation season. Jock Wallace allowed him to leave early in the 1978/9 campaign, and he retired as a player the following summer. Subsequently George has held various coaching positions with Aston Villa, Fulham, Enderby Town, Middlesbrough, QPR and Worcester City, and in both Norway and Kuwait.
Apps: 14+1 Lge; 1 FAC; 1 LC.
Goals: 1 FAC.

ASHBY, HENRY RADFORD
b.
Derby Athletic/cs 1896:Burton Swifts/
cs 1899:Brighton United/Nov 1899:not known/
cs 1901:Burton United/
cs 1904:Plymouth Argyle/July 1905:FOSSE.
debut: 2.9.05 v.Clapton Orient (H).

A full-back of genuine class, Harry had his career tragically cut short by a serious leg-break sustained at Hull in 1907 which necessitated early retirement. At the time of his injury, he had missed only a single Fosse game from the date of his signing, and took a deservedly profitable benefit in recompense from a Midland League game against Hull City reserves in March 1908. Earlier, he had been tried briefly as an emergency centre-forward by Burton Swifts, and indeed scored a hat-trick against Burnley in his first game as an attacker.
Apps: 66 Lge; 2 FAC.

ATHERLEY, R.
b.
Nov 1901:FOSSE.
debut: 28.3.02 v.Blackpool (A).

An as yet untraceable centre-forward whose only appearance was to deputise for Rab King in the above 0-4 Good Friday defeat.
Apps: 1 Lge.

ATHERTON, JAMES
b.
South Shore/cs 1894:Blackpool/
cs 1895:FOSSE/Aug 1896:Kettering/
cs 1898:New Brompton.
debut: 28.9.95 v.Burton Wanderers (H).

A promising Lancastrian centre-half - a regular for the Blackpool side who finished as Lancashire League runners-up in 1895, and a member of the South Shore team from that same town which Fosse had removed from the Cup a season earlier - James was unfortunate to find himself understudying the consistent Jack Walker during his year with Fosse.
Apps: 2 Lge.

ATTER, JAMES
b. Stamford, 1870.
Mill Hill House/1890:FOSSE/
cs 1892:Crouch End/Feb 1893:FOSSE/
cs 1893:Crouch End/Corinthians.
debut (comp): 4.10.1890
v.Burton Wanderers (H) FAC.

A star amateur outside-left for Fosse when their fixture list still consisted primarily of friendlies, Jimmy was simultaneously one of the committee men who secured the club's election to the Midland League, and he played in Fosse's inaugural games in both that competition and in the FA Cup, as well as scoring the club's first goal at Filbert Street. Business commitments - Jimmy was a solicitor - led to him playing his football in London for a spell, but he returned to lend his all-round skills to both Fosse and Leicestershire CCC (having earlier scored heavily as a local cricketer with Leicester Ivanhoe, Leicester Banks and Egerton Park). Moving back South again, he was

awarded the prestigious cap and badge of the London FA, and later represented both the famous Corinthians and the Middlesex county soccer team.
Apps: 2 FAC; 24 ML.
Goals: 6 ML.

ATTERBURY, SEPTIMUS
b. Allestree, Derby, 18.10.1880.
d. Coalville, 13.3.1964.
Jan 1899:Loughborough/cs 1899:Barnsley/
cs 1901:Wellingborough/Aug 1902:FOSSE/
cs 1903:Swindon Town/
May 1907:Plymouth Argyle.
debut: 25.12.02 v.Gainsborough Trinity (H).

Fosse's steady left-back in the latter half of 1902/3 (and, indeed, again as a guest player during WW1), Sep had earlier tasted Southern League football with Wellingborough, but it was his record in that sphere after leaving Filbert Street which is most noteworthy. For after 115 appearances for Swindon, he completed a then monumental tally of 330 games for Plymouth (champions in 1913), winning Southern League representative honours against the Irish League in 1913 and the Welsh League in 1921. At this point, the veteran Sep ceased playing, but continued in the position of Argyle trainer until 1937.
Apps: 21 Lge.

SEP ATTERBURY

B

AYTON, JAMES
b. Barrhead, 15.10.1923.
d. Leicester, 25.8.1988.
Neilston Victoria/1944:Third Lanark/
Oct 1948:CITY/June 1951:Shrewsbury Town/
cs 1952:Bedford Town.
debut: 30.10.48 v.Barnsley (H).

A then-record signing for City at £7,750,
Jimmy was disappointingly plagued by illness
and injury during his Leicester sojourn, initially
making five inside-left appearances in
succession before succumbing to a bout of
jaundice. In the opening reserve match of 1949/
50 he cracked a bone in his jaw, and an injury
received on his first team comeback resulted in
a cartilage operation. Though noted from his
Scottish League days as a powerful shot as well
as a stylist, Jimmy found it impossible to
compete with newcomer Arthur Rowley when
he did finally regain fitness.
Apps: 8 Lge.
Goals: 1 Lge.

BACON, ERNEST FREDERICK
b. Leicester, 19.2.1896.
d. Aylestone, 9.1.1972.
St.Andrews/Aug 1919:CITY/
May 1920:Watford/
July 1921:Charlton Athletic/Erith & Belvedere/
1929:Callendar Athletic.
debut: 13.9.19 v.Fulham (H).

A pre-war schoolboy international who guested
for Coventry City during WW1, Ernest was
given his League baptism at right-half by Peter
Hodge, but was largely consigned to reserve
football during his City season. He went on to
represent Watford in their first-ever Football
League game, and also turned out intermittently as a full-back for his two Third Division
clubs.
Apps: 4 Lge.

BAILEY, HORACE PETER
b. Derby, 3.7.1881.
d. Biggleswade, 1.8.1960.
Sept 1899:Derby County/1903:Ripley Athletic/
1905:Leicester Imperial/
Jan 1907:FOSSE/
Apr 1910:Derby County/
Feb 1911:Birmingham.
debut: 9.9.07 v.Wolverhampton Wanderers (H).

A brilliant amateur goalkeeper who gained
near-immediate full international recognition
for his valuable contribution to Fosse's
successful promotion effort - thereby becoming
the club's first England cap - 'H.P.' climaxed
the busy year of 1908 by also appearing for the
victorious United Kingdom XI in the football
final of the Olympic Games. His departure, after
collecting five senior and four amateur caps
while with Fosse, was solely aimed at helping
the Rams out of an injury crisis (he had failed to
make a single first team appearance for them in
his first spell), and the bulk of his remaining
career was then played out at St.Andrews.
Throughout his playing years, Horace was
employed by the Midland Railway Company at
Derby as a rating official.
Apps: 68 Lge; 2 FAC.

BAILEY, WILLIAM HENRY
b. Melton Mowbray, 2.10.1869.
d. Leicester, 19.10.1930.
Melton Rovers/1891:FOSSE.
debut (comp): 12.9.91
v.Derby Junction (H) ML.

A Fossil from the pre-Midland League days,
Harry was a popular, stalwart full-back who
became the recipient of the club's first benefit
pay-out - from a friendly against prestigious
London amateurs, Casuals, on Boxing Day
1893. In fact, Harry was at left-back for Fosse's
opening games in both the Midland and
Football Leagues. It looked as if he had made
his final senior appearance in January 1897, but
when he turned up to watch Fosse at Walsall in
September 1899, he was asked to perform in
goal, and was beaten only once as the team
notched a rare away win! Such versatility was
wholly in character, though, for Harry was also
for several years on the books of Leicestershire
CCC as a batsman. His brother Herbert was
also a Fossil of Midland League vintage.
Apps: 47 Lge; 17 FAC; 61 ML.

BAILLIE, JOSEPH
b. Dumfries, 26.2.1929.
St.Roch's/1946:Celtic/
Nov 1954:Wolverhampton Wanderers/
June 1956:Bristol City/June 1957:CITY/
June 1960:Bradford Park Avenue.
debut: 16.11.57 v.Preston North End (H).

The regular left-back in City's late-50s
struggles to survive and establish themselves in
the First Division, Joe had initially arrived in
England with Scottish League representative
honours, a Scotland 'B' cap and a Scottish Cup-
winners medal (1951) already to his name. He
nonetheless found it impossible to secure a
breakthrough at Molineux, making only a
single League appearance before rebuilding his
confidence at Ashton Gate. Joe's cultured
coolness in the No.3 shirt for Leicester was a
forceful reminder that he had begun his career
in the Parkhead half-back line.
Apps: 75 Lge; 5 FAC.

BAINES, STANLEY N.
b. Syston, 28.7.1920.
Coalville Town/Nov 1937:CITY/
July 1946:Northampton Town.
debut: 10.9.38 v.Preston North End (H).

A young outside-left who briefly stood in for
Eric Stubbs during the final pre-war season,
Stan had his football progress completely
marred by WW2 disruptions. City allowed his
registration to lapse in the close season of 1946,
and he was then only able to add a single
League appearance for the Cobblers to his
record as a Northampton 'guest'.
Apps: 7 Lge.
Goals: 1 Lge.

BAIRD, JOHN
b. Dumbartonshire.
Vale of Leven/1889:Aston Villa/
1889:Kidderminster Olympic/
1890:Kidderminster/
cs 1891:Aston Villa/

July 1895:FOSSE.
debut: 7.9.95 v.Burton Swifts (H).

A versatile defender who had appeared in the
last Cup final to be held at Kennington Oval, as
left-half in the 1892 Villa side defeated by
West Brom, and had won a League championship medal in 1894, John was unfortunate with
injuries during his Fosse season, when he vied
for a full-back place with Harry Davy and
Harry Bailey. Earlier, John had also assisted an
unbeaten Kidderminster Olympic to the
inaugural championship of the Birmingham &
District League, before that club disappeared in
an over-ambitious and short-lived merger with
the local Harriers.
Apps: 13 Lge; 1 FAC.

BALDWIN, JAMES J.
b. Blackburn, 12.1.1922.
d. Blackburn, 13.2.1985.
Mill Hill St.Peters/1945:Blackburn Rovers/
Feb 1950:CITY/
Apr 1956:Great Yarmouth (p/mgr).
debut: 25.2.50 v.Luton Town (H).

Signed from his home-town club for £10,000
by Norman Bullock, Jimmy was the regular
right-half, and occasional inside-right, of City's
sides of the early 50s. A slight, prematurely
balding forager whose stamina belied his
physique, he was a shrewd, unostentatious
operator who earned a championship medal
from City's 1953/4 Division Two campaign.
After his playing days were over, Jimmy also
managed Yeovil for a spell.
Apps: 180 Lge; 10 FAC.
Goals: 4 Lge.

BALL, ALFRED
b.
1893:Preston North End/Kettering/
May 1897:FOSSE/cs 1900:Nelson.
debut: 4.9.97 v.Luton Town (H).

An ever-present at right-half in his first two
seasons with Fosse, Alf was a model of
defensive consistency who had earlier had a
brief taste of First Division fare at Deepdale,
just as proud Preston were losing their aura of
invincibility, and had scored one of the
Kettering goals which removed Fosse from the
Cup in 1896/7.
Apps: 75 Lge; 6 FAC.
Goals: 3 Lge.

BALLARD, FRANK
b.
Long Eaton Rangers/
cs 1898:FOSSE.
debut: 15.10.98 v.Manchester City (A).

A full-back recruited from Midland League
football, Frank failed to mount a convincing
challenge to either Jack Walker or George
Swift, and managed only a single senior game
on either flank in place of his vastly more
experienced clubmates.
Apps: 2 Lge.

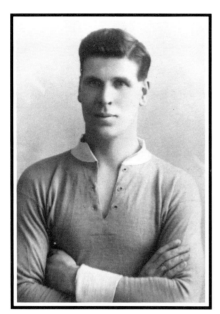

JOHN BAMBER

BAMBER, JOHN
b. Peasley Cross, 11.4.1895.
d. Peasley Cross, 1971.
St.Helens Recreational/Alexander Vics/
Heywood/St.Helens Town/
Dec 1915: Liverpool/Feb 1924:CITY/
cs 1927:Tranmere Rovers/
Aug 1930:Prescot Cables.
debut: 9.2.24 v.Sheffield Wednesday (H).

An Anfield regular at half-back in both wartime
and the first two post-war League seasons, and
then honoured with an England cap, two
Football League appearances, and two games
for the FA touring side in South Africa, John
curiously missed out on the medals as
Liverpool went on to twice take the League
championship in 1922 and 1923. The move to
Filbert Street revitalised his career, with John a
fixture at left-half as City raced to promotion,
an ever-present in their initial season in the top
flight, and a member of the first team to perch
the club (however briefly) on the League's
pinnacle. Displaced shortly thereafter by
expensive import Sid Bishop, John returned to
Merseyside to end his career.
Apps: 113 Lge; 7 FAC.
Goals: 7 Lge.

BANKS, GORDON
b. Sheffield, 30.12.1938.
Millspaugh Steelworks/Rawmarsh Welfare/
Millspaugh Steelworks/Sept 1955:Chesterfield/
May 1959:CITY/Apr 1967:Stoke City/
Mar 1977:Fort Lauderdale Strikers.
debut: 9.9.59 v.Blackpool (H).

First noticed in Chesterfield's unexpected
progress to the FA Youth Cup Final in 1956,
the goalkeeping genius inevitably dubbed
'Banks of England' was, only a decade later, a
national hero for his significant role in his
country's World Cup win. Still a raw youngster
when Matt Gillies signed him for £7,000 after
only 23 League games for the Spireites, Gordon
developed quickly at Filbert Street, basing his

game on an uncanny sense of positioning and
an acute appreciation of the value of solidity
over the gratuitously spectacular. He engendered supreme confidence amongst his
defenders yet he could also call on superb
reflexes and agility when required. Gordon's
second Cup Final appearance for City in 1963
was a very rare shaky performance, but he'd
already broken Liverpool hearts almost single-
handedly in the semi-final to book City's
Wembley ticket, and had also by then won the
first of his 73 full England caps to add to
Under-23 and Football League honours. The
rise to contention of Peter Shilton spelt a
premature end to Gordon's Leicester career,
and when West Ham dropped their promised
option on his transfer (honourably - they had in
the interim committed to buy Kilmarnock's
Bobby Ferguson), he moved to Stoke for
£50,000. His England career peaked again in
1970, when a reflex save from Pele's header
became probably TV's most re-run piece of
goalkeeping action, and the civil honour of an
OBE followed. At club level, Gordon inspired
Stoke to their first-ever trophy, the League Cup
(repeating his major City success for the team
he'd helped beat in 1964), and earned himself
the accolade of 1972 Footballer of the Year, but
his world was shattered that October when a car
crash cost him the sight of one eye. Adherence
to his own high standards precluded a League
comeback after recovery, but stints of coaching
at Stoke and Port Vale, and a spell as manager
of Telford United, bracketed a brief return to
playing in the transatlantic NASL, where he
was voted Goalkeeper of the Year. Gordon
returned to Filbert Street in 1986 as chairman
of the club's short-lived 'Lifeline' fund-raising
operation.
Apps: 293 Lge; 34 FAC; 25 LC; 4 ECWC.

GORDON BANKS

IAN BANKS

BANKS, IAN FREDERICK
b. Mexborough, 9.1.1961.
Jan 1979:Barnsley/June 1983:CITY/
Sept 1986:Huddersfield Town/
July 1988:Bradford City/
Mar 1989:West Bromwich Albion.
debut: 27.8.83 v.Notts County (H).

A stocky but skilful midfielder with an
explosive long-range shot, Ian suffered injury
problems shortly after Gordon Milne paid
£100,000 to bring him to City from Oakwell,
and took time to settle. Never a wholly
automatic choice thereafter, probably because
difficult to motivate to consistent peak
involvement, he nonetheless turned in some
excellent performances on the left, alternating
pin-point driven crosses with a knack of
shuffling inside for a telling strike. Ian's
penalty goal in the final game of 1985/6
clinched City's First Division survival for
another year, but he moved back to Yorkshire
shortly after Bryan Hamilton's arrival. Ian was
the Terriers' skipper when they nosedived to
Division Three in 1988, but he earned himself a
big-money transfer back to the Second at
Valley Parade, and was the subject of another
six-figure deal during the deadline week of
1989.
Apps: 78+15 Lge; 6 FAC; 3+1 LC.
Goals: 14 Lge; 1 LC.

BANNISTER, WILLIAM
b. Burnley, 1879.
d. Leicester, 26.3.1942.
Earley/1899:Burnley/
Nov 1901:Bolton Wanderers/
Dec 1902:Woolwich Arsenal/
May 1904:FOSSE/Sept 1910:Burnley/
1912:Leicester Imperial.
debut: 3.9.04 v.Blackpool (A).

A tough, towering ex-international centre-half
(twice capped for England and twice representing the Football League while with his
Lancashire clubs), Billy served Fosse for six
seasons after his record £300 transfer from
Arsenal, and skippered the side in the promotion season of 1907/8. His attacking instincts,

occasionally deemed somewhat reckless for a pivot, were supplemented by a noteworthy long-range shot, and he was awarded a benefit at Christmas 1909 (a reserve fixture with Nottingham Forest), just over a week before his final first team appearance. Billy later ran pubs in both Burnley and Leicester.
Apps: 149 Lge; 11 FAC.
Goals: 15 Lge; 3 FAC.

BARLOW, HERBERT
b. Kilnhurst, 22.7.1916.
Silverwood Colliery/July 1935:Barnsley/ June 1938:Wolverhampton Wanderers/ Feb 1939:Portsmouth/Dec 1949:CITY/ June 1952:Colchester United.
debut: 17.12.49 v.Sheffield Wednesday (H).

A creative inside-forward who also knocked in over 70 League goals during his near-20-year senior career, Bert first hit the headlines in 1939. Unable to make a first-team breakthrough at Molineux, he moved to Fratton Park on the 'never-never', scored a Cup semi-final goal to take otherwise struggling Pompey to Wembley, and there struck again in the 31st minute to help his underdog team to a shock 4-1 win over Wolves! Ten years later, Bert again had Wembley (and a possible Cup/League double) in his sights as champions Portsmouth expected a Highbury semi-final cakewalk - only to find their calculations upset by an inspired, giant-killing City side. Joining Leicester only a matter of months later, Bert lent his wily experience for three Second Division campaigns, and did not retire until, at the age of 38, he'd given two further seasons of all-out effort to Colchester.
Apps: 42 Lge; 2 FAC.
Goals: 9 Lge.

BARLOW, JOHN
b. Prescot, 1876.
Prescot/1897:Everton/1899:Reading/ cs 1901:Tottenham Hotspur/1903:Reading/ May 1903:FOSSE.
debut: 5.9.03 v.Barnsley (A).

A Lancastrian wanderer who totted up only four League appearances in two seasons at Goodison, and then sampled Southern League fare at Elm Park and White Hart Lane, John appeared without conspicuous success at both inside and outside-left in Fosse's appalling 1903/4 campaign, which ended with the club seeking re-election.
Apps: 22 Lge; 5 FAC.
Goals: 2 Lge; 1 FAC.

BARNETT, CHARLES
b. Derby.
Feb 1913:FOSSE/cs 1920:Mansfield Town.
debut: 26.4.13 v.Hull City (A).

The goalkeeping understudy to both Brebner and Bown, Charles was recruited from Derbyshire League junior football, and also briefly helped out Derby County as a guest player in 1915/16. He was only six times on a winning side with Fosse, and failed to appear in a single senior game for City.
Apps: 20 Lge.

BARRATT, ALFRED E.
b. Oadby.
Aug 1914:FOSSE.
debut: 2.4.1915 v.Lincoln City (A).

A local outside-left whose sole senior appearance lent him the rather marginal distinction of being the last player to make a League debut for the Fosse, prior to the upheavals of war and reconstruction.
Apps: 1 Lge.

BARRATT, ALFRED GEORGE
b. Corby, 13.4.1920.
July 1938:Northampton Town/ Sept 1939:Stewart & Lloyds (Corby)/ Sept 1946:CITY/ July 1950:Grimsby Town/ July 1951:Southport.
debut: 17.4.48 v.West Ham United (H).

Having played a single League game as a youngster with the Cobblers, Alf returned from WW2 action as a Marine Commando to become a reserve-team fixture in his four post-war seasons at Filbert Street, yet missed the 1947/8 Combination Cup Final while making his third appearance in a week as senior centre-half. Only one further City run-out followed, at right-back the following season, but this tall, well-built stopper finally came into his own at Southport, totting up over 200 games for the Third Division (North) side.
Apps: 4 Lge.

BARRETT, WILLIAM HENRY
b. Nuneaton.
Nuneaton Town/Army football/ 1918:Hinckley United/ Apr 1919:CITY/ July 1925:Derby County.
debut: 30.8.19 v.Wolverhampton Wanderers (H).

Noted by Fosse in the pre-war days as a likely prospect, right-back Billy proved he had lost none of his pluck, speed or first-time tackling power in a short spell with Hinckley, and was snapped up for the resumption of League competition. He gave fine service across five seasons, but was only a covering reserve when City finally secured promotion, and sadly failed to get a first-team look-in at Derby as the Rams followed them up the next year. Billy's only goals for City came from penalties in the final games he played in each senior competition.
Apps: 143 Lge; 9 FAC.
Goals: 1 Lge; 1 FAC.

BARRON, CHARLES W.
b.
Sept 1914:FOSSE.
debut: 2.1.15 v.Birmingham (A).

A right-back introduced to Fosse's hapless struggle of the final pre-war season, when the defence had been shipping goals in sixes and sevens, Charles, noted as 'a North Country lad', helped stave off all but the final embarrassment of the club having to go to the re-election vote.
Apps: 16 Lge.

BARRY, LEONARD JAMES
b. Sneinton, 27.10.1901.
d. Mapperley, 17.4.1970.
May 1920:Notts County/ Sept 1927:CITY/ Aug 1933:Nottingham Forest.
debut: 1.10.27 v.Manchester United (H).

Initially an amateur with the Magpies, while he completed RAF service at Cranwell, Len was capped at that level (v.Ireland in 1923/4) before turning professional. However, it was his consistent cleverness as an old-fashioned dribbling left-winger in the City side that finished successively third and second in Division One which earned him five full England honours in 1928 and 1929. His lengthy and profitable partnership with Arthur Lochhead provided an object lesson in the effective employment of complementary ball-control skills, and while Len's personal contributions to the score-sheet were often of a spectacular nature, he is at least as well remembered for his unselfish service to the more prolific Chandler and Hine. He was approaching the veteran stage when Danny Liddle inherited his role, and featured only briefly in Forest's struggling Second Division side.
Apps: 203 Lge; 11 FAC.
Goals: 25 Lge; 1 FAC.

BAUCHOP, WILLIAM FOTHERINGHAM
b. Alloa, 18.1.1882.
Alloa Athletic/cs 1905:Plymouth Argyle/ May 1906:Heart of Midlothian/ Carlisle United/ June 1909:Stockport County/ Aug 1911:FOSSE/ Aug 1912:Norwich City/cs 1913:Fulham/ Jan 1914:Grimsby Town.
debut: 2.9.11 v.Gainsborough Trinity (A).

A jinky Scottish outside-left signed to partner Frank Rollinson, but soon displaced by the youthful promise of George Harrison, Willie then followed belatedly in the Norwich-bound bootprints of his more successful brother Jimmy, who had previously won fame with Celtic, Derby and Spurs, and was by then with Bradford. Willie himself had briefly tasted the big time, as one of the Hearts side beaten 0-3 by Celtic in the 1907 Scottish Cup Final, and would be noted later as one of the Canaries who embarrassed Fosse in the Cup in 1912/13. He played first-team football for neither of his last two clubs, however.
Apps: 18 Lge; 3 FAC.
Goals: 1 Lge.

BAXTER, JAMES
b. Glasgow.
Parkhead/Aug 1925:CITY/ June 1929:Reading/Nov 1930:Torquay United.
debut: 24.4.26 v.Bury (A).

A patient reserve wing-half whose half-dozen senior appearances were spread across four seasons when City were at their strongest as a consistent First Division force.
Apps: 6 Lge.
Goals: 1 Lge.

BEADSWORTH, ARTHUR

b. Leicester, 1876.
Hinckley Town/May 1900:FOSSE/
cs 1901:Preston North End/
Oct 1902:Manchester United/
cs 1903:Swindon Town/
cs 1905:New Brompton/
Aug 1906:Burton United.
debut: 29.9.1900 v.Newton Heath (H).

A utility forward with both Fosse and the newly-rechristened Manchester United - his right-wing debut against his future club was followed by three games in the inside-left berth - Arthur had his best spell with Swindon, where he made 54 Southern League appearances (11 goals) while earning the then substantial wage of £2 per week. He made no senior appearances for Preston, while Burton United were set for their final Football League season when he joined them, and his own fate (scoreless in 18 games as a forward) rather accurately mirrored theirs.
Apps: 4 Lge.

BEARDSLEY, GODFREY LEONARD

b. Barrow-on-Soar, 1879.
d. Erpingham, June 1912.
Rossal School/Dec 1896:Loughborough/
Sept 1898:FOSSE/(1901:Corinthians).
debut: 10.9.98 v.Woolwich Arsenal (A).

A gentleman goalkeeper from a sporting family, Godfrey interrupted his law studies to turn professional and was soon, ironically, at the centre of a major row between Loughborough and Leicester over the legality of his transfer. Eventually the FA found Fosse guilty of 'poaching' the player, fined the club £50, and suspended secretary/manager W.D.Clark *sine die*, but allowed Godfrey to continue as a Fossil. He distinguished himself between the Filbert Street sticks until December 1900 (once saving a thrice-taken penalty at Small Heath in March 1899), then resumed his law practice and reverted to amateur status, occasionally assisting the Corinthians before his tragically early death. One of his brothers was a founder of Loughborough Corinthians, for years Leicestershire's foremost amateur club; but it has not been possible to establish conclusively whether Godfrey was also in any way related to Fred Beardsley, the former Forest goalkeeper who went on to found Arsenal.
Apps: 69 Lge; 7 FAC.

BEBY, JOHN VICTOR

b. Gillingham, 23.8.1907.
d. Rochester, 8.4.1976.
am:Charlton Athletic/Army football/
Dec 1929:Gillingham/Apr 1930:CITY/
June 1932:Ashford/Oct 1932:Bristol Rovers/
July 1933:Crystal Palace/
Mar 1934:Darlington/
Mar 1936:Exeter City.
debut: 3.5.30 v.Birmingham (A).

A six-foot goalkeeper who had served with the Grenadier Guards, John lost out in his tussles with Jim McLaren for the green jersey at Leicester, and then experienced mixed fortunes with his Third Division clubs: in and out at

Eastville; failing to make the first-team at Selhurst; but becoming an ever-present at Feethams for 1934/5, after helping Darlington take the Division Three (North) Cup at the end of the previous season. After WW2 he qualified as a coach, having spells with AEK Athens and Blida (Algeria) as well as in Germany and India. John returned to take over the Cricketers' pub in Gillingham.
Apps: 29 Lge; 1 FAC.

BEDFORD, GEORGE

b. Chesterfield, 1918.
Temple Normanton/trials-Chesterfield/
Jan 1935:CITY/
Mar 1941:Northampton Town.
debut: 14.12.35 v.Barnsley (A).

A stalwart reserve centre-half for City in the late 30s, who nevertheless made two of his senior appearances in the forward line, George lost his chance of footballing progress with the declaration of war. His final City games were played in regional competitions, latterly as a guest, following his official move to the County Ground. He similarly assisted Mansfield Town.
Apps: 4 Lge.

BEEBY, OLIVER

b. Leicester, 2.10.1934.
May 1953:CITY/June 1959:Notts County/
cs 1961:Oxford United.
debut: 5.9.55 v.Doncaster Rovers (A).

An England Youth international full-back, local lad Oliver showed admirable patience during his six-year stint with City's junior and reserve sides, breaking through to senior action only once, in a humbling 2-6 defeat at Belle Vue. Unfortunately, at Meadow Lane he received little better reward, being released after only 13 League outings.
Apps: 1 Lge.

BELL, JOHN

b. Dundee, 1877.
Dundee Wanderers/Renton/Bacup/
cs 1894:Wolverhampton Wanderers/
cs 1895:Grimsby Town/
June 1899:Chesterfield/
cs 1901:Millwall/May 1903:FOSSE.
debut: 5.9.03 v.Barnsley (A).

A forward in his Wolves season (3 goals in 6 League games), Scottish nomad John was converted to centre-half by Grimsby and had built a substantial reputation as a constructive pivot by the time he joined Fosse, shortly after Millwall's surprise run to the Cup semi-finals. Yet he was unable to take much pressure off a leaky defence as Leicester found themselves rooted in the re-election zone, and he was not retained.
Apps: 21 Lge; 1 FAC.

BELL, WILLIAM JOHN

b. Backworth, nr.Newcastle, 1906.
Blyth Spartans/Chopwell Institute/
Dec 1923-trials-Aston Villa/
Aug 1924:Lincoln City/
May 1925:Mansfield Town/
Feb 1926:CITY/

July 1930:Torquay United.
debut: 27.2.26 v.West Bromwich Albion (A).

Elevated from Mansfield's successful Midland League side straight into the First Division, William was soon vying earnestly with Harold Wadsworth for the role of City's left-flank attacker, and indeed held it on merit for some time until Len Barry arrived. He improved on his City goal tally over the course of a single season at Plainmoor, but failed to impress future City boss Frank Womack sufficiently to earn himself another contract.
Apps: 41 Lge.
Goals: 5 Lge.

BELL, WILLIAM JOHN

b. Johnstone, 3.9.1937.
Neilston/1957:Queens Park/
July 1960:Leeds United/Sept 1967:CITY/
June 1969:Brighton & Hove Albion (p/coach).
debut: 30.9.67 v.Everton (H).

Already in possession of two Scottish amateur caps from his Hampden Park half-back days, Willie earned a matching pair of full international honours as left-back with Don Revie's Leeds. He also picked up medals from their 1964 Division Two championship campaign, the 1965 FA Cup Final and the 1967 Fairs Cup Final before making way for Terry Cooper and being lined up as a £45,000 City replacement for Richie Norman. The hefty defender failed to survive Matt Gillies' departure, though, and headed for the South Coast after Frank O'Farrell had taken City to Wembley without him. After a spell of coaching at St.Andrews (Blues were fined for employing Willie in this capacity while he was still a registered player with Brighton), he became manager of both Birmingham and Lincoln City, but resigned from the latter in 1978 to join an evangelical religious crusade in the USA.
Apps: 49 Lge; 6 FAC; 2 LC.

WILLIE BELL

BELTON, THOMAS
b. 1879.
d. 1944
Woodhouse United/Whitwick White Cross/
cs 1902:FOSSE/
cs 1904:Coventry City/
Loughborough Corinthians.
debut: 6.9.02 v.Small Heath (H).

Fosse were in a sad Second Division tailspin
when Tom joined them, but his efforts from the
various inside-forward berths at least delayed
the ignominy of a re-election application by a
season, for he was second top scorer in his first
campaign, and a spirited trier. A decade on,
Tom was still appearing regularly as a centre-
half for Loughborough Corinthians, alongside
his brother Jack.
Apps: 49 Lge; 5 FAC.
Goals: 12 Lge; 5 FAC.

TOMMY BENFIELD

BENFIELD, THOMAS CHARLES
b. Leicester, 1889.
d. France, 10.11.1918.
Army football/pro July 1910:FOSSE/
June 1914:Derby County.
debut: 12.11.10 v.Hull City (H).

A corporal in the Leicestershire Regiment who
had trials with Fosse reserves in February and
October 1907 while stationed at Glen Parva
barracks, Tommy became in 1909 the first
county soldier to take part in the then-
prestigious annual Army v.Navy match. He
signed for Fosse upon demob, and played in
four of the five forward positions over the next
four seasons, at a time when such versatility
was rare. His gradual development as a pacy
marksman was noted by the newly-relegated
Rams, and he contributed 15 goals as an ever-
present inside-right in their 1915 Division Two
championship side. With Britain at war,
however, he briefly returned to guest for Fosse,
then found he could not resist a recall to the
colours. Sadly he was killed by a sniper's bullet
shortly before Armistice Day, and before his
footballing talent could truly blossom.
Apps: 106 Lge; 5 FAC.
Goals: 23 Lge.

BENNETT, A.
b.
1891:FOSSE.
debut (comp): 12.9.1891
v.Derby Junction (H) ML.

A centre-forward who struggled - with, it
should be said, most of his clubmates - to make
the transition from local friendly fare to the first
season of Midland League competition.
Apps: 1 FAC; 5 ML.
Goals: 2 ML.

BENNETT, JOHN W.
b. Liverpool, 1880.
Wavertree/1900:Lincoln City/
Wellingborough/cs 1901:Northampton Town/
cs 1903:Luton Town/May 1904:FOSSE/
Apr 1905:Blackburn Rovers.
debut: 3.9.04 v.Blackpool (A).

A fine right-back who had rebuilt his career in
the Southern League after being released by
Lincoln, Jack joined Fosse's concerted attempt
to bounce back from the re-election reprieve of
1904, and impressed so much that he earned
himself a move to First Division Blackburn
before season's end. His role there, though, was
primarily to understudy international Bob
Crompton, and his chances were severely
limited.
Apps: 27 Lge; 7 FAC.
Goals: 1 Lge.

BENSKIN, F.S.
b. Leicester.
Leicester Old Boys/Apr 1902:FOSSE/
1904:South Wigston Albion.
debut: 24.1.03 v.Burnley (A) (1 goal).

The goalscoring half of the Benskin brothers
partnership: an amateur inside or outside-left
who could surely have done with an extended
first-team trial. Apart from scoring in his only
League game, he also hit a hat-trick in the first
of his senior friendlies, at Ripley in April 1902.
Apps: 1 Lge.
Goals: 1 Lge.

BENSKIN, WILLIAM EWART
b. Leicester, 8.4.1880.
d. Leicester, 1.6.1956.
Leicester Old Boys/May 1901:FOSSE/
1904:South Wigston Albion.
debut: 25.1.02 v.Burslem Port Vale (H).

A faithful reserve centre- or left-half for Fosse
across three seasons of Second Division
struggle, 'Benny' was another to write his name
in bolder print across the records of the County
cricket club. A fast bowler who had two spells
with Leicestershire between 1906 and 1924,
bracketing a stint representing Perthshire and
Scotland, he performed the summer game hat-
trick against Essex at Southend, in the very first
of his 100 County Championship matches.
Renowned as a joker, 'Benny' later worked as
an upholsterer at the Royal Infirmary. (It is
suspected, but unconfirmed, that he also turned
out in the Southern League for Northampton
Town in 1906/7).
Apps: 11 Lge.

BERRINGTON, W.A.
b.1888.
Army football/
1912:Aberdare/cs 1913:FOSSE.
debut: 7.2.14 v.Leeds City (H).

A former Grenadier Guardsman whom Fosse
had spotted during his brief spell of Southern
League football in Wales, Berrington played in
all five matches of the 1913 Swedish tour, but
subsequently was restricted to only two Second
Division games as left-back deputy for Sam
Currie.
Apps: 2 Lge.

BERRY, A.
b.
Dec 1900:FOSSE.
debut: 16.3.01 v.New Brighton Tower (H).

A steady reserve right-half for Fosse across
four fairly uninspiring seasons; Berry's origins
and destiny unfortunately remain a mystery.
Apps: 24 Lge.

BETTS, HERBERT
b. Leicester.
Leicester Imperial/
(Mar 1902-trial-FOSSE).
debut: 31.3.02 v.Preston North End (H).

A left-half briefly landed in poverty-stricken
Fosse's rather desperate end-of-season trawl of
local talent, and soon thrown back to the Imps.
Apps: 2 Lge.

BICKNELL, STEPHEN JOHN
b. Stockton, nr.Rugby, 28.11.58.
VS Rugby/app July 1975/
pro Nov 1976:CITY/
Aug 1978:Torquay United/
cs 1979:Southam United.
debut: 9.4.77 v.Newcastle United (A).

A young winger tossed into the First Division
deep-end by Jimmy Bloomfield late in his final
campaign at the helm (as high hopes of
European qualification again receded fast),
Steve failed to impress, and had scant
opportunity to rebuild his confidence as City
slithered the following season. His Plainmoor
record consisted only of three substitute
appearances, and he quickly returned to minor-
grade football.
Apps: 6+1 Lge.

BINNEY, JOHN
b.
June 1902:FOSSE/
cs 1903:Worksop Town/
cs 1904:Denaby United.
debut: 6.9.02 v.Small Heath (H).

Impressive in pre-season practice, and chosen
for Fosse's opening pair of games for 1902/3,
this inside-left then never again made the
Filbert Street first team; though he found his
level in Midland League football.
Apps: 2 Lge.

ALAN BIRCHENALL

BIRCHENALL, ALAN JOHN

b. East Ham, 22.8.1945.
Thorneywood Thistle/
June 1963:Sheffield United/
Nov 1967:Chelsea/
June 1970:Crystal Palace/
Sept 1971:CITY/
(Mar 1976-loan-Notts County)/
(Apr 1977-loan-San Jose Earthquakes)/
Sept 1977:Notts County/
Apr 1978:Memphis Rogues/
Sept 1978:Blackburn Rovers/
Mar 1979:Luton Town/
Oct 1979:Hereford United/
cs 1980:Trowbridge (p/mgr).
debut: 2.10.71 v.Crystal Palace (H).

An extrovert blond striker who gained four
England Under-23 caps before making a trio of
heftily-valued transfers, Alan had initially come
to notice as a skilful foil for Mick Jones at
Bramall Lane, and was Dave Sexton's first
major buy at Stamford Bridge. Jimmy
Bloomfield eventually added him to the rapidly
burgeoning community of transplanted
Cockneys at Leicester, where Alan gradually
assumed a deeper-lying schemer's role as
attack-oriented City's fortunes ebbed and
flowed entertainingly in the early 70s. Again
inclining to the nomadic life, Alan then carried
both his boots and his ever-ready smile around
the lower Divisions for a while but returned to
Filbert Street in 1983 as an energetic public
relations officer. He is still attempting to
rewrite his own legend with his 'Geriatric
Megastars', a popular charity-supporting team
of former City favourites.
Apps: 156+7 Lge; 14 FAC; 6 LC.
Goals: 12 Lge; 1 FAC; 1 LC.

BISHOP, MATTHEW

b. Melton Mowbray.
Aug 1895:FOSSE/cs 1897:Warmley/
Feb 1899:FOSSE.
debut: 12.10.95
v.Hinckley Town (H) FAC (1 goal).

A young outside-left whose senior progress was
initially stymied by the return of old favourite
Billy Dorrell, Matt himself became another
player to twice sign on to the Fosse payroll,
albeit with hardly greater success second time
around. His interim spell with Bristol-based
Warmley coincided with that club's promotion
to the Southern League's First Division, and
ended when the club resigned part-way through
1898/9.
Apps: 13 Lge; 6 FAC.
Goals: 2 Lge; 2 FAC.

BISHOP, SIDNEY MACDONALD

b. Stepney, 10.2.1900.
d. Chelsea, 4.5.1949.
Ilford/RAF/(trials-Crystal Palace)/
May 1920:West Ham United/
Nov 1926:CITY/
June 1928:Chelsea.
debut: 6.11.26 v.Derby County (A).

A former Hammers skipper, a player in the first
Wembley FA Cup Final in 1923, and the bearer
of the Upton Park nickname 'Sticks' on account
of his slender frame, Sid was a cultured,
constructive wing-half who fitted in perfectly
with City's ascending First Division side,
winning himself suitable recognition by way of
four England caps (one goal) and one Football
League honour. Indeed, only injury prevented
Sid captaining his country against Scotland in
1928. He was far from keen, however, on living
outside London, and was quite prepared to drop
a Division to move (for £3,800) to Stamford
Bridge, where he helped Chelsea to promotion
in his second season.
Apps: 49 Lge; 4 FAC.
Goals: 7 Lge.

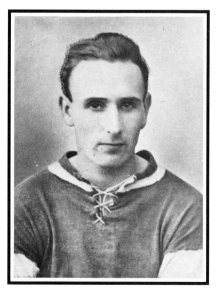

SID BISHOP

ADAM BLACK

BLACK, ADAM HUDSON

b. Denny, 18.2.1898.
d. Leicester, 30.8.1981.
Bathgate/Jan 1920:CITY.
debut: 24.1.20 v.Hull City (H).

Holder of the record for the highest number of
League appearances for City, Adam was
ever-present in four of his sixteen playing
seasons, and missed but a single game in each
of three more. His consistent, unostentatious
brilliance at full-back - he alternated for several
years between left and right flanks before
settling on the latter side - cried out for
international recognition, but the nearest Adam
got to a cap was an appearance for the
Anglo-Scots against the Home Scots in March
1923, the penultimate time the Scottish trial
took place in this popular format. Perhaps his
slight build and stature deceived the selectors,
but his resilience and bravery had already won
him the DCM during his wartime service with
the Argyll and Sutherland Highlanders before
Peter Hodge swooped for his signature from
little Bathgate (soon to become a Scottish
League team themselves). Adam won a
Second Division championship medal in 1925
and then starred for a decade in the top flight
before retiring to run a Leicester newsagent's
shop, having earned three cash benefits for
loyalty from a grateful City. Adam's younger
brother moved from Denny Hibs to
Sunderland in 1921, after representing
Scotland at Junior level, but played only a
couple of League games at inside-forward for
the Rokerites before moving on to Third
Division (North) champions-to-be Nelson.
Apps: 528 Lge; 29 FAC.
Goals: 4 Lge.

BLACKETT, JOSEPH

b. Newcastle, 1875.
Newcastle United/Gateshead/
June 1896:Loughborough/
May 1897:Wolverhampton Wanderers/
Mar 1900:Derby County/Apr 1901:Sunderland/
Oct 1901:Middlesbrough/cs 1905:Luton Town/
July 1906:FOSSE/cs 1909:Rochdale (p/mgr)/
cs 1912:Barrow.
debut: 1.9.06 v.Burslem Port Vale (A).

Though he started his League career as an
outside-left, and even had the odd game at
centre-forward for Derby, Joe had forged a fair
reputation as an uncompromising full-back by
the time Fosse expended a sizeable £115 fee on
his transfer. (As was the custom then, the fee
was paid to Middlesbrough, who had retained
Joe's League registration, rather than to
Southern League Luton). He gave good value,
too; turning out on either flank as required to
stiffen the Fosse defence and add conviction to
the promotion drive, and then going on to take
part in the club's First Division (mis) adventure
in his final season. Joe represented the English
XI in the Players' Union international at Ibrox
in March 1900, and was selected as travelling
reserve for the Football League's game in
Belfast in October 1904. He first experienced
promotion with Boro' in 1902 and, later, in his
initial season as player-manager at Rochdale,
he led his team into the top flight of the
Lancashire Combination, and to the championship of that competition a year later. Joe was a
trainer at Reading from 1913, and enlisted for
WW1 service in May 1915.
Apps: 78 Lge; 3 FAC.

BLESSINGTON, JAMES

b. Linlithgow, 28.2.1874.
d. Newton Abbott, 18.4.1939.
1890:Leith Hibernians/1891:Leith Athletic/
1892:Celtic/Mar 1898:Preston North End/
June 1899:Derby County/
Oct 1899:Bristol City/Aug 1900:Luton Town/
May 1903:FOSSE.
debut: 5.9.03 v.Barnsley (A).

The epitome of those tough, thoughtful and
often shrewdly skilled Scots who did so much
to change the face of early English professional
football, Jimmy had been a member of three
Celtic championship teams, had picked up two
Scottish Cup runners-up medals, and earned
four full caps and five selections for the
Scottish League side before he crossed the
border. Curiously, his spell at Derby was
notably short (only two League games), but he
lit up the forward lines of his two Southern
League clubs, and was an ever-present in the
inside-right berth in his first season at
Leicester, having joined the remarkably heavy
transfer traffic of the time between Luton and
Fosse. Jimmy was still a valuable player when
he additionally assumed the onus of becoming
the club's first ever Team Manager in January
1907 - decades before managers as such were
granted any credit for feats like Fosse's 1908
promotion - and he continued selflessly to pass
on his experience to the Fosse reserves between
his increasingly sporadic League appearances.
He certainly earned the profits from his benefit

match - a Boxing Day 1908 reserve fixture
against Leeds City. In 1913, some years after
leaving Fosse, he was appointed coach to
Belfast Celtic, and also served as an athletics
handicapper in Ireland; while in the inter-war
years he became a West Country licensee.
Apps: 100 Lge; 12 FAC.
Goals: 18 Lge; 3 FAC.

BLOCKLEY, JEFFREY PAUL

b. Leicester, 12.9.1949.
June 1967:Coventry City/Oct 1972:Arsenal/
Jan 1975:CITY/
(Feb 1978-loan-Derby County)/
June 1978:Notts County/1981:Gloucester City.
debut: 1.2.75 v.Chelsea (H).

A team-mate of Peter Shilton's in Leicester
Boys' Trophy-winning team of 1965, Jeff was
initially overlooked by his home-town club. His
cool, strong centre-half play soon, however,
saw him through the ranks at Highfield Road,
and to the first of his ten England Under-23
caps; yet it was only after a big-money move to
Highbury that he received a full England call-
up. Matters soured somewhat at Arsenal, with
Frank McLintock unready to relinquish his
place, and the crowd unforgiving after Jeff
turned in a below-par performance in his club's
1973 Cup semi-final defeat by Sunderland.
However, what seemed a desperation purchase
on Jimmy Bloomfield's part in fact worked
wonders for both player and club, as City
escaped an apparently inevitable relegation spot
thanks to the inspirational successes of Jeff at
the back and Chris Garland up front.
Injuries unfortunately dogged much of Jeff's
subsequent Leicester career, but when he gave
up his role as defensive cornerstone, it was to
the high promise of young Steve Sims. Jeff
returned to the county on retirement, was
briefly manager of Southern League club
Leicester United, and from April to May 1989
took the reins at Hinckley Athletic.
Apps: 75+1 Lge; 7 FAC; 2+1 LC.
Goals: 2 Lge.

BOWERS, JOHN WILLIAM ANSLOW

b. Santon, nr.Scunthorpe, 22.2.1908.
d. Allestree, Derby, 4.7.1970.
Appleby Works/
Dec 1927:Scunthorpe United/
May 1928:Derby County/
Nov 1936:CITY.
debut: 21.11.36 v.Swansea Town (A) (1 goal).

A genuine goalscoring giant, of impeccable
thrusting bravery, Jack started as he meant to
go on - stepping up from the Midland League
with Scunthorpe to score on his Derby debut
and add a hat-trick in his second game. Record-
breaking years followed, with Jack the First
Division's top scorer for three consecutive
seasons in the early 30s. He notched three goals
in his two Football League representative
games, and two in his three full England
matches, and only a serious knee injury in 1934
brought a hiccup to his exploits. Nonetheless,
Jack already had twelve goals in the bag for
1936/7 when Derby accepted struggling City's

£7,500 transfer offer - and amazingly he was to
add no less than 33 more before the season had
ended with City acclaimed as Division Two
champions. To talk of hero worship from the
fans in this context is almost to understate
Jack's popular status, but there can be no
denying his transformational effect on the club.
Understandably, his scoring rate decreased a
little back in the top flight, but when the war
put an end to Jack's 'official' statistics, he
could look back on a career total of 219 goals
in only 282 League games. He briefly coached
at Notts County, then returned to the Baseball
Ground as assistant trainer and physiotherapist.
His son, John, also made a playing career with
the Rams.
Apps: 79 Lge; 5 FAC.
Goals: 52 Lge; 4 FAC.

JACK BOWERS

BOWN, HERBERT ARTHUR

b. East Ham, 3.5.1893.
d. Leicester, 11.2.1959.
Romford Town/(trials-West Ham United)/
Apr 1913:FOSSE/May 1922:Halifax Town/
Jan 1925:Hull City.
debut: 8.11.13 v.Notts County (H).

A calm, reliable 'keeper who yet retained a
taste for drama - he took a couple of penalties
for Fosse during WW1, and also got on the
scoresheet for Halifax during his two ever-
present seasons in the Third Division (North) -
Herbert saw off several challenges for his place
between the Fosse sticks before the war and
those of City after it. Having represented Essex
as an amateur, he only signed professional for
Fosse after taking part in their first overseas
tour, to Sweden in the summer of 1913.
During the first post-war season, Herbert set
one City record which still stands: keeping a
clean sheet in seven consecutive League games.
He had retired to his fish and poultry business
in Leicester for several months when Hull
called on him for a four-game spell during an
injury crisis.
Apps: 143 Lge; 11 FAC.

BRACEY, FREDERICK CECIL
b. Derby, 20.7.1887.
d. Derby, 28.3.1960.
Small Heath/Holbrook Swifts/
Nov 1905:FOSSE/
July 1908:Bradford Park Avenue/
cs 1909:Rochdale.
debut: 7.12.05 v.Hull City (H).

Able to play on both wings, Fred unfortunately couldn't hold down either position for long at Filbert Street, though former team-mate Joe Blackett was sufficiently impressed by his reserve form to take him eventually to Rochdale. In the interim, he made seven appearances for Park Avenue in their initial League season. He is better remembered as a Derbyshire cricketer, with 77 first-class matches as a bowler to his credit between 1906 and 1914, taking 132 wickets.
Apps: 10 Lge.

BRADLEY, GORDON
b. Scunthorpe, 20.5.1925.
am:Scunthorpe United/Nov 1942:CITY/
Feb 1950:Notts County/
Aug 1958:Cambridge City/Glentoran.
debut (postwar): 21.12.46
v.West Bromwich Albion (A).

Given the nod over the younger Leslie Major when injury ruled out Ian McGraw, Gordon was City's luckless goalkeeper in the 1949 Cup Final. He had joined City, on 'Digger' Maw's recommendation, during WW2, when he also guested for Grimsby Town and Notts County, and built a reputation for agility and quick reflexes that may well have been connected with his all-round sporting prowess: he was Leicestershire table-tennis champion and also played lawn tennis professionally. At Meadow Lane, Gordon totted up 192 League appearances and scored one goal - against City in 1956, from an outfield position after he'd injured a hand.
Apps: 69 Lge; 5 FAC.

BRADSHAW, THOMAS DICKINSON
b. Hambleton, 15.3.1879.
Apr 1896:Preston North End/
Dec 1896:Blackpool/May 1897:Sunderland/
Jan 1898:Nottingham Forest/Mar 1899:FOSSE/
cs 1900:New Brighton Tower/
cs 1901:Swindon Town/Oct 1901:Reading/
cs 1902:Preston North End/
1903:Wellingborough/Southport Central/
Accrington Stanley/Oct 1905:FOSSE/
May 1907:Glossop.
debut: 3.4.99 v.Grimsby Town (H).

A well-travelled outside or inside-right who had two separate spells with Fosse, Tom was also a cricket professional with Preston CC and a coach at Harrow School. His League bow had come with Blackpool during their initial League season (when Tom had scored against Fosse), and his First Division baptism at Roker, but his wanderlust rather mirrored the lack of concentration he was sometimes accused of displaying on the pitch. His temperament was

also suspect, and he was said to be under suspension by Glossop (for whom he never played a League game) when criminally charged and found guilty of wife-beating in 1908.
Apps: 43 Lge; 5 FAC.
Goals: 9 Lge; 1 FAC.

BRASH, ARCHIBALD
b. Edinburgh.
St.Mirren/cs 1894:Sheffield Wednesday/
cs 1898:Crewe Alexandra/
cs 1899:Sheffield Wednesday/
June 1900:FOSSE.
debut: 1.9.1900 v.Stockport County (H).

A small Scottish right-winger who starred for Wednesday in the 1896 Cup Final (his quickly-taken throw-in led to them gaining a 30-second opening goal), and returned for their 1900 promotion campaign, Archie did not quite live up to his advance billing with Fosse. Yet he did manage one purple passage, belatedly opening his Leicester scoring account by netting four times against Burton Swifts in December 1900.
Apps: 14 Lge.
Goals: 5 Lge.

BREBNER, RONALD GILCHRIST
b. Darlington, 23.9.1881.
d. 11.11.1914.
(am:throughout career:Edinburgh University/
Northern Nomads/London Caledonians)/
also: cs 1905:Sunderland/Feb 1906:Rangers/
Oct 1906:Chelsea/1907:Darlington/
1907:Elgin City/Feb 1910:Queens Park/
Aug 1911:Huddersfield Town/
Aug 1912:Chelsea/May 1913:FOSSE.
debut: 3.9.13 v.Nottingham Forest (A).

The second of Fosse's peerless amateur goalkeepers, 'R.G.' won a total of 23 England amateur caps, and had followed Horace Bailey into the United Kingdom Olympic side, matching the latter's achievement by playing in the gold-medal team at the 1912 Stockholm Games. A trained dental surgeon, he also appeared in a full England trial (South v.North, November 1912), and represented the Amateurs v.Professionals in the 1913 Charity Shield match. Having played in all but two of Fosse's first twenty matches in 1913/14 (and having picked up his final pair of caps on the dates of his absences), he was carried off the field at Lincoln with an injury that finished his career and was said to have contributed significantly to his early death ten months later.
Apps: 18 Lge.

BRIEN, ANTHONY JAMES
b. Dublin, 10.2.1969.
app/pro Feb 1987:CITY/Dec 1988:Chesterfield.
debut: 30.9.87 (sub) v.Ipswich Town (H).

The cool, thoughtful central defensive pivot of the City side which fought through to the semi-finals of the FA Youth Cup in 1987, Tony made an impressive early League bow when replacing Phil Horner after only a couple of minutes of the Ipswich game, and was soon adding to his senior experience as a reliable stand-in in both the right-back and centre-back

positions. One of the first City players to have his contract extended by the incoming David Pleat, Tony nonetheless soon found himself displaced in the club's 'shadow squad' by Grant Brown, though the £90,000 laid out by Third Division strugglers Chesterfield for the services of the 19-year-old testified to his evident promise.
Apps: 12+4 Lge; 1 FAC; 1 LC; 3 FMC.
Goals: 1 Lge.

MARK BRIGHT

BRIGHT, MARK ABRAHAM
b. Stoke-on-Trent, 6.6.1962.
Leek Town/1981:Port Vale/June 1984:CITY/
Nov 1986:Crystal Palace.
debut: 25.8.84 v.Newcastle United (H).

A late scoring burst for Port Vale at the end of 1983/4 brought Mark to Gordon Milne's attention, and a complex, appearance-related deal, fixed by the League's transfer tribunal and payable in £33,000 instalments, landed the tall striker at Filbert Street. His first season saw him as a regular occupant of the sub's bench - he had, in fact, claimed each of his first four Vale goals in a No.12 shirt - but he was unable to add a first-team goal to his fine Central League record of 28 in 27 games. A spectacular brace against champions Everton on the opening day of 1985/6 looked like opening the floodgates, but Mark still struggled to fill the front role vacated by the summer transfer of local favourite Gary Lineker, and faced a rare degree of hostility (some of it sadly racist) from the Leicester crowd. After turning down mooted transfers to Hull and Walsall, Mark eventually moved to Selhurst, rebuilt his confidence, and hit the goal trail in earnest, winning a Golden Boot as the Second Division's top scorer in 1988, and helping Palace up into Division One in 1989.
Apps: 26+16 Lge; 1 FAC; 3+1 LC.
Goals: 6 Lge.

BRODIE, MURRAY

b. Glasgow, 26.9.1950.
Cumbernauld United/Nov 1968:CITY/
Sept 1970:Aldershot/
cs 1983:Basingstoke Town.
debut: 4.10.69 v.Watford (H) (1 goal).

Murray's first-team career at City was
compressed into a single week in October 1969,
as the strongly built forward made an
unexpected debut against Watford, scoring
once. He netted again, spectacularly, in a
midweek fixture against Middlesbrough, and
limped off injured during the following
Saturday's match at Preston. Unable to regain a
place upon recovery, Murray moved, along
with reserve full-back Jimmy Burt, to
Aldershot, and set about a successful assault on
that club's aggregate appearance record, being
eventually freed thirteen years, 461 League
games, 84 League goals, and a well-merited
Testimonial game later.
Apps: 3 Lge.
Goals: 2 Lge.

BROOKS, JOSEPH ERNEST

b. Heanor, 20.11.1892.
d. Heanor, 1975.
Langley Heanor/May 1919:Grimsby Town/
cs 1920:Shirebrook/June 1921:CITY.
debut: 9.2.22 v.Clapton Orient (H).

A diminutive winger who came probably too
late to League football after WW1 - he was
almost 27 when making the first of his three
appearances for the Mariners - Ernie failed to
reproduce at Filbert Street the form which had
prompted Peter Hodge to give him a second
chance.
Apps: 4 Lge.

BROWN, ALISTAIR

b. Musselburgh, 12.4.1951.
app Oct 1966/pro Apr 1968:CITY/
Mar 1972:West Bromwich Albion/
(May 1981-loan-Portland Timbers)/
Mar 1983:Crystal Palace/Aug 1983:Walsall/
June 1984:Port Vale.
debut: 5.5.69 v.Sunderland (H) (2 goals).

The tall, elegant striker who made a teenage
dream debut in the tense, relegation-delaying
game against Sunderland, Ally went on to
become the club's top scorer as City returned to
the top flight via the Division Two championship in 1971 (when his goal at Bristol City
clinched the title), and earned both Scottish
Youth caps and an Under-23 trial appearance
while at Filbert Street. He then repeated his
experiences of relegation and promotion during
an eleven-year stint at the Hawthorns, in which
he made over half of his career total of 495
League appearances (141 goals), and struck up
a useful partnership with his namesake Tony as
Albion sought European glory. Ally had
retreated to the middle line by the time he
commenced his late wanderings, but helped
Port Vale to a 1986 Fourth Division promotion
slot in his final season in senior football.
Apps: 93+8 Lge; 7+2 FAC; 10+1 LC.
Goals: 32 Lge; 2 FAC; 1 LC.

ALLY BROWN

BROWN, GRAHAM FREDERICK

b. Leicester, 5.11.50.
app June 1967/pro Nov 1968:CITY/
cs 1971:Burton Albion.
debut: 4.4.70 (sub) v.Aston Villa (H).

A prolific reserve-team scorer, local lad
Graham earned his first-team break after
claiming all four City goals in a testimonial
friendly at Plymouth. Having only once leapt
from the sub's bench into the League fray,
however, he now has to share with Malcolm
Clarke and Kevin Reed the dubious honour of
the shortest-ever senior career at City.
Apps: 0+1 Lge.

GRANT BROWN

BROWN, GRANT ASTLEY

b. Sunderland, 19.11.1969.
YTS July 1986/pro July 1987:CITY.
debut: 30.4.1988 v.Bradford City (A).

One of several members of City's 1986/7
Youth Cup squad to make an early senior bow,
central defender Grant had a harsh baptism at
Valley Parade as the home side went full-
throttle towards the play-offs, but he impressed
David Pleat sufficiently to be given the nod
over experienced newcomer Steve Thompson
for the opening games of 1988/9, and gained in
poise and pacing during an extended first-team
run in the No.6 shirt over the next few months.
Solid form in City reserves' late-season revival
in the Central League also won him an
encouraging last-match senior recall.
Apps (to 13.5.89): 14 Lge; 2 LC.

BROWN, JAMES

b. Renton.
d. c1923.
Renton Union/Renton Thistle/Renton/
cs 1890:Aston Villa/
Oct 1893:FOSSE/
Sept 1899:Loughborough.
debut: 4.11.93 v.Mansfield Town (H) FAC.

A moustachio'd Scottish 'professor' who joined
Fosse during their final Midland League season
as a wing-half or free-scoring centre-forward,
Jimmy also gave stalwart Division Two service
at centre-half, astutely prompting the attack and
eventually earning himself a benefit from a
friendly with Southampton in September 1898.
A year later his veteran skills were briefly
employed in the hard-up Luffs' precarious and
eventually fatal struggle to retain League status;
while in 1902 he became a League referee.
Early Fosse team photos show Jimmy wearing
a cap marked 'SFA'. As he is apparently not to
be confused with the J.Brown of Cambuslang
who played for Scotland v.Wales in 1890, the
assumption is that he must have been a junior
international.
Apps: 116 Lge; 23 FAC; 14 ML.
Goals: 4 Lge; 3 FAC; 14 ML.

BROWN, JOHN THOMAS

b. Eastwood.
Kirby Colliery/
Aug 1922:CITY/
Aug 1931:Wrexham.
debut: 10.10.25 v.Aston Villa (H).

A patient understudy for either full-back slot
over several seasons, latterly standing in
successfully for both Adam Black and Reg
Osborne, Jack finally made the left-back berth
his own during the 1928/9 season when City
made their most concerted attempt ever for
Division One honours. A former Notts miner,
he presented a physical and temperamental
contrast to his stylish partner Black, but was no
less effective against First Division wingers.
In 1933 he assisted Wrexham to what was then
also their highest League placing, runners-up
spot in Division Three (North).
Apps: 114 Lge; 3 FAC.

BROWN, PAUL ANDREW
b. Birmingham, 19.9.1964.
app:Aston Villa/Sept 1982:CITY/
May 1983:Nuneaton Borough/Stourbridge/
Alvechurch/Willenhall Town.
debut: 8.1.83 v.Notts County (H) FAC.

Capped by England Schools as an outside-left, Paul had become an apprentice left-back with Villa by the time England Youth honours came his way. Signed as a pro by City after trials (he scored in the pre-season Bass Charity Vase Final), Paul was called up for his Cup-tie debut in the wake of Tommy Williams' second leg-break, but appeared overawed as Notts County took City apart, and suffered a subsequent loss of confidence. Recently he has become a nomad on the West Midlands non-league scene.
Apps: 1 FAC.

BROWN, THOMAS
b. Beith.
Glenbuck/Aug 1899:FOSSE/
Dec 1901:Chesterfield/cs 1902:Lanark/
Nov 1902:FOSSE/cs 1903:Portsmouth/
Sept 1904:Dundee.
debut: 2.9.99 v.Woolwich Arsenal (A) (1 goal).

A brother of the goal-hungry Scottish international Sandy Brown (whose clubs included Preston, Portsmouth, Spurs, Middlesbrough and Luton), Tommy was also a bustling centre-forward. He fell foul of the Fosse directorate half-way through his third season, when suspended for breaches of training discipline, but was forgiven within a year and returned for a second stint, before moving on to replace his brother at Fratton Park. Despite the hiatus in his Fosse career, Tommy was the club's top scorer for three seasons running.
Apps: 72 Lge; 5 FAC.
Goals: 38 Lge; 3 FAC.

BRUCE, DAVID
b. Perth.
Dundee East Craigie/Aug 1935:CITY/
May 1936:Bristol Rovers/Aug 1937:St.Mirren/
1940:Airdrieonians.
debut: 25.4.36 v.Burnley (A).

Plucked from Scottish junior football, outside-right David had only a single try-out at senior level with City, shortly before he was allowed to move on to Eastville in a joint deal with Tommy Mills. He fared little better with Rovers, but at least got on the scoresheet twice in 12 League games before returning north of the border, where he played the bulk of his games at full-back.
Apps: 1 Lge.

BRUNTON, MATTHEW
b. Burnley, 20.4.1878.
d. Burnley, 29.12.1962.
Army football/Aug 1899:Preston North End/
cs 1900:Accrington Stanley/July 1901:Burnley/
1903:Accrington Stanley/May 1904:FOSSE/
Feb 1905:Nelson/cs 1905:Accrington Stanley/
July 1906:Oldham Athletic/
cs 1908:Southport Central/1909:Haslingden/
Oct 1910:Darwen/
Nov 1910:Accrington Stanley.
debut: 3.9.04 v.Blackpool (A).

A centre-forward who failed either to readjust to League football from the Lancashire Combination, or to settle for long outside his home county. While Matthew inspired Oldham to the championship of the Combination in his first season at Boundary Park, he made only a single appearance for them after their resultant election to Division Two. His best campaign had been with Burnley, when he occupied all five forward positions in 30 Second Division games, scoring eight times. He was later on the training staffs of both Accrington and Burnley.
Apps: 5 Lge; 1 FAC.

DAVID BUCHANAN

BUCHANAN, DAVID
b. Newcastle, 23.6.1962.
app July 1978/pro June 1979:CITY/
(Oct 1982-loan-Northampton Town)/
July 1983:Peterborough United/
1984:North Shields/1984:Blyth Spartans/
July 1986:Sunderland/
(Sept 1987-loan-York City)/
(Apr 1988-trials-Middlesbrough)/
May 1988:(Norway)/1988:Newcastle Blue Star.
debut: 1.1.79 v.Oldham Athletic (H) (1 goal).

City's youngest-ever League player, David made his scoring debut (on the same day as Bobby Smith and Gary Lineker) at the age of 16 years and 192 days, as Jock Wallace turned to the juniors in his efforts to avert the spectre of a second successive relegation. The slender, light-haired striker - a good close dribbler, yet direct - justifiably became an immediate crowd favourite, but a succession of injuries and the club's desire not to rush his development contributed to David suffering a degree of disenchantment and a loss of appetite for the game over the next few seasons. After an unsuccessful spell at London Road, he dropped out of senior football altogether to build a career in leisure centre management, but his evident ability and increased maturity while playing part-time in the Northern League (and winning England caps at semi-pro level) nudged Lawrie McMenemy into offering him another senior chance at Roker.
Apps: 24+9 Lge; 4+1 FAC.
Goals: 7 Lge; 1 FAC.

BUCKLEY, JOHN WILLIAM
b. Glasgow, 18.5.1962.
Queens Park/1979:Celtic/
cs 1983:Partick Thistle/
July 1984:Doncaster Rovers/
July 1986:Leeds United/
(Mar 1987-loan-CITY)/
(Oct 1987-loan-Doncaster Rovers)/
Nov 1987:Rotherham United.
debut: 4.4.87 (sub) v.Newcastle United (A).

An old-fashioned ball-playing winger of the unpredictable type, John was twice bought by Billy Bremner (presumably motivated by memories of Eddie Gray) after making his Scottish League mark with Partick, but barely got a chance to shine at Elland Road, and came to City on extended loan for the fateful run-in to eventual relegation in 1987. Surprisingly, he spent more time on the bench than in action, for he gave brief, tantalising glimpses of genuine crowd-pleasing dribbling talent. John returned to Leeds when it looked possible that City might face them in the First/Second Division play-offs, then started a second circuit of Yorkshire clubs. At Millmoor, he won a Fourth Division championship medal in 1989.
Apps: 1+4 Lge.

BULLING, JAMES
b. West Bridgford.
jnr:Nottingham Forest/Shirebrook/
May 1930:CITY/June 1932:Wrexham/
June 1936:Shrewsbury Town.
debut: 15.11.30 v.Liverpool (A).

A nephew of the Forest full-back Harold Bulling, Jim was a wing-half who had a couple of brief spells as deputy for George Ritchie or Bill Findlay, but found his level more comfortably in the Third Division, over four seasons at the Racecourse.
Apps: 12 Lge.

BUNCE, PAUL ERIC
b. Coalville, 7.1.1967.
app July 1983/pro Jan 1985:CITY/
Mar 1987:Northampton Town/
cs 1988:Weymouth.
debut: 11.10.86 v.Nottingham Forest (H).

A teenage winger who progressed through the City ranks to be given a senior break by Bryan Hamilton, Paul failed adequately to assert himself in the First Division, and proved to be no answer to City's desperate need for attacking width in the relegation season of 1986/7. After a £5,000 deadline-day move to Northampton, already booked for the Fourth Division championship, he had to wait until the final games of that season for a look-in, but scored in his first full game. Paul was, however, freed by the Cobblers in 1988.
Apps: 5+1 Lge.

BURBECK, RONALD THOMAS
b. Leicester, 27.2.1934.
May 1952:CITY/Oct 1956:Middlesbrough/
Aug 1963:Darlington.
debut: 15.9.52 v.West Ham United (A).

An England Youth international winger who

stood in once for Tom Dryburgh during his first season as a pro (while on National Service in the RAF), and then waited over three years for another brief chance, Ron had to go north to escape the abundance of experienced flankmen on City's books in the mid-50s. He made 138 League appearances for the Ayresome club, chiefly as provider for the prolific Brian Clough and Alan Peacock.
Apps: 3 Lge.

BURGESS, T.
b.
Leicester Imperial/cs 1901:FOSSE/
cs 1902:Leicester Imperial.
debut: 23.11.01
v.Stockport County (H) (1 goal).

A local outside or inside-right who impressed in the August trials but found it difficult to dislodge the then established Fosse partnership of Webb and Richards during his season with the professionals.
Apps: 3 Lge.
Goals: 1 Lge.

BURTON, HORACE ARTHUR
b. Melton Mowbray, 1887.
d. Sept 1969.
Holwell Works/Oct 1910:FOSSE/
1919:Loughborough Corinthians.
debut: 1.4.11 v.Bradford Park Avenue (A).

A burly, two-footed wing-half and loyal clubman for Fosse, never guaranteed a senior place during his five pre-war seasons, Horace often forced his way back into the team at the expense of more experienced imports. He was one of Arsenal's guests in 1963 when they marked the 50th anniversary of the opening of Highbury and the first fixture there against the Fosse, in which Horace played left-half.
Apps: 78 Lge; 4 FAC.
Goals: 1 Lge.

BUSHELL, WILLIAM
b. Wednesbury.
Darlaston/cs 1926:West Bromwich Albion/
1927:Willenhall/May 1928:CITY/
cs 1931:Walsall.
debut: 17.10.29 v.Birmingham (H) (1 goal).

A luckless understudy to Hughie Adcock during his three years at Filbert Street, this right winger at least set aside his liking for West Midlands clubs long enough to score the winning goal against Birmingham on his City debut. He had failed to gain a first-team place in Albion's relegated side during his season there, but later managed to notch four goals in his 30 League games at Fellows Park.
Apps: 3 Lge.
Goals: 1 Lge.

BUTLER, RICHARD
b. Shepshed.
Shepshed Albion/cs 1909:Nottingham Forest/
Dec 1910:FOSSE.
debut: 31.12.10 v.Bolton Wanderers (A).

For a couple of seasons one of Teddy King's chief rivals for a Fosse wing-half slot, Richard

had previously made but a single First Division appearance for Forest.
Apps: 26 Lge; 2 FAC.

BYRNE, PATRICK JOSEPH
b. Dublin, 15.5.1956.
1974:Bohemians/Mar 1978:Philadelphia Fury/
1978:Shelbourne/July 1979:CITY/
July 1981:Heart of Midlothian/
Aug 1983:Shamrock Rovers/
cs 1988:Shelbourne (p/mgr).
debut: 11.8.79 v.Rotherham United (H) LC.

Already broadly experienced in Irish football (he had played in European competition and in the 1976 FAI Cup Final) when Jock Wallace signed him shortly after his brief NASL sojourn, Pat contributed some tenacious midfield performances to City's 1980 promotion push, offering the option of attacking width on the right. In his First Division season he was less able to perk a struggling side, but chose suitably dramatic stages at Anfield and White Hart Lane for his rare goals. Pat helped Hearts to promotion in his second season, by which time he was commuting weekly from Dublin after his wife had failed to settle in Edinburgh, and then he returned with significant success to League of Ireland football. In his first four years as Shamrock skipper, he led them as a virtual ever-present to the championship in 1984 and, remarkably, to the League/FAI Cup double in each of the next three seasons. Pat won his first of four caps for Eire in 1984.
Apps: 31+5 Lge; 3 FAC; 2 LC.
Goals: 3 Lge.

CALDER, JOHN
b. Glengarnock.
Dalry Thistle/July 1931:CITY/
St.Johnstone/Falkirk/Morton/
Feb 1937:Bolton Wanderers/
cs 1938:Barnsley/1939:Morton/
cs 1941:Albion Rovers/
Apr 1942:Morton.
debut: 19.9.31 v.Grimsby Town (A).

A rapid, but all too brief step up from Scottish junior football to deputise for Arthur Chandler was Jack's lot in his Filbert Street year. Yet later, after a morale-boosting return north of the border, the record books beckoned for the tall centre-forward. For Morton against Raith in April 1936 he netted no less than eight goals, and a succession of lesser, if still impressive, goalscoring feats earned him another crack at the English game. Bolton were a lowly First Division side at the time, but Barnsley became Third Division champions with Jack as a valuable fringe member of their squad.
Apps: 1 Lge.

CALDER, WILLIAM CARSON
b. Glasgow, 28.9.1934.
Port Glasgow/Aug 1955:CITY/Apr 1959:Bury/
Nov 1963:Oxford United/Nov 1966:Rochdale.
debut: 23.8.58 v.Everton (H).

Returning from National Service to understudy Derek Hogg, Bill was given the latter's vacant

No.11 shirt at the start of 1958/9, but proved unable to hold it against the new challenge of Gordon Wills. Subsequently, though, he made a substantial reputation as a robust, free-scoring right winger at Bury (Third Division champions in 1961) and totalled 96 League goals before retirement.
Apps: 3 Lge.

CALLACHAN, HARRY
b. Kirkintilloch.
Celtic/Sept 1927:CITY/
Aug 1931:Burton Town.
debut: 7.4.28 v.Newcastle United (A).

A tall young left-back who could yet barely see over such obstacles in his path to the first team as Reg Osborne and Jack Brown. Reserve-team football had been Harry's lot at Parkhead, too.
Apps: 3 Lge.

JOE CALVERT

CALVERT, JOSEPH WILLIAM
b. Bullcroft, 3.2.1907.
Owston Park Rangers/Frickley Colliery/
May 1931:Bristol Rovers/May 1932:CITY/
Jan 1948:Watford/July 1948:Brush Sports.
debut: 27.8.32 v.Sheffield United (H).

An ever-present in his Eastville season, then a fine fifteen-year servant to City, goalkeeper Joe made only sporadic first-team appearances in his pre-war Filbert Street campaigns, briefly displacing one McLaren (Jim) only to be sidelined by another (Sandy). Advancing years hardly affected his mobility, though, and after 62 wartime appearances for City (and several RAF representative games in India and Burma) he was the most consistent choice between the sticks in 1946/7 when League soccer resumed. He played his last game for City when over the age of 40 years and ten months: an occasion that marks him as most probably having been the club's oldest senior player. Joe then joined the mass transfer-and-loan exodus that took five City players to Watford on the same day, and was still demonstrating true veteran prowess for his final, Loughborough-based team as they lifted the Leicestershire Senior Cup in May 1949.
Apps: 72 Lge; 8 FAC.

CAMPBELL, JAMES
b.
Celtic/Oct 1943:CITY/Oct 1946:Walsall.
debut (postwar): 5.1.46 v.Chelsea (A) FAC.

A wartime signing who claimed eleven goals from 46 appearances in regional football, Jim played at outside-right in the Stamford Bridge leg of the first post-war Cup tie, in the only season that the competition operated on a two-leg basis. He subsequently managed 15 League games in his two seasons at Fellows Park, and scored once.
Apps: 1 FAC.

CAMPBELL, JOHN
b. Stevenston, Ayrshire, 1910.
1930:Dalry Thistle/July 1931:CITY/
Dec 1933:Lincoln City.
debut: 17.12.32 v.Birmingham (H) (1 goal).

Accompanied to Filbert Street by his Scottish junior clubmate Jack Calder, centre-forward John took longer to taste first-team football, but could count himself unlucky not to have had a longer tenure. His goals-per-game ratio was impressive, but competition from Jim Paterson, and the advent of George Dewis, restricted his chances. In compensation - or perhaps to demonstrate to City their mistake in letting him go - John raced to a century of League goals for the Sincil Bank club before the war. He had also used his time at Filbert Street to continue studying, passing exams in Edinburgh that qualified him as a chemist and druggist.
Apps: 21 Lge; 1 FAC.
Goals: 12 Lge; 2 FAC.

KENNY CAMPBELL

CAMPBELL, KENNETH
b. Cambuslang, 6.9.1892.
d. Macclesfield, 28.4.1977.
Rutherglen Glencairn/Cambuslang Rangers/
May 1911:Liverpool/Apr 1920:Partick Thistle/
June 1922:New Brighton/Mar 1923:Stoke City/
Nov 1925:CITY/Nov 1929:New Brighton.
debut: 14.11.25 v.Sunderland (H).

A medallist from Cup Finals on both sides of the border (a 1914 loser with Liverpool; a 1921 winner with Partick), and holder of eight post-war caps for Scotland to add to one Scottish League appearance, Kenny maintained his reputation for modesty and quiet efficiency throughout his spell between the City posts. A cool, reliable custodian who was already reaching the veteran stage on his arrival at Leicester to aid First Division consolidation, he managed to stretch his peacetime career out to 370 senior games with two final seasons for the Rakers in the Third Division (North), before opening a sports shop in Wallasey.
Apps: 79 Lge; 2 FAC.

WILLIE CARLIN

CARLIN, WILLIAM
b. Liverpool, 6.10.1940.
May 1958:Liverpool/Aug 1962:Halifax Town/
Oct 1964:Carlisle United/
Sept 1967:Sheffield United/
Aug 1968:Derby County/
Oct 1970:CITY/Sept 1971:Notts County/
Nov 1973:Cardiff City.
debut: 20.10.70 v.Birmingham City (A).

A single Anfield appearance and a nosedive from Third to Fourth Division at the Shay were hardly accurate auguries for the remarkable motivational career Willie was later to forge. Nor, really, were the contrasts in his experiences at Carlisle (Third Division champs in 1965) and with the Blades (relegated from the First in 1968). But a £60,000 move to Brian Clough's Derby set the tone from then on, as the pint-sized midfielder inspired the Rams to the top of the Second, and to fourth place on their return to the top flight. £35,000 of that fee was returned by Frank O'Farrell for Willie's signature, and his all-action, true-grit approach duly helped seal City's promotion; just as it was to do for Notts County (from Third to

Second in 1973) after Jimmy Bloomfield had perhaps over-hastily discarded the little dynamo. O'Farrell, at least, was not one to underestimate Willie's infectiously enthusiastic influence, taking him to Cardiff to spark another of that club's then-annual Second Division survival acts before his retirement in May 1974.
Apps: 31 Lge; 6 FAC.
Goals: 1 Lge.

CARNELLY, ALBERT
b. Nottingham, 29.12.1870.
d. Nottingham, Aug 1920.
1889:Notts Mapperley/1890:Notts County/
1891:Loughborough/
May 1894:Nottingham Forest/
May 1896:FOSSE/cs 1897:Bristol City/
cs 1898:Ilkeston/Nov 1898:Bristol City/
cs 1899:Thames Ironworks/
cs 1900:Millwall/
cs 1901:Ilkeston.
debut: 5.9.96 v.Darwen (H).

A goalscoring inside-forward who leapt from Midland League to First Division and finished as Forest's top scorer in his first year on Trentside, Albert then only missed two games during his Fosse season. He joined Bristol City (along with Harry Davy) for their first Southern League season, and their first under that name, scoring 4 goals in their first-ever FA Cup tie; while Thames Ironworks were in their final season under that name when Albert moved there (the club becoming West Ham United in 1900).
Apps: 28 Lge; 3 FAC.
Goals: 10 Lge.

CARR, EVERTON DALE
b. Antigua, West Indies, 11.1.1961.
app July 1977/pro Jan 1979:CITY/
July 1981:Halifax Town/
Mar 1983:Rochdale/
cs 1983:Nuneaton Borough/
July 1987:Weymouth/
Oct 1987:Bath City/
Nov 1987:Barnet/
Jan 1988:Nuneaton Borough/
1988:Oadby Town.
debut: 28.4.79 (sub) v.Fulham (A).

A pacy, harrying full-back who played as an 18-year-old in the final three games of 1978/9, Everton was unfortunate enough to be sent off in the last of them, an ill-refereed affair at Bramall Lane that represented Sheffield United's farewell to the Second Division. He stood in once for Dennis Rofe during the following season, and had a brief run of First Division games in 1980/1, but had to move to The Shay for a regular League spot. He later revived his occasional City partnership with Willie Gibson at both Nuneaton and Weymouth; and while with the latter was involved in an amusing incident in a Conference game at Maidstone. Entering the fray as a half-time substitute he failed to report his presence to the referee, who booked him a full 25 minutes later after finally noticing the only black player on the pitch!
Apps: 11+1 Lge; 2 LC.

CARR, GEORGE

b. Redcar, 19.1.1899.
Nov 1916:Bradford Park Avenue/
cs 1919:Middlesbrough/
Feb 1924:CITY/
Aug 1932:Stockport County/
May 1933:Nuneaton Town (p/mgr).
debut: 23.2.24 v.Coventry City (H) (1 goal).

A beefy, hard-shooting inside-forward
when he came to Leicester - having played
First Division football at Ayresome
alongside his brothers Jackie and Billy -
George scored the goal (against Bradford
City) which guaranteed City's 1925
promotion, and proved a splendid linkman
between left-winger Wadsworth and
spearhead Chandler. It was not long,
however, before George's invaluable
versatility became apparent, for after
recovering from a broken leg he assumed
the pivotal position of centre-half as if born
to the role (he had, in fact, played there as a
teenager for Bradford in wartime football),
and provided the solid bedrock from which
City's best-ever First Division attack
launched its near-miss assaults on the title.
George had pre-war spells managing
Cheltenham Town and coaching Stockton,
and was a post-war scout for City.
Apps: 179 Lge; 13 FAC.
Goals: 24 Lge; 1 FAC.

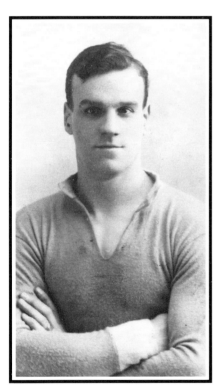

GEORGE CARR

CARRIGAN, PATRICK

b. Cleland, 5.7.1898.
Douglas Water Thistle/Oct 1923:CITY/
Mar 1930:Sheffield United/
(Sept 1933-trials-Southend United).
debut: 2.1.24 v.Bury (A).

City's regular first-choice centre-half for
only one full season, Pat was nonetheless
due a lot of credit for his sturdy efforts
towards securing the 1925 Second Division
championship. He was a fine successor to
Mick O'Brien and, after his year of glory, a
loyal reserve to the likes of Norman Watson
and George Carr. Pat then extended his top
flight career by three seasons at Bramall
Lane, following a £1,750 move.
Apps: 75 Lge; 7 FAC.
Goals: 3 Lge.

PAT CARRIGAN

CARROLL, JAMES (TONY)

b. Glasgow.
d. (lost at sea), March 1944.
Strathclyde/Newry Town/
Belfast Celtic/
cs 1931:Shelbourne/
cs 1933:Clyde/
Feb 1935:CITY/
June 1938:Luton Town.
debut: 23.2.35 v.Preston North End (A).

A late recruit by Arthur Lochhead to City's
eventually futile attempt to avoid relegation
in 1935, Tony was a small, nippy outside-
right with an eye for goal (15 in 1935/6
alone), whose more orthodox crossing skills
provided Jack Bowers with many an
opening as City bounced back up in 1937.
He made 13 appearances for Luton before
the war ended his senior career and, indeed,
took his life.
Apps: 94 Lge; 3 FAC.
Goals: 25 Lge; 1 FAC.

CARTER, ROGER

b.
Hugglescote Robin Hoods/
Aug 1898:FOSSE.
debut: 3.2.1900 v.Burslem Port Vale (A).

A local keeper who kept a clean sheet while
standing in for Godfrey Beardsley in the above
match, but then reportedly showed such poor
form for the reserves that only a month later,
when Beardsley again had to drop out, the
Fosse selectors overlooked him and instead
chose inside-forward Lyon as replacement
goalie!
Apps: 1 Lge.

CHALMERS, LEONARD

b. Corby, 4.9.1936.
Corby Town/Jan 1956:CITY/
June 1966:Notts County.
debut: 26.4.58 v.Birmingham City (A).

Forever remembered for two dramatic games
- his nerve-wracking senior debut, when City
needed a last-match win at St.Andrews to avoid
the drop; and the 1961 Cup Final, when the
crippling injury he suffered proved to be the
turning point - Len actually gave over a
decade's fine service to Leicester. Switching
from wing-half to make the right-back slot his
own for four seasons, he was an incisive tackler
who was tagged with the affectionate nickname
'Chopper' some time before Chelsea's Ron
Harris earned a similar dubbing; though Len
also showed a compensatory concern for his
fellow players' welfare as City's PFA representative, being actively involved in the 1961
maximum-wage negotiations. He went on to
make 51 League appearances during his two
years at Meadow Lane, and at least one source
has him as manager of Dunstable Town from
1968.
Apps: 171 Lge; 20 FAC; 9 LC; 4 ECWC.
Goals: 4 Lge.

LEN CHALMERS

CHANDLER, ARTHUR CLARENCE HILLIER

b. Paddington, 27.11.1895.
d. Leicester, 18.6.1984.
Handley Page/
1920:Queens Park Rangers/
June 1923:CITY/
June 1935:Notts County.
debut: 25.8.23 v.Hull City (A).

Rivalled only by Arthur Rowley for the title of
City's greatest-ever marksman - 'Channy'
notched the highest aggregate; the other Arthur
had the better scoring ratio - this Cockney
centre-forward was an inspired purchase by
Peter Hodge, especially as he had less than 20
senior goals to his credit before arriving at
Filbert Street, and on grounds of age alone
might have been regarded as past his peak.
Hard and courageous, but resilient, too - Arthur
made 118 consecutive appearances from the
date of his City debut - he bulged nets in both
top Divisions with strikes delivered from every
angle and distance, though oddly enough for
such a sure-shot, never contributed a single
penalty goal to his career total. He equalled
Fred Shinton's long-standing seasonal scoring
record for the club in the 1925 promotion drive,
eclipsed it with 34 goals in both 1928 and 1929,
and also equalled Johnny Duncan's record of
six goals in a game (while inaugurating the
legend of the six swans flying overhead).
Clearly he deserved the international recognition that was inexplicably denied him. Three
times Arthur played in the annual England trial
game (once for the North v.South; twice for
The Rest v.England) and each time he scored;
but a single appearance for the Football League
- when they met the Scottish League at Filbert
Street in 1927, and when for once 'Channy'
failed to register a goal - and a place on the
1929 FA tour of South Africa were his only
tangible honours. A consistently cheery
character - this photograph from his own
collection is captioned on the back "Special
Training at Skegness!" - Arthur hung up his
boots after adding half a dozen goals to his haul
as a Magpie, but was then involved in one
backroom capacity or another with City until
well past retirement age. In this sense, Arthur's
true honour was in embodying for successive
generations of City players and fans the very
best traditions of both the club and the game.
Apps: 393 Lge; 26 FAC.
Goals: 259 Lge; 14 FAC.

CHAPMAN, VERNON WILLIAM

b. Leicester, 9.5.1921.
1940:CITY/
July 1947:Leyton Orient/
1949:Brush Sports.
debut: 12.4.47 v.Swansea Town (H).

A local lad who played in several wartime
games, Vernon deputised only once for Mal
Griffiths at outside-right after League soccer
recommenced. He had slightly better fortune at
Brisbane Road, making 31 appearances and
scoring seven goals in the Third Division
(South) after a £550 move.
Apps: 1 Lge.

ARTHUR CHANDLER

CHARLES, GARY ANDREW

b. London, 13.4.70.
app/pro1987:Nottingham Forest/
(Mar 1989-loan-CITY).
debut: 25.3.89 (sub) v.Birmingham City (H).

A young full-back given his initial two-game
Trentside break by Brian Clough as an
emergency right-winger, Gary joined City on
a month's loan as defensive cover when
Tony Spearing was facing imminent
suspension, and rapidly displayed a
surprising amount of mature confidence and
coolness both on and off the ball as he
earned himself an extension to his Leicester
sojourn until the end of the season. Indeed,
his form was sufficiently exciting to earn
him an England Under-21 squad call-up after
only seven weeks at Filbert Street.
Apps: 5+3 Lge.

CHEATER, J.

b.
South Wigston Albion/
Jan 1904:FOSSE/
cs 1904:Countesthorpe.
debut: 16.1.04 v.Stockport County (H).

One of three local full-backs called up for
Second Division try-outs following George
Mountain's sending-off in Fosse's 1903/4
FA Cup exit, but soon released.
Apps: 6 Lge.

CHEESEBROUGH, ALBERT

b. Burnley, 17.1.1935.
Jan 1952:Burnley/June 1959:CITY/
July 1963:Port Vale/
July 1965:Mansfield Town.
debut: 22.8.59 v.West Ham United (A).

Having stepped into League football with his
home-town club at the age of 17, Albert had
played 140 First Division games, scoring 36
goals (including a hat-trick against City), and
had won one England Under-23 cap by the time
Matt Gillies laid out £19,775 to bring him to
Filbert Street. A left-winger converted to
inside-forward at Turf Moor, he was
temporarily converted back again by City for
his most important matches, standing in for
injury victim Gordon Wills in five games of the
1961 Cup run, including the Final. Albert also
played as a pacy support striker in almost half
the games of the 1962/3 Double-chasing
season, but missed out on a second trip to
Wembley, and was shortly off on lower
division travels.
Apps: 122 Lge; 11 FAC; 4 LC; 1 ECWC.
Goals: 40 Lge; 2 FAC; 1 LC.

CHENEY, DENNIS

b. Coalville, 30.6.1924.
Coalville Town/am Mar 1940/
pro Nov 1941:CITY/(Jan 1948-loan-Watford)/
Oct 1948:Bournemouth & Boscombe Athletic/
June 1954:Aldershot/Aug 1956:Dorchester.
debut (postwar): 30.8.47 v.Fulham (H).

A youthful discovery in wartime football
(22 goals in 42 games), Dennis was a deputy
for Charlie Adam in the No.11 shirt once before
and once after his loan spell at Vicarage Road
(marked by a scoring debut), but switched with
greater success to centre-forward with his
subsequent clubs, eventually claiming a total of
71 goals from 228 League games.
Apps: 2 Lge.

CHISHOLM, KENNETH McTAGGART

b. Glasgow, 12.4.1925.
Feb 1941:Queens Park/cs 1946:Partick Thistle/
Jan 1948:Leeds United/Dec 1948:CITY/
Mar 1950:Coventry City/
Mar 1952:Cardiff City/Dec 1953:Sunderland/
Aug 1956:Workington/
Jan 1958:Glentoran (p/mgr).
debut: 1.1.49 v.Coventry City (H).

An inveterate wanderer who picked up the
nomadic habit upon returning to civvy street
from service as an RAF bomber pilot, Ken
guested for City, Chelsea, Portsmouth and
Bradford Park Avenue in 1945/6 as well as
turning in good enough performances at
Hampden to earn a call-up for Scotland's 1946
'Victory International' against Ireland. A hefty,
bustling inside- forward with fine heading
ability, he represented City's record investment
at the time Johnny Duncan pushed through the
cash-plus-player deal which saw Ray Iggleden
and an £11,000 cheque on their way to Leeds.
Soon regarded as very much the joker of the

KEN CHISHOLM

City pack, Ken helped the club to both Wembley and Second Division survival in 1949, though he contributed to a muted controversy some 36 years later with the publication of his allegations of match fixing at the time. When he moved on from Filbert Street, a player-exchange was again part of the deal, with Jack Marsh joining City from Highfield Road. Ken eventually topped the 150 mark in League goals while at Workington, and ended his playing career in the USA.
Apps: 42 Lge; 7 FAC.
Goals: 17 Lge; 2 FAC.

CHRISTENSEN, TOMMY
b. Aarhus, Denmark, 20.9.1961.
AGF (Aarhus)/1979:PSV Eindhoven/
AGF (Aarhus)/Vejle Boldklub/Feb 1985:Elche/
(Nov 1985-loan-CITY)/
(Nov 1985-loan-Portsmouth)/1986:Brondby/
1987:Vejle Boldklub.
debut: 9.11.85 (sub) v.Southampton (H).

Both of Danish international forward Tommy's loan spells with League clubs were teasingly inconclusive. With City the compact blond striker made an immediate impact as he came on for 30 minutes to bring the best out of Peter Shilton in the opposing goal, but a week later he shared in an unconvincing struggle on Loftus Road's artificial surface. After an additional three reserve appearances (1 goal), City tried to extend his loan period, but either Tommy or his Spanish club wanted a definite deal. Then, at Fratton Park, Tommy knocked in two goals in three League games, but suffered an injury which shortened his stay.
Apps: 1+1 Lge.

CHRISTIE, TREVOR
b. Newcastle, 28.2.1959.
app Sept 1975/pro Dec 1976:CITY/
June 1979:Notts County/
June 1984:Nottingham Forest/
Feb 1985:Derby County/
Aug 1986:Manchester City/Oct 1986:Walsall/
Mar 1989:Mansfield Town.
debut: 25.2.78
v.Wolverhampton Wanderers (H).

Given a break by Frank McLintock almost as an early 19th birthday present, gangling striker Trevor went on to become City's top scorer during Jock Wallace's first season in charge (albeit with only 8 goals). His front-running, heading and ball-shielding skills only really developed, though, after his move to Meadow Lane. A number of his 64 League goals for the Magpies helped them into the First Division, while another three harshly greeted City back into the top flight on the opening day of 1983/4. Brian Clough invested £165,000 to take Trevor across the Trent, but soon offloaded him to Derby, for whom his 100th aggregate League goal was scored late in the Third Division promotion campaign of 1986. Then surprisingly swapped for Mark Lillis, Trevor had only a short stay at Maine Road before joining Walsall, and contributed to both their fine 1987 Cup run and their 1988 promotion.
Apps: 28+3 Lge; 1 LC.
Goals: 8 Lge.

TREVOR CHRISTIE

CLARK, WILLIAM
b. Airdrie.
Port Glasgow Athletic/
May 1904:Bristol Rovers/
May 1908:Sunderland/
Oct 1910:Bristol City/
Aug 1911:FOSSE.
debut: 2.9.11 v.Gainsborough Trinity (A).

A Scottish right-winger with considerable English experience (a Southern League championship medal in his first Eastville season, alongside Pudan and Dunkley, on his way to a 133-game, 35-goal record; two terms in the top flight for Sunderland; and a relegation campaign at Ashton Gate), Willie soon lost his Fosse place to Tommy Benfield, and simply had to bow to the younger player's greater consistency and pace.
Apps: 6 Lge.
Goals: 1 Lge.

CLARKE, ALLAN JOHN
b. Willenhall, 31.7.1946.
app 1961/pro Aug 1963:Walsall/
Mar 1966:Fulham/
June 1968:CITY/
June 1969:Leeds United/
June 1978:Barnsley (p/mgr).
debut: 10.8.68
v.Queens Park Rangers (A) (1 goal).

An instinctive goalscorer whose transfers to and from City both broke the existing British record (at £150,000 and £165,000 respectively), Allan began his Filbert Street year as a tangible symbol of the club's ambition, soon ingratiated himself with the fans with a hat-trick among his early goal flow, but increasingly came to look something of a luxury as 1968/9 unexpectedly developed into an earnest relegation struggle. He was clearly a man for the big occasion (scoring the Cup semi-final winner; taking the Man of the Match award at Wembley), but his apparently leisurely style seemed at odds with the requirements of a scramble for safety points. The slim striker added one England Under-23 cap to his burgeoning representative tally while with City, but only made the breakthrough to full international honours after being snapped up by Don Revie. Nicknamed 'Sniffer' at Elland Road in recognition of his clinical penalty-area poaching skills, Allan played in three FA Cup Finals for Leeds (scoring their winner in 1972), won a championship medal in 1974, and was also a scorer in their Fairs Cup victory of 1971. He led Barnsley out of the Fourth Division in his first year of management, then returned to Leeds as boss; subsequently also managing Scunthorpe United and Barnsley again. Allan's brothers Frank, Derek, Kelvin and Wayne each also carved out football careers at League level, and the latter became another expensive City purchase in June 1989, after building a fine goalscoring record with Wolves, Birmingham and Everton.
Apps: 36 Lge; 8 FAC; 2 LC.
Goals: 12 Lge; 1 FAC; 3 LC.

ALLAN CLARKE

CLARKE, BERNARD M.
b. Leicester.
St.Peters/Dec 1919:CITY/
cs 1921:Halifax Town.
debut: 28.8.20 v.Clapton Orient (A).

A right-back who spent much of the first post-WW1 season as an amateur in City's reserves, Bernard then signed professional forms and played in the first three matches of 1920/1, only to be permanently sidelined thereafter by the stronger claims of Billy Barrett and Adam Black. Unfortunately, he made little impact at The Shay, either.
Apps: 3 Lge.

CLARKE, MALCOLM McQUEEN G.
b. Clydebank, 29.6.1944.
Johnstone Burgh/Aug 1964:CITY/
Aug 1967:Cardiff City/July 1969:Bristol City/
July 1970:Hartlepool.
debut: 18.9.65 (sub) v.Leeds United (H).

Dubiously distinguished by having had the shortest-ever first-team career with City, reserve wing-half Malcolm came on as No.12 in the 89th minute of his sole League game - curiously, as John Sjoberg and Derek Dougan simultaneously left the field injured - and was reliably reported not to have touched the ball during the remainder of play! Partial compensation for such frustration came during Malcolm's two-year Ninian Park spell, when he claimed a goal in the Welsh Cup Final of 1968 and then aided Cardiff's surprising progress to the semi-finals of the European Cup Winners Cup.
Apps: 0+1 Lge.

CLARKE, PATRICK
b. Dundalk.
Dundalk/
May 1934:CITY/
July 1938:Sligo Rovers.
debut: 2.2.35 v.Manchester City (A).

An Irish left-back whose single League chance came when both Adam Black and Sandy Wood were unable to turn out in the above game, a 3-6 Maine Road defeat, Pat then returned to League of Ireland football.
Apps: 1 Lge.

CLAY, THOMAS
b. Leicester, 19.11.1892.
d. Southend, 21.2.1949.
Belvoir Street SS/
Apr 1911:FOSSE/
Jan 1914:Tottenham Hotspur/
cs 1929:Northfleet (p/coach).
debut: 25.11.11 v.Bradford Park Avenue (A).

A teenage prodigy as an unflappable full-back in local football circles, Tommy rapidly stepped up to Second Division action when Billy Henry moved to Manchester City. A cultured thinker and passer of the ball in an age of hoof-happy defenders, he shone regularly in Fosse's struggling side, and after the epic FA Cup tussles with Spurs in 1914 he and Harry Sparrow were together snapped up by the

victors. At White Hart Lane, Tommy was in the promotion side of 1920 and the Cup-winning team of 1921, and was even chosen in one game as goalkeeper, while after playing 318 League games (plus 106 wartime matches) in Spurs' colours, he was entrusted with inspiring the youngsters at their 'nursery' club. Tommy won four full England caps after WW1, and represented the Football League once, but the oft-repeated claim that he was the first Leicester-born man to play for his country is erroneous - that honour had fallen to Small Heath Alliance goalkeeper C.C.Charsley in 1893. Tommy closed his active involvement in football with a spell as coach at St.Albans from 1931.
Apps: 63 Lge; 6 FAC.

TOMMY CLAY

COCHRANE, MICHAEL
b. Belfast.
Milltown/Distillery/May 1900:FOSSE/
Mar 1901:Middlesbrough/
cs 1901:Distillery.
debut: 8.9.1900 v.Small Heath (A).

Coming to Leicester only two years after Glasgow Celtic had vainly offered £200 to Distillery for his services, Irish international right-back Mick was a Fosse ever-present from the date of his debut to that of his transfer - a period which also saw him win the last of his eight caps. During his first stint in Belfast, he had also represented the Irish League on four occasions.
Apps: 27 Lge; 1 FAC.

CODD, T.H.
b.
Goole Town/Dec 1914:FOSSE.
debut: 26.12.14 v.Arsenal (A).

A well-respected outside-left in the Midland League, Codd had anything but a happy introduction to Second Division football - his first two games were both 0-6 defeats. Nonetheless, he retained his position for the bulk of the rest of the ignominious final pre-war season, closing his career in a 5-1 victory!
Apps: 13 Lge.

COLES, DONALD STRATTON
b. Plymouth, 1879.
Ardingly College/Brighton & Hove Rangers/
cs 1901:Brighton & Hove Albion/
Aug 1902:FOSSE/
(Sussex amateur football).
debut: 13.9.02 v.Chesterfield (A).

A full-back who impressed in pre-season trials, but was given only one chance to perform at League level - in a 0-5 defeat - Donald had previously gained a little experience in the Southern League Second Division under former Fosse trainer John Jackson. He later regained amateur status and represented his adopted county.
Apps: 1 Lge.

COLLINS, W. ARTHUR
b. Leicester, 1883.
Leicester Old Boys/Sept 1901:FOSSE/
July 1905:Fulham/cs 1914:Norwich City.
debut: 28.3.02 v.Blackpool (A).

A consistent Fosse performer as an elegantly constructive centre or left-half, Arthur really made his name in London, where he helped Fulham to two successive Southern League championships and into the Second Division. A popular hero dubbed 'Prince Arthur' by the Craven Cottage crowd, he came close to England honours when playing in the 1906 Professionals v.Amateurs international trial, and by 1909 was on the management committee of the Players Union. After 197 League games for Fulham, he moved back into the Southern League for the 1914/15 season, then returned to play 47 wartime games for Fosse. Arthur was a son of Fosse director Tom Collins, who served the board for ten years prior to his death in June 1913.
Apps: 82 Lge; 14 FAC.
Goals: 5 Lge.

CONNACHAN, JAMES
b.
Celtic/Sept 1898:Newton Heath/
Feb 1899:Glossop North End/
May 1900:FOSSE.
debut: 1.9.1900 v.Stockport County (H) (1 goal).

A roving forward tried everywhere in the front line by Fosse except at outside-left, this Scot was hardly prolific, but at least managed to score against his two previous League clubs during his single season at Leicester.
Apps: 29 Lge.
Goals: 6 Lge.

COOPER, PAUL DAVID
b. Brierley Hill, 21.12.1953.
app/pro July 1971:Birmingham City/
Mar 1974:Ipswich Town/July 1987:CITY/
Mar 1989:Manchester City.
debut: 12.9.87 v.Crystal Palace (A).

Not the tallest of goalkeepers, but certainly one of the more agile and quick-witted, Paul carved out a thirteen-year career of well over 500 senior games for Ipswich, winning both FA

Cup and UEFA Cup winner's medals after initially joining the Suffolk club on loan from Birmingham. Understandably keen to downplay his long-standing popular reputation as a spectacular penalty-save expert and instead place merited stress on his all-round stability in the six-yard box, Paul joined City as an out-of-contract free agent, and soon renewed his old defensive partnership with Russell Osman after displacing the out-of-sorts Ian Andrews. His rapid, accurate distribution was in fact every bit as noteworthy as his persistent prowess at keeping out spot-kicks, and he soon convinced David Pleat, too, of his right to the senior City berth after the mid-season managerial change. Martin Hodge's early injury allowed Paul another lengthy spell as No.1 during 1988/9, but a shaking received in a car crash sidelined him for a few weeks; his recovery coincided with Hodge's, and he became a deadline-week mover to augment the successful Maine Road promotion challenge.
Apps: 56 Lge; 1 FAC; 9 LC; 4 FMC.

PAUL COOPER

CORBETT, WILLIAM R.
b. Falkirk, 31.8.1922.
Maryhill/cs 1941:Celtic/
June 1948:Preston North End/Aug 1949:CITY/
July 1950:Yeovil Town/
1951:Dunfermline Athletic.
debut: 1.10.49 v.Bury (A).

'Capped' in the wartime international against England in 1942, and a subsequent guest player for West Ham while on military service away from Parkhead, Bill was bought for £7,000 by Johnny Duncan to challenge Tom McArthur and Norman Plummer for the City centre-half spot. However, he had barely made a breakthrough when the manager departed, and was soon on his way himself after failing to convince Norman Bullock that he could marshall City's defence as well as he had done Celtic's in the immediate post-war period.
Apps: 16 Lge; 1 FAC.

COULSON, ERNEST
b.
Dec 1898:FOSSE/Nov 1901:Burton United/
Nov 1902:Chesterfield/Aug 1903:FOSSE.
debut: 23.1.04 v.Chesterfield (A).

The outside-right of a pair of Fosse amateurs whom it seems fair to presume (on the evidence of their almost always moving in tandem) to have been brothers, Ernest scored the winner in his first senior friendly appearance against Reading, and earned a single shot at League action some seven months later.
Apps: 1 Lge.

COULSON, HENRY WILLIAM
b.
Jan 1898:FOSSE/Nov 1901:Burton United/
Nov 1902:Chesterfield/Apr 1903:FOSSE.
debut: 12.2.98 v.Lincoln City (H) (1 goal).

Of the nigh-inseparable Coulsons, Henry was first on the Fosse scene with his occasional appearances in the inside-forward berths in friendlies and charity cup games, but could still never improve on his record of a single Second Division selection. The pair played together for Fosse reserves on occasions, and presumably did so too at Burton and Chesterfield: for neither played even once at League level at either club!
Apps: 1 Lge.
Goals: 1 Lge.

COUTTS, WILLIAM F.
b. Edinburgh.
Edinburgh Ashton/Dunbar United/
Aug 1930:Heart of Midlothian/
(Feb 1932-loan-Leith Athletic)/
May 1934:CITY.
debut: 25.8.34
v.Wolverhampton Wanderers (H) (1 goal).

A tricky Scottish inside-forward or wing-half who cost £950 and then made irregular appearances in each of the last five up-and-down seasons before the war, Billy also turned out in regional fare for Northampton Town in 1939/40. He had been a team-mate of Archie Gardiner with Hearts, for whom he played in the Scottish Cup semi-final of 1932/3. Billy marked the fiftieth anniversary of his City debut by appearing as a still sprightly guest at the club's Centenary celebrations.
Apps: 48 Lge; 2 FAC.
Goals: 4 Lge.

COX, WILLIAM JAMES
b.
Feb 1903:Bury/May 1904:Plymouth Argyle/
Aug 1905:FOSSE/
Oct 1905:Accrington Stanley/
Jan 1906:Preston North End/
May 1906:Dundee/
Apr 1907:Heart of Midlothian/
Nov 1907:Bradford Park Avenue.
debut: 2.9.05 v.Clapton Orient (H).

Fosse didn't take long to decide that this centre-forward wouldn't fit the bill. He was dropped after the first three games of 1905/6, and within

a month was on his way north. His new team did, however, take the championship of the Lancashire Combination that season. After his initially successful stint in Scotland (top scoring with 18 League goals at Dundee), William became one of the first players engaged by the newly-formed Bradford club, which had to play its first season, incongruously, in the Southern League, prior to its election to Division Two.
Apps: 3 Lge.

CRAWFORD, JAMES CHERRIE
b Bellshill, 27.9.1930.
Oct 1947:CITY/March 1954:Plymouth Argyle/
cs 1956:Peterborough United.
debut: 26.12.50 v.Grimsby Town (H).

A ball-playing Scottish inside-forward whose Filbert Street progress was hampered by a spell of National Service, Jimmy made isolated appearances in four forward positions over a four season span, and then found himself similarly cast as a utility reserve at Home Park.
Apps: 10 Lge; 1 FAC.
Goals: 2 Lge.

CREWS, ALEXANDER N.
b. Devon.
Green Waves/cs 1910:Plymouth Argyle/
Aug 1912:Chelsea/Sept 1912:FOSSE/
Sept 1913:Stockport County.
debut: 12.10.12 v.Grimsby Town (A).

Whether unlucky or just unsuitable, this Devonian pivot got only the one chance to impress in a season when Fosse tried six different centre-halves. Records show that Alex had had little more opportunity to shine nearer home, having played at most a couple of games for Argyle in the Southern League some two years before, and having lasted only a month in the Stamford Bridge reserves.
Apps: 1 Lge.

CROSS, GRAHAM FREDERICK
b. Leicester, 15.11.1943.
Nov 1960:CITY/(Mar 1976-loan-Chesterfield)/
June 1976:Brighton & Hove Albion/
July 1977:Preston North End/
cs 1978:Enderby Town/
Mar 1979:Lincoln City.
debut: 29.4.61 v.Birmingham City (H) (1 goal).

Falling just short of Adam Black's club record League appearance total, but bettering his aggregate tally to stand, with 599 senior games for City, as Leicester's most consistent servant ever, Graham also proved himself one of the most versatile over his sixteen seasons. It was often said that his regular switching of position cost him an England place (especially in the days when little premium was put on zonal adaptability), but Graham's failure to add senior international honours to his eleven Under-23 caps nevertheless seemed more a case of culpable oversight on the part of the national team's management. As early as 1962/3, Matt Gillies' tactical interchanging of Graham and Frank McLintock was a match-

GRAHAM CROSS

winning ploy, though a later tendency to shuttle Graham between defence, midfield and the striking line could occasionally be put down to desperate expediency. Eventually, when the twin centre-back game became the norm, it was in defence that Graham settled - if that's the right word, given his relentless energy and enthusiasm. Four Cup Final appearances, a Second Division championship medal and a 1973 Testimonial game were the tangible mementos of his City career but, for supporters, other memories jostle: of the 18-year-old playing like a veteran in City's gallant European exit in Madrid; of the cool back-heel that won a Cup replay at Blackburn; of the 'hat-trick' against Forest, consisting of 'one for them, two for us'; of numerous bustling forays forward, and of countless opposing strikers cowed into frustration by Graham's sturdy shadowing and solid tackle. His football prowess - several times coveted by Brian Clough - probably cost him a much more successful county cricket career than he actually managed (as, naturally, a Leicester-shire all-rounder), but the winter game kept a hold on him for some time after his final departure from Filbert Street. He was ever-present in Brighton's runaway rise from Third to Second Division in 1977, and then inspired Preston to take the same promotional route a year later. It was wholly unfitting that when he answered Lincoln's emergency call in 1979, even Graham couldn't save them from relegation. A spell coaching and then managing Hinckley Athletic marked the final phase of his soccer involvement.
Apps: 495+3 Lge; 59 FAC; 40 LC; 2 ECWC.
Goals: 29 Lge; 6 FAC; 2 LC.

CROSS,
NICHOLAS JEREMY ROLAND
b. Birmingham, 7.2.1961.
app 1977/pro Feb 1979:West Bromwich Albion/Aug 1985:Walsall/Jan 1988:CITY/ June 1989:Port Vale.
debut: 30.1.1988 v.Reading (A).

Initially a young rival for an Albion striking role with the likes of Ally Brown and Peter Eastoe, Nicky later partnered Trevor Christie at Fellows Park as he gradually improved his goals-per-game ratio and developed his characteristic penalty area control. A well-balanced, eager bustler, superb at shielding and turning with the ball in tight positions, he was, at £65,000, a shrewd short-term David Pleat buy to play in support of Mike Newell, and indeed, proved resilient enough to see off the challenge of international Jimmy Quinn during the following season.
Apps: 54+4 Lge; 1 FAC; 3+2 LC; 1 FMC.
Goals: 15 Lge; 1 LC.

CUNNINGHAM, LAURENCE PAUL
b. Archway, 8.3.1956.
July 1974:Orient/
Mar 1977:West Bromwich Albion/
June 1979:Real Madrid/
(Mar1983-loan-Manchester United)/
Aug 1983:Sporting Gijon/
cs 1984:Olympique Marseilles/
(Oct 1985-loan-CITY)/
July 1986:Rayo Vallecano/
1987:RSC Charleroi/Feb 1988:Wimbledon/
July 1988:Rayo Vallecano.
debut: 23.11.85 v.Manchester United (H).

A superbly skilful, confidently confrontational winger with six caps at each of Under-21 and full England levels, Laurie initially moved to Spain for just under £1 million, and tasted both sides of the hysterical success ethic on the continent, falling a little from popular favour after helping Real to the Spanish championship, and the European Cup semi-final and Final in his first two years. Later, unsettled in Marseilles, he had an extended loan period with City which, despite being injury-strewn, was inspirationally instrumental in keeping them in Division One in 1986. Some of his once-electrifying pace had gone, but little of the ball-juggling cockiness, and Laurie genuinely lit up Filbert Street for a while with his bursts of extrovert and effective footballing skills. In the midst of further continental wanderings, he again briefly returned to London, and appeared at Wembley as substitute for FA Cup winners Wimbledon in 1988.
Apps: 13+2 Lge.

CUNNINGHAM, WILLIAM EDWARD
b. Mallusk, Antrim, 20.2.1930.
Tranent Juniors/1948:St.Mirren/
Nov 1954:CITY/
Sept 1960:Dunfermline Athletic.
debut: 11.12.54
v.Wolverhampton Wanderers (H).

Ironically earning several of his 30 Irish caps while a regular in City's reserves, Willie had learned his football in Scotland, and had

already won international recognition for his stylish defensive play with St.Mirren when City laid out £4,750 for him. He settled well initially, shuttling between the two full-back berths, but was then squeezed out by the Stan Milburn/John Ogilvie partnership which saw City through the 1957 promotion year. He returned for three seasons of First Division battling but, again ironically, only ever played twice for City in the centre-half position he held for Northern Ireland throughout the 1958 World Cup. The eventual move to Dunfermline worked well for Willie: he played in their 1961 Scottish Cup victory, and was manager when the Pars returned to Hampden in 1965, having had a spell coaching under Jock Stein in the interim. He sold Jackie Sinclair to City before moving on for further spells of management at Falkirk and St.Mirren, and in 1971 turned down the Scottish FA's offer of the national team manager's post.
Apps: 127 Lge; 11 FAC.
Goals: 4 Lge.

CURRIE, SAMUEL
b. Kilwinning, 22.11.1889.
Kilwinning Rangers/May 1909:FOSSE/
July 1922:Wigan Borough.
debut: 19.3.10 v.Birmingham (A).

Fosse's regular left-back for six seasons before the war, and City's for three campaigns after it, Sam displaced Dick Pudan and went on to forge useful partnerships in hard times with Tommy Clay, Billy Barrett and Adam Black; in each case sharing the benefits of his experience with younger players. His signing actually cost him a medal, for Fosse swooped between the drawn Final of the Scottish Junior Cup in 1909 and its replay, which Kilwinning won. One of Fosse's several early union activists, Sam played in December 1910 for the Players Union XI against a combined Manchester United/City side - scoring an own goal and being injured badly enough to miss the next eight Fosse games! He took a well-merited club benefit from the League game with South Shields in November 1919, and only dropped into the Third Division (North) at the end of his City career. An older brother was a Bury inside-forward before WW1.
Apps: 236 Lge; 12 FAC.
Goals: 4 Lge; 2 FAC.

CURRIE, WALTER
b. Lochgelly.
East Fife/
1916:Raith Rovers/Dec 1919:CITY/
May 1922:Bristol Rovers.
debut: 14.2.20 v.Stockport County (A).

One of several players plucked by City from Starks Park as a result of return visits by former Raith boss Peter Hodge, 'Wattie' had impressed in wartime football as a skilful wing-half. Yet although he played quite a few games in front of his unrelated namesake, he could never secure a regular middle-line place over his three seasons at Leicester. He was, however, an ever-present in his Third Division campaign at Eastville.
Apps: 32 Lge.
Goals: 1 Lge.

CUSACK, NICHOLAS JOHN
b. Rotherham, 24.12.1965.
Birmingham Polytechnic/Long Eaton United/
Alvechurch/June 1987:CITY/
July 1988:Peterborough United.
debut: 15.8.87 v.Shrewsbury Town (H).

As a tall ex-student centre-forward signing
from Alvechurch, young Nick was rather
overburdened from the day of his arrival by
wishful comparisons to the recently-departed
Alan Smith, and not exactly aided by being
plunged straight into the first team on the
season's opening day. His development back in
the reserves was encouraging enough to earn
him an extended contract, but it promised to be
an uphill struggle for Nick to compete with
Newell, Cross, Reid and newcomer Quinn for a
senior slot. Posh were clearly impressed by his
spectacular strike against them in a Testimonial
friendly in April 1988, and three months later
he moved to London Road in the deal which
brought Alan Paris to Leicester.
Apps: 5+11 Lge; 0+1 FAC; 1+1 FMC.
Goals: 1 Lge.

DAINTY, HERBERT CHARLES
b. Geddington, 2.6.1879.
Kettering/Aug 1899:FOSSE/
May 1900:New Brighton Tower/
Aug 1901:FOSSE/cs 1902:Northampton Town/
May 1903:Notts County/
May 1904:Southampton/May 1905:Dundee/
May 1911:Bradford Park Avenue/
Oct 1913:Ayr United (p/mgr)/
Apr 1915:Dundee Hibernian (p/mgr).
debut: 23.9.99 v.Luton Town (A).

A sturdy Northamptonshire pivot, Herbert had
two spells as Fosse's centre-half around the
turn of the century, and became a noted
wanderer around the League and Southern
League scene. It was in Scotland, however, that
he really distinguished himself. One of four
Englishmen in Dundee's first (and only)
Scottish Cup-winning team of 1910, he also
represented the Scottish League that year, and
became something of a legendary figure on
Tayside. He returned as player/manager and
even (for a while in 1922) as chairman of the
local Hibernians - soon to change their name to
Dundee United - and also had his own team,
Dainty's XI, which played regularly for
charities throughout the WW1 period. After
having spent some time coaching in South
America, Herbert became Ipswich Town trainer
for two years from 1932.
Apps: 53 Lge; 5 FAC.
Goals: 3 Lge.

DALY, GERARD ANTHONY
b. Cabra, Dublin, 30.4.1954.
Bohemians/Apr 1973:Manchester United/
Mar 1977:Derby County/
(May 1978 & May 1979-loans-New England
Tea Men)/
Aug 1980:Coventry City/
(Jan 1983-loan CITY)/
July 1984:Birmingham City/
Oct 1985:Shrewsbury Town/
Mar 1987:Stoke City/
July 1988:Doncaster Rovers.
debut: 5.2.83 v.Carlisle United (A).

A vital midfield cog in Tommy Docherty's
mid-70s reconstruction of Manchester United,
Gerry later clashed verbally with the volatile
manager at both Old Trafford and the Baseball
Ground, and seemed happier with the quieter
style of Gordon Milne, who not only signed
him for Coventry (for £300,000), but also
called on him to contribute to City's 1983
promotion push as a loan player. The slim,
multi-capped Eire international responded
magnificently, and City only lost once after he
joined the fray, with the forwards gratefully
latching on to his intelligent promptings and
judiciously varied distribution, and Gerry
himself showing a fine battling commitment. It
was a genuine surprise when Milne decided to
face First Division rigours without him, but
Gerry simply got on with helping Birmingham
out of the Second in the very next season.
Apps: 17 Lge.
Goals: 1 Lge.

GERRY DALY

DARBY, ERNEST W.
b.
Leicester Nomads/am Oct 1908/
am Apr 1910:FOSSE/
cs 1910:Loughborough Corinthians/
cs 1911:Belvoir St.SS.
debut: 14.4.10 v.Hull City (A).

An amateur goalkeeper who continued to play
for his first club while assisting Fosse's
reserves, Ernest briefly stood in for the absent
Starbuck and Bailey at the tail-end of 1909/10.
He had previously had trials with Woolwich
Arsenal as a teenager.
Apps: 4 Lge.

DAVIES, BENJAMIN E.
b. Middlesbrough.
d. Middlesbrough, 1970.
cs 1910:Middlesbrough/May 1920:Cardiff City/
June 1923:CITY/
June 1924:Bradford Park Avenue.
debut: 8.12.23 v.South Shields (A).

A tall, slim keeper whose top flight experience
at Ayresome was limited by the form of
England international Tim Williamson, Ben

joined Cardiff for their initial season in the
League, and by the end of it had assisted them
to promotion. As a Bluebird, he proved an
insurmountable barrier to City in their 1922/3
FA Cup exit at Cardiff's hands, but within less
than a year Ben was standing in briefly for
George Hebden in the Filbert Street goal. At
Park Avenue he failed to win a first-team call.
Apps: 3 Lge.

DAVIES, RICHARD
b. Quarrington Hill, 1876.
Nov 1894:Manchester City/1895:Hanley Town/
Aug 1895:FOSSE/cs 1896:not known/cs
1897:Glossop North End/May 1898:Wolver-
hampton Wanderers/cs 1899:Reading.
debut: 21.9.95 v.Darwen (A).

Signed by Fosse as a youthful centre-forward
after he'd joined Hanley's sole season in The
Combination from Manchester City's reserves,
Richard showed rather more versatility across
the Leicester forward line than he did striking
success, and after a while his first team
appearances were confined to friendlies. He left
Glossop on the eve of their election to the
League, and flattered to deceive with Wolves,
scoring twice in his first game, but never again.
Apps: 7 Lge; 3 FAC.
Goals: 4 Lge.

DAVIES, ROGER
b. Wolverhampton, 25.10.1950.
Bridgnorth Town/Worcester City/
Sept 1971:Derby County/
(Aug 1972-loan-Preston North End)/
July 1976:Bruges/Dec 1977:CITY/
Mar 1979:Tulsa Roughnecks/
Sept 1979:Derby County/
Mar 1980:Seattle Sounders/
Apr 1983:Fort Lauderdale Strikers/
(Sept 1983-trial-Burnley)/
Nov 1983:Darlington/
Feb 1984:Gresley Rovers/
Nov 1985:Stapenhill.
debut: 10.12.77 v.Derby County (H).

Frank McLintock's City were already
struggling when Roger returned to Division
One from Belgium with a club record £250,000
transfer fee and high expectations to live up to.
Unfortunately, the lanky striker needed time to
play himself back into the pace of English
football, and that was a commodity City's
predicament (and the crowd's short patience)
excluded. Roger could recover neither goal
touch nor general form, and of the four efforts
that ironically gave him the joint top-scorer
position for the season, one was a penalty and
another, his first, might less charitably have
been credited as a Norwich own goal. Even
when Jock Wallace took over, City fans saw
little of the razor-sharpness and awkward un-
orthodoxy that had marked Roger's first spell at
Derby with some spectacular goals (all five
against Luton in the Rams' championship
season of 1974/5; a memorable hat-trick in a
televised Cup replay with Spurs) and had won
him an England Under-23 cap.
Apps: 22+4 Lge; 2 FAC; 0+1 LC.
Goals: 6 Lge.

DAVIS, HERBERT
b. Bradford, 11.8.1906.
Guiseley/Nov 1927:Bradford Park Avenue/
Apr 1932:Sunderland/Dec 1936:CITY/
June 1937:Crystal Palace.
debut: 12.12.36 v.Chesterfield (A).

Only 5ft.4ins tall, Bert nonetheless posed a
rather large threat to opposing defences, who
worried far more about his scoring record -
remarkably prolific for an orthodox winger -
than ever he did about his diminutive stature.
He had won a Third Division (North) championship medal in his first season with his home-
town club, and was a Roker regular right up
until they claimed the First Division title in
1936, but at Filbert Street he rather quickly lost
his battle with Tony Carroll for the outside-
right slot as City rocketed to promotion in
1937. Bert saw his final action as a wartime
guest back at Park Avenue.
Apps: 8 Lge; 1 FAC.

DAVIS, WILLIAM
b.
1889:FOSSE/1893:Hinckley Town.
debut (comp): 4.10.90
v. Burton Wanderers (H) FAC.

An amateur defender who played at left-back in
Fosse's initial Cup tie, and at centre-half in
their first Midland League game, but spent the
bulk of his Leicester career thereafter turning
out for the Fosse Rovers. He was, however, still
representing Leicestershire in inter-county fare
in 1895, and was at left-back for Hinckley in
the County Cup Final of 1897.
Apps: 1 FAC; 5 ML.

D'AVRAY, JEAN MICHEL
b. Johannesburg, South Africa, 19.2.1962.
May 1979:Ipswich Town/
(Feb 1987-loan-CITY).
debut: 14.2.87 v.Liverpool (A).

A tall striker of massive but largely unrealised
scoring potential by the time he arrived for a
brief loan spell with City, Mich had emerged
from the shadow of Paul Mariner at Ipswich,
yet never convincingly assumed the latter's
goal mantle. Naturalised in 1983, he had won
two England Under-21 caps despite finding
himself a regular occupant of the Portman Road
subs' bench, and while with Leicester appeared
either ill-briefed as to how to play alongside
Alan Smith, or simply unable to adapt to such a
twin-spearhead role. He has subsequently
reverted to a deeper-lying position at Portman
Road.
Apps: 3 Lge.

DAVY, HARRY
b. Padiham, 1872.
Padiham/Heywood Central/1892:Blackpool/
Apr 1895:FOSSE/cs 1897:Bristol City.
debut: 7.9.95 v.Burton Swifts (H).

Signed after accruing substantial Lancashire
League experience with his two previous clubs,
Harry became a sound, strong-kicking right-
back for two seasons with Fosse, welding an
ever-present partnership with George Swift in

1896/7. He then joined former team-mate
Albert Carnelly and Fossil-to-be Jack Hamilton
for Bristol City's inaugural Southern League
season.
Apps: 50 Lge; 6 FAC.

DAW, EDWIN CHARLES
b. Doncaster, 1876.
d. Doncaster, 1944.
Doncaster Congregationals/
Hexthorpe Wanderers/(trials-Sheffield United)/
Nov 1896:Grimsby Town/
cs 1897:Barnsley St.Peters/cs 1898:Rushden/
Aug 1899:Luton Town/May 1900:FOSSE/
cs 1902:New Brompton/cs 1903:not known/
Nov 1904:Doncaster Rovers/
Dec 1905:Bradford City/
May 1906:Oldham Athletic (-1907)/
Apr 1910:FOSSE.
debut: 1.10.1900 v.Burton Swifts (A).

A 6ft-tall goalkeeper who had already packed
in quite a bit of experience before joining Fosse
for the first time, Teddy had in fact made his
League debut for Grimsby against Fosse in
1896/7, then played in Barnsley's last Midland
League line-up prior to their Second Division
election; for Rushden against Fosse in the Cup;
and for Luton in the season they temporarily
lost League status. Teddy took over from
Godfrey Beardsley for Fosse and was a
capable, consistent custodian until his
wanderlust reasserted itself, and he moved to
the club we now know as Gillingham. At
Bradford City, he eventually lost his place to
22-stone giant Willie Foulke (who had kept him
out of the Blades first team a decade before),
while at Oldham he played in the Lancashire
Combination championship team that also
earned immediate elevation to the League.
Teddy gamely returned to help out Fosse in one
game in 1910, but showed his rustiness in conceding six goals to Stockport.
Apps: 56 Lge; 2 FAC.

DAWKINS, DEREK ANTHONY
b. Edmonton, 29.11.1959.
pro Oct 1977:CITY/Dec 1978:Mansfield Town/
Dec 1981:Bournemouth/
July 1983:Torquay United.
debut: 22.4.78 v.Derby County (A).

Given a run out at right-back in the final three
games of 1977/8 by caretaker boss Ian
MacFarlane, as already-relegated City looked
for a bit of belated pride and some pointers for
the future, Derek was still a teenager when
released by Jock Wallace to Mansfield. He
subsequently built a lengthy career in the lower
Divisions, with 73 League games at Field Mill
and 175 at Plainmoor, where he converted to a
midfield marking role and even popped up with
some valuable goals (such as the winner against
Spurs in a 1987/8 Littlewoods Cup tie).
Apps: 3 Lge.

DAWSON, JAMES E.
b. Stoneyburn, 21.12.1927.
Polkemmet/May 1946:CITY/
June 1949:Portsmouth/
Sept 1951:Northampton Town/Sept
1952:Southend United.
debut: 12.9.46 v.Birmingham City (H).

Signed as a pro by City after leaving the RAF,
Jimmy was groomed in the reserves as an
outside-left, though two of his limited first team
appearances were as an emergency right-half. A
move to reigning League champions
Portsmouth seemed to promise progress, but
Jimmy played only one League game as
Pompey repeated their Division One winners
act, and failed to make a single senior
appearance for either of his two subsequent
clubs.
Apps: 5 Lge.

DEWIS, GEORGE
b. Burbage, 22.1.1913.
Nuneaton Town/Nov 1933:CITY/
cs 1950:Yeovil Town.
debut: 9.12.33 v.West Bromwich Albion (H).

Carefully nurtured as a likely heir to Arthur
Chandler after George Carr had spotted him
playing for Nuneaton, George gave early
evidence of his potential centre-forward
prowess, based on strength and aerial ability, as
City used him sparingly over his first five
seasons. He was nearing his peak as a bustling
leader of the line when war was declared - and
George's wartime tally of 62 goals, scored in
the 81 games he managed to fit in during Army
service, instanced both his and the club's loss.
George's best years were effectively behind
him when peacetime football resumed, even if
an aggregate 19 goals in 1946/7 represented
City's top individual tally. He gave three more
years' service as a player, and was soon back
from his West Country non-league stint (he had
also guested for Yeovil during 1945/6) to start a
second Filbert Street career, initially as
assistant coach, then as trainer to the reserve
and youth teams. The dedication he lavished on
successive waves of City youngsters deserves
high tribute - and thankfully has drawn grateful
public testimony from the likes of Peter
Shilton. Rather like Arthur Chandler, George
would not let even his pension-book keep him
away from Filbert Street, where he remained as
kitman until 1983.
Apps: 116 Lge; 13 FAC.
Goals: 45 Lge; 6 FAC.

DICKSON, ADAM
b. Hamilton, 4.1.1929.
Thorniewood United/June 1951:CITY/
cs 1955:Peterborough United.
debut: 27.10.51 v.West Ham United (A).

An understudy to fellow Scottish 'keeper
Johnny Anderson throughout his City career,
Adam was a safe-handling, reliable reserve who
was unlucky not to find another League club,
and more unfortunate still in failing to win the
first-team jersey with a Posh side steaming to
the first of its many Midland League championships.
Apps: 16 Lge; 1 FAC.

DILKS, THOMAS FRANK
b.
1901:Northampton Town/cs 1903:Reading/
Oct 1903:FOSSE/cs 1904:not known/
cs 1905:Northampton Town.
debut: 24.10.03 v.Grimsby Town (H).

Signed after a mere three-game spell with Southern League Reading, Dilks became the third of eight outside-lefts tried by Fosse in the barrel-scraping, rock-bottom season of 1903/4, and fared little better than any other.
Apps: 8 Lge; 1 FAC.

DIXON, ARTHUR
b. Middleton, 17.11.1921.
Baillieston Juniors/May 1940:Queens Park/
cs 1945:Clyde/1947:Heart of Midlothian/
Nov 1949:Northampton Town/Oct 1951:CITY/
cs 1953:Kettering Town.
debut: 6.10.51 v.Bury (H).

An English-born, Scottish raised inside-forward who made a rapid goalscoring impact at Northampton, and earned the nickname 'Rubberneck' from Cobblers' fans impressed by his heading ability, Arthur could only briefly shift Fred Worthington from the first team at Filbert Street, and never got another look-in after City signed Johnny Morris. He was once chosen for a Scottish representative side during the war, but dropped out when his birthplace became known.
Apps: 11 Lge.

DOHERTY, JOHN
b. Manchester, 12.3.1935.
pro Mar 1952:Manchester United/
Oct 1957:CITY/cs 1958:Rugby Town (p/mgr).
debut: 5.10.57 v.Everton (II).

A genuine 'Busby Babe', nurtured through United's junior squads for a League debut at 18, John eventually found competition for an inside-forward place at Old Trafford unbearably intense. He had scored for United on a rare senior outing only two weeks before City swooped for his £6,500 transfer, but it soon became evident that he was carrying an old injury which recurred after twelve successive games had given City cause for optimism about his progress. John took medical advice to avoid the stresses of the League game, and became the Southern League's youngest ever player/manager at the age of 23. In the early 80's, he was noted as being Burnley's chief scout.
Apps: 12 Lge.
Goals: 5 Lge.

DONNELLY, JAMES
b. South Bank, 1882.
South Bank/Darlington St.Augustine's/
Oct 1902:Sheffield United/May 1907:FOSSE/
cs 1910:Darlington.
debut: 7.9.07 v.Leeds City (H).

A £150 signing who contributed tellingly to Fosse's only promotion campaign from both right flank forward positions, Jimmy remains best remembered as the scorer of the club's opening First Division goal. Indeed, he finished that unfortunate top-flight season as top scorer, and then turned selfless provider as Fred Shinton raced to a record seasonal goal haul in 1909/10. Jimmy was a member, as was Ronald Brebner, of the Darlington squad which reached the last 16 of the FA Cup in 1911 (beating his former First Division club Sheffield United along the way) and he was still active when

they took the North Eastern League championship in 1913.
Apps: 74 Lge; 2 FAC.
Goals: 26 Lge; 1 FAC.

DORRELL, WILLIAM
b. Coventry.
1889:Singer's/cs 1892:FOSSE/
Apr 1894:Aston Villa/Mar 1896:FOSSE.
debut: 17.9.92 v.Mansfield Town (A) ML.

Billy actually made his Fosse bow a fortnight before the above-cited match, in the first friendly of the new season, and contributed a goal to the 10-1 demolition of his former club - the one we now know as Coventry City. He had been the crowd's hero there, and was to become one (twice!) with Fosse, despite taking the left-wing spot from the popular Jimmy Atter. Speedy and incisive, he was tempted to Villa after scoring Fosse's final Midland League goal, but with England internationals Smith and Athersmith acting as obstacles to him gaining a regular first team spot on either wing, Billy's chances at Perry Barr were limited. He nonetheless scored five goals in only 11 League appearances, added a brace in his only FA Cup game as Villa progressed to the 1895 Final, and was chosen for the Football League against the Irish League. The welcome on his return to Fosse was heartfelt - and Billy obliged his fans by scoring in the first League game of his three-year second spell, during which he turned in a number of scintillating displays on both flanks. He even once tested his pace in a 440-yard challenge race with a visiting American athlete, and won, before the kick-off of the home game with Darwen in February 1898. Billy took a benefit from the prestigious friendly against the touring Corinthians in December 1898. He became a Villa scout in the 20s, by which stage his son Arthur was starring both for that club and England.
Apps: 59 Lge; 14 FAC; 43 ML.
Goals: 20 Lge; 11 FAC; 16 ML.

DORRELL, WILLIAM (Jnr)
b. Small Heath.
Dec 1919:CITY/cs 1920:Hinckley United/
Loughborough Corinthians.
debut: 6.12.19 v.Rotherham County (H).

Though it has not been possible to prove definitively a family connection with former Fosse star Billy, it is assumed this right-winger was his son, and therefore brother to Arthur. Peter Hodge clearly thought there was no chance of him carving an equally illustrious career, however, for he got only the one opportunity to deputise for George Douglas in the initial post-WW1 season. He was twice in County Cup-winning sides: for City Reserves in 1920, and for Loughborough Corinthians in 1923.
Apps: 1 Lge.

DOUGAN, ALEXANDER DEREK
b. Belfast, 20.1.1939.
Distillery/Aug 1957:Portsmouth/
Mar 1959:Blackburn Rovers/
July 1961:Aston Villa/
June 1963:Peterborough United/
May 1965:CITY/

Mar 1967:Wolverhampton Wanderers.
debut: 21.8.65 v.Liverpool (H).

DEREK DOUGAN

Reversing the usual dynamic by which a modern 'personality' is constructed, Derek achieved a remarkable about-turn in his career and his image midway through his playing days. A process begun at Peterborough, accelerated at Leicester and completed at Wolves actually provided a rare example of a caricature turning into a genuine character. Too many of Derek's early energies had been spent in establishing a rebellious persona as joker and wilful controversialist - often to the detriment of his football - before he found a mature balance between showmanship and soccer. He'd been to Wembley with Blackburn (in 1960, when he posted a transfer request on the morning of the Cup Final) and his standing as a Northern Ireland regular seemed assured no matter what, but the trajectory of his striking career seemed permanently stalled when Villa let him go to London Road, after he'd amused many with his adoption of a shaven head, and scared more with his propensity for off-field scrapes. Perhaps a spell in the Third Division helped restore a sense of perspective, or perhaps a renewed burst of media interest in 'The Doog' when Posh met Arsenal in the Cup rekindled ambitions. At any rate, Derek took a pay cut to join City back in the top flight, and proceeded to justify Matt Gillies' gamble as he managed both to put a smile back on City's game and to link with fellow-newcomer Jackie Sinclair in a lethal finishing partnership. Brilliant in the air, and with a remarkably sure and subtle first touch for a tall striker, Derek led City's forward line with unique flair, and lapped up the crowd's adulation - not least on such occasions as when he knocked in a flamboyant hat-trick against former club Villa, or when he led a bemused close marker *behind* the goal while awaiting a City corner! The Doog's departure was the cause of much ill-feeling between the club and its supporters, centred on the belief that City had merely,

unimaginatively, cashed in on the first offer to doubly recoup their investment; and City fans were irked even more when Derek made an immediate impact at Molineux, where his goals ensured promotion within a couple of months. Settling with Wolves for 300+ games and 100+ goals over almost eight years, Derek also won there his only victor's trophy, for the 1974 League Cup. An articulate chairman of the PFA, a stimulating author and easeful TV pundit, he surprised few when he later moved into management (albeit with Kettering, where he clashed with the FA over shirt sponsorship), or even when, in 1983, he led a consortium of businessmen in rescuing and reconstructing Wolves after they had fallen into receivership.
Apps: 68 Lge; 5 FAC; 3 LC.
Goals: 35 Lge; 1 FAC; 5 LC.

DOUGAN, MAXWELL SPALDING
b. Stoneyburn, 23.5.1938.
cs 1962:Queens Park/Sept 1963:CITY/
Dec 1966:Luton Town.
debut: 27.11.63 v.Gillingham (H) LC.

A Scottish amateur international centre-half, Max made his City debut as an emergency centre-forward, helping the club past one hurdle on their way to League Cup glory, and later being rewarded with a half-back place in the first leg of the Final at Stoke. His Filbert Street chances were severely limited by the consistency of Ian King and John Sjoberg, but it was his occasional experience at full-back which stood Max in good stead for his subsequent years as a rugged, unceremonious No.2 with Luton, who he helped from the Fourth Division basement to the verge of Division Two.
Apps: 9 Lge; 2 LC.

MAX DOUGAN

DOUGLAS, GEORGE HAROLD
b. Forest Gate, 18.8.1893.
d. Tunbridge Wells, 1979.
Ilford/May 1912:FOSSE/Feb 1921:Burnley/
May 1922:Oldham Athletic/
Aug 1926:Bristol Rovers/
July 1928:Tunbridge Wells Rangers (p/mgr).
debut: 21.12.12 v.Hull City (H).

GEORGE DOUGLAS

Having graduated from West Ham schools football to become an outside-right - and occasional goalscoring centre-forward - in the Isthmian League, George was on the fringe of the amateur international squad when he joined Fosse. Retaining unpaid status for his first season (and winning two England amateur caps during that period), he re-signed in 1913 as a professional and gave fine right-wing service on both sides of WW1; though in the final game Fosse ever played under that name, a 1919 friendly against the B.E.F. (France) XI, George was in the opposing team, and even missed a penalty. Four months later he scored the first League goal attributed to Leicester City. He took his benefit from the League game against Birmingham in September 1920, then moved on to play First Division football with both his Lancashire clubs.
Apps: 127 Lge; 6 FAC.
Goals: 10 Lge; 1 FAC.

DRYBURGH, THOMAS JAMES DOUGLAS
b. Kirkcaldy, 23.4.1923.
Lochgelly Albert/June 1947:Aldershot/
July 1948:Rochdale/Aug 1950:CITY/
May 1954:Hull City/July 1955:King's Lynn/
Aug 1957:Oldham Athletic/
Nov 1957:Rochdale.
debut: 4.9.50 v.Notts County (H).

A former ice-hockey star with Kirkcaldy Fliers, and a Scottish junior international winger in his Lochgelly days, Tom then tasted life in both Sections of the Third Division before signing for City at a £6,500 fee. Taking over from Charlie Adam, he became Arthur Rowley's first regular left-wing partner, and maintained a decent scoring rate himself, but lost his place to Peter Small in the 1954 promotion season, and never quite recovered his effective dash with his subsequent League clubs.
Apps: 95 Lge; 4 FAC.
Goals: 29 Lge; 1 FAC.

DUFFY, CHRISTOPHER FRANCIS
b. Jarrow, 1885.
1904:Brentford/cs 1905:Middlesbrough/
Aug 1906:Newcastle United/May 1908: Bury/
July 1914:North Shields Athletic/
cs 1919:not known/Dec 1919:CITY.
debut: 6.4.20 v.Bristol City (H) (1 goal).

Quite a veteran by the time he joined City for a brief run out as a left-sided forward late in the initial post-WW1 season, Chris had many years before won a reputation as an athletic sprinter, and had used his pace as a winger to carve a reasonable career on Teesside, Tyneside and at Gigg Lane. Upon retirement, he became a headmaster in Newcastle.
Apps: 4 Lge.
Goals: 1 Lge.

DUFFY, MICHAEL KEVIN
b. Leicester, 12.6.1961.
July 1978:CITY/May 1981:Enderby Town/
Wigston Town/Shepshed Charterhouse/
Corby Town.
debut: 9.9.78 v.Notts County (H).

One of the City youngsters unexpectedly elevated to an early first team spot by Jock Wallace, Mick was a busy inside-forward with a useful junior-team scoring rate, and had a neat headed 'goal' dubiously disallowed on his debut. He later laid on Gary Lineker's initial first team goal in the return game with the Magpies, and scored himself in the final match of 1978/9, but was only ever to make one further substitute appearance in senior football.
Apps: 7+5 Lge.
Goals: 1 Lge.

DUMBRELL, GEORGE
b. Catford.
Nunhead/Dartford/May 1928:Brentford/
May 1930:CITY/
Nov 1933:Bournemouth & Boscombe Athletic/
Aug 1934:Brentford.
debut: 2.3.31 v.Blackburn Rovers (A).

A reserve full-back in both his Griffin Park spells (retiring in 1938 with an aggregate of only 17 League appearances for the Bees), George nonetheless cost City £1,750 when bought as cover for Reg Osborne. In fact he made light work of bridging the gulf between his background as a Third Division 'stiff' and the exigencies of performing in the top flight whenever he was called upon to partner Adam Black in City's back line. Strangely enough, George had made his name as a goalscorer at Dartford.
Apps: 37 Lge; 2 FAC.

DUNCAN, JOHN
b. Lochgelly, 14.2.1896.
d. Leicester, 14.3.1966.
Denbeath Star/Lochgelly United/
1916:Raith Rovers/July 1922:CITY.
debut: 26.8.1922
v.Stockport County (A) (2 goals).

A scheming but far from shot-shy inside-forward of authentically high class, Johnny had already led Raith to their highest-ever Scottish League placing (3rd) in 1922 when City expended £1500 to bring him and his brother Tom to Filbert Street. Peter Hodge had overseen his first few wartime appearances for the Kirkcaldy club, and kept close track of his progress, correctly identifying the strongly-built artist who'd been nicknamed 'Tokey' as the potential lynch-pin of City's sustained scrap for

League honours. Johnny responded with both goals and graft as City missed promotion on goal average at the end of his first season, and was to parade his play-making skills for five campaigns in the First Division after he'd finally chivvied City up in 1925. That year he'd added 30 League goals to Arthur Chandler's 32, and had become the first scorer of six goals in a single game for the club as they pasted Port Vale 7-0 on Christmas Day. The inevitable, well-merited Scottish cap came in October 1925, with Johnny scoring the opening goal against Wales, but inexplicably it wasn't followed by subsequent selections. The maestro eventually retreated into the half-back line, the better to orchestrate City's championship assaults, and indeed had lost little effectiveness when, in 1930, he found himself at loggerheads with the City directors over their refusal to sanction his running a pub. Over this point of principle, the Turk's Head on Welford Road acquired a genial landlord, and City lost one of their greats - though Johnny's footballing intelligence couldn't be allowed to idle for too long. In March 1946, it was to Johnny that City turned for a manager to succeed Tom Bromilow and to prepare the club for the return to League football; and it was he who proudly led out his team at Wembley in 1949. Unfortunately, another argument with the board occurred that October, and with the same principled abruptness, Johnny returned to his pumps. Something of the man's managerial character is affectionately sketched in Don Revie's 1955 autobiography; but it is in City's cherished reputation over the years as a 'footballing' side wherein resides the best testimony to the influence of Johnny's playing personality.
Apps: 279 Lge; 16 FAC.
Goals: 88 Lge; 7 FAC.

TOM DUNCAN

DUNCAN, THOMAS KERR
b. Lochgelly, 1.9.1897.
d. Leicester, 9.2.1940.
Lochgelly United/1920:Raith Rovers/
July 1922:CITY/Sept 1924:Halifax Town/
cs 1926:Bristol Rovers.
debut: 4.9.22 v.Rotherham County (A).

For some time the right-flank partner to his elder brother Johnny at both Raith and

Leicester, Tom had nothing like as illustrious a career, but was somewhat unlucky to be in direct competition for the City winger's role with Hughie Adcock, and then to find his more delicate skills a little overwhelmed by the harsher rigours of Third Division soccer.
Apps: 41 Lge; 1 FAC.
Goals: 6 Lge.

DUNKLEY, ALBERT E.
b. Northampton, 1877.
1897:Northampton Town/May 1900:FOSSE/
Feb 1901:Northampton Town/
cs 1901:New Brompton/Queens Park Rangers/
May 1903:Blackburn Rovers/
cs 1904:Bristol Rovers/Aug 1906:Blackpool.
debut: 1.9.1900 v.Stockport County (H).

Outside-left in the first side ever fielded by Northampton, and top scorer in their initial competitive season (in the Northants League), Albert had only a brief liaison with Fosse, moving on almost immediately after surrendering his left-wing spot to Tommy Allsopp, and then building quite a reputation as a nomad. He won a Southern League championship medal in his first season with Bristol Rovers, playing alongside future Fossils Clark and Pudan.
Apps: 10 Lge; 1 FAC.

DUNNE, JAMES PETER
b. Dublin, 16.3.1935.
Sept 1953:CITY/cs 1956:St.Patrick's Athletic/
July 1960:Peterborough United/
cs 1963:Cambridge United.
debut: 16.4.55 v.Sheffield Wednesday (A).

A young Irish inside-left who briefly deputised for Arthur Rowley, but never found himself on a winning City side at senior level, Jimmy nonetheless found FAI Cup glory with St.Patrick's in 1959.
Apps: 4 Lge.

DUNNE, THOMAS
b. Dublin, 19.3.1927.
d. Southport, 23.1.1988.
Home Farm/St.Patrick's Athletic/
1945:Shamrock Rovers/
Nov 1949:CITY/
July 1954:Exeter City/
Aug 1956:Shrewsbury Town/
July 1957:Southport.
debut: 17.2.51 v.Cardiff City (A).

Having followed his Shamrock team-mate, international 'keeper Tommy Godwin, to Leicester, wing-half Tommy had to wait somewhat longer for a first team breakthrough as the City management passed into the hands of Norman Bullock, and had to content himself with becoming the sure-shot penalty expert of the Football Combination side. Though he eventually displaced Johnny King to claim the No.6 shirt for a fair run of Second Division games in 1953, he lost out himself to newcomer Eddie Russell midway through the 1954 promotion campaign. A nephew of the former Sheffield United, Arsenal, Southampton and Ireland goalscorer Jimmy Dunne, Tommy later became a Southport licensee.
Apps: 33 Lge; 1 FAC.

DURRANT,
ARTHUR FRANCIS (JAMIE)
b. Luton, 1878.
d. Luton, 6.4.1927.
Luton Stanley/Mar 1898:Luton Town/
May 1904:FOSSE/Sept 1909:Leyton/
cs 1913:Luton Town.
debut: 3.9.04 v.Blackpool (A).

The epitome of the orthodox outside-right, rarely wandering from his narrow corridor of operation, but patrolling it with pace and a rich repertoire of trickery, Jamie gave Fosse five seasons of valuable service, culminating in the roller-coaster experience of successive promotion and relegation. At Luton, he had learned good footballing habits from Jimmy Blessington, who he followed to Filbert Street, while later, as a senior player at Southern League Leyton, he was in turn mentor to the young Charles Buchan, who acknowledged the debt he owed Jamie in his autobiography. It was another contemporary, however, who came up with the rather fanciful description of how Jamie "ran with amazing speed in a soft-footed manner reminiscent of a wolf"!
Apps: 140 Lge; 13 FAC.
Goals: 24 Lge; 3 FAC.

EARLE, STEPHEN JOHN
b. Feltham, 1.11.1945.
pro Nov 1963:Fulham/Nov 1973:CITY/
(Nov 1977-loan-Peterborough United)/
Mar1978:Detroit Express/
July 1978:Tulsa Roughnecks/
Oct 1978:Telford United/
Mar 1979:Tulsa Roughnecks/
1980:Wichita Wings.
debut: 1.12.73
v.Tottenham Hotspur (H) (1 goal).

A prolific scorer in three Divisions for Fulham (his 98 League goals for them included a hat-trick in the 1966 relegation decider at Northampton, and a personal nap-hand at Halifax in September 1969), Steve was also a one-time striking partner of Allan Clarke, and was bought by Jimmy Bloomfield to lift some of the scoring burden from Frank Worthington. After helping City dispose of his former club on the way to the 1974 FA Cup semi-final in his first season, Steve ironically then suffered something of a goal drought himself, and was displaced for a spell by Chris Garland, before returning to hit 13 goals in 1976/7. He took a belated Craven Cottage testimonial (Fulham v.City) in October 1975, and in 1979 returned to City with NASL club Tulsa for a friendly.
Apps: 91+8 Lge; 13 FAC; 3 LC.
Goals: 20 Lge; 6 FAC.

EASTOE, PETER R.
b. Tamworth, 2.8.1953.
June 1971:Wolverhampton Wanderers/
Nov 1973:Swindon Town/
Mar 1976:Queens Park Rangers/
Mar 1979:Everton/
Aug 1982:West Bromwich Albion/
(Oct 1983-loan-CITY)/
(Mar 1984-loan-Huddersfield Town)/
(Aug 1984-loan-Walsall)/
(Oct 1984-loan-CITY)/
(Feb 1985-loan-Wolverhampton Wanderers)/

July 1985:Sporting Farense/1986:not known/
cs 1988:Atherstone United.
debut: 19.10.83 v.Norwich City (A) (1 goal).

A much-travelled striker taken twice on loan by
City from West Brom, largely to support Gary
Lineker during Alan Smith's then-annual slow
start to the season, Peter actually made his
Filbert Street bow in the game with Southampton which was abandoned during a torrential
downpour. He proceeded to make a good
impression, but then suffered a double fracture
of the jaw in a game against Manchester
United. Adept at shielding and laying off the
ball in attack, Peter had suffered a diminishing
goal rate since his time at Swindon, but his
second goal for City - in the first match of his
second spell - was the 95th League strike of his
career. He had played in European competitions
for three of his clubs, and extended his career in
Portugal after a remarkable total of five loan-
outs from the Hawthorns.
Apps: 11 Lge; 1 LC.
Goals: 2 Lge.

EATON, SAMUEL L.
b. Derby, 1881.
Derby St.James/Derby County/Hinckley Town/
Feb 1898:FOSSE/cs 1900:not known/
June 1901:Stockport County/Jan 1902:FOSSE/
cs 1903:Luton Town/May 1905:Watford/
cs 1906:Earlestown/Accrington Stanley/
Maidstone United.
debut: 12.2.98 v.Lincoln City (H).

Sam's first two games as a teenager for Fosse
were at outside-right, but it was in the inside-
right position that he made sufficient impact to
earn a brief recall in 1902, and in which he had
been a very junior apprentice to Steve Bloomer
at Derby. His first season at Luton coincided
with Jamie Durrant's last, while other
teammates there included Tommy Allsopp,
Jack Bennett and Harry Moody.
Apps: 52 Lge; 5 FAC.
Goals: 12 Lge; 1 FAC.

ECCLES, PETER EDWARD
b. Dublin, 24.8.1962.
Shamrock Rovers/
Aug 1988:Kingston Olympic/
Oct 1988:Dundalk/Oct 1988:CITY.
debut: 8.4.89 v.Blackburn Rovers (A).

A tall central defender who won a fistful of
League of Ireland championship and FAI Cup
medals with Shamrock, and made an international appearance as substitute for the Republic
against Uruguay in 1986 (alongside Daly,
Langan and clubmate Pat Byrne), Peter joined
City shortly after returning from a summer stint
in Australian football. He received some fine
notices for his Central League performances,
and earned his senior call-up in place of the
injured Steve Walsh, but was unfortunately
somewhat embarrassed by the pace of his only
Second Division sortie, which ended unhappily
at half-time with an injury. The greater
potential shown by younger prospects Grant
Brown and Richard Smith was behind the
decision to release him in May 1989.
Apps: 1 Lge.

EDMUNDS, PAUL
b. Doncaster, 2.12.1957.
Troston Welfare/pro Apr 1979:CITY/
May 1981:Bournemouth/
cs 1982:Bentley Victoria/
Grantham/Burton Albion.
debut: 8.3.80 v.Sunderland (A).

All but one of Paul's League appearances were
made in promotion seasons. The red-haired
right winger contributed two cracking
individual goals as a latecomer to City's 1980
Second Division championship effort before
breaking his wrist at Wrexham, but played
again for Jock Wallace only in the initial top
flight game of the following season. Then, at
Bournemouth, his fourteen games helped the
Cherries out of the Fourth Division in 1982, but
failed to gain him a contract renewal. A
qualified schoolteacher, Paul continued to play
on a part-time basis in non-league football.
Apps: 8 Lge.
Goals: 2 Lge.

EDWARDS, H.R.
b.
Singers/cs 1892:Small Heath/Oct 1893:FOSSE/
Aug 1894:Derby County/
1895:Wolverton L.& N.W.R./
Dec 1898:Watford/cs 1899:Bedford Queens.
debut: 21.10.93
v.Mansfield Town (H) ML (1 goal).

Briefly renewing acquaintance with old Singers
team-mate Billy Dorrell during Fosse's final
Midland League season, Edwards was a
constructive inside-right who had joined Small
Heath for their initial Second Division
campaign. At Derby he failed to make a senior
appearance, but Wolverton were still a force in
Southern League football when he joined them
as an attacking centre-half.
Apps: 6 FAC; 12 ML.
Goals: 2 ML.

EDWARDS, LESLIE
b. Nuneaton, 1912.
Folkestone Town/Dec 1930:CITY/
cs 1932:Folkestone Town/
May 1933:Crystal Palace/
May 1936:Newport County.
debut: 12.12.1931 v.Blackburn Rovers (A).

A right-half who played his trio of City games
away from home, and had the misfortune to
make his debut in a 0-6 thrashing, Leslie at
least managed to tot up 65 League appearances
for his two Third Division (South) clubs. He
also guested during WW2 for Reading.
Apps: 3 Lge.

EDWARDS, WALTER THOMAS
b. Llanelli, 13.3.1923.
Workington/Aug 1946:Fulham/Mar
1948:Southend United/Dec 1948:CITY/
cs 1949:Bath City/May 1952:Walsall/
cs 1953:Oswestry Town.
debut: 18.12.48 v.Leeds United (A) (1 goal).

Another hapless pretender to Charlie Adam's
first team No.11 shirt, freed by Johnny Duncan

after only five months on City's books. He had
barely left Filbert Street before another Walter
Edwards, also an outside-left, signed for City
from Leeds United; but this latter failed to
make a League breakthrough at all during his
year with the club.
Apps: 3 Lge.
Goals: 1 Lge.

EGGLESTON, THOMAS
b. Mitcham, 21.2.1920.
am Dec 1936/pro Feb 1937:Derby County/
July 1946:CITY/Jan 1948:Watford.
debut: 31.8.46 v.Manchester City (H).

Though wartime Royal Navy service left him
short of senior playing experience (he had
guested for Southampton, and was an emergency choice for one of the ties which saw
Derby through to the 1946 FA Cup Final),
Tommy became City's regular left-half in the
first postwar League season. He lost his battle
for selection against John King, however, early
in 1947/8, and became part of the remarkable
five-man transfer to Vicarage Road, where he
was to make 177 League appearances before
retirement. Tommy nonetheless stayed in the
game until his pension book became due:
coaching at Brentford, Watford, Sheffield
Wednesday and Everton; managing Mansfield
Town and Greek club Ethnikos; and acting as
physiotherapist to Plymouth Argyle and
Ipswich Town. He lives in retirement in
Tockwith, Yorkshire.
Apps: 34 Lge.
Goals: 2 Lge.

ENGLISH, THOMAS STEVEN
b. Cirencester, 18.10.1961.
June 1979:Coventry City/Sept 1982:CITY/
Aug 1984:Rochdale/
Sept 1984:Plymouth Argyle/
Nov 1984:Colchester United/
cs 1985:Canberra City Olympians/
Sept1985:Colchester United/
cs 1987:Wealdstone/cs 1988:Bishops Stortford.
debut: 18.9.82 v.Blackburn Rovers (A).

TOM ENGLISH

An England Youth international forward upgraded from his Highfield Road apprenticeship by Gordon Milne, Tom struck an early League scoring partnership with Mark Hateley, and managed a hat-trick against City in March 1981. However, he was dogged with domestic troubles which unfortunately continued to distract him after a controversial move to Filbert Street, when Milne acquired him in a straight swap deal for popular Jim Melrose. Tom failed to impress an accordingly highly critical Leicester crowd, despite his contribution to the 1983 promotion effort, and despite an eventual move from the firing line into a deeper midfield role. Upon his release, he played for three clubs in a season on a non-contract basis, spent a summer in Australia, and then returned to Colchester to play regularly alongside his younger brother, Tony. In a rare occurrence in 1985/6, both brothers were sent off during a match at Crewe.
Apps: 29+15 Lge; 0+1 FAC; 2+1 LC.
Goals: 3 Lge; 1 LC.

ESSOM, WALTER
b. Leicester, 1895.
Leicester Imperial/cs 1919:CITY/
cs 1920:Ashby Town.
debut: 13.9.19 v.Fulham (H).

A local left-back who briefly displaced Sam Currie to play in the successive home and away fixtures with Fulham in 1919/20.
Apps: 2 Lge.

EVENSON, ISAAC
b. Manchester, Nov 1882.
d. 1954.
Tonge/cs 1901:Stockport County/
July 1903:FOSSE/July 1905:Clapton Orient/
Apr 1907:West Bromwich Albion/
May 1908:Plymouth Argyle.
debut: 5.9.03 v.Barnsley (A).

Signed as a centre-forward by Fosse, but settling at inside-left, Ike was one of the few successes of the disastrous 1903/4 season, finishing as top scorer and remaining to help lift the re-elected club a few rungs up the Second Division ladder the following year. Having previously been Stockport's joint top scorer in their first season playing at Edgeley Park, Ike subsequently moved on to assist Orient in their first-ever League campaign, and even took on the additional responsibility of caretaker-managership of that financially-ailing club for three months in 1906; while on his later travels he became better known as a middle-line schemer than as a spearhead.
Apps: 42 Lge; 10 FAC.
Goals: 14 Lge; 6 FAC.

FARMER, JOHN
b. Biddulph, 31.8.1947.
Chatterley BC/Jan 1965:Stoke City/
(July 1972-loan-West Bromwich Albion)/
(Dec 1974-loan-CITY)/
cs 1976:Northwich Victoria.
debut: 7.12.74 v.Everton (H).

Despite managing 163 League games in goal for Stoke and winning himself England Under-23 recognition, John spent much of his Victoria

Ground career in the shadow of Gordon Banks, and was just having to come to terms with the start of another spell as understudy - this time to Peter Shilton - when he answered the call to alleviate a City goalkeeping emergency. With Mark Wallington injured and Carl Jayes as yet inexperienced, John was a decidedly classy stopgap, but ironically he was injured himself in his second match, and returned to Stoke just as Wallington embarked on his monumental record of consecutive City appearances. John's earlier loan spell, at West Brom, had been somewhat more leisurely: consisting of three friendly matches on a Swedish tour.
Apps: 2 Lge.

FARMER, KEVIN JOHN
b. Ramsgate, 24.1.1960.
app July 1976/pro Oct 1977:CITY/
Aug 1979:Northampton Town/
cs 1982:Bedworth.
debut: 17.12.77 v.Ipswich Town (A).

City were anchored to the bottom of the First Division when Frank McLintock threw both Kevin and Mark Goodwin into the limelight at Ipswich, and for the young striker it was his sole opportunity in the first team. Grandson of a QPR director, Kevin was released by Jock Wallace and went on to make 77 League appearances (scoring 12 goals) in three seasons with the Cobblers, whom he represented at centre-back as well as up front. He has more recently been involved with Senior League outfit Kirby Muxloe.
Apps: 1 Lge.

FARRINGTON, JOHN ROBERT
b. Lynemouth, 19.6.1947.
app Sept 1963/
pro June 1965:Wolverhampton Wanderers/
Oct 1969:CITY/Nov1973:Cardiff City/
Oct 1974:Northampton Town/
cs 1980:AP Leamington/
Shepshed Charterhouse.
debut: 18.10.69 v.Bristol City (H).

A direct right-winger who made his Molineux debut whilst still an apprentice and later laid on several goals there for Derek Dougan, John was a £30,000 Frank O'Farrell purchase who started as he meant to go on, providing a pinpoint centre for Rodney Fern's goal in his first City match, and soon assisting materially in the 1971 Second Division championship campaign. With John on the right and Len Glover on the left, City's quick-break style was based on an attack of genuine width and pace, and the Northumbrian pigeon-fancier's finishing wasn't bad, either, with some of his best goals reserved for the Cup competitions. O'Farrell called back for John when attempting to keep Cardiff out of the Third Division, and the winger managed a valuable League hat-trick, a Welsh Cup Final appearance and a European game during his short spell at Ninian Park. Then former City coach Bill Dodgin took him to Northampton, where a 232-game spell as schemer ended his 15-year League career. John also briefly managed AP Leamington.
Apps: 115+3 Lge; 16 FAC; 9+2 LC.
Goals: 18 Lge; 6 FAC; 3 LC.

JOHN FARRINGTON

FEELEY, ANDREW JAMES
b. Hereford, 30.9.1961.
app 1978/
pro Aug 1979:Hereford United/
(Mar 1980-loan-Chelsea)/
cs 1980:Trowbridge/
Jan 1984:CITY/
July 1987:Brentford/June 1989:Bury.
debut: 10.3.84 v.Manchester United (A).

Andy made his Hereford debut while still an apprentice midfielder, and entered the record books at the age of 17 as the youngest-ever captain of a League team. However, a succession of disciplinary and injury problems led to him dropping into the non-league sphere after 51 games, while still in his 'teens. City were the third League club to offer him another chance - partly on the recommendation of former Trowbridge boss Alan Birchenall - and Andy's Old Trafford baptism showed the value of their investment in his tigerish tackling and committed attitude, which soon led to his establishment as a regular at right-back. His uncomplicated spirit and application would have been useful to City's cause in the relegation year of 1987, but injury again sidelined him at a crucial stage, and when he refused new contract terms he was allowed to move on to Griffin Park as a free agent.
Apps: 74+2 Lge; 6 FAC; 4 LC.

RODNEY FERN

FERN, RODNEY ALAN
b. Burton-on-Trent, 13.12.1948.
Measham SW/Dec 1966:CITY/
June 1972:Luton Town/
(Jan 1973-loan-Coventry City)/
July 1975:Chesterfield/
June 1979:Rotherham United.
debut: 3.2.68 v.Leeds United (H).

A popular utility forward who mixed flashes of
creative inspiration with moments of almost
endearing clumsiness, Rodney was given his
first team break by coach Bert Johnson (while
Matt Gillies was on sick leave), and played out
his first season in an unlikely-looking but
effective striking partnership with Frank Large.
It was Rodney's 44th-minute goal, in only his
third game, which prompted City's hoodoo-
breaking FA Cup fightback against Manchester
City in 1968, and indeed it was the Cup which
regularly brought the best out of him. The Sixth
Round winner at Mansfield helped City
towards Wembley in 1969, while his headed
'goal' at Arsenal in 1971 might have opened
the way to another medal for Rodney had it not
been controversially disallowed. He was City's
top scorer in 1969/70, but it was a superb
playmaking performance in the crucial Easter
game at Luton in the next promotion campaign
which probably earned Rodney his later
(£45,000) move to Kenilworth Road. He had a
mixed time there until the goal ratio increased
again at Chesterfield, but it was as a veteran at
Rotherham - using his (now-balding) head to
save his legs, and still striking regularly - that
he enjoyed renewed success; twice embarrassing City in the 1979 League Cup and winning a
Third Division championship medal in 1981.
He retired in 1983, with a career aggregate of
124 League goals, and became a publican.
Apps: 133+19 Lge; 22+1 FAC; 12 LC.
Goals: 32 Lge; 5 FAC; 3 LC.

FINCHAM, GORDON RICHARD
b. Peterborough, 8.1.1935.
Fletton/Nov 1952:CITY/
June 1958:Plymouth Argyle/
July 1963:Luton Town.
debut: 6.4.53 v.Rotherham United (A).

Good judges rated Gordon one of the most
highly-promising centre-halves City had ever
had, but after learning his trade as understudy
to Matt Gillies and claiming a regular first team
spot in 1955/6, he was stricken by serious
injuries, and only managed one subsequent
League appearance for the club, with Tony
Knapp and Ian King vaulting over him in the
queue. Gordon was able, however, to partially
rebuild his career at Plymouth (Third Division
champions in his first season), and played many
games there alongside former Filbert Street
clubmates Dave MacLaren and John Newman.
After leaving Luton, he emigrated to
South Africa.
Apps: 50 Lge; 4 FAC.

FINDLAY, WILLIAM
b. Wishaw, c1900.
d. Braunstone, 11.6.1949.
1922:Musselburgh Bruntonians/
1923:Third Lanark/Aug 1924:Liverpool/
May 1925:CITY/June 1932:Watford.
debut: 19.9.25 v.Newcastle United (A).

A Scottish wing-half who provided valuable
cover for City over seven First Division
seasons, playing in a third of the League games
during that period, Billy doggedly refused to be
overawed at the prospect of substituting for the
likes of internationals Johnny Duncan, John
Bamber or Sid Bishop. A member of
Musselburgh's Scottish Junior Cup-winning
side of1923, he had been unable to make a first-
team breakthrough at Anfield but, on leaving
City, Billy played for five years at Vicarage
Road, and then took over the Watford
manager's chair for just short of a decade. A
qualified physiotherapist, he was manager of
Edgware Town at the time of his death.
Apps: 100 Lge; 4 FAC.

FLANAGAN, WILLIAM
b.
Oct 1896:Burton Wanderers/Aug 1897:FOSSE.
debut: 27.11.97 v.Burton Swifts (A).

An inside-forward who had scored only once in
nine Second Division games at Derby Turn, in
Wanderers' final season in the League, William
got even fewer chances to impress after joining
Fosse, who released him before the season was
out.
Apps: 4 Lge.

FLETCHER, THOMAS
b. Heanor, 15.6.1881.
d. Derby, 29.9.1954.
Hill's Ivanhoe/Derby Nomads/
Apr 1902:FOSSE/Nov 1904:Derby County.
debut: 12.4.02 v.Doncaster Rovers (A) (1 goal).

A well-known amateur forward who first
turned out for Fosse, along with his brother, in
Billy Dorrell's testimonial friendly against the

Corinthians at Christmas 1898, Tommy then
made sporadic senior appearances at either
inside or outside-left over three League seasons
from 1901/2 and, with the Rams, proceeded to
amass a total of 33 League games in all five
forward positions between 1904-06. He also
made one County Championship appearance as
a cricketing all-rounder for Derbyshire CCC.
Apps: 5 Lge.
Goals: 2 Lge.

FLINT, J.
b.
debut (comp): 4.10.90
v.Burton Wanderers (H) FAC.

One of the amateur pioneers of Fosse's
pre-league days, Flint was outside-right in
the club's initial foray into the FA Cup
competition, but made only the odd appearance
in friendly matches following the club's
elevation to the Midland League.
Apps: 1 FAC.

FORD, GARY
b. York, 8.2.1961.
app/pro Feb 1979:York City/June 1987:CITY/
Dec 1987:Port Vale.
debut: 15.8.87 v.Shrewsbury Town (H).

A veteran of 426 senior games for his home-
town club, midfielder Gary was bought by
Bryan Hamilton to play as an out-and-out
winger for City, and knuckled down to the role
with commendable enthusiasm and energy,
despite an early injury setback. An almost
invariable tendency to drift inside with the ball,
though, evidenced his discomfort at being
isolated on the flank, and Gary became the first
player to depart under the David Pleat regime,
to become immediately involved in Vale's
1988 FA Cup giant-killing of Spurs.
Apps: 15+1 Lge; 1+1 LC; 2 FMC.
Goals: 2 Lge; 1 FMC.

FOSTER, JAMES
b.
1899:Northampton Town/May 1900:FOSSE/
cs 1901:Kettering.
debut: 1.9.1900 v.Stockport County (H).

A half-back signed after one Midland League
season in Northampton's colours, and
originally ear-marked to replace Herbert
Dainty, Foster was allowed to move on when
Dainty returned.
Apps: 20 lge; 1 FAC.

FRAME, WILLIAM
b. Carluke, 7.5.1912.
Shawfield Juniors/Oct 1933:CITY/
cs 1950:Rugby Town (p/coach).
debut: 6.10.34 v.Tottenham Hotspur (A).

Signed from Glasgow junior football at the
same time as Johnny Grogan, Billy was,
precisely one year later, pitched into First
Division action at White Hart Lane in Adam
Black's stead, and promptly netted an own
goal. The right-back was however quick to
recover from this potentially unnerving
experience, becoming a regular in time to gain
a medal from City's 1937 promotion campaign,

and going on to give almost 17 years service. Billy played more games in wartime competitions than any other City player (220), and was still an automatic choice when a Christmas injury sadly robbed him of the chance to play a major role in City's 1949 Wembley bid.
Apps: 220 Lge; 19 FAC.

FREEBAIRN, WILLIAM
b.
Partick Thistle/cs 1895:Abercorn/
May 1896:FOSSE.
debut: 5.9.96 v.Darwen (H) (1 goal).

Willie joined Fosse after helping Abercorn to the championship of the Scottish Second Division, and soon made the outside-right spot his own. Discipline was, though, clearly not his strongest suit, as he became the first Fosse player to be sent off in League football - for insulting a linesman at Lincoln - and was later one of six players suspended by the club for unspecified offences in February 1898. He never played for Fosse again, and is believed to have returned to Scotland (possibly with East Stirlingshire). A brother, Archie, also played for Partick and had a long career as a half-back and skipper at Bolton.
Apps: 44 Lge; 4 FAC.
Goals: 14 Lge; 3 FAC.

FREEMAN, -.
b.
cs 1892:FOSSE.
debut: 17.9.92 v.Mansfield Town (A) ML.

Not so much as an initial has turned up in so far futile research on this player, the Fosse inside-left for the early months of the second Midland League season; a fact which would at least seem to indicate he enjoyed professional status.
Apps: 4 FAC; 10 ML.
Goals: 2 FAC; 5 ML.

PAUL FRIAR

FRIAR, JOHN PAUL
b. Govan, 6.6.1963.
Woodhill BC/app 1979/pro June 1980:CITY/
Feb 1983:Rotherham United/
(Nov1983-loan-Motherwell)/
July 1984:Charlton Athletic/
(Mar 1986-loan-Northampton Town)/
cs 1986:Aldershot/Oct 1987:Dover/
Nov 1987:Welling United/Dec 1987:Dartford/
1988:Crawley/1988:Aylesbury United/
1988:Enfield.
debut: 17.1.81 v.Leeds United (H).

A Scottish Youth international who got an early shot at filling City's problematic left-back position, Paul vied for three seasons with Billy Gibson and Norman Leet for selection, and was then displaced by Bobby Smith halfway through the 1983 promotion season, quickly moving on. A competent enough tackler, willing to mix it with heftier opponents, Paul was also a speedy overlapper, but his crossing control often let him down. At the end of his first Millmoor season, Rotherham dropped into Division Three, and Paul was out of favour at Charlton as they rose to Division One, but in 1987 he helped Aldershot up from the Fourth via the play-offs before his surprising release.
Apps: 56+2 Lge; 6 FAC; 2 LC.

FROGGATT, JACK
b.Sheffield, 17.11.1922.
RAF football/Sept 1945:Portsmouth/
Mar 1954:CITY/
Nov 1957:Kettering Town (p/coach; p/mgr).
debut: 6.3.54 v.Bury (H).

Capped by England at both outside-left and centre-half, the masterfully versatile, always ebullient Jack had twice picked up First Division championship medals with Pompey and, after Bert Barlow, was another of the beaten Portsmouth semi-finalists of 1949 to find his way to Filbert Street. He became the final link - a virtual insurance policy against run-in jitters - in the 1954 promotion side, then switched positions and shirts with effective, unruffled ease thereafter until settling as ever-present centre-half and captain for the 1957 Division Two championship season. Utterly dominant in the air, Jack also continued to lean on his attacking experience to become a superb distributor of the ball from the back. He moved to Kettering for £6,000, and was player/manager for successive relegation and promotion teams before reverting to the playing ranks only. He retired in 1962, and took a pub back in Portsmouth. Jack's cousin, Redfern Froggatt of Sheffield Wednesday, was also an England international.
Apps: 143 Lge; 5 FAC.
Goals: 18 Lge.

FULWOOD, BENJAMIN
b.
Long Eaton Rangers/Aug 1898:FOSSE.
debut: 8.10.98 v.Gainsborough Trinity (H).

A young outside-left who contributed to Fosse's near-miss promotion effort of 1898/9, vying for the flank position with Welsh international Alfred Watkins, and occasionally

partnering him. Bennie was later followed from Long Eaton by a younger brother who had unsuccessful trials with Fosse reserves in 1906.
Apps: 11 Lge; 2 FAC.
Goals: 3 Lge; 2 FAC.

FURR, HAROLD
b. Hitchin.
Croydon Common/Brentford/
May 1912:FOSSE.
debut: 28.9.12 v.Huddersfield Town (A).

One of two brothers who moved within weeks of each other from Brentford to Fosse, having previously played for manager Bartlett at Croydon, Harold was a goalkeeper who stood in for Fred Mearns on several occasions, but unhappily found himself picking the ball out of his net 27 times. At Brentford he had under-studied former Fosse 'keeper Archie Ling.
Apps: 8 Lge.

FURR, WILLIAM S.
b. Hitchin.
Croydon Common/Brentford/
July 1912:FOSSE/
(Aug 1913-trial-Luton Town)/1913:not known/
1919:Luton Town.
debut: 28.9.12 v.Huddersfield Town (A).

Outside-right Willie's League baptism came in the same game as brother Harold's, but led to no further chances at Filbert Street (where he'd faced Fosse in the Cup in 1911/12). Even when switched to the left-wing in the reserves, he was unable to get past the ever-present George Harrison during his Fosse season, and then failed to win a contract at Luton. He did, however, make one Southern League appearance for the Hatters in 1919/20.
Apps: 1 Lge.

GALBRAITH, THOMAS D.
b. Vale of Leven.
Vale of Leven/Jan 1898:Sunderland/
Aug 1898:FOSSE.
debut: 3.9.98 v.Lincoln City (H).

Whilst he only contributed briefly to the Sunderland campaign that saw them occupying the Division One runners-up spot in 1898, Tommy became a free-scoring right-winger for the Fosse team that just missed out on promotion in 1899. However, his goal touch deserted him the following season, despite a shift to the inside-right position.
Apps: 62 Lge; 6 FAC.
Goals: 17 Lge; 1 FAC.

GALLACHER, HUGH
b. Maybole.
1890:Preston North End/
Jan 1893:Sheffield United/Aug 1894:FOSSE/
cs 1896:not known/cs 1897:New Brompton.
debut: 8.9.94 v.Rotherham Town (H) (1 goal).

A fine outside-left whose early English career had all been in the top flight, Hugh had joined Preston just as they were losing their 'Invincibles' tag, but helped them to runners-up spot in the League for three successive seasons. He had then moved to Bramall Lane for the

Blades' initial season in Division One, played in the first Sheffield derby at League level, and had become noted for the eccentricity of chewing his way through an ounce of 'twist' tobacco per game - half an ounce per half! With Fosse he regularly patrolled the left flank over the first two seasons in the Second Division, but found his days numbered when Billy Dorrell returned from Aston Villa. At New Brompton he briefly renewed his partnership with fellow ex-Fossil David Skea.
Apps: 47 Lge; 7 FAC.
Goals: 11 Lge; 4 FAC.

GARDINER, ARCHIBALD
b. Glasgow, 17.3.1913.
Burnbank/Penicuik/(trial-Clapton Orient)/
May 1931:Heart of Midlothian/Feb1934:CITY/
Oct 1934:Wrexham.
debut: 21.2.34 v.Portsmouth (A) (4 goals).

The instant impact centre-forward Archie made on his transfer south is unlikely to be bettered in City annals; a four-goal debut in a 5-3 away win, followed two matches later by a home hat-trick! Another two matches later he was in City's first-ever FA Cup semi-final team, yet after three games in the following season, he was allowed to move on. The turn-around in fortunes was remarkable, yet Archie was not entirely new to disappointment, having for some time understudied the Scottish international goalscoring legend Barney Battles at Tynecastle, and dropped back into Hearts reserves, no matter how successful, whenever the senior man returned to the side. With the senior centre-forward at Leicester still Arthur Chandler, it was very much a case of 'as you were'. Perhaps predictably, though, Archie managed to mark his Wrexham home debut with a hat-trick. His father, Harry, was a former Bolton Wanderers centre-half who had represented the Football League in their first (1892) clash with the Scottish League. (There is much unresolved debate among club historians over what happened to Archie after leaving Wrexham; several claims have been advanced that he joined Nottingham Forest in September 1935, moved to Mansfield Town in the 1938 close season and was killed in action in North Africa during the War. Doubts are cast over such claims, however, by alternative identification of the Forest and Mansfield player as Charlie Gardiner, originally signed from junior football in Perth).
Apps: 18 Lge; 1 FAC.
Goals: 11 Lge.

GARDINER, WILLIAM SILCOCK
b. Larbert, 15.8.1929.
1949:Rangers/Aug 1955:CITY/
Nov 1958:Reading.
debut: 5.9.55 v.Doncaster Rovers (A) (1 goal).

Another prolific scorer who spent much of his early career in Scottish reserve football (nonetheless claiming one Scotland 'B' cap), Willie moved for £4,000 from Ibrox - as David Halliday's first purchase - to play alongside Arthur Rowley, and even managed the unlikely feat of outgunning his new partner in his first year, averaging better than a goal a game. The tall, fair-haired centre-forward lost his place to

Derek Hines in the 1957 promotion campaign, but returned to help City survive their first fraught season back in Division One. Unfortunately, a succession of leg injuries, culminating in a bad break, marred Willie's two-year stay at Elm Park.
Apps: 69 Lge; 2 FAC.
Goals: 48 Lge; 1 FAC.

CHRIS GARLAND

GARLAND, CHRISTOPHER STEPHEN
b. Bristol, 24.4.1949.
pro May 1966:Bristol City/Aug 1971:Chelsea/
Mar 1975:CITY/Nov 1976:Bristol City.
debut: 15.3.75 v.Coventry City (A).

A teenage local hero at Ashton Gate, blond striker Chris had won one England Under-23 cap when Chelsea laid out a six-figure fee for him, and he appeared for the Blues in their 1972 League Cup Final defeat. His move to City had an inspirational effect on a struggling side, and his eight goals in ten games at the end of 1974/5 did much to avert the very real threat of relegation. Sent off in the opening game of the following season, Chris bounced back in a hard-working support role to Frank Worthington, and had only just lost his first team place in Jimmy Bloomfield's last campaign when Bristol City's offer to take him home and refund City's outlay was accepted. Injuries dogged his second spell there, and indeed his contract was twice cancelled, but Chris refused to lie down, and was still turning out on a non-contract basis in 1982/3, to take his Bristol City appearance record over the 200 mark, and his career aggregate League and Cup scoring record to 101 goals.
Apps: 52+3 Lge; 3 FAC; 5 LC.
Goals: 15 Lge; 3 FAC; 1 LC.

GARRATY, WILLIAM
b. Saltley, 6.10.1878.
d. Birmingham, 6.5.1931.
Highfield Villa/Aston Shakespeare/
cs 1897:Aston Villa/Sept 1908:FOSSE/
Oct 1908:West Bromwich Albion/
Dec 1910:Lincoln City.
debut: 12.9.08 v.Bristol City (H).

A veteran goalscoring centre-forward who had been capped for England in 1903, and won both

League championship and FA Cup medals from his 256 game, 111 goal career with Villa, Billy stayed with Fosse only a matter of some seven weeks when signed to augment their First Division forces. He was hardly over the hill - as his twenty goals for West Brom over the next two years evidenced - and the wisdom of Fosse letting him go (at £270, representing £20 profit) had to be questioned in view of their subsequent nosedive to relegation. They had lost only once with Billy in the side, despite his own inability to get off the scoring mark. Back in the early days of his senior career, Billy took part in the notorious ten and a half minute match between Sheffield Wednesday and Villa - the Football League had demanded that a game abandoned in November 1898 had to be completed almost four months later, and Billy, who wasn't in the side for the first 79 minutes and 30 seconds, had made his breakthrough in the interim!
Apps: 6 Lge.

GARVEY, JAMES
b. Paisley, 4.6.1919.
cs 1939:Northampton Town/
June 1946:CITY.
debut: 24.5.47 v.Burnley (H).

Having played in one League game for the Cobblers in the abandoned 1939/40 season - an appearance then expunged from official records - Jim had little more luck after becoming a postwar City signing. The Scottish left-half or inside-left was valued for his constructive approach work, but niggling knee injuries held him back whenever he looked about to make a sustained first team breakthrough. His final senior outing was in the crucial last game of 1948/9 at Cardiff, when the point gained kept City out of Division Three.
Apps: 15 Lge; 1 FAC.

GIBSON, DAVID WEDDERBURN
b. Winchburgh, 23.9.1938.
Livingston United/1955:Hibernian/
Jan 1962:CITY/
Sept 1970:Aston Villa/
Jan 1972:Exeter City.
debut: 3.2.62 v.Fulham (H).

One of the very finest ball-playing footballers to have graced Filbert Street since the war, Davie had still to complete his National Service when Matt Gillies paid Hibs £25,000 for his signature, but as soon as he turned full-time to City's cause, he forged an unforgettable early partnership with Mike Stringfellow on the left wing. His elegant control and visionary passing skills were a major factor behind City's Wembley visits in 1963 and 1969, and Davie found the net himself with pleasing regularity, scoring in both legs of the 1964 League Cup final against Stoke, and knocking in three goals in his seven full Scottish international appearances. His artistry was barely on the wane when he left to give a veteran's course in midfield style at Villa and Exeter, and while with the former club he returned to Wembley as substitute for the 1971 League Cup Final.
Apps: 274+6 Lge; 29 FAC; 30 LC.
Goals: 41 Lge; 5 FAC; 7 LC.

DAVID GIBSON

GIBSON, GEORGE
b. Biddulph.
Frickley Colliery/Apr 1932:Sunderland/
Nov 1934:CITY/(Jan 1936-loan-Distillery)/
June 1937:Workington.
debut: 10.11.34 v.Stoke City (H).

Brought down from Roker when City were
searching for both short and long-term
replacements for Arthur Chandler in 1934/5,
George held a briefer purchase than most on the
old goalgetter's centre-forward shirt, only
playing in two heavy defeats within ten days of
his transfer. A bustler of the old brylcreem-and-
centre-parting style, he had indeed only played
twice previously at senior level for Sunderland,
and eventually returned to North Eastern
League football.
Apps: 2 Lge.

GIBSON, Dr.THOMAS
b. Denistoun, Glasgow.
May 1926:CITY.
debut: 12.3.28 v.West Ham United (A).

The last of the old-school amateur players to
turn out for City in League football, 'Doctor
Tom' was an inside-forward who occasionally
filled in for Ernie Hine or Arthur Lochhead -
though his limited career consisted entirely of
away matches, and he was never on a winning
City side at senior level.
Apps: 4 Lge.
Goals: 1 Lge.

GIBSON, WILLIAM
b. Lanark, 24.6.1959.
Easthouses BC/Mar 1979:CITY/
Oct 1982:Nuneaton Borough/
cs 1987:Weymouth.
debut: 16.8.80 v.Ipswich Town (H).

Left-back Billy impressed Jock Wallace on a
1980 close-season tour of Germany and
Holland, and surprisingly found himself pitched
into City's opening game on their First Division
return, holding his place as an enthusiastic

harrier for half of that season of struggle
against the drop. He lost out, though, in the
three-cornered fight with fellow youngsters
Paul Friar and Norman Leet early in the next
campaign, and was soon to drop out of League
football.
Apps: 28 Lge; 1 FAC; 3 LC.

GILL, ERNEST HARRY
b. Mountsorrel, 1877.
d. Hull, 1950.
Freemantle/Poole Town/1899:Southampton/
May 1901:FOSSE.
debut: 26.10.01 v.Gainsborough Trinity (A).

Best known as a professional right-arm fast-
medium bowler with Leicestershire CCC (for
whom he played a handful of first-class
matches in the summer of 1901, and for whom
his brother George also featured), Ernest had
previously played football for several years in
the Hampshire League, and turned out in one
Southern League match for Southampton. For
Fosse he impressed in a couple of friendlies,
and replaced George Swift at left-back in the
above match, only to have his career abruptly
terminated a month later by a serious leg-break
suffered in an acrimonious reserve-team
'friendly' at Ilkeston.
Apps: 1 Lge.

GILLIES, ALEXANDER
b.
Lochgelly United/Oct 1895:Bolton Wanderers/
Feb 1896:Manchester City/
Aug 1896:Heart of Midlothian/
Feb 1897:Sheffield Wednesday/
Aug 1897:FOSSE.
debut: 18.9.97 v.Grimsby Town (A).

A Scottish forward well and truly bitten by the
wandering bug, Alec briefly deposed Johnny
McMillan at Leicester, largely on his record of
scoring at least once in each of his six friendly
games. Yet, ironically, he contrived to extend
throughout his stay with Fosse an unenviable
record of failing to notch a single goal for any
of his Football League clubs in that competition. He was one of several players whose
services were dispensed with in February 1898.
Apps: 4 Lge.

GILLIES, MATTHEW MUIRHEAD
b. Loganlea, 12.8.1921.
1942:Bolton Wanderers/Jan 1952:CITY.
debut: 26.1.52 v.Doncaster Rovers (H).

A medical student who signed for Bolton while
on RAF service during the war and later
became their skipper, Matt had been on
Motherwell's books as an amateur, and had
guested for Arsenal, QPR and Chelsea. He
joined City for £9,500 to bolster the central
defensive position, and was the regular pivot,
thoughtful but solid, in the 1954 Second
Division championship season. Despite his on-
field influence as a steadying senior pro,
however, it was beyond the playing arena that
Matt was really to make his mark on City
history. Becoming coach in April 1956, he
assumed the role of acting manager in
November 1958 (on David Halliday's

resignation), and was entrusted with the full
managerial reins in January 1959. Directing
City's generally upbeat fortunes for almost a
decade, Matt twice led his team out at
Wembley, twice took them to the League Cup
final, and thoroughly earned for himself a
reputation as both a shrewd market operator
and a good judge of character. He became a
local Justice of the Peace while still in office at
Filbert Street, though his primary commitment
to his club's continuing honours chase even led
to him suffering a lengthy spell of stress-related
ill-health towards the end of his regime, making
something of a nonsense of the occasionally
voiced criticism that he was 'too gentlemanly'
for the purported rat-race of modern football.
Matt was nonetheless quick to pass the lion's
share of credit for City's tactical innovations of
the 60s to his coach Bert Johnson, and it was
little surprise to anyone when he immediately
resigned in the wake of Johnson's sacking.
What did surprise many was that he then took
another managerial post, at Nottingham Forest;
but even an apparent 'defection' to City's local
rivals failed to diminish Matt's standing for
those who recognised his crucial contribution to
the process of turning a club with a long-
standing 'yoyo' reputation into one with a
sustained 'First Division' image.
Apps: 103 Lge; 8 FAC.

GLOVER, LEONARD
b. Kennington, 31.1.1944.
May 1962:Charlton Athletic/Nov 1967:CITY/
May 1976:Tampa Bay Rowdies/
Oct 1976:Kettering Town/
Apr 1977:Tampa Bay Rowdies/
Sept 1977:Kettering Town.
debut: 18.11.67 v.Arsenal (H).

A series of niggling injuries spoiled both the
beginning and end of Lenny's City career, but
in the interim seasons his left-wing skills and
pace bemused many an opposing full-back, and
it was a genuine tribute to both his ability and
personality that he became a firm favourite of
the usually highly critical Popular Side
supporters, whose anticipatory roar whenever
Lenny received the ball must equally have
unnerved many an adversary. He had first faced
City as a Charlton teenager in the League Cup,
and the £80,000 fee Matt Gillies paid for him
five years later represented at the time an
English record for a winger. Lenny's goals saw
City through the first two rounds of their 1969
Cup run to Wembley, though his fitness to play
in the Final was always in doubt, and two years
later he regularly ripped Second Division
defences apart as City sped to promotion. Back
in the top flight he laid on many of Frank
Worthington's goals, and when City's
entertaining 'nearly' team reached the Cup
semi-finals in 1974, Lenny claimed the
consolation goal in the replay against Liverpool. After returning from America, he was
involved in one last FA Cup campaign, with the
oddest of results. Having played for Kettering
in a First Round victory over Tilbury in
November 1977, Lenny had his eligibility
officially queried by the losers - and Kettering
eventually went out of the Cup after a replay
had been ordered by the FA! Subsequently

retiring to the role of publican, Lenny still managed to amaze the crowd at Tommy Williams' 1986 Testimonial game with a display of wing-play arts only rarely glimpsed at Filbert Street since his departure.
Apps: 245+7 Lge; 35+1 FAC; 17 LC.
Goals: 38 Lge; 8 FAC; 2 LC.

ALBERT GODDERIDGE

GODDERIDGE, ALBERT EDWARD
b. Tamworth, 1903.
Two Gates/May 1922:CITY/
June 1927:Barnsley.
debut: 29.3.24 v.Fulham (H).

Wresting the first team goalkeeper's jersey from George Hebden, Albert became the sturdy last line of defence in City's successful 1925 promotion push, but found himself back in the reserves after the squad charged with establishing the club in the top flight had been augmented by the arrival of the vastly experienced Kenny Campbell. Then, at Oakwell, he again had to knuckle down to being regarded primarily as an understudy, this time to the consistent Tommy Gale.
Apps: 50 Lge; 6 FAC.

GODWIN, THOMAS FERGUS
b. Dublin, 20.8.1927.
Home Farm/Shamrock Rovers/
Sept 1949:CITY/
June 1952:Bournemouth & Boscombe Athletic/
June 1963:Dorchester Town.
debut: 26.11.49 v.Swansea Town (H).

Signed only days after starring for the Republic of Ireland in a shock 2-0 win over England at Goodison Park, Tommy was another of City's international goalkeepers to fit the traditional mould of unspectacular soundness. A master of the high ball, and no mean shot-stopper, he was nonetheless no stranger to misfortune: a broken leg in an FAI Cup semi-final with Shamrock had cost him both a Final place and more early representative honours, while during his City sojourn his place was constantly under pressure from prospective Scottish international Johnny Anderson. Indeed, City's confidence in the younger 'keeper contributed to Tommy's early departure. He had won four Eire caps while at

Filbert Street, and added another four (to take his total to 13) after settling at Dean Court, where he built a total of 357 League appearances over ten seasons.
Apps: 45 Lge; 1 FAC.

GOLDIE, WILLIAM
b. Hurlford, 1878.
Hurlford Thistle/Mar 1898:Liverpool/
Dec 1903:Fulham/Aug 1908:FOSSE.
debut: 1.9.08 v.Sheffield Wednesday (H).

A dour, tough-tackling left-half with a slide-rule pass, Billy followed his elder brother Archie (a former Clyde full-back) to Anfield and there, in the middle of one spell of 119 consecutive appearances, became an ever-present in Liverpool's first Championship-winning side of 1901. He helped lift Fulham from the Southern League to the Second Division, and then joined Fosse for their First Division debut, staying three seasons. On leaving he ran a pub, but still turned out occasionally for Leicester Imperial, though how East Midlands patrons coped with his notoriously near-impenetrable Scottish accent is unrecorded: an FA disciplinary committee had once,when dealing with Billy, felt the need to employ an interpreter!
Apps: 82 Lge; 6 FAC.
Goals: 1 Lge.

JIMMY GOODFELLOW

GOODFELLOW, JAMES BOYD
b. Edinburgh, 30.7.1938.
Third Lanark/May 1963:CITY/
Mar 1968:Mansfield Town/
cs1971:Weymouth/Nuneaton Borough/
AP Leamington.
debut: 7.9.63 v.Stoke City (A).

A nippy, neatly-balanced 'cruiserweight' striker picked up on a free transfer from Thirds when economy measures dictated that the ill-fated Glasgow club divest itself of a superbly skilful forward-line, Jimmy gave excellent inside-forward support to City's mid-60's front line, and notched several useful goals - including one in the first leg of the 1965 League Cup

Final, and an 18-yard header in one match against Forest. He entered the record book indelibly, however, with his 35th League appearance for City - as the club's first-ever official No.12, on the opening day that the rules allowed substitutes for injured players. At Field Mill, Jimmy renewed an effective partnership with Nick Sharkey that had first been forged in City's Combination side, and was a stylish prompter of Mansfield's 1969 Cup run which City ended in the Sixth Round. His only senior representative honour was selection for the Scottish League against Scotland in February 1962, when Frank McLintock was amongst the opposition.
Apps: 96+2 Lge; 9 FAC; 14 LC.
Goals: 26 Lge; 3 FAC; 7 LC.

GOODWIN, MARK ADRIAN
b. Sheffield, 23.2.1960.
app July 1976/pro Oct 1977:CITY/
Mar 1981:Notts County/July 1987:Walsall.
debut: 17.12.77 v.Ipswich Town (A).

Given a first-team break by Frank McLintock only months after turning professional, blond midfielder Mark pumped some genuine enthusiasm into a City side almost resigned to its relegation fate, and gave a remarkable display of unrestrained joy on opening his goal account at Old Trafford. Occasionally looking a little overwhelmed by the physical rigours of Second Division struggle, Mark was often used on the sub's bench by Jock Wallace, but his spells of service as ball-winner, distributor and even full-back made him a suitably versatile understudy for almost any eventuality. He moved to Meadow Lane as the last link in County's promotion-winning side of 1981, alongside Trevor Christie, and passed the 200 mark in League appearances for the Magpies early in 1986/7, before once more rejoining Christie at Fellows Park for successive promotion and relegation campaigns.
Apps: 69+22 Lge; 4+1 FAC; 3 LC.
Goals: 8 Lge.

GORDON, ROBERT
b.
July 1893:Heart of Midlothian/
May 1894:Aston Villa/Oct 1894:FOSSE/
June 1895:Woolwich Arsenal/
cs 1896:Reading.
debut: 3.11.94 v.Kimberley (H) FAC (2 goals).

A well-built bustler of a centre-forward, but none too speedy - the 'Daily Post' rather harshly described him as 'cumbrous' - Bob was the fifth attack leader tried by Fosse within the first two months of their initial League season. He'd already notched two goals in four League appearances for Villa that season (plus one in their game against the Football League, played as a benefit for League founder William McGregor), and forged a prolific inside trio partnership with David Skea and Billy McArthur for Fosse before taking his shooting boots to Plumstead. In February 1897, Bob represented the Southern League against the London FA, scoring twice.
Apps: 21 Lge; 4 FAC.
Goals: 12 Lge; 2 FAC.

GORMAN, JAMES
b. Middlesbrough, 1882.
South Bank/Darlington St.Augustine's/
Darlington/Mar 1906:Liverpool/
May 1908:FOSSE.
debut: 3.10.08 v.Manchester City (A).

A highly-rated centre-half whose Anfield role
was to understudy Scottish international Alec
Raisbeck, James suffered appalling fortune
with Fosse - being so badly injured on his debut
that he was unable to return until the club's
relegation fate was already settled. To rub salt
into the wound, the second match of his
comeback, and his final Fosse appearance, was
the ignominious 0-12 defeat by Forest.
Apps: 3 Lge.

GOUDIE, A. PETER
b. Derby.
Derby Nomads/Jan 1899:FOSSE/
cs 1899:Derby Nomads.
debut: 14.1.99 v.Luton Town (A).

An amateur goalkeeper - in fact a reporter on a
Derby newspaper by profession - who stood in
for Godfrey Beardsley in the above match, after
having faced the Corinthians in a friendly three
weeks previously. There can't have been many
players who've made their senior bow in a 6-1
away win and never been picked again, but
Peter was one.
Apps: 1 Lge.

GOULD, WILLIAM
b. Burton-on-Trent.
Mar 1904:Burton United/June 1905:FOSSE/
May 1906:Bristol Rovers/May 1907:Glossop/
Sept 1908:Bradford City/
May 1909:Manchester City.
debut: 16.9.05 v.Leeds City (H).

Top scorer at Peel Croft in 1904/5, Willie had
to vie at Leicester for his favoured inside-left
spot with fellow Fosse newcomer Harry
Moody, and was soon sidelined when he failed
to deliver in the finishing stakes. He became an
ever-present on the left-wing at Eastville, and
remained a useful flank player for his subsequent League clubs.
Apps: 6 Lge.
Goals: 1 Lge.

GRAHAM, HARRY
b. Edinburgh, 16.12.1887.
Granton Oakvale/Nov 1908:St.Bernards/
Apr 1910:Bradford City/Oct 1911:Birmingham/
Sept 1912:Raith Rovers/
cs 1913:Heart of Midlothian/Dec 1920:CITY/
Nov 1924:St.Bernards/cs 1925:Reading.
debut: 25.12.20 v.Stoke (H).

After relatively uneventful spells south of the
border, Harry earned both a runners-up medal
and a move to Hearts from Raith's Scottish Cup
Final appearance in 1913, and starred for the
Edinburgh club on both sides of WW1, being
chosen for the Scottish League in October
1914. A qualified dentist, he was exempt from
military call-up, but volunteered and fought
with the Gloucestershire Regiment before
returning to football action, latterly alongside

Arthur Lochhead at Tynecastle. A creative
inside-forward, Harry prompted Jock Paterson
to a hat-trick in his City debut match, and held
his place in an otherwise regularly changing
front-line until the arrival of George Carr. It
was slightly ironic that he should eventually
return to the Edinburgh-based Scottish League
club St.Bernards, who had attempted to block
his move from Birmingham to Raith by
petitioning the authorities that they still had a
claim on Harry's Scottish registration, and were
due a fee.
Apps: 110 Lge; 6 FAC.
Goals: 14 Lge; 2 FAC.

GRANT, ALEXANDER FRANK
b. Camerton, 11.8.1916.
am:Doncaster Rovers/am:Sheffield United/
Aug 1937:Bury/May 1938:Aldershot/
Dec 1941:CITY/Nov 1946:Derby County/
Nov 1948:Newport County/
Aug 1949:Leeds United/Mar 1950:York City.
debut (postwar): 31.8.46
v.Manchester City (H).

A dependable reserve 'keeper for most of his
clubs, Alick was probably at his peak during
the war years, when he guested for Derby,
Nottingham Forest and Mansfield as well as
turning out regularly (97 apps) for City. Indeed,
his trio of guest appearances for Derby included
both legs of the 1944/5 Midland Cup Final
against Villa. Alick unfortunately had to pick
the ball out of the net seven times in City's first
two postwar League games, and soon moved
'officially' to the Baseball Ground, where a
unique contract for 1947/8 gave him a 'wage'
of threepence per week while he took schoolteaching exams he'd missed during the war!
Apps: 2 Lge.

GRAVER, ANDREW MARTIN
b. Craghead, 12.9.1927.
Willington Athletic/Annfield Plain/
Sept 1947:Newcastle United/
Sept 1950:Lincoln City/Dec 1954:CITY/
July 1955:Lincoln City/Nov 1955:Stoke City/
cs 1957:Boston United/Oct 1958:Lincoln City/
July 1961:Skegness Town.
debut: 18.12.54 v.Chelsea (A) (1 goal).

Given only one League chance on Tyneside,
centre-forward Andy soon made up for lost
time at Sincil Bank, knocking in 107 goals in
172 games during his first spell there, including
six in one game against Crewe as Lincoln raced
to the 1952 championship of Division Three
(North). City paid a club record fee in the hope
that Andy's goal touch would keep them in
Division One, but despite scoring in each of his
first two games, he failed to spark alongside
Arthur Rowley, and returned to Lincoln during
the close season, after Derek Hines had
reclaimed the City No.9 shirt. Press rumours of
the time intimated that City had lost heavily on
the deals, but in fact Andy's moves both
constituted club records (in the same way that
Allan Clarke's would later).He arrived for
£27,000 plus Eric Littler (valued at £600), and
departed for £26,000. By the time Andy had
finished his third spell with the Imps, he had
created (and still holds) that club's aggregate

scoring record of 144 League goals. His father,
Fred, had played as a forward for Grimsby,
Leeds and Southend in the 20s.
Apps: 11 Lge; 1 FAC.
Goals: 3 Lge.

GREATOREX, GEORGE ARTHUR
b. Huthwaite, 1900.
Sutton Junction/May 1921:CITY/
cs 1922:Mansfield Town.
debut: 27.8.21 v.Bradford Park Avenue (A).

An inside-right who had impressed City while
playing Central Alliance football against the
reserves, and started the 1921/2 season in
support of Jock Paterson, George scored on his
first two home appearances. Only 5ft. 5ins tall,
yet sturdily-built, he was quickly dubbed
'Baby' by the Leicester crowd, but soon faded
from the picture as Peter Hodge sought a promotion-winning combination. His move to
Mansfield took him back into the Central
Alliance, which was then the Stags' station.
Apps: 11 Lge.
Goals: 2 Lge.

GREENHALGH, BRIAN ARTHUR
b. Chesterfield, 20.2.1947.
app/pro Feb 1965:Preston North End/
Sept 1967:Aston Villa/Feb 1969:CITY/
June 1969:Huddersfield Town/
July 1971:Cambridge United/
Feb 1974:Bournemouth/
(Aug 1974-loan-Torquay United)/
Mar 1975:Watford/cs 1976:Dartford/
Staines Town/Carshalton Athletic (p/mgr).
debut: 1.4.69 (sub) v.Coventry City (A).

A youthful striking partner for Brian Godfrey at
both Deepdale and Villa Park, Brian was
brought to Filbert Street by Frank O'Farrell, but
barely given a chance to contribute to City's
1969 relegation struggle. He was involved in a
crucial denied penalty incident on his first
substitute appearance in the tense game at
Highfield Road, and was never, in fact, on a
winning City side. Brian played fifteen times
alongside Frank Worthington as Huddersfield
rose to the First Division, then rediscovered his
long-dormant scoring touch at Cambridge, and
commenced a series of southern travels, which
also took in coaching spells with Maidenhead
United and Chesham United.
Apps: 2+2 Lge.

GREW, MARK STUART
b. Bilston, 15.2.1958.
app 1975/pro June 1976:West Bromwich
Albion/(Dec 1978-loan-Wigan Athletic)/
(Mar 1979-loan-Notts County)/
July 1983:CITY/
(Oct 1983-loan-Oldham Athletic)/
Mar 1984:Ipswich Town/
(Sept 1985-loan-Fulham)/
(Jan 1986-loan-West Bromwich Albion)/
(Mar 1986-loan-Derby County)/
June 1986:Port Vale.
debut: 27.8.83 v.Notts County (H).

When City laid out £60,000 for goalkeeper
Mark while Mark Wallington was in contractual dispute, the newcomer had just completed
eight years at the Hawthorns, during which he

had patiently understudied Tony Godden for all but 33 League games. Mark's West Brom debut had, in fact, been a real oddity, coming on as substitute keeper in a 1978/9 UEFA Cup tie against Galatasaray. At Filbert Street, he had an unnerving introduction, being beaten by a succession of long-range power shots as City struggled to find their First Division feet, and gave way to Wallington after five straight defeats. Mark fared little better at Portman Road in the shadow of Paul Cooper, but seemed set fair to establish some sort of record for the number of loan deals he had been involved in. He suffered a serious knee injury early in his Port Vale spell, but returned to perform heroically in their 1988 Cup run and 1989 promotion campaign.
Apps: 5 Lge.

GREWCOCK, NEIL
b. Leicester, 26.4.1962.
app June 1978/pro June 1979:CITY/
Mar 1982:Gillingham/
June 1983:Shepshed Charterhouse/
Aug 1984:Burnley.
debut: 3.3.79 v.Cardiff City (H) (1 goal).

Still a sixteen-year-old apprentice when Jock Wallace gave him a goal-crowned League baptism, Neil had to bide his time for another crack at senior action, having one short spell on either wing near the beginning and end of the 1980/1 First Division campaign. Short but stocky, Neil didn't quite develop the pace necessary to maintain a flank position, and drifted into a midfield role for Gillingham. He then returned to Leicestershire with his League career apparently at an end, but was offered a lifeline back at Turf Moor by John Bond, which he grasped eagerly. His performances were a rare bright element of Burnley's near-disastrous 1987 cliff-hanger, and his goal in the final Fourth Division game of that season helped ward off the prospect of the old club dropping out of the League.
Apps: 7+1 Lge; 0+1 LC.
Goals: 1 Lge.

GRIEVE, ROBERT
b. Greenock, 28.3.1884.
Morton/Aug 1906:Manchester City/
Nov 1909:Accrington Stanley/
Dec 1910:FOSSE/cs 1911:Southport Central.
debut: 7.1.11
v.Wolverhampton Wanderers (H) (2 goals).

A Scottish centre-forward whose 44 League games for Manchester City produced 18 goals, Robert had regained amateur status by the time he was snapped up from Lancashire Combination football by Fosse to replace the departed Jack Hall. He had the ill-fortune, however, to arrive at Filbert Street less than a month before Fred Shinton returned from Bolton, and his first team tenure was accordingly short. It was marked by one oddity, though, which points to the idiosyncracy of then-prevailing registration rules: only a week after his Fosse debut, he played for Accrington in their First Round FA Cup tie against Wolves! (There is an unconfirmed suspicion that Robert was the Scottish junior cap who moved from Duntocher Hibs to

Belfast Distillery in the 1904 close season).
Apps: 4 Lge.
Goals: 2 Lge.

GRIFFITHS, MALWYN WILLIAM
b. Merthyr Tydfil, 8.3.1919.
Merthyr Thursday/May 1936:Arsenal/
(1937-loan-Margate)/Sept 1938:CITY/
cs 1956:Burton Albion.
debut: 24.9.38 v.Bolton Wanderers (H).

Plucked from Welsh junior football by Arsenal, and then loaned out to their own 'nursery' club for experience, right winger Mal made his senior Highbury bow against City in February 1938, and contributed five goals in nine appearances as the Gunners raced to the First Division title that year. Rivalries for first team shirts at Arsenal were fierce, however, and only a bargain £750 transfer to City opened the door to a regular position - one Mal was still holding some 18 years later. He 'lost' one League appearance and one goal when the 1939/40 season was abandoned after only three fixtures, and City somehow contrived to lose touch with Mal himself during the war, at the end of which a director had to be despatched to Wales to persuade him to resume his career. Thereafter, Mal's consistency made him the one automatic choice in an ever-changing City front line, and his steady goalscoring record peaked at two crucial times: when he added to his six strikes on City's 1949 Cup run the club's first-ever goal at Wembley, and when he notched his own best seasonal League total of eleven during the 1954 Division Two championship effort. City played an invited International XI at the end of their next promotion campaign in a testimonial match for Mal, who had represented his own country eleven times (scoring twice) between 1947 and 1954.
Apps: 373 Lge; 36 FAC.
Goals: 66 Lge; 10 FAC.

GROGAN, JOHN
b. Paisley, 30.10.1915.
Shawfield Juniors/Oct 1933:CITY/
Sept 1947:Mansfield Town.
debut: 19.10.35 v.Newcastle United (A).

Another player who was robbed of his best footballing years by the war, Johnny was Sep Smith's understudy at right-half during the four League seasons before the break, and then had to vie with the same player for the centre-half shirt when League competition resumed. As a trusty reserve, he made several appearances for the London Combination representative XI (which then had regular fixtures against the likes of the Central League); while as a wartime guest he also turned out for Northampton Town and Grimsby Town. It was suspected that Johnny was nearing retirement when City let him move to Field Mill, but he kept going there for another five years, scoring his sole League goal in one of 202 appearances for the Stags.
Apps: 46 Lge; 6 FAC.

GROSVENOR, PERCY
b. Evesham, 17.3.1911.
Evesham Town/Feb 1933:CITY.
debut: 30.12.33 v.Aston Villa (H).

A left-half from a footballing family - his father had been on Wolves' books, two brothers (of whom Tom was an England cap) played League soccer during the 30s, and another was briefly on City's roster as a junior - Percy had been passed over by West Brom after trials when City took him on as a likely understudy to George Ritchie. He had played thirteen League and Cup games during his first season before appearing in a beaten side - that being in the club's first FA Cup semi-final in 1934 - and went on to inherit Ritchie's shirt as a regular from 1935/6 to the outbreak of war, showing both fight and finesse in City's up-and-down travails of the time.
Apps: 168 Lge; 12 FAC.
Goals: 1 Lge.

PERCY GROSVENOR

GROVES, PAUL
b. Derby, 28.2.1966.
Belper Town/Nov 1986:Burton Albion/
Apr 1988:CITY.
debut: 2.5.88 (sub)
v.Huddersfield Town (H) (1 goal).

A former part-timer with Burton, whom he helped to the Wembley Final of the FA Trophy in 1987 (also scoring their consolation goal in a replay defeat), Paul was offered the chance to drop his bricklaying day-job when signed by David Pleat after the 1988 transfer deadline. The strongly-built attacking midfielder cost £12,000 and the promise of a visit from City to play a friendly under Burton's new floodlights, while Pleat received Football League sanction to name him amongst the thirteen players for the season's penultimate game, against an already-relegated Huddersfield. Paul's fine header made him the first City substitute to score on his debut, and another headed goal, in the Littlewoods Cup replay at Nottingham Forest, proved the high point of his first full season as a City squad player. He turned down a mooted move to Peterborough in March 1989.
Apps (to 13.5.89): 7+9 Lge;
0+1 FAC; 1 LC; 0+1 FMC.
Goals: 1 Lge; 1 LC.

GURRY, JOHN WILLIAM

b. Barking, 17.7.1907.
d. Leicester, 1.10.1983.
am:West Ham United/Barking/
Mar 1930:CITY/July 1935:Southampton/
cs 1936:Chester.
debut: 12.11.32 v.Leeds United (A).

Brought out of the Athenian League by City
(after his job in the hosiery trade had led him to
Leicester), Jack was utilised as a reserve right-
half or inside-forward, but suffered like several
players of his era from an inability to dislodge
the consistent Sep Smith. He fared little better
at either of his subsequent League clubs, but
did end his career with three goals to his credit
- all scored for Chester against Lincoln City in
a 7-3 win in November 1936!
Apps: 23 Lge.

GWYNNE, ERNEST

b.
Aug 1903:FOSSE.
debut: 26.10.03 v.Woolwich Arsenal (A).

A centre-forward from junior football in the
Birmingham area, Ernest could have asked for
better luck in making his one and only League
appearance for Fosse - the above match ended
in a 0-8 defeat.
Apps: 1 Lge.

HACKETT, A.

b.
Sept 1901:FOSSE/Leicester Imperial.
debut: 6.1.02 v.West Bromwich Albion (A).

An inside-left who played in the last two trial
matches of August 1901 and impressed
sufficiently to earn a professional contract, he
nonetheless failed to spark his senior forward
colleagues into an effective scoring response in
two away defeats during 1901/2.
Apps: 2 Lge.

HADLEY, ARTHUR

b. 1877.
cs 1895:Reading/cs 1898:Notts County/
Aug 1902:FOSSE/Dec 1906:Notts County.
debut: 6.9.02 v.Small Heath (H).

A goalscoring outside-right in both the
Southern and Football Leagues, Arthur was a
member of the first Reading side to play at Elm
Park, and the second Magpies team to reach
third place in the First Division (their highest
position ever). His goal supply, however, rather
dried up as Fosse slithered towards the Second
Division basement, even if Arthur was a
popularly regarded provider. He was a loyal
one, too, for he came back in April 1905 briefly
to help out the club which had released him in
the 1904 close season.
Apps: 64 Lge; 7 FAC.
Goals: 4 Lge; 3 FAC.

HAIG, PAUL

b. Nottingham.
Mapperley/cs 1907:Eastwood Rangers/
Feb 1911:FOSSE/
cs 1911:Mansfield Mechanics/cs
1912:Eastwood Rangers/

Aug 1913:Notts County.
debut: 25.2.11 v.Huddersfield Town (H).

An outside-left who briefly stepped up from
Notts & Derbyshire League football at a fee of
£25, and quickly dropped down again to the
Central Alliance, Paul later made one League
appearance for the Magpies.
Apps: 12 Lge.
Goals: 2 Lge.

HAINES, JOHN T.W.

b. Wickhamford, 24.4.1920.
d. Evesham, 19.3.1987.
Evesham Town/Cheltenham Town/
(1938-trials-Liverpool)/
June 1939:Swansea Town/
July 1947:CITY/
Mar 1948:West Bromwich Albion/
Dec 1949:Bradford Park Avenue/
Oct 1953:Rochdale/July 1955:Chester/
cs 1957:Wellington Town/
cs 1958:Kidderminster Harriers/
Oct 1958:Evesham Town.
debut: 23.8.47 v.Leeds United (A).

His early career stymied by the outbreak of
war, Jack made his long-delayed League debut
with Swansea in 1946/7, and impressed Johnny
Duncan as a forceful linkman. The City
manager seemed unsure of how best to utilise
Jack at Filbert Street, however - handing him
shirts numbered 4, 6, 8, 9 and 10 in his limited
spell with City, before swapping him for Peter
McKennan. Jack was used exclusively in the
forward line at the Hawthorns, and soon won an
England cap, scoring twice against Switzerland.
Albion were promoted back to the top flight in
1949, but Jack was tasting more bitter fortunes
the next season, as Bradford dropped from the
Second to the Third Division (North). Harry
Catterick paid a club record of £2,000 to take
Jack to Rochdale as he continued to play out his
career in the League's lower echelons.
Apps: 12 Lge; 3 FAC.
Goals: 3 Lge; 1 FAC.

HALES, A.

b.
Aug 1902:FOSSE.
debut: 27.9.02 v.Burnley (H).

An outside-left, this Fossil is another whose
sole senior game represents a flicker in a
surrounding obscurity that research has failed
to penetrate.
Apps: 1 Lge.

HALL, BENJAMIN

b. Ecclesfield, 6.3.1879.
d. 1963.
Jan 1900:Grimsby Town/
Aug 1903:Derby County/Aug 1911:FOSSE/
cs 1912:Hyde/cs 1913:South Shields.
debut: 2.9.11 v.Gainsborough Trinity (A).

An inside-right with the Mariners, Ben was
taken on by Derby to replace the charismatic
Archie Goodall at centre-half, when that role
was effectively the midfield lynchpin of the
side, and skill and vision were more important
requisites than brawn. He made 245 League

appearances for the Rams (scoring 11 times),
but had lost much of his pace by the time he
joined Fosse, and could not for long hold off
the challenge of the younger Percy Hanger for
the pivot's position. Ben became manager of
Bristol Rovers in May 1920, later led Loughborough Corinthians, and was still involved in
the game, scouting for Southend United, after
WW2. He had three brothers who also played
League football: Ellis, Fretwell and Harry.
Apps: 14 Lge.

HALL, JOHN HENRY

b. Newark (?)
Newark/Oct 1904:Stoke/
May 1906:Brighton & Hove Albion/
Apr 1908:Middlesbrough/
June 1910:FOSSE/
Dec 1910:Birmingham.
debut: 3.9.10
v.Bolton Wanderers (H) (2 goals).

The top scorer for each of his respective clubs
from 1905/6 onwards (outshooting even Steve
Bloomer during his three years at Ayresome),
Jack had only a short spell as leader of Fosse's
attack before the directorate accepted a
'substantial' bid from Birmingham for his
services. He had certainly engendered high
expectations among the Fosse faithful: in the
four public trial matches of August 1910, he
scored eleven goals, including three hat-tricks!
Jack also rewarded Birmingham with a goal in
each of his first six League games, scored two
for them against Fosse the following season
and, in 1912/13, hit a treble against his former
team. (It has yet to be established conclusively
whether it was this Jack Hall, or another of that
name, who coached Feyenoord to the Dutch
championship in the late 1920s, and had a
second spell at the helm of the Rotterdam club
on the eve of WW2).
Apps: 15 Lge.
Goals: 5 Lge.

JACK HALL

HALTON, REGINALD LLOYD

b. Buxton, 11.7.1916.
d. Mar 1988.
1936:Manchester United/cs 1937:Notts County/
Nov 1937:Bury/Dec 1948:Chesterfield/
Sept 1950:CITY/
Feb 1953:Scarborough (p/mgr)/
cs 1954:Goole Town.
debut: 30.9.50 v.Cardiff City (H).

Starting his career as an outside-left at Old
Trafford, Reg soon settled down as a constructive left-half at Gigg Lane, and may well have
developed to international level if the war had
not interrupted his career. As it was, he guested
for Portsmouth and Fulham, and also played
perhaps his most memorable match before
League football resumed - in the Arsenal side
which met Moscow Dynamo in a classic of
propaganda and prestige in November 1945.
Reg was 34 when former Bury boss Norman
Bullock signed him for the second time to add
experience to City's middle line, and he gave
two seasons' staunch service before taking the
reins (and a centre-forward role!) at Scarborough, from where he sent the young Colin
Appleton to Filbert Street.
Apps: 64 Lge; 3 FAC.
Goals: 3 Lge.

HAMILL, STEWART

b. Glasgow, 22.1.1960.
Anniesland United/Possil YM/Pollok/
Sept 1980:CITY/
(Mar 1982-loan-Scunthorpe United)/
Sept 1982:Kettering Town/Nuneaton Borough/
Mar 1986:Northampton Town/
cs 1986:Altrincham/Mar 1987:Scarborough/
cs 1988:Boston United.
debut: 8.11.80 v.Manchester City (H).

Winger or midfielder Stewart made a rapid rise
from part-time Scottish junior football - and a
job as a Co-Op van driver - to the First
Division, and held his place in Jock Wallace's
young side for eight games. He didn't then
return until the second match of the 1981/2
Second Division season, but was unfortunate to
be limited to two games, especially as he scored
the winning goal in each of them. Scunthorpe
failed to take up their option on Stewart's
signature after his 4-game loan spell, and he
dropped into non-league football. Former
Nuneaton manager Graham Carr gave him a
brief chance at a return to the League fray with
Northampton, but a contract was not forthcoming despite Stewart scoring after a mere 35
seconds of his Cobblers debut at Tranmere.
However, a year later, he joined Scarborough at
precisely the time they were overtaking Barnet
to become the first side automatically promoted
from the top of the non-league pyramid to the
Fourth Division.
Apps: 10 Lge.
Goals: 2 Lge.

HAMILTON, A. JOHN

b. Ayrshire, 1872.
Ayr/June 1894:Wolverhampton Wanderers/
cs 1895:Loughborough/cs 1897:Bristol City/
Sept 1900:FOSSE/June 1901:Watford/
cs 1902:Wellingborough/cs 1903:Fulham.
debut: 15.9.1900 v.Grimsby Town (H).

Reportedly leaving Ayr 'in consequence of the
dullness of trade', Jack became an early victim
of serious injury at Wolves, an ever-present at
left-half in Loughborough's inaugural League
season, and the tough-tackling skipper of
Bristol City for the last of his Southern League
years there, when he played alongside the likes
of Harry Davy, Albert Carnelly, Billy Langham
and Jimmy Stevenson. He took the pivot's role
during his Fosse season, when the failings of
the forward line were more marked than those
of the defence, and, after further Southern
League ramblings, remained at Craven Cottage
on the training staff until 1910, then returned to
Ashton Gate as reserve trainer and, during
WW1, manager. (Greater efforts have probably
been made to sort out Jack's career details than
expended on any other player of the era; for
three recently-published League club histories
have each set out divergent, and impossibly
conflated, career biographies for 'their' John
Hamilton's. We are now fairly confident that
the above is accurate, having refuted to our
satisfaction claims that 'our' Jack played
additionally for Derby County and/or Gainsborough Trinity, Brentford and Leeds City).
Apps: 28 Lge; 1 FAC.

HAMILTON, NEVILLE ROY

b. Leicester, 19.4.1960.
app Nov 1976/pro Oct 1977:CITY/
Jan 1979:Mansfield Town/cs 1981:Rochdale/
cs 1984:Wolverhampton Wanderers.
debut: 27.12.1977 v.Manchester United (A).

A teenage midfielder given one game by Frank
McLintock and three more by caretaker boss
Ian MacFarlane after City's 1978 relegation
had become a foregone conclusion, Nev raised
£25,000 when sold to Field Mill by Jock
Wallace, and went on to play 163 League
games for Mansfield and Rochdale before
Tommy Docherty took him to Molineux for a
shot at Second Division football. Tragically,
though, Nev suffered a heart attack during pre-
season training with Wolves, and was forced to
retire on medical advice before kicking a ball in
anger for them. More happily, after recovery,
he qualified as a full FA coach in August 1986.
Apps: 4 Lge.

HAMMOND, WALTER HENRY

b. Chorlton, 1868.
d. Bolton, Dec 1921.
June 1892:Sheffield United/
cs 1897:New Brighton Tower/
May 1900:FOSSE.
debut: 9.2.01 v.Nottingham Forest (A) FAC.

A centre-forward whose Filbert Street season
seemed to be jinxed, Harry had no sooner
signed from Fosse's Division Two rivals New
Brighton than he was hospitalised with typhoid
fever, and when he finally regained fitness
some five months later, he had to lead a side in
the middle of an eleven-game run without a
win. Previously, Harry had been a prolific
goalscorer for the Blades, and had easily topped
New Brighton's scoring charts in his final
season there despite spending most of it in the
centre-half berth. One amusing story attaches to
Harry from his Sheffield days: in becoming the

first player from that club to be sent off in a
League match, for fighting a Crewe defender,
he so incensed the crowd that a panicky flight
from the ground seemed the wisest option to
him. His team-mates eventually found him
hiding on Crewe station some time after the
match; still wearing his kit!
Apps: 4 Lge; 1 FAC.
Goals: 1 Lge.

HANGER, PERCY

b. Kettering.
Kettering St.Mary's/Kettering/
Apr 1910:FOSSE/cs 1913:Kettering.
debut: 23.4.10 v.Burnley (H).

A centre-half of boundless stamina who
understudied both Andy Aitken and Ben Hall
before securing a regular first team slot for
himself, Percy had first played trial games for
Fosse reserves in December 1908, and was a
member of a noted Northamptonshire
footballing family, of whom Harry was a
Bradford City half-back from 1906-09.
Apps: 54 Lge; 3 FAC.
Goals: 1 FAC.

HARPER, ERNEST

b.
Hugglescote United/Aug 1904:FOSSE/
Mar 1905:Derby County.
debut: 21.1.05 v.Burton United (A).

An amateur full-back who was elevated from
the reserves for Fosse's first away win of
1904/5, but could not thereafter claim a place
against the heavy competition of Bennett,
Oakes, Robinson and Pollock. He made no
League appearances for Derby.
Apps: 1 Lge.

HARPER, WILLIAM E.

b. Nechells, Birmingham, 1876.
d. Weston, 1944.
Smethwick Wesleyan Rovers/
Oct 1899:West Bromwich Albion/
Sept 1903:FOSSE.
debut: 26.9.03 v.Chesterfield (H).

Another Fossil who failed to appear on a
winning side, Billy was a tall, speedy outside-
left with a modicum of previous experience at
Albion, having played seven times in their 1902
promotion side, but only once in Division One.
He had represented 'England' in 1899 in the
little-known series of Junior international
matches against Scotland - as there was no
precise equivalent south of the border to
Scottish junior football (a non-league set-up
that still exists, and confusingly has nothing to
do with the ages of the players), the 'national'
representative side was then drawn almost
wholly from minor West Midland clubs.
Apps: 4 Lge.

HARRISON, ALBERT

b. Leigh, 15.2.1904.
Chorley/Mar 1927:Nottingham Forest/
Dec 1929:CITY/May 1931:Dundalk/
cs 1932:Drumcondra/
July 1933:Wigan Athletic.
debut: 7.12.29 v.Derby County (H).

A tall blond centre-half who took over the pivotal berth from George Carr, Albert had been chosen the summer previously for the FA team touring South Africa, when he played in one 'Test Match' behind Arthur Chandler. His first team tenure at Filbert Street was however not a long one - effectively, he carried the can for a 2-8 mauling at Grimsby in November 1930, and then found himself displaced by the up-and-coming Roger Heywood. He was invariably known throughout his career as 'Snowy'.
Apps: 32 Lge; 1 FAC.
Goals: 1 Lge.

HARRISON, DEREK
b. Littlethorpe, Leics, 9.2.1950.
app Aug 1965/pro Feb 1967:CITY/
Feb 1971:Torquay United/
June 1975:Colchester United/cs 1976:Dawlish.
debut: 10.9.69 v.Bristol City (H) LC.

A tall, commanding centre-half and skipper for City reserves, Derek was unlucky to be understudying the consistent John Sjoberg for the bulk of his Filbert Street career, and to be effectively queue-jumped by the more versatile Malcolm Manley. Derek's two League Cup appearances came 13 months apart, and with his chances clearly limited he moved to Plainmoor after a loan spell to tot up 127 League games. Bobby Roberts then took him on at Layer Road, but he failed to make much impression there, and dropped into non-league football.
Apps: 2 LC.

GEORGE HARRISON

HARRISON, GEORGE
b. Church Gresley, 18.7.1892.
d. Derby, 12.3.1939.
Gresley Rovers/Feb 1911:FOSSE/
Apr 1913:Everton/
Dec 1923:Preston North End/
Nov 1931:Blackpool.
debut: 22.4.11 v.Leeds City (H).

A hefty, direct outside-left who soon showed with Fosse that he was worthy of a much higher grade of football, George was ever-present in 1912/13 and then signed for Everton two days after the final game. At Goodison he won a

First Division championship medal in 1915, and his continuing reliability as a provider of quality crosses earned him two full England caps after the war. George's stamina was almost as remarkable as his touchline skill, and he was nearly forty when he retired from the League game; initially to run a pub in Preston. He was a licensee back in his native village at the time of his early death.
Apps: 59 Lge; 1 FAC.
Goals: 9 Lge.

HARRISON, JAMES CHARLES
b. Leicester, 12.2.1921.
Wellington Victoria/Dec 1940:CITY/
July 1949:Aston Villa/July 1951:Coventry City/
July 1953:Corby Town.
debut (postwar): 21.9.46 v.Fulham (A) (1 goal).

A local signing during WW2, Jimmy served in the forces in India and Burma and guested for Reading before making his League bow for City as a centre-forward - a position to which he occasionally reverted in emergencies from his more regular slot at full-back. His bulk and enthusiasm appeared to suit him for forward forays, but the fact Jimmy had only ever added one other first team counter to his debut goal made his selection in the No.9 shirt for City's first Wembley Final something of a desperate gamble - albeit one partly dictated by circumstance. The crucial face-saving game at Cardiff a week after the Cup Final was Jimmy's last for City, as Villa stepped in with a £12,000 bid during the close season. He was only, however, to make eight League appearances for them (scoring once) before moving on again to Highfield Road, where a team with an average age of 31 dropped from the Second to the Third Division (North), yet still thrashed City in the FA Cup. Jimmy now runs a successful haulage business from a Wigston base.
Apps: 81 Lge; 11 FAC.
Goals: 1 Lge; 1 FAC.

HARRISON, WALTER EDWARD
b. Coalville, 16.1.1923.
Coalville Town/Navy football/am June 1945/
pro Aug 1945:CITY/Dec 1950:Chesterfield/
1953:Corby Town.
debut: 7.9.46 v.West Ham United (A).

A tall, wiry right-half who had guested for Kilmarnock while on Navy service during the war, Walter soon gained the nickname 'Spider' from the Filbert Street fans, and had his intelligent prompting recognised with two England 'B' caps in May 1949, immediately after helping City to Wembley and picking up a runners-up medal alongside his unrelated namesake. Walter excelled at the wall-pass game, but is still remembered by more senior City supporters for a 50-yard dribble past five men that ended with him scoring a Cup goal against Sheffield Wednesday in 1948. Chesterfield recruited him for £8,500 to their unsuccessful fight against relegation from the Second Division in 1951, but he went on to make 75 League appearances (13 goals) for the Saltergate side.
Apps: 125 Lge; 18 FAC.
Goals: 3 Lge; 2 FAC.

JIM HARROLD

HARROLD, JAMES GEORGE WILLIAM
b. Poplar, 26.3.1892.
d. Epsom, 7.10.1950.
1909:Custom House/
(Jan 1912-trials-Huddersfield Town)/
(1912-am registration-West Ham United)/
Feb 1913:FOSSE/
July 1923:Millwall.
debut: 15.2.13 v.Grimsby Town (H).

Fosse were in such a hurry to play this England amateur international centre-half they were subsequently fined two guineas by the FA for fielding him before the completion of transfer formalities (one week after he'd first appeared for his country, and less than a fortnight before he won his only other cap). The tall Londoner, blessed with brilliant heading ability and a seemingly telescopic tackle, soon proved his worth, and signed as a professional during the 1913 close season. Jim went on to give superb service on both sides of WW1, and took a benefit from the home game with Blackpool in December 1920. After moving back to London, he also started a parallel career with Essex CCC, for whom he played occasional first-class cricket until 1929.
Apps: 206 Lge; 12 FAC.
Goals: 7 Lge.

HARROLD, SIDNEY
b. Stourbridge, 5.6.1895.
Wednesbury/1918:FOSSE/
May 1920:Nottingham Forest/
cs 1922:Accrington Stanley.
debut (postwar): 30.8.19 v.Wolverhampton Wanderers (H).

Unrelated to Jim, Sidney was an outside left who joined Fosse during the final season of WW1 football. He appeared in the side for City's first League outing after reconstruction, but found himself out of favour with Peter Hodge before the term was over. He later made 13 appearances in Forest's Second Division championship campaign of 1921/2.
Apps: 18 Lge.
Goals: 2 Lge.

HASTIE, GEORGE

b. Glasgow.
Govan Glentoran/July 1906:Ashfield/
June 1909:Kilmarnock/
June 1910:Bristol Rovers/Bath City/
Nov 1911:Kilmarnock/Aug 1912:St Johnstone/
Nov 1912:Abercorn/July 1914:FOSSE/
1919:Abercorn/Sept 1920:Johnstone.
debut: 2.9.14 v.Lincoln City (H).

A Scottish inside-left caught up with understandable bewilderment in Fosse's plummet to
the Second Division re-election zone in the
war-shadowed season of 1914/15. A Junior
international, George had previously claimed
six goals in 20 Southern League games for
Bristol Rovers, and a Scottish Qualifying Cup
winner's medal with Abercorn in 1912/13.
Apps: 17 Lge; 1 FAC.
Goals: 1 Lge.

HAZELL, ROBERT JOSEPH

b. Kingston, Jamaica, 14.6.1959.
app/pro May 1977:Wolverhampton Wanderers/
Sept 1979:Queens Park Rangers/
Sept 1983:CITY/(May 1985-loan-Kilfa AIK)/
(Sept 1985-loan-Wolverhampton Wanderers)/
Aug 1986-trial-Luton Town/
Oct 1986-trial-Leeds United/
Nov 1986:Reading/Dec 1986:Port Vale.
debut: 1.10.83 v.Birmingham City (A).

A valuable and popular contributor to City's
First Division survival struggles of 1983/4 and
1984/5, Bob came to Leicester after the upward
trajectory of his career seemed temporarily to
have stalled at Loftus Road. England honours at
youth, Under-21 and 'B' levels had come the
way of the big central defender, and he had
starred for Rangers in the 1982 FA Cup Final,
though his disciplinary record was far from
unsullied, and Filbert Street regulars had
witnessed one of his dismissals after a clash
with Mark Goodwin. There was, however,
general approval when Gordon Milne signed
Bob to play alongside John O'Neill, and delight
in the way he combined an intimidatory
presence with some almost delicate ball skills.
The sight of him strolling forward with the ball
as opponents hesitated over the wisdom of
attempting a tackle was certainly one to relish.
Unfortunately, off the field, Bob soon had
disagreements with Milne over both training
and tactics, and never played again for the first
team after being substituted in a match at Forest
in November 1984. A series of injuries then set
him back severely, with a ruptured achilles
tendon in the opening game of a loan spell back
at Wolves keeping him out for nine months.
After City freed him in 1986, Bob had a
month's trial at Luton again invalidated by
injury, but proved his fitness on a non-contract
basis at Reading (where he was sent off on his
debut!), and then signed up at Vale Park.
Apps: 41 Lge; 1 FAC; 4 LC.
Goals: 2 Lge.

HEATH, RICHARD TERENCE

b. Leicester, 17.11.1943.
app/pro Nov 1961:CITY/May 1964:Hull City/
Mar 1968:Scunthorpe United/
Feb 1973:Lincoln City.
debut: 10.11.62 v.West Ham United (H).

A teenage inside-forward with a good scoring
record in the reserves, Terry was a valuable
squad member as City mounted their attempt on
the Double in 1962/3, when one of his goals
proved decisive in separating Leicester and
Manchester United at Filbert Street after hat-
tricks from Keyworth and Law had cancelled
each other out. A first team place proved more
elusive the following season, but Terry left the
club on a high note, playing in the first leg of
the League Cup Final at Stoke. Gradually
withdrawing to a scheming role, he nonetheless
scored some important goals for his subsequent
clubs, including two for Hull in a memorable
Cup giant-killing of Forest, and 50 in 177
League games for Scunthorpe, where he played
alongside Kevin Keegan. His career unfortunately ended through injury after two knee
operations in less than a year, and, as a
technicality prevented any compensation
payment, Lincoln very honourably held a
Testimonial match against Ipswich on Terry's
behalf in March 1976. He was last heard of as
proprietor of a Newquay guest house.
Apps: 8 Lge; 1 LC.
Goals: 2 Lge.

HEATHCOCK, JOSEPH BERTY

b. Cradley Heath, 5.12.1903.
Leamington Town/Oct 1923:CITY/
June 1928:Nottingham Forest/
June 1930:Cradley Heath/
Sept 1931:Hereford United.
debut: 19.3.27 v.Sheffield United (A) (2 goals).

Another City player who could feel justifiably
frustrated at his lack of senior opportunities,
Bert stood in once at centre-forward for Arthur
Chandler, scored twice in a 3-0 away win, yet
never got another League chance at Filbert
Street. His opportunities after a £150 move to
Forest were also limited, but two spectacular
scoring bursts in his first season there brought a
13-goal haul. Bert is thus best remembered for
notching nine of City Reserves' record 22 goals
against Ibstock Colliery in the Senior Cup
during his first Leicester season.
Apps: 1 Lge.
Goals: 2 Lge.

HEBBERD, TREVOR NEIL

b. Alresford, 19.6.1958.
Alresford/app/pro July 1976:Southampton/
(Mar 1981-loan-Washington Diplomats)/
(Sept 1981-loan-Bolton Wanderers)/
(Nov 1981-loan-CITY)/
Mar 1982:Oxford United/
Aug 1988:Derby County.
debut: 28.11.81
v.Cambridge United (H) (1 goal).

Often the man to drop out of Southampton's
first team whenever one of Lawrie McMenemy's imports arrived, Trevor suffered for his
own versatility at The Dell, regularly warming
the bench before coming on as striker, wide-
man or midfield prompter. Jock Wallace
brought him to Filbert Street on loan shortly
after he'd faced City at Burnden Park, but his
elegant, deceptively casual style on the left of
midfield failed to impress the boss despite
Trevor never being in a losing City line-up. At

Oxford, alongside former City reserve Malcolm
Shotton, he was a major force in the team that
raced from Division Three to establish itself in
the top flight, and he scored the opening goal
at Wembley as United captured the 1986 Milk
Cup. Trevor also took the 'Man of the Match'
award from that game.
Apps: 4 Lge.
Goals: 1 Lge.

HEBDEN,
GEORGE HORACE ROBERT

b. West Ham, 2.6.1900.
d. Leicester, 16.8.1973.
Barking Town/May 1920:CITY/
May 1925:Queens Park Rangers/
July 1927:Gillingham.
debut: 9.4.21 v.Hull City (H).

A schoolboy international goalkeeper, George
was elevated from London League amateur
football to understudy his fellow East Ender,
Herbert Bown, at Filbert Street. By 1922 he had
made the first team position his own with a
string of instinctively fearless performances,
yet was himself displaced midway through the
1925 promotion season by the calmer Albert
Godderidge.
Apps: 101 Lge; 3 FAC.

HEDLEY, GEORGE THOMAS

b. Co. Durham, 1882.
d. 1937.
West Stanley/cs 1905:Middlesbrough/Chester/
Jan 1906:Heart of Midlothian/
Mar 1906:Hull City/Apr 1908:FOSSE/
cs 1909:Luton Town.
debut: 4.4.08 v.Fulham (A).

Bought for £275 to boost Fosse's full-back
strength during the final promotion push of
1908, 'Tot' was the regular right-back in the ill-
fated First Division campaign which followed,
and the only player besides Jim Gorman and
Bob Pollock to make his final appearance in the
infamous 0-12 drubbing by Forest, which he
helped explain away to the satisfaction of the
League commission of enquiry. He had
previously tasted League football with both
'Boro (3 games) and Hull (78 apps), and
despite the ruffling he received while with
Fosse, was still noted for coolness in clearing
his lines while playing a season of Southern
League fare at Luton. His appetite for the game
was such that he was still turning out for
Brandesburton in 1924.
Apps: 35 Lge; 3 FAC.
Goals: 1 Lge.

HENDERSON, JOHN

b. Dumfries.
1894:Dumfries/May 1898:Lincoln City/
Dec 1900:FOSSE/Mar 1901:Small Heath.
debut: 15.12.1900 v.Woolwich Arsenal (H).

In a stay of just over three months at Filbert
Street, John played five times at outside-left
and eight times at inside-right, but failed to
provide the valuable commodity - goals - which
he had been signed to supply. Perhaps
surprisingly, Small Heath still saw him as a
likely candidate to buttress their squad in the

succesful run-in to their 1901 promotion bid, though he only managed four games for them alongside Johnny McMillan.
Apps: 13 Lge.

HENDERSON, WILLIAM MARTIN MELVILLE
b. Kirkcaldy, 3.5.1956.
1973:Rangers/(Oct 1977-loan-Hibernian)/ Apr 1978:Philadelphia Fury/Oct 1978:CITY/ Sept 1981:Chesterfield/Oct 1983:Port Vale.
debut: 14.10.78 (sub) v.Charlton Athletic (H).

One of the few non-internationals in Jock Wallace's Ibrox squad, Martin was a striker with a goal-every-three-games habit and a winner's medal from the 1976 Scottish Cup Final when he joined the then-annual exodus to the NASL. Wallace brought him back from Philadelphia to Filbert Street and showed remarkable patience with the ever-willing but occasionally clumsy forward as his scoring ratio dropped to less than one-in-six; but it was as foil to his one-time Kirkcaldy schoolboy partner Alan Young that Martin found his most useful support role when City climbed back from Division Two in 1980. Martin later knocked in 23 goals in 87 League games for Chesterfield (relegated in 1983), but his career ended in an acrimonious contract dispute after a second successive relegation season at Port Vale.
Apps: 79+12 Lge; 5 FAC; 3+1 LC.
Goals: 12 Lge; 4 FAC.

BILLY HENRY

HENRY, WILLIAM ARMSTRONG
b. Glasgow, 6.9.1884.
Blantyre Victoria/cs 1906:Rangers/ cs 1908:Falkirk/June 1909:FOSSE/ Nov 1911:Manchester City/ July 1920:St Bernards.
debut: 1.9.09 v.Wolverhampton Wanderers (H).

Missing only a single game during his spell with Fosse of over two seasons, right-back Billy matched consistency with evident class, and came very close to a Scottish cap, appearing for the Anglo-Scots against the

Home Scots in the international trial of March 1911. His successive back-line partnerships with Dick Pudan and Sam Currie considerably tightened a Fosse defence still smarting from its First Division thrashings, and his form soon attracted an irresistible bid from top flight Manchester City, for whom he made 142 League appearances on both sides of WW1, many of them in front of former Fosse 'keeper Walter Smith. Billy's single League goal was a 40-yard match-winner for Man. City at Meadow Lane on the opening day of 1912/13. He did gain one 'unofficial' honour during WW1, when Scotland met England at Goodison Park in a 'Grand Military International' in May 1916.
Apps: 89 Lge; 7 FAC.

HENRYS, ARTHUR
b.
cs 1891:Newton Heath/Mar 1893:FOSSE/ June 1896:Notts County.
debut: 1.4.93 v.Newark (A) ML.

An outside-left in his first Football Alliance season with the team which would later be known as Manchester United, Arthur converted to defensive roles as he played at three different levels over the next three seasons - making 3 First Division appearances for the Heathens in 1892/3 before his move to Leicester, where he became the regular Fosse centre-half in the Midland League, and took the left-half berth in the inaugural Second Division campaign. After moving on, Arthur found a place in the Magpies' side hard to maintain, dropping out after only seven games of a season that would end with the Second Division championship.
Apps: 37 Lge; 14 FAC; 23 ML.
Goals: 1 Lge; 1 ML.

HERNON, JAMES
b. Cleland, 6.12.1924.
Mossvale Strollers/Apr 1942:CITY/ Sept 1948:Bolton Wanderers/ Aug 1951:Grimsby Town/July 1954:Watford/ July 1956:Hastings United.
debut (postwar): 7.6.47 v.Fulham (H).

A teenage signing from Paisley junior football during the war, Jimmy had to wait until his Army demob in 1947 for a League bow, on the only occasion City's official programme has stretched into June. A lightweight inside-forward who seriously challenged Don Revie for the scheming role at Leicester, he raised the then-highest fee for an outgoing transfer from the club when Bolton invested £14,750 in his late-blossoming talent, but the subtler delicacies of his style of play could, unfortunately, be all too easily nullified by close physical attention. Strangely enough, though, Jimmy claimed a respectable goal-tally in the supposedly 'harder' lower divisions with Grimsby and Watford.
Apps: 31 Lge; 3 FAC.
Goals: 7 Lge.

HERROD, E.
b.
cs 1891:FOSSE.
debut (comp): 12.9.91 v.Derby Junction (H) ML.

A right-sided forward who took the flank position in Fosse's first Midland League game, but faded from the scene shortly after the move from Aylestone Road to Filbert Street.
Apps: 1 FAC; 7 ML.
Goals: 1 FAC.

HEYES, GEORGE
b. Bolton, 16.11.1937.
Apr 1956:Rochdale/July 1960:CITY/ Sept 1965:Swansea Town/July 1969:Barrow/ cs 1970:Hereford United.
debut: 11.3.61 v.West Bromwich Albion (A).

A reliably unflappable stand-in for Gordon Banks over six seasons, whenever the England 'keeper was either injured or absent on international duty, George had his lengthiest first team run at the start of 1965/6, as Banks recovered from a broken wrist - yet moved on within weeks as it became obvious he would have to relinquish even his Combination position to 16-year-old Peter Shilton. George then played over a hundred senior games for the Swans (earning a Welsh Cup-winner's medal in 1966) before seeing out his League career at Holker Street. He clearly passed on some useful tips to his son Darren, an England schoolboy 'keeper who faced City for Scunthorpe United in the Littlewoods Cup during 1987/8.
Apps: 25 Lge; 2 LC.

ROGER HEYWOOD

HEYWOOD, ROGER
b. Chorley, 4.5.1909.
d. Leicester, 30.12.1985.
Chorley/Nov 1929:CITY.
debut: 3.5.30 v.Birmingham (A).

Bought for a bargain £575 from the club which had taken the Lancashire Combination title two seasons running, Roger was a towering stopper centre-half who served City for twelve years, and also appeared as a wartime guest for Northampton Town shortly before his retirement. The bulk of his appearances came in City's early 30's years of First Division struggle, and it was somewhat sadly ironic that his first team fortunes should revive (in a wing-

half slot) during the final pre-war relegation season. Contributing to a great City tradition, one of Roger's rare goals was an Anfield winner. He used to spend his summers playing League cricket back in Lancashire.
Apps: 228 Lge; 12 FAC.
Goals: 2 Lge.

HIBBERD, JOHN TURNER
b.
Oct 1895:FOSSE.
debut: 2.11.95
v.Hucknall St.Johns (H) FAC (1 goal).

One of the several cases of a 'blink-and-you-missed-it' senior Fosse career - there's not even a record of this inside-right playing in any of the club's then-numerous friendly matches to supplement the above isolated appearance against an obscure Nottinghamshire team of Cup hopefuls. John did, however, notch the Fosse Rovers' winning goal in the Leicester-shire Senior Cup Final of the same season; and had represented the county a year previously.
Apps: 1 FAC.
Goals: 1 FAC.

HILL, JOHN
b.
Leith Rangers/Leith Athletic/
1892:Middlesbrough Ironopolis/cs
1893:FOSSE/cs 1895:Glossop North End/
Oct 1897:West Herts.
debut: 9.9.93 v.Burton Wanderers (H) ML.

A team-mate of McArthur and Seymour in the Ironopolis team which reached the quarter-finals of the FA Cup in 1893, outside right Jacky moved to Leicester with the latter for what proved to be the final season of Midland League competition, and was soon joined by the former. When Archie Hughes then later joined his former fellows, it meant four ex-Nops' were assisting Fosse in their initial assault on the Second Division. A Scottish junior international (1891), Jacky eventually teamed up with the club we now know as Watford, and indeed became a director of the renamed club in 1909, when he was running a newsagent/tobacconist business in Watford High Street.
Apps: 20 Lge; 13 FAC; 20 ML.
Goals: 2 Lge; 7 FAC; 7 ML.

HINE, ERNEST WILLIAM
b. Smithy Cross, 9.4.1900.
d. Huddersfield, 1974.
Staincross Station/Apr 1921:Barnsley/
Jan 1926:CITY/May 1932:Huddersfield Town/
Feb 1933:Manchester United/
Dec 1934:Barnsley.
debut: 16.1.26 v.Burnley (H) (2 goals).

Eventually notching more than 300 senior goals (286 in the League) over a 17-year career span, former miner Ernie was another prolific marksman to announce his intentions early - scoring on his Barnsley debut in a Cup replay at Norwich and averaging the classic ratio of a goal every two games in his first Oakwell stint. He even hit two in his first game in City colours after a £3,000 move. A First Division regular at inside-right thereafter, he was the only one of City's trio of all-time top scorers to receive halfway decent recognition of his sharpshooting prowess: graduating from Football League honours (5 games; 2 goals) to international trials (4 games and 2 goals, in the England v.The Rest series) to the full England side (6 caps; 4 goals). Twice Ernie topped the 30 goals per season mark for City (saving his best effort for the Division One runners-up season of 1928/9, when he cracked in 32 goals in 35 games), and he was still severely embarrassing top flight defences when City surprisingly allowed him to move for £4,000 back to Yorkshire. His first goal for the Terriers was actually against the City, but neither at Leeds Road nor Old Trafford could Ernie quite recapture his deadly touch, and it took a transfer back 'home' to Oakwell for the veteran to settle back into his old scoring habits. With an eventual overall Barnsley total of 123 League goals, he remains that club's record aggregate scorer to date.
Apps: 247 Lge; 12 FAC.
Goals: 148 Lge; 8 FAC.

HINES, DEREK JABEZ
b. Moira, 8.2.1931.
Moira United/am June 1947/
pro Mar 1948:CITY/
Nov 1961:Shrewsbury Town.
debut: 27.3.48 v.Tottenham Hotspur (A).

A genuine teenage prodigy, playing (on trial) in Southend United's reserve team at the age of 15, centre-forward Derek was given an early baptism by City and then nursed gradually into regular first team football while still winning England Youth international caps and, later, Army representative honours. Though his scoring rate was somewhat eclipsed by that of striking partner Arthur Rowley, Derek proved a wonderful forager, and made an inestimable contribution to both the promotion seasons of 1954 and 1957. After winning his first Division Two championship medal, he played and scored for Young England against England in the then-annual eve-of-Cup-Final game, but was subsequently passed over by the selectors. He was also unlucky in missing out on City's first two Wembley Finals: being regarded as a lucky mascot reserve in 1949 and a veteran calming influence on the 1961 squad. A short while after answering Arthur Rowley's invitation for a brief reunion at Gay Meadow, Derek returned to Filbert Street as youth team coach.
Apps: 299 Lge; 18 FAC.
Goals: 116 Lge; 1 FAC.

HODGE, MARTIN JOHN
b. Southport, 4.2.1959.
app Sept 1975/pro Feb 1977:Plymouth Argyle/
July 1979:Everton/
(Dec 1981-loan-Preston North End)/
(July 1982-loan-Oldham Athletic)/
(Jan 1983-loan-Gillingham)/
(Feb 1983-loan-Preston North End)/
Aug 1983:Sheffield Wednesday/
Aug 1988:CITY.
debut: 27.8.88 v.West Bromwich Albion (H).

A £135,000 Goodison import from Plymouth, goalkeeper Martin nonetheless made and sustained his first real impact at Hillsborough after a bargain £50,000 move. Wednesday were promoted at the end of his first ever-present season, and he went on to amend the Owls' record for consecutive appearances until missing his first game for them in September 1987. He enjoyed a spell as skipper, and was noted almost as much for the contribution of his kicking to their favoured long-ball game as for his penalty-area command. David Pleat expended two-thirds of the £300,000 he had recently received for Ian Andrews to bring Martin to Filbert Street in a literally eve-of-season deal but, ironically and sadly, the new No.1 suffered a serious stomach injury only minutes into his debut game, and was sidelined for months thereafter until an operation finally fixed the muscle trouble. Martin then made a somewhat shaky return to senior action, but has since given evidence of becoming a usefully settling influence on the City defence, and a courageous master of last-ditch, one-on-one situations.
Apps (to 13.5.89): 19 Lge.

HODGKINSON, ALBERT VICTOR
b. Pembroke Dock, 4.8.1885.
d. Stone, Staffs, 1.11.1959.
Old Normanton/Hinckley Town/Derby County/
Nov 1903:Grimsby Town/
May 1904:Plymouth Argyle/May 1905:FOSSE/
June 1906:Bury/cs 1907:Southampton/
cs 1909:Croydon Common/
Mar 1911:Southend United.
debut: 2.9.05 v.Clapton Orient (H).

Barely 20 when Fosse became his fourth senior club (after much haggling with Grimsby over his League registration and transfer fee), Albert was a clever Welsh winger who suffered somewhat at Leicester from the club's inability to settle on a regular inside-left partner for him. He had failed to win a breakthrough at Derby, where his brother William made a brief impact at centre-forward, and instead took his League bow with the Mariners after a trial spell. His outward transfer to Bury brought about the sort of situation which still mightily confuses researchers, for he took over there directly from another outside-left named Hodgkinson (Joseph, transferred to Crystal Palace); but at least the Welsh selectors knew they had the right man when awarding him a cap against Ireland after he had helped Southampton to the FA Cup semi-finals in his initial season at The Dell. Albert was also a noted baseball player.
Apps: 33 Lge; 1 FAC.
Goals: 5 Lge.

HODGSON, WILLIAM
b. Glasgow, 9.7.1935.
1954:St.Johnstone/(loan-Guildford City)/
May 1957:Sheffield United/Sept 1963:CITY/
June 1965:Derby County/
Sept 1967:Rotherham United/
Dec 1967:York City.
debut: 14.9.63 v.Bolton Wanderers (A).

A diminutive, enthusiastically industrious and virtually tireless utility forward who wore four different forward shirts at Filbert Street but made most of his appearances at Howard Riley's expense, Billy had been an old

adversary of City's during his Bramall Lane days, appearing against them in the FA Cup semi-final marathon of 1961. He gained further semi-final experience at Leicester, in the League Cup campaigns of 1964 and 1965, missing out on a winner's tankard in the first season, but taking a runners-up memento from the Final against Chelsea. Billy became a Baseball Ground regular at outside left, and a veteran inspiration for York, before taking coaching appointments with both the Blades and the Minstermen.
Apps: 46 Lge; 5 FAC; 13 LC.
Goals: 10 Lge; 5 LC.

BILLY HODGSON

HOGG, CHARLES
b.
St.Andrews/Feb 1915:FOSSE.
debut: 27.2.15 v.Blackpool (H) (1 goal).

Initially a triallist then, in April 1915, the last player to sign as a Fosse professional before the WW1 break, this two-footed inside-forward earned his brief stab at League football with a prolific scoring record in the local Mutual League. He continued with Fosse during the wartime season of 1915/16, scoring 4 times in 13 appearances.
Apps: 7 Lge.
Goals: 2 Lge.

HOGG, DEREK
b. Stockton, 4.11.1930.
Lostock Hall/(trials-Preston North End)/
Chorley/Oct 1952:CITY/
Apr 1958:West Bromwich Albion/
Oct 1960:Cardiff City/
July 1962:Kettering Town.
debut: 14.2.53 v.Leeds United (H).

Signed from Lancashire Combination football as a potential right-wing successor to Mal Griffiths, Derek claimed a regular first-team spot with City only after switching to the left flank at the start of the 1954/5 First Division

season. By October 1955 his usually effective (but occasionally over-elaborate) close-dribbling style had earned him a call-up for the Football League against the Scottish League, and he became a key contributor to City's 1957 Division Two championship effort, working in effective harness with Arthur Rowley. West Brom invested £20,000 in Derek's confident talent to boost their First Division challenge, then he moved on after two full seasons to make a scoring Ninian Park debut against City.
Apps: 161 Lge; 4 FAC.
Goals: 26 Lge.

HOLDING, WILLIAM
b.
Castle Donington/Feb 1909:FOSSE.
debut: 27.2.09 v.Sheffield United (A).

Pitched into the Fosse first team only two weeks after scoring on his reserve debut, this inexperienced outside-right impressed enough to be retained for 1909/10, but dropped out of the picture soon afterwards, never having appeared for a winning Fosse side. Indeed, his 'middle' senior game was the record 0-12 thrashing at Forest.
Apps: 3 Lge.

HOLMES, JAMES PAUL
b. Dublin, 11.11.1953.
St.John Bosco/Nov 1970:Coventry City/
Mar 1977:Tottenham Hotspur/
Mar 1981:Vancouver Whitecaps/
Oct 1982-trial-CITY/Feb 1983-trial-Brentford/
Mar 1983:Torquay United/
Nov 1983:Peterborough United (p/asst.mgr)/
Dec 1985:Nuneaton Borough (p/mgr)/
1987:Leicester United/
1987:Hitchin Town (p/mgr)/
1988:Northampton Town (coach)/
1989:Bedworth United (p/co-mgr).
debut: 30.10.82 v.Sheffield Wednesday (H).

Eire's youngest-ever international (at 17 years, 200 days), skilful full-back Jimmy showed precocious class at Highfield Road, playing in a Youth Cup Final and winning the first of 30 full caps before making his League bow against Leicester. He went on to attract numerous bids until Gordon Milne accepted Spurs' six-figure fee. A horrific leg-break suffered in an international in Bulgaria threatened to end Jimmy's career, but after a year out of the game he returned to the fray alongside Johnny Giles in Canada. Milne gave his former charge a brief trial with City, when the Second Division pace seemed too much for him, yet Jimmy managed a total of 78 more League games as he accomplished a transition to coaching and managerial roles, most recently with Coventry Sporting. He received a Dublin Testimonial game in August 1985.
Apps: 2 Lge.

HOOPER, HAROLD
b. Brierley Hill,1900.
Brierley Hill Alliance/May 1921:Southampton/
May 1924:CITY/
Aug 1926:Queens Park Rangers.
debut: 30.8.24 v.Manchester United (A).

A dour, resolute defender who had arrived in an exchange deal which saw Fred Price and Dennis Jones departing for The Dell, Harry won his personal duel with Reg Osborne for the City left-back slot for the larger part of the 1925 promotion season, but couldn't keep his rival out for long once the First Division campaign got under way.
Apps: 33 Lge; 6 FAC.

HARRY HOOPER

HORNER, PHILIP MATTHEW
b. Leeds, 10.11.1966.
app 1983/pro Nov 1984:CITY/
(Mar 1986-loan-Rotherham United)/
July 1988:Halifax Town.
debut: 3.1.87 (sub) v.Sheffield Wednesday (H).

A tall reserve striker for over two seasons, capped at Youth level and also used up front in his four League games on loan at Rotherham, Phil was experimentally transformed into a central defender just before his emergency elevation to the first team bench, and coolly slotted into that position as sub for John O'Neill in City's 6-1 win against the Owls. A couple of his subsequent senior run-outs proved, however, to be nightmarish affairs in defensive terms (at Tottenham, and against Crystal Palace), and Phil failed to make David Pleat's first retained list in 1988. He initially took the No.3 shirt at The Shay, and has also been noted as sweeper there.
Apps: 7+3 Lge; 0+1 FAC; 1 LC.

HOUGHAM, H.
b.
South Wigston Albion/Apr 1904:FOSSE.
debut: 16.4.04 v.Bradford City (H).

A local trialist who played at outside left in Fosse's final two defeats of the dismal 1903/4 season, but failed to break through again after being retained for the following season.
Apps: 2 Lge.

HOUGHTON, WILLIAM GASCOIGNE

b. Hemsworth, 20.2.1939.
Aug 1957:Barnsley/July 1964:Watford/
June 1966:Ipswich Town/July 1969:CITY/
Jan 1970:Rotherham United.
debut: 9.8.69 v.Birmingham City (H).

A vastly experienced defender, Billy had the
shortest spell of his 507-game League career at
Filbert Street, joining Frank O'Farrell's Second
Division team as a motorway commuter after
moving house from Ipswich back to his native
Barnsley. He had been a schoolboy prodigy and
England youth international left-half while at
Oakwell, and in 1968 had won a Second
Division championship medal as a left-back at
Portman Road, but he was hard pressed with
City to keep out Alan Woollett, and a small fee
took him back to Yorkshire to play as well as
reside.
Apps: 6+1 Lge; 3 LC.

HOWE, HERBERT ALEXANDER

b. Rugby, 1.4.1916.
Leicester Nomads/Feb 1937:CITY/
July 1947:Notts County.
debut: 4.5.39 v.Wolverhampton Wanderers (H).

Forced to mark time in WW2 regional football
between his debut at left-half and his immediate
postwar stint at left-back - in fact he made 209
interim appearances for City as well as guesting
for Northampton Town - Bert was effectively
robbed of the opportunity to fulfil his evident
potential at Filbert Street. Twice in 1946/7 Bert
had to take over the injured Joe Calvert's
goalkeeping jersey, but such gameness could
not prevent City letting him drop into the Third
Division. The larger part of his 52-game spell at
Meadow Lane, however, was ironically played
out before huge crowds and in the full glare of
media attention attracted by the presence of his
new team-mate Tommy Lawton. Upon
retirement through injury, Bert became trainer
to Rugby Town.
Apps: 28 Lge; 3 FAC.

HOWES, ARTHUR

b.
Sept 1896:FOSSE/Nov 1897:Reading/
cs 1898:FOSSE/cs 1899:Brighton United/
cs 1901:Dundee/
cs 1902:Brighton & Hove Albion/
cs 1904:Queens Park Rangers.
debut: 27.2.97 v.Blackpool (A).

An alert and agile goalkeeper who loyally
played out the bulk of three seasons in the
shadows of Jimmy Thraves, Charlie Saer and
Godfrey Beardsley, Arthur later joined the
substantial number of English players (Herbert
Dainty and Charles Webb among them) to
assist Dundee - a club seemingly intent on
single-handedly reversing the usual cross-
border flow of football talent around the turn of
the century. The lure of the South Coast sea air
then exerted itself again, before Arthur took cap
and gloves to QPR's imposing-sounding home
of the time: the Agricultural Society Grounds,
Park Royal.
Apps: 15 Lge; 1 FAC.

HUBBARD, ARCHIBALD

b. Leicester, 1884.
d. 1967.
Leicester Imperial/St.Andrews/
Aug 1904:FOSSE/May 1907:Fulham/
Jan 1908:Watford/May 1909:Norwich City/
Nov 1910:Grimsby Town/
Aug 1912:Lincoln City/
Sept 1913:Leicester Imperial.
debut: 12.11.04
v.Gresley Rovers (H) FAC (2 goals).

Invariably but inexplicably known as 'Ranji'
throughout his Fosse career, Archie was
switched regularly around the central attacking
positions before settling into the centre-forward
berth he was to occupy until the advent of the
unrelated Shirley Hubbard. A crowd favourite
for his dashing enthusiasm, he went on to
appear in Fulham's first-ever League team
(alongside ex-Fossil Arthur Collins and Fossils-
to-be Billy Goldie and Fred Threlfall); then
moved through Southern League and Midland
League football until Grimsby were re-elected
to the League in 1911 - for a season in which
Archie was top scorer.
Apps: 58 Lge; 2 FAC.
Goals: 21 Lge; 2 FAC.

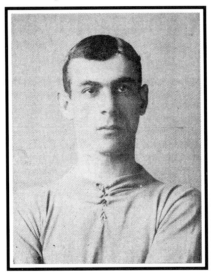

SHIRLEY HUBBARD

HUBBARD, SHIRLEY

b. Leicester.
St.Andrews/Army football/Leicester Imperial/
Feb 1907:FOSSE/May 1913:Darlington/
cs 1919:CITY/cs 1920:Ashby Town (p/coach).
debut: 29.3.07 v.Burton United (A).

Still a soldier in the Leicestershire Regiment
when he made his League bow with Fosse in
place of namesake Archie, Shirley had only
recently returned from a couple of years of
service in India. In fact, the two Hubbards (who
also had two local junior teams in common, but
reputedly no close kinship) only appeared
together once in Fosse's first team, when both
scored in the final game of 1906/7. Thereafter,
Shirley fought off a series of imported attack
leaders, persistently re-emerging in the forward
line as he sampled promotion, relegation and

Second Division struggle from the sharp end.
On Christmas Day 1912, while his benefit
match (a reserve fixture against Long Eaton
St.Helens) was taking place at Filbert Street, he
was being led off the Clapton Orient pitch with
a broken collarbone; characteristically, though,
he was back in senior action before the season
was out. Even if the Fosse directorate were
content to let him move on in 1913, many of
the same men on the new City board were
pleased to see him return with an offer of
experienced help in 1919, and he capped his
brief comeback with one last goal.
Apps: 140 Lge; 14 FAC.
Goals: 36 Lge; 3 FAC.

HUFTON, S.

b.
Aug 1891:FOSSE.
debut: 3.10.91 v.Small Heath (H) FAC.

The hapless pivot when Midland Leaguers
Fosse made their first-hurdle FA Cup exit in
1891/2, Hufton was also occasionally thrust
into a more overtly forward role as the club
stumbled through its initial season of regular
competitive fare.
Apps: 1 FAC; 16 ML.
Goals: 1 ML.

HUGHES, ARCHIBALD

b. Renfrewshire.
Barrhead/cs 1892:Middlesbrough Ironopolis/
cs 1893:Bolton Wanderers/Aug 1894:FOSSE/
cs 1895:Glossop North End.
debut: 1.9.94 v.Grimsby Town (A).

Preparing for their first tilt at League football,
Fosse signed Archie to assume their 'playmaker' role and, according to the usual tactical
custom of the day, handed him either the
centre-half or inside-forward position from
which to direct midfield operations. He had
built quite a reputation at Bolton, but had
unfortunately spent all but the first five minutes
of their 1894 FA Cup Final defeat by Notts
County as a limping, ineffectual passenger. His
track record with Fosse, however, was
interrupted for different reasons, as Archie
twice found himself suspended by the
committee for breaches of training regulations,
and it was little surprise when his registration
was not renewed at the end of the season.
Apps: 18 Lge; 3 FAC.
Goals: 2 Lge.

HUGHES, BERNARD

b.
Aug 1904:FOSSE.
debut: 14.4.06 v.Hull City (A).

An amateur right-half retained as a professional
after impressing in the three trial matches of
August 1905 (in the second of which he had to
take over from the injured goalkeeper), Bernard
spent almost the whole of his Fosse career in
reserve to the experienced William Morgan.
Apps: 1 Lge.

HUGHES, WILLIAM

b. Coatbridge, 30.12.1948.
Coatbridge Jnrs/Dec 1965:Sunderland/

Aug 1977:Derby County/Dec 1977:CITY/
(Sept 1979-loan-Carlisle United)/
Apr 1980:San Jose Earthquakes/Corby Town.
debut: 26.12.77 v.Middlesbrough (H).

Despite totting up the years at Roker, Billy had his modest achievements overshadowed for a long time by those of his brother, Celtic's John 'Yogi' Hughes. He eventually righted that particular imbalance when making a valuable contribution to Sunderland's underdog FA Cup-winning side of 1973. The strongly-built forward with the surprisingly subtle touch finally left Roker after 11 seasons and a testimonial game, having won one cap as a substitute for Scotland in 1975, and was hitting his goalscoring stride at Derby when Frank McLintock tempted him to help dig City out of the relegation mire. Understandably, Billy was not up to that specific task, but remained at the club as a utility forward throughout Jock Wallace's first season in charge, before drifting off for a brief taste of Stateside football.
Apps: 36+1 Lge; 1 FAC; 1 LC.
Goals: 5 Lge.

BILLY HUGHES

HUMPHREYS, PERCY
b. Cambridge, 3.12.1880.
d. Stepney, 13.4.1959.
Cambridge St.Mary's/
1900:Queens Park Rangers/
cs 1901:Notts County/June 1907:FOSSE/
Feb 1908:Chelsea/
Dec 1909:Tottenham Hotspur/
Oct 1911:FOSSE/
cs 1912:West Hartlepool (p/mgr)/
Nov 1914:Norwich City.
debut: 7.9.07 v.Leeds City (H).

Having represented England and the Football League once apiece in 1903, and having totalled 66 League goals for the Magpies, centre-forward Percy made a whirlwind goalscoring contribution to Fosse's promotion effort, establishing himself as their seasonal top scorer with 19 goals in 26 games before being spirited away to Stamford Bridge for £350 (the

precise ceiling for transfer fees then - briefly - in force between League clubs). His impressive goal ratio dropped a little with Chelsea, then perked up again with Spurs, but when Percy returned for a second Filbert Street stint, it was unfortunately with a mediocre side which he was unable to lift. At the time war was declared, he was about to take up a three-year appointment as player/coach with a Swiss club, but instantly returned home.
Apps: 40 Lge; 4 FAC.
Goals: 21 Lge; 4 FAC.

HUTCHINS, DONALD
b. Middlesbrough, 8.5.1948.
Stockton Juniors/Feb 1966:CITY/
July 1969:Plymouth Argyle/
July 1972:Blackburn Rovers/
June 1974:Bradford City.
debut: 15.4.68 v.Burnley (A).

An orthodox outside-left who found it hard to displace either Len Glover or Mike Stringfellow, Don got only one chance to impress new manager Frank O'Farrell, who released him after only a few months in charge. Don's natural pace and exuberant skills came to the fore, however, in 96 League games at Plymouth and, two moves later, in Bradford City's 1977 promotion from the Fourth Division. At Valley Parade, in fact, he totalled 256 League appearances, and stretched his career goals total to a very respectable 74.
Apps: 4 Lge.

HYETT, JAMES
b.
Stapleford Town/Jan 1905:FOSSE.
debut: 28.1.05 v.Liverpool (H).

Another of the elusive 'Fossil-for-a-fortnight' brigade, seemingly destined for obscurity after the briefest of senior try-outs in the centre-forward berth.
Apps: 1 Lge.

IGGLEDEN, HORATIO
b. Hull, 17.3.1925.
am Sept 1941/pro Mar 1942:CITY/
Dec 1948:Leeds United/July 1955:Exeter City/
Aug 1956:Goole Town.
debut (postwar): 5.10.46 v.Luton Town (A).

A Royal Marine who signed for City after guesting for Grimsby Town, Ray was a versatile forward who made sporadic first team appearances in four attacking positions, and was still looked on as a fine goalscoring prospect when he was involved in the part-exchange deal with Leeds which brought Ken Chisholm to Filbert Street. His pace and shooting power brought him exactly 50 League and Cup goals at Elland Road, including a hat-trick against City in January 1954, by which time he was the regular inside-left partner to the great John Charles.
Apps: 11 Lge.
Goals: 2 Lge.

JACKSON, RONALD
b. Crook, 15.10.1919.
d. Lincolnshire, Mar 1980.
1945:Wrexham/Dec 1949:CITY/

July 1955:Kettering Town/Rugby Town.
debut: 24.12.49 v.Hull City (A).

Norman Bullock's second signing (at a cost of £9,000), Ron was a left-back noted for his speed in recovery and a remarkable heading ability for a man only 5ft.7ins tall. A games master at a Leicester school (as indeed he had been in Wrexham), he appeared to be on his way out of the first team reckoning after a lengthy contract dispute in 1952, but returned to hold down his position as an ever-present in the 1954 promotion season. The highlight of that season for Ron, however, was in the first game of the Cup quarter-final marathon with Preston, when he outplayed Tom Finney and still managed to get forward to score his only City goal.
Apps: 161 Lge; 12 FAC.
Goals: 1 FAC.

JACKSON, WILLIAM
b. Farnworth, 5.7.1902.
d. 1974.
Leyland/May 1924:Sunderland/
Sept 1925:Leeds United/
May 1927:West Ham United/
Feb 1928:Chelsea/May 1931:CITY/
May 1932:Bristol Rovers/
May 1934:Cardiff City/Jan 1935:Watford.
debut: 12.9.31 v.Liverpool (H).

Two-footed winger Billy spent a lot of time in reserve football with his first five League clubs, proving unable to make a breakthrough at all at Roker. He played 38 times (scoring twice) for Leeds, only twice for the Hammers, and only 26 times (6 goals) over almost four seasons at Stamford Bridge. His spell with City saw him understudying Hughie Adcock, but Billy found a more regular slot (and a short-lived goalscoring touch) at Eastville.
Apps: 4 Lge.

JAKEMAN, LESLIE
b. Nuneaton, 14.3.1930.
Atherstone/June 1947:Derby County/
cs 1949:Hinckley Athletic/May 1951:CITY/
cs 1954:Hinckley Athletic/Sept 1954:CITY/
Feb 1955:Coventry City.
debut: 6.9.54 v.Burnley (A).

A junior released by Derby back to the Midland non-league scene, Les was then nurtured further through the ranks at City as a wing-half or inside-forward, and 'farmed out' to Hinckley to add to his experience. His sudden recall for a surprise first-team bow at Turf Moor in the No.4 shirt caused quite a fuss - City were soon afterwards fined by the League for fielding him while he was still officially registered as a Hinckley player. Les unfortunately then failed to add any further senior appearances during his short spell at Highfield Road.
Apps: 1 Lge.

JAMES, ROBERT MARK
b. Swansea, 23.3.1957.
app Mar 1973/pro Apr 1974:Swansea City/
July 1983:Stoke City/
Oct 1984:Queens Park Rangers/
June 1987:CITY/Jan 1988:Swansea City.
debut: 15.8.87 v.Shrewsbury Town (H).

A 16-year-old apprentice when he made his Vetch Field debut, Robbie went on to play in all four divisions for his home-town club as they rose to join the elite, and knocked in 110 senior goals as he matured from a hefty front runner into a powerful Welsh international midfielder. Sizeable fees took him via Stoke to Loftus Road, where he developed another string to his bow by holding down a full-back spot, and where City were reminded of his long-range shooting prowess during their 1987 FA Cup exit. Bryan Hamilton saw in Robbie the sort of experienced campaigner who could help settle a predominantly youthful Second Division defence, but many of his efforts were negated by a lack of pace, and some of the vigour seemed to leave his game after Wales were eliminated from the European Championships. A couple of particularly lacklustre performances in front of new City boss David Pleat resulted in a rapid departure for Robbie, who re-signed for the Swans and immediately assumed their captaincy, leading them to promotion from the Fourth Division via the 1988 play-offs, and to Welsh Cup victory (as a Final goalscorer) in 1989.
Apps: 21+2 Lge; 4 LC; 1 FMC.

ROBBIE JAMES

JARVIE, JOHN
b. Old Monkland, 19.10.1900.
Bellshill Athletic/1923:Third Lanark/
Aug 1925:CITY/Oct 1926:Portsmouth/
Mar 1928:Southend United/
(July 1929-trials-Watford)/
Aug 1929:Norwich City/Aug 1930:Chester/
Aug 1931:Shrewsbury Town.
debut: 16.9.25 v.Manchester United (A).

Compensating for his lack of height through notable agility and clean handling, John impressed City as a likely goalkeeping deputy to Albert Godderidge, and in fact got an early first team run as the side started its First Division campaign rather shakily. Unfortunately unable to stem a rising goal-deficit

column, however, he was edged out definitively by the signing of his international compatriot, Kenny Campbell. At Portsmouth, John's four League games included the demoralising experiences of having seven (Middlesbrough) and eight (Liverpool) goals whizz past him, but he fared better in Division Three (South), before curiously leaving Norwich in 1930 despite being an ever-present in League and Cup games during his season there.
Apps: 5 Lge.

JAYES, BRIAN
b. Leicester, 13.12.1932.
am/pro July 1954:CITY/
July 1956:Mansfield Town/
July 1960:Ramsgate.
debut: 31.8.55 v.Nottingham Forest (A).

Bad timing rather afflicted right-half Brian as he made his first team bow. The injury crisis that had offered him a place was in fact quite widespread, and a depleted City side shipped 15 goals in the three successive away defeats in which he played near the beginning of 1955/6. Brian subsequently became a regular at Field Mill, making 115 League appearances and scoring once.
Apps: 3 Lge.

JAYES, CARL GEOFFREY
b. Leicester, 15.3.1954.
app Mar 1969/pro July 1971:CITY/
Nov 1977:Northampton Town/
cs 1980:AP Leamington.
debut: 5.2.72 v.Orient (H) FAC.

Capped seven times for England schoolboys, and an occasional City reserve team goalkeeper while still at school, Carl looked set to eventually follow Peter Shilton's route to the top. His unexpected debut was a nightmare, however, as City found themselves in the position of felled giants, with Carl dropping Orient's second goal over his head into the net. He waited patiently for more than two years for another chance, briefly but efficiently deputising for Mark Wallington just prior to that 'keeper embarking on his record marathon run of consecutive appearances. Carl was a regular for the Cobblers until accompanying John Farrington to Leamington, and after a year there hung up his boots to become a policeman.
Apps: 5 Lge; 1 FAC.

JELLY, HORACE EDWARD
b. Leicester, 28.8.1921.
Belgrave United/Navy football/am Jan 1944/
pro May 1946:CITY/
Aug 1951:Plymouth Argyle.
debut: 26.5.47 v.Southampton (A).

A teenage right-winger who converted to full-back while on wartime Navy service, Ted first signed for City while on leave and became a professional when demobbed. Very much a reserve for the first two postwar seasons, he timed his New Year's Day re-entry perfectly in 1949, holding his place in the No.2 shirt throughout the glory run to Wembley. A regular in the following season, Ted lost out when City signed Arthur Lever, and unluckily

had his Plymouth career curtailed by a cartilage injury. Ted held an FA coaching badge, but when he could not find a senior club, turned his energies to setting up a thriving electrical business back in Leicester.
Apps: 56 Lge; 9 FAC.
Goals: 1 Lge.

GEORGE JOBEY

JOBEY, GEORGE
b. Heddon, 1885.
d. Chaddesden, 9.3.1962.
Morpeth Harriers/Apr 1906:Newcastle United/
May 1913:Arsenal/
June 1914:Bradford Park Avenue/
Aug 1919:CITY/
May 1920:Northampton Town (p/mgr).
debut: 6.9.19 v.Wolverhampton Wanderers (A).

A robust half-back and occasional centre-forward for his local League club, George played in the latter position when taking a runners-up medal from the 1911 FA Cup Final, and when he made his Arsenal debut (against Fosse) in the first game at Highbury - an occasion he also marked by scoring; by being carried off injured; and by making an undignified exit from the half-built stadium on a milk cart! During WW1 he turned out for Hamilton Academicals, then signed for City when peace and League football returned. After three games up front, the veteran resumed his old half-back position, but was not retained after his slowness had become apparent. It was initially announced he had assumed the player/manager role at Ebbw Vale, but George disappointed the Welshmen by changing his mind and taking the reins at Northampton, also there adding another 77 League games to his considerable appearance aggregate. In 1922 George became manager of Wolves, and from 1925 to 1941 was the boss at Derby County. Renowned there as a disciplinarian who bought big, George got the Rams promotion in 1926, and took them to the championship runners-up spot twice in the 30's, but he was eventually suspended by a joint FA/League commmission for alleged complicity in the over-payment of bonuses and signing-on fees. When his ban was finally lifted, George took charge for 1952/3 at Mansfield, but reportedly his heart was no longer in the game.
Apps: 30 Lge; 4 FAC.

JOBLING, KEVIN ANDREW
b. Sunderland, 1.1.1968.
app July 1984/pro Jan 1986:CITY/
Feb 1988:Grimsby Town.
debut: 4.4.87 v.Newcastle United (A).

A tidy teenage midfielder who seemed to lack the necessary confidence to express himself with more flair on his intermittent senior opportunities with City, Kevin was one of several players to be given a break by Bryan Hamilton and then quickly to be assessed as not meeting David Pleat's standards. Perhaps unfortunately, Kevin reserved his most forceful display for the Full Members (Simod) Cup tie at Charlton in 1987/8, when his match-winning two-goal performance was watched by hardly more spectators than he was used to playing before in City's reserves. It was Bobby Roberts who snapped up his signature in part-exchange when City moved for Phil Turner, but Kevin couldn't keep Grimsby from slipping into Division Four by the season's end.
Apps: 4+5 Lge; 0+1 FAC; 3 FMC.
Goals: 2 FMC.

JOHNSON, EDWARD
b.
debut (comp): 4.10.90
v.Burton Wanderers (H) FAC.

The inside-left in Fosse's first two FA Cup tie defeats, Teddy played with the club he had joined around 1889 for the initial Midland League season but, like many of his fellow pioneers, found the regular competitive demands of the club's new station a little too much for him.
Apps: 2 FAC; 18 ML.
Goals: 1 ML.

JOHNSON, JAMES
b.
debut (comp): 4.10.90
v.Burton Wanderers (H) FAC.

A popular right-half who had taken over the Fosse captaincy in 1889, Jimmy led his men into their first FA Cup foray, and was also involved alongside his brother Teddy in the first two County Cup-winning sides.
Apps: 1 FAC.

JOHNSTON, JAMES C.
b. Aberdeen, 12.4.1923.
Peterhead/Feb 1947:CITY/May 1950:Reading/
Mar 1953:Swindon Town/
June 1955:Merthyr Tydfil (p/mgr).
debut: 15.9.48 v.Brentford (A).

A wiry, tough-tackling left-half signed from the Highland League after trials, Jimmy found his first team breakthrough delayed by a niggling foot injury, and was then edged out of the Wembley running by Johnny King's consistency. The pair vied for the senior No.6 shirt throughout the following season, but Norman Bullock let Jimmy move on to Elm Park, where he was immovable for three seasons and 120 games. He added 75 more Third Division (South) appearances at Swindon.
Apps: 35 Lge; 1 FAC.

DAI JONES

JONES, DAVID ORMOND
b. Cardiff, 28.10.1910.
Ely United/Ebbw Vale/1929-trials-Millwall/
1931:Clapton Orient/May 1933:CITY/
Oct 1947:Mansfield Town/
cs 1949:Hinckley Athletic (p/mgr).
debut: 26.8.33 v.Aston Villa (A).

A bargain buy from penurious Orient at only £200, and initially signed to partner Adam Black, Dai was an outstanding full-back who soon walked into the Welsh international side, and won a total of seven caps. An ever-present in the 1937 promotion campaign, he went on to play throughout the war for City, Notts County and West Ham, and was still a Filbert Street regular throughout the first peacetime season, in which he notched the club's opening goal. Almost 37-years-old when he moved to Field Mill, Dai still stamped his authoritative class on another 74 League games before moving down to Birmingham Combination level.
Apps: 226 Lge; 12 FAC.
Goals: 4 Lge.

JONES, DENNIS
b. Shirebrook, 14.5.1894.
d. Bolsover, 12.9.1961.
Shirebrook/June 1921:CITY/
May 1924:Southampton/
June 1925:Mansfield Town.
debut: 5.11.21 v.Barnsley (H).

A centre-half for his Central Alliance club, Dennis made the bulk of his City appearances on the right of the middle line, deposing the veteran Teddy King and holding the position until Billy Newton arrived, then going south as part of the deal which brought Harry Hooper to Filbert Street. He made only seven League appearances for the Saints, though, before commencing a lengthy stint at Field Mill, where he was still employed as assistant trainer in the late 40's.
Apps: 64 Lge; 3 FAC.
Goals: 2 Lge.

JONES, ROBERT
b. Coventry, 17.11.1964.
app June 1981:Manchester City/
Sept 1982:CITY/Aug 1986:Walsall/
cs 1987:Kidderminster Harriers.
debut: 7.5.83 v.Oldham Athletic (A) (1 goal).

An England schoolboy international who failed to win a contract at Maine Road, Robbie then took advantage of parental links to become the possessor of Welsh youth caps shortly after arriving at Filbert Street as a professional. He made a stunning impact when standing in for Gary Lineker in the crucial, televised promotion tussle at Boundary Park, scoring the first goal as City grabbed an invaluable win. When he next scored to help City to their belated opening First Division point, a rosy future looked assured for the young striker, but despite his close control, willing running and impressive reserve-team scoring ratio, Robbie's diminutive stature eventually told against him at the highest level, and he was freed by Gordon Milne at the end of 1985/6.
Apps: 12+3 Lge; 2 LC.
Goals: 3 Lge.

JONES, ROBERT SAMUEL (DICK)
b. Wrexham, 1868.
Wrexham Grosvenor/June 1888:Everton/
June 1894:Manchester City/
July 1895:South Shore/May 1897:FOSSE/
Aug 1901:Burton United/cs 1902:not known/
1904:Leeds City.
debut: 4.9.97 v.Luton Town (H).

First chosen for Wales in 1894 while on Everton's books (though not in their first team), Dick picked up his second and last cap in March 1898 when he and Fosse team-mate Alfred Watkins both faced Scotland. Dick had well earned the recognition with some stalwart displays at left-half, and when Fosse just missed out on promotion a year later, he was absent only once from a steadfast defence. He had disciplinary problems at Burton (and it is believed he may have dropped down to Lancashire Combination fare with White Star Wanderers shortly afterwards), but later, when the newly-formed Leeds City embarked on a series of high-class friendlies as a means of angling for League election, the now-veteran Dick was in their side which faced Fosse at Elland Road.
Apps: 104 Lge; 9 FAC.
Goals: 1 Lge.

JOPLING, JOSEPH
b. South Shields, 21.4.1951.
Aug 1969:Aldershot/Sept 1970:CITY/
(Jan 1974-loan-Torquay United)/
Mar 1974:Aldershot.
debut: 10.10.70 v.Sunderland (H).

Rejected by Sunderland after youth team trials, but a teenage regular in his first season with the Shots, full-back Joe was regarded by Frank O'Farrell as very much an investment for the future when he arrived in a deal which sent £30,000 plus Murray Brodie and Jimmy Burt south. He made an early bow in place of David Nish, but got few chances to impress Jimmy

Bloomfield over the next three seasons, and eventually returned to Aldershot to stay. By the time Joe retired, he had proved his all-round defensive versatility at the Recreation Ground in an aggregate of over 400 League and Cup games.
Apps: 2+1 Lge.

KEECH, WILLIAM
b. Irthlingborough, 1872.
Oct 1895:Liverpool/cs 1896:Barnsley/
cs 1897:Blackpool/Feb 1898:FOSSE/
Feb 1899:Loughborough/
cs 1899:Queens Park Rangers/
cs 1902:Brentford/cs 1904:Kensal Rise United.
debut: 26.2.1898 v.Walsall (A).

A hat-trick in a friendly against old rivals Loughborough two days before his League debut immediately endeared centre-forward William to the Fosse followers. But after leading the attack for the rest of 1897/8 and the beginning of the next season, he struggled to find a first team place, and ironically became one more hand to the pumps for the terminally floundering Luffs. He next turned up at right-half, however, in QPR's first professional team in the Southern League, and remained in the middle line until finishing his career in that sphere with the then-lowly Bees.
Apps: 15 Lge.
Goals: 5 Lge.

KEELEY, ERNEST
b. Ellesmere Port, 1913.
Ellesmere Port Town/Sept 1931:Chester/
Feb 1932:CITY.
debut: 18.2.32 v.West Ham United (H).

A product of Cheshire junior football, wing-half Ernie was signed up in time to play in Chester's first-ever League side, and had barely had time to adjust to this elevation when City slapped in a bid of £2,500 to give him a lightning glimpse of Division One football. Looked upon as a longer-term contender for the problematic right-half position, Ernie unfortunately never got much chance to lay claim to it, being injured so badly early the next season that he was forced to quit the game entirely in 1933. His father had been Chester's goalkeeper when they won the Welsh Cup in 1908, while Ernie's younger brother Arthur was truly ill-fated, moving optimistically up in status as a forward from Chester to Portsmouth in 1939, but being killed in action during the war.
Apps: 4 Lge.

KELLARD, ROBERT SYDNEY WILLIAM
b. Southend, 1.3.1943.
Mar 1960:Southend United/
Sept 1963:Crystal Palace/
Nov 1965:Ipswich Town/
Mar 1966:Portsmouth/July 1968:Bristol City/
Aug 1970:CITY/Sept 1971:Crystal Palace/
Dec 1972:Portsmouth/
(Jan 1975-loan-Hereford United)/
Sept 1975:Torquay United.
debut: 15.8.70 v.Cardiff City (H).

A combative midfielder with an alert brain to complement his ball-winning skills, Bobby was the mainspring of City's 1971 promotion side, and as soon as he linked with Willie Carlin, the club's upward ambitions achieved an immovable foundation. Chipping in with some valuable goals on the way to that championship, Bobby was unfortunate not to consolidate his First Division career with City, but new boss Jimmy Bloomfield soon had him crossing paths with Alan Birchenall as the club's tactical emphasis changed. His League career had begun at the age of 16, and England youth caps had come his way before he embarked on his travels. The alacrity with which former clubs Palace and Pompey welcomed the mature player back for second spells was testimony to the value placed on his tenacious talent. At the end of his playing career, Bobby briefly took the manager's chair at Chelmsford City, and then entered the antiques business.
Apps: 48 Lge; 6 FAC; 6 LC.
Goals: 8 Lge.

BOBBY KELLARD

KELLY, BERNARD
b. Carfin, 21.10.1932.
Law Hearts/1951:Muirkirk Juniors/
Oct 1951:Raith Rovers/July 1958:CITY/
Apr 1959:Nottingham Forest/
cs 1959:Aberdeen/Aug 1960:Raith Rovers.
debut: 30.8.58 v.Arsenal (A).

A hefty goalscoring inside-forward who developed a formidable reputation at Starks Park and garnered due recognition in 1957 at Scotland 'B' and Scottish League levels, Bernie came south as a David Halliday purchase with a record of 92 League and Cup goals from 207 games. He was soon on the goal trail again at Filbert Street, sniping successfully during a typically entrenched rearguard campaign for the club, but sadly failed to settle off the pitch. A brief stay on Trentside did nothing to ameliorate Bernie's home-sickness, but he never quite recaptured former glories after returning to Scotland. He currently works in a solar heating business in Canada.
Apps: 24 Lge; 3 FAC.
Goals: 13 Lge; 2 FAC.

EDDIE KELLY

KELLY, EDWARD PATRICK
b. Glasgow, 7.2.1951.
Possilpark/app 1966/pro Feb 1968:Arsenal/
Sept 1976:Queens Park Rangers/
July 1977:CITY/July 1980:Notts County/
Aug 1981:Bournemouth/Dec 1981:CITY/
Mar 1983:Kettering Town/Melton Town/
Oct 1984:Torquay United.
debut: 20.8.77 v.Manchester City (A).

Frank McLintock's first and probably most valuable signing, Eddie was a former team-mate of his new boss during the glory years at Highbury as well as at Loftus Road. A scorer in the 1970 Fairs Cup Final, Eddie had gone on to contribute mightily to Arsenal's 1971 Double, entering the record books as the first substitute to score in an FA Cup Final, and winning Scotland Under-23 honours. His compact midfield style was somewhat overwhelmed in City's 1978 plummet, but he reacted well as mature anchorman to Jock Wallace's young promotion side, and it was a genuine surprise when greater efforts to retain his services were not made in 1980, after his contract had expired. Eddie's immediate success in inspiring Notts County to swap divisions with City seemed a sad irony to Leicester supporters, but it was not in fact long before Wallace called him back to the Second Division fray, for Leicester once more had to lean a little on his experience. In 1984 David Webb, too, signed Eddie for a second time to add another reviving jolt to his career.
Apps: 119 Lge; 8+1 FAC; 5 LC.
Goals: 3 Lge.

KELLY, ROBERT ANTHONY
b. Birmingham, 21.12.1964.
app Oct 1981/pro Dec 1982:CITY/
(Dec 1984-loan-Tranmere Rovers)/

Feb 1987:Wolverhampton Wanderers.
debut: 12.5.84 v.Sunderland (H).

A Brummie midfielder whose parentage qualified him to play as an Eire youth international, Robert clearly possessed useful ball skills, but occasionally appeared less well equipped for the robust physical challenge of top-class football. A loan spell with Bryan Hamilton's Tranmere (2 goals in five games) seemed to signal City's willingness to jettison him after only one first team run-out, but Robert was in Gordon Milne's line-up at the start of 1985/6, and was also a squad member under Hamilton the following season, distinguishing himself with a neatly chipped goal against Manchester United. With his Filbert Street development at something of a standstill, though, the club accepted Wolves' £30,000 fee for Robert, who helped steer the Molineux side into the 1987 Third/Fourth Division play-offs, but then sustained a serious back injury which kept him out of Wolves' successful promotion sides of the following two years.
Apps: 17+7 Lge; 1+2 LC.
Goals: 1 Lge.

KEMBER, STEPHEN DENNIS
b. Croydon, 8.12.1948.
app July 1965/pro Dec 1965:Crystal Palace/
Sept 1971:Chelsea/July 1975:CITY/
(Apr 1978-loan-Vancouver Whitecaps)/
Oct 1978:Crystal Palace/
Mar 1980:Vancouver Whitecaps.
debut: 16.8.75 v.Birmingham City (H).

A tigerish midfielder who made an early impression at Selhurst, and was part of the first Palace side to reach Division One, Steve moved to Chelsea for £170,000 - then a club record - just as Dave Sexton's side were going into decline. By the time he came to Filbert Street, on the heels of Chelsea's eventual relegation, Steve had already totted up nearly 350 League games (and had won three England Under-23 caps), but there was no sign of tiredness in his play as he chased and prompted among his fellow London exiles with City. The 1978 debacle took much out of him, though, and Steve didn't last long into the Wallace regime. A £50,000 move saw him back at Selhurst for two more playing seasons, and successive stints as youth coach and caretaker manager.
Apps: 115+2 Lge; 5 FAC; 6 LC.
Goals: 6 Lge.

KENNEDY,
MICHAEL FRANCIS MARTIN
b. Salford, 9.4.1961.
app cs 1977/pro Jan 1979:Halifax Town/
Aug 1980:Huddersfield Town/
Aug 1982:Middlesbrough/
June 1984:Portsmouth/Jan 1988:Bradford City/
Mar 1989:CITY.
debut: 18.3.89 v.Plymouth Argyle (A).

Having brought Halifax their then-record incoming fee of £50,000 as a teenage midfielder, Mick developed his ball-winning skills in several hard-knocks schools throughout the 80's, drawing admiration from many for

his drive and commitment (and winning two caps for the Republic of Ireland in May 1986), but also attracting censure during his Pompey days for some ill-judged verbal revelling in his hard-man image. Having helped Portsmouth into Division One in 1987, and Bradford City into the play-offs in 1988, he arrived at Filbert Street shortly before the 1989 transfer deadline, in a straight swap with Jimmy Quinn, and immediately assumed Paul Ramsey's midfield anchoring role.
Apps (to 13.5.89): 9 Lge.

KEOGH, GEORGE
b.
Leicester Imperial/Oct 1905:FOSSE/
Sept 1907:Leicester Imperial/Hinckley United.
debut: 20.1.06 v.Leeds City (A).

A local left-back who showed promise in trials and friendlies, but only got a lone crack at senior level, replacing the injured Oakes in a 1-4 defeat at Leeds.
Apps: 1 Lge.

KEYWORTH, KENNETH
b. Rotherham, 24.2.1934.
am:Wolverhampton Wanderers/
Jan 1952:Rotherham United/May 1958:CITY/
Dec 1964:Coventry City/
Aug 1965:Swindon Town.
debut: 23.8.58 v.Everton (H).

One risks describing the supposedly 'typical' Yorkshireman in attempting to characterise Ken. Rugged, dour, and an honest grafter, he gave City seven seasons of unflashy commitment as he developed from left-half to centre-forward, playing all his Filbert Street games in the First Division and capping his career with the superb diving header that proved the 1963 side's only moment of Wembley glory. Ken almost joined Wolves as a junior, but became a home-town Millmoor regular after finishing his National Service. His only representative honour was at wing-half for a Sheffield Select team against England 'B', and he cost City a bargain £9,000 a couple of seasons before Matt Gillies and Bert Johnson began experimenting with him up front. Ken wore the No.10 shirt in the 1961 Cup Final, No.9 two years later, and was still the club's central striker in both legs of the 1964 League Cup Final. Injuries received in a car crash severely blunted his effectiveness thereafter, and his free transfer move to Jimmy Hill's Coventry was ironically completed on the same day City slaughtered them 8-1 at Highfield Road on the way to another League Cup Final.
Apps: 177 Lge; 23 FAC; 11 LC; 4 ECWC.
Goals: 63 Lge; 7 FAC; 4 LC; 3 ECWC.

KING, EDWIN
b. Leicester, 1884.
d. Braunstone, 7.7.1952.
Aylestone Swifts/St.Andrews/
Leicester Imperial/May 1906:FOSSE.
debut: 6.4.07 v.West Bromwich Albion (A).

Serving his sole senior club for eighteen seasons until retiring to become City's coach at the age of 40, Teddy was a hard-working

worrier of a half-back who would fit in wherever Fosse or City required his whole-hearted reliability. He waited longer for a regular first team place than many of his peers, having only 15 appearances to his name before 1910, after which he successively held down the pivotal position, both wing-half spots, and even, in 1914/15, the centre-forward berth, with his ten goals making him Fosse's second-top scorer that season. Teddy's versatility was just as invaluable after the war, and it was at this juncture that he also became the regular wicketkeeper for Leicestershire's Second XI, eventually making a belated County break-through for two matches in 1925. A distinctly well-earned club benefit came his way from the League game with Stockport County in February 1920, while Teddy also wrote his name indelibly into the City record as coach to the side which came so close to the First Division title in 1929.
Apps: 227 Lge; 9 FAC.
Goals: 26 Lge.

KING, GEORGE
b. Coalville.
Coalville Town/Aug 1909:FOSSE.
debut: 10.12.10 v.Gainsborough Trinity (H).

A reserve left-back for two seasons with Fosse, George was described as possessing a 'pretty style' but appearing 'fragile' when making his sole League appearance. His 1909 contract, still on City's files, gives some insight into a footballer's conditions at the time, with George taking home the princely sum of £1.7s.6d per week from April to September, with no guarantee of any summer wages whatever if his registration wasn't renewed.
Apps: 1 Lge.

KING, HARRY EDWIN
b. Northampton.
Nov 1907:Birmingham/Worcester/
cs 1910:Crewe Alexandra/
June 1911:Northampton Town/
May 1914:Arsenal/Oct 1919:CITY/
Sept 1920:Brentford.
debut: 18.10.19 v.Huddersfield Town (A).

A free-scoring centre-forward who came to prominence in the Cobblers' Southern League days, with 67 goals in only 99 games, Harry then continued to hit the net regularly at Highbury, where his tally included a four-goal haul from the last game Arsenal ever played in the Second Division. He could not claim a senior spot there immediately after the war, however, and came to Leicester in a package deal with forward partner Billy Spittle. Though both scored in their first home match, neither settled down with City. Yet Harry was to go on to create more goal records at Griffin Park, finishing as top scorer in Brentford's initial League season, and notching their first hat-trick at that level.
Apps: 8 Lge.
Goals: 1 Lge.

IAN KING

KING, IAN AITKEN
b. Loanhead, 27.5.1937.
Broughton Star/Arniston Rangers/
June 1957:CITY/Mar 1966:Charlton Athletic.
debut: 11.9.57 v.Sheffield Wednesday (A).

A Scottish schoolboy international surprisingly
released from a provisional contract with
Hearts, Ian was a Matt Gillies discovery who
eventually won a lengthy personal battle with
England prospect Tony Knapp for the City
No.5 berth. The rugged pivot in all four of
City's early 60s Cup Final sides (missing only
the second leg of the League Cup Final against
Chelsea), he was also a composed distributor
who spread the ball forward with some poise
and vision. When Ian finally surrendered his
position to John Sjoberg, he soon found himself
in familiar company at The Valley, playing
alongside Colin Appleton, and when he retired
as a player he returned to live locally, spending
time coaching at both Enderby Town and
Burton Albion, and managing Thringstone.
Apps: 244 Lge; 27 FAC; 22 LC; 4 ECWC.
Goals: 6 Lge; 1 LC.

KING, JOHN
b. Birmingham.
Hinckley United/Jan 1922:CITY/
July 1924:Halifax Town.
debut: 9.2.22 v.Clapton Orient (H).

Kept in the reserves primarily by Harry
Graham's consistency, Jack was an inside-left
who managed a respectable goal ratio on his
sporadic senior appearances during 1921/2 and
1923/4, yet who later lasted less than a season
at The Shay after moving with Tommy Duncan
and scoring on his Halifax debut.
Apps: 7 Lge.
Goals: 4 Lge.

KING, JOHN CHARLES
b. Great Gidding, 5.11.1926.
am Sept 1943/pro Sept 1944:CITY/

July 1955:Kettering Town.
debut (postwar): 31.8.46
v.Manchester City (H).

Signed as a part-timer during the war after
impressing in Peterborough schools football,
Johnny was a left-half and occasional inside-
forward who maintained the unusual dual
professions of footballer and farmer throughout
his career. The youngest and smallest player of
the 1949 Cup team, he could not have been
further from the rustic stereotype, for his wiry
physique was driven by a shrewd footballing
intelligence which served City well for nine
postwar seasons.
Apps: 197 Lge; 21 FAC.
Goals: 5 Lge.

KING, ROBERT
b.
1895:Airdrieonians/Aug 1897:FOSSE/
Apr 1900:Glossop/Aug 1901:FOSSE/
cs 1902:Hamilton Academicals.
debut: 11.9.97 v.Small Heath (A).

A versatile forward in both his spells with
Fosse, Rab alternated primarily between the
outside-left and centre-forward positions, and
was top scorer in the season before he first
moved on to Second Division rivals Glossop.
One of his meagre two goals for the Derbyshire
side was against Fosse, and when Rab returned,
he played through 1901/2 as an ever-present.
Apps: 115 Lge; 9 FAC.
Goals: 34 Lge; 5 FAC.

KING, WILLIAM
b.
Hull City/Sept 1911:FOSSE/
cs 1912:Goole Town.
debut: 16.9.11 v.Nottingham Forest (A).

'His only defect was lack of weight', summed
up the Daily Post's critic when Fosse released
young forward Willie after his season's shot at
League football - a level he had failed
previously to reach with Hull. He joined Goole
as they prepared for their first season in the
Midland League.
Apps: 7 Lge; 1 FAC.
Goals: 4 Lge.

KIRKMAN, NORMAN
b. Bolton, 6.6.1920.
1941:Burnley/Sept 1946:Rochdale/
Dec 1947:Chesterfield/Aug 1949:CITY/
July 1950:Southampton/
Mar 1952:Exeter City (p/mgr).
debut: 27.8.49 v.Hull City (H).

Freed by Burnley without playing a peacetime
League game, Norman became a sought-after
full-back at Rochdale, and earned that club its
then-record fee from a Chesterfield management keen to improve on their recent highest-
ever Second Division placing. Johnny Duncan
paid £8,500 to bring him to Leicester, but he
was soon asking new manager Norman Bullock
for a transfer after failing to hang on to the
senior No.3 shirt. Two seasons at The Dell saw
a similar in-and-out record develop, and
Norman's subsequent managerial stints were

also of fairly short duration: a year at Exeter,
and just under two holding the reins at Bradford
Park Avenue. Much later, in the mid-60s, he
was boss at Northwich Victoria.
Apps: 12 Lge.

KNAPP, ANTHONY
b. Newstead, 13.10.1936.
Newstead Colliery/am:Nottingham Forest/
Bentinck Juniors/Dec 1953:CITY/
Aug 1961:Southampton/
Aug 1967:Coventry City/
Mar 1968:Los Angeles Wolves/
Mar 1969:Bristol City/
Oct 1969:Tranmere Rovers/
July 1971:Poole Town (p/mgr).
debut: 11.2.56 v.Stoke City (A).

A classy young centre-half who made rapid
strides after 1958 and was soon fringeing the
England side - being once chosen as travelling
reserve for the national team, and once
appearing for the Football League against the
Scottish League in March 1960 - Tony had the
ill-fortune to lose his place through injury and
find such a capable rival as Ian King barring his
way back. The disappointment of missing out
on the 1961 Cup run led to an almost inevitable
move, but in the course of a 233-game League
career for the Saints, Tony's sole tangible
honour was to help that club into Division One
for the first time in 1966. Coventry sent out a
desperate call to Tony to replace broken-leg
victim George Curtis after only two games of
their first-ever top flight season, and he
eventually saw out his senior playing days in
the Third with Tranmere, before learning the
managerial ropes with Poole Town in 1971. It
has, however, been abroad that Tony has made
his biggest impact, managing the Icelandic
national side as well as four leading Norwegian
clubs: Viking Stavanger, Fredrikstad, Vidar
Stavanger and Brann Bergen.
Apps: 86 Lge; 4 FAC; 2 LC.

KRUSE, PATRICK KARL
b. Arlesey, 30.11.1953.
Arlesey Town/app June 1970/pro Feb1972:
CITY/(Sept 1974-loan-Mansfield Town)/
Mar 1975:Torquay United/Mar 1977:Brentford/
(Feb 1982-loan-Northampton Town)/
cs 1982:Barnet.
debut: 27.4.74 v.Tottenham Hotspur (A).

Like Derek Harrison, another 'home-grown'
centre-half edged out of the first team
reckoning by the similar internal promotions of
the likes of Munro and Sims, Pat got his only
City chances in the final games of 1973/4, then
actually replaced Harrison at Plainmoor. It was
towards the end of his 79-game spell with
Torquay that Pat unwillingly put himself in the
record books - as scorer of the fastest-ever own
goal in League history, after only six seconds of
the Torquay v.Cambridge United game of
January 1977. He totalled 186 League games
for Brentford after being signed by former City
coach Bill Dodgin, scoring 12 goals at the right
end, but his experience could not help lift
Northampton out of the re-election zone during
his extended loan spell at the County Ground.
Apps: 2 Lge.

KYLE, PETER
b. Glasgow, 1878.
cs 1899:Liverpool/May 1900:FOSSE/
1901:Wellingborough/West Ham United/
Kettering/cs 1902 not known/
cs 1904:Port Glasgow Athletic.
debut: 1.9.1900 v.Stockport County (H).

An inside-forward whose Anfield record
amounted to four barren League games, and
one in the Cup, Peter had one Fosse season in
which his scoring rate was hardly more prolific,
and then made three rapid moves around the
Southern League. (There is no firm evidence
either way, but it is suspected that 'our' man
was not the same Peter Kyle who moved from
Larkhall Thistle to Tottenham in 1905, and then
on to Woolwich Arsenal, Aston Villa, Sheffield
United, Royal Albert and Watford).
Apps: 31 Lge; 1 FAC.
Goals: 3 Lge; 1 FAC.

LANE, WILLIAM HARRY CHARLES
b. Tottenham, 23.10.04.
d. Chelmsford, 10.11.1985.
Gnome Athletic/Park Avondale/Barnet/
Northfleet/cs 1924:Tottenham Hotspur/
Nov 1926:CITY/May 1928:Reading/
May 1929:Brentford/May 1932:Watford/
Jan 1936:Bristol City/July 1937:Clapton Orient.
debut: 6.11.26 v.Derby County (A) (1 goal).

Signed for £2,250 after showing goalscoring
potential with Spurs (7 goals in 26 games),
Billy spent an almost inevitably frustrating
couple of seasons with City as understudy to
Arthur Chandler, scoring in the first two of his
extremely limited outings in the centre-forward
berth. By the time he got to Griffin Park,
though, Billy was really ready to let loose -
notching 84 strikes in only 114 games for the
Bees. Seventy-two more goals followed at
Watford, including a hat-trick scored inside a
three-minute spell in a game against Clapton
Orient - ironically to become his last club. Billy
went on to serve a managerial apprenticeship at
Guildford City, and was guiding the fortunes of
Brighton & Hove Albion when they took the
Third Division (South) championship in 1958.
He later managed Gravesend & Northfleet, and
scouted for Arsenal and Brighton.
Apps: 5 Lge.
Goals: 2 Lge.

LANG, JOHN
b. Kilbirnie, Ayrshire, 16.8.1882.
Co-Operative United (Glasgow)/Govan/
cs 1902:Barnsley/Feb 1903:Sheffield United/
Sept 1909:FOSSE/cs 1910:Denaby United.
debut: 18.9.09 v.Lincoln City (A).

The right-wing partner of Jimmy Donnelly for
several of his early seasons with the Blades,
John was a candidate for full international
honours when chosen for the Anglo-Scots
against the Home Scots in March 1905, having
earned Junior caps some years previously. He
briefly resumed his old Bramall Lane liaison at
Filbert Street, though as often as not the former
team-mates were effectively in competition for
the outside-right spot during Fosse's highest-
scoring season. John's transfer itself was a far
from straightforward affair: not only was the

£75 fee to rise by another £25 should John be
retained for a second season; but Fosse's
cheque for the lower amount actually bounced
on first presentation!
Apps: 17 Lge.
Goals: 2 Lge.

LANGAN, DAVID FRANCIS
b. Dublin, 15.2.1957.
app/pro June 1976:Derby County/
July 1980:Birmingham City/
July 1984:Oxford United/
(Oct 1987-loan-CITY)/
Nov 1987:Bournemouth/
July 1988:Peterborough United.
debut: 24.10.87 v.Hull City (H).

A regular right-back choice for Eire over
almost a decade, David played all his football
for both the Rams and Blues (for whom he
represented a record purchase) in the First
Division, and aided Oxford's ascent to that
status within a year of being freed from
St.Andrews, going on to win a Milk Cup medal
in 1986. A tenacious tackler with an adventurous streak, he briefly added his experience to
Bryan Hamilton's struggling Second Division
side, but Oxford's demand for a transfer fee
precluded a permanent move to Filbert Street.
Within days of his loan spell coming to an end,
Second Division rivals Bournemouth invested
£25,000 in his defensive acumen.
Apps: 5 Lge.

LANGFORD, WALTER
b. Wolverhampton.
Wellington Town/May 1928:CITY/
Aug 1933:Queens Park Rangers.
debut: 2.2.29 v.Newcastle United (H).

Another of the several City reserves of decent
class left champing frustratedly at the bit during
the club's First Division heyday of the late
20's, Walter was the deputy for Arthur
Lochhead at inside-left, and eventually grabbed
rare first team chances at wing-half, too. Mick
O'Brien signed him for QPR.
Apps: 13 Lge; 2 FAC.
Goals: 5 Lge; 1 FAC.

LANGHAM, WILLIAM
b. Nottingham.
1894:South Shore/cs 1896:Notts County/
cs 1898:Bristol City/Nov 1900:FOSSE/
cs 1901:Doncaster Rovers/
cs 1903:Gainsborough Trinity/
cs 1906:(Irish football)/Mar 1907:Lincoln City.
debut: 15.12.1900 v.Woolwich Arsenal (H).

A well-travelled outside-right who spent his
shortest spell with one club at Filbert Street,
deposing Archie Brash, Billy then moved on to
assist Doncaster through their first two seasons
in the League. Previously he had helped Notts
County to Division One in 1897, scoring the
winning goal in one of the Test Matches that
then decided promotion and relegation issues,
and had played alongside Blessington,
Carnelly, Davy, Hamilton, Pollock and
Stevenson in Bristol.
Apps: 14 Lge; 1 FAC.
Goals: 2 Lge.

LARGE, FRANK
b. Leeds, 26.1.1940.
British Railways (Halifax)/
June 1959:Halifax Town/
June 1962:Queens Park Rangers/
Feb 1963:Northampton Town/
Mar 1964:Swindon Town/
Sept 1964:Carlisle United/
Dec 1965:Oldham Athletic/
Dec 1966:Northampton Town/
Nov 1967:CITY/June 1968:Fulham/
Aug 1969: Northampton Town/
Nov 1972:Chesterfield/
Apr 1974:Baltimore Comets/
Sept 1974:Kettering Town.
debut: 11.11.67 v.Manchester City (A).

Retiring in 1974 with 209 League goals under
his belt and presumably an expert knowledge of
the geography of Britain, Frank was one of the
old have-boots-will-travel brigade; an
anachronistically effective bustling centre-
forward who could terrify goalkeepers with
nothing more than a smile in their direction. It
looked a desperate measure for City to give him
his first break in the top flight, but the two-
thirds of a season he spent leading the Filbert
Street attack remain utterly memorable - for his
bravery, his unselfish lay-offs, his aerial power,
and his sheer infectious delight that First
Division defences were as susceptible to his
barnstorming style as had been those at lower
levels. When City included Frank in the
package deal which secured Allan Clarke there
was a distinct sense of loss to be set against the
excitement of a record buy - and the club's
history might have been very different if Frank
had been around for the relegation battles of
1969. As it was, he was soon back at the
County Ground for a third stint with the
Cobblers. With Northampton, he had previously won a Third Division championship
medal and had experienced relegation back,
while he had repeated those contrasting
achievements at other junctures with Carlisle
and Fulham respectively. Frank now runs a
farm in Ireland.
Apps: 26 Lge; 6 FAC.
Goals: 8 Lge; 3 FAC.

LEE, ALAN ROBERT
b. Wegberg, W.Germany, 19.6.1960.
1975:Rangers/Apr 1978:Philadelphia Fury/
Jan 1979:CITY/
cs 1981:Kidderminster Harriers.
debut: 28.4.79 v.Fulham (A).

A tall, sandy-haired winger, born on an RAF
base in Germany but brought up in Scotland,
Alan had been a youth team player under Jock
Wallace at Ibrox, and was the third City signing
from Philadephia within a year, following Pat
Byrne and Martin Henderson to Filbert Street.
Unfortunately, he made minimal impact on his
senior outings, at the end of 1978/9 and the
opening of the next season, as a left-sided
attacker.
Apps: 6 Lge.

LEE, ALBERT GEORGE
b.
Oxford Victoria (Leicester)/Aug 1904:FOSSE/

Leicester Imperial.
debut: 18.3.05 v.Lincoln City (A).

A local amateur inside-forward who deputised for Arthur Mounteney in the above game, a 1-5 defeat, and whose only other senior game was a friendly against Coventry City a year later.
Apps: 1 Lge.

JACK LEE

LEE, JACK
b. Sileby, 4.11.1920.
Quorn Methodists/am Dec 1940/
pro Feb 1941:CITY/June 1950:Derby County/
Nov 1954:Coventry City.
debut (postwar): 5.10.46
v.Luton Town (A) (2 goals).

City's main marksman in the immediate postwar years, after he left the RAF, Jack overcame a couple of serious injury setbacks to show international class striking prowess, though it was not until he became a Derby player that he actually gained his England cap, scoring in a 4-1 win in Belfast in 1950. Kenilworth Road must have been Jack's favourite away ground - apart from his debut-game double, he notched four there in the epic 5-5 Cup-tie of 1949 - the year he contributed eight Cup goals to City's Wembley progress. Lethal with both head and feet, he was a distinct crowd favourite, and there was uproar when the club accepted Derby's £16,000 bid - even if hindsight suggests City got the better of that day's dealings, with Arthur Rowley arriving as a replacement. Jack was second-top scorer in the First Division at the end of his first Baseball Ground season, but soon suffered more injuries which restricted his appearances thereafter. His aggregate League goal total when he finally left Highfield Road was 136 (in 232 games). Also a Leicestershire cricketer, Jack only made one County Championship appearance, in 1947 - despite taking a wicket with the first ball he bowled!
Apps: 123 Lge; 14 FAC.
Goals: 74 Lge; 10 FAC.

LEE, ROBERT GORDON
b. Melton Mowbray, 2.2.1953.
app July 1971/pro Feb 1972:CITY/
(Aug 1974-loan-Doncaster Rovers)/
Sept 1976:Sunderland/
Aug 1980:Bristol Rovers/
July 1981:Carlisle United/
Mar 1983:Southampton/Aug 1983:Darlington/
(cs 1984:Hong Kong)/1984:Boston United.
debut: 18.3.72 (sub) v.Derby County (A).

Sustained only by the memories of one-and-a-bit senior games for City over almost three years (and probably haunted by recall of a missed 'sitter' on his brief debut appearance), rangy striker Bob might have been forgiven for feeling he was on his way out when loaned to Doncaster at the beginning of 1974/5. Yet a decent run of League football reinvigorated his play, and a two-goal City comeback at Loftus Road on Boxing Day 1974 eased him into a regular support role to Frank Worthington and Chris Garland. In fact, Bob himself headed City's scoring list in 1975/6 as he began to make his powerful physique pay dividends in opposing penalty areas, but he was soon off to Roker in a big-money deal after Sunderland had failed to land Worthington. He played through relegation seasons for both Sunderland and Bristol Rovers, and a promotion year for Carlisle, but Bob actually had his proudest moment in non-league football, virtually ending his career at Wembley after scoring two semi-final goals to take Boston United to the FA Trophy Final in 1985.
Apps: 55+8 Lge; 3+1 FAC; 4 LC.
Goals: 17 Lge; 2 FAC.

LEECH, WILLIAM
b. Newcastle-under-Lyme, 1875.
Newcastle Swifts/cs 1898:Tottenham Hotspur/
cs 1899:Burslem Port Vale/cs 1900:Stoke/
cs 1903:Plymouth Argyle/July 1906:FOSSE.
debut: 1.9.06 v.Burslem Port Vale (A).

A defensive half-back broadly experienced in Potteries football, Billy was tempted south for a second time to play in Plymouth's inaugural season, and stayed three years in Southern League combat before joining Fosse. Missing only two League games in his first season in Fosse's right-half berth, and an ever-present in the 1908 promotion campaign, Billy then patiently coaxed along the reserves, occasionally deputising for his successor, Arthur Randle, until re-engaged as the senior club trainer; a position he held until WW1.
Apps: 84 Lge; 3 FAC.
Goals: 3 Lge.

LEEK, KENNETH
b. Ynysybwl, 26.7.1935.
Pontypridd/Aug 1952:Northampton Town/
Apr 1958:CITY/June 1961:Newcastle United/
Nov 1961:Birmingham City/
Dec 1964:Northampton Town/
Nov 1965:Bradford City/Aug 1968:Rhyl/
1970:Ton Pentre.
debut: 23.8.58 v.Everton (H) (1 goal).

Ironically best remembered for the game he didn't play for City, Ken was a fine centre-forward who may have developed a truly stellar career if the blow of being dropped on the eve of the 1961 Cup Final hadn't hit him so hard. Already a Welsh Under-23 cap at Fourth Division Northampton, Ken joined City in the top flight initially as an inside or outside-left, but was soon vying with Derek Hines for the No.9 shirt, winning the first six of his eventual 17 full Welsh caps, and accelerating his chance-taking ratio - to the point where he had scored in every round of the FA Cup before City incomprehensibly took the field at Wembley without him. A move was inevitable after that, and Ken became a noted marksman at St.Andrews following his brief spell on Tyneside, claiming two goals in Blues' League Cup Final win over Villa in 1963. He returned to his first club to help the Cobblers up into the First Division, and fetched a club record £10,000 fee from Bradford City shortly afterwards. By the time he moved back to Wales, Ken had totted up 147 League goals.
Apps: 93 Lge; 17 FAC; 1 LC.
Goals: 34 Lge; 9 FAC.

LEET, NORMAN DAVID
b. Leicester, 13.3.1962.
Shepshed Charterhouse/June 1980:CITY/
Feb 1983:Shepshed Charterhouse/Oadby Town.
debut: 2.5.81 v.Norwich City (A).

A sturdily-built, no-frills defender who had been an England schoolboy international at centre-half, Norman held down the left-back spot for a couple of spells during 1981/2 under Jock Wallace. He had only one first team chance to impress Gordon Milne, however, and was soon released. He was then denied through a combination of injury and employment difficulties even a decent part-time career in senior non-league football.
Apps: 19 Lge; 3 LC.

LEGGE, A.
b. London.
Custom House/July 1914:FOSSE/
cs 1915:Croydon Common.
debut: 13.3.15 v.Glossop (A).

A reserve centre-forward who followed Jim Harrold's path from London League football to the Fosse, but met with little success, finding himself only the sixth selection as attack leader during the club's last, dismal pre-war season. In common with City's Dennis Cheney, he had the odd experience of appearing only in an away win and a home defeat.
Apps: 2 Lge.

LEIGHTON, JOHN
b.
Hibernian/July 1896:FOSSE.
debut: 5.9.96 v.Darwen (H).

Initially vying with Jack Lord for the left-half spot during his Fosse season, John invariably completed an all-Scottish half-back line (with Brown and Walker or Proudfoot) whenever he appeared. He was reported as returning north of the border in 1897, but there is no record of him playing subsequently at Scottish League level.
Apps: 14 Lge.

LEVER, ARTHUR RICHARD
b. Cardiff, 25.3.1920.
Cardiff Corinthians/cs 1943:Cardiff City/
Sept 1950:CITY/July 1954:Newport County.
debut: 9.9.50 v.Sheffield United (H).

Always popularly known as 'Buller', right-back
Arthur was an ever-present member of the
Cardiff side which took the Third Division
(South) title in 1946/7, and was soon knocking
on the door of the First. A club record buy for
City at £15,000, Arthur was entrusted by
Norman Bullock with the team captaincy, and
exhibited a cool defensive acumen, though for
his last two seasons he had to fight hard with
Stan Milburn for the Filbert Street senior berth.
He won his sole Welsh cap in October 1952,
against Scotland, and later returned to his
homeland to assist Newport for three years.
Apps: 119 Lge; 5 FAC.

LEWIS, ALBERT EDWARD TALBOT
b. Bedminster, 20.1.1877.
d. Bristol, 22.2.1956.
Jan 1896:Bedminster/cs 1897:Bristol City/
1898:Everton/1899:Bristol City/1901:Walsall/
1902:Sheffield United/Aug 1904:Sunderland/
cs 1905·Luton Town/Aug 1906:FOSSE/
Oct 1907:Bristol City.
debut: 1.9.06 v.Burslem Port Vale (A).

Usually known simply as 'Tal', this tall,
athletic goalkeeper was an ever-present for
Fosse as they narrowly missed out on promotion in 1906/7 - making his career-best
unbroken run of first-class games - and it was a
major surprise that he was not retained for the
following campaign. Certainly, First Division
Bristol City had no qualms about re-signing
him for a third spell on their books, though
after a season there, 'Tal' retired to concentrate
on his parallel career as a Somerset cricketer,
going on to score one double-century championship innings. Much later, in 1920, he coached
the summer game in India. Prior to his Fosse
sojourn, he had managed 23 League games for
the Blades and 4 at Roker Park (after signing in
a joint deal with Alf Common), but his time at
both Everton and Luton had been spent entirely
in reserve football. Until the turn of the century,
most of his recorded appearances had been as a
full-back!
Apps: 38 Lge; 1 FAC.

LEWIS, GEORGE
b. Chasetown, 1876.
Nov 1894:Walsall Town Swifts/
Wellingborough/Feb 1897:Notts County/
cs 1902:Bristol City/cs 1903:Stourbridge/
Oct 1903:FOSSE.
debut: 10.10.03 v.Burnley (H).

A left-back with a lot of accumulated First
Division experience from his Magpies days
(129 games), George came to Leicester via
Ashton Gate to contest his defensive berth with
Walter Robinson, but showed few signs of
being able to reverse the team's precipitous
drop into the re-election zone, and rather too
obvious signs of advancing age. As an aside
relevant to changing trends in football fashion,
George was invariably photographed with his

hands in his shorts pockets!
Apps: 10 Lge; 5 FAC.

LEWIS, WILLIAM J.
b.
Feb 1894:Small Heath/cs 1898:not known/
Stourbridge/May 1902:FOSSE.
debut: 6.9.02 v.Small Heath (H) (1 goal).

All five members of the Fosse front line were
making their club debut when this veteran
centre-forward made his scoring bow against
his former team, and he was one of only three
who saw out the season, albeit at inside-right
and with a fairly dismal goalgetting record.
Apps: 30 Lge; 1 FAC.
Goals: 3 Lge.

DANNY LIDDLE

LIDDLE,
DANIEL HAMILTON SNEDDON
b. Bo'ness, 17.2.1912.
d. Wigston, 9.6.1982.
Bo'ness/East Fife/May 1932:CITY/
July 1946:Mansfield Town.
debut: 27.8.32 v.Sheffield United (H).

A small, tricky left-winger with a fair eye for
goal, Danny became the first East Fife player to
be capped for his country, and had turned out
three times for Scotland in the year before he
trekked south to Filbert Street. A remarkably
consistent performer for City up to and through
the war, and occasionally an electric one,
Danny was twice the club's top scorer in the
years of First Division struggle, switching to
the inside-left berth to accommodate Eric
Stubbs in the 1937 promotion effort. He also
assisted Northampton, Notts County and
Mansfield in wartime competition, and after
nominally retiring in May 1946, came back for
one final League game with the Stags.
Apps: 255 Lge; 19 FAC.
Goals: 64 Lge; 7 FAC.

LIGGINS, JOHN GRANVILLE
b. Altrincham, 26.3.1906.
d. Hyde, 22.2.1976.
Hyde/Dec 1933:CITY/Nov 1935:Burnley.
debut: 24.11.34 v.Leeds United (H) (1 goal).

A former railway worker whose Cheshire
League scoring exploits attracted City's
envious gaze, Jack became another pretender to
the mantle of the ageing Arthur Chandler, and
was doubly unfortunate to suffer an early
broken collar-bone and to be fighting for his
place in a relegation-bound team, for his strike
rate was good given his limited opportunities.
After moving to fellow Second Division team
Burnley for £640, he again walked into a
difficult situation, with the 16-year-old Tommy
Lawton pressing his irresistible claim to the
first team leader's role, and Jack missed out
once more.
Apps: 8 Lge.
Goals: 5 Lge.

LIGHTBODY, THOMAS
b. Motherwell.
Dec 1911:FOSSE/cs 1913:Peebles Rovers.
debut: 9.4.12 v.Clapton Orient (H).

A young Scottish centre-half who found
himself understudying Percy Hanger at
Leicester, and moved on after Jim Harrold had
arrived to claim the regular pivotal role. Each
of Tom's appearances were in home victories.
Apps: 3 Lge.

LINEKER, GARY WINSTON
b. Leicester, 30.11.1960.
app July 1977/pro Dec 1978:CITY/
June 1985:Everton/July 1986:Barcelona/
June 1989:Tottenham Hotspur.
debut: 1.1.79 v.Oldham Athletic (H).

Although now regarded as one of the world's
foremost strikers, Gary made a rather stumbling
start to his first-team career with City, who
initially struggled to harness the youngster's
remarkable pace to a coherent tactical role.
Indeed, Gary was quite often played wide in his
early days, until his alert goal-poaching habit
began truly to blossom during 1981/2. There
were still distinct gaps in his footballing
repertoire when City fought their way back to
Division One in 1983, but Gary gradually
refined his ball-holding and control skills while
leading the Filbert Street scoring list for four
seasons running on quick-witted predatory
instinct, and became an inevitable England
choice up front despite City's lowly status in
the top flight. Equally inevitable, perhaps, was
a move, and it was to reigning champions
Everton that Gary went in return for an
£800,000 cheque. Thirty League goals, ten
more in Cup competitions (including one at
Wembley in the FA Cup Final), and both
versions of the Footballer of the Year award
made up Gary's individual tally from his
Goodison season, when he also emerged as an
unexpectedly fine header of the ball, though the
Toffees finished runners-up to Liverpool in
both major domestic competitions. Gary's
value escalated dramatically again, however,
following his summer exploits in the 1986
World Cup, when his hat-trick against Poland
made him a national hero and his total of six
goals won him the competition's Golden Boot
award as top scorer. Terry Venables' Barcelona
laid out some £2,750,000 in pesetas for Gary's
now globally-famous talent, with City benefit-

ing from a negotiated percentage of Everton's profit (amounting to £250,000), and the quicksilver striker maintained his fine scoring record at both club and international level, though neither of his partnerships with fellow exiles Mark Hughes or Steve Archibald could quite prompt Barcelona higher than second place in the Spanish League in 1987. Gary picked up his first-ever winner's medal from the 1988 Spanish Cup Final, but took the first real knock to his modestly-handled prestige when, suffering from the onset of hepatitis, he shared in England's poor European Championship displays that summer. Perhaps ironically, his rehabilitation at Barcelona under Johan Cruyff's management entailed an enforced return to virtually orthodox wing play, with his cross from the right providing the opening goal in the Catalans' European Cup Winners Cup victory of 1989. A comeback to characteristic scoring form for England, and a second big money signing for Terry Venables, then heralded Gary's return to the Football League.
Apps: 187+7 Lge; 13 FAC; 9 LC.
Goals: 95 Lge; 6 FAC; 2 LC.

GARY LINEKER

LING, ARTHUR SAMUEL (ARCHIE)
b. Cambridge.
Cambridge/June 1902:FOSSE/
cs 1905:Swindon Town/cs 1909:Brentford.
debut: 6.9.02 v.Small Heath (H).

The regular goalkeeper, over-exposed behind a flimsy defence, during two lowly seasons of Second Division struggle at Fosse, Archie loyally returned in December 1904 to deputise for the injured Walter Smith, despite having been released some months before. At Swindon, he was a Southern League custodian for four years and 140 games, although only a registration wrangle had stopped him moving to Norwich in 1907. With Brentford, in the same competition, Archie also showed commendable consistency, and is credited by some sources

with scoring two goals for them during 1910/11. He additionally played a reasonable standard of Minor Counties cricket for Cambridgeshire.
Apps: 59 Lge; 7 FAC.

LITTLER, JOSEPH ERIC
b. St.Helens, 14.4.1929.
Stubshaw Cross/May 1951:CITY/
Dec 1954:Lincoln City/June 1955:Wrexham/
Dec 1955:Crewe Alexandra/Aug 1956:Chorley.
debut: 26.4.52 v.Notts County (H) (1 goal).

Plucked from the lower reaches of Lancashire Combination football, Eric was a stubborn trier of a centre-forward who made sporadic appearances over the course of four seasons as deputy to Derek Hines, then moved on in part-exchange for Andy Graver. His inability to command a regular berth was repeated with his three subsequent clubs, and Eric compiled an aggregate of only 28 League appearances and five goals after leaving Filbert Street.
Apps: 5 Lge; 1 FAC.
Goals: 2 Lge.

LOCHHEAD, ANDREW LORIMAR
b. Milngavie, 9.3.1941.
Renfrew Juniors/Dec 1958:Burnley/
Oct 1968:CITY/Feb 1970:Aston Villa/
Aug 1973:Oldham Athletic/
(Apr 1974-loan-Denver Dynamo).
debut: 2.11.68 v.Newcastle United (A).

A six-foot, bullet-domed central striker who made his First Division mark as a superb header of the ball, Andy had won one Scotland Under-23 cap in 1963 and gone on to amass more than a century of League goals for Burnley prior to his £80,000 move to Leicester. Though he had once totally frustrated a City attack when serving as a stand-in centre-half for Burnley at Filbert Street, it was definitely his goal-touch that the soon-to-depart Matt Gillies coveted as City struggled in 1968/9, and which would help pave the way to Wembley during that season of contrasts. Andy gloried in the Fifth Round Anfield winner, but rather muffed his Cup Final chance of even greater fame with a miscued shot from a fine position. He started the following season with a quick-fire goal spree, but couldn't maintain the momentum, and after Frank O'Farrell let him move on to Villa Park, Andy proved unable to save his new club from their embarrassing drop into the Third Division. He did, however, assist them to the League Cup Final in 1971 and then to promotion in 1972, and also prompted Oldham up to the Second in his initial season at Boundary Park. Andy later coached the Latics and managed Padiham.
Apps: 40+4 Lge; 12+1 FAC; 6 LC.
Goals: 12 Lge; 3 FAC; 4 LC.

LOCHHEAD, ARTHUR WILLIAM
b. Busby, 8.12.1897.
Mar 1919:Heart of Midlothian/
June 1921:Manchester United/Oct 1925:CITY.
debut: 17.10.25
v.West Bromwich Albion (H) (2 goals).

Another of Peter Hodge's key signings, Arthur

was bought from Old Trafford for £3,300 to add his guile in both the scoring and scheming departments to City's initial attempts at First Division consolidation - and the inside-left duly delivered in a nine-year playing span at Filbert Street which ended with his elevation to the manager's chair in October 1934. Arthur had shown sufficient early promise at Hearts (as top scorer in the same team as Harry Graham) to merit a Scottish trial in the Home Scots v.Anglo-Scots fixture in March 1920, and was still displaying consistent high class stealth when chosen to represent the Anglos in the equivalent game eight years later, while he was simultaneously helping City to their highest-ever top flight positions and holding down a job as a schoolmaster. In the interim, he had experienced both relegation and promotion with United while establishing the goal-every-three-games ratio he would maintain with City - though he would not again be associated with a relegated side until persuaded by the City board to swap his veteran player status for that of manager following Peter Hodge's death in 1934. A City side whose central figures had aged together went down in 1935 despite Arthur's attempts to turn over the staff, yet it was a surprise when he resigned shortly after the start of the 1936/7 season, as his reshaped team had finished a respectable sixth in the Second Division the term before.
Apps: 303 Lge; 17 FAC.
Goals: 106 Lge; 8 FAC.

LONIE, THOMAS
b.
Dundee Harp/Jan 1894:Notts County/
July 1894:Darwen/Dundee Wanderers/Dundee/
Oct 1895:Stoke/Aug 1896:FOSSE.
debut: 5.9.96 v.Darwen (H) (1 goal).

A Fosse centre-forward for a little over two months, Tom claimed a hat-trick in the second public trial match of 1896, scored each of his Second Division goals against his former Darwen club-mates, and had his abrupt departure later described in the secretary's report as a 'defection'.
Apps: 7 Lge.
Goals: 2 Lge.

LORD, JACK
b.
Derby St.Luke's/cs 1891:FOSSE.
debut: 12.9.91 v.Derby Junction (H) ML.

A veteran of Fosse's first Midland League fixture, and a stalwart at half-back for all three seasons in that competition, as well as the first three in the Second Division, Jack was invariably described as a dogged, rather than brilliant player, but was clearly esteemed as the sort of clubman essential to the temperamental blend of a squad. Accordingly, he took a well-supported benefit from a friendly against Burton Wanderers in September 1897.
Apps: 29 Lge; 16 FAC; 56 ML.
Goals: 2 Lge; 2 FAC; 3 ML.

LORNIE, JOHN
b. Aberdeen, 2.3.1939.
Banks O'Dee/Mar 1958:CITY/

June 1961:Luton Town/
June 1963:Carlisle United/
June 1964:Tranmere Rovers/
Sept 1966:Ross County.
debut: 7.2.59
v.West Bromwich Albion (A) (1 goal).

A Scottish schoolboy international and holder
of a winner's medal from the 1957 Scottish
Junior Cup Final, Jack spent three seasons at
Filbert Street as reserve centre-forward, getting
few chances to shine despite claiming a goal
from each of his first two games, and eventually moved to Kenilworth Road without having
once appeared in a winning City line-up at
senior level. His brother Jim was the St.Mirren
goalkeeper in the 1955 Scottish League Cup
final, while his grandfather, James Lamb, had
long before found goalkeeping fame of the
wrong sort - as the Bon Accord 'keeper beaten
a record 36 times by the Arbroath forwards in
the notorious Scottish Cup tie of 1885.
Apps: 8 Lge; 1 LC.
Goals: 3 Lge.

JACK LORNIE

LOVATT, HAROLD A.
b. Audley, Staffs., Feb 1906.
Port Vale/cs 1924:Preston North End/
Sept 1925:Crewe Alexandra/
Mar 1926:Bradford City/Nov 1926:Wrexham/
cs 1927:Scarborough/May 1928:CITY/
Dec 1930:Notts County/
Oct 1931:Northampton Town/
cs 1932:Macclesfield/Stafford Rangers.
debut: 21.2.29 v.Cardiff City (H) (1 goal).

Centre-forward Harry could hardly have done
more to lay claim to a first team berth at City -
his limited outings were marked by two First
Division hat-tricks - yet there was still no
question of him displacing a fit Arthur
Chandler for any lengthy spell. Strangely, his
Filbert Street stay was the longest of his first-
class career, which had effectively started with
an impressive goal-rush at Crewe. Harry failed
to settle at either of his last two League clubs,
despite three goals in nine games for the
Magpies and seven in fourteen for the
Cobblers.
Apps: 10 Lge.
Goals: 9 Lge.

LOWE, W.
b.
Loughborough/cs 1892:FOSSE/
cs 1893:Long Eaton Rangers/
cs 1895:Loughborough.
debut: 17.9.92
v.Mansfield Town (A) ML (1 goal).

Known throughout his Fosse spell as 'Kiddy' -
though whether in acknowledgement of his
youth, his on-field trickery or his sense of
humour, we are unsure - this right-sided
forward made the first of his three appearances
in League football at Filbert Street, albeit in the
colours of the Luffs, in October 1895. Earlier,
he had made his Midland League bow for Fosse
as emergency goalkeeper, when Jimmy Thraves
arrived 35 minutes late for the game at
Mansfield, then resumed his place up front and
claimed Fosse's consolation goal.
Apps: 4 FAC; 20 ML.
Goals: 2 FAC; 9 ML.

LOWERY, EDWARD
b. Walker-on-Tyne, 1909.
Walker Park/Usworth Colliery/
Dec 1930:East Fife/May 1932:CITY/
Yeovil Town/July 1934:Torquay United/
cs 1936:Darlington/cs 1937:Frickley Colliery.
debut: 27.8.32 v.Sheffield United (H).

A Geordie inside-right who had learnt the
graces of Scottish style before coming to Filbert
Street, Ted was City's first-choice schemer for
the first ten games of 1932/3, and looked every
inch another of Peter Hodge's subtly effective
cross-border purchases, when successive illness
and injuries ruined his progress to such an
extent that soon he was only able to parade his
talents in a Third Division context.
Apps: 14 Lge.
Goals: 1 Lge.

LYNES, JAMES
b.
Nov 1895:FOSSE/May 1896:Lincoln City.
debut: 2.11.95 v.Hucknall St.Johns (H) FAC.

'A West Country lad' signed from a junior club
in the Birmingham area, James rejoiced in the
nickname 'Trilby', and made intermittent
appearances during 1895/6 at both outside-right
and centre-forward. For some unfathomed
reason, he utilised his forename as a pseudony-
mous surname on each of his first three Fosse
outings - a friendly, a Cup-tie and a League
game at Anfield. The last of his four Second
Division goals for Lincoln proved to be the
winner against Fosse in April 1897.
Apps: 7 Lge; 3 FAC.
Goals: 3 Lge.

LYNEX, STEPHEN CHARLES
b. West Bromwich, 23.1.1958.
Sandwell/app 1974/
pro Jan 1976:West Bromwich Albion/
cs 1977-trial-Sligo Rovers/
Aug 1977:Shamrock Rovers/
Apr 1979:Birmingham City/Feb 1981:CITY/
(Oct 1986-loan-Birmingham City)/
Mar 1987:West Bromwich Albion/
cs 1988:Cardiff City.
debut: 14.2.81 v.Sunderland (A).

Despite having only a limited League career at
St.Andrews, where he rapidly gained a
reputation as 'super-sub', Steve also had two
cup-winning medals to his name by the time
Jock Wallace paid £60,000 to bring him to
Leicester - from West Brom's Youth Cup
victory in 1976, and from Shamrock's FAI Cup
win in 1978. In fact, the speedy winger's
confidence-building sojourn in Irish football
got off to a uniquely unpromising start - with a
gunman offering Steve a persuasive reason not
to prolong his trial period with Sligo - but
Johnny Giles soon gave him a second chance
after having been responsible for freeing him
from the Hawthorns only weeks before. At
Filbert Street he developed quickly with regular
top-flight football, soon assuming the mantle of
penalty-taker and going on to claim about half
his respectable goal tally from the spot. For
most of his City days the only orthodox winger
on the club's books, Steve suffered occasionally from either instructions or an inclination to
make himself more of an all-round midfield
player, and sometimes appeared strangely
reticent to play to his pacy, dribbling strengths.
Even so, the sight of him taking on his marker
close to either touchline or by-line, and leaving
him flailing, brightened many an early-80's
afternoon. However, a combined loss of form
and, apparently, motivation led to a marked
drop in Steve's valuation: he moved back to his
home-town club for a merely nominal fee only
a year after City had held out for a six-figure
price from Albion.
Apps: 200+13 Lge; 12 FAC; 14+1 LC.
Goals: 57 Lge; 1 FAC; 2 LC.

STEVE LYNEX

LYON,
HERBERT ERNEST SAXON
BERTIE CORDEY
b. Yorkshire, 1877.
Gresley Rovers/Jan 1898:FOSSE/
cs 1900:Nelson/June 1901:Watford/
cs 1902:Reading/cs 1903:West Ham United/

cs 1904:Brighton & Hove Albion/
cs 1905:Swindon Town/
cs 1906:Carlisle United/
cs 1907:Swindon Town/June 1908:Blackpool.
debut: 14.1.99 v.Luton Town (A) (1 goal).

Primarily an inside-forward, Bertie makes the Leicester record books as the only outfield player actually selected in advance by the club to play a full first-class game as goalkeeper - and he kept a clean sheet against Bolton Wanderers in March 1900, after only three reserve outings between the sticks, before once more reverting to his attacking duties. Otherwise he is renowned for his mouthful of Christian names (note the parental affectation that lumbered him with a corruption of 'coeur-de-lion' to live up to!), and for his habit of switching clubs on an annual basis. Fosse actually picked up £35 from Blackpool for his League registration eight years after he had left the club.
Apps: 15 Lge; 1 FAC.
Goals: 5 Lge; 2 FAC.

GARY McALLISTER

McALLISTER, GARY
b. Motherwell, 25.12.1964.
Fir Park BC/1981:Motherwell/Aug 1985:CITY.
debut: 28.9.85 v.Ipswich Town (H).

Notionally 'a buy for the future' when included in a joint transfer deal with the more experienced Ali Mauchlen, attacking midfielder Gary very soon displayed a refreshing and remarkably mature regard for the value of accurate passing to feet, and rapidly gained confidence to express a pleasingly ambitious range of skills on the ball as he adapted to regular First Division football. Indeed, by his second City season he was justifiably attracting the attention of Scottish international boss Andy Roxburgh - but with mixed results when it came to being honoured. Gary scored the equaliser on his debut for Scotland 'B' against France in April 1987, but also picked up the injury which kept his much-needed talent out of City's vital last

three games prior to their eventual relegation. Given by Bryan Hamilton the rather back-handed tribute of being expected to function effectively in a variety of midfield and forward roles, Gary found his form suffering for a while, but perked up under David Pleat's guidance, and his elegant playmaking abilities were soon drawing envious glances from several clubs of higher status. A distinctly erratic successor to Steve Lynex as City's regular penalty taker, he has nonetheless boosted his goal tally to respectable levels with a few blindingly executed strikes from rather less favourable positions. The only ever-present player in 1988/9, Gary remains the nub of constant transfer speculation.
Apps (to 13.5.89): 156+2 Lge; 4 FAC; 12+1 LC; 4 FMC.
Goals: 36 Lge; 2 FAC; 3 LC.

McARTHUR, THOMAS
b. Neilston, 23.4.1925.
Neilston Thistle/Neilston Victoria/
Jan 1947:CITY/Jan 1954:Plymouth Argyle/
cs 1954:Brush Sports/Enderby Town.
debut: 17.5.47 v.Chesterfield (A).

A tall, tough, former Scots Guardsman, centre-half Tom made first team appearances across eight Second Division seasons, commanding the position only during 1950/1, yet loyally and reliably understudying Sep Smith, Norman Plummer and Matt Gillies in succession while skippering the Reserves. Moving on immediately after being given a rare runaround in a 1-7 defeat, his stay at Home Park was brief (only two League games), and he returned to the county and settled in the Narborough area.
Apps: 97 Lge; 2 FAC.

McARTHUR, WILLIAM
b.
Renton/Sunderland Albion/
Middlesbrough Ironopolis/
cs 1893:Bolton Wanderers/
Apr 1894:FOSSE/
cs 1896:Dundee/
May 1898:Brighton United/
(Apr 1900:Army service)/1901:Worthing.
debut: 28.4.94 v.Grantham Rovers (A) ML.

Unable to break into Bolton's FA Cup Final side of 1894, centre or inside-forward William joined Fosse in time to play in the club's final match in the Midland League. In fact, a fortnight before that fixture, he won over Fosse supporters with a hat-trick performance in a friendly against old rivals Loughborough, and there was little doubt he would be re-registered for the first assault on the Second Division - to which he duly contributed as second-top scorer to David Skea, and during which he notched four goals in Fosse's record 13-0 FA Cup win over Notts Olympic. He went one better in 1895/6, as leading goalgetter, but then moved back north of the border. William terminated his stint with Brighton by signing up with the Royal Sussex Regiment to fight in the Boer War, and was then reinstated as an amateur on his return.
Apps: 55 Lge; 10 FAC; 1 ML.
Goals: 27 Lge; 9 FAC.

MACAULEY, JAMES LOWRY
b. Portarlington, 1889.
d. Preston, 8.10.1945.
Cliftonville/Oct 1910:Huddersfield Town/
May 1914:Preston North End/July 1919:CITY/
June 1920:Grimsby Town/
cs 1921:Lancaster Town/cs 1923:Morecambe.
debut: 30.8.19
v.Wolverhampton Wanderers (H).

Five times chosen for the Irish League, and six times as a full Irish international after moving to Huddersfield during that club's initial season in the League, James lent his considerable experience to City's first campaign after WW1, plying his artistry in the inside-left position. His goals came in successive home and away fixtures with Grimsby, who were sufficiently impressed to later take him on for a further season of Second Division fare - a sphere in which he had played all his English football to that date, as war had delayed Preston's ascent after 1915.
Apps: 19 Lge; 4 FAC.
Goals: 2 Lge.

McCULLOCH, DAVID
b. Hamilton, 5.10.1911.
d. Hamilton, May 1979.
Hamilton Amateurs/Shotts United/
1932:Third Lanark/
June 1934:Heart of Midlothian/
Nov 1935:Brentford/Oct 1938:Derby County/
July 1946:CITY/Dec 1946:Bath City/
Aug 1949:Waterford (p/coach)/
1951:Alloa Athletic (p/mgr).
debut: 31.8.46 v.Manchester City (H).

Unfortunately looking well past his best when briefly turning out for City in the first postwar League season, Dave had been a centre-forward in the classic mould throughout the 30's, leading the Scottish scorers' list in 1934/5 (with 38 goals) and winning his first honours while averaging a goal per game at Tynecastle. He scored in his only Scottish League representative game, then added three goals while winning seven full caps, and also played in one wartime international for Scotland at a juncture when he was guesting regularly for the likes of Falkirk, Aldershot, Bath City, Swansea Town and Brentford. The latter club had originally paid £6,000 for his aerial ability and all-action foraging, and got 85 First Division goals in return out of Dave's pre-war total of 178. He had been Derby's record signing at £9,500, and joined City with Tom Eggleston for a joint fee of £3,100. As a real veteran, Dave led the League of Ireland scoring chart at the end of his first season with Waterford, and in later years worked for Rolls Royce at East Kilbride.
Apps: 4 Lge.
Goals: 2 Lge.

McDERMENT, WILLIAM STIRLING
b. Paisley, 5.1.1943.
Johnstone Burgh/May 1961:CITY/
July 1967:Luton Town/
May 1969:Notts County/1970:Morton.
debut: 15.5.63 v.Aston Villa (A).

A reliable reserve half-back who made sporadic appearances across five First Division seasons

in the mid-60's, Billy could never quite lay claim to a regular senior berth, and perhaps the closest he came to a moment of glory in English football was in getting one hand on the Football Combination Cup in 1967 as skipper of the City reserves side which shared that trophy with Spurs. He briefly partnered Max Dougan in Luton's Fourth Division promotion side, but fared better back in Scotland after failing to click at Meadow Lane.
Apps: 20+3 Lge; 2 FAC; 5 LC.
Goals: 1 Lge.

McDONALD, DAVID
b.
Dundee Wanderers/cs 1895:Dundee/ cs 1896:Everton/Oct 1896:FOSSE.
debut: 7.11.96 v.Lincoln City (H).

Unable to make a Goodison Park breakthrough, Scottish inside-right Davie was signed by Fosse as an instant early-season replacement for his former Dundee team-mate, Lonie, but lost his goal-touch after an early burst of deadly finishing. He had been Dundee's top scorer in the Scottish First Division in 1895/6.
Apps: 16 Lge; 2 FAC.
Goals: 7 Lge.

MacDONALD, KEVIN DUNCAN
b. Inverness, 22.11.1960.
Inverness Caledonian/May 1980:CITY/ Nov 1984:Liverpool/(Dec 1987-loan-CITY)/ (Nov 1988-loan-Rangers).
debut: 29.11.80 (sub) v.Norwich City (H).

Striding into the First Division after only two seasons of Highland League football, midfielder Kevin impressed immediately with his combativeness and almost cocky confidence. The latter attribute stuck with him throughout his City career from the moment he stepped up to take a crucial penalty in his first full home game, and was later evidenced by some memorably cool defensive work (including a number of heart-stopping back headers to Mark Wallington) when he filled in for Larry May during the 1983 promotion run-in. Indeed, once Kevin had mastered his occasionally fiery temper, he proved himself a genuinely classy operator, with only a marginal lack of pace detracting from his repertoire of control, vision and ball-winning ability. A £400,000 cheque took him to Anfield, where injuries cruelly hampered his progress in a formidably strong squad. Even so, he picked up an FA Cup winner's medal in 1986, before a broken leg once more heralded a long lay-off. Kevin had still to return to the senior Liverpool line-up when he came back to Filbert Street for a loan spell under caretaker manager Peter Morris, and unfortunately showed every sign of rustiness in the three defeats in which he played. He was freed by Liverpool in May 1989.
Apps: 136+5 Lge; 4 FAC; 10 LC.
Goals: 8 Lge.

McDONALD, THOMAS
b. Glasgow, 24.5.1930.
Hibernian/
Apr 1954:Wolverhampton Wanderers/
July 1956:CITY/cs 1960:Dunfermline Athletic/

Dec 1962:Raith Rovers/
cs 1963:Queen of the South/
Dec 1963:Stirling Albion.
debut: 18.8.56
v.Doncaster Rovers (H) (2 goals).

Initially understudy to, and then replacement for, the great Gordon Smith at Hibs, Tommy won one Scotland 'B' cap and then found himself stuck in Wolves' reserves for much of his Molineux stay. David Halliday paid £6,000 to bring the outside-right to Leicester, and he got the 1956/7 promotion effort off to a flying start, though eventually missed out on the run-in. For three seasons thereafter he battled Howard Riley for the No.7 shirt, having his best scoring season (13 League and Cup goals) just prior to moving back to Scotland. Ill-luck dogged him there, especially when he went down with appendicitis virtually on the eve of the 1961 Scottish Cup Final, though he subsequently played in European competition for Dunfermline along with Willie Cunningham.
Apps: 113 Lge; 5 FAC.
Goals: 27 Lge; 2 FAC.

MacFARLANE, IAN
b. Lanark, 26.1.1933.
Aberdeen/Aug 1956:Chelsea/May 1958:CITY/ July 1959:Bath City.
debut: 4.10.58 v.Luton Town (H).

A tough, hefty full-back who probably set the Doug Rougvie mould at both Pittodrie and Stamford Bridge, yet who only got one chance to deputise for Willie Cunningham at Leicester after a £9,000 move, Ian moved on to partner Tony Book in Bath's 1960 Southern League championship side. He later embarked on a much more successful coaching career, which saw him return to Filbert Street as assistant manager to both Frank McLintock and Jock Wallace between 1977 and 1982. In the interim, Ian had fulfilled second-in-command duties at Middlesbrough, Manchester City and Sunderland, and had held the full managerial reins at Carlisle; it is perhaps fair to say that on the whole he tended to be associated with highly-motivated yet essentially dour sides.
Apps: 1 Lge.

McFARLANE, PETER
b. Motherwell.
Carfin/1894:Motherwell/Dec 1894:FOSSE.
debut: 12.1.95 v.Crewe Alexandra (A).

A 'sturdy' full-back who matched his single Scottish League appearance for Motherwell with one senior game south of the border, Peter was described as 'too prone to dribble' in an era when the back line positions were dominated by big kickers specialising in first-time clearances.
Apps: 1 Lge.

McGRAW, IAN
b. Glasgow, 30.8.1926.
Arbroath/Dec 1948:CITY/
cs 1951:Corby Town.
debut: 25.12.48 v.Tottenham Hotspur (H).

Ian's was a tragically truncated City career following his £4,200 signing by Johnny Duncan. The easefully authoritative young Scottish 'keeper had really endeared himself to City supporters with his performances in the 1949 Cup run, and had helped rebuff Portsmouth in the semi-final, when he was seriously injured a week later in the rough-house League game with Grimsby. A broken little finger not only kept him out of the Wembley line-up, but also developed complications which led to the necessity of amputation. At that stage, Ian had made eight appearances in each of the League and Cup competitions, and while he bravely came back to add another five games in 1950/1 despite his handicap, he could not for long displace internationals Tommy Godwin or Johnny Anderson. He was, however, granted a Testimonial game in April 1953: a City friendly against Wolves.
Apps: 13 Lge; 8 FAC.

McGREGOR, WILLIAM
b. Paisley, 1.12.1923.
Mossvale YMCA/April 1947:CITY/
Sept 1953:Mansfield Town.
debut: 27.3.48 v.Tottenham Hotspur (A).

A spirited, compact, quick-tackling reserve right-back for six seasons at Filbert Street, Willie picked up a medal from the 1948 Combination Cup win, but got few chances to shine in the Second Division before joining the colony of ex-City men at Field Mill, where in contrast he played 118 League games across three seasons.
Apps: 9 Lge; 1 FAC.

McILMOYLE, HUGH
b. Cambuslang, 29.1.1940.
Port Glasgow Juniors/Aug 1959:CITY/
July 1962:Rotherham United/
Mar 1963:Carlisle United/
Oct 1964:Wolverhampton Wanderers/
Mar 1967:Bristol City/
Sept 1967:Carlisle United/
Sept 1969:Middlesbrough/
July 1971:Preston North End/
cs 1973:Morton/July 1974:Carlisle United/
cs 1975:Morton (p/coach).
debut: 3.4.61 v.West Ham United (H) (1 goal).

The centre of a major City controversy when chosen in Ken Leek's No.9 shirt for the 1961 Cup Final after only seven League games, Hugh was in no way overawed by the Wembley occasion, playing an intelligent deep-lying role and looking City's most dangerous forward, but was then subjected to perhaps over-intense scrutiny from a sceptical crowd as he struggled to maintain a first team striker's role the following season. The sense of too much responsibility being heaped upon the slender youngster too soon was borne out by his future development into a fine and versatile servant for a host of other clubs. His first of three spells at Brunton Park saw Hugh top the Football League scoring charts with 39 goals in Carlisle's 1964 rise from the Fourth Division, and he helped them into the Second Division a year later. Subsequent moves attracted some hefty transfer fees, with Hugh's heading

abilities in particular much in demand, and he matured eventually into a perceptive attacking midfielder, bowing out of the senior game with a career aggregate of 161 League goals.
Apps: 20 Lge; 1 FAC; 1 ECWC.
Goals: 5 Lge; 1 ECWC.

HUGH McILMOYLE

MACKAY, ROBERT
b. Harthill, 6.5.1948.
Whitburn Bluebells/Harthill Juniors/
Apr 1965:CITY/cs 1970:Boston United/
cs 1971:Kidderminster Harriers.
debut: 21.8.68 v.Manchester City (H).

A versatile defensive midfielder who looked set for a useful run in City's first team, Bobby suffered a definitive knock to his progress in the first game he played for new manager Frank O'Farrell, being stretchered off in the Third Round tie at Barnsley as City embarked on their 1969 Wembley run. Only one League Cup game followed his cartilage operation, and Bobby's senior career came to a premature end. At Kidderminster he briefly linked up with former City reserves John and Jim Flanagan.
Apps: 6+1 Lge; 1 FAC; 1+1 LC.
Goals: 1 Lge.

McKENNA, JAMES PETER
b. Blackpool, 18.4.1910.
d. 27.8.1986.
Feb 1930:CITY/cs 1932:Bath City.
debut: 26.3.32 v.Birmingham (H).

The third-choice City 'keeper behind Jim McLaren and John Beby, Jim got but one chance to exhibit his prowess at senior level, and moved on to help Bath to the championship of the Southern League's Western Division in 1933.
Apps: 1 Lge.

McKENNAN, PETER STEWART
b. Airdrie, 16.7.1918.
Whitburn Juniors/July 1935:Partick Thistle/
Oct 1947:West Bromwich Albion/
Mar 1948:CITY/Sept 1948:Brentford/
May 1949:Middlesbrough/

July 1951:Oldham Athletic/
July 1954:Coleraine (p/coach).
debut: 13.3.48 v.Cardiff City (A).

A fascinating character who barely settled at Filbert Street at all, inside-forward Peter was known throughout his career by the nickname 'Ma Ba' ('My Ball'), after his habitually confident on-field shout for possession - all the more noticeable for his voice's honing on the wartime parade grounds he'd commanded as a sergeant-major in the Royal Welsh Fusiliers. At that period, having already gained near-legendary status at Firhill, he also guested for Wolves, West Brom, Chelsea and Brentford, and assisted Irish side Glentoran throughout 1941 - winning Irish League representative honours to add to his two pre-war Scottish League selections. Peter came to Leicester as the more highly-valued component of the part-exchange deal that took Jack Haines to the Hawthorns, and left within a month of the new season starting, signing for Brentford for £7,000 on the day City beat them at Griffin Park. As a veteran, he inspired Oldham to the Third Division (North) championship in 1953, then finished his active career back in Ireland. His repute lives on in Glasgow however, where stories still circulate of how the gate for the St.Mirren v. City friendly of April 1948 was boosted by several hundred Partick supporters who made the trip just to see their former hero perform.
Apps: 18 Lge.
Goals: 7 Lge.

MACKIE, ROBERT
b. Dalry, Ayrshire, Aug 1882.
Stenhousemuir/May 1904:Heart of Midlothian/
Aug 1905:Chelsea/Nov 1907:FOSSE/
cs 1909:Airdrieonians.
debut: 23.11.07 v.Derby County (H).

'Ungainly but obstinate', Bob was a full-back signed by Chelsea for their first-ever League season, and became a vital defensive cog in Fosse's promotion season, before suffering along with his team-mates some of the First Division embarrassments of 1908/9. Returning to Scottish football to settle at Broomfield, he received an Airdrie benefit from a game against Albion Rovers in 1914.
Apps: 33 Lge; 3 FAC.

MACKLEWORTH, COLIN
b. Bow, 24.3.1947.
app 1962/pro Apr 1964:West Ham United/
Nov 1967:CITY/cs 1971:Kettering Town/
Metropolitan Police/Clapton.
debut: 9.3.68 v.Rotherham United (A) FAC.

A capable reserve 'keeper for both his League clubs, Colin won a Youth Cup medal with the Hammers in 1963, but only turned out three times for their first team. Brought to Filbert Street as cover for Peter Shilton, he faced a high-pressure debut in the Cup tie at Millmoor, and also saw City through the replay before making his League bow. For another three seasons he bore the frustrations of regular Combination football and highly irregular senior opportunities, then left for Southern League

fare before joining the police force.
Apps: 6 Lge; 3 FAC.

McLAREN, ALEXANDER
b. Tibbermore, 25.12.1910.
d. 5.2.1960.
Dec 1927:St.Johnstone/Feb 1933:CITY/
Oct 1940:Morton/Nov 1945:St.Johnstone.
debut: 8.3.33 v.Everton (A).

Taking over the City green jersey from namesake Jim, former blacksmith and Scottish international 'keeper Sandy must have wondered what had hit him on his debut, as a Dixie Dean hat-trick accounted for only half the Everton goals which flew past him that afternoon. Nonetheless, he went for 102 consecutive games between the City sticks from that date, and was still very much the first-choice custodian when war brought a halt to League football over six years later. Noted particularly for his unflappability and the prodigious strength of his punch, Sandy was unfortunate not to add to his tally of five caps while with City (he had remarkably won the first at the age of 18), and took a Second Division championship medal in 1937 as the only tangible honour from a superb Leicester career. After a wartime spell as a taxi driver, and a stint with Morton, he returned to his first senior club.
Apps: 239 Lge; 17 FAC.

SANDY McLAREN

MacLAREN, DAVID
b. Auchterarder, 12.6.1934.
St Johnstone Juniors/RAF/Feb 1956:Dundee/
Jan 1957:CITY/May 1960:Plymouth Argyle/
June 1965:Wolverhampton Wanderers/
Sept 1966:Southampton/
July 1967:Worcester City.
debut: 2.2.57 v Notts County (A).

Though unrelated to either of City's other goalkeeping McLarens, Dave was clearly destined for fame as a custodian; brothers Jimmy and Roy both kept goal in League football (the former for Berwick, Chester and Carlisle, the latter for St Johnstone, Bury and Sheffield Wednesday), and another brother,

Monty, was a Liverpool reserve. An emergency buy from Dundee when Johnny Anderson got injured partway through the 1957 promotion campaign, Dave thereafter shaded the rivalry for the green jersey on a regular basis until the advent of Gordon Banks. His soundness then saw him through five Second Division seasons at Home Park and Molineux, and made him an ideal choice to shore up Southampton's defence in their first-ever Division One season. Way back in 1954, while on RAF service, Dave had won both the 'Sportsman of the Year' award and unofficial representative honours in Malaya, and in 1970 returned there as a coach, assuming the management role for the Malaysian national team in 1972. He also coached the Australian side Hakoah in the early 70's.
Apps: 85 Lge; 5 FAC.

McLAREN, JAMES
b. Falkirk, 12.7.1897.
d. Leicester, Nov 1975.
Bonnybridge Heatherbell/1920:Stenhousemuir/ May 1922:Bradford City/May 1927:CITY/ Oct 1933:Watford.
debut: 7.5.27 v Newcastle United (H).

The son of a former Scottish champion racing cyclist, Jim had been, in 1911, the goalkeeper in the first schoolboy international played by Scotland, and distinguished himself with a penalty save. After WW1, he helped Sten-housemuir into, and through, their first season in the Scottish League, then built a good reputation in a struggling Bradford City side which was relegated from Division Two in 1927 - his transfer to City helping to relieve some of the severe financial embarrassment the Valley Parade outfit were then suffering. At Leicester, Jim displaced fellow-countryman Kenny Campbell as City mounted their most convincing assaults on the First Division title, and held his key position for all but a few games until succeeded in turn by namesake Sandy. By the time he retired from Vicarage Road in 1939, Jim had amassed a career total of 517 League games, and had become only the second player in League history to receive benefit payments from three separate clubs.
Apps: 170 Lge; 10 FAC.

McLEOD, RODERICK
b. Kilsyth, Feb 1872.
d. Lambeth, Dec 1931.
Westburn/Partick Thistle/ Jan 1891:West Bromwich Albion/ Aug 1897:FOSSE/May 1898:Brighton United/ Apr 1899:Southampton/Aug 1900:Brentford.
debut: 4.9.97 v Luton Town (H).

A baby-faced, classy inside-forward whose successful stint with West Brom had brought him 60 League goals and appearances in both the 1892 and 1895 FA Cup Finals, Roddie was Fosse's leading marksman in his only season, but was soon to join the Southern League roundabout onto which so many early players leapt from Leicester (in this case, accompanied by Fosse trainer John Jackson). Roddie left Southampton in pique after being dropped from their 1900 Cup Final team, but won a Southern

League Division Two medal with the Bees.
Apps: 28 Lge; 1 FAC.
Goals: 13 Lge; 1 FAC.

McLINTOCK, FRANCIS
b. Glasgow, 28.12.1939.
Shawfield Juniors/Jan 1957:CITY/ Oct 1964:Arsenal/ June 1973:Queens Park Rangers.
debut: 14.9.59 v Blackpool (A).

Brought down from the Gorbals and nurtured at Filbert Street as a probing wing-half, Frank possessed the rare combination of toughness and elegance and soon became a key element in City's then-revolutionary midfield strategies of the early 60's. Whether switching roles in mid-match with Graham Cross or creating cross-field magic with Davie Gibson, he oozed footballing class. It was no surprise either when he graduated to full Scottish honours or when Billy Wright's Arsenal eventually paid City their then-record outgoing transfer fee of £80,000 for his services. Frank took some time to settle at Highbury, and extended his apparent Wembley hoodoo in the late 60's (following heartbreak FA Cup Final defeats for City in 1961 and 1963 with a pair of losing League Cup Final appearances for Arsenal in 1968 and 1969) even after settling to the role of central defender. Then, though, he experienced a couple of years of genuine glory; skippering the Gunners to their 1970 Fairs Cup win, and to the domestic Double a year later, as well as picking up both the 1971 'Footballer of the Year' award and a CBE, and re-establishing himself as an influential international. Subsequently, it looked a certain case of Frank being written off too early when he was allowed to move cheaply to QPR, and assisted them to a near-miss title bid in 1976. It was however, equally evident that after 609 League games, he was handed too much backroom responsibility too soon when engaged as City manager in 1977 in succession to Jimmy Bloomfield. Too many of his transfer-market dealings bore the stamp of desperation, too few of his tactical ideas translated effectively to on-field practice, and Frank's unwillingness to commit to living again in Leicester (or to leaving behind his London business interests) hardly helped his cause. His City team were already certainties for relega-tion when he resigned in April 1978, and he returned to the capital as, successively, adviser on the atrocious soccer-themed movie 'Yesterday's Hero', youth coach at QPR, broadcaster, Brentford manager and assistant boss at Millwall.
Apps: 168 Lge; 20 FAC; 11 LC; 1 ECWC.
Goals: 25 Lge; 3 LC.

McMILLAN, JOHN STUART
b. Port Glasgow, 16.2.1871.
d. Birkdale, 3.11.1941.
Port Glasgow Athletic/cs 1890:St Bernards/ Nov 1890:Derby County/May 1896:FOSSE/ Jan 1901:Small Heath/ May 1903:Bradford City/ May 1906:Glossop (p/mgr).
debut: 5.9.96 v Darwen (H) (1 goal).

A prodigy in Scottish junior football, appearing

regularly from the age of 14, Johnny made only one appearance for his first senior side, leaving the Edinburgh-based St Bernards in a bitter row over professionalism, but then gave fine service to Derby, scoring 50 League and Cup goals over six seasons. With Fosse, the versatile forward led by example, maintaining a high scoring ratio while demonstrating a rare degree of creative flair, and prompting the club to its first serious promotion challenge in 1899. He took a club benefit from a friendly with Notts County in December 1900, and moved to Small Heath only a month later, there to experience promotion, relegation and promotion again during an eventful stay. Johnny was handed the role of captaining Bradford City for their inaugural League season, and gradually prepared himself for a managerial career, which he picked up again after WW1 with two seasons in charge at Gillingham. His Leicester-born son, Stuart, was also a player with Derby, Wolves, Chelsea, Clapton Orient and Bradford City, and managed Derby to their 1946 FA Cup win.
Apps: 122 Lge; 9 FAC.
Goals: 43 Lge; 5 FAC.

McNALLY, OWEN
b. Denny.
Denny Hibs/Celtic/(Sept 1927-loan-Arthurlie)/ Hamilton Academicals/ cs 1930:Bray Unknowns/cs 1931:Cardiff City/ cs 1932:Bray Unknowns/1933:Laussanne/ cs 1934:Sligo Rovers/cs 1935:Distillery/ Jan 1936:CITY/Aug 1937:Racing Club de Paris.
debut: 30.1.36 v Nottingham Forest (A).

Born in the same Scottish town as Adam Black, centre-forward Owen was certainly possessed of rather more wanderlust than his eminently settled predecessor. A frustrated reserve to record scorer Jimmy McGrory at Celtic, he once took out his ire in a Scottish Second Division match for Arthurlie against Armadale to the tune of eight goals, and then soon started collecting clubs and countries in almost equal proportion. The trek from Scotland through Ireland, Wales and Switzerland might have satisfied many a footballing mercenary, but the 5ft 7ins Owen maintained his rolling stone status for some years yet; playing again on both sides of the Irish border, and gathering the 'moss' of a scoring appearance for the Irish League against the Football League in September 1935. Shortly thereafter, signing for £1,000, he had a spirited bash at solving City's centre-forward problem, at that time being wrestled with by centre-half Fred Sharman, but soon to be comprehensively resolved by the advent of Jack Bowers. Accordingly, nothing daunted, Owen simply got out his passport again....
Apps: 16 Lge; 1 FAC.
Goals: 7 Lge; 1 FAC.

McNEILL, IAN McKEAND
b. Bailleston, Glasgow, 24.2.1932.
Bridgetown Waverley/1950:Aberdeen/ Mar 1956:CITY/ Mar 1959:Brighton & Hove Albion/ July 1962:Southend United.
debut: 2.4.56 v Sheffield Wednesday (H).

Signed jointly with Joe O'Neil from City boss David Halliday's former club, inside-forward Ian soon made an impact at Filbert Street, contributing 18 goals to the 1957 Second Division Championship campaign. He found goals, and a regular place, somewhat harder to come by in the top flight against the challenges of John Doherty, Jimmy Walsh and Bernie Kelly, but it was nonetheless Ian's invaluable strike in the final game of 1957/8 which saved City from an immediate drop back. Later, on the South Coast, he adopted a deeper-lying schemer's role in 116 games for Brighton and 41 for Southend. Ian entered management with Highland League outfit Ross County, then took the reins at Wigan Athletic before becoming assistant manager at Chelsea in the early 80's. He is currently boss at Shrewsbury Town.
Apps: 72 Lge; 4 FAC.
Goals: 26 Lge; 1 FAC.

McWHIRTER, DOUGLAS
b. Erith, 13.8.1886.
d. Plumstead, 14.10.1966.
Bromley/Mar 1912:Fosse/
cs 1914:Southend United.
debut: 30.3.12 v Bradford (H).

A valuable right-half during Fosse's pre-war years of steep decline, Douglas was a newly-capped amateur international when Fosse signed him, and went on to add mementos of three more England appearances to the winner's medals he gained from both the 1911 FA Amateur Cup Final (for Bromley) and the 1912 Olympic Games football Final (for the United Kingdom). Having eventually turned professional, though, he was refused reinstatement as an amateur by the FA in 1921.
Apps: 58 Lge; 2 FAC.
Goals: 2 Lge.

McWHIRTER, PETER
b. Scotland, c1871.
d. 1943.
(Toronto football)/Morton/Oct 1895:FOSSE/
cs 1897:Warmley/cs 1898:Brighton United/
Oct 1899:FOSSE.
debut: 26.10.95 v Darwen (H).

An outside-right signed from Scottish reserve-team football, Peter only briefly held his position during Fosse's second season in the League, and was next heard of sailing for Canada in December 1896 to rejoin his emigrant family. He nevertheless swiftly returned, to link up with former Fosse inside-forward partners Manson and McArthur at Southern League Warmley and Brighton respectively. His second stint with Fosse was almost entirely played out in the reserves, and spiced only with an outing in Jack Walker's benefit friendly against Everton.
Apps: 17 Lge; 1 FAC.
Goals: 1 Lge.

MAJOR, LESLIE DENNIS
b. Yeovil, 25.1.1926.
RAF football/Loughborough Corinthians/
am June 1943/pro Dec 1944:CITY/
May 1949:Plymouth Argyle.
debut: 25.8.47 v Plymouth Argyle (H).

Trained as a PT instructor and based at Loughborough, Les represented the RAF on several occasions as a goalkeeper, as well as playing wartime football for City and Notts County. On demob he became Gordon Bradley's rival for the City's custodianship, having one run of 15 games at the beginning of 1947/8, and then being pitched into the anti-relegation scuffles of 1949, but being overlooked for the 'keeper's job at Wembley that year. Almost immediately, Les moved to Home Park for £1,800 and played 75 League games for the Pilgrims across seven seasons, before injury cut short his career. He returned to Leicestershire for a stint as a village publican, and is now living in Madeley, Staffs.
Apps: 26 Lge.

MANDY, LEONARD AUBREY
b. Transvaal, South Africa.
Transvaal/Oct 1929:CITY.
debut: 26.12.29 v Grimsby Town (H).

Briefly preferred to Joe Wright as stand-in keeper for Jim McLaren, South African trialist Aubrey kept a clean sheet on his Boxing Day debut, but saw in the New Year with seven Sheffield United goals whistling past him, and was never chosen again. He was originally recommended to City by Reg Osborne and Arthur Chandler, who had faced him on the FA tour the previous summer.
Apps: 3 Lge.

MALCOLM MANLEY

MANLEY, MALCOLM RICHARDSON
b. Johnstone, 1.12.1949.
Johnstone Burgh/Jan 1969:CITY/
Dec 1973:Portsmouth.
debut: 20.4.68 v Southampton (H).

Equally adept at the centre of the back four or playing just in front of it (and even once utilised as a scoring spearhead), Malcolm had his youthful versatility traded into a fairly regular position on the City substitute's bench - from where he joined the action in three crucial Cup-ties in 1969, including the Wembley Final.

When he did make the starting line-up on a more regular basis, Malcolm was living testimony to the redundancy of the conventional shirt numbering system, and some of his most useful defensive contributions to the 1971 promotion effort came when he was wearing a No.11. For a couple of First Division seasons he vied strongly with John Sjoberg and Alan Woollett for a pivotal berth, then lost his hard-won place with the advent of Malcolm Munro. A £50,000 move to Fratton Park looked promising, but a serious injury cut short Malcolm's career after only 11 League games for Pompey. Eventually, in April 1976, Portsmouth and City played a Testimonial friendly on his behalf.
Apps: 109+11 Lge; 1+4 FAC; 11 LC.
Goals: 5 Lge; 1 LC.

MANSHIP, E.
b.
Jan 1903:FOSSE.
debut: 28.2.1903 v Burton United (H).

A local inside-left, unimpressive in his only game, and utterly elusive to all further research.
Apps: 1 Lge.

MANSON, DAVID G.
b. Glasgow.
(Scottish football)/cs 1894:Rotherham Town/
Apr 1895:FOSSE/Oct 1896:Lincoln City/
cs 1897:Warmley/Feb 1899:Gravesend United.
debut: 7.9.95 v Burton Swifts (H).

Initially tried by Fosse at outside-right, Davie met with more success in the inside position, and was re-signed for the 1896/7 season. After only one senior game that term, though, he was suspended as an internal disciplinary measure by the directorate, and swiftly packed his bags. He later joined fellow ex-Fossils Bishop and McWhirter for Warmley's brief Southern League honeymoon - promotion, then mid-season disbandment.
Apps: 24 Lge; 1 FAC.
Goals: 8 Lge; 1 FAC.

MARSH, JOHN KIRK
b. Mansfield, 8.10.1922.
Mansfield BC/Aug 1942:Notts County/
Sept 1948:Coventry City/Mar 1950:CITY/
Sept 1950:Chesterfield/Aug 1951:Workington.
debut: 18.3.50 v Sheffield United (A).

One of three City acquisitions on the same deadline day, Jack figured in the part-exchange deal which took Ken Chisholm to Highfield Road, and made his bow in a reconstructed City front line that also included Peter Small and Ian Wilson for the first time. Luckless in front of goal by the end of 1949/50, the inside-left started the following season with a couple of double strikes, but then had to drop out to accommodate Arthur Rowley's shift from the No.9 to the No.10 shirt. Jack had never really been able to recapture the burst of scoring form he had found alongside the inspirational Tommy Lawton at Meadow Lane, and drifted out of the League game altogether in 1951.
Apps: 14 Lge.
Goals: 4 Lge.

MARSHALL, ARTHUR G.
b. Liverpool, 1880.
Crewe Alexandra/May 1901:FOSSE/
Jan 1902:Stockport County/
cs 1902:Manchester United/
May 1903:Portsmouth/cs 1904:Hull City.
debut: 7.9.01 v Woolwich Arsenal (A).

Reputedly a highly promising inside-left with
Fosse, Arthur nonetheless moved on immediately after the club signed Jimmy Stevenson,
and had been converted to full-back by the time
he joined United. He only got six League
games there, though, and made only a solitary
appearance in the Southern League for Pompey
before joining the newly-formed Hull, who
played only friendlies in the season prior to
their League election.
Apps: 15 Lge; 1 FAC.
Goals: 5 Lge.

MATTHEWS, PAUL WILLIAM
b. Leicester, 30.9.1946.
app Aug 1963/pro Aug 1964:CITY/
(Sept 1972-loan-Southend United)/
Dec 1972:Mansfield Town/
Oct 1977:Rotherham United/
(Mar 1979-loan-Northampton Town)/
Heanor Town/Oadby Town.
debut: 19.4.65 v Aston Villa (H).

Deceptively frail-looking, Paul initially
developed as an orthodox outside-right and
stood in several times for Jackie Sinclair before
seeming to drop out of the senior reckoning for
a year or so. He returned to the fray, however,
in City's desperate late attempts to beat the
drop in 1969, and came closest to establishing a
regular first team place in midfield during the
following season, when he assumed the nigh-
impossible task of replacing Davie Gibson. His
mature playmaking skills were better valued,
however, at Field Mill, where in the course of a
124-game stay he helped prompt the Stags from
the Fourth to the Second Division.
Apps: 56+5 Lge; 4 FAC; 6+3 LC.
Goals: 5 Lge.

MAUCHLEN, ALISTER HENRY
b. Kilwinning, 29.6.1960.
Irvine Meadow/1978:Kilmarnock/
Oct 1982: Motherwell/Aug 1985:CITY.
debut: 24.8.85 (sub) v Oxford United (A).

A terrier-like, ball-winning midfielder, Ali was
originally a Jock Wallace purchase for
Motherwell, then, like Gary McAllister, a key
member of the 'Well team which won the
Scottish First Division Championship and took
Celtic to a replay in the Scottish Cup semi-final
in 1985. The pair moved together for a quarter
of a million pounds to Leicester, and neither
looked out of place in the English top flight,
with Ali settling to the more defensively-
inclined role, and linking well with Ian Wilson
in a neat, if diminutive, partnership. His goal in
the final game of 1985/6 helped keep City up,
and he shed a lot of honest sweat in toiling
vainly to repeat the feat a year later. Bryan
Hamilton had tried him a few times as an
emergency full-back, and Ali settled in that
position when David Pleat arrived, or at least

used it effectively as a starting block for his
forays forward. Very much a crowd favourite
for his intense commitment.
Apps (to 13.5.89): 136+5 Lge;
3+1 FAC; 12 LC; 1 FMC.
Goals: 8 Lge; 1 LC.

MAW, ARTHUR W.
b. Frodingham.
Frodingham Athletic/Scunthorpe United/
Mar 1929:Notts County/July 1932:CITY/
July 1939:Scunthorpe United.
debut: 7.1.33 v Wolverhampton Wanderers (H).

Always known as 'Digger', inside-forward
Arthur got off to a good start with City, topping
the 1932/3 scorers list with 14 goals from only
18 games, and maintained his form at the
beginning of the following season at such a
level that he was chosen as travelling reserve
for England's game in Belfast in October. It
was poor reward for his consistently dangerous
efforts during City's mid-30's struggles (top
scorer again in 1936) that he should miss out on
the Second Division championship medals in
1937, his leanest season; but Arthur bounced
back to commit his foraging skills to the club
until just before the outbreak of war - during
which he also guested for Grimsby Town.
Apps: 179 Lge; 10 FAC.
Goals: 58 Lge; 6 FAC.

MAY, LAWRENCE CHARLES
b. Sutton Coldfield, 26.12.1958.
app July 1975/pro Sept 1976:CITY/
(cs 1978-loan-New England Tea Men)/
Aug 1983: Barnsley/
Feb 1987:Sheffield Wednesday/
Sept 1988:Brighton & Hove Albion.
debut: 26.3.77 v Bristol City (H).

Given the briefest of teenage opportunities by
both Jimmy Bloomfield and Frank McLintock,
Larry began to exhibit his central defensive
skills and strength most forcefully under Jock
Wallace's management. He supplied the pace in
a fine partnership with John O'Neill, and got
forward to claim some vital goals in the
promotion seasons of 1980 (including the
championship clincher) and 1983, and on the
Cup semi-final trail of 1982. Larry's aerial
prowess and acute reading of the game were
much appreciated by a Leicester crowd that was
accordingly somewhat baffled when Gordon
Milne accepted £110,000 from Barnsley for his
talents on the very eve of 1983/4. Three and a
half years and 133 League games later, Larry's
transfer value had almost doubled as the Owls
swooped for his signature and returned him to
the First Division stage, and the price was again
high when the newly-promoted Seagulls took
on Larry to plug their leaky Second Division
defence.
Apps: 180+7 Lge; 12 FAC; 8 LC.
Goals: 12 Lge; 3 FAC.

MEARNS, FREDERICK CHARLES
b. Sunderland, 31.3.1879.
d. Sunderland, 22.1.1931.
Selbourne/Jan 1901:Sunderland/
May 1902:Kettering/
Mar 1903:Tottenham Hotspur/
May 1904:Bradford City/cs 1905:Barrow/

May 1906:Bury/cs 1908:Hartlepools United/
cs 1909:Barnsley/Jan 1911:FOSSE/
cs 1913:Newcastle City.
debut: 11.2.11 v.Glossop (H).

A well-travelled goalkeeper who started his
senior career as understudy to the long-serving
Scottish international Teddy Doig at Roker
Park, Fred had sampled the game at numerous
levels before joining Fosse in an exchange deal
which took forward George Travers to
Barnsley. Kettering and Spurs were of equal
Southern League status when he assisted them
between the sticks, while Hartlepools United
had just been formed and admitted to the
Northern League when Fred signed for them.
He was Barnsley's 'keeper in both games of the
1910 FA Cup Final, and gave Fosse fine service
as a hefty last liner for more than two years,
after which he moved homeward into the North
Eastern League. He later also acted as trainer to
Durham City.
Apps: 68 Lge; 2 FAC.

GEORGE MEEK

MEEK, GEORGE
b. Glasgow, 15.2.1934.
Thorniewood United/Hamilton Academicals/
Aug 1952:Leeds United/
(Jan 1954-loan-Walsall)/Aug 1960:CITY/
July 1961:Walsall/Mar 1965:Dudley/
cs 1965:Rushall Olympic.
debut: 20.8.60 v.Blackpool (H).

Almost invariably described by contemporary
commentators as a 'big-hearted little 'un',
George was not one to let his limited stature in
any way diminish his effectiveness as a darting
winger, and he was a regular thorn in City's
flesh for Leeds throughout the 50's. He had 230
League games under his belt by the time Matt
Gillies brought him to Leicester, but he
struggled to displace either Howard Riley or
Gordon Wills, and was soon grateful to return
for a second spell at Fellows Park, encompassing Walsall's heady Second Division days.
George eventually played on in West Midlands
football until the age of 50.
Apps: 13 Lge.

JIM MELROSE

MELROSE, JAMES MILLSOPP
b. Glasgow, 7.10.1958.
Eastercraigs/1975:Partick Thistle/
July 1980:CITY/Sept 1982:Coventry City/
Aug 1983:Celtic/
(Sept 1984-loan-Wolverhampton Wanderers)/
Nov 1984:Manchester City/
Mar 1986:Charlton Athletic/
Sept 1987:Leeds United/
Feb 1988:Shrewsbury Town.
debut: 16.8.80 v.Ipswich Town (H).

Capped eight times at Scotland Under-21 level,
and once for the Scottish League, Jim
developed a nippy striking profile at Firhill, and
became City's third £250,000 buy when Jock
Wallace judged him a likely foil for target man
Alan Young. He initially struggled to adapt to
the pace of the First Division - as did many of
his youthful team-mates in 1980/1 - but picked
up a few useful goals as City belatedly battled
against their relegation fate, and signed off his
first term with a cheeky hat-trick at Norwich
which doomed the Canaries as well. Jim
developed into a crowd favourite during the
next season, and many were critical that his
enforced role as 'super-sub' kept him for too
long out of the important action (like the FA
Cup semi-final against Spurs); while almost all
were vocal in their condemnation of the
exchange deal involving Tommy English which
Gordon Milne engineered early in his Filbert
Street tenure. Maintaining a decent scoring
record, Jim has nonetheless subsequently
become something of a wanderer, but at Celtic
he made substitute appearances in the Finals of
both Scottish knockout competitions of 1984,
and he assisted both Manchester City and
Charlton into the First Division. Indeed, his
goals for the latter in the 1987 promotion/
relegation play-offs did a lot to keep them up.
While at Shrewsbury (initially on loan), Jim
was the victim of an assault by Swindon's
Chris Kamara that eventually saw the latter
player become the first to face legal prosecution
for such an act.
Apps: 57+15 Lge; 2+6 FAC; 6 LC.
Goals: 21 Lge; 4 FAC; 1 LC.

MERCER, JOHN THOMPSON
b. Belfast, 1879.
d. Jan 1947.
Linfield Swifts/Distillery/
May 1899:Brighton United/Feb 1900:FOSSE/
cs 1900:Linfield/Feb 1903:Distillery/

Oct 1903:Derby County.
debut: 24.2.1900 v.Chesterfield.

A 'dashing' Irish international outside-right
(capped four times before first sampling
English football, and a further seven after
leaving Fosse), Johnny had impressed in
Brighton's Southern League line-up, but failed
to bolster Fosse's still-viable promotion
prospects after his mid-season arrival. Further
glory back in Belfast (including two Irish Cup
medals) encouraged Derby to give him another
chance at League level, but a more experienced
Johnny was only a little more successful with
the Rams in Division One. He later had lengthy
spells as a director at each of Glentoran and
Distillery, and was chairman of the Irish
League in 1941/2.
Apps: 9 Lge.
Goals: 2 Lge.

MERCER, STANLEY
b. Tranmere, 11.9.19.
am Jan 1944:Blackpool/am July 1944/
pro Nov 1944:CITY/
Jan 1947:Accrington Stanley/
Oct 1948:Mansfield Town.
debut (postwar): 5.1.46 v.Chelsea (A) FAC.

A wartime signing who notched 13 goals in 27
regional games for City and also guested for
Accrington and Manchester United, Stan was a
handy centre-forward who hardly got a break at
Filbert Street when peace returned, but who
knocked in a total of 42 goals in 80 League
games for his subsequent two clubs after
earning £750 for the City coffers. Between
1953 and 1955, Stan occupied the manager's
chair at Mansfield, in succession to George
Jobey.
Apps: 1 Lge; 2 FAC.

MESSER, ROBERT
b. Edinburgh.
Bo'ness/May 1910:FOSSE.
debut: 24.9.10 v.Clapton Orient (A).

A tall young Scottish outside-right, one of no
less than nine players tried in that problematic
position during 1910/11, and not a conspicuous
success.
Apps: 2 Lge.

MIDDLETON, FRANCIS
b. Whitwick.
Whitwick White Cross/
Nov 1901:Derby County/Aug 1906:FOSSE.
debut: 1.9.06 v.Burslem Port Vale (A) (1 goal).

An outstanding outside-left whose top-class
promise was first signalled when Derby paid
£100 to his local Midland League club for his
signature, Frank stepped straight into the Rams'
First Division front line alongside the near-
legendary likes of Steve Bloomer. After 65
League games he had confirmed his chief role
as provider by scoring only three goals, yet
upon moving to Leicester he notched one
counter in each of his first four games before
suffering injury. Frank contributed some fine
wing performances in the first half of Fosse's
promotion season, but was sorely distressed by
the tragic death of his young child in January

1908, and dropped out of contention soon after.
Apps: 49 Lge; 3 FAC.
Goals: 10 Lge.

MIDDLETON, JOHN
b. Sunderland.
Herrington Swifts/Lambton Star/May
1922:CITY/May 1925:Queens Park Rangers/
cs 1927:Aldershot.
debut: 28.4.23 v.Bury (H).

Elevated from Wearside League football, Jack
was a skilful reserve inside-right who deputised
for several of City's stars in the early 20's, but
could never quite claim a regular Filbert Street
role. With QPR, he occasionally played in front
of both George Hebden and Hugh Richmond,
while he returned to Aldershot in the mid-30's
as trainer/coach.
Apps: 12 Lge; 1 FAC.
Goals: 3 Lge.

MILBURN, STANLEY
b. Ashington, 22.10.1926.
Ashington/Jan 1947:Chesterfield/
Feb 1952:CITY/Jan 1959:Rochdale/
cs 1965:Spotland Methodists/TBA(Rochdale).
debut: 22.3.52 v.Sheffield United (A).

A member of the remarkable Geordie footballing dynasty of Milburn's and Charlton's, Stan
followed three of his brothers in exhibiting an
affinity for the full-back position, and took little
time at Saltergate in impressing the various
selection panels who honoured him with one
England 'B' cap, two Football League
appearances, and a place on the FA XI tour of
Canada, all in 1950. Norman Bullock expended
£10,000 in bringing him to Leicester, where his
sterling defensive work was a feature for seven
seasons, including the promotion campaigns of
1954 and 1957. Stan was an ever-present in the
latter season, scoring his only City goal in a 5-4
win at Bury, and kept Irish international Willie
Cunningham on the sidelines. Then, after
bowing out of the First Division fray at an age
when many players would be contemplating retirement, he took his boundless enthusiasm to
little Rochdale, playing on for seven more
seasons, skippering his side to the 1962 League
Cup Final, and completing his first-class career
with an aggregate of 589 League games.
Characteristically, though, Stan was still
turning out in local football in Rochdale in the
early 80's!
Apps: 173 Lge; 10 FAC.
Goals: 1 Lge.

MILES, IDRIS
b. Swansea.
d. 1983.
Nov 1930:Cardiff City/
May 1931:Yeovil & Petters United/
Oct 1932:CITY/May 1934:Clapton Orient/
cs 1937:Exeter City/1938:Worcester City.
debut: 22.10.32 v.Everton (H) (1 goal).

A tiny right-winger who had been released by
Cardiff after only three League games, Idris
briefly assumed Hughie Adcock's position with
City, but suffered appalling fortune in twice
breaking his collar-bone in the course of his
first Filbert Street season. Failing to get another

chance, he moved on in the part-exchange deal with Orient that brought fellow-Welshman Tommy Mills to Leicester, and for the club then playing at Lea Bridge Speedway he totted up 73 League games across three seasons, scoring six times.
Apps: 7 Lge.
Goals: 1 Lge.

MILLER, WILLIAM
b.
cs 1893:FOSSE/cs 1895:Kettering.
debut: 9.9.93 v.Burton Wanderers (H) ML.

An inside or centre-forward who impressed sufficiently as an ever-present in the final Midland League season to be retained for the first shot at the Second Division. William's goal tally in the latter sphere could have been higher. He missed the first penalty awarded to Fosse in the League, against Newcastle in October 1894 - which would have given him a hat-trick! On dropping back into Midland League football, he assisted Kettering to their first-ever championship in 1896.
Apps: 10 Lge; 9 FAC; 20 ML.
Goals: 2 Lge; 5 FAC; 7 ML.

MILLS, ANDREW
b. Knighton, Radnorshire, 1878.
cs 1897:Blackburn Rovers/
cs 1898:Swindon Town/
cs 1899:Brighton United/May 1900:FOSSE.
debut: 1.9.1900 v.Stockport County (H).

A versatile defender who settled best in Fosse's right-back position in partnerships with old hands George Swift or Walter Robinson, Andy ironically came closest to international recognition just as he was fading from the first team picture at Leicester. In fact he was stretchered out of the Welsh trial game of February 1903, and subsequently made only one further Fosse appearance. Two of Andy's goals were penalties; the other a lofted shot from his own half!
Apps: 64 Lge; 3 FAC.
Goals: 3 Lge.

MILLS, GARY ROLAND
b. Northampton, 11.11.1961.
pro Nov 1978:Nottingham Forest/
(Mar 1982-loan-Seattle Sounders)/
(Oct 1982-loan-Derby County)/
(Apr 1983-loan-Seattle Sounders)/
Aug 1987:Notts County/Mar 1989:CITY.
debut: 4.3.89 v.Walsall (H).

The son of former Northampton stalwart Roly Mills, Gary made a prodigious impact in his early years on Trentside, earning a winner's medal from Forest's second European Cup triumph in 1980 while still a teenager, and picking up two England Under-21 caps to add to his youth international honours. The attacking midfielder later fell foul, however, of the League's attempts to tighten up the regulations regarding loan and transfer deals with American clubs in the NASL, and a combination of such difficulties and severe injury problems kept Gary away from the City Ground limelight for some time. By the time he

made the short move to Meadow Lane, Gary had been somewhat edged out of the picture by a new generation of Brian Clough discoveries, but his consistency on the Magpies' flanks encouraged David Pleat to regard him as a likely belated replacement for Peter Weir at Filbert Street, and he became a City player in a part-exchange deal that saw Phil Turner depart for Nottingham. As yet, he has not proved as penetrative as was hoped, but should settle to a renewed promotion-seeking campaign.
Apps (to 13.5.89): 13 Lge.

MILLS, THOMAS JAMES
b. Ton Pentre, 28.12.1911.
d. Bristol, 15.5.1979.
Trocadero Restaurant/cs 1929:Clapton Orient/
May 1934:CITY/May 1936:Bristol Rovers.
debut: 3.9.34 v.Everton (H) (1 goal).

The scorer of one of Wales' winning goals against England in November 1933, inside-forward Tommy doubled his tally of caps to four while on City's books, but struggled with several less nominally illustrious rivals for a regular place in the club's relegation-bound side, and then failed to make his mark in the initial attempt to climb back. His £575 move to Eastville, in company with David Bruce, revived his career a little, and he managed 99 League games for Rovers before retirement in 1939. Tommy had originally joined Orient as an amateur, after being spotted playing for the staff team of the Trocadero Hotel.
Apps: 17 Lge; 1 FAC.
Goals: 5 Lge.

MILLS, WILLIAM
b. Hackney, 1891.
Barnet Alston/Vicar of Wakefield/
Dec 1911:FOSSE.
debut: 16.12.11
v.Stockport County (H) (1 goal).

An enthusiastic inside-forward who cost Fosse a £5 signing-on fee from London junior football, Billy felt the wrath of the game's hidebound establishment almost as soon as he arrived - receiving a draconian two months suspension for the heinous offence of having played Sunday football in London after registering with Leicester. Thankfully not overly discouraged by such pettiness, Billy continued to assist Fosse until the outbreak of war, and was top scorer in the disastrous 1914/15 season. Unfortunately, he suffered serious wounds in the conflict in France, and City played a benefit friendly on his behalf in October 1919 against a Select XI.
Apps: 77 Lge; 2 FAC.
Goals: 20 Lge; 1 FAC.

MILNES, FREDERICK HOUGHTON
b.
Sheffield Wycliffe/Sheffield/
(May 1902:Sheffield United)/
(Oct 1904:West Ham United)/
(Mar 1906:Manchester United)/
(Feb 1907:FOSSE)/(Sept 1908:Norwich City).
debut: 27.4.07 v.Lincoln City (A).

A classy amateur international right-back

whose primary allegiance was to the long-established Sheffield Club - for whom he scored a penalty in their 1904 FA Amateur Cup win - Fred was always ready to lend his assistance on a non-contract basis to almost any senior club who asked, having short spells with all those mentioned above, and probably more besides. For Fosse he only turned out in a home friendly against Stockport County and in the above League match, yet the local press reaction to his appearance was little short of ecstatic. He also played at Filbert Street against a Leicestershire XI in 1907, as a member of the Pilgrims, an amateur combination about to tour Canada and the United States.
Apps: 1 Lge.

MITCHELL, J.
b. Belfast.
Royal Field Artillery/(Apr 1912:FOSSE)/
(Mar 1913:FOSSE).
debut: 27.4.12 v.Leeds City (H).

A serving bombardier who occasionally turned out for Fosse reserves when stationed nearby, and was given a senior break at left-half in the final game of 1911/12, along with fellow squaddie Sharpley. (It is suspected he may also have played for Coventry in the Southern League during 1912/13).
Apps: 1 Lge.

MITTEN, JOHN
b. Manchester, 30.3.1941.
am:1957:Mansfield Town/am:1958/
pro Sept 1960:Newcastle United/
Sept 1961:CITY/
(Apr 1963-trials-Manchester United)/
Aug 1963:Coventry City/
Jan 1967:Plymouth Argyle/
July 1968:Exeter City/cs 1971:Bath City/
Tiverton Town.
debut: 30.9.61 v.West Ham United (A).

The son of former Manchester United and Fulham player Charlie Mitten, and honoured by England at both schoolboy and youth levels, John was managed by his father at both Mansfield and Newcastle - and hardly endeared himself to a Geordie crowd already whispering of nepotism when he missed a penalty on his debut as a 17-year-old. He came to Leicester initially on trial, being signed permanently only after his first team debut at outside-left. He played in four senior competitions in a four-month spell, but then had his City progress comprehensively blocked by the arrival of Mike Stringfellow. In the meantime, John was also making his mark in Leicestershire cricket as a useful wicket-keeper, with 14 first-class matches to his name between 1961 and 1963. Eventually he joined Jimmy Hill's Sky Blue revival at Coventry, and then settled for several seasons of West Country football.
Apps: 12 Lge; 1 FAC; 1 LC, 2 ECWC.
Goals: 1 LC.

MOODY, HERBERT B.
b. Luton, 1880.
Luton Stanley/cs 1901:Luton Town/
Aug 1905:FOSSE/cs 1907:Luton Town/
June 1912:Millwall.

debut: 2.9.05 v.Clapton Orient (H) (1 goal).

Six times chosen for the Southern League representative side between 1910 and the outbreak of war, this clever inside or centre-forward, usually known as Harry, was equally adept at creating and collecting chances; though his most prolific scoring days were still in front of him after two seasons in an improving Fosse side building towards its promotion challenge. In both his first spell with Luton and his Fosse days, Harry benefited enormously from the tutelage of Jimmy Blessington, and was also able to exploit for Fosse his familiarity with Jamie Durrant's style and strengths. He left Millwall just before they became one of the founder members of Division Three in 1920, having totalled over 350 Southern League games in his career, and having claimed about 125 goals.
Apps: 54 Lge; 1 FAC.
Goals: 11 Lge; 1 FAC.

MORALEE, MATTHEW W.
b. Mexborough. 21.2.1912.
1929:Denaby United/
cs 1930:Gainsborough Trinity/
Feb 1931:Grimsby Town/
Oct 1936:Aston Villa/Nov 1937:CITY/
July 1939:Shrewsbury Town.
debut: 13.11.37 v.Preston North End (H).

An intelligent, prompting inside-forward who never quite bore out his early promise, Matt had been bought by Villa from Blundell Park as a likely candidate to help lift them from the ignominy of their first-ever season in Division Two, but he got few chances to shine as they failed to rebound immediately. At Filbert Street, it was primarily a hectic, eventually un-successful battle to help keep City in Division One which Matt joined, and despite a few sparkling displays he was released into Midland League football on the eve of war. Appearances as a guest player for Grimsby, Doncaster Rovers and Rotherham United followed, before Matt saw out his active career back at Denaby.
Apps: 38 Lge; 5 FAC.
Goals: 6 Lge.

MORAN, EDWARD
b. Cleland, 20.7.1930.
Cleland BC/Sept 1947:CITY/
Oct 1951:Stockport County/
Feb 1957:Rochdale/
Sept 1958:Crewe Alexandra/
Aug 1959:Flint Town United/
1963:Glossop (p/coach).
debut: 2.4.49 v.Grimsby Town (H).

Another of the skilful young Scots snapped up in Johnny Duncan's regular cross-border raids of the immediate postwar years, Eddie was a ball-playing inside-right who was initially noted for coming unscathed through his teenage debut game - a veritable battle with Grimsby in which eight City men suffered injuries of varying severity. A brief run in Bert Barlow's shirt in 1950/1 was the pinnacle of Eddie's senior career at Leicester, but the schemer also found his shooting boots at Edgeley Park,

knocking in 42 League goals in 110 games, and then remained in the North West to see out his senior playing days.
Apps: 8 Lge.
Goals: 1 Lge.

MORAN, JAMES
b. Cleland, 6.3.1935.
Wishaw Juniors/Dec 1955:CITY/
Nov 1957:Norwich City/
Jan 1961:Northampton Town/
Aug 1962:Darlington/July 1963:Workington/
May 1966:Lowestoft Town (p/coach).
debut: 19.4.57 v.Leyton Orient (A) (1 goal).

Jimmy's City career was short but relatively sweet - his League bow coming in the game at Brisbane Road which clinched the Second Division championship of 1957. There seemed little chance of the inside-right deposing Ian McNeill for long, however, and his transfer to Norwich looked merely a wise career move until the Canaries introduced a note of teasing mystery to the proceeedings - playing Jimmy in a floodlit friendly against Aberdeen under the pseudonym of 'Johnstone' prior to signing him. After up and down spells with both Cobblers and Quakers, Jimmy settled to a century of League games at Workington, then later returned to East Anglia. He had a spell managing Yarmouth Town, still lives in Norwich and, until July 1988, ran a local team there, Coltishall HV.
Apps: 3 Lge.
Goals: 1 Lge.

MORAN, JOSEPH
b.
Doncaster Rovers/Sept 1904:FOSSE.
debut: 19.11.04 v.Lincoln City (H).

Discarded by Doncaster on their re-election to the League, this left-winger proved an unimpressive one-off deputy for Tommy Allsopp on Fosse's flank.
Apps: 1 Lge.

MORAN, STEVEN JAMES
b. Croydon, 10.1.1961.
app/pro Aug 1979:Southampton/
Sept 1986:CITY/Nov 1987:Reading.
debut: 13.9.86
v.Sheffield Wednesday (A) (1 goal).

Bought for £300,000 to help consolidate City's seemingly well-established First Division position, record signing Steve unfortunately extended a dismal sequence. His predecessors with the 'most-expensive' tag, Allan Clarke and Roger Davies, had each arrived for relegation seasons, and Bryan Hamilton's team duly made the drop in 1987 despite Steve's goals. In fact, Steve's City spell has to be adjudged a disappointment overall, for only in sporadic flashes did Filbert Street fans witness the incisive opportunism which had established him at the Dell and won England Under-21 selection, and he proved unable to strike up an effective partnership with any of the club's other front-men, as he had previously for the Saints with Mike Channon and Kevin Keegan. Lawrie McMenemy spotted Steve as a

schoolboy, offered him a new pair of boots if he collected a second-half hat-trick in a Sunday junior game; duly coughed up when the feat was achieved, and signed him shortly after-wards. He made a scoring substitute's debut for Southampton, and his mercurial progress thereafter was hampered only by a couple of lengthy spells on the treatment table. It was, however, inconsistency rather than injury which prompted his in-and-out status at Leicester, and even after a £200,000 move to Reading (a record for that club, too), Steve's frustrations continued. He was cup-tied and therefore sidelined as the Royals took the Simod Cup at Wembley, and was then unable to stop them sliding into Division Three.
Apps: 35+8 Lge; 1 FAC; 5+2 LC; 0+1 FMC.
Goals: 14 Lge; 3 LC.

STEVE MORAN

MORGAN, SIMON CHARLES
b. Birmingham, 5.9.1966.
app July 1983/pro Nov 1984:CITY.
debut: 6.10.85 v.Coventry City (A).

A left-back of seemingly unbounded promise when he joined the City defensive ranks as a teenager, Simon settled quickly to his responsibilities in a struggling side, showing the sort of style and spirit which made Under-21 honours for his country an inevitability. Both his anticipation and tackling skills marked the fair-haired Brummie as the first apparent specialist No.3 to hold a regular City place since Dennis Rofe, but squad-system exigen-cies soon saw his mettle tested in roles all across the back four (and even behind it, in Bryan Hamilton's short-lived tactical experi-ments utilising a sweeper). A degree of inconsistency was an understandable result, and Simon also suffered fitness problems for several months in 1987/8, but more recently his value as a utilitarian defender has been re-emphasised with a number of sterling displays in the centre-back berth.
Apps (to 13.5.89): 133+10 Lge;
4 FAC; 12 LC; 3 FMC.
Goals: 2 Lge; 1 LC.

MORGAN, WILLIAM
b.
1896:Newton Heath/
Mar 1903:Bolton Wanderers/cs 1903:Watford/
Aug 1904:FOSSE/cs 1906:New Brompton.
debut: 3.9.04 v.Blackpool (A).

A long-serving stalwart of the Manchester club which had been officially re-christened as United before he left them, William was retrieved by Fosse from the lower reaches of the Southern League's Second Division to give two seasons' worth of consistent, grafting effort at either right-half or centre-forward.
Apps: 66 Lge; 7 FAC.
Goals: 9 Lge; 3 FAC.

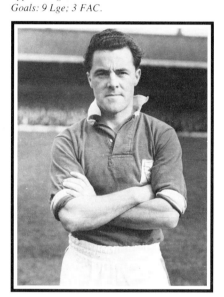

JOHNNY MORRIS

MORRIS, JOHN
b. Radcliffe, 27.9.1924.
Radcliffe/Aug 1939:Manchester United/
Mar 1949:Derby County/Oct 1952:CITY/
May 1958:Corby Town (p/mgr)/
cs 1961:Kettering Town (p/mgr).
debut: 4.10.52 v.Plymouth Argyle (H).

On the Old Trafford books as a junior from the age of 15, Johnny made his senior bow in wartime football while still a month short of his 17th birthday, and by the time peace returned he had also guested for Bolton and Charlton while on leave from his Royal Armoured Corps tank crew. A skilful, thoughtful dribbler at inside-forward, and blessed with a thunderous shot, he helped engineer United's 1948 FA Cup victory, and had won the first of five Football League representative honours when, after disagreeing with Matt Busby on tactics, he attracted a British record fee of £24,500 from Derby. His form with the Rams won him three full England caps (and three international goals to go with them), and his capture by Second Division City (at a club record of £21,500) was regarded with some surprise. A regular at inside-right for four seasons (with a Division Two championship medal from 1954), Johnny then switched to right-half and was an ever-present inspiration to the next table-topping promotion side of 1957. His off-field relations

with the club management were not always of the most cordial variety, but Johnny's most notorious brush with authority came when he managed to get himself sent off for insulting the referee during City's public practice match in August 1957, and picked up a 14-day suspension to interrupt the early part of his final Leicester season. Following his Southern League player/manager days (taking over from Jack Froggatt at Kettering), he also held the executive reins at both Great Harwood and Oswestry Town. Johnny's younger brother, William, had a brief League career at Rochdale.
Apps: 206 Lge; 14 FAC.
Goals: 33 Lge; 1 FAC.

MORTIMER, FREDERICK ERNEST
b.
Grenadier Guards/1912:Crystal Palace/
May 1913:FOSSE/May 1914:Swansea Town/
cs 1920:Rugby Town.
debut: 20.9.13 v.Birmingham (A).

A former soldier who proved the goalscoring success of Fosse's tour of Sweden in the summer of 1913, and claimed 29 reserve-team goals in 1913/14, Mortimer also hit a hat-trick in his first senior home game, but was generally unable to perk up a struggling side, and followed manager Bartlett to Southern League Swansea. Previously in that sphere he had made but a single appearance for Palace.
Apps: 22 Lge; 2 FAC.
Goals: 8 Lge; 1 FAC.

MOUNTAIN, GEORGE
b. Grimsby, 1874.
d. Grimsby, 10.7.1936.
1889:Grimsby White Star/Waltham Hornets/
Aug 1895:Grimsby Town/Grimsby All Saints/
1897:Grimsby Town/May 1903:FOSSE/
cs 1904:Grimsby Rangers.
debut: 5.9.03 v.Barnsley (A).

A hearty, play-anywhere man who eventually settled to the right-back spot after breaking his football career in 1895 to go to sea, 'Bodge' totted up 152 League games for the Mariners, helping them win the Second Division championship in 1901, accepting a benefit game against Lincoln City, and only leaving after their relegation in 1903. Thoughts of frying pans and fires must have crossed his mind, though, as Fosse slumped into the re-election mire, and for all his fighting spirit (literally expressed in the FA Cup defeat by Burton United, when he was sent off), 'Bodge' was unable to effect a turnaround in their fortunes before he returned to the fishing town. Grimsby had applied to the FA to let George pocket Fosse's transfer fee himself, but had been refused.
Apps: 26 Lge; 4 FAC.

MOUNTENEY, ARTHUR
b. Belgrave, Leicester, 11.2.1883.
d. Leicester, 1.6.1933.
Leicester Imperial/Nov 1903:FOSSE/
Apr 1905:Birmingham/
Apr 1909:Preston North End/
July 1911:Grimsby Town/
Dec 1912:Portsmouth/

cs 1914:Hinckley Athletic.
debut: 30.1.04 v.Bolton Wanderers (H).

Joining Fosse when they were at their lowest ebb, 'Pecker' was one of the young local forward prospects on whom the club pinned hopes of a revival, and he did not let them down, winning a regular place shortly after the start of 1904/5 and ending that season as top scorer. It was, though, his Cup hat-trick which simultaneously destroying West Brom and alerting top flight clubs to his potential, made it certain that Fosse could not hope to hang on to him. In the First Division with both Birmingham and Preston he developed into a coolly precise all-round forward, with a calculating approach to tactics befitting the son of a county cricket strategist - a status 'Pecker' would soon enjoy himself, appearing for Leicestershire in 144 first-class matches between 1911 and 1924. When his dual playing careers ended, he became cricket coach at Stoneygate School.
Apps: 30 Lge; 4 FAC.
Goals: 11 Lge; 10 FAC.

MOYES, DAVID
b. Cowdenbeath.
Kingseat Juniors/1919:Raith Rovers/
Aug 1926:CITY/Aug 1927:Cowdenbeath.
debut: 23.10.26 v.Liverpool (A).

A veteran of 218 Scottish League games for the Kirkcaldy side, and the beneficiary of a Raith v.Darlington friendly in April 1925, left-back Davie spent most of his Filbert Street season in the shadow of Reg Osborne and, not wishing to serve a belated reserve-team apprenticeship, was glad to return to the east of Scotland to extend his senior career.
Apps: 3 Lge.

MUGGLETON, CARL DAVID
b. Leicester, 13.9.1968.
app cs 1985/pro Sept 1986:CITY/
(Sept 1987-loan-Chesterfield)/
(Feb 1988-loan-Blackpool)/
(Oct 1988-loan-Hartlepool United).
debut: 21.1.89 v.West Bromwich Albion (A).

A fine local goalkeeping prospect, Carl was initially denied senior experience at Filbert Street by the presence of Ian Andrews and Paul Cooper, but took several on-loan opportunities to prove his worth at League level, showing a confident command of his area with the Spireites (for whom his 17-game spell literally ended with a last-minute penalty save at Fulham), and later playing twice for Blackpool, seven times for Hartlepool and, as a guest, starring for Luton's youth team in a continental tournament. Accordingly, there was little surprise when Carl made such a nerveless City debut at the Hawthorns, and he held his place on merit until Martin Hodge regained fitness, having shown admirably clean handling behind a none-too-steadfast defence.
Apps (to 13.5.89): 3 Lge.

MUNCIE, WILLIAM
b. Carluke, 28.8.1911.
Shettleston/Aug 1934:CITY/May
1938:Southend United/Mar 1944:CITY/

Oct 1946:Crewe Alexandra.
debut: 20.10.34 v.Middlesbrough (A).

A reliable stand-in winger on either flank, and the final player signed by Peter Hodge before his death, William was unfortunate to be stuck in the queues behind Hughie Adcock and Tony Carroll for the right-wing berth, and Danny Liddle and Eric Stubbs for that on the left. The war then cut severely into his latter playing years, and he was able to make only the odd appearance in regional fare for both City and Northampton until discovering that his pace had deserted him when he attempted to make a League comeback at Crewe.
Apps: 42 Lge; 1 FAC.
Goals: 11 Lge.

MUNRO, MALCOLM GEORGE

b. Melton Mowbray, 21.5.1953.
app July 1968/pro May 1970:CITY.
debut: 11.9.71 v.Ipswich Town (A).

With only a handful of senior appearances to his name up to that point, young central defender Malcolm assumed the first team No.5 shirt at the beginning of 1973/4 and held it almost solidly until Jeff Blockley arrived a season and a half later, welding a rigid partnership with Graham Cross, and helping secure City's route to the Cup semi-finals. An England cap at school and youth levels, the slender and extremely speedy defender actually did well to recover from the mishap of scoring an own goal on his 1973 breathrough day, but he was less mature about showing patience when Blockley displaced him - walking out on his contract to emigrate to Canada. City retained his registration until July 1980, when it became evident he would not return.
Apps: 69+1 Lge; 9 FAC; 5 LC.
Goals: 1 Lge; 1 LC.

MURDOCH, JAMES

b.
1888:FOSSE.
debut (comp): 4.10.90
v.Burton Wanderers (H) FAC.

The Victorian equivalent of a midfield playmaker, this Fosse pioneer lined up in the first County Cup-winning side in the pivotal centre-half position (scoring a long-distance fourth goal in the Final replay), and was at inside-right for the club's first-ever FA Cup tie.
Apps: 1 FAC.

NEWELL, MICHAEL COLIN

b. Liverpool, 27.1.1965.
am:Liverpool/Sept 1983:Crewe Alexandra/
Dec 1983:Wigan Athletic/
Jan 1986:Luton Town/Sept 1987:CITY/
June 1989:Everton.
debut: 16.9.87 v.Oldham Athletic (H) (1 goal).

One of Bryan Hamilton's proteges at Wigan (and a Wembley scorer in Athletic's 1985 Freight/Rover Trophy victory), Mike then became an expensive David Pleat signing at Luton, and forged a useful striking partnership with Mick Harford. The tall, slim forward then swapped the dubious delights of artificial turf

for the Filbert Street sward in a club record £350,000 deal, and rapidly headed himself into the good graces of City fans before succumbing to a bout of the inertia which spread itself alarmingly over the struggling Second Division side in mid-season. Mike experienced continuing spells of frustration in front of goal even after David Pleat's takeover at Leicester, and twice let his temper boil over to earn himself dismissals, but after allying his remarkable ball control and mobility to an admirable work-rate he was awarded the City captaincy midway through 1988/9 - a season he finished as top scorer, with flashes of form that earned him a highly-valued move to Goodison. Mike was also a fine cricketing prospect, representing Lancashire at both Under-18 and Under-25 levels.
Apps: 81 Lge; 2 FAC; 9 LC; 4 FMC.
Goals: 21 Lge; 5 LC.

NEWMAN, JOHN HENRY GEORGE

b. Hereford, 13.12.1933.
jnr:Hereford United/St.Andrews Athletic/
Mar 1951:Birmingham City/Nov 1957:CITY/
Jan 1960:Plymouth Argyle/
Oct 1967: Exeter City.
debut: 9.11.57 v.Burnley (A).

Limited to 59 League games with Birmingham, but an emergency choice at right-half for the Blues in their 1956 Cup Final defeat, Johnny stepped straight into the pivot's role at Leicester as City fought to establish themselves back in the First Division, and must have quickly doubted the wisdom of his £12,000 move as he stood at the centre of a defence which shipped 29 goals in his first eight games, including seven on his debut! He gratefully gave back the No.5 shirt to Ian King after that little whirlwind, but after helping assure top flight survival in the crunch match back at his old St.Andrews stamping ground, he was immovable from the right-half position throughout the whole of the next consolidatory term, until finally giving way to the promise of Frank McLintock in September 1959. Johnny amassed almost 300 League appearances as Plymouth skipper, and close to another hundred at Exeter, where he also embarked on a managerial career that has subsequently taken in Grimsby Town, Derby County and Hereford United, plus an assistant's role at Notts County. It was at Plymouth in November 1964 that he fuelled countless 'fancy that' snippets in the press by actually passing a penalty kick a few feet forward for team-mate Mike Trebilcock to score.
Apps: 61 Lge; 4 FAC.
Goals: 2 Lge.

NEWTON, ROBERT A.

b. Earl Shilton, 19.1.1946.
app Dec 1962/pro Aug 1963:CITY/
May 1965:Bradford City/
cs 1966:Wellington Town/cs 1968:Tamworth.
debut: 25.9.63 v.Aldershot (H) LC (1 goal).

A rangy teenage outside-left who briefly understudied Mike Stringfellow, Bob took his only real Filbert Street consolation from firing the opening goal of City's eventually successful

League Cup campaign of 1963/4. A season at Valley Parade (also marked by a debut goal, and by an occasional partnership with Ken Leek) closed his League career, and by the time Bob appeared in little Tamworth's FA Cup runs of the late 60's and early 70's, he had been converted to a full-back role.
Apps: 2 Lge; 1 LC.
Goals: 1 LC.

BILLY NEWTON

NEWTON, WILLIAM

b. Cramlington, 14.5.1893.
d. Stockport, 29.4.1973.
Hartford Colliery/cs 1919:Newcastle United/
cs 1920:Cardiff City/May 1922:CITY/
May 1926:Grimsby Town/
June 1927:Stockport County/
July 1931:Hull City.
debut: 13.10.23 v.Bradford City (A).

A tough-tackling Geordie whose senior career got off to a slow start, Billy showed remarkable stamina in remaining involved in football until he was in his seventies, returning to Edgeley Park in 1932 for a 30-year-plus stint on Stockport's coaching and training staff. He could hardly have looked forward to such a lengthy professional life when Newcastle released him without a senior game to his name, but he made sufficient sporadic wing-half appearances in Cardiff's first two seasons in the League to attract Peter Hodge's attention. Another reserve-team season followed, but Billy was soon to displace Dennis Jones from the City right-half berth, and hold it through the 1925 promotion campaign and on into the First Division. Thereafter, though Grimsby and Hull each got a season's commitment out of him, he devoted his considerable enthusiasm to Stockport on an almost lifelong basis.
Apps: 87 Lge; 8 FAC.
Goals: 1 Lge.

NISH, DAVID JOHN

b. Burton-on-Trent, 26.9.1947.
Measham/am/pro July 1966:CITY/
Aug 1972:Derby County/
Feb 1979:Tulsa Roughnecks/
Mar 1980:Seattle Sounders/

Shepshed Charterhouse/
June 1982:Gresley Rovers (p/mgr)/Stapenhill.
debut: 3.12.66 v.Stoke City (H) (1 goal).

A teenage prodigy who won numerous England youth honours and was once chosen as first team substitute by City while still at school, David exhibited amazing versatility over his first few seasons in City's senior squad, appearing as a creative midfielder and a defensive wing-half before settling as an attacking left-back. By this time his natural ease and cool authority had made him ideal material for the team captaincy, and when City got to Wembley in 1969, David became the youngest-ever Cup Final skipper at 21. Rarely missing a game, and amassing ten England Under-23 caps and several Football League honours in recognition of his elegant effectiveness, he led City back to the top flight in 1971 and looked set for a lengthy Leicester career when reigning champions Derby came in with a British record fee of £250,000 to take him to the Baseball Ground. Five full England caps and a League championship medal (1975) deservedly came David's way, but he subsequently suffered a series of knee injury problems and left for the less demanding sphere of NASL football when he felt he was slipping from his own high standards of performance. A Testimonial game between current Rams and their championship-winning predecessors in December 1979 was Derby's fitting adieu to him, but he rejoined former team-mates Bruce Rioch and Colin Todd on the coaching staff at Middlesbrough in July 1988.
Apps: 228 Lge; 28 FAC; 16 LC.
Goals: 25 Lge; 4 FAC; 2 LC.

DAVID NISH

NOBLE, ROBERT
b. Buckhaven, 29.9.1891.
d. Newcastle, 1.5.1976.
Bromley/May 1912:FOSSE/
Nov 1912:Millwall/1921:London Caledonians.
debut: 7.9.12 v.Nottingham Forest (H).

A civil servant who played as an amateur throughout his career - and had been a team-mate of Douglas McWhirter in Bromley's Amateur Cup-winning side of 1911 - this inside-forward failed to impress the Fosse directorate in his brief, early-season try-out, but was presumably happier anyway to assist Southern League Millwall and cut down on the

travelling from his capital base. (It is suspected Robert may have been registered with both Aston Villa and QPR while still a teenager, but he made senior appearances for neither).
Apps: 4 Lge.

NORMAN, ALFRED
b.
Leicester Imperial/Aug 1906:FOSSE/
cs 1907:Leicester Imperial.
debut: 24.11.06 v.Bradford City (A).

A local outside-right who twice deputised in League games for Jamie Durrant during 1906/7, and once in a friendly against Luton.
Apps: 2 Lge.
Goals: 1 Lge.

NORMAN, RICHARD
b. Newcastle, 5.9.1935.
Ferryhill Athletic/
cs 1958:Horden Colliery Welfare/
Nov 1958:CITY/
June 1968:Peterborough United.
debut: 23.1.60 v.Newcastle United (A).

A steady, unflamboyant Geordie left-back, overlooked by his home-town League club despite starring for Ferryhill's Northern League championship team of 1958, Richie only needed a couple of chances to deputise for Willie Cunningham to develop an unshakeable grip on City's No.3 shirt. From April 18th, 1960 to the end of February 1964 he never missed a match, shattering the then-standing City record for consecutive League and Cup appearances, and matching consistency to fitness through 194 games, including two FA Cup Finals and City's brief European adventure. Richie was not to miss many games over the next four seasons either, playing in both League Cup Finals, and leaving an abiding impression of cheerful sportsmanship. After a brief stint with Posh, Richie turned to coaching and training duties at Burton Albion, Derby County, Northampton Town and Northamptonshire CCC.
Apps: 303 Lge; 30 FAC; 28 LC; 4 ECWC.
Goals: 2 Lge; 3 LC.

NORTH, MARC VICTOR
b. Ware, 25.9.1966.
app/pro 1983:Luton Town/
(Mar 1985-loan-Lincoln City)/
(Jan 1987-loan-Scunthorpe United)/
(Mar 1987-loan-Birmingham City)/
Aug 1987:Grimsby Town/Mar 1989:CITY.
debut: 25.3.89 (sub) v.Birmingham City (H).

Initially signed as a teenage goalkeeper by David Pleat, and later taken on as a striker at Blundell Park by Bobby Roberts, Marc rejoined both as a deadline-day City signing, just a couple of months after hitting the goalscoring headlines in Grimsby's giant-killing Cup run. Marc had, in fact, taken his conversion from last-liner to front-man in stages, making his League debut as a defender while on loan at Lincoln, before briefly partnering Mike Newell and Mick Harford at Kenilworth Road. With City, he has yet to get the chance to impress over 90 minutes, for his belated full senior debut saw him carried off with a broken shin

after he had opened the scoring against Crystal Palace with a fine header.
Apps (to 13.5.89): 1+7 Lge.
Goals: 1 Lge.

NORTON, JOSEPH P.
b. Leicester.
Leicester Imperial/cs 1911:Stockport County/
cs 1912: not known/
Jan 1914:Manchester United/July 1919:CITY/
May 1920:Bristol Rovers/
cs 1922:Swindon Town/
June 1923:Kettering Town.
debut: 1.9.19 v.Tottenham Hotspur (A).

A First Division regular at Old Trafford immediately before WW1, Joe returned to his home town to guest for Fosse in wartime football and then signed on for the reconstructed club's first League season. A winger who happily turned out on either flank after making his City debut as an emergency centre-forward, Joe nonetheless seemed to carry a jinx with him during his Filbert Street season - in only three of the twelve games he played did City manage even to score! At Eastville, Joe helped Rovers to their first-ever League win with one of his own rare goals; another, back in 1911, had been the very first strike he registered at League level, for Stockport against Fosse!
Apps: 11 Lge; 1 FAC.

NUTTALL, ERNEST A.
b. Leicester.
Mill Hill House/1889:FOSSE.
debut (comp): 4.10.90
v.Burton Wanderers (H) FAC.

An amateur wing-half signed prior to Fosse's initial foray into the FA Cup, and elected club captain for the first assault on the Midland League, having previously represented the Leicestershire FA in Inter-County fare. Always known as 'Snooks', he actually claimed the club's first-ever FA Cup goal (in their second tie) and was still turning out in the occasional Fosse friendly in 1893/4 as the club embraced professionalism ever more firmly.
Apps: 3 FAC; 35 ML.
Goals: 1 FAC; 2 ML.

OAKES, W.H.
b.
Clapton/Feb 1904:West Ham United/
May 1904:FOSSE.
debut: 3.9.04 v.Blackpool (A).

A well-regarded full-back, noted for the length and accuracy of his clearances, Oakes signed after 14 Southern League appearances for West Ham, just prior to that club's move to Upton Park. He had two seasons with Fosse, contesting the left-back position with Walter Robinson and Bob Pollock.
Apps: 40 Lge; 1 FAC.

O'BRIEN, MICHAEL TERENCE
b. Kilcock, Dublin, 10.8.1893.
d. Uxbridge, 21.9.1940.
Walker Celtic/Wallsend/Blyth Spartans/
Newcastle East End/Celtic/Alloa Athletic/
Brentford/May 1919:Norwich City/
Dec 1919:South Shields/
May 1920:Queens Park Rangers/

Mar 1922:CITY/June 1924:Hull City/
May 1926:Brooklyn Wanderers/
Dec 1926:Derby County/June 1928:Walsall/
May 1929:Norwich City/June 1931:Watford.
debut: 18.3.22 v.Notts County (H).

Mick was a virtually legendary figure in inter-war football, whose itchy feet and love of the blarney could scarcely disguise a genuine talent for classical centre-half play. One of his claims was that he had never kicked a football until the age of 18 when, shortly before he joined the Army, his family moved from Ireland to the North East. Nonetheless, he quickly became a footballing mercenary before the outbreak of war, served during the hostilities in both the Navy and the Royal Flying Corps, and then resumed his soccer wanderings in 1919. After almost two seasons easing QPR into the League, and having won both his first Irish cap and selection for the Football League against the Army (November 1921), Mick brought his 6ft.1in. presence and his outsize personality to Leicester. Further caps came his way as firstly he played alongside Jim Harrold in a daunting defensive pairing, then usurped his partner's pivotal role. Eventually, a £750 cheque took him to Hull, and his subsequent moves even included an inquisitive taste of early Stateside soccer. When Mick finally hung up his boots (alongside 10 caps for Ireland and 4 as the Republic's skipper), he moved straight into management: at QPR for two years from 1933, as assistant at Brentford for a season, and then in control at Ipswich Town in their final season of Southern League football. Unfortunately, at this time personal problems (including the loss of his wife) began to overwhelm Mick, and within a couple of years his remarkably full life ended.
Apps: 65 Lge; 2 FAC.
Goals: 6 Lge.

O'CALLAGHAN, EUGENE
b. Ebbw Vale, 6.10.1906.
d. London, 4.7.1956.
Ebbw Vale/Victoria United/
1922:Barnet/Northfleet/
1926:Tottenham Hotspur/
Mar 1935:CITY/Oct 1937:Fulham.
debut: 2.3.35 v.Middlesbrough (H).

An outstanding Welsh international inside-right who earned eleven caps while scoring 93 League goals in 252 games with Spurs, 'Taffy' had experienced both relegation and promotion at White Hart Lane, and it was ironic that his move to Filbert Street should be a desperate strategem to help City avoid their fate of accompanying Spurs in the big drop to Division Two. Gene nonetheless soon knuckled down to the task of prompting City back up again, and earned his 1937 championship medal as second-top scorer behind Jack Bowers. Reaching the veteran stage, though, he was soon content to join Fulham in the lower echelon, and eventually retired after a few games of wartime football, including a nostalgic return to Tottenham as a guest player. For ten postwar years, until his death, Gene was reserve-team trainer at Craven Cottage.
Apps: 84 Lge; 5 FAC.
Goals: 30 Lge; 1 FAC.

OGILVIE, JOHN FORREST
b. Motherwell, 28.10.1928.
Thorniewood United/Hibernian/
(Aug 1955-trials-Sheffield United)/
Oct 1955:CITY/Jan 1960:Mansfield Town.
debut: 12.11.55 v.Swansea Town (H).

Denied his true share of the glory as a valuable defensive member of Hibernian's 1951 Scottish championship squad - he broke a leg after 15 minutes of that season's Scottish Cup semi-final - John found it difficult subsequently to pick up the pieces of his career at Easter Road, and was freed in 1955. Bramall Lane briefly beckoned, but it was David Halliday who offered John a firm contract, and the left-back settled into sound partnerships, first with Willie Cunningham, and then, throughout the 1957 promotion campaign, with Stan Milburn. In the years of First Division consolidation, Ogie's place was not quite so secure, but even with an in-and-out senior record and a series of injuries, he remained the chief dressing-room joker and morale-booster among the club's large Scottish contingent. His two penalty goals came in his final two senior City games. Now back in Leicester, in the knitwear trade, he helps manage Alan Birchenall's team of self-avowedly geriatric ex-City players.
Apps: 82 Lge; 3 FAC.
Goals: 2 Lge.

OLD, S.
b.
cs 1891:FOSSE.
debut: 12.9.91 v.Derby Junction (H) ML.

Fosse's first goalkeeper in the Midland League, Old saw the club through its brief tenancy of the Aylestone Road cricket ground, and on to Filbert Street, but lost his place at Christmas 1891 and drifted away.
Apps: 1 FAC; 7 ML.

O'NEIL, JOSEPH
b. Glasgow, 15.8.1931.
Bridgeton Waverley/1950:Aberdeen/
(Nov 1952-loan-Southend United)/
Mar 1956:CITY/Oct 1957:Northampton Town/
July 1959:Bath City.
debut: 24.8.57 v.Manchester United (H).

Never a Pittodrie regular, Joe nonetheless drew startled admiration from Dons followers for one particular show of bravery, bordering on recklessness. Three weeks before the 1954 Scottish Cup semi-final against Rangers, Joe suffered a depressed skull fracture - yet played on the big day and contributed a hat-trick to Aberdeen's 6-0 win. Further injury problems unfortunately ruled the tall forward out of the Hampden Final line-up. He accompanied clubmate Ian McNeill to Filbert Street, to renew acquaintance with former Dons boss David Halliday, but had to wait over a season for his first team bow, briefly figuring at wing-half during City's shaky start to 1957/8, then swiftly moving to the County Ground before re-uniting at Bath with another ex-Aberdonian, Ian MacFarlane.
Apps: 5 Lge.
Goals: 2 Lge.

O'NEILL, JOHN PATRICK
b. Derry, 11.3.1958.
Derry BC/
non-contract Mar 1976/
pro Feb 1979:CITY/
July 1987:Queens Park Rangers/
Dec 1987:Norwich City.
debut: 19.8.78 v.Burnley (A).

John was still a Loughborough undergraduate, playing for City on a non-contract basis while completing his economics studies, when Jock Wallace gave him an unexpected first team nod for the opening game of 1978/9. The gamble soon paid off, for John quickly developed into a cool, polished central defender. Already capped at Under-21 level for Northern Ireland prior to his League bow, he soon began adding full caps on a regular basis as his fine reading of the game brought him the added responsibility of the City captaincy. Occasionally criticised for an apparently over-casual on-field approach, and sometimes embarrassed by a relative lack of pace, John nonetheless saved Leicester many a goal against with his intelligent interventions, and the experience gained in two World Cup campaigns for his country stood City's defence in good stead during the up and down struggles of the early 80's. In 1986, he surpassed Gordon Banks' record as the most-capped City player, but a year later was allowed to move on to Loftus Road for £150,000. As QPR enjoyed a brief flurry of Division One success, John was restricted to only two League appearances, and then hit even worse fortune. He suffered a crippling knee injury after only 34 minutes of his Norwich debut at Wimbledon, and some months later had to concede his career was at a sadly premature end. Norwich very honorably arranged a Testimonial game on his behalf, attended by many City fans, in May 1989.
Apps: 313 Lge; 19 FAC; 13 LC.
Goals: 10 Lge; 1 FAC; 1 LC.

OSBORN, FREDRICK
b. Leicester, 10.11.1889.
d. Leicester, 11.10.1954.
Avondale/Hinckley United/
Apr 1910:FOSSE/
May 1913:Preston North End.
debut: 22.10.10 v.Huddersfield Town (A).

A local inside or centre-forward who developed a fine reputation for marksmanship, Freddie was top scorer for Fosse in 1913, and was soon snapped up for £250 by First Division Preston. At Deepdale he experienced relegation and promotion in his first two seasons, and then attempted to play on in the top flight after the war despite having received a bullet through the thigh while on active service. Ironically, it was the form of Fosse's wartime discovery Tom Roberts, sold to Preston in the 1919 close season and destined to become an England international, which was largely responsible for Freddie failing to hold his place there. Another of Leicester's amazingly numerous breed of footballer/cricketers, Freddie was also a stylish batsman for the County before the war.
Apps: 67 Lge; 4 FAC.
Goals: 28 Lge; 2 FAC.

OSBORNE, JOHN
b. Renfrew, 14.10.19.
Linwood Thistle/Sept 1938:CITY/
Jan 1948:Watford.
debut (postwar): 5.1.46 v.Chelsea (A) FAC.

A right-half who arrived at Filbert Street from Scottish junior football on the same day as Charlie Adam, Johnny made his first team breakthrough on the first day of the abandoned 1939/40 season, and thus had his only League appearance expunged from all official records. He did not return to Leicester until the transitional year of 1945, but was back in the No.4 shirt for both legs of the FA Cup tie with Chelsea. Johnny later became a component of the extraordinary mass transfer deal with Watford, for whom he made 34 League appearances, scoring thirteen times.
Apps: 2 FAC.

REG OSBORNE

OSBORNE, REGINALD
b. Wynberg, South Africa, 23.7.1898.
d. Hounslow, 1977.
Army football/Feb 1923:CITY/
Nov 1933:Folkestone.
debut: 2.4.23 v.Fulham (H).

A stylish left-back whose football prowess came to light while he was serving with the RAMC, Reg first attracted City's attention when starring for England in the amateur international against Ireland played at Filbert Street in 1921. When he left the service, the club were instrumental in finding him a job with the Watling Street Boot Company in the city, and deemed him a likely full-back partner for Adam Black. His debut found him in direct opposition to his brother Frank, Fulham's England winger, and it was only four years before Reg himself stepped up to full international status, winning one cap in a home defeat by Wales, and later touring the land of his birth with an FA party. Nevertheless, he came under pressure for his senior jersey at Leicester on several occasions (from the likes of Harry Hooper and Jack Brown), and there was much

to commend in the loyalty which kept him with City for more than a decade. Both his goals were penalties; both were scored against Sunderland.
Apps: 240 Lge; 9 FAC.
Goals: 2 Lge.

RUSSELL OSMAN

OSMAN, RUSSELL CHARLES
b. Repton, 14.2.1959.
app/pro Mar 1976:Ipswich Town/
July 1985:CITY/June 1988:Southampton.
debut: 17.8.85 v.Everton (H).

The son of Rex Osman, a Derby County reserve half-back of the 50's, Russell made great strides as an Ipswich youngster, winning an FA Youth Cup winners' medal in 1975 and only just missing out on a place in the 1978 FA Cup side. Established at club and eventually England level in a resolute centre-back partnership with Terry Butcher, he was also a member of Bobby Robson's victorious UEFA Cup team of 1981, but his once meteoric career, founded equally on strength and skill, appeared to be standing still during his latter years at Portman Road. Russell cost Gordon Milne a £240,000 fee when arriving to stiffen City's First Division defence, and expressed the hope that he would hit high enough form to start adding to his personal tally of eleven full caps (which had been preceded by seven Under-21 call-ups). The latter ambition failed to materialise, but Russell's energetic efforts to keep City in the top flight could hardly be faulted. He assumed the captaincy for the beginning of the 1987/8 campaign, and his coolness and comfort on the ball stood out pleasingly against a Second Division backdrop, but his retention of higher ambitions led to him moving to The Dell on the expiry of his contract.
Apps: 108 Lge; 2 FAC; 8 LC; 2 FMC.
Goals: 8 Lge.

OSVOLD, KJETIL
b. Aalesund, Norway, 5.6.1961.
Lillestrom/Apr 1987:Nottingham Forest/
(Dec 1987-loan-CITY)/

Apr 1988:Djurgaarden/
Apr 1989:PAOK Thessalonikis.
debut: 5.12.87 v.Middlesbrough (H).

One of Bryan Hamilton's last acts as City manager was to bring Norwegian cap Kjetil to Filbert Street on loan, but the blond midfielder looked as unhappy in the left-flank problem position as had most previous candidates, especially as his time in a blue shirt coincided with City's lengthy Second Division goal drought. A few months earlier, Brian Clough had paid £100,000 for 'Ossie', whose international career had previously peaked in 1986 when he claimed the winning goal for Norway against Argentina; but the Forest boss gave him few first-team opportunities, and soon accepted £70,000 from Sweden for his unsettled import. A further move to Greece followed a year later.
Apps: 3+1 Lge.

OWEN, ALFRED SYDNEY
b. Stoke.
(North Stafford Nomads/
Northern Nomads)/
Jan 1907:Stoke/
July 1907:Stockport County/
Apr 1908:Stoke/
Sept 1908:FOSSE/
(cs 1911:English Wanderers)/
July 1911:Blackpool/
Nov 1912:Stoke.
debut: 7.11.08 v.Nottingham Forest (H).

A noted amateur who signed for Fosse just before completing his chartered accountancy exams, and after Stoke had resigned from the Football League, Syd was one of the few individual successes of Fosse's relegation-bound team of 1909, and continued to turn out for the club as a forceful inside or outside-left over the next two seasons whenever business commitments - or amateur international fixtures - would permit. Originally he had been a full-back at Stoke, but took to the advanced role so well that he was chosen for the senior England trial match of January 1910, scoring once in the Whites v. Stripes fixture at Anfield but failing subsequently to win a full cap. On leaving Fosse, he toured Eastern Europe with a crack combination of English amateurs, and while at Blackpool became a controversial secretary of the Players' Union, taking part in the first legal action around the League's retain and transfer system ('The Kingaby Case'), then resigning in February 1913 to take up a commercial appointment in Budapest.
Apps: 43 Lge; 8 FAC.
Goals: 12 Lge; 1 FAC.

OWEN, S.
b.
1891:FOSSE.
debut: 5.12.91
v.Wednesbury Old Athletic (A) ML.

A right-back partner to Harry Bailey during the first two Midland League seasons; unfortunately otherwise still cloaked in the obscurity that adheres to so many of his fellow early Fossils.
Apps: 4 FAC; 18 ML.

PARIS, ALAN DAVID
b. Slough, 15.8.1964.
Slough Town/Nov 1982:Watford/
Aug 1985:Peterborough United/
July 1988:CITY.
debut: 29.8.88 v.Portsmouth (A).

Never a first-teamer at Watford, Alan built himself a fine reputation as a footballing full-back with Posh, and joined City's Second Division squad in the deal which took Nick Cusack to London Road. It has been as a central defender that he has made his Filbert Street mark, however, allying pace and determination to an evident relish for playing his way out of trouble whenever possible, and winning over an initially sceptical crowd which now regularly hails him with his dressing-room nickname of 'Delbert'. Indeed, Alan won the Supporters Club 'Player of the Year' award for 1989.
Apps (to 13.5.89): 37 Lge;
1 FAC; 4+1 LC; 1 FMC.
Goals: 1 Lge.

PARKER, JOHN FRANCIS
b. Ellistown, 16.1.1896.
d. Newhall, 2.11.1973.
Midway Athletic/Newhall Swifts/
Army football/Sept 1919:CITY/
May 1920:Norwich City.
debut: 20.9.19 v.Fulham (A).

A compact centre-forward whose lack of inches counted against him in an era of towering leaders, John had to act as understudy to Harry King and Jock Paterson for most of his season with City, and best distinguished himself in the reserve side, scoring six in the 11-2 Leicestershire Senior Cup final victory over Moira Athletic. After a £50 move, he led Norwich's attack in their inaugural Football League game, but managed only two goals in 20 games for the Canaries.
Apps: 5 Lge.
Goals: 1 Lge.

PARRY, MAURICE PRYCE
b. Oswestry, 1878.
d. Bootle, 24.3.1935.
Oswestry/Aug 1898:FOSSE/
Feb 1899:Loughborough/
May 1899:Brighton United/cs 1900:Liverpool/
May 1909:Partick Thistle.
debut: 10.9.98 v.Woolwich Arsenal (A).

Although a half-back from a footballing family (his brother Thomas won Welsh caps while remaining with Oswestry), Maurice came to Leicester primarily to find work in the engineering trade, and had to be persuaded to try his luck as a professional. Nonetheless, he got only one chance with Fosse to displace his countryman Dick Jones, and was soon on his way to assist the ailing Luffs. He was a Southern League regular at Brighton before that club withdrew from the competition, then embarked on a fine nine-year career at Anfield, making 207 League appearances as a tough ball-winner, and collecting championship medals from both top Divisions as well as sixteen Welsh caps. Maurice, an organ-playing

advocate of tee-totalism, was later a member of the first Partick team to play at Firhill. He suffered the lingering after-effects of wartime gassing, but coached in South Africa, Liverpool, Jersey and Cologne.
Apps: 1 Lge.

PARTRIDGE, MALCOLM
b. Calow, Chesterfield, 28.8.50.
app/pro Sept 1968:Mansfield Town/
Sept 1970:CITY/
(Jan 1972-loan-Charlton Athletic)/
Mar 1975:Grimsby Town/
July 1979:Scunthorpe United/
Mar 1982:Skegness Town.
debut: 19.9.70 v.Charlton Athletic (A) (1 goal).

A tall striker who impressed Frank O'Farrell as a teenage goalscorer at Field Mill (where he had made his debut in the same game as Nick Sharkey and Jimmy Goodfellow), Malcolm cost £50,000 when added to City's 1971 promotion-chasing squad. He was just settling alongside Ally Brown when a broken arm interrupted his progress, and thereafter he struggled to hold down a regular senior place, despite a useful habit of scoring in Cup ties. Malcolm nevertheless worked hard on developing other aspects of his game, and at both Grimsby (in 138 League games) and Scunthorpe (in 97) he was successful as a deeper-lying attacker.
Apps: 25+11 Lge; 3+1 FAC; 1+2 LC.
Goals: 4 Lge; 3 FAC; 1 LC.

JIM PATERSON

PATERSON, JAMES
b. Stirling, 1907.
Camelon Juniors/Jan 1927:Everton/
cs 1927:St.Johnstone/cs 1930:Cowdenbeath/
May 1932:CITY/July 1935:Reading/
July 1938:Clapton Orient.
debut: 27.8.32 v.Sheffield United (H) (1 goal).

Though he was unable to get a look-in at Goodison, with Dixie Dean blocking his senior chances, Jim rebuilt his confidence quickly

back in Scotland, winning three caps in 1931 while notching 53 goals in only 74 games for Cowdenbeath. A comparatively lightweight centre-forward, but blessed with great pace and bravery, Jim was not quite so prolific after his second move south of the border, and could never quite shake off the challenge of the veteran Arthur Chandler at Leicester. City experimented with him in different forward positions during the 1935 relegation season, and he settled at Reading as an inside-left, claiming 23 goals in 73 League games, before taking his boots to Orient and then bowing out of the senior game.
Apps: 48 Lge; 1 FAC.
Goals: 17 Lge; 1 FAC.

PATERSON, JOHN
b. Dundee, 14.12.1896.
Fort Hill/Dundee North End/Army football/
Dundee/Dec 1919:CITY/Mar 1922:Sunderland/
Oct 1924:Preston North End/
Sept 1925:Mid-Rhondda/
cs 1928:Mansfield Town.
debut: 20.12.19 v.Stoke City (H) (1 goal).

Another of Peter Hodge's shrewd postwar signings, Jock had proven his fitness at Dundee after having been wounded five times while serving with the Black Watch in France, and was soon among the goals at Filbert Street. He claimed the reconstructed club's first League hat-trick a week before scoring for the Anglo-Scots in the international trial, and was then chosen to face England a month later. Top scorer in each of the following two seasons in the City centre-forward role, Jock attracted an irresistible £3,790 bid from Sunderland, and subsequently led the Roker team to second and third positions in the First Division with 37 goals in 74 games. Preston, however, were relegated at the end of his season there, and Jock dropped into Southern League football.
Apps: 81 Lge; 8 FAC.
Goals: 34 Lge; 3 FAC.

PATERSON, THOMAS A.
b. Lochore, 3.4.1927.
Raith Rovers/Lochgelly Albert/
Mar 1948:CITY/June 1950:Newcastle United/
July 1952:Watford/July 1955:Berwick Rangers.
debut: 15.9.48 v.Brentford (A) (1 goal).

Tom had a few outings for Raith in wartime football, but had reverted to the junior ranks when Johnny Duncan spotted him on a trip home. A play-anywhere forward with an expressed preference for the inside-right spot, Tom effectively had to settle for becoming Charlie Adam's understudy for the No.11 shirt. He got only two chances to impress on Tyneside after a £2,500 move, but made 45 League appearances (7 goals) for Watford before assisting Berwick in their first assault on the Scottish 'B' Division. (Tom should not be confused with his later City namesake, who left Filbert Street without a senior appearance to his name, but played League football in the 70's for Middlesbrough, Bournemouth and Darlington).
Apps: 17 Lge.
Goals: 4 Lge.

PEAKE, ANDREW MICHAEL
b. Market Harborough, 1.11.1961.
app July 1978/pro Jan 1979:CITY/
Aug 1985:Grimsby Town/
Sept 1986:Charlton Athletic.
debut: 6.1.79 v.Norwich City (H) FAC.

Another teenager given a deep-end dunking by
Jock Wallace, midfielder Andy performed with
remarkable maturity on his televised Cup debut
and proceeded to establish himself as an
exciting linkman of prodigious promise,
winning numerous England Youth caps, a
Second Division championship medal, and one
Under-21 honour. A series of injuries, and
City's early desire not to rush his development,
occasionally kept Andy out of the limelight, but
his inventive playmaking and mastery of the
long ball could never be overlooked for long,
and his knack of scoring spectacular long-range
goals was a valuable feature of City's attacking
options in the early 80's. It was regrettable that
Andy's departure (for £110,000) seemed to set
the seal on growing suspicions that he had
failed quite to live up to his early potential, but
at least he was back in top flight football within
a year, battling to keep Charlton clear of
relegation.
Apps: 141+6 Lge; 9 FAC; 5+1 LC.
Goals: 13 Lge.

PEERS, SAMUEL
b.
Coventry City/Apr 1902:FOSSE/
Nov 1903:Swindon Town.
debut: 19.4.02 v.Lincoln City (H).

A trialist centre-half who impressed sufficiently
in his debut game to win a contract for the
following season, Sam vied with Arthur Collins
for the position of attack-minded pivot, and
then demonstrated his versatility by briefly
challenging for Fosse's outside-left spot.
Swindon Town accounts show him earning the
princely sum of £1.15s. per week for his
Southern League season there.
Apps: 14 Lge; 2 FAC.
Goals: 1 Lge.

PEPPER, WILLIAM
b.
Sheppey United/Jan 1913:FOSSE/
cs 1913:Gillingham.
debut: 8.2.13 v.Leeds City (A)

A young trialist goalkeeper plucked from the
Kent League, William kept a clean sheet in a
senior friendly at Gillingham, and a week later
was given the chance to deputise for Fred
Mearns at League level, when unfortunately
five goals whistled past him at Elland Road.
His subsequent Southern League career with
the Gills was equally brief.
Apps: 1 Lge.

PERKINS, GEORGE
b.
Market Harborough/May 1904:FOSSE.
debut: 19.11.04 v.Lincoln City (H).

In signing this young 'keeper, Fosse might well
have been trying to console him for a recent

major embarrassment - he had been the hapless
Harborough last-line who had conceded ten
goals when the Fossils removed his Northants
League team from the previous season's FA
Cup. His Filbert Street role, however, was to
understudy the consistent Walter Smith, and he
got only a solitary senior chance to display his
capabilities.
Apps: 1 Lge.

PERRY, RICHARD
b.
1889:FOSSE.
*debut (comp): 4.10.90
v.Burton Wanderers (H) FAC.*

A Fossil from 1889 onwards, Dick played (and
was injured) in the first, drawn final of the 1890
County Cup, and was at centre-half when the
club made its FA Cup bow during the following
season. He also managed a handful of games
during the initial Midland League campaign.
Apps: 1 FAC; 5 ML.

PHILP, JOHN B.
b. Kelty.
Inverkeithing/July 1932:CITY/
July 1934:Rhyl Athletic.
debut: 9.9.33 v.Tottenham Hotspur (H).

Another addition to the club's solo appearance
ranks, this Scottish right-half briefly attempted
to fill Sep Smith's boots in the above home
defeat.
Apps: 1 Lge.

PICKARD, J.W.
b.
Sept 1895:FOSSE.
debut: 5.10.95 v.Loughborough (H).

A young outside-right whose initial senior
game was Fosse's first in the Football League
against their old local rivals, the newly-elected
Luffs. Apparently the 5-0 scoreline here, and
that of a 4-1 Cup romp the following week,
satisfied more than did the lad's performances,
for his only other mark on the Fosse record
came when he turned out in the Christmas Day
friendly against the club's first Irish guests,
Cliftonville.
Apps: 1 Lge; 1 FAC.

PILKINGTON, SAVILLE H.
b.
Loughborough Corinthians/
(Dec 1913-trials-FOSSE).
debut: 17.1.14 v.Birmingham (H).

An outside-left taken on trial from the reigning
champions of the Leicestershire Senior League,
he played only in the above League game and
in an embarrassing friendly defeat at Northampton a fortnight later.
Apps: 1 Lge.

PLUMMER, NORMAN LEONARD
b. Leicester, 12.1.1924.
ATC football/am July 1942/
pro Nov 1942:CITY/
July 1952:Mansfield Town/
Aug 1956:Kettering Town.
debut (postwar): 25.12.47 v.Brentford (A).

A former RAF sports officer, and a play-
anywhere enthusiast after his wartime signing,
Norman made his first and last senior City
appearances as a centre-forward, but it was his
interim adherence to the central defensive role
which was to make his name. He inherited the
team captaincy from Sep Smith early in the
1948/9 season of radical contrasts, getting
plenty of hard work in City's desperate struggle
to avoid the drop into Division Three, and
earning appropriate acclaim for the qualities of
undemonstrative leadership which saw the club
through to Wembley. Strangely enough,
Norman was soon having to fight for his place
with the likes of Tom McArthur and Bill
Corbett, and eventually followed the well-worn
path from Filbert Street to Field Mill shortly
after Matt Gillies had arrived to assume the
City No.5 shirt. He made 166 League appearances (5 goals) for the Stags, then assisted
Kettering to the Southern League championship
of 1957.
Apps: 66 Lge; 9 FAC.
Goals: 1 Lge.

NORMAN PLUMMER

POLLOCK, ROBERT
b.
cs 1899:Bristol City/cs 1900:Kettering/
cs 1901:Notts County/Sept 1902:FOSSE/
cs 1909:Leyton/cs 1910:Leicester Imperial.
debut: 4.10.02 v.Preston North End (A).

A veteran of Southern League fare at Bristol
and Kettering, Bob failed to make a first-team
breakthrough with the First Division Magpies,
but proved a remarkably resilient and versatile
defender with Fosse over seven seasons. He
favoured the wing-half positions, building long
runs of appearances on either flank, but could
slot into a full-back role whenever the necessity
arose. It was fitting that his benefit match -
against Grimsby in February 1908; the first
time a League match had been set aside for
such a purpose by the Fosse - should come in
the season which climaxed in the promotion he
had laboured so hard to secure. His total of
senior appearances constituted a Fosse record;
as, incidentally, did his aggregate haul of
fourteen successful penalties.
Apps: 211 Lge; 19 FAC.
Goals: 14 Lge; 5 FAC.

POTTS, BRIAN

b. Sunderland, 3.9.1948.
app Aug 1964/pro Sept 1965:CITY/
July 1969:Peterborough United.
debut: 3.4.68 (sub) v.Newcastle United (A).

A teenage member of City reserves' Combination Cup-winning side of 1967, Brian finally got a substantial first team chance during the last months of Matt Gillies' managerial tenure at Leicester, filling in for Peter Rodrigues in the right-back spot as City began their slide into the relegation zone. Frank O'Farrell released him at the end of the season, but he put together a 50-game career with Posh.
Apps: 9+1 Lge; 1 LC.

PRICE, ERNEST CLIFFORD

b. Market Bosworth, 13.6.1900.
Coalville Swifts/am Jan 1917:FOSSE/
(Nov 1919-loan-Coalville Swifts)/
pro Oct 1920:CITY/June 1922:Halifax Town/
Dec 1923:Southampton/
cs 1926:Nottingham Forest/
Oct 1928:Loughborough Corinthians.
debut: 11.9.19
v.Tottenham Hotspur (H) (2 goals).

Having claimed 33 goals for the Fosse in wartime competitions, to make himself leading scorer for the period, Cliff was finally persuaded to turn professional by Peter Hodge over a year after making his League bow at inside-left and hitting three counters in his first two games. The local lad did not, however, find it easy to compete for a senior slot with imports like Macauley and Graham, and eventually moved on to make his mark elsewhere - as a goalscorer in Division Three, and as a more studious contributor to the attacks of the Saints and Forest.
Apps: 28 Lge.
Goals: 8 Lge.

PRICE, FREDERICK THOMAS

b. Ibstock, 24.10.1901.
Whitwick Imperial/May 1921:CITY/
May 1924:Southampton/
cs 1925:Wolverhampton Wanderers/
cs 1927:Chesterfield.
debut: 26.2.23 v.South Shields (H).

A clever outside-left, Fred was unfortunate to find himself third in line for the City first team shirt behind Alex Trotter and Percy Tompkin, and moved to The Dell, along with Dennis Jones, as part of the deal which brought Harry Hooper to Leicester. Fred's brother Jack played as a full-back for City reserves, Bristol Rovers, Swindon Town and Torquay United, while Cliff (see above) was his uncle and, briefly, his forward partner at The Dell.
Apps: 4 Lge.

PRIESTMAN, J.

b.
Mar 1893:FOSSE.
debut: 11.3.93 v.Long Eaton Rangers (A) ML.

A versatile reserve forward who turned out in all the front-line positions for Fosse across the final two Midland League seasons and the first in the Second Division, appearing at outside-left in the club's initial League fixture. Another early Fossil to elude further researches; it is suspected he may have earlier played for Melton Rovers.
Apps: 8 Lge; 7 ML.
Goals: 2 Lge; 3 ML.

PRINDIVILLE, STEVEN ALAN

b. Harlow, 26.12.1968.
YTS July 1985/pro Jan 1987:CITY/
cs 1988:Chesterfield.
debut: 16.1.88 (sub) v.Shrewsbury Town (A).

A scorer in City's FA Youth Cup semi-final in 1987, full-back Steve made a brief step up to senior level during the early days of David Pleat's management, and looked confidently adventurous in his Simod Cup outing, but was freed in the summer of 1988. At Saltergate he has been a regular, linking again at various times with Robert Alleyne and Tony Brien.
Apps: 0+1 Lge; 1 FMC.

PROCTOR, JAMES F.

b. London.
Custom House/cs 1911:Huddersfield Town/
Nov 1912:FOSSE/cs 1913:Stockport County.
debut: 30.11.12 v.Fulham (H).

Briefly one of Dick Pudan's charges during his stint as manager at Leeds Road, this inside-right then played a few games in front of his former boss when the latter resumed his playing career with the Fosse. James had also been a former amateur team-mate of Jim Harrold, but made nothing like the same impact at Leicester.
Apps: 7 Lge; 1 FAC.
Goals: 1 Lge; 1 FAC.

PROCTOR, NORMAN

b. Blaydon.
Scotswood/Blyth Spartans/
1922:Rotherham County/
cs 1923:West Ham United/June 1924:CITY/
May 1925:Tranmere Rovers/
Sept 1927:Halifax Town.
debut: 30.8.24 v.Manchester United (A).

A deep-lying, scheming inside-forward who first came to notice in the County Durham schools side, Norman found himself unexpectedly elevated in status during the 1923 close season: as the Rotherham team he left had just been relegated from the Second, promoted West Ham were preparing for their initial First Division term. He only managed seven games for the Hammers, though, and then had an even shorter senior career at Filbert Street, definitively losing his place after four of the first five games of 1924/5 had seen City scoreless. Norman's best spell came with the Shaymen, for whom he made 126 appearances.
Apps: 5 Lge.

PROUDFOOT, DAVID

b.
Partick Thistle/Dec 1896:FOSSE/
cs 1898:Bedminster/cs 1899:Partick Thistle.
debut: 5.12.96 v.Grimsby Town (H).

A skilful centre-half from a footballing family - his brother John also trekked south from Partick to play for Blackburn, Everton and Watford - David failed to complete his second season with Fosse. One of six players suspended by the club as a disciplinary measure in February 1898, he never played again in Leicester colours.
Apps: 25 Lge; 2 FAC.

PUDAN, ALBERT ERNEST (DICK)

b. West Ham.
Clapton/cs 1900:West Ham United/
cs 1902:Bristol Rovers/
July 1906:Newcastle United/May 1909:FOSSE/
Aug 1910:Huddersfield Town (mgr)/
Nov 1912:FOSSE.
debut: 1.9.09 v.Wolverhampton Wanderers (H).

Universally known throughout his career as Dick, this extremely cultured full-back stood out in an age of hefty kickers by dint of his thoughtful and constructive approach to the game. He joined West Ham as an amateur for their initial Southern League season under that name, and won a championship medal in that sphere in 1905 while totting up 116 appearances for Bristol Rovers. Dick also took an FA Cup runners-up medal from Newcastle's 1908 Final defeat. His Fosse full-back partnership with Henry was the classiest the club had fielded, and Dick became a sure-shot penalty taker, but Huddersfield, newly elected to the League, offered him an early chance to preach tactics rather than play, and he directed their fortunes from the sidelines for two seasons before briefly returning to Leicester and donning his boots again to partner the young Tommy Clay. When the club was reconstructed as Leicester City in 1919, Dick - described on registration documents as a hosiery manufacturer - was among the new directors; though as he had been a professional player, it took until March 1921 for the FA to sanction his appointment in that capacity. He remained on the board until the Second World War, and briefly took the chair - the only former player so to serve the club.
Apps: 46 Lge; 5 FAC. Goals: 7 Lge.

PUTTNAM, DAVID PAUL

b. Leicester, 3.2.1967.
Kirby Muxloe/cs 1985:Leicester United/
Feb 1989:CITY.
debut: 11.4.89 (sub) v.Barnsley (H).

A reserve-team trialist who scored one goal and made two more on his Central League debut, David soon signed up from City's Blaby-based Southern League neighbours as David Pleat sought to fill the left-wing gap occasioned by Peter Weir's return to Scotland. His five-minute introduction to senior action briefly raised spirits in a listless home defeat, and his willingness to take on his full-back for pace and skill provided some optimistic pointers from the final two games of 1988/9.
Apps (to 13.5.89): 2+1 Lge.

PYNEGAR, ALBERT E.

b. Eastwood, 24.9.1895.
d. Basford, 1978.
Sutton Town/May 1920:CITY/
Jan 1924:Coventry City/

July 1925:Oldham Athletic/Jan 1929:Port Vale/
Oct 1930:Chesterfield/
Aug 1932:Rotherham United.
debut: 2.9.20 v.Bury (H) (2 goals).

A veritable goal machine, Albert was unfortunate to be edged out of the senior reckoning so
often with City by Jock Paterson, George Waite
and Arthur Chandler. He could hardly be
faulted for the vigour with which he pressed his
claims, though: swapping Central Alliance
football with Sutton for record-breaking action
in the same league with City reserves, he scored
six times on his debut and finished 1920/1 with
49 goals from only 25 appearances, to add to
his six counters for the first team. A prematurely balding bustler who actually preferred
the inside-forward positions to the leader's role,
Albert indexed his goal-knack again in 1922/3,
with eleven goals from only fourteen Second
Division games, yet still was not assured of a
regular place. At Coventry he was top scorer in
a relegated team; then twice topped Oldham's
Second Division charts before helping both
Vale and Chesterfield to the Third Division
(North) championship in successive seasons.
Apps: 44 Lge; 4 FAC.
Goals: 20 Lge; 1 FAC.

JIMMY QUINN

QUINN, JAMES MARTIN
b. Belfast, 18.11.1959.
Whitchurch Alport/Oswestry Town/
Dec 1981:Swindon Town/
Aug 1984:Blackburn Rovers/
Dec 1986:Swindon Town/June 1988:CITY/
Mar 1989:Bradford City.
debut: 27.8.88 (sub)
v.West Bromwich Albion (H).

Often an international teammate of John
O'Neill and Paul Ramsey, Jimmy had collected
18 Northern Ireland caps as a striker by the
time City signed him for a tribunal-set fee of
£210,000. A relatively late entrant to senior
football, he had quickly built a reputation as an
elegant front-runner, but it was not until the
1987/8 season, when he played alongside hefty
target-man Dave Bamber at Swindon, that he
revealed a really prolific predatory knack.

Three goals against City had featured in his
sizeable haul that term but, having arrived at
Filbert Street, he proved unable to convince
David Pleat that he merited a regular spearhead
role in lieu of either Nicky Cross or Mike
Newell. Jimmy accordingly suffered much
frustration on the subs' bench during his short
City spell, despite three times coming on and
scoring. Indeed, he was able to offer only tantalising glimpses of his aerial power and dead-
ball accuracy, and soon had to accept he was
something of a tactical fish out of water with
Leicester, moving on to Valley Parade in the
exchange deal which brought Mick Kennedy in
the opposite direction. Perhaps predictably,
Jimmy claimed Bradford's late winner against
City a month later.
Apps: 13+18 Lge;
0+1 FAC; 2+1 LC; 0+1 FMC.
Goals: 6 Lge.

RAMSEY, PAUL CHRISTOPHER
b. Derry, 3.9.1962.
Derry Athletic YC/app 1979/
pro Apr 1980:CITY.
debut: 7.3.81 (sub) v.Arsenal (H).

One of many latter-day City midfielders also
utilised extensively as a full-back, Paul
developed his ball-winning skills during the
club's Second Division stint of the early 80's,
wearing the No.2 shirt throughout the 1983
promotion campaign, and timing his first goal -
in the crucial game at Oldham - to perfection.
He won the first of several Northern Ireland
caps in September 1983, though injuries and
spells of in-and-out form have occasionally left
him sidelined from both domestic and
international action. Probably strongest in a
man-marking role, and least effective as the
fulcrum of a passing game, Paul nonetheless
claimed the City Supporters' 'Goal of the
Season' award for a precise piece of opportunism against QPR in 1986/7. He was handed the
team captaincy on the arrival of new manager
David Pleat, and granted a Testimonial year in
1989, yet City were ready to bid him farewell
in a mooted exchange deal with Walsall's
Craig Shakespeare before that year's transfer
deadline. Paul opted to stay and fight for his
place against the new challenge of Mick
Kennedy, but his Filbert Street future currently
seems uncertain.
Apps (to 13.5.89): 227+4 Lge;
8 FAC; 16 LC; 1+1 FMC.
Goals: 10 Lge; 1 FAC; 1 LC.

RANDLE, ARTHUR JOHN
b. West Bromwich, 3.12.1880.
d. West Bromwich, 29.9.1913.
Lyng Rovers/Oldbury Town/Darlaston/
cs 1901:West Bromwich Albion/
May 1908:FOSSE.
debut: 1.9.08 v.Sheffield Wednesday (H).

An experienced wing-half who had made 132
League appearances during his seven-year stint
as a Throstle, Arthur signed on for Fosse's
fateful First Division bow, and shook off the
disappointments of that campaign to complete
five years' service in the right-half berth as a
defensive lynchpin. When Fosse released him
in 1913, he became licensee of 'The Golden

Cup' back in his home town, but within months
succumbed to cancer at the age of 32. All
proceeds from the South Eastern League game
between Fosse and Brentford reserves were
donated to Arthur's widow. Arthur was another
West Midlander to have been selected early in
his career as a 'junior international'.
Apps: 123 Lge; 10 FAC.
Goals: 2 Lge.

RANTANEN, JARI JUHANI
b. Helsinki, 31.12.1961.
HJK (Helsinki)/Estoril/Beerschot/
1986:IFK Gothenburg/Aug 1987:CITY/
(Dec 1988-loan-Belenenses).
debut: 12.9.87 v Crystal Palace (A).

A peripatetic international striker whose goal
earned Finland a draw against England in 1985,
and who had gained wide experience in
Portuguese, Belgian and Swedish football, Jari
joined City after a week's training-ground
'trial' and despite the fact that Bryan Hamilton
had never seen him play a senior game! He had
been omitted from Gothenburg's UEFA Cup
Final side despite leading their scoring list in
the competition, and the move to England
initially reinvigorated his career, with the City
fans soon overcoming their incredulity about
the circumstances of his signing to hail 'The
Mighty Finn'. A handful of bustling,
goalscoring appearances also indicated that the
hefty frontman possessed a fair amount of
vision and finesse on the ball, but an ankle
injury and a subsequent loss of confidence
denied Jari the chance to develop his initially
promising partnership with Mike Newell,
which was never renewed again by David Pleat.
The latter's attempts to offload Jari were for a
long time frustrated - the terms of his work
permit precluded sale or loan to a British club,
while the demands of the player's agent
scuppered a deal with Bundesliga club Koln.
Jari had been out of first-team action for almost
a year prior to his unsuccessful trial spell in
Lisbon, but continued to add caps to his tally
throughout this unhappy period on Leicester's
books.
Apps (to 13.5.89): 10+3 Lge;
2+1 LC; 2+1 FMC.
Goals: 3 Lge; 1 LC.

REED, KEVIN DAVID
b. Leicester, 22.9.1960.
app July 1977/pro May 1978:CITY.
debut: 22.11.78 (sub) v.Wrexham (H).

A diminutive winger, Kevin made his solitary
senior appearance under faintly farcical
circumstances. Larry May's car broke down on
the way to an evening match, nominated
substitute Peter Welsh stepped into the vacant
defensive berth, and Kevin was plucked from
the stand to wear the No.12 shirt despite having
only one reserve game's experience to his
credit at the time. The inevitable happened
when Trevor Christie suffered injury, and
Kevin almost made his bow a scoring one when
hitting the Wrexham bar with his first shot.
Never again in contention, though, he was
released in July 1979.
Apps: 0+1 Lge.

REEDAY, MAURICE J.
b. Darwen.
Darwen/1934:Blackpool/
cs 1936:Accrington Stanley/Mar 1937:CITY.
debut: 11.9.37 v.Arsenal (H).

The full-back always popularly known as 'the man Stanley Matthews couldn't beat', Maurice has often been given confirmatory credit as such by his frustrated victim, who never relished the ultra-tight marking that was Maurice's trademark, whether in League, Cup or wartime football. Though he had never made a senior breakthrough at Bloomfield Road, Maurice showed sufficient promise in his 22 games at Accrington to tempt a £900 bid from Frank Womack, and in the final two pre-war seasons regularly displaced either Dai Jones or Billy Frame in showing that his defensive capabilities could be adapted to either flank. Another player to 'lose' three appearances from the abandoned 1939/40 season, Maurice ended his career as a guest player back in Lancashire, for Accrington, Blackburn and Burnley.
Apps: 74 Lge; 5 FAC.
Goals: 2 Lge.

REID, PAUL ROBERT
b. Warley, 19.1.1968.
app July 1984/pro Jan 1986:CITY.
debut: 7.3.87 v.Southampton (A).

A competitive, nimble teenage striker whose promise was first recognised by Bryan Hamilton, Paul found his career given a major boost when new boss David Pleat decided to play him as a left-footed right-winger. He thrived initially on this unorthodox tactical switch, especially when able to exploit his penchant for cutting inside and across a defence before unleashing a powerful shot, but the predictability of the manoeuvre and Paul's often ineffectual efforts to vary it by going outside his marker have more recently led to a lull in his progress. Some fine goals have accrued to his career to date, though, with a brilliant solo effort at Blackburn taking the 1988 'Goal of the Season' award from the supporters.
Apps (to 13.5.89): 71+6 Lge;
2 FAC; 8 LC; 2 FMC.
Goals: 11 Lge; 3 LC.

RENNIE, DAVID
b. Edinburgh, 29.8.1964.
app July 1980/pro May 1982:CITY/
Jan 1986:Leeds United.
debut: 3.9.83 v.West Bromwich Albion (A).

An almost automatic choice for Scotland at youth international level, David looked set for a long Filbert Street career as a coolly elegant defender in the Alan Hansen mould. But City's constant need for experience at the back in their First Division rearguard campaigns allowed scant opportunities for him to play himself into the side in his favoured berth, and a series of lack-lustre performances when David was experimentally shoe-horned into midfield or full-back roles did little to aid his confidence. His only goal for City, though, was a landmark - the club's 5,000th in the League. Sold to Elland Road for £45,000, David initially had to get used once more to his versatility being exploited for tactical purposes, and had been sidelined for some time when he popped up with Leeds' first goal in their 1987 FA Cup semi-final. Subsequently he has claimed central defensive responsibilities there with much success.
Apps: 21 Lge; 2 LC.
Goals: 1 Lge.

REVIE, DONALD GEORGE
b. Middlesbrough, 10.7.1927.
d. Edinburgh, 26.5.1989.
Middlesbrough Swifts/Aug 1944:CITY/
Nov 1949:Hull City/Oct 1951:Manchester City/
Nov 1956:Sunderland/Dec 1958:Leeds United.
debut (postwar): 31.8.46
v.Manchester City (H).

Though the controversies of his managerial career seem to have set the tone of posterity's harsh judgement on him, Don was no stranger to acrimony even in his early days at Leicester. A teenage signing from City's short-lived North-Eastern 'nursery' club, who was taken under Sep Smith's wing and taught the basics of constructive inside-forward play, Don was an early victim of the City crowd's occasional propensity for giving 'stick' to their own players, with his thoughtful style initially deemed ponderous by spectators wanting the ball delivered into the box rather more speedily. He turned City hero, however, with his efforts in the 1949 Cup run, culminating in his two semi-final goals against Portsmouth, and it was tragic that he had to miss out on the Wembley showpiece after broken blood vessels in his nose almost cost him his life. Several transfer requests later, a £20,000 fee took him to Hull, to learn more of the game's finer points alongside player-manager Raich Carter, and then at Maine Road he hit the headlines as the tactical architect of the so-called 'Revie Plan', which represented a domestic response to recently rubbed-in lessons from the Hungarians. Don played as a deep-lying centre-forward in both the 1955 and 1956 FA Cup Finals, picked up the 'Footballer of the Year' award for 1955, and won recognition at both Football League (two games, six goals) and full England levels (six caps, four goals). He had rather less playing success at either Roker or Elland Road, but assumed the Leeds player-manager's role in March 1961, dropped the on-field responsibility in May 1963, and thereafter led his uncompromising side through a lengthy catalogue of successes and near-misses in League, Cup and European competitions. He was thrice heralded as 'Manager of the Year' (in 1969, 1970 and 1972), was awarded the OBE in 1970, and took over the England manager's reins in 1974. Don shouldered much criticism for his safety-first approach and his legendary dossiers on the national side's opposition, and was then accused of everything short of treason when secretly negotiating himself a massively-paid coaching job in the United Arab Emirates from July 1977. Ultimately, the last few years of his life were sadly blighted by incurable illness.
Apps: 96 Lge; 14 FAC.
Goals: 25 Lge; 4 FAC.

DON REVIE

REYNOLDS, W.
b. Leicester.
Belvoir Street SS/Oct 1912:FOSSE/
cs 1913:Leicester Imperial.
debut: 18.1.13 v.Birmingham (A).

An outside-right from the same local club as Tommy Clay, Reynolds understudied Tommy Benfield and George Douglas for a few months, and made his sole senior appearance in a heavy defeat at St.Andrews.
Apps: 1 Lge.

RICHARDS, CHARLES HENRY
b. Burton-on-Trent, 1875.
d. Burton-on-Trent.
Gresley Rovers/cs 1895:Notts County/
Jan 1896:Nottingham Forest/
Jan 1899:Grimsby Town/June 1901:FOSSE/
Aug 1902:Manchester United/
Mar 1903:Doncaster Rovers.
debut: 7.9.01 v.Woolwich Arsenal (A).

Though he featured at inside-right in Fosse's most goal-shy attack ever, Charles had a fair scoring record behind him. 1898 had seen him win his sole England cap (in place of Steve Bloomer) and help Forest to FA Cup victory, and he had claimed 42 goals in 80 League games at Grimsby, leaving after helping them into Division One. He later notched the first League goal scored by the newly-rechristened Manchester United, but failed in his late bid to save Doncaster from an unsuccessful re-election application. (It is believed he may have been a printer by trade, taking over the family business which held copyright in both the Notts County and Forest team-sheet 'programmes' of the late Victorian era).
Apps: 25 Lge; 1 FAC.
Goals: 5 Lge.

RICHARDS, PERCY
b. Merthyr Tydfil.
Merthyr Town/Jan 1931:CITY/
cs 1932:Coventry City/Apr 1934:Bath City.
debut: 5.2.31 v.Arsenal (H).

A Welsh outside-left who understudied Len Barry during his City days, and experienced distinct ups and downs: his first two appearances were in a 2-7 defeat and a 6-0 victory! (There is dissension amongst football historians as to whether Percy had a Football League pedigree prior to his City spell: it is quite possible that he had previously served Cardiff City from 1926 and Tranmere Rovers from 1928; feasible that he was at Newport County in 1929; but unlikely that 'our' Percy was the man at Plymouth Argyle from 1927. Informed clarification would be, as ever, welcomed by the authors!)
Apps: 10 Lge.
Goals: 2 Lge.

RICHARDSON, DAVID
b. Billingham, 11.3.1932.
Nov 1949:CITY/June 1955:Grimsby Town/ June 1960:Swindon Town/July 1961:Barrow.
debut: 18.9.54 v.Newcastle United (H).

Recruited from Teesside junior football, Dave developed into a versatile reserve defender who had the misfortune to get his patiently awaited senior break while Eddie Russell was still firm favourite for the No.6 shirt, and just after Colin Appleton had given notice of his claim on the same position. In his first season at Grimsby, where he eventually totalled 175 League games, Dave helped the Mariners to the championship of Division Three (North). Despite the coincidence of name and north-eastern origins, he should not be confused with City's youth coach of the 80's.
Apps: 2 Lge.

RICHMOND, HUGH
b. Kilmarnock.
Kilbirnie Ladeside/July 1913:Kilmarnock/ Army/Galston/Arthurlie/Mar 1919:FOSSE/ (Jan 1920-loan-Nuneaton Town)/ May 1922:Coventry City/ May 1925:Queens Park Rangers/ July 1926:Blyth Spartans.
debut (postwar): 30.8.19 v.Wolverhampton Wanderers (H).

Bought as an inside-forward towards the end of Fosse's final season of wartime football, Hugh soon demonstrated a facility at centre-half too, but then had to play second fiddle to Jim Harrold for the bulk of his stay. He skippered the City reserve team in the Central Alliance, then built a more substantial senior reputation at Coventry, where his aerial ability earned him the nickname 'Rubberneck', as well as a 16-goal return. During WW1, Hugh had served with the Seaforth Highlanders; he never appeared at senior level for Killie.
Apps: 24 Lge.
Goals: 2 Lge.

RIDLEY, FRED
b.
Barnet Alston/June 1913:FOSSE.
debut: 20.9.13 v.Birmingham (A).

One of several outside-lefts tried out following the departure of George Harrison, this experienced amateur had been a squad member when Barnet Alston won the London League championship in 1907.
Apps: 1 Lge.

RIDLEY, JOHN
b. Consett, 27.4.1952.
Sheffield University/Aug 1973:Port Vale/ (Apr 1978-loan-Fort Lauderdale Strikers)/ Oct 1978:CITY/Aug 1979:Chesterfield/ Aug 1982:Port Vale/ Aug 1985:Stafford Rangers (p/coach).
debut: 28.10.78 v.Bristol Rovers (H).

Signed by Jock Wallace to stiffen the City midfield during the manager's first, crucial 'holding' season in the Second Division, John performed his short-term function well, with some gritty displays in front of the back four, and exercised a useful calming influence on the predominantly younger players around him. Subsequently, he helped Chesterfield take the Anglo-Scottish Cup in 1981, was a valuable member of Port Vale's Division Four promotion side of 1983, and led Stafford to Bob Lord Trophy success in 1986.
Apps: 17+7 Lge; 2 FAC.

HOWARD RILEY

RILEY, HOWARD
b. Wigston, 18.8.1938.
Wigston Old Boys/Aug 1955:CITY/ Dec 1965:Walsall/Apr 1967:Atlanta Chiefs/ July 1968:Barrow/Rugby Town/Burton Albion/ Ibstock Penistone Rovers/Midland Athletic/ Wigston Old Boys.
debut: 22.8.1955 v.Nottingham Forest (H).

A first-teamer within months of leaving Kibworth School, Howard came from a fine local sporting family. His grandfather Edwin and father Harold had both been County cricketers, and the latter had been a City reserve in 1924, as would be Howard's brother Bob in the 60's. His energetic performances at outside-right earned him the crowd's nickname of 'Puffer', as well as two England Under-23 caps to add to his youth international honours, and Howard was the only Leicestershire-born player in the 1961 Cup Final team. He maintained his place as an orthodox speedy winger throughout the 1963 run to Wembley, and scored the winning goal in the 1964 League Cup Final, at a time when he was effectively a part-timer, training for and then following a parallel teaching career. Following a brief stint in the FIFA-outlawed National Professional Soccer League in America (forerunner of the NASL), his League days ended with Colin Appleton at Holker Street, but Howard remained active in local soccer for some years, most recently as manager of Wigston Town.
Apps: 193 Lge; 24 FAC; 12 LC; 4 ECWC.
Goals: 38 Lge; 5 FAC; 4 LC.

RITCHIE, GEORGE THOMPSON
b. Maryhill, 16.1.1904.
d. Leicester, 10.9.1978.
Maryhill/cs 1923:Blackburn Rovers/ cs 1924:Falkirk/Sept 1928:CITY/ Aug 1937:Colchester United.
debut: 29.9.28 v.Burnley (H).

Having quickly bounced back from an abortive spell at Ewood as a youthful centre-forward, George developed into a classy left-half at Falkirk, and never looked in danger of disappointing on his second sortie into English football. Signing shortly after he had starred for a Scottish League XI in a Filbert Street friendly for the benefit of Leicestershire CCC, he soon took a grip on the wing-half spot vacated by Sid Bishop and forged a fine triangular link on City's left flank with Arthur Lochhead and Len Barry as the club rose to runners-up position in the top flight. Eight seasons of poised performances followed, with George captaining the side until his place was put under pressure by Percy Grosvenor. The promotion campaign of 1937 was his last with City, for he joined the newly-formed Colchester United and led them to the Southern League Cup and championship in successive seasons. Appointed coach at Ipswich on the eve of WW2, George was then to be found on the training staff back at Filbert Street between 1946 and 1950.
Apps: 247 Lge; 14 FAC.
Goals: 12 Lge; 1 FAC.

ROBERTS, JEREMY
b. Middlesbrough, 24.11.1966.
1983:Hartlepool United/June 1984:CITY/ Oct 1986:Luton Town/ Mar 1987:Darlington/ Sept 1988:Brentford/ (Oct 1988-loan-Maidenhead).
debut: 12.10.85 v.West Bromwich Albion (H).

A non-contract player on a Youth Opportunities scheme at Hartlepool, goalkeeper Jerry made his senior bow as a 16-year-old in an FA Cup tie at Rotherham, and subsequently played in the replay and one Fourth Division game before being released. He followed Ian Andrews into the England youth team's yellow jersey shortly after arriving at Filbert Street, and understudied his international predecessor for the first team custodianship after Mark Wallington moved on. His contract was cancelled by mutual consent, however, in October 1986, and Jerry returned to the North East to resume his League career after a brief spell in Luton's reserves.
Apps: 3 Lge.

ROBERTS, ROBERT
b. Edinburgh, 2.9.1940.
1958:Motherwell/Sept 1963:CITY/
Sept 1970:Mansfield Town/
cs 1972:Coventry City (coach)/
July 1973:Colchester United (p/coach).
debut: 21.9.63 v.Fulham (H).

City's record signing at the time, Bobby cost £41,000 as Matt Gillies outbid Ipswich Town for his services. Primarily an attacking linkman, with one appearance for each of Scotland Under-23 and the Scottish League to his credit, he struggled initially to justify high expectations at Filbert Street, especially as City employed him successively at left-half, inside-right and centre-forward, and he missed out on the 1964 League Cup Final despite scoring in both legs of the semi-final classic against West Ham. Bobby really clicked, however, when he inherited Frank McLintock's No.4 shirt, rolling up his sleeves and becoming City's midfield anchorman throughout the mid and late-60's, and finally gaining a modicum of reward as an ever-present in the 1969 Cup run. Much valued for his 100 per cent effort and skilful prompting, he had one trait that became almost perversely endearing - rarely finishing a game without having endangered the crowd with at least one thunderbolt shot way over the bar! He later gave two seasons' and 80 games' service to Mansfield, and twice returned to the League fray when coaching at Colchester, where he assumed his first managerial role in June 1975 and met much success. Subsequently, as boss at Wrexham, Bobby was forced to make one last return to action - playing in a Welsh Cup tie as a goalkeeper! (His dubious qualifications for this amounted to the fact that he had temporarily replaced the injured Peter Shilton at Old Trafford in 1967, and had even earlier guarded the net behind Ian St.John in a trophy-winning Motherwell 5-a-side team!). Bobby later coached the El Shabar side in Kuwait, managed Grimsby Town during their 1987/8 relegation season, and then returned to Leicester in June 1988 to assume Peter Morris' position on the City coaching staff.
Apps: 224+5 Lge; 30 FAC; 21+1 LC.
Goals: 26 Lge; 4 FAC; 6 LC.

ROBERTSON, ARCHIBALD LAMOND
b. Paisley, 27.9.1947.
Sept 1966:Burnley/June 1968:Bury/
Feb 1969:Halifax Town/
Dec 1972:Brighton & Hove Albion/
May 1974:Exeter City/
(Apr 1976-loan-Chicago Sting)/
Sept 1977:CITY/
Sept 1978:Peterborough United/
Jan 1979:Bradford City/
July 1981:Northwich Victoria (p/mgr)/Darwen.
debut: 17.9.77 v.Arsenal (A).

A junior at Turf Moor, midfielder Lammie got his League break with Bury and helped Halifax clinch their first-ever promotion in 1969. He dropped from Division Two to Three in his first season at Brighton, and prompted Exeter to rise from the basement to Division Three in 1977. Then Frank McLintock moved in to bring him to Filbert Street (on a recommendation from Davie Gibson), but his top flight experience

was brief. Lammie found it impossible to settle in a City line-up then changing shape almost weekly, and faced a sceptical crowd who had got hold of the rumour that McLintock had originally bid for his Exeter team-mate Alan Beer, and had not wished to come away empty-handed. Accordingly, his occasionally delicate ball skills were exhibited largely in a reserve team context until he resumed his travels.
Apps: 6+1 Lge.

ROBERTSON, HUGH
b.
Partick Thistle/cs 1890:Everton/
cs 1894:Millwall Athletic/June 1985:Burnley/
cs 1897:Lincoln City/cs 1899:Millwall/
cs 1900:Dundee/Nov 1900:FOSSE.
debut: 1.12.1900 v.Burton Swifts (H) (1 goal).

An experienced Scottish centre-forward deemed not to fit the bill for Fosse at the end of his month's trial, Hugh previously had been Lincoln's Second Division top scorer for both his seasons at Sincil Bank, and had fitted in two Southern League spells with Millwall. There is debatable evidence about his early contribution to Everton's cause, for he is often confused with his contemporary there, a wing-half named Hope-Robertson who moved on to Bootle.
Apps: 5 Lge.
Goals: 1 Lge.

ROBINSON, WALTER L.
b. Irthlingborough.
Finedon/Irthlingborough Town/
Aug 1898:FOSSE/Aug 1905:Burton United.
debut: 17.12.98 v.Newton Heath (H).

A dogged, hard-tackling defender, Walter inherited the Fosse pivot's role from Jimmy Brown and over seven seasons turned out in all five full and half-back positions, battling his way back past countless interim signings after several times appearing to have dropped out of the senior reckoning. His loyalty was rewarded, and his popularity acknowledged, with a benefit game in 1903 (a Christmas friendly against Clapton), and his fighting spirit was recognised by Burton United, who he skippered through their final two seasons in the Football League.
Apps: 177 Lge; 17 FAC.
Goals: 3 Lge.

ROBSON, KEITH
b. Hetton-le-Hole, 15.11.1953.
May 1971:Newcastle United/
Sept 1974:West Ham United/
(May 1977-loan-Team Hawaii)/
Aug 1977:Cardiff City/
Feb 1978:Norwich City/Sept 1981:CITY/
(Mar 1983-loan-Carlisle United)/
Sept 1983:(Hong Kong)/Wroxham/
Norwich Busmen/Corinthians/Wroxham.
debut: 12.9.81 v.Derby County (A).

The luckless understudy to Malcolm MacDonald on Tyneside, Keith became something of a Cup-tie specialist at Upton Park after a £60,000 move, scoring in the 1976 European Cup Winners' Cup Final, and briefly forming a twin striking partnership with his namesake and fellow North-Easterner, 'Pop'.

Two moves later, Jock Wallace bought him to inject some extra experience and weight into City's youthful promotion challenge, but his first team tenure as a left-sided attacker was brief. He returned to East Anglia after a short spell in Hong Kong football, and remained active in local football in the Norwich area, latterly as coach to Sunday side Mackintosh.
Apps: 8+1 Lge; 1+1 FAC; 1 LC.
Goals: 1 LC.

PETER RODRIGUES

RODRIGUES, PETER JOSEPH
b. Cardiff, 21.1.1944.
May 1961:Cardiff City/Dec 1965:CITY/
Oct 1970:Sheffield Wednesday/
July 1975:Southampton/Romsey Town.
debut: 1.1.66 v.Stoke City (H).

At his peak the undisputed master of the sliding tackle, Peter was already an established Welsh international right-back, with additional experience in Cardiff's initial Cup Winners' Cup forays, when he became a New Year's Eve signing for City at the new record fee of £42,500. Thereafter, his pace, overlapping inclinations and that trademark method of dispossession brought a new dimension to received notions of Filbert Street full-back play, and his City career would surely have stretched much further had it not been for the exciting emergence of Steve Whitworth. Only one sad incident - a missed close-range goal chance in the 1969 FA Cup Final - remotely shadowed Peter's stay at Leicester, but he firmly obliterated that particular Wembley memory when, after being freed by the Owls and having won the last of his 40 caps, he skippered underdogs Southampton to Cup victory over Manchester United in 1976. Peter is currently landlord of a Hampshire pub.
Apps: 139+1 Lge; 18+1 FAC; 11+1 LC.
Goals: 6 Lge.

ROFE, DENNIS
b. Epping, 1.6.1950.
app/pro Feb 1968:Orient/Aug 1972:CITY/
Feb 1980:Chelsea/July 1982:Southampton.
debut: 26.8.72 v.Coventry City (H).

Lined up to rejoin his former manager Jimmy Bloomfield at Leicester on the very day David Nish left, Dennis cost about half the £250,000 fee City received. Comparisons between the left-backs, if invidious, were inevitable, but sound judgement saw that what City had lost in sheer elegance, they had gained in cheery enthusiasm and wholehearted vigour. Dennis justifiably became a fixture in City's No.3 shirt, quick into the tackle and quick to augment the attack, and was unlucky to win only one Under-23 cap. The dressing room joker among City's Cockney colony of the mid-70's, he faced his on-field responsibilities with determined seriousness, and took the team captaincy when Frank McLintock arrived. The majority of his small tally of goals remain utterly memorable: a last-minute solo waltz from the halfway line to clinch a 4-3 away win over Birmingham; a flukey free kick from his own half that floated over QPR's Phil Parkes; and a pair of hot shots at Swansea that hit, and almost broke, the same stanchion. Later, Dennis unfortunately misjudged the relative promotion potentials of City and Chelsea when leaving for Stamford Bridge, but returned to the top flight at The Dell, where he remains as coach.
Apps: 290 Lge; 22 FAC; 12 LC.
Goals: 6 Lge.

ROLLINSON, FRANK
b. Sheffield.
Heeley/1906:Sheffield Wednesday/
Aug 1911:FOSSE/Feb 1912:Portsmouth/
Sept 1913:Luton Town.
debut: 2.9.11 v.Gainsborough Trinity (A).

A goal-hungry inside-left for the Owls, Frank rather lost his scoring touch at Leicester and, after leaving the field in the notorious match at Grimsby which ended with only five Fossils on the pitch, he promptly departed for pastures new. He helped both of his subsequent Southern League clubs to promotion, and got back to some serious scoring form at Luton.
Apps: 17 Lge.
Goals: 2 Lge.

ROSEVEAR, C.
Sept 1900:FOSSE.
debut: 29.3.02 v.Newton Heath (A).

One of three local centre-forwards tried out at the tail end of the goal-drought season of 1901/2, Rosevear had earlier entered the Fosse record books as the club's first (albeit unofficial) substitute, when he replaced the injured Wragg during Johnny McMillan's benefit friendly against Notts County on Christmas Eve 1900, and scored the third goal.
Apps: 3 Lge.

ROULSTON, ARTHUR
b. Castle Donington.
Jan 1896:Loughborough/cs 1900:Kettering/
May 1901:FOSSE/
cs 1903:Whitwick White Cross.
debut: 7.9.01 v.Woolwich Arsenal (A).

Originally a winger with the Luffs, who he served throughout their Football League career, Arthur had long since converted to the left-half

position by the time he reached Leicester, and he proved a consistently sound, steady defender as an ever-present throughout two fairly nondescript Second Division seasons.
Apps: 68 Lge; 3 FAC.
Goals: 1 Lge.

ROWELL, THOMAS
b. Birtley.
Birtley/Aug 1897:FOSSE.
debut: 16.10.97 v.Walsall (H).

A tough right-back from Northern Alliance football, Tom briefly covered absences in four different defensive positions during his Fosse season after finding Jack Walker virtually immovable from his favoured berth. Like many fringe players of his era, he fared better in the club's then-heavy programme of friendlies and minor cup games, playing in eleven of the season's 20 such matches, and scoring once in the Burford Cup semi-final.
Apps: 5 Lge.

ROWLEY, GEORGE ARTHUR
b. Wolverhampton, 21.4.1926.
Blackhall St.Lukes/
am:Wolverhampton Wanderers/
Apr 1944:West Bromwich Albion/
Dec 1948:Fulham/June 1950:CITY/
June 1958:Shrewsbury Town (p/mgr).
debut:19.8.50 v.Bury (A)(1 goal).

The most prolific scorer the Football League has known, Arthur clearly gave early promise of feats to come despite Wolves' failure to sign him on professional forms. He made his senior debut, alongside his brother Jack and only five days after his 15th birthday, in a wartime Manchester United fixture at Anfield; and also turned out as a guest player for Brighton and Lincoln before military service in Germany and Palestine. His introduction to League combat, however, was a slow process at the Hawthorns (4 goals in 24 apps; including one 60-minute stint as stand-in goalkeeper against Leicester in February 1948), and it was not until he reached Craven Cottage, and gunned Fulham into the First Division, that his reputation began to rise. There was still much disquiet among City fans, though, when Arthur arrived as an instant, cheaper replacement for the well-liked Jack Lee; but the imminent event of the first of his sixteen Leicester hat-tricks and a first seasonal total of 28 goals rather smoothed his integration, and his smashing of Arthur Chandler's seasonal scoring record with 38 the following term duly conferred on him heroic status. Arthur went one goal better in 1953, rifled home thirty in the 1954 promotion campaign, 23 more in the First Division, then was actually toppled from the peak of the club's league goals chart for one season by Willie Gardiner's 34 (Arthur following with 29). The Second Division championship year of 1957 was a matter of numerous club records for City, so Arthur just had to help himself to one that would last: 44 strikes in an ever-present season. A haul of only (!) 20 back in the top flight was considered such a lapse from his standards that the club rather crazily allowed Arthur to slip away to Shrewsbury, there to continue his path

towards a career total of 434 League goals from 619 games. At the risk of representing the burly, lion-hearted inside-left as a merely statistical construct, it can be added that he scored in all four Divisions (50 in One; 232 in Two; 114 in Three; and 38 in the basement, from which he lifted the Shrews at the first attempt); that he was the League's top individual scorer in both 1953 and 1957, and, incidentally, holds the City record for most penalties converted (41 in League and Cup). That he never added full England honours to his single appearances for each of the 'B' team and the Football League (both in 1956) was a clear injustice (his less prolific brother Jack won 6 caps); and that City will probably never again see a forward with quite such an appetite for hitting the back of the net is an inescapable inference. Arthur's managerial career after hanging up his shooting boots was comparatively unremarkable, taking him from Gay Meadow to spells at Sheffield United, Southend United and Oswestry Town; and it was sad that his second, belated Testimonial game in 1977 was such a low-key affair between Southend and City. (Twelve years earlier the celebratory participants had been Shrewsbury and Wolves). But nothing could dim the Leicester folk memory of 'The Gunner' rampaging through helplessly flailing defenders, bringing his thunderbolt left peg into lethal action, and giving the Goalkeepers' Union a collective backache.
Apps: 303 Lge; 18 FAC.
Goals: 251 Lge; 14 FAC.

ARTHUR ROWLEY

ROWLEY, WILLIAM SPENCER
b. Hanley, 1865.
Hanley Orion/1883:Stoke/Burslem Port Vale/
cs 1887:Stoke/Aug 1898:FOSSE.
debut: 3.9.98 v.Lincoln City (H).

Fosse just could not escape controversy with their newly-signed goalkeeping choices for the start of the 1898/9 season. Not only did the 'poaching' of Godfrey Beardsley land them in

deep trouble, but their engagement of this former England and Football League custodian also had them carpeted before the football establishment. William had retired from playing some two years previously, and had had to seek reinstatement as an amateur to serve Stoke as secretary. Yet Fosse paid him a signing-on fee after he had negotiated his own transfer, and prior to his single appearance. It was only a month later that the FA's wrath descended upon all parties concerned, with Fosse fined £10, and Rowley and Fosse secretary/manager W.D.Clark each suspended for 12 months for such unethical practice. William later became a Potteries postman, and then emigrated to the USA.
Apps: 1 Lge.

ROWSON, S.
b.
1889:FOSSE.
debut (comp): 4.10.90
v.Burton Wanderers (H) FAC.

Another of the pioneer Ancients, a right-back who turned out in each of the club's first two ill-fated stabs at FA Cup glory, then faded from the scene during the initial Midland League season. He did, however, play in both of Fosse's Leicestershire Senior Cup-winning teams of 1890 and 1891.
Apps: 2 FAC; 6 ML.

ROXBURGH, ANDREW
b. Granton, Edinburgh.
Rugby Town/June 1920:CITY.
debut: 28.8.20 v.Clapton Orient (A).

The elder of two Scottish-born, Rugby-educated brothers who contemporaneously assisted City as amateurs, Andrew was a ball-playing inside forward and, it is believed, remains the only man to have played at first-team level for both of Leicester's senior football clubs, having also turned out as a fly-half for the Tigers in several fixtures during 1922. (Former City reserve winger Richard Pell was, in the mid-80's, the most recent successful convert to the Rugby Union code, while several City players over the years have won junior recognition at the oval ball game prior to turning professional).
Apps: 19 Lge.
Goals: 2 Lge.

ROXBURGH, JOHN A.
b. Granton, Edinburgh, 10.11.1901.
Rugby Town/June 1920:CITY/
Oct 1922:Aston Villa/Feb 1924:Stoke/
Aug 1925:Sheffield United/Sheffield.
debut: 9.10.20 v.West Ham United (H).

More single-minded about a soccer career than his brother Andrew, John was actually selected for an England amateur international before his birthplace became known. After making a teenage League debut for City, this jinky outside-right went on to tot up around 80 League appearances for his four senior clubs. The Roxburgh brothers appeared in the same City side together on only five occasions, and it was somewhat ironic that each should have

effectively surrendered their positions to one of the Duncan brothers. A third Roxburgh sibling, Walter, played in City's pre-season trials of 1921.
Apps: 48 Lge; 2 FAC.
Goals: 2 Lge; 1 FAC.

RUSSELL, ANDREW
b. Airdrie.
Airdrieonians/Dec 1927:CITY/
Sept 1928:Falkirk/Morton/
July 1931:Queen of the South/
July 1934:Coleraine.
debut: 14.4.28 v.Birmingham (H).

Brought South to bolster City's reserve half-back strength during the push for the First Division title, Andy got just the one chance to deputise for Billy Findlay, and was soon heading back over the border (in the company of fellow reserve George Wyness) in the part-exchange deal that brought George Ritchie to Leicester. As a regular for Queen of the South, he assisted them to their first-ever promotion in 1932/3, and to their highest-ever Division One placing of 4th a year later, before trying his luck in Ireland. Andy had originally qualified as an engineer during his Airdrie days.
Apps: 1 Lge.

RUSSELL, EDWARD THOMAS
b. Cranwell, 15.7.1928.
St.Chad's College/
1946:Wolverhampton Wanderers/
Dec 1951:Middlesbrough/Oct 1953:CITY/
Aug 1958:Notts County.
debut: 14.11.53 v.Notts County (A).

One of several City players over the years to have simultaneously followed a schoolteaching career, Eddie was a tall left-half, hard-tackling yet constructive. He toured Canada with the FA party in 1950, but was certain of a first-team place at neither Molineux nor Ayresome. An £8,000 fee gave him the chance, however, to contribute to City's 1954 promotion push, and he was the regular No.6 in the ensuing top-flight campaign. Eddie missed out entirely on the 1957 championship effort, but bounced back again in the First Division before having a brief spell at Meadow Lane.
Apps: 90 Lge; 11 FAC.
Goals: 5 Lge.

RUSSELL, MARTIN CHRISTOPHER
b. Dublin, 27.4.1967.
Belvedere YC/1983:Manchester United/
(Oct 1986-loan-Birmingham City)/
(Jan 1987-loan-Norwich City)/Mar 1987:CITY/
Feb 1989:Scarborough.
debut: 18.4.87 v.West Ham United (H).

Honoured at Under-21 level by Eire both before and after his £25,000 move to Filbert Street, Martin built a fair reputation in the Old Trafford reserves as an attacking midfielder, but left United without a senior game to his credit. In fact, his only League experience had come during his brief St.Andrews loan spell, and it had not really equipped him with sufficient assertiveness for the left-flank role which Bryan Hamilton initially asked him to

fill for City's relegation-bound side. Martin's neat footwork and silky changes of direction were put briefly to better use in the midfield department of David Pleat's Second Division squad, though a tendency to get too easily hustled out of his stride still limited his senior chances. The valuation of his outward move at £105,000 raised a few eyebrows, and represented by some margin Scarborough's record fee.
Apps: 13+7 Lge; 3+1 LC; 1 FMC.

RUSSELL, WILLIAM
b.
West Norwood/Dec 1913:FOSSE.
debut: 20.12.13 v.Huddersfield Town (A).

An amateur outside-right, noted as 'a sprinter', William was elevated from Isthmian League football to cover briefly for the injured George Douglas. He had also played representative matches for both Surrey and London.
Apps: 5 Lge.

SAER, CHARLES
b.
Fleetwood Rangers/
Feb 1897:Blackburn Rovers/
Sept 1897:FOSSE/cs 1898:Stockport County.
debut: 18.9.97 v.Grimsby Town (A).

A cheerfully charismatic but ultra-competent goalkeeper, Charlie earned much due credit for helping Fosse to create their best defensive record during his single season with the club. After moving on into Lancashire League football, he became centrally involved in early activism among professional players, and was voted secretary of the first Players' Union during 1898.
Apps: 28 Lge; 1 FAC.

SALMONS, GEOFFREY
b. Mexborough, 14.1.1948.
Feb 1966:Sheffield United/
July 1974:Stoke City/
(Sept 1977-loan-Sheffield United)/
Oct 1977:CITY/Aug 1978:Chesterfield/
cs 1982:Gainsborough Trinity.
debut: 15.10.77 v.Coventry City (H).

A regular alongside Tony Currie in the exciting Blades midfield which helped them to promotion behind City in 1971, Geoff cost Stoke a hefty £180,000 fee as he continued his top-flight progress. Three seasons later, though, with the Potters relegated, he commenced successive loan spells at Bramall Lane and Filbert Street, where his thrusting displays in Frank McLintock's struggling side soon earned him a full transfer. Though it was an all-too-typical reflection on a disastrous season that Geoff's four goals made him the club's joint top scorer, it was surprising that Jock Wallace deemed him surplus to City's revivalist requirements at the start of the following term.
Apps: 25+1 Lge; 2 FAC.
Goals: 4 Lge.

SAMMELS, JONATHAN CHARLES
b. Ipswich, 23.7.1945.
app/pro Aug 1962:Arsenal/July 1971:CITY/

Mar 1978:Vancouver Whitecaps/
Nuneaton Borough (p/coach)/
Trowbridge Town.
debut: 14.8.71 v.Huddersfield Town (A).

Though having gained immense top-level
experience at Highbury, and having shared in
some of Arsenal's greatest glory days, Jon had
also suffered a rare measure of disappointment
before arriving at Leicester for £100,000 as
Jimmy Bloomfield's first purchase. To set
against his winning of one Football League
honour and nine England Under-23 caps, his
Wembley League Cup trips had both ended in
defeat, while his winning goal in Arsenal's
1970 Fairs Cup triumph seemed to herald a
brighter future for Jon than the fate of being
sidelined for much of the following Double
season. The elegant midfielder soon, though,
shrugged off any ill-effects on his morale as he
set about helping re-establish City as a First
Division force and, in his first senior game,
indeed prompted them to capture the FA
Charity Shield. Adept at slowing the pace of a
game, Jon did not always endear himself to an
impatient crowd, but was blessed with a sharp
eye for a telling long pass and could also
unleash a fair long-distance shot, as well as
showing a willingness to play guinea-pig at the
centre of some of Bloomfield's more extrovert
tactical experiments. (Remember the short-
lived 'S Plan' with Jon cast in a Beckenbauer-
like sweeper's role?) His consistency over
more than six seasons in the top flight was
admirable, and it was notable that the team's
precipitate decline in 1977/8 coincided with the
waning influence of Jon on the City attack.
After spells in the NASL and in senior non-
league football, Jon returned to Leicester to
open a driving school.
Apps: 236+5 Lge; 17+1 FAC; 12 LC.
Goals: 21 Lge; 1 FAC; 3 LC.

JON SAMMELS

SANDERCOCK, KENNETH L.
b. Plymouth, 31.1.1951.
app/pro Jan 1969:Torquay United/
Nov 1969:CITY/
Nov 1971:Torquay United.
debut: 8.11.69 (sub) v.Blackpool (A).

A youth-team player under Frank O'Farrell at
Plainmoor, Ken followed his former manager to
Filbert Street and found an early senior squad
place for his compact midfield skills and
tenacity. His Bloomfield Road bow as
substitute gave him more time to impress than
did his first 'full' match - for Ken was carried
off only moments into the next game at Bolton.
Thereafter he alternated between the half-back
line and the bench for a while, but failed to get
a look-in during the following promotion push,
and eventually returned to Torquay, where he
often played alongside his brother Phil.
Apps: 5+5 Lge.

SANDY SCOTT

SCOTT, ALEX MacNAUGHTON
b. Kingsbarns, Fife, 17.11.1922.
Lochgelly Albert/Mar 1947:CITY/
Jan 1950:Carlisle United/
July 1956:South Shields.
debut: 3.1.48 v.Fulham (A).

A strongly-built inside or outside-left when
signed from Scottish junior football, Sandy was
soon converted to left-back by Johnny Duncan,
and then went through his forward to defender
transformation all over again in the course of
City's 1949 Cup run, during which he was
notably successful in the Highbury semi-final
against Portsmouth. New manager Norman
Bullock let him go for £1,500 halfway through
the next season, though, after signing Ron
Jackson for the No.3 berth, and it was left to
Bill Shankly to recognise Sandy's fighting
qualities by taking him to Brunton Park, where
he totted up 203 League appearances in six
years.
Apps: 31 Lge; 10 FAC.
Goals: 1 Lge.

SCOTT, GEOFFREY SAMUEL
b. Birmingham, 31.10.1956.
app:Aston Villa/Solihull Borough/
Highgate United/Apr 1977:Stoke City/
Feb 1980:CITY/Feb 1982:Birmingham City/
Oct 1982:Charlton Athletic/

Aug 1984-trial-Middlesbrough/
Sept 1984:Northampton Town/
July 1985:Cambridge United.
debut: 20.2.80 v.Swansea City (H).

The regular left-back in Stoke's 1979 promotion side, Geoff replaced the departed Dennis
Rofe for the run-in to City's Second Division
championship the following season. His form,
though, was far from convincing, and it was as
an emergency central defender that he played
his best games for City in their attempts to
retain top-flight status. Almost exclusively a
one-footed player, Geoff could appear
ungainly, but his new-found effectiveness in the
middle of the back four earned him a £50,000
move back into the First Division with
Birmingham. Later, serious injury marred his
Charlton spell and threatened his career, finally
forcing him to retire midway through his first
season as Cambridge skipper. Geoff eventually
returned to Midland Combination minnows
Highgate United as manager.
Apps: 39 Lge; 2 FAC; 3 LC.

SEALY, ANTHONY JOHN
b. Hackney, 7.5.1959.
app/pro May 1977:Southampton/
Mar 1979:Crystal Palace/
(Feb 1980-loan-Port Vale)
/Mar 1981:Queens Park Rangers/
(Feb 1982-loan-Port Vale)/
(Dec 1983-loan-Fulham)/cs 1984:Fulham/
Sept 1985:CITY/
(Feb 1987-loan-Bournemouth)/
July 1987:Sporting Lisbon/Mar1989:Brentford.
debut: 21.9.85 v.Birmingham City (A)(1 goal).

A well-travelled striker, neat and speedy, Tony
too often found that his lack of height and
weight in the box made him a likely candidate
to step down from the front-line; at least to the
sub's bench. Indeed, it was in short bursts of
energetic and enthusiastic harrying that Tony
proved most effective for each of his clubs, and
rather symptomatic of his stop-start career that
his most treasured moment should remain his
brief Wembley appearance as Southampton's
No.12 in their 1979 League Cup defeat. He did,
though, play important roles in promotion
pushes at both QPR and Bournemouth, and impressed sufficiently with both City and the
Cherries for Keith Burkinshaw to whisk him off
to Portugal, where he formed a useful striking
partnership with the Brazilian Cascavel.
Apps: 28+11 Lge; 2+2 LC.
Goals: 7 Lge.

SEED, ANGUS CAMERON
b. Whitburn, 6.2.1893.
d. Barnsley, 7.3.1953.
Seaham Harbour/(Dec 1913-trials-Everton)/
Jan 1914:FOSSE/July 1914:Reading/
Nov 1916:St.Bernards/Dec 1919:Mid-Rhondda/
cs 1921:Workington.
debut: 21.2.14 v.Glossop (H).

Briefly tried out as a right-back replacement for
the Tottenham-bound Tommy Clay, Angus was
destined to follow a career at both playing and
managerial levels that was largely overshadowed by the achievements of his brother
Jimmy. Angus' glory was to come during

WW1, when, after a season as a Southern League reserve at Elm Park, he joined the Footballers' Battalion and was decorated with the Military Medal for valorous service at Vimy Ridge. But while he was making a return to football in, successively, Scottish wartime fare, the Southern League and the North Eastern League (becoming first trainer, then manager, at Workington), Jimmy was winning England caps as a Spurs schemer; and even when Angus moved on for lengthy spells in the boss's chair at Aldershot and Barnsley, Jimmy was taking the limelight in a similar capacity at, first, Clapton Orient and then, for a record 23 years, at Charlton.
Apps: 3 Lge.

SEYMOUR, THOMAS
b. (Scotland).
Middlesbrough Ironopolis/cs 1893:FOSSE.
debut: 9.9.93 v.Burton Wanderers (H) ML.

A right-half who served Fosse throughout the final season of Midland League football and into the initial Second Division season, Tom had left the 'Nops' (the first professional club on Teesside) just before their own one and only League campaign. He was badly injured at Burton in February 1895, and was said to be returning to his native Scotland to recuperate when Fosse released him.
Apps: 19 Lge; 13 FAC; 20 ML.
Goals: 1 Lge; 1 FAC; 1 ML.

SHANKS, THOMAS
b. New Ross, Co.Wexford, 1880.
Wexford/Derby West End/
Apr 1898:Derby County/Oct 1901:Brentford/
Dec 1902:Woolwich Arsenal/
May 1904:Brentford/Oct 1906:FOSSE/
cs 1909:Leyton.
debut: 13.10.06 v.Clapton Orient (A).

Best remembered as the man who schemed Fosse into the First Division, and as scorer of the winner in the crucial promotion decider at Stoke in 1908, Tommy was an Irish international inside-forward (capped three times between 1903-5) who had played his first League football alongside Steve Bloomer for the Rams, and had also shot Arsenal to promotion in 1904 - as top scorer and penalty expert - between his two spells with Southern League Brentford.
Apps: 57 Lge; 2 FAC.
Goals: 16 Lge.

SHARKEY, DOMINIC
b. Helensburgh, 4.5.1943.
May 1958:Sunderland/Oct 1966:CITY/
Mar 1968:Mansfield Town/
July 1970:Hartlepool.
debut: 30.11.66 v.Manchester United (H).

A diminutive striker who inherited Brian Clough's No.9 shirt at Roker and helped shoot Sunderland back into Division One in 1964, earning for himself two Scottish Under-23 selections, Nick arrived at Filbert Street with better than a goal-every-other-game scoring ratio to his credit. Initially, it was intended that he would take some of the attacking weight

from Derek Dougan, but the pair played together only once, and it was the end of the 1967 season before Nick grabbed another chance with characteristic goal flair. He soon lost his place the following term, though, and it was his prolific reserve-team partnership with Jimmy Goodfellow, later continued at League level after both had moved to Field Mill, which most memorably marked his City career.
Apps: 6 Lge.
Goals: 5 Lge.

SHARMAN, FREDERICK
b. Loughborough, 23.11.1912.
Brush Sports/Loughborough Corinthians/
May 1933:CITY.
debut: 1.2.34 v.Liverpool (H).

The son of a former Notts County and Grimsby player, whose turn-of-the-century League experience had amounted to only two senior games for the Magpies, Fred was a versatile and muscular stalwart of City's up-and-down struggles of the 30's. Primarily a defender, standing in for and then displacing Roger Heywood at centre-half, he also took the right-back spot from time to time, and had one lengthy spell at centre-forward during 1935/6, with no mean success as a bustling goalscorer. Fred won a Second Division championship medal as pivot in 1937, and was still going strong when war broke out, making a further 54 appearances during the hostilities and also guesting for Notts County and his old Brush Sports side, before retiring in 1944. He later returned briefly to Filbert Street as reserve-team trainer.
Apps: 190 Lge; 10 FAC.
Goals: 18 Lge.

FRED SHARMAN

SHARP, BUCHANAN
b. Alexandria, Dumbartonshire, 2.11.1894.
d. Bolton, 1956.
Vale of Leven/Nov 1919:Chelsea/
Mar 1923:Tottenham Hotspur/Jan 1925:CITY/
June 1926:Nelson/Oct 1928:Southport.
debut: 24.1.25 v.Coventry City (H) (1 goal).

A tricky Scottish inside-forward who was just

getting into his goal-scoring stride at Stamford Bridge when Spurs leapt in for his signature, Buchanan then found his progress somewhat stymied at White Hart Lane, where he only managed three League appearances. Peter Hodge recruited him as an experienced back-up to Johnny Duncan during City's 1925 promotion push, but after a few games in the top-flight during the following campaign he moved on to complete his League career in Lancashire, netting 21 goals in his first season at Nelson.
Apps: 12 Lge.
Goals: 2 Lge.

SHARP, W.A.
b. Leicester.
Leicester Imperial/Apr 1902:FOSSE.
debut: 10.1.03 v.Chesterfield (H).

There is a time-honoured tradition in football journalism that even a disastrous debut by a player is commented on with an indulgent epithet of the order of 'promising', or some such. 'Observer' of the Leicester Daily Post well and truly broke ranks, though, in summing up this outside-right on his sole senior run-out: 'a total failure' and 'very weak' constituted his assessment on the local lad after a particularly dispiriting home defeat.
Apps: 1 Lge.

SHARPLEY, WILLIAM
b.
Army football/(Mar 1912-trials-FOSSE).
debut: 27.4.12 v.Leeds City (H).

An Army corporal given the briefest of League breaks in the final game of the 1911/12 season, at left-back behind fellow squaddie and trialist Mitchell, when he still had two years to serve in the Essex Regiment.
Apps: 1 Lge.

SHEARD, FRANK
b. Spilsby, 29.1.1922.
Skegness Town/Nov 1940:CITY/
May 1946:Southend United/
Aug 1956:Gravesend & Northfleet.
debut (postwar): 5.1.46 v.Chelsea (A) FAC.

A hefty young centre-half signed on during the second season of wartime football, Frank held the senior pivot's position for both legs of the first postwar FA Cup tie, but had moved on to Southend before the resumption of Football League action, in which he totted up 180 games over seven seasons.
Apps: 2 FAC.

SHEFFIELD, JOHN D.
b. Coalville.
Coalville Albion/Whitwick White Cross/
Oct 1902:Burton United/
cs 1903:Coalville Town/July 1904:FOSSE/
cs 1905:Ibstock Albion/Coalville Town.
debut: 1.10.04 v.Liverpool (A).

Outside-right Jack clearly did not fancy taking his football talents far from home, as his list of clubs in the North Leicestershire area indicates, yet he also managed to fit a spell of far-flung

military service during the Boer War into the above chronology. He managed twelve Second Division appearances for the Peel Croft club, but was effectively debarred from greatly extending his experience at that level with Fosse by the consistency of Jamie Durrant.
Apps: 2 Lge.

SHEPHERD, JOHN
b.
Apr 1912:FOSSE.
debut: 20.4.12 v.Stockport County (A).

A trialist inside-left of so-far-untraced origin; though stated at the time to be 'well recommended from the South'.
Apps: 1 Lge.

PETER SHILTON

SHILTON, PETER LESLIE
b. Leicester, 18.9.1949.
app June 1965/pro Sept 1966:CITY/
Nov 1974:Stoke City/
Sept 1977:Nottingham Forest/
Aug 1982:Southampton/
June 1987:Derby County.
debut: 4.5.66 v.Everton (H).

It is almost the case that however far back into Peter's superb goalkeeping career one delves for perspective, one could have safely predicted the heights it would reach. A schoolboy prodigy, his dedication to working on the practice and psychology of his destined profession (and even on building the correct physique for it) was evident while he was helping Leicester Boys to their 1965 Trophy win, and picking up his first international recognition with England Schools. At Filbert Street there was immediate acknowledgement of Peter's precocious talent, and he became City's youngest-ever First Division debutant when characteristically keeping a clean sheet against Cup-winners-to-be Everton. Barely another year had elapsed before a queue of top clubs was forming, ready to snatch Peter (now an automatic choice for England Youth) from the Filbert Street shadow of Gordon Banks, and an unenviable choice soon faced Matt Gillies over which of his top-rank 'keepers to part

with. He elected to invest in the younger man's ability and ambition, and it was not too long before his judgement was substantiated by Peter's assumption of Banks' place in the international arena. In the interim, City experienced a Cup Final, a relegation and a promotion (with Peter's shot-stopping solidity, aerial agility, uncanny sense of positioning and absolute command of his area in large part responsible for the club creating its best-ever defensive record during 1970/1). Rarely out of the public eye - his adoption of an all-white playing kit and his long-distance scoring success at Southampton at various times assuring that - Peter was inevitably now adding full international mementos to his thirteen England Under-23 caps, but also becoming less than enchanted with City's trophy-winning prospects. Jimmy Bloomfield accepted a £325,000 cheque from Stoke for the unsettled star, and the move ironically threatened to rebound on Peter as the Potters themselves struggled, and he found himself only sharing the yellow jersey of England with Ray Clemence. But when Stoke dropped into Division Two, Peter was the subject of a typically shrewd bit of Brian Clough business, and in five years of almost uninterrupted success in domestic and European competitions with Forest, he once more re-established himself as the country's undisputed No.1. Maintaining his impeccable, highly self-critical standards at The Dell (after another £325,000 move), Peter became the most-capped England 'keeper of all time, skippering the national side on occasion, and earning the civil honour of the MBE in 1986. Then, after another big-money transfer to the Baseball Ground, he set about creating a further series of major career landmarks: surpassing Terry Paine's all-time record for the highest number of League appearances with his 825th game in April 1988, and overtaking Bobby Moore's record total of England caps when gaining his 109th such honour against Denmark in June 1989. Nearing 40 years of age, Peter shows every sign of continuing to represent a highly intimidatory barrier for top-class forwards for some years to come.
Apps: 286 Lge; 33 FAC; 20 LC.
Goals: 1 Lge.

SHINTON, FREDERICK
b. Wednesbury, Mar 1883.
d. West Bromwich, 11.4.1923.
Hawthorn Villa/Moxley White Star/
Wednesbury Old Athletic/Hednesford Town/
Apr 1905:West Bromwich Albion/
Nov 1907:FOSSE/cs 1910:Bolton Wanderers/
Jan 1911:FOSSE.
debut: 30.11.07 v.Lincoln City (A) (1 goal).

Fosse decidedly got the best of the bargain from the part-exchange deal which took Harry Wilcox and £125 to The Hawthorns and brought inside-forward Fred to Leicester partway through what turned out to be the club's first promotion season; for the latter also went on to become Fosse's first true goalscoring hero. His strike rate at West Brom was already mightily impressive (46 goals in 64 league games), and ten goals towards the promotion target did much to endear the

enthusiastic bustler to his new supporters. Strangely, Fred got fewer chances to enliven Fosse's struggling front-line in the top flight, but when they tried to bounce straight back up again in 1909/10, Fred weighed in with a 32-goal haul from the centre-forward berth that remained a club record until the days of Arthur Chandler. His brave, almost reckless style of headlong assault earned him the Filbert Street nickname of 'Nutty' (he had been known as 'Tickler' or 'Appleyard' at West Brom), while it was often remarked how much his fair-haired, handsome looks appealed to Fosse's fairly substantial female support. A brief, unhappy spell at Bolton interrupted Fred's progress and seemed to take the gloss off his game, for despite a scoring comeback for Fosse, he failed to earn a new contract for the following season. A younger brother, Arthur, signed for City in 1919, but never made the grade.
Apps: 92 Lge; 9 FAC.
Goals: 55 Lge; 3 FAC.

SILVESTER, -.
b.
cs 1892:FOSSE.
debut: 17.9.92 v.Mansfield Town (A) ML.

A centre-half taken on to add creative wit to Fosse's middle-line after the embarrassments of the initial Midland League season. (It is by no means certain, but it is believed this player may have been Alfred H.Silvester, who represented Birmingham St.George's, West Bromwich Albion reserves, Kidderminster Harriers and Small Heath Old Edwardians around this period).
Apps: 4 FAC; 11 ML.
Goals: 1 ML.

SIMMS, SAMUEL
b. Atherton.
cs 1912:Everton/June 1913:Swindon Town/
June 1914:FOSSE/1919:Swindon Town/
cs 1921:Gillingham.
debut: 2.9.14 v.Lincoln City (H) (2 goals).

Essentially a reserve centre-forward at each of his previous clubs, Sam had scored on the first of his two First Division appearances for Everton, and had thrice stepped in as under-study leader for Swindon during their Southern League championship season of 1914. He got off on the right foot with Fosse, but then had to vie with near-namesake Stephen Sims for a regular forward berth in what proved the worst season ever for the club.
Apps: 16 Lge; 1 FAC.
Goals: 5 Lge.

SIMPSON, FRANK L.
b.
Syston Victoria/(Oct 1902-trials-FOSSE)/
Leicester Imperial/Aug 1903:FOSSE/
cs 1904:Leicester Imperial/
cs 1907:Leicester Nomads.
debut: 7.12.03
v.Burton United (at Derby) FAC.

A local amateur outside-left who came back from a dispiriting setback during his first spell with the club - he broke his collarbone in a

rough-house reserve match at Whitwick, after which Fosse director Collins was suspended for a month by the FA for his incautious comments and behaviour. Familiarly known as Sandy, he eventually had only a brief brush with the senior game, and was later alongside ex-Fossil Ernest Vickerstaffe in helping found Leicester Nomads as the town's first-class amateur combination.
Apps: 2 Lge; 1 FAC.

SIMPSON, HENRY C.
b. Aberdeenshire.
Peterhead/Oct 1907:St.Bernards/
Mar 1910:FOSSE/July 1910:St.Bernards.
debut: 2.4.10 v.Oldham Athletic (A).

A member of St.Bernards' 1907/8 Qualifying Cup-winning side, and well experienced in Scottish Second Division football (playing alongside Harry Graham on occasion), Harry joined Fosse as an inside-right partner to Fred Shinton just at the unfortunate point when their efforts to bounce straight back into the First Division were beginning to founder. In fact the tiny forward failed to appear in a winning Fosse side during his brief stay, and returned to Edinburgh for a fee of £45.
Apps: 7 Lge.
Goals: 1 Lge.

SIMPSON, THOMAS
b. Keyworth, 13.8.1879.
d. Oldham, 19.12.1961.
1899:Notts County/Oct 1902:FOSSE/
May 1903:Everton.
debut: 18.10.02 v.Barnsley (A).

An outside-left who only really came into his own while at Leicester, Tom had totted up only seven League appearances for the Magpies prior to his Fosse stint, and would play but one senior game for the Toffees while understudying the noted amateur and England international, Harold Hardman. Yet his left-wing thrusts and his brief scoring burst did much to save Fosse from the embarrassment of a re-election application (albeit only for one year), and earned him at least the promise of elevation from the League's basement to its heights. Tom was also a Nottinghamshire cricketer.
Apps: 27 Lge; 1 FAC.
Goals: 5 Lge.

SIMS, STEPHEN
b. Bedminster, 11.12.1895.
d. Weston, 1973.
Bath City/Aug 1914:FOSSE/
cs 1919:Bristol Rovers/July 1922:Burnley/
cs 1924:not known/Bristol City/
cs 1926:Bristol Rovers/
cs 1927:Newport County.
debut: 2.9.14 v.Lincoln City (H).

A prolific scorer for 1914 Western League runners-up Bath, Stephen unfortunately proved to be another of Louis Ford's signings for the final post-war League season who could do little to halt the Fosse's disastrous decline. By the time his career resumed after the war, however, Stephen had switched to the centre-half berth, and impressed sufficiently in Bristol Rovers' first season in Division Three to attract

a bid from top-flight Burnley.
Apps: 11 Lge.
Goals: 2 Lge.

SIMS, STEVEN FRANK
b. Lincoln, 2.7.1957.
app Aug 1973/pro July 1974:CITY/
Dec 1978:Watford/Sept 1984:Notts County/
Oct 1986:Watford/June 1987:Aston Villa.
debut: 20.8.75 v.Manchester City (A).

Like Fred Sharman before him and Russell Osman more recently, Steve was a City centre-half with a footballing father: in his case, Frank, a good Lincoln City clubman in the 50's. After a rapid rise through the City junior ranks, Steve made his League bow as replacement for the injured Jeff Blockley, and established himself during the last year of Jimmy Bloomfield's managership as a central defender of some class, whose evident brawn was simply a highly useful adjunct to his astute intelligence. He became an England Under-21 regular (10 caps; 1 goal) and appeared once for England 'B', and even came out of the 1978 relegation farrago with some credit. Yet he did not last long into the Jock Wallace era, moving on to Vicarage Road at a fee of £175,000, a then-record outlay by a Third Division club. Watford were, though, in the middle of their meteoric rise up the League and, as an unfussily effective exponent of their long-ball tactics, Steve eventually had two seasons in the top flight with them, plus a taste of European competition, until transferring to Meadow Lane after a series of injuries. He again tasted relegation with the Magpies, but was soon reunited with his former manager and mentor, Graham Taylor, both in the First Division with Watford and in Villa's successful 1988 promotion drive.
Apps: 78+1 Lge; 3 FAC; 5 LC.
Goals: 3 Lge.

SINCLAIR, HARVEY PATRICK
b. Bournemouth, 30.11.1933.
am:Bournemouth & Boscombe Athletic/
Dec 1950:Fulham/Cambridge United/
Aug 1956:CITY/Sept 1958:Bristol Rovers/
July 1959:Fulham.
debut: 26.1.57 v.Grimsby Town (H).

More familiarly known as Harry, this luckless goalkeeper must have been heartily sick of reserve-team football by the time he finished his wanderings. His belated League debut was for City, following an injury to Johnny Anderson, but within days the club had bought Dave MacLaren to see out the rest of the 1957 promotion season. Some two years later, he ended his League career with a solitary appearance for Bristol Rovers.
Apps: 1 Lge.

SINCLAIR, JOHN EVENS WRIGHT
b. Culross, Fife, 21.7.1943.
Blairhall Colliery/
cs 1960:Dunfermline Athletic/May 1965:CITY/
Dec 1967:Newcastle United/
Dec 1969:Sheffield Wednesday/
(Mar 1973-loan-Chesterfield)/
cs 1973:Durban (SA)/

Aug 1973:Dunfermline Athletic/
cs 1975:Stenhousemuir.
debut: 21.8.65 v.Liverpool (H) (1 goal).

A Jock Stein signing for Dunfermline, Jackie was a nippy, goalscoring winger who had already come close to glory in both European competition and the 1965 Scottish Cup Final when Matt Gillies brought him to Filbert Street for £25,000 to forge an instantly successful little-and-large striking partnership with Derek Dougan. The adjective 'dynamic' seemed coined for Jackie as he adapted his killing pace and shooting instincts to service on either flank, and it was no surprise that he won a full Scotland cap at the end of his first City season (making up for the earlier disappointment of being chosen for a postponed Scottish League representative game). After two years in the First Division, Jackie was still bettering the classic striker's average of a goal-every-other-game, and though his scoring ratio dropped off a little during 1967/8, it seemed he was being jettisoned with undue haste at the wave of a Newcastle cheque for £67,500. He met less overall success on Tyneside, despite contributing crucially to the Geordies' 1969 Fairs Cup victory, and was eventually exchanged for Sheffield Wednesday's David Ford, linking up again at Hillsborough with former City team-mate Peter Rodrigues. Later Jackie found his way back to East End Park, and ended his career with an aggregate of 115 League goals to his name. His older brother Willie played for Falkirk, Huddersfield, Tranmere and Halifax, while his uncle was Tommy Wright, Sunderland's Scottish international of the 50's.
Apps: 103 Lge; 5 FAC; 5 LC.
Goals: 50 Lge; 2 FAC; 1 LC.

JACKIE SINCLAIR

SJOBERG, JOHN
b. Aberdeen, 12.6.1941.
Banks O'Dee/Aug 1958:CITY/
June 1973:Rotherham United.
debut: 28.10.60 v.Cardiff City (A).

A teenage centre-half when he followed Jack

Lornie's route to Filbert Street, John made his initial impact for City's first team as a right-back, taking over from Len Chalmers just prior to the start of the 1963 Cup run, and climaxing his first season as a regular with a Wembley appearance. He was a stalwart of the League Cup campaigns of the next two years, and was still shuttling between the Nos. 2 and 5 shirts with effective ease until the arrival of Peter Rodrigues to hold down the former position. Settling thereafter to a memorable central defensive partnership with Graham Cross, John displayed a craggy consistency and imposed his aerial mastery on many a First Division game. This quality tempted Matt Gillies into giving him one spell at centre-forward, but John's back-four abilities were more vital to City's strength and shape, and it was notable that the club's 1969 relegation occurred in a season when niggling injuries severely limited John's appearances, and indeed kept him out of the Cup Final line-up. Two years later, he was a key member of the Second Division promotion side, and took his Testimonial game after the championship had been secured. During his latter Leicester days, he had started a printing business, and it was to this that John returned after a very brief spell of six League games at Millmoor.
Apps: 334+1 Lge; 44 FAC; 34 LC.
Goals: 15 Lge; 1 FAC; 3 LC.

JOHN SJOBERG

SKEA, DAVID F.
b.
Arbroath/cs 1892:Aston Villa/
July 1893:Darwen/1893:Bury/
Aug 1894:FOSSE/cs 1896:Swindon Town/
cs 1897:New Brompton.
debut: 1.9.94 v.Grimsby Town (A) (2 goals).

A skilful hot-shot of an inside-left to whom a number of the club's Football League 'firsts' attach, David notched Fosse's initial goal in the competition, and became the scorer of each of the club's first hat-tricks and penalties at this level. Unsurprisingly, his marksmanship

granted him the honour of being the Fosse's first seasonal top-scorer (with a creditable 23 goals from a maximum 30 games), and his tally stood as a record until Fred Shinton's goal-rush in 1909/10. Clearly, he suffered closer attentions from Second Division defences the following term, and his goal rate dropped accordingly, but David could still accept limited opportunities with a rare alacrity, as his 5 goals from only 6 Southern League games for Swindon would indicate. His original bow in English football had been a scoring one, but one game and one goal represented the extent of his Villa Park career; while his promising spell with Swindon was actually cut short as a disciplinary measure after he had arrived for training 'in an intoxicated condition'. Transfer-listed at £25, David spent over six months out of the game, until Swindon finally accepted £10 for his registration from New Brompton.
Apps: 45 Lge; 7 FAC.
Goals: 29 Lge; 8 FAC.

SLACK, A.
b.
cs 1892:FOSSE.
debut: 17.9.92 v.Mansfield Town (A) ML.

Fosse's ever-present centre-forward during 1892/3, but an irregular reserve the following season, Slack claimed the club's first hat-trick at Midland League level, during the 7-1 demolition of Newark which constituted Fosse's best win in that competition.
Apps: 4 FAC; 26 ML.
Goals: 1 FAC; 11 ML.

SLACK, RODNEY
b. Farcet, 11.4.1940.
Fletton YC/Sept 1958:CITY/
Mar 1961:Queens Park Rangers/
cs 1962:Cambridge United.
debut: 12.10.60 v.Mansfield Town (H) LC.

Standing in for Gordon Banks in City's first-ever League Cup tie, Rodney kept a clean sheet on what proved to be his only senior outing, but was soon back in third-team football behind Banks and George Heyes. His spell with QPR resulted in only one League appearance, but he served Cambridge consistently well in their Southern League battles, culminating in a 1969 Double win.
Apps: 1 LC.

SMALL, PETER VICTOR
b. Horsham, 23.10.1924.
Horsham Town/Aug 1947:Luton Town/
Mar 1950:CITY/Sept 1954:Nottingham Forest/
July 1957:Brighton & Hove Albion.
debut: 18.3.50 v.Sheffield United (A).

A compact, strong winger who was nicknamed 'The Horsham Flier', and had faced City in the epic Luton Cup ties of 1949, prior to switching clubs for £6,000, Peter had to be content to spend the majority of his Filbert Street days in the shadow of Mal Griffiths. It was only during the 1954 promotion season, when he starred mainly on the left flank and contributed the bulk of his City goals, that he was able to make a substantial breakthrough, and even this run was soon curtailed by the pressing claims of

young Derek Hogg. Peter was somewhat luckier in his three years on Trentside (87 apps; 20 goals), and was a squad member for Forest when they accompanied City back into the First Division in 1956/7.
Apps: 65 Lge; 7 FAC.
Goals: 16 Lge; 4 FAC.

ALAN SMITH

SMITH, ALAN MARTIN
b. Birmingham, 21.11.1962.
Alvechurch/June 1982:CITY/
Mar 1987:Arsenal/
(Mar-May 1987:loan back to CITY).
debut: 28.8.82 v.Charlton Athletic (H).

Capped by England at semi-pro level while playing as a left-sided striker for Alvechurch's successful Southern League side, Alan became the final signing of the Jock Wallace era at City, and a bargain inheritance for Gordon Milne, who immediately paired the tall, elegant attacker with Gary Lineker. Though the latter initially hogged the headlines for his scoring exploits as City returned to the First Division and set about their battle for consolidation, Alan soon proved an unselfish foil, creating numerous chances with his excellent ball control and vision, and snapping up a fair quotient himself. Displaying a rare combination of stylishness and ready willingness to chase and harry, and posing an effective striking threat both in the air and on the ground, Alan also stood out for that even rarer commodity of sportsmanship: for while neither his bravery nor commitment could be questioned, his record of a single booking over five seasons was positively remarkable in a current context of so much 'professional' niggling. On Lineker's departure, Alan determinedly shouldered the responsibility as City's primary goal-getter, and after he finally shrugged off his reputation as a sluggish seasonal starter in 1986/7, there was as much inevitability in the upsurge of million-pound transfer rumours as there was credit in the player's modestly-expressed desire to honour his Leicester contract. Indeed, when his big-money move to Highbury was finally negotiated, he agreed on

an instant loan-back to City, to aid their eventually futile fight to stay in the top rank. Alan's initial season with the Gunners brought mixed fortunes under intense scrutiny, though he scored one of their consolation goals in the Littlewoods Cup Final of 1988 and finished as the club's top scorer; but it was his goal burst at the start of 1988/9 which elevated him into the England squad. He won his first cap as a substitute in Saudi Arabia, heralding a brief international renewal of his old Filbert Street partnership with Lineker. May 1989 saw Alan score one and lay on the other of the Arsenal strikes at Anfield which gave the Gunners the First Division championship by the narrowest possible of goal margins.
Apps: 190+10 Lge; 8 FAC; 8+1 LC.
Goals: 76 Lge; 4 FAC; 4 LC.

SMITH, ARTHUR ERIC
b. Whetstone, Leics, 5.9.1921.
Whetstone Athletic/
Wolverhampton Wanderers/Feb 1941:CITY/
June 1948:West Bromwich Albion/
Aug 1952:Plymouth Argyle/
June 1954:Crewe Alexandra.
debut (postwar): 25.1.47 v.Brentford (A) FAC.

Arthur was a locally-born inside-left who impressed City with some convincingly crafty performances in wartime football, claiming 33 goals from 74 games after his step up from the then-inoperative Wolves' juniors (a move which cost City a small Football League fine, for they had in fact fielded him in ignorance of his Wolves registration). He nonetheless found his first-team chances limited by the partnership of Dewis and Lee when League football resumed, and then at the Hawthorns briefly found his way barred by Jack Haines, who had preceded him from Leicester to West Brom a few months earlier. Arthur did however tot up 49 League appearances (12 goals) there before moving to Plymouth (28 games; 8 goals) and ending his career with a four-game spell at Gresty Road.
Apps: 17 Lge; 5 FAC.
Goals: 3 Lge; 2 FAC.

SMITH, ARTHUR HUGH
b. Bury.
May 1935:Bury/May 1938:CITY.
debut: 27.8.38 v.Stoke City (H).

A right-winger bought on the eve of the final pre-war League season, Arthur soon lost his place to newcomer Mal Griffiths, and barely got a look-in thereafter. He claimed two goals in the first match of the 1939/40 season, but promptly 'lost' them from official records when that campaign was abandoned, and soon he disappeared from senior football entirely.
Apps: 8 Lge.

SMITH, DEAN
b. Leicester, 28.11.1958.
app Apr 1975/pro Dec 1976:CITY/
(Apr 1978-loan-Houston Hurricane)/
Oct 1978:Brentford/
Feb 1981:Nuneaton Borough/Enderby Town/
Corby Town/Shepshed Charterhouse.
debut: 10.9.77 (sub) v.Everton (H).

Another of the several City teenagers unlucky enough to be thrown into the deep mire of the 1977/8 relegation farce, and then find themselves either at odds with, or superfluous to the plans of, incoming manager Jock Wallace. Dean was a strong, combative and mobile striker who nonetheless failed to bear out his high promise after a £20,000 move to Griffin Park, and returned to the local non-league arena after scoring 16 goals in 54 League games for the Bees.
Apps: 8+2 Lge.
Goals: 1 Lge.

SMITH, ERIC T.H.
b. Tamworth, 3.11.1921.
Castle Bromwich/cs 1945:CITY/
Jan 1947:Bath City.
debut (postwar): 31.8.46
v.Manchester City (H).

A young centre-half whose promise, shown in 13 games of the transitional season of 1945/6, tempted City into releasing Frank Sheard on the resumption of peacetime football. Eric held the No.5 berth for the initial postwar quintet of Second Division matches, but soon dropped out of the senior game altogether.
Apps: 5 Lge.

SMITH, GEORGE H.
b.
Hinckley Athletic/Dec 1892:FOSSE/
(Aug 1895-trials-Preston North End).
debut: 17.12.92 v.Doncaster Rovers (A) ML.

A sure-footed stalwart right-back for Fosse in the last two Midland League seasons, plus the initial campaign in the Second Division, George failed to earn a Deepdale contract after his release.
Apps: 24 Lge; 12 FAC; 35 ML.

SMITH, HARRY
b.
Berwick Rangers/Aug 1897:FOSSE/
cs 1898:Bedminster.
debut: 4.9.97 v.Luton Town (H).

Harry led the Fosse attack during the early stages of 1897/8 without conspicuous success, after joining from the Birmingham & District League club who would later become Worcester City (i.e. not the Scottish League club of the same name). He fared even less well with his subsequent Southern League club, failing to make a senior appearance for them.
Apps: 15 Lge.
Goals: 4 Lge.

SMITH, ISAAC
b. Wednesbury.
Oldbury Town/June 1919:CITY.
debut: 30.8.19 v
.Wolverhampton Wanderers (H).

A young left-half who failed to live up to the demands of post-WW1 League football, Ike at least makes the record books as a member of Leicester City's first side to play under that title. He had previously played half a dozen wartime games for Fosse during 1918/19.
Apps: 2 Lge.

BOBBY SMITH

SMITH, ROBERT NISBET
b. Dalkeith, 21.12.1953.
1970:Hibernian/Dec 1978:CITY/
(Feb 1982-loan-Peterborough United)/
(Nov 1982-loan-Hibernian)/
Oct 1986:Hibernian/
Sept 1987:Dunfermline Athletic.
debut: 1.1.79 v.Oldham Athletic (H) (1 goal).

Basically an attacking midfielder, Bobby had proven his versatility at Easter Road by leading Hibs' seasonal scoring list and then converting to left-back in the course of a year, and Jock Wallace chased his signature for some six months before an £85,000 deal was struck in time for Bobby to share a League bow with both Gary Lineker and David Buchanan. He settled well at Filbert Street as an aggressive prompter, opportunist and penalty expert, and was second-top scorer in the 1980 promotion campaign. Yet a lean spell followed, when City seemed willing to offload Bobby at the end of either of his loan-outs, and it was at full-back that he surprisingly re-established himself, contributing to the 1983 promotion effort, and holding his place in Gordon Milne's line-ups for much of the next three seasons. Eventually, another Easter Road loan did lead to Bobby rejoining his first club on a free transfer; though Hibs pocketed a decent fee when he shifted Premier Division bases. Dunfermline made a presentation to Bobby midway through their 1988/9 promotion season to mark his 500th senior game.
Apps: 175+6 Lge; 10 FAC; 8+1 LC.
Goals: 21 Lge; 1 FAC.

SMITH, SEPTIMUS CHARLES
b. Whitburn, 13.3.1912.
Whitburn/Mar 1929:CITY.
debut: 31.8.29 v.Huddersfield Town (A).

Still many veteran followers' notion of the best all-round City player ever, Sep was unarguably one of the club's most loyal servants, ending his magnificent twenty-year playing span with a brief spell as coach. From a fanatical footballing background (of seven brothers, five played at League level, with Tom also turning out for Leicester, Joe moving from City reserves to Watford, and Jack and Willie both spending the bulk of lengthy careers at Portsmouth), Sep was an England Schoolboys star in 1926 and clearly destined to join the top echelon of creative midfielders. His early games as a City teenager were at inside-forward, where he exhibited a fair scoring prowess to supplement his cool distributive skills, but it was at right-half that Sep truly made his mark throughout the club's turbulent times of the mid and late-30's. His repute was national, yet his representative honours' tally looks comparatively derisory: only one full cap, one appearance as second-half substitute in the 1935 Jubilee international against Scotland, and one game for the Football League. For club honours, too, Sep had to make do with only meagre reward for his inspirational captaincy, by way of a Second Division championship medal in 1937. He managed 213 wartime games (scoring 48 goals), and was still holding together City's postwar efforts as a veritable veteran of a pivot, constantly taking younger players like Don Revie under his tutelary wing, aiding Johnny Duncan's tactical preparations for City's 1949 Wembley trip, and finally hanging up his boots after seeing the club's Second Division future assured in the crucial last-match tussle at Cardiff.

Apps: 350 Lge; 23 FAC.
Goals: 35 Lge; 2 FAC.

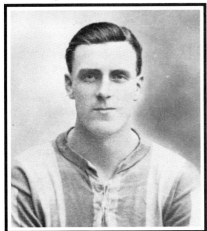

TOM SMITH

SMITH, THOMAS GABLE
b. Whitburn, 18.10.1900.
d. Whitburn, 21.2.1934.
Marsden Villa/Whitburn/
cs 1919:South Shields/Dec 1919:CITY/
Jan 1924:Manchester United/
June 1927:Northampton Town/
May 1930:Norwich City/Feb 1931:Whitburn.
debut: 20.12.19 v.Stoke (H).

Another of the footballing Smith clan, and the first to taste League football with South Shields (as did Jack and Willie, but not Sep), Tom was an inside-forward purchase by Peter Hodge whose attacking versatility ironically militated

against him holding down a regular first-team berth with City across the first five post-war seasons. He turned out in each of the forward positions except outside-left as City sought a promotion-worthy blend, yet he had to move to Old Trafford to up his status, as United accompanied City out of the lower sphere in 1925. Indeed, Tom's United debut in the inside-right slot he held for 83 matches (12 goals) was against City. Then as a Cobbler he totted up another 112 League appearances (22 goals), before finishing his career with a single game for Norwich. He should not be confused with the Tom Smith who became manager of Northampton for nine years from 1939.
Apps: 72 Lge; 9 FAC.
Goals: 12 Lge; 3 FAC.

SMITH, WALLACE
b. Allerton, 1883.
d. Worksop, 3.7.1917.
Rothwell/1901:Kettering Town/
cs 1904:Northampton Town/
May 1905:Bradford City/Jan 1909:FOSSE/
Mar 1909:Hull City.
debut: 9.1.09 v.Bristol City (A).

A Yorkshireman whose first senior experience came in the Southern League with two Northamptonshire clubs, Wally was a gutsy inside or centre-forward who won a Division Two championship medal with Bradford City in 1908, when they just pipped Fosse for the title, and cost the latter club a hefty £625 fee when enlisted to the ensuing, vain relegation struggle. Less than two months later, Wally was on his way again for the reduced sum of £500, and managed 33 goals in 90 League games for Hull before injury put paid to his playing career in early 1912. He still made one further appearance at Filbert Street, though: as emergency linesman for the first-half of the Fosse v. Hull fixture of March 1912. Wally had become a Worksop licensee when he died, aged only 33.
Apps: 5 Lge; 1 FAC.

SMITH, WALTER ERNEST
b. Leicester, 25.3.1884.
Leicester Imperial/Feb 1904:FOSSE/
May 1906:Manchester City/
Oct 1920:Port Vale/cs 1922:Plymouth Argyle/
Jan 1923:Grimsby Town.
debut: 25.2.04 v.Bristol City (H).

The first of Leicester's star-quality goalkeepers to be generally recognised as such, Walter initially joined Fosse as an amateur, but turned pro in September 1904, and missed only three games thereafter until his £600 move to Hyde Road. In the interim he had helped restore defensive confidence to Fosse's re-elected side and shift them several notches up the Second Division table, gaining a reputation as the Division's best 'keeper for his agility and resilience, with his lack of height (5ft.8ins) proving no handicap, but his hefty frame presenting an awkward barrier for rampaging, charge-happy forwards. In 1907 the 'Athletic News' correspondent was dubbing Walter 'the only first-class goalkeeper in the country who disdains training', with his subject opting to

follow his plumbing business rather than indulge in such 'unnecessary' practice. Walter totted up 233 League games for the Mancunians (bracketing wartime spells when he returned to assist Fosse as a guest in 24 fixtures, and also played for Fulham), was honoured once for the Football League against the Scots in 1915, and was still exhibiting a clean pair of hands in senior football until the close season of 1923. Something of an all-round sportsman himself (a schoolboy rugby star, and a wicketkeeper for both Leicester Temperance and the County seconds), this non-smoker and complete tee-totaller had a son, Walter A.Smith, who captained Combined Universities at both rugby and cricket and also played both sports for Leicestershire.
Apps: 79 Lge; 8 FAC.

SOO, FRANK
b. Buxton, 8.3.1914.
Prescot Cables/1933:Stoke City/
Sept 1945:CITY/July 1946:Luton Town/
cs 1948:Chelmsford City.
debut: 5.1.46 v.Chelsea (A) FAC.

Reputed to be the first player of Chinese extraction to play League football when he made his breakthrough as a professional with Stoke, Frank was a midfield ball-artist whose skills both complemented and contrasted with those of his great pre-war team-mate, Stanley Matthews. He was on the verge of full international recognition in 1939, and indeed won a total of eight wartime and Victory caps, the last being gained during his single season on City's books. Frank had also guested for the likes of Everton, Chelsea and Brentford while hostilities continued, but it was to join his former Stoke boss Tom Mather that he accepted a £4,600 move to less fashionable City for the transitional post-war campaign. Frank impressed City supporters immensely with his craft and trickery, but he failed to settle to the prospect of a new regime after Mather left, and the club recouped £3,000 of its outlay in banking Luton's cheque for his services. After 71 League games for Luton (4 goals) and some Southern League success, Frank had spells as manager of both Scunthorpe United and St.Albans City, and coached extensively in Sweden.
Apps: 2 FAC.

SPARROW, F.HENRY
b. Faversham, 13.6.1889.
d. Lincoln, 13.6.1973.
Faversham Thursday/1909:Portsmouth/
cs 1911:Sittingbourne/
Oct1911:Croydon Common/Feb 1912:FOSSE/
Jan 1914:Tottenham Hotspur.
debut: 10.2.12 v.Bristol City (A) (1 goal).

Clearly a player for whom Cup tie defeats brought on itchy feet, centre-forward Harry was a £90 signing for Fosse immediately after they had removed Croydon Common from the competition, and two seasons later moved with Tommy Clay to Spurs the day after that club had k.o.'d Fosse at the second attempt. Harry had struggled to find a Southern League place with Pompey, making only five scoreless appearances over two seasons, but flourished at Croydon under manager J.W.Bartlett, who rejoined him at Leicester only a month later and oversaw his immediate rise to the top of the Fosse scoring chart. Harry maintained his excellent goal ratio until whisked off to White Hart Lane, where he got fewer opportunities to shine (18 games, 7 goals) before the outbreak of war.

Apps: 48 Lge; 3 FAC.
Goals: 29 Lge.

SPEARING, ANTHONY
b. Romford, 7.10.1964.
app/pro Oct 1982:Norwich City/
(Nov 1984-loan-Stoke City)/
(Feb 1985-loan-Oxford United)/
July 1988:CITY.
debut: 27.8.88 v.West Bromwich Albion (H).

A former England Youth skipper and a graduate of Norwich's 1983 FA Youth Cup win, Tony had become a Carrow Road regular at left-back in the First Division (despite a debut own-goal, and a broken leg suffered shortly afterwards), and surprised many observers when electing to step down a grade to join City for £100,000 and challenge Simon Morgan for the No.3 shirt. Re-emphasising his credentials as a nippy and tenacious defender, he proved an unobtrusively adept performer in a backline which often strained for collective cohesion during 1988/9.
Apps (to 13.5.89): 36 Lge; 1 FAC; 2 LC; 1 FMC.

SPITTLE, WILLIAM ARTHUR
b. Southfields, 1893.
1912:Woolwich Arsenal/Oct 1919:CITY/
May 1921:Nuneaton Town.
debut: 18.10.19 v.Huddersfield Town (A).

Partnering Harry King in a joint move from Highbury, Billy was a scheming forward who had totalled only seven Second Division games for Arsenal in the two seasons before the war, and unfortunately failed to establish himself to Peter Hodge's satisfaction in several shots at holding down City's inside-right position in the two seasons after it. He was not helped, though, by the need to undergo a cartilage operation in April 1920.
Apps: 26 Lge.
Goals: 3 Lge.

SPRIGGS, F.
b.
Leicester Imperial/
Apr 1902:FOSSE.
debut: 19.4.02 v.Lincoln City (H) (2 goals).

A local young centre-forward who made quite an impact in the final game of 1901/2, yet thereafter only got one more first-team chance, in a near-embarrassing Cup qualifying tie at Irthlingborough, before being released in 1904. (The difficulty of researching players of this era, however, leaves open the outside possibility that this Fossil and his namesake following were in fact one and the same person).
Apps: 1 Lge; 1 FAC.
Goals: 2 Lge.

SPRIGGS, FRANK
b.
Sept 1909:FOSSE/cs 1910:Merthyr Town/
cs 1911:Rochdale.
debut: 2.10.09 v.Blackpool (A).

A centre-forward who partnered Fred Shinton in the above away win, but played the rest of his senior football in, successively, the lower reaches of the Southern League and (for a trio of games under ex-Fossil and 'Dale player-manager Joe Blackett) the Lancashire Combination.
Apps: 1 Lge.

STAPLES, JOHN WILLIAM
b.
Whitwick White Cross/May 1902:FOSSE/
1903:Whitwick White Cross.
debut: 6.9.02 v.Small Heath (H).

An outside-left whose brief elevation from the Midland League was already being judged a failure at the time Fosse were forced to pay a £10 fine for having made an illegal transfer approach to him the previous April.
Apps: 5 Lge.

'JONTY' STARBUCK

STARBUCK, JONATHAN
b. Measham, 1884.
d. Burton-on-Trent, 18.4.1939.
Measham/cs 1905:Burton United/
June 1907:FOSSE/cs 1912:Ilkeston United.
debut: 7.9.07 v.Leeds City (H).

A tall 'keeper who joined Fosse after Burton's demise, 'Jonty' gave five seasons of loyal service despite regularly being cast in the role of reserve to H.P.Bailey and Fred Mearns. His safe handling helped Fosse through several tricky encounters on the route to promotion in 1908, and he was hardly to blame for either their immediate return to the lower Division or any failure to bounce back. He finished his playing days in the Central Alliance.
Apps: 77 Lge; 12 FAC.

STARKEY, A.E.
b. Coalville.
Shepshed Albion/Mar 1911:FOSSE.
debut: 25.3.11 v.Fulham (H).

A local outside-right who had an extended first-team trial at the end of 1910/11, but failed to win a contract for the next season.
Apps: 8 Lge.

STEPHENSON, ROY
b. Crook, 27.5.1932.
Sunnyside Jnrs/June 1949:Burnley/
Sept 1956:Rotherham United/
Nov 1957:Blackburn Rovers/Mar 1959:CITY/
July 1960:Ipswich Town/
June 1965:Lowestoft Town.
debut: 14.3.59 v.Chelsea (H).

Though he had racked up a fair number of League games as a utility forward in the top flight, had picked up some good habits from the likes of Jimmy McIlroy and Jimmy Adamson, and had been a regular for the Millers in the Second Division, Roy appeared to be facing something of a late career crisis when he found himself sidelined for all but two games of his second season at Filbert Street. Matt Gillies had paid £8,000 to add Roy's inside-forward skills to City's successful attempt to ward off relegation, but he was then edged out of the reckoning for his favoured No.7 shirt by Tommy McDonald and Howard Riley. One move, though, revived Roy's enthusiasm and effectiveness at a stroke: with Alf Ramsey adding him to the Ipswich team-building jigsaw as the right-wing provider for the Crawford/ Phillips goal combine which sensationally saw the East Anglians to the championships of Division Two and One in successive seasons, and into the European Cup.
Apps: 12 Lge.

STEVENS, GREGOR
b. Glasgow, 13.1.1955.
1974:Motherwell/May 1979:CITY/
Sept 1979:Rangers/
(Jan 1984-loan-Heart of Midlothian)/
cs 1984:Motherwell/Nov 1984:Partick Thistle/
Aug 1986:Brechin City.
debut: 11.8.79 v.Rotherham United (H) LC.

All too evidently ill-at-ease with English football, Gregor struggled through only a handful of shaky performances as a City central defender before Jock Wallace somehow managed shrewdly to recoup his £125,000 investment in a second cross-border deal. Gregor had begun his Motherwell career as a midfielder, but had developed as a tough-tackling sweeper to win Scottish League and Under-21 honours; though he was definitely to overdo the toughness when he got to Ibrox, where he revelled in the nickname 'Igor' and, in February 1982, received a shaming six months suspension after his fifth sending-off in two years. He also, however, picked up Scottish Cup medals from the Finals of 1980 (loser's) and 1981 (winner's).
Apps: 4 Lge; 2 LC.

STEVENSON, JAMES
b. Paisley, 1876.
Clyde/Jan 1895:Derby County/
Oct 1898:Newcastle United/
cs 1900:Bristol City/Sept 1901:Grimsby Town/
Jan 1902:FOSSE/Oct 1902:Clyde.
debut: 18.1.02 v.Burton United (A).

A Cup Finalist with Derby in 1898, and then described as 'a wizard of the leather', James was a noted dribbler as an inside-left, as well as a fair marksman (31 goals in 73 League games for the Rams), and fetched the handsome transfer fee of £225 from newly-promoted Newcastle. He began his wanderings as his goal-touch waned, though, and his brief spell at Leicester ended in acrimony, with James one of several Fosse players suspended as an internal disciplinary measure within two months of signing on. (He should not be confused with the James Stevenson who played for Morton, Nottingham Forest and New Brompton in the early years of the century).
Apps: 7 Lge.
Goals: 1 Lge.

STEWART, ALEXANDER

b. (Scotland)
Morton/1889:Burnley/Dec 1892:Everton/
cs 1893:Nottingham Forest/
Mar 1897:Notts County/cs 1898:Bedminster/
cs 1899:Northampton Town/
Aug 1901:Burnley/Aug 1902:FOSSE.
debut: 10.4.03 v.Glossop (A) (1 goal).

The scorer of both Burnley's goals when they beat FA Cup-holders Blackburn in the 1890 Final of the prestigious Lancashire Cup, and an Evertonian FA Cup Finalist in 1893 as a wing-half, Alick had a full and successful playing career which was supposed to be over when he signed on as Fosse's trainer in 1902. Yet injury crises conspired to force him to don his boots again in the above match, and his goal from inside-left pointed the way to a welcome away win that did much to avert the threat of an enforced application for re-election. Alick also turned out in three friendly fixtures to demonstrate his own fitness to his charges, and remained at Filbert Street until 1905.
Apps: 1 Lge.
Goals: 1 Lge.

STIRLING, JAMES

b.
Third Lanark/Oct 1894:FOSSE/
Apr 1895:Burnley.
debut: 27.10.94 v.Newton Heath (A).

Despite his debut being at centre-forward, James was essentially an outside-right, but could never command a regular spot during Fosse's initial Second Division campaign or, indeed, at Burnley (where he managed only two League appearances). He had been signed in a joint deal with Thirds' inside-forward James Milliken, whose own Fosse career was restricted to friendlies and games in the short-lived United Counties League competition, but who at least managed a reasonable Southern League season with Spurs in 1896/7.
Apps: 4 Lge.
Goals: 1 Lge.

STOODLEY, CLAUDE HENRY

b.
Walthamstow Grange/Oct 1912:Glossop/
Aug 1913:FOSSE/May 1914:Merthyr Town/
Nov 1920:Norwich City.
debut: 20.9.13 v.Birmingham (A).

Hardly a prolific scorer during his Fosse season at inside right, Claude must have rather startled himself by belatedly opening his goal account with a hat-trick in the classic 5-5 Cup tie draw with Tottenham. This was very much his only moment of glory, however as Fosse barely kept their heads above the re-election zone.
Apps: 25 Lge; 2 FAC.
Goals: 3 Lge; 3 FAC.

STRAUGHTON, JAMES H.

b. Workington.
Army football/Sept 1912:FOSSE/
Aug 1914:Pontypridd/Leicester Imperial.
debut: 16.11.12
v.Wolverhampton Wanderers (H).

A Cumbrian centre-forward whose football prowess was noted while he was soldiering in the Border Regiment, James turned out to be something of a goal-shy attack leader for Fosse, and was regarded as very much third choice behind Sparrow and Mortimer. Indeed, the whole team failed to score on the five occasions he played during 1913/14. His brother Joe also had a few games for Fosse reserves in 1912/13 before joining Workington Central and dying only months later in an industrial accident.
Apps: 15 Lge.
Goals: 2 Lge.

STRICKLAND, DEREK

b. Stoneyburn, 7.11.1959.
1976:Rangers/Sept 1979:CITY/
May 1981:Heart of Midlothian/
Feb 1983:East Stirlingshire.
debut: 22.9.79 (sub) v.Fulham (H).

A Scottish schoolboy international, and a youth-team forward at Ibrox under Jock Wallace, Derek came to Filbert Street as part of the deal which returned Gregor Stevens north of the border. He had had only two senior games for Rangers, and found his City opportunities limited, but acted as a virtual lucky mascot for the promotion-bound side of 1980, never appearing on a losing side, and contributing the only goal of a crucial win at Notts County. Derek moved to Hearts alongside Pat Byrne, but managed only one substitute appearance for the Tynecastle club's first team.
Apps: 4+3 Lge.
Goals: 2 Lge.

STRINGFELLOW, MICHAEL DAVID

b. Kirkby in Ashfield, 27.1.1943.
Feb 1960:Mansfield Town/Jan 1962:CITY/
cs 1975:Nuneaton Borough.
debut: 20.1.62 v.Everton (A).

To attempt to characterise Mike's fourteen seasons with City is to risk an unfortunately not over-glib analogy with the footballing cliche: 'It's a game of two halves'. For seven years after his £25,000 move from Mansfield the lanky outside-left was one of the most feared attackers in the country, forming a lethal left-wing partnership with Davie Gibson and racking up a healthy goal tally. He was also taking a disproportionate amount of 'stick', though, from defenders otherwise at a loss to curb his pace and strength; and the legacy was a further seven years of courageous struggle and

determination as Mike fought off a succession of near-crippling injuries (and a sometimes sadly unsympathetic crowd) to continue to give his all for City. Mike had developed at Field Mill under Raich Carter, making his League bow at 17 alongside Ken Wagstaffe, and soon impressing Matt Gillies as a likely successor to Gordon Wills. He hit 19 League and Cup goals in his first full season at Leicester, including the looping header past Liverpool's Tommy Lawrence which assured City of a 1963 Wembley appearance, and for five years thereafter his seasonal goal tally never dropped below double figures, while the number of strikes attributable to his crosses was countless. Injury problems really began to bite, however, during the 1968/9 relegation/Cup Final campaign, and a catalogue of operations, comebacks, breakdowns and sheer frustrations ensued. Yet all this time even a semi-fit 'Stringy' was a valuable squad member, and his April 1975 Testimonial game against Wolves was barely adequate recognition of the club's debt to his early excellence and later against-the-odds example. Mike's spell with Nuneaton was brief, and he became a local licensee.
Apps: 292+23 Lge; 26+2 FAC; 26+1 LC.
Goals: 82 Lge; 7 FAC; 8 LC.

MIKE STRINGFELLOW

STUBBS, PHILIP ERIC GORDON

b. Chester, 10.9.1912.
Bolton Wanderers/Sept 1934:Wrexham/
cs 1935:Nottingham Forest/Nov 1936:CITY/
Dec 1945:Chester.
debut: 14.11.36 v.Southampton (H).

Something of a prototype for Mike Stringfellow in terms of stature and style, Eric was also an outside left who had a dramatic impact on City's fortunes on arrival. Again it was a matter of a 'natural' partnership, for where Mike preceded Davie Gibson into the City side by a week, so Eric became Frank Womack's first major signing a week before Jack Bowers joined the club, and the powerful pair set about transforming a mundane Second Division season into a convincing championship win.

Eric held his place for much of the following two top-flight seasons, but never turned out for City again after war had caused the 1939/40 season to be abandoned, guesting instead for Wrexham (with whom he had originally made his League bow) and Chester (for whom he signed on the eve of the transitional 1945/6 season).
Apps: 74 Lge; 4 FAC.
Goals: 14 Lge; 1 FAC.

SUMMERS, JOHN LAWRENCE
b. Manchester, 8.2.1915.
Tunbridge Wells Rangers/Apr 1934:CITY/
May 1935:Derby County/
Oct 1936:Southampton.
debut: 1.9.34 v.Chelsea (A) (1 goal).

A young right-winger who was given two spells during City's 1935 relegation season in which to lay claim to the place of the ageing Hughie Adcock, John then departed to learn more of the tricks of his trade in the shadow of another international, Sammy Crooks, at Derby. Such high-class tutelage at least bore a modicum of fruit at The Dell, where John notched seven League goals in 31 outings. He retired prematurely in 1938 to join the police force.
Apps: 11 Lge.
Goals: 2 Lge.

SVARC, ROBERT LOUIS
b. Leicester, 8.2.1946.
app Oct 1961/pro Mar 1963:CITY/
Dec 1968:Lincoln City/
(Sept 1970-loan-Barrow)/
cs 1972:Boston United/
Dec 1972:Colchester United/
Oct 1975:Blackburn Rovers/
(Sept 1977-loan-Watford).
debut: 23.9.64 v.Peterborough United (H) LC.

A free-scoring reserve striker who initially got a chance to take over the City centre-forward slot from Ken Keyworth, Bobby then had to wait another three seasons for his next few opportunities to impress. A tough forager rather than a target man, he always looked likelier to make the grade at a lower League level, and after he had briefly been part of the Barrow side which failed to get re-elected to the Fourth Division in 1971, he made a fine League comeback at Colchester, with 59 goals in 116 games, assisting the U's to promotion in 1974, and earning himself a further elevation with a move to Second Division Blackburn. Bobby finished his senior career, only four goals short of his League century, after suffering injury in his sole game for Watford.
Apps: 13 Lge; 1 FAC; 4 LC.
Goals: 2 Lge.

SWEENIE, THOMAS THORNTON
b. Paisley, 15.7.1945.
Johnstone Burgh/June 1963:CITY/
(July 1968-trials-Arsenal)/
(Aug 1968-trials-Huddersfield Town)/
Oct 1968:York City/1969:Burton Albion.
debut: 27.11.63 v.Gillingham (H) LC.

A teenage inside-forward of unbounded promise, possessing a firecracker left-foot shot

which drew earnest, if exaggerated, comparisons with Puskas from the football press, Tom tragically had his top-class progress cut short by injury. Matt Gillies was determined to nurture Tom's career slowly after his explosive two-goal League bow at Blackpool (and after Liverpool had been pipped for his signature), but a lengthy stint as a deep-lying attacker seemed assured until a bad tackle at Forest in February 1967 caused severe damage to his knee, which remained weakened thereafter. In the interim Tom had won a League Cup tankard and also put himself in the records as City's first-ever scoring substitute. Released from Filbert Street in June 1968, he was offered a short-term contract by Arsenal but, after testing his fitness with Billy Hodgson's York, sadly gave up the senior game.
Apps: 50+1 Lge; 1 FAC; 4 LC.
Goals: 11 Lge; 1 FAC.

TOM SWEENIE

SWIFT, GEORGE HAROLD
b. St.Georges, Wellington.
St.Georges Swifts/
1885:Wellington Town/
(1886-trials-Stoke)/
Wellington St.Georges/
1888:Crewe Alexandra/
cs 1891:Wolverhampton Wanderers/
cs 1894:Loughborough/Aug 1896:FOSSE/
June 1902:Notts County/cs 1904:Leeds City.
debut: 5.9.96 v.Darwen (H).

A fine left-back who showed early promise in Shropshire football, played in the Football Alliance for Crewe, and stepped up to the top flight with Wolves, George appeared for the latter club in the Cup Final of 1893, then became the only Loughborough player ever to win senior representative honours when playing for the Football League against the Irish League in 1895. He proved an inspirationally consistent captain for Fosse, being ever-present in four of his six seasons, and almost leading them into the First Division in 1899. He took a well-earned benefit from an October 1900 friendly against Wolves, and eventually moved on to Notts County where the promise of the trainer's role awaited his eventual retirement. He then took on the trainer's duties at newly-founded Leeds City, yet had to don playing kit once more in an emergency when Leeds played at Chelsea in March 1906. George became

manager of Chesterfield in 1908, and of Southampton in 1911.
Apps: 186 Lge; 14 FAC.
Goals: 4 Lge; 2 FAC.

TAYLOR, A.
b. Earl Shilton.
Earl Shilton/Jan 1914:FOSSE.
debut: 19.9.14 v.Huddersfield Town (H).

A local left-back who initially had trials with Fosse in January 1914, then vied with Sam Currie for a first-team place during the disastrous final pre-war season. He also had the unfortunate experience of seeing six Derby County goals whizzing past him after he had replaced the injured Herbert Bown between the sticks during that year's Baseball Ground fixture.
Apps: 14 Lge.

TAYLOR, HARRY
b.
Small Heath/cs 1891:FOSSE/
cs 1894:Hinckley Town.
debut: 23.1.1892
v.Long Eaton Rangers (A) ML.

A versatile reserve defender for Fosse in both the first and third Midland League campaigns, Harry was an ever-present in the half-back line in 1892/3.
Apps: 4 FAC; 30 ML.
Goals: 1 ML.

TEARSE, DAVID JAMES
b. Newcastle, 11.8.1951.
North Kenton Boys Club/May 1969:CITY/
Nov 1971:Torquay United/
(Jan 1975-loan-Reading).
debut: 11.10.69 (sub) v.Preston North End (A).

A teenage Geordie striker given an early chance by Frank O'Farrell, David played his first full game for City as an emergency right-back at Ewood Park, and then had a brief run in competition with Ally Brown and Murray Brodie as a candidate for Andy Lochhead's target man role. After two further isolated appearances, he made an early departure when Jimmy Bloomfield started applying the cheque-book to rebuilding his First Division forward line. David scored 23 goals in 77 League games across four seasons at Plainmoor.
Apps: 7+1 Lge; 1+2 FAC; 0+1 LC.
Goals: 1 Lge.

TEWLEY, ALAN BERNARD
b. Leicester, 22.1.1945.
app/pro July 1962:CITY/
(Aug 1964-loan-Rugby Town)/
Nov 1969:Bradford Park Avenue/
Oct 1970:Crewe Alexandra/
cs 1973:Boston United.
debut: 6.5.67 (sub) v.Newcastle United (H).

A patient reserve winger, effective on either flank, Alan picked up some useful goals after his belated City breakthrough, but suffered badly from the shift in tactical thinking that saw the employment of even one orthodox flanker as something of a luxury; for City already had

Len Glover operating on the left and Rodney Fern emerging as a versatile attacker in the No.7 shirt. Alan's sense of a rather cruel fate must have been compounded when Park Avenue dropped out of the bottom of the Fourth Division, but at least he got a decent run of League games at Gresty Road, and was part of the Boston side which fought its way to the Third Round of the Cup and almost embarrassed the mighty Derby, leaving the Baseball Ground with a scoreless draw after Alan's header had hit the post and run along the line.
Apps: 15+3 Lge; 1+1 LC.
Goals: 5 Lge.

ALAN TEWLEY

THOMAS, BARRIE ERNEST
b. Measham, 19.5.1937.
Measham Imperial/July 1954:CITY/
June 1957:Mansfield Town/
Sept 1959:Scunthorpe United/
Jan 1962:Newcastle United/
Nov 1964:Scunthorpe United/
Nov 1966:Barnsley.
debut: 25.12.54 v.Sheffield United (A).

A precocious former pit-boy who made a First Division breakthrough at 17 as deputy for Johnny Morris, became an England Youth international, and signed off the 1954/5 season with a hat-trick, Barrie was clearly jettisoned inadvisedly early by City after his return from National Service, for he went on to build a substantial striking reputation until injury curtailed his career in 1968. There were few frills to his game, but a brave, direct style brought him a phenomenal haul of League goals, and he was once called up for an England training squad while at Newcastle. He was first noticed claiming 48 goals from 72 games with the Stags, then grabbing 67 in 88 games for Second Division Scunthorpe. A fee of over £40,000 took him to Tyneside (48 goals in 73 apps), and half that amount constituted Scunthorpe's transfer record when he returned there. A nagging knee problem brought his exploits to a halt at Oakwell with a career League aggregate of 210 goals from 335 games, and Barnsley met

Newcastle in a Testimonial for Barrie in November 1968, by which time he was back at Measham SW, in the Leicestershire Senior League, as manager.
Apps: 7 Lge.
Goals: 3 Lge.

THOMPSON, R. ARTHUR
b.
debut: 26.11.92 v.Grantham Rovers (H) ML.

An amateur to the core, this right-back represented Fosse over several seasons, captaining the reserve team (Fosse Rovers, as they were for some time known) and regularly turning out in the more prestigious friendly games, especially if the opposition themselves were amateurs. He also played for Leicestershire in inter-county competition. (Fosse signed another full-back named Arthur Thompson from Castle Donington in April 1899, but we are nonetheless fairly confident that it was this veteran who took his last senior bow in the game against Small Heath that month).
Apps: 4 Lge; 1 ML.

THOMPSON, ROBERT
b. Bells Close, Newcastle, 1890.
d. Liverpool, 1958.
1909:Scotswood/May 1911:FOSSE/
Apr 1913:Everton/cs 1921:Millwall/
cs 1922:Tranmere Rovers.
debut: 16.9.11 v.Nottingham Forest (A).

A Geordie full-back who vied with both Tommy Clay and Sam Currie for a first-team berth during his two Leicester seasons, Bob was snapped up by Everton in a joint transfer deal with winger George Harrison, and went on to serve at Goodison throughout the WW1 period, making 83 League appearances on either side of the conflict, and winning a First Division championship medal in 1915.
Apps: 27 Lge; 1 FAC.

THOMSON, DAVID L.
b. Bothkennar, 2.2.1938.
Bo'ness United/cs 1959:Dunfermline Athletic/
Aug 1961:CITY/cs 1963:Queen of the South.
debut: 30.4.62
v.Tottenham Hotspur (H) (1 goal).

The hero of Dunfermline's 1961 Scottish Cup win - as an unexpected selection for the replay against Celtic, he scored the first goal with a diving header - centre-forward David was snapped up by Matt Gillies as a possible replacement for Ken Leek, but in two seasons managed only the one senior outing (and that at inside-left) while the City No.9 shirt was being swapped around with some abandon.
Apps: 1 Lge.
Goals: 1 Lge.

THOMSON, WILLIAM
b. Glasgow.
Clyde/Sept 1914:FOSSE/1915:Arthurlie/
cs 1919:CITY/Oct 1924:Bristol Rovers.
debut: 12.9.14 v.Grimsby Town (A).

By the time he left for Eastville, Billy was the last of the pre-war Fossils still to be active for

the reconstructed City. Having originally signed from Shawfield as a tough wing-half, and suffered Fosse's plunge to the nadir of their fortunes, he returned from Scotland for City's reinvigorated assault on the Second Division, and became a strong defensive anchor for Peter Hodge's predominantly attack-minded team-building efforts, partnering Jim Harrold and Mick O'Brien in succession until displaced by John Bamber.
Apps: 197 Lge; 12 FAC.
Goals: 3 Lge.

THORNTON, WILLIAM
b. Birmingham.
Bathurst Works/May 1919:CITY.
debut: 30.8.19
v.Wolverhampton Wanderers (H)

Signed from a Birmingham factory team in time for City's first match under their new title, William was an inside right who failed to satisfy Peter Hodge's rigorous standards, and moved on after one season.
Apps: 11 Lge.
Goals: 2 Lge.

THORPE, HAROLD CHEETHAM
b New Whittington, Chesterfield, 1880.
d. New Whittington, 16.9.1908.
1900:Chesterfield/
May 1903:Woolwich Arsenal/cs 1904:Fulham/
Aug 1907:FOSSE.
debut: 7.9.07 v.Leeds City (H).

A left-back of some skill and power, Harry had built up a solid body of top-class experience before joining Fosse, playing Second Division football for his home-town club, helping Arsenal gain promotion from that sphere in 1904, and assisting Fulham to two Southern League championships in 1906 and 1907. His defensive capabilities were a major boost to Fosse's successful promotion effort, but Harry sadly failed to finish the season, having contracted a debilitating strain of influenza after a game at Glossop in March 1908. Tragically, he never recovered, and died at his family home within months. Several Fosse players acted as pall bearers at his funeral.
Apps: 26 Lge; 2 FAC.

THORPE, JOHN
b. Skegby, Mansfield.
Mansfield Mechanics/May 1911:FOSSE.
debut: 21.10.11 v.Huddersfield Town (H).

A young right-half who failed to make the transition from Notts & Derbyshire League football to the demands of Second Division fare.
Apps: 2 Lge.

THRAVES, JAMES
b.
1890:Notts County/cs 1892:FOSSE/
Sept 1897:Long Eaton Rangers.
debut: 17.9.92 v.Mansfield Town (A) ML.

Notts County's FA Cup Final goalkeeper in 1891 despite having only two previous League games to his credit, Jimmy even ended his stint with the Magpies having played in more Cup

matches than League! He then got off to a strange start with Fosse, missing a train connection and turning up 35 minutes late for his Midland League debut at Mansfield, but rather compensated by being an ever-present between the sticks for the next four and a half seasons. A measure of his ability as much as his consistency was that his frustrated understudy during the first League season, T.Chappell, was good enough to win himself an eventual move to Manchester City; while the man in his shadow during 1895/6, Strachan, even took to playing the odd game in the half-back line to try to win a first-team breakthrough. Goalkeeping in those days was very much an art of first-time clearances, with any 'keeper foolish enough to hold onto the ball liable to rough handling, but Jimmy was an early master. For a couple of years he also pursued a unique parallel career as Fosse groundsman. He benefited from a friendly against Luton in September 1896, and played his last competitive Fosse game in the 1897 Burford Cup Final victory over Notts County.
Apps: 80 Lge; 24 FAC; 44 ML.

FRED THRELFALL

THRELFALL, FREDERICK
b. Preston, 1879.
June 1898:Manchester City/cs 1905:Fulham/
July 1909:FOSSE.
debut: 1.9.09
v.Wolverhampton Wanderers (H) (1 goal).

A deft, speedy winger whose Manchester City mentor was the great Billy Meredith, Fred was one of the few 'innocents' on the Hyde Road payroll when the FA uncovered a mesh of financial irregularities there and slapped massive fines and suspensions on a majority of the players and management, almost causing the club to fold. His move to Craven Cottage brought him immediate success, as Fulham raced to the Southern League championship in 1906 and 1907, and won election to the League. Fred played in the Professionals v.Amateurs international trial (alongside Arthur Collins) in 1906, and was regarded a prize capture by Fosse as they attempted to bounce straight back

into Division One. He turned in some scintillating displays on either flank, and off the field was a member of the management committee of the Players' Union. He later became trainer to the Irish team Cliftonville.
Apps: 50 Lge; 6 FAC.
Goals: 6 Lge; 4 FAC.

TIMSON, DAVID Y.
b. Leicester, 24.8.1947.
app Dec 1962/pro Sept 1964:CITY/
Aug 1967:Newport County.
debut: 11.4.64 v.Blackpool (H).

Until fellow goalkeeper Peter Shilton broke his record, David was the youngest City debutant, having made a single stand-in appearance at the age of sixteen when Gordon Banks was on England duty and regular reserve George Heyes was injured. Ironically, David was not to don the first-team green jersey again until Shilton had become the established No.1; playing in the final two games of 1966/7 while Shilton was on an England Youth tour. He then managed 23 games at Somerton Park before departing the senior game.
Apps: 3 Lge.

TOMLIN, DAVID
b. Nuneaton, 9.2.1953.
app Aug 1970/pro Oct 1971:CITY/
Apr 1977:Torquay United/Aug 1978:Aldershot/
cs 1981:Andover/Godalming.
debut: 16.10.71 v.Huddersfield Town (H).

A young winger who persistently fringed Jimmy Bloomfield's squads of the early 70's, and regularly warmed the sub's bench, David is chiefly remembered for one inspired performance in his first season, when he ran England full-back Terry Cooper ragged in a home game against Leeds. It was the sort of form David could not maintain, however, and his role became that of occasional stand-in for Len Glover. He managed 38 games at Torquay and 30 at Aldershot, scoring twice for each club.
Apps: 19+7 Lge; 1+2 FAC; 1 LC.
Goals: 2 Lge.

MAURICE TOMPKIN

TOMPKIN, MAURICE
b. Countesthorpe, 17.2.1919.
d. Leicester, 27.9.1956
Mar 1938:CITY/Dec 1945:Bury/
Sept 1946:Huddersfield Town/
1947:Kettering Town.
debut: 7.5.38 v.Birmingham (H).

The son of former City winger Percy, and an outside-right himself, Maurice made a pre-war teenage debut, but played no more senior football until appearing in 20 games for Bury during the transitional 1945/6 season, and going on to make ten First Division starts at Huddersfield. Maurice was always happier as a cricketer, though; starring as a prolific, stylish batsman for Leicestershire from 1938 to the time of his tragically early death, and amassing 29 centuries amongst his 18,590 runs.
Apps: 1 Lge.

TOMPKIN, PERCY LORD
b. Salford, 28.1.1894.
d. Countesthorpe, 25.2.1948.
Countesthorpe/Leicester Imperial/
(Apr 1913-trials-FOSSE)/
Sutton Junction/Nuneaton Town/Army football/
cs 1919:Huddersfield Town/June 1920:CITY/
cs 1925:Nuneaton Town.
debut: 2.9.20 v.Bury (H) (1 goal).

The pacy, left-sided, senior member of the Tompkin duo, Percy rejoiced in the non-derogatory nickname of 'Fairy', and battled for four seasons with Alex Trotter for the City's outside-left spot, with honours roughly even between them. He had previously played but a single League game for the powerful Terriers side which won promotion and reached the Cup Final in the same season.
Apps: 87 Lge; 3 FAC.
Goals: 4 Lge.

TOWERS, WILLIAM HARRY
b. Leicester, 13.7.1920.
am Aug 1944/pro Jan 1945:CITY/
Oct 1946:Torquay United/Sept 1956:Minehead.
debut: 5.1.46 v.Chelsea (A) FAC.

A local left-half who had played a handful of Regional League games for City in 1940/1, a few years prior to signing, Bill eventually totalled 44 wartime appearances and scored 2 goals. He briefly shared in the return to Second Division football, and was then allowed to join former City trainer/coach Jack Butler, by now Torquay manager, at Plainmoor. He stayed with Torquay for 10 years, making 274 League appearances, and prompting City to visit Devon for his 1952 benefit match.
Apps: 4 Lge; 2 FAC.

TRAINER, HARRY
b. Wrexham, 1872.
d. Wrexham, 1924.
Wrexham Victoria/Westminster Rovers/
cs 1894:Wrexham/
(1894-trials-West Bromwich Albion)/
cs 1895:FOSSE/cs 1897:Sheppey United/
cs 1899:not known/Feb 1900:Wrexham.
debut: 7.9.95 v.Burton Swifts (H).

International centre-forward Harry first cropped

up in the Fosse annals in November 1894, when the club received an FA censure for illegally approaching and registering him. But they got their man eventually, after he had led Wales in all three home internationals of March 1895 (scoring twice against Ireland), and had picked up his second successive Welsh Cup consolation medal. Harry nonetheless proved an inconsistent marksman in the Second Division, and a nap hand of goals in an 8-0 demolition of Rotherham Town provided precisely half his first seasonal League tally. Unable thereafter to command a regular attacking role, he moved on for a couple of seasons to Sheppey, then enjoying an elevated status in the Southern League's top echelon, and bowed out of the game when 'knee failure' ended his second Wrexham stint. He was a cousin of the oft-capped Welsh 'keeper Jim Trainer.
Apps: 31 Lge; 4 FAC.
Goals: 12 Lge; 4 FAC.

TRAVERS, JAMES EDWARD (GEORGE)
b. Birmingham, 1888.
d. Smethwick, 31.8.1946.
Bilston United/cs 1907:Birmingham/
Dec 1908:Aston Villa/
cs 1909:Queens Park Rangers/
Aug 1910:FOSSE/Jan 1911:Barnsley/
Feb 1914:Manchester United/
cs 1919:Swindon Town/June 1920:Millwall/
Oct 1920:Norwich City/June 1921:Gillingham/
1923:Nuneaton Town/
Nov 1928:Cradley Heath/1929:Bilston United.
debut: 3.9.10
v.Bolton Wanderers (H) (2 goals).

A merry wanderer of an inside-forward, George was best known before his arrival in Leicester for having scored a hat-trick on his Villa debut. He had claimed seven goals in 34 Southern League matches for QPR, and was showing only occasional signs of adding significantly to Fosse's firepower when he was exchanged for goalkeeper Fred Mearns. He appeared in Barnsley's victorious 1912 Cup Final team, played 21 pre-war First Division games for United, and returned from Army service to resume his country-wide meanderings. He was in Millwall's first-ever League line-up, and in the same season scored the goal which gave Norwich their belated first-ever League win.
Apps: 12 Lge.
Goals: 5 Lge.

TROTTER, ALEXANDER E.
b. Jarrow.
Ashington/cs 1920:CITY/
May 1924:South Shields/May 1927:Port Vale.
debut: 2.9.20 v.Bury (H) (1 goal).

Essentially an outside-left, Sandy made his City bow in the centre-forward berth after stepping up from North Eastern League football, and managed quite a few more games as a makeshift leader while attempting to shrug off Percy Tompkin's challenge for the flank position. He exhibited flair and dash in City's attempts to rise from the Second Division, but by the time they achieved that feat he was in the middle of a three-season spell with South

Shields, which ended with relegation to the Third Division (North) and presaged that club's later lock, stock and barrel uprooting to Gateshead. (Some sources claim that Sandy had additionally played in WW1 football with both Rangers and Dumbarton).
Apps: 96 Lge; 4 FAC.
Goals: 10 Lge; 1 FAC.

TROUGHEAR, WILLIAM B.
b. Workington, 1885.
Workington/May 1909:Sunderland/
May 1914:FOSSE.
debut: 2.9.14 v.Lincoln City (H).

Right-back Billy made exactly a century of League appearances for Sunderland, but only the final six of them had been in the year of their 1912/13 First Division title win. An England trialist in 1910/11 (Whites v. Stripes), he was approaching the veteran stage when he brought his dour defensive qualities to Leicester, and was no better equipped than his team-mates to stem the tide of humiliating results which left Fosse clutching at the re-election straw before the wartime abandonment of the League.
Apps: 15 Lge; 1 FAC.

TRUEMAN, ALBERT HARRY
b. Leicester, 1882.
am Aug 1899:FOSSE/Grasmere Swifts/
Hinckley Town/Coalville Town/
Aug 1905:FOSSE/cs 1908:Southampton/
Mar 1911:Sheffield United/cs 1913:Darlington.
debut: 2.9.05 v.Clapton Orient (H).

Inexplicably known to all and sundry throughout his career as 'Nigger', this local left-half was on Fosse's books from an early age, represented the county at juvenile level, and faced Notts County in a benefit friendly at Christmas 1900, but also played for several local sides before settling to a regular challenging role at Filbert Street. He wrestled for three seasons with Bob Pollock for a first-team place, and also patiently captained the reserves as Fosse headed for promotion. He flourished with Southampton, though, winning representative honours for the Southern League and scoring the winning goal for that combination when they beat the Football League in November 1910 at White Hart Lane, on the way to a clean sweep of that season's Inter-League tournament. After further travels, he made a nostalgic, if reluctant, return to Filbert Street action in September 1916, when persuaded from the stands to make up the numbers in a wartime game against Grimsby Town.
Apps: 43 Lge; 1 FAC.
Goals: 2 Lge.

TURNER, PHILIP
b. Sheffield, 12.2.1962.
pro Feb 1980:Lincoln City/
Aug 1986:Grimsby Town/Feb 1988:CITY/
Mar 1989:Notts County.
debut: 19.3.1988 (sub) v.Blackburn Rovers (A).

Arriving in the part-exchange deal that took Kevin Jobling to Blundell Park, and departing in the two-way transaction that brought Gary

Mills to Leicester, Phil also found in the interim his tactical role in David Pleat's Second Division side being swapped around on a fairly regular basis. Stints at full-back, in midfield and as an auxiliary winger hardly allowed him to settle, but his neat skills on the ball were unfortunately supplemented neither by exceptional pace nor a great deal of penetration - though a magnificent 30-yard strike against Blackburn, bringing him his first City goal, will live long in the memory. Phil had totted up 242 League appearances for Lincoln, and built a fine playmaking reputation in his season-and-a-half at Grimsby.
Apps: 18+6 Lge; 1 FAC; 1+1 LC.
Goals: 2 Lge.

TURNER, RICHARD WILLIAM
b. Leicester.
Leicester Imperial/Feb 1906:FOSSE/
Aug 1910:Portsmouth/Aug 1911:Leyton.
debut: 24.3.06 v.Bradford City (H).

Despite making an earlier first-team break-through than his brother, inside-left Billy then had to spend a rather longer apprenticeship in Fosse's reserves, and barely got a game until Bob moved on. Indeed, the only occasion on which the pair turned out together (after their joint introduction in an April 1905 friendly against Forest) was the game at Chesterfield in the promotion season. Billy later had a none-too-successful spell in Southern League football, making 34 appearances in a relegated Pompey side (6 goals) after a £25 move, and starting only twice (scoring once) for Leyton.
Apps: 14 Lge.
Goals: 3 Lge.

TURNER, ROBERT FREWIN
b. Leicester, 15.7.1885.
d. Darlington, 15.2.1959.
Leicester Imperial/Mar 1905:FOSSE/
Apr 1909:Everton/
July 1911:Preston North End/
cs 1912:Darlington/June 1914:Coventry City.
debut: 22.9.06 v.Barnsley (H).

The younger and more successful of the Turner brothers, Bob - or 'Leggy' as he was usually known - also led the more colourful career. Not only was he a speedy outside-left with Fosse, good enough to take over from Frank Middleton halfway through the 1908 promotion season and hold his place in the top flight, but he also emulated his father Frew as a cricketing all-rounder for Leicestershire (1909-11). His transfer to Everton, when Fosse's relegation fate was already settled, was a truly controversial affair, with Bob's new club reporting him to the FA for demanding an illicit £100 signing-on fee, and the player finding himself suddenly somewhat worse off after a £50 fine. Undaunted, however, he made a scoring Goodison debut in the Liverpool derby and set about making final preparations for his impending marriage - the notoriously celebrated affair attended by most of the Fosse team on the eve of their 0-12 defeat at Nottingham Forest. As if Bob had not wrought enough havoc for one month, he then assisted Everton to a 4-2 win over a rather more sober Fosse only three days

later. His subsequent efforts for a relegated Preston side and for North Eastern League champions Darlington inevitably seem mundane by comparison!
Apps: 56 Lge; 3 FAC.
Goals: 7 Lge; 1 FAC.

MARK VENUS

VENUS, MARK
b. Hartlepool, 6.4.1967.
cs 1984:Hartlepool United/Aug 1985:CITY/ Mar 1988:Wolverhampton Wanderers.
debut: 31.3.86 v.Aston Villa (A).

Recruited on a YTS scheme by his home-town club after he had spurned approaches by Barnsley and Coventry, left-back Mark made four League appearances as a non-contract player, and came to Leicester as a free agent when United wanted him to continue on that basis. Reserve-team 'Player of the Year' by the end of his first season, Mark had also made a single appearance in Simon Morgan's stead prior to finding himself the regular senior No.3 from the start of 1986/7. Though he understandably betrayed occasional defensive naivete in City's First Division struggles, he also demonstrated commendable accuracy with his crosses from advanced positions, and laid on several of the goals which lifted the club to an unaccustomed early mid-table slot. Thereafter, suffering as something of a regular scapegoat for a frustrated crowd, Mark nonetheless stuck doggedly to his defensive tasks, and his single goal for City was a memorable last-minute volley that won the game against Swindon in 1987/8. David Pleat allowed Mark to move on for £40,000 to Fourth Division leaders Wolves for their championship run-in, and he was a Third Division medallist a year later, too.
Apps: 58+3 Lge; 2 FAC; 3 LC; 2+1 FMC.
Goals: 1 Lge.

VICKERSTAFFE, ERNEST B.
b. Hanley.
Cheltenham Town/Eastville Athletic/ (trials-Bristol City)/Leicester Old Boys/ Dec 1902:FOSSE/1904:Leicester Old Boys/ cs 1907:Leicester Nomads/ cs 1909:Hinckley United.
debut: 27.2.04 v.Burslem Port Vale (A).

A well respected amateur full-back, raised in Leicester, and then showing a belated homing instinct after starting his football career in the West, Ernest suffered the cruellest of luck on his senior debut, breaking his leg in two places. Fortunately he eventually recovered ('guesting' for Fosse in an April 1906 friendly against Notts County), and went on to become captain of the all-amateur Leicester Nomads in their inaugural season.
Apps: 1 Lge.

VILLIERS, HENRY G.
b. Bedford.
Bedford Town/Army/cs 1919:Rugby Town/ July 1920:CITY/Hinckley United.
debut: 28.8.20 v.Clapton Orient (A).

A wing-half in whom high hopes were invested at the start of 1920/1, Henry failed to bridge the considerable gulf between the Birmingham Combination and the Second Division, and was released after two seasons of understudying Teddy King and Billy Thomson, having made considerably less impact than his former Rugby team-mates, the Roxburghs.
Apps: 5 Lge.

VINCETT, JOHN HERBERT
b. Hastings, 24.5.1883.
d. Lambeth, 28.12.1953.
Hastings & St.Leonards/ Aug 1907:Grimsby Town/Aug 1908:FOSSE/ Jan 1909:Barnsley/cs 1909:not known/ Dec 1910:Tottenham Hotspur.
debut: 12.12.08 v.Manchester United (A).

Noted for his powerful, lengthy kicking, John was a tall, weighty full-back who had been a regular in his Mariners season, but his essentially unsophisticated defensive style was deemed not to be up to the First Division mark after his £100 transfer, and he was allowed to move on within a month of his sole senior game. For twelve summers from 1907 he was a professional medium-pace bowler with Sussex, and also turned out twice for Surrey in 1921.
Apps: 1 Lge.

WADDLE, ALAN
b. Wallsend, 9.6.1954.
Nov 1971:Halifax Town/July 1973:Liverpool/ Sept 1977:CITY/May 1978:Swansea City/ Dec 1980:Newport County/ Aug 1982:Mansfield Town/ cs 1983:Hartlepool United/ Oct 1983:Peterborough United/ Jan 1985:Hartlepool United/ Mar 1985:Swansea City.
debut: 24.9.77 v.Nottingham Forest (H).

A tall striker who had only scored 4 goals in 40 games when added to the Anfield investment collection for £45,000, Alan failed to make the grade on Merseyside despite scoring the winning goal in his first Goodison derby, and had become accustomed to Central League

football when Frank McLintock asked him to help turn around City's atrocious start to the 1977/8 season. Within a couple of months, though, it was evident that neither Alan's confidence nor mobility were up to the task at hand, and it was only during his first spell at Swansea, under John Toshack, that Alan began to score with any regularity. He assisted the Swans up to the Second Division (on their whirlwind rise from Fourth to First), then cost Newport their all-time record outlay of £80,000. His subsequent wanderings brought mixed fortunes; perhaps best summed up in Alan's experience in the Mansfield v. Crewe fixture of October 1982, when he scored for both sides and was then sent off! His return to the Vetch sparked a successful fightback against relegation on the part of the Swans, and though Alan was due to join Barry Town for the 1986/7 season, he was instead offered a post running Swansea's commercial operations.
Apps: 11 Lge.
Goals: 1 Lge.

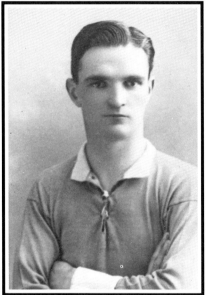

HAROLD WADSWORTH

WADSWORTH, HAROLD
b. Bootle, 1.10.1898.
d. Chesterfield, 2.11.1975.
1918:Liverpool/Jun 1924:CITY/ Apr 1927:Nottingham Forest/ June 1928:Millwall.
debut: 30.8.24 v.Manchester United (A).

Harold joined his older brother, long-serving centre-half Walter, at Anfield during the final season of WW1 football, and soon etched a reputation as a raiding winger, but was then relegated to reserve status for the bulk of both Liverpool championship seasons of 1922 and 1923. The move to Filbert Street, however, brought him immediate recompense (albeit in a minor key), as his ever-present record on City's left wing immeasurably aided the 1925 promotion success, and his continuing consistency as partner to George Carr or Arthur Lochhead contributed sturdily to First Division consolidation. Harold's rather lowly goal ratio

picked up appreciably during his Forest season, and he then helped establish newly-promoted Millwall as a Second Division force over the following four years.
Apps: 98 Lge; 8 FAC.
Goals: 7 Lge.

WAITE, GEORGE H.

b. Bradford, 1.3.1894.
d. Bradford, 1972.
cs 1915:Bradford Park Avenue/
May 1920:Raith Rovers/Jan 1921:Clydebank/
cs 1921:Pontypridd/May 1922:CITY/
Mar 1923:Clapton Orient/
July 1926:Hartlepools United/
cs 1927:York City.
debut: 6.5.22 v.Sheffield Wednesday (A).

Briefly a team-mate of Davie Moyes and the Duncans at Raith, where he scored 11 Scottish League goals in a rapid burst, George was a centre-forward who relied more on speed than brawny bustling. But in attempting to fill Jock Paterson's boots at Leicester, he was always aware of the persistent challenge of Albert Pynegar for City's chief scoring mantle. Curiously, his own marksmanship was set aside at Orient, where he adopted the role of provider over three Second Division seasons.
Apps: 28 Lge; 2 FAC.
Goals: 12 Lge.

WALKER, CHARLES J.

b.
debut (comp): 4.10.1890
v.Burton Wanderers (H) FAC.

One of the Fosse pioneers from the pre-Midland League days, Charlie was the goalkeeper in both the first victorious County Cup campaign and the club's initial FA Cup encounter. He was also the embarrassed centre of the 'lost in the fog' incident, when belatedly discovered still guarding his goal some time after the end of a mist-enshrouded Fosse v. Loughborough friendly. Charlie's three first-class games, all defeats, resulted in his conceding eleven goals.
Apps: 1 FAC; 2 ML.

WALKER, DAVID

b. Walsall, 1884.
d. Oct 1935.
Walsall White Star/Birchfield Villa/
1904:Wolverhampton Wanderers/
cs 1905:Bristol Rovers/
Apr 1907:West Bromwich Albion/
May 1908:FOSSE/June 1911:Bristol Rovers/
1912:Willenhall Swifts/1914:Walsall.
debut: 1.9.08 v.Sheffield Wednesday (H).

A new signing (jointly with Randle for £700) for Fosse's inaugural campaign in the First Division, Dave held one of the three inside-forward positions for almost three seasons at Leicester, without quite replicating the scoring form which had first brought him to the directorate's attention. He had briefly tasted top flight fare at Molineux (2 apps), had scored 25 Southern League goals in 61 games during his first Eastville spell, and claimed 15 strikes in his Second Division season with West Brom;

while the irony of his Fosse scoring record was that his third and least prolific season (when he was also sent off after scoring in a rough encounter with Clapton Orient) nonetheless saw him as the club's top marksman with only seven counters. Dave's later travels took him back via the Southern League to the Birmingham & District League, where in fact Walsall were then playing on par status with Willenhall.
Apps: 73 Lge; 9 FAC.
Goals: 27 Lge; 2 FAC.

DAVE WALKER

WALKER, DAVID CLIVE ALLAN

b. Watford, 24.10.1945.
Nov 1962:CITY/Oct 1966:Northampton Town/
July 1969:Mansfield Town/
cs 1975:Chelmsford City/Gravesend.
debut: 18.4.64 v.Aston Villa (A).

A youthful understudy at right-back to John Sjoberg and Len Chalmers, Clive was a quick-tackling defender who had to follow the rather well-worn trails to both the County Ground and Field Mill to really establish his League name. He turned out in 72 games during the Cobblers' vertiginous plummet to the Fourth Division, but made sufficient impression as an influentially cool strategist to be recalled there for successive spells as coach and manager after a lengthy interim 229-game stint with Mansfield. Clive's solitary League Cup appearance for City earned him a loser's tankard from the second leg of the 1965 Final against Chelsea.
Apps: 17 Lge; 1 LC.

WALKER, DONALD HUNTER

b. Edinburgh, 10.9.1935.
Tranent Juniors/Nov 1955:CITY/
Oct 1959:Middlesbrough/
Sept 1963:Grimsby Town/
(July 1964-trial-Workington).
debut: 19.10.57 v.Nottingham Forest (H).

A nephew of Hearts, Chelsea and Scotland star Tommy Walker, Don helped City re-establish themselves in the First Division with a series of playmaking midfield performances at both wing-half and inside-forward, but his claim to

the No.6 shirt soon crumpled against the vigorous competition of Ken Keyworth and Colin Appleton. His occasionally fastidious style subsequently guaranteed him a first-team place at neither Ayresome nor Blundell Park, but he totalled 24 League games with Boro' and 15 with Grimsby.
Apps: 32 Lge; 2 FAC.
Goals: 1 Lge.

WALKER, ERNEST EDWIN

b. Hinckley, 24.11.1889.
Hinckley United/Oct 1919:CITY/
cs 1924:Hinckley United.
debut: 18.10.19 v.Huddersfield Town (A).

Quite what a second stint of military discipline did to Ernie's sense of attacking adventure is hard to discern, but after this Army reservist was called up again in April 1921, with over thirty games as an inside-forward or outside left already to his credit, he re-emerged as a left-back challenger to Adam Black, and won selection in an equivalent number of games as an out-and-out defender. During his first spell in the uniform of the Leicestershire Regiment, before and during the war, he was better known as a successful rugby player, chosen for numerous representative fifteens.
Apps: 64 Lge; 9 FAC.
Goals: 3 Lge; 2 FAC.

WALKER, JOHN

b. Alexandria, Dumbartonshire.
Vale of Leven/1891:Grimsby Town/
cs 1893:Everton/Oct 1894:Manchester City/
May 1895:FOSSE.
debut: 7.9.95 v.Burton Swifts (H).

A versatile Scottish defender who joined Grimsby during their Football Alliance days and stayed with them into the League, Jack scored on his First Division debut for Everton, but played only two further games for them at centre-half before joining the newly-formed Manchester City (that club being reconstructed from the debris of Ardwick). Moving on again to Leicester, Jack settled as an ever-present pivot in Fosse's second League season, and indeed missed few games over four seasons - the latter two at right-back - until he suffered a broken shin in an April 1899 fixture against Grimsby which ended his career. He was awarded a benefit friendly against Everton in October of that year, which not only raised about £75 but also a storm of protest about Fosse's unpublicised decision to field an under-strength side, by all accounts flattered by only a 1-4 reverse.
Apps: 113 Lge; 12 FAC.
Goals: 1 Lge.

WALKER, JOSEPH NICOL

b. Aberdeen, 29.9.1962.
Elgin City/(1979-loan-Keith)/
(1980-loan-Inverness Caledonian)/
July 1980:CITY/Jan 1983:Motherwell/
Dec 1983:Rangers/(Dec 1986-loan-Falkirk)/
(Dec 1987-loan-Dunfermline Athletic).
debut: 9.3.82 v.Chelsea (A).

Another of Jock Wallace's recruits from the

Highland League, 6ft.3in. goalkeeper Nicky had once toured Holland in the same Caley youth team as Kevin MacDonald, and was soon winning Scottish international honours at that level after his move to Filbert Street. He briefly stepped up for Second Division action after Mark Wallington's record-breaking run of consecutive appearances came to an end through injury, and impressed with his confidence and clean handling after a shaky start at Stamford Bridge. Nicky was then signed twice more by Jock Wallace, developing into an Ibrox regular until displaced by England international Chris Woods.
Apps: 6 Lge.

WALLINGTON, FRANCIS MARK
b. Sleaford, 17.9.1952.
am/pro Oct 1971:Walsall/Mar 1972:CITY/
July 1985:Derby County/
Aug 1988:Lincoln City.
debut: 11.3.72 v.West Ham United (H).

Faced with the initially daunting and thankless task of succeeding Banks and Shilton between the Leicester posts, Mark more than made up for a comparative lack of charismatic flair by dint of a dogged consistency and willingness to work at the raw edges of his game, eventually building a monumental club record for consecutive appearances as testament to his awesome reliability. He was very much a goalkeeping tyro when bought for £30,000 by Jimmy Bloomfield as cover for Shilton, having made only eleven League appearances as a Fellows Park discovery, but having impressed mightily with a spectacular televised perform-ance in a Cup tie at Everton. Indeed, for several seasons he continued to learn his trade while very much in the England 'keeper's shadow, only stepping up for an extended first-team run at the beginning of 1974/5 when Shilton's determination to move was becoming irresistible. It was ironic that Mark should suffer injury only weeks after his predecessor's sale to Stoke, for his return to the fray in the Third Round FA Cup tie with Oxford in January 1975 became the start of a run in which he was never again absent until March 1982: a spell of 294 League games, 22 FA Cup encounters, and 15 League Cup ties (331 senior games in all). During this time he had added two England Under-23 caps to his haul of schools and amateur youth honours, experi-enced two relegation seasons and one Second Division championship, and become one of the select band of goalkeeper-captains in League football; while one of the more remarkable aspects of his unbroken run of appearances was that he had actually been prevented from training for several years in the middle of his career by a skin affliction. Even after a sickening collision with Shrewsbury's Chic Bates had sidelined Mark for the first time in years, he came back to tot up another invalu-able ever-present contribution to City's 1983 promotion season (picking up a deserved Testimonial on the way), to see off the imported challenge of Mark Grew whilst briefly in contract dispute with the club, and finally to be displaced from the City six-yard box only by the youthful promise of Ian

Andrews. Mutterings about the veteran's apparent loss of sharpness - prompted as much by superficial judgements about thinning hair and a widening girth as by genuine signs of creakiness - were still proven somewhat premature, though, as his rearguard experience materially assisted new club Derby to successive promotions from the Third to the First Division in the first two years following his £25,000 transfer. It was hardly apt reward, then, when Mark subsequently found himself once more stuck in reserve behind Peter Shilton at the Baseball Ground. A return to his native county coincided with the Red Imps' return to League football following their one-year exile in the GM Vauxhall Conference.
Apps: 412 Lge; 25 FAC; 23 LC.

MARK WALLINGTON

WALSH, JAMES
b. Glasgow, 3.12.1930.
Bo'ness/1950:Celtic/Nov 1956:CITY/
cs 1964:Rugby Town.
debut: 23.3.57 v.Fulham (H).

A scorer in the Finals of both the 1953 Coronation Cup and the 1955 Scottish Cup, and capped once for Scotland Under-23's, Jimmy was yet never quite assured of his inside-forward place for Celtic at a time when the likes of Fernie, Tully, Mochan and Bobby Collins were also in front-line contention. He became the subject of one of David Halliday's regular cross-border transfer raids, but played only his debut game in the 1957 Second Division championship effort, reserving his substantial striking energies for the next six years of top flight combat, during which he was twice City's top scorer. Jimmy claimed a hat-trick in the club's first-ever League Cup tie (indeed, the first registered in that competition), and later that season led his team out at Wembley as skipper, having contributed the breakthrough goal in the drawn-out FA Cup semi-final series against Sheffield United. Another scoring milestone was Jimmy's

opening of City's account in European competition, but his quick-witted, darting elegance was later offset by a diminishing effectiveness in front of goal, and through a combination of problems with injuries and eyesight (Jimmy was one of the first footballers to play regularly in contact lenses), he had lost his place by the time the 1963 Wembley return was achieved. On leaving Rugby, Jimmy moved into the newsagent's business in Leicester in which he is still occupied.
Apps: 176 Lge; 18 FAC; 4 LC; 1 ECWC.
Goals: 79 Lge; 5 FAC; 5 LC; 2 ECWC.

WALSH, STEVEN
b. Fulwood, 3.11.1964.
1982:Wigan Athletic/June 1986:CITY.
debut: 23.8.86 v.Luton Town (H).

A strapping central defender who followed Bryan Hamilton from Wigan as the manager's initial City purchase (£100,000), Steve immediately deposed the unsettled John O'Neill in Leicester's back line, and showed great promise of becoming an aerially dominant stopper, but displayed an occasionally naive impetuosity against First Division forwards which threatened to cost the club dear. His second City season started with his dismissal for an ugly attack on Shrewsbury's David Geddis, but he returned from a lengthy suspension with a much cooler and more mature outlook, and began to show himself additionally as a useful goalscorer. Indeed, Steve took the Supporters Club 'Player of the Year' award in 1988 to index his rehabilitation, but ill-luck with injuries hampered his progress the following term.
Apps: (to 13.5.89): 82+1 Lge;
1 FAC; 10 LC; 3 FMC.
Goals: 9 Lge; 1 LC.

WALTERS, VICTOR
b.
Gravesend/Walthamstow Grange/
Oct 1913:FOSSE.
debut: 20.12.13 v.Huddersfield Town (A).

Fosse manager Bartlett was almost as partial as his later City counterpart Jimmy Bloomfield to players with London or South-East footballing credentials: this amateur left-winger being another of his signings to attempt to make the leap from London League fare to Second Division struggles. In common with such exact or near contemporaries as Russell, Ridley and Legge, though, Victor failed to register with sufficient impact at the higher level.
Apps: 11 Lge.
Goals: 2 Lge.

WARD, PATRICK
b. Dumbarton, 28.12.1926.
Renton Guild/Glasgow Perthshire/
1948:Hibernian/Sept 1955:CITY/
June 1958:Crewe Alexandra/
Sept 1960:Rugby Town.
debut: 22.10.55 v.Fulham (A).

An early purchase by David Halliday as City regrouped for a fresh assault on the Second Division, Pat was a sturdy, fair-haired left-half

whose Easter Road experience had largely been gained in the central defensive berth. Signed for £3,500, he took the City No.6 shirt from Eddie Russell, and for some time thwarted the first-team progress of the teenage Colin Appleton; yet after contributing some fine tight-marking performances to the 1957 promotion success, Pat only got an isolated trio of opportunities to impress at the top level in England. His stay at Gresty Road brought him 31 Fourth Division appearances and one goal.
Apps: 57 Lge; 1 FAC.

PAT WARD

WARNER, REGINALD OWEN
b. Anstey, 1.3.1931.
Anstey Methodists/Apr 1949:CITY/
Mar 1955:Mansfield Town/
cs 1957:Hinckley Athletic.
debut: 8.11.52 v.Swansea Town (A).

An England Youth international centre-forward, Reg became a versatile utility defender as he struggled to fulfil his potential at League level. At wing-half he was used as an occasional deputy for either Johnny King or Jimmy Baldwin, and made a small contribution to the 1954 promotion drive before hitting the well-worn Field Mill trail for a run of 33 League games.
Apps: 7 Lge; 1 FAC.

WARREN, GEORGE
b.
Hinckley Town/Dec 1903:FOSSE/
cs 1904:Gresley Rovers/Nuneaton Town/
1907:Coventry City/
Oct 1911:Stockport County/
1912:Hinckley United.
debut: 12.12.03 v.Glossop (H).

As would the on-loan Peter Eastoe precisely eighty years later, George had the curiously frustrating experience of making his club debut in a match which was abandoned: in this centre-forward's case the disappointment was doubled by the fact that he had already notched a goal in the fog-halted away fixture against

Manchester United in December 1903. He was, however, to hold his line-leading position for most of the rest of the humbling 1903/4 season, despite appearing in a winning side only five times. George picked up the nickname 'Tubby' at Coventry (who he joined in their Birmingham & District League days, and starred for in their early Southern League campaigns), and later made a brief return to League soccer at Edgeley Park. A recent Coventry history asserts that he died during WW1.
Apps: 21 Lge.
Goals: 7 Lge.

WATERALL, THOMAS
b. Radford, Nottingham, 1884.
d. Nottingham, 8.11.1951.
1904:Radford Institute/1905:Eleanor United/
Apr 1906:Notts County/
June 1908:Bradford Park Avenue/
cs 1909:Mansfield Mechanics/
July 1913:FOSSE/July 1914:Watford/
cs 1921:Gillingham/1922:Sittingbourne.
debut: 3.9.13 v.Nottingham Forest (A) (1 goal).

An outside-left who cost Fosse a £10 transfer fee, and kept bouncing back into first-team contention despite manager Bartlett's several attempts to replace him, Tom was one of a trio of brothers to play as top-level forwards, with Ike following him into the Notts County side and later moving to Millwall, and Albert leaving Meadow Lane to build a substantial reputation with Stockport County. Tom himself found his moment of glory in the final pre-war season of Southern League football, assisting Watford to the championship.
Apps: 31 Lge; 2 FAC.
Goals: 6 Lge.

WATERS, JOSEPH J.W.
b. Limerick, 20.9.1953.
app Apr 1969/pro Sept 1970:CITY/
Jan 1976:Grimsby Town.
debut: 9.3.74
v.Queens Park Rangers (A) FAC (2 goals).

Joe's explosive entry into the City annals - joining the 1974 Cup fray as a last-minute replacement for Alan Birchenall, and ensuring the club a semi-final place with two cracking goals before a national television audience - perhaps inevitably overshadowed all his subsequent efforts on Leicester's behalf. The little midfielder, already capped at schools and youth level, earned himself a near-immediate call-up to the full Eire squad for a South American tour, and then showed himself to be an astute and energetic prompter on his sporadic returns to the City first team after Birchenall's recovery. But Jimmy Bloomfield's side was at its most settled when Joe was ready for regular senior football, and the apparent backslide to Blundell Park was in fact a shrewd move. In eight years with Grimsby, Joe established himself as an inspirational skipper, eventually leading his team back into Division Two from the basement depths, and was limited to a mere couple of Eire caps mainly by the competing claims of Johnny Giles and Liam Brady. In 357 League games for the Mariners, he also claimed 65 goals, before moving into a

coaching role in America in the 1984 close season.
Apps: 11+2 Lge; 2 FAC; 1 LC.
Goals: 1 Lge; 2 FAC.

WATKIN, FRANK H.
b.
Leeds City/Newark Castle Rovers/
Oct 1910:FOSSE/Aug 1912:Notts County.
debut: 28.1.11 v.Clapton Orient (H).

A left-wing understudy to Sydney Owen, Frank had no sooner laid claim to the amateur international's flank position than he was himself displaced by a fellow capture from Nottinghamshire junior football, Paul Haig. He played no senior football for either Leeds or the Magpies.
Apps: 4 Lge.
Goals: 1 Lge.

WATKINS, ALFRED ERNEST
b. Llanwnog, 1878.
d. Barking, 7.12.1957.
Oswestry/Oct 1897:FOSSE/
Apr 1899:Aston Villa/
Feb 1901:Grimsby Town/
cs 1901:Millwall/
cs 1906:Southend United.
debut: 5.2.98 v.Darwen (H).

Holding jointly with Dick Jones the record of being the first player to win a full cap while on Fosse's books, Alfred had, by the time of the Welsh international against Scotland on 19th March 1898, played only a single senior game for the club! Indeed, by the time the close season came round, his appearances for club and country evened out at two apiece. At least the inside or outside-left became a Fosse regular in the near-miss promotion effort of 1898/9, showing a useful goal touch, turning down further Welsh honours to help the League cause, and attracting an unrefusable offer from Villa at season's end. With the First Division giants, however, his internationals-to-League-games ratio looked even more disproportionate - Alfred twice representing Wales, but only once turning out for Villa's seniors. He gained the last of his five caps in 1904, playing alongside his brother W.M.Watkins, of Stoke, Villa and Sunderland fame. After leaving the game, Alfred was an assistant station-master, and then a cemetary caretaker. He died in a fire at his home.
Apps: 31 Lge; 4 FAC.
Goals: 12 Lge; 2 FAC.

WATKINS, ALFRED W.
b.
Nelson/May 1904:FOSSE/
Nov 1904:Blackburn Rovers.
debut: 3.9.04 v.Blackpool (A).

Joining Fosse after building a high-scoring reputation in the Lancashire Combination, this inside-right experienced none of the success of his namesake with Fosse, and failed even to make a first-team appearance after his move to Ewood.
Apps: 4 Lge; 1 FAC.
Goals: 2 FAC.

WATSON, NORMAN

b. Chester-le-Street, 21.12.1899.
Chester-le-Street/May 1922:CITY/
June 1932:Notts County/
Aug 1934:Wigan Athletic.
debut: 14.4.23 v.Manchester United (H).

A sturdy half-back who exhibited versatility
and patience in equal measure when sporadically backing up City's early-20's promotion
efforts, Norman was rewarded with a lengthy
run in the pivot's role as soon as Division One
was reached, and thereafter shuttled left and
right across the middle line (with odd excursions to outside-right and full-back) for another
seven top-flight seasons as a semi-regular.
Eventually moving to Meadow Lane as a
veteran, he made only five League starts before
dropping into non-league football.
Apps: 173 Lge; 5 FAC.
Goals: 1 Lge.

WEBB, CHARLES

b. Higham Ferrers, 4.3.1879.
d. Jan 1939.
Higham Ferrers/Rushden/cs 1900:Kettering/
May 1901:FOSSE/cs 1902:Wellingborough/
cs 1903:Kettering/May 1904:Southampton/
July 1905:Dundee/Mar 1908:Manchester City/
June 1909:Airdrieonians.
debut: 7.9.01 v.Woolwich Arsenal (A).

The regular outside-right in Fosse's somewhat
goal-shy attack of 1901/2, Charles exhibited a
marked affinity for playing alongside that other
Northamptonshire-born soccer wanderer,
Herbert Dainty - the pair appearing together for
both Southampton (Southern League) and
Dundee (Scottish League) as well as for Fosse
in the Second Division.
Apps: 32 Lge; 1 FAC.
Goals: 3 Lge.

WEBB, DAVID JAMES

b. East Ham, 9.4.1946.
am:West Ham United/
May 1963:Leyton Orient/
Mar 1966:Southampton/
Feb 1968:Chelsea/
July 1974:Queens Park Rangers/
Sept 1977:CITY/Dec 1978:Derby County/
May 1980:Bournemouth (p/coach; then mgr)/
Feb 1984:Torquay United (p/mgr).
debut: 1.10.77
v.Wolverhampton Wanderers (A).

Best remembered as a chunkily piratical figure
at the heart of Chelsea's defence, whose
occasional forward rampages brought about
such magical moments as the winning goal in
the replayed 1970 FA Cup Final, and whose
try-anything enthusiasm even saw him chosen
as goalkeeper for a League game against
Ipswich in December 1971, Dave started his
lengthy career as a crew-cut full-back at
Brisbane Road and The Dell, and only later
developed into such a swashbuckling stopper.
Dave's first move helped seal Southampton's
1966 promotion to the First Division, but most
of his club honours accrued while he was on the
Stamford Bridge books, including a victor's
medal from the 1971 European Cup Winners'

Cup. A six-figure transfer to Loftus Road saw
him partnering Frank McLintock at the back as
QPR came within a whisker of championship
success, and the pair were reunited at Filbert
Street as manager McLintock attempted to
shore up City's hard-pressed defence with
Dave's combative experience. The disappointment of relegation was part of his lot at both
Leicester and Derby, but Dave was back on the
promotion trail at Bournemouth during his first
stint of management. His final appearances as a
player came at Torquay, some time after his
nominal retirement, and subsequently he also
occupied the managerial chair at Southend.
Apps: 32+1 Lge; 2 FAC.

WEBB, HARRY

b.
Stafford Rangers/Oct 1888:FOSSE.
debut (comp): 4.10.90
v.Burton Wanderers (H) FAC.

Fosse's first professional player, initially
engaged at the princely sum of 2s.6d per week,
Harry was a versatile forward who drew
particular plaudits for his heading prowess, and
remained a loyal leading attacker for the club
until the end of the second Midland League
season.
Apps: 6 FAC; 26 ML.
Goals: 5 FAC; 8 ML.

WEBB, WILLIAM

b. Mexborough, 7.3.1932.
Wath/May 1951:Rochdale/June 1951:CITY/
June 1957:Stockport County/
cs 1963:Hyde United.
debut: 27.8.51 v.Sheffield Wednesday (A).

A teenage first-teamer at Leicester within
months of his surprise £1,250 elevation from
Rochdale (where he played only a single senior
friendly in his brief stay), Bill assumed Ron
Jackson's No.3 shirt for what proved to be the
longest run of appearances in his six-year City
sojourn. National Service soon beckoned, and
Bill represented the Army alongside Derek
Hines, but following his return to full-time
football he could never quite shake the tag of
reliable stand-in. His main asset was pace, and
a couple of his intermittent senior run-outs were
in the outside-left spot, but it was back in
defence that Bill later clocked up 243 League
games for Stockport.
Apps: 47 Lge; 2 FAC.

WEBB, WILLIAM G.

b. Glasgow.
Cambuslang Rangers/Sept 1925:CITY/
cs 1927:St.Johnstone/
May 1930:Bournemouth & Boscombe Athletic/
May 1933:Ramsgate.
debut: 6.2.26 v.Bolton Wanderers (A).

A young outside-left unlucky enough to find
himself third in line for a first-team slot behind
Wadsworth and Bell, Willie had to return to
Scotland for an effective relaunch of his career,
then managed three seasons in the Third
Division (South) at Dean Court after his third
cross-border move, scoring 7 times in 57
League appearances.
Apps: 1 Lge.

WEBSTER, FRANCIS R.

b.
Shepshed Albion/Dec 1908:FOSSE.
debut: 12.12.08 v.Manchester United (A).

A local centre-half who understandably
struggled to make the quickfire transition from
the Leicestershire Senior League to the First
Division when flung into the midst of Fosse's
fateful season of top-flight struggle; briefly
holding the pressurised pivotal role after
England international Bannister and before
Scottish cap Aitken.
Apps: 7 Lge; 3 FAC.

PETER WEIR

WEIR, PETER RUSSELL

b. Johnstone, Renfrewshire, 18.1.1958.
Neilston Juniors/1978:St.Mirren/
May 1981:Aberdeen/Jan 1988:CITY/
Nov 1988:St.Mirren.
debut: 16.1.88 v.Shrewsbury Town (A).

A tall, deceptively shuffling left-flank forward
with notable dead-ball skills and crossing
acumen, Peter won the first four of his six
Scottish caps while dazzling the Love Street
faithful, and was soon involved in a part-
exchange deal which valued him at £330,000
and set a new transfer record between two
Scottish clubs. With the Dons he hit occasionally devastating form and shared in most of the
glories of their 80's renaissance, earning
medals from two Premier Division championship campaigns, three Scottish Cup wins, and
the classic European Cup Winners' Cup Final
triumph over Real Madrid in 1983. Becoming
David Pleat's first signing for Leicester a week
before his 30th birthday, Peter quickly slotted
into a reorganised midfield, linking elegantly
with Gary McAllister and occasionally
delighting those nostalgic for the intricacies of
the touchline dribbling art. Unfortunately,
Peter's family found it difficult to settle in the
South; but his £135,000 homeward move was
profitable recognition of the significance of his
role in City's Second Division revival.
Apps: 26+2 Lge; 1 LC; 1 FMC.
Goals: 2 Lge.

WELLER, KEITH
b. Islington, 11.6.1946.
Jan 1964:Tottenham Hotspur/
June 1967:Millwall/
May 1970:Chelsea/
Sept 1971:CITY/
(Apr 1978-loan-New England Tea Men)/
Feb 1979:New England Tea Men/
July 1980:Fort Lauderdale Strikers.
debut: 2.10.71 v.Crystal Palace (H).

A marvellously talented, sometimes temperamental individualist who lent forceful right-
flank panache to Jimmy Bloomfield's elegant
teams of the early 70's, Keith could usually be
relied upon to deliver a tellingly spectacular
contribution to the most mundane of games.
City fans were treated to regular displays of
both his midfield and striking skills, while
national television audiences also gasped at
some of his exploits: a 'Goal of the Season' at
Luton in the Cup (and a long-range own-goal
on the same ground a year later!), a thunderbolt
volley against Newcastle, and Keith's final City
goal - when he dazzled Norwich defenders with
his white tights - among them. Keith won four
England caps (scoring once with a rare header)
and once represented the Football League while
with City, yet his sole honour at club level
remained his medal from Chelsea's European
Cup Winners' Cup victory of 1971. His
occasional frustrations at Leicester peaked in
the notorious incident when he refused to take
the field for the second half of a League game
against Ipswich in December 1974, and his last
couple of Filbert Street seasons were marred by
knee injuries that sadly cut short his career, but
memories of his cool brilliance predominate.
Keith settled longer than most in Stateside
football, moving into club management, and
more recently coaching Dallas Sidekicks in the
indoor soccer league there.
Apps: 260+2 Lge; 24 FAC; 11 LC.
Goals: 37 Lge; 3 FAC; 3 LC.

KEITH WELLER

WELSH, PETER MARTIN
b. Coatbridge, 19.7.1959.
Caldervale YC/Aug 1976:CITY/
(Apr 1978-loan-Houston Hurricane)/
July 1982:Hibernian/Nov 1983:Falkirk/
Mar 1984:Alloa Athletic/Wigston Town/
Lutterworth Town.
debut: 14.5.77 v.Tottenham Hotspur (A).

'Blooded' as a teenage midfielder in Jimmy
Bloomfield's penultimate game in charge at
City, Peter had to wait patiently for a call-up
from Jock Wallace for further League
experience. A versatile reserve, Peter employed
his strong build best in defensive situations,
filling in at various stages in all the back four
positions, yet could also move forward with
effective purpose, making him a useful choice
for the sub's bench. A late burst of goalscoring
unfortunately failed either to gain City
promotion in 1982 or indeed to win Peter a
renewed contract, and his subsequent experiences in Scottish football were not of the
happiest, comprising only a total of thirty
senior games for his three clubs. More recently,
he has returned to Leicester and still turns out
in local circles.
Apps: 24+17 Lge.
Goals: 4 Lge.

WESLEY, GEORGE THOMAS
b.
(Army football)/Leicester Imperial/
(Jan 1907-trials-FOSSE).
debut: 26.1.07 v.Barnsley (A).

An amateur centre-forward, still attached to the
Army officers' mess at Portsmouth when given
a brief trial by Fosse after starring for the local
Imps.
Apps: 1 Lge.

WEST, ALFRED
b.
Feb 1903:FOSSE.
debut: 25.2.04 v.Bristol City (H).

A stand-in full-back whose individual potential
was somewhat overwhelmed by the collective
malaise of a Fosse side bound for the re-
election zone.
Apps: 3 Lge.

WEST, JAMES
b. Enderby.
Enderby Town/Aug 1908:FOSSE/
Aug 1910:Leyton.
debut: 9.4.09 v.Notts County (A).

A local outside-left who played his initial first-
team game in the floodlit friendly with
Blackburn at Burton in October 1908, and then
took the First Division flank position after the
departure of 'Leggy' Turner. Unable to hold his
place against the challenge of Fred Threlfall,
however, James made less than a handful of
appearances the following season before
reuniting with Jamie Durrant and Tommy
Shanks at Southern League Leyton.
Apps: 10 Lge.
Goals: 2 Lge.

WHITE, ERIC WINSTON
b. Leicester, 26.10.1958.
app July 1975/pro Oct 1976:CITY/
Mar 1979:Hereford United/
Apr 1983:(Hong Kong)/
Sept 1983:Chesterfield/
Oct 1983:Port Vale/
Nov 1983:Stockport County/Dec 1983:Bury/
(Oct 1986-loan-Rochdale)/
Mar 1987:Colchester United/Oct 1988:Burnley.
debut: 19.3.77 v.Stoke City (A).

A speedy orthodox winger whose dozen City
games encompassed selection by three different
managers and gave notice of genuine potential,
Winston exhibited remarkable resilience in
extending his career past several stiff setbacks.
General upheavals at Filbert Street meant he
had few chances to consolidate the promise of a
debut in which he laid on Frank Worthington's
winning goal, though a fine performance at
Anfield shone through the relegation-haunted
gloom of the following season, a year before
Jock Wallace accepted Hereford's £15,000 bid.
Then, after 175 League games at Edgar Street
(21 goals), Winston was freed for a summer of
Far East football, but fixed himself up with a
series of trials on his return; the fourth of which
paid off in the form of a contract offer from
Bury. He was ever-present in the Shakers'
successful 1985 promotion push from the
Fourth Division; later strengthened the
Colchester squad which narrowly failed to
repeat that feat in 1987, when they reached the
play-offs; and was still deemed worth a five-
figure fee when moving on to Turf Moor with
over 400 senior games already under his belt.
Apps: 10+2 Lge.
Goals: 1 Lge.

WHITE, IAN S.
b. Glasgow, 20.12.1935.
Port Glasgow Hibs/St.Anthony's/Petershill/
Apr 1956:Celtic/July 1958:CITY/
June 1962:Southampton/
July 1967:Hillingdon Borough/
June 1968:Portals (p/mgr).
debut: 7.11.59 v.Sheffield Wednesday (H).

Never given a senior break at Parkhead, despite
a fine playing record in Scottish Junior football,
Ian initially found himself similarly stuck in
City's reserve team, albeit the 1959 Combination championship side, as Johnny Newman
held on to the first-team No.4 shirt. Then, even
though he grasped every opportunity to display
his wing-half skills, the unassuming redhead
was unfortunate enough to be vying for his
place with the younger and more flamboyantly
talented Frank McLintock, and it was not really
until he resumed his occasional partnership
with Tony Knapp down at The Dell that Ian
could claim a regular League selection.
Apps: 47 Lge; 3 FAC; 4 ECWC.
Goals: 1 Lge.

WHITEHEAD, HARRY
b. Barlestone, 19.9.1874.
d. Leicester, 14.9.1944.
1896:Loughborough/cs 1897:Hinckley Town/
May 1902:FOSSE/cs 1903:Hinckley Town.
debut: 6.9.02 v.Small Heath (H).

Harry's trio of right-back appearances for Fosse, each in a losing side, were rather emphatically overshadowed by his cricketing record of 380 first-class matches for Leicestershire between 1898 and 1922. His prowess as an opening batsman and medium-pace bowler was recognised by selection for the Players v. Gentlemen fixture at the Oval in 1907, and it was the opinion of County historian E.E.Snow that only Harry's 'light-hearted' and somewhat 'impetuous' approach to the game prevented him gaining higher honours. He scored over 15,000 runs and took over 100 wickets for Leicestershire.
Apps: 3 Lge.

WHITELAW, ANDREW
b. Jamestown, Dumbartonshire, 19.5.1865.
d. Mansfield, 1938.
Vale of Leven/cs 1891:Notts County/
cs 1893:Heanor Town/Aug 1894:FOSSE/
cs 1895:Heanor Town.
debut: 8.9.94 v.Rotherham Town (H).

Twice capped for Scotland while with Vale of Leven, and a Scottish Cup finalist with that team in 1890, Andrew was a rather more mobile exponent of full-back play than many of his hefty peers, and apparently more thoughtful about his distribution. His 42-game League experience with Notts recommended him to the Fosse for their first assault on the Second Division, but afterwards he played out the rest of his career in the Midland League.
Apps: 16 Lge; 5 FAC.

WHITFIELD, NORMAN
b. Prudhoe, Northumberland, 3.4.1896.
d. 1970.
Jarrow Croft/cs 1913:FOSSE/
cs 1920:Hednesford Town/
cs 1922:Chesterfield.
debut: 28.2.14 v.Stockport County (A).

A Geordie inside-forward signed as a 17-year-old, Norman sporadically served Fosse before and during WW1 and City afterwards. He was primarily a schemer, though occasionally pressed into the central attacking role as the club sought desperately for firepower, yet it was not until later, at Saltergate, that he delivered the goods in this respect, with 57 goals over five seasons.
Apps: 24 Lge.
Goals: 6 Lge.

WHITWORTH, STEPHEN
b. Ellistown, 20.3.1952.
app July 1968/pro May 1969:CITY/
Mar 1979:Sunderland/
Oct 1981:Bolton Wanderers/
July 1983:Mansfield Town/cs 1985:Barnet.
debut: 2.9.70 v.Bristol City (H).

An immaculately cool and perceptive right-back, perfectly suited in his adventurous adaptability to a game in which tactical developments meant he was only rarely in direct opposition to an orthodox winger, Steve won his first-team spurs as an early-season stand-in for the injured Peter Rodrigues in Frank O'Farrell's promotion-bound side, and

missed only three games throughout the entire span of Jimmy Bloomfield's subsequent managerial reign. His consistently classy performances (one run of 198 consecutive appearances at the time creating a club record) made international selection look inevitable, and Steve duly won seven full caps to add to six at Under-23 level and complete his English representative set, following numerous schools and youth selections. A temporary loss of form during his Testimonial season preceded Steve's £120,000 move to Roker, but the carrot-haired defender continued to display his pace and tackling ability at League level for another six years, when also finally laying to rest the idiosyncratic jinx that may have earned him one of the most unwanted records in football. For while Steve's close-range goal had won for City the Charity Shield in 1971, and he had also got on the scoresheet for England Under-23's, he had never registered a strike in League or Cup football until converting a penalty for Mansfield against Hereford in March 1985 - in his 570th League game, and nearly 15 years after his debut! The irony here is that it was as an overlapping auxiliary attacker that Steve had first made his name! He was in promoted sides at Leicester and Sunderland, and experienced relegation with both City and Bolton; then, at Barnet, was player-coach in the near-miss attempt to become the first club to gain automatic elevation from the Vauxhall Conference to the Fourth Division.
Apps: 352+1 Lge; 29 FAC; 18 LC.

STEVE WHITWORTH

WIGGINS, JOSEPH ALBERT
b. Wembley, 1911.
Grays-Thurrock/Aug 1927:Brentford/
May 1928:CITY/July 1934:Gillingham/
July 1935:Rochdale/
May 1936:Oldham Athletic/
Feb 1937:Stalybridge Celtic/Apr 1937:Hurst.
debut: 21.3.1931 v.Liverpool (H).

A promising Griffin Park reserve who had scored twice in his four Brentford League games, Joe was recruited at £1,400 as centre-forward cover for Arthur Chandler, but spent a frustrating six years at Filbert Street, finally

converting to the left-back berth in an attempt to claim a first-team place. It was in defence that Gillingham then employed him, while Rochdale got 13 goals out of Joe during his single Spotland season.
Apps: 9 Lge.

WILCOX, HARRY MELBOURNE
b. Hackney, 1878.
d. Plymouth, 21.7.1937.
cs 1898:Small Heath/July 1900:Watford/
cs 1901:Preston North End/
cs 1905:Plymouth Argyle/Aug 1906:FOSSE/
Nov 1907:West Bromwich Albion/
July 1908:Plymouth Argyle.
debut: 1.9.06 v.Burslem Port Vale (A) (1 goal).

Fosse's top scorer in 1906/7, when utilised mainly at centre-forward, Harry had first made his mark as a prolific inside-right with Preston, helping shoot them back into Division One in 1904. He missed out on a further promotion success at Leicester when Fosse and West Brom agreed to exchange attackers, and Fred Shinton arrived as the bargain half of the deal, to score twice as many goals for the elevated Fosse as Harry did for fifth-placed Albion. Harry then made his final move, back to Southern League Plymouth, where he converted into a masterful centre-half and went on to complete a club aggregate of almost 300 games before retirement. He captained the Argyle championship side of 1913, and won representative honours for the Southern League against the Irish League in 1911, playing alongside fellow ex-Fossils Trueman and Moody and scoring the first goal in a 4-0 win.
Apps: 44 Lge; 1 FAC.
Goals: 16 Lge.

WILD, ARTHUR
b.
Feb 1903:FOSSE.
debut: 26.3.03 v.Stockport County (H).

The eighth of nine occupants of the Fosse inside-left berth during 1902/3, and another so-far untraceable one-shot player.
Apps: 1 Lge.

WILKINSON, STEPHEN JOHN
b. Lincoln, 1.9.1968.
app July 1985/pro Sept 1986:CITY/
(Aug 1988-loan-Rochdale)/
(Sept 1988-loan- Crewe Alexandra).
debut: 28.3.87 (sub) v.Manchester City (H).

Working his way through the City ranks as a prolific teenage goalscorer, Steve took encouragement from a brief taste of First Division action, and assumed Mark Bright's burden as chief Central League striker, topping the Reserves' goals chart in 1987/8. That same season he claimed his first League strike with the equaliser in the 4-4 home draw with Crystal Palace, but his next senior joy did not come until he notched two counters during a five-game loan spell with Crewe. Another reserve-team scoring burst (once more giving him leading scorer status) earned Steve a 45 minute run-out at Roker on the final day of 1988/9.
Apps (to 13.5.89): 3+4 Lge; 1 FAC.
Goals: 1 Lge.

WILLIAMS, DARREN

b. Birmingham, 15.12.1968.
app July 1985/pro Dec 1986:CITY.
debut: 4.10.88 v.Hull City (A) (1 goal).

Like Simon Morgan, Paul Reid and Robert
Alleyne, another acquisition by courtesy of
youth coach Dave Richardson's Brummie
scouting network, Darren found himself
surprisingly elevated from his reserve-team
midfield slot for a senior debut on City's left
wing, and slotted home a fine drive to cap the
occasion. Subsequently he has had a few
chances to show that his skills are neat and tidy
rather than flamboyant, and has even been
utilised at full-back in the Central League, but
he remains a fine prospect for the future.
Apps (to 13.5.89): 4+2 Lge; 2 LC.
Goals: 1 Lge.

TOMMY WILLIAMS

WILLIAMS, THOMAS EDWARD

b. Winchburgh, 18.12.1957.
app July 1974/pro Dec 1975:CITY/
July 1986:Birmingham City/
cs 1988:Grimsby Town.
debut: 5.10.77 v.Chelsea (A).

Born in Scotland but raised in Leicester,
Tommy often had to call on his reserves of
native grit to see him through a lengthy City
spell as one of the club's most versatile yet ill-
fated players of recent years. Pitched into the
senior game in the midst of the 1977/8
relegation struggle, and asked to play in central
defence, at full-back and in midfield during his
first few months as a first-teamer, Tommy
responded with boundless enthusiasm and no
little skill, going on to establish himself as a
regular utility player under Jock Wallace, and
eventually settling to the right-back role.
Having experienced a Second Division
championship and a second relegation term,
Tommy was at the heart of City's bid to secure
a promotion/Cup double in 1982 when he
suffered a broken leg during the Villa Park

semi-final against Spurs, and the cost to the
club was inestimable as both targets disappeared in his absence. Worse, however, was to
follow, for after a comeback of only four senior
games, Tommy broke the same leg again in
training, and faced another gruelling period of
recovery. It was characteristic that he bounced
back into First Division football with full-
blooded fervour, and his efforts in the centre-
back role in 1984/5 did much to secure City's
continued top-flight status. Despite Tommy's
move to St.Andrews, he enjoyed a deservedly
profitable Testimonial at Filbert Street in
December 1986, when City Present met a team
of former Leicester stars.
Apps: 236+5 Lge; 18 FAC; 12 LC.
Goals: 10 Lge.

WILLIAMSON, BRIAN WILLIAM

b. Blyth, 6.10.1939.
Seaton Delaval/Oct 1958:Gateshead/
July 1960:Crewe Alexandra/
Dec 1962:Leeds United/
Feb 1966:Nottingham Forest/
(Aug 1967-loan-CITY)/Dec 1968:Fulham.
debut: 30.8.67 v.Sheffield Wednesday (H).

Borrowed by City from Forest after Peter
Shilton had suffered an injury at Old Trafford
and the club were caught without experienced
cover, Brian was an experienced 'keeper who
had nonetheless spent some five years in the
reserve teams of both Leeds and Forest,
understudying Gary Sprake and Peter Grum-
mitt. He did not endear himself to City
supporters with his habit of punching almost
every aerial ball, but otherwise performed
adequately during his short spell between the
Filbert Street sticks, to which he returned the
following May as the Forest goalie past whom
City uncharitably put four. Earlier, Brian had
racked up 55 League games for each of
Gateshead and Crewe; later he would manage
only a dozen for Fulham before retiring to go
into the security business.
Apps: 6 Lge; 1 LC.

WILLIAMSON, WILLIAM M.

b. Longton.
Sept 1905:Stoke/Crewe Alexandra/
May 1910:FOSSE/June 1911:Stoke.
debut: 27.12.10 v.Barnsley (H).

An outside-right who barely got a look-in over
Fred Threlfall's shoulder during his Fosse
season. Billy's father was a director at Stoke.
Apps: 2 Lge.

WILLS, GORDON FRANCIS

b. West Bromwich, 24.4.1934.
am:West Bromwich Albion/
Dec 1951:Wolverhampton Wanderers/
Aug 1953:Notts County/May 1958:CITY/
June 1962:Walsall/cs 1964:Sankeys.
debut: 30.8.58 v.Arsenal (A).

A National Serviceman in the RAF who had
been unable to break through the ranks at
Molineux, Gordon had made his League bow
with the Magpies and notched 47 goals in 154
Second Division games before Matt Gillies
plucked him from a relegated side for £9,000

and installed him on City's top-flight left flank.
The tall winger helped City through the panics
which attended their first few seasons back in
Division One, and contributed a lot to the 1961
Cup run with his willingness to augment the
attacking spearhead as well as maintain
pressure on his full-back. Occasionally injury-
prone, Gordon picked up a severe knock in the
first semi-final tie of 1961, yet insisted on
continuing until the whistle despite the
eventually-realised danger that he would miss
the Final. The advent of Mike Stringfellow
spelled the end of Gordon's days with City, and
the residual toll of his injuries then restricted
him to only two seasons at Fellows Park (35
games; 1 goal).
Apps: 111 Lge; 10 FAC; 3 LC; 4 ECWC.
Goals: 30 Lge; 2 FAC; 1 ECWC.

GORDON WILLS

WILSON, IAN G.

b. Fife, 11.2.1923.
Sept 1946:Forfar Athletic/
Nov 1946:Preston North End/
June 1948:Burnley/Mar 1950:CITY/
Oct 1951:Chesterfield/
May 1953:Rotherham United/
July 1956:Boston United/
1957:Vancouver St.Andrews.
debut: 18.3.50 v.Sheffield United (A).

One of the objects of Norman Bullock's pre-
deadline spending spree of 16th March 1950
(along with Jack Marsh and Peter Small),
£7,000-buy Ian was a calculating outside-left
who had never quite borne out the promise
Preston had discerned during his brief
introduction to the senior game with Forfar. Six
goals in 16 League games had been his lot at
Deepdale, while Ian's Turf Moor memories
focussed more on the way his goals had won
Burnley a last-gasp Central League championship than on his 19 games in their first-team.
Ian was soon deemed below par at Leicester,
too; succumbing to the joint challenge of the
veteran No.11 Charlie Adam and newcomer
Tom Dryburgh. Yet he turned out in 77 League
matches for Chesterfield (19 goals), and
became a great favourite at Millmoor, where he

helped knock City out of the Cup in 1955, and where he contributed four goals to the final League game of that season in a bold attempt to push Rotherham to the double-figure score they needed to gain promotion to Division One on goal average. (In fact they beat Liverpool 6-1 and stayed down). After 108 games and 44 goals for the Millers, and a brief spell with Boston, Ian emigrated to Canada, where he continued playing and coaching into the 60's.
Apps: 12 Lge.
Goals: 2 Lge.

IAN WILSON

WILSON, IAN WILLIAM
b. Aberdeen, 27.3.1958.
jnr:Aberdeen/jnr:Dundee/Elgin City/
Apr 1979:CITY/Sept 1987:Everton.
debut: 11.8.79 v.Rotherham United (H) LC.

Blending constructive and combative play in the middle of the park, Ian caught Jock Wallace's eye in Highland League football, and arrived for a £30,000 fee, which he repaid many times over with his influential prompting and playmaking skills. A key member of both Wallace's and Gordon Milne's promotion sides, Ian impressed most in the latter, adopting an advanced role which saw him coming in late behind Lineker and Smith and claiming a fair tally of eight goals, including the crucial winner at Fulham in April 1983. He fell victim to the recent City habit of selecting midfielders in full-back positions during the next two seasons, but re-emerged as a mature motivator and anchor-man, long forgiven by even his most grudging critics for his unfortunate own-goal contribution to City's 1982 Cup semi-final defeat. Belated but deserved international recognition came Ian's way at the age of 29, when he followed his call-up at 'B' level in April 1987 with two full Scottish caps a month later, but the combined experience of this personal elevation and City's relegation unsettled him, and a transfer became inevitable. Nonetheless, Ian saved one of his finest performances for his final Filbert Street game: scoring once and laying on two more goals against Plymouth on the day before his

£300,000 move to Goodison. With Everton he received an FA Cup runners-up medal as a 1989 Wembley substitute.
Apps: 276+9 Lge; 15 FAC; 18 LC.
Goals: 17 Lge; 1 FAC; 1 LC.

WILSON, W.T.
b.
Alfreton/Aug 1901:FOSSE.
debut: 14.9.01 v.Barnsley (H).

Fosse's reserve goalkeeper for two seasons, understudying Teddy Daw and Archie Ling in succession.
Apps: 5 Lge.

WISE, HAROLD A.
b. London.
Custom House/July 1914:FOSSE/
cs 1915:Croydon Common.
debut: 21.9.14 v.Huddersfield Town (A).

Another Fosse signing of the immediate pre-war days from the London League; an amateur inside-forward whose gentlemanly attitude was somewhat at odds with the club's scrabbling necessity for points at all cost to haul themselves out of the re-election zone.
Apps: 11 Lge.
Goals: 1 Lge.

WOOD, ALEXANDER LOCHIAN
b. Lochgelly, 12.6.1907.
(USA)/Feb 1933:CITY/
May 1936:Nottingham Forest.
debut: 30.3.33 v.Blackpool (H).

A well-travelled full-back, Sandy had won a Scottish schoolboy cap just before his family sailed to try their fortune in the United States. He became a naturalised American, and appeared in a full international for USA v. Uruguay, then had to play for some time on a Home Office permit after signing for City, until he was officially repatriated. For just over three seasons at Filbert Street he vied principally with Dai Jones for the left-back spot, assisting City to their first-ever Cup semi-final in 1934, but was then allowed to move on to Trentside for £750.
Apps: 52 Lge; 5 FAC.

WOOD, CECIL JOHN BURDETT
b. Northampton, 21.11.1875.
d. Leicester, 5.6.1960.
Leicester YMCA/Oct 1896:FOSSE.
debut: 20.3.97 v.Walsall (A) (1 goal).

Yet another Fossil better known for his prowess at the summer game, C.J.B. was a Leicester-shire stalwart between 1896 and 1923, captaining the County in 1914, 1919 and 1920, having also played for London County (opening the batting with W.G.Grace) and, four times, for the Gentlemen v. Players. He carried his bat through an innings on 17 occasions for Leics, including the time he managed the feat in both innings in a 1911 game against Yorkshire. He also, in later life, had a spell as secretary to the club during the Second World War. Next to all this, his amateur football exploits seem rather a sideshow, with his Fosse first-team

appearances being made some three years apart. Yet C.J.B. also scored in the annual Christmas fixture against the powerful Corinthians in 1899, and occasionally deserted his favoured positions of inside-forward or wing-half to assist Fosse reserves in goal.
Apps: 3 Lge.
Goals: 1 Lge.

WOODVINE, ALBERT
b. Kirk Sandall, Yorks.
Nov 1937:CITY.
debut: 5.2.38 v.Brentford (A).

A City junior whose prospects were wrecked by the eruption of WW2, this outside right made a brief comeback in the last two seasons of regional football, but was freed in 1946.
Apps: 1 Lge.

WOODWARD, MAURICE
b. Enderby, 1892.
Enderby Town/Aug 1912:FOSSE/
cs 1914:Southend United/
1920:Wolverhampton Wanderers/
cs 1922:Bristol Rovers.
debut: 28.2.14 v.Stockport County (A).

A young local wing-half who had to move into Southern League football on either side of WW1 to gain substantial experience, and then made a brief return to Second Division fare at Molineux, Maurice was later kept out of the League side at Eastville by ex-City man Walter Currie.
Apps: 2 Lge.

ALAN WOOLLETT

WOOLLETT, ALAN HOWARD
b. Wigston, 4.3.1947.
app Aug 1963/pro Aug 1964:CITY/
July 1978:Northampton Town/
cs 1979:Corby Town.
debut: 22.4.67 (sub) v.Sheffield United (H).

All too often in his early days the scapegoat of an impatient City crowd, Alan was a tenacious central defender and a resilient character, belying his almost diffident appearance with a steely determination both in tackling opponents

and in building a more amicable rapport with his vociferous critics. A single off-colour game, albeit in a vital Cup-tie with Everton, set the crowd on Alan's back (and some even went so far as to blame him for Manchester City's goal in the 1969 Cup Final, when he stood in for injury victim John Sjoberg), yet subsequently there were countless occasions when the central defender earned much more than grudging cheers for his sterling back-line performances. Over the course of several seasons Alan looked as if he would have to settle for becoming merely a fringe utility member of the first-team squad, but each time he bounced back to reclaim a senior berth, and he was probably at his peak almost ten years after his debut, when regularly partnering Jeff Blockley during 1975/6. The loyal clubman took a deserved Testimonial from a friendly against Chelsea in May 1977, and eventually closed his career with a season at Northampton, in the familiar company of coach Clive Walker and on-loan Paul Matthews. Alan is now a prison officer.
Apps: 213+15 Lge; 15 FAC; 17 LC.

WOOLLISCROFT, ARTHUR

b. Salford, 17.2.1904.
d. 1977.
Manchester Docks/
Sept 1926:Manchester City/
1928:Caernarvon Athletic/Mar 1929:CITY/
Jan 1930:Watford/Sept 1933:Newport County.
debut: 2.11.29 v.Sheffield Wednesday (A).

A junior at Maine Road who made no first-team breakthrough, Arthur was simultaneously employed as a hand on cargo boats on the Manchester Ship Canal, then moved into the Welsh National League with his former manager D.G.Ashworth, to play alongside former City reserve Chris Hackett. After one season City paid £400 for Arthur's inside-forward services, but he only got a single chance to stand in for Ernie Hine before being offloaded. He netted 14 League goals for Watford, but failed to score in 15 appearances for Newport. (His surname was generally spelt with a single 'L' during his playing career, but appears as above in birth and death registrations).
Apps: 1 Lge.

WOOLRIDGE, JOHN

b.
Hanley Swifts/May 1900:FOSSE.
debut: 8.9.1900 v.Small Heath (A).

A winger from the Potteries given a brief run-out on the Fosse flanks and soon jettisoned, without appearing before the home crowd.
Apps: 3 Lge.

WORTHINGTON, FRANK STEWART

b. Halifax, 23.11.1948.
app/pro Nov 1966:Huddersfield Town/
Aug 1972:CITY/Sept 1977:Bolton Wanderers/
(May 1979-loan-Philadelphia Fury)/
Nov 1979:Birmingham City/
(Apr 1981-loan-Tampa Bay Rowdies)/
Mar 1982:Leeds United/Dec 1982:Sunderland/
June 1983:Southampton/
May 1984:Brighton & Hove Albion/

July 1985:Tranmere Rovers (p/mgr)/
Feb 1987:Preston North End/
Nov 1987:Stockport County/
Apr 1988:Cape Town Spurs/Oct 1988:Chorley/
Dec 1988:Stalybridge Celtic/
Feb 1989:Galway United.
debut: 23.8.72
v.Manchester United (A) (1 goal).

FRANK WORTHINGTON

At a time when the concepts of 'personality' and 'charisma' first underwent their continuing devaluation in the hands of the 'build-'em-up; shoot-'em-down' media, and when sports commentators in particular seemed desperate to assign 'character' status to random workhorses, Frank remained an original: mainly because his outsize image was always harnessed to an outsize talent. Off-field flamboyance ever had its footballing concomitant as Frank's consistent practise of the attacking arts graced the League sphere for over two decades, and one has to reach for a paradoxical construct to try to sum up his striker's impact for City and his numerous other clubs: something like 'casually lethal' might do the trick. The elegant thrust, alternately subtle and spectacular, was an integral part of his repertoire - along with the incisive flick, the arrogant ball control and the deceptively lazy stride - from the time he helped Huddersfield into the First Division in 1970. City made an early move for 'Wortho' as the Terriers began to slide, but an England Under-23 tour intervened, pushing up the likely fee and alerting Liverpool to Frank's quality. A failed medical test quashed Anfield interest, though, and Jimmy Bloomfield jumped at the second chance, watching with glee as his six-figure investment accrued compound interest over five seasons of entertaining 'total football' (or thereabouts) from City. Frank was a popular choice for the national side, winning eight England caps (2 goals) while at his most prolific with City, yet his best single season as a scorer came at Burnden, after Frank McLintock had allowed him to slip away, when

he headed the 1979 First Division list with 24. His St.Andrews debut came against City, and then in the 80's Frank's wanderings began in earnest, with his disdain for the predictable spicing the rather bland tactical recipes of a host of aspiring clubs, and the personal 200-goal landmark being easily surpassed. He briefly shouldered managerial responsibility, too, at Prenton Park until balance-sheet politics edged him onwards into Preston's 1987 promotion run-in, and Frank left Stockport for South Africa with the record of having scored League goals in each of 21 successive seasons. Brothers Dave and Bob had lengthy League careers, too; each launching off from Halifax as hefty full backs.
Apps: 209+1 Lge; 18 FAC; 10+1 LC.
Goals: 72 Lge; 4 FAC; 2 LC.

WORTHINGTON, FRED

b. Manchester, 6.1.1924.
July 1947:Bury/Mar 1951:CITY/
July 1955:Exeter City/
July 1956:Oldham Athletic/
cs 1957:Chorley (p/coach)/June 1958:Mossley.
debut: 31.3.1951 v.Leeds United (A).

Belatedly following manager Norman Bullock from Gigg Lane to complete a City inside trio with Hines and Rowley, Fred became the thoughtful, deeper-lying prompter of the forward line for some eighteen months, until the arrival of the classier Johnny Morris consigned him to a regular diet of reserve football. As something of a veteran following his brief contribution to City's 1954/5 First Division campaign, he subsequently found his opportunities limited in each of his seasons at Exeter (16 apps; 1 goal) and Oldham (10;1).
Apps: 55 Lge; 2 FAC.
Goals: 9 Lge.

WRAGG, WILLIAM A.

b. 1875.
Apr 1896:Nottingham Forest/
Mar 1899:FOSSE/Jan 1901:Small Heath/
Aug 1901:Watford/cs 1902:Hinckley Town/
Aug 1903:Chesterfield/cs 1904:not known/
Sept 1905:Brighton & Hove Albion.
debut: 1.4.99 v.Blackpool (A).

The left-half in Forest's FA Cup-winning side of 1898 (and creator of the first goal of the Final despite the handicap of a leg injury), William joined Fosse just as they were about to suffer the disappointment of missing promotion by one place and one point. Fosse used his versatile talents primarily in the right-back berth, but before he moved on he had served in all five of the defensive positions, and proved himself a genuine hot-shot of a free-kick specialist.
Apps: 49 Lge; 4 FAC.
Goals: 5 Lge.

WRIGHT, JOSEPH

b. Gateshead, 1907.
d. Newton Abbott, 20.11.36.
Birtley/Apr 1929:CITY/
July 1930:Torquay United/
July 1932:Brighton & Hove Albion.
debut: 2.9.1929 v.Manchester United (H).

A Geordie goalkeeper who made a remarkably rapid leap from the Second Division of the North-Eastern League into top-flight League fare, Joe leapfrogged over regular reserve 'keeper John Beby to become Jim McLaren's stand-in for the 1929/30 season, and accumulated an unexpected amount of experience. Much of it, however, was back-bending, despite City's reasonable League position, and Joe's final game was the exhilarating 6-6 draw with Cup-finalists Arsenal. Two seasons as first choice at each of Plainmoor and the Goldstone Ground ensued, but ill-health cut short Joe's career, and he died at the age of 29.
Apps: 15 Lge.

WRIGHT, WILLIAM JOHN
b. Blackpool, 4.3.1931.
May 1950:Blackpool/Aug 1955:CITY/
July 1958:Newcastle United/
Aug 1959:Plymouth Argyle/
Aug 1961:Hull City/Aug 1961:Millwall/
cs 1962:Tonbridge.
debut: 10.9.55 v.Barnsley (H).

Understandably frustrated as understudy to Stanley Matthews at Bloomfield Road, where he had managed only 15 League games and 2 goals over four seasons, Billy then found his high hopes of a regular place with City (after a £1,500 move) soon looking bleak against the challenge of the club's mid-50's superabundance of wingers. He could hardly be accused of not grasping the main chance when it presented itself, though: entering the 1956/7 promotion fray on Christmas Day, and contributing ten goals to the championship success from 17 games on either flank. It was somewhat surprising that Billy did not start the following campaign as an automatic choice; less so, in this light, that Newcastle jumped in with £7,500 for his signature. He suffered cruelly from injuries while on Tyneside, though, and moved south with a record of only five games; three goals. A full season at Home Park fuelled his wanderlust, but his spell at The Den ended a League career marked more by might-have-been's and if-only's than by potential fulfilled.
Apps: 27 Lge; 2 FAC.
Goals: 10 Lge.

YATES, STEPHEN
b. Measham, 8.12.1953.
app July 1970/pro Mar 1972:CITY/
Nov 1977:Southend United/
Dec 1983:Doncaster Rovers/
(Feb 1985-loan-Darlington)/
(Mar 1985-loan-Chesterfield)/
Aug 1985:Stockport County/
Sept 1985-trial-Burnley/
Oct 1985:Shepshed Charterhouse.
debut: 23.3.74 (sub) v.Newcastle United (A).

A cousin of David Nish who had shown all-round sporting ability as a schoolboy - representing England at cricket, and holding the national record for discus-throwing - Steve was a heftily built full-back who made the majority of his City appearances as a competent stand-in for Dennis Rofe, but stood little chance of displacing the ebullient No.3 on a regular basis.

At Southend, however, he gradually converted into a central defender during the course of a run of exactly 250 League and Cup games, and contributed immense solidity to their 1981 Fourth Division championship side. At left-back again, he also assisted Doncaster to promotion from the League basement in 1984; while his final two senior games came during a non-contract spell at Stockport.
Apps: 12+7 Lge; 1 FAC; 1 LC.

ALAN YOUNG

YOUNG, ALEXANDER FORBES (ALAN)
b. Kirkcaldy, 26.10.1955.
Kirkcaldy YMCA/July 1974:Oldham Athletic/
May 1979:CITY/Aug 1982:Sheffield United/
Aug 1983:Brighton & Hove Albion/
Sept 1984:Notts County/Aug 1986:Rochdale/
Mar 1988:Shepshed Charterhouse (p/coach).
debut: 11.8.79
v.Rotherham United (H) LC (1 goal).

Scorer of the hat-trick by which Oldham removed City from the FA Cup in 1979, Alan became one of the first players to be transferred under the new freedom-of-contract regulations and have his transfer fee set by an independent tribunal. The £250,000 move upset Oldham while still equalling City's then-record fee, but appeared more of a bargain as Alan led the club's charge towards Division One with a fair goalscoring verve and no little delicacy of skill for a forward so apparently forceful. His scoring touch deserted him somewhat thereafter, though, and it occasionally looked as if he was more intent on backchatting his way through a game than getting on and playing it. Fitness problems also marred the picture, though Jock Wallace stood by Alan despite the striking challenge of Jim Melrose, and it was not until the very eve of the next season, by which time Gordon Milne had taken over, that Alan was on his way to Bramall Lane for

£200,000. Seven League goals for the Blades, twelve for the Seagulls and thirteen for the Magpies subsequently represented a one-in-three scoring ratio, but Alan's spells on the treatment table, especially for a nagging back ailment, were becoming more frequent, and severely limited his contribution to Rochdale's Fourth Division struggles. He returned to Leicestershire as player/coach at Shepshed, and to help run the indoor cricket and soccer centre at Thurmaston.
Apps: 102+2 Lge; 10 FAC; 5 LC.
Goals: 26 Lge; 2 FAC; 1 LC.

YOUNG, ARCHIBALD W.
b. Twechar, Dumbartonshire.
Dunipace/Dunfermline Athletic/
Apr 1932:CITY/July 1935:Bristol Rovers/
June 1936:Exeter City/May 1937:Gillingham/
Sept 1938:Rochdale.
debut: 29.10.32 v.Arsenal (A).

A creative inside-left or wing-half, Archie did not make the happiest of entries to English senior football: standing in for Arthur Lochhead in a crushing 2-8 Highbury defeat by Herbert Chapman's champions-to-be. Undaunted, however, he proved a useful reserve for three First Division seasons. His subsequent Third Division wanderings still left him goal-less, and the Gills failed to win re-election at the end of Archie's initial season there. He made only a single appearance at Spotland.
Apps: 14 Lge; 1 FAC.

MIDLAND LEAGUE WHO'S WHO

The following players made senior appearances for Fosse in the Midland League (1891-94) only; never turning out in either a Football League Match or FA Cup tie.

	Apps/Gls		Apps/Gls
A. Atkins (OL)	1/-	C. Lisle (OR)	1/-
C. Atter (OR)	1/-	C. Mabbott (IR)	2/1
Herbert Bailey (CF)	5/1	E. Mouel (OR)	15/5
-. Carter (IF)	4/1	J. Rickus (IF)	3/-
T. DeVille (GK)	10/-	-. Shaw (IL)	1/-
G. Frettingham (IL)	1/-	-. Stott (CF)	1/-
F. Gardner (LH)	1/-	A. Vickers (LH)	4/-
W. Hardy (OR)	11/2	E. Wilkins (CF)	1/-
W.H. Harris (GK)	1/-	R.E. Winter (OL)	1/-
J. King (CF)	2/-	A. Wood (LB)	2/-
R. Lewis (CH)	3/-	A. Worrall (CF)	4/3

Research into the careers of Fossils of this era has proved extremely difficult, and unfortunately it is possible to offer only the following incomplete annotations on the above list:

Atkins was a triallist from Hemington, near Castle Donington. He may previously have played for Notts Olympic. **C.Atter** and **Herbert Bailey** were brothers of fellow-Fossils Jimmy and Harry respectively; and Herbert had previously turned out for each of Birmingham St.Georges, Wolverhampton Wanderers and Melton Town. **DeVille** was in his second spell with Fosse, initially joining in 1886, and having kept goal for Loughborough in the interim. **Frettingham** was a triallist from Newark, who also had trials with Nottingham Forest in 1892/3; we presume him to have been a relative of John Abel Frettingham, who later played for Lincoln City and New Brompton.
Frank Gardner was the Fosse secretary, forced to turn out to make up the numbers at Doncaster in 1891/2.

Harris was another former Loughborough goalkeeper, who had joined the Luffs from Leicester Teachers in 1890. **Mabbott** was a product of the strong Nottingham works side, Mellors Ltd, and had played for Forest reserves and Kettering before his Fosse stint. Some records list him as later assisting Notts County, but if so we have the wrong initial for him above, as Magpies statisticians list him as John Mabbott. **Rickus** was a former West Bromwich Albion reserve, who later played for Gravesend United in the Southern League.

Shaw was a local signing from the London Road team; **Vickers** a four-year servant from 1889. **Winter** was an amateur on the books of Nottingham Forest; and we believe **Wood** had assisted Kettering before his 1891 signing. **Arthur Worrall** was by far the best known of this particular group of Fossils: he had previously played for a couple of seasons with each of Wolverhampton Wanderers and Burton Swifts, and left Fosse after his goalscoring start to the 1893/4 season (he also hit 6 goals in 3 friendlies) to join Woolwich Arsenal. He later served Stockport County and Barnsley.

THE NEARLY MEN

Over the years, the club has been served, of course, by numerous reserve players who failed to make a single breakthrough into senior competitive football at Leicester. A few of these have been players with prior experience at senior level; a greater number have gone on to build variably lengthy careers with subsequent clubs. A small percentage of 'those who got away' have proved sufficiently successful elsewhere to embarrass or haunt the club which discarded them. Overleaf we index a representative cross-section of players whose careers peaked, statistically at least, away from Filbert Street.

New Zealand-born centre-forward **Reg Boyne**, who was on Aston Villa's books before WW1, and played for Fosse during the hostilities, moved on to Brentford in 1919, where he claimed the Bees' first League goal a year later. **T.Chappell** was a goalkeeping understudy to the ever-present Jimmy Thraves: he signed from Buxton in 1894, moved on to non-league West Manchester in 1895, and then joined Manchester City, for whom he played 8 League games, including two against Fosse. Another goalkeeper, **Billy Coventry**, joined Fosse in 1906 from Chester: he appeared at League level both before and afterwards with Crewe Alexandra.

Outside-right **Jack Crisp** was a Fosse reserve in 1913/14, but moved back to Birmingham on the outbreak of war. He was later to win a League championship medal with West Bromwich Albion during a nine-year stint at the Hawthorns, and also played for Blackburn Rovers, Coventry City and Birmingham. **William Cummings** was a reserve half-back for Fosse in 1907/8: a former Ashington, Reading and Norwich player, he moved on to Chelsea, but failed to get a look-in there, either. The same season, the left-back for Fosse reserves was **Harry Davies**, who had played previously for Wolves, Shrewsbury, Gainsborough Trinity, Doncaster Rovers and Grimsby Town.

H.Ekroth and **Karl Gustafssen** were both Swedish international wing-halves/inside forwards who turned out regularly for Fosse reserves before WW1. The former came on trial to Filbert Street after Fosse's 1913 Swedish tour, while the latter had faced both Gillingham and Barrow in senior friendlies during 1912/13. **William Hogan** was a Fosse signing from Fleetwood Rangers in 1895, who turned out for Grimsby Town once in 1896/7: he was more famous at the time, however, as a baseball pitcher with both Preston North End and Derby.

W.Lavery was another trialist full-back in 1907/8: the previous season he had played 14 League games for Preston, and indeed later extended his career at Deepdale. **Edward J.Leahy** was a goalkeeper signed by J.W.Bartlett from Walthamstow Grange, who went on to serve both Southend United and Aberdare Athletic, where he became player-manager. **Arthur Leonard** was a Wigston youngster who, following his release in December 1901, built the beginnings of a senior career in Ireland, then became a successful forward at Small Heath, Stoke, St.Bernards, Clapton Orient and Plymouth Argyle. Half-back **Matt Lockhead** signed for Fosse in 1909 from Swindon Town: he had previously played for St.Mirren, and would subsequently have a reserve spell at Manchester City before moving back south to Swindon, Bath City and Reading.

Scottish forward **James Milliken** arrived from Third Lanark in 1894, but found senior action only in friendlies and United Counties League matches. He then dropped out of sight for a season, and reappeared with Spurs in the Southern League in 1896/7. **W.Roberts**, a reserve triallist in November 1907, had played twice at inside forward for Preston North End the season before; while his near-namesake, **W.Tommy Roberts**, went in the opposite direction immediately after WW1: a Fosse discovery during wartime, the centre-forward went on to play for England and the Football League, earned an FA Cup Final appearance, and also served Burnley.

Former Sheffield Wednesday left-half **J.Taylor** was a Fosse trialist in 1910/11. Birmingham-born full-back **Harry Turner** was with Fosse in 1903, having previously had two spells with Portsmouth and a stint in the League with New Brighton Tower. Amateur centre-forward **Bernard Vann** was another unsuccessful Fossil of 1907: both he and his brother had turned out for Derby County, and the two would later also play for both Northampton Town and Burton United. Another amateur, full back or centre-half **George Webber**, followed manager Bartlett from Croydon Common, represented Fosse in each game of their 1913 Swedish tour, and then followed his boss again, to Swansea Town for 1914/15; while another full-back who failed to make a Fosse breakthrough was Galston-born **John White**, who had played 50 times for Newcastle United, and had spells with Kilmarnock, St.Mirren, Clyde and Dundee before his frustrating 1899/1900 term at Leicester.

*Between the wars, City maintained a fairly sizeable professional squad, but released few potential stars without at least one first-team outing. They turned down **Raich Carter** after trials, and once had future Scottish international **Billy Steel** on their groundstaff, but the bulk of their untried discards subsequently performed at a less exalted level.*

Inside-forward **John Allen** was a 1925 signing from Scottish juniors Parkhead, who made 8 appearances for Manchester City after a move in March 1927. **J.Cairns** was a forward who could not add to his Brentford record of one appearance, one goal following his 1928 signing (though he did pop up again briefly at Rochdale during 1933/4, after stints with Kettering, Margate and Portsmouth reserves), while another reserve front-runner, **W.Clarke**, played for Exeter City during 1937/8, and fleetingly for Southampton the following season. Creative inside-forward **Jimmy Dickson** was a £200 buy from Dunfermline Athletic in 1930, but got no senior break with City.

Outside-left **Stanley Duff** picked up League experience with Tranmere Rovers and New Brighton after leaving City in 1937. **Tommy Dutton** signed for City from Chorley in 1931, but left unrewarded for his reserve efforts in 1934, going on to score six times for Queens Park Rangers, ten times for Doncaster Rovers, and twelve times for Mansfield Town. He also made one appearance for Rochdale during 1939/40. Goalkeeper **Ted Gaskell** sought first-team football with a move to Brentford in 1937, yet had to wait no less than ten years for his League bow - ironically against City! He went on to tot up 34 appearances, and shared in a Testimonial at Griffin Park in 1954.

Full-back **C.T.Gellatly**, a signing from Shirebrook in 1930, moved on a year later for a three-season stint at Gillingham. Outside-right **George Gibbs** had two spells with Barnsley after leaving Filbert Street in 1928, and half-back **S.High** left a year later for Torquay United, having originally been signed from Easington Colliery. Inside-left **Syd Kearney** had a lengthy career after leaving City for Tranmere Rovers in 1937, going on to play for Accrington Stanley on both sides of the war, and then totting up 65 games in the left-half position for Bristol City.

Edwin R.MacLachlan had been on the books of Queens Park and Hibernian before signing as an outside-left for City in January 1927, though it wasn't until he moved to Nottingham Forest less than four months later that he got a League debut. He later played for Mansfield Town and Northampton Town, but it was in football administration that 'Mac' made his biggest mark locally, as a long-serving secretary to the Leicestershire Senior League and, between 1963 and 1970, as chairman of the County FA.

Young forward **John Hamilton McNeil** signed for City from Ayr United, but was another to move on quickly: to become a decent goalscorer at both Hull City and Bury. One of the few City men of this era to end a distinguished career as a Filbert Street reserve was **J.F.Mitchell**, the bespectacled amateur goalkeeper who had represented Preston in the 1922 Cup Final, and who arrived as cover for Kenny Campbell in November 1926 from Manchester City. Forward **R.Mullaney** was a youngster who reached no such heights, but he did knock in a couple of League goals for Barrow after a 1937 move.

George Norton lost his career to the war: on the heels of his City release, his sole appearance at inside-left for Bradford Park Avenue was in the second game of the abandoned 1939/40 League season. More fortunate was **Jack Price**, brother of first-teamer Fred, who played as a full-back at Bristol Rovers, Swindon Town and Torquay United after his 1923 move.

Goalkeeper **Albert Smith** joined City from Wombwell in 1928 and moved on a year later, playing five League games during a month's trial at Watford, but declining the proffered contract. Full-back **Joe Smith** was a contemporary, but this member of the Whitburn brotherhood failed to emulate Tom or Sep with a senior career at Filbert Street, and instead made his mark with two seasons at Watford after a 1930 move.

Geordie full-back **J.W.Traynor** was unable at either Leicester or Crystal Palace to win a first-team place, but he finally made League appearances for Gateshead in 1934/5. **Ted Udall** followed him into the City reserve side in 1932, but left two years later, to play 81 League games for a Derby County side which he helped to runners-up spot in Division One in 1935/6.

Archie Waterston was a wanderer: City became his first senior club after he'd starred alongside Billy Findlay in Musselburgh Bruntonians' 1923 Scottish Junior Cup win (scoring twice in the Final), but he returned north to Cowdenbeath in 1926 without a first-team game to his credit. Subsequent goal-hauls for Newport County (35), Southampton (1), Tranmere Rovers (17), Southport (44), Doncaster Rovers (27) and Aldershot (4) at least bore out the promise City had initially discerned.

George Wyness, a Geordie from Jarrow who joined City from Houghton CW and then moved on to Falkirk, later returned to Football League action as a defensive half-back throughout the 30's with Southport, Chester, Rochdale, Notts County and Gateshead.

Since WW2, the list of 'nearly men' has been supplemented by players from several categories: those on the books during wartime who had to move on to make League break-throughs; young apprentices who've reached professional status elsewhere; players on loan either to or from City; and, more recently, by out-of-contract 'free agents' undergoing trials with the club.

Scottish full-back **David Agnew** left City in 1961, played once for Scunthorpe, then carved out an 85-game career at Notts County. Striker **Johnny Allen** was an early Jock Wallace buy from Hinckley Athletic who was freed in 1980 for a season at Port Vale, and then returned to Hinckley. **Bob Atkins** failed to earn a contract after his City apprenticeship, but the defensive midfielder soon stepped up from Enderby Town to Sheffield United, and moved to Preston in 1985.

Forward **Mick Balmer** managed 28 games for Halifax (9 goals) after being released in 1965, and then moved to Derry City. Full-back **Peter Bebbington**, signed from Oswestry Town in 1965, made over 50 League appear-ances for Barrow (where he faced City in the Cup in 1968) and 17 more for Stockport. Forward **Mick Betteridge** was a Loughborough Colleges student who signed amateur forms for City in December 1942, and had a peacetime League career with West Brom, Swindon and Chester. **Brian Billington** had a brief spell with Notts County in 1969/70, and then joined Enderby Town.

City's goalkeeper for the 1975/6 Youth Cup campaign was trialist **Pat Bonner**, later to win considerable fame with both Celtic and the Republic of Ireland. **Ken Brandon** was already experienced at League level with Swindon and Chester before supplementing City's squad in 1956: he had to wait two years for a move to Darlington, though, before adding to his senior appearance tally. Young Irish forward **Bobby Bruce** arrived from Larne in March 1950, but his sole League game came after a move to Leyton Orient in November 1951.

Released from Filbert Street in 1985, defender **Scott Burnside** had brief spells with each of Berwick Rangers, East Stirlingshire and Cowdenbeath. Full-back **Jimmy Burt** moved to Aldershot along with Murray Brodie in 1970: he had 24 League outings there, followed by spells at Northampton and Rochdale.

Young centre-forward **David Cartlidge** left Filbert Street in 1961, and played for both Bradford City and Chester within a season. **Mervyn Cawston** was a much-travelled goalkeeper who had a brief loan spell with City

in 1975/6, and served each of Norwich, Southend, Newport, Gillingham, Chicago Sting and Maidstone United at first-team level.

Winger **Peter Chamberlain** was a City reserve during 1956/7, but made 78 appear-ances in five years at Swindon, and then served Aldershot for 46 games. Goalkeeper **Trevor Churchill** started his career with Yorkshire Amateurs, played ten games for Reading in 1946/7, had two years as a City reserve, then went on to play 110 times for Rochdale and on eleven more occasions for Swindon. City changed their mind about releasing forward **Barry Cliff** in 1984, but he was still on his way a year later without senior experience; and it was not until he reached Stranraer for the 1986/7 season that he found first-team football, despite an interim spell with Hibernian.

Forward-cum-midfielder **Robert Codner** played youth and reserve football for both Tottenham and City in the early 80's, then made his reputation with Barnet, earning a £115,000 move to Brighton in September 1988. **Robert Cooper** was loaned out for a five-game spell with Preston during 1985/6, but released by City at the end of that term.

Full-back **Paul Crawford** won Scottish Youth honours while at Filbert Street, but had to move back north in 1982 for first-team football: initially with Dunfermline, and then East Stirlingshire. **Paul Culpin** was City's reserve 'Player of the Year' and top scorer during 1981/2, but was released to pick up his career with Nuneaton Borough. This he did with a vengeance, smashing scoring records at the top of the non-league pyramid with 131 goals in 150 appearances, and earning a £50,000 move to Coventry in June 1985. He has subsequently played for Northampton.

John Currie came to Leicester in 1957 with Scottish Schoolboy caps to his name, but was unable to claim a senior wing-half position until moving to Workington in 1961. He also turned out later for Chester. Forward **Fred Cutting**, having won the Military Medal during WW2, made a few appearances for City in the transitional 1945/6 season, spent the following campaign in Norwich's reserves, and looked to have blown his League chances by joining Colchester in 1947. However, he was an integral part of their FA Cup giant-killing team which reached the last 16 that season, and was still a regular when the Layer Road outfit found itself elected to the League in 1950/1.

Former Scottish international goalkeeper **Bobby Ferguson** briefly helped out City's reserves during a loan spell from West Ham in March 1974. **Michael Ford** (son of one-time Bristol City star Tony) drifted away to Devizes Town after completing his City apprenticeship, but joined Cardiff in 1984 as a utility player, and earned himself a £150,000 transfer to Oxford in June 1988.

Another striker of the 80's was **Mark Forster**, on Middlesbrough's books as an amateur until signed by City in 1983, but playing for Darlington's League side before the season was out, and eventually notching 13 goals in 38 League games after his loan move to Feethams was made permanent. **Mike Foster** was also a forward on City's books from 1959: he played his League football subsequently for

Colchester and Millwall.

Young winger **Jason Garwood** was loaned out for League experience at Northampton during the early months of 1988/9, and made seven senior appearances. After a further loan spell at Leicester United, he was released by David Pleat to Burton Albion in March 1989.

Brothers **Andy Geddes** and **Paul Geddes** both joined City in 1979 from Scottish junior football. Midfielder Andy won a £20,000 move to Dundee in November 1980, and within a month was appearing in the Scottish League Cup Final. He left Dens Park amid much acrimony in 1984 to play in South Africa. Defender Paul meanwhile had also returned to Scotland, but found no more joy at Hibernian than he had at Filbert Street. He did, however, play two League games while on trial at Wimbledon.

Midfielder **Adie Green** had a loan spell with Rochdale in 1977/8 to prepare him for the step up to City's senior squad, but was released to Aldershot shortly after Jock Wallace's arrival. Little forward **Bobby Greig** got a brief League run at Workington after leaving City in February 1968, while Scottish full-back **Steve Hamilton** had to return home for senior football: with Hearts from 1980, East Fife from 1981 and East Stirling from 1983.

Central defender **Nigel Hart** (a son of ex-Manchester City star Johnny, and a brother of Leeds, Forest and Sheffield Wednesday centre-back Paul) had played one League game for Wigan Athletic before joining City in 1979, but it wasn't until two years later, after a move to Blackpool, that he extended his senior career. Subsequent spells with Crewe, Bury and Stockport have followed. Inside-forward **Tom Hartley** had only a month with City's reserves, from 27th December 1947, when he signed from North Shields, to 28th January 1948, when he joined the mass transfer move to Watford. He had started his career at Gateshead in 1935/6, and also had a wartime spell with Chesterfield. It was Chesterfield who gave a five-game break during 1983/4 to midfielder **Mike Higginbottom**, whom City had freed in 1981.

The former City reserve to make the biggest mark on the transfer market to date has been **Richard Hill**. Released to Nuneaton Borough in 1983, the strongly-built attacking midfielder joined Northampton Town two years later, and was the Fourth Division's top scorer in 1986/7, before a £240,000 move to Watford. He has subsequently moved on again, to Oxford United. Aberdonian **John Hillard** was a 1942 signing from Northampton, whose postwar League career consisted of a septet of games for Torquay during 1946/7. **Mick Hollis** was another City reserve forward to wander. After three years of frustration at Filbert Street, he joined Barrow in 1969, and subsequently also served Chester, Stockport and Reading in an almost 250-game League career.

Prolific reserve scorer **Alan Hoult** made the City sub's bench at Hull for the FA Cup tie of 1978, but was not called on. Yet months later he was turning out for Hull on loan. He also played on loan at Lincoln, but managed only one League Cup appearance after a transfer to Bristol Rovers. Goalkeeper **Steve Humphries** had two spells with City in the shadow of the immovable Mark Wallington. He picked up League appearances, though, at Doncaster, Cardiff and Wrexham in the early 80's, and after interim spells with Kettering Town and Vancouver Whitecaps, joined Steve Whitworth and Robert Codner at Barnet. There his consistent performances won him recognition at England semi-professional level.

Mark Hutchinson was a 1983 signing for City, after he had been released from his Aston Villa apprenticeship. The midfielder, however, had to wait for a move a year later to Carlisle before making his League bow; he also featured briefly for Northampton before joining the colony of one-time City players at Nuneaton. **Peter Jackson** was top scorer for City reserves in 1975/6: he never made the League game, but had a helping of glory in assisting St.Patrick's Athletic to the semi-final of the FAI Cup while on loan in Ireland during 1974/5.

Gordon Jayes, a 16-year-old debutant for City during the war and a schoolboy international, managed only 27 League appearances for Notts County when peace returned, but scored seven goals. Another to be released from Filbert Street in 1946 was defender **Ralph Jones**, who went on to play for Newport and Bristol Rovers. There was certainly no suspicion of nepotism at City when **Dave Johnston** was freed in 1962, untried, to play for Exeter and Stockport: the young reserve was coach Bert Johnston's son.

Some would dispute that **Tom Kilkelly** ought to qualify for inclusion in the Who's Who of senior players: but his only first-team run-out for City was in the 3rd/4th place play-off of the FA Cup in 1973/4, a game not counted towards any other player's official statistics in this book. The midfielder won Irish Youth caps while with City, and played four League games for Northampton on loan during 1974/5, but was freed the next summer. He subsequently played for Burton Albion, Shamrock Rovers and in South Africa before returning to the Midlands non-league scene.

Fred Kilshaw was a wartime City discovery whose brief League career amounted to a mere eight games at inside-forward for New Brighton during 1946/7. **Tony Lee** was a prolific youth and reserve scorer for City between 1965 and 1967, but notched only three goals in a subsequent brief League career at Bradford City and Darlington. A more potent goal-poacher at League level was **Gordon Livie**, who netted 25 goals from 53 appearances for Mansfield after a 1952 move. Full-back **John Loughlan** waited patiently but in vain for a City breakthrough in the early 60's, but starred for Morton, Crystal Palace and Wrexham thereafter. At Selhurst he shared in the 1969 promotion campaign which lifted Palace to Division One for the first time. His son Tony was a YTS trainee with City from 1986-88.

Inside-forward **Gerry McCaffrey** won an Irish Under-23 cap while on City's books in 1962/3, and was later honoured with four appearances for the Irish League after picking up his senior career with Distillery, Glentoran and Drogheda. Another Irishman, Derry City full-back **Ray McGuinness**, had a reserve trial

with City in December 1988, and contrived to get himself sent off on his debut at Old Trafford.

Striker **Dixie McNeil** became something of a goalscoring legend after leaving Filbert Street in 1966, claiming an aggregate of 239 League goals from a wandering career that took in Exeter, Northampton, Lincoln, Hereford (twice) and Wrexham. He became manager of the latter club in April 1985. Lanky forward **Pat McShane** moved from City to Hearts in 1979, but his few senior games all came in the Edinburgh club's 1980/1 relegation season.

Winger **Dick Marshall** notched seven goals in 31 League appearances for Southport after a 1965 move; goalkeeper **Keith Mason** got 30 League chances in five years at Huddersfield from 1982; half-back **Ken Mellor** managed two seasons at each of Mansfield and Swindon after his 1957 release. Central defender **David Needham** and goalkeeper-turned-full-back **Gordon Nisbet** were both City trialists in the mid-60's: the former went on to star for Notts County, QPR and Nottingham Forest and won England B caps; while the latter was capped at Under-23 level while with West Brom and before moves to Hull, Plymouth and Exeter.

Young forward **Tom Paterson** turned out for Middlesbrough, Bournemouth and Darlington between 1974 and 1979 following a City apprenticeship, while defender **Jess Payne** had a 25-game stint with Torquay from December 1977, and then gave long service to Yeovil Town. Barnet winger **Lee Payne** began a City trial in September 1988 with a Central League outing against Newcastle: it was the visitors, however, who immediately snapped him up on a League contract at a substantial fee. He moved on to Reading in March 1989.

Full-back **Jon Pearson** did not taste League football after his City release in 1986, but within 12 months he was appearing at Wembley as a substitute for Kidderminster Harriers on their way to FA Trophy triumph. Winger **Brendan Phillips** got only a single chance with Peterborough after moving from City in 1973, but after travelling the non-league circuit and winning England semi-professional caps while at Boston United, he cost Fourth Division Mansfield a £15,000 fee in 1980. Forward **Doug Pimbley** was a City amateur from December 1945: his postwar professional record ran to a couple of games for Birmingham City and 23 for Notts County.

Goalkeeper **Gary Plumley**, son of former City secretary Eddie, got his chance after leaving Leicester with Newport, for whom he played European soccer, and to whom he returned thrice amid and after spells with Hereford, Cardiff and Hong Kong's Happy Valley FC. Gary came out of virtual retirement in 1987 to play for injury-hit Watford in their FA Cup semi-final against Spurs at Villa Park, but was beaten four times.

Former England Youth international **Brian Punter** had been on Wolves' books before joining City as a reserve winger from Bromsgrove in 1958, but it was at Lincoln a year later that he made his League bow, going on to score 21 goals in 75 games. **Sean Rafter** was another goalkeeper to suffer a frustrating spell as cover to Mark Wallington: he had built

his reputation with Southend, and later got a few chances with Orient. Full-back **Barry Reed** was for four years on City's roster as an amateur, and two as a professional, but his release in 1961 earned him only a single League game at Luton. Wing-half **Peter Rushworth** fared somewhat better: signed in 1951 from Cheltenham, he moved in 1953 for 88 games with Bournemouth. Forward **Alan Russell** managed 14 games with Peterborough after his 1971 release.

Hefty defender **Malcolm Shotton** was another City cast-off to rebuild his confidence at Nuneaton. He moved on to skipper Oxford in their rise from the Third to the First Division, and in 1986 received the Milk Cup at Wembley for them. Rapid moves thereafter took him to Portsmouth, Huddersfield and Barnsley. Striker **John Stalker** was sold by Jock Wallace to Darlington in October 1979 and went on to score 36 League goals in 116 games there, though he had less success in subsequent short spells with Hartlepool United, Meadowbank Thistle and East Fife. England schoolboy international half-back **Len Staples**, the only member of the 1948 Combination Cup-winning side not to taste first-team football with City, took partial compensation from a 164-game career with Newport.

Northern Ireland international winger **Ian Stewart**, previously with QPR and Newcastle, had a couple of games with City's Central League side in December 1988, following his release by Portsmouth, but failed to earn a contract. Experienced **Steve Thompson** was bought by David Pleat in June 1988 as a likely replacement for Russell Osman, but the hefty central defender, who had skippered Lincoln and had been instrumental in helping keep Charlton in the top flight, wore a senior City shirt only in a pre-season friendly at Cambridge, and was allowed to move to Sheffield United after only five months at Filbert Street.

Reserve 'keeper **George Torrance** left Filbert Street in 1956, and collected a handful of senior appearances with Oldham, Rochdale and Albion Rovers; **Harry Walton** turned out once for Southend in peacetime soccer after having joined City in September 1942; full-back **Dick Walton** totted up almost 200 games for Leyton Orient and Exeter after his 1948 departure. Striker **Derek Watts**, who made the City sub's bench during 1971/2 but failed to get into the action, managed a single appearance as No.12 for Northampton while on loan during 1973/4, then had a season with Miami Toros.

Jimmy Wilson was a close-season signing in 1954 from Alloa, but he moved on to Mansfield in March 1955 for an 18-game spell in which he claimed one League goal. Forward **Brian Wright** has occasionally been errone-ously credited with two senior appearances for City that were in fact made by his contempo-rary, Billy Wright, but at least he got a brief breakthrough with Lincoln after a January 1959 move. Wartime signing **Harold Wyles** was a full-back sold to Gateshead in February 1948, who went on to tot up 235 League appearances.

LEICESTER FOSSE
SECRETARY/MANAGERS

1884 - 1892:	Frank Gardner
1892 - 1894:	Ernest A.Marson
1894 - Nov 1895:	J.Lee
Nov 1895 - Jul 1897:	Henry S.Jackson
Jul 1897 - Sep 1898:	William D.Clark
Sep 1898 - Jan 1912:	George Johnson
Mar 1912 - Mar 1914:	John William Bartlett
Apr 1914 - Jan 1915:	Louis Ford

During George Johnson's tenure as secretary, Fosse gave player Jimmy Blessington the title of team manager between January 1907 and April 1909; and Andy Aitken the title of player-manager from April 1909 to May 1911. Directors S.Scattergood and J.M.Hawkes both had short spells as honorary secretary in the interim periods before the professional appointments of Bartlett and Ford, while director Harry Linney held that post for the end of Fosse's League days and throughout the World War One period.

Secretary/managers during the Fosse era were primarily administrators, possessing only limited autonomy, if that, in team matters. It is unclear how much leeway many of the above gentlemen had in player recruitment; certainly they tended to leave tactics (however rudimentary) to the club trainer, and team selection was primarily a matter for the Committee or (after 1897) the Directors.

Messrs. **Gardner** and **Marson** were elected to their posts by fellow club committee members; the former had been a player, the latter became a director, and both later acted as League referees. **Mr.Lee** (about whom it has not been possible to discover anything) was the first 'professional' football administrator to be employed by the club.

Henry 'Swin' Jackson was a former Staffordshire cricketer who had been general secretary of West Bromwich Albion from 1892-94. After leaving Fosse he became secretary at Luton Town, then emigrated to Canada, where he became a parish registrar and postmaster.

William D.Clark had been associated with Derby County before becoming secretary/manager with Burton Wanderers from 1894. Appointed to the Fosse post when the club became a Limited Company, he evinced both an eye for gimmickry and a blind eye for League and FA rules (see narrative text), which earned him an indefinite suspension from the game from September 1898. When this was rescinded, he found himself back in Burton, with the amalgamated United, between 1901-04.

George Johnson was the longest-serving of Fosse's secretaries. Originally a Rugby follower, and a former honorary secretary of the Leicester branch of the National Cyclists Union, he came to the Fosse post with the credentials of having run their annual fund-raising Sports Days. He eventually retired to concentrate on his partnership in a printing business, and was later to benefit from a specially arranged friendly at Filbert Street between Bradford City and Steve Bloomer's XI.

John William Bartlett, born in Forest Gate, had joined Croydon Common as a player in 1898, and taken the manage-

rial reins two years later, elevating his club into the Southern League, where they competed with some success until the First World War caused their disbandment. By this time Mr.Bartlett had completed two years with Fosse, had turned down an offer to coach in Germany and, in May 1914, had become manager of Swansea Town.

Louis Ford was a veteran of football administration by the time he found himself at Leicester. He was honorary financial secretary of West Bromwich Albion from 1887, their general secretary from 1890-92, and then a director until 1896. In that year he joined Walsall as secretary, but by 1900 was acting as a League referee. He was an FA councillor from 1890-93, served on the Football League Management Committee, and was Vice-President of that body between 1894-97, though ironically it was the League's assessment of Fosse's internal problems in 1915 that led to his early resignation.

LEICESTER FOSSE
TRAINERS & COACHES

The men who had more influence on Fosse's on-field efforts received scant publicity at the time. Research has thrown up so little detail about the club's trainers that it is not even known for sure if the listing is complete.

The first such gentlemen noted are the otherwise anonymous Messrs **Smith** and **Brown**, who coached Fosse through their final Midland League seasons of 1892/3 and 1893/4 respectively. **Bob Roberts**, who took the trainer's role for the initial Division Two campaign, was a former Welsh international who had played for Druids and Bolton Wanderers. His successor in 1895 was **Joe Newton**, who also left after a single season, heading for Dundee.

John Jackson was the next man charged with directing Fosse's fitness and fortunes. Born in Aston, Birmingham in 1861, he had been assistant trainer to Wolves when they won the Cup in 1893, had guided Loughborough for two years (1893-95), and trained Liverpool throughout 1895/6. He moved on from Leicester to help form Brighton United in 1898, taking several players with him, and commenced a long tenure as licensee of a Brighton pub when the club collapsed in April 1900. Only a year later, though, he was appointed manager/trainer to the new Brighton & Hove Albion club, and remained with them until 1905. His pub duties then occupied him, apart from one brief return to football as Blackpool manager in 1907, until his death in June 1931.

Bob Dunmore, who later moved on to become trainer of Woolwich Arsenal, stayed at Filbert Street for a couple of seasons until being replaced by another mysterious **Mr.Brown**, who in turn was succeeded by **Alick Stewart**, whose career details are included in the Player's Who's Who by dint of his single League appearance.

Harley Thompson, the man accused of enticing six Fossils from the pitch at Grimsby in 1912, had been with the club since at least 1905, and stayed on as assistant when **Billy Leech** became the first Fossil to be elevated from the playing ranks to the position of head trainer.

LEICESTER CITY
MANAGERS

*(Between June 1986 and May 1987, Milne was designated as
General Manager and Hamilton as Team Manager).
(Caretaker or acting managers have included Bert Johnson,
Ian MacFarlane and Peter Morris).*

PETER HODGE

Rightly regarded as the primary architect of City's rise to First
Division respectability in the 20's, Peter clearly commanded
greater respect from his board than his Fosse predecessors had
done in the same nominal joint role of secretary/manager; and
equally clearly exercised a greater degree of autonomy in his
involvement with matters of selection and tactics. Though he
was not actually at the helm for the pinnacle years of City's
championship pursuit, he had gradually built up many of the
systems and much of the side which saw the club go so close to
its grail.

Entering football administration in his home town of Dunfermline with a juvenile team in 1890, he then combined the
role of secretary for Dunfermline Juniors with refereeing duties
in the Scottish League's Second Division, which he carried out
from 1897 to 1906. Peter was honorary secretary to Dunfermline Athletic when Raith Rovers appointed him as their
first manager in April 1907, and he remained at Starks Park
until October 1912, when he was ousted by an ambitious
director two years after taking Raith into the Scottish First
Division. In June 1914 he took over at Stoke, and led them to
the top of the Southern League's Second Division. They
promptly applied for re-election to the Football League, and
were successful runners-up to Leicester Fosse in the vote,
though the wartime break meant that they then could not take
their place until 1919. By this time, Peter was back in
Kirkcaldy, as both a local recruiting officer and, once more, as
manager of Raith, who he rebuilt for peacetime football from
1916 onwards.

After the reconstruction of Leicester City, the new board began
negotiations for Peter to take over at Leicester almost immedi-

ately, and the formalities of his resignation from Raith and
official appointment at Filbert Street took place during the first
two weeks of September 1919. Not surprisingly, the new boss
returned north of the border for a fair proportion of his key
signings, several of whom had experienced his management at
Raith. Peter experimented and dabbled shrewdly in the bargain
end of the market with a single-minded aim to get City into
Division One; yet his appreciation of footballing artistry never
left him. He finally turned out a side of Second Division
champions in 1925, and altered it only slightly into one which
consolidated its new, elevated status. Then, however, in May
1926, he was tempted away by Manchester City, who had
reached the previous season's FA Cup Final, but had also been
relegated. His new charges missed out by one place on an
instant return, but were promoted as champions next time out,
and Peter also helmed them to third place in the top flight
during his Maine Road stay (further distinguished by his
signing of the young Matt Busby). But in March 1932, with
Leicester perilously close to the drop, he returned to Filbert
Street.

The stars of City's recent heyday were now ageing, and
replacements of similar calibre were hard to come by on a
limited budget. Peter helped them stay up by the skin of their
teeth in 1932 and 1933, and lifted them two places to 17th
position in 1934, but suffered illness as he prepared for the new
campaign, and died in August 1934, still in office. Several of
his City charges acted as pall-bearers at his funeral.

WILLIE ORR

The man who inherited Peter Hodge's First Division City side,
Willie fine-tuned it to the extent that it sat for two seasons
proudly, if slightly frustratedly, in its highest-ever top flight
placings: third in 1927/8 and second in 1928/9.

Willie was born in Shotts, Lanarkshire, on 20.6.1873. In his
playing days a fine defender with Airdrieonians, Preston North
End and, for ten years from 1897, with Celtic, he won three full
Scottish caps, four Scottish League championship medals, and

five Scottish Cup medals, three as a winner. In 1909 he became a director back at Airdrie, and served as such until 1921, when he took over the manager's chair there. His side took the Scottish Cup in 1924, missing the Double by one League placing, and his reputation was high enough for City to take him on a month after Hodge's departure. Jim McLaren, Sid Bishop and Len Barry were among his Filbert Street purchases who contributed to the championship pursuit; while Sep Smith was a later junior recruit. As City began to struggle for First Division survival, though, things began to sour for Willie. He left Leicester in March 1932, as distress signals were being transmitted north for the return of Peter Hodge; and while he soon found new employment as secretary/manager of Falkirk, it was not long before he was definitively disgraced. For in April 1935 the Scottish League banned him for life after he had been charged with bribery, and found guilty of paying £3 to Ayr United player Robert Russell to miss a crucial relegation game against Falkirk. (The game in question was ordered to be replayed). Willie died in February 1946.

ARTHUR LOCHHEAD
(See Players' Who's Who).

FRANK WOMACK

Remembered mainly for his success in turning round City's fortunes in his first season at the helm with one decisive flurry of transfer-market action, Frank pushed the club from the Second Division depths to its championship within a matter of months on the heels of his purchases of Eric Stubbs and, especially, Jack Bowers.

A Sheffielder by birth (16.9.1888), Frank spent the entirety of a lengthy playing career as a Birmingham full-back, and played in an England trial match in 1913. He served his managerial apprenticeship with Worcester City, and then bossed Torquay United (1929-32) and Grimsby Town (1932-36; Second Division champs in 1934) before succeeding Arthur Lochhead at Filbert Street, and tasting instant glory. His perception in recognising what it took to get out of Division Two did not, though, extend to any brilliant insights as to how to keep City afloat in the top flight, and he resigned in May 1939 after the club tumbled back down again on the eve of war. A sad epilogue to his Leicester regime was provided in 1940 by the authorities, who handed him a one year suspension for his implication in the irregularities then found in City's pre-war books; but Frank bounced back to take charge of Notts County from July 1942 to March 1944, and of Oldham Athletic from February 1945 until April 1947. In 1951 he spent a few brief months as caretaker manager of Grimsby once more, and he was living in retirement in Caistor when he died in 1968.

TOM BROMILOW

Tom prepared City for a new Second Division campaign throughout the summer of 1939, saw the season abandoned after only three League games, and stayed at the helm throughout the uncertain days of wartime competition until May 1945. To him fell the twin tasks of keeping the club going as a morale booster on the home front and coping with the vicissitudes of fielding eleven recognised footballers each week, and it was to his credit that sufficient attractive 'guest' players turned out in the blue and white during that period to fulfil both functions.

Tom (b. Liverpool, 7.10.1894) had an eleven-year, 341-game playing career as a constructive left-half at Anfield during the immediate postwar seasons, and was recognised as the brains behind Liverpool's championship wins of 1922 and 1923. He won five England caps and represented the Football League on six occasions, then turned to management: with Burnley, in Holland, and then twice at Crystal Palace. He joined City from Selhurst, and was later manager at Newport County for four years until 1950. Later still, Tom returned to Filbert Street as an 'A' team trainer and as chief scout, in which capacity he was acting for City when he died at Nuneaton, returning by train from a Welsh Cup tie on 4.3.1959. His son George was an England amateur international forward who played League football for Southport in the mid-50's.

TOM MATHER

City's boss for the transitional postwar season of 1945/6, Tom never so much as selected a team for League duty, was frustrated (predominantly by financial constraints) in attempting to rebuild a City side in the image of his pre-war teams, and resigned after only nine months in March 1946.

Born in 1888, Tom had entered football administration in 1910, as secretary at Bolton Wanderers. After serving in the Navy in WW1, he became secretary/manager of Southend United in 1921, and assumed the managerial position at Stoke in October 1923, there giving Stanley Matthews his senior break. From June 1935 to the outbreak of WW2, he was boss at Newcastle United; while a year after leaving Leicester he helmed Kilmarnock for most of the 1947/8 season, and then returned south. He died in March 1957.

JOHN DUNCAN
(See Players' Who's Who).

NORMAN BULLOCK

The man who bought Arthur Rowley, and who pointed City to their first postwar promotion in 1954, Norman rather lost control of his charges as the First Division adventure turned sour, and was ushered out of his post in February 1955.

It was September 1920 when a £10 signing-on fee to Sedgeley Park landed young centre-forward Norman at Bury, and eighteen years before he left the club whose League appearance and goalscoring records he still holds (506 games; 124 goals). Three times capped by England, he led the Shakers to promotion in 1924, and to fourth position in Division One two years later; briefly held the player/manager's dual responsibility, and then opted for management as a full-time activity in June 1935. His bid for complete control over the team brought him into conflict with certain members of the Gigg Lane board in 1938, though, and he shifted allegiance to Chesterfield. Norman had been out of managerial harness for some four years when he succeeded Johnny Duncan at Leicester in November 1949, but he soon created something of a whirlwind of activity on the arrivals and departures front as he re-ordered both the playing and backroom staffs. His scouting net was cast far and wide (Matt Gillies, Johnny Morris and Jack Froggatt were among his other successful purchases after Rowley; Andy Graver the last of several conspicuously less so), but his style of man-management was becoming worrying to the board at the time incidents of indiscipline in a Whitley Bay hotel brought matters to a head. Norman's accordingly rolled. He never again sought a similar job, and died in October 1970.

DAVID HALLIDAY

Stirring a few more Scots into the playing blend inherited from Norman Bullock, and keeping a much firmer grip on them, David took two seasons to get City back into the top flight after their tumble in 1955 - and his championship-winning side of 1957 proved a record-breaking one as well as they piled on the goals and considerably heightened the Filbert Street entertainment quotient. That David clearly cared more to see his team going forward than defending with any security was, perhaps inevitably, his downfall when First Division attacks began exploiting the gaps his tactical plans did not cover.

It's not hard to pin down the origins of David's attacking inclinations. As a player, the Dumfries-born centre-forward successfully scorched his way towards goal with admirable regularity. His football in the immediate post-WW1 era was played with Queen of the South and Dundee, and he represented the Scottish League against the Football League in 1924. Then he came south of the border, claiming 153 League goals for Sunderland at a ratio of only a little under one a game, and winning a £6,000 move to Arsenal. He could not get a regular place at Highbury, and exactly half of his League goals as a Gunner came in one match against City: the 6-6 draw of 1930 in which he netted four, and which proved to be his last Arsenal outing before a move to Manchester City. For them he netted 47 goals, and for Clapton Orient a further 33, until taking the player/manager post at Yeovil in 1935. He became boss at Aberdeen in January 1938, and took over at Leicester in July 1955. Several of his former Pittodrie charges joined him at Filbert Street over the next few years, and he also introduced surprise packages like Willie Gardiner to the Leicester scene. David took much due credit for his marshalling of the 1957 promotion side, and at least ensured last-gasp First Division survival the following term, but his days were numbered as soon as 1958/9 looked like developing into a similar uphill battle, and he and the club parted company in October 1958. He died in January 1970.

MATT GILLIES
(See Players' Who's Who)

FRANK O'FARRELL

Narrowly winning the board's vote over Allan Brown of Luton as City quickly sought Matt Gillies' successor, Frank took over a relegation-bound team, yet led them to Wembley as a distinctly consoling diversion. The softly-spoken Irishman then remoulded the club for a rapid return to the top flight, achieved after two seasons on a basis of intelligent pragmatism, when his management methods even justified the scrutiny of a series of educational documentary television programmes. Perhaps unfortunately for City, Manchester United must have watched the latter, for they spirited Frank away with the proverbial offer he couldn't refuse.

Cork-born Frank was first introduced to English football by West Ham, who signed him as a wing-half from Cork United in January 1948. He soon became an Eire international and, presciently, joined the unofficial Hammers 'Academy' then being informally tutored by Malcolm Allison. After 197 League games, Frank moved on to Preston North End for 118 more, and then assumed the player/manager's role at Weymouth, who he eventually helmed to the Southern League championship in 1964/5. Torquay United then stepped in with an offer of the manager's chair, and it was from Plainmoor that Frank moved to Leicester. Several of his early City purchases were of questionable value, but the signings of Bobby Kellard and Willie Carlin to energise and motivate the push to the 1971 Second Division championship were masterstrokes. Frank and his coach Malcolm Musgrove (another ex-Hammer) were less happily employed at Old Trafford, though, where the shadow of Matt Busby and the demand for instant success from a transitional team weighed heavily upon them. Frank later took over at Cardiff for a crucial five months of anti-relegation struggle during 1973/4, had a spell coaching in Iran, and returned for a couple of stints back at Torquay as general and caretaker manager.

JIMMY BLOOMFIELD

If, under David Halliday and Matt Gillies, the predominant dressing-room accent was Scottish, then under Jimmy it became Cockney. Expensive exiles from London clubs abounded as Jimmy waved the City cheque book around with effective abandon and built a superbly entertaining First Division side in the early and mid-70's. Leicester at that time were essentially a 'nearly' team; always threatening to gain a place in European competition yet, somehow, finding 7th to be their highest end-of-season ranking, and a semi-final replay defeat their best FA Cup performance. Jimmy's oft-expressed penchant for attacking football was nonetheless interpreted with some intriguing and genuinely aesthetic variations by his adventurous teams, and regular (if inconsistent) displays of pace and improvisatory skill were almost ample compensation for the lack of tangible success in the eyes of City fans.

Jimmy, born in Kensington (15.2.1934), started his playing career as a constructive inside-forward with Hayes, and went on to give fine service between 1952 and 1969 with Brentford (twice), Arsenal, Birmingham City, West Ham United, Plymouth Argyle and Orient, amassing 496 League appearances and claiming 93 goals from them, and even managing to play in two Fairs Cup Finals (for London and Birmingham). Graduating to the managerial office at Orient in 1969, he pointed his team to the Third Division championship, and a year later found himself preparing Leicester for their Charity Shield win and their return to the top flight. Following his six seasons' tenure at Filbert Street, Jimmy returned to Orient as boss, but ill-health forced him to resign prematurely, and he was acting as a part-time Luton scout at the time of his tragically early death in April 1983.

FRANK McLINTOCK

(See Players' Who's Who).

JOCK WALLACE

Deserving of heartfelt thanks for taking a dispirited club by the scruff of the neck, shaking it back to self-respect and infusing its representative teams with a battling swagger, Jock quickly built his own mythology at Leicester, but in many ways became unproductively trapped within it before he left. It might justifiably be argued that his feat in stopping the side falling into Division Three in 1978/9 was a greater triumph than the Second Division championship success he prompted the following season; and there is a case to be made that his embarrassment when City dropped straight back was primarily a consequence of the club tightening its belt and not providing adequate financial resources. But in that top flight term, and the subsequent unsuccessful attempt to bounce straight back, the conflicting strengths and weaknesses of the patented Wallace approach became more and more obvious. A great motivator, a shrewd judge of a player's commitment, and always one to encourage youthful talent, Jock could nonetheless appear a rather naive tactician; and it did not help on this score that his assistant, Ian MacFarlane, seemed cut from the same craggy rock. The abiding memory of the latter years of the Wallace regime, which would end in acrimony when Jock broke his contract to join Motherwell in August 1982 (prompting legal action and belated out-of-court settlement), was of Jock and Ian together rising from the City bench, snarling and shaking their fists to demand more frenetic effort, rather than attempting to convey to their charges any subtler shift in playing pattern.

The son of a goalkeeper (also Jock, who turned out for Raith Rovers, Blackpool and Derby on either side of WW2), Jock himself performed between the sticks for a motley collection of clubs of varying status after finishing his army service. Initially a young amateur with Blackpool, he joined Workington in 1952, making five League appearances, and then played for Ashton United and Airdrieonians before joining West Brom in 1959. After 69 League games at the Hawthorns, Jock moved on again, to Bedford Town, Hereford United and, as player/manager, to Berwick Rangers, where he took part in the classic giant-killing of their Glasgow namesakes. He had a spell coaching at Hearts, and then took over the Ibrox manager's office in June 1972. Remarkable success for Rangers followed, with the pinnacles of Jock's career coming in 1976 and 1978, when the domestic Treble was captured. Almost deified by the Ibrox faithful, Jock genuinely shocked British football when joining City, where the contrast in recent fortunes could not have been more extreme. And it is worth reiterating that, although Jock left City in the same nominal Second Division grade as when he joined them, his gruffly populist, up-and-at-'em approach had in the interim given the club back its pride.

The row over Jock's 'poaching' by Motherwell had hardly died down when he left Fir Park to return to Ibrox. Success in his second spell at his spiritual home was, however, harder to come by, and in April 1986 he again bade farewell to Glasgow. A couple of months later, Jock was installed as boss at Spanish League club Seville, but was somewhat out of his element during this brief continental sojourn. He then remained in semi-retirement in Spain until answering an SOS to return to management in January 1989 at Colchester United, then 92nd in the League and apparently Conference-bound. Predictably, Jock roused them to survival by an 8-point margin.

GORDON MILNE

Decidedly less charismatic than his predecessor Jock Wallace, Gordon quietly edged City into the promotion frame at the end of his first season in charge, and somehow contrived to keep them in the top flight against the odds for three seasons, before closing the Leicester chapter of his career with a year as General Manager, working in harness with new team boss Bryan Hamilton. Gordon's public image throughout his stay was of a man whose first priority was to perform the increasingly difficult task of balancing the City books. His essentially safety-first approach to club management may well have been the most appropriate response to the shifting economic structure of modern top flight football, but it also appeared to many supporters that perhaps Gordon gained rather more respect from the boardroom than he did from the dressing room, and certainly more than he did from the terraces. Nonetheless, he marshalled his on-field resources with relative success, and rode with dignity the storms of criticism which met decisions like the Melrose/English swap, the failure to retain Gerry Daly, or the attempted conversion to full-back of seemingly the entire midfield complement.

Again a man with football in his blood, Gordon started his League career at Deepdale, where his father Jimmy had been a pre-war star and was then manager. After 81 League games for Preston as a right-half, he moved to Anfield and took a regular

berth in Bill Shankly's first great Liverpool side, helping them to promotion and on to two League championships, winning 14 England caps, and only moving on to Blackpool in 1967 after 236 League games (18 goals). His managerial career started a couple of years later at then-non-league Wigan Athletic, and he took up the reins at Coventry in June 1972, in partnership for two years with Joe Mercer, then as solo manager and, finally, as chief executive when Dave Sexton arrived to assume team manager duties. He was as well used, therefore, to the system of dual responsibility which operated for the first time at Leicester in his final season, as he was to keeping a club of limited means in the First Division. Some two months after his contract with City expired in May 1987, Gordon surprised many by accepting an offer to manage the Turkish club Besiktas, who finished as League runners-up in his first season there.

BRYAN HAMILTON

Brought in to work in tandem with Gordon Milne and attempt to reverse the mid-80's pattern of First Division brinkmanship at Leicester, Bryan got off to a fine start as his infectious enthusiasm caught the imagination of both the Filbert Street crowd and, unfortunately less sustainedly, his playing staff. His initial months in the post saw City move into the top half of the First Division table for the first time in a decade, yet by the end of that switchback 1986/7 season the club found itself relegated, and Bryan proved unable to reverse, or even halt, a slide which threatened to lead to the ignominy of the Third Division. Twice he broke the club transfer record, in signing Steve Moran and Mike Newell, but there was otherwise little conviction evident in either his team-building dealings or his attempts at morale-lifting motivation.

Born in Belfast in December 1946, Bryan started his playing career with Distillery, and earned the first of his 50 Northern Ireland caps while starring for Linfield, before Ipswich Town won the race for his in-demand attacking midfield services in August 1971. Over four years and 153 League games later, Everton paid a substantial fee to take him to Goodison, and he appeared in the 1977 League Cup Final before moving on to Millwall, and then to Swindon, where he entertained thoughts of retirement to concentrate on coaching. In October 1980, however, Bryan assumed the player/manager's job at Tranmere Rovers, and clocked up another 109 League appearances before hanging up his boots. Working on the proverbial shoestring, Bryan saw several crises through at Prenton Park before leaving in February 1985 and taking up the manager's role at Wigan. A Freight/Rover Trophy win at Wembley in May 1985 was a highlight of Bryan's stay there, and in June 1986, after impressing on a World Cup TV panel with his easy manner and analytical shrewdness, he topped the shortlist for the City team manager's job. Questions over the precise division of responsibilities between the new man and general manager Gordon Milne were temporarily shelved as City made their best start to a campaign in years, but the rapport Bryan built with the fans was not matched by that with his players as City tumbled. He survived a boardroom vote of confidence following relegation, and was in sole control for the start of the Second Division campaign of 1987/8, but dissension in the ranks soon became evident, and there was tangible distaste from several players over the positional and tactical roles they were being asked to perform. City were in truly desperate straits when, unsurprisingly, the axe fell on Bryan in December 1987. Shortly afterwards, he seemed to have tacitly acknowledged his limitations as a track-suited boss when returning to Wigan as chief executive, but subsequently Bryan has again assumed control of team matters at Springfield Park.

DAVID PLEAT

Both City and David Pleat were at a low ebb when the latter inherited Bryan Hamilton's managerial duties at Filbert Street. City were nudging the bottom of the Second Division, and were in the midst of their record run of seven League matches without a goal, while David was still suffering from the outcry following a gutter-press smear campaign which led to his departure from Tottenham. By the end of his first term in charge, though, both club and boss were very much rehabilitated, for David had rapidly assessed City's tactical shortcomings, appraised their personnel's potential, turned around the

side's fortunes, and had them playing some of the most attractive football seen from a Leicester team in some time. That 1988/9 did not see City maintain this progressive momentum was clearly as much of an intensely irritating mystery to David as it was to the club's fans.

David, born in Nottingham in January 1945, won England honours at both schools and youth level as a speedy winger, but found it hard to make a sustained first-team challenge with Forest, and moved on while still only 19 to Luton Town. There, a series of injuries cut down his reliance on sheer pace, and forced him into a more studiously constructive game, which served him well through subsequent moves to Shrewsbury Town, Exeter City and Peterborough United. He became player/manager at Nuneaton Borough for a spell, then took on a series of backroom jobs with Luton, which culminated with him rising through the coaching hierarchy and eventually assuming the managerial reins in early 1978. He returned the Hatters to the top-flight in 1982, kept them there the following term when his delight at a last-gasp reprieve was evident to the TV millions who saw his jig across the Maine Road pitch, and had them well-established as an entertaining playing force when he left to meet the challenge of raising Spurs to the heights coveted by their ambitious board. David saw Tottenham to the 1987 FA Cup Final, but his future became unsure as press agitation for the return of Terry Venables mounted, and the coincidental appearance of unsubstantiated tabloid allegations about David's private life effectively enforced his resignation. In these difficult circumstances, there was courage evident on the parts of both the City board and David himself when his Leicester appointment was made, but vindication came early where it mattered: on the pitch.

LEICESTER CITY TRAINERS, COACHES & ASSISTANT MANAGERS

Aside from the several former players who have hung up their boots to concentrate on coaching and training duties at Filbert Street, or have returned to do so (amongst whom are numbered Teddy King, George Ritchie, Sep Smith, George Dewis, Arthur Chandler, Matt Gillies, Derek Hines, Ian MacFarlane and Bobby Roberts), the following have also served City in such roles under various titles:

DAVE GARDNER

Dave Gardner was City trainer from 1919-31, serving under Peter Hodge and Willie Orr throughout the club's First Division heyday, and died on a golf course in November 1931 while still in post. Capped for Scotland as a Third Lanark player in 1897, Dave had in the interim been a solid left-back for Newcastle United, Grimsby Town, West Ham United and Croydon Common. His assistants on the staff at Leicester included **Ernest Nixon** (who briefly succeeded him as senior trainer) and blind masseur **Bill Fox**.

A teaming of **Laurie Edwards** and **Willie McLean** saw City through to the outbreak of war, and the latter returned afterwards for three years. Edwards had previously served under George Jobey at Derby County, while the bespectacled McLean, once a Powderhall sprinter, had held similar posts with St.Mirren and Doncaster Rovers, and was to go to Wembley with Leicester in 1949.

Jack Butler coached City throughout the war years. His sixteen-year stint as an Arsenal centre-half had earned him one England cap, and he had finished his playing career with Torquay United before joining Daring FC of Belgium as a coach. On leaving Filbert Street he became successively manager of Torquay, Crystal Palace, Daring again, and

Colchester United, and also contrived an interim stint as coach to the Danish FA.

Jim Metcalfe, formerly with Preston North End, had two short spells as trainer with City, initially arriving on the eve of war in 1939, then returning in 1949/50, when Sep Smith held the coaching role. New manager Norman Bullock, however, brought in his former Bury team-mate **David Jones** in the summer of 1950. Jones, also a former Nottinghamshire bats-man, similarly had two spells at Leicester, as head trainer until 1956, and then as assistant from 1958-78. His own second-in-command from 1954 was former Everton and Derby goalkeeper **Frank King**, who left City to take up the senior trainer's position at Luton in 1958.

Alec Dowdells came in to head the staff in 1956 after 14 years with Celtic and a spell as trainer to the Scottish national side. On his retirement ten years later, a Scotland XI came to Filbert Street for his Testimonial game. For many of these years he was partnered with Jones and coach **Bert Johnson**, a former Charlton player who had guested for Bolton during the war alongside Matt Gillies. The latter employed Johnson in 1959, initially as head scout, after he had managed non-league Bexleyheath and Cambridge United, and Johnson eventually stood in as acting team manager in 1968 while Gillies was absent ill. It was Johnson's sacking later that year that prompted Gillies' resignation, and the pair were soon afterwards reunited at Nottingham Forest.

Frank O'Farrell brought former West Ham and Leyton Orient winger **Malcolm Musgrove** from a coaching role at Aston Villa to be his assistant, and also took him to Old Trafford when he departed. Musgrove, who had substantially helped to dump City out of the FA Cup in 1964, later had spells as Torquay manager and coaching with Connecticut Bi-Centennials, Chicago Sting, Exeter City and Plymouth Argyle.

ALEC DOWDELLS

David Coates also joined the training staff under O'Farrell, and stayed through the Bloomfield and McLintock years. A former player with Hull, Mansfield and Notts County, he has subsequently worked with David Pleat at Luton, and as youth coach at Oxford United.

Other coaches utilised by Jimmy Bloomfield were **Bill Dodgin Jnr** (1972-73) and **Mike Everitt** (1975-77). Dodgin was a former England Under-23 cap who had played for Fulham and Arsenal, coached Millwall and QPR, and returned to Craven Cottage as both coach and manager. Less than a year after arriving at Filbert Street, though, he was off for the first of two spells managing Northampton Town. In the interim, he became boss at Brentford. Everitt had been a player with Arsenal, Northampton, Plymouth and Brighton; player-manager at non-league Wimbledon; and one of Dodgin's predecessors at Brentford.

Frank McLintock brought Ian MacFarlane back as his assistant, and Jock Wallace kept him on in that capacity, while introducing **Eddie May** as reserve team coach. May had a long League career at centre-half with Southend, Wrexham and Swansea City, plus a spell in America with Chicago Sting, and went on to coach at Charlton after four years with Leicester. He became manager of Newport County in July 1988, after their relegation to the Vauxhall Conference, but stayed less than a month at the crisis-racked club before being recruited by the club who had taken their League place, Lincoln. Another Wallace appointment was that of youth coach **Dave Richardson**, who completely reorganised City's junior scouting and recruitment network over a successful six-year spell until Bryan Hamilton passed him over for promotion in 1987, when he departed to assist Graham Taylor at Aston Villa.

Gerry Summers was Gordon Milne's assistant for four years from 1982. A former West Brom, Sheffield United, Hull and Walsall player, Gerry had previously coached at Wolves and West Brom, and had six-year spells as manager at both Oxford and Gillingham. Milne also instituted a regime of specialised goalkeeping coaching, and brought in former Sheffield United and England 'keeper **Alan Hodgkinson** to work with the likes of Ian Andrews and Carl Muggleton.

On the breaking up of the Milne/Hamilton managerial tandem, the latter recruited his one-time Ipswich team-mate **Peter Morris** as coach. Morris had become player-manager of Mansfield in his second spell there, assistant manager at Newcastle, and boss at both Peterborough and Crewe before his year-long stint at Filbert Street. He took over the manager-ship of Kettering in July 1988. Morris was joined on the City coaching staff by another former Ipswich star, **Cyril Lea**, whose playing career had started at Leyton Orient, peaked with two Welsh caps, and who had coached at both Ipswich and Stoke before taking the manager's job at Colchester. With City Lea assumed the youth development role.

The backroom staff was buttressed further in January 1988, when David Pleat took on **Gordon Lee** as coach. The one-time Villa and Shrewsbury full-back had been working abroad (with KR Reykjavik, and in the Middle East) after stints in the manager's chair at each of Port Vale, Blackburn Rovers, Newcastle United, Everton and Preston North End. Pleat then showed he intended to persevere with a back-up team of three coaches when appointing former City favourite Bobby Roberts to the staff on Peter Morris' departure. Further changes during the 1989 close season saw Cyril Lea's exit and the arrival of former Luton player, coach and manager **John Moore**.

DAVE RICHARDSON

PHYSIOTHERAPISTS

Until the late 60's, it was usual for the head trainer both to act as match-day sponge-man and to run the club's treatment room. Increasing sophistication in the healing skills associated with football injuries then brought about the fairly widespread employment of specialists; and City joined the ranks of those clubs utilising qualified physiotherapists on their own staffs when appointing **George Preston** in 1968. George's father had been involved with Peterborough United for over 20 years, but his own grounding as a sports physio had come with Kent County Cricket Club. He remained at Filbert Street until January 1977, when former Stirling Albion and St.Johnstone physio **Jim Peacock** took over. The latter's stay was only brief, however (he subsequently rejoined St.Johnstone), and ten months later, **John McVey** was tempted away from his NHS practise to take over at Leicester. Despite being Scots-born, John also performed physio duties for the Northern Ireland national team for several years. He left Filbert Street to take up a private practice in May 1989, to be replaced the following month by **Mark Geeson**, the former Kettering and Grimsby Town physiotherapist.

CHAIRMEN
& DIRECTORS

Leicester Fosse Committee Members (1891 -1897)

J.P.Angrave, T.S.Ashmole, F.Ashwell (president), J.Atter,
J.A.Barfoot, W.J.Brierley, J.E.Carpenter, H.Chitham,
J.Coleman, M.A.Cook, W.J.Cooper, J.J.Curtis, F.Gardner,
G.H.Geeson, F.W.Green, J.H.Grinen, Dr.Halkyard, J.D.Harris,
W.H.Harris, J.A.Hartopp, S.Hudson, E.Johnson, James Johnson,
Joseph Johnson, W.G.Jones, C.W.Kilby, E.A.Marson,
G.Palmer, A.T.Porter, S.Reid, T.Salisbury, T.Seddon,
J.Simmons, H.Simpson, A.W.Staines, A.J.Stubbs, C.Walker,
A.West, W.A.Wilbourne, T.H.Woollerton.
(Prior to 1891, the club president had been Sir Thomas Wright.)

Leicester Fosse Directors (1897-1919)

E.J.Benn, C.Bentley, J.S.Blackwell, G.W.Boylan, L.H.Burridge,
H.Collins, T.Collins, W.J.Cooper, C.Crossland, J.J.Curtis,
J.A.Hartopp, J.M.Hawkes, S.Hudson (ch 1897-99),
W.Hutchinson, J.Lewis, H.Linney, J.H.Linthwaite, E.A.Marson,
S.W.Matthews, F.C.Norman, G.T.Oldershaw, A.Pickering,
S.Reid, A.Rice, M.J.Rice, J.Richards, S.Scattergood, T.Seddon,
W.H.Shaw, J.H.Smedley, S.C.Smith, W.Smith (ch 1911-15),
W.H.Squires (ch 1905-11, 1915-19), A.W.Staines,
W.E.Stevens, A.Tomkins, A.H.Vass (ch 1899-1905), P.Wilson,
G.Woodford, C.Wright, F.W.Wright, O.J.Wright.
(Presidents 1897-1919: Sir J.F.L.Rolleston, A.H.Vass,
M.J.Rice).

Leicester City Directors (from 1919)
(previously on Fosse board)*

L.H.Burridge (* 1919-1940) (ch 1927-1929; 1933-1935)
H.Collins (* 1919-1921)
C.Crossland (* 1919-1928)
W.A.Jennings (1919-1921) (ch 1919-1921)
H.Linney (* 1919-1924)
A.Needham (1919-1931; 1936-1939)
A.E.Pudan (1919-1940) (ch 1929-1931)
W.H.Squires (* 1919-1936;1936-1940) (ch 1925-1927; 1931-
1933; pres 1933-1936)
W.Tompkins (1919-1932)
M.J.Rice (* pres 1919-1925; ch 1921-1925; dir 1929-1931)
J.Carter (1921-1924)
A.Rice (* 1921-1940)
E.Gregson (1921-1940) (ch 1935-1938)
W.A.Tompkins (1933-1940) (ch 1938-1940)
W.S.G.Needham, OBE (1936-1940; 1941-1979) (ch 1961-1964;
1975-1978)
F.S.Smith (1936-1940)
L.L.Green (1939-1940;1940-1946)
L.T.Shipman, CBE (1939-1979) (ch 1948-1956; 1970-73)
A.E.Pallett (1939-1979) (ch 1940-1948; 1967-1970)
G.McDonald (1940)
W.A.Wileman (1940-1968) (ch 1956-1958)
T.S.Bloor (1941-1978) (ch 1958-1961; 1973-1975)
D.E.Sharp (1946-1983) (ch 1964-1967; 1978-1981)
J.H.Burridge (1959-1974)
T.W.Shipman (1966-date) (ch 1981-date)

T.E.Bloor (1974-1986)
C.McLeod (1976-1978)
W.G.Page (1976-date)
W.K.Shooter (1979-date)
T.Smeaton (1979-date)
T.L.Bennett (vice-pres 1983; pres 1984-date)
M.F.George (vice-pres 1983; dir 1983-date)
J.M.Elsom (vice-pres 1983; dir 1984-date)
K.R.Brigstock (vice-pres 1985-date)

SECRETARIES

The post of secretary was not nominally separated from that of manager until 1936, when **George Smith** was promoted from the role of assistant secretary he had held since Willie Orr arrived in 1926. Smith discharged his administrative duties until the end of the war (having done much to keep the club going during the hostilities), when **Charles Maley** was appointed in his stead.

A seemingly dour Scot from a footballing family (his uncle Willie managed Celtic to glory, while his father Tom was secretary-manager at Manchester City and Bradford Park Avenue), Charles arrived from Bradford City in 1945, ran a fairly formal and faintly forbidding administration, and stayed until retirement in 1962. He died in January 1965.

Eddie Plumley was his successor, immediately noted for a greater dynamism and a rather more sophisticated grasp of public relations principles. Originally a young goalkeeper on the books of Birmingham City, Eddie had shifted to the St.Andrews office as an assistant in 1955. He found himself with a Cup Final on his hands in his first season at Leicester, and coped well with the changing demands on a football administrator throughout the 60's; moving on to Coventry in 1969, and later to the role of Chief Executive at Watford.

City looked far afield for their next appointment, bringing **John Smith** back to England after a stint as business manager of the New York Generals (the club which later became the Cosmos). John had learnt the office ropes at Leyton Orient, the Football Combination and Queens Park Rangers before his Stateside sojourn, and was noted as something of a progressive thinker at Leicester throughout the 70's, when the club's commercial base had to be efficiently diversified. He moved on in 1979 to become Chief Executive at Luton Town, and has since been centrally involved in a host of Kenilworth Road controversies over relocation, artificial pitches, and bans on away supporters.

Alan Bennett, appointed in February 1979 and still in post, experienced a three month 'handover' period with Smith, while still functioning as secretary of Aston Villa. He had begun his administrative career with the Football Association, and had been assistant secretary at Chelsea before taking over the Villa Park office. He is noted, especially via his programme column, for striking a fine diplomatic balance between the demands of communication and confidentiality.

The authors would like to express sincere thanks
to all those companies and individuals
whose subscriptions to this book helped make
publication possible.

PATRONS
ROLL OF HONOUR

McCHRYSTALS SOLICITORS

71, King Street, Leicester

NATIONAL WESTMINSTER BANK PLC

2, St.Martins, Leicester

NATIONAL WESTMINSTER BANK PLC

2, St.Martins, Leicester

F.W.HEWITT & SON (1927) LTD

St.George Street, Leicester

PARK ASSOCIATES LTD

13, Victoria Street, Nottingham

KILBY BRIDGE MOTORS

Kilby Bridge, Wigston, Leicester

TALBOGRAPHIC SYSTEMS LTD

James House, Welford Road, Leicester

ANSELLS SALES LTD

Aldridge Road, Perry Barr, Birmingham

MIDLAND INSULATION SUPPLIES LTD

1, Mill Ind. Estate, Quarry Lane, Enderby

ACE WINDOWS

23a, Leicester Road, Anstey, Leicester

GCM PRINT & PACKAGING SERVICE LIMITED

16, East Park Road, Leicester

CENTRAL MOTOR COMPANY (LEICESTER) LTD

Foundry Square, Belgrave Gate, Leicester

FRESHA BAKERIES LTD

Humberstone Lane, Leicester

LOUGHBOROUGH & DISTRICT L.C.F.C. SUPPORTERS CLUB

87, Brookfield Avenue, Loughborough, Leics

TRAVEL FORCE LIMITED

High Street, Leicester

McHUGH (CIVIL ENGINEERING) LIMITED

637, Melton Road, Thurmaston, Leicester

SUBSCRIBERS

1	LEICESTER CITY FOOTBALL CLUB	62	DAVID STEPHEN KENDALL, Wigston Meadows, Leics
2	THE FOOTBALL LEAGUE	63	STEPHEN ROSS, Leicester
3	T.L.BENNETT, President, Leicester City F.C.	64	JOHN TRELEVEN, West Kensington, London
4	T.W.SHIPMAN, Chairman, Leicester City F.C.	65	BEN BIGGS
5	L.T.SHIPMAN C.B.E., Life Member, Leicester City F.C.	66	MICHAEL J. ATKINSON, Kilby, Leics
6	KEN BRIGSTOCK, Vice President, Leicester City F.C.	67	ERNEST TENCH, Lynwood, Western Australia
7	MARTIN GEORGE, Vice Chairman, Leicester City F.C.	68	SIMON LANE, Glenfield, Leicester
8	JOHN ELSOM, Director, Leicester City F.C.	69	Miss CHERYL AMANDA HOLMES
9	BILL PAGE, Director, Leicester City F.C.	70	PETER GREEN, Melton Mowbray, Leics
10	BILL SHOOTER, Director, Leicester City F.C.	71	Cpl. S. NYSZCZOTA, Bassingbourn Barracks, Herts
11	TOM SMEATON, Director, Leicester City F.C.	72	COLIN EVERETT, Leicester
12	ALAN BENNETT, General Secretary, Leicester City F.C.	73	CHARLES HINE, South Wigston, Leicester
13	DAVID PLEAT, Manager, Leicester City F.C.	74	Mrs P. MORAN
14	PETER HILL, Commercial Manager, Leicester City F.C.	75	ARTHUR ATKINS, Toronto, Ontario, Canada
15	ALAN BIRCHENALL, Public Relations, Leicester City F.C.	76	MICHAEL P. DONOGHUE, W.V.A. U.S.A.
16	JACK CURTIS, Youth Liaison Officer, Leicester City F.C.	77	BRIAN JAMES, Glen Parva, Leicester
17	JOANNA POOL, Leicester City F.C.	78	J.W.GREATOREX, Anstey, Leicester
18	CHARLIE ADAM, Leicester	79	DAVID KEATS, Thornton Heath, Surrey
19	MIKE DAVAGE, Old Catton, Norwich	80	TREVOR NUNN, Spondon, Derbys
20	THE ASSOCIATION OF FOOTBALL STATISTICIANS	81	PADDY, CHRIS & JONATHAN BUCKLEY, Derbys
21	KAREN LEVENS, Vienna, Austria	82	WALTER FREARSON, Earl Shilton, Leics
22	ROLAND ORTON, Great Bowden, Leics	83	GEOFFREY TURNER, Scarborough, N.Yorkshire
23	CLARICE LAXTON, Burnmoor St., Leicester	84	CLIVE GUNBY, Bromley, Kent
24	NEVILLE CHADWICK PHOTOGRAPHY,Wigston, Leicester	85	MICHAEL McCONKEY, Luton, Beds
25	DANNY McKEOWN, Leicester Forest East	86	COLIN J.S.ONIONS, Fleckney, Leics
26	K.S.E.CHERRY, Braunstone, Leicester	87	J.GARNER, Leicester
27	R.HEIGHWAY, Low Fell, Tyne & Wear	88	Miss STEPHANIE BOSWORTH, Glen Parva, Leicester
28	K.N. & H.A.BASKCOMB, Worth Matravers, Dorset	89	PHILLIP M.EVANS
29	NEIL FOWLER, Brassington, Derbys	90	CHRIS KERSLAKE, Swindon, Wilts
30	NORMAN GREENOP, Gamblesby, Cumbria	91	STEPHEN R.SMITH
31	BRIAN AUSTICK, Otley, W.Yorkshire	92	ANDREW JAMES SIBSON
32	P.LOWE, Whitwick, Leics	93	D.E.DURRAN, Shearsby, Leics
33	Mrs B.TAYLOR, Littlethorpe,Leics	94	CRAIG BIRD, Wigston Magna, Leicester
34	ANDREW DAVY, Tathwell, Lincs	95	K.EVANS, Measham, Burton on Trent, Derbys
35	ADRIAN P.WOOD, Duston, Northampton	96	ADRIAN GASCOIGNE, Barwell, Leics
37	IAN DAVIDSON, Glastonbury, Somerset	97	MICHAEL T.I'ANSON, Hinckley, Leics
38	WILLIAM R.DAVIDSON, Rugby, Warks	98	ANDREW GREATOREX, Glenfield, Leicester
39	MICKEY STRETTON, Leicester	99	GARY BRANSTON, Thurnby, Leicester
40	EDGAR ARTHUR ASKHAM,	100	NATHAN THOMAS, Leicester
41	DAVID ASKHAM, Wigston Magna,Leicester	101	JOHN HAMILTON, Enderby, Leics
42	SUSAN STANHOPE, Glen Parva, Leicester	102	T.J.MUGGLETON, Syston, Leics
43	IAN BLACKHURST, Glen Parva, Leicester	103	NICK ATKINS,Wollaton Park, Nottingham
44	NEIL BLACKHURST, Glen Parva, Leicester	104	LIAM BENFORD, Eyres Monsell, Leicester
45	ANDREW SHERRIFF,	105	A.L.EARP, Chilton, Devon
46	NIGEL LEWIS, Leicester	106	NEIL C GOODFELLOW, Leicester
47	R.T.PAGE, Oadby, Leicester	107	NEIL C.GOODFELLOW, Leicester
48	DAVID BISHOP, Basildon, Essex	108	ANDREW D.JARRAM, Groby, Leicester
49	DAVID WILLCOX, Huncote, Leics	109	TERENCE JOHN O'CONNOR, Leicester
50	M. J. FARMER, Carington Arms, Ashby Folville, Leics	110	GRAHAM PENDERED, Rushden, Northants
51	R.F.WILLCOCKS, Sileby, Leics	111	TONY ROBINSON, Earl Shilton, Leics
52	S.S.GODDARD, Leicester	112	DAVID WALLIS
53	GERALD PICKERING, Leicester	113	KEITH ELLIS, Kirby Muxloe, Leics
54	WILLIAM PICKERING, Leicester	114	DAVID BROOKS, Thurmaston, Leicester
55	CHRISTOPHER ROBIN BERWICK, Blaby, Leicester	115	ROBERT MARTIN GREGORY, Stoke-on-Trent, Staffs
56	DANIEL ABELL,	116	P.R.NAYLOR, Melton Mowbray, Leics
57	BRYAN PLANT, Leicester	117	MICHAEL JACKSON, Stoneygate, Leicester
58	HANNU SUOJANEN, Turku, Finland	118	GARY A.KIRK, Braunstone, Leicester
59	A.P.TRIGG, Corby, Northants	119	GRAEME MALCOLM NORRIS, Kettering, Northants
60	BARRY CARLISLE,	120	D.P.RICHENS, Dursley, Gloucestershire
61	DAVID CARLISLE, Coalville, Leics	121	FRANK DARLING, Deptford, London

122 JASON FINDLEY, Western Park, Leicester
123 DAVID KIRKBY, Shepshed, Leics
124 STEPHEN SKELTON, Wildwood, Stafford
125 MARC GUNBY, Walthamstow, London
126 BRIAN TOMLINSON, Wigston, Leicester
127 KEVIN TAYLOR, Narborough, Leics
128 NIGEL PETER WILBY, Bath, Avon
129 PHILIP JOHN WALLAM, Shepshed, Leics
130 NEIL BULLOUS, Wigston Meadows, Leicester
131 DOUGLAS M.KEMP, Walthamstow, London
132 D.NORTON, Quedgeley, Gloucestershire
133 JULIAN C.SUTHERLEY
134 PAUL RICHARD STRATFORD, Kettering, Northants
135 BERT, BRIAN & MARK EVEREST, Leicester
136 BERT, BRIAN & MARK EVEREST, Leicester
137 RONALD JOHNSON, Wellingborough, Northants
138 JOHN McDONAGH, Milton Keynes, Bucks
139 TERRY MATZK, St.Neots, Huntingdon
140 IAN HARRINGTON, East Goscote, Leics
141 JUSTIN PRESTON, Thurcaston, Leicester
142 JOHN PRATT, Leicester
143 GAVIN EVANS, Leicester
144 CHRISTOPHER J.BELL, Knighton, Leicester
145 PHILIP HABERFIELD, Canada
146 TERENCE HABERFIELD
147 KEN HABERFIELD, Loughborough, Leics
148 HOWARD NURSE, Thurcaston, Leicester
149 THOMAS JOHN DAY
150 DARRELL JAMES SUTTON
151 MATTHEW SOADY
152 PAUL SOADY, Brackley, Northants
153 PAUL V.SYKES, Evington, Leicester
154 THE BEDFORD FAMILY, Market Harborough, Leics
155 R.W.BRATT, Leicester
156 ARTHUR BIRD, Kirby Muxloe, Leics
157 KEVIN WARREN, Radcliffe on Trent, Notts
158 GARETH MILLER, Leicester
159 IAN MICHAEL GILLARD, Loughborough, Leics
160 TIMOTHY JOHN PICKETT, Aylestone, Leicester
161 A.P.HOLYOAK, Market Harborough, Leics
162 C.I.HUNT, Birstall, Leicester
163 ROGER AUSTIN, Bourne, Lincs
164 SIMON BROWN, Knighton, Leicester
165 Miss ANNE BONEHAM, Loughborough, Leics
166 MAURICE ALAN BENNETT, Dordon, Staffs
167 PAUL MICHAEL DAY, Castle Donington, Derbys
168 BRIAN GOODGER, Leicester
169 DAVID PAYNE, Cleveleys, Lancs
170 ALAN JOSELIN, Leicester
171 IAN DAVID SILVESTER, Leicester
172 ANN STEWART, Leicester
173 ANDREW PHILIP KNIGHT, Raunds, Northants
174 D.J.HARDY, Anstey, Leicester
175 ROY G.JONES, Market Bosworth, Warks
176 LAURENCE FORD, Kings Heath, Birmingham
177 STAFFORD ROBERT BUCK, Fleckney, Leics
178 STEPHEN INGALL, Cosby, Leics
179 PAUL INGALL, Eyres Monsell, Leicester
180 ANDREW INGALL, Wigston Fields, Leicester
181 D.C.MAYER, Wigston Fields, Leicester
182 HAROLD RICHARDSON, New Parks, Leicester
183 BRIAN W.SMITH, Evington, Leicester
184 IAN D.SMITH, Corby, Northants
185 TOM FALL, Leicester
186 K.BONSER, Hinckley, Leics
187 PETER W.BAXTER, Leicester
188 PETER NEVILLE JOHNSON, Markfield, Leics
189 GAVIN STRETTON, Leicester
190 DAVID ANTONY SMITH, Leicester
191 NEIL STRETTON, Lochmaben, Dumfriesshire
192 Mr.M.S. & Mrs.J.L.KNOTT, Nottingham
193 JOHN MAY, Stevenage, Herts

194 JOHN MACKANESS, Priors Hardwick, Warks
195 STEVE WALTON, Melton Mowbray, Leics
196 RONALD WILTON, Cropston, Leics
197 GRAHAME WOODROFFE, Leicestershire
198 KEVIN WINTERTON, Measham, Staffs
199 IAN NEWHAM, Melton Mowbray, Leics
200 Miss C.N.FINCHAM, Wigston, Leicester
201 PHIL & STEVE BROWN, Leicester Forest East
202 ROBERT TWYCROSS, Leicester
203 ALAN & BRETT BRAY, Selston, Notts
204 NICHOLAS HILL, Newcastle-under-Lyme, Staffs
205 C.W.HOPPER, Ravenshead, Notts
206 TERRY MORGAN, Glen Parva, Leicester
207 JACQUELINE A.MARKLEY
208 G.T.WEBB, Kirby Muxloe, Leics
209 MARTIN JOHN WHEELER, Melton Mowbray, Leics
210 LOUISE TAYLOR, Leicester
211 ANDREW EMLYN GRAHAM RICHARDS, Leicester
212 JAMES OSBORNE, Kegworth, Derbys
213 ROB O'DONNELL, Wigston, Leicester
214 Miss LISA BROWN, Leicester
215 STUART BAILEY, Enderby, Leics
216 GRAHAM RICHARDS, Trent Bridge, Nottingham
217 NEIL T.BROOKES, Melton Mowbray, Leics
218 DAVID CRITCHLOW, Leicester
219 STEVE MATTHEWS, Leicester
220 RICHARD NEIL BREWIN, Huncote, Leics
221 CHRISTOPHER BROWN, Bognor Regis, W.Sussex
222 LAWRENCE H.COTTERILL
223 JIM W.ATKINSON, Leicester
224 KAREN QUILTER, Anstey, Leics
225 I.S.PERKINS, Burbage, Leics
226 NIGEL WATTAM, Bourne, Lincs
227 DAVID WALLWORK, Broughton Astley, Leics
228 PETER WARREN, Ibstock, Leics
229 JAMES R.WOOLLARD, Southborne, Dorset
230 PETER H.FLAVELL, Sapcote, Leics
231 PETER H.FLAVELL, Sapcote, Leics
232 GARY BOWN, Glenfield, Leics
233 STEVEN R.BOTTING, Groby, Leicester
234 IAN HAFFORD, 16 Signal Regiment, BFPO 35
235 SHANE HULL, Bourne, Lincs
236 ADRIAN GARNER, Cotgrave, Nottingham
237 PATRICK SHEEHAN, Shipton on Cherwell, Oxon
238 JOHN WILLIAM SPIERS, Bradway, Sheffield
239 STEPHEN HILL, Wigston Magna, Leicester
240 DEREK MARSHALL, New Parks, Leicester
241 WILLIAM ANTHONY GREEN, Wigston, Leicester
242 PHIL ARNOLD, Winchmore Hill, London
243 T.MOWLE, Melton Mowbray, Leics
244 E.J.C.WOOD, Leicestershire
245 KEVIN WELLS, Harlow, Essex
246 DAVID FEARN, Bilton, Rugby, Warks
247 D.P.JACKSON, Blackpool, Lancs
248 PETE HOLT, Desborough, Northants
249 NIGEL HILL, Bengeo, Hertford, Herts
250 BARRY DOWNES, Wigston Fields, Leicester
251 GREGORY BEAVEN, Leicester
252 GERARD BOLAND, Buckingham, Bucks
253 KEVIN PATRICK WARD, Quorn, Leics
254 K.J. & S.J. & D.E.WAIT, Melton Mowbray, Leics
255 DAVID FREDERICK THOMPSON, Andover, Hants
256 ELAINE MOORE, The Meadows, Nottingham
257 LINDA & ROBERT WORTLEY, Braunstone, Leicester
258 ROBERT WALKER, Stoney Stanton, Leics
259 IAN C.THOMPSON, Newtown Linford, Leics
260 R.A.BREWIN, Hinckley, Leics
261 CAROLINE E.AKERS, Rowley Fields, Leicester
262 IAN CHESTER, Alcester, Warks
263 P.ROBINSON
264 J.WOODWARD, Lutterworth, Leics
265 RICHARD PATRICK WHITTINGTON, Leicester

266 J.D.THOMAS, Geraldton, Western Australia
267 PAUL JACKSON, Portsmouth, Hants
268 D.JONES, Hinckley, Leics
269 JOHN A.FORMAN, Leicester
270 ANDREA DUNION
271 TONY PEARSON, Market Harborough, Leics
272 JOHN PAGE, Abbey Rise, Leicester
273 PAUL J.OSBORNE, Easton-on-the-hill, Lincs
274 ROGER GREW, Barrow-on-Soar, Leics
275 JOHN ROY WEST, Barwell, Leics
276 MARK WILSON, Wilbarston, Leics
277 JAMES ROBERT CORAH,
278 ROBERT CORAH, Castle Donington, Derbys
279 ADAM STEVEN CHARLTON, Leicester
280 ANNE FAIRHURST, Pemberton, Wigan, Lancs
281 HAROLD GREEN
282 PATRICK DUNCAN, London W12
283 D.N.DENTON, Blaby, Leicester
284 JAMES AUGUSTUS, Groby, Leicester
285 T.N.H.BRUTNALL, Oadby, Leicester
286 M.J.BURFORD, Sheffield, South Yorks
287 TANIA L.DENNISON, Sheffield, South Yorks
288 KENNETH COOMBS, Leicester
289 TIMOTHY MARK AHRONSON, Narborough, Leicester
290 DAVE RYAN, Leicester
291 BARRY R.ORTON, Leicester
292 CHRIS BALDERSTONE
293 DENNIS HENRY
294 STEWART HENRY, London SE5
295 RICHARD ROGERS, Glenfield, Leicester
296 Miss SAMANTHA McCARTHY, Leicester
297 TERRY MOSS, Melton Mowbray, Leics
298 ROBERT JAMES UPTON, Syston, Leics
299 PAUL JOHN BRADSHAW, South Wigston, Leicester
300 M.J.HORNSBY, London NW1
301 M.J.HORNSBY, London NW1
302 M.J.HORNSBY, London NW1
303 M.J.HORNSBY, London NW1
304 M.J.HORNSBY, London NW1
305 M.J.HORNSBY, London NW1
306 DAVID N. LUMB, Leicester
307 BRIAN, MICHELLE & PAUL LEES, Leicester
308 S.D.HODSON, Coleorton, Leics
309 C.D.BOCKROSS, New Parks, Leicester
310 DAVE CHRISTIAN, Melton Mowbray, Leics
311 MICHAEL L.POPE, Thurmaston, Leicester
312 RICHARD PYATT, Leicester
313 ANDREW POTTER, New Parks, Leicester
314 PHILIP PASSINGHAM, Market Harborough, Leics
315 J.C.OSBORNE, Hinckley, Leics
316 L.C.F.C.SUPPORTERS' CLUB, (Hinckley Branch)
317 L.C.F.C.SUPPORTERS' CLUB, (Hinckley Branch)
318 PHILLIP BRADLEY, Whitwick, Leics
319 F.D.WALKER, Thurmaston, Leicester
320 G.S.WHITE, Braunstone, Leicester
321 A.SMITH, Countesthorpe, Leics
322 MARTIN SPENCER, Kettering, Northants
323 SHEILA JACOBS, Leicester
324 MICK BALE, Birstall, Leicester
325 ANDREW M.BURNHAM
326 Mrs JANICE M.DRUCE, Fleckney, Leics
327 RICHARD CAVE, Fleckney, Leics
328 GERALD JOHN HUTCHINSON, Leicester
329 JOHN LUCAS, Kibworth, Leics
330 MAURICE LABRAM, Lutterworth, Leics
331 VINCENT JOHN MADDEN, Atherstone, Warks
332 JONATHAN HURST, Thurnby, Leics
333 ALISON MARY LENTON, Blaby, Leics
334 DAVID JOHN HENRY LENTON, Blaby, Leics
335 E.S.THOMAS, Braunstone, Leicester
336 MARK ROBERT TAYLOR, Edgware, Middlesex
337 MICHAEL WILBUR, Crystal Palace, London

338 ANTHONY WILBY, Nuneaton, Warks
339 W.P.DOYLE, Edmonton, London
340 HENRYK CYNKAR, Rushey Mead, Leicester
341 MARK COATES, Aylestone, Leicester
342 PATRICK DUFFY
343 MALCOLM C.CLAPHAM, Wigston, Leicester
344 NEAL HALFPENNY, South Wigston, Leicester
345 IAN R.REYNOLDS, Wellingborough, Northants
346 J.S.ROBINSON, Hinckley, Leics
347 HAROLD PUTT, Loughborough, Leics
348 STEVE PORTER, Loughborough, Leics
349 DEE & GRAHAM CLARKE, Glen Parva, Leicester
350 SHARON CHAMBERLAIN, Wigston Magna, Leicester
351 NIGEL RICHES, Loughborough, Leics
352 PETER SMITH, Coalville, Leics
353 ELIZABETH ANN SMITH, Oadby, Leicester
354 K.T.H.PORTER, Gilmorton, Leics
355 CRAIG POLLARD, Leicester
356 GEOFFREY LOVETT, Burbage, Leics
357 T.HANGER, Kettering, Northants
358 GRAHAM JORDISON, Blackburn, Lancs
359 Mrs KAREN CROSSLEY, Leicester
360 RAYMOND J.HALL, Claybrooke Magna, Leics
361 DEREK M.CURTIS, Market Harborough, Leics
362 JOHN ROBERT WOODLAND, Humberstone, Leicester
363 NATHAN WORRALL, Ratby, Leics
364 DANIEL COTTERELL, Hinckley, Leics
365 ELAINE TRINDER, Leicester
366 PETER HALL, Syston, Leics
367 JAMES F.L.WESTWOOD, Towcester, Northants
368 A.C.WALSOM, Braunstone, Leicester
369 EDWARD GEORGE WALE, Leicester
370 DENIS MANNING, South Africa
371 JONATHON ISON
372 BRADLEY ILIFFE
373 JAMES E.G.JOHNSON, Bradford, W.Yorkshire
374 GEOFFREY W.HANDS, Market Harborough, Leics
375 CHRISTOPHER J.WIGGINGTON, London SW1
376 G.L.WOOD, Culcavey, Hillsborough, Co. Down, N.Ireland
377 T.WORMLEIGHTON, Glen Parva, Leicester
378 DOMINIC JAMES PATRICK WILLIAMS, Keighley, Yorks
379 SYDNEY H.LEE, Halesowen, W.Midlands
380 ROBERT LEE, Leicester
381 F.J.LUCE, Bexleyheath, Kent
382 DAVID LAYHE, Worksop, Notts
383 KEITH BACKUS,
384 DAVID LONG, West Knighton, Leicester
385 SEAN LINNELL, Glen Parva, Leicester
386 DAVID CULLEN, New Parks, Leicester
387 DARREN CHENELER, Polesworth, Staffs
388 MARK CAIN, Happy Valley, Hong Kong
389 STEVE LAMBDEN, Sports Ed. Central T.V.
390 CENTRAL T.V.SPORT, Nottingham
391 CENTRAL T.V.SPORT, Nottingham
392 CENTRAL T.V.SPORT, Nottingham
393 MARTYN COE, Leicester
394 GRAHAM J.COOK, Rowley Fields, Leicester
395 SHAUN MOLLOY, Leicester
396 GARY MILLS, Earls Barton, Northants
397 WAYNE MILLS, Earls Barton, Northants
398 REG PARRY, Anstey, Leicester
399 MARTYN MORTON, Leicester
400 CHRISTOPHER MORRIS, Perry Barr, Birmingham
401 PAUL MANSON, Whitwick, Leics
402 DAVID J.PICK, Thurnby Lodge Estate, Leicester
403 BARRY GOULD
404 PEACHY Snr.
405 C.VENABLES
406 R.FREESTONE
407 MATTHEW CORT
408 DAVID G.LEEDHAM
409 MARK LORD

410 DAVID MARVIN	482 Master CRAIG TURNER, Grantham, Lincs
411 RICKY VARNEY	483 L.EXTON, Bedford
412 DENIS MOORE, Hatfield, Herts	484 MARIE RILEY, Melton Mowbray, Leics
413 LEE MIDDLETON, Oadby, Leicester	485 PAUL RILEY, Melton Mowbray, Leics
414 KEITH W.McLAUGHLIN, (Accountant) Markfield, Leics	486 GUY WILLIAM STANHOPE, Cosby, Leics
415 KEITH W.McLAUGHLIN, (Accountant) Markfield, Leics	487 BOYD EDWARD STANHOPE, Cosby, Leics
416 KEITH W.McLAUGHLIN, (Accountant) Markfield, Leics	488 Mrs E.M.HARRISON, Leicester
417 CHRISTOPHER D. MOORE & Co, Rothley, Leics	489 IN MEMORY OF ROSEMARY FORRESTER
418 STEVEN MACKANESS, Priors Hardwick, Warks	490 THE DRAYCOTT FAMILY of Thurmaston, Leicester
419 JOHN BELTON, LOUGHBOROUGH DYNAMO F.C.	491 ØIVIND SMESTAD, Skårer, Norway
420 MARK RICHARDSON,Leicester	492 NEIL PARK, Queniborough, Leics
421 ANDY ROBINSON	493 NIGEL, NEIL, RICHARD & JAMES BROWNE, Leicester
422 TIM ROBINSON	494 LINDA GINNETTA, Leicester
423 JOHN C.ROBINSON	495 PAUL GREENLEES, Cheadle, Cheshire
424 JOHN ROBINSON, Hinckley, Leics	496 PHILLIP PARKER, Thurnby Lodge, Leicester
425 JASON DAVID RADCLIFFE	497 ROBERT G.PRESSLER, Ullesthorpe, Leics
426 CHRISTOPHER SLOAN	498 GEORGE ERNEST WILES, Rossington, S.Yorkshire
427 D.L.SMITH, Flitwick, Bedfordshire	499 DON HALES, Holwell, Hitchin, Herts
428 ANDREW JOHN LANG	500 MIKE & DIANA CARR, Oreland, Pennsylvania,U.S.A.
429 PAUL ANTHONY STACEY, Thatcham, Berks	501 P.J.HUNT, Loughborough, Leics
430 A.K.STEVENS, Brewood, Staffs	502 RALPH MORTIMER, London NW4
431 RICHARD SPOONER	503 P.T.WILSON, Leicester Forest East
432 BRENDAN TYRRELL, Kibworth Beauchamp, Leics	504 CARL HULLS, Saffron Lane, Leicester
433 J.UNWIN, Quorn, Leics	505 MICHAEL WESTON, Leicester
434 MARK NORTON, Leicester	506 GLENN JONES, Leicester
435 CHRISTOPHER NORTON, Oadby, Leicester	507 MARY EARP, Oadby, Leicester
436 T.W.HYSLOP, Corby, Northants	508 LISA CAVEN, Saffron Lane, Leicester
437 CHRISTOPHER IAN SMITH, Wigston, Leicester	509 STUART J.FOWLER, Leicester
438 DAVID S.HUMBERSTON, Leicester	510 D.C.WHEATLEY, Ilford, Essex
439 JOHN KERR & MASTER I.KERR, Melton Mowbray, Leics	511 JOHN PASIECZNIK, Belgrave, Leicester
440 NIGEL DOWNES, Wigston, Leicester	512 ALAN JACKSON, Radcliffe-on-Trent, Notts
441 ANDREW WILBY, Rushden, Northants	513 TREVOR C.CLEAVER, King's Lynn, Norfolk
442 PAUL TOMPKINS, Kettering, Northants	514 M.C.WIDDOWSON, Countesthorpe, Leics
443 A.C.JUDSON, Asfordby, Leics	515 MARK EASON, Wigston Meadows, Leicester
444 A.C.JUDSON, Asfordby, Leics	516 N.M.MASTERS, Daventry, Northants
445 GRAHAM PARKER, Markfield, Leics	517 R.TURBITT, Darlington, Co.Durham
446 CARL & GORDON HARRISON, Mountsorrel, Leics	518 ERIC CLEAVER, Clacton-on-Sea, Essex
447 I.SHARMAN, Burbage, Leics	519 BARRIE ANTHONY BARNETT, Evesham, Worcs
448 THOMAS LENNON, Leicester	520 ROGER ELM-ABBOT, London NW3
449 T.J.GRANT, Saffron Walden, Essex	521 ANTHONY W.LAYWOOD, Knipton, Lincs
450 JOHN R.TAYLOR, Lower Sydenham, London	522 PAUL MARTIN ELLIS, Mottingham, London SE9
451 A.W.PICKER, INCHLINES LTD, Leicester	523 M.WAGSTAFF, Bishops Waltham, Hants
452 A.W.PICKER, INCHLINES LTD, Leicester	524 J.RINGROSE, Romford, Essex
453 R.A.CLARKE, RICH & CARR, Leicester	525 DAVID LUMB, Bolton, Lancs
454 D.P.CHRISTIAN, RICH & CARR, Leicester	526 DEREK HYDE, Swansea, West Glamorgan
455 DAVID BOWLER, TOPS TARPAULIN M'FTRS, Leicester	527 L.A.ZAMMIT, Fareham, Hants
456 ANONYMOUS SUPPORTER, Eyres Monsell, Leicester	528 MOIRA & FREDERICK FURNESS, North Shields
457 ANONYMOUS SUPPORTER, Leicester Forest East	529 A.& J.A.WATERMAN, Grays, Essex
458 DAVID BUTTERISS, Wigston, Leicester	530 STEPHEN PEARS, Croft, Leics
459 B.S.DHADLI, London SW1	531 HARRY KAY, Bingley, West Yorkshire
460 IAN MICHAEL FREEMAN, Wellingborough, Northants	532 WADE MARTIN, Sandbach, Cheshire
461 CHRIS SWISTAK, Acton, London W3	533 SCOTT KENNEY, R.A.F.Wildenrath, B.F.P.O. 42
462 MARK HEALEY, Groby, Leicester	534 B.H.STANDISH, Banbury, Oxon
463 B.MOORE, Leicester	535 FREDERICK JOHN LEE, Plymouth, Devon
464 ANDREW PETER SMYTHE, Bishop Waltham, Hants	536 G.T.ALLMAN, Essington, Wolverhampton
465 MAURICE CANN, Maidenhead, Berks	537 JOHN NORTHCUTT, Great Baddow, Essex
466 S.DREWERY, Belgrave, Leicester	538 GEORGE A.HIGHAM, Bebington, Wirral
467 ANDREW J.BRENNAN, Cosby, Leics	539 SEAN JOHN BURTON, Claybrooke Magna, Leics
468 IAN CLEMENTS, Leicester	540 LEE GOLDING, Broughton Astley, Leics
469 Mr PETER & Miss SAMMI GREGORY, Leicester	541 DAVID COULSON, Nuneaton, Warks
470 IAN D.NESBITT, Glenfield, Leicester	542 GERALD HILL, Stoke-on-Trent, Staffs
471 PAUL E.HOLE, Narborough, Leicester	543 TONY BLUFF, Thurnscoe, South Yorks
472 MARK ODAMS, Brentwood, Essex	544 DAFYDD WILLIAMS, Northfield, Birmingham
473 MICHAEL TOPLIS, Long Eaton, Notts	545 D.A.R.H.WEBSTER, Ashford, Middlesex
474 MICK HORN, Wigston Magna, Leicester	546 JOHN NORMAN, Wigston, Leicester
475 LEICESTER HANDBALL CLUB '73	547 MICHAEL CAMPBELL, Kingsbury, London NW9
476 PAUL WHEATLEY, Retford, Notts	548 R.K.SHOESMITH, Cranham, Upminster, Essex
477 J.W.CANEY, Beaumont Leys, Leicester	549 DAVID R.LEAKE, Countesthorpe, Leics
478 MATTHEW H. LIQUORISH, Mountsorrel, Leics	550 NICHOLAS TEBBUTT, Leicester
479 MALC, BEN & TOM SNELL, Thrussington, Leics	551 ANDY PATEMAN, Leicester
480 IAN & JAMES HUGHES, Thrussington, Leics	552 JOHN BEGGIE, Leicester
481 B.V.MURPHY, Maidenhead, Berks	553 DARREN CARTLIDGE, Leicester

554 LINDA BONE, Gosport, Hants
555 A.R.HARTSHORN, Leicester
556 B.HOURSTON, St.Ola, Orkney
557 DAVID W.RUSH, Reading, Berkshire
558 A.WILKINSON, Colchester, Essex
559 N.F.WEBSTER (Builders), Oundle, Peterborough
560 SHAUN McGRADY, Hinckley, Leics
561 J.MOTSON, St Albans, Herts
562 ALAN EVERITT, Leicester
563 CHRISTOPHER DEAN SMITH, Wigston, Leicester
564 VICKY BIRCH, Northampton
565 FRANK GRANDE, Whitehills, Northampton
566 GEOFFREY WRIGHT, Ware, Herts
567 DAVID J. McGREGOR, Rugby, Warks
568 CLIFF GARNER, Nuneaton, Warks
569 ANDREW JOYCE, Ratby, Leics
570 COLIN COLLINGWOOD, Edingale, Staffs
571 STUART CONOPO, Kilsby, Warks
572 KEN DILKES, Leicester
573 CHRIS YORK, Thurmaston, Leicester
574 STEPHEN SMITH, Wigston, Leicester
575 COLIN JOHNSON, Coalville, Leics
576 MICHAEL P.COSGROVE, Askham, Notts
577 ANDY CLAYTON, Braunstone, Leicester
578 SIMON CLENT, Cosby, Leics
579 R.C.STEADMAN, Barrow-on-Soar, Leics
580 NIGEL DEVENEY
581 GUY H.REVIS, Gilmorton, Leics
582 Miss DEBORAH BILLS, Newbold Verdon, Leics
583 ROBIN HOLDER, Glen Parva, Leicester
584 BEN HAYWOOD, Barwell, Leics
585 SIDNEY JOHN BENNETT, Hinckley, Leics
586 JAMES W.HOLLAND, South Wigston, Leicester
587 SHAUN SIBSON, Mountsorrel, Leics
588 A.W.C.TAYLOR, Spalding, Lincs
589 PHILIP SWALES, Stoneygate, Leicester
590 MICHAEL MILLS, Beaumont Leys, Leicester
591 NORMAN KERR, Eyres Monsell, Leicester
592 WALTER HIGGINS,O.B.E.,J.P. Great Glen, Leics
593 ASHLEY HEVER, Coalville, Leics
594 A.V.WARD, Aylestone, Leicester
595 PIPPA MALLABAND, Burgess Hill, West Sussex
596 A.N.DAVIS, Nuneaton, Warks
597 S.COLLINGS, Leicester
598 J.A.HARRIS, Enfield, Middlesex
599 SIMON J.BATTERBEE, Rotterdam, Holland
600 Dr.JOHN E.BATTERBEE, Rotterdam, Holland
601 DAVID HART, Hemel Hempstead, Herts
602 RICHARD HART, Hemel Hempstead, Herts
603 B.FREESTONE, Atherstone, Warks
604 DAVID ROBERT EARNSHAW, Belper, Derbys
605 SIMON TUFF, Glenfield, Leicester
606 K.MOULDEN, Reading, Berks
607 JAMES MICHAEL MOORE, Oakham, Leics
608 JIM READ, London E5
609 STEPHEN KIERAN BYRNE, Bristol, Avon
610 CHARLES STANDLEY, Thorpe Langton, Leics
611 CLIVE RICHARDS, Wigston, Leicester
612 P.J.COOKE, Braunstone, Leicester
613 RICHARD CONNOLLY, Leicester
614 LEONARD COOK, Leicester
615 OLLIE PARDO, Chesterfield, Derbys
616 DEAN WALTON, Gilmorton, Leics
617 MARK HULLS, Leicester
618 RAY KIRBY, Wigston Magna, Leicester
619 JUSTIN & MATTHEW GANDY,Birstall, Leicester
620 ROGER H.GANDY, Birstall, Leicester
621 RICHARD D.N.WELLS, Kingston-upon-Thames, Surrey
622 ALLAN GEARY, Coalville, Leics
623 MICHAEL KEAVENY, Goodwood, Leicester
624 MARTIN WHITLOCK, Roade, Northants
625 MARTIN W.MILLER, Coventry, Warks

626 LARS-OLOF WENDLER, Hoganas, Sweden
627 MARK JOHNSON, Leicester
628 ALAN WARD, Nuneaton, Warks
629 CHRISTIAN REICHLING, Leicester
630 DAVID PANTHER, Belgrave, Leicester
631 KEVIN PARKER, Stamford, Lincs
632 IAIN DUNLOP, Barwell, Leics
633 RICKY ARMS, Hinckley, Leics
634 M.HERWORTH, Leicester
635 CRAIG MUSSON,East Leake, Leics
636 B.E.WARDLE, Shepshed, Leics
637 NEIL F.JENSEN, Hitchin, Herts
638 PAUL FRANCIS LOVELOCK, Newfoundpool, Leicester
639 J.M.& M.J. & J.F.CARTER, Birstall, Leicester
640 J.M.& M.J. & J.F.CARTER, Birstall, Leicester
641 DAVID JOHN COLEMAN, Coalville, Leics
642 M.J.WARD, Leicester
643 S.C.NASH, Narborough, Leics
644 J.S.WREN, Shepshed, Leics
645 COLIN DAVIS, New York City, U.S.A.
646 ALAN PETCHER, Cirencester, Glos
647 JASON NIXON, Thurnby Lodge, Leicester
648 DAVID AYRE, Wigston Magna, Leicester
649 ANDREW IWASZKO, Leicester
650 ANDREW IWASZKO, Leicester
651 ANTHONY RICHARD OWEN, Birstall, Leicester
652 DAVID C.PARKER, Leicester
653 CLIVE CHEAL, Lancing, Sussex
654 A.HARDING, Swindon, Wilts
655 DARRYL JOHNATHON HOY, Oadby, Leicester
656 REV.CANON GORDON SEALY, Leicester
657 Mrs E.WELLS, Leicester
658 W.D.PHILLIPS, Frogmore, Devon
659 MARK POOLE, Ibstock, Leics
660 TROND ISAKSEN, Vevelstad, Norway
661 STANLEY A.ROBINSON, Bexleyheath, Kent
662 KEITH DUCKER, Norwich
663 W.E.BROMBLEY & SONS, Loughborough, Leics
664 W.E.BROMBLEY & SONS, Loughborough, Leics
665 G.J.DUCHARME, Leicester
666 ANDREW DAVID MAYNEORD, Alcester, Warks
667 W.J.BELL, Ailsworth, Peterborough
668 SIMON CRUICKSHANK, Weldon, Northants
669 PETER & WENDY JONES, Bury St.Edmunds, Suffolk
670 R.HUTCHINSON, Loughborough, Leics
671 PETER FELL, Mansfield, Notts
672 DAVID WAYTE, Thringstone, Leics
673 SIMON JOHN GUILDFORD, Birstall, Leicester
674 JOHN EATON, Kettering, Northants
675 STUART COE, Leicester
676 NEIL HORSLEY, Rowley Fields, Leicester
677 BARRY ROGER ALLEN, Rothwell, Northants
678 LEE PAYNE, Cropston, Leics
679 NIGEL JOHN GREEN, Coalville, Leics
680 CHRIS EYRE, Wendover, Bucks
681 DAVID BAILEY, Kettering, Northants
682 MARK O'NEILL, Wymondham, Leics
683 MATT COX, Glen Parva, Leicester
684 BARRY MAX THRAVES, Leicester
685 CARL BROOMHEAD, Blaby, Leics
686 SIMON KIMBER, Cosby, Leics
687 RICHARD SMITH, Dublin, Republic of Ireland
688 TONY BILLING, Costock, Leics
689 MATTHEW COLIN HASELTON, Leicester
690 ROBERT SINKINSON, Leicester
691 ROBERT BUTLIN, Market Harborough, Leics
692 PHILIP YORK, Hinckley, Leics
693 BEN FLETCHER, London NW6
694 PHILLIP DARREN SMITH, Ashby-de-la-Zouch,Leics
695 SERBIA FOOTBALL CLUB, Evington, Leicester
696 RICHARD STOCKEN, Holmes Chapel, Cheshire
697 DAVID BERRIDGE, Newton Abbot, Devon

698	STAN ALLEN
699	ROBERT TOWERS, Hinckley, Leics
700	RICHARD C.STANIFORTH,Corston, Malmesbury, Wilts
701	HARLEY LAWER, Plymouth, Devon
702	M.SWART, En Wieringerwerf, The Netherlands
703	DAVID DOWNS, Reading, Berks
704	PHILIP HARRY WHITEHEAD, Blackburn, Lancs
705	GARETH M.DAVIES, Holyhead, Gwynedd
706	WILLIAM DONNACHIE, Edinburgh
707	IAN BLAIR, Bath, Avon
708	H.BERRY, Chorley, Lancs
709	ROGER HUDSON, Thames Ditton, Surrey
710	JOHN MUSGROVE, Gateshead, Tyne & Wear
711	DONALD NOBLE, Dunkeld, Perthsire
712	PAUL CURETON, Telford, Shropshire
713	DAVID HELLIWELL, Sheffield, S.Yorkshire
714	GRAHAM & JANET CARTER, Needham Market, Suffolk
715	NORMAN KINCAID, Upper Norwood, London
716	DAVID FAGGIANI, Manchester
717	STUART BEESON, Alvaston, Derbys
718	ANDREW ANDERSON, Dorchester, Dorset
719	DONALD ASHWOOD, Armadale, West Lothian
720	JOE WATERS, South Ockendon, Essex
721	PETER READ, Barlestone, Nuneaton, Warks
722	IAN GRIFFITHS, Wrexham, Clwyd
723	MALCOLM MAIN, Ketton, Nr Stamford, Lincs
724	R.D.KING, Bexleyheath, Kent
725	MATTHEW PHIPPS, Leicester
726	ORTONS SERVICE STATION, Carlton, Nuneaton
727	P.A.& G.A.JEPSON, Narborough, Leics
728	RUSSELL JARVIS, Shepshed, Leics
729	JOHN HANN, Helensburgh, Dunbartonshire
730	TERRY FROST, Wyke,Bradford, West Yorkshire
731	ANDREW CASSIE, C.I.B.LTD, Thames Ditton, Surrey
732	IAN CASSIE, STILETTO LTD, Twickenham, London
733	PETER DRIVER, Syston, Leicester
734	STEVEN MARK SPENCER, Syston, Leicester
735	LEE RICHARD SPENCER, Syston, Leicester
736	PATRICK CLEALL, Snaresbrook, London
737	P.A.CASWELL, Braunstone, Leicester
738	PETER DAVID GINNS, Leicester
739	MARTIN GOULD, Loughborough, Leics
740	ALAN R.BEEBE, Burbage, Leics
741	CHRIS JINKS, Wigston Harcourt, Leics
742	Miss AMANDA EARP, Barnstone, Notts
743	CLIVE A.MAJOR, Loughborough, Leics
744	JOHN PRESTON, Huncote, Leics
745	TIM PRESTON, Huncote, Leics
746	STEVEN BOURNE, Burton upon Trent, Staffs
747	KEVIN PAUL HEIRCOCK, Eyres Monsell, Leicester
748	CHARLES THOMAS BAILEY, Rugby, Warks
749	JOHN WESTON, South Kilworth, Leics
750	STEWART M.OSBORNE, Kettering, Northants
751	DAVID JOHN MARTIN, Haywards Heath, Sussex
752	DANIEL CLEMENTS, Wigston Magna, Leicester
753	PETER LUNN, Catford, London
754	J.E.GARDINER, Lewes, East Sussex
755	ALAN WICKES, East Goscote, Leics
756	PAUL WICKES, Croft, Lincs
757	DUNCAN WATT, Sleaford, Lincs
758	L.DAVIES, Huncote, Leics
759	JAMES MARLOW, St.Marks, Leicester
760	SAMUEL MARK FAIRGRIEVE, Stoney Stanton, Leics
761	DAVID STONELEIGH, HALCYON F.C. Scarborough, N.Yorks
762	ROBERT TINGLEY, Long Clawson, Leics
763	PETER DENNIS THURMAN, Shepshed, Leics
764	CHRIS BRIGHTMORE, Hinckley, Leics
765	BRUCE S.BATEMAN, Beaumont Leys, Leicester
766	JOHN DAVIES, Hathern, Leics
767	J.T.FINN, Queniborough, Leics
768	DAVID SHEPHERD, Hugglescote, Leics
769	ROBERT BERRIDGE, Melton Mowbray, Leics
770	Miss S.A.MATTS, Wigston Fields, Leicester
771	W.V.MATTS, Wigston Fields, Leicester
772	STEPHEN GEARY, Glenfield, Leicester
773	NICHOLAS HANGER, Kettering, Northants
774	CHRISTINA FOX, South Wigston, Leicester
775	KELVIN KNIGHT, Earl Shilton, Leics
776	P.C.TURNER, Keyworth, Notts
777	STUART HOWSIN, Huncote, Leics
778	RICHARD WILBY, Leicester
779	RITA HALL, Market Harborough, Leics
780	DENNIS JAMES, Leicester
781	HOWARD FOREMAN, Stocking Farm Estate, Leicester
782	PETER HOGG, Market Harborough, Leics
783	GREG WILSON, South Wigston, Leicester
784	JEFFREY HILL, Leicester
785	SANDRA & TRACY CRITCHLOW, Leicester
786	T.C.HOLLAND, Atherstone, Warks
787	DAVID FELL, Leicester
788	PAUL & KAREN GIBSON, Leicester
789	HOWARD READER, Glen Parva, Leicester
790	SIDNEY RAYMOND HEATHCOTE(Ray), Leicester
791	JAMES D.WEAVER, Wigston, Leicester
792	KÅRE M.TORGRIMSEN, Stavanger, Norway
793	DEAN BEVANS, Leicester
794	H.W.COATES, Cosby, Leics
795	T.BONHAM, Shepshed, Leics
796	SIMON KING, Rugby, Warks
797	BRIAN SMITH, Great Glen, Leicester
798	M.R.BURDETT, Staines, Middlesex
799	IAN KEW, Leicester Forest East
800	GLENN WILLIS, Newbold Verdon, Leics
801	DAVID ALLEN SKEVINGTON, Hinckley, Leics
802	JOHN BYRNE, Barrhead, Glasgow
803	NEIL HAMMONDS, Leicester
804	CHRISTOPHER DYSON, Sheepy Magna, Warks
805	Mrs BALBI MURRELL, Maidstone, Kent
806	PETE NUNWA
807	GLENN MURRELL, Maidstone, Kent
808	JOHN FLETCHER, Shepshed, Leics
809	MICHAEL COWALL, Rugby, Warks
810	B.G.PRIEST, Swinford, Lutterworth, Leics
811	PAUL ADDISON, Rugby, Warks
812	IAN ADDISON, Catthorpe, Leics
813	CALUM CAMBRON, Wigston Harcourt, Leicester
814	JAMES WHITE, Oadby Grange, Leicester
815	FRANK HARRIS, Oadby, Leicester
816	KEITH HEATH, Hinckley, Leics
817	DENISE CROUCHER, Leicester
818	M.J.HACKETT, Swinford, Lutterworth, Leics
819	L.SYLVESTER, Loughborough, Leics
820	SIMON BOOR, Birstall, Leicester
821	PATRICK JOHN TILER, Braunston, Rutland
822	KEVIN REYNOLDS, Loughborough, Leics
823	DAVID ALLAN TONES, South Wigston, Leicester
824	DARREN FINNEY, Earl Shilton, Leics
825	ROBERT HESKINS, Wigston Magna, Leicester
826	STEPHEN PERKINS, Loughborough, Leics
827	BRIAN JOHN STRATFORD, Hillmorton, Warks
828	PAUL FRAZER CLARKE, Birstall, Leicester
829	DEAN CREESE, Fleckney, Leics
830	BRIAN CREESE, Fleckney, Leics
831	ADRIAN MARK BURNS, Braunstone, Leicester
832	DARREN GREENHILL, Western Park, Leicester
833	CHRISTOPHER HORNER, Chiswick, London
834	SIMON TOMLINSON, Grantham, Lincs
835	JOHN & JUDY OSWIN, Birstall, Leicester
836	A.& I.WILLETT, Desford, Leics
837	KEVIN VERNON, Burbage, Leics
838	TERENCE I.WARWICK, Redditch, Worcs
839	MARTIN HARRISON, Kibworth Beauchamp, Leics
840	A.W.HEATH, THORNTON INTERIORS LTD., Leicester
841	JEREMY CRAMP, Kibworth Beauchamp, Leics

842 ANDY KNOTT, Arthingworth, Leics
843 MARK WILLIAMS, Norwich
844 COLIN MURRANT, East Carlton, Leics
845 RYAN MURRANT, East Carlton, Leics
846 TIMOTHY MURRANT, East Carlton, Leics
847 LEE EDGELEY, Leicester
848 KEVIN LOCK, Syston, Leics
849 MARCO SWINFIELD, Leicester
850 STEPHEN HINDS, Anstey, Leicester
851 TERRY LACEY, Oadby, Leicester
852 ANDREW POWELL, Loughborough, Leics
853 RAY BECK, Gislingham, Suffolk
854 MARTIN HALL, Earl Shilton, Leics
855 PHILIP TURNER, Kirby Muxloe, Leics
856 NEVILLE GREEN, Leicester
857 W.D.WILKINS, South Wigston, Leicester
858 RONALD BEET, Kibworth Beauchamp, Leics
859 JON ALLEN, Clarendon Park, Leicester
860 ANTHONY WALTERS, Beeston, Notts
861 STEVEN WARDLE, Ashby-de-la-Zouch, Leics
862 D.M.L.MARTIN, Bleasby, Notts
863 MICHAEL KELLAM, Frankly, Birmingham
864 JAMES HAND, Saffron Lane, Leicester
865 BARRY WHITMORE, Countesthorpe, Leics
866 ALAN PETER TUFFLEY, Wigston, Leicester
867 Master DANE WOODWARD, Ryhall, Lincs
868 STEVEN FRENCH, Kibworth, Leics
869 SIMON BODYCOTE, Croft, Leics
870 RYAN BETTS, Leicester
871 DAVE CATTLE, Leicester Forest East
872 MICHAEL IAN TURNER, Littlethorpe, Leics
873 MARTYN SMITH, Leicester
874 DAVID WARD, Shepshed, Leics
875 J.R.GOODALL, Leicester Forest East
876 JOHN KASPEREK, Kelvedon, Colchester, Essex
877 K.D.JOHNSON, Shepshed, Leics
878 Mrs A.FORD, Leicester
879 FRANK KOPKA, Northampton
880 Miss KIRSTINE MOWBRAY, Melton Mowbray, Leics
881 RICHARD GRAVES, Loughborough, Leics
882 SIMON CHALLANDS, Scotswood, Newcastle upon Tyne
883 J.L.B.HILL, Long Buckby, Northants
884 RAYMOND SMITH, Stockingford,Nuneaton, Warks
885 JIM WATTAM, Cambridge
886 DAVID McGRAW, Great Doddington, Northants
887 RICHARD A.CREASEY, Syston, Leics
888 CHRISTOPHER PAUL KNIFTON, Whitwick, Leics
889 R.G.SHILCOCK, Narborough, Leics
890 TIM MOORE, Bournemouth, Dorset
891 T.C.PENNINGTON, Newton Harcourt, Leics
892 JOSEPH BYRNE, Wellingborough, Northants
893 P.A.BARKER, Boothville, Northampton
894 PETER MARKS, Dovercourt, Essex
895 STEPHEN PAUL NEEDHAM, Coalville, Leics
896 ROGER WASH, Newmarket, Suffolk
897 PAUL JOANNOU, Stockbridge, Edinburgh
898 EDWIN ERNEST KNIGHT, Groby, Leicester
899 DAVID RICHARDS, Whitwick, Leics
900 ANNE & MARTYN BULMAN, Blaby, Leics
901 THOMAS MAWSON, Rugby, Warks
902 DONALD STUART ANGUS, Edgbaston, Birmingham
903 PAUL STILLWELL, Pitstone, Leighton Buzzard, Beds
904 RAY WILLARS, Oadby, Leicester
905 KEVIN PAUL DARBY, Desborough, Northants
906 MARK REDHEAD, Broughton Astley, Leics
907 CHRISTOPHER J.ROBINSON, Burbage, Leics
908 BRIAN W.MELLERICK, Beaumont Leys, Leicester
909 ROGER IAN CAVEN, Northampton
910 J.CARROTTE, Kirby Muxloe, Leics
911 PATRICIA ARNOLD, Leicestershire
912 PAUL J.WEBB, Stanton-by-Dale, Derbys
913 CHRIS BONEHAM, Gilmorton, Leics

914 PAUL JEROME, Lower Wanborough, Wilts
915 PATRICIA & JOHN BENNETT, Glenfield, Leicester
916 STEVEN DAVID GREEN, Leicester
917 KEVIN BOURGAULT, Leicester
918 LISA WILLETT, Botcheston, Desford, Leics
919 GERALD CAUSON, Desford, Leics
920 ALAN OSTLER
921 PETER BAXTER, Reading, Berks
922 DAVID CHENEY, Countesthorpe, Leics
923 KEITH HARRINGTON, Syston, Leics
924 DAVID HUNT
925 REGINALD HUNT
926 NEIL HUNT, Chesterfield, Derbys
927 HUGH JONATHAN McGREGOR, Desford, Leics
928 TONY GREASLEY, Wellingborough, Northants
929 Mr C. & Mrs K.PERKINS, Loughborough, Leics
930 ROBERT HURST, Leicester
931 LANCE TOMLYN, Northampton
932 ANTHONY SHARMAN, Blaby, Leics
933 K.P.WOOD, Ipswich, Suffolk
934 P.W.STEVENSON, Sutton in Ashfield, Notts
935 F.J.BURTON, Rothley, Leics
936 MICHAEL E.GARDNER, Norwich, Norfolk
937 THAO PANTER, Burton Latimer, Northants
938 J.KEENAN, Saffron Lane, Leicester
939 JOYCE & NELLIE MOORE, Castle Donington, Derbys
940 ROB KELLY, Tunbridge Wells, Kent
941 MARK G.BATTY (Surveyor), Kibworth Harcourt, Leics
942 CARL ANTHONY BODYCOTT, Anstey, Leicester
943 BRIAN & SHELLEY PICK, Exmouth, Devon
944 R.J.MATCHETT, Whitwick, Leics
945 COLIN CAMERON, Sidcup, Kent
946 CHRISTOPHER HINSLEY, Narborough, Leics
947 GARRY STOKES, Loughborough, Leics
948 SIMON CURLEY, Syston, Leicester
949 LEE SMITH, Ibstock, Leics
950 MARK CUNNOLD, Blaby, Leics
951 JAMES WILLIAM LADKIN, Eyres Monsell, Leicester
952 NEIL DAVID CROSSLAND, Halifax, W.Yorkshire
953 M.J.O'CONNOR, St.Johns, Worcester
954 MICHAEL PAYNE, Dunton Bassett, Leics
955 STEVE GILBY, Adelaide, South Australia
956 ANTONY LYONS, Rugby, Warks
957 GEIR JUVA, Drammen, Norway
958 PER TANDBERG, Drammen, Norway
959 CHRISTER SVENSSON, Odeshog, Sweden
960 JON SAMMELS, Countesthorpe, Leics
961 JONATHAN POOK, Syston, Leicester
962 JONATHAN POOK, Syston, Leicester
963 JONATHAN POOK, Syston, Leicester
964 ANTONY CHRISTIAN SMALLSHAW, Sharnford, Leics
965 KEITH BUTTERISS, Wigston Magna, Leicester
966 ROBERT P.AUCOTT, Knighton, Leicester
967 KEVIN KEY, South Wigston, Leicester
968 NICK WRIGHT, Leicester
969 S.W.CHAMBERS, Desborough, Northants
970 KEVIN JOHN SMITH, Wigston Fields, Leicester
971 A.W.RICHARDS, Leicester
972 CLIVE WILLIAM SPENCER, Swadlincote, Staffs
973 LAWRENCE JOHN VEASEY, Swadlincote, Staffs
974 C.J.FREER, Saxilby, Lincoln
975 TIM JEWITT, Oadby, Leics
976 Dr. NEIL GEORGE HANSFORD, Weymouth, Dorset
977 DANIEL & RACHEL CARR, Seagrave, Leics
978 MITCHELL EVINSON, Braunstone, Leicester
979 ADAM P.BROWN, Wigston Magna, Leicester
980 N.PITTARD, Leicester
981 Mrs J.ADCOCK, Birstall, Leicester
982 JOHN W.E.HAYES, Beeston, Nottingham
983 PAUL MILES, Billesdon, Leics
984 IAN HARRIS, Gamlingay, Cambridgeshire
985 CHRIS BALLARD, Knighton, Leicester

986 J.M.OWEN, Evington, Leicester
987 ANDREW KENT, Anstey, Leics
988 GORDON L.SMITH, South Wigston, Leicester
989 J.R.W.HOLT, Stamford, Lincs
990 HELEN A.CAVE, Market Harborough, Leics
991 Miss J.E.GAMBLE, Broughton Astley, Leics
992 CHRISTOPHER CARTER, Loughborough, Leics
993 ANNE LUDLAM, Heather, Leicester
994 JAMES ANTHONY KERAN, Leicester
995 JOHN KEVIN PROTHEROE, Leicester
996 ANDREW P.J.GREEN, Mountsorrel, Leics
997 NEIL R.COLLEDGE, Evington, Leicester
998 CRAIG BREWIN, Bounds Green, London
999 JOHN SJOBERG, Kirby Muxloe, Leics
1000 Mrs ELAINE MONK, Anstey, Leicester
1001 PETER HOLMES, Leicester
1002 COLIN HOLMES, Leicester
1003 PETER DAVID WILSON, Northampton
1004 ADRIAN THOMAS HYDE, Telford, Shropshire
1005 NEIL ADAMSON, Newport, Gwent, S.Wales
1006 SIMON J.MESSENGER, Woburn Sands, Beds
1007 MICHAEL CHAMBERS, Sileby, Leics
1008 COLIN BANNER, Leicester
1009 MICHAEL LOUGHRAN, Thurmaston, Leicester
1010 LYNTON GUEST, London, W10
1011 PETER JOHNSON, Bristol, Avon
1012 DAVID MASTERS, Birstall, Leicester
1013 R.H.BENT, Western Park, Leicester
1014 K.W.BRANT, Evington, Leicester
1015 PAUL COCKAYNE, Braunstone, Leicester
1016 RICHARD JOHN COOK, Cosby, Leics
1017 ALAN de HARO, Melton Mowbray, Leics
1018 ROY ILIFFE, Leicester
1019 C.G.LOWSON, Leicester
1020 DEAN MASON, Oadby, Leicester
1021 CHRISTOPHER JOHN CAMPBELL, Leicestershire
1022 ALAN CHARLES PYKETT, Leicester
1023 LEE ALAN SARGENT, Braunstone, Leicester
1024 ROBERT BROWN, Melton Mowbray, Leics
1025 PHILIP CORLESS, Ibstock, Leics
1026 PATRICK J. & MARTIN G.BISHOP, Humberstone, Leicester
1027 T.E.FORWARD, Wellingborough, Northants
1028 P.E.FORWARD, Wellingborough, Northants
1029 Miss ROSEMARY ANN HARVEY, Nuneaton, Warks
1030 PHILLIP N.SHAW, Maidenhead, Berks
1031 ADRIAN J.SANSOME, Burbage, Leics
1032 CHRISTOPHER LEWITT, Leicester
1033 S.W.KIRK & Miss J. BAKER, Burton Overy, Leics
1034 KEVIN O'BRIEN, Leicester
1035 DEREK A.PEARSON, Leicester
1036 RODNEY DUNBAR, Burton Latimer, Northants
1037 RICHARD HOFFMAN, Leicester
1038 SIMON HALLAM, Leicester
1039 JOHN LEES, Newbold Verdon, Leics
1040 MICHAEL F.DOWNIE, Chilwell Beeston, Notts
1041 M.G.HADDON, Hinckley, Leics
1042 R.L.HADDON, Hinckley, Leics
1043 I.N.CAMPBELL, Hinckley, Leics
1044 J.GOODFELLOW, Stoney Stanton, Leics
1045 TOM SWEENIE (Carpet Fitting Specialist), Sapcote, Leics
1046 MARK STOCKER, Leicester
1047 KARL A.DURHAM, Lincoln
1048 ROBERT HAILSTONES, Husbands Bosworth, Leics
1049 JOHN BODKIN, Abbey Rise, Leicester
1050 R.BETTS, Willesden, London
1051 STUART WILLIAM POYNOR, Ratby, Leics
1052 KEITH COBURN, Cambridge
1053 MICHAEL BARRS, Thornton, Leicester
1054 ROBERT EDWARD TAYLOR, Broughton Astley, Leics
1055 DAVID STATHAM, Leicester
1056 JOHN BELCHER, Rowley Fields, Leicester
1057 Miss DIANE WESTON, South Wigston, Leicester

1058 R.A.COTTERELL. Ashby de la Zouch, Leics
1059 MARTIN FISHER, Mickleover, Derbys
1060 G.E.ROBINSON, Stapleford, Notts
1061 J.P.HENNESSEY, Cosby, Leics
1062 DESMOND BILLINGHAM, Leicester
1063 TOM WORMLEIGHTON, Leicester
1064 A.B.THORBURN, Melton Mowbray, Leics
1065 R.A.UNDERWOOD, Leicestershire
1066 G.RIDDLESTON, Western Park, Leicester
1067 NIGEL TYERS, Oakham, Rutland
1068 MARTIN JARVIS, Wellingborough, Northants
1069 J.E.SHARP, Great Glen, Leicester
1070 PAUL DYSON, Long Eaton, Notts
1071 ANDY KNAPP, Leicester Forest East
1072 PAUL BUTTERFIELD, Barlestone, Warks
1073 TREVOR HAROLD BRAY, Hinckley, Leics
1074 BRIAN H.HOBBS, Thornbury, Bristol
1075 SIMON KISBY, Blaby, Leics
1076 K.M.POLE, Leicester
1077 MARK PHILIP GULLIFORD, Braunstone Frith, Leicester
1078 KEVIN LINNELL, Glen Parva, Leicester
1079 DAVID LAKEY, Melton Mowbray, Leics
1080 JOHN LAKEY, Keighley, West Yorkshire
1081 ANTHONY MANSELL, Oadby, Leicester
1082 IAN PURCHASE, Swadlincote, Staffs
1083 PETER S.GORE, Hounslow, Middlesex
1084 PAUL R.HATTON, Milton Ernest, Beds
1085 KIM BAILEY, Leicester
1086 DARRELL J.QUINN, Aylestone, Leicester
1087 PAUL WELCH, Barlestone, Warks
1088 PAUL ANTHONY BROWN, Leicester
1089 GREGORY DROZDZ, Crystal Palace, London
1090 CROSSLAND, OTTER, HUNT, Sheffield
1091 MICHAEL JOHN LUCAS, Hinckley, Leics
1092 MICHAEL DAVID LUCAS, Hinckley, Leics
1093 M.A.WATSON, Barwell, Leics
1094 ALAN JAMES STABLES, Lee, London SE12
1095 PETER READ, Wigston Fields, Leicester
1096 CHRIS ELLIOTT, Barrow-upon-Soar, Leics
1097 DAVID COBLEY, Beaumont Leys, Leicester
1098 PETER C.MAYES, Kettering, Northants
1099 GORDON NASH, Shepshed, Leics
1100 PETER ANDREW HILL, Sileby, Leics
1101 HOWARD RILEY, Wigston Magna, Leicester
1102 JAMES & RACHEL STEVENS, Leicester
1103 MARIA PRIME, Aylestone, Leicester
1104 DAVID YOUNG, Wigston, Leicester
1105 SEAN YOUNG, Wigston, Leicester
1106 DAVID MONK, Market Harborough, Leics
1107 Mrs M.CHESTER, Coalville, Leics
1108 NORMAN GEORGE BARLOW, Leicester
1109 CRAIG PEARSON, Beaumont Leys, Leicester
1110 ANDREW SIVELL, Loughborough, Leics
1111 BARRY REEVES, Queniborough, Leics
1112 GLYNN MARSHALL, South Wigston, Leicester
1113 TREVOR MARSHALL, South Wigston, Leicester
1114 DARREN THOMPSON, Wigston Magna, Leicester
1115 DAVID WATCHORN, Saffron Lane, Leicester
1116 STUART ILIFFE, Leicester
1117 TERRY POTTER, Leicester
1118 J.G.MORTIMER, Ilkeston, Derbys
1119 ANTON RIPPON, Mickleover, Derbys
1120 LESTER CHARLES COLLYER, Welwyn Garden City, Herts
1121 DAVID ROBBINS, London SW4
1122 JOSEPH ROBBINS
1123 ROBERT DAVID FAGG, Ibstock, Leics
1124 BARRIE BAKER, Barwell, Leics
1125 MICK HARDY, Norwich, Norfolk
1126 MICK HARDY, Norwich, Norfolk
1127 RAYMOND RANDLE, Leicester
1128 PETER A.HAWES, Woodgate, Leicester
1129 ROBERT FARMER STANIFORTH, Anstey, Leics

1130 ANDREJ KURBALIJA, Leicester
1131 IAN KIRWAN, Syston, Leicester
1132 PAUL KIRWAN, Denby Dale, West Yorks
1133 STEPEHN MARK PORT, Surbiton, Surrey
1134 Miss K.A.MORRELL, Hertford Heath, Herts
1135 T.WOODCOCK
1136 J.BLANKLEY
1137 JOHN EASTWOOD, Ipswich, Suffolk
1138 ANDREW ROSBOROUGH, Corby, Northants
1139 P.E.DUNKLEY, Fleckney, Leics
1140 DUNCAN & MARGARET CLARKE, Groby, Leicester
1141 ADRIAN I'ANSON, Enderby, Leicester
1142 ALEXANDER STROUD, Holland Park, London
1143 MICHAEL FRANCIS, Sandy, Beds
1144 PETER JOHN SHOEBOTHAM, Wigston Magna, Leicester
1145 LEONARD W.MITCHELL, Arnesby, Leics
1146 ANTHONY JOHN HARRISON, Hugglescote, Leics
1147 R.N.SMALLEY, Mountsorrel, Leics
1148 MIKE CHEETHAM, Evington, Leicester
1149 NICHOLAS CLIVE JARVIS, Shepshed, Leics
1150 PETER HUMPHREY, PRINTSTREAM, Whetstone, Leics
1151 DARREN SPENCER, Narborough, Leicester
1152 ANN McGIBBON, Kibworth, Leics
1153 GERALD TOON, Scraptoft, Leicester
1154 GEORGE TOON, Scraptoft, Leicester
1155 ALEX KINNAIRD, Aylestone Park, Leicester
1156 NEIL KINNAIRD, Lutterworth, Leics
1157 DAVE WILLIAMS, Gilmoreton Estate, Leicester
1158 DAVE KENNELL, New Parks, Leicester
1159 DAVE KENNELL, New Parks, Leicester
1160 ROGER BROWN, Aylestone, Leicester
1161 JOHN HATTON, Oadby, Leicester
1162 NIGEL MANN, Uppingham Road, Leicester
1163 DAVE MONAGHAN, Leicester
1164 PAUL SHARMAN, Leicester
1165 STAN GRANT, Mowmacre Hill, Leicester
1166 C.C.HILL, Deeping St.James, Peterborough
1167 MARK BEECROFT, Walthamstow, London
1168 DINO KYPRIANOU, Leicester
1169 PAUL RICHARDSON, Glen Parva, Leicester
1170 ROBERT BEADMAN, New Parks, Leicester
1171 Mr & Mrs R.W.DICKENS, Nuneaton, Warks
1172 ALAN P.CRAFT, Kingston-upon-Thames, Surrey
1173 ROBERT A.CRAFT
1174 S.P.TOMLIN, Sedlescombe, Battle, East Sussex
1175 JIM REID, Kibworth Beauchamp, Leics
1176 JOHN S.NOON, Leicester Forest East
1177 GIMSON TIMBER GROUP, Leicester
1178 LEICESTER SOUND, Leicester
1179 NICK GODRICH, Sileby, Leics
1180 AUDNEL GROUP, Syston, Leicester
1181 TELEGAMES, Kilby Bridge, Leicester
1182 BBC RADIO LEICESTER, Leicester
1183 CRIPPS of KIBWORTH, Kibworth, Leics
1184 PETER SMITH, Loughborough, Leics
1185 SIMON C.FAULKS, Barwell, Leics
1186 STUART HAMPTON, Warrington, Cheshire
1187 GARETH HYATT, Wigston, Leicester
1188 K.MASON, Kimberley, Nottingham
1189 SARAH & DONNA BARTON, Banbury, Oxon
1190 ALAN DAVIES, Worcester
1191 IAIN STURCH, Acocks Green, Birmingham
1192 IAN D.MILES, Leicester
1193 KEVIN SHELDON, Beaumont Leys, Leicester
1194 MARTIN SIMONS, Bekkevoort, Belgium
1195 JOHN BRYSON, Ilford, Essex
1196 STUART MILLS, West Knighton, Leicester
1197 NORMAN GREEN, Ipswich, Suffolk
1198 GORDON SMALL, Preston, Lancs
1199 KEVIN COLEY, Glen Parva, Leicester
1200 CANDIDA F.V.BASKCOMB, Amsterdam, Holland
1201 MICHAEL TAYLOR, Owlthorpe, Sheffield, S.Yorkshire

1202 DAVID GEOFFREY SMITH, Oadby, Leicester
1203 PHIL GIBSON, Maidenhead, Berkshire
1204 PHILIP N.PARSLOW, Worcester
1205 ANTONY WALTON, Leicester
1206 JOHN M.MOORE, Hatton, Warwick
1207 GRAHAM ROBSON, Loughborough, Leics
1208 GEORGE ROBINSON, Leicester
1209 CLIVE WESTON, Wigston Fields, Leicester
1210 PETER PICKUP, Pudsey, West Yorkshire
1211 MALCOLM HARTLEY, Bradford, West Yorkshire
1212 STEPHEN & ELAINE ROBERTS, Rothley, Leics
1213 JASON BOWERS, Stamford, Lincs
1214 DAVID ADCOCK, Tamworth, Staffs
1215 FRANK (MAX) MALIN, Market Harborough, Leics
1216 ANDREW L. HENSON, Thurmaston, Leicester
1217 M.J.SMITH, Leicester Forest East
1218 J.STEWART, Leicester
1219 ROBERT HAMPSON, Oadby, Leicester
1220 ROBERT BOYALL, Leicester
1221 SHIRAAZ WALA, Leicester
1222 VINCENT DUDDY, Oadby, Leicester
1223 DERMOT CLINTON, Atherstone, Warks
1224 ROBERT DALY, Newbold Verdon, Leics
1225 MALCOLM BECKWITH, St.Matthews, Leicester
1226 RAY GOBLE, West Ashling, Sussex
1227 PER PERSSON, Borlänge, Sweden
1228 JOSEPH GAYDECKI, Dulwich, London
1229 IAN CHAMBERLAIN, Knighton, Leicester
1230 P.K.REDHEAD, Leicester
1231 ALFRED SMITH, Leicester
1232 DEAN WALTON, Leicester
1233 NEIL WALTON, Leicester
1234 ANDREW ARNOLD, Stenson Fields, Derby
1235 IAN & OWEN TWELLS, Coalville, Leics
1236 MICHAEL DEAN, Long Marston, Herts
1237 ALBERT CHARLTON, Loughborough, Leics
1238 IAN PARKER, Peatling Magna, Leics
1239 BARRY EDWARDS, Newbold Verdon, Leics
1240 STEPHEN KEENAN, Earl Shilton, Leics
1241 ROB BRUCE, Gretton, Northants
1242 NICK GIANNINI, Enderby, Leicester
1243 RICHARD AUSTEN SMITH, Ipswich, Suffolk
1244 IAN M.ILIFFE, Leicester
1245 WAYNE A.ILIFFE, Leicester
1246 NIGEL SHIER (Nuthall Lighting), Dinnington, Sheffield
1247 ADRIAN TAYLOR, Market Bosworth, Warks
1248 M.A.HIGGINS, Stow on the Wold, Glos
1249 Miss J.K.TURLAND, Loughborough, Leics
1250 JOHN DINGWALL, Wigston Magna, Leicester
1251 LUCILLE WEAVER, Worcester
1252 SYDNEY PRICE, Burton upon Trent, Staffs
1253 STEVE MUNTON (Munton's Bakery), Fenton, Stoke on Trent
1254 Cpl.J.F.NEWELL, B.F.P.O. 807
1255 PAUL RUSSELL, Market Harborough, Leics
1256 BRIAN A.SMITH, Finchfield, Wolverhampton
1257 ROLAND A.DAKIN, The Travellers Rest, Caversham, Berks
1258 NIGEL HADDON, Macclesfield, Cheshire
1259 MICHAEL G.HOLTOM, Stratford upon Avon, Warks
1260 PAUL STEVENSON, Glenfield, Leicester
1261 ANTHONY MILLS, Hove, East Sussex
1262 A.J.BRAKER, Queniborough, Leics
1263 ROBERT W.GASCOIGNE, Upper Norwood, London
1264 JOHN & NEIL OGILVIE, Wigston Magna, Leicester
1265 STEPHEN LEWIN, Randburg, South Africa
1266 JOHN FOLEY, Glen Parva, Leicester
1267 DAVID G.ROSSELL, Glen Parva, Leicester
1268 JOHN KNOX, Earl Shilton, Leics
1269 VINCE & ELIZABETH FOLEY, Cricklade, Wilts
1270 STEPHEN WANN, Morecambe, Lancs
1271 DAVID MICHAEL WOODS, Redfield, Bristol
1272 COLIN ROBERT MARTIN, Staines, Middlesex
1273 MICHAEL HEWITT, Wigston Magna, Leicester

1274 C.BOULTER, Barwell, Leics
1275 W.T.BOULTER, Barwell, Leics
1276 J.ABBOTT, Earl Shilton, Leics
1277 P.LIVING, Ipswich, Suffolk
1278 GLENN MITCHELL STEWART, Narborough, Leicester
1279 KEITH LOWE, Victoria, British Columbia, Canada
1280 A.SEYMOUR, Wakes Meadow, Northampton
1281 PAUL MIDDLETON, Oadby, Leicester
1282 TONY REYNOLDS, Loughborough, Leics
1283 CLARE PURSER, Elton, Peterborough
1284 NEIL A.PRATT, Hinckley, Leics
1285 WILLIAM WYLES, Loughborough, Leics
1286 MICHAEL ALLEN, Loughborough, Leics
1287 MARTIN RYAN, Braunstone, Leicester
1288 ANDY BROWN, Beaumont Leys, Leicester
1289 R.F.OSBORNE, Burton upon Trent, Staffs
1290 ANDREW BARBER, Barwell, Leics
1291 BRUCE TARRY, South Wigston, Leicester
1292 PETER MICHAEL ROPER, Market Harborough, Leics
1293 BRIAN DAVID HILL, Warwick
1294 DERRICK WALE, Glen Parva, Leicester
1295 MERVYN RICHARD WARING, Church Gresley, Staffs
1296 PAUL HARRIS, Loughborough, Leics
1297 MARK A.PICKERING, Melton Mowbray, Leics
1298 TOM NORDON, Tavistock, Devon
1299 IAN LANE, Altrincham, Cheshire
1300 Miss JANE MANSELL, Morden, Surrey
1301 CARL MEADS, Wigston, Leicester
1302 BARRY ELLIOTT, Wigston, Leicester
1303 PHILIP WRIGHT, Tonbridge, Kent
1304 S.BECK, Braunstone, Leicester
1305 JOHN NORMAN, Nuneaton, Warks
1306 ALAN NORMAN, Stockingford, Nuneaton, Warks
1307 Mrs ZERIN REYNOLDS, Corby, Northants
1308 TERRY BUCK, Measham, Staffs
1309 CHARLES STEWART VEASEY, Burbage, Leics
1310 A.R.& D.NICHOLLS, Ross-on-Wye, Herefordshire
1311 C.W.M.WOOD, Oadby, Leicester
1312 ANDREW BOTT, Thurmaston, Leicester
1313 GREGORY SCOTT BILLSON, Stocking Farm, Leicester
1314 GRAHAM BROWN, Wigston, Leicester
1315 TONY GREEN, Thurnby, Leicester
1316 DAVID ROBERT WELLS, Oakham, Leics
1317 NICK SHARPE, Basingstoke, Hants
1318 HELGA LENGA, Leicester
1319 PETER LENGA, Leicester
1320 TIM HAYES, Wigston, Leicester
1321 J.J.HAWKES, Oadby, Leicester
1322 R.M.SMITH, Hunstanton, Norfolk
1323 MARK FORD, Leicester
1324 ANDREW DALES, Houghton le Spring, Tyne & Wear
1325 ROBERT A.ROWLETT, Shutford, Banbury, Oxon
1326 MALCOLM UPTON, Coalville, Leics
1327 RON EVANS, Inkersall, Chesterfield, Derbys
1328 ANGIE STURGIS, Market Harborough, Leics
1329 DAVID J.MOONEY, Thames Ditton, Surrey
1330 DAVID SLACK, Leicester Forest East
1331 KEITH FAULKES, Thurmaston, Leicester
1332 CLIVE CREASEY, Grantham, Lincs
1333 VAUGHN CRAXTON, Chapel Brampton, Northampton
1334 RICHARD MORRIS, Oadby, Leicester
1335 KEVIN BROWN, Groby, Leics
1336 C.E.GOWTAGE, Burton upon Trent, Staffs
1337 GARY DEAN LEWIN, Wigston Harcourt, Leicester
1338 RIKKI MARLON LEWIN, Wigston Harcourt, Leicester
1339 F.D.FRAZER, Leicester
1340 P.J.NEVILLE, Wigston, Leicester
1341 Miss STACY.D.NICHOLLS, Dunton Bassett, Leics
1342 P.S.BUTLER, Anstey, Leicester
1343 KEVIN GOUGH, Swadlincote, Staffs
1344 IAN BOULTER, Glenfield, Leicester
1345 RAYMOND SHAW, Sutton in Ashfield, Notts

1346 Dr R.GARNER, Leicester
1347 ANDREW GARNER, Leicester
1348 Miss HELEN SPAWTON, Melton Mowbray, Leics
1349 JEAN HUGHES, Finningley, Doncaster
1350 PAUL & JUDITH SHARRATT, Markfield, Leicester
1351 WAYNE RUSSELL, South Wigston, Leicester
1352 WILLY BACH, Walcote, Lutterworth, Leics
1353 SIMON ASHLEY BLANCHARD, Werrington, Peterborough
1354 Master GUY SALMON, Leicestershire
1355 CHRISTOPHER STEPHEN MEADOWS, Glenfield, Leicester
1356 STEWART FELL, Radcliffe, Manchester
1357 D.C.ROSE
1358 ROBERT TERPILOWSKI, Redbridge, Ilford, Essex
1359 D.F.R.LORD, Husbands Bosworth, Leics
1360 KEITH GRIFFIN, Burbage, Leics
1361 STEPHEN HUMPHREY, Kirby Muxloe, Leics
1362 SEAN RINGROSE, Narborough, Leics
1363 MATTHEW BOZEAT, Evington, Leicester
1364 BARRY ELLIS, Oadby, Leicester
1365 ALEXANDER LOVETT, Syston, Leics
1366 STUART REVELL, Luton, Beds
1367 C.GEARY & SONS, Ratby, Leicester
1368 STEVE RADWAN, Oadby, Leicester
1369 L.WOODWARD, Brackley, Northants
1370 CAROLE JONES, Cosby, Leics
1371 Mr & Mrs W.CRANE, Eyres Monsell, Leicester
1372 ROBERT & THOMAS HIBBERT, Enderby, Leicester
1373 STEPHEN FREDERICK HOLMAN, Oadby, Leicester
1374 SUSAN TAIT, Leicester
1375 JOHN McWHIRTER, Leicester
1376 BERNARD SPIERS, Leicester
1377 DAVE MAKINS, Barwell, Leics
1378 TREV MAKINS, Melton Mowbray, Leics
1379 JAMES HUNT, West Bridgford, Nottingham
1380 ROBERT HUNT, Stoneygate, Leicester
1381 TOM CONSTABLE, Oadby, Leicester
1382 MIKE & RUSS LOASBY, Humberstone, Leicester
1383 SIMON HODGETT, Desborough, Northants
1384 Mrs JENNIFER WHITE, Leicester
1385 Miss SHEILA WALLACE, Leicester
1386 MARTIN PRIME, Loughborough, Leics
1387 LUKE WRIGHT, Mountsorrel, Leics
1388 LEE TURNER, Kirby Muxloe, Leics
1389 MICHAEL J.TAYLOR, Yatton, Bristol, Avon
1390 STEVE OSWIN, Solihull, West Midlands
1391 JAMES GODFREY, Thurlby, Bourne, Lincs
1392 MARK TOLLINGTON, Knighton, Leicester
1393 PAUL NELSON, Tettenhall, Wolverhampton
1394 JOHN BARBER, Earl Shilton, Leics
1395 TONY McMAHON, Addlestone, Weybridge, Surrey
1396 GERALD DRAKE, Glen Parva, Leicester
1397 D.B.ANDERSON, Deeping St.James, Lincs
1398 K.E.WOOSTER, Thurnby, Leicester
1399 PETER TAYLORSON, South Woodford, London
1400 PETER TAYLORSON, South Woodford, London
1401 SPORTS MARKETING(AUSTRALIA), Adelaide, Sth Australia
1402 ANDREW TAYLOR, Loughborough, Leics
1403 ROBERT BRUCE, Loughborough, Leics
1404 TONY T.PEARCE, Leicester
1405 TIM DAVIES, London W14
1406 WAYNE DAVID FRISBY, Corby, Northants
1407 GRAHAM SPACKMAN, Pinner, Middlesex
1408 MICHAEL WOOLLEY, Reading, Berks
1409 D.GRAY, Harrogate, North Yorkshire
1410 D.GRAY, Harrogate, North Yorkshire
1411 LANCE WARD, West Bridgford, Nottingham
1412 JOHN SIBSON, Abbots Langley, Herts
1413 STEVE LACEY, Rectory Farm, Northampton
1414 GEOFFREY BUTLER, Witham, Essex
1415 G.EAMES(Joiners & Builders), Houghton on the Hill, Leics
1416 R.PHILLIPS, South Wigston, Leicester
1417 SHANE DOWNS, Loughborough, Leics

1418 RYAN LAKEY, Keighley, West Yorkshire
1419 JOHN LAKEY, Keighley, West Yorkshire
1420 PETER FOSTER, Melton Mowbray, Leics
1421 CYRIL GEORGE, Aberfan, Merthyr Tydfil, Glamorgan
1422 BHARAT & NATALIE PATEL, Queniborough, Leics
1423 MICK ANDREWS, Market Harborough, Leics
1424 ROBERT McKNIGHT, Woodbridge, Suffolk
1425 MARK BLABER, Corby, Northants
1426 MARTIN NEIL BICKMORE, Glen Parva, Leicester
1427 PAUL WISDISH, Leicester
1428 SEAN J.D.McCARTHUR, Rugby, Warks
1429 Cpl. ANDREW MILLER, Syston, Leicester
1430 R.WARD, Braunstone, Leicester
1431 LEICESTERSHIRE RECORD OFFICE, Leicester
1432 PAUL WATTS, Kettering, Northants
1433 DAVID FLEETWOOD, Barnehurst, Bexleyheath, Kent
1434 JOHNNY GREEN, Queniborough, Leics
1435 WARWICK KAY, Thurnby, Leicester
1436 ALISON WINDER, Groby, Leicester
1437 ROBERT FERGUSON, Syston, Leicester
1438 A.J.HAMILTON, Midsomer Norton, Bath, Avon
1439 SIMON C.WEST, Wigston Harcourt, Leicester
1440 DOUGLAS LAMMING, North Ferriby, North Humberside
1441 JAMES LOWRY, Dronfield Woodhouse, Sheffield
1442 IAN GENTRY, Sharnford, Leics
1443 STUART TEASDALE, Leicester
1444 LEE TEASDALE, Leicester
1445 STEVEN WOODCOCK, Syston, Leics
1446 Ms. M.STEVENS, Newbold Verdon, Leics
1447 W.F.HOWARD, South Braunstone, Leicester
1448 PETE CAMPBELL, Aylestone, Leicester
1449 KRISTIAN JON WARD, Higham-on-the-hill, Warks
1450 BOB BROWN, SPORTS FORUM, Perth, W.Australia
1451 RICHARD CLARKE, Washington, D.C.,U.S.A.
1452 ALISTAIR MICHAEL WOOD, Countesthorpe, Leicester
1453 MIKE L.PURKISS, Hoo, Rochester, Kent
1454 G.GLENTON, Sale, Manchester
1455 M.PUGH, M & M ROOFING CO., Croft, Leics
1456 BOB LAMBERT, Rugby, Warks
1457 KENNETH WEBB, Bedford
1458 RICHIE TYLEY, Liphook, Hants
1459 ROBERT COX, Carlton, Nuneaton, Warks
1460 R.A.HAWES, Loughborough, Leics
1461 SIMON CHRISTOPHER MAXFIELD, Gainsborough, Lincs
1462 Mrs CHRISTINE HARTOPP, Glenfield, Leicester
1463 PHILIP R.BIRD, Colchester, Essex
1464 PHILIP R.BIRD, Colchester, Essex
1465 PETER ELLIOTT, Oadby, Leicester
1466 NICHOLAS F.BLANKLEY, Ealing, London
1467 FRED BLANKLEY
1468 ROBERT CLIVE SMITH, Enderby, Leics
1469 A.G.C.LANE, Solihull, West Midlands
1470 GAIL NICHOLLS, Dunton Bassett, Leics
1471 STEVEN HITCHCOX, Banbury, Oxon
1472 MATTHEW TRUMPESS, Oakham, Leics
1473 PETER, JANE, MATTHEW & CATHERINE PRESTON, Warks
1474 ROBERT LOCKWOOD, Solihull, West Midlands
1475 STEVE SMITH, Lutterworth, Leics
1476 NIGEL KIRK, Burton Lazars, Leics
1477 RICHARD TEBBUTT (Distrib.Northern Dairies), Loughborough
1478 KEVIN DURKIN, Leicester
1479 MICHAEL DURKIN, Leicester
1480 TERENCE DURKIN, Leicester
1481 CHRISTINE HOWKER, Wigston Fields, Leicester
1482 ROBERT CRAWFORD, Leicester
1483 ADRIAN BRADBURY, Aylestone, Leicester
1484 MALCOLM MOORE, Loughborough, Leics
1485 PETER RICHARDSON, Thurnby, Leicester
1486 TOM DEVLIN, Newtonnards, Co.Down, Northern Ireland
1487 ADRIAN FLYNN, Corby, Northants
1488 ANTHONY JONES, Wembley, Middlesex
1489 CAMILLA BASKCOMB & DAVE GILLAN, Battersea, London

1490 LYNN CAVE, Thurlaston, Leics
1491 PETER SIKES, Syston, Leicester
1492 ANDREW SIKES, Syston, Leicester
1493 P.G.GILBERT, Buxton, Derbyshire
1494 RICHARD JAMES PITTS, Narborough, Leics
1495 P.A.CRANE, Carpenter & Joiner, Leicester
1496 GARY TOWERS, Wigston Fields, Leicester
1497 Mrs H.E.INGHAM, Whitwick, Leics
1498 COLIN HALL, Leicester
1499 MICHAEL JAMES HUGHES, Thurmaston, Leicester
1500 TERRY CROFT, Leicester
1501 JOHN NOSELEY, Belgrave, Leicester
1502 JACK NOSELEY, Leicester
1503 CHRIS MILLARD, Leicester
1504 DAVID PITCHER, Leicester
1505 PAUL STONE, Leicester
1506 COLIN STONE, Leicester
1507 ROBERT W.FREEMAN, Ashby-de-la-Zouch, Leics
1508 JAMES CHATFIELD, Hadleigh, Suffolk
1509 STEPHEN CARR, Tipton, Staffs
1510 DAVID JEFFERY, Harpenden, Herts
1511 STEPHEN J.SMITH, Bradford, West Yorkshire
1512 DAVID DALBY, Wigston, Leicester
1513 GARY R.BENTLEY & JULIE M.GLOVER, Whitwick, Leics
1514 HOLYWELL FOOTWEAR LTD, Holywell, Stamford, Lincs
1515 HOLYWELL FOOTWEAR LTD, Holywell, Stamford, Lincs
1516 JOHN DUNCAN, Ewell, Surrey
1517 MAXWELL CARRUTHERS, Oadby, Leicester
1518 PATRICK CARRUTHERS, Oadby, Leicester
1519 LEE CARRUTHERS, Oadby, Leicester
1520 SHIRLEY CARRUTHERS, Oadby, Leicester
1521 CHRISTOPHER DEWEY, Thurmaston, Leicester
1522 PAUL GIBSON, Woodgate, Leicester
1523 THE THOMAS ORGANISATION, Silver Street, Leicester
1524 R.P.CHILDS, Birmingham
1525 MICHAEL MAIER, London NW3
1526 D.J.FILBY, Bridlington, East Yorkshire
1527 BRIAN TABNER, Forton, Preston, Lancs
1528 STEWART R.GREEN, Stamford, Lincs
1529 STEWART R.GREEN, Stamford, Lincs
1530 JEREMY BALL, Toronto, Canada
1531 JOHN P.RICHARDSON, London
1532 ROY SPROULE, Hamilton, New Zealand
1533 BARRY, RICHARD & MATTHEW BOURNE, Heswall, Wirral
1534 GARRY ROOST, Brixton, London
1535 GARRY ROOST, Brixton, London
1536 GEOFF GREATOREX, Braunstone Frith, Leicester
1537 DEREK BAUSER, Leicester
1538 M.J.THOMPSON, Burbage, Leics
1539 LIONEL WILLETT, Botcheston, Desford, Leics
1540 KEITH J.ROWLETT, Lower Waterford, Vermont, U.S.A.
1541 DAVE SMITH, Oadby, Leicester
1542 HELEN SMITH, Oadby, Leicester
1543 THOMAS SMITH, Oadby, Leicester
1544 JENNIFER SMITH, Oadby, Leicester
1545 PAUL SMITH, Oadby, Leicester
1546 SALLY SMITH, Oadby, Leicester
1547 PAUL TAYLOR, London N22
1548 ROWENA TAYLOR, London N22
1549 KATE TAYLOR, London N22
1550 HELEN TAYLOR, London N22
1551 PHILIP LINK, Tinwell, Stamford, Lincs
1552 EAMON C.HEIGHWAY, Thurmaston, Leicester
1553 JULIAN BASKCOMB, Leicester